HISTORY

OF

WOMAN SUFFRAGE

HISTORY

OF

WOMAN SUFFRAGE

VOLUME I

EDITED BY

ELIZABETH CADY STANTON,
SUSAN B. ANTHONY, AND
MATILDA JOSLYN GAGE.

Source Book Press

HISTORY

OF

WOMAN SUFFRAGE

EDITED BY

ELIZABETH CADY STANTON,
SUSAN B. ANTHONY, AND
MATILDA JOSLYN GAGE.

ILLUSTRATED WITH STEEL ENGRAVINGS.

IN THREE VOLUMES.

VOL. I.

1848–1861.

———

" GOVERNMENTS DERIVE THEIR JUST POWERS FROM THE CONSENT OF THE GOVERNED."

———

SECOND EDITION.

SUSAN B. ANTHONY.
ROCHESTER, N. Y.: CHARLES MANN.
LONDON: 25 HENRIETTA STREET, COVENT GARDEN.
PARIS: G. FISCHBACHER, 33 RUE DE SEINE.
1889.

THESE VOLUMES

ARE

AFFECTIONATELY INSCRIBED

TO THE

Memory of

MARY WOLLSTONECRAFT,
FRANCES WRIGHT, LUCRETIA MOTT, HARRIET MARTINEAU, LYDIA MARIA CHILD,
MARGARET FULLER, SARAH AND ANGELINA GRIMKÉ, JOSEPHINE S. GRIFFING,
MARTHA C. WRIGHT, HARRIOT K. HUNT, M.D., MARIANA W. JOHNSON,
ALICE AND PHEBE CAREY, ANN PRESTON, M.D., LYDIA MOTT,
ELIZA W. FARNHAM, LYDIA F. FOWLER, M.D.,
PAULINA WRIGHT DAVIS,

Whose Earnest Lives and Fearless Words, in Demanding
Political Rights for Women, have been,
in the Preparation of these Pages,
a Constant Inspiration

TO

The Editors.

LIST OF ENGRAVINGS.

Vol. I.

PREFACE.

In preparing this work, our object has been to put into permanent shape the few scattered reports of the Woman Suffrage Movement still to be found, and to make it an arsenal of facts for those who are beginning to inquire into the demands and arguments of the leaders of this reform. Although the continued discussion of the political rights of woman during the last thirty years, forms a most important link in the chain of influences tending to her emancipation, no attempt at its history has been made. In giving the inception and progress of this agitation, we who have undertaken the task have been moved by the consideration that many of our co-workers have already fallen asleep, and that in a few years all who could tell the story will have passed away.

In collecting material for these volumes, most of those of whom we solicited facts have expressed themselves deeply interested in our undertaking, and have gladly contributed all they could, feeling that those identified with this reform were better qualified to prepare a faithful history with greater patience and pleasure, than those of another generation possibly could.

A few have replied, "It is too early to write the history of this movement; wait until our object is attained; the actors themselves can not write an impartial history; they have had their discords, divisions, personal hostilities, that unfit them for the work." Viewing the enfranchisement of woman as the most important demand of the century, we have felt no temptation to linger over individual differences. These occur in all associations, and may be regarded in this case as an evidence of the growing self-assertion and individualism in woman.

Woven with the threads of this history, we have given some personal reminiscences and brief biographical sketches. To the few who, through ill-timed humility, have refused to contribute any of their early experiences we would suggest, that as each brick in a magnificent structure might have had no special value alone on the road-side, yet, in combination with many others, its size, position, quality, becomes of vital consequence; so with the actors in any great reform, though they may be of little value in themselves; as a part of a great movement they may be worthy of mention—even important to the completion of an historical record.

To be historians of a reform in which we have been among the chief actors, has its points of embarrassment as well as advantage. Those who fight the battle can best give what all readers like to know—the impelling motives to action; the struggle in the face of opposition; the vexation under ridicule; and the despair in success too long deferred. Moreover, there is an interest in history written from a subjective point of view, that may compensate the reader in this case for any seeming egotism or partiality he may discover. As an autobiography is more interesting than a sketch by another, so is a history written by its actors, as in both cases we get nearer the soul of the subject.

We have finished our task, and we hope the contribution we have made may enable some other hand in the future to write a more complete history of " the most momentous reform that has yet been launched on the world—the first organized protest against the injustice which has brooded over the character and destiny of one-half the human race."

CONTENTS.

(9)

CHAPTER VI.

OHIO.

CHAPTER VII.

REMINISCENCES BY CLARINA I. HOWARD NICHOLS.

CHAPTER VIII.

MASSACHUSETTS.

CHAPTER IX.

INDIANA AND WISCONSIN.

CHAPTER X.

PENNSYLVANIA.

CHAPTER XI.

LUCRETIA MOTT.

CHAPTER XII.

NEW JERSEY.

CHAPTER XIII.

MRS. STANTON'S REMINISCENCES.

CHAPTER XIV.

NEW YORK.

CHAPTER XV.

WOMAN, CHURCH, AND STATE.

INTRODUCTION.

The prolonged slavery of woman is the darkest page in human history. A survey of the condition of the race through those barbarous periods, when physical force governed the world, when the motto, "might makes right," was the law, enables one to account for the origin of woman's subjection to man without referring the fact to the general inferiority of the sex, or Nature's law.

Writers on this question differ as to the cause of the universal degradation of woman in all periods and nations.

One of the greatest minds of the century has thrown a ray of light on this gloomy picture by tracing the origin of woman's slavery to the same principle of selfishness and love of power in man that has thus far dominated all weaker nations and classes. This brings hope of final emancipation, for as all nations and classes are gradually, one after another, asserting and maintaining their independence, the path is clear for woman to follow. The slavish instinct of an oppressed class has led her to toil patiently through the ages, giving all and asking little, cheerfully sharing with man all perils and privations by land and sea, that husband and sons might attain honor and success. Justice and freedom for herself is her latest and highest demand.

Another writer asserts that the tyranny of man over woman has its roots, after all, in his nobler feelings; his love, his chivalry, and his desire to protect woman in the barbarous periods of pillage, lust, and war. But wherever the roots may be traced, the results at this hour are equally disastrous to woman. Her best interests and happiness do not seem to have been consulted in the arrangements made for her protection. She has been bought and sold, caressed and crucified at the will and pleasure of her master. But if a chivalrous desire to protect woman has always been the mainspring of man's dominion over her, it should have prompted him to place in her hands the same weapons of defense he has found to be most effective against wrong and oppression.

It is often asserted that as woman has always been man's slave—subject—inferior—dependent, under all forms of government and religion, slavery must be her normal condition. This might have some weight had not the vast majority of men also been enslaved for centuries to kings and popes, and orders of nobility, who, in the progress of civilization, have reached complete equality. And did we not also see the great changes in woman's condition, the marvelous transformation in her character, from a toy in the Turkish harem, or a drudge in the German fields, to a leader of thought in the literary circles of France, England, and America!

In an age when the wrongs of society are adjusted in the courts and at the ballot-box, material force yields to reason and majorities.

Woman's steady march onward, and her growing desire for a broader outlook, prove that she has not reached her normal condition, and that society has not yet conceded all that is necessary for its attainment.

Moreover, woman's discontent increases in exact proportion to her development. Instead of a feeling of gratitude for rights accorded, the wisest are indignant at the assumption of any legal disability based on sex, and their feelings in this matter are a surer test of what her nature demands, than the feelings and prejudices of the sex claiming to be superior. American men may quiet their consciences with the delusion that no such injustice exists in this country as in Eastern nations, though with the general improvement in our institutions, woman's condition must inevitably have improved also, yet the same principle that degrades her in Turkey, *insults* her in this republic. Custom forbids a woman there to enter a mosque, or call the hour for prayers; here it forbids her a voice in Church Councils or State Legislatures. The same taint of her primitive state of slavery affects both latitudes.

The condition of married women, under the laws of all countries, has been essentially that of slaves, until modified, in some respects, within the last quarter of a century in the United States. The change from the old Common Law of England, in regard to the civil rights of women, from 1848 to the advance legislation in most of the Northern States in 1880, marks an era both in the status of woman as a citizen and in our American system of jurisprudence. When the State of New York gave married women certain rights of property, the individual existence of the wife was recognized, and the old idea that "husband and wife are one, and that one the husband," received its death-blow. From that hour the statutes of the several States have been steadily diverging from the old English codes. Most of the Western States copied the advance legislation of New York, and some are now even more liberal.

The broader demand for political rights has not commanded the thought its merits and dignity should have secured. While complaining of many wrongs and oppressions, women themselves did not see that the political disability of sex was the cause of all their special grievances, and that to secure equality anywhere, it must be recognized everywhere. Like all disfranchised classes, they begun by asking to have certain wrongs redressed, and not by asserting their own right to make laws for themselves.

Overburdened with cares in the isolated home, women had not the time, education, opportunity, and pecuniary independence to put their thoughts clearly and concisely into propositions, nor the courage to compare their opinions with one another, nor to publish them, to any great extent, to the world.

It requires philosophy and heroism to rise above the opinion of the wise men of all nations and races, that to be *unknown*, is the highest testimonial woman can have to her virtue, delicacy and refinement.

A certain odium has ever rested on those who have risen above the conventional level and sought new spheres for thought and action, and especially on the few who demand complete equality in political rights. The leaders in this movement have been women of superior mental and physical organization, of good social standing and education, remarkable alike for their domestic virtues, knowledge of public affairs, and rare executive ability; good speakers and writers, inspiring and conducting the genuine reforms of the day; everywhere exerting themselves to promote the best interests of society; yet they have been uniformly ridiculed, misrepresented, and denounced in public and private by all classes of society.

Woman's political equality with man is the legitimate outgrowth of the fundamental principles of our Government, clearly set forth in the Declaration of Independence in 1776, in the United States Constitution adopted in 1784, in the prolonged debates on the origin of human rights in the anti-slavery conflict in 1840, and in the more recent discussions of the party in power since 1865, on the 13th, 14th, and 15th Amendments to the National Constitution; and the majority of our leading statesmen have taken the ground that suffrage is a natural right that may be regulated, but can not be abolished by State law.

Under the influence of these liberal principles of republicanism that pervades all classes of American minds, however vaguely, if suddenly called out, they might be stated, woman readily perceives the anomalous position she occupies in a republic, where the government and religion alike are based on individual conscience and judgment—where the natural rights of all citizens have been exhaustively discussed, and repeatedly declared equal.

From the inauguration of the government, representative women have expostulated against the inconsistencies between our principles and practices as a nation. Beginning with special grievances, woman's protests soon took a larger scope. Having petitioned State legislatures to change the statutes that robbed her of children, wages, and property, she demanded that the Constitutions—State and National—be so amended as to give her a voice in the laws, a choice in the rulers, and protection in the exercise of her rights as a citizen of the United States.

While the laws affecting woman's civil rights have been greatly improved during the past thirty years, the political demand has made but a questionable progress, though it must be counted as the chief influence in modifying the laws. The selfishness of man was readily enlisted in securing woman's civil rights, while the same element in his character antagonized her demand for political equality.

Fathers who had estates to bequeath to their daughters could see the advantage of securing to woman certain property rights that might limit the legal power of profligate husbands.

Husbands in extensive business operations could see the advantage of allowing the wife the right to hold separate property, settled on her in time of prosperity, that might not be seized for his debts. Hence in the several States able men championed these early measures. But political rights, involving in their last results equality everywhere, roused all the antagonism of a dominant power, against the self-assertion of a class hitherto subservient. Men saw that with political equality for woman, they could no longer keep her in social subordination, and "the majority of the male sex," says John Stuart Mill, "can not yet tolerate the idea of living with an equal." The fear of a social revolution thus complicated the discussion. The Church, too, took alarm, knowing that with the freedom and education acquired in becoming a component part of the Government, woman would not only outgrow the power of the priesthood, and religious superstitions, but would also invade the pulpit, interpret the Bible anew from her own stand-point, and claim an equal voice in all ecclesiastical councils. With fierce warnings and denunciations from the pulpit, and false interpretations of Scripture, women have been intimidated and misled, and their religious feelings have been played upon for their more complete subjugation. While the general principles of the Bible are in favor of the most enlarged freedom and equality of the race, isolated texts have been used to block the wheels of progress in all periods; thus bigots have defended capital punishment, intemperance, slavery, polygamy, and the subjection of woman. The creeds of all nations make obedience to man the corner-stone of her religious character. Fortunately, however, more liberal minds are now giving us higher and purer expositions of the Scriptures.

As the social and religious objections appeared against the demand for political rights, the discussion became many-sided, contradictory, and as varied as the idiosyncrasies of individual character. Some said, " Man is woman's natural protector, and she can safely trust him to make laws for her." She might with fairness reply, as he uniformly robbed her of all property rights to 1848, he can not safely be trusted with her personal rights in 1880, though the fact that he did make some restitution at last, might modify her distrust in the future. However, the calendars of our courts still show that fathers deal unjustly with daughters, husbands with wives, brothers with sisters, and sons with their own mothers. Though woman needs the protection of one man against his whole sex, in pioneer life, in threading her way through a lonely forest, on the highway, or in the streets of the metropolis on a dark night, she sometimes needs, too, the protection of all men against this one. But even if she could be sure, as she is not, of the ever-present, all-protecting power of one strong arm, that would be weak indeed compared with the subtle, all-pervading influence of just and equal laws for all women. Hence woman's need of the ballot, that she may hold in her own right hand the weapon of self-protection and self-defense.

Again it is said: " The women who make the demand are few in number, and their feelings and opinions are abnormal, and therefore of no weight in considering the aggregate judgment on the question." The number is larger than appears on the surface, for the fear of public ridicule, and the loss of private favors from those who shelter, feed, and clothe them, withhold many from declaring their opinions and demanding their rights. The ignorance and indifference of the majority of women, as to their status as citizens of a republic, is not remarkable, for history shows that the masses of all oppressed classes, in the most degraded conditions, have been stolid and apathetic until partial success had crowned the faith and enthusiasm of the few.

The insurrections on Southern plantations were always defeated

2

by the doubt and duplicity of the slaves themselves. That little band of heroes who precipitated the American Revolution in 1776 were so ostracised that they walked the streets with bowed heads, from a sense of loneliness and apprehension. Woman's apathy to the wrongs of her sex, instead of being a plea for her remaining in her present condition, is the strongest argument against it. How completely demoralized by her subjection must she be, who does not feel her personal dignity assailed when all women are ranked in every State Constitution with idiots, lunatics, criminals, and minors; when in the name of Justice, man holds one scale for woman, another for himself; when by the spirit and letter of the laws she is made responsible for crimes committed against her, while the male criminal goes free; when from altars where she worhips no woman may preach; when in the courts, where girls of tender age may be arraigned for the crime of infanticide, she may not plead for the most miserable of her sex; when colleges she is taxed to build and endow, deny her the right to share in their advantages; when she finds that which should be her glory—her possible motherhood—treated everywhere by man as a disability and a crime! A woman insensible to such indignities needs some transformation into nobler thought, some purer atmosphere to breathe, some higher stand-point from which to study human rights.

It is said, " the difference between.the sexes indicates different spheres." It would be nearer the truth to say the difference indicates different duties in the same sphere, seeing that man and woman were evidently made for each other, and have shown equal capacity in the ordinary range of human duties. In governing nations, leading armies, piloting ships across the sea, rowing life-boats in terrific gales; in art, science, invention, literature, woman has proved herself the complement of man in the world of thought and action. This difference does not compel us to spread our tables with different food for man and woman, nor to provide in our common schools a different course of study for boys and girls. Sex pervades all nature, yet the male and female tree and vine and shrub rejoice in the same sunshine and shade. The earth and air are free to all the fruits and flowers, yet each absorbs what best ensures its growth. But whatever it is, it requires no special watchfulness on our part to see that it is maintained. This plea, when closely analyzed, is generally found to mean woman's inferiority.

The superiority of man, however, does not enter into the demand for suffrage, for in this country all men vote; and as the lower orders of men are not superior, either by nature or grace, to the higher orders of women, they must hold and exercise the right of self-government on some other ground than superiority to women.

Again it is said, " Woman when independent and self-asserting will lose her influence over man." In the happiest conditions in life, men and women will ever be mutually dependent on each other. The complete development of all woman's powers will not make her less capable of steadfast love and friendship, but give her new strength to meet the emergencies of life, to aid those who look to her for counsel and support. Men are uniformly more attentive to women of rank, family, and fortune, who least need their care, than to any other class. We do not see their protecting love generally extending to the helpless and unfortunate ones of earth. Wherever the skilled hands and cultured brain of woman have made the battle of life easier for man, he has readily pardoned her sound judgment and proper self-assertion. But the prejudices and preferences of man should be a secondary consideration, in presence of the individual happiness and freedom of woman. The formation of her character and its influence on the human race, is a larger question than man's personal liking. There is no fear, however, that when a superior order of women shall grace the earth, there will not be an order of men to match them, and influence over such minds will atone for the loss of it elsewhere.

An honest fear is sometimes expressed " that woman would degrade politics, and politics would degrade woman." As the influence of woman has been uniformly elevating in new civilizations, in missionary work in heathen nations, in schools, colleges, literature, and in general society, it is fair to suppose that politics would prove no exception. On the other hand, as the art of government is the most exalted of all sciences, and statesmanship requires the highest order of mind, the ennobling and refining influence of such pursuits must elevate rather than degrade woman. When politics degenerate into bitter persecutions and vulgar court-gossip, they are degrading to man, and his honor, virtue, dignity, and refinement are as valuable to woman as her virtues are to him.

Again, it is said, " Those who make laws must execute them ; government needs force behind it,—a woman could not be sheriff or a policeman." She might not fill these offices in the way men do, but she might far more effectively guard the morals of society, and the sanitary conditions of our cities. It might with equal force be said that a woman of culture and artistic taste can not keep house, because she can not wash and iron with her own hands, and clean the range and furnace. At the head of the police, a woman could direct her forces and keep order without ever using a baton or a pistol in her own hands. "The elements of sovereignty," says Blackstone, "are three: wisdom, goodness, and power." Conceding to woman wisdom and goodness, as they are not strictly masculine virtues, and substituting moral power for physical force, we have the necessary elements of government for most of life's emergencies. Women manage families, mixed schools, charitable institutions, large boarding-houses and hotels, farms and steam-engines, drunken and disorderly men and women, and stop street fights, as well as men do. The queens in history compare favorably with the kings.

But, "in the settlement of national difficulties," it is said, "the last resort is war; shall we summon our wives and mothers to the battle-field?" Women have led armies in all ages, have held positions in the army and navy for years in disguise. Some fought, bled, and died on the battle-field in our late war. They performed severe labors in the hospitals and sanitary department. Wisdom would dictate a division of labor in war as well as in peace, assigning each their appropriate department.

Numerous classes of men who enjoy their political rights are exempt from military duty. All men over forty-five, all who suffer mental or physical disability, such as the loss of an eye or a fore-finger; clergymen, physicians, Quakers, school-teachers, professors, and presidents of colleges, judges, legislators, congressmen, State prison officials, and all county, State and National officers; fathers, brothers, or sons having certain relatives dependent on them for support,—all of these summed up in every State in the Union make millions of voters thus exempted.

In view of this fact there is no force in the plea, that "if women vote they must fight." Moreover, war is not the normal state of the human family in its higher development, but merely a feature of barbarism lasting on through the transition of the race, from the savage to the scholar. When England and America settled the *Alabama* Claims by the Geneva Arbitration, they pointed the way for the future adjustment of all national difficulties.

Some fear, "If women assume all the duties political equality implies, that the time and attention necessary to the duties of home life will be absorbed in the affairs of State." The act of voting occupies but little time in itself, and the vast majority of women will attend to their family and social affairs to the neglect of the State, just as men do to their individual interests. The virtue of patriotism is subordinate in most souls to individual and family aggrandizement. As to offices, it is not to be supposed that the class of men now elected will resign to women their chances, and if they should to any extent, the necessary number of women to fill the offices would make no apparent change in our social circles. If, for example, the Senate of the United States should be entirely composed of women, but two in each State would be withdrawn from the pursuit of domestic happiness. For many reasons, under all circumstances, a comparatively smaller proportion of women than men would actively engage in politics.

As the power to extend or limit the suffrage rests now wholly in the hands of man, he can commence the experiment with as small a number as he sees fit, by requiring any lawful qualification. Men were admitted on property and educational qualifications in most of the States, at one time, and still are in some—so hard has it been for man to understand the theory of self-government. Three-fourths of the women would be thus disqualified, and the remaining fourth would be too small a minority to precipitate a social revolution or defeat masculine measures in the halls of legislation, even if women were a unit on all questions and invariably voted together, which they would not. In this view, the path of duty is plain for the prompt action of those gentlemen who fear universal suffrage for women, but are willing to grant it on property and educational qualifications. While those who are governed by the law of expediency should give the measure of justice they deem safe, let those who trust the absolute right proclaim the higher principle in government, " equal rights to all."

Many seeming obstacles in the way of woman's enfranchisement will be surmounted by reforms in many directions. Co-operative labor and co-operative homes will remove many difficulties in the way of woman's success as artisan and housekeeper, when admitted to the governing power. The varied forms of progress, like parallel lines, move forward simultaneously in the same direction. Each reform, at its inception, seems out of joint with all its surroundings ; but the discussion changes the conditions, and brings them in line with the new idea.

The isolated household is responsible for a large share of woman's ignorance and degradation. A mind always in contact with children and servants, whose aspirations and ambitions rise no higher than the roof that shelters it, is necessarily dwarfed in its proportions. The advantages to the few whose fortunes enable them to make the isolated household a more successful experiment, can not outweigh the difficulties of the many who are wholly sacrificed to its maintenance.

Quite as many false ideas prevail as to woman's true position in the home as to her status elsewhere. Womanhood is the great fact in her life; wifehood and motherhood are but incidental relations. Governments legislate for men; we do not have one code for bachelors, another for husbands and fathers; neither have the social relations of women any significance in their demands for civil and political rights. Custom and philosophy, in regard to woman's happiness, are alike based on the idea that her strongest social sentiment is love of children; that in this relation her soul finds complete satisfaction. But the love of offspring, common to all orders of women and all forms of animal life, tender and beautiful as it is, can not as a sentiment rank with conjugal love. The one calls out only the negative virtues that belong to apathetic classes, such as patience, endurance, self-sacrifice, exhausting the brain-forces, ever giving, asking nothing in return; the other, the outgrowth of the two supreme powers in nature, the positive and negative magnetism, the centrifugal and centripetal forces, the masculine and feminine elements, possessing the divine power of creation, in the universe of thought and action. Two pure souls fused into one by an impassioned love—friends, counselors—a mutual support and inspiration to each other amid life's struggles, must know the highest human happiness;—this is marriage; and this is the only cornerstone of an enduring home. Neither does ordinary motherhood, assumed without any high purpose or preparation, compare in sentiment with the lofty ambition and conscientious devotion of the artist whose pure children of the brain in poetry, painting, music, and science are ever beckoning her upward into an ideal world of beauty. They who give the world a true philosophy, a grand poem, a beautiful painting or statue, or can tell the story of every wandering star; a George Eliot, a Rosa Bonheur, an Elizabeth Barrett Browning, a Maria Mitchell—whose blood has flowed to the higher arches of the brain,—have lived to a holier purpose than they whose children are of the flesh alone, into whose minds they have breathed no clear perceptions of great principles, no moral aspiration, no spiritual life.

Her rights are as completely ignored in what is adjudged to be woman's sphere as out of it; the woman is uniformly sacrificed to the wife and mother. Neither law, gospel, public sentiment, nor domestic affection shield her from excessive and enforced maternity, depleting alike to mother and child;—all opportunity for mental improvement, health, happiness—yea, life itself, being ruthlessly sacrificed. The weazen, weary, withered, narrow-minded wife—

mother of half a dozen children—her interests all centering at her fireside, forms a painful contrast in many a household to the liberal, genial, brilliant, cultured husband in the zenith of his power, who has never given one thought to the higher life, liberty, and happiness of the woman by his side; believing her self-abnegation to be Nature's law.

It is often asked, "if political equality would not rouse antagonisms between the sexes?" If it could be proved that men and women had been harmonious in all ages and countries, and that women were happy and satisfied in their slavery, one might hesitate in proposing any change whatever. But the apathy, the helpless, hopeless resignation of a subjected class can not be called happiness. The more complete the despotism, the more smoothly all things move on the surface. "Order reigns in Warsaw." In right conditions, the interests of man and woman are essentially one; but in false conditions, they must ever be opposed. The principle of equality of rights underlies all human sentiments, and its assertion by any individual or class must rouse antagonism, unless conceded. This has been the battle of the ages, and will be until all forms of slavery are banished from the earth. Philosophers, historians, poets, novelists, alike paint woman the victim ever of man's power and selfishness. And now all writers on Eastern civilization tell us, the one insurmountable obstacle to the improvement of society in those countries, is the ignorance and superstition of the women. Stronger than the trammels of custom and law, is her religion, which teaches that her condition is Heaven-ordained. As the most ignorant minds cling with the greatest tenacity to the dogmas and traditions of their faith, a reform that involves an attack on that stronghold can only be carried by the education of another generation. Hence the self-assertion, the antagonism, the rebellion of woman, so much deplored in England and the United States, is the hope of our higher civilization. A woman growing up under American ideas of liberty in government and religion, having never blushed behind a Turkish mask, nor pressed her feet in Chinese shoes, can not brook any disabilities based on sex alone, without a deep feeling of antagonism with the power that creates it. The change needed to restore good feeling can not be reached by remanding woman to the spinning-wheel, and the contentment of her grandmother, but by conceding to her every right which the spirit of the age demands. Modern inventions have banished the spinning-wheel, and the same law of progress makes the woman of to-day a different woman from her grandmother.

With these brief replies to the oft-repeated objections made by the opposition, we hope to rouse new thoughts in minds prepared to receive them. That equal rights for woman have not long ago been secured, is due to causes beyond the control of the actors in this reform. " The success of a movement," says Lecky, " depends much less upon the force of its arguments, or upon the ability of its advocates, than the predisposition of society to receive it."

CHAPTER I.

As civilization advances there is a continual change in the standard of human rights. In barbarous ages the right of the strongest was the only one recognized ; but as mankind progressed in the arts and sciences intellect began to triumph over brute force. Change is a law of life, and the development of society a natural growth. Although to this law we owe the discoveries of unknown worlds, the inventions of machinery, swifter modes of travel, and clearer ideas as to the value of human life and thought, yet each successive change has met with the most determined opposition. Fortunately, progress is not the result of pre-arranged plans of individuals, but is born of a fortuitous combination of circumstances that compel certain results, overcoming the natural inertia of mankind. There is a certain enjoyment in habitual sluggishness ; in rising each morning with the same ideas as the night before ; in retiring each night with the thoughts of the morning. This inertia of mind and body has ever held the multitude in chains. Thousands have thus surrendered their most sacred rights of conscience. In all periods of human development, thinking has been punished as a crime, which is reason sufficient to account for the general passive resignation of the masses to their conditions and evironments.

Again, " subjection to the powers that be " has been the lesson of both Church and State, throttling science, checking invention, crushing free thought, persecuting and torturing those who have dared to speak or act outside of established authority. Anathemas and the stake have upheld the Church, banishment and the scaffold the throne, and the freedom of mankind has ever been sacrificed to the idea of protection. So entirely has the human will been enslaved in all classes of society in the past, that monarchs have humbled themselves to popes, nations have knelt at the feet of monarchs, and individuals have sold themselves to others under the subtle promise of " protection "—a word that simply means release from all responsibility, all use of one's own faculties—a word that has ever blinded people to its true significance. Under authority and this false promise of " protection," self-reliance, the first incentive to freedom, has not only been lost, but the aversion of mankind for responsibility has been fostered by the few, whose greater bodily strength, superior intellect, or the inherent law of self-development has impelled to active exertion. Obedience and self-sacrifice—the virtues prescribed for subordinate classes, and which naturally grow out of their condition—are alike opposed to the theory of individual rights and self-government. But as even the inertia of mankind is not proof against the internal law of progress, certain beliefs have been inculcated, certain crimes invented, in order to intimidate the masses. Hence, the Church made free thought the worst of sins, and the spirit of inquiry the worst of blasphemies ; while the State proclaimed her temporal power of divine origin, and all rebellion high treason alike to God and the king, to be speedily and severely punished. In this union of Church and State mankind touched the lowest depth of degradation. As late as the time of Bunyan the chief doctrine inculcated from the pulpit was obedience to the temporal power.

All these influences fell with crushing weight on woman ; more sensitive, helpless, and imaginative, she suffered a thousand fears and wrongs where man did one. Lecky, in his " History of Rationalism in Europe," shows that the vast majority of the victims of fanaticism and witchcraft, burned, drowned, and tortured, were women. Guizot, in his " History of Civilization," while decrying the influence of caste in India, and deploring it as the result of barbarism, thanks God there is no system of caste in Europe ; ignoring the fact that in all its dire and baneful effects, the caste of sex everywhere exists, creating diverse codes of morals for men and women, diverse penalties for crime, diverse industries, diverse religions and educational rights, and diverse relations to the Government. Men are the Brahmins, women the Pariahs, under our existing civilization. Herbert Spencer's " Descriptive Sociology of England," an epitome of English history, says : " Our laws are based on the all-sufficiency of man's rights, and society exists to-day for woman only in so far as she is in the keeping of some man." Thus society, including our systems of jurisprudence, civil and political theories, trade, commerce, education, religion, friendships, and family life, have all been framed on the sole idea of man's rights. Hence, he takes upon himself the responsibility of directing and controlling the powers of woman, under that all-sufficient excuse of tyranny, " divine right." This same cry of divine authority created the castes of India ; has for ages separated its people into bodies, with different industrial, educational, civil, religious, and political rights ; has maintained this separation for the benefit of the superior class, and sedulously taught the doctrine that any change in existing conditions would be a sin of most direful magnitude.

The opposition of theologians, though first to be exhibited when any change is proposed, for reason that change not only takes power from them, but lessens the reverence of mankind for them, is not in its final result so much to be feared as the opposition of those holding political power. The Church, knowing this, has in all ages aimed to connect itself with the State. Political freedom guarantees religious liberty, freedom to worship God according to the dictates of one's own conscience, fosters a spirit of inquiry, creates self-reliance, induces a feeling of responsibility.

The people who demand authority for every thought and action, who look to others for wisdom and protection, are those who perpetuate tyranny. The thinkers and actors who find their authority within, are those who inaugurate freedom. Obedience to outside authority to which woman has everywhere been trained, has not only dwarfed her capacity, but made her a retarding force in civilization, recognized at last by statesmen as a dangerous element to free institutions. A recent writer, speaking of Turkey, says : " All attempts for the improvement of that nation must prove futile, owing to the degradation of its women ; and their elevation is hopeless so long as they are taught by their religion that their condition is ordained of heaven." Gladstone, in one of his pamphlets on the revival of Catholicism in England, says : " The spread of this religion is due, as might be expected, to woman ; " thus conceding in both cases her power to block the wheels of progress. Hence, in the scientific education of woman, in the training of her faculties to independent thought and logical reasoning, lies the hope of the future.

The two great sources of progress are intellect and wealth. Both represent power, and are the elements of success in life. Education frees the mind from the bondage of authority and makes the individual self-asserting. Remunerative industry is the means of securing to its possessor wealth and education, transforming the laborer to the capitalist. Work in itself is not power; it is but the means to an end. The slave is not benefited by his industry ; he does not receive the results of his toil ; his labor enriches another— adds to the power of his master to bind his chain still closer. Although woman has performed much of the labor of the world, her industry and economy have been the very means of increasing her degradation. Not being free, the results of her labor have gone to build up and sustain the very class that has perpetuated this injustice. Even in the family, where we should naturally look for the truest conditions, woman has always been robbed of the fruits of her own toil. The influence the Catholic Church has had on religious free thought, that monarchies have had on political free thought, that serfdom has had upon free labor, have all been cumulative in the family upon woman. Taught that father and husband stood to her in the place of God, she has been denied liberty of conscience, and held in obedience to masculine will. Taught that the fruits of her industry belonged to others, she has seen man enter into every avocation most suitable to her, while she, the uncomplaining drudge of the household, condemned to the severest labor, has been systematically robbed of her earnings, which have gone to build up her master's power, and she has found herself in the condition of the slave, deprived of the results of her own labor. Taught that education for her was indelicate and irreligious, she has been kept in such gross ignorance as to fall a prey to superstition, and to glory in her own degradation. Taught that a low voice is an excellent thing in woman, she has been trained to a subjugation of the vocal organs, and thus lost the benefit of loud tones and their well-known invigoration of the system. Forbidden to run, climb, or jump, her muscles have been weakened, and her strength deteriorated. Confined most of the time to the house, she has neither as strong lungs nor as vigorous a digestion as her brother. Forbidden to enter the pulpit, she has been trained to an unquestioning reverence for theological authority and false belief upon the most vital interests of religion. Forbidden the medical profession, she has at the most sacred times of her life been left to the ignorant supervision of male physicians, and seen her young children die by thousands. Forbidden to enter the courts, she has seen her sex unjustly tried and condemned for crimes men were incapable of judging.

Woman has been the great unpaid laborer of the world, and although within the last two decades a vast number of new employments have been opened to her, statistics prove that in the great majority of these, she is not paid according to the value of the work done, but according to sex. The opening of all industries to woman, and the wage question as connected with her, are most subtle and profound questions of political economy, closely interwoven with the rights of self-government.

The revival of learning had its influence upon woman, and we find in the early part of the fourteenth century a decided tendency toward a recognition of her equality. Christine of Pisa, the most eminent woman of this period, supported a family of six persons by her pen, taking high ground on the conservation of morals in opposition to the general licentious spirit of the age. Margaret of Angoulême, the brilliant Queen of Navarre, was a voluminous writer, her Heptaméron rising to the dignity of a French classic. A paper in the *Revue des Deux Mondes*, a few years since, by M. Henri Baudrillart, upon the "Emancipation of Woman," recalls the fact that for nearly four hundred years, men, too, have been ardent believers in equal rights for woman.

In 1509, Cornelius Agrippa, a great literary authority of his time, published a work of this character. Agrippa was not content with claiming woman's equality, but in a work of thirty chapters devoted himself to proving "the superiority of woman." In less than fifty years (1552) Ruscelli brought out a similar work based on the Platonic Philosophy. In 1599, Anthony Gibson wrote a book which in the prolix phraseology of the times was called, "A Woman's Worth defended against all the Men in the World, proving to be more Perfect, Excellent, and Absolute, in all Virtuous Actions, than any man of What Quality Soever." While these sturdy male defenders of the rights of woman met with many opponents, some going so far as to assert that women were beings not endowed with reason, they were sustained by many vigorous writers among women. Italy, then the foremost literary country of Europe, possessed many women of learning, one of whom, Lucrezia Morinella, a Venetian lady, wrote a work entitled, "The Nobleness and Excellence of Women, together with the Faults and Imperfections of Men."

The seventeenth century gave birth to many essays and books of a like character, not confined to the laity, as several friars wrote upon the same subject. In 1696, Daniel De Foe wished to have an institute founded for the better education of young women. He said: "We reproach the sex every day for folly and impertinence, while I am confident had they the advantages of education equal to us, they would be guilty of less than ourselves." Alexander's History of Women, John Paul Ribera's work upon Women, the two huge quartos of De Costa upon the same subject, Count Ségur's "Women: Their Condition and Influence," and many other works showed the drift of the new age.

The Reformation, that great revolution in religious thought, loosened the grasp of the Church upon woman, and is to be looked upon as one of the most important steps in this reform. In the reign of Elizabeth, England was called the Paradise of Women When Elizabeth ascended the throne, it was not only as queen, but she succeeded her father as the head of the newly-formed rebellious Church, and she held firm grasp on both Church and State during the long years of her reign, bending alike priest and prelate to her fiery will. The reign of Queen Anne, called the Golden Age of English Literature, is especially noticeable on account of Mary Astell and Elizabeth Elstob. The latter, speaking nine languages, was most famous for her skill in the Saxon tongue. She also replied to current objections made to woman's learning. Mary Astell elaborated a plan for a Woman's College, which was favorably received by Queen Anne, and would have been carried out, but for the opposition of Bishop Burnett.

During the latter part of the eighteenth century, there were public discussions by women in England, under the general head of Female Parliament. These discussions took wide range, touching upon the entrance of men into those industries usually assigned to women, and demanding for themselves higher educational advantages, and the right to vote at elections, and to be returned members of Parliament.

The American Revolution, that great political rebellion of the ages, was based upon the inherent rights of the individual. Perhaps in none but English Colonies, by descendants of English parents, could such a revolution have been consummated. England had never felt the bonds of feudalism to the extent of many countries; its people had defied its monarchs and wrested from them many civil rights, rights which protected women as well as men, and although its common law, warped by ecclesiasticism, expended its chief rigors upon women, yet at an early day they enjoyed certain ecclesiastical and political powers unknown to women elsewhere. Before the Conquest, abbesses sat in councils of the Church and signed its decrees; while kings were even dependent upon their consent in granting certain charters. The synod of Whitby, in the ninth century, was held in the convent of the Abbess Hilda, she herself presiding over its deliberations. The famous prophetess of Kent at one period communicated the orders of Heaven to the Pope himself. Ladies of birth and quality sat in council with the Saxon Witas—*i. e.*, wise men—taking part in the Witenagemot, the great National Council of our Saxon ancestors in England. In the seventh century this National Council met at Baghamstead to enact a new code of laws, the queen, abbesses, and many ladies of quality taking part and signing the decrees. Passing by other similar instances, we find in the reign of Henry III. that four women took seats in Parliament, and in the reign of Edward I. ten ladies were called to Parliament, while in the thirteenth century, Queen Elinor became keeper of the Great Seal, sitting as Lord Chancellor in the *Aula Regia*, the highest court of the Kingdom. Running back two or three centuries before the Christian era, we find Martia, her seat of power in London, holding the reins of government so wisely as to receive the surname of Proba, the Just. She especially devoted herself to the enactment of just laws for her subjects, the first principles of the common law tracing back to her; the celebrated laws of Alfred, and of Edward the Confessor, being in great degree restorations and compilations from the laws of Martia, which were known as the "Martian Statutes."

When the American colonies began their resistance to English tyranny, the women—all this inherited tendency to freedom surging in their veins—were as active, earnest, determined, and self-sacrificing as the men, and although, as Mrs. Ellet in her " Women of the Revolution" remarks, "political history says but little, and that vaguely and incidentally, of the women who bore their part in the revolution," yet that little shows woman to have been endowed with as lofty a patriotism as man, and to have as fully understood the principles upon which the struggle was based. Among the women who manifested deep political insight, were Mercy Otis Warren, Abigail Smith Adams, and Hannah Lee Corbin; all closely related to the foremost men of the Revolution. Mrs. Warren was a sister of James Otis, whose fiery words did so much to arouse and intensify the feelings of the colonists against British aggression. This brother and sister were united to the end of their lives in a friendship rendered firm and enduring by the similarity of their intellects and political views. The home of Mrs. Warren was the resort of patriotic spirits and the headquarters of the rebellion. She herself wrote, " By the Plymouth fireside were many political plans organized, discussed, and digested." Her correspondence with eminent men of the Revolution was extensive and belongs to the history of the country. She was the first one who based the struggle upon " inherent rights," a phrase afterward made the corner-stone of political authority. Mrs. Warren asserted that " 'inherent rights' belonged to all mankind, and had been conferred on all by the God of nations." She numbered Jefferson among her correspondents, and the Declaration of Independence shows the influence of her mind. Among others who sought her counsel upon political matters were Samuel and John Adams, Dickinson, that pure patriot of Pennsylvania, Jefferson, Gerry, and Knox. She was the first person who counseled separation and pressed those views upon John Adams, when he sought her advice before the opening of the first Congress. At that time even Washington had no thought of the final independence of the colonies, emphatically denying such intention or desire on their part, and John Adams was shunned in the streets of Philadelphia for having dared to hint such a possibility. Mrs. Warren sustained his sinking courage and urged him to bolder steps. Her advice was not only sought in every emergency, but political parties found their arguments in her conversation. Mrs. Warren looked not to the freedom of man alone, but to that of her own sex also.

England itself had at least one woman who watched the struggle of America with lively interest, and whose writings aided in the dissemination of republican ideas. This was the celebrated Catharine Sawbridge Macaulay, one of the greatest minds England has ever produced—a woman so noted for her republican ideas that after her death a statue was erected to her as the "Patroness of Liberty." During the whole of the Revolutionary period, Washington was in correspondence with Mrs. Macaulay, who did much to sustain him during those days of trial. She and Mrs. Warren were also correspondents at that time. She wrote several works of a republican character, for home influence; among these, in 1775, "An Address to the people of England, Scotland, and Ireland, on the present Important Crisis of Affairs," designed to show the justice of the American cause. The gratitude Americans feel toward Edmund Burke for his aid, might well be extended to Mrs. Macaulay.

Abigail Smith Adams, the wife of John Adams, was an American woman whose political insight was worthy of remark. She early protested against the formation of a new government in which woman should be unrecognized, demanding for her a voice and representation. She was the first American woman who threatened rebellion unless the rights of her sex were secured. In March, 1776, she wrote to her husband, then in the Continental Congress, "I long to hear you have declared an independency, and, by the way, in the new code of laws which I suppose it will be necessary for you to make, I desire you would remember the ladies, and be more generous and favorable to them than your ancestors. Do not put such unlimited power into the hands of husbands. Remember, all men would be tyrants if they could. If particular care and attention are not paid to the ladies, we are determined to foment a rebellion, and will not hold ourselves bound to obey any laws in which we have no voice or representation." Again and again did Mrs. Adams urge the establishment of an independency and the limitation of man's power over woman, declaring all arbitrary power dangerous and tending to revolution. Nor was she less mindful of equal advantages of education. " If you complain of education in sons, what shall I say in regard to daughters, who every day experience the want of it?" She expressed a strong wish that the new Constitution might be distinguished for its encouragement of learning and virtue. Nothing more fully shows the dependent condition of a class than the methods used to secure their wishes. Mrs. Adams felt herself obliged to appeal to masculine selfishness in showing the reflex action woman's education would have upon man. "If," said she, "we mean to have heroes, statesmen, and philosophers, we should have learned women." Thus did the Revolutionary Mothers urge the recognition of equal rights when the Government was in the process of formation. Although the first plot of ground in the United States for a public school had been given by a woman (Bridget Graffort), in 1700, her sex were denied admission. Mrs. Adams, as well as her friend Mrs. Warren, had in their own persons felt the deprivations of early educational advantages. The boasted public school system of Massachusetts, created for boys only, opened at last its doors to girls, merely to secure its share of public money. The women of the South, too, early demanded political equality. The counties of Mecklenberg and Rowan, North Carolina, were famous for the patriotism of their women. Mecklenberg claims to have issued the first declaration of independence, and, at the centennial celebration of this event in May, 1875, proudly accepted for itself the derisive name given this region by Tarleton's officers, "The Hornet's Nest of America." This name—first bestowed by British officers upon Mrs. Brevard's mansion, then Tarleton's headquarters, where that lady's fiery patriotism and stinging wit discomfited this General in many a sally— was at last held to include the whole county. In 1778, only two years after the Declaration of Independence was adopted, and while the flames of war were still spreading over the country, Hannah Lee Corbin, of Virginia, the sister of General Richard Henry Lee, wrote him, protesting against the taxation of women unless they were allowed to vote. He replied that " women were already possessed of that right," thus recognizing the fact of woman's enfranchisement as one of the results of the new government, and it is on record that women in Virginia did at an early day exercise the right of voting. New Jersey also specifically secured this right to women on the 2d of July, 1776—a right exercised by them for more than a third of a century. Thus our country started into governmental life freighted with the protests of the Revolutionary Mothers against being ruled without their consent. From that hour to the present, women have been con-

3

tinually raising their voices against political tyranny, and demanding for themselves equality of opportunity in every department of life.

In 1790, Mary Wollstonecraft's "Vindication of the Rights of Women," published in London, attracted much attention from liberal minds. She examined the position of woman in the light of existing civilizations, and demanded for her the widest opportunities of education, industry, political knowledge, and the right of representation. Although her work is filled with maxims of the highest morality and purest wisdom, it called forth such violent abuse, that her husband appealed for her from the judgment of her contemporaries to that of mankind. So exalted were her ideas of woman, so comprehensive her view of life, that Margaret Fuller, in referring to her, said : " Mary Wollstonecraft—a woman whose existence proved the need of some new interpretation of woman's rights, belonging to that class who by birth find themselves in places so narrow that, by breaking bonds, they become outlaws." Following her, came Jane Marcet, Eliza Lynn, and Harriet Martineau—each of whom in the early part of the nineteenth century, exerted a decided influence upon the political thought of England. Mrs. Marcet was one of the most scientific and highly cultivated persons of the age. Her "Conversations on Chemistry," familiarized that science both in England and America, and from it various male writers filched their ideas. It was a text-book in this country for many years. Over one hundred and sixty thousand copies were sold, though the fact that this work emanated from the brain of a woman was carefully withheld. Mrs. Marcet also wrote upon political economy, and was the first person who made the subject comprehensive to the popular mind. Her manner of treating it was so clear and vivid, that the public, to whom it had been a hidden science, were able to grasp the subject. Her writings were the inspiration of Harriet Martineau, who followed her in the same department of thought at a later period. Miss Martineau was a remarkable woman. Besides her numerous books on political economy, she was a regular contributor to the London *Daily News*, the second paper in circulation in England, for many years writing five long articles weekly, also to Dickens' *Household Words*, and the *Westminster Review*. She saw clearly the spirit and purpose of the Anti-Slavery Movement in this country, and was a regular contributor to the *National Anti-Slavery Standard*, published in New York. Eliza Lynn, an Irish lady, was at this time writing leading editorials for political papers. In Russia, Catharine II., the absolute and irresponsible ruler of that vast nation, gave utterance to views, of which, says La Harpe, the revolutionists of France

and America fondly thought themselves the originators. She caused her grandchildren to be educated into the most liberal ideas, and Russia was at one time the only country in Europe where political refugees could find safety. To Catharine, Russia is indebted for the first proposition to enfranchise the serfs, but meeting strong opposition she was obliged to relinquish this idea, which was carried to fruition by her great-grandson, Alexander.

This period of the eighteenth century was famous for the executions of women on account of their radical political opinions, Madame Roland, the leader of the liberal party in France, going to the guillotine with the now famous words upon her lips, " Oh, Liberty, what crimes are committed in thy name ! " The beautiful Charlotte Corday sealed with her life her belief in liberty, while Sophia Lapiérre barely escaped the same fate ; though two men, Siéyes and Condorcét, in the midst of the French Revolution, proposed the recognition of woman's political rights.

Frances Wright, a person of extraordinary powers of mind, born in Dundee, Scotland, in 1797, was the first woman who gave lectures on political subjects in America. When sixteen years of age she heard of the existence of a country in which freedom for the people had been proclaimed ; she was filled with joy and a determination to visit the American Republic where the foundations of justice, liberty, and equality had been so securely laid. In 1820 she came here, traveling extensively North and South. She was at that time but twenty-two years of age. Her letters gave Europeans the first true knowledge of America, and secured for her the friendship of LaFayette. Upon her second visit she made this country her home for several years. Her radical ideas on theology, slavery, and the social degradation of woman, now generally accepted by the best minds of the age, were then denounced by both press and pulpit, and maintained by her at the risk of her life. Although the Government of the United States was framed on the basis of entire separation of Church and State, yet from an early day the theological spirit had striven to unite the two, in order to strengthen the Church by its union with the civil power. As early as 1828, the standard of " The Christian Party in Politics " was openly unfurled. Frances Wright had long been aware of its insidious efforts, and its reliance upon women for its support. Ignorant, superstitious, devout, woman's general lack of education made her a fitting instrument for the work of thus undermining the republic. Having deprived her of her just rights, the country was now to find in woman its most dangerous foe. Frances Wright lectured that winter in the large cities of the West and Middle States, striving to rouse the nation to the new danger which threatened it. The clergy at once became her most bitter opponents. The cry of "infidel" was started on every side, though her work was of vital importance to the country and undertaken from the purest philanthropy. In speaking of her persecutions she said : " The injury and inconvenience of every kind and every hour to which, in these days, a really consistent reformer stands exposed, none can conceive but those who experience them. Such become, as it were, excommunicated after the fashion of the old Catholic Mother Church, removed even from the protection of law, such as it is, and from the sympathy of society, for whose sake they consent to be crucified."

Among those who were advocating the higher education of women, Mrs. Emma Willard became noted at this period. Born with a strong desire for learning, she keenly felt the educational disadvantages of her sex. She began teaching at an early day, introducing new studies and new methods in her school, striving to secure public interest in promoting woman's education. Governor Clinton, of New York, impressed with the wisdom of her plans, invited her to move her school from Connecticut to New York. She accepted, and in 1819 established a school in Watervleit, which soon moved to Troy, and in time built up a great reputation. Through the influence of Governor Clinton, the Legislature granted a portion of the educational fund to endow this institution, which was the first instance in the United States of Government aid for the education of women. Amos B. Eaton, Professor of the Natural Sciences in the Rensselaer Institute, Troy, at this time, was Mrs. Willard's faithful friend and teacher. In the early days it was her custom, in introducing a new branch of learning into her seminary, to study it herself, reciting to Professor Eaton every evening the lesson of the next day. Thus she went through botany, chemistry, mineralogy, astronomy, and the higher mathematics. As she could not afford teachers for these branches, with faithful study she fitted herself. Mrs. Willard's was the first girls' school in which the higher mathematics formed part of the course, but such was the prejudice against a liberal education for woman, that the first public examination of a girl in geometry (1829) created as bitter a storm of ridicule as has since assailed women who have entered the law, the pulpit, or the medical profession. The derision attendant upon the experiment of advancing woman's education, led Governor Clinton to say in his message to the Legislature: " I trust you will not be deterred by commonplace ridicule from extending your munificence to this meritorious institution." At a school convention in Syracuse, 1845, Mrs. Willard suggested the employment of women as superintendents of public schools, a measure since adopted in many States. She also projected the system of normal schools for the higher education of teachers. A scientific explorer as well as student, she wrote a work on the "Motive Power in the Circulation of the Blood," in contradiction to Harvey's theory, which at once attracted the attention of medical men. This work was one of the then accumulating evidences of woman's adaptation to medical study.

In Ancient Egypt the medical profession was in the hands of women, to which we may attribute that country's almost entire exemption from infantile diseases, a fact which recent discoveries fully authenticate. The enormous death-rate of young children in modern civilized countries may be traced to woman's general enforced ignorance of the laws of life, and to the fact that the profession of medicine has been too exclusively in the hands of men. Though through the dim past we find women still making discoveries, and in the feudal ages possessing knowledge of both medicine and surgery, it is but recently that they have been welcomed as practitioners into the medical profession. Looking back scarcely a hundred years, we find science much indebted to woman for some of its most brilliant discoveries. In 1736, the first medical botany was given to the world by Elizabeth Blackwell, a woman physician, whom the persecutions of her male compeers had cast into jail for debt. As Bunyan prepared his "Pilgrim's Progress" between prison walls, so did Elizabeth Blackwell, no-wise disheartened, prepare her valuable aid to medical science under the same conditions. Lady Montague's discovery of a check to the small-pox, Madam Boivin's discovery of the hidden cause of certain hemorrhages, Madam de Coudray's invention of the manikin, are among the notable steps which opened the way to the modern Elizabeth Blackwell, Harriot K. Hunt, Clemence S. Lozier, Ann Preston, Hannah Longshore, Marie Jackson, Laura Ross Wolcott, Marie Zakrzewska, and Mary Putnam Jacobi, who are some of the earlier distinguished American examples of woman's skill in the healing art.

Mary Gove Nichols gave public lectures upon anatomy in the United States in 1838. Paulina Wright (Davis) followed her upon physiology in 1844, using a manikin in her illustrations.* Mari-

---

* As showing woman's ignorance and prejudice, Mrs. Davis used to relate that when she uncovered her manikin some ladies would drop their veils because of its indelicacy, and others would run from the room ; sometimes ladies even fainted.

ana Johnson followed Mrs. Davis, but it was 1848 before Elizabeth Blackwell—the first woman to pass through the regular course of medical study—received her diploma at Geneva.* In 1845–6, preceding Miss Blackwell's course of study, Dr. Samuel Gregory and his brother George issued pamphlets advocating the education and employment of women-physicians, and, in 1847, Dr. Gregory delivered a series of lectures in Boston upon that subject, followed in 1848 by a school numbering twelve ladies, and an association entitled the "American Female Medical Education Society." In 1832, Lydia Maria Child published her "History of Woman," which was the first American storehouse of information upon the whole question, and undoubtedly increased the agitation. In 1836, Ernestine L. Rose, a Polish lady— banished from her native country by the Austrian tyrant, Francis Joseph, for her love of liberty—came to America, lecturing in the large cities North and South upon the "Science of Government." She advocated the enfranchisement of woman. Her beauty, wit, and eloquence drew crowded houses. About this period Judge Hurlbut, of New York, a leading member of the Bar, wrote a vigorous work on "Human Rights,"† in which he advocated political equality for women. This work attracted the attention of many legal minds throughout that State. In the winter of 1836, a bill was introduced into the New York Legislature by Judge Hertell, to secure to married women their rights of property. This bill was drawn up under the direction of Hon. John Savage, Chief-Justice of the Supreme Court, and Hon. John C. Spencer, one of the revisers of the statutes of New York. It was in furtherance of this bill that Ernestine L. Rose and Paulina Wright at that early day circulated petitions. The very few names they secured show the hopeless apathy and ignorance of the women as to their own rights. As similar bills ‡ were pending in New York until finally passed in 1848, a great educational work was accomplished in the constant discussion of the topics involved. During the winters of 1844–5–6, Elizabeth Cady Stan-

---

* The writer's father, a physician, as early as 1843–4, canvassed the subject of giving his daughter (Matilda Joslyn Gage) a medical education, looking to Geneva—then presided over by his old instructor—to open its doors to her. But this bold idea was dropped, and Miss Blackwell was the first and only lady who was graduated from that institution until its incorporation with the Syracuse University and the removal of the college to that city.

† Judge Hurlbut, with a lawyer's prejudice, first prepared a paper against the rights of woman. Looking it over, he saw himself able to answer every argument, which he proceeded to do—the result being his "Human Rights."

‡ In the New York chapter a fuller account of the discussion and action upon these bills will be given.

ton, living in Albany, made the acquaintance of Judge Hurlbut and a large circle of lawyers and legislators, and, while exerting herself to strengthen their convictions in favor of the pending bill, she resolved at no distant day to call a convention for a full and free discussion of woman's rights and wrongs.

In 1828, Sarah and Angelina Grimke, daughters of a wealthy planter of Charleston, South Carolina, emancipated their slaves and came North to lecture on the evils of slavery, leaving their home and native place forever because of their hatred of this wrong. Angelina was a natural orator. Fresh from the land of bondage, there was a fervor in her speech that electrified her hearers and drew crowds wherever she went. Sarah published a book reviewing the Bible arguments the clergy were then making in their pulpits to prove that the degradation of the slave and woman were alike in harmony with the expressed will of God. Thus women from the beginning took an active part in the Anti-Slavery struggle. They circulated petitions, raised large sums of money by fairs, held prayer-meetings and conventions. In 1835, Angelina wrote an able letter to William Lloyd Garrison, immediately after the Boston mob. These letters and appeals were considered very effective abolition documents.

In May, 1837, a National Woman's Anti-Slavery Convention was held in New York, in which eight States were represented by seventy-one delegates. The meetings were ably sustained through two days. The different sessions were opened by prayer and reading of the Scriptures by the women themselves. A devout, earnest spirit prevailed. The debates, resolutions, speeches, and appeals were fully equal to those in any Convention held by men of that period. Angelina Grimke was appointed by this Convention to prepare an appeal for the slaves to the people of the free States, and a letter to John Quincy Adams thanking him for his services in defending the right of petition for women and slaves, qualified with the regret that by expressing himself " adverse to the abolition of slavery in the District of Columbia," he did not sustain the cause of freedom and of God. She wrote a stirring appeal to the Christian women of the South, urging them to use their influence against slavery. Sarah also wrote an appeal to the clergy of the South, conjuring them to use their power for freedom.

Among those who took part in these conventions we find the names of Lydia Maria Child, Mary Grove, Henrietta Sargent, Sarah Pugh, Abby Kelley, Mary S. Parker, of Boston, who was president of the Convention; Anne Webster, Deborah Shaw, Martha Storrs,

Mrs. A. L. Cox, Rebecca B. Spring, and Abigail Hopper Gibbons, a daughter of that noble Quaker philanthropist, Isaac T. Hopper.

Abby Kelley was the most untiring and the most persecuted of all the women who labored throughout the Anti-Slavery struggle. She traveled up and down, alike in winter's cold and summer's heat, with scorn, ridicule, violence, and mobs accompanying her, suffering all kinds of persecutions, still speaking whenever and wherever she gained an audience; in the open air, in school-house, barn, depot, church, or public hall; on week-day or Sunday, as she found opportunity. For listening to her, on Sunday, many men and women were expelled from their churches. Thus through continued persecution was woman's self-assertion and self-respect sufficiently developed to prompt her at last to demand justice, liberty, and equality for herself.

In 1840, Margaret Fuller published an essay in the *Dial*, entitled "The Great Lawsuit, or Man *vs.* Woman: Woman *vs.* Man." In this essay she demanded perfect equality for woman, in education, industry, and politics. It attracted great attention and was afterward expanded into a work entitled "Woman in the Nineteenth Century." This, with her parlor conversations, on art, science, religion, politics, philosophy, and social life, gave a new impulse to woman's education as a thinker.*

"Woman and her Era," by Eliza Woodson Farnham, was another work that called out a general discussion on the status of the sexes, Mrs. Farnham taking the ground of woman's superiority. The great social and educational work done by her in California, when society there was chiefly male, and rapidly tending to savagism, and her humane experiment in the Sing Sing (N. Y.), State Prison, assisted by Georgiana Bruce Kirby and Mariana Johnson, are worthy of mention.

In the State of New York, in 1845, Rev. Samuel J. May preached a sermon at Syracuse, upon "The Rights and Conditions of Women," in which he sustained their right to take part in political life, saying women need not expect "to have their wrongs fully redressed, until they themselves have a voice and a hand in the enactment and administration of the laws."

In 1847, Clarina Howard Nichols, in her husband's paper, addressed to the voters of the State of Vermont a series of editorials, setting forth the injustice of the property disabilities of married women.

In 1849, Lucretia Mott published a discourse on woman, delivered

---

* See Appendix.

in the Assembly Building, Philadelphia, in answer to a Lyceum lecture which Richard H. Dana, of Boston, was giving in many of the chief cities, ridiculing the idea of political equality for woman. Elizabeth Wilson, of Ohio, published a scriptural view of woman's rights and duties far in advance of the generally received opinions. At even an earlier day, Martha Bradstreet, of Utica, plead her own case in the courts of New York, continuing her contest for many years. The temperance reform and the deep interest taken in it by women; the effective appeals they made, setting forth their wrongs as mother, wife, sister, and daughter of the drunkard, with a power beyond that of man, early gave them a local place on this platform as a favor, though denied as a right. Delegates from woman's societies to State and National conventions invariably found themselves rejected. It was her early labors in the temperance cause that first roused Susan B. Anthony to a realizing sense of woman's social, civil, and political degradation, and thus secured her life-long labors for the enfranchisement of woman. In 1847 she made her first speech at a public meeting of the Daughters of Temperance in Canajoharie, N. Y. The same year Antoinette L. Brown, then a student at Oberlin College, Ohio, the first institution that made the experiment of co-education, delivered her first speech on temperance in several places in Ohio, and on Woman's Rights, in the Baptist church at Henrietta, N. Y. Lucy Stone, a graduate of Oberlin, made her first speech on Woman's Rights the same year in her brother's church at Brookfield, Mass.

Nor were the women of Europe inactive during these years. In 1824 Elizabeth Heyrick, a Quaker woman, cut the gordian knot of difficulty in the anti-slavery struggle in England, by an able essay in favor of immediate, unconditional emancipation. At Leipsic, in 1844, Helene Marie Weber—her father a Prussian officer, and her mother an English woman—wrote a series of ten tracts on "Woman's Rights and Wrongs," covering the whole question and making a volume of over twelve hundred pages. The first of these treated of the intellectual faculties; the second, woman's rights of property; the third, wedlock—deprecating the custom of woman merging her civil existence in that of her husband; the fourth claimed woman's right to all political emoluments; the fifth, on ecclesiasticism, demanded for woman an entrance to the pulpit; the sixth, upon suffrage, declared it to be woman's right and duty to vote. These essays were strong, vigorous, and convincing. Miss Weber also lectured in Vienna, Berlin, and several of the large German cities. In England, Lady Morgan's "Woman and her Master" appeared;—a work filled with philosophical reflections, and of the same general bearing as Miss Weber's. Also an "Appeal of Women," the joint work of Mrs. Wheeler and William Thomson—a strong and vigorous essay, in which woman's limitations under the law were tersely and pungently set forth and her political rights demanded. The active part women took in the Polish and German revolutions and in favor of the abolition of slavery in the British West Indies, all taught their lessons of woman's rights. Madam Mathilde Anneke, on the staff of her husband, with Hon. Carl Schurz, carried messages to and fro in the midst of danger on the battle-fields of Germany.

Thus over the civilized world we find the same impelling forces, and general development of society, without any individual concert of action, tending to the same general result; alike rousing the minds of men and women to the aggregated wrongs of centuries and inciting to an effort for their overthrow.

The works of George Sand, Frederika Bremer, Charlotte Bronté, George Eliot, Catharine Sedgwick, and Harriet Beecher Stowe, in literature; Mrs. Hemans, Mrs. Sigourney, Elizabeth Barrett Browning, in poetry; Angelica Kauffman, Rosa Bonheur, Harriet Hosmer, in art; Mary Somerville, Caroline Herschell, Maria Mitchell, in science; Elizabeth Fry, Dorothea Dix, Mary Carpenter, in prison reform; Florence Nightingale and Clara Barton in the camp—are all parts of the great uprising of women out of the lethargy of the past, and are among the forces of the complete revolution a thousand pens and voices herald at this hour.

CHAPTER II.

IN newspaper literature woman made her entrance at an early period and in an important manner. The first *daily* newspaper in the world was established and edited by a woman, Elizabeth Mallet, in London, March, 1702. It was called *The Daily Courant.* In her salutatory, Mrs. Mallet declared she had established her paper to "spare the public at least half the impertinences which the ordinary papers contain." Thus the first daily paper was made reformatory in its character by its wise woman-founder.

The first newspaper printed in Rhode Island was by Anna Franklin in 1732. She was printer to the colony, supplied blanks to the public officers, published pamphlets, etc., and in 1745 she printed for the colonial government an edition of the laws comprising three hundred and forty pages. She was aided by her two daughters, who were correct and quick compositors. The woman servant of the house usually worked the press. The third paper established in America was *The Mercury*, in Philadelphia. After the death of its founder, in 1742, it was suspended for a week, when his widow, Mrs. Cornelia Bradford, revived it and carried it on for many years, making it both a literary and a pecuniary success. The second newspaper started in the city of New York, entitled the *New York Weekly Journal*, was conducted by Mrs. Zeuger for years after the death of her husband. She discontinued its publication in 1748. The *Maryland Gazette*, the first paper in that colony, and among the oldest in America, was established by Anna K. Greene in 1767. She did the colony printing and continued the business till her death, in 1775. Mrs. Hassebatch also established a paper in Baltimore in 1773. Mrs. Mary K. Goddard published the *Maryland Journal* for eight years. Her editorials were of so spirited and pronounced a character that only her sex saved her from sound floggings. She took in job work. She was the first postmaster after the Revolution, holding the office for eight years. Two papers were

(43)

early published in Virginia by women. Each was established in Williamsburg, and each was called *The Virginia Gazette.* The first, started by Clementina Reid, in 1772, favored the Colonial cause, giving great offense to many royalists. To counteract its influence, Mrs. H. Boyle, of the same place, started another paper in 1774, in the interests of the Crown, and desirous that it should seem to represent the true principles of the colony, she borrowed the name of the colonial paper. It lived but a short time. The Colonial *Virginia Gazette* was the first paper in which was printed the Declaration of Independence. A synopsis was given July 19th, and the whole document the 26th. Mrs. Elizabeth Timothee published a paper in Charleston, South Carolina, from 1773 to 1775, called *The Gazette.* Anna Timothee revived it after the Revolution, and was appointed printer to the State, holding the office till 1792. Mary Crouch also published a paper in Charleston, S. C., until 1780. It was founded in special opposition to the Stamp Act. She afterward removed to Salem, Mass., and continued its publication for several years. Penelope Russell printed *The Censor* in Boston, Mass., in 1771. She set her own type, and was such a ready compositor as to set up her editorials without written copy, while working at her case. The most tragical and interesting events were thus recorded by her. The first paper published in America, living to a second issue, was the *Massachusetts Gazette and North Boston News Letter.* It was continued by Mrs. Margaret Draper, two years after the death of her husband, and was the only paper of spirit in the colony, all but hers suspending publication when Boston was besieged by the British. Mrs. Sarah Goddard printed a paper at Newport, R. I., in 1776. She was a well-educated woman, and versed in general literature. For two years she conducted her journal with great ability, afterward associating John Carter with her, under the name of Sarah Goddard & Co., retaining the partnership precedence so justly belonging to her. *The Courant* at Hartford, Ct., was edited for two years by Mrs. Watson, after the death of her husband, in 1777. In 1784 Mrs. Mary Holt edited and published the *New York Journal,* continuing the business several years. She was appointed State printer. In 1798, *The Journal and Argus* fell into the hands of Mrs. Greenleaf, who for some time published both a daily and semi-weekly edition. In Philadelphia, after the death of her father in 1802, Mrs. Jane Aitkins continued his business of printing. Her press-work bore high reputation. She was specially noted for her correctness in proof-reading. The *Free Enquirer,* edited in New York by Frances Wright in 1828, " was the first periodical established in the United States for the purpose of fearless and unbiased inquiry on all subjects." It had already been published two years under the name of *The New Harmony Gazette*, in Indiana, by Robert Dale Owen, for which Mrs. Wright had written many leading editorials, and in which she published serially "A Few Days in Athens."

Sarah Josepha Hale established a ladies' magazine in Boston in 1827, which she afterward removed to Philadelphia, there associating with herself Louis Godey, and assuming the editorship of *Godey's Lady's Book*. This magazine was followed by many others, of which Mrs. Kirkland, Mrs. Osgood, Mrs. Ellet, Mrs. Sigourney, and women of like character were editors or contributors. These early magazines published many steel and colored engravings, not only of fashions, but reproductions of works of art, giving the first important impulse to the art of engraving in this country.

Many other periodicals and papers by women now appeared over the country. Mrs. Anne Royal edited for a quarter of a century a paper called *The Huntress*. In 1827 Lydia Maria Child published a paper for children called *The Juvenile Miscellany*, and in 1841 assumed the editorship of *The Anti-Slavery Standard*, in New York, which she ably conducted for eight years. *The Dial*, in Boston, a transcendental quarterly, edited by Margaret Fuller, made its appearance in 1840 ; its contributors, among whom were Ralph Waldo Emerson, Bronson Alcott, Theodore Parker, Wm. H. Channing, and the nature-loving Thoreau, were some of the most profound thinkers of the time. Charlotte Fowler Wells, the efficient coadjutor of her brothers and husband for the last forty-two years in the management of *The Phrenological Journal* and Publishing House of Fowler & Wells in New York city, and since her husband's death in 1875 the sole proprietor and general manager, has also conducted an extensive correspondence and written occasional articles for the *Journal*. *The Lowell Offering*, edited by the "mill girls" of that manufacturing town, was established in 1840, and exercised a wide influence. It lived till 1849. Its articles were entirely written by the girl operatives, among whom may be mentioned Lucy Larcom, Margaret Foley, the sculptor, who recently died in Rome ; Lydia S. Hall, who at one time filled an important clerkship in the United States Treasury, and Harriet J. Hansan, afterward the wife of W. S. Robinson (Warrington), and herself one of the present workers in Woman Suffrage. Harriet F. Curtis, author of two popular novels, and Harriet Farley, both "mill girls," had entire editorial charge during the latter part of its existence. In Vermont, Clarina Howard Nichols edited the *Windham County Democrat* from 1843 to 1853. It was a political paper of a pronounced character; her husband was the publisher. Jane G. Swisshelm edited *The Saturday Visitor*, at Pittsburg, Pa., in 1848. Also the same year *The True Kindred* appeared, by Rebecca Sanford, at Akron, Ohio. *The Lily*, a temperance monthly, was started in Seneca Falls, N. Y., in 1849, by Amelia Bloomer, as editor and publisher. It also advocated Woman's Rights, and attained a circulation in nearly every State and Territory of the Union. *The Sybil* soon followed, Dr. Lydia Sayre Hasbrook, editor; also *The Pledge of Honor*, edited by N. M. Baker and E. Maria Sheldon, Adrian, Michigan.

In 1849, *Die Frauen Zeitung*, edited by Mathilde Franceska Anneke, was published in Milwaukee, Wisconsin. In 1850, Lydia Jane Pierson edited a column of the *Lancaster* (Pa.) *Gazette;* Mrs. Prewett edited the *Yazoo* (Miss.) *Whig*, in Mississippi; and Mrs. Sheldon the *Dollar Weekly.* In 1851, Julia Ward Howe edited, with her husband, *The Commonwealth*, a newspaper dedicated to free thought, and zealous for the liberty of the slave. In 1851, Mrs. C. C. Bentley was editor of the *Concord Free Press*, in Vermont, and Elizabeth Aldrich of the *Genius of Liberty*, in Ohio. In 1852, Anna W. Spencer started the *Pioneer and Woman's Advocate*, in Providence, R. I. Its motto was, " Liberty, Truth, Temperance, Equality." It was published semi-monthly, and advocated a better education for woman, a higher price for her labor, the opening of new industries. It was the earliest paper established in the United States for the advocacy of Woman's Rights. In 1853, *The Una*, a paper devoted to the enfranchisement of woman, owned and edited by Paulina Wright Davis, was first published in Providence, but afterward removed to Boston, where Caroline H. Dall became associate editor. In 1855, Anna McDowell founded *The Woman's Advocate* in Philadelphia, a paper in which, like that of Mrs. Anna Franklin, the owner, editor, and compositors were all women. About this period many well-known literary women filled editorial chairs. Grace Greenwood started a child's paper called *The Little Pilgrim* ; Mrs. Bailey conducted the *Era*, an anti-slavery paper, in Washington, D. C., after her husband's death.

In 1868, *The Revolution*, a pronounced Woman's Rights paper, was started in New York city; Susan B. Anthony, publisher and proprietor, Elizabeth Cady Stanton and Parker Pillsbury, editors. Its motto, " Principles, not policy; justice, not favor; men, their rights and nothing more; women, their rights and nothing less." In 1870 it passed into the hands of Laura Curtis Bullard, who edited it two years with the assistance of Phebe Carey and Augusta Larned, and in 1872 it found consecrated burial in *The Liberal Christian*, the leading Unitarian paper in New York. From the advent of *The Revolution* can be dated a new era in the woman suffrage movement. Its brilliant, aggressive columns attracted the comments of the press, and drew the attention of the country to the reform so ably advocated. Many other papers devoted to the discussion of woman's enfranchisement soon arose. In 1869, *The Pioneer*, in San Francisco, Cal., Emily Pitts Stevens, editor and proprietor. *The Woman's Advocate*, at Dayton, O., A. J. Boyer and Miriam M. Cole, editors, started the same year. *The Sorosis* and *The Agitator*, in Chicago, Ill., the latter owned and edited by Mary A. Livermore, and *The Woman's Advocate*, in New York, were all alike short-lived. *L'Amérique*, a semi-weekly French paper published in Chicago, Ill., by Madam Jennie d'Héricourt, and *Die Neue Zeit*, a German paper, in New York, by Mathilde F. Wendt, this same year, show the interest of our foreign women citizens in the cause of their sex. In 1870, *The Woman's Journal* was founded in Boston, Lucy Stone, Julia Ward Howe, and Henry B. Blackwell, editors. *Woodhull and Claflin's Weekly*, an erratic paper, advocating many new ideas, was established in New York by Victoria Woodhull and Tennie C. Claflin, editors and proprietors. *The New Northwest*, in Portland, Oregon, in 1871, Abigail Scott Duniway, editor and proprietor. *The Golden Dawn*, at San Francisco, Cal., in 1876, Mrs. Boyer, editor.

The Ballot-Box was started in 1876, at Toledo, O., Sarah Langdon Williams, editor, under the auspices of the city Woman's Suffrage Association. It was moved to Syracuse in 1878, and is now edited by Matilda Joslyn Gage, under the name of *The National Citizen and Ballot-Box*, as an exponent of the views of the National Woman Suffrage Association. Its motto, " Self-government is a natural right, and the ballot is the method of exercising that right." Laura de Force Gordon for some years edited a daily democratic paper in California. In opposition to this large array of papers demanding equality for woman, a solitary little monthly was started a few years since, in Baltimore, Md., under the auspices of Mrs. General Sherman and Mrs. Admiral Dahlgren. It was called *The True Woman*, but soon died of inanition and inherent weakness of constitution.

In the Exposition of 1876, in Philadelphia, the *New Century*, edited and published under the auspices of the Woman's Centennial Committee, was made-up and printed by women on a press of their own, in the Woman's Pavilion. In 1877 Mrs. Theresa Lewis started *Woman's Words* in Philadelphia. For some time, Penfield,

N. Y., boasted its thirteen-year-old girl editor, in Miss Nellie Williams. Her paper, the *Penfield Enterprise*, was for three years written, set up, and published by herself. It attained a circulation of three thousand.

Many foreign papers devoted to woman's interests have been established within the last few years. The *Women's Suffrage Journal*, in England, Lydia E. Becker, of Manchester, editor and proprietor; the *Englishwoman's Journal*, in London, edited by Caroline Ashurst Biggs; *Woman and Work* and the *Victoria Magazine*, by Emily Faithful, are among the number. Miss Faithful's magazine having attained a circulation of fifty thousand. *Des Droits des Femmes*, long the organ of the Swiss woman suffragists, Madame Marie Goegg, the head, was followed by the *Solidarite*. *L'Avenir des Femmes*, edited by M. Leon Richer, has Mlle. Maria Dairésmes, the author of a spirited reply to the work of M. Dumas, *fils*, on Woman, as its special contributor. *L'Éspérance*, of Geneva, an Englishwoman its editor, was an early advocate of woman's cause. *La Donna*, at Venice, edited by Signora Gualberti Aläide Beccari (a well-known Italian philanthropic name); *La Cornelia*, at Florence, Signora Amelia Cunino Foliero de Luna, editor, prove Italian advancement. Germany, Spain, and the Netherlands must not be omitted from the list of those countries which have published Woman's Rights papers. In Lima, Peru, we find a paper edited and controlled entirely by women; its name, *Alborada*, *i. c.*, the Dawn, a South American prophecy and herald of that dawn of justice and equality now breaking upon the world. The Orient, likewise, shows progress. At Bukarest, in Romaine, a paper, the *Dekebalos*, upholding the elevation of woman, was started in 1874. The *Euridike*, at Constantinople, edited by Emile Leonzras, is of a similar character. The *Bengalee Magazine*, devoted to the interests of Indian ladies, its editorials all from woman's pen, shows Asiatic advance.

In the United States the list of women's fashion papers, with their women editors and correspondents, is numerous and important. For fourteen years *Harper's Bazaar* has been ably edited by Mary L. Booth; other papers of similar character are both owned and edited by women. *Madame Demorest's Monthly*, a paper that originated the vast pattern business which has extended its ramifications into every part of the country and given employment to thousands of women. As illustrative of woman's continuity of purpose in newspaper work, we may mention the fact that for fifteen years Fanny Fern did not fail to have an article in readiness each week for the *Ledger*, and for twenty years Jennie June (Mrs. Croly) has edited *Demorest's Monthly* and contributed to many other papers throughout the United States. Mary Mapes Dodge has edited the *St. Nicholas* the past eight years. So important a place do women writers hold, *Harper's Monthly* asserts, that the exceptionally large prices are paid to women contributors. The spiciest critics, reporters, and correspondents to-day, are women—Grace Greenwood Louise Chandler Moulton, Mary Clemmer. Laura C. Holloway is upon the editorial staff of the Brooklyn *Eagle*. The New York *Times* boasts a woman (Midi Morgan) cattle reporter, one of the best judges of stock in the country. In some papers, over their own names, women edit columns on special subjects, and fill important positions on journals owned and edited by men. Elizabeth Boynton Harbert edits "The Woman's Kingdom" in the *Inter-Ocean*, one of the leading dailies of Chicago. Mary Forney Weigley edits a social department in her father's—John W. Forney—paper, the *Progress*, in Philadelphia. The political columns of many papers are prepared by women, men often receiving the credit. Among the best editorials in the New York *Tribune*, from Margaret Fuller to Lucia Gilbert Calhoun, have been from the pens of women.

If the proverb that "the pen is mightier than the sword" be true, woman's skill and force in using this mightier weapon must soon change the destinies of the world.

4

CHAPTER III.

THE WORLD'S ANTI-SLAVERY CONVENTION, LONDON, JUNE 12, 1840.

Individualism rather than Authority—Personal appearance of Abolitionists—Clerical
attempt to silence Woman—Double battle against the tyranny of sex and color—
Bigoted Abolitionists—James G. Birney likes freedom on a Southern plantation, but
not at his own fireside—John Bull never dreamt that Woman would answer his call
—The venerable Thomas Clarkson received by the Convention standing—Lengthy
debate on "Female" delegates—The "Females" rejected—William Lloyd Garrison
refused to sit in the Convention.

In gathering up the threads of history in the last century, and
weaving its facts and philosophy together, one can trace the liberal
social ideas, growing out of the political and religious revolutions
in France Germany, Italy, and America; and their tendency to
substitute for the divine right of kings, priests, and orders of nobility, the higher and broader one of individual conscience and judgment in all matters pertaining to this life and that which is to come.
It is not surprising that in so marked a transition period from the
old to the new, as seen in the eighteenth century, that women,
trained to think and write and speak, should have discovered that
they, too, had some share in the new-born liberties suddenly announced to the world. That the radical political theories, propagated in different countries, made their legitimate impress on the
minds of women of the highest culture, is clearly proved by their
writings and conversation. While in their ignorance, women are
usually more superstitious, more devoutly religious than men; those
trained to thought, have generally manifested more interest in political questions, and have more frequently spoken and written on
such themes, than on those merely religious. This may be attributed, in a measure, to the fact that the tendency of woman's mind,
at this stage of her development, is toward practical, rather than
toward speculative science.

Questions of political economy lie within the realm of positive
knowledge; those of theology belong to the world of mysteries and
abstractions, which those minds, only, that imagine they have compassed the known, are ambitious to enter and explore. And yet, the

(50)

quickening power of the Protestant Reformation roused woman, as well as man, to new and higher thought. The bold declarations of Luther, placing individual judgment above church authority, the faith of the Quaker that the inner light was a better guide than arbitrary law, the religious idealism of the Transcendentalists, and their teachings that souls had no sex, had each a marked influence in developing woman's self-assertion. Such ideas making all divine revelations as veritable and momentous to one soul, as another, tended directly to equalize the members of the human family, and place men and women on the same plane of moral responsibility.

The revelations of science, too, analyzing and portraying the wonders and beauties of this material world, crowned with new dignity, man and woman,—Nature's last and proudest work. Combe and Spurzheim, proving by their Phrenological discoveries that the feelings, sentiments, and affections of the soul mould and shape the skull, gave new importance to woman's thought as mother of the race. Thus each new idea in religion, politics, science, and philosophy, tending to individualism, rather than authority, came into the world freighted with new hopes of liberty for woman.

And when in the progress of civilization the time had fully come for the recognition of the feminine element in humanity, women, in every civilized country unknown to each other, began simultaneously to demand a broader sphere of action. Thus the first public demand for political equality by a body of women in convention assembled, was a link in the chain of woman's development, binding the future with the past, as complete and necessary in itself, as the events of any other period of her history. The ridicule of facts does not change their character. Many who study the past with interest, and see the importance of seeming trifles in helping forward great events, often fail to understand some of the best pages of history made under their own eyes. Hence the woman suffrage movement has not yet been accepted as the legitimate outgrowth of American ideas—a component part of the history of our republic—but is falsely considered the willful outburst of a few unbalanced minds, whose ideas can never be realized under any form of government.

Among the immediate causes that led to the demand for the equal political rights of women, in this country, we may note three:

1. The discussion in several of the State Legislatures on the property rights of married women, which, heralded by the press with comments grave and gay, became the topic of general interest around many fashionable dinner-tables, and at many humble fire-

sides. In this way all phases of the question were touched upon, involving the relations of the sexes, and gradually widening to all human interests—political, religious, civil, and social. The press and pulpit became suddenly vigilant in marking out woman's sphere, while woman herself seemed equally vigilant in her efforts to step outside the prescribed limits.

2. A great educational work was accomplished by the able lectures of Frances Wright, on political, religious, and social questions. Ernestine L. Rose, following in her wake, equally liberal in her religious opinions, and equally well informed on the science of government, helped to deepen and perpetuate the impression Frances Wright had made on the minds of unprejudiced hearers.

3. And above all other causes of the " Woman Suffrage Movement," was the Anti-Slavery struggle in this country. The ranks of the Abolitionists were composed of the most eloquent orators, the ablest logicians, men and women of the purest moral character and best minds in the nation. They were usually spoken of in the early days as " an illiterate, ill-mannered, poverty-stricken, crazy set of long-haired Abolitionists." While the fact is, some of the most splendid specimens of manhood and womanhood, in physical appearance, in culture, refinement, and knowledge of polite life, were found among the early Abolitionists. James G. Birney, John Pierpont, Gerrit Smith, Wendell Phillips, Charles Sumner, Maria Weston Chapman, Helen Garrison, Ann Green Phillips, Abby Kelly, Paulina Wright Davis, Lucretia Mott, were all remarkably fine-looking.

In the early Anti-Slavery conventions, the broad principles of human rights were so exhaustively discussed, justice, liberty, and equality, so clearly taught, that the women who crowded to listen, readily learned the lesson of freedom for themselves, and early began to take part in the debates and business affairs of all associations. Woman not only felt every pulsation of man's heart for freedom, and by her enthusiasm inspired the glowing eloquence that maintained him through the struggle, but earnestly advocated with her own lips human freedom and equality. When Angelina and Sarah Grimke began to lecture in New England, their audiences were at first composed entirely of women, but gentlemen, hearing of their eloquence and power, soon began timidly to slip into the back seats, one by one. And before the public were aroused to the dangerous innovation, these women were speaking in crowded, promiscuous assemblies. The clergy opposed to the abolition movement first took alarm, and issued a pastoral letter, warning their congregations against the influence of such women. The clergy identified with anti-slavery associations took alarm also, and the initiative steps to silence the women, and to deprive them of the right to vote in the business meetings, were soon taken. This action culminated in a division in the Anti-Slavery Association. In the annual meeting in May, 1840, a formal vote was taken on the appointment of Abby Kelly on a business committee and was sustained by over one hundred majority in favor of woman's right to take part in the proceedings of the Society. Pending the discussion, clergymen in the opposition went through the audience, *urging every woman who agreed with them, to vote against* the motion, thus asking them to do then and there, what with fervid eloquence, on that very occasion, they had declared a sin against God and Scripture for them to do anywhere. As soon as the vote was announced, and Abby Kelly's right on the business committee decided, the men, two of whom were clergymen, asked to be excused from serving on the committee.

Thus Sarah and Angelina Grimke and Abby Kelly, in advocating liberty for the black race, were early compelled to defend the right of free speech for themselves. They had the double battle to fight against the tyranny of sex and color at the same time, in which, however, they were well sustained by the able pens of Lydia Maria Child and Maria Weston Chapman. Their opponents were found not only in the ranks of the New England clergy, but among the most bigoted Abolitionists in Great Britain and the United States. Many a man who advocated equality most eloquently for a Southern plantation, could not tolerate it at his own fireside.

The question of woman's right to speak, vote, and serve on committees, not only precipitated the division in the ranks of the American Anti-Slavery Society, in 1840, but it disturbed the peace of the World's Anti-Slavery Convention, held that same year in London. The call for that Convention invited delegates from all Anti-Slavery organizations. Accordingly several American societies saw fit to send women, as delegates, to represent them in that august assembly. But after going three thousand miles to attend a World's Convention, it was discovered that women formed no part of the constituent elements of the moral world. In summoning the friends of the slave from all parts of the two hemispheres to meet in London, John Bull never dreamed that woman, too, would answer to his call. Imagine then the commotion in the conservative anti-slavery circles in England, when it was known that half a dozen of those terrible women who had spoken to promiscuous assemblies, voted on men and measures, prayed and petitioned against slavery, women who had been mobbed, ridiculed by the press, and denounced by the pulpit, who had been the cause of setting all American Abolitionists by the ears, and split their ranks asunder, were on their way to England. Their fears of these formidable and belligerent women must have been somewhat appeased when Lucretia Mott, Sarah Pugh, Abby Kimber, Elizabeth Neal, Mary Grew, of Philadelphia, in modest Quaker costume, Ann Green Phillips, Emily Winslow, and Abby Southwick, of Boston, all women of refinement and education, and several, still in their twenties, landed at last on the soil of Great Britain. Many who had awaited their coming with much trepidation, gave a sigh of relief, on being introduced to Lucretia Mott, learning that she represented the most dangerous elements in the delegation. The American clergymen who had landed a few days before, had been busily engaged in fanning the English prejudices into active hostility against the admission of these women to the Convention. In every circle of Abolitionists this was the theme, and the discussion grew more bitter, personal, and exasperating every hour.

The 12th of June dawned bright and beautiful on these discordant elements, and at an early hour anti-slavery delegates from different countries wended their way through the crooked streets of London to Freemasons' Hall. Entering the vestibule, little groups might be seen gathered here and there, earnestly discussing the best disposition to make of those women delegates from America. The excitement and vehemence of protest and denunciation could not have been greater, if the news had come that the French were about to invade England. In vain those obdurate women had been conjured to withhold their credentials, and not thrust a question that must produce such discord on the Convention. Lucretia Mott, in her calm, firm manner, insisted that the delegates had no discretionary power in the proposed action, and the responsibility of accepting or rejecting them must rest on the Convention.

At eleven o'clock, the spacious Hall being filled, the Convention was called to order. The venerable Thomas Clarkson, who was to be President, on entering, was received by the large audience standing; owing to his feeble health, the chairman requested that there should be no other demonstrations. As soon as Thomas Clarkson withdrew, Wendell Phillips made the following motion:

"That a Committee of five be appointed to prepare a correct list of the members of this Convention, with instructions to include in such list, all persons bearing credentials from any Anti-Slavery body."

This motion at once opened the debate on the admission of women delegates.

Mr. Phillips: When the call reached America we found that it was an invitation to the friends of the slave of every nation and of every clime. Massachusetts has for several years acted on the principle of admitting women to an equal seat with men, in the deliberative bodies of anti-slavery societies. When the Massachusetts Anti-Slavery Society received that paper, it interpreted it, as it was its duty, in its broadest and most liberal sense. If there be any other paper, emanating from the Committee, limiting to one sex the qualification of membership, there is no proof; and, as an individual, I have no knowledge that such a paper ever reached Massachusetts. We stand here in consequence of your invitation, and knowing our custom, as it must be presumed you did, we had a right to interpret "friends of the slave," to include women as well as men. In such circumstances, we do not think it just or equitable to that State, nor to America in general, that, after the trouble, the sacrifice, the self-devotion of a part of those who leave their families and kindred and occupations in their own land, to come three thousand miles to attend this World's Convention, they should be refused a place in its deliberations.

One of the Committee who issued the call, said: As soon as we heard the liberal interpretation Americans had given to our first invitation, we issued another as early as Feb. 15, in which the description of those who are to form the Convention is set forth as consisting of "gentlemen."

Dr. Bowring: I think the custom of excluding females is more honored in its breach than in its observance. In this country sovereign rule is placed in the hands of a female, and one who has been exercising her great and benignant influence in opposing slavery by sanctioning, no doubt, the presence of her illustrious consort at an anti-slavery meeting. We are associated with a body of Christians (Quakers) who have given to their women a great, honorable, and religious prominence. I look upon this delegation from America as one of the most interesting, the most encouraging, and the most delightful symptoms of the times. I can not believe that we shall refuse to welcome gratefully the co-operation which is offered us.

The Rev. J. Burnet, an Englishman, made a most touching appeal to the American ladies, to conform to English prejudices and custom, so far as to withdraw their credentials, as it never did occur to the British and Foreign Anti-Slavery Society that they were inviting ladies. It is better, said he, that this Convention should be dissolved at this moment than this motion should be adopted.

The Rev. Henry Grew, of Philadelphia: The reception of women as a part of this Convention would, in the view of many, be not only a violation of the customs of England, but of the ordinance of Almighty God, who has a right to appoint our services to His sovereign will.

Rev. Eben Galusha, New York: In support of the other side of this question, reference has been made to your Sovereign. I most cordially approve of her policy and sound wisdom, and commend to the consideration of our American female friends who are so deeply interested in the subject, the example of your noble Queen, who by sanctioning her consort, His Royal Highness Prince Albert, in taking the chair on an occasion not dissimilar to this, showed her sense of propriety by putting her Head foremost in an assembly of gentlemen. I have no objection to woman's being the neck to turn the head aright, but do not wish to see her assume the place of the head.

George Bradburn, of Mass.: We are told that it would be outraging the customs of England to allow women to sit in this Convention. I have a great respect for the customs of old England. But I ask, gentlemen, if it be right to set up the customs and habits, not to say prejudices of Englishmen, as a standard for the government on this occasion of Americans, and of persons belonging to several other independent nations. I can see neither reason nor policy in so doing. Besides, I deprecate the principle of the objection. In America it would exclude from our conventions all persons of color, for there customs, habits, tastes, prejudices, would be outraged by *their* admission. And I do not wish to be deprived of the aid of those who have done so much for this cause, for the purpose of gratifying any mere custom or prejudice. Women have furnished most essential aid in accomplishing what has been done in the State of Massachusetts. If, in the Legislature of that State, I have been able to do anything in furtherance of that cause, by keeping on my legs eight or ten hours day after day, it was mainly owing to the valuable assistance I derived from the women. And shall such women be denied seats in this Convention? My friend George Thompson, yonder, can testify to the faithful services rendered to this cause by those same women. He can tell you that when "gentlemen of property and standing" in "broad day" and "broadcloth," undertook to drive him from Boston, putting his life in peril, it was our women who made their own persons a bulwark of protection around him. And shall such women be refused seats here in a Convention seeking the emancipation of slaves throughout the world? What a misnomer to call this a World's Convention of Abolitionists, when some of the oldest and most thorough-going Abolitionists in the world are denied the right to be represented in it by delegates of their own choice.

And thus for the space of half an hour did Mr. Bradburn, six feet high and well-proportioned, with vehement gesticulations and voice of thunder, bombard the prejudices of England and the hypocrisies of America.

George Thompson: I have listened to the arguments advanced on this side and on that side of this vexed question. I listened with profound attention to the arguments of Mr. Burnet, expecting that from him, as I was justified in expecting, I should hear the strongest arguments that could be adduced on this, or any other subject upon which he might be pleased to employ his talents, or which he might adorn with his eloquence. What are his arguments? Let it be premised, as I speak in the presence of American friends, that that gentleman is one of the best controversialists in the country, and one of the best authorities upon questions of business, points of order, and matters of principle. What are the strongest arguments, which one of the greatest champions on any question which he chooses to espouse, has brought forward? They are these:

1st. That English phraseology should be construed according to English usage.

2d. That it was never contemplated by the anti-slavery committee that ladies should occupy a seat in this Convention.

3d. That the ladies of England are not here as delegates.

4th. That he has no desire to offer an affront to the ladies now present.

Here I presume are the strongest arguments the gentleman has to adduce, for he never fails to use to the best advantage the resources within his reach. I look at these arguments, and I place on the other side of the question, the fact that there are in this assembly ladies who present themselves as delegates from the oldest societies in America. I expected that Mr. Burnet would, as he was bound to do, if he intended to offer a successful opposition to their introduction into this Convention, grapple with the constitutionality of their credentials. I thought he would come to the question of title. I thought he would dispute the right of a convention assembled in Philadelphia, for the abolition of slavery, consisting of delegates from different States in the Union, and comprised of individuals of both sexes, to send one or all of the ladies now in our presence. I thought he would grapple with the fact, that those ladies came to us who have no slavery from a country in which they have slaves, as the representatives of two millions and a half of captives. Let gentlemen, when they come to vote on this question, remember, that in receiving or rejecting these ladies, they acknowledge or despise [loud cries of No, no]. I ask gentlemen, who shout " no," if they know the application I am about to make. I did not mean to say you would despise the ladies, but that you would, by your vote, acknowledge or despise the parties whose cause they espouse. It appears we are prepared to sanction ladies in the employment of all means, so long as they are confessedly unequal with ourselves. It seems that the grand objection to their appearance amongst us is this, that it would be placing them on a footing of equality, and that would be contrary to principle and custom. For years the women of America have carried their banner in the van, while the men have humbly followed in the rear. It is well known that the National Society solicited Angelina Grimke to undertake a mission through New England, to rouse the attention of the women to the wrongs of slavery, and that that distinguished woman displayed her talents not only in the drawing-room, but before the Senate of Massachusetts. Let us contrast our conduct with that of the Senators and Representatives of Massachusetts who did not disdain to hear her. It was in consequence of her exertions, which received the warmest approval of the National Society, that that interest sprung up which has awakened such an intense feeling throughout America. Then with reference to efficient management, the most vigorous anti-slavery societies are those which are managed by ladies.

If now, after the expression of opinion on various sides, the motion should be withdrawn with the consent of all parties, I should be glad.

But when I look at the arguments against the title of these women to sit amongst us, I can not but consider them frivolous and groundless. The simple question before us is, whether these ladies, taking into account their credentials, the talent they have displayed, the sufferings they have endured, the journey they have undertaken, should be acknowledged by us, in virtue of these high titles, or should be shut out for the reasons stated.

Mr. Phillips, being urged on all sides to withdraw his motion, said: It has been hinted very respectfully by two or three speakers that the delegates from the State of Massachusetts should withdraw their credentials, or the motion before the meeting. The one appears to me to be equivalent to the other. If this motion be withdrawn we must have another. I would merely ask whether any man can suppose that the delegates from Massachusetts or Pennsylvania can take upon their shoulders the responsibility of withdrawing that list of delegates from your table, which their constituents told them to place there, and whom they sanctioned as their fit representatives, because this Convention tells us that it is not ready to meet the ridicule of the morning papers, and to stand up against the customs of England. In America we listen to no such arguments. If we had done so we had never been here as Abolitionists. It is the custom there not to admit colored men into respectable society, and we have been told again and again that we are outraging the decencies of humanity when we permit colored men to sit by our side. When we have submitted to brick-bats, and the tar tub and feathers in America, rather than yield to the custom prevalent there of not admitting colored brethren into our friendship, shall we yield to parallel custom or prejudice against women in Old England? We can not yield this question if we would; for it is a matter of conscience. But we would not yield it on the ground of expediency. In doing so we should feel that we were striking off the right arm of our enterprise. We could not go back to America to ask for any aid from the women of Massachusetts if we had deserted them, when they chose to send out their own sisters as their representatives here. We could not go back to Massachusetts and assert the unchangeableness of spirit on the question. We have argued it over and over again, and decided it time after time, in every society in the land, in favor of the women. We have not changed by crossing the water. We stand here the advocates of the same principle that we contend for in America. We think it right for women to sit by our side there, and we think it right for them to do the same here. We ask the Convention to admit them; if they do not choose to grant it, the responsibility rests on their shoulders. Massachusetts can not turn aside, or succumb to any prejudices or customs even in the land she looks upon with so much reverence as the land of Wilberforce, of Clarkson, and of O'Connell. It is a matter of conscience, and British virtue ought not to ask us to yield.

Mr. Ashurst: You are convened to influence society upon a subject connected with the kindliest feelings of our nature; and being the first assembly met to shake hands with other nations, and employ your combined efforts to annihilate slavery throughout the world, are you to com mence by saying, you will take away the rights of one-half of creation ? This is the principle which you are putting forward.

The Rev. A. Harvey, of Glasgow: It was stated by a brother from America, that with him it is a matter of conscience, and it is a question of conscience with me too. I have certain views in relation to the teaching of the Word of God, and of the particular sphere in which woman is to act. I must say, whether I am right in my interpretations of the Word of God or not, that my own decided convictions are, if I were to give a vote in favor of females, sitting and deliberating in such an assembly as this, that I should be acting in opposition to the plain teaching of the Word of God. I may be wrong, but I have a conscience on the subject, and I am sure there are a number present of the same mind.

Captain Wanchope, R. N., delegate from Carlisle: I entreat the ladies not to push this question too far. I wish to know whether our friends from America are to cast off England altogether. Have we not given £20,000,000 of our money for the purpose of doing away with the abominations of slavery? Is not that proof that we are in earnest about it?

James C. Fuller: One friend said that this question should have been settled on the other side of the Atlantic. Why, it was there decided in favor of woman a year ago.

James Gillespie Birney: It has been stated that the right of women to sit and act in all respects as men in our anti-slavery associations, was decided in the affirmative at the annual meeting of the American Anti-Slavery Society in May, 1839. It is true the claim was so decided on that occasion, but not by a large majority; whilst it is also true that the majority was swelled by the votes of the women themselves. I have just received a letter from a gentleman in New York (Louis Tappan), communicating the fact, that the persistence of the friends of promiscuous female representation in pressing that practice on the American Anti-Slavery Society, at its annual meeting on the twelfth of last month, had caused such disagreement among the members present, that he and others who viewed the subject as he did, were then deliberating on measures for seceding from the old organization.

Rev. C. Stout: My vote is that we confirm the list of delegates, that we take votes on that as an amendment, and that we henceforth entertain this question no more. Are we not met here pledged to sacrifice all but everything, in order that we may do something against slavery, and shall we be divided on this *paltry question* and suffer the whole tide of benevolence to be stopped by *a straw ?* No ! You talk of being men, then be men ! Consider what is worthy of your attention.

Rev. Dr. Morrison: I feel, I believe, as our brethren from America and many English friends do at this moment, that we are treading on the brink of a precipice; and that precipice is the awaking in our bosoms by this discussion, feelings that will not only be averse to the great object for which we have assembled, but inconsistent, perhaps, in some degree, with the Christian spirit which, I trust, will pervade all meetings connected with the Anti-Slavery cause. We have been unanimous against the common foe, but we are this day in danger of creating division among heartfelt friends. Will our American brethren put us in this position?

Will they keep up a discussion in which the delicacy, the honor, the respectability of those excellent females who have come from the Western world are concerned? I tremble at the thought of discussing the question in the presence of these ladies—for whom I entertain the most profound respect—and I am bold to say, that but for the introduction of the question of woman's rights, it would be impossible for the shrinking nature of woman to subject itself to the infliction of such a discussion as this.

As the hour was late, and as the paltry arguments of the opposition were unworthy much consideration—as the reader will see from the specimens given—Mr. Phillips' reply was brief, consisting of the correction of a few mistakes made by different speakers. The vote was taken, and the women excluded as delegates of the Convention, by an overwhelming majority.

George Thompson: I hope, as the question is now decided, that Mr. Phillips will give us the assurance that we shall proceed with one heart and one mind.

Mr. Phillips replied: I have no doubt of it. There is no unpleasant feeling in our minds. I have no doubt the women will sit with as much interest behind the bar* as though the original proposition had been carried in the affirmative. All we asked was an expression of opinion, and, having obtained it, we shall now act with the utmost cordiality.

Would there have been no unpleasant feelings in Wendell Phillips' mind, had Frederick Douglass and Robert Purvis been refused their seats in a convention of reformers under similar circumstances? and, had *they* listened one entire day to debates on their peculiar fitness for plantation life, and unfitness for the forum and public assemblies, and been rejected as delegates on the ground of color, could Wendell Phillips have so far mistaken their real feelings, and been so insensible to the insults offered them, as to have told a Convention of men who had just trampled on their most sacred rights, that "they would no doubt sit with as much interest behind the bar, as in the Convention"? To stand in that august assembly and maintain the unpopular heresy of woman's equality was a severe ordeal for a young man to pass through, and Wendell Phillips, who accepted the odium of presenting this question to the Convention, and thus earned the sincere gratitude of all womankind, might be considered as above criticism, though he may have failed at one point to understand the feelings of woman. The fact is important to mention, however, to show that it is

---

* The ladies of the Convention were fenced off behind a bar and curtain, similar to those used in churches to screen the choir from the public gaze.

almost impossible for the most liberal of men to understand what
liberty means for woman. This sacrifice of human rights, by men
who had assembled from all quarters of the globe to proclaim universal emancipation, was offered up in the presence of such women
as Lady Byron, Anna Jameson, Amelia Opie, Mary Howitt,
Elizabeth Fry, and our own Lucretia Mott. The clergy with
few exceptions were bitter in their opposition. Although, as Abolitionists, they had been compelled to fight both Church and Bible
to prove the black man's right to liberty, conscience forbade them
to stretch those sacred limits far enough to give equal liberty to
woman.

The leading men who championed the cause of the measure
in the Convention and voted in the affirmative, were Wendell
Phillips, George Thompson, George Bradburn, Mr. Ashurst, Dr.
Bowring, and Henry B. Stanton. Though Daniel O'Connell was
not present during the discussion, having passed out with the
President, yet in his first speech, he referred to the rejected delegates, paying a beautiful tribute to woman's influence, and saying
he should have been happy to have added the right word in the
right place and to have recorded his vote in favor of human equality.

William Lloyd Garrison, having been delayed at sea, arrived
too late to take part in the debates. Learning on his arrival
that the women had been rejected as delegates, he declined
to take his seat in the Convention ; and, through all those interesting discussions on a subject so near his heart, lasting ten days,
he remained a silent spectator in the gallery. What a sacrifice for
a principle so dimly seen by the few, and so ignorantly ridiculed by
the many ! Brave, noble Garrison ! May this one act keep his
memory fresh forever in the hearts of his countrywomen !

The one Abolitionist who sustained Mr. Garrison's position, and sat
with him in the gallery, was Nathaniel P. Rogers, editor of the *Herald
of Freedom*, in Concord, New Hampshire, who died in the midst of
the Anti-Slavery struggle. However, the debates in the Convention had the effect of rousing English minds to thought on the
tyranny of sex, and American minds to the importance of some
definite action toward woman's emancipation.

As Lucretia Mott and Elizabeth Cady Stanton wended their way
arm in arm down Great Queen Street that night, reviewing the exciting scenes of the day, they agreed to hold a woman's rights convention on their return to America, as the men to whom they had
just listened had manifested their great need of some education on
that question. Thus a missionary work for the emancipation of

woman in "the land of the free and the home of the brave" was then and there inaugurated. As the ladies were not allowed to speak in the Convention, they kept up a brisk fire morning, noon, and night at their hotel on the unfortunate gentlemen who were domiciled at the same house. Mr. Birney, with his luggage, promptly withdrew after the first encounter, to some more congenial haven of rest, while the Rev. Nathaniel Colver, from Boston, who always fortified himself with six eggs well beaten in a large bowl at breakfast, to the horror of his host and a circle of æsthetic friends, stood his ground to the last—his physical proportions being his shield and buckler, and his Bible (with Colver's commentaries) his weapon of defence.*

The movement for woman's suffrage, both in England and America, may be dated from this World's Anti-Slavery Convention.

---

* Some of the English clergy, dancing around with Bible in hand, shaking it in the faces of the opposition, grew so vehement, that one would really have thought that they held a commission from high heaven as the possessors of all truth, and that all progress in human affairs was to be squared by their interpretation of Scripture. At last George Bradburn, exasperated with their narrowness and bigotry, sprang to the floor, and stretching himself to his full height, said: "Prove to me, gentlemen, that your Bible sanctions the slavery of woman—the complete subjugation of one-half the race to the other—and I should feel that the best work I could do for humanity would be to make a grand bonfire of every Bible in the Universe."

CHAPTER IV.

NEW YORK.

The First Woman's Rights Convention, Seneca Falls, July 19–20, 1848—Property Rights of Women secured—Judge Fine, George Geddes, and Mr. Hadley pushed the Bill through—Danger of meddling with well-settled conditions of domestic happiness—Mrs. Barbara Hertell's will—Richard Hunt's tea-table—The eventful day—James Mott President—Declaration of sentiments—Convention in Rochester—Clergy again in opposition with Bible arguments.

NEW YORK with its metropolis, fine harbors, great lakes and rivers; its canals and railroads uniting the extremest limits, and controlling the commerce of the world; with its wise statesmen and wily politicians, long holding the same relation to the nation at large that Paris is said to hold to France, has been proudly called by her sons and daughters the Empire State.

But the most interesting fact in her history, to woman, is that she was the first State to emancipate wives from the slavery of the old common law of England, and to secure to them equal property rights. This occurred in 1848. Various bills and petitions, with reference to the civil rights of woman, had been under discussion twelve years, and the final passage of the property bill was due in no small measure to two facts. 1st. The constitutional convention in 1847, which compelled the thinking people of the State, and especially the members of the convention, to the serious consideration of the fundamental principles of government. As in the revision of a Constitution the State is for the time being resolved into its original elements in recognizing the equality of all the people, one would naturally think that a chance ray of justice might have fallen aslant the wrongs of woman and brought to the surface some champion in that convention, especially as some aggravated cases of cruelty in families of wealth and position had just at that time aroused the attention of influential men to the whole question. 2d. Among the Dutch aristocracy of the State there was a vast amount of dissipation; and as married women could hold neither property nor children under the common law, solid, thrifty Dutch fathers were daily confronted with the fact that the inheritance of their daughters, carefully accumulated, would at marriage pass into the hands of dissipated, impecunious husbands, reducing them and their children to poverty and dependence. Hence this influential class of citizens heartily seconded the efforts of reformers, then demanding equal property rights in the marriage relation. Thus a wise selfishness on one side, and principle on the other, pushed the conservatives and radicals into the same channel, and both alike found anchor in the statute law of 1848. This was the death-blow to the old Blackstone code for married women in this country, and ever since legislation has been slowly, but steadily, advancing toward their complete equality.

Desiring to know who prompted the legislative action on the Property Bill in 1848, and the names of our champions who carried it successfully through after twelve years of discussion and petitioning, a letter of inquiry was addressed to the Hon. George Geddes of the twenty-second district—at that time Senator—and received the following reply:

FAIRMOUNT, ONONDAGA CO., N. Y., }
November 25, 1880. }

MRS. MATILDA JOSLYN GAGE:

Dear Madam :—I was much gratified at the receipt of your letter of the 22d inst., making inquiries into the history of the law of 1848 in regard to married women holding property independently of their husbands. That the "truth of history" may be made plain, I have looked over the journals of the Senate and Assembly, and taken full notes, which I request you to publish, if you put any part of this letter in print.

I have very distinct recollections of the whole history of this very radical measure. Judge Fine, of St. Lawrence, was its originator, and he gave me his reasons for introducing the bill. He said that he married a lady who had some property of her own, which he had, all his life, tried to keep distinct from his, that she might have the benefit of her own, in the event of any disaster happening to him in pecuniary matters. He had found much difficulty, growing out of the old laws, in this effort to protect his wife's interests.

Judge Fine was a stately man, and of general conservative tendencies, just the one to hold on to the past, but he was a just man, and did not allow his practice as a lawyer, or his experience on the bench, to obscure his sense of right. I followed him, glad of such a leader.

I, too, had special reasons for desiring this change in the law. I had a young daughter, who, in the then condition of my health, was quite likely to be left in tender years without a father, and I very much desired to protect her in the little property I might be able to leave. I had an elaborate will drawn by my old law preceptor, Vice-Chancellor Lewis H. Sandford, creating a trust with all the care and learning he could bring to my aid. But when the elaborate paper was finished, neither he or I felt satisfied with it. When the law of 1848 was passed, all I had to do was to burn this will.

In this connection I wish to say that the Speaker of the Assembly, Mr. Hadley, gave aid in the passage of this law that was essential. Very near the end of the session of the Legislature he assured me that if the bill passed the Senate, he would see that it passed the House. By examining my notes of the Assembly's action, you will see that the bill never went to a committee of the whole in that body, but was sent directly to a select committee to report complete. It was the power of the Speaker that in this summary manner overrode the usual legislative forms. The only reason Mr. Hadley gave me for his zeal in this matter, was that it was a good bill and ought to pass.

I believe this law originated with Judge Fine, without any outside prompting. On the third day of the session he gave notice of his intention to introduce it, and only one petition was presented in favor of the bill, and that came from Syracuse, and was due to the action of my personal friends—I presented it nearly two months after the bill had been introduced to the Senate.

The reception of the bill by the Senate showed unlooked-for support as well as opposition. The measure was so radical, so extreme, that even its friends had doubts; but the moment any important amendment was offered, up rose the whole question of woman's proper place in society, in the family, and everywhere. We all felt that the laws regulating married women's, as well as married men's rights, demanded careful revision and adaptation to our times and to our civilization. But no such revision could be perfected then, nor has it been since. We meant to strike a hard blow, and if possible shake the old system of laws to their foundations, and leave it to other times and wiser councils to perfect a new system.

We had in the Senate a man of matured years, who had never had a wife. He was a lawyer well-read in the old books, and versed in the adjudications which had determined that husband and wife were but one person, and the husband that person; and he expressed great fears in regard to meddling with this well-settled condition of domestic happiness. This champion of the past made long and very able arguments to show the ruin this law must work, but he voted for the bill in the final decision.

The bill hung along in Committee of the Whole until March 21st, when its great opponent being absent, I moved its reference to a select Committee, with power to report it complete; that is, matured ready for its passage. So the bill was out of the arena of debate, and on my motion was ordered to its third reading.

In reply to your inquiries in regard to debates that preceded the action of 1848, I must say I know of none, and I am quite sure that in our long discussions no allusion was made to anything of the kind. Great measures often occupy the thoughts of men and women, long before they take substantial form and become things of life, and I shall not dispute any one who says that this reform had been thought of before 1848. But I do insist the record shows that Judge Fine is the author of the law which opened the way to clothe woman with full rights, in regard to holding, using, and enjoying in every way her own property, independently of any husband.

I add the following extracts taken from the journals of the Senate and Assembly of 1848, viz:

Senate journal for 1848, p. 35. January 7th. "Mr. Fine gave notice that he would, at an early day, ask leave to introduce a bill for the more effectual protection of the property of married women."

Jan. 8th, p. 47. "Mr. Fine introduced 'the bill,' and it was referred to the Judiciary Committee," which consisted of Mr. Wilkin, Mr. Fine, and Mr. Cole.

Feb. 7th, p. 157. Mr. Wilkin reported the bill favorably, and it was sent to the Committee of the Whole.

Feb. 23d. Mr. Geddes presented the petition of three hundred citizens of Syracuse praying for the passage of a law to protect the rights of married women.

March 1st, p. 242. "The Senate spent some time in Committee of the Whole" on the bill, and reported progress, and had leave to sit again.

March 3d, p. 250. The Senate again in Committee of the Whole on this bill.

March 15th, p. 314. The Senate again in Committee of the Whole on this bill.

March 21st, p. 352. Mr. Lawrence, from Committee of the Whole, reported the bill with some amendments. "Thereupon ordered that said bill be referred to a Select Committee consisting of Mr. Fine, Mr. Geddes, and Mr. Hawley to report complete."

March 21st, p. 354. "Mr. Geddes, from the Select Committee, reported complete, with amendments, the bill entitled 'An Act for the more effectual protection of the property of married women,' which report was laid on the table."

March 28th, p. 420. "On motion of Mr. Geddes, the Senate then proceeded to the consideration of the report of the Select Committee on the bill entitled '(as above)', which report was agreed to, and the bill ordered to a third reading."

March 29th, p. 443. The bill entitled "(as above)" was read the third time, and passed—ayes, 23; nays, 1, as follows:

Ayes—Messrs. Betts, Bond, Brownson, Burch, Coffin, Cole, Cook, Cornwell, Fine, Floyd, Fox, Fuller, Geddes, S. H. P. Hall, Hawley, Johnson, Lawrence, Little, Martin, Smith, Wallon, Wilkin, Williams, 23.

Nays—Clark, 1.

April 7th, p. 541. The bill was returned from the Assembly with its concurrence.

Its history in the Assembly (*see its Journal*):

March 29th, p. 966. A message from the Senate, requesting the concurrence of the Assembly to "An Act for the more effectual protection of the property of married women." On motion of Mr. Campbell, the bill was sent to a Committee consisting of Messrs. Campbell, Brigham, Myers, Coe, and Crocker, to report complete (*see page 967*).

April 1st, page 1025. Mr. Campbell reported in favor of its passage, p. 1026. Report agreed to by the House.

April 6, p. 1129. Mr. Collins moved to recommit to a Select Committee for amendment. His motion failed, and the bill passed (p. 1130). Ayes, 93. Nays, 9.

The Governor put his name to the bill and thus it became a law.

Please reply to me and let me know whether I have made this matter clear to you.

Very respectfully,

GEO. GEDDES.

When the first bill was introduced by Judge Hertell in 1836, he made a very elaborate argument in its favor, covering all objections, and showing the incontestable justice of the measure. Being too voluminous for a newspaper report it was published in pamphlet form. His wife, Barbara Amelia Hertell, dying a few years since, by her will left a sum for the republication of this exhaustive argument, thus keeping the memory of her husband green in the hearts of his countrywomen, and expressing her own high appreciation of its value.

Step by step the Middle and New England States began to modify their laws, but the Western States, in their Constitutions, were liberal in starting. Thus the discussions in the constitutional convention and the Legislature, heralded by the press to every school district, culminated at last in a woman's rights convention.

The *Seneca County Courier*, a semi-weekly journal, of July 14, 1848, contained the following startling announcement:

SENECA FALLS CONVENTION.

WOMAN'S RIGHTS CONVENTION.—A Convention to discuss the social, civil, and religious condition and rights of woman, will be held in the Wesleyan Chapel, at Seneca Falls, N. Y., on Wednesday and Thursday, the 19th and 20th of July, current; commencing at 10 o'clock A.M. During the first day the meeting will be exclusively for women, who are earnestly invited to attend. The public generally are invited to be present on the second day, when Lucretia Mott, of Philadelphia, and other ladies and gentlemen, will address the convention.

This call, without signature, was issued by Lucretia Mott, Martha C. Wright, Elizabeth Cady Stanton, and Mary Ann McClintock. At this time Mrs. Mott was visiting her sister Mrs. Wright, at Auburn, and attending the Yearly Meeting of Friends in Western New York. Mrs. Stanton, having recently removed from Boston to Seneca Falls, finding the most congenial associations in Quaker families, met Mrs. Mott incidentally for the first time since her residence there. They at once returned to the topic they had so often discussed, walking arm in arm in the streets of London, and Boston, "the propriety of holding a woman's convention." These four ladies, sitting round the tea-table of Richard Hunt, a prominent Friend near Waterloo, decided to put their long-talked-of resolution into action, and before the twilight deepened into night, the call was written, and sent to the *Seneca County Courier.* On Sunday morning they met in Mrs. McClintock's parlor to write their declaration, resolutions, and to consider subjects for speeches.* As the convention was to assemble in three days, the time was short for such productions; but having no experience in the *modus operandi* of getting up conventions, nor in that kind of literature, they were quite innocent of the herculean labors they proposed. On the first attempt to frame a resolution; to crowd a complete thought, clearly and concisely, into three lines; they felt as helpless and hopeless as if they had been suddenly asked to construct a steam engine. And the humiliating fact may as well now be recorded that before taking the initiative step, those ladies resigned themselves to a faithful perusal of various masculine productions. The reports of Peace, Temperance, and Anti-Slavery conventions were examined, but all alike seemed too tame and pacific for the inauguration of a rebellion such as the world had never before seen. They knew women had wrongs, but how to state them was the difficulty, and this was increased from the fact that they themselves were fortunately organized and conditioned; they were neither "sour old maids," "childless women," nor "divorced wives," as the newspapers declared them to be. While they had felt the insults incident to sex, in many ways, as every proud, thinking woman must, in the laws, religion, and literature of the world, and in the invidious and degrading sentiments and customs of all nations, yet they had not in their own experience endured the coarser forms of tyranny resulting from unjust laws, or association with immoral and unscrupulous men, but they had souls large enough to feel the wrongs of others, without being scarified in their own flesh.

After much delay, one of the circle took up the Declaration of 1776, and read it aloud with much spirit and emphasis, and it was at once decided to adopt the historic document, with some slight changes such as substituting "all men" for "King George." Knowing that women must have more to complain of than men under any circumstances possibly could, and seeing the Fathers had eighteen grievances, a protracted search was made through statute

---

* The antique mahogany center-table on which this historic document was written now stands in the parlor of the McClintock family in Philadelphia.

books, church usages, and the customs of society to find that exact number. Several well-disposed men assisted in collecting the grievances, until, with the announcement of the eighteenth, the women felt they had enough to go before the world with a good case. One youthful lord remarked, "Your grievances must be grievous indeed, when you are obliged to go to books in order to find them out."

The eventful day dawned at last, and crowds in carriages and on foot, wended their way to the Wesleyan church. When those having charge of the Declaration, the resolutions, and several volumes of the Statutes of New York arrived on the scene, lo! the door was locked. However, an embryo Professor of Yale College was lifted through an open window to unbar the door; that done, the church was quickly filled. It had been decided to have no men present, but as they were already on the spot, and as the women who must take the responsibility of organizing the meeting, and leading the discussions, shrank from doing either, it was decided, in a hasty council round the altar, that this was an occasion when men might make themselves pre-eminently useful. It was agreed they should remain, and take the laboring oar through the Convention.

James Mott, tall and dignified, in Quaker costume, was called to the chair; Mary McClintock appointed Secretary, Frederick Douglass, Samuel Tillman, Ansel Bascom, E. W. Capron, and Thomas McClintock took part throughout in the discussions. Lucretia Mott, accustomed to public speaking in the Society of Friends, stated the objects of the Convention, and in taking a survey of the degraded condition of woman the world over, showed the importance of inaugurating some movement for her education and elevation. Elizabeth and Mary McClintock, and Mrs. Stanton, each read a well-written speech; Martha Wright read some satirical articles she had published in the daily papers answering the diatribes on woman's sphere. Ansel Bascom, who had been a member of the Constitutional Convention recently held in Albany, spoke at length on the property bill for married women, just passed the Legislature, and the discussion on woman's rights in that Convention. Samuel Tillman, a young student of law, read a series of the most exasperating statutes for women, from English and American jurists, all reflecting the *tender mercies* of men toward their wives, in taking care of their property and protecting them in their civil rights.

The Declaration having been freely discussed by many present, was re-read by Mrs. Stanton, and with some slight amendments adopted.

When, in the course of human events, it becomes necessary for one portion of the family of man to assume among the people of the earth a position different from that which they have hitherto occupied, but one to which the laws of nature and of nature's God entitle them, a decent respect to the opinions of mankind requires that they should declare the causes that impel them to such a course.

We hold these truths to be self-evident: that all men and women are created equal; that they are endowed by their Creator with certain inalienable rights; that among these are life, liberty, and the pursuit of happiness; that to secure these rights governments are instituted, deriving their just powers from the consent of the governed. Whenever any form of government becomes destructive of these ends, it is the right of those who suffer from it to refuse allegiance to it, and to insist upon the institution of a new government, laying its foundation on such principles, and organizing its powers in such form, as to them shall seem most likely to effect their safety and happiness. Prudence, indeed, will dictate that governments long established should not be changed for light and transient causes; and accordingly all experience hath shown that mankind are more disposed to suffer, while evils are sufferable, than to right themselves by abolishing the forms to which they were accustomed. But when a long train of abuses and usurpations, pursuing invariably the same object evinces a design to reduce them under absolute despotism, it is their duty to throw off such government, and to provide new guards for their future security. Such has been the patient sufferance of the women under this government, and such is now the necessity which constrains them to demand the equal station to which they are entitled.

The history of mankind is a history of repeated injuries and usurpations on the part of man toward woman, having in direct object the establishment of an absolute tyranny over her. To prove this, let facts be submitted to a candid world.

He has never permitted her to exercise her inalienable right to the elective franchise.

He has compelled her to submit to laws, in the formation of which she had no voice.

He has withheld from her rights which are given to the most ignorant and degraded men—both natives and foreigners.

Having deprived her of this first right of a citizen, the elective franchise, thereby leaving her without representation in the halls of legislation, he has oppressed her on all sides.

He has made her, if married, in the eye of the law, civilly dead.

He has taken from her all right in property, even to the wages she earns.

He has made her, morally, an irresponsible being, as she can commit many crimes with impunity, provided they be done in the presence of her husband. In the covenant of marriage, she is compelled to promise obedience to her husband, he becoming, to all intents and purposes, her master—the law giving him power to deprive her of her liberty, and to administer chastisement.

He has so framed the laws of divorce, as to what shall be the proper causes, and in case of separation, to whom the guardianship of the children shall be given, as to be wholly regardless of the happiness of women—the law, in all cases, going upon a false supposition of the supremacy of man, and giving all power into his hands.

After depriving her of all rights as a married woman, if single, and the owner of property, he has taxed her to support a government which recognizes her only when her property can be made profitable to it.

He has monopolized nearly all the profitable employments, and from those she is permitted to follow, she receives but a scanty remuneration. He closes against her all the avenues to wealth and distinction which he considers most honorable to himself. As a teacher of theology, medicine, or law, she is not known.

He has denied her the facilities for obtaining a thorough education, all colleges being closed against her.

He allows her in Church, as well as State, but a subordinate position, claiming Apostolic authority for her exclusion from the ministry, and, with some exceptions, from any public participation in the affairs of the Church.

He has created a false public sentiment by giving to the world a different code of morals for men and women, by which moral delinquencies which exclude women from society, are not only tolerated, but deemed of little account in man.

He has usurped the prerogative of Jehovah himself, claiming it as his right to assign for her a sphere of action, when that belongs to her conscience and to her God.

He has endeavored, in every way that he could, to destroy her confidence in her own powers, to lessen her self-respect, and to make her willing to lead a dependent and abject life.

Now, in view of this entire disfranchisement of one-half the people of this country, their social and religious degradation—in view of the unjust laws above mentioned, and because women do feel themselves aggrieved, oppressed, and fraudulently deprived of their most sacred rights, we insist that they have immediate admission to all the rights and privileges which belong to them as citizens of the United States.

In entering upon the great work before us, we anticipate no small amount of misconception, misrepresentation, and ridicule; but we shall use every instrumentality within our power to effect our object. We shall employ agents, circulate tracts, petition the State and National legislatures, and endeavor to enlist the pulpit and the press in our behalf. We hope this Convention will be followed by a series of Conventions embracing every part of the country.

The following resolutions were discussed by Lucretia Mott, Thomas and Mary Ann McClintock, Amy Post, Catharine A. F. Stebbins, and others, and were adopted:

WHEREAS, The great precept of nature is conceded to be, that "man shall pursue his own true and substantial happiness." Blackstone in his

Commentaries remarks, that this law of Nature being coeval with mankind, and dictated by God himself, is of course superior in obligation to any other. It is binding over all the globe, in all countries and at all times; no human laws are of any validity if contrary to this, and such of them as are valid, derive all their force, and all their validity, and all their authority, mediately and immediately, from this original; therefore,

Resolved, That such laws as conflict, in any way, with the true and substantial happiness of woman, are contrary to the great precept of nature and of no validity, for this is " superior in obligation to any other."

Resolved, That all laws which prevent woman from occupying such a station in society as her conscience shall dictate, or which place her in a position inferior to that of man, are contrary to the great precept of nature, and therefore of no force or authority.

Resolved, That woman is man's equal—was intended to be so by the Creator, and the highest good of the race demands that she should be recognized as such.

Resolved, That the women of this country ought to be enlightened in regard to the laws under which they live, that they may no longer publish their degradation by declaring themselves satisfied with their present position, nor their ignorance, by asserting that they have all the rights they want.

Resolved, That inasmuch as man, while claiming for himself intellectual superiority, does accord to woman moral superiority, it is pre-eminently his duty to encourage her to speak and teach, as she has an opportunity, in all religious assemblies.

Resolved, That the same amount of virtue, delicacy, and refinement of behavior that is required of woman in the social state, should also be required of man, and the same transgressions should be visited with equal severity on both man and woman.

Resolved, That the objection of indelicacy and impropriety, which is so often brought against woman when she addresses a public audience, comes with a very ill-grace from those who encourage, by their attendance, her appearance on the stage, in the concert, or in feats of the circus.

Resolved, That woman has too long' rested satisfied in the circumscribed limits which corrupt customs and a perverted application of the Scriptures have marked out for her, and that it is time she should move in the enlarged sphere which her great Creator has assigned her.

Resolved, That it is the duty of the women of this country to secure to themselves their sacred right to the elective franchise.

Resolved, That the equality of human rights results necessarily from the fact of the identity of the race in capabilities and responsibilities.

Resolved, therefore, That, being invested by the Creator with the same capabilities, and the same consciousness of responsibility for their exercise, it is demonstrably the right and duty of woman, equally with man, to promote every righteous cause by every righteous means; and especially in regard to the great subjects of morals and religion, it is self-evidently her right to participate with her brother in teaching them, both in private and in public, by writing and by speaking, by any instrumentalities proper to be used, and in any assemblies proper to be held; and this being a self-evident truth growing out of the divinely implanted principles of human nature, any custom or authority adverse to it, whether modern or wearing the hoary sanction of antiquity, is to be regarded as a self-evident falsehood, and at war with mankind.

At the last session Lucretia Mott offered and spoke to the following resolution :

Resolved, That the speedy success of our cause depends upon the zealous and untiring efforts of both men and women, for the overthrow of the monopoly of the pulpit, and for the securing to woman an equal participation with men in the various trades, professions, and commerce.

The only resolution that was not unanimously adopted was the ninth, urging the women of the country to secure to themselves the elective franchise. Those who took part in the debate feared a demand for the right to vote would defeat others they deemed more rational, and make the whole movement ridiculous.

But Mrs. Stanton and Frederick Douglass seeing that the power to choose rulers and make laws, was the right by which all others could be secured, persistently advocated the resolution, and at last carried it by a small majority.

Thus it will be seen that the Declaration and resolutions in the very first Convention, demanded all the most radical friends of the movement have since claimed—such as equal rights in the universities, in the trades and professions ; the right to vote ; to share in all political offices, honors, and emoluments; to complete equality in marriage, to personal freedom, property, wages, children ; to make contracts ; to sue, and be sued ; and to testify in courts of justice. At this time the condition of married women under the Common Law, was nearly as degraded as that of the slave on the Southern plantation. The Convention continued through two entire days, and late into the evenings. The deepest interest was manifested to its close.

The proceedings were extensively published, unsparingly ridiculed by the press, and denounced by the pulpit, much to the surprise and chagrin of the leaders. Being deeply in earnest, and believing their demands pre-eminently wise and just, they were wholly unprepared to find themselves the target for the jibes and jeers of the nation. The Declaration was signed by one hundred men, and women, many of whom withdrew their names as soon as the storm of ridicule began to break. The comments of the press were carefully preserved,* and it is curious to see that the same old arguments, and objections rife at the start, are reproduced by the press

---

* See Appendix.

of to-day. But the brave protests sent out from this Convention touched a responsive chord in the hearts of women all over the country.

Conventions were held soon after in Ohio, Massachusetts, Indiana, Pennsylvania, and at different points in New York.

Mr. Douglass, in his paper, *The North Star*, of July 28, 1848, had the following editorial leader :

THE RIGHTS OF WOMEN.—One of the most interesting events of the past week, was the holding of what is technically styled a Woman's Rights Convention at Seneca Falls. The speaking, addresses, and resolutions of this extraordinary meeting were almost wholly conducted by women; and although they evidently felt themselves in a novel position, it is but simple justice to say that their whole proceedings were characterized by marked ability and dignity. No one present, we think, however much he might be disposed to differ from the views advanced by the leading speakers on that occasion, will fail to give them credit for brilliant talents and excellent dispositions. In this meeting, as in other deliberative assemblies, there were frequent differences of opinion and animated discussion; but in no case was there the slightest absence of good feeling and decorum. Several interesting documents setting forth the rights as well as grievances of women were read. Among these was a Declaration of Sentiments, to be regarded as the basis of a grand movement for attaining the civil, social, political, and religious rights of women. We should not do justice to our own convictions, or to the excellent persons connected with this infant movement, if we did not in this connection offer a few remarks on the general subject which the Convention met to consider and the objects they seek to attain. In doing so, we are not insensible that the bare mention of this truly important subject in any other than terms of contemptuous ridicule and scornful disfavor, is likely to excite against us the fury of bigotry and the folly of prejudice. A discussion of the rights of animals would be regarded with far more complacency by many of what are called the *wise* and the *good* of our land, than would be a discussion of the rights of women. It is, in their estimation, to be guilty of evil thoughts, to think that woman is entitled to equal rights with man. Many who have at last made the discovery that the negroes have some rights as well as other members of the human family, have yet to be convinced that women are entitled to any. Eight years ago a number of persons of this description actually abandoned the anti-slavery cause, lest by giving their influence in that direction they might possibly be giving countenance to the dangerous heresy that woman, in respect to rights, stands on an equal footing with man. In the judgment of such persons the American slave system, with all its concomitant horrors, is less to be deplored than this *wicked* idea. It is perhaps needless to say, that we cherish little sympathy for such sentiments or respect for such prejudices. Standing as we do upon the watch-tower of human freedom, we can not be deterred from an expression of our approbation of any movement, however humble, to improve and elevate the character of any members of the human family. While it is impossible for us to go into this subject at length, and dispose of the various objections which are often urged against such a doctrine as that of female equality, we are free to say that in respect to political rights, we hold woman to be justly entitled to all we claim for man. We go farther, and express our conviction that all political rights which it is expedient for man to exercise, it is equally so for woman. All that distinguishes man as an intelligent and accountable being, is equally true of woman; and if that government only is just which governs by the free consent of the governed, there can be no reason in the world for denying to woman the exercise of the elective franchise, or a hand in making and administering the laws of the land. Our doctrine is that " right is of no sex." We therefore bid the women engaged in this movement our humble Godspeed.

THE ROCHESTER CONVENTION, AUGUST 2, 1848.

Those who took part in the Convention at Seneca Falls, finding at the end of the two days, there were still so many new points for discussion, and that the gift of tongues had been vouchsafed to them, adjourned, to meet in Rochester in two weeks. Amy Post, Sarah D. Fish, Sarah C. Owen, and Mary H. Hallowell, were the Committee of Arrangements. This Convention was called for August 2d, and so well advertised in the daily papers, that at the appointed hour, the Unitarian Church was filled to overflowing.

Amy Post called the meeting to order, and stated that at a gathering the previous evening in Protection Hall, Rhoda De Garmo, Sarah Fish, and herself, were appointed a committee to nominate officers for the Convention, and they now proposed Abigail Bush, for President; Laura Murray, for Vice-President; Elizabeth McClintock, Sarah Hallowell, and Catherine A. F. Stebbins, for Secretaries. Mrs. Mott, Mrs. Stanton, and Mrs. McClintock, thought it a most hazardous experiment to have a woman President, and stoutly opposed it.

To write a Declaration and Resolutions, to make a speech, and debate, had taxed their powers to the uttermost; and now, with such feeble voices and timid manners, without the slightest knowledge of Cushing's Manual, or the least experience in public meetings, how could a woman preside? They were on the verge of leaving the Convention in disgust, but Amy Post and Rhoda De Garmo assured them that by the same power by which they had resolved, declared, discussed, debated, they could also preside at a public meeting, if they would but make the experiment. And as the vote of the majority settled the question on the side of woman, Abigail Bush took the chair, and the calm way she assumed the duties of the office, and the admirable manner in which she discharged them, soon reconciled the opposition to the seemingly ridiculous experiment.

The proceedings were opened with prayer, by the Rev. Mr. Wicher, of the Free-will Baptist Church. Even at that early day, there were many of the liberal clergymen in favor of equal rights for women. During the reading of the minutes of the preliminary meeting by the Secretary, much uneasiness was manifested concerning the low voices of women, and cries of " Louder, louder!" drowned every other sound, when the President, on rising, said:

Friends, we present ourselves here before you, as an oppressed class, with trembling frames and faltering tongues, and we do not expect to be able to speak so as to be heard by all at first, but we trust we shall have the sympathy of the audience, and that you will bear with our weakness now in the infancy of the movement. Our trust in the omnipotency of right is our only faith that we shall succeed.

As the appointed Secretaries could not be heard, Sarah Anthony Burtis, an experienced Quaker school-teacher, whose voice had been well trained in her profession, volunteered to fill the duties of that office, and she read the reports and documents of the Convention with a clear voice and confident manner, to the great satisfaction of her more timid coadjutors.

Several gentlemen took part in the debates of this Convention. Some in favor, some opposed, and others willing to make partial concessions to the demands as set forth in the Declaration and Resolutions. Frederick Douglass, William C. Nell, and William C. Bloss advocated the emancipation of women from all the artificial disabilities, imposed by false customs, creeds, and codes. Milo Codding, Mr. Sulley, Mr. Pickard, and a Mr. Colton, of Connecticut, thought " woman's sphere was home," and that she should remain in it ; he would seriously deprecate her occupying the pulpit.

Lucretia Mott replied, that the gentleman from New Haven had objected to woman occupying the pulpit, and indeed she could scarcely see how any one educated in New Haven, Ct., could think otherwise than he did. She said, we had all got our notions too much from the clergy, instead of the Bible. The Bible, she contended, had none of the prohibitions in regard to women ; and spoke of the " honorable women not a few," etc., and desired Mr. Colton to read his Bible over again, and see if there was anything there to prohibit woman from being a religious teacher. She then complimented the members of that church for opening their doors to a Woman's Rights Convention, and said that a few years ago, the Female Moral Reform Society of

Philadelphia applied for the use of a church in that city, in which to hold one of their meetings; they were only allowed the use of the basement, and on condition that none of the women should speak at the meeting. Accordingly, a D.D. was called upon to preside, and another to read the ladies' report of the Society.

Near the close of the morning session, a young bride in traveling dress,* accompanied by her husband, slowly walked up the aisle, and asked the privilege of saying a few words, which was readily granted. Being introduced to the audience, she said, on her way westward, hearing of the Convention, she had waited over a train, to add her mite in favor of the demand now made, by the true women of this generation :

It is with diffidence that I speak upon this question before us, not a diffidence resulting from any doubt of the worthiness of the cause, but from the fear that its depth and power can be but meagerly portrayed by me. . . . . Woman's rights—her civil rights—equal with man's—not an equality of moral and religious influence, for who dares to deny her that?—but an equality in the exercise of her own powers, and a right to use all the sources of erudition within the reach of man, to build unto herself a name for her talents, energy, and integrity. We do not positively say that our intellect is as capable as man's to assume, and at once to hold, these rights, or that our hearts are as willing to enter into his actions; for if we did not believe it, we would not contend for them, and if men did not believe it, they would not withhold them with a smothered silence. . . . . In closing, she said: There will be one effect, perhaps unlooked for, if we are raised to equal administration with man. It will classify intellect. The heterogeneous triflings which now, I am very sorry to say, occupy so much of our time, will be neglected; fashion's votaries will silently fall off; dishonest exertions for rank in society will be scorned; extravagance in toilet will be detested; that meager and worthless pride of station will be forgotten; the honest earnings of dependents will be paid; popular demagogues crushed; impostors unpatronized; true genius sincerely encouraged; and, above all, pawned integrity redeemed! And why? Because enfranchised woman then will feel the burdens of her responsibilities, and can strive for elevation, and will reach all knowledge within her grasp. . . . . If all this is accomplished, man need not fear pomposity, fickleness, or an unhealthy enthusiasm at his dear fireside; we can be as dutiful, submissive, endearing as daughters, wives, and mothers, even if we hang the wreath of domestic harmony upon the eagle's talons.

Thus for twenty minutes the young and beautiful stranger held her audience spell-bound with her eloquence, in a voice whose pathos thrilled every heart. Her husband, hat and cane in hand, remained standing, leaning against a pillar near the altar, and

---

* Rebecca Sanford, now Postmaster at Mt. Morris, N. Y.

seemed a most delighted, nay, reverential listener. It was a scene never to be forgotten, and one of the most pleasing incidents of the Convention.

Sarah Owen read an address on woman's place and pay in the world of work. In closing, she said :

An experienced cashier of this city remarked to me that women might be as good book-keepers as men; but men have monopolized every lucrative situation, from the dry-goods merchant down to whitewashing. Who does not feel, as she sees a stout, athletic man standing behind the counter measuring lace, ribbons, and tape, that he is monopolizing a woman's place, while thousands of rich acres in our western world await his coming ? This year, a woman, for the first time, has taken her place in one of our regular medical colleges. We rejoice to hear that by her dignity of manner, application to study, and devotion to the several branches of the profession she has chosen, she has secured the respect of her professors and class, and reflected lasting honor upon her whole sex. Thus we hail, in Elizabeth Blackwell, a pioneer for woman in this profession.

It is by this inverted order of society that woman is obliged to ply the needle by day and by night, to procure even a scanty pittance for her dependent family. Let men become producers, as nature has designed them, and women be educated to fill all those stations which require less physical strength, and we should soon modify many of our social evils. I am informed by the seamstresses of this city, that they get but thirty cents for making a satin vest, and from twelve to thirty for making pants, and coats in the same proportion. Man has such a contemptible idea of woman, that he thinks she can not even sew as well as he can; and he often goes to a tailor, and pays him double and even treble for making a suit, when it merely passes through his hands, after a woman has made every stitch of it so neatly that he discovers no difference. Who does not see gross injustice in this inequality of wages and violation of rights ? To prove that woman is capable of prosecuting the mercantile business, we have a noble example in this city in Mrs. Gifford, who has sustained herself with credit. She has bravely triumphed over all obloquy and discouragement attendant on such a novel experiment, and made for herself an independent living.

In the fields of benevolence, woman has done great and noble works for the safety and stability of the nation. When man shall see the wisdom of recognizing a co-worker in her, then may be looked for the dawning of a perfect day, when woman shall stand where God designed she should, on an even platform with man himself.

Mrs. Roberts, who had been requested to investigate the wrongs of the laboring classes, and to invite that oppressed portion of the community to attend the Convention, and take part in its deliberations, made some appropriate remarks relative to the intolerable servitude and small remuneration paid to the working-class of women. She reported the average price of labor for seamstresses to be from 31 to 38 cents a day, and board from $1.25 to $1.50 per week to be deducted therefrom, and they were generally obliged to take half or more in due bills, which were payable in goods at certain stores, thereby obliging them many times to pay extortionate prices.

Mrs. Galloy corroborated the statement, having herself experienced some of the oppressions of this portion of our citizens, and expressed her gratitude that the subject was claiming the attention of this benevolent and intelligent class of community. It did not require much argument, to reconcile all who took part in the debates, to woman's right to equal wages for equal work, but the gentlemen seemed more disturbed as to the effect of equality in the family. With the old idea of a divinely ordained head, and that, in all cases, the man, whether wise or foolish, educated or ignorant, sober or drunk, such a relation to them did not seem feasible. Mr. Sully asked, when the two heads disagree, who must decide? There is no Lord Chancellor to whom to apply, and does not St. Paul strictly enjoin obedience to husbands, and that man shall be head of the woman?

Lucretia Mott replied that in the Society of Friends she had never known any difficulty to arise on account of the wife's not having promised *obedience* in the marriage contract. She had never known any mode of decision except an appeal to reason; and, although in some of the meetings of this Society, women are placed on an equality, none of the results so much dreaded had occurred. She said that many of the opposers of Woman's Rights, who bid us to obey the bachelor St. Paul, themselves reject his counsel. He advised them not to marry. In general answer she would quote, "One is your master, even Christ." Although Paul enjoins silence on women in the Church, yet he gives directions how they should appear when publicly speaking, and we have scriptural accounts of honorable women not a few who were religious teachers, viz: Phebe, Priscilla, Tryphena, Triphosa, and the four daughters of Philip, and various others.

Mrs. Stanton thought the gentleman might be easily answered; saying that the strongest will or the superior intellect now governs the household, as it will in the new order. She knew many a woman, who, to all intents and purposes, is at the head of her family.

Mr. Pickard asked who, after marriage, should hold the property, and whose name should be retained. He thought an umpire necessary. He did not see but all business must cease until the consent of both parties be obtained. He saw an impossibility of introducing such rules into society. The Gospel had established the unity and oneness of the married pair.

Mrs. Stanton said she thought the Gospel, rightly understood, pointed to a oneness of equality, not subordination, and that property should be jointly held. She could see no reason why marriage by false creeds should be made a degradation to woman; and, as to the name, the custom of taking the husband's name is not universal. When a man has a bad name in any sense, he might be the gainer by burying himself under the good name of his wife. This last winter a Mr. Cruikshanks applied to our Legislature to have his name changed. Now, if he had taken his wife's name in the beginning, he might have saved the Legislature the trouble of considering the propriety of releasing the man from such a burden to be entailed on the third and fourth generation. When a slave escapes from a Southern plantation, he at once takes a name as the first step in liberty—the first assertion of individual identity. A woman's dignity is equally involved in a life-long name, to mark her individuality. We can not overestimate the demoralizing effect on woman herself, to say nothing of society at large, for her to consent thus to merge her existence so wholly in that of another.

A well-written speech was read by William C. Nell, which Mrs. Mott thought too flattering. She said woman is now sufficiently developed to prefer justice to compliment.

A letter was read from Gerrit Smith, approving cordially of the object of the Convention.

Mrs. Stanton read the Declaration that was adopted at Seneca Falls, and urged those present who did not agree with its sentiments, to make their objections then and there. She hoped if there were any clergymen present, they would not keep silent during the Convention and then on Sunday do as their brethren did in Seneca Falls — use their pulpits throughout the city to denounce them, where they could not, of course, be allowed to reply.

The resolutions* were freely discussed by Amy Post, Rhoda De Garmo, Ann Edgeworth, Sarah D. Fish, and others. While Mrs. Mott and Mrs. Stanton spoke in their favor, they thought they were too tame, and wished for some more stirring declarations. Elizabeth McClintock read, in an admirable manner, a spirited poetical reply, from the pen of Maria Weston Chapman, to "A Clerical Appeal" published in 1840. Mrs. Chapman was one of the grand women in

---

* See Appendix.

Boston, who, during the early days of Anti-Slavery, gave her unceasing efforts to that struggle. Her pen was a power in the journals and magazines, and her presence an inspiration in their fairs and conventions. When Abby Kelly, Angelina Grimke, and Lucretia Mott first began to speak to promiscuous assemblies in Anti-Slavery Conventions, "a clerical appeal" was issued and sent to all the clergymen in New England, calling on them to denounce in their pulpits this unmannerly and unchristian proceeding. Sermons were preached, portraying in the darkest colors the fearful results to the Church, the State, and the home, in thus encouraging women to enter public life.

"PASTORAL LETTER."

Extract from a Pastoral Letter of "the General Association of Massachusetts (Orthodox) to the Churches under their care"—1837:

III. We invite your attention to the dangers which at present seem to threaten the female character with wide-spread and permanent injury. The appropriate duties and influence of woman are clearly stated in the New Testament. Those duties and that influence are unobtrusive and private, but the source of mighty power. When the mild, dependent, softening influence of woman upon the sternness of man's opinions is fully exercised, society feels the effects of it in a thousand forms. The power of woman is her dependence, flowing from the consciousness of that weakness which God has given her for her protection, (!) and which keeps her in those departments of life that form the character of individuals, and of the nation. There are social influences which females use in promoting piety and the great objects of Christian benevolence which we can not too highly commend.

We appreciate the unostentatious prayers and efforts of woman in advancing the cause of religion at home and abroad; in Sabbath-schools ; in leading religious inquirers to the pastors (!) for instruction; and in all such associated effort as becomes the modesty of her sex; and earnestly hope that she may abound more and more in these labors of piety and love. But when she assumes the place and tone of man as a public reformer, our care and protection of her seem unnecessary; we put ourselves in self-defence (!) against her; she yields the power which God has given her for her protection, and her character becomes unnatural. If the vine, whose strength and beauty is to lean upon the trellis-work, and half conceal its clusters, thinks to assume the independence and the overshadowing nature of the elm, it will not only cease to bear fruit, but fall in shame and dishonor into the dust. We can not, therefore, but regret the mistaken conduct of those who encourage females to bear an obtrusive and ostentatious part in measures of reform, and countenance any of that sex who so far forget themselves as to itinerate in the character of public lecturers and teachers. We especially deplore the intimate acquaintance and promiscuous conversation of females with regard to

things which ought not to be named; by which that modesty and delicacy which is the charm of domestic life, and which constitutes the true
influence of woman in society, is consumed, and the way opened, as we
apprehend, for degeneracy and ruin.

We say these things not to discourage proper influences against sin,
but to secure such reformation (!) as we believe is Scriptural, and will be
permanent.

William Lloyd Garrison, in a cordial letter, accompanying the
above extract, which he had copied for us with his own hand from
the files of *The Liberator*, said : " This ' Clerical Bull ' was fulmi-
nated with special reference to those two noble South Carolina wom-
en, Sarah M. and Angelina E. Grimke, who were at that time publicly pleading for those in bonds as bound with them, while on a
visit to Massachusetts. It was written by the Rev. Dr. Nehemiah
Adams, of Boston, author of ' A South-side View of Slavery.' "

Maria Weston Chapman's amusing answer in rhyme, shows that
the days for ecclesiastical bulls were fast passing away, when women,
even, could thus make light of them.

MRS. CHAPMAN'S POEM.

"THE TIMES THAT TRY MEN'S SOULS."

Confusion has seized us, and all things go wrong,
    The women have leaped from "their spheres,"
And, instead of fixed stars, shoot as comets along,
    And are setting the world by the ears!
In courses erratic they're wheeling through space,
In brainless confusion and meaningless chase.

In vain do our knowing ones try to compute
    Their return to the orbit designed;
They're glanced at a moment, then onward they shoot,
    And are neither "to hold nor to bind;"
So freely they move in their chosen ellipse,
The "Lords of Creation" do fear an eclipse.

They've taken a notion to speak for themselves,
    And are wielding the tongue and the pen;
They've mounted the rostrum; the termagant elves,
    And—oh horrid!—are talking to men!
With faces unblanched in our presence they come
To harangue us, they say, in behalf of the dumb.

They insist on their right to petition and pray,
    That St. Paul, in Corinthians, has given them rules
For appearing in public; despite what those say
    Whom we've trained to instruct them in schools;

But vain such instructions, if women may scan
And quote texts of Scripture to favor their plan.

Our grandmothers' learning consisted of yore
    In spreading their generous boards;
In twisting the distaff, or mopping the floor,
    And *obeying the will of their lords.*
Now, misses may reason, and think, and debate,
Till unquestioned submission is quite out of date.

Our clergy have preached on the sin and the shame
    Of woman, when out of " her sphere,"
And labored *divinely* to ruin her fame,
    And shorten this horrid career;
But for spiritual guidance no longer they look
To Fulsom, or Winslow, or learned Parson Cook.

Our wise men have tried to exorcise in vain
    The turbulent spirits abroad;
As well might we deal with the fetterless main,
    Or conquer ethereal essence with sword;
Like the devils of Milton, they rise from each blow,
With spirit unbroken, insulting the foe.

Our patriot fathers, of eloquent fame,
    Waged war against tangible forms;
Aye, *their* foes were men—and if ours were the same,
    We might speedily quiet their storms;
But, ah! their descendants enjoy not such bliss—
The assumptions of Britain were nothing to this.

Could we but array all our force in the field,
    We'd teach these usurpers of power
That their bodily safety demands they should yield,
    And in the presence of manhood should cower;
But, alas! for our tethered and impotent state,
Chained by notions of knighthood—we can but debate.

Oh! shade of the prophet Mahomet, arise!
    Place woman again in " her sphere,"
And teach that her soul was not born for the skies,
    But to flutter a brief moment here.
This doctrine of Jesus, as preached up by Paul,
If embraced in its spirit, will ruin us all.

                    —*Lords of Creation.*

On reading the " Pastoral Letter," our Quaker poet, John Greenleaf Whittier, poured out his indignation on the New England
clergy in thrilling denunciations. Mr. Whittier early saw that
woman's only protection against religious and social tyranny, could

be found in political equality. In the midst of the fierce conflicts
in the Anti-Slavery Conventions of 1839 and '40, on the woman
question *per se*, Mr. Whittier remarked to Lucretia Mott, " *Give
woman the right to vote*, and you end all these persecutions by reform and church organizations.'

THE PASTORAL LETTER.

So, this is all—the utmost reach
  Of priestly power the mind to fetter!
When laymen think—when women preach—
  A war of words—a " Pastoral Letter! "
Now, shame upon ye, parish Popes!
  Was it thus with those, your predecessors,
Who sealed with racks, and fire, and ropes
  Their loving-kindness to transgressors ?

A " Pastoral Letter," grave and dull—
  Alas! in hoof and horns and features,
How different is your Brookfield bull,
  From him who bellows from St. Peter's!
Your pastoral rights and powers from harm,
  Think ye, can words alone preserve them ?
Your wiser fathers taught the arm
  And sword of temporal power to serve them.

Oh, glorious days—when Church and State
  Were wedded by your spiritual fathers!
And on submissive shoulders sat
  Yours Wilsons and your Cotton Mathers.
No vile " itinerant " then could mar
  The beauty of your tranquil Zion,
But at his peril of the scar
  Of hangman's whip and branding-iron.

Then, wholesome laws relieved the Church
  Of heretic and mischief-maker,
And priest and bailiff joined in search,
  By turns, of Papist, witch, and Quaker!
The stocks were at each church's door,
  The gallows stood on Boston Common,
A Papist's ears the pillory bore—
  The gallows-rope, a Quaker woman!

Your fathers dealt not as ye deal
  With " non-professing " frantic teachers;
They bored the tongue with red-hot steel,
  And flayed the backs of " female preachers."

Old Newbury, had her fields a tongue,
 And Salem's streets could tell their story,
Of fainting woman dragged along,
 Gashed by the whip, accursed and gory!

And will ye ask me, why this taunt
 Of memories sacred from the scorner?
And why with reckless hand I plant
 A nettle on the graves ye honor?
Not to reproach New England's dead
 This record from the past I summon,
Of manhood to the scaffold led,
 And suffering and heroic woman.

No—for yourselves alone, I turn
 The pages of intolerance over,
That, in their spirit, dark and stern,
 Ye haply may your own discover!
For, if ye claim the "pastoral right,"
 To silence freedom's voice of warning,
And from your precincts shut the light
 Of Freedom's day around ye dawning;

If when an earthquake voice of power,
 And signs in earth and heaven, are showing
That forth, in the appointed hour,
 The Spirit of the Lord is going!
And, with that Spirit, Freedom's light
 On kindred, tongue, and people breaking,
Whose slumbering millions, at the sight,
 In glory and in strength are waking!

When for the sighing of the poor,
 And for the needy, God hath risen,
And chains are breaking, and a door
 Is opening for the souls in prison!
If then ye would, with puny hands,
 Arrest the very work of Heaven,
And bind anew the evil bands
 Which God's right arm of power hath riven,—

What marvel that, in many a mind,
 Those darker deeds of bigot madness
Are closely with your own combined,
 Yet "less in anger than in sadness"?
What marvel, if the people learn
 To claim the right of free opinion?
What marvel, if at times they spurn
 The ancient yoke of your dominion?

A glorious remnant linger yet,
  Whose lips are wet at Freedom's fountains,
The coming of whose welcome feet
  Is beautiful upon our mountains!
Men, who the gospel tidings bring
  Of Liberty and Love forever,
Whose joy is an abiding spring,
  Whose peace is as a gentle river!

But ye, who scorn the thrilling tale
  Of Carolina's high-souled daughters,
Which echoes here the mournful wail
  Of sorrow from Edisto's waters,
Close while ye may the public ear—
  With malice vex, with slander wound them—
The pure and good shall throng to hear,
  And tried and manly hearts surround them.

Oh, ever may the power which led
  Their way to such a fiery trial,
And strengthened womanhood to tread
  The wine-press of such self-denial,
Be round them in an evil land,
  With wisdom and with strength from Heaven,
With Miriam's voice, and Judith's hand,
  And Deborah's song, for triumph given!

And what are ye who strive with God
  Against the ark of His salvation,
Moved by the breath of prayer abroad,
  With blessings for a dying nation?
What, but the stubble and the hay
  To perish, even as flax consuming,
With all that bars His glorious way,
  Before the brightness of His coming?

And thou, sad Angel, who so long
  Hast waited for the glorious token,
That Earth from all her bonds of wrong
  To liberty and light has broken—
Angel of Freedom! soon to thee
  The sounding trumpet shall be given,
And over Earth's full jubilee
  Shall deeper joy be felt in Heaven!

In answer to the many objections made, by gentlemen present, to granting to woman the right of suffrage, Frederick Douglass replied in a long, argumentative, and eloquent appeal, for the complete equality of woman in all the rights that belong to any human soul. He thought the true basis of rights was the capacity of individuals ; and as for himself, he should not dare claim a right that he would not concede to woman.

This Convention continued through three sessions, and was crowded with an attentive audience to the hour of adjournment. The daily papers made fair reports, and varied editorial comments, which, being widely copied, called out spicy controversies in different parts of the country. The resolutions and discussions regarding woman's right to enter the professions, encouraged many to prepare themselves for medicine and the ministry. Though few women responded to the demand for political rights, many at once saw the importance of equality in the world of work.

The Seneca Falls Declaration was adopted, and signed by large numbers of influential men and women of Rochester and vicinity, and at a late hour the Convention adjourned, in the language of its President, " with hearts overflowing with gratitude."

CHAPTER V.

REMINISCENCES.

EMILY COLLINS.

The first Suffrage Society—Methodist class-leader whips his wife—Theology enchains the soul—The status of women and slaves the same—The first medical college opened to women, Geneva, N. Y.—Petitions to the Legislature laughed at, and laid on the table—Dependence woman's best protection; her weakness her sweetest charm—Dr. Elizabeth Blackwell's letter.

I WAS born and lived almost forty years in South Bristol, Ontario County—one of the most secluded spots in Western New York; but from the earliest dawn of reason I pined for that freedom of thought and action that was then denied to all womankind. I revolted in spirit against the customs of society and the laws of the State that crushed my aspirations and debarred me from the pursuit of almost every object worthy of an intelligent, rational mind. But not until that meeting at Seneca Falls in 1848, of the pioneers in the cause, gave this feeling of unrest form and voice, did I take action. Then I summoned a few women in our neighborhood together and formed an Equal Suffrage Society, and sent petitions to our Legislature; but our efforts were little known beyond our circle, as we were in communication with no person or newspaper. Yet there was enough of wrong in our narrow horizon to rouse some thought in the minds of all.

In those early days a husband's supremacy was often enforced in the rural districts by corporeal chastisement, and it was considered by most people as quite right and proper—as much so as the correction of refractory children in like manner. I remember in my own neighborhood a man who was a Methodist class-leader and exhorter, and one who was esteemed a worthy citizen, who, every few weeks, gave his wife a beating with his horsewhip. He said it was necessary, in order to keep her in subjection, and because she scolded so much. Now this wife, surrounded by six or seven little children, whom she must wash, dress, feed, and attend to day and night, was obliged to spin and weave cloth for all the garments of the family. She had to milk the cows, make butter and cheese, do all the cooking, washing, making, and mending for the family, and, with the pains of maternity forced upon her every eighteen months, was whipped by her pious husband, " because she scolded." And pray, why should he not have chastised her? The laws made it his privilege—and the Bible, as interpreted, made it his duty. It is true, women repined at their hard lot; but it was thought to be fixed by a divine decree, for " The man shall rule over thee," and " Wives, be subject to your husbands," and " Wives, submit yourselves unto your husbands as unto the Lord," caused them to consider their fate inevitable, and to feel that it would be contravening God's law to resist it. It is ever thus; where Theology enchains the soul, the Tyrant enslaves the body. But can any one, who has any knowledge of the laws that govern our being—of heredity and pre-natal influences—be astonished that our jails and prisons are filled with criminals, and our hospitals with sickly specimens of humanity? As long as the mothers of the race are subject to such unhappy conditions, it can never be materially improved. Men exhibit some common sense in breeding all animals except those of their own species.

All through the Anti-Slavery struggle, every word of denunciation of the wrongs of the Southern slave, was, I felt, equally applicable to the wrongs of my own sex. Every argument for the emancipation of the colored man, was equally one for that of woman; and I was surprised that all Abolitionists did not see the similarity in the condition of the two classes. I read, with intense interest, everything that indicated an awakening of public or private thought to the idea that woman did not occupy her rightful position in the organization of society; and, when I read the lectures of Ernestine L. Rose and the writings of Margaret Fuller, and found that other women entertained the same thoughts that had been seething in my own brain, and realized that I stood not alone, how my heart bounded with joy! The arguments of that distinguished jurist, Judge Hurlburt, encouraged me to hope that men would ultimately see the justice of our cause, and concede to women their natural rights.

I hailed with gladness any aspiration of women toward an enlargement of their sphere of action; and when, in the early part of 1848, I learned that Miss Elizabeth Blackwell had been admitted as a student to the medical college at Geneva, N. Y., being the first lady in the United States that had attained that privilege, and knowing the tide of public sentiment ,she had to stem, I could not **refrain**

from writing her a letter of approval and encouragement. In return I received the following:

PHILADELPHIA, *August* 12, 1848.

DEAR MADAM:—Your letter, I can assure you, met with a hearty welcome from me. And I can not refrain from writing to you a warm acknowledgment of your cordial sympathy, and expressing the pleasure
with which I have read your brave words. It is true, I look neither for
praise nor blame in pursuing the path which I have chosen. With firm religious enthusiasm, no opinion of the world will move me, but when I
receive from a woman an approval so true-hearted and glowing, a recognition so clear of the motives which urge me on, then my very soul bounds
at the thrilling words, and I go on with renewed energy, with hope, and
holy joy in my inmost being.

My whole life is devoted unreservedly to the service of my sex. The
study and practice of medicine is in my thought but one means to a great
end, for which my very soul yearns with intensest passionate emotion,
of which I have dreamed day and night, from my earliest childhood, for
which I would offer up my life with triumphant thanksgiving, if martyrdom could secure that glorious end : — the true ennoblement of
woman, the full harmonious development of her unknown nature, and
the consequent redemption of the whole human race. "Earth waits for
her queen." Every noble movement of the age, every prophecy of future
glory, every throb of that great heart which is laboring throughout
Christendom, call on woman with a voice of thunder, with the authority
of a God, to listen to the mighty summons to awake from her guilty
sleep, and rouse to glorious action to play her part in the great drama of
the ages, and finish the work that man has begun.

Most fully do I respond to all the noble aspirations that fill your letter.
Women are feeble, narrow, frivolous at present: ignorant of their own
capacities, and undeveloped in thought and feeling; and while they remain so, the great work of human regeneration must remain incomplete;
humanity will continue to suffer, and cry in vain for deliverance, for
woman has her work to do, and no one can accomplish it for her. She
is bound to rise, to try her strength, to break her bonds;—not with
noisy outcry, not with fighting or complaint; but with quiet strength,
with gentle dignity, firmly, irresistibly, with a cool determination that
never wavers, with a clear insight into her own capacities, let her do her
duty, pursue her highest conviction of right, and firmly grasp whatever
she is able to carry.

Much is said of the oppression woman suffers; man is reproached with
being unjust, tyrannical, jealous. I do not so read human life. The exclusion and constraint woman suffers, is not the result of purposed injury
or premeditated insult. It has arisen naturally, without violence, simply because woman has desired nothing more, has not felt the soul too
large for the body. But when woman, with matured strength, with
steady purpose, presents her lofty claim, all barriers will give way, and
man will welcome, with a thrill of joy, the new birth of his sister spirit,
the advent of his partner, his co-worker, in the great universe of being.

If the present arrangements of society will not admit of woman's free development, then society must be remodeled, and adapted to the great wants of all humanity. Our race is one, the interests of all are inseparably united, and harmonic freedom for the perfect growth of every human soul is the great want of our time. It has given me heartfelt satisfaction, dear madam, that you sympathize in my effort to advance the great interests of humanity. I feel the responsibility of my position, and I shall endeavor, by wisdom of action, purity of motive, and unwavering steadiness of purpose, to justify the noble hope I have excited. To me the future is full of glorious promise, humanity is arousing to accomplish its grand destiny, and in the fellowship of this great hope, I would greet you, and recognize in your noble spirit a fellow-laborer for the true and the good.   ELIZABETH BLACKWELL.
MRS. EMILY COLLINS.

But, it was the proceedings of the Convention, in 1848, at Seneca Falls, that first gave a direction to the efforts of the many women, who began to feel the degradation of their subject condition, and its baneful effects upon the human race. They then saw the necessity for associated action, in order to obtain the elective franchise, the only key that would unlock the doors of their prison. I wrote to Miss Sarah C. Owen, Secretary of the Women's Protective Union, at Rochester, as to the line of procedure that had been proposed there. In reply, under date of October 1, 1848, she says:

Your letter has just reached me, and with much pleasure I reply to the echo of inquiry, beyond the bounds of those personally associated with us in this enterprise. It is indeed encouraging to hear a voice from South Bristol in such perfect unison with our own.

Possibly, extracts from my next letter to Miss Owen, dated Oct. 23, 1848, will give you the best idea of the movement:

I should have acknowledged the receipt of yours of the 1st inst. earlier, but wished to report somewhat of progress whenever I should write. Our prospects here are brightening. Every lady of any worth or intelligence adopts unhesitatingly our view, and concurs in our measures. On the 19th inst. we met and organized a Woman's Equal Rights Union. Living in the country, where the population is sparse, we are consequently few; but hope to make up in zeal and energy for our lack of numbers. We breathe a freer, if not a purer atmosphere here among the mountains, than do the dwellers in cities,—have more independence, —are less subject to the despotism of fashion, and are less absorbed with dress and amusements. . . . . A press entirely devoted to our cause seems indispensable. If there is none such, can you tell me of any paper that advocates our claims more warmly than the *North Star?**

* Published by Frederick Douglass, the first colored man that edited a paper in this country. His press was presented to him by the women of England, who sympathized with the anti-slavery movement.

A lecturer in the field would be most desirable; but how to raise funds to sustain one is the question. I never really wished for Aladdin's lamp till now. Would to Heaven that women could be persuaded to use the funds they acquire by their sewing-circles and fairs, in trying to raise their own condition above that of "infants, idiots, and lunatics," with whom our statutes class them, instead of spending the money in decorating their churches, or sustaining a clergy, the most of whom are striving to rivet the chains still closer that bind, not only our own sex, but the oppressed of every class and color.

The elective franchise is now the one object for which we must labor; that once attained, all the rest will be easily acquired. Moral Reform and Temperance Societies may be multiplied *ad infinitum,* but they have about the same effect upon the evils they seek to cure, as clipping the top of a hedge would have toward extirpating it. Please forward me a copy of the petition for suffrage. We will engage to do all we can, not only in our own town, but in the adjoining ones of Richmond, East Bloomfield, Canandaigua, and Naples. I have promises of aid from people of influence in obtaining signatures. In the meantime we wish to disseminate some able work upon the enfranchisement of women. We wish to present our Assemblyman elect, whoever he may be, with some work of this kind, and solicit his candid attention to the subject. People are more willing to be convinced by the calm perusal of an argument, than in a personal discussion. . . . .

Our Society was composed of some fifteen or twenty ladies, and we met once in two weeks, in each other's parlors, alternately, for discussion and interchange of ideas. I was chosen President; Mrs. Sophia Allen, Vice-President; Mrs. Horace Pennell, Treasurer; and one of several young ladies who were members was Secretary. Horace Pennell, Esq., and his wife were two of our most earnest helpers. We drafted a petition to the Legislature to grant women the right of suffrage, and obtained the names of sixty-two of the most intelligent people, male and female, in our own and adjoining towns, and sent it to our Representative in Albany. It was received by the Legislature as something absurdly ridiculous, and laid upon the table. We introduced the question into the Debating Clubs, that were in those days such popular institutions in the rural districts, and in every way sought to agitate the subject. I found a great many men, especially those of the better class, disposed to accord equal rights to our sex. And, now, as the highest tribute that I can pay to the memory of a husband, I may say that during our companionship of thirty-five years, I was most cordially sustained by mine, in my advocacy of equal rights to women. Amongst my own sex, I found too many on whom ages of repression had wrought their natural effect, and whose ideas and aspirations were narrowed down to the confines of "woman's sphere," beyond whose limits it was not only impious, but infamous to tread. "Woman's sphere" *then*, was to discharge the duties of a housekeeper, ply the needle, and teach a primary or ladies' school. From press, and pulpit, and platform, she was taught that "to be unknown was her highest praise," that "dependence was her best protection," and "her weakness her sweetest charm." She needed only sufficient intelli gence to comprehend her husband's superiority, and to obey him in all things. It is not surprising, then, that I as often heard the terms "strong-minded" and "masculine" as opprobrious epithets used against progressive women, by their own sex as by the other ; another example only of the stultifying effect of subjection, upon the mind, exactly paralleled by the Southern slaves, amongst many of whom the strongest term of contempt that could be used was "*Free Nigger.*" Our Equal Rights Association continued to hold its meetings for somewhat over a year, and they were at last suspended on account of bad weather and the difficulty of coming together in the country districts. We, however, continued to send petitions to the Legislature for the removal of woman's disabilities.

From 1858 to 1869 my home was in Rochester, N. Y. There, by brief newspaper articles and in other ways, I sought to influence public sentiment in favor of this fundamental reform. In 1868 a Society was organized there for the reformation of abandoned women. At one of its meetings I endeavored to show how futile all their efforts would be, while women, by the laws of the land, were made a subject class ; that only by enfranchising woman and permitting her a more free and lucrative range of employments, could they hope to suppress the "social evil." My remarks produced some agitation in the meeting and some newspaper criticisms. In Rochester, I found many pioneers in the cause of Woman Suffrage, and from year to year we petitioned our Legislature for it.

Since 1869 I have been a citizen of Louisiana. Here, till recently, political troubles engrossed the minds of men to the exclusion of every other consideration. They glowed with fiery indignation at being, themselves, deprived of the right of suffrage, or at having their votes annulled, and regarded it as an intolerable outrage ; yet, at the same time, they denied it to all women, many of whom valued the elective franchise as highly, and felt as intensely, as did men, the injustice that withheld it from them. In 1879, when the Convention met to frame a new Constitution for the State, we strongly petitioned it for an enlargement of our civil rights and for the ballot. Mrs. Elizabeth L. Saxon was indefatigable in her efforts, and went before the Convention in person and plead our cause. But the majority of the members thought there were cogent reasons for not granting our petitions; but they made women eligible to all school offices—an indication that Louisiana will not be the last State in the Union to deny women their inalienable rights.   EMILY COLLINS.

The newspaper comments on Elizabeth Blackwell as a physician, both in the French and American papers, seem very ridiculous to us at this distance of time. *The American,* Rochester, N. Y., July, 1848 :

A NOVEL CIRCUMSTANCE.—Our readers will perhaps remember that some time ago a lady, Miss Elizabeth Blackwell, applied for admission as a student in one of the medical colleges of Philadelphia, her purpose being to go through an entire course of the study of medicine. The application was denied, and the lady subsequently entered the Geneva Medical College, where, at the Annual Commencement on the 23d instant, she graduated with high honors and received the degree of M.D., the subject of her thesis being "ship fever." On receiving her diploma she thus addressed the President: "With the help of the Most High, it shall be the effort of my life to shed honor on this diploma." Professor Lee, who delivered the customary oration, complimented the lady by saying that she had won the distinction of her class by attending faithfully to every duty required of candidates striving for the honor. Eighteen young gentlemen received the degree of M.D. at the same time.

After graduating with high honors in this country, Dr. Elizabeth Blackwell went to France to secure still higher advantages of education than could be found here. What was thought of her there will be seen by the following letter of a Paris correspondent in the New York *Journal of Commerce:*

AN AMERICAN DOCTRESS. — The medical community of Paris is all agog by the arrival of the celebrated American doctor, Miss Blackwell. She has quite bewildered the learned faculty by her diploma, all in due form, authorizing her to dose and bleed and amputate with the best of them. Some of them think Miss Blackwell must be a socialist of the most rabid class, and that her undertaking is the entering wedge to a systematic attack on society by the whole sex. Others, who have seen her, say that there is nothing very alarming in her manner; that, on the contrary, she is modest and unassuming, and talks reasonably on other subjects. The ladies attack her in turn. One said to me a few days since, "Oh, it is too horrid! I'm sure I never could touch her hand! Only to think that those long fingers of hers had been cutting up dead people." I have seen the doctor in question, and must say in fairness, that her appearance is quite prepossessing. She is young, and rather good-looking; her manner indicates great energy of character, and she seems to have entered on her singular career from motives of duty, and encouraged by respectable ladies of Cincinnati. After about ten days' hesitation, on the part of the directors of the Hospital of Maternity, she has at last received permission to enter the institution as a pupil.

ERNESTINE L. ROSE.

BY L. E. BARNARD.

Ernestine L. Rose—maiden name Siismund Potoski—was born January 13, 1810, at Pyeterkow, in Poland. Her father, a very pious and learned rabbi, was so conscientious that he would take no pay for discharging the functions of his office, saying he would not convert his duty into a means of gain. As a child she was of a reflective habit, and though very active and cheerful, she scarcely ever engaged with her young companions in their sports, but took great delight in the company of her father, for whom she entertained a remarkable affection.

At a very early age she commenced reading the Hebrew Scriptures, but soon became involved in serious difficulties respecting the formation of the world, the origin of evil, and other obscure points suggested by the sacred history and cosmogony of her people. The reproofs which met her at every step of her biblical investigations, and being constantly told that " little girls must not ask questions," made her at that early day an advocate of religious freedom and woman's rights ; as she could not see, on the one hand, why subjects of vital interest should be held too sacred for investigation, nor, on the other, why a " little girl " should not have the same right to ask questions as a little boy. Despite her early investigation of the Bible, she was noted for her strict observance of all the rites and ceremonies of the Jewish faith, though some of them, on account of her tender age, were not demanded of her. She was, however, often painfully disturbed by her " carnal reason " questioning the utility of these multifarious observances. As an illustration, she one day asked her father, with much anxiety, why he fasted* so much more than others, a habit which was seriously impairing his health and spirits ; and being told that it was to please God, who required this sacrifice at his hands, she, in a serious and most emphatic tone, replied, " If God is pleased in making you sick and unhappy, I hate God." This idea of the cruelty of God toward her father had a remarkable influence upon her ; and at the age of four-

---

* Fasting with Jews meant abstaining from food and drink from before sunset one evening, until after the stars were out the next evening.

teen she renounced her belief in the Bible and the religion of her father, which brought down upon her great trouble and persecution alike from her own Jewish friends and from Christians. At the age of sixteen she had the misfortune to lose her mother. A year afterward her father married again, and through misdirected kindness involved her in a lawsuit, in which she plead her own case and won it ; but she left the property with her father, declaring that she cared nothing for it, but only for justice, and that her inheritance might not fall into mercenary hands. She subsequently traveled in Poland, Russia, the Germanic States, Holland, Belgium, France, and England ; during which time she witnessed and took part in some interesting and important affairs. While in Berlin she had an interview with the King of Prussia concerning the right of Polish Jews to remain in that city. The Jews of Russian Poland were not permitted to continue in Prussia, unless they could bring forward as security Prussian citizens who were holders of real estate. But even then they could get a permit to tarry only on a visit, and not to transact any business for themselves. Mlle. Potoski, being from Poland and a Jewess, was subject to this disability. Though she could have obtained the requisite security by applying for it, she preferred to stand upon her natural rights as a human being. She remonstrated against the gross injustice of the law, and obtained the right to remain as long as she wished, and to do what she pleased.

In Hague, she became acquainted with a very distressing case of a poor sailor, the father of four children, whose wife had been imprisoned for an alleged crime of which he insisted she was innocent. Inquiring into the case, Mlle. Potoski drew up a petition which she personally presented to the King of Holland, and had the satisfaction of seeing the poor woman restored to her family. She was in Paris during the Revolution of July, 1830, and witnessed most of its exciting scenes. On seeing Louis Phillipe presented by Lafayette to the people of Paris from the balcony of the Tuilleries, she remarked to a friend, " That man, as well as Charles X., will one day have good reason to wish himself safely off the throne of France."

In England she became acquainted with Lord Grosvenor and family, with Frances Farrar, sister of Oliver Farrar, M.P., the Miss Leeds, and others of the nobility ; also with many prominent members of the Society of Friends, among them Joseph Gurney and his sister Elizabeth Fry, the eminent philanthropist, in whose company she visited Newgate Prison. In 1832 she made the acquaintance of Robert Owen, and warmly espoused his principles. In 1834 she presided at the formation of a society called " The Association of all

Ernestine L. Rose

Classes of all Nations, without distinction of sect, sex, party condition, or color." While in England she married William E. Rose, and in the spring of 1836, came to the United States, and resided in the city of New York. Soón after her arrival she commenced lecturing on the evils of the existing social system, the formation of human character, slavery, the rights of woman, and other reform questions.

At a great public meeting in the Broadway Tabernacle to consider the necessity of an improved system of Free Schools, J. S. Buckingham, M.P., of England, and Rev. Robert Breckenridge, of Kentucky, were among the speakers. Mrs. Rose, sitting in the gallery, called the reverend gentleman to order for violating the sense of the audience, in entirely overlooking the important object which had called the people together, and indulging in a violent clerical harangue against a class whom he stigmatized as infidels. This bold innovation of a woman upon the hitherto unquestioned prerogatives of the clergy, at once caused a tremendous excitement. Loud cries of " Throw her down!" " Drag her out!" " She's an infidel!" resounded in all parts of the building. She, however, held her ground, calm and collected while the tumult lasted, and after quiet was restored, continued her remarks in a most dignified manner, making a deep impression upon all present. Certain religious papers declared it a forewarning of some terrible calamity, that a woman should call a minister to account, and that, too, in a church.

Mrs. Rose has lectured in not less than twenty-three different States of the Union. Some of them she has visited often, and on several occasions she has addressed legislative bodies with marked effect, advocating the necessity of legal redress for the wrongs and disabilities to which her sex are subject. As an advocate of woman's rights, anti-slavery and religious liberty, she has earned a worldwide celebrity. For fifty years a public speaker, during which period she has associated with the influential classes in Europe and America, and borne an active part in the great progressive movements which mark the present as the most glorious of historical epochs, Ernestine L. Rose has accomplished for the elevation of her sex and the amelioration of social conditions, a work which can be ascribed to few women of our time.

In the spring of 1854, Mrs. Rose and Miss Anthony took a trip together to Washington, Alexandria, Baltimore, Philadelphia, speaking two or three times in each place. This was after the introduction of the Kansas-Nebraska Bill in Congress, and the excitement of the country upon the slavery question was intense. Mrs. Rose's

7

third lecture in Washington was on the "Nebraska Question." This lecture was scarcely noticed, the only paper giving it the least report, being *The Washington Globe*, which, though it spoke most highly of her as a lecturer, misrepresented her by ascribing to her the arguments of the South. *The National Era*, the only anti-slavery paper in Washington, was entirely silent, taking no notice of the fact that Mrs. Rose had spoken in that city against the further spread of slavery. Whether this was due to editorial prejudice against sex, or against freedom of religious belief, is unknown.

In the winter of 1855, Mrs. Rose spoke in thirteen of the fifty-four County Conventions upon woman suffrage held in the State of New York, and each winter took part in the Albany Conventions and hearings before the Legislature, which in 1860 resulted in the passage of the bill securing to women the right to their wages and the equal guardianship of their children.

Mrs. Rose was sustained in her work by the earnest sympathy of her husband, who gladly furnished her the means of making her extensive tours, so that through his sense of justice she was enabled to preach the Gospel of Woman's Rights, Anti-Slavery, and Free Religion without money and without price.

The Boston Investigator of January 15, 1881, speaking of a letter just received from her, says: "Thirty years ago Mrs. Rose was in her prime—an excellent lecturer, liberal, eloquent, witty, and we must add, decidedly handsome—'the Rose that all were praising.' Her portrait, life-size and very natural, hangs in Investigator Hall, and her intelligent-looking and expressive countenance, and black glossy curls, denote intellect and beauty. As an anti-slavery lecturer, a pioneer in the cause of woman's rights, and an advocate of Liberalism, she did good service, and is worthy to be classed with such devoted friends of humanity and freedom as Frances Wright, Harriet Martineau, Lucretia Mott, and Lydia Maria Child, who will long be pleasantly remembered for their ' works' sake.' "

LONDON, *January* 9, 1877.

MY DEAR MISS ANTHONY:—Sincerely do I thank you for your kind letter. Believe me it would give me great pleasure to comply with your request, to tell you all about myself and my past labors; but I suffer so much from neuralgia in my head and general debility, that I could not undertake the task, especially as I have nothing to refer to. I have never spoken from notes; and as I did not intend to publish anything about myself, for I had no other ambition except to work for the cause of humanity, irrespective of sex, sect, country, or color, and did not expect that a Susan B. Anthony would wish to do it for me, I made no memorandum of places, dates, or names; and thirty or forty years ago the press was not sufficiently educated in the rights of woman, even to notice, much less to report speeches as it does now; and therefore I have not anything to assist me or you.

All that I can tell you is, that I used my humble powers to the uttermost, and raised my voice in behalf of Human Rights in general, and the elevation and Rights of Woman in particular, nearly all my life. And so little have I spared myself, or studied my comfort in summer or winter, rain or shine, day or night, when I had an opportunity to work for the cause to which I had devoted myself, that I can hardly wonder at my present state of health.

Yet in spite of hardships, for it was not as easy to travel at that time as now, and the expense, as I never made a charge or took up a collection, I look back to that time, when a stranger and alone, I went from place to place, in high-ways and by-ways, did the work and paid my bills with great pleasure and satisfaction; for the cause gained ground, and in spite of my heresies I had always good audiences, attentive listeners, and was well received wherever I went.

But I can mention from memory the principal places where I have spoken. In the winter of 1836 and '37, I spoke in New York, and for some years after I lectured in almost every city in the State; Hudson, Poughkeepsie, Albany, Schenectady, Saratoga, Utica, Syracuse, Rochester, Buffalo, Elmira, and other places; in New Jersey, in Newark and Burlington; in 1837, in Philadelphia, Bristol, Chester, Pittsburg, and other places in Pennsylvania, and at Wilmington in Delaware; in 1842, in Boston, Charlestown, Beverly, Florence, Springfield, and other points in Massachusetts, and in Hartford, Connecticut; in 1844, in Cincinnati, Dayton, Zanesville, Springfield, Cleveland, Toledo, and several settlements in the backwoods of Ohio, and also in Richmond, Indiana; in 1845 and '46, I lectured three times in the Legislative Hall in Detroit, and at Ann Arbor and other places in Michigan; and in 1847 and '48, I spoke in Charleston and Columbia, in South Carolina.

In 1850, I attended the first National Woman's Rights Convention in Worcester, and nearly all the National and State Conventions since, until I went to Europe in 1869. Returning to New York in 1874, I was present at the Convention in Irving Hall, the only one held during my visit to America.

I sent the first petition to the New York Legislature to give a married woman the right to hold real estate in her own name, in the winter of 1836 and '37, to which after a good deal of trouble I obtained five signatures. Some of the ladies said the gentlemen would laugh at them; others, that they had rights enough; and the men said the women had too many rights already. Woman at that time had not learned to know that she had any rights except those that man in his generosity allowed her; both have learned something since that time which they will never forget. I continued sending petitions with increased numbers of signatures until 1848 and '49, when the Legislature enacted the law which granted to woman the right to keep what was her own. But no sooner did it become legal than all the women said, "Oh! that is right! We ought always to have had that."

During the eleven years from 1837 to 1848, I addressed the New York Legislature five times, and since 1848 I can not say positively, but a good many times; you know all that better than any one else.

Your affectionate friend,   ERNESTINE L. ROSE.

In collecting the reminiscences of those who took the initiative steps in this movement, Mrs. Rose was urged to send us some of her experiences, but in writing that it was impossible for her to do so, and yet giving us the above summary of all she has accomplished, *multum in parvo*, she has in a good measure complied with our request.

All through these eventful years Mrs. Rose has fought a double battle; not only for the political rights of her sex as women, but for their religious rights as individual souls; to do their own thinking and believing. How much of the freedom they now enjoy, the women of America owe to this noble Polish woman, can not be estimated, for moral influences are too subtle for measurement.

Those who sat with her on the platform in bygone days, well remember her matchless powers as a speaker; and how safe we all felt while she had the floor, that neither in manner, sentiment, argument, nor repartee, would she in any way compromise the dignity of the occasion.

She had a rich musical voice, with just enough of foreign accent and idiom to add to the charm of her oratory. As a speaker she was pointed, logical, and impassioned. She not only dealt in abstract principles clearly, but in their application touched the deepest emotions of the human soul.

CHAPTER VI.

OHIO.

The promised land of fugitives—"Uncle Tom's Cabin"—Salem Convention, 1850—Akron, 1851—Massilon, 1852—The address to the women of Ohio—The Mohammedan law forbids pigs, dogs, women, and other impure animals to enter a Mosque—The *New York Tribune*—Cleveland Convention, 1853—Hon. Joshua R. Giddings—Letter from Horace Greeley—A glowing eulogy to Mary Wollstonecroft—William Henry Channing's Declaration—The pulpit responsible for public sentiment—President Asa Mahan debates—The Rev. Dr. Nevin pulls Mr. Garrison's nose—Antoinette L. Brown describes her exit from the World's Temperance Convention—Cincinnati Convention, 1855—Jane Elizabeth Jones' Report, 1861.

THERE were several reasons for the early, and more general agitation of Woman's Rights in Ohio at this period, than in other States. Being separated from the slave border by her river only, Ohio had long been the promised land of fugitives, and the battle-ground for many recaptured victims, involving much litigation.

Most stringent laws had been passed, called "the black laws of Ohio," to prevent these escapes through her territory. Hence, this State was the ground for some of the most heated anti-slavery discussions, not only in the Legislature, but in frequent conventions. Garrison and his followers, year after year, had overrun the "Western Reserve," covering the north-eastern part of the State, carrying the gospel of freedom to every hamlet.

A radical paper, called *The Anti-Slavery Bugle*, edited by Oliver Johnson, was published in Salem. It took strong ground in favor of equal rights for woman, and the editor did all in his power to sustain the conventions, and encourage the new movement.

Again, Abby Kelly's eloquent voice had been heard all through this State, denouncing "the black laws of Ohio," appealing to the ready sympathies of woman for the suffering of the black mothers, wives, and daughters of the South. This grand woman, equally familiar with the tricks of priests and politicians, the action of Synods, General Assemblies, State Legislatures, and Congresses, who could maintain an argument with any man on the slavery question, had immense influence, not only in the anti-slavery conflict, but by her words and example she inspired woman with new self-respect.

These anti-slavery conventions, in which the most logical reasoners, and the most eloquent, impassioned orators the world ever produced, kept their audiences wrought up to the highest pitch of en-

thusiasm hour after hour, were the school in which woman's rights
found its ready-made disciples. With such women as Frances D.
Gage, Hannah Tracy Cutler, Josephine S. Griffing, J. Elizabeth
Jones, Mariana Johnson, Emily Robinson, Maria Giddings, Betsey
Cowles, Caroline M. Severance, Martha J. Tilden, Rebecca A. S.
Janney, to listen to the exhaustive arguments on human rights,
verily the seed fell on good ground, and the same justice, that in
glowing periods was claimed for the black man, they now claimed
for themselves, and compelled the law-makers of this State to give
some consideration to the wrongs of woman.

Again, in 1850, Ohio held a Constitutional Convention, and these
women, thoroughly awake to their rights, naturally thought, that if
the fundamental laws of the State were to be revised and amended,
it was a fitting time for them to ask to be recognized.

In 1851, Harriet Beecher Stowe commenced the publication of
" Uncle Tom's Cabin " in the *National Era*, in Washington, D. C.,
which made Ohio, with its great river, classic soil, and quickened the
pulsations of every woman's heart in the nation.

Reports of the New York Conventions, widely copied and ridiculed in leading journals, from Maine to Texas, struck the key-note
for similar gatherings in several of the Northern States. Without
the least knowledge of one another, without the least concert of action, women in Ohio, Indiana, Pennsylvania, and Massachusetts,
sprang up as if by magic, and issued calls for similar conventions.
The striking uniformity in their appeals, petitions, resolutions, and
speeches; making the same complaints and asking the same redress
for grievances, shows that all were moved by like influences. Those
who made the demand for political freedom in 1848, in Europe
as well as America, were about the same age. Significant facts to
show that new liberty for woman was one of the marked ideas of
the century, and that as the chief factor in civilization, the time had
come for her to take her appropriate place.

The actors in this new movement were not, as the London and
New York journals said, " sour old maids," but happy wives and
faithful mothers, who, in a higher development, demanded the rights
and privileges befitting the new position. And if they may be
judged by the vigor and eloquence of their addresses, and the
knowledge of parliamentary tactics they manifested in their conventions, the world must accord them rare common-sense, good
judgment, great dignity of character, and a clear comprehension of
the principles of government. In order to show how well those who
inaugurated this movement, understood the nature of our republican

institutions, and how justly they estimated their true position in a republic, we shall give rather more of these early speeches and letters than in any succeeding chapters.

In 1849, Mrs. Elizabeth Wilson, of Cadiz, Ohio, aroused some attention to the general question, by the publication of "A Scriptural View of Woman's Rights and Duties," clearly demonstrating the equality of man and woman in the creation, as well as the independent, self-reliant characteristics sanctioned in woman, by the examples of the sex given in the Bible. As woman has ever been degraded by the perversion of the religious element of her nature, the scriptural arguments were among the earliest presentations of the question. When opponents were logically cornered on every other side, they uniformly fell back on the decrees of Heaven. The ignorance of women in general as to what their Bibles really do teach, has been the chief cause of their bondage. They have accepted the opinions of men for the commands of their Creator. The fulminations of the clergy against the enfranchisement of woman, were as bitter and arrogant as against the emancipation of the African, and they defended their position in both cases by the Bible. This led Abolitionists and women to a very careful study of the Scriptures, and enabled them to meet their opponents most successfully. No clergyman ever quoted Scripture with more readiness and force than did Lucretia Mott and William Lloyd Garrison, who alike made the Bible a power on the side of freedom.

SALEM CONVENTION.

In 1850 the first convention in Ohio was held at Salem, April 19th and 20th, in the Second Baptist Church.* The meeting convened at 10 o'clock, and was called to order by Emily Robinson, who proposed Mariana W. Johnson as President *pro tem.*, Sarah Coates, Secretary *pro tem.* On taking the chair, Mrs. Johnson read the following call :

We, the undersigned, earnestly call on the women of Ohio to meet in Convention, on Friday, the 19th of April, 1850, at 10 o'clock A.M., in the town of Salem, to concert measures to secure to all persons the recognition of equal rights, and the extension of the privileges of government without distinction of sex, or color; to inquire into the origin and design of the rights of humanity, whether they are coeval with the human race, of universal inheritance and inalienable, or merely conventional, held by

---

* Years before the calling of this Convention, Mrs. Frances D. Gage had roused much thought in Ohio by voice and pen. She was a long time in correspondence with Harriet Martineau and Mrs. Jane Knight, who was energetically working for reduced postage rates, even before the days of Rowland Hill.

sufferance, dependent for a basis on location, position, color, and sex, and like government scrip, or deeds of parchment, transferable, to be granted or withheld, made immutable or changeable, as caprice, popular favor, or the pride of power and place may dictate, changing ever, as the weak and the strong, the oppressed and the oppressor, come in conflict or change places. Feeling that the subjects proposed for discussion are vitally important to the interests of humanity, we unite in most earnestly inviting every one who sincerely desires the progress of true reform to be present at the Convention.

The meeting of a convention of men to amend the Constitution of our (?) State, presents a most favorable opportunity for the agitation of this subject. Women of Ohio! we call upon you to come up to this work in womanly strength and with womanly energy. Don't be discouraged at the prospect of difficulties. Remember that contest with difficulty gives strength. Come and inquire if the position you now occupy is one appointed by wisdom, and designed to secure the best interests of the human race. Come, and let us ascertain what bearing the circumscribed sphere of woman has on the great political and social evils that curse and desolate the land. Come, for this cause claims your most invincible perseverance; come in single-heartedness, and with a personal self-devotion that will yield everything to Right, Truth, and Reason, but not an iota to dogmas or theoretical opinions, no matter how time-honored, or by what precedent established.

Randolph—Elizabeth Steadman, Cynthia M. Price, Sophronia Smalley, Cordelia L. Smalley, Ann Eliza Lee, Rebecca Everit. New Garden— Esther Ann Lukens. Ravenna—Lucinda King, Mary Skinner, Frances Luccock.

The officers of the Convention were: Betsey M. Cowles, President; Lydia B. Irish, Harriet P. Weaver, and Rana Dota, Vice-Presidents. Caroline Stanton, Ann Eliza Lee, and Sallie B. Gove, Secretaries. Emily Robinson, J. Elizabeth Jones, Josephine S. Griffing, Mariana Johnson, Esther Lukens, Mary H. Stanton, Business Committee.

Mrs. Jones read a very able speech, which was printed in full in their published report, also a discourse of Lucretia Mott's, "On Woman," delivered Dec. 17, 1849, in the Assembly Building in Philadelphia. Interesting letters were read from Mrs. Mott, Lucy Stone, Sarah Pugh, Lydia Jane Pierson, editor of the Lancaster *Literary Gazette*, Elizabeth Cady Stanton, and Harriet N. Torrey.* Twenty-two resolutions, covering the whole range of woman's political, religious, civil, and social rights, were discussed and adopted. The following memorial to the Constitutional Convention, was presented by Mariana Johnson:

---

* See Appendix.

MEMORIAL.

We believe the whole theory of the Common Law in relation to woman is unjust and degrading, tending to reduce her to a level with the slave, depriving her of political existence, and forming a positive exception to the great doctrine of equality as set forth in the Declaration of Independence. In the language of Prof. Walker, in his "Introduction to American Law": "Women have no part or lot in the foundation or administration of the government. They can not vote or hold office. They are required to contribute their share, by way of taxes, to the support of the Government, but are allowed no voice in its direction. They are amenable to the laws, but are allowed no share in making them. This language, when applied to males, would be the exact definition of political slavery." Is it just or wise that woman, in the largest and professedly the freest and most enlightened republic on the globe, in the middle of the nineteenth century, should be thus degraded?

We would especially direct the attention of the Convention to the legal condition of married women. Not being represented in those bodies from which emanate the laws, to which they are obliged to submit, they are protected neither in person nor property. "The merging of woman's name in that of her husband is emblematical of the fate of all her legal rights." At the marriage-altar, the law divests her of all distinct individuality. Blackstone says: "The very being or legal existence of the woman is suspended during marriage, or at least incorporated or consolidated into that of her husband." Legally, she ceases to exist, and becomes emphatically a new creature, and is ever after denied the dignity of a rational and accountable being. The husband is allowed to take possession of her estates, as the law has proclaimed her legally dead. All that she has, becomes legally his, and he can collect and dispose of the profits of her labor without her consent, as he thinks fit, and she can own nothing, have nothing, which is not regarded by the law as belonging to her husband. Over her person he has a more limited power. Still, if he render life intolerable, so that she is forced to leave him, he has the power to retain her children, and "seize her and bring her back, for he has a right to her society which he may enforce, either against herself or any other person who detains her" (Walker, page 226). Woman by being thus subject to the control, and dependent on the will of man, loses her self-dependence; and no human being can be deprived of this without a sense of degradation. The law should sustain and protect all who come under its sway, and not create a state of dependence and depression in any human being. The laws should not make woman a mere pensioner on the bounty of her husband, thus enslaving her will and degrading her to a condition of absolute dependence.

Believing that woman does not suffer alone when subject to oppressive and unequal laws, but that whatever affects injuriously her interests, is subversive of the highest good of the race, we earnestly request that in the New Constitution you are about to form for the State of Ohio, women shall be secured, not only the right of suffrage, but all the political and legal rights that are guaranteed to men.

After some discussion the memorial was adopted. With the hope of creating a feeling of moral responsibility on this vital question, an earnest address* to the women of the State was also presented, discussed, and adopted.

ADDRESS TO THE WOMEN OF OHIO.

How shall the people be made wiser, better, and happier, is one of the grand inquiries of the present age. The various benevolent associations hold up to our view special forms of evil, and appeal to all the better feelings of our nature for sympathy, and claim our active efforts and co-operation to eradicate them. Governments, at times, manifest an interest in human suffering; but their cold sympathy and tardy efforts seldom avail the sufferer until it is too late. Philanthropists, philosophers, and statesmen study and devise ways and means to ameliorate the condition of the people. Why have they so little practical effect? It is because the means employed are not adequate to the end sought for. To ameliorate the effects of evil seems to have been the climax of philanthropic effort. We respectfully suggest that lopping the branches of the tree but causes the roots to strike deeper and cling more closely to the soil that sustains it. Let the amelioration process go on, until evil is exterminated root and branch; and for this end the people must be instructed in the Rights of Humanity;—not in the rights of men and the rights of women; the rights of the master and those of the slave;—but in the perfect equality of the Rights of Man. The rights of man! Whence came they? What are they? What is their design? How do we know them? They are of God! Those that most intimately affect us as human beings are life, liberty, and the pursuit of happiness. Their design is happiness. The human organization is the charter deed by which we hold them. Hence we learn that rights are coeval with the human race, of universal heritage, and inalienable; that every human being, no matter of what color, sex, condition, or clime, possesses those rights upon perfect equality with all others. The monarch on the throne, and the beggar at his feet, have the same. Man has no more, woman no less.

Rights may not be usurped on one hand, nor surrendered on the other, because they involve a responsibility that can be discharged only by those to whom they belong, those for whom they were created; and because, without those certain inalienable rights, human beings can not attain the end for which God the Father gave them existence. Where and how can the wisdom and ingenuity of the world find a truer, stronger, broader basis of human rights. To secure these rights, says the Declaration of Independence, "Governments were instituted among men, deriving their just powers from the consent of the governed;" and "whenever any form of government becomes destructive of those ends, it is the right of the people to alter or abolish it, and to substitute a new government, laying its foundation on such principles, and organizing its powers in such form, as to them shall

---

* Said to have been written by J. Elizabeth Jones.

seem most likely to effect their safety and happiness." The Government of this country, in common with all others, has never recognized or attempted to protect women as persons possessing the rights of humanity. They have been recognized and protected as appendages to men, without independent rights or political existence, unknown to the law except as victims of its caprice and tyranny. This government, having therefore exercised powers underived from the consent of the governed, and having signally failed to secure the end for which all just government is instituted, should be immediately altered, or abolished.

We can not better describe the political condition of woman, than by quoting from a distinguished lawyer of our own State. Professor Walker, in his "Introduction to American Law," says

OF HUSBAND AND WIFE,

"We have a few statutory provisions on the' subject, but for the most part the law of husband and wife is *Common Law*, and you will find that it savors of its origin in all its leading features. The whole theory is a slavish one, compared even with the civil law. I do not hesitate to say, by way of arousing your attention to the subject, that the law of husband and wife, as you gather it from the books, is a disgrace to any civilized nation. I do not mean to say that females are degraded in point of fact. I only say, that the theory of the law degrades them almost to the level of slaves." We thank Prof. Walker for his candor. He might have added that the practice of the law does degrade woman to the level of the slave. He also says: "With regard to political rights, females form a positive exception to the general doctrine of equality. They have no part nor lot in the formation or administration of government. They can not vote or hold office. We require them to contribute their share in the way of taxes for the support of government, but allow them no voice in its direction. We hold them amenable to the laws when made, but allow them no share in making them. This language applied to males, would be the exact definition of political slavery; applied to females, custom does not teach us so to regard it."

Of married women he says: "The·legal theory is, marriage makes the husband and wife one person, and that person is the husband. He the substantive, she the adjective. In a word, there is scarcely a legal act of any description that she is competent to perform. If she leaves him without cause, (legal) he may seize and bring her back, for he has a right to her society, which he may enforce, either against herself, or any other person. All her personality in regard to property becomes the husband's by marriage, unless the property has been specially secured to her. If the property be not in his possession, he may take measures to reduce it to possession. He can thus dispose of it in spite of her. If debts were due to her, he may collect them. If he was himself the debtor, the marriage cancels the debt. If she has earned money during marriage, he may collect it. In regard to realty (real estate) he controls the income, and without her consent he can not encumber, or dispose of the property beyond his own life." Women, married or single, have no political rights whatever. While single, their legal rights are the same as

those of men; when married, their legal rights are chiefly suspended.
" The condition of the wife may be inferred from what has already been
said. She is almost at the mercy of her husband; she can exercise no
control over his property or her own. As a general rule, she can make
no contracts binding herself or him. Her contracts are not merely void-
able, but absolutely void. Nor can she make herself liable for his contracts, torts, or crimes. Her only separate liability is for her own crimes.
Her only joint liability, is for her own torts committed without his participation, and for contracts for which the law authorizes her to unite
with him. She has no power over his person, and her only claim upon
his property is for a bare support. In no instance can she sue or be sued
alone in a civil action; and there are but few cases in which she can be
joined in a suit with him. In Ohio, but hardly anywhere else, is she allowed to make a will, if haply she has anything to dispose of."

Women of Ohio! Whose cheek does not blush, whose blood does not
tingle at this cool, lawyer-like recital of the gross indignities and wrongs
which Government has heaped upon our sex? With these marks of
inferiority branded upon our persons, and interwoven with the most sacred relations of human existence, how can we rise to the true dignity of
human nature, and discharge faithfully the important duties assigned us
as responsible, intelligent, self-controlling members of society? No
wonder that so many of our politicians are dough-faced serviles, without
independence or manhood; no wonder our priests are time-serving
and sycophantic; no wonder that so many men are moral cowards
and cringing poltroons. What more could be expected of a progeny
of slaves? Slaves are we, politically and legally. How can we, who,
it is said, are the educators of our children, present to this nation
anything else but a generation of serviles, while we, ourselves, are in a
servile condition, and padlocks are on our lips? No! if men would be
men worthy of the name, they must cease to disfranchise and rob their
wives and mothers; they must forbear to consign to political and legal
slavery their sisters and their daughters. And, would we be women
worthy the companionship of true and noble men, we must cease longer
to submit to tyranny. Let us rise in the might of self-respect, and assert
our rights, and by the aid of truth. the instincts of humanity, and a just
application of the principles of equality, we shall be able to maintain them.

You ask, would you have woman, by engaging in political party bick-
erings and noisy strife, sacrifice her integrity and purity? No, neither
would we have men do it. . . . . We hold that whatever is essentially
wrong for woman to do, can not be right for man. If deception and
intrigue, the elements of political craft, be degrading to woman, can
they be ennobling to man? If patience and forbearance adorn a woman,
are they not equally essential to a manly character? If anger and tur-
bulence disgrace woman, what can they add to the dignity of man?
Nothing; because nothing can be morally right for man, that is morally
wrong for woman. Woman, by becoming the executioner of man's vengeance on his fellow-man, could inflict no greater wrong on society than
the same done by man; but it would create an intenser feeling of shuddering horror, and would, we conceive, rouse to more healthful activity

man's torpid feelings of justice, mercy, and clemency. And so, also, if woman had free scope for the full exercise of the heavenly graces that men so gallantly award her, truth, love, and mercy would be invested with a more sacred charm. But while they continue to enforce obedience to arbitrary commands, to encourage love of admiration and a desire for frivolous amusements; while they crush the powers of the mind, by opposing authority and precedent to reason and progress; while they arrogate to themselves the right to point us to the path of duty, while they close the avenues of knowledge through public institutions, and monopolize the profits of labor, mediocrity and inferiority must be our portion. Shall we accept it, or shall we strive against it?

Men are not destitute of justice or humanity; and let it be remembered that there are hosts of noble and truthful ones among them who deprecate the tyranny that enslaves us; and none among ourselves can be more ready than they to remove the mountain of injustice which the savagism of ages has heaped upon our sex. If, therefore, we remain enslaved and degraded, the cause may justly be traced to our own apathy and timidity. We have at our disposal the means of moral agitation and influence, that can arouse our country to a saving sense of the wickedness and folly of disfranchising half the people. Let us no longer delay to use them.

Let it be remembered too, that tyrannical and illiberal as our Government is, low as it places us in the scale of existence, degrading as is its denial of our capacity for self-government, still it concedes to us more than any other Government on earth. Woman, over half the globe, is now and always has been but a chattel. Wives are bargained for, bought and sold, as other merchandise, and as a consequence of the annihilation of natural rights, they have no political existence. In Hindostan, the evidence of woman is not received in a court of justice. The Hindu wife, when her husband dies, must yield implicit obedience to the oldest son. In Burmah, they are not allowed to ascend the steps of a court of justice, but are obliged to give their testimony outside of the building. In Siberia, women are not allowed to step across the footprints of men or reindeer. The Mohammedan law forbids pigs, dogs, women, and other impure animals to enter the Mosque. The Moors, for the slightest offense, beat their wives most cruelly. The Tartars believe that women were sent into the world for no other purpose than to be useful, convenient slaves. To these heathen precedents our Christian brethren sometimes refer to prove the inferiority of woman, and to excuse the inconsistency of the only Government on earth that has proclaimed the equality of man. An argument worthy its source.

In answer to the popular query, "Why should woman desire to meddle with public affairs?" we suggest the following questions:

1st. Is the principle of taxation without representation less oppressive and tyrannical, than when our fathers expended their blood and treasure, rather than submit to its injustice?

2d. Is it just, politic, and wise, that universities and colleges endowed by Government should be open only to men?

3d. Is it easier for Government to reform lazy, vicious, ignorant, and hardened felons, than for enlightened humanity — loving parents, to "train up a child in the way it should go"?

4th. How can a mother, who does not understand, and therefore can not appreciate the rights of humanity, train up her child in the way it should go?

5th. Whence originates the necessity of a penal code?

6th. It is computed that over ten millions of dollars are annually expended in the United States for the suppression of crime. How much of this waste of treasure is traceable to defective family government?

7th. Can antiquity make wrong right?

In conclusion, we appeal to our sisters of Ohio to arise from the lethargy of ages; to assert their rights as independent human beings; to demand their true position as equally responsible co-workers with their brethren in this world of action. We urge you by your self-respect, by every consideration for the human race, to arise and take possession of your birthright to freedom and equality. Take it not as the gracious boon tendered by the chivalry of superiors, but as your *right*, on every principle of justice and equality.

The present is a most favorable time for the women of Ohio to demand a recognition of their rights. The organic law of the State is about to undergo a revision. Let it not be our fault if the rights of humanity, and not alone those of "free white male citizens," are recognized and protected. Let us agitate the subject in the family circle, in public assemblies, and through the press. Let us flood the Constitutional Convention with memorials and addresses, trusting to truth and a righteous cause for the success of our efforts.

This Convention had one peculiar characteristic. It was officered entirely by women ; not a man was allowed to sit on the platform, to speak, or vote. *Never did men so suffer.* They implored just to say a word ; but no ; the President was inflexible—no man should be heard. If one meekly arose to make a suggestion he was at once ruled out of order. For the first time in the world's history, men learned how it felt to sit in silence when questions in which they were interested were under discussion. It would have been an admirable way of closing the Convention, had a rich banquet been provided, to which the men should have had the privilege of purchasing tickets to the gallery, there to enjoy the savory odors, and listen to the after-dinner speeches. However, the gentlemen in the Convention passed through this severe trial with calm resignation ; at the close, organized an association of their own, and generously endorsed all the ladies had said and done.

Though the women in this Convention were unaccustomed to public speaking and parliamentary tactics, the interest was well sustained for two days, and the deliberations were conducted with dignity and order. It was here Josephine S. Griffing uttered her first brave words for woman's emancipation, though her voice had long been heard in pathetic pleading for the black man's rights. This Convention, which was called and conducted by Mrs. Emily Robinson, with such aid as she could enlist, was largely attended and entirely successful.

A favorable and lengthy report found its way into the *New York Tribune* and other leading journals, both East and West, and the proceedings of the Convention were circulated widely in pamphlet form. All this made a very strong impression upon the public mind. From the old world, too, the officers of the Convention received warm congratulations and earnest words of sympathy, for the new gospel of woman's equality was spreading in England as well as America.

AKRON CONVENTION,

The advocates for the enfranchisement of woman had tripled in that one short year. The very complimentary comments of the press, and the attention awakened throughout the State, by the presentation of "the memorial" to the Constitutional Convention, had accomplished a great educational work. Soon after this, another convention was called in Akron. The published proceedings of the first convention, were like clarion notes to the women of Ohio, rousing them to action, and when the call to the second was issued, there was a generous response. In 1851, May 28th and 29th, many able men and women rallied at the stone church, and hastened to give their support to the new demand, and most eloquently did they plead for justice to woman.

Frances D. Gage, Hannah Tracy Cutler, Jane G. Swisshelm, Caroline M. Severance, Emma R. Coe, Maria L. Giddings, Celia C. Burr (afterward Burleigh), Martha J. Tilden, and many other noble women who were accustomed to speaking in temperance and anti-slavery meetings, helped to make this Convention most successful. Frances D. Gage was chosen President of the Convention. On taking the chair she said:

I am at a loss, kind friends, to know whether to return you thanks, or not, for the honor conferred upon me. And when I tell you that I have never in my life attended a regular business meeting, and am entirely inexperienced in the forms and ceremonies of a deliberative body, you will not be surprised that I do not feel remarkably grateful for the position. For though you have conferred an honor upon me, I very much fear I shall not be able to reflect it back. I will try.

When our forefathers left the old and beaten paths of New England, and struck out for themselves in a new and unexplored country, they went forth with a slow and cautious step, but with firm and resolute hearts. The land of their fathers had become too small for their children. Its soil answered not their wants. The parents shook their heads and said, with doubtful and foreboding faces: "Stand still, stay at home. This has sufficed for us; we have lived and enjoyed ourselves here. True, our mountains are high and our soil is rugged and cold; but you won't find a better; change, and trial, and toil, will meet you at every step. Stay, tarry with us, and go not forth to the wilderness."

But the children answered: "Let us go; this land has sufficed for you, but the one beyond the mountains is better. We know there is trial, toil, and danger; but for the sake of our children, and our children's children, we are willing to meet all." They went forth, and pitched their tents in the wilderness. An herculean task was before them; the rich and fertile soil was shadowed by a mighty forest, and giant trees were to be felled. The Indians roamed the wild, wide hunting-grounds, and claimed them as their own. They must be met and subdued. The savage beasts howled defiance from every hill-top, and in every glen. They must be destroyed. Did the hearts of our fathers fail? No; they entered upon their new life, their new world, with a strong faith and a mighty will. For they saw in the prospection a great and incalculable good. It was not the work of an hour, nor of a day; not of weeks or months, but of long struggling, toiling, painful years. If they failed at one point, they took hold at another. If their paths through the wilderness were at first crooked, rough, and dangerous, by little and little they improved them. The forest faded away, the savage disappeared, the wild beasts were destroyed, and the hopes and prophetic visions of their far-seeing powers in the new and untried country, were more than realized.

Permit me to draw a comparison between the situation of our forefathers in the wilderness, without even so much as a bridle-path through its dark depths, and our present position. The old land of moral, social, and political privilege, seems too narrow for our wants; its soil answers not to our growing, and we feel that we see clearly a better country that we might inhabit. But there are mountains of established law and custom to overcome; a wilderness of prejudice to be subdued; a powerful foe of selfishness and self-interest to overthrow; wild beasts of pride, envy, malice, and hate to destroy. But for the sake of our children and our children's children, we have entered upon the work, hoping and praying that we may be guided by wisdom, sustained by love, and led and cheered by the earnest hope of doing good.

I shall enter into no labored argument to prove that woman does not occupy the position in society to which her capacity justly entitles her. The rights of mankind emanate from their natural wants and emotions. Are not the natural wants and emotions of humanity common to, and shared equally by, both sexes? Does man hunger and thirst, suffer cold and heat more than woman? Does he love and hate, hope and fear, joy and sorrow more than woman? Does his heart thrill with a deeper pleasure in doing good? Can his soul writhe in more bitter agony under the consciousness of evil or wrong? Is the sunshine more glorious, the air more quiet, the sounds of harmony more soothing, the perfume of flowers more exquisite, or forms of beauty more soul-satisfying to his senses, than to hers? To all these interrogatories every one will answer, No! Where then did man get the authority that he now claims over one-half of humanity? From what power the vested right to place woman—his partner, his companion, his helpmeet in life—in an inferior position? Came it from nature? Nature made woman his superior when she made her his mother; his equal when she fitted her to hold the sacred position of wife. Does he draw his authority from God, from the language of holy writ? No! For it says that "Male and female created he *them*, and gave *them* dominion." Does he claim it under law of the land? Did woman meet with him in council and voluntarily give up all her claim to be her own law-maker? Or did the majesty of might place this power in his hands?—The power of the strong over the weak makes man the master! Yes, there, and there only, does he gain his authority.

In the dark ages of the past, when ignorance, superstition, and bigotry held rule in the world, might made the law. But the undertone, the still small voice of Justice, Love, and Mercy, have ever been heard, pleading the cause of humanity, pleading for truth and right; and their low, soft tones of harmony have softened the lion heart of might, and, little by little, he has yielded as the centuries rolled on; and man, as well as woman, has been the gainer by every concession. We will ask him to yield still; to allow the voice of woman to be heard; to let her take the position which her wants and emotions seem to require; to let her enjoy her natural rights. Do not answer that woman's position is now all her natural wants and emotions require. Our meeting here together this day proves the contrary; proves that we have aspirations that are not met. Will it be answered that we are factious, discontented spirits, striving to disturb the public order, and tear up the old fastnesses of society? So it was said of Jesus Christ and His followers, when they taught peace on earth and good-will to men. So it was said of our forefathers in the great struggle for freedom. So it has been said of every reformer that has ever started out the car of progress on a new and untried track.

We fear not man as an enemy. He is our friend, our brother. Let woman speak for herself, and she will be heard. Let her claim with a calm and determined, yet loving spirit, her place, and it will be given her. I pour out no harsh invectives against the present order of things —against our fathers, husbands, and brothers; they do as they have been taught; they feel as society bids them; they act as the law requires. Woman must act for herself.

Oh, if all women could be impressed with the importance of their own action, and with one united voice, speak out in their own behalf, in behalf of humanity, they could create a revolution without armies, without bloodshed, that would do more to ameliorate the condition of mankind, to purify, elevate, ennoble humanity, than all that has been done by re-formers in the last century.

When we consider that Mrs. Gage had led the usual arduous domestic life, of wife, mother, and housekeeper, in a new country, overburdened with the care and anxiety incident to a large family reading and gathering general information at short intervals, taken from the hours of rest and excessive toil, it is remarkable, that she should have presided over the Convention, in the easy manner she is said to have done, and should have given so graceful and appropriate an extemporaneous speech, on taking the chair. Maria L. Giddings, daughter of Joshua R. Giddings, who represented Ohio many years in Congress, presented a very able digest on the common law. Betsey M. Cowles gave a report equally good on "Labor," and Emily Robinson on "Education."

In all the early Conventions the resolutions were interminable. It was not thought that full justice was done to the subject, if every point of interest or dissatisfaction in this prolific theme was not condensed into a resolution. Accordingly the Akron Convention presented, discussed, and adopted fifteen resolutions. At Salem, the previous year, the number reached twenty-two.

Letters were read from Amelia Bloomer, Elizabeth Wilson, Lydia F. Fowler, Susan Ormsby, Elsie M. Young, Gerrit Smith, Henry C. Wright, Paulina Wright Davis, Elizabeth Cady Stanton, Clarina Howard Nichols, and others. The Hutchinson family enlivened this Convention with such inspiring songs as "The Good Time Coming." Ever at the post of duty, they have sung each reform in turn to partial success. Jesse expressed his sympathy in the cause in a few earnest remarks.

This Convention was remarkable for the large number of men who took an active part in the proceedings. And as we have now an opportunity to express our gratitude by handing their names down to posterity, and thus make them immortal, we here record Joseph Barker, Marius Robinson, Rev. D. L. Webster, Jacob Heaton, Dr. K. G. Thomas, L. A. Hine, Dr. A. Brooke, Rev. Mr. Howels, Rev. Geo. Schlosser, Mr. Pease, and Samuel Brooke. The reports of this Convention are so meagre that we can not tell who were in the opposition; but from Sojourner Truth's speech, we fear that the clergy, as usual, were averse to enlarging the boundaries of freedom.

In those early days the sons of Adam crowded our platform, and often made it the scene of varied pugilistic efforts, but of late years we invite those whose presence we desire. Finding it equally difficult to secure the services of those we deem worthy to advocate our cause, and to repress those whose best service would be silence, we ofttimes find ourselves quite deserted by the "stronger sex" when most needed.

Sojourner Truth, Mrs. Stowe's "Lybian Sibyl," was present at this Convention. Some of our younger readers may not know that

Sojourner Truth was once a slave in the State of New York, and carries to-day as many marks of the diabolism of slavery, as ever scarred the back of a victim in Mississippi. Though she can neither read nor write, she is a woman of rare intelligence and common-sense on all subjects. She is still living, at Battle Creek, Michigan, though now 110 years old. Although the exalted character and personal appearance ot this noble woman have been often portrayed, and her brave deeds and words many times rehearsed, yet we give the following graphic picture of Sojourner's appearance in one of the most stormy sessions of the Convention, from

REMINISCENCES BY FRANCES D. GAGE.

SOJOURNER TRUTH.

The leaders of the movement trembled on seeing a tall, gaunt black woman in a gray dress and white turban, surmounted with an uncouth sun-bonnet, march deliberately into the church, walk with the air of a queen up the aisle, and take her seat upon the pulpit steps. A buzz of disapprobation was heard all over the house, and there fell on the listening ear, "An abolition affair!" "Woman's rights and niggers!" "I told you so!" "Go it, darkey!"

I chanced on that occasion to wear my first laurels in public life as president of the meeting. At my request order was restored, and the business of the Convention went on. Morning, afternoon, and evening exercises came and went. Through all these sessions old Sojourner, quiet and reticent as the "Lybian Statue," sat crouched against the wall on the corner of the pulpit stairs, h r sun-bonnet shading her eyes, her elbows on her knees, her chin resting upon her broad, hard palms. At intermission she was busy selling the "Life of Sojourner Truth," a narrative of her own strange and adventurous life. Again and again, timorous and trembling ones came to me and said, with earnestness, "Don't let her speak, Mrs. Gage, it will ruin us. Every newspaper in the land will have our cause mixed up with abolition and niggers, and we shall be utterly denounced." My only answer was, "We shall see when the time comes."

The second day the work waxed warm. Methodist, Baptist, Episcopal, Presbyterian, and Universalist ministers came in to hear and discuss the resolutions presented. One claimed superior rights and privileges for man, on the ground of "superior intellect"; another, because of the "manhood of Christ; if God had desired the equality of woman, He would have given some token of His will through the birth, life, and death of the Saviour." Another gave us a theological view of the "sin of our first mother."

There were very few women in those days who dared to "speak in meeting"; and the august teachers of the people were seemingly getting the better of us, while the boys in the galleries, and the sneerers among the pews, were hugely enjoying the discomfiture, as they supposed, of the "strong-minded." Some of the tender-skinned friends were on the point of losing dignity, and the atmosphere betokened a storm. When, slowly from her seat in the corner rose Sojourner Truth, who, till now, had scarcely lifted her head. "Don't let her speak!" gasped half a dozen in my ear. She moved slowly and solemnly to the front, laid her old bonnet at her feet, and turned her great speaking eyes to me. There was a hissing sound of disapprobation above and below. I rose and announced " Sojourner Truth," and begged the audience to keep silence for a few moments.

The tumult subsided at once, and every eye was fixed on this almost Amazon form, which stood nearly six feet high, head erect, and eyes piercing the upper air like one in a dream. At her first word there was a profound hush. She spoke in deep tones, which, though not loud, reached every ear in the house, and away through the throng at the doors and windows.

" Wall, chilern, whar dar is so much racket dar must be somethin' out o' kilter. I tink dat 'twixt de niggers of de Souf and de womin at de Norf, all talkin' 'bout rights, de white men will be in a fix pretty soon. But what's all dis here talkin' 'bout ?

" Dat man ober dar say dat womin needs to be helped into carriages, and lifted ober ditches, and to hab de best place everywhar. Nobody eber helps me into carriages, or ober mud-puddles, or gibs me any best place ! " And raising herself to her full height, and her voice to a pitch like rolling thunder, she asked. " And a'n't I a woman ? Look at me ! Look at my arm ! (and she bared her right arm to the shoulder, showing her tremendous muscular power). I have ploughed, and planted, and gathered into barns, and no man could head me ! And a'n't I a woman ? I could work as much and eat as much as a man—when I could get it—and bear de lash as well ! And a'n't I a woman ? I have borne thirteen chilern, and seen 'em mos' all sold off to slavery, and when I cried out with my mother's grief, none but Jesus heard me ! And a'n't I a woman ?

" Den dey talks 'bout dis ting in de head ; what dis dey call it ? " (" Intellect," whispered some one near.) " Dat's it, honey. What's dat got to do wid womin's rights or nigger's rights ? If my cup won't hold but a pint, and yourn holds a quart, wouldn't ye be mean not to let me have my little half-measure full ? " And she-pointed her significant finger, and sent a keen glance at the minister who had made the argument. The cheering was long and loud.

" Den dat little man in black dar, he say women can't have as much rights as men, 'cause Christ wan't a woman ! Whar did your Christ come from ? " Rolling thunder couldn't have stilled that crowd, as did those deep, wonderful tones, as she stood there with outstretched arms and eyes of fire. Raising her voice still louder, she repeated, " Whar did your Christ come from? From God and a woman ! Man had nothin' to do wid Him." Oh, what a rebuke that was to that little man.

Turning again to another objector, she took up the defense of Mother Eve. I can not follow her through it all. It was pointed, and witty, and solemn ; eliciting at almost every sentence deafening applause ; and she ended by asserting : " If de fust woman God ever made was strong enough to turn de world upside down all alone, dese women togedder (and she glanced her eye over the platform) ought to be able to turn it back, and get it right side up again ! And now dey is asking to do it, de men better let 'em." Long-continued cheering greeted this. " 'Bleeged to ye for hearin' on me, and now ole Sojourner han't got nothin' more to say."

Amid roars of applause, she returned to her corner, leaving more than one of us with streaming eyes, and hearts beating with gratitude. She had taken us up in her strong arms and ca ried us safely over the slough of difficulty turning the whole tide in our favor. I have never in my life seen anything like the magical influence that subdued the mobbish spirit of the day, and turned the sneers and jeers of an excited crowd into rotes of respect and admiration. Hundreds rushed up to shake hands with her, and congratulate the glorious old mother, and bid her God-speed on her mission of " testifyin' agin concerning the wickedness of this 'ere people."

WOMAN'S RIGHTS MEETING IN A BARN—" JOHN'S CONVENTION."

MRS. M. E. J. GAGE:

DEAR MADAM:—Your postal and note requesting items of history of the almost forgotten doings of thirty years ago, is at hand.

In 1850 Ohio decided by the votes of her male population to " alter and amend her Constitution." The elected delegates assembled in Cincinnati in the spring of that year.

In view of affecting this legislation the " Woman's Rights Convention " at Salem, Columbiana Co., was called in April, 1850, and memorialized the Delegate Convention, praying that Equal Rights to all citizens of the State be guaranteed by the new Constitution. In May a county meeting was called in McConnelsville, Morgan Co., Ohio. Mrs. H. M. Little, Mrs. M. T. Corner, Mrs. H. Brewster, and myself, were all the women that I knew in that region, even favorable to a movement for the help of women. Two of these only asked for more just laws for married women. One hesitated about the right of suffrage. I alone in the beginning asked for the ballot,* and equality before the law for all adult citizens of sound minds, without regard to sex or color. The Freemasons gave their hall for our meeting, but no men were admitted. I drew up a memorial for signatures, praying that the words " white " and " male " be omitted in the new Constitution. I also drew up a paper copying the unequal laws on our statute books with regard to women. We met, Mrs. Harriet Brewster presiding. Some seventy ladies of our place fell in through the day. I read my paper, and Mrs. M. T. Corner gave a historical account of noted women of the past. It was a new thing. At the close, forty names were placed on the memorial. For years I had been talking and writing, and people were used to my " craziness." But who expected Mrs. Corner and others to take such a stand ! Of course, we were heartily abused.

This led to the calling of a county meeting at Chesterfield, Morgan County. It was advertised to be held in the M. E. Church. There were only present some eight ladies, including the four above mentioned We four " scoffers " hired a hack and rode sixteen miles over the hill, before 10 A.M., to be denied admittance to church or school-house Rev. Philo Matthews had found us shelter on the threshing-floor of a fine barn, and we found about three or four hundred of the farmers, and their wives, sons, and daughters, assembled. They were nearly all

---

* My notoriety as an Abolitionist made it very difficult for me to reach people at home, and, consequently, I had to work through press and social circle; women dared not speak then. But the seed was sown far and wide, now bearing fruit.

"Quakers" and Abolitionists, but then not much inclined to "woman's rights." I had enlarged my argument, and there the "ox-sled" speech was made, the last part of May, 1850, date of day not remembered. A genuine "Quaker Preacher" said to me at the close, "Frances, thee had great Freedom. The ox-cart inspired thee." The farmers' wives brought huge boxes and pans of provisions. Men and women made ꭓeeches, and many names were added to our memorial. On the whole, ꭓe had a delightful day. It was no uncommon thing in those days for ꭓbolitionist, or Methodist, or other meetings, to be held under the trees, or in large barns, when school-houses would not hold the people. But to shut up doors against women was a new thing.

In December of 1851 I was invited to attend a Woman's Rights Convention at the town of Mount Gilead, Morrow Co., Ohio. A newspaper call promised that celebrities would be on hand, etc. I wrote I would be there. It was two days' journey, by steamboat and rail. The call was signed "John Andrews," and John Andrews promised to meet me at the cars. I went. It was fearfully cold, and John met me. He was a beardless boy of nineteen, looking much younger. We drove at once to the "Christian Church." On the way he cheered me by saying "he was afraid nobody would come, for all the people said nobody would come for his asking." When we got to the house, there was not one human soul on hand, no fire in the old rusty stove, and the rude, unpainted board benches, all topsy-turvy. I called some boys playing near, asked their names, put them on paper, five of them, and said to them, "Go to every house in this town and tell everybody that 'Aunt Fanny' will speak here at 11 A.M., and if you get me fifty to come and hear, I will give you each ten cents." They scattered off upon the run. I ordered John to right the benches, picked up chips and kindlings, borrowed a brand of fire at the next door, had a good hot stove, and the floor swept, and was ready for my audience at the appointed time. John had done his work well, and fifty at least were on hand, and a minister to make a prayer and quote St. Paul before I said a word. I said my say, and before 1 P.M., we adjourned, appointing another session at 3, and one for 7 P.M., and three for the following day. Mrs. C. M. Severance came at 6 P.M., and we had a good meeting throughout.

John's Convention was voted a success after all. He died young, worn out by his own enthusiasm and conflicts.

FRANCES D. GAGE.

In September, 1851, a Woman's Temperance Convention was held in Cincinnati, Ohio, in Foster Hall, corner of Fifth and Walnut Streets. Mrs. Mary B. Slough, President ; Mrs. George Parcells, Vice-President ; Mrs. William Pinkham, Secretary. Resolutions were discussed, and a Declaration of Independence adopted. Mrs. Slough was the "Grand Presiding Sister of Ohio." This meeting was held to raise funds for a banner, they had promised the firemen, Co. No. 1, if they would vote the Temperance ticket.

Of the temperance excitement in the State, Mrs. Gage says :

In the winter of 1852–53, there was great excitement on the Temperance question in this country, originating in Maine and spreading West. Some prominent women in Ohio, who were at Columbus, the State capital, with their husbands—who were there from all parts of the State, as Senators, Representatives, jurists, and lobbyists—feeling a great interest, as many of them had need to, in the question, were moved to call a public meeting on the subject. This resulted in the formation of a "Woman's State Temperance Society," which sent out papers giving their by-laws and resolutions, and calling for auxiliary societies in different parts of the State. This call in many places met with hearty responses.

In the following autumn, 1853, officers of the State Society, Mrs. Professor Coles, of Oberlin, President, called a convention of their members and friends of the cause, at the city of Dayton, Ohio.

The famous "Whole World's Convention" had just been held in New York City, followed by the "World's Convention," at which the Rev. Antoinette L. Brown was expelled from the platform, simply because she was a woman. The Hon. Samuel Carey presented a resolution, which I quote from memory, something as follows :

"*Resolved,* That we recognize women as efficient aids and helpers in the home, but not on the platform."

This was not perhaps the exact wording, but it was the purport of the resolution, and was presented while Neal Dow, the President of the Convention, was absent from the chair, and after much angry and abusive discussion, it was passed by that body of great men.

The Committee of Arrangements, appointed at Dayton, could find no church, school-house, or hall in which to hold their convention, till the Sons of Temperance consented to yield their lodge-room, provided there were no men admitted to their meetings. Alas ! the Committee consented. I traveled two hundred miles, and, on reaching Dayton at a late hour, I repaired at once to the hall. Our meeting was organized. But hardly were we ready to proceed when an interruption occurred. I had been advertised for the first speech, and took my place on the platform, when a column of well-dressed ladies, very fashionable and precise, marched in, two and two, and spread themselves in a half circle in front of the platform, and requested leave to be heard.

Our President asked me to suspend my reading, to which I assented, and she — a beautiful, graceful lady—bowed them her assent. Forthwith they proceeded to inform us, that they were delegated by a meeting of Dayton ladies to come hither and read to us a remonstrance against "the unseemly and unchristian position" we had assumed in calling conventions, and taking our places upon the platform, and seeking notoriety by making ourselves conspicuous before men. They proceeded to shake the dust from their own skirts of the whole thing. They discussed wisely the disgraceful conduct of Antoinette L. Brown at the World's Temperance Convention, as reported to them by Hon. Samuel Carey, with more of the same sort, which I beg to be excused from trying to recall to mind, or to repeat. When their mission was ended, in due form they filed out of the low dark door, descended the stair-way, and disappeared from our sight.

When we had recovered our equilibrium after such a knock-down surprise,

Mrs. Bateman requested me to proceed. I rose, and asked leave to change my written speech for one not from my pen, but from my heart. The protest of the Dayton "Mrs. Grundys" had been well larded with Scripture, so I added: "Out of the abundance of the heart the mouth speaketh," and never before, possibly never since, have I had greater liberty in relieving my mind, as the Quakers would say. I had been at New York and had boarded with Antoinette L. Brown, so I knew whereof I was bearing testimony, when I assured my hearers that Samuel Carey had certainly been lying—under a mistake. I gave my testimony, not cringingly, but as one who knew, and drew a comparison between Antoinette L. Brown, modestly but firmly standing her ground as a delegate from her society, with politicians and clergymen crying, "Shame on the woman," and stamping and clamoring till the dust on the carpet of the platform enveloped them in a cloud. Meanwhile, her best friends, William H. Channing, William Lloyd Garrison, Oliver Johnson, Wendell Phillips. and others stood by her, bidding her stand firm. The conduct of these ladies in marching through the streets of Dayton, in the most crowded thoroughfares, in the midst of a State fair, to tell some other women that they were making themselves "conspicuous." What I said, or how it was said, mattereth not.

That evening, the Sons of Temperance Hall, which our committee had promised to "keep clear of men," was well filled with women. But all around the walls, and between the benches, on the platform—and in the aisles, there were men from every part of the State. These ladies had given us a grand advertisement.

The following is the report of said meeting clipped from the *Evening Post* twenty-seven years ago, by Mrs. Gage:

THE OHIO WOMEN'S CONVENTION.

DAYTON, *Sept.* 24, 1853.

To-day the Ohio State Women's Temperance Society held a meeting at this place. The attendance was not large, but was respectable, both in number and talents. Mrs. Bateman, of Columbus, presided, and a good officer she made. Parliamentary rules prevailed in governing the assembly, and were enforced with much promptness and dignity. She understood enough of these to put both sides of the question—an attainment which, I have noticed, many Mr. Presidents have often not reached.

The enactment of the Maine law in Ohio is the principal object at which they appeared to aim. Its constitutionality and effect were both discussed, decisions of courts criticised, and all with much acuteness and particularly happy illustrations. In reference to the practicability of enforcing it, when once passed, one woman declared, that "if the men could not do it, the women would give them effectual aid."

In the course of the meeting, two original poems were read, one by Mrs. Gage, formerly of this State, and now of St. Louis, and one by Mrs. Hodge, of Oberlin. There were also delivered three formal addresses, one by Mrs. Dryer, of Delaware County. Ohio, one by Mrs. Griffing, of Salem, Ohio, and the other by Mrs. Gage, either of which would not have dishonored any of our public orators if we consider the matter, style, or manner of delivery. Men can deal in statistics and logical deductions, but women only can describe the horrors of intemperance—can draw aside the curtain and show us the wreck it makes of domestic love and home enjoyment—can paint the anguish of the drunkard's wife and the miseries of his children. Wisdom would seem to dictate that those who feel the most severely the effects of any evil, should best know how to remove it. If this be so, it would be difficult to give a reason why women should not act, indeed lead off. in this great temperance movenrent.

A most exciting and interesting debate arose on some resolutions introduced by the Secretary, Mrs. Griffing, condemnatory of the action of the World's Temperance Convention in undelegating Miss Brown, and excluding her from the platform.

These resolutions are so pithy, that I can not refrain from furnishing them in full. They are as follows :

" *Resolved*, That we regard the tyrannical and cowardly conformation to the ' usages of society,' in thrusting woman from the platform in the late so-called, but mis-called World's Temperance Convention, as a most daring and insulting outrage upon all of womankind ; and it is with the deepest shame and mortification that we learn that our own State of Ohio furnished the delegate to officiate in writing and presenting the resolutions, and presiding at the session when the desperate act was accomplished.

" *Resolved*, That our thanks are due to the Hon. Neal Dow, of Maine, the President of the Convention, for so manfully and persistently deciding and insisting upon and in favor of the right of all the friends of temperance, duly delegated, to seats and participation in all the proceedings."

The friends of General Carey rallied, and with real parliamentary tact moved to lay the resolutions on the table. There was much excitement and some nervousness. The remarks made *pro* and *con* were pithy and to the point. The motion to lay on the table was lost by a large majority. Mrs. Griffing supported her resolutions with much coolness and conscious strength. The General had few defenders, and most of those soon abandoned him to his fate, and fell back upon the position of deprecating the introduction of what they called the question of Woman's Rights into the Convention. All, however, was of no avail ; the resolutions passed by a large majority, and amid much applause.

After recess an attempt was made to reconsider this vote. The President urged some one who voted in the affirmative to move a reconsideration, that a substitute might be offered, condemning the action of the World's Convention in reference to Miss Brown, " as uncourteous, unchristian, and unparliamentary." The motion was made evidently from mere courtesy; but, when put to vote, was lost by a very large majority. The delegates from Oberlin, and some others, joined in the following protest :

" We beg leave to request that it be recorded in the minutes of the meeting, that the delegation from Oberlin, and some others, a'though we regard as uncourteous, unchristian, and unparliamentary, the far-famed proceedings at New York, yet we can not endorse the language of censure as administered by our most loved and valued sisters."

Thus fell General Carey, probably mortally wounded. His vitality, indeed, must be very great, if he can outlive the thrusts given him on this occasion. What rendered his conduct in New York more aggravating is the fact that heretofore, he has encouraged the women of Ohio in their advocacy of temperance, and promised to defend them.

It is not, however, for Ohio men to interfere in this matter. Ohio women have shown themselves abundantly able to take care of themselves and the General too.

LETTERS FROM FRIENDS IN OHIO.

Mrs. R. A. S. Janney, in reply to our request for a chapter of her recollections, said :

The agitation of "Woman's Rights" began in Ohio in 1843 and '44, after Abby Kelly lectured through the State on Anti-slavery.

The status of the public mind at that time is best illustrated by the fact that Catharine Beecher, in 1846, gave an address in Columbus on education, by sitting on the platform and getting her brother Edward to read it for her.

In 1849, Lucy Stone and Antoinette L. Brown, then students at Oberlin College, lectured at different places in the State on "Woman's Rights."

In 1850 a Convention was held at Salem; Mariana Johnson presented a memorial, which was numerously signed and sent to the Constitutional Convention. The same week Mrs. F. D. Gage called a meeting in Masonic Hall, McConnellsville, and drew up a memorial, which was also largely signed, and presented to the Constitutional Convention. Memorials were sent from other parts of the State, and other county conventions held.

The signatures to the petition for "Equal Rights," numbered 7,901, and for the Right of Suffrage, 2,106.

The discussions in the Constitutional Convention were voted to be dropped from the records, because they were so low and obscene. Dr. Townsend, of Lorain, and William Hawkins, of McConnellsville, were our friends in the Convention.

MRS. CORNER'S LETTER.

CLEVELAND, O., *Nov.* 14, 1876.

DEAR MRS. BLOOMER:—Your postal recalls to mind an event which occurred before the women of Ohio had in any sense broken the cords which bound them. A wife was not then entitled to her own earnings, and if a husband were a drunkard, or a gambler, no portion of his wages could she take, without his consent, for the maintenance of herself and family.

Some small gain has been attained in the letter of the law, and much in public opinion. Less stigma rests upon one who chooses an avocation suited to her own taste and ability. We have struggled for little; but it is well for us to remember that the world was not made in a day.

The meeting to which you allude was held in Chesterfield, Morgan County, Ohio. I went in company with Mrs. Gage, and remember well what a spirited meeting it was. When it was found that the church could not be had, the ladies of the place secured a barn, made it nice and clean, had a platform built at one end of the large floor for the speakers and invited guests, and seats arranged in every available place.

The audience was large and respectful, as well as respectable. The leading subjects were : The injustice of the laws, as to property and children, in their results to married women ; the ability of woman to occupy positions of trust now withheld from her; her limited means for acquiring an education ; etc.

Mrs. Gage spoke with great enthusiasm and warmth. I think it must have been almost her first effort, to be followed by years of persistent work by voice and pen, to secure a wider field of labor for her sex, and to spur dull woman to do for herself; to make use of the means within her grasp; to become fit to bear the higher responsibilities which the coming years might impose

Her dear voice is almost silent now, still she lingers as if to catch some faint glimpse of hoped-for results, ere she drops this mortal coil.

Very truly yours,   MARY T. CORNER.

MASSILON CONVENTION.

On May 27, 1852, another State Convention was held in Massilon. We give the following brief notice from the *New York Tribune :*

The third Woman's Rights Convention of Ohio has just closed its session. It was held in the Baptist church, in this place, and was numerously attended, there being a fair representation of men, as well as women; for though the object of these, and similar meetings, is to secure woman her rights, as an equal member of the human family, neither speaking nor membership was here confined to the one sex, but *all* who had sentiments to utter in reference to the object of the Convention—whether for or against it—were invited to speak with freedom, and those who wished to aid the movement to sit as members, without distinction of sex. All honorable classes were represented, from the so-called highest to the so-called lowest—the seamstress who works for twenty-five cents a day; the daughters of the farmer, fresh from the dairy and the kitchen; the wives of the laborer, the physician, the lawyer, and the banker, the legislator, and the minister, were all there—all interested in one common cause, and desirous that every right God gave to woman should be fully recognized by the laws and usages of society, that every faculty he has bestowed upon her should have ample room for its proper development. Is this asking too much? And yet this is the sum and substance of the Woman's Rights Reform—a movement which fools ridicule, and find easier to sneer at than meet with argument.

Before they separated they organized " The Ohio Woman's Rights Association," and chose Hannah Tracy Cutler for President.

The first annual meeting of this Association was held at Ravenna, May 25th and 26th, 1853. In the absence of the President, Mrs. Caroline M. Severance presided. The speakers were Rev. Antoinette L. Brown, Mrs. Lawrence, Emma R. Coe, Josephine S. Griffing, Martha J. Tilden, and many others. Emily Robinson presented an able and encouraging report on the progress of the work. Mrs. Severance was appointed to prepare a memorial to the Legislature, which was presented March 23, 1854, laid on the table and ordered to be printed. This document is found in the June number of *The Una,* 1854, and is a very carefully written paper on the legal status of woman.

CLEVELAND NATIONAL CONVENTION.

In 1853, October 6th, 7th, and 8th, the Fourth National Convention was held in Cleveland. There were delegates present from New York, Pennsylvania, Massachusetts, Connecticut, Ohio, Michigan, Indiana, and Missouri. The *Plain Dealer* said all the ladies prominent in this movement were present, some in full Bloomer costume. At the appointed time Lucretia Mott arose and said :

As President of the last National Convention at Syracuse, it devolves on me to call this meeting to order. It was decided in a preliminary gathering last evening, that Frances D. Gage, of St. Louis, was the suitable person to fill the office of President on this occasion.

Mrs. GAGE, being duly elected, on taking the chair, said: Before proceeding farther, it is proper that prayer should be offered. The Rev. Antoinette L. Brown will address the throne of grace.

She came forward and made a brief, but eloquent prayer. It was considered rather presumptuous in those days for a woman to pray in public, but as Miss Brown was a graduate of Oberlin College, had gone through the theological department, was a regularly orda:ned preacher, and installed as a pastor, she felt quite at home in al the forms and ceremonies of the Church.

The Cleveland *Journal*, in speaking of her, said: She has one distinction, she is the handsomest woman in the Convention. Her voice is silvery, and her manner pleasing. It is generally known that she is the pastor of a Congregational church in South Butler, N. Y.

In her opening remarks, Mrs. GAGE said: It is with fear and trembling that I take up the duties of presiding over your deliberations; not fear and trembling for the cause, but lest I should not have the capacity and strength to do all the position requires of me. She then gave a review of what had been accomplished since the first Convention was held in Seneca Falls, N. Y., July 19, 1848, and closed by saying: I hope our discussions will be a little more extensive than the call would seem to warrant, which indicates simply our right to the political franchise.

To which, Mrs. MOTT replied: I would state that the limitation of the discussions was not anticipated at the last Convention. The issuing of the call was left to the Central Committee, but it was not supposed that they would specify any particular part of the labor of the Convention, but that the broad ground of the presentation of the wrongs of woman, the assertion of her rights, and the encouragement to perseverance in individual and combined action, and the restoration of those rights, should be taken.

After which, Mrs. GAGE added: I would remark once for all, to the Convention, that there is perfect liberty given here to speak upon the subject under discussion, both for and against; and that we urge all to do so. If there are any who have objections, we wish to hear them

If arguments are presented which convince us that we are doing wrong, we wish to act upon them. I extremely regret that while we have held convention after convention, where the same liberty has been given, no one has had a word to say against us at the time, but that some have reserved their hard words of opposition to our movement, only to go away and vent them through the newspapers, amounting, frequently, to gross misrepresentation. I hope every one here will remember, with deep seriousness, that the same Almighty finger which traced upon the tablets of stone the commands, "Thou shalt not kill," "Thou shalt not steal," traced also these words, "Thou shalt not bear false witness against thy neighbor."

The other officers of the Convention were then elected, as follows:

Vice-Presidents—Antoinette L. Brown, New York; Lucretia Mott, Pennsylvania; Caroline M. Severance, Ohio; Joseph Barker, Ohio; Emily Robinson, Ohio; Mary B. Birdsall, Indiana; Sibyl Lawrence, Michigan; Charles P. Wood, New York; Amy Post, New York.

Secretaries—Martha C. Wright, New York; Caroline Stanton, Ohio; H. B. Blackwell, Ohio.

Treasurer—T. C. Severance, Ohio.

Business Committee—Ernestine L. Rose, New York; James Mott, Pennsylvania; Lucy Stone, Massachusetts; Wm. Lloyd Garrison, Mass.; Abby Kelly Foster, Mass.; Mary T. Corner, Ohio; C. C. Burleigh, Connecticut; Martha J. Tilden, Ohio; John O. Wattles, Indiana.

Finance Committee—Susan B. Anthony, Rochester; Phebe H. Merritt, Michigan; H. M. Addison, Ohio; Hettie Little, Ohio; E. P. Heaton, Ohio.

Letters were read from distinguished people. Notably the following from Horace Greeley:

NEW YORK, *Oct.* 2, 1853.

DEAR MADAM:—I have received yours of the 26th, this moment. I do not see that my presence in Cleveland could be of any service. The question to be considered concerns principally woman, and women should mostly consider it. I recognize most thoroughly the right of woman to choose her own sphere of activity and usefulness, and to evoke its proper limitations. If she sees fit to navigate vessels, print newspapers, frame laws, select rulers—any or all of these—I know no principle that justifies man in interposing any impediment to her doing so. The only argument entitled to any weight against the fullest concession of the rights you demand, rests in the assumption that woman does not claim any such rights, but chooses to be ruled, guided, impelled, and have her sphere prescribed for her by man.

I think the present state of our laws respecting property and inheritance, as respects married women, show very clearly that woman ought not to be satisfied with her present position; yet it may be that she is so. If all those who have never given this matter a serious thought are to be

considered on the side of conservatism, of course that side must prepon-
derate. Be this as it may, woman alone can, in the present state of the
controversy, speak effectively for woman, since none others can speak
with authority, or from the depths of a personal experience.

Hoping that your Convention may result in the opening of many eyes,
and the elevation of many minds from light to graver themes,

I remain yours,

Mrs. C. M. SEVERANCE,   HORACE GREELEY.
Cleveland, Ohio.

And here let us pay our tribute of gratitude to Horace Greeley. In
those early days when he, as editor of the *New York Tribune*, was
one of the most popular men in the nation, his word almost law to the
people, his journal was ever true to woman. No ridicule of our
cause, no sneers at its advocates, found a place in *The Tribune;* but
more than once, he gave columns to the proceedings of our conventions.

To this letter, Henry B. Blackwell, brother of Dr. Elizabeth Blackwell, and the future husband of Lucy Stone, pertinently replied,
saying:

It is suggested that woman's cause should be advocated by women
only. The writer of that letter is a true friend of this reform, and yet I
feel that I owe you no apology for standing on this platform. But if I do,
this is sufficient, that I am the son of a woman, and the brother of a
woman. I know that this is their cause, but I feel that it is mine also.
Their happiness is my happiness, their misery my misery.

The interests of the sexes are inseparably connected, and in the elevation of one lies the salvation of the other. Therefore I claim a part in
the last and grandest movement of the ages; for whatever concerns
woman concerns the race. In every human enterprise the sexes should
go hand in hand. Experience sanctions the statement. I know of but
few movements in history, which have gone on successfully without the
aid of woman. One of these is war—the work of human slaughter. Another has been the digging of gold in California. I have yet to learn
what advantages the world has derived from either. Whenever the sexes
have been severed in politics, in business, in religion, the result has been
demoralization.

Mr. Blackwell spoke with great eloquence for nearly an hour, advocating the political, civil, and moral equality of woman. He
showed the power of the ballot in combating unjust laws, opening
college doors, securing equal pay for equal work, dignifying the
marriage relation, by making woman an equal partner, not a subject.
He paid a glowing eulogy to Mary Wollstonecroft. He said:

We need higher ideas of marriage. There is scarcely a young man
here who does not hope to be a husband and a father; nor a young woman

who does not expect to be a wife and a mother. But who does not revolt at the idea of perpetuating a race inferior to ourselves? For myself I could not desire a degenerate family. I would not wish for a race which would not be head and shoulders above what I had been. Let me say to men, select women worthy to be wives. The world is overstocked with these mis-begotten children of undeveloped mothers. No man who has ever seen the symmetrical character of a true woman, can be happy in a union with such. Ladies! the day is coming when men who have seen more well-developed women, will scorn the present standard of female character. Will you not teach them to do so? You may have to sacrifice much, but you will be repaid. This history of the world is rich with glorious examples. Mary Wollstonecroft, the writer of that brave book, "The Rights of Woman," published two generations ago, dared to be true to her convictions of duty in spite of the prejudices of the world. What was the result? She attained a noble character. She found in Godwin a nature worthy of her own, and left a child who became the wife and worthy biographer of the great poet Shelley. Let us imitate that child of glorious parents—parents who dared to make all their relations compatible with absolute right, to give all their powers the highest development.

People say a married woman can not have ulterior objects; that her position is incompatible with a high intellectual culture; that her thoughts and sympathies must be restricted to the four walls of her dwelling. Why, if I were a woman (I speak only as a man) and believed this popular doctrine, that she who is a wife and a mother, being that, must be nothing more, but must cramp her thoughts into the narrow circle of her own home, and indulge no grander aspirations for universal interests—believing that, I would forswear marriage. I would withdraw myself from human society. and go out into the forest and the prairie to live out my own true life in the communion and sympathy of my God. So far as I was concerned, the race might become worthily extinct—it should never be unworthily perpetuated. I could do no otherwise. For we are not made merely to eat and drink, and give children to the world. We are placed here upon the threshold of an immortal life. We are but the chrysalis of the future. If immortality means anything, it means unceasing progress for individuals and for the race.

Mr. Blackwell complimented those women who were just inaugurating a movement for a new costume, promising greater freedom and health. He thought· the sneers and ridicule so unsparingly showered on the "Bloomers," might with more common sense be turned on the "tight waists, paper shoes, and trailing skirts of the fashionable classes."

The facts of history may as well be stated here in regard to the "Bloomer" costume. Mrs. Bloomer was among the first to wear the dress, and stoutly advocated its adoption in her paper, *The Lily*, published at Seneca Falls, N. Y. But it was introduced by Elizabeth Smith Miller, the daughter of the great philanthropist, Gerrit Smith, in 1850. She wore it for many years, even in the most fashionable circles of Washington during her father's term in Congress

Lucy Stone, Miss Anthony, and Mrs. Stanton, also wore it a few years. But it invoked so much ridicule, that they feared the odium attached to the dress might injure the suffrage movement, of which they were prominent representatives. Hence a stronger love for woman's political freedom, than for their own personal comfort, compelled them to lay it aside. The experiment, however, was not without its good results. The dress was adopted for skating and gymnastic exercises, in seminaries and sanitariums. At Dr. James C. Jackson's, in Dansville, N. Y., it is still worn. Many farmers' wives, too, are enjoying its freedom in their rural homes.

Mrs. Bloomer, editor of *The Lily*, at Seneca Falls, New York, was introduced at the close of Mr. Blackwell's remarks, and read a well-prepared digest of the laws for married women.

Reporting one of the sessions, the *Plain Dealer* said:

Mrs. Gage, ever prompt in her place, called the Convention to order at the usual hour. The Melodean at this time contained 1,500 people. We think the women may congratulate themselves on having most emphatically "made a hit" in the forest city.

Of the *personnel* of the Convention, it says:

Mrs. Mott is matronly-looking, wearing the Quaker dress, and apparently a good-natured woman. Her face does not indicate her character as a fiery and enthusiastic advocate of reform. Mrs. Gage is not a handsome woman, but her appearance altogether is prepossessing. You can see genius in her eye. She presided with grace at all the sessions of the Convention. The house was thronged with intelligent audiences. The President frequently contrasted the order, decorum, and kindness of the Cleveland audiences, with the noisy and tumultuous demonstrations which recently disgraced the city of New York, at the Convention held there.

Hon. JOSHUA R. GIDDINGS, on being called to the stand, remarked:

That he was present to express, and happy of the opportunity to express, his sincere interest in the cause, and regard for the actors in this movement; but that on almost any other occasion he could speak with less embarrassment than here, with such advocates before him; and as he had not come prepared to address the Convention, declined occupying its time longer.

In reading over the debates of these early Conventions, we find the speakers dwelling much more on the wrongs in the Church and the Home, than in the State. But few of the women saw clearly, and felt deeply that the one cause of their social and religious degradation was their disfranchisement, hence the discussions often turned on the surface-wrongs of society.

Many of the friends present thought the Convention should issue an original Declaration of Rights, as nothing had been adopted as yet, except the parody on the Fathers' of '76. Although that, and the one William Henry Channing prepared, were both before the Convention, it adjourned without taking action on either.

As so many of these noble leaders in the anti-slavery ranks have passed away, we give in this chapter large space to their brave words. Also to the treatment of Miss Brown, in the World's Temperance Convention, for its exceptional injustice and rudeness.

Miss Brown read a letter from William H. Channing, in which he embodied his ideas of a Declaration. Lucy Stone also read a very able letter from Thomas Wentworth Higginson. Both of these letters contain valuable suggestions for the adoption of practical measures for bringing the wrongs of woman to the notice of the world.

MR. CHANNING'S LETTER.

ROCHESTER, N. Y., *Oct.* 3, 1853.

To the President and Members of the Woman's Rights Convention :

As I am prevented, to my deep regret, from being present at the Convention, let me suggest in writing what I should prefer to speak. First, however, I would once again avow that I am with you heart, mind, soul, and strength for the Equal Rights of Women. This great reform will prove to be, I am well assured, the salvation and glory of this Republic, and of all Christian and civilized States:

> " And if at once we may not
> Declare the greatness of the work we plan,
> Be sure at least that ever in our eyes
> It stands complete before us as a dome
> Of light beyond this gloom—a house of stars
> Encompassing these dusky tents—a thing
> Near as our hearts, and perfect as the heavens.
> Be this our aim and model, and our hands
> Shall not wax faint, until the work is done."

The Woman's Rights Conventions, which, since 1848, have been so frequently held in New York, Ohio, Massachusetts, Pennsylvania, etc., have aroused respectful attention, and secured earnest sympathy, throughout the United States. It becomes the advocates of the Equal Rights of Women, then, to take advantage of this wide-spread interest and to press the Reform, at once, onward to practical results.

Among other timely measures, these have occurred to me as promising to be effective:

I. There should be prepared, printed, and widely circulated, A DECLARATION OF WOMAN'S RIGHTS.

This Declaration should distinctly announce the inalienable rights of women:

9

1st. As human beings,—irrespective of the distinction of sex—actively to co-operate in all movements for the elevation of mankind.

2d. As rational, moral, and responsible agents, freely to think, speak, and do, what truth and duty dictate, and to be the ultimate judges of their own sphere of action.

3d. As women, to exert in private and in public, throughout the whole range of Social Relations, that special influence which God assigns as their appropriate function, in endowing them with feminine attributes.

4th. As members of the body politic, needing the protection, liable to the penalties, and subject to the operation of the laws, to take their fair part in legislation and administration, and in appointing the makers and administrators of the laws.

5th. As constituting one-half of the people of these free and United States, and as nominally, free women, to possess and use the power of voting, now monopolized by that other half of the people, the free men.

6th. As property holders, numbered and registered in every census, and liable to the imposition of town, county, state, and national taxes, either to be represented if taxed, or to be left untaxed if unrepresented, according to the established precedent of No taxation without representation.

7th. As producers of wealth to be freed from all restrictions on their industry; to be remunerated according to the work done, and not the sex of the workers, and whether married or single, to be secured in the ownership of their gains, and the use and distribution of their property.

8th. As intelligent persons, to have ready access to the best means of culture, afforded by schools, colleges, professional institutions, museums of science, galleries of art, libraries, and reading-rooms.

9th. As members of Christian churches and congregations, heirs of Heaven and children of God, to preach the truth, to administer the rites of baptism, communion, and marriage, to dispense charities, and in every way to quicken and refine the religious life of individuals and of society

The mere announcement of these rights, is the strongest argument and appeal that can be made, in behalf of granting them. The claim to their free enjoyment is undeniably just. Plainly such rights are inalienable, and plainly too, woman is entitled to their possession equally with man. Our whole plan of government is a hypocritical farce, if one-half the people can be governed by the other half without their consent being asked or granted. Conscience and common sense alike demand the equal rights of women. To the conscience and common sense of their fellow-citizens, let women appeal untiringly, until their just claims are acknowledged throughout the whole system of legislation, and in all the usages of society.

And this introduces the next suggestion I have to offer.

II. Forms of petition should be drawn up and distributed for signatures, to be offered to the State Legislatures at their next sessions. These petitions should be directed to the following points:

1st. That the right of suffrage be granted to the people, universally, without distinction of sex; and that the age for attaining legal and political majority, be made the same for women as for men.

2d. That all laws relative to the inheritance and ownership of property, to the division and administration of estates, and to the execution of Wills, be made equally applicable to women and men.

3d. That mothers be entitled, equally with fathers, to become guardians of their children.

4th. That confirmed and habitual drunkenness, of either husband or wife, be held as sufficient ground for divorce ; and that the temperate partner be appointed legal guardian of the children.

5th. That women be exempted from taxation until their right of suffrage is practically acknowledged.

6th. That women equally with men be entitled to claim trial before a jury of their peers.

These petitions should be firm and uncompromising in tone ; and a hearing should be demanded before Committees specially empowered to consider and report them. In my judgment, the time is not distant, when such petitions will be granted, and when justice, the simple justice they ask, will be cordially, joyfully rendered.

I call then for the publication of a Declaration of Woman's Rights, accompanied by Forms of Petitions, by the National Woman's Rights Convention at their present session. In good hope,

Your friend and brother, WILLIAM HENRY CHANNING.

Miss BROWN remarked :

There is one of these demands, the fourth, which for myself, I should prefer to have amended thus—instead of the word " divorce," I would insert " legally separated." The letter otherwise meets my cordial and hearty approbation.

MR. HIGGINSON'S LETTER.

WORCESTER, *Sept.* 15, 1853.

DEAR FRIEND :—In writing to the New York Woman's Rights Convention, I mentioned some few points of argument which no opponents of this movement have ever attempted to meet. Suffer me, in addressing the Cleveland Convention, to pursue a different course, and mention some things which the friends of the cause have not yet attempted to do.

I am of a practical habit of mind, and have noticed with some regret that most of the friends of the cause have rested their hopes, thus far, chiefly upon abstract reasoning. This is doubtless of great importance, and these reasonings have already made many converts; because the argument is so entirely on one side that every one who really listens to it begins instantly to be convinced. The difficulty is, that the majority have not yet begun to listen to it, and this, in great measure, because their attention has not been called to the facts upon which it is founded.

Suppose, now, that an effort were made to develop the facts of woman's wrongs. For instance :

1st. We say that the laws of every State of this Union do great wrong to woman, married and single, as to her person and property, in her private and public relations. Why not procure a digest of the laws on these subjects, then ;

prepared carefully, arranged systematically, corrected up to the latest improve-ments, and accompanied by brief and judicious commentaries? No such work exists, except that by Mansfield, which is now obsolete, and in many respects defective.

2d. We complain of the great educational inequalities between the sexes. Why not have a report, elaborate, statistical, and accurate, on the provision for female education, public and private, throughout the free States of this Union, at least? No such work now exists.

3d. We complain of the industrial disadvantages of women, and indicate at the same time, their capacities for a greater variety of pursuits. Why not ob-tain a statement, on as large a scale as possible, first, of what women are doing now, commercially and mechanically, throughout the Union (thus indicating their powers); and secondly, of the embarrassments with which they meet, the inequality of their wages, and all the other peculiarities of their position, in these respects? An essay, in short, on the Business Employments and Interests of Women; such an essay as Mr. Hunt has expressed to me his willingness to publish in his *Merchants' Magazine.* No such essay now exists.

Each of these three documents would be an arsenal of arms for the Woman's Rights advocate. A hundred dollars, appropriated to each of these, would more than repay itself in the increased subscriptions it would soon bring into the treasury of the cause. That sum would, however, be hardly sufficient to repay even the expenses of correspondence and traveling necessary for the last two essays, or the legal knowledge necessary for the first.

If there is, however, known to the Convention at Cleveland any person qual-ified and ready to undertake either of the above duties for the above sum (no person should undertake more than one of the three investigations), I would urge you to make the appointment. It will require, however, an accurate, clear-headed, and industrious person, with plenty of time to bestow. Better not have it done at all, than not have it done thoroughly, carefully, and dispassion-ately. Let me say distinctly, that I can not be a candidate for either duty, in my own person, for want of time to do it in; though I think I could render some assistance, especially in preparing materials for the third essay. I would also gladly subscribe toward a fund for getting the work done.

Permit me, finally, to congratulate you on the valuable results of every Con-vention yet held to consider this question. I find the fact everywhere remark-ed, that so large a number of women of talent and character have suddenly come forward into a public sphere. This phenomenon distinguishes this reform from all others that have appeared in America, and illustrates with new meaning the Greek myth of Minerva, born full-grown from the head of Jove. And if (as some late facts indicate) this step forward only promotes the Woman's Rights movement from the sphere of contempt into the sphere of hostility and perse-cution—it is a step forward, none the less. And I would respectfully suggest to the noble women who are thus attacked, that they will only be the gainers by such opposition, unless it lead to dissensions or jealousies among themselves.

Yours cordially,

Miss Lucy Stone.   Thomas Wentworth Higginson.

Lucy Stone remarked: This letter, you see, proposes that we shall find some way, if possible, by which our complaints may be spread before the people. We find men and women in our conventions, earnest and thoughtful, who are not drawn by mere curiosity, but from a conscious want of just such a movement as this. They go away and carry to their villages and hamlets the ideas they have gathered here; and it is a cause for thankfulness to God that so many go away to repeat what they have heard. But we have wanted the documents to scatter among the people, as the Tract Society scatters its sheets. And now Mr. Higginson proposes that we have these essays.

The President of Oberlin College, Rev. Asa Mahan, was present during all the sessions of the Convention, and took part in the debates. On the subject of the Seneca Falls Declaration, he said:

I can only judge of the effect of anything upon the public mind, by its effect upon my own. It has been suggested that that Declaration is a parody. Now you can not present a parody, without getting up a laugh; and wherever it goes, it will never be seriously considered. If a declaration is to be made, it should be one that will be seriously considered by the public. I would suggest that the Declaration of this Convention be entirely independent of the other.

I have a remark to make upon a sentiment advanced by Mrs. Rose. I have this objection to the Declaration upon which she commented. It is asserted there, that man has created a certain public sentiment, and it is brought as a charge against the male sex. Now I assert, that man never created that sentiment. I say it is a wrong state of society totally, when, if woman shall be degraded, a man committing the same offense shall not be degraded also. There is perfect agreement between us there. But, that Declaration charges that sentiment upon man. Now I assert that it is chargeable upon woman herself; and that as she was first in man's original transgression, she is first here.

Mrs. Rose: I heartily agree that we are both in fault; and yet we are none in fault. I also said, that woman, on account of the position in which she has been placed, by being dependent upon man, by being made to look up to man, is the first to cast out her sister. I know it and deplore it; hence I wish to give her her rights, to secure her dependence upon herself. In regard to that sentiment in the Declaration, our friend said that woman created it. Is woman really the creator of the sentiment? The laws of a country create sentiments. Who make the laws? Does woman? Our law-makers give the popular ideas of morality.

Mr. Barker: And the pulpit.

Mrs. Rose: I ought to have thought of it: not only do the law-makers give woman her ideas of morality, but our pulpit preachers. I beg pardon—no, I do not either—for Antoinette L. Brown is not a priest. Our priests have given us public sentiment called morals, and they have always made or recognized in daily life, distinctions between man and woman. Man, from the time of Adam to the present, has had utmost license, while woman must not commit the slightest degree of "impropriety," as it is termed. Why, even to cut her skirts shorter than the fashion, is considered a moral delinquency, and stigmatized as such by more than one pulpit, directly or indirectly.

You ask me who made this sentiment; and my friend yonder, says woman. She is but the echo of man. Man utters the sentiment, and woman echoes it. As I said before—for I have seen and felt it deeply—she even appears to be quite flattered with her cruel tyrant, for such he has been made to be—she is quite flattered with the destroyer of woman's character—aye, worse than that, the destroyer of woman's self-respect and peace of mind—and when she meets him, she is flattered with his attentions. Why should she not be? He is admitted into Legislative halls, and to all places where men "most do congregate;" why, then, should she not admit him to her parlor? The woman is admitted into no such places; the Church casts her out; and a stigma is cast upon her, for what is called the slightest "impropriety." Prescribed by no true moral law, but by superstition and prejudice, she is cast out not only from public places, but from private homes. And if any woman would take her sister to her heart, and warm her there again by sympathy and kindness, if she would endeavor once more to infuse into her the spark of life and virtue, of morality and peace, she often dare not so far encounter public prejudice as to do it. It requires a courage beyond what woman can now possess, to take the part of the woman against the villain. There are few such among us, and though few, they have stood forward nobly and gloriously. I will not mention names, though it is often a practice to do so; I must, however, mention our sister, Lucretia Mott, who has stood up and taken her fallen sister by the hand, and warmed her at her own heart. But we can not expect every woman to possess that degree of courage.

ABBY KELLY FOSTER: I want to say here that I believe the law is but the writing out of public sentiment, and back of that public sentiment, I contend lies the responsibility. Where shall we find it? "'Tis education forms the common mind." It is allowed that we are what we are educated to be. Now if we can ascertain who has had the education of us, we can ascertain who is responsible for the law, and for public sentiment. Who takes the infant from its cradle and baptizes it " in the name of the Father, Son, and Holy Ghost;" and when that infant comes to childhood, who takes it into Sabbath-schools; who on every Sabbath day, while its mind is "like clay in the hands of the potter," moulds and fashions it as he will; and when that child comes to be a youth, where is he found, one-seventh part of the time; and when he comes to maturer age, does he not leave his plow in the furrow, and his tools in the shop, and one-seventh part of the time go to the place where prayer is wont to be made? On that day no sound is heard but the roll of the carriage wheels to church; all are gathered there, everything worldly is laid aside, all thoughts are given entirely to the Creator; for we are taught that we must not think our own thoughts, but must lay our own wills aside, and come to be moulded and fashioned by the priest. It is "holy time," and we are to give ourselves to be wholly and entirely fashioned and formed by another. That place is a holy place, and when we enter, our eye rests on the "holy of holies;" he within it is a "divine." The "divines" of the thirteenth century, the "divines" of the fifteenth century, and the "divines" of the nineteenth century, are no less "divines."

What I say to-day is taken for what it is worth, or perhaps for less than it is worth, because of the prejudice against me; but when he who edu- cates the people speaks, "he speaks as one having authority," and is not to be questioned. He claims, and has his claim allowed, to be spe- cially ordained and specially anointed from God. He stands mid-way between Deity and man, and therefore his word has power.

Aye, not only in middle age does the man come, leaving everything behind him; but, in old age, "leaning on the top of his staff," he finds himself gathered in the place of worship, and though his ear may be dull and heavy, he leans far forward to catch the last words of duty—of duty to God and duty to man. Duty is the professed object of the pulpit, and if it does not teach that, what in Heaven's name does it teach? This anointed man of God speaks of moral duty to God and man. He teaches man from the cradle to the coffin; and when that aged form is gathered within its winding-sheet, it is the pulpit that says, "Dust to dust and ashes to ashes."

It is the pulpit, then, which has the entire ear of the community, one- seventh part of the time. If you say there are exceptions, very well, that proves the rule. If there is one family who do not go to church, it is no matter, its teachings are engendered by those who do go; hence I would say, not only does the pulpit have the ear of the community one-seventh part of the time of childhood, but it has it under circumstances for form- ing and moulding and fashioning the young mind, as no other educating influence can have it. The pulpit has it, not only under these circum- stances; it has it on occasions of marriage, when two hearts are welded into one; on occasions of sickness and death, when all the world beside is shut out, when the mind is most susceptible of impressions from the pulpit, or any other source.

I say, then, that woman is not the author of this sentiment against her fallen sister, and I roll back the assertion on its source. Having the public ear one-seventh part of the time, if the men of the pulpit do not educate the public mind, who does educate it? Millions of dollars are paid for this education, and if they do not educate the public mind in its morals, what, I ask, are we paying our money for? If woman is cast out of society, and man is placed in a position where he is respected, then I charge upon the pulpit that it has been recreant to its duty. If the pulpit should speak out fully and everywhere, upon this subject, would not woman obey it? Are not women under the special leading and direc- tion of their clergymen? You may tell me, that it is woman who forms the mind of the child; but I charge it back again, that it is the minister who forms the mind of the woman. It is he who makes the mother what she is; therefore her teaching of the child is only conveying the instruc- tions of the pulpit at second hand. If public sentiment is wrong on this (and I have the testimony of those who have spoken this morn- ing, that it is), the pulpit is responsible for it, and has the power of changing it. The clergy claim the credit of establishing public schools. Granted. Listen to the pulpit in any matter of humanity, and they will claim the originating of it, because they are the teachers of the people. Now, if we give credit to the pulpit for establishing public schools, then

I charge them with having a bad influence over those schools; and if the charge can be rolled off, I want it to be rolled off; but until it can be done, I hope it will remain there.

Mr. MAHAN: No class of persons had better be drawn into our discussions to be denounced, unless there is serious occasion for it. I name the pulpit with solemn awe, and unless there is necessity for it, charges had better not be made against it. Now, I say that no practice and no usage in the Church can be found, by which a criminal man, in reference to the crimes referred to, may be kept in the Church and a criminal woman cast out. There is no such custom in any of the churches of God. After twenty years' acquaintance with the Church, I affirm that the practice does not exist. Now, in regard to the origin of public sentiment, can a pulpit be found, will the lady who has just sat down, name a pulpit in the wide world, where the principle is advocated, that a criminal woman should be excluded, and the man upheld? Whatever faults may be in it, that fault is not there.

Mrs. ROSE: Not in theory, but in practice.

Mr. MAHAN: Neither in theory nor in practice. Where a wrong state of society exists, the pulpit may be in fault for not reprobating it.

ABBY K. FOSTER: I do not wish to mention names, or I could do so. I could give many cases where ministers have been charged with such crimes, and where the evidence of guilt was almost insurmountable, and yet they were not disciplined. They were afraid it would injure the Church. I remember one minister who was brought up for trial, and meantime they suspended him from office, and paid him only half his salary, but retained him as a church member; when, if it had been the case of a woman, and had the slightest shade of suspicion been cast upon her, they would not have waited even for trial and judgment. They would have cast her out of the church at once.

WILLIAM LLOYD GARRISON said: I have but a few words to submit to the meeting at the present time. In regard to the position of the Church and clergy, on the subject of purity, I think it is sufficient to remind the people here, that whatever may be the external form observed by the Church toward its members, pertaining to licentiousness, one thing is noticeable, and that is, that the marriage relation is abolished among three and a half millions of people; and the abolition of marriage on that frightful scale, is in the main sanctioned and sustained by the American Church and clergy. And if this does not involve them in all that is impure, and licentious, and demoralizing, I know not what can do so.

As it respects the objection to our adopting the Declaration of Independence as put forth at Seneca Falls, on the ground that it is a parody, and that, being a parody, it will only excite the mirthfulness of those who hear or read it in that form; I would simply remark, that I very much doubt, whether, among candid and serious men, there would be any such mirthfulness excited. At the time that document was published, I read it, but I had forgotten it till this morning, and on listening to it, my mind was deeply impressed with its pertinacity and its power. It seemed to me, the *argumentum ad hominum*, to this nation. It was measuring the people of this country by their own standard. It was taking their own words and applying their own principles to women, as they have been applied to men. At the same time, I liked the suggestion that we had better present an original paper to the country; and on conferring with the Committee after the adjournment, they agreed that it would be better to have such a paper; and that paper will undoubtedly be prepared, although we are not now ready to lay it before the Convention.

It was this morning objected to the Declaration of sentiments, that it implied that man was the only transgressor, that he had been guilty of injustice and usurpation, and the suggestion was also made, that woman should not be criminated, in this only, but regarded rather as one who had erred through ignorance; and our eloquent friend, Mrs. Rose, who stood on this platform and pleaded with such marked ability, as she always does plead in any cause she undertakes to speak upon, told us her creed. She told us she did not blame anybody, really, and did not hold any man to be criminal, or any individual to be responsible for public sentiment, as regards the difference of criminality of man and woman.

For my own part, I am not prepared to respect that philosophy. I believe in sin, therefore in a sinner; in theft, therefore in a thief; in slavery, therefore in a slaveholder; in wrong, therefore in a wrong-doer; and unless the men of this nation are made by woman to see that they have been guilty of usurpation, and cruel usurpation, I believe very little progress will be made. To say all this has been done without thinking, without calculation, without design, by mere accident, by a want of light; can anybody believe this who is familiar with all the facts in the case? Certainly, for one, I hope ever to lean to the charitable side, and will try to do so. I, too, believe things are done through misconception and misapprehension, which are injurious, yes, which are immoral and unchristian; but only to a limited extent. There is such a thing as intelligent wickedness, a design on the part of those who have the light to quench it, and to do the wrong to gratify their own propensities, and to further their own interests. So, then, I believe, that as man has monopolized for generations all the rights which belong to woman, it has not been accidental, not through ignorance on his part; but I believe that man has done this through calculation, actuated by a spirit of pride, a desire for domination which has made him degrade woman in her own eyes, and thereby tend to make her a mere vassal.

It seems to me, therefore, that we are to deal with the consciences of men. It is idle to say that the guilt is common, that the women are as deeply involved in this matter as the men. Never can it be said that the victims are as much to be blamed as the victimizer; that the slaves are to be as much blamed as the slaveholders and slave-drivers; that the women who have no rights, are to be as much blamed as the men who have played the part of robbers and tyrants. We must deal with conscience. The men of this nation, and the men of all nations, have no just respect for woman. They have tyrannized over her deliberately, they have not sinned through ignorance, but theirs is not the knowledge that saves. Who can say truly, that in all things he acts up to the light he enjoys, that he does not do something which he knows is not the very thing, or the best thing he ought to do? How few there are among mankind who are able to say this with regard to themselves. Is not the light all around us? Does not this nation know how great its guilt is in enslaving one-sixth of its people? Do not the men of this nation know ever since the landing of the pilgrims, that they are wrong in making subject one-half of the people? Rely upon it, it has not been a mistake on their part. It has been sin. It has been guilt; and they manifest their guilt to a demonstration, in the manner in which they receive this movement. Those who do wrong ignorantly, do not willingly continue in it, when they find they are in the wrong. Ignorance is not an evidence of guilt certainly. It is only an evidence of a want of light. They who are only ignorant, will never rage, and rave, and threaten, and foam, when the light comes; but being interested and walking in the light, will always present a manly front, and be willing to be taught, and be willing to be told they are in the wrong.

Take the case of slavery: How has the anti-slavery cause been received? Not argumentatively, not by reason, not by entering the free arena of fair discussion and comparing notes; the arguments have been rotten eggs, and brickbats and calumny, and in the southern portion of the country, a spirit of murder, and threats to cut out the tongues of those who spoke against them. What has this indicated on the part of the nation? What but conscious guilt? Not ignorance, not that they had not the light. They had the light and rejected it.

How has this Woman's Rights movement been treated in this country, on the right hand and on the left? This nation ridicules and derides this movement, and spits upon it, as fit only to be cast out and trampled underfoot. This is not ignorance. They know all about the truth. It is the natural outbreak of tyranny. It is because the tyrants and usurpers are alarmed. They have been and are called to judgment, and they dread the examination and exposure of their position and character.

Women of America! you have something to blame yourselves for in this matter, something to account for to God and the world. Granted. But then you are the victims in this land, as the women of all lands are, to the tyrannical power and godless ambition of man; and we must show who are responsible in this matter. We must test everybody here. Every one of us must give an account of himself to God. It is an individual testing of character. Mark the man or the woman who derides this movement, who turns his or her back upon it; who is disposed to let misrule keep on, and you will find you have a sure indication of character. You will find that such persons are destitute of principles; for if you can convict a man of being wanting in principle anywhere, it will be everywhere. He who loves the right for its own sake, loves the right everywhere. He who is a man of principle, is a man of principle always. Let me see the man who is willing to have any one of God's rational creatures sacrificed to promote anything, aside from the well-being of that creature himself, and I will show you an unprincipled man.

It is so in this movement. Nobody argues against it, nobody pretends to have an argument. Your platform is free everywhere, wherever these Conventions are held. Yet no man comes forward in a decent, re-spectable manner, to show you that you are wrong in the charges you bring against the law-makers of the land. There is no argument against it. The thing is self-evident. I should not know how to begin to frame an argument. That which is self-evident is greater than argument, and beyond logic. It testifies of itself. You and I, as human beings, claim to have rights, but I never think of going into an argument with anybody, to prove that I ought to have rights. I have the argument and logic here, it is in my own breast and consciousness; and the logic of the schools becomes contemptible beside these. The more you try to argue, the worse you are off. It is not the place for metaphysics, it is the place for affirmation. Woman is the counterpart of man; she has the same divine image, hav-ing the same natural and inalienable rights as man. To state the propo-sition is enough; it contains the argument, and nobody can gainsay it, in an honorable way.

I rose simply to say, that though I should deprecate making our plat-form a theological arena, yet believing that men are guilty of intentional wrong, in keeping woman subject, I believe in having them criminated. You talk of injustice, then there is an unjust man somewhere. Even Mrs. Rose could talk of the guilt of society. Society! I know nothing of society. I know the guilt of individuals. Society is an abstract term: it is made up of individuals, and the responsibility rests with individuals. So then, if we are to call men to repentance, there is such a thing as wrong-doing intelligently, sinning against God and man, with light enough to convict us, and to condemn us before God and the world. Let this cause then be pressed upon the hearts and consciences, against those who hold unjust rights in their possession.

Mrs. Rose: I want to make a suggestion to the meeting. This is the afternoon of the last day of our Convention. We have now heard here the Bible arguments on both sides, and I may say to them that I agree with both, that is, I agree with neither. A gentleman, Dr. Nevin, I be-lieve, said this morning that he also would reply to Mr. Barker, this aft-ernoon. We have already had Mr. Barker answered. If any one else speaks farther on Miss Brown's side, somebody will have to reply upon the other. "There is a time and a season for everything," and this is no time to discuss the Bible. I appeal to the universal experience of men, to sustain me in asking whether the introduction of theological quibbles, has not been a firebrand wherever they have been thrown? We have a political question under discussion; let us take that question and argue it with reference to right and wrong, and let us argue it in the same way that your fathers and mothers did, when they wanted to throw off the British yoke.

Dr. Nevin: It will be unjust, not to permit me to speak.

Mrs. Mott moved that he be allowed, since he had already got the floor, without attempting to limit him at all; but that immediately after, the Convention should take up the resolutions.

Mrs. Rose objected, because, if a third person should speak, then a fourth must speak, or plead injustice, if not permitted to do so.

Considerable confusion ensued, Dr. Nevin, however, persisting in speaking, whereupon the President invited him to the platform. He took the stand, assuring the President and officers, as he passed them, that he wished only to reply to some misinterpretations of Mr. Barker's, and would take but little of the time which they so much needed for business. After commencing, however, with Bible in hand, he launched out into an irrelevant eulogium upon "his Christ," etc.; from that to personalities against Mr. Barker and his associates upon the platform, calling him a "renegade priest," "an infidel from foreign shores, who had come to teach Americans Christianity!"

Mr. GARRISON rose to a point of order, with regard to the speaker's personalities as to the nativity of anybody.

Dr. NEVIN retorted: The gentleman has been making personalities against the whole priesthood.

Mr. BARKER: I expressly and explicitly made exceptions. I only wish that Mr. Nevin may not base his remarks upon a phantom.

Dr. NEVIN continued wandering on for some time, when Stephen S. Foster rose, to a point of order, as follows: "The simple question before us, is whether woman is entitled to all the rights to which the other sex is entitled. I want to say, that the friend is neither speaking to the general question, nor replying to Mr. Barker." Mr. Foster continued his remarks somewhat, when Dr. Nevin demanded that the Chair protect him in his right to the floor. The Chair decided that Mr. Foster was out of order, in continuing to speak so long upon his point of order.

Mr. FOSTER said he would not appeal to the house from the decision of the Chair, because he wished to save time. He continued a moment longer, and sat down.

Dr. NEVIN proceeded, and in the course of his remarks drew various unauthorized inferences, as the belief of Mr. Barker, in the doctrines of Christ. Mr. Barker repeatedly corrected him, but Dr. Nevin very ingeniously continued to reaffirm them in another shape. Finally, Mr. Garrison, in his seat, addressing the President, said: "It is utterly useless to attempt to correct the individual. He is manifestly here in the spirit of a blackguard and rowdy." (A storm of hisses and cries of "down!" "down!")

Dr. NEVIN: I am sorry friend Garrison has thought fit to use those words. He has been in scenes and situations like these, and has himself stood up and spoken in opposition to the opinions of audiences, too often not to have by this time been taught patience.

Mrs. CLARK: Mr. Garrison is accustomed to call things by their right names.

Dr. NEVIN: Very well, then I should call him—turning upon Mr. G.— worse names than those. Only one word has fallen from woman in this Convention, to which I can take exception, and that fell from the lips of a lady whom I have venerated from my childhood—it was, that the pulpit was the castle of cowards.

Mrs. MOTT: I said it was John Chambers' cowards' castle; and I do say, that such ministers make it a castle of cowards; but I did not wish to make the remark general, or apply it to all pulpits.

Dr. NEVIN continued some time longer.

Mrs. FOSTER asked, at the close of his remarks, if he believed it was right for woman to speak what she believed to be the truth, from the pulpit; to which he replied affirmatively, "there and everywhere."

Mrs. ROSE: I might claim my right to reply to the gentleman who has just taken his seat. I might be able to prove from the arguments he brought forward, that he was incorrect in the statements he made, but I waive that right, the time has been so unjustly consumed already. To one thing only, I will reply. He charged France with being licentious, and spoke of the degraded position of French women, as the result of the infidelity of that nation. I throw back the slander he uttered, in regard to French women. I am not a French woman, but if there is no other here to vindicate them, I will do it. The French women are as moral as any other people in any country; and when they have not been as moral, it has been because they have been priest-ridden. I love to vindicate the rights of those who are not present to defend themselves.

STEPHEN S. FOSTER: Our "reverend" friend spoke of *dragging* infidelity into this Convention, as though infidelity had to be "dragged" here. I want to know if Christianity has been "dragged" here, when the speakers made it the basis of their arguments. Who ever dreamed of "dragging" Christianity here when they came to advocate the rights of woman in the name of Christ? Why then should any one stand up here and charge a speaker with "dragging" infidelity when he advocates the rights of woman under the name of an infidel. I supposed that Greek and Jew, Barbarian and Scythian, Christian and Infidel had been invited to this platform. One thing I know, we have had barbarians here, whether we invited them or not; and I like to have barbarians here; I know of no place where they are so likely to be civilized. I have never yet been in a meeting managed by men when there was such conflict of feelings, where there was not also ten times as much confusion. And I think this meeting a powerful proof of the superiority of our principles over those who oppose us.

Tell me if Christianity has not ever held the reins in this country; and what has it done for woman? I am talking now of the popular idea of Christianity. What has Christianity done for woman for two hundred years past? Why, to-day, in this Christian nation, there are a million and a half of women bought and sold like cattle; a million and a half of women who can not say who are the fathers of their children! I ask, are we to depend on a Christianity like that to restore woman her rights? I am speaking of your idea of Christianity—of Dr. Nevin's idea of Christianity—I shall come to the true Christianity by and by.

One of two things is certain. The Church and Government deny to woman her rights. There is not a denomination in this country which places woman on an equality with man. Not one. Can you deny it?

Mrs. MOTT: Except the Progressive Friends.

Mr. FOSTER: They are not a denomination, they have broken from all bands and taken the name of the Friends of Progress. I say there is not a religious society, having an organized body of ministers, which admits woman's equality in the Gospel. Now, tell me, in God's name, what we are to hope from the Church, when she leaves a million and a half of women liable to be brought upon the auction-block to-day? If the Bible is against woman's equality, what are you to do with it? One of two things: either you must sit down and fold up your hands, or you must discard the divine authority of the Bible. Must you not? You must acknowledge the correctness of your position, or deny the authority of the Bible. If you admit the construction put upon the Bible by friend Barker, to be a false one, or Miss Brown's construction to be the true one, what then? Why, then, the priesthood of the country are blind leaders of the blind. We have got forty thousand of them, Dr. Nevin included with the rest. He stands as an accredited Presbyterian, giving the hand of fellowship to the fraternity, and withholding it from Garrison and others—he could not even pray a few years ago in an anti-slavery meeting. Now, either the Bible is against the Church and clergy, or else they have misinterpreted it for two hundred years, yes, for six thousand years. You must then either discard the Bible or the priesthood, or give up Woman's Rights.

A friend says he does not regret this discussion. Why, it is the only thing we have done effectively since we have been here. When we played with jack-straws, we were hail-fellow with those who now oppose us. When you come to take up the great questions of the movement, when you propose to man, to divide with woman the right to rule, then a great opposition is aroused. The ballot-box is not worth a straw until woman is ready to use it. Suppose a law were passed to-morrow, declaring woman's rights equal with those of men, why, the facts would remain the same. The moment that woman is ready to go to the ballot-box, there is not a Constitution that will stand in the country. In this very city, in spite of the law, I am told that negroes go to the ballot-box and vote, without let or hindrance; and woman will go when she resolves upon it. What we want for woman is the right of speech; and in Dr. Nevin's reply to Mrs. Foster, does he mean that he would be willing to accord the right of speech to woman and admit her into the pulpit? I don't believe he would admit Antoinette Brown to his pulpit. I was sorry Mrs. Foster did not ask him if he would. I don't believe he dares to do it. I would give him a chance to affirm or deny it. I hope some other friend will give him that opportunity, and that Antoinette Brown may be able to say that she was invited by the pastor of one of the largest churches in this beautiful city, to speak to his people in his pulpit; but if he does it, he is not merely one among a thousand, but one among ten thousand.

I wish to have it understood that an infidel is as much at home here. as a Christian; and that his principles are no more "dragged" here than those of a Christian. For myself, I claim to be a Christian. No man ever heard me speak of Christ or of His doctrines, but with the profoundest reverence. Still, I welcome upon this platform those who differ as far as possible from me. And the Atheist no more "drags" in his Atheism, provided he only shows that Atheism itself demands woman's equality, and is no more out of order than I, when I undertake to show that Christianity preaches one law, one faith, and one line of duty for all.

Mrs. MOTT: We ought to thank Dr. Nevin for his kindly fears, lest we women should be brought out into the rough conflicts of life, and overwhelmed by infidelity. I thank him, but at the same time I must say, that if we have been able this afternoon to sit uninjured by the hard conflict in which he has been engaged, if we can maintain our patience at seeing him so laboriously build up a man of straw, and then throw it down and destroy it, I think we may be suffered to go into the world and bear many others unharmed.

Again, I would ask in all seriousness, by what right does Orthodoxy give the invidious name of Infidel, affix the stigma of infidelity, to those who dissent from its cherished opinions? What right have the advocates of moral reform, woman's rights, abolition, temperance, etc., to call in question any man's religious opinions? It is the assumption of bigots. I do not want now to speak invidiously, and say sectarian bigots, but I mean the same kind of bigotry which Jesus rebuked so sharply, when He called certain men " blind leaders of the blind."

Now, we hold Jesus up as an example, when we perceive the assumption of clergymen, that all who venture to dissent from a given interpretation, must necessarily be infidels; and thus denounce them as infidels; for it was only by inference, that one clergyman this afternoon made Joseph Barker deny the Son of God. By inference in the same way, he might be made to deny everything that is good, and praiseworthy, and true.

I want we should consider these things upon this platform. I am not troubled with difficulties about the Bible. My education has been such, that I look to that Source whence all the inspiration of the Bible comes. I love the truths of the Bible. I love the Bible because it contains so many truths; but I never was educated to love the errors of the Bible; therefore it does not startle me to hear Joseph Barker point to some of those errors. And I can listen to the ingenious interpretation of the Bible, given by Antoinette Brown, and am glad to hear those who are so skilled in the outward, when I perceive that they are beginning to turn the Bible to so good an account. It gives evidence that the cause is making very good progress. Why, my friend Nevin has had to hear the temperance cause denounced as infidel, and proved so by Solomon; and he has, no doubt, seen the minister in the pulpit, turning over the pages of the Bible to find examples for the wrong. But the Bible will never sustain him in making this use of its pages, instead of using it rationally, and selecting such portions of it as would tend to corroborate the right; and these are plentiful; for notwithstanding the teaching of theology, and men's arts in the religious world, men have ever responded to righteousness and truth, when it has been advocated by the servants of God, so that we need not fear to bring truth to an intelligent examination of the Bible. It is a far less dangerous assertion to say that God is unchangeable, than that man is infallible.

In this debate on the Bible-position of woman, Mr. Garrison having always been a close student of that Book, was so clear in his positions, and so ready in his quotations, that he carried the audience triumphantly with him. The Rev. Dr. Nevin came out of the contest so chagrined, that, losing all sense of dignity, on meeting Mr. Garrison in the vestibule of the hall, at the close of the Convention, he seized him by the nose and shook him vehemently. Mr. Garrison made no resistance, and when released, he calmly surveyed his antagonist and said, " Do you feel better, my friend? do you hope thus to break the force of my argument?" The friends of the Rev. Mr. Nevin were so mortified with his ungentlemanly behavior that they suppressed the scene in the vestibule as far as possible, in the Cleveland journals, and urged the ladies who had the report of the Convention in charge, to make no mention of it in their publication. Happily, the fact has been resurrected in time to point a page of history.

A question arising in the Convention as to the colleges, Antoinette Brown remarked :

That much and deeply as she loved Oberlin, she must declare that it has more credit for liberality to woman than it deserves. Girls are not allowed equal privileges and advantages there; they are not allowed instructions in elocution, nor to speak on commencement day. The only college in the country that places all students on an equal footing, without distinction of sex or color, is McGrawville College in Central New York. Probably Antioch College, Ohio (President Horace Mann), will also admit pupils on the same ground.

Mrs. Rose said she knew of no college where both sexes enjoyed equal advantages. It matters not, however, if there be. We do not deal with exceptions, but with general principles.

A sister has well remarked that we do not believe that man is the cause of all our wrongs. We do not fight men—we fight bad principles. We war against the laws which have made men bad and tyrannical. Some will say, "But these laws are made by men." True, but they were made in ignorance of right and wrong, made in ignorance of the eternal principles of justice and truth. They were sanctioned by superstition, and engrafted on society by long usage. The Declaration issued by the Seneca Falls Convention is an instrument no less great, no less noble than that to which it bears a resemblance.

In closing she alluded to that portion of Mr. Channing's Declaration which referred to the code of morals by which a fallen woman is forever ruined, while the man who is the cause of, or sharer in her crime, is not visited by the slightest punishment. "It is time to consider whether what is wrong in one sex can be right in another. It is time to consider why if a woman commits a fault, too often from ignorance, from inexperience, from poverty, because of degradation and oppression—-aye! because of designing, cruel man; being made cruel by ignorance of laws and institutions,—why such a being, in her helplessness, in her ignorance, in her inexperience and dependency—why a being thus situated, not having her mind developed, her faculties called out: and not allowed to mix in society to give her experience, not being acquainted with human nature, is drawn down, owing often to her best and tenderest feelings; in consequence also of being accustomed to look up to man as her superior, as her guardian, as her master,—why such a being should be cast out of the pale of humanity, while he who committed the crime, or who is, if not the main, the great secondary cause of it,—he who is endowed with superior advantages of education and experience, he who has taken advantage of that weakness and confiding spirit, which the young always have,—I ask, if the victim is cast out of the pale of society, shall the despoiler go free?" The question was answered by a thunder of "No! no! no!" from all parts of the house. A profound sensation was observable. "And yet," said Mrs. Rose, "he does go free!!"

Ernestine L. Rose, says the *Plain Dealer*, is the master-spirit of the Convention. She is described as a Polish lady of great beauty, being known in this country as an earnest advocate of human liberty. Though a slight foreign accent is perceptible, her delivery is effective. She spoke with great animation. The impression made by her address was favorable both to the speaker and the cause. In speaking of the *personnel* of the platform, it says:

Mrs. Lydia Ann Jenkins, of New York, who made an effective speech, is habited in the Bloomer costume, and appears to much advantage on the stage. Her face is amiable, and her delivery excellent. She is as fine a female orator as we have heard. The address embodied the usual arguments offered in favor of this cause, and were put in a forcible and convincing manner. We say convincing, because such a speaker would convince the most obdurate unbeliever against his will.

Miss Stone is somewhat celebrated for an extraordinary enthusiasm in the cause of her sex, and for certain eccentricities of speech and thought, as well as of outward attire. She is as independent in mind as in dress. She is as ready to throw off the restraints society seems to have placed on woman's mind, as she is to cast aside what she considers an absurd fashion in dress. Without endorsing the eliminated petticoats, we can not but admire Miss Stone's "stern old Saxon pluck," and her total independence of the god, Fashion. Her dress is first a black velvet coat with collar, fastened in front with buttons, next a skirt of silk, reaching to the knees, then "she wears the breeches" of black silk, with neat-fitting gaiters. Her hair is cut short and combed straight back. Her face is not beautiful, but there is mind in it; it is earnest, pleasant, prepossessing. Miss Stone must be set down as a lady of no common abilities, and of uncommon energy in the pursuit of a cherished idea. She is a marked favorite in the Conventions.

During the proceedings, Miss Brown, in a long speech on the
10

Bible, had expounded many doctrines and passages of Scripture in regard to woman's position, in direct opposition to the truths generally promulgated by General Assemblies, and the lesser lights of the Church. Mrs. Emma R. Coe took an equally defiant position toward the Bench and the Bar, coolly assuming that she understood the spirit of Constitutions and Statute Laws. Some lawyer had made a criticism on the woman's petition then circulating in Ohio, and essayed to give the Convention some light on the laws of the State, to all of which Mrs. Coe says:

I have very little to say this evening beyond reading a letter, received by me to-day. (Here follows the letter). I beg leave to inform the gentleman, if he is present, that I believe I understand these laws, and this point particularly, very nearly as well as himself; and that I am well acquainted with the laws passed since 1840, as with those enacted previous to that time. I would also inform him that the committee, some of whom are much better read in law than myself, were perfectly aware of the existence of the statutes he mentions, but did not see fit to incorporate them into the petition, not only on account of their great length, but because they do not at all invalidate the position which the petition affects to establish, viz: the inequality of the sexes before the law. Their insertion, therefore, would have been utterly superfluous. This letter refers, evidently, to that portion of the petition which treats of the equalization of property, which I will now read. (Then follows the reading of one paragraph of the petition). Again I refer you to the letter, the first paragraph of which is as follows:

"Mrs. Emma R. Coe, will you look at Vol. 44, General Laws of Ohio, page 75, where you will find that the property of the wife can not be taken for the debts of her husband, etc.; and all articles of household furniture, and goods which a wife shall have brought with her in marriage, or which shall have come to her by bequest, gift, etc., after marriage, or purchased with her separate money or other property, shall be exempt from liability for the debts of her husband, during her life, and during the life of any heir of her body."

Very true: we readily admit the law of which the gentleman has given an abstract; and so long as the wife holds the property in her hands, just as she received it, it can not be taken for the husband's debts, but the moment she permits her husband to convert that property into another shape, it becomes his, and may be taken for his debts. The gentleman I presume will admit this at once.

The next paragraph of the letter reads thus: "Also in Vol. 51, General Laws of Ohio, page 449, the act regulating descent, etc., provides, that real estate, which shall have come to the wife by descent, devise, or gift, from her ancestor, shall descend—first, to her children, or their legal representatives. Second, if there be no children, or their legal representatives living, the estate shall pass to the brothers and sisters of the intestate, who may be of the blood of the ancestor from whom the estate came, or their legal representatives," etc. True again: So long as the wife holds real estate in her own name, in title, and in title only, it is hers; for her husband even then controls its profits, and if she leave it so, it will descend to her heirs so long as she has an heir, and so long as she can trace the descent. But if she suffers her husband to sell that property and receive the money, it instantly becomes his; and instead of descending to her heirs, it descends to his heirs. This the gentleman will not deny. Now, we readily admit, that while the wife abides by the statutes, of which our article has given us an abstract, her husband can not take the property from her, he can only take the use of it. But the moment she departs from the statute, she comes under the provisions of the common law; which, when they do not conflict, is equally binding in Ohio, as the statute law. And in this case the common and statute laws do not conflict. Departing from the statute, that is, suffering her property to be exchanged, the provision is thus: (Here follows the common law, taken from the petition). I have nothing further to add on this point, but will quote the last paragraphs in the letter.

"If you would know what our laws are, you must refer to the laws passed in Ohio since 1840."

This has already been answered.

"You said last night, that the property of the wife passed to the husband, even to his sixteenth cousin! Will you correct your error? And oblige   A BUCKEYE."

I should be extremely happy to oblige the gentleman, but having committed no error there is nothing to correct; and I do not, therefore, see that I can in conscience comply with his request. I am, however, exceedingly thankful for any expression of interest from that quarter. There are other laws which might be mentioned, which really give woman an apparent advantage over man; yet, having no relevancy to the subject in the petition, we did not see fit to introduce them. One of these is, that no woman shall be subject to arrest and imprisonment for debt; while no man, that is, no ordinary man, none unless he has a halo of military glory around his brow, is held sacred from civil process of this kind. But this exemption is of very little benefit to woman, since, if the laws were as severe to her as to man, she would seldom risk the penalty. For this there are two very good reasons. One is, that conscious of her inability to discharge obligations of this kind, she has little disposition to run deeply into debt; and the other is, that she has not the credit to do it if she wished! If, however, she does involve herself in this way, the law exempts her from imprisonment. This, perhaps, is offered as a sort of palliation for the disabilities which she suffers in other respects. The only object of the petition is, I believe, that the husband and wife be placed upon a legal and political equality. If the law gives woman an advantage over man, we deprecate it as much as he can. Partiality to either, to the injury of the other, is wrong in principle, and we must therefore oppose it. We do not wish to be placed in the position which the husband now occupies. We do not wish that control over his interests, which he may now exercise over the interests of the wife. We would no sooner intrust this power to woman than to man. We would never place her in authority over her husband.

The question of woman's voting, of the propriety of woman's appearing at the polls, is already settled. See what has been done in Detroit: On the day of the late election, the women went to the offices and stores of gentlemen, asking them if they had voted. If the reply happened to be in the negative, as was often the case, the next question was, "Will you be kind enough to take this vote, sir, and deposit it in the ballot-box for me?" Which was seldom, if ever, refused. And so, many a man voted for the "Maine Law," who would not, otherwise, have voted at all. But this was not all; many women kept themselves in the vicinity of the polls, and when they found a man undecided, they ceased not their entreaties until they had gained him to the Temperance cause. More than this, two women finding an intemperate man in the street, talked to him four hours, before they could get him to promise to vote as they wished. Upon his doing so, they escorted him, one on each side, to the ballot-box, saw him deposit the vote they had given him, and then treated him to a good supper.

Now, this is more than any Woman's Rights advocate ever thought of proposing. Yet no one thinks of saying a word against it, because it was done for temperance. But how much worse would it have been for those women to have gone to the polls with a brother or husband, instead of with this man? Or to have deposited two votes in perhaps five minutes' time, than to have spent four hours in soliciting some other person to give one? Why is it worse to go to the ballot-box with our male friends, than to the church, parties, or picnics, etc.? If a man should control the political principles of his wife, he should also control her religious principles.

CHARLES C. BURLEIGH: Among the resolutions which have been acted upon and adopted by this meeting is one which affirms that for man to attempt to fix the sphere of woman, is cool assumption. I purpose to take that sentiment for the text of a few words of remark this evening, for it is just there that I think the whole controversy hinges. It is not so much what is woman's appropriate sphere; it is not so much what she may do and what she may not do, that we have to contend about; as whether one human being or one class of human beings is to fix for another human being, or another class of human beings, the proper field of action and the proper mode of employing the faculties which God has given them. If I understand aright the principles of liberty, just here is the point of controversy, between the despot and the champion of human rights, in any department. Just when one human being assumes to decide for another what is that other's sphere of action, just then despotism begins. Everything else is but the legitimate consequence of this.

I have said it is not so much a matter of controversy what woman may do or may not do. Why, it would be a hard matter to say what has been recognized by men themselves, as the legitimate sphere of woman. We have a great deal of contradiction and opposition nowadays when woman attempts to do this, that, or the other thing, although that very thing has sometime or other, and somewhere or other, been performed or attempted to be performed by woman, with man's approval. If you talk about politics, why, woman's participation in politics is no new thing, is no mere assumption on her part, but has been recognized as right and proper by men.

You have already been told of distinguished women who have borne a very prominent part in politics, both in ancient and modern times, and yet the multitude of men have believed and acknowledged that it was all right; and are now acknowledging it with all the enthusiasm of devoted loyalty. They are now acknowledging it in the case of an Empire on which it has been said that the sun never sets—an Empire, "The morning drumbeat of whose military stations circles the earth with one continued peal of the martial airs of England." It is recognized, too, not by the ignorant and thoughtless only, or the radical and heretical alone, but also by multitudes of educated and pious men. That bench of Bishops, sitting in the House of Lords, receiving its very warrant to act politically, from the hands of a woman, listening to a speech from a woman on the throne, endorses every day the doctrine that a woman may engage in politics.

If you seize the young tree, when it just begins to put forth to the air and sunshine and dews, and bend it in all directions for fear it will not grow in proper shape, do not hold the tree accountable for its distortion. There is no danger that from acorns planted last year, pine trees will grow, if you do not take some special care to prevent it. There is no danger that from an apple will grow an oak, or, from a peach-stone an elm; leave nature to work out her own results, or, in other words, leave God to work out His own purpose, and be not so anxious to intrude yourselves upon Him and to help Him govern the Universe He has made. Some of us have too high an estimation of His goodness and wisdom to be desirous of thrusting ourselves into His government. We are willing to leave the nature of woman to manifest itself in its own aptitudes. Try it. Did one ever trust in God and meet with disappointment? Never! Tyrants always say it is not safe to trust their subjects with freedom. Austria says it is not safe to trust the Hungarian with freedom. Man says woman is not safe in freedom, she will get beyond her sphere.

After having oppressed her for centuries, what wonder if she should rebound, and at the first spring, even manifest that law of reaction somewhat to your inconvenience, and somewhat even beyond the dictates of the wisest judgment. What then? Is the fault to be charged to the removal of the restraint; or is it to be charged to the first imposition of the restraint? The objection of our opponents remind one of the Irishman walking among the bushes just behind his companion, who caught hold of a branch, and passing on, let it fly back into the face of his friend; "Indade I am thankful to ye!" said the injured man, "for taking hold of that same; it a'most knocked the brains out of me body as it was, an' sure, if ye hadn't caught hold of it, it would have kilt me intirely!"

The winds come lashing over your lake, the waters piling upon each other, wave rolling upon wave, and you may say what a pity we could not bridge the lake over with ice, so as to keep down these billows which may rise so high as to submerge us. But stand still! God has fixed the law upon the waters, "thus far shalt thou come"; and as you watch the ever piling floods, it secures their timely downfall. When they come as far as their appointed limits, the combing crest of the wave tells that the hour of safety has arrived, proving that God was wiser than you in writing down laws for His creation. We need not bridge over woman's nature with the ice of conventionalism, for fear she will swell up, aye, and overflow the continent of manhood. There is no danger. Trust to the nature God has given to humanity, and do not except the nature He has given to this portion of humanity.

But I need not dwell upon such an argument before an audience who have witnessed the bearing of women in this Convention. It is a cool, aye, insolent assumption for man to prescribe the sphere of woman. What is the sphere of woman? Clearly, you say, her powers, her natural instincts and desires determine her sphere. Who, then, best knows those instincts and desires? Is it he who has all his knowledge at second-hand, rather than she who has it in all her consciousness?

If, then, you find in the progress of the race hitherto, that woman has revealed herself pure, true, and beautiful, and lofty in spirit, just in proportion as she has enjoyed the right to reveal herself; if this is the testimony of all past experience, I ask you where you will find the beginning of an argument against the claim of woman to the right to enlarge her sphere yet more widely, than she has hitherto done. Wait until you see some of these apprehended evils, aye, a little later even, than that, until you see the natural subsidence of the reaction from the first out-bound of their oppression, before you tell us it is not safe or wise to permit woman the enlargement of her own sphere.

The argument which I have thus based upon the very nature of man, and of humanity and God, is confirmed in every particular—is most impregnably fortified on every point, by the facts of all past experience and all present observation; and out of all this evidence of woman's right and fitness to determine her own sphere, I draw a high prophecy of the future. I look upon this longing of hers for a yet higher and broader field, as an evidence that God designed her to enter upon it.

> "Want, is the garner of our bounteous Sire;
> Hunger, the promise of its own supply."

I might even add the rest of the passage as an address to woman herself, who still hesitates to assert the rights which she feels to be hers and longs to enjoy; I might repeat to her in the words of the same poet:

> "We weep, because the good we seek is not,
> When but for *this* it is not, that we weep;
> We creep in dust to wail our lowly lot,
> Which were *not* lowly, if we scorned to creep;
> That which we *dare* we shall be, when the will
> Bows to prevailing Hope, its would-be to fulfill."

It can be done. This demand of woman can be nobly and successfully asserted. It can be, because it is but the out-speaking of the divine sentiment of woman. Let us not then tremble, or falter, or despair—I know we shall not. I know that those who have taken hold of this great work, and carried it forward hitherto, against obloquy, and persecution, and contempt, will not falter now. No! Every step is bearing us to a higher eminence, and thus revealing a broader promise of hope, a brighter prospect of success. Though they who are foremost in this cause must bear obloquy and reproach, and though it may seem to the careless looker-on, that they advance but little or not at all; they know that the instinct which impels them being divine, it can not be that they shall fail. They know that every quality of their nature, every attribute of their Creator, is pledged to their success.

> "They never fail who gravely plead for right,
> God's faithful martyrs can not suffer loss.
> Their blazing faggots sow the world with light,
> Heaven's gate swings open on their bloody cross."

Pres. MAHAN: If I would not be interrupting at all, there are a few thoughts having weight upon my mind which I should be very happy to express. I have nothing to say to excite controversy at all, but there are things which are said, the ultimate bearing of which I believe is not always understood. I have heard during these discussions, things said which bear this aspect—that the relation of ruler and subject is that of master and slave. The idea of the equality of woman with man, seems to be argued upon this idea. I am not now to speak whether it is lawful for man to rule the woman at all; but I wish to make a remark upon the principles of governor and governed. The idea seems to be suggested that if the wife is subject to the husband, the wife is a slave to the man—if He has said, in the sense in which some would have it, even that the woman should be subject to the man, and the wife to the husband, you will find that in no other position will woman attain her dignity; for God has never dropped an inadvertent thought, never penned an inadvertent line. There is not a law or principle of His being, that whoever penned that Book did not understand. There is not a right which that Book does not recognize; and there is not a duty which man owes to woman, or woman to man, that is not there enjoined. It is my firm conviction, that there is but one thing to be done on this subject— if the women of this State want the elective franchise, they can have it. I don't believe it is in the heart of man to refuse it. Only spread the truth, adhere to Woman's Rights, and adhere to that one principle, and when the people are convinced that her claim is just, it will be allowed.

Of Charles C. Burleigh the *Plain Dealer* says:

This noble poet had not said much in the Convention. He had taken no part in the interferences and interruptions of other gentlemen, Mr. Barker and Mr. Nevin for instance.

When at length he took the stand he did indeed speak out a noble defense of woman's rights. It was the only speech made before the Convention by man in which the cause of woman was advocated exclusively. When Mr. Burleigh arose, two or three geese hissed; when he closed, a shower of applause greeted him.

We hope the reader will not weary of these debates. As the efforts of many of our early speakers were extemporaneous, but

little of what they said will be preserved beyond this generation
unless recorded now. These debates show the wit, logic, and readiness of our women ; the clear moral perception, the courage, and
honesty of our noble Garrison ; the skill and fiery zeal of Stephen
Foster ; the majesty and beauty of Charles Burleigh ; and, in Asa
Mahan, the vain struggles of the wily priest, to veil with sophistry
the degrading slavery of woman, in order to reconcile her position
as set forth in certain man-made texts of Scripture with eternal
justice and natural law. Mr. Mahan would not have been willing
himself, to accept even the mild form of subjection he so cunningly
assigns to woman. The deadliest opponents to the recognition of
the equal rights of woman, have ever been among the orthodox
clergy as a class.

WORLD'S TEMPERANCE CONVENTION.

Just previous to this, two stormy Conventions had been held in
the city of New York ; one called to discuss Woman's Rights, the
other a World's Temperance Convention. Thus many of the leaders of each movement met for the first time to measure their powers of logic and persuasion.

Antoinette L. Brown was appointed a delegate by two Temperance associations. Her credentials were accepted, and she took her
seat as a member of the Convention ; but when she arose to speak
a tempest of indignation poured upon her from every side. As this
page in history was frequently referred to in the Cleveland Convention, we will let Miss Brown here tell her own story :

Why did we go to that World's Convention ? We went there because
the call was extended to " the world." On the 12th of May a preliminary
meeting had been held at New York—the far-famed meeting at the Brick
Chapel. There, because of the objection taken by some who were not
willing to have the " rest of mankind " come into the Convention, a part
of those present withdrew. They thought they would have a " Whole
World's Temperance Convention," and they thought well, as the result
proved. When it was known that such a Convention would be called,
that all persons would be invited to consider themselves members of the
Convention, who considered themselves members of the world, some of
the leaders of the other Convention—the half world's Convention—felt that
if it were possible, they would not have such a meeting held; therefore
they took measures to prevent it. Now, let me read a statement from
another delegate to that Convention, Rev. Wm. H. Channing, of Rochester. (Miss Brown read an extract from the *Tribune,* giving the facts in
regard to her appointment as delegate, by a society of long standing, in
Rochester, and extracts, also, of letters from persons prominent in the
Brick Chapel meeting, urging Mr. Greeley to persuade his party to aban-

don the idea of a separate Convention, a part of such writers pleading that it was an unnecessary movement, as the call to the World's Temperance Convention was broad enough, and intended to include all). This appointment was made without my knowledge or consent, but with my hearty endorsement, when I knew it was done. Let me state also, that a society organized and for years in existence in South Butler, N. Y., also appointed delegates to that Convention, and myself among the number. They did so because, though they knew the call invited all the world to be present, yet they thought it best to have their delegations prepared with credentials, if being prepared would do any good.

When we reached New York, we heard some persons saying that women would be received as delegates, and others saying they would not. We thought we ought to test that matter, and do it, too, as delicately and quietly as possible. There were quite a number of ladies appointed delegates to that meeting, but it was felt that not many would be necessary to make the test of their sincerity.

We met at the Woman's Rights Convention on the day of the opening of the half world's Temperance Convention, and had all decided to be content with our own Temperance Convention, which had passed off so quietly and triumphantly. Wendell Phillips and I sat reconsidering the whole matter. I referred him to the fact, which had come to me more than once during the few last days, that the officials of the Convention in session at Metropolitan Hall, and others, had been saying that women would be received no doubt; that the Brick Chapel meeting was merely an informal preliminary meeting, and its decisions of no authority upon the Convention proper; and that the women were unjust in saying, that their brethren would not accept their co-operation before it had been fairly tested. Then, said Phillips, " Go, by all means; if they receive you, you have only to thank them for rebuking the action of the Brick Chapel meeting. Then we will withdraw and come back to our own meeting. If, on the other hand, they do not receive you, we will quietly and without protest, withdraw, and, in that case, not be gone half an hour." I turned and invited one lady, now on this platform, as gentle and lady-like as woman can be, Caroline M. Severance, of your own city, to go with me. She said: "I am quite willing to go, both in compliance with your wish, and from interest in the cause itself. But I am not a delegate, and I have in this city venerated grandparents, whose feelings I greatly regard, and would not willingly or unnecessarily wound; so that I prefer to go in quietly, but take no active part in what will seem to them an antagonistic position for woman, and uncalled for on my part. In that way I am quite ready to go." And so we went out from our own meeting, Mr. Phillips, Mrs. S., and myself; none others went with us, nor knew we were going.

After arriving at Metropolitan Hall, accompanied by these friends, I did quietly what we had predetermined was the best to do. The Secretary was sitting upon the platform. I handed him my credentials from both societies. He said: "I can not now tell whether you will be received or not. There is a resolution before the house, stating, in substance, that they would receive all delegates without distinction of color or sex. If this resolution is adopted, you can be received." I then left my credentials in his hands, and went down from the platform. It was rather trying, in the sight of all that audience, to go upon the platform and come down again; and I shall not soon forget the sensations with which I stepped off the platform. After a little time they decided that the call admitted all delegates. I thought this decision settled my admission, and I went again upon the platform. In the meantime a permanent organization was effected. I went there, for the purpose of thanking them for their course, and merely to express my sympathy with the cause and their present movement, and then intended to leave the Hall. I arose, and inquired of the President, Neal Dow, if I was rightly a member of the Convention. He said, "Yes, if you have credentials from any abstinence societies." I told him I had, and then attempted to thank him. There was no appeal from the President's decision, but yet they would not receive my expression of thanks; therefore I took my seat and waited for a better opportunity.

And now let me read a paragraph again from this paper, the temperance organ of your State. The writer is still Gen. Carey. (The extract intimated that Miss Brown, supported and urged on by several others, made an unwomanly entrance into the Convention, and upon the platform itself, which was reserved for officers, and as it would imply, already filled). There were only the two other persons I mentioned who went with me to that Convention, but they took their seats back among the audience, and did not approach the platform. There were friends I found in that audience to sustain me, but none others came with me for that purpose. The platform was far from being full; it is a large platform, and there might a hundred persons sit there, and not incommode each other at all.

(Here Miss Brown read another extract from the same article, in which Gen. Carey implies, that concerted measures had been set on foot at the Woman's Rights meeting at the Tabernacle, the evening after Miss Brown's first attempt at a hearing before the Temperance Convention, for coming in upon them again *en masse*, and revengefully).

Not a word was said that night upon the subject, in the Convention at the Tabernacle, except what was said by myself; and I said what I did, because some one inquired whether I was hissed on going upon the platform. As to that matter, when I went upon the platform I was not hissed, at others times I did not know whether they hissed me or others, and

"Where ignorance is bliss, 'tis folly to be wise."

I stated some of the facts to our own Convention, but I did not refer to this resolution (the one which was to exclude all but officers or invited guests from the platform), for I was not entirely clear with regard to the nature of it, it was passed in so much confusion. I did state this, that there had been a discussion raised upon such a resolution, and that it was decided that only officers and invited guests should sit upon the platform; but that they had received me as a delegate, and had thus revoked the action of the Brick Chapel meeting, and that on the morrow Neal Dow might invite me to sit upon the platform. That was the substance of my remarks, and not one word of objection was taken, or reply made by our Convention.

I read again from this paper. (An extract implying that among the measures taken to browbeat the Convention into receiving Miss Brown, was the forming of a society instantly, under the special urgency of herself and friends, for this especial object, etc.) That again is a statement without foundation. I intend to-night to use no harsh words, and I shall say nothing with regard to motives. You may draw your own conclusions in regard to all this. I shall state dispassionately, the simple, literal facts as they occurred, and they may speak for themselves.

When Wendell Phillips went out of the Convention, he told persons with whom he came in contact, that a delegate had been received by the President, and that delegate had been insulted, and nobody had risen to sustain her. He said to me, too, "I shall not go to-morrow, but do you go. I can do nothing for you, because I am not a delegate." There were a few earnest friends in New York, however, who felt that the rights of a delegate were sacred. They organized a society and appointed just three delegates to that Temperance Convention. Those three persons were Wendell Phillips, of Boston; Mr. Cleveland, one of the editors of the *Tribune;* and Mr. Gibbon, son-in-law of the late venerated Isaac T. Hopper. The last two were men from New York City. The question was already decided that women might be received as delegates to that Convention; therefore there was no need of appointing any one to insist upon woman's right to appear, and no one was appointed for that purpose.

The next morning we went there with Mr. Phillips, who presented his credentials. During the discussion, Mr. Phillips took part, and persisted in holding the Convention to parliamentary rules. He carried in his hand a book of rules, which is received everywhere as authority, and when he saw that they were wrong, he quoted the standard authority to them. After a while the preliminary business was disposed of, and various resolutions were brought forward. I arose, and the President said I had the floor. I was invited upon the stand, and was therefore an "invited guest" within their own rules; but when once there, I was not allowed to speak, although the President said repeatedly that the floor was mine. The opposition arose from a dozen or more around the platform, who were incessantly raising "points of order"—the extempore bantlings of great minds in great emergencies. For the space of three hours I endeavored to be heard, but they would not hear me (although as a delegate, and I spoke simply as a delegate), I could have spoken but ten minutes by a law of the house. Twice the President was sustained in his decision by the house; but finally some one insisted that there might be persons voting in the house who were not delegates, and it was decided that the Hall should be cleared by the police, and that those who were delegates might come in, one by one, and resume their seats.

There were printed lists of the delegates of the Convention, but there were several new delegates whose names were not on the lists. Wendell Phillips and his colleagues were among them. He went to the President and said: "I rely upon you to be admitted to the Hall, for we know that our names are not yet on the list." The President assented. As the delegates returned, the names upon the printed lists were called, and while the rest of us were earnest to be admitted to the house, and while they were examining our credentials and deciding whether or not we should be received, Neal Dow had gone out of the Hall, and Gen. Carey had taken the Chair! The action of a part of the delegates who were in the house while the other part were shut out, was like to nothing that ever had occurred in the annals of parliamentary history. Those persons who came in afterward, asked what was the business before the house, and on being informed, moved that it be reconsidered. The President decided upon putting it to the house, that they had not voted in the affirmative, and would not reconsider. Gen. Samuel F. Carey is a man of firmness, and I could not but admire the firmness with which he presided, although I felt that his decisions were wrong. "Gentlemen," said he, "there can be no order when you are raising so many points of order; take your seats!" and they took their seats.

Previous to the adjournment, a question was raised about Wendell Phillips' credentials, and again next morning they raised it and decided it against him, so that he felt all further effort vain, and left the Hall. After this, there came up a multitude of resolutions, which were passed so rapidly that no one could get the opportunity of speaking to them. A resolution also written by Gen. Carey, was presented by him, as follows:

"*Resolved*, That the common usages have excluded women from the public platform," etc.

That resolution, amid great confusion, was declared as passed. Of course, then soon after, I left the Hall. I ought to say, in regard to Mr. Phillips' credentials, that they had been referred to a committee, who decided that he had not properly been sent to the Convention, for no reason in the world, but because the society who sent him, had been organized only the night before; while I know positively, and others knew, that there were societies organized one week before, for the very purpose of sending delegates to that Convention; which societies will never be heard of again, I fear. But the Neal Dow Association, of New York, exists yet. Their society shall not die; so good comes out of evil often.

A motion was also made by some one, as better justice to Mr. Phillips, to refer the credentials of all the delegates of Massachusetts to the Committee on Credentials, but for very obvious and prudent reasons, it was not suffered to have a moment's hearing or consideration. (Miss Brown here read a few additional lines from the same article, asserting that she was merely the tool of others, and thrust by them upon the platform; and charging all the disorder and disturbance of that Convention to herself and friends, etc.) I needed no thrusting upon the platform. I was able to rise and speak without urging or suggestion. And as to the disorder which prevailed throughout the Convention, who made that disorder? I said not a word to cause it, for they gave me no opportunity to say a word, and the other delegates with me, sat quietly. No mention is made in this paper that I had credentials. It is stated that throughout Ohio the impression is that I had none; and it is generally believed that I went there without proper credentials.

One word more as to Mr. Carey. He says, "The negro question was not discussed as Greeley & Co. wished it to be. O Greeley, how art thou fallen!" These are Gen. Carey's words, not mine. Mr. Greeley has risen greatly in my estimation, and not fallen. A colored delegate* did take his credentials to the Convention, but he was not received. I saw him myself, and asked him what could be done about it. He folded up his hands and said it was too late. And this was a " World's Temperance Convention!"

And this paper says that the *New York Tribune*, which has usually been an accredited sheet, has most shamefully misrepresented the whole affair, and refers to what was said in the *Tribune*, as to what the Convention had accomplished: "The first day, crowding a woman from the platform; second day, gagging her; and the third day voting she should stay gagged;" and asserts that it is a misrepresentation.

The evenings of that Convention were not devoted to this discussion, and were not noisy or fruitless. There were burning words spoken for temperance during the evenings; but whether the *Tribune's* report of the day-sessions be correct or not, you yourselves can be the judges. I must say, however, the *Tribune* did not misrepresent that affair in its regular report; and I call upon Gen. Carey, in all kindness and courtesy, to point out just what the misstatements are—and upon any one acquainted with the facts, to show the false statement, if it can be shown.

And now I leave the action of the Convention to say what were our motives in going there. From what I have related of the circumstances which conspired to induce us to go, and the manner of our going, you can but see that no absurd desire for notoriety, no coveting of such unenviable fame as we know must await us, were the inducements. And as a simple fact, there was nothing so very important in a feeble woman's going as a delegate to that Convention; but the fact was made an unpleasant one in the experience of that delegate, and was blown into notoriety by the unmanly action of that Convention itself. But what were our reasons for going to that Convention? Did we go there to forward the cause of Temperance or to forward the cause of woman, or what were our motives in going? Woman was pleading her own cause in the Convention at the Tabernacle, and she had no need that any should go there to forward her cause for her; and much as I love temperance, and love those poor sisters who suffer because of intemperance, it was not especially to plead their cause that I went there. I went to assert a principle, a principle relevant to the circumstances of the World's Convention to be sure, but one, at the same time, which, acknowledged, must forward all good causes, and, disregarded, must retard them. I went there, asking no favor as a woman, asking no special recognition of the woman-cause. I went there in behalf of the cause of humanity. I went there, asking the indorsement of no ism, and as the exponent of no measure, but as a simple item of the world in the name of the world, claiming that all the sons and daughters of the race should be received in that Convention, if they went there

* James McCune Smith.

with the proper credentials. I simply planted my feet upon the rights of a delegate. I asked for nothing more, and dare take nothing less. The principle which we were there to assert, was that which is the soul of the Golden Rule, the soul of that which says, "All things whatsoever ye would that men should do unto you, do ye even so unto them." I went there to see if they would be true to their own call, and recognize delegates without distinction of color, sex, creed, party, or condition; to see if they would recognize each member of the human family, as belonging to the human family; to see if they would grant the simple rights of a delegate to all delegates.

And do you ask, did this not retard the cause of Temperance? No; it carried it forward, as it carries every good cause forward. It awakened thought, and mankind need only to be aroused to thought, to forever destroy all wrong customs, and among them the rum traffic. They need only to think to the purpose, and when this shall be done, all good causes are bound to go forward together. Christianity is the heart and soul of them all, and those reforms which seek to elevate mankind and better their condition, cling around our Christianity, and are a part of it. They are like the cluster of grapes, all clinging about the central stem.

A wrong was done in that Convention to a delegate, and many people saw and felt that wrong, and they began to inquire for the cause of it; and so the causes of things were searched more nearly than before, and this was a good which promoted temperance. It is absurd to believe that any man or woman is any less a temperance man or woman, or a "Maine law" man or woman now, than before. If ever they loved that cause they love it now as before.

Water is the very symbol of democracy! a single jet of it in a tube will balance the whole ocean. We went there, only to claim in the name of Democracy and Christianity, that all be treated alike and impartially. The human soul is a holy thing; it is the temple of living joy or sorrow. It is freighted with vital realities. It can outlengthen Heaven itself, and it should be reverenced everywhere, and treated always as a holy thing. We only went there in the name of the world, in the name of humanity, to promote a good cause; and it is what I pledge myself now anew to do, at all times and under all circumstances, when the opportunity shall present itself to me. It was a good act, a Christian duty, to go there under those circumstances.

But let me now leave this matter, and say something which may have a direct bearing upon the circumstances of our Convention, and show why it is proper to bring up these facts here. Let us suppose ourselves gathered in Metropolitan Hall. It is a large hall, with two galleries around its sides. I could see men up there in checked blouses, who looked as though they might disturb a Convention, but they looked down upon the rowdyism of the platform, a thing unprecedented before, with simple expressions of wonder, while they were quiet. Well, here we are upon the platform. The President is speaking.

PRESIDENT: "Miss Brown has the floor."

A DELEGATE: "Mr. President, I rise to a point of order."

PRESIDENT: "State your point of order."

It is stated, but at the same time, in the general whirl and confusion all around, another voice from the floor exclaims: "I rise to a point of order!"

The PRESIDENT: "State it!"

But while these things are going on, a voice arises, "She sha'n't speak!"

another, " She sha'n't be heard ! " another, " You raise a point of order when
he is done, and I will raise another." In the confusion I hear something
almost like swearing, but not swearing, for most of those men are " holy men,"
who do not think of swearing. The confusion continues. Most of this time I
am standing, but presently a chair is presented me, and now a new class of
comforters gathers around me, speaking smooth, consoling words in my ear
while upon the other side are angry disputants, clinching their fists and growing red in the face. Are the former good Samaritans, pouring into my wounded
heart the oil and the wine ? Listen. "I know you are acting conscientiously ;
but now that you have made your protest, do, for your own sake, withdraw from
this disgraceful scene."

"I can not withdraw," I say ; "it is not now the time to withdraw; here is
a principle at stake."

"Well, in what way can you better the cause ? Do you feel you are doing
any good ?" Another voice chimes in with: "Do you love the Temperance
cause ? Can you continue here and see all this confusion prevailing around
you ? Why not withdraw, and then the Convention will be quiet;" and all
this in most mournful, dolorous tones. I think if the man cries, I shall certainly cry too.

But then a new interval of quiet occurs, and so I rise to get the floor. I
fancy myself in a melting mood enough to beg them, with prayers and tears,
to be just and righteous; but no, " this kind goeth not out by prayer and fasting," and so I stand up again. Directly Rev. John Chambers points his
finger at me, and calls aloud: "Shame on the woman! Shame on the woman!"
Then I feel cool and calm enough again, and sit down until his anger has way.
Again the "friends" gather around me, and there come more appeals to me,
while the public ear is filled with "points of order"; and the two fall together,
in a somewhat odd, but very pointed contrast, somewhere in the center of my
brain. "Do you think," says one, "that Christ would have done so?" spoken
with a somewhat negative emphasis. "I think He would," spoken with a positive emphasis. "Do you love peace as well as Christ loved it, and can you
do thus ?"

What answer I made I know not, but there came rushing over my soul the
words of Christ: "I came not to send peace, but a sword." It seems almost to
be spoken with an audible voice, and it sways the spirit more than all things
else. I remember that Christ's doctrine was, "first pure, then peaceable ;" that
He, too, was persecuted. So are my doctrines good ; they ask only for the
simple rights of a delegate, only that which must be recognized as just, by the
impartial Father of the human race, and by His holy Son. Then come these
mock pleading tones again upon my ear, and instinctively I think of the Judas
kiss, and I arise, turning away from them all, and feeling a power which may,
perhaps, never come to me again. There were angry men confronting me, and
I caught the flashing of defiant eyes ; but above me, and within me, and all
around me, there was a spirit stronger than they all. At that moment not the
combined powers of earth and hell could have tempted me to do otherwise
than to stand firm. Moral and physical cowardice were subdued, thanks to
that Washington delegate for the sublime strength roused by his question :
" Would Christ have done so ? "

That stormy scene is passed ; that memorable time when chivalrous men forgot the deference, which according to their creed is due to woman, and forgot it as they publicly said, because a woman claimed a right upon the platform ; and so they neither recognized her equality of rights, nor her conceded courtesy as a lady. This was neither just nor gallant, but to me it was vastly preferable to those appeals made to me as a lady—appeals which never would have been made to a man under the same circumstances; and which only served to show me the estimation in which they held womanhood. It reminded me of a remark which was made concerning the Brick Chapel meeting : "If you had spoken words of flattery, they would have done what you wanted."

Let the past be the past. " Let the dead bury their dead," contains truths we well may heed. Is God the impartial Father of humanity? Is He no respecter of persons? Is it true that there is known neither male nor female in Christ Jesus ? In my heart of hearts, I believe it is all true. I believe it is the foundation of the Golden Rule. And now let me tell you in conclusion : if it be true, this truth shall steal into your souls like the accents of childhood ; it shall come like a bright vision of hope to the desponding ; it shall flash upon the incredulous ; it shall twine like a chain of golden arguments about the reason of the skeptic.

WM. LLOYD GARRISON, having listened to the narration of the action of the World's Convention in New York, said : I rise to offer some resolutions by which the sense of this Convention may be obtained. I happened to be an eyewitness of these proceedings, and I bear witness to the accuracy of the account given us this evening by Miss Brown. I have seen many tumultuous meetings in my day, but I think on no occasion have I ever seen anything more disgraceful to our common humanity, than when Miss Brown attempted to speak upon the platform of the World's Temperance Convention in aid of the glorious cause which had brought that Convention together. It was an outbreak of passion, contempt, indignation, and every vile emotion of the soul, throwing into the shade almost everything coming from the vilest of the vile, that I have ever witnessed on any occasion or under any circumstances ; venerable men, claiming to be holy men, the ambassadors of Jesus Christ, losing all self-respect and transforming themselves into the most unmannerly and violent spirits, merely on account of the sex of the individual who wished to address the assembly.

Miss Brown was asked while standing on the platform, " Do you love the temperance cause ? " What could have been more insulting than such a question as that at that moment ? What but the temperance cause had brought her to the Convention ? Why had she been delegated to take her seat in that body except on the ground that she was a devoted friend of the temperance enterprise, and had an interest in every movement pertaining to the total abstinence cause ? She had been delegated there by total abstinence societies because of her fitness as a temperance woman to advocate the temperance cause, so dear to the hearts of all those who love perishing humanity. Was it the love of the temperance cause that raised the outcry against her ? or was it not simply contempt of woman, and an unwillingness that she should stand up anywhere to bear her testimony against popular wrongs and crimes, the curses of the race?

Miss BROWN: Allow me to state one incident. A Doctor of Divinity was present at the meeting. His son and daughter-in-law stated to me the fact. " I said to my father, you had stormy times at the Convention to-day." " Yes," said the father, "stormy times." Said the son, "Why didn't you allow her to speak?" "Ah," said the Doctor, "it was the principle of the thing!" But it so happened that the son and daughter thought the principle a wrong one.

Mr. GARRISON : Yes, it was the principle that was at stake. It was not simply the making of a speech at that Convention, by a woman. By her speaking something more was implied, for if woman could speak there and for that object, she might speak elsewhere for another object, and she might, peradventure, as my friend does, proceed to occupy a pulpit and settle over a congregation. In fact, there is no knowing where the precedent would lead ; reminding me of the man who hesitated to leave off his profanity, because having left that off he should have to leave off drinking, and if he left off drinking he should have to leave off his tobacco and other vile habits. He liked symmetry of character, and so he was unwilling to take the first step toward reform.

The principle for which Miss Brown contended, was this : every society has a right to determine who shall represent it in convention. Invitation was given to the "whole world" to meet there in convention, to promote the cause of Temperance. Our friend needed no credentials under the call. It is true all societies were invited to send delegates, but in addition to that all the friends of Temperance throughout the world were expressly and earnestly invited to be present, and under that last express invitation she had a right to come in as an earnest friend of the cause, and take her seat in the Convention. When a body like that comes together, the principle is this, each delegate stands on the same footing as every other delegate, and no one delegate nor any number of delegates has a right to exclude any other delegate who has been sent there by any like society. Our friend had credentials from two societies, and thus was doubly armed ; but she was put down by a most disgraceful minority of the Convention, who succeeded in carrying their point. In view of all this, I would present for the action of this Convention the following resolutions :

WHEREAS, a cordial invitation having been extended to all temperance societies and all the friends of temperance throughout the world, to meet personally or by delegates in a "World's Temperance Convention" in the city of New York, Sept. 6th and 7th, 1853 ;

And whereas, accepting this invitation in the spirit in which it was apparently given, the "South Butler Temperance Association," and the "Rochester Toronto Division of the Sons of Temperance," duly empowered the Rev. Antoinette L. Brown, to act in that Convention as their delegate, representative, and advocate.

And whereas, on presenting herself at the time specified, her credentials were received by the Committee on the roll of the Convention, but on rising to address the assembly (though declared by the President to be entitled to the floor, and although his decision was repeatedly sustained by a majority of the delegates) she was met with derisive outcries, insulting jeers, and the most rowdyish manifestations, by a shameless minority, led on by the Rev. John Chambers, of Philadelphia, and encouraged by Gen. Carey, of Ohio, and other professed friends of the temperance cause—so as to make it impossible for her to be heard, and thus virtually excluding her from the Convention in an ignominious manner, solely on account of her being a woman ; therefore,

Resolved, That in the judgment of this Convention, the treatment received by the Rev. Antoinette L. Brown in the "World's Temperance Convention" (falsely so called) was in the highest degree disgraceful to that body, insulting to

11

the societies whose credentials she bore, worthy only of those who are filled with strong drink, and a scandal to the temperance movement.

Resolved, That the thanks of this Convention be given to Miss Brown, for having accepted the credentials so honorably proffered to her by the temperance societies aforesaid, and claiming a right, not as a woman, but as a duly authorized delegate, an eloquent and devoted advocate of the temperance enterprise, to a seat and voice in the " World's Temperance Convention; " and for the firm, dignified, and admirable manner in which she met the storm of opprobrium and insult which so furiously assailed her on her attempting to advocate the beneficent movement for the promotion of which the Convention was expressly called together.

Hon. JOSHUA R. GIDDINGS : Ladies and gentlemen, although I had designed to take no active part in the proceedings, I can not avoid rising, to second that resolution. When I learned of the appointing of this Convention, it brought a thrill of joy to me. I had read the transactions to which the lady has made such feeling allusion. I had read and mourned over them, and I rejoiced that an opportunity was to be given to the people of Cleveland, and this Western Reserve, to tender their thanks to this Convention, which had been appointed to meet upon the shores of Lake Erie; and that they also might see what sort of a greeting the friends of the rights of woman would receive here. And I now rejoice at the hearty manner in which the Convention has proceeded. I rejoice at the treatment the Convention has received. Then I was about to say, the fogies of New York, if they could see and know all that they might see here, would not be like some spirits, whom Swedenborg says he saw in the other world. He found spirits who had been departed several years, who had not yet learned that they were dead. I think Rev. John Chambers would now look down and begin to suspect that he had departed.

My friends, I know not how the remarks of Miss Brown fell upon your ears. I can only say that they struck me with deep feelings of mortification, that at this noontide of the nineteenth century any human being, who can give her' thoughts to an assembly in the eloquent manner in which she has spoken to us, has been treated as she was ; and when this resolution of reproof by my friend from Massachusetts was presented, I resolved to rise and second it, and express myself willing that it be sent out in the report, that I most heartily concur in the expressions contained in these resolutions.

WILLIAM L. GARRISON : I wish to make one statement in regard to General Carey, to show that he does not himself act on consistent principles, in this matter. The last number of the *Pennsylvania Freeman* contains an account of a temperance gathering held in Kennett Square. That square is for that region the headquarters of Abolitionists, Liberals, Come-outers, and so forth. In that meeting women were appointed for Vice-Presidents and Secretaries with men, and there was a complete mixture throughout the committees without regard to sex ; and who do you think were those who spoke on that occasion recognizing that woman was equal with man in that gathering ? The first was G. W. Jackson, of Boston, who made himself very conspicuous in the exclusion of women from the "World's Convention"; second, Judge O'Neil, of South Carolina, who spoke at New York, and who was also very active in the efforts to exclude Miss Brown ; last of all was General Carey, of Ohio ; and three days afterward they wended their way to New York, and there conspired with others to prevent a delegate from being admitted, on the ground of being a woman; showing that while at old Kennett they were willing to conform, finding it would be popular; in New York they joined in this brutal proscription of a woman, only because she was a woman.

Lucy Stone : I know it is time to take the question upon these resolutions, but I wish to say one word. When a world's convention of any kind is called —when the Rev. Drs. Chambers, Hewett, Marsh, and I don't know how many more, backed up by a part of those who were in that convention, are ready to ignore the existence of woman, it should show us something of the amount of labor we have to do, to teach the world even to know that we are a part of it; and when women tell us they don't want any more rights, I want them to know that they are held to have no right in any world's convention. I took up a book the other day, written by the Rev. Mr. Davis, in which he sketches the events of the last fifty years. He states that the Sandwich Islands at one time had one missionary at such a station; Mr. Green—and his wife ! Then he went on to state another where there were nineteen, and—their wives ! Now these are straws on the surface, but they indicate " which way the wind blows," and indicate, in some sense, the estimation in which woman is held. I mention these facts so that we may see something of the length of the way we must tread, before we shall even be recognized.

The reader will see from these debates the amount of prejudice, wickedness, and violence, woman was compelled to meet from all classes of men, especially the clergy, in those early days, and on the other hand the wisdom, courage, and mild self-assertion with which she fought her battle and conquered. There is not a man living who took part in that disgraceful row who would not gladly blot out that page in his personal history. But the few noble men— lawyers, statesmen, clergymen, philanthropists, poets, orators, philosophers—who have remained steadfast and loyal to woman through all her struggles for freedom—have been brave and generous enough to redeem their sex from the utter contempt and distrust of all womankind.

NATIONAL CONVENTION AT CINCINNATI, OHIO.

In 1855, October 17th and 18th, the people of Cincinnati, Ohio, were summoned to the consideration of the question of Woman's Rights. A brief report in the city journals, is all we can find of the proceedings. From these we learn that the meetings were held in Nixon's Hall, that some ladies wore bloomers, and some gentlemen shawls, that the audiences were large and enthusiastic, that the curiosity to see women who could make a speech was intense. Martha C. Wright, of Auburn, a sister of Lucretia Mott, was chosen President. On the platform sat Mrs. Mott, Hannah Tracy Cutler, Josephine S. Griffing, Mary S. Anthony, of Rochester, N. Y.; Einestine L. Rose, Adeline Swift, Joseph Barker, an Englishman, an ex-member of Parliament, Lucy Stone and her husband, Henry B. Blackwell, recently married. Mrs. Stone did not take her husband's name, because she believed a woman had a right to an individual existence, and an individual name to designate that existence.

After the election of officers,* the President stated the object of the Convention to be to secure equality with man in social, civil, and political rights. It was only seven years, she said, since this movement commenced, since our first Convention was called, in timidity and doubt of our own strength, our own capacity, our own powers; now, east, west, north, and even south, there were found advocates of woman's rights. The newspapers which ridiculed and slandered us at first, are beginning to give impartial accounts of our meetings. Newspapers do not lead, but follow public opinion; and doing so, they go through three stages in regard to reforms; they first ridicule them, then report them without comment, and at last openly advocate them. We seem to be still in the first stage on this question.

Mrs. CUTLER said: "Let there be light, and there was light," "And many shall run to and fro, and knowledge shall be increased." This light, this increase of knowledge, we are seeking. Men have always applied the last text to themselves, and did not expect woman to run to and fro and increase in knowledge. They objected to her raising her voice on this platform in the pursuit or diffusion of knowledge; but when she is employed upon the stage to minister to everything that pollutes and degrades man, no voice was raised against it. It was but a few years ago that a French queen brought over with her to the British Isles, a male mantua-maker. It was not supposed then that woman was capable of fitting woman's clothes properly. She has since advanced to have the charge of man's wardrobe; and it will be right when the time comes, for man to take care of himself. Conservatism opposes this now; but I love conservatism; it is guarding our institutions until the new mother is prepared to take the charge.

I desire that marriage shall not be simply a domestic union as in early days, or a social one as it has now become, but a complete and perfect union, conferring equal rights on both parties. I desire light from the source of light. The question is frequently asked, "What more do these women want?" A lady in Cincinnati told me that she did not desire any change, for she thought we had now entirely the best of it; while the men toiled in their shops and offices, the women walked the streets splendidly dressed, or lounged at home with nothing to do but spend the money their husbands earned. I never understood the elevating effect of the elective franchise until I went to England, where so few enjoy it. I attended a political meeting during the canvass of Derby, as a reporter for three or four political papers in the United States. One of the candidates proposed to legislate for universal suffrage; his opponent

---

* See Appendix.

replied by showing the effect of it upon France, which he declared was the only country in which it existed. "You forget," exclaimed one, "America!" "America! never name her! a land of three millions of slaves." The multitude would not believe this; they shouted in derision, whenever the speaker attempted to resume. America was their last hope. If that country was given up to slavery, they could only despair. Party leaders rose and tried to calm them as Christ calmed the sea, but they could do nothing. "You are an American," said one near me; "get up and defend your country!" What could I say? I spoke, however, and pledged them that the stain of slavery should be wiped out.

Mr. WISE, of North Carolina, made a long and learned address, treating principally of geology and women. He claimed for woman more even than she for herself. He said: "Women are generally more competent to vote than their husbands, and sisters better fitted to be judges than their brothers, the mother more capable of wisely exercising the elective franchise than her booby son."

LUCY STONE said: The last speaker alluded to this movement as being that of a few disappointed women. From the first years to which my memory stretches, I have been a disappointed woman. When, with my brothers, I reached forth after the sources of knowledge, I was reproved with "It isn't fit for you; it doesn't belong to women." Then there was but one college in the world where women were admitted, and that was in Brazil. I would have found my way there, but by the time I was prepared to go, one was opened in the young State of Ohio—the first in the United States where women and negroes could enjoy opportunities with white men. I was disappointed when I came to seek a profession worthy an immortal being—every employment was closed to me, except those of the teacher, the seamstress, and the housekeeper. In education, in marriage, in religion, in everything, disappointment is the lot of woman. It shall be the business of my life to deepen this disappointment in every woman's heart until she bows down to it no longer. I wish that women, instead of being walking show-cases, instead of begging of their fathers and brothers the latest and gayest new bonnet, would ask of them their rights.

The question of Woman's Rights is a practical one. The notion has prevailed that it was only an ephemeral idea; that it was but women claiming the right to smoke cigars in the streets, and to frequent bar-rooms. Others have supposed it a question of comparative intellect; others still, of sphere. Too much has already been said and written about woman's sphere. Trace all the doctrines to their source and they will be found to have no basis except in the usages and prejudices of the age. This is seen in the fact that what is tolerated in woman in one country is not tolerated in another. In this country women may hold prayer-meetings, etc., but in Mohammedan countries it is written upon their mosques, "Women and dogs, and other impure animals, are not permitted to enter." Wendell Phillips says, "The best and greatest thing one is capable of doing, that is his sphere." I have confidence in the Father to believe that when He gives us the capacity to do anything He does not make a blunder. Leave women, then, to find their sphere. And do not tell us before we are born even, that our province is to cook dinners, darn stockings, and sew on buttons. We are told woman has all the rights she wants; and even women, I am ashamed to say, tell us so. They mistake the politeness of men for rights—seats while men stand in this hall to-night, and their adulations; but these are mere courtesies. We want rights. The flour-merchant, the house-builder, and the postman charge us no less on account of our sex; but when we endeavor to earn money to pay all these, then, indeed, we find the difference. Man, if he have energy, may hew out for himself a path where no mortal has ever trod, held back by nothing but what is in himself; the world is all before him, where to choose; and we are glad for you, brothers, men, that it is so. But the same society that drives forth the young man, keeps woman at home—a dependent—working little cats on worsted, and little dogs on punctured paper; but if she goes heartily and bravely to give herself to some worthy purpose, she is out of her sphere and she loses caste. Women working in tailor-shops are paid one-third as much as men. Some one in Philadelphia has stated that women make fine shirts for twelve and a half cents apiece; that no woman can make more than nine a week, and the sum thus earned, after deducting rent, fuel, etc., leaves her just three and a half cents a day for bread. Is it a wonder that women are driven to prostitution? Female teachers in New York are paid fifty dollars a year, and for every such situation there are five hundred applicants. I know not what you believe of God, but I believe He gave yearnings and longings to be filled, and that He did not mean all our time should be devoted to feeding and clothing the body. The present condition of woman causes a horrible perversion of the marriage relation. It is asked of a lady, "Has she married well?" "Oh, yes, her husband is rich." Woman must marry for a home, and you men are the sufferers by this; for a woman who loathes you may marry you because you have the means to get money which she can not have. But when woman can enter the lists with you and make money for herself, she will marry you only for deep and earnest affection.

I am detaining you too long, many of you standing, that I ought to apologize, but women have been wronged so long that I may wrong you a little. (Applause). A woman undertook in Lowell to sell shoes to ladies. Men laughed at her, but in six years she has run them all out, and has a monopoly of the trade. Sarah Tyndale, whose husband was an importer of china, and died bankrupt, continued his business, paid off his debts, and has made a fortune and built the largest china warehouse in the world. (Mrs. Mott here corrected Lucy. Mrs. Tyndale has not the largest china warehouse, but the largest assortment of china in the world). Mrs. Tyndale, herself, drew the plan of her warehouse. and it is the best plan ever drawn. A laborer to whom the architect showed it, said: "Don't she know e'en as much as some men?" I have seen a woman at manual labor turning out chair-legs in a cabinet-shop, with a dress short enough not to drag in the shavings. I wish other women would imitate her in this. It made her hands harder and broader, it is true, but I think a hand with a dollar and a quarter a day in it, better than one with a crossed ninepence. The men in the shop didn't use tobacco, nor swear—they can't do those things where there are women, and we owe it to our brothers to go wherever they work to keep them decent. The widening of woman's sphere is to improve her lot. Let us do it, and if the world scoff, let it scoff—if it sneer, let it sneer—but we will go on emulating the example of the sisters Grimke and Abby Kelly. When they first lectured against slavery they were not listened to as respectfully as you listen to us. So the first female physician meets many difficulties, but to the next the path will be made easy.

Lucretia Mott has been a preacher for years ; her right to do so is not questioned among Friends. But when Antoinette Brown felt that she was commanded to preach, and to arrest the progress of thousands that were on the road to hell ; why, when she applied for ordination they acted as though they had rather the whole world should go to hell, than that Antoinette Brown should be allowed to tell them how to keep out of it. She is now ordained over a parish in the State of New York, but when she meets on the Temperance platform the Rev. John Chambers, or your own Gen. Carey (applause) they greet her with hisses. Theodore Parker said : "The acorn that the school-boy carries in his pocket and the squirrel stows in his cheek, has in it the possibility of an oak, able to withstand, for ages, the cold winter and the driving blast." I have seen the acorn men and women, but never the perfect oak ; all are but abortions. The young mother, when first the new-born babe nestles in her bosom, and a heretofore unknown love springs up in her heart, finds herself unprepared for this new relation in life, and she sends forth the child scarred and dwarfed by her own weakness and imbecility, as no stream can rise higher than its fountain.

We find no report of the speeches of Frances D. Gage, Lydia Ann Jenkins, Ernestine L. Rose, Euphemia Cochrane, of Michigan, nor J. Mitchell, of Missouri, editor of the *St. Louis Intelligencer*, nor of the presence of James Mott, whose services were always invaluable on the committees for business and resolutions.

In 1857, the Legislature of Ohio passed a bill enacting that no married man shall dispose of any personal property without having first obtained the consent of his wife ; the wife being empowered in case of the violation of such act, to commence a civil suit in her own name for the recovery of said property ; and also that any married woman whose husband shall desert her or neglect to provide for his family, shall be entitled to his wages and to those of her minor children. These amendments were warmly recommended by Gov. Salmon P. Chase in his annual message. The Select Committee* of the Senate on the petition asking the right of suffrage for woman, reported in favor of the proposed amendment, recommending the adoption of the following resolution :

Resolved, That the Judiciary Committee be instructed to report to the Senate a bill to submit to the qualified electors at the next election for Senators and Representatives an amendment to the Constitution, whereby the elective franchise shall be extended to the citizens of Ohio without distinction of sex.

But the bill was defeated in the Senate by a vote of 44 to 44. The petition had received 10,000 signatures. We give this able report in full.†

The proceedings of these early Conventions might be read with pride and satisfaction by the women of Ohio to-day, with all their

---

* J. D. Cattell and H. Canfield.   † See Appendix.

superior advantages of education. Frances D. Gage was a natural orator. Her wit and pathos always delighted her audiences, and were highly appreciated by those on the platform. Her off-hand speeches, ready for any occasion, were exactly complemented by J. Elizabeth Jones, whose carefully prepared essays on philosophy, law, and government, would do honor to any statesman. Together they were a great power in Ohio. From this time Conventions were held annually for several years, the friends of woman suffrage being thoroughly organized; J. Elizabeth Jones was made General Agent. In her report of May 16th, 1861, she says :

And through the earnest efforts of Mrs. Robinson, Mrs. Gage, Mrs. Wilson, Mrs. Tilden, and many others, the Legislature was petitioned from year to year for a redress of legal and political wrongs. At a later period, the indefatigable exertions of Mrs. Adeline T. Swift sustained the interest and the agitation in such portions of the State as she could reach. As the fruit of her labor, many thousands of names, pleading for equality, have been presented to the General Assembly, which labor has been continued to the present time.

Our last effort, of which I am now more particularly to speak, was commenced early in the season, by extensive correspondence to enlist sympathy and aid in behalf of petitions. As soon as we could get the public ear, several lecturing agents were secured, and they did most efficient service, both with tongue and with pen. One of these was Mrs. C. I. H. Nichols, of Kansas, formerly of Vermont ; and perhaps no person was ever better qualified than she. Ever ready and ever faithful, in public and in private, and ever capable, too, whether discussing the condition of woman with the best informed members of the legal profession, or striving at the fireside of some indolent and ignorant sister, over whose best energies " death is creeping like an untimely frost," to waken in her heart a desire for that which is truly noble and good.

Of another of our agents—Mrs. Cutler, of Illinois—equally as much can be said of her qualifications and her efficiency. Having been very widely acquainted with the sorrowful experiences of women, both abroad and in our own country, which have been caused by their inferior position, and by legal disabilities ; and lamenting, too, as only great and elevated natures can, the utter wreck of true, noble womanhood in the higher circles of society, a necessity is thus laid upon her to do all in her power to lift both classes into a freer, better life.

Mrs. Frances D. Gage, of Ohio, deeply interested herself in this question in the beginning, and has never failed in faithful testimony and timely word, to promote its success. Although not identified with us as an agent, yet we had her active co-operation during the campaign. Her editorial connection with the press, and her lectures on the West India Islands, gave her abundant opportunity, which she did not fail to embrace, of circulating petitions and advocating the cause to which she has so largely given her energies.

Besides the General Agent, whose time was divided between correspondence, lecturing, and the general details of the movement, there were other and most efficient workers, especially in canvassing for signatures. We are indebted to Mrs. Anne Ryder, of Cincinnati, for much labor in this direction ; and also to

Mrs. Howard, of Columbus, for similar service. Miss Olympia Brown, a graduate of Antioch College, canvassed several towns most successfully—adding thousands of names to the lists heretofore obtained. Equally zealous were women, and men also, in various sections of the State. By means of this hearty co-operation, both branches of the Legislature were flooded with Woman's Rights petitions during the first part of the session—a thousand and even two thousand names were presented at a time.

Our main object this year, as heretofore, has been to secure personal property and parental rights, never ignoring, however, the right to legislate for ourselves. We were fortunate in the commencement in enlisting some of the leading influences of the State in favor of the movement. Persons occupying the highest social and political position, very fully endorsed our claims to legal equality, and rendered valuable aid by public approval of the same. We took measures at an early period to obtain the assistance of the press; and by means of this auxiliary our work has been more fully recognized, and more generally appreciated than it could otherwise have been. Without exception, the leading journals of the State have treated our cause with consideration, and generously commended the efforts of its agents.

So numerous were the petitions, and so largely did they represent the best constituency of the State, that the committees in whose hands they were placed, felt that by all just parliamentary usage, they were entitled to a candid consideration. Accordingly they invited several of us who had been prominent, to defend our own cause in the Senate chamber, before their joint Committee and such of the General Assembly and of the public, as might choose to come and listen. From the reports of the numerous letter-writers who were present, I will place one extract only upon record.

"The Senate chamber was filled to overflowing to hear Mrs. Jones, Cutler, and Gage, and hundreds went away for want of a place to stand. Columbus has seldom seen so refined and intelligent an audience as that which gathered round those earnest women, who had none of the charm of youth or beauty to challenge admiration, but whose heads were already sprinkled with the frosts of life's winter. Earnest, truthful, womanly, richly cultivated by the experiences of practical life, those women, mothers, and two of them grandmothers, pleaded for the right of woman to the fruit of her own genius, labor, or skill, and for the mother her right to be the joint guardian of her own offspring. I wish I could give you even the faintest idea of the brilliancy of the scene, or the splendor of the triumph achieved over the legions of prejudice, the cohorts of injustice, and the old national guard of hoary conservatism. If the triumph of a prima donna is something to boast, what was the triumph of these toil-worn women, when not only the members of the Committee, but Senators and Members of the House, crowded around them with congratulations and assurances that their able and earnest arguments had fully prevailed, and the prayers of their petitioners must be granted."

The address of the first speaker was a written argument on legal rights. It was solicited by members of the General Assembly for publication, and distributed over the State at their expense.

The change in public sentiment, the marked favor with which our cause began to be regarded in the judicial and legislative departments, encouraged us to hope that if equal and exact justice were not established, which we could hardly expect, we should at least obtain legal equality in many particulars. The Senate committee soon reported a bill, drafted by one of their number— Judge Key—and fully endorsed by all the judges of the Supreme Court, securing to the married woman the use of her real estate, and the avails of her own separate labor, together with such power to protect her property, and do business in her own name, as men possess. The last provision was stricken out and the bill thus amended passed both Houses, the Senate by a very large majority.

Although this secures to us property rights in a measure only, yet it is a great gain. He, who in abject bondage has striven with his fetters, rejoices to have the smallest amount of their weight removed. We have, therefore, reason to be grateful not only for the benefits we shall derive from this Act, but for the evidence of a growing sense of justice on the part of those who claim for themselves the exclusive right to legislate. Senator Parish had already prepared a Bill for Guardianship, and to change the Laws of Descent, that something more than a paltry dower should be secured to the widow in the common estate; but the press of business, and the sudden commencement of open hostilities between the North and South, precluded all possibility of further legislation in our behalf. While Judge Key has deservedly received universal thanks from the women of Ohio, for proposing and carrying through the Legislature the Property Bill, they are no less indebted to the Hon. Mr. Parish for his faithful defense of their cause, not only during the present session, but in years past. If all the Honorable Senators and Representatives who have given their influence in favor of it were to be mentioned, and all the faithful men and earnest women who have labored to promote it, the list would be long and distinguished. J. ELIZABETH JONES.

Thus, in a measure, were the civil rights of the women of Ohio secured. Some of those who were influential in winning this modicum of justice have already passed away; some, enfeebled by age, are incapable of active work; others are seeking in many latitudes that rest so necessary in the declining years of life.

The question naturally suggests itself, where are the young women of Ohio, who will take up this noble cause and carry it to its final triumph? They are reaping on all sides the benefits achieved for them by others, and they in turn, by earnest efforts for the enfranchisement of woman, should do what they can to broaden the lives of the next generation.

In Ohio, as elsewhere, the great conflict between the North and South turned the thoughts of women from the consideration of their own rights, to the life of the nation. Many of them spent their last days and waning powers in the military hospitals and sanitariums, ministering to sick and dying soldiers; others at a later period in the service of the freedmen, guiding them in their labors, and instructing them in their schools; all alike forgetting that justice to woman was a more important step in national safety than freedom or franchise to any race of men.

CHAPTER VII.

REMINISCENCES BY CLARINA I. HOWARD NICHOLS.

VERMONT : Editor *Windham County Democrat*—Property Laws, 1847 and 1849—Ad-dressed the Legislature on school suffrage, 1852.
WISCONSIN : Woman's State Temperance Society—Lydia F. Fowler in company—Op-position of Clergy—"Woman's Rights" wouldn't do—Advertised "Men's Rights."
KANSAS : Free State Emigration, 1854—Gov. Robinson and Senator Pomeroy—Woman's Rights speeches on Steamboat, and at Lawrence—Constitutional Convention, 1859—State Woman Suffrage Association—John O. Wattles, President—Aid from the Francis Jackson Fund—Canvassing the State—School Suffrage gained.
MISSOURI : Lecturing at St. Joseph, 1858, on Col. Scott's invitation—Westport and the John Brown raid, 1859—St. Louis, 1854—Frances D. Gage, Rev. Wm. G. Eliot, and Rev. Mr. Weaver.

IN gathering up these individual memories of the past, we feel there will be an added interest in the fact that we shall thus have a subjective, as well as an objective view of this grand movement for woman's enfranchisement. To our older readers, who have known the actors in these scenes, they will come like the far-off whispers of by-gone friends; to younger ones who will never see the faces of the noble band of women who took the initiative in this struggle, it will be almost as pleasant as a personal introduction, to have them speak for themselves; each in her own peculiar style recount the experiences of those eventful years. As but few remain to tell the story, and each life has made a channel of its own, there will be no danger of wearying the reader with much repetition.

To Clarina Howard Nichols the women of Kansas are indebted for many civil rights they have as yet been too apathetic to exercise.

Her personal presence in the Constitutional Convention of 1859, secured for the women of that State liberal property rights, equal guardianship of their children, and the right to vote on all school questions. She is a large-hearted, brave, faithful woman, and her life speaks for itself. Her experiences are indeed the history of all that was done in the above-mentioned States.

VERMONT.

I was born in Townshend, Windham County, Vermont, January 25, 1810.

From 1843 to 1853 inclusive, I edited *The Windham County*

Democrat, published by my husband, Geo. W. Nichols, at Brattle-boro.

Early in 1847, I addressed to the voters of the State a series of editorials setting forth the injustice and miserable economy of the property disabilities of married women. In October of the same year, Hon. Larkin Mead, of Brattleboro, "moved," as he said, "by Mrs. Nichols' presentation of the subject" in the *Democrat,* intro-duced in the Vermont Senate a bill securing to the wife real and personal property, with its use, and power to defend, convey, and devise as if "sole." The bill as passed, secured to the wife real estate owned by her at marriage, or acquired by gift, devise, or in-heritance during marriage, with the rents, issues, and profits, as against any debts of the husband ; but to make a sale or conveyance of either her realty or its use valid, it must be the joint act of hus-band and wife. She might by last will and testament dispose of her lands, tenements, hereditaments, and any interest therein descend-able to her heirs, as if "sole." A subsequent Legislature added to the latter clause, moneys, notes, bonds, and other assets, accruing from sale or use of real estate. And this was the first breath of a legal civil existence to Vermont wives.

In 1849, Vermont enacted a Homestead law. In 1850, a bill em-powering the wife to insure, in her own interest, the life, or a term of the life of her husband ; the annual premium on such insurance not to exceed $300 ; also an act giving to widows of childless hus-bands the whole of an estate not exceeding $1,000 in value, and half of any amount in excess of $1,000 ; and if he left no kin, the whole estate, however large, became the property of the widow. Prior to this Act, the widow of a childless husband had only half, however small the estate, and if he left no kindred to claim it, the remaining half went into the treasury of the State, whose gain was the town's loss, if, as occasionally happened, the widow's half was not sufficient for her support.*

In 1852, I drew up a petition signed by more than 200 of the most substantial business men, including the staunchest conserva-tives, and tax-paying widows of Brattleboro, asking the Legislature to make the women of the State voters in district school meetings.

Up to 1850 I had not taken position for suffrage, but instead of

---

* Mrs. Nichols had written up a case occurring among the subscribers to the *Democrat,* in which $500, the whole estate, was divided, the half of that amount being all the law allowed for the support of a woman, then in the decline of life, and sent fifty marked copies of the paper to members of the Legislature elect. One of them introduced the bill, which passed the first day of the session.

disclaiming its advocacy as improper, I had, since 1849, shown the absurdity of regarding suffrage as unwomanly. Having failed to secure her legal rights by reason of her disfranchisement, a woman must look to the ballot for self-protection. In this cautious way I proceeded, aware that not a house would be opened to me, did I demand the suffrage before convicting men of legal robbery, through woman's inability to defend herself.

The petition was referred to the Educational Committee of the House, whose chairman, editor of the *Rutland Herald,* was a bitter opponent, and I felt that he would, in his report, lampoon " Woman's Rights " and their most prominent advocates, thus sending his poison into all the towns ignorant of our objects, and strengthening the already repellant prejudices of the leading women at the capital. I wrote to Judge Thompson, editor of the *Green Mountain Freeman* (a recent accession to the press of the State and friendly to our cause), what I feared, and asked him to plead before the Committee and interest influential members to protect woman's cause against abuse before the House. He counseled with leading members of the three political parties—Whig, Free-Soil, and Democrat—including the Speaker of the House, and they advised, as the best course, that " Mrs. Nichols come to Montpelier, and they would invite her, by a handsome vote, to speak to her petition before the House." " When," added Judge T., " you can use your privilege to present the whole subject of Woman's Rights. Come, and I will stick by you like a brother." I went. The resolution of invitation was adopted with a single dissenting vote, and that from the Chairman of the Educational Committee, who unwittingly made the vote unanimous by the unfortunate exclamation, " If the lady wants to make herself ridiculous, let her come and make herself as ridiculous as possible and as soon as possible, but I don't believe in this scramble for the breeches ! "

In concluding my plea before the House (in which I had cited the statutes and decisions of courts, showing that the husband owned even the wife's clothing), I thanked the House for its resolution, and referred to the concluding remark of the Chairman of the Educational Committee, and said that though I " had earned the dress I wore, my husband owned it — not of his own will, but by a law adopted by bachelors and other women's husbands," and added : " I will not appeal to the gallantry of this House, but to its manliness, if such a taunt does not come with an ill grace from gentlemen who have legislated our skirts into their possession ? And will it not be quite time enough for them to taunt us with being after their wardrobes, when they shall have restored to us the legal right to our own?"

With a bow I turned from the Speaker's stand, when the profound hush of as fine an audience as earnest woman ever addressed, was broken by the muffled thunder of stamping feet, and the low, deep hum of pent-up feeling loosed suddenly from restraint. A crowd of ladies from the galleries, who had come only at the urgent personal appeal of Judge Thompson, who had spent the day calling from house to house, and who a few months before had utterly failed to persuade them to attend a course of physiological lectures from Mrs. Mariana Johnson, on account of her having once presided over a Woman's Rights Convention, these women met me at the foot of the Speaker's desk, exclaiming with earnest expressions of sympathy: "We did not know before what Woman's Rights were, Mrs. Nichols, but we are for Woman's Rights."

Said Mrs. Thompson to me upon our return to her home: "I broke out in a cold perspiration when your voice failed and you leaned your head on your hand."* "I thought you were going to fail," continued Mrs. Thompson. "Yes," said the Judge, "I was very doubtful how it would come out when I saw how sensitive Mrs. Nichols was. But," (turning to me), "you have had a complete triumph! That final expression of your audience was perfect. *Mr. Herald* with his outside recruits did not come forward with the suit of male attire at the close, as he had advertised he would, (I did not tell Mrs. N. this, my dear," said the Judge.) "He'll catch it now, in the House and out." And he did "catch it."

The effort brought me no reproach, no ridicule from any quarter, but instead, cordial recognition and delicate sympathy from unexpected quarters, and even from those who had heard but the report of persons present. The editorial criticism of the Chairman of the Educational Committee, paid me the high compliment of saying, that "in spite of her efforts Mrs. Nichols could not unsex herself; even her voice was full of womanly pathos." The report of the Committee was adverse to my petition, but not disrespectful. Though the petition failed, the favorable impression created was regarded as a great triumph for woman's rights.

---

* The violent throbbing of Mrs. Nichols' heart, caused by her unusual position and her intense anxiety that her plea might be successful, had stopped her speaking at the close of a brief preface to her plea. She, however, soon rallied, though her voice was tremulous throughout, from the conviction that only an eminently successful presentation of her subject, could spike the enemy's batteries and win a verdict of "just and womanly." Mrs. Nichols hoped no further than that. She did not expect conservative Vermont to yield at once for what she asked, as she stood alone with her paper among the press; and there was no other advocate in the State to take the field.

From the time I spoke at the Worcester Convention, 1850, until I left for Kansas, October, 1854, I responded to frequent calls from town and neighborhood committees and lyceums—in the county and adjoining territory of New Hampshire and Massachusetts as well as Vermont, to lecture or join in debate with men and women, the women voting me their time, on the subject of woman's legal and political equality. In these neighborhood lyceums, ministers and deacons and their wives and daughters took part. Generally wives were appointed in opposition to their husbands, and from their rich and varied experience did excellent execution. In order to secure opposition, I used to let the negative open and close, otherwise the debate was sure to be tame or no debate at all. In all my experience it was the same; the "affirmative" had the merit and the argument.

The clergy often spoke—always when present—and in the negative, if it was their first hearing; and without a single exception they faced the audience at the close with a cordial endorsement of the cause. Said one such: " I told you, ladies and gentlemen, that I had given little attention to the subject, and you see that I told the truth. Mrs. Nichols has made out her case, and let her and the women laboring like her, persevere, and woman will gain her rights." " Let your wife go all she can," said one of these converts to Mr. Nichols, " she is breaking down prejudices and making friends for your paper. Your political opponents have represented her as a masculine brawler for rights, and those who have never met her know no better. I went to hear her, full of misgivings that it might be so."

In the winter of 1852 I went as often as twice a week—late P.M. and returned early A.M.—from six to twenty miles. I was sent for where there was no railroad. I often heard of " ready-made pants," and once of a " rail," but the greater the opposition, the greater the victory.

On a clear, cold morning of January, 1852, I found myself some six miles from home at a station on the Vermont side of the Massachusetts State line, on my way to Templeton, Mass., whither I had been invited by a Lyceum Committee to lecture upon the subject of " Woman's Rights." I had scarcely settled myself in the rear of the saloon for a restful, careless two hours' ride, when two men entered the car. In the younger man I recognized the sheriff of our county. Having given a searching glance around the car, the older man, with a significant nod to his companion, laid his hand upon the saloon door an instant, and every person in the car had risen to his feet, electrified by the wail of a "Rachel mourning for her children." "O father! she's *my* child! *she's my child!*" I reached the door, which was guarded by the sheriff, in a condition of mental exaltation (or concentration), which to this day reflects itself at the recollection of that agonizing cry of the beautiful young mother, set upon by the myrmidons of the law whose base inhumanity shames the brute! "Who is it?" "What is it?" "What does it all mean?" were the anxious queries put up on all sides. I answered: "It means, my friends, that a woman has no legal right to her own babies; that the law-makers of this *Christian country* (!) have given the custody of the babies to the father, drunken or sober, and he may send the sheriff—as in this case—to arrest and rob her of her little ones! You have heard sneers at 'Woman's Rights.' This is one of the rights—a mother's right to the care and custody of her helpless little ones!"

From that excited crowd—all young men and grown boys, I being the only woman among them—rose thick and fast—"*They've no business with the woman's babies!*" "*Pitch 'em overboard!*" "*I'll help.*" "*Good for you; so'll I!*" "All aboard." (The conductor had come upon the scene). "*All aboard.*" "Wait a minute till he gets the other child," cries the old man, rushing out of the saloon with a little three-year-old girl in his arms, while the sheriff rushed in. Standing behind the old man, I beckoned to the conductor, who knew me, to "*go on,*" and in five minutes we were across the Massachusetts line, and I was in the saloon. With his hand on her child, the sheriff was urging the mother to let go her hold. "Hold on to your baby," I cried, "he has no right to take it from you, and is liable to fine and imprisonment for attempting it. Tell me, Mr. C——, are you helping the other party as a favor, or in your official capacity? In the latter case you might have taken her child in Vermont, but we are in Massachusetts now, quite out of your sheriff's beat." "The grandfather made legal custodian by the father, was he? That would do in Vermont, sir, but under the recent decision of a Massachusetts Court, given in a case like this, *only the father* can take the child from its mother, and in attempting it you have made yourselves liable to fine and imprisonment." Thus the "sheriffalty" was extinguished, and mother and child took their seat beside me in the car.

Meantime the conductor had made the old gentleman understand that they could get off at the next station, where they might take the "up train," and get back to their "team" on the Vermont side of the "line." As they could get no carriage at the bare little station, and with the encumbrance of the child, could not foot it six miles in the cold and snow, they must wait some three or four hours for the train, which suggested the possibility of a rescue. I could not stop over a train, but I could take the baby along with me, if some one could be found—The conductor calls. The car stops. As the child robbers step out (the little girl, clutched in the old grandfather's arms) 'mid the frantic cries of the mother and the execrations of the passengers, two middle-aged gentlemen of fine matter-of-fact presence, entered. I at once met their questioning faces with a hurried statement of facts, and the need of some intelligent, humane gentleman to aid the young mother in the recovery of her little girl. Having spoken together aside, the younger man introduced " Dr. B——, who lives in the next town, where papers can be made out, and a sheriff be sent back to bring the men and child; the lady can go with the doctor, and the baby with Mrs. Nichols. I would stop, but I must be in my seat in the Legislature." " I have no money, only my ticket to take me to my friends," exclaimed the anxious mother. " I will take care of that," said the good doctor; " you won't need any." " They will have to pay," I whispered. . . . .

I gave my lecture at Templeton to a fine audience; accepted an invitation to return and give a second on the same subject, and having left the dear little toddler happy and amply protected, at noon next day found myself back at Orange, where I had left the mother. Here the conductor, who by previous arrangement, left a note from me telling her where to go for her baby, reported that the party had been brought to Orange for trial, spent the night in care of the sheriff, and were released on giving up the little girl and paying a handsome sum of the needful to the mother. He had scarcely ended his report when the pair entered the car, like myself, homeward bound. The old gentleman, care-worn and anxious, probably thinking of his team left standing at the Vermont station, looked straight ahead, but the kind-hearted sheriff caught my eye and smiled. In my happiness I could not do otherwise than give smile for smile.

Arrived at home, I found the affair, reported by the conductor of the evening train, had created quite an excitement, sympathy being decidedly with the mother. I was credited with being privy to the escapade and the pursuit, and as having gone purposely to the rescue. Had this been true, I could not have managed it better, for a good Providence went with me. I received several memorial " hanks " of yarn, with messages from the donors that " they

12

would keep me in knitting-work while preaching woman's rights on the railroad "—a reference to my practice of knitting on the cars, and the report that I gave a lecture on the occasion to my audience there.

And thus was the seed of woman's educational, industrial, and political rights sown in Vermont, through infinite labor, but in the faith and perseverance which bring their courage to all workers for the right.

WISCONSIN.

In September and October, 1853, I traveled 900 miles in Wisconsin, as agent of the Woman's State Temperance Society, speaking in forty-three towns to audiences estimated at 30,000 in the aggregate, people coming in their own conveyances from five to twenty miles. I went to Wisconsin under an engagement to labor as agent of the State Temperance League, an organization composed of both sexes and officered by leading temperance men—at the earnest and repeated solicitations of its delegates whom I met at the " Whole World's Temperance Convention," held in New York City in September, and who were commissioned by the League to employ speakers to canvass the State; the object being to procure the enactment of a " Maine Law " by the next Legislature. These delegates had counseled, among others, with Horace Greeley, who advised my employment, curiosity to hear a woman promising to call out larger audiences and more votes for temperance candidates in the pending election.

I, at first, declined to make the engagement, on the ground that I could not be spared from my newspaper duties; but to escape further importunity, finally consented to " ask my husband at home," and report at New York, where one of the gentlemen would await my answer, and myself, if I decided to accept their proposition. My husband's cheerful, " Go, wife, you will be doing just the work you love, and enjoying a journey which you have not means otherwise to undertake," and a notice from Mrs. Lydia F. Fowler, that she would join us in the trip with a view to arranging for physiological lectures at eligible points in the State, decided me to go. Mrs. F.'s company was not only a social acquisition, but a happy insurance against pot-house witlings on the alert to impale upon the world's dread laugh, any woman who, to accomplish some public good, should venture for a space to cut loose from the marital " buttons ' and go out into the world alone !

In making the engagement, I had taken it for granted, that the right and propriety of woman's public advocacy of temperance was a settled question in the field to which I was invited. But arrived at Milwaukee, I found that the popular prejudice against women as public speakers, and especially the advocacy of Woman's Rights, with which I had for years been identified, had been stirred to its most disgusting depths by a reverend gentleman who had preceded us, and who had for years been a salaried " agent at large," of the New York State Temperance Society. A highly respectable minority of the Executive Committee of the League endorsed the action of their delegation, but were overruled by a numerical majority, and I found myself in the position of agent " at large," while the reverend traducer secured his engagement in my place.

This turn of affairs, embarrassing at first, proved in the end providential—a timely clearance for a more congenial craft—since the women of the State had organized a Woman's State Temperance Society, and advertised a Convention to meet the following week at Delavan, the populous shire town of Walworth County, fifty miles distant in the interior. Thither the friendly Leaguers proposed to take us. Meantime it was arranged that Mrs. F. and I should address the citizens of Milwaukee. A capacious church was engaged for Sabbath evening, from which hundreds went away unable to get in. But neither clergyman nor layman could be found willing to commit himself by opening the services ; and with " head uncovered," in a church in which it was "a shame for a woman to speak," I rested my burden with the dear Father, as only burdens are rested with Him, in conscious unity of purpose.

Mrs. F. addressed the audience on the physiological effects of alcoholic drinks. I followed, quoting from the prophecy of King Lemuel, that " his mother taught him," Proverbs xxxi., verses 4, 5, 8, 9, " Open thy mouth for the dumb ; in the cause of all such as are appointed to destruction. Open thy mouth, judge righteously and plead the cause of the poor and needy." The spirit moved audience and speaker. We forgot ourselves ; forgot everything but " the poor and needy," the drunkard's wife and children " appointed to destruction " through license laws and alienated civil rights.

At Delavan we met a body of earnest men and women, indignant at the action of the Executive Committee of the League, to which many of them had contributed funds for the campaign, and ready to assume the responsibility of my engagement, and the expenses of Mrs. F., who in following out her original plan, generously consented to precede my lectures with a brief physiological dissertation apropos to the object of the canvass. The burden of the speaking, as planned, rested with me, provided my hitherto untested physical ability proved equal, as it did, to the daily effort.

In counsel with Mrs. R. Ostrander, President of the Society, and her sister officials, women of character and intelligence, I could explain, as I could not have done to any body of equally worthy men, that in justice to ourselves, to them, and to the cause we had at heart, we must make the canvass in a spirit and in conditions above reproach. "I can not come down from my work," said Miss Lyon, founder of Mount Holyoke Female Seminary, when importuned to rebut some baseless scandal. To fight our way would be to mar the spirit and effect of our work. We must place the opposition at a disadvantage from the first; then we could afford to ignore it altogether and rise to a level with the humane issues of the campaign. It was accordingly arranged that the friends should make appointments and secure us suitable escort to neighboring towns; and to distant and less accessible points a gentleman was engaged to take us in a private carriage,—his wife, a woman of rare talent and fine culture, to accompany us. A programme which was advertised in the local papers and happily carried out.

From Delavan we returned to Milwaukee to perfect our arrangements. From thence our next move was to Waukesha, the shire town of Waukesha County, twenty miles by rail, to a Temperance meeting advertised for " speaking and the transaction of business." The meeting was held in the Congregational church, the pastor acting as chairman. The real business of the meeting was soon disposed of, and then was enacted the most amusing farce it was ever my lot to witness. The chairman and his deacon led off in a long-drawn debate on sundry matters of no importance, and of less interest to the audience, members of which attempted in vain, by motions and votes, to cut it short. When it had become sufficiently apparent that the gentlemen were " talking against time " to prevent speaking, there were calls for speakers. The chairman replied that it was a " business meeting, but Rev. Mr. ——, from Illinois, would lecture in the evening." Several gentlemen rose to protest. One said he " had walked seven miles that his wife and daughters might ride, to hear the ladies speak." Another had " ridden horseback twelve miles to hear them." A storm was impending; the chairman was prepared; he declared the meeting adjourned and with his deacon left the house.

There was a hurried consultation in the ante-room, which resulted in an urgent request for " Mrs. Nichols to remain and speak in the evening." The speaker noticed for the evening, joined heartily in the request ; "half an hour was all the time he wanted." But when the evening came, he insisted that I should speak first, and when I should have given way for him, assured me that he "had made arrangements to speak the next evening," and joined in the "go on, go on!" of the audience. So it was decided that I should remain over the Sabbath, and Mrs. F. return with the friends to Milwaukee.

Meantime it had transpired that in the audience were several Vermonters from a settlement of fourteen families from the vicinity of my home; among them a lady from my native town ; we had been girls together. "We know all about Mrs. N.," said one. "We take the *Tribune,* and friends at home send us her paper." So the good Father had sent vouchers for His agent at large. But this was not all. I had a pleasant reserve for the evening. I had recognized in the deacon, a friend from whom I had parted twenty-one years before in Western New York. In the generous confidence of youthful enthusiasm we had enlisted in the cold-water army; together pledged ourselves to fight the liquor interest to the death. And here my old friend, whose début on the Temperance platform I had aided and cheered, had talked a full hour to prevent me from being heard! Was I indignant? Was I grieved? Nay! It was not a personal matter. Time's graver had made us strange to each other. His name and voice had revealed him to me ; but the name I bore was not that by which he had known me. Besides, I remembered that twenty-one years before, I could not have been persuaded to hear a woman speak on any public occasion, and I had nothing to forgive,—my friend had only stood still where I had left him. Such, suppressing his name, was the story I told my audience on that evening. And with his puzzled and kindly face intently regarding me, I assured my hearers that I had not a doubt of his whole-souled and manly support in my present work. Nor was I disappointed.

Next morning, (Sabbath) I listened to a scholarly sermon on infidel issues and innovations from the chairman of the "business meeting" of the previous afternoon, he having stayed away from my lecture to prepare it. In the evening, after the temperance lecture of my Illinois friend, I improved the opportunity of a call from the audience, the Rev. Chairman being present, to meet certain points of the sermon, personal to myself and the advocates of rights for women, closing with a brief confession of my faith in Christ's rule of love and duty as impressing every human being into the service of a common humanity—the right to serve being commensurate with the obligation, as of God and not of man.

One week later, another business meeting was held in the same house, and in its published proceedings was a resolution introduced by the Rev. Chairman, endorsing Mrs. Nichols, and inviting her "to be present and speak" at a County Convention appointed for a subsequent day. Not long after he sent me, through a brother clergyman, an apology that would have disarmed resentment, had I felt any, toward a man who, having opposed me without discourtesy and retracted by a published resolution, was yet not satisfied without tendering a private apology.

I had achieved a grateful success; license to "plead the cause of the poor and needy," where, *how* to do so, without offending old-time ideas of woman's sphere, had seemed to the women under whose direction I had taken the field, the real question at issue. In consideration of existing prejudices, they had suggested the prudence of silence on the subject of Woman's Rights. And here, on the very threshold of the campaign, I had been compelled to vindicate my right to speak for woman; as a woman, to speak for her from any stand-point of life to which nature, custom, or law had assigned her. I had no choice, no hope of success, but in presenting her case as it stood before God and my own soul. To neither could I turn traitor, and do the work, or satisfy the aspirations of a true and loving woman.

For more than a quarter of a century earnest men had spoken, and failed to secure justice to the poor and needy, "appointed to destruction" by the liquor traffic. They had failed because they had denied woman's right to help them, and taken from her the means to help herself. In speaking for woman, I must be heard from a domestic level of legal pauperism disenchanted of all political prestige. In appealing to the powers that be, I must appeal from sovereigns drunk to sovereigns sober,—with eight chances in ten that the decision would be controlled by sovereigns drunk.

To impress the paramount claim of women to a no-license law, without laying bare the legal and political disabilities that make them "the greatest sufferers," the helpless victims of the liquor traffic, was impossible. It would have been stupidly unwise to withhold what with a majority of voters is the weightier consideration, that in alienating from women their earnings, governments impose upon community taxes for the support of the paupered children of drunken fathers, whose mothers would joyfully support and train them for usefulness; and who, as a rule, have done so when by the death or divorce of the husband they have regained the control of their earnings and the custody of their children. Thus proving, that man, by his disabling laws, has made woman helpless and dependent, and not God, who has endowed her with capabilities equal to the re. sponsibilities He has imposed.

Worse than unwise would it have been to allow an unjust preju- dice against Woman's Rights, to turn the edge of my appeals for a law in the interest of temperance, when by showing the connection, as of cause and effect, between men's rights and women's wrongs, between women's *no*-rights and their helplessness and dependence, I could disarm that prejudice and win an intelligent support for both temperance and equal rights. On such a showing I based my appeals to the noble men and women of Wisconsin. I assured my audiences, that I had not come to talk to them of " Woman's Rights," that in- deed I did not find that women had any rights in the matter, but to "suffer and be still; to die and give no sign." But I had come to them to speak of *man's rights* and *woman's needs*.

From the Lake Shore cities, from the inland villages, the shire towns, and the mining communities of the Mississippi, whose churches, court-houses, and halls, with two or three exceptions, could not hold the audiences, much less seat them; the responses were hearty, and when outspoken, curiously alike in language as well as sentiment on the subject of rights. " I like Mrs. Nichols' idea of talking man's rights; the result will be woman's rights," said a gentleman rising in his place in the audience at the close of one of my lectures. On another occasion, " Let Mrs. Nichols go on talking men's rights and we'll have women's rights." " Mrs. Nichols has made me ashamed of myself—ashamed of my sex! I didn't know we had been so mean to the women," was the outspoken conclusion of a man who had lived honored and respected, his threescore years and ten. This reaction from the curiosity and doubt which every- where met us in the expressive faces of the people, often reminded me of an incident in my Vermont labors for a Maine law.

In accepting an invitation to address an audience of ladies in the aristocratic old town of C——, in an adjoining county, I had sug- gested, that as it was votes we needed, I would prefer to address an audience of both sexes. Arrived at C——, I found that the ladies of the committee, having acted upon my suggestion, were intensely anxious as to the result. " An audience," they said, "could not be collected to listen to woman's rights; the people were sensitive even to the innovation of a mixed audience for a woman, and they felt that I ought to be informed of the facts." And I felt in every nerve, that they were suffering from fear lest I should fail to vindi- cate the womanliness of our joint venture. But the people came, a church full; intelligent, expectant, and curious to hear a woman The resident clergyman, of my own faith, declined to be present and open with prayer. A resident Universalist clergyman present, declined to pray. A young Methodist licentiate in the audience, not feeling at liberty to decline, tried. His ideas stumbled; his words hitched, and when he prayed: " Bless thy serv—a'hem—thy handmaid, and a'hem—and let all things be done decently and in order;" we in the committee pew felt as relieved as did the young Timothy when he had achieved his amen!

Utterly unnerved by the anxious faces of my committee, I turned to my audience with only the inspiration of homes devastated and families paupered, to sustain me in a desperate exhibit of the need and the "determination of women, impelled by the mother-love that shrinks neither from fire or flood, to rescue their loved ones from the fires and floods of the liquor traffic, though to do so they must make their way through every platform and pulpit in the land!" " Thank God!" exclaimed the licentiate on my right. " Amen!" emphasized the chairman on my left. My committee were radiant. My audience had accepted woman's rights in her wrongs; and I —— only woman's recording angel can tell the sensations of a disfranchised woman when her "declaration of intentions" is endorsed by an Anti-Woman's Rights audience with fervent thanks to God!

Latter-day laborers can have little idea of the trials of the early worker, driven by the stress of right and duty against popular prejudices, to which her own training and early habits of thought have made her painfully sensitive. St. Paul, our patron saint, I think had just come through such a trial of his nerves when he wrote: " The spirit is willing, but the flesh is weak." The memory of the beautiful scenery, the charming Indian summer skies, the restful companionship of our family party in the daily drive, and the generous hospitality of the people of Wisconsin, is one of the pleasantest of a life, as full of sweet memories as of trials, amid and through which they have clung to me with a saving grace.

The Temperance majority in the ensuing election, so far as influenced by canvassing agents, was due to the combined efforts of all who labored for it, and of these it was my good fortune to meet a younger brother of William H. and C. C. Burleigh, who from his man's stand-point of precedents and statistics did excellent service.

The law enacted by the Legislature securing to the wives of drunkards their earnings and the custody and earnings of their minor children, I think I may claim as a result of appeals from the home stand-point of woman's sphere. As a financial measure diverting the supplies and lessening the profits of the liquor traffic, this law is a civil service reform of no mean promise for the abatement of pauper and criminal taxes. In a plea of counsel for defendant in a case of wife-beating to which I once listened, said the gentlemanly attorney : " If Patrick will let the bottle alone"— " Please, your honor," broke in the weeping wife, " if you will stop Misthur Kelly from filling it."

KANSAS.

In October, 1854, with my two eldest sons, I joined a company of two hundred and twenty-five men, women, and children, emigrants from the East to Kansas. In our passage up the Missouri River I gave two lectures by invitation of a committee of emigrants and Captain Choteau and brother, owners of the boat. A pious M.D. was terribly shocked at the prospect, and hurried his young wife to bed, but returned to the cabin himself in good time to hear. As the position was quite central, and I wished to be heard distinctly by the crowd which occupied all the standing room around the cabin, I took my stand opposite the Doctor's berth. Next morning, poor man ! his wife was an outspoken advocate of woman's rights. The next evening she punched his ribs vigorously, at every point made for suffrage, which was the subject of my second lecture.

The 1st of November, 1854—a day never to be forgotten—heaven and earth clasped hands in silent benedictions on that band of immigrants, some on foot, some on horseback, women and children, seventy-five in number, with the company's baggage, in ox-carts and wagons drawn by the fat, the broken-down, and the indifferent " hacks" of wondering, scowling Missouri, scattered all along the prairie road from Kansas City to Lawrence, the Mecca of their pilgrimage.

In advance of all these, at 11 o'clock A.M., Mrs. H—— and myself were sitting in front of the Lawrence office of the New England Emigrant Aid Company, in the covered wagon of Hon. S. C. Pomeroy, who had brought us from Kansas City, and entered the office to announce the arrival of our company ; when a hilarious explosion of several voices assured us that good lungs as well as brave hearts were within. Directly Col. P. and Dr. (Governor) Robinson came out. " Did you hear the cheering ?" asked the Doctor. " I did, and was thinking when you came out, what a popular man the Colonel must be to call forth such a greeting !" " But the cheers were for Mrs. Nichols," was the reply ; and the Doctor proceeded to tell us that, " the boys" had been hotly discussing women's rights, when one of their advocates who had heard her lecture, expressed a wish that his opponents could hear Antoinette Brown on the subject ; a second wished they could hear Susan B. Anthony ; and a third wished they could hear Mrs. Nichols. On the heels of these wishes, the announcement of Colonel Pomeroy, that " Mrs. Nichols was at the door," was the signal for triumphant cheering. " The boys " wanted a lecture in the evening. The Doctor said : " No ; Mrs. Nichols is tired. To-morrow the thatching of the church will be completed, and she can dedicate the building."

Thus truths sown broadcast among the stereotyped beliefs and prejudices of the old and populous communities of the East, had wrought a genial welcome for myself and the advocacy of woman's cause on the disputed soil of Kansas. But, alas ! for the " stony ground." One of " the boys " didn't stay to the " dedication." He had " come to Kansas to get away from the women," and left at once for Leavenworth. I wonder if the Judge—he is that now, and a benedict—remembers ? I still regret that lost opportunity for making his acquaintance.

At Lawrence, the objective point of all the Free State immigration, where I spent six weeks in assisting my sons to make a home for the winter, I mingled freely with the incoming population, and gave several lectures to audiences of from two to three hundred, the entire population coming together at the ringing of the city dinner-bell. I returned to Vermont early in January, 1855, and in April following, with two hundred and fifty emigrants (my husband and younger son accompanying me), rejoined my other sons in the vicinity of Baldwin City, where we took claims and commenced homes. I presented the whole subject of Woman's Rights on the boats in going and returning, as at first, by invitation. In the summer of 1855, delegates were elected to a Constitutional Convention, which later convened at Topeka. Governor Robinson, who with six other delegates voted for the exclusion of the word " male " from qualification for elector, sent me an invitation to attend its sessions, speak before it for woman's equality, and they would vote me a secretary's or clerk's position in the Convention. My husband's fatal illness prevented me from going.

In January, 1856, I returned from Kansas to Vermont, widowed and broken in health, to attend to matters connected with my husband's estate. Prevented by the ruffian blockade of the Missouri from returning as intended, I spent some time in the summer and all of the autumn of 1856 and January, 1857, lecturing upon Kansas, the character and significance of its political involvements, its promise and importance as a free or slave State, and its claims to an efficient support in the interest of freedom. In September, being appealed to by the "Kansas National Aid Committee," at the instance of Horace Greeley, I engaged for two months in a canvass of Western New York, lecturing and procuring the appointment of committees of women to collect supplies for the suffering people of Kansas; my two oldest sons, C. H. and A. O. Carpenter being among its armed defenders, the latter having been wounded in the fight between the invaders under Captain Pate and the forces under John Brown and Captain S. Shores, at Black Jack.

Between May, 1856, and February, 1857 (not counting my engagement with the Aid Committee), I gave some fifty Kansas lectures in the States of Vermont, New Hampshire, Massachusetts, Connecticut, Pennsylvania, and New York, followed occasionally by one or two lectures on the legal and political disabilities of women; receiving more invitations on both subjects than I could possibly fill.

My experiences in these semi-political labors were often racy, never unsatisfactory. In a public conveyance one day, an honest old Pennsylvania farmer asked if I was " the lady who made an appointment to speak in his place on Kansas, and did not come ? " I replied that I had filled all the appointments made for me with my knowledge ; that I made a point of keeping my promises. " I believe you, ma'am," said he. " I suspicioned then it was jest a republican trick. You see, ma'am, our folks all are dimocrats and wouldn't turn out to hear the republican speakers; so they appointed a meeting for *you* and everybody turned out, for we'd hearn of your lectures. But instid of you, General D—— and Lawyer C—— came, and we were mad enough. I was madder, 'cause I'd opened my house, seein' as it was the largest and most convenient in the neighborhood."

Occasionally I stumbled on a loose segment of woman's sphere, even among the friends of " free Kansas." In a populous Vermont village, at a meeting called for the purpose, a committee was appointed to invite me to speak, composed of the two clergymen of the village and Judge S——. Reverend W—— excused himself from the service on the ground of " conscientious scruples as to the propriety of women speaking in public." Judge S——, a man who for a quarter of a century had, by a racy combination of wit and logic, maintained his ground against the foes of temperance and freedom, with inimitable gravity thanked the audience for the honor conferred on him ; adding, " I have no conscientious scruples about getting desirable information wherever I can find it."

In Sinclairville, Chautauque County, New York, where I arrived late, in consequence of a railroad accident, I found a crowded church. A gentleman introduced to me as " Mr. Bull " was sitting at a table in the extreme front corner of the spacious platform, recording the names and advance payments of a class in music, which, as I had been told outside, was being organized by a gentleman who had arrived with the news of my probable detention.

During the next half hour gentlemen rose at three several times and requested Mr. B—— to " postpone the class business till the close of the lecture: that people had come from a distance to hear the lecture, and were anxious to return home, the night being dark and rainy." " I will be through soon. I like to finish a thing when I begin." " There'll be time enough," were the several replies, given in a tone and with an emphasis that suggested to my mind a doubt of the speaker's sympathy with my subject. When the clock pointed to eight, I quietly took my seat in the desk and was smoothing my page of notes when there fell on my astonished ear—" I was about to introduce the lady speaker, but she has suddenly disappeared." Stepping forward, I said, " Excuse me, sir; as the hour is very late I took my place to be in readiness when you should be through with your class." " Madam, you will speak on this platform." " I noticed, sir, that I could not see my audience from the platform, also that the desk was lighted for me." " Madam, you can't speak in that pulpit!" " This is very strange. Will you give me your reasons?" " It's none of your business!" " Indeed, sir, I do not understand it. Will you give me your authority?" " It's my pulpit, and if you speak in this house to-night you speak from this platform!" " Excuse me, sir; I mistook you for the music-teacher, who, as I was told, was organizing a class in music." And stepping quickly to the platform to restore the equanimity of the house, I remarked, as indicating my position, that my self-respect admonished me to be the lady always, no matter how ungentlemanly the treatment I might receive; that the cause of humanity, the cause of suffering Kansas was above all personal considerations, and proceeded with my lecture.

At the close, Mr. B—— arose and said: " I owe this audience an apology for my ungentlemanly language to Mrs. Nichols. I am aware that I shall get into the public prints, and I wish to set myself right." A gentleman in the audience rose and moved, " that we excuse the Rev. R. B—— for his ungentlemanly language to Mrs. Nichols to-night, on the score of his ignorance." The motion was seconded with emphasis by a man of venerable presence.

" Friends," I appealed, " this is a personal matter; it gives me no concern. It will affect neither me nor my work. Please name suitable women for the committee of relief which I am here to ask." Business being concluded, I turned to Mr. B——, who was shut in with me by a press of sympathizing friends, and expressed my regret, that he should have said anything to place him under the necessity of apologizing, adding, " but I hope in future you will remember the words of Solomon : ' Greater is he that controlleth his own spirit, than he that taketh a city.' Good-night, sir." I learned that a few months before he had prevented his people from inviting Antoinette Brown to speak to them on Temperance, by declaring that " he would never set his foot in a pulpit that had been occupied by a woman." When three weeks later I heard of his dismissal from his charge in S——, I could appreciate the remark of his brother clergyman in a neighboring town, to whom I related the incident, that " Brother B—— is rather given to hooking with those horns of his, but he's in hot water now."

In the winter and spring of 1856, I had, by invitation of its editor, written a series of articles on the subject of woman's legal disabilities, preparatory to a plea for political equality, for the columns of the Kansas *Herald of Freedom*, the last number of which went down with the "*form*" and press of the office to the bottom of the Kansas river, when the Border ruffians sacked Lawrence in 1856.

In March, 1857, I again returned to Kansas, and with my daughter and youngest son, made a permanent home in Wyandotte County.

The Constitution was adopted in November, 1859, by popular vote. In January, 1860, Kansas having been admitted to the Union, the first State Legislature met at Topeka, the capital of the new State. I attended its sessions, as I had those of the Convention, and addressed both in behalf of justice for the women of the State, as delegate of the Kansas Woman's Rights Association. This Association was formed in the spring of 1859 with special reference to the Convention which had already been called to meet in the July following, in the city of Wyandotte.

The Association—if I recollect aright—numbered some twenty-five earnest men and women of the John Brown type, living in Moneka, Linn County ; John O. Wattles, President ; Susan Wattles, Secretary. Wendell Phillips, treasurer of the Francis Jackson Woman's Rights Fund, guaranteed payment of expenses, and the Association sent me, with limited hopes and unstinted blessings, to canvass the principal settlements in the Territory, obtain names to petitions and represent them—if allowed by courtesy of the Convention—in behalf of equal civil and political rights for the women of the State to be organized. I was appealed to as the only woman in the Territory who had experience and could take the field, which was I believe true.

We had no material for Conventions, and the population was so sparse, distances so great, and means of conveyance and communication so slow and uncertain, that I felt sure an attempt at Conventions would be disastrous, only betraying the weakness of our reserves, for I must have done most, if not all the speaking.

It was the policy of the Republicans to " keep shady," as a party. John Wattles came to Wyandotte before I addressed the Convention, counseled with members, and reported to me that " I didn't need him, that it was better that no man appear in it."

After spending some four weeks in the field, I went to the Convention, and with a very dear friend, Mrs. Lucy B. Armstrong, of Wyandotte, was given a permanent seat beside the chaplain, Rev. Mr. Davis, Presiding Elder of the Methodist Episcopal Church of the District, which I occupied till the adjournment of the Convention, laboring to develop an active and corresponding interest in outsiders as well as members, until my petitions had been acted upon and the provisions finally passed ; purposely late in the session.

Having at the commencement, only two known friends of our cause among the delegates to rely upon for its advocacy, against the compact opposition of the sixteen Democratic members, and the bitter prejudices of several of the strongest Republicans, including the first Chief Justice of the new State and its present unreconstructed Senator Ingalls, an early report upon our petitions would have been utter defeat. Persistent " button-holing " of the delegates, any " unwomanly obtrusiveness " of manners, a vague apprehension of which, at that period of our movement, was associated in the minds of even good men and women, with the advocacy of the cause, was the " big-'fraid " followed by more than one " little 'fraid," that made my course one of anxiety, less only than my faith in the ultimate adoption of the provisions named.

Of political suffrage I had, as I confidentially told my friends of the Association, no hope, and for the very reason given me later by members of the Convention who consented to school suffrage; viz : " even if endorsed by popular vote, such a provision would probably defeat admission to the Union." None the less, however, was the necessity for disarming the prejudices and impressing upon delegates and citizens the justice of the demand for political enfranchisement

Fortunately, the hospitable tea-table of Mrs. Armstrong, with whom I was domiciled for the session, offered abundant womanly opportunity for conference and discussion with delegates; and in the homes of leading citizens I met a hearty sympathy which I can never forget.

During a recess of the Convention, a friendly member introduced me to Governor Medary, as " the lady who, by vote of the Convention, will speak here this evening in behalf of equal Constitutional rights for the women of Kansas." " But, Mrs. Nichols, you would not have women go down into the muddy pool of politics ? " asked the Governor. " Even so, Governor, I admit that you know best how muddy that pool is, but you remember the Bethesda of old ; how the angel had to go in and trouble the waters before the sick could be healed. So I would have the angels trouble this muddy pool that it may be well with the people ; for you know, Governor Medary, that this people is very sick. But here is a petition to which I am adding names as I find opportunity ; will you place your name on the roll of honor ? " " Not now, Madam, not now. I will *sign the bill.*" And the Governor, quite unconscious of his mistake, with a smile and a bow, hurried away amid the good-natured raillery of the little circle that had gathered around us. But it was Governor Robinson, the life-long friend of woman and a free humanity, that had the pleasure of " signing the bills."

In compliance with the earnest request of delegates, supported by the action of the Association, I labored from the adjournment of the Convention till the vote on the adoption of the Constitution, to " remove the prejudices "—as the delegates expressed it—" of their constituents, against the Woman's Rights provisions " of that document. The death of Mr. Wattles on the eve of the campaign sent me alone into the lecture field. For with the exception of Hon. Charles Robinson, our first State Governor, and always an outspoken friend of our cause, the politicians in the field either ignored or ridiculed the idea of women being entitled under the school provision to vote.

At Bloomington, when I had presented its merits in contrast with existing legal provisions, a venerable man in the audience rose and remarked that the Hon. James H. Lane, in addressing them a few days before, denied that the provision regarding Common Schools meant anything more than equal educational privileges, and that the Courts would so decide. That it would never do to allow women to vote, for only vile women would go to the polls. And now, added the old gentleman, " I would like to hear what Mrs. Nichols has to say on this point?" Taking counsel only of my indignation, I replied: "Mrs. Nichols has to say, that vile men who seek out vile women elsewhere, may better meet them at the polls under the eyes of good men and good women:" and dropped into my seat 'mid a perfect storm of applause, in which women joined as heartily as men.

Policy restrained the few Republican members who had voted against the provisions* from open opposition, and the more that everywhere Democrats, whom I appealed to as "friends in political disguise," treated me with marked courtesy; often contributing to my expenses. One such remarked, "There, Mrs. Nichols, is a Democratic half-dollar; I like your Woman's Rights."

At Troy, Don. Co., sitting behind the closed shutters of an open window, I heard outside a debate between Republicans and Democrats One of the latter, an ex-Secretary of the Territory, at one time acting Governor, and a member of the Constitutional Convention, who had dwelt much on the superior prerogatives of the Anglo-Saxon race, was saying, "You go for political equality with the negro; we Democrats won't stand that, it would demoralize the white man." On my way to lecture in the evening, a friend forewarned me that the ex-Secretary, with two or three of his political stripe, had engaged a shrewd Democratic lawyer, by getting him half drunk, to reply to me. So when in my concluding appeal I turned as usual to the Democrats, I narrated the above incident and bowed smilingly to the ex-Secretary, with whom I was acquainted, and said, "Gentlemen who turn up their 'Anglo-Saxon' noses at the idea of 'political equality with the negro,' as demoralizing to the white man, forget that in all these years the white woman has been 'on a political equality with the negro'; they forget, that in keeping their own mothers, wives and daughters in the negro pew, to save them from demoralization by political equality with the white man, they are paying themselves a sorry compliment." The drunken lawyer was quietly hustled out by his friends, the Democrats themselves joining the audience in expressions of respect at the close of my lecture. But

* The head and front of the opposition was Judge Kingman, Chairman of the Judiciary Committee, to which, with the Committee on Elections, my petition was referred. He wrote the Report against granting our demand, and of those who signed it all but (Gen.) Blunt and himself were Democrats. The report was adopted by a solid vote of the Democrats (16), and enough Republicans to make a majority. Thirty-six Republicans and 16 Democrats comprised the whole delegation. If my memory is not at fault, 27 Republicans voted in caucus for the provisions which were ultimately carried in our behalf, which was a majority of the whole Convention. In caucus a majority were in favor of political rights; but only a minority, from conviction that Woman Suffrage would prevent admission to the Union, would vote it in Convention.

Clarina I. Howard Nichols

these from hundreds of telling incidents must suffice to initiate you in the spirit of that ever memorable campaign.

In 1854, when I was about leaving Vermont for Kansas, an earnest friend of our cause protested that I was " going to bury myself in Kansas, just as I had won an influence and awakened a public sentiment that assured the success of our demand for equal rights." I replied that it was a thousand times more difficult to procure the repeal of unjust laws in an old State, than the adoption of just laws in the organization of a new State. That I could accomplish more for woman, even the women of the old States, and with less effort, in the new State of Kansas, than I could in conservative old Vermont, whose prejudices were so much stronger than its convictions, that justice to women must stand a criminal trial in every Court of the State to win, and then pay the costs.

My husband went to Kansas for a milder climate ; my sons to make homes under conditions better suited than the old States to their tastes and means. I went to work for a Government of " equality, liberty, fraternity," in the State to be.

I had learned from my experience with the legal fraternity, that as a profession they were dead-weights on our demands, and the reason why. When pressed to logical conclusions, which they were always quick to see, and in fair proportion to admit, were in our favor, they almost invariably retreated under the plea that the reforms we asked " being fundamental, would destroy the harmony of the statutes ! " And I had come to the conclusion that it would cost more time and effort to disrupt the woman's " disabilities " attachment from the legal and political harmonicons of the old States, than it would to secure vantage ground for legal and political equality in the new. I believed then and believe now that Woman Suffrage would have received a majority vote in Kansas if it could have been submitted unembarrassed by the possibility of its being made a pretext for keeping Kansas out of the Union. And but for Judge Kingman, I believe it would have received the vote of a majority in convention. He played upon the old harmonicon, " organic law," and " the harmony of the statutes."

My pleas before the Constitutional Convention and the people, were for equal legal and political rights for women. In detail I asked :

1st. Equal educational rights and privileges in all the schools and institutions of learning fostered or controlled by the State.

2d. An equal right in all matters pertaining to the organization and conduct of the Common Schools.

13

3d. Recognition of the mother's equal right with the father to the control and custody of their mutual offspring.

4th. Protection in person, property, and earnings for married women and widows the same as for men.

The first three were fully granted. In the final reading, Kingman changed the wording of the fourth, so as to leave the Legislature a chance to preserve the infamous common law right to personal services. There were too many old lawyers in the Convention. The Democracy had four or five who pulled with Kingman, or he with them against us. Not a Democrat put his name to the Constitution when adopted.

The debate published in the Wyandotte *Gazette* of July 13, 1859, on granting Mrs. Nichols a hearing in the Constitutional Convention, and the Committee's report on the Woman's Petition, furnishes a page of history of which some of the actors, at least, will have no reason to read with special pride.

REPORT OF JUDICIARY FRANCHISE COMMITTEE ON WOMAN SUFFRAGE PETITIONS.

The Committee on the Judiciary, to whom in connection with the Committee on Franchise was referred the petition of sundry citizens of Kansas, " protesting against any constitutional distinctions based on difference of sex," have had the same under consideration, and beg leave to make the following report :

Your Committee concede the point in the petition upon which the right is claimed, that " the women of the State have individually an evident common interest with its men in the protection of life, liberty, property, and intellectual culture, and are not disposed to deny, that sex involves greater and more complex responsibilities, but the Committee are compelled to dissent from conclusion of petition; they think the rights of women are safe in present hands. The proof that they are so is found in the growing disposition on the part of different Legislatures to extend and protect their rights of property, and in the enlightened and progressive spirit of the age which acts gently, but efficiently upon the legislation of the day. Such rights as are natural are now enjoyed as fully by women as men. Such rights and duties as are merely political they should be relieved from, that they may have more time to attend to those greater and more complicated responsibilities which petitioners claim, and which your Committee admit devolves upon woman.

All of which is respectfully submitted.

SAM. A. KINGMAN, GEO. H. LILLIE, P. S. PARKS, JOHN P. SLOUGH, SAM. A. STINSON, JOHN F. BURNS, J. D. GREER, G. BLUNT, BEN. WRIGLEY.

MISSOURI.

In the spring of 1858, having arranged my home affairs, I set about the prosecution of a plan for widening the area of woman's work and influence on the Missouri border. Separated only by the

steam-plowed river from my Kansas home, Missouri towns and hamlets lay invitingly before me. For more than three years I had held
my opportunity in reserve. The time to improve it seemed to have
come.

When our company landed at Kansas City, October, 1854, members of a Missouri delegation opposed to the Free State emigration
to that Territory met us. More than half the company that preceded ours had been turned back by their representations without a
look at the territory. As our boat touched the landing, Col. Scott,
of St. Joseph, stepped on board, and commenced questioning Hon.
E. M. Thurston, of Maine, who, as Committee of Arrangements for
the transfer of the company's baggage, excused himself, and turning
to me, added : " Here, sir, is a lady who can give you the information you desire—Mrs. Nichols, editor of the *Windham County
Democrat*." In accepting the introduction, I caught the surprised
and quizzical survey of a pair of keen, black eyes, culminating in
an unmistakable expression of humorous anticipation ; and, certain
that my interviewer was intelligent and a gentleman, I resolved to
follow his lead in kind. " Madam," he inquired, " can you tell me
where all these people are from, and where they are going ? " They
are from the New England States, and are going to Kansas. " And
what are they going to do in Kansas ? " Make homes and surround
themselves with the institutions, social and political, to which they
are accustomed. " But, madam, they can't make homes on the Kansas prairies with free labor ; it is impossible ! "

Why, sir, our ancestors felled the primitive forests and cleared
the ground to grow their bread, but Kansas prairies are ready for
the plow ; their rank grasses invite the flocks and herds. Do you
know what a country we come from ? did you never hear how in
New Hampshire and Vermont the sheeps' noses have to be sharpened, so that they can pluck the spires of grass from between the
rocks ?

With a humorous, give-it-up sort of laugh, he remarked, abruptly :
" You are an editor ; do you ever lecture ? " Sometimes I do.
" On what subjects ? " Education, Temperance, Woman's Rights—
" Oh, woman's rights ! Will you go to St. Joseph and lecture on
woman's rights ? Our people are all anxious to hear on that subject." Why, sir, I am an Abolitionist, and they would tar and
feather me ! " You don't say anything about slavery in your woman's rights' lectures, do you ? " No, sir ; I never mix things.

After a sharp, but good natured tilt on the slavery question, the
Colonel returned to the lecture, about which he was so evidently in

earnest—guaranteeing "a fine audience, courteous treatment, and ample compensation"; that I gave a promise to visit St. Joseph on my return if there should be time before the closing of navigation, a promise I was prevented from fulfilling. And now after three years, in which the emigrants had made homes and secured them against the aggressions of the slave power, I wrote him that if the people of St. Joseph still wished to hear, and it pleased him to renew his guarantees of aid and protection, I was at leisure to lecture on woman's rights. His reply was prompt; his assurances hearty. I had "only to name the time," and I would find everything in readiness. That the truce-like courtesy of the compact between us may be appreciated, I copy a postscript appended to his letter and a postscript in reply added to my note of appointment; with the explanation, that in our Kansas City interview, the Colonel had declared the negro incapable of education, and that emancipation would result in amalgamation.

Postscript No. 1.—Have you tried your experiment of education on any little nigger yet?   J. S.

Postscript No. 2.—No, I have not tried my educational experiment, for the reason that the horrid amalgamationists preceded us, and so bleached the "niggers" that I have not been able to find a pure-blood specimen.   C. I. H. N.

The subject of slavery was not again mentioned between us. And when we shook hands in the cabin of the steamer at parting, he remarked, with a manly frankness in grateful contrast with the covert contempt felt, rather than expressed, in his previous courtesies, that he thought it proper I should know, that my audiences, composed of the most intelligent and respectable people of St. Joseph, were pleased with my lectures. One of its most eminent citizens had said to him, that he "had not thought of the subject in the light presented, but he really could see no objection to women voting."

Only one lecture had been proposed. By a vote of my audience I gave a second, and had reason to feel that I had effectually broken ground in Missouri; that I had not only won a respectful consideration for woman's cause and its advocacy, but improved my opportunity to vindicate New England training, in face of Southern prejudices. One little episode, as rich in its significance, as in the inspiration it communicated, will serve to round out my St. Joseph experience.

In introducing me to my audience, the Colonel—remembering, perhaps, that I did not "mix things," or feeling that he might trust my consciousness of being cornered on the slavery question—re-marked in a vein of courteously concealed irony : " It looks very strange to us for a lady to speak in public, but we must remember that in the section of country from which this lady comes, the necessity of self-support bears equally upon women, and crowds them out of domestic life into vocations more congenial to the sterner sex. Happily our domestic institutions, by relieving women of the necessity to labor, protect them in the sacred privacy of home."

In his ignorance of the subject, my friend had unwittingly resined the bow. In bringing his "domestic institution" to the front, he had so "mixed things," that in my showing of the legal disabilities of women, of the *no*-right of the white wife and mother to herself, her children, and her earnings, my audience could not fail to appreciate the anomalous character of a " protection " so pathetically suggestive of the legal level of the slave woman, to which man, in his greed of wealth and power, had "crowded" both.

Some months later, at the breakfast-table of a Missouri River steamer, a gentleman of St. Joseph recognized me, and reported my lectures to ex-Governor Rollins, who was also on board, and asked an introduction. After a long and pleasant discussion with the Governor, who entered at once upon the subject, in its legal, political, and educational aspects, it was agreed that I should lecture at my earliest convenience in several of the principal towns of the State, the capital included ; the Governor himself proposing to com-municate with influential citizens to make the necessary arrange-ments.

An early compliance with my promise was prevented by the Kan-sas movement for a constitutional convention ; my connection with which left me no leisure till late in the autumn, when I commenced my proposed lecture course in Missouri by an appointment at West-port, by arrangement of a gentleman of that place, whose acquaint-ance I had made in my Kansas campaign. Arrived at the Westport hotel, where my entertainment had been bespoken, I was taken by the landlady to her own cosy sitting-room, and made pleasantly at home. Later in the day I became aware of considerable excitement in the bar-room and street of the town. The landlord held several hurried consultations with his wife in the ante-room. My dinner was served in the private room, it " being more pleasant," my hostess said, " than eating at the public table with a lot of strange men." An hour after time, the gentleman who was to call for myself and the landlady, announced an assembly of a " dozen rude boys," and that in consequence of the news of John Brown's raid at Harper's Ferry (of which I had not before heard), the excitement was such that he could not persuade the ladies to come out. With some hesitation he added, that it "had even been suggested that I might be an emissary or accomplice, in what was suspected to be a general and preconcerted abolition movement." This explained the questionings of my hostess, and the provision against any possible rudeness which I might have received from the "strange men" at the public table. Thus ended my projected campaign in Missouri. For every city and hamlet in the State was so haunted by the marching spirit of the Kansas hero, that to have suggested a lecture on any subject from a known Abolitionist, would have ruined the political prospects of even an ex-Governor.

Three years later, assisted by a former resident of Kansas, I lectured to a very small, but respectful audience in Kansas City ; and in the spring of 1867 was invited by a committee of ladies to lecture at a Fair of the Congregational Society of that city, with accompanying assurances from the pastor and his wife, of their confidence in the salutary influence of such a lecture, on a community which had been recently treated to an unfriendly presentation of the woman's rights movement and its advocates. I was too ill at the time to leave home, but the difference between my anxious efforts three years before to be heard, and this more than cordial assurance of a waiting audience, was a happy tonic. It was from persons who knew me only through my advocacy of woman's equality, and evidenced the progress of our cause.

In December, 1854, on my return from Kansas to Vermont, I spent several days in St. Louis, in the pleasant family of my friend, Mrs. Frances D. Gage, who, very much to my regret, was away in Illinois. The Judge having recently removed to the city, the family were comparatively strangers; Abolitionists in a pro-slavery community. Mrs. Gage, I think, had broken ground for temperance, but they could tell me of no friends to woman's rights. Rev. Mr. Elliot was not then one of us, as I learned through a son of Mrs. Gage, who called on him in my behalf for the use of his lecture-room. I felt instinctively that, unfettered by home and business interests, I was less constrained than my friend, and resolved, if possible, to win a hearing for woman. Having secured a hall, I called at the business office of a gentleman of wealth and high social position—a slave-holder and opposed to free Kansas, with whom I had formed a speaking acquaintance in Brattleboro'—and procured from him a voucher for my respectability. Armed with this I called on the editors of the *Republican* (pro-slavery), and secured a paid notice of my lecture. The editor of the *Democrat*, who had an interest in free Kansas, and was glad of news items from its immigrants, received me cordially, and gave the "lady lecturer" a handsome "personal," though he had no more interest in my subject than either of the other gentlemen, and gave me little encouragement of an audience. Nevertheless, when the evening came, I met an audience intelligent and respectful, and larger than I had ventured to expect, but not numerous enough to warrant the venture of a second lecture in the expensive hall, which from the refusal of church lecture-rooms, I had been obliged to occupy. But here, as often before and after, a good Providence interposed. Rev. Mr. Weaver, Universalist, claimed recognition as "a reader in his boyhood of Mrs. Nichols' paper"—his father was a patron of the *Windham County Democrat*—and tendered the use of his church for further lectures. I had found a friend of the cause. The result was a full house, and hearty appeals for "more."

As isolated, historical facts, how very trivial all these "reminiscences" appear! How egotistical the pen that presumes upon anything like a popular interest in their perusal! But to the social and political reformer, as to the Kanes and Livingstons, trifles teach the relations of things, and indicate the methods and courses of action that result in world-wide good or evil. Seeds carried by the winds and waves plant forests and beautify the waste places of the earth. Truths that flowed from the silent nib of my pen in Vermont, had been garnered in a boy's sympathies to yield me a man's welcome and aid in St. Louis. How clear the lesson, that for seed-sowing, all seasons belong to God's truth!

The autumn and winter of 1860–61 I spent in Wisconsin and Ohio; in Wisconsin, visiting friends and lecturing. In Ohio, Mrs. Frances D. Gage, Mrs. Hannah Tracy Cutler, and myself were employed under direction of Mrs. Elizabeth Jones, of Salem, to canvass the State, lecturing and procuring names to petitions to the Legislature for equal legal and political rights for the women of the State. The time chosen for this work was inopportune for immediate success—the opening scenes of the rebellion alike absorbing the attention of the people and their Legislature. Women in goodly numbers came out to hear, but men of all classes waited in the streets, or congregated in public places to hear the news and discuss the political situation.

From December, 1863, to March, 1866, I was in Washington, D. C., writing in the Military or Revenue Departments, or occupying the position of Matron in the Home for Colored Orphans, which had been opened in the second year of the rebellion, by the help of the Government and the untiring energy of a few noble women intent on saving the helpless waifs of slavery cast by thousands upon the bare sands of military freedom.

In the autumn of 1867, the Legislature of Kansas having submitted to the voters of the State a woman suffrage amendment to its Constitution, I gave some four weeks to the canvass, which was engaged in by some of the ablest friends of the cause from other States, among them Lucy Stone, Rev. Olympia Brown, Elizabeth Cady Stanton, and Susan B. Anthony. In our own State, among others, Governor Robinson, John Ritchie, and S. N. Wood of the old Free State Guard, rallied to the work. With the canvass of Atchison and Jefferson Counties, and a few lectures in Douglass, Shawnee, and Osage Counties, I retired from a field overlaid with happy reminders of past trials merged in present blessings. The work was in competent hands, but the time was ill-chosen on account of the political complications with negro suffrage, and failure was the result.

Since December, 1871, my home has been in California, where family cares and the infirmities of age limit my efforts for a freer and a nobler humanity to the pen. Trusting that love of God and man will ever point it with truth and justice, I close this *exposé* of my public life.

CHAPTER VIII.

MASSACHUSETTS.

Women in the Revolution—Anti-Tea Leagues—Phillis Wheatley—Mistress Anne Hutchinson—Heroines in the Slavery Conflict—Women Voting under the Colonial Charter—Mary Upton Ferrin Petitions the Legislature in 1848—Woman's Rights Conventions in 1850, '51—Letter of Harriet Martineau from England—Letter of Jeannie Deroine from a Prison Cell in Paris—Editorial from *The Christian Inquirer*—*The Una*, edited by Paulina Wright Davis—Constitutional Convention in 1853—Before the Legislature in 1857—Harriet K. Hunt's Protest against Taxation—Lucy Stone's Protest against the Marriage Laws—Boston Conventions—Theodore Parker on Woman's Position.

DURING the Revolutionary period, the country was largely indebted to the women of Massachusetts. Their patriotism was not only shown in the political plans of Mercy Otis Warren,* and the sagacious counsels of Abigail Smith Adams, but by the action of many other women whose names history has not preserved. It was a woman who sent Paul Revere on his famous ride from Boston to Concord, on the night of April 18, 1775, to warn the inhabitants of the expected invasion of the British on the morrow. The church bells pealing far and near on the midnight air, roused tired sleepers hurriedly to arm themselves against the invaders of their homes.

During the war two women of Concord dressed in men's clothing, captured a spy bearing papers which proved of the utmost importance to the patriot forces.

---

* Mercy Otis, born at Barnstable, Mass., September 25, 1728, married James Warren, about 1754. Reference has been made to her correspondence with the eminent men of the Revolution. Aside from her patriotism, Mrs. Warren was a woman of high literary ability. She wrote several dramatic and satirical works in 1773, against the royalists, which, with two tragedies, were included in a volume of Dramatic and Miscellaneous Poems, published in 1790. She also wrote "A History of the Rise, Progress, and Termination of the American Revolution, interspersed with Biographical, Political, and Moral Observations," in three volumes, published in Boston, 1805. Mrs. Warren lived quite into the present century, dying October 19, 1814.

Mrs. Ellet, "Queens of Society," says: "In point of influence, Mercy Warren was the most remarkable woman who lived in the days of the American Revolution."

Rochefoucauld, "Tour in the United States," says: "Seldom has a woman in any age acquired such ascendency by the mere force of a powerful intellect, and her influence continued through her life."

Generals Lee and Gates were among her correspondents; Knox wrote: "I should be happy to receive your counsels from time to time." Mrs. Washington was frequently entertained by Mrs. Warren, at one time when the former was in Massachusetts with the General, Mrs. Warren going with her chariot to headquarters at Cambridge for her.

(201)

During these early days, the women of various Colonies—Virginia, New York, Rhode Island, Massachusetts—formed Anti-Tea Leagues. In Providence, R. I., young ladies took the initiative; twenty-nine daughters of prominent families, meeting under the shade of the sycamore trees at Roger Williams' spring, there resolving to drink no more tea until the duty upon it was repealed. The name of one of these young ladies, Miss Coddington, has been preserved, to whose house they all adjourned to partake of a frugal repast; hyperion* taking the place of the hated bohea. In Newport, at a gathering of ladies, where both hyperion and bohea were offered, every lady present refused the hated bohea, emblem of political slavery. In Boston, early in 1769, the matrons of three hundred families bound themselves to use no more tea until the tax upon it was taken off. The young ladies also entered into a similar covenant, declaring they took this step, not from personal motives, but from a sense of patriotism and a regard for posterity.† Liberty, as alone making life of value, looked as sweet to them as to their fathers. The Women's Anti-Tea Leagues of Boston were formed nearly five years previous to the historic "Boston Tea Party," when men disguised as Indians, threw the East India Company's tea overboard, and six years before the declaration of war.

American historians ignoring woman after man's usual custom, have neglected to mention the fact that every paper in Boston was suspended during its invasion by the British, except the chief rebel newspapers of New England, *The Massachusetts Gazette* and *North Boston News-Letter*, owned and edited by a woman, Margaret Draper.

They make small note of Women's Anti-Tea Leagues, and the many instances of their heroism during the Revolutionary period, equaling, as they did, any deeds of self-sacrifice and bravery that man himself can boast.

The men of Boston, in 1773, could with little loss to themselves, throw overboard a cargo of foreign tea, well knowing that for the last five years this drink had not been allowed in their houses by the women of their own families. Their reputation for patriotism was

---

* Dried leaves of the raspberry.—LOSSING.

† Lossing, "Field-Book of the Revolution," says: "On February 9, 1769, the Mistresses of three hundred families met and formed a league, and upon the second day the young ladies assembled in great numbers, signing the following covenant: 'We, the daughters of those patriots who have, and do now, appear for public interest, and in proper regard for their posterity as such, do, with pleasure, engage with them in denying ourselves the drink of foreign tea, in hopes to frustrate a plan which tends to deprive a whole country of all that is valuable in life.'"

thus cheaply earned in destroying what did not belong to them and what was of no use to them. Their wives, daughters, mothers, and sisters drank raspberry, sage, and birch, lest by the use of foreign tea they should help rivet the chains of oppression upon their country. Why should not the American Revolution have been successful, when women so nobly sustained republican principles, taking the initiative in self-sacrifice and pointing the path to man by patriotic example.

In Massachusetts, as in other States, were also formed associations known as " Daughters of Liberty."* These organizations did much to fan the nascent flames of freedom.

The first naval battle of the Revolution was fought at Machias, Maine, then a part of Massachusetts. An insult having been offered its inhabitants, by a vessel in the harbor, the men of the surrounding country joined with them to avenge this indignity to their " Liberty Tree," arming themselves, from scarcity of powder, with scythes, pitchforks, and other implements of peace. At a settlement some twenty miles distant, a quantity of powder was discovered, after the men had left for Machias. What was to be done, was the immediate question. Every able-bodied man had already left, only small boys and men too aged or too infirm for battle having remained at home. Upon that powder reaching them the defeat of the British might depend. In this emergency the heroism of woman was shown. Two young girls, Hannah and Rebecca Weston, volunteered their services. It was no holiday excursion for them, but a trip filled with unseen dangers. The way led through a trackless forest, the route merely indicated by blazed trees. Bears, wolves, and wild-cats were numerous. The distance was impossible to be traversed in a single day; these young girls must spend the night in that dreary wilness. Worse than danger from wild animals, was that to be apprehended from Indians, who might kill them, or capture and bear them away to some distant tribe. But undauntedly they set out on their perilous journey, carrying twenty pounds of powder. They reached Machias in safety, before the attack on the British ship, finding their powder a most welcome and effective aid in the victory which soon crowned the arms of the Colonists. The heroism of these young girls was far greater than if they had fought in the

---

* Lossing's " Field-Book of the Revolution " states that on the 12th of June, 1769, the " Daughters of Liberty," met at the house of pastor Moorehead, in such numbers that in one afternoon they spun two hundred and ninety skeins of fine yarn, which they presented to him. After supper they were joined by many " Sons of Liberty," who united with the " Daughters " in patriotic songs.

ranks, surrounded by companions, 'mid the accompaniments of beating drums, waving flags, and all the paraphernalia of war.

In the war of 1812 two young girls of Scituate, Rebecca and
Abigail W. Bates, by their wit and sagacity, prevented the landing
of the enemy at this point.* Congress, during its session of 1880,
nearly seventy years afterward, granted them pensions, just as from
extreme age they were about to drop into the grave.

Though it is not considered important to celebrate the virtues of
the Pilgrim Mothers in gala days, grand dinners, toasts, and speeches,
yet a little retrospection would enable us to exhume from the past,
many of their achievements worth recording. More facts than we
have space to reproduce, testify to the heroism, religious zeal, and literary industry of the women who helped to build up the early civilization of New England. Their writings, for some presumed on authorship, are quaint and cumbrous; but in those days, when few men
published books, it required marked courage for women to appear in
print at all. They imitated the style popular among men, and received much attention for their literary ability. Charles T. Cong-
don, as the result of his explorations through old book-stores, has
brought to light some of these early writers.

In 1630, Mrs. Anne Bradstreet, known as quite a pretentious
writer, came to Boston with her husband, Simon Bradstreet, Governor of Massachusetts. Her first work was entitled "The Tenth
Muse lately sprung up in America." The first edition was published in London in 1650, and the first Boston edition was published
in 1678. If Mrs. Bradstreet loved praise, she was fortunate in her
time and position. It would have been in bad taste, as it would
have been bad policy, not to eulogize the poems of the Governor's
wife. She was frequently complimented in verse as bad as her own.
Her next great epic was entitled "A Complete Discourse and Description of the Four Elements, Constitutions, Ages of Man, Seasons
of the Year, together with an exact epitome of the Four Monarchies,
viz: the Assyrian, Persian, Grecian, and Roman." "Glad as we
were," says the owner, "to obtain this book at a considerable price,

---

* These girls, then only about twelve and fourteen years of age, saw the enemy making preparations to land at an isolated point. No men were near to defend the place,
or to whom warning could be given. A bright thought struck one of the girls. Accustomed to play the drum, she well knew how to beat the call to arms, and no sooner had
this thought entered her mind, than she began a tattoo, calling her sister to take the fife
as an accompaniment. Together they marched toward the shore, careful to keep hidden
by the rocks, among whose intricacies they wound back and forth, the sound of their instruments falling upon the enemy's ears, now far, now near, as though a force of many
hundred men was marching down upon them, and thoroughly frightened, they beat a
retreat to their boats.

we are still gladder of the privilege of closing it." Although this lady had eight children, about whom she wrote some amusing rhymes, she found time in the wilds of America to perpetuate also these ponderous-titled poems.

Phillis Wheatly, a colored girl, also wrote poetry in Colonial Boston, years before our Declaration of Independence startled the world. She was brought from Africa, and sold in the slave market of Boston, when only six years old. Mr. Sparks, the biographer of Washington, thinks "that the poems contained in her published volume, exhibit the most favorable evidence on record, of the capacity of the African intellect for improvement." When the Rev. George Whitefield died, at Newburyport, Mass., in 1770, the same writer from whom we quote these facts, says: "It was quite natural, his demise being much talked of in religious families, that our sable Phillis should burst into monody. That expression of grief I have before me. Of the most rhetorical preacher of his age, it is not inspiring to read:

> "He prayed that grac in every heart might dwell.
> He longed to see A nerica excel."

Phillis married badly, and died at the age of thirty-one, in 1784, utterly impoverished, leaving three little children. Her own copy of her poems is in the library of Harvard College. When she died it was sold for her husband's debts.

In a letter thanking her for an acrostic on himself, General Washington said: "If you should ever come to Cambridge, or near headquarters, I shall be happy to see a person so gifted by the muses, and to whom Nature has been so liberal and beneficent in her dispensations."

Was there ever any story, which had such a hold upon the readers of a generation, as "Charlotte Temple"? It is said 25,000 copies were sold soon after publication—an enormous sale for that day. Mrs. Rowson, who wrote the book, was a daughter of a lieutenant in the Royal Navy; she was an actress in Philadelphia, and afterward kept a school in Boston for young ladies, where she died, in 1824. Her seminary was highly recommended.

Women in the last age naturally drifted into the didactic. They should have the credit of trying always to be useful. They go through so many pages, seeking to give the little people some notion of botany, of natural history, of other branches of human intelligence. There is no book cleverer in its way than Miss Hannah Adams' "History of New England," of which the second edition was published in Boston in 1807. The object of this lady was, as she tells us in the preface, "to impress the minds of young persons with veneration for those eminent men to whom their posterity are so highly indebted." All the tradition is that Miss Adams was a wonderfully learned lady. She is best known by her "History of the Jews." She wrote pretty good English, of which this may be considered a specimen : "Exalted from a feeble state to opulence and independence, the Federal Americans are now recognized as a nation throughout the globe." To a sentence so admirably formed, possibly there is nothing to add.

MISTRESS ANNE HUTCHINSON.

Mistress Anne Hutchinson, founder of the Antinomian party of New England, was a woman who exerted great influence upon the religious and political free thought of those colonies. She was the daughter of an English clergyman, and with her husband, followed Pastor Cotton, to whom she was much attached, to this country in 1634, and was admitted a member of the Boston church, becoming a resident of Massachusetts one hundred and forty years before the Revolutionary war. She was of commanding intellect, and exerted a powerful influence upon the infant colony.

It was a long established custom for the brethren of the Boston church to hold, through the week, frequent public meetings for religious exercises. Women were prohibited from taking part in these meetings, which chafed the free spirit of Mistress Hutchinson, and soon she called meetings of the sisters, where she repeated the sermons of the Lord's day, making comments upon them. Her illustrations of Scripture were so new and striking that the meetings were rendered more interesting to the women than any they had attended. At first the clergy approved, but as the men attracted by the fame of her discourses, crowded into her meetings, they began to perceive danger to their authority ; the church was passing out of their control. Her doctrines, too, were alarming. She taught the indwelling of the Holy Spirit in each believer, its inward revelations, and that the conscious judgment of the mind should be the paramount authority. She was the first woman in America to demand the right of individual judgment upon religious questions. Her influence was very great, yet she was not destined to escape the charge of heresy.

The first Synod in America was called upon her account. It convened August 30, 1637, sat three weeks, and proclaimed eighty-two errors extant ; among them the tenets taught by Mistress

Hutchinson. She was called before the church and ordered to retract upon twenty-nine points. The infant colony was shaken by this discussion, which took on a political aspect.* Mistress Hutchinson remained steadfast, and was sustained by many important people, among whom was the young Governor Vane.

Church and State became united in their opposition to Mistress Anne Hutchinson. The fact that she presumed to teach men, was prominently brought up, and in November, 1637, she was arbitrarily tried before the Massachusetts General Court upon a joint charge of sedition and heresy. She was examined for two days by the Governor and prominent members of the clergy. The Boston Church, which knew her worth, sustained her, with the exception of five members, one of them the associate pastor, Wilson. But the country churches and clergy were against her, and she was convicted and sentenced to imprisonment and banishment.

As the winter was very severe, she was allowed to remain in Roxbury until spring, when she joined Roger Williams in Rhode Island, where she helped form a body-politic, democratic in principle, in which no one was "accounted delinquent for doctrine." Mistress Hutchinson thus helped to dissever Church and State, and to found religious freedom in the United States.

After her residence in Rhode Island, four men were sent to reclaim her, but she would not return. Upon the death of her husband she moved, for greater security, to "The Dutch Colony," and died somewhere in the State of New York.

Thus, through the protracted struggle of the American Colonies for religious and political freedom, woman bravely shared the dangers and persecutions of those eventful years. As spy in the enemy's camp; messenger on the battle-field; soldier in disguise; defender of herself and children in the solitude of those primeval forests; imprisoned for heresy; burned, hung, drowned as a witch: what suffering and anxiety has she not endured! what lofty heroism has she not exemplified!

And when the crusade against slavery in our republic was inaugurated in 1830, another Spartan band of women stood ready for the battle, and the storm of that fierce conflict, surpassing in courage, moral heroism, and conscientious devotion to great principles, all

---

* "This dispute infused its spirit into everything. It interfered with the levy of troops for the Pequot war; it influenced the respect shown to the magistrates, the distribution of town lots, the assessment of rates, and at last the continued existence of the two parties was considered inconsistent with the public peace."—Bancroft, "History of the United States."

that woman in any age had done or dared. With reverent lips we mention the names of Sarah and Angelina Grimke, Lydia Maria Child, Maria Weston Chapman, Mary S. Parker, Abby Kelly, whose burning words of rebuke aroused a sleeping nation to a new-born love of liberty. To their brave deeds, pure lives, and glowing eloquence, we pay our tributes of esteem and admiration.

To such as these let South Carolina and Massachusetts build future monuments, not in Quincy granite, or Parian marble, but in more enduring blessing to the people; inviolable homesteads for the laborer; free schools and colleges for boys and girls, both black and white; justice and mercy in the alms-house, jail, prison, and the marts of trade, thus securing equal rights to all.

WOMAN'S EARLY POLITICAL RIGHTS.

In Massachusetts, women voted at an early day. First, under the Old Province Charter, from 1691 to 1780, for all elective officers; second, they voted under the Constitution for all elective officers except the Governor, Council, and Legislature, from 1780 to 1785. The Bill of Rights, adopted with the Constitution of 1780, declared that all men were born free and equal. Upon this, some slaves demanded their freedom, and their masters yielded.[*] Restrictions upon the right of suffrage were very great in this State; church membership alone excluded for thirty years three-fourths of the male inhabitants from the ballot-box.[†]

That women exercised the right of suffrage amid so many restrictions, is very significant of the belief in her right to the ballot, by those early Fathers.[‡]

THE FIRST STEP IN MASSACHUSETTS.

Woman's rights petitions were circulated in Massachusetts as early as 1848. Mary Upton Ferrin, of Salem, in the spring of that year, consulting Samuel Merritt, known as "the honest lawyer of Salem," in regard to the property rights of married women, and the divorce laws, learned that the whole of the wife's personal property belonged to the husband, as also the improvements upon her real estate; and that she could only retain her silver and other small valuables by

---

[*] *Atlantic Monthly*, June, 1871.

[†] In three New England colonies church membership was required for the franchise.—Frothingham, "Rise of the Republic."

[‡] Dr. John Weis, of New York, now an aged gentleman, well remembers his grandmother saying, that at an early day women were allowed to vote in all the New England colonies.

secreting them, or proving them to have been loaned to her. To such deception did the laws of Massachusetts, like those of most States, based on the Old Common Law idea of the wife's subjection to the husband, compel the married woman in case she desired to retain any portion of her own property.

Mrs. Ferrin reported the substance of the above conversation to Mrs. Phebe King,* of Danvers, who at once became deeply interested, saying, " If such are the laws by which women are governed, every woman in the State should sign a petition to have them altered."

" Will you sign one if drawn up ? " queried Mrs. Ferrin.

" Yes," replied Mrs. King, " and I should think every woman would sign such a petition."

As the proper form of petitions was something with which women were then quite unfamiliar, the aid of several gentlemen was asked, among them Hon. D. P. King and Judge John Heartley, but all refused.

Miss Betsy King then suggested that Judge Pitkin † possessed sufficient influence to have the laws amended without the trouble of petitioning the Legislature. Strong in their faith that the enactment of just laws was the business of legislative bodies, these ladies believed they but had to bring injustice to the notice of a law-maker in order to have it done away. Therefore, full of courage and hope, Judge Pitkin was respectfully approached. But, to their infinite astonishment, he replied :

" The law is very well as it is regarding the property of married women. Women are not capable of taking care of their own property ; they never ought to have control of it. There is already a law by which a woman can have her property secured to her."

" But not one woman in fifty knows of the existence of such a law," was the reply.

" They ought to know it ; it is no fault of the law if they don't. I do not think the Legislature will alter the law regarding divorce. If they do, they will make it more stringent than it now is."

Repulsed, but not disheartened, Mrs. Ferrin herself drew up several petitions, circulated them, obtaining many hundred signatures of old and young ; though finding the young more ready to ask for change than those inured to ill-usage and injustice. Many

---

* Mother of the late Daniel P. King, at that time a member of the Massachusetts Legislature, and since then a Representative in Congress.

† Benj. C. Pitkin, of Salem, at that time State Senator.

persons laughed at her; but knowing it to be a righteous work, and deeming laughter healthful to those indulging in it, Mrs. Ferrin continued to circulate her petitions.

They were presented to the Legislature by Rev. John M. Usher, a Universalist minister of Lynn, and member of the lower House. Although too late in the session for action, these petitions form the initiative step for Woman Suffrage in Massachusetts.

Early the next fall, similar petitions were circulated. It was determined to attack the Legislature in such good season, that lateness of time would not again be brought up as an excuse for non-attention to the prayers of women. Mrs. King's interest continued unabated, and through her advice, Mrs. Ferrin prepared an address to accompany the petitions. Hon. Charles W. Upham, minister of the First Unitarian church of Salem, afterward Representative in Congress, was State Senator that year. From him they received much encouragement. "I concur with you in every sentiment," said he, "but please re-write your address, making two of it; one in the form of a memorial to the Legislature, and the other, an address to the Judiciary Committee, to whom your petitions will be referred." These two documents will be found to suggest most of the important demands, afterward made in every State, for a change of laws relating to woman. The fallacy of "sacredness" for these restrictive laws was shown; the rights of humanity as superior to any outside authority, asserted; and justice made the basis of the proposed reformation. The right of woman to trial by a jury of her peers was claimed, followed by the suggestion that woman is capable of making the laws by which she is governed. The memorial excited much attention, and was printed by order of the Legislature, though the possibility of a woman having written it was denied.*

But in 1850, as in 1849, no action was taken, the petitioners having "leave to withdraw." Petitions of a similar character were again circulated throughout Salem and Danvers, in 1850, '51, '52, '53, making six successive years, in each of which the petitioners had "leave to withdraw," as the only reply to their prayers for relief. The Hon. Mr. Upham, however, remained woman's steadfast friend through all this period, and Mrs. Phebe Upton King was as constantly found among the petitioners.

In 1852 the petitions were signed only by ladies over sixty years of age, women of large experience and matured judgment, whose

---

* Hon. Mr. Upham saying: "A great many of the members told me they didn't believe a woman wrote it."

prayers should have received at least respectful consideration from the legislators of the State. We give the appeal accompanying their petition :

GENTLEMEN:—Your petitioners, who are tax-payers and originators of these petitions, are upwards of three-score years; ten of them are past three-score years and ten; three of them three-score and twenty. If length of days, a knowledge of the world and the rights of man and woman entitle them to a respectful hearing, few, if any, have prior or more potent claims, for reason has taught them what individual rights are, experience, what woman and her children suffer for the want of just protection in those, and humanity impels them once more to appear before you, it may be for the last time. Let not their gray hairs go down in sorrow to the grave for the want of this justice in your power to extend, as have several of their number whose names are no longer to be found with theirs, whose voices can plead never more in behalf of your own children and those of your constituents.

In 1853 a petition* bearing only Mrs. King's name was presented. In 1854 the political organization called the "Know Nothings" came into power, and although no petition was presented, a bill securing the control of their own property to all women married subsequent to the passage of the law, was passed. The power to make a will without the husband's consent, was also secured to wives, though not permitted to thus will more than one-half of their personal property. This law also gave to married women having no children, whose husbands should die without a will, five thousand dollars, and one-half of the remainder of the husband's property. The following year the Divorce Law† was amended, and shortly thereafter two old ladies, nearly seventy years of age, having no future marriage in view, but solely influenced by a desire to secure their own property to their own children, which without such divorce they would be unable to do, although one of their husbands had not provided for his wife in twenty years, nor the other in thirty years, availed themselves of its new privileges.

The first change in the tyrannous laws of Massachusetts was really due to the work of this one woman, Mary Upton Ferrin, who for six years, after her own quaint method, poured the hot shot of her ear-

---

* This petition was put in the hands of a gentleman to secure his mother's name (who had signed numbers of petitions before), and those of certain other ladies, but unfaithful to this trust, he forwarded the petition with but its single name, which, Mrs. Ferrin remarks, was powerful in itself.

† James W. North, a lawyer, of Augusta, Maine, to his honor be it said, assisted Mrs. Ferrin, by perfecting the divorce petition, in circulation during her six years of petition work.

nest conviction of woman's wrongs into the Legislature. In circulating petitions, she traveled six hundred miles, two-thirds of this
distance on foot. Much money was expended besides her time and
travel, and her name should be remembered as that of one of the
brave pioneers in this work.

Although two thousand petitions were sent into the Constitutional
Convention of 1853, from other friends of woman's enfranchisement in the State, Mrs. Ferrin totally unacquainted with that step,
herself petitioned this body for an amendment to the Constitution
securing justice to women, referring to the large number of petitions
sent to the Legislature during the last few years for this object.
Working as she did, almost unaided and alone, Mrs. Ferrin is an
exemplification of the dissatisfaction of women at this period with
unjust laws.*

MRS. FERRIN'S ADDRESS TO THE JUDICIARY COMMITTEE OF THE MASSA-
CHUSETTS LEGISLATURE IN 1850.

Long have our liberties and our lives been lauded to the skies, to our
amusement and edification, and until our sex has been as much regaled as
has the Southern slave, with "liberty and law." But, says one, "Women are
free." So likewise are slaves free to submit to the laws and to their masters.
"A married woman is as much the property of her husband, likewise her
goods and chattels, as is his horse," says an eminent judge, and he might have
added, many of them are treated much worse. No more apt illustration could
have been given. Though man can not beat his wife like his horse, he can
kill her by abuse—the most pernicious of slow poisons; and, alas, too often
does he do it. It is for such unfortunate ones that protection is needed.
Existing laws neither do nor can protect them, nor can society, on account of
the laws. If they were men, society would protect and defend them. Long,
silently, and patiently have they waited until forbearance ceases to be a virtue.

Should a woman make her will without her husband's consent in writing, it
is of no use. It is as just and proper that a woman should dispose of her own
property to her own satisfaction as that a man should dispose of his. In many
cases she is as competent, and sadly to be pitied if not in many cases more so.
And even with her husband's consent she can not bequeath to him her real

---

* A lady commenting upon unjust legislation, said: "When the laws were made regarding women and children, the most impotent men were employed to make them; decent men had other business to do."

From time to time, Mrs. Ferrin sent in memorials and addresses with the petitions she
yearly forwarded. One of these in reply to the oft-made boast of man's unsolicited
amelioration of woman's condition, carried the following retort: "The Powers tell us
much has been done to ameliorate the condition of woman without any effort on
woman's part. It would add a huge feather to their caps should they give us the history
of the cause of the need of such reformation. It can not be because woman placed herself
in so degrading a position. So, the merit of the up-lifting hardly reaches the demerit of
the down-treading."

estate. She can sell it with his consent, but the deeds must pass and be recorded, and then, if the husband pleases, he can take the money and buy the property back again. Does justice require that a man and his wife should use so much deception, and be at so much unnecessary expense and trouble, to settle their own private affairs to their own satisfaction—affairs which do not in the least affect any other individual? Reason, humanity, and common sense answer—No!

" All men are created free and equal," and all women are born subject to laws which they have neither the power to make or to repeal, but which they are taxed, directly or indirectly, to support, and many of which are a disgrace to humanity and ought to be forthwith abolished. A woman is compelled by circumstances to work for less than half an ordinary man can earn, and yet she is as essential to the existence, happiness, and refinement of society as is man.

We are told " a great deal has already been done for woman; " in return we would tender our grateful acknowledgments, with the assurance that when ours is the right, we will reciprocate the favor. Much that has been done, does not in the least affect those who are already married; and not one in ten of those who are not married, will ever be apprised of the existence of the laws by which they might be benefited. Few, if any, would marry a man so incompetent as in their opinion to render it necessary to avail themselves of such laws; neither would any spirited man knowingly marry a woman who considered him so incompetent; hence, instead of being a blessing, much labor and expense accrue to those who desire to avail themselves of their benefit; and such a step often induces the most bitter contention.

We are told " the Bible does not provide for divorce except for one offence." Neither does the Bible prohibit divorce for any other justifiable cause. Inasmuch as men take the liberty to legislate upon other subjects of which the Bible does, and does not, take particular notice, so likewise are they equally at liberty to legislate and improve upon this, when the state of society demands it. . . . . A woman who has a good husband glides easily along under his protection, while those who have bad husbands, of which, alas! there are too many, are not aware of the depths of their degradation until they suddenly and unexpectedly find themselves, through the influence of the law, totally destitute, condemned to hopeless poverty and servitude, with an ungrateful tyrant for a master. No respectable man with a decent woman for a wife, will ever demean himself so much as to insult or abuse his wife. Wherever such a state of things exists, it is a disgrace to the age and to society, by whomsoever practiced, encouraged, or protected, whether public or private—whether social, political, or religious.

A very estimable and influential lady, whose property was valued at over $150,000, married a man, in whom she had unbounded, but misplaced confidence, as is too often the case; consequently the most of her property was squandered through intemperance and dissipation, before she was aware of the least wrong-doing. So deeply was she shocked by the character of her husband, that she soon found a premature grave, leaving several small children to be reared and educated upon the remnant of her scattered wealth.

Nearly twelve years since, a woman of a neighboring town, whose husband had forsaken her, hired a man to carry her furniture in a wagon to her native place, with her family, which consisted of her husband's mother, herself, and six children, the eldest of which was but twelve years old. On her arrival there, she had only food enough for one meal, and nine-pence left. During the summer, in consequence of hardships and deprivations, she was taken violently sick, being deprived of her reason for several weeks. Her husband had not, as yet, appeared to offer her the least assistance, although apprised of her situa ion. But, being an uncommonly mean man, he had sold her furniture, piece by piece, and reduced her to penury, so that nothing but the aid of her friends and her own exertions, saved her and her family from the alms-house.

Says the law to this heroic woman, "What, though your property is squandered, your health and spirits broken, and you have six small children, besides yourself and your husband's mother to support! After five years of incessant toil in humility and degradation, why should not your lord and master intrude his loathsome person, like a blood-sucker upon your vitals, never offering you any assistance; and should your precarious life be protracted to that extent of time, for twenty dollars you can buy a divorce from bed and board, and have your property secured to you. Such, Madam, is your high privilege. Complain then not to us, lest instead of alleviating your sufferings, we strengthen the cords that already bind you."

The moral courage of the "Hero of the Battle-field" would shrink in horror from scenes like these; but such is the fate of woman, to whom God grant no future "hell."

In case a man receives a trifle from a departed friend or any other source, the wife's signature is not required. Recently a poor man left his daughter twenty dollars, of which her husband allowed her ten, retaining the remainder for acknowledging its receipt. It was probably the only ten dollars the woman ever received, except for her own exertions, which were constantly required to supply the necessities of her family, her husband being very intemperate and abusive, often pulling her by the ears so as to cause the blood to flow freely.

No bodily pain, however intense, can compare with the mental suffering which we witness and experience, and which would long since have filled our Insane Asylums to overflowing, were it not for the unceasing drudgery to which we are subjected, in order to save ourselves and families from starvation.

Often does the drunkard bestow upon his wife from one to a dozen children to rear and support until old enough to render her a little assistance, when they are compelled to seek service in order to clothe themselves decently, and often are their earnings, with those of their mother, appropriated to pay for rum, tobacco, gambling, and other vices. "Say not that we exaggerate these evils; neither tongue nor pen can do it!" says the unfortunate wife of a man whose moral character, so far as she knew, was unimpeachable, but who proved to be an insufferable tyrant, depriving her of the necessaries of life, and often ordering her out of the house which her friends provided for them to live in, using the most abusive epithets which ingenuity, or the want of it, could suggest. Intemperance degraded the character of the man with whom she lived as long as apprehensions for the safety of her life would warrant; from the fact that her health was rapidly failing under the severity and deprivation to which she was subjected, and the repeated threats of violence to her own life and that of her friends. "But one step farther and you drive us to desperation! Sooner would I pour out my heart's blood, drop by drop, than suffer again what I have hitherto experienced, or that my female friends should suffer as I have done, and I know that many of them do. Yet, neither sacrifice, sympathy, argument, or influence can avail us anything under existing circumstances."

Such an appeal from helpless, down-trodden humanity, though it were made to a council of the most benighted North American savages, would not pass unheeded. Shall it be made in vain to you?

To many of us death would be a luxury compared to what we suffer in consequence of the abusive treatment we receive from unprincipled men, which existing laws sanction and encourage by their indiscriminate severity, and with which we are told " it would be difficult to meddle on account of their sacredness and sublimity." The idea is sufficiently ludicrous to excite the risibility of the most grave. Though the sublime and the ridiculous may be too nearly allied for females to distinguish the difference, unjust inequality is to them far more contemptible than sacred, having thus far been ungraciously subjected to it. Well may we be called " the weaker sex " if the error in judgment is ours, although we have intellect and energy enough not to respect the circumstances under which we are placed, nor the powers which would designedly inflict such injustice upon us.

Debased indeed would a man consider himself to employ a woman to plead his cause, with a woman for judge and twelve women for jurors. How much less degraded are women when exposed to a similar assembly of men, who have for them neither interest, sympathy, nor respect, subjected as they are to insolent questions and the uncharitable remarks of an indifferent multitude.

It is urged that women are ignorant of the laws. They are sufficiently enlightened to comprehend the meaning of justice—a far more important thing— which admits of neither improvement nor modification, but is applicable to every emergency. With the perceptibility that some can boast, it would require but a short time for them to enact laws sufficient to govern themselves, which is all that the most aspiring can covet; convinced as they are that, as in families, so likewise in government, the mild, indulgent parent who would consult the greatest good of the greatest number, is rewarded with agreeable and honorable children ; while the one who is unjust, partial, and severe, is proportionably recompensed for his indiscretion.

In regard to unjust imprisonment we are told, " It is of too rare occurrence to require legal enactments." How many a devoted wife, mother, and child can tell a far different story. Who of us or our children is secure from false accusation and imprisonment, or, perhaps, an ignominious death upon the gallows, to screen some miserable villain from justice ? Witnesses, lawyers, judges, jurors, and executioners are paid for depriving innocent persons of their time, liberty, health, and reputation, which, to many, is dearer than life, while the guilty one escapes, and society, when too late, laments the sad catastrophe. The life-blood of many a victim demands not only justice for the guilty, but protection for the innocent.

FIRST NATIONAL CONVENTION IN WORCESTER,
October 23d and 24th, 1850.

The Conventions in New York and Ohio, though not extensively advertised, nor planned with much deliberation, for in both cases they were hastily decided upon, yet their novelty attracted much attention, and drew large audiences. Those who had long seen and felt woman's wrongs, were now, for the first time inspired with the hope that something might be done for their redress by organized action. When Massachusetts decided to call a convention, the initiative steps were well considered, as there were many men and women in that State trained in the anti-slavery school, skilled in managing conventions, who were also interested in woman's enfranchisement. But to the energy and earnestness of Paulina Wright Davis, more than to any other one person, we may justly accord the success of the first Conventions in Massachusetts.

In describing the preliminary arrangements in a report read in the second decade meeting in New York in 1870, she says:

"In May, 1850, a few women in Boston attending an Anti-Slavery meeting, proposed that all who felt interested in a plan for a National Woman's Rights Convention, should consult in the ante-room. Of the nine who went out into that dark, dingy room, a committee of seven were chosen to do the work. Worcester was the place selected, and the 23d and 24th of October the appointed time. However, the work soon devolved upon one person.* Illness hindered one, duty to a brother another, duty to the slave a third, professional engagements a fourth, the fear of bringing the gray hairs of a father to the grave prevented another from serving; but the pledge was made, and could not be withdrawn.

"The call was prepared, an argument in itself, and sent forth with earnest private letters in all directions. It covered the entire question, as it now stands before the public. Though moderate in tone, carefully guarding the idea of the absolute unity of interests and of the destiny of the two sexes which nature has established, it still gave the alarm to conservatism.

"Letters, curt, reproachful, and sometimes almost insulting, came with absolute refusals to have the names of the writers used, or added to the swelling list already in hand. There was astonishment at the temerity of the writer in presenting such a request.

"Some few there were, so cheering and so excellent, that it is but justice to give extracts from them:

"'I doubt whether a more important movement has ever been launched, touching the destiny of the race, than this in regard to the equality of the sexes. You are at liberty to use my name.   WILLIAM LLOYD GARRISON.'

---

* Mrs. Davis herself.

" 'You do me but justice in supposing me deeply interested in the question of woman's elevation.   CATHERINE M. SEDGWICK.'

" 'The new movement has my fullest sympathy, and my name is at its service
                              " 'WILLIAM HENRY CHANNING.'

" None came with such perfect and entire fullness as the one from which I quote the closing paragraph :

" 'Yes, with all my heart I give my name to your noble call.
                              " 'ELIZABETH CADY STANTON.'

" 'You are at liberty to append my own and my wife's name to your admirable call,   " 'ANN GREEN PHILLIPS,
                              " 'WENDELL PHILLIPS.'

" Rev. Samuel J. May's letter, full of the warmest sympathy, well deserves to be quoted entire, but space forbids; suffice it that we have always known just where to find him.

" 'Your business is to launch new ideas—not one of them will ever be wrecked or lost. Under the dominion of these ideas, right practice must gradually take the place of wrong, and the first we shall know we shall find the social swallowing up the political, and the whole governing its parts.
              " 'With genuine respect, your co-worker,
" 'MRS. PAULINA W. DAVIS.   ELIZUR WRIGHT.'

" Letters from Gerrit Smith, Joshua R. Giddings, John G. Whittier, Ralph Waldo Emerson, A. Bronson Alcott, Caroline Kirkland, Ann Estelle Lewis, Jane G. Swisshelm, William Elder, Rev. Thomas Brainard, and many others, expressive of deep interest, are before us.

" The Convention came together in the bright October days, a solemn, earnest crowd of noble men and women.

" One great disappointment fell upon us. Margaret Fuller, toward whom many eyes were turned as the future leader in this movement, was not with us. The 'hungry, ravening sea,' had swallowed her up, and we were left to mourn her guiding hand— her royal presence. To her, I, at least, had hoped to confide the leadership of this movement. It can never be known if she would have accepted it; the desire had been expressed to her by letter; but be that as it may, she was, and still is, a leader of thought; a position far more desirable than a leader of numbers.

" The Convention was called to order by Mrs. Sarah H. Earl,* of Worcester, and a permanent list of officers presented in due order, and the whole business of the Convention was conducted in a par-

---

* Wife of John Milton Earl, editor of the *Worcester Spy.*

liamentary manner.   Mrs. Earl, to whose memory we pay tribute to-day as one gone before, not lost, was one of the loveliest embodiments of womanhood I have ever known.   She possessed a rare combination of strength, gentleness, and earnestness, with a childlike freedom and cheerfulness.   I miss to-day her clear voice, her graceful self-poise, her calm dignity.

"From our midst another is missing: Mrs. Sarah Tyndale, of Philadelphia—one of the first to sign the call.   Indeed, the idea of such a convention had often been discussed in her home, more than two years before, a home where every progressive thought found a cordial welcome.   To this noble woman, who gave herself to this work with genuine earnestness, it is fitting that we pay a tribute of affectionate respect.   She was, perhaps, more widely known than any other woman of her time for her practical talents; having conducted one of the largest business houses in her native city for nearly a quarter of a century.   Genial and largely hospitable, there was for her great social sacrifice in taking up a cause so unpopular; but she had no shrinking from duty, however trying it might be.   Strong and grand as she was, in her womanly nature, she had nevertheless the largest and tenderest sympathies for the weak and erring.   She was prescient, philosophical, just, and generous.   The mother of a large family, who gathered around to honor and bless her, she had still room in her heart for the woes of the world, and the latter years of her life were given to earnest, philanthropic work.   We miss to-day her sympathy, her wise counsel, her great, organizing power.

"Many others there are, whose names well deserve to be graven in gold, and it is cause of thanksgiving to God that they are still present with us, their lives speaking better than words.   Some are in the Far West, doing brave service there; others are across the water; others are withheld by cares and duties from being present; but we would fain hope none are absent from choice.

"Profound feeling pervaded the entire audience, and the talent displayed in the discussions, the eloquence of women who had never before spoken in public, surprised even those who expected most. Mrs. C. I. H. Nichols, of Vermont, made a profound impression. There was a touching, tender pathos in her stories which went home to the heart; and many eyes, all unused to tears, were moistened as she described the agony of the mother robbed of her child by the law.

"Abby H. Price, large-hearted and large-brained, gentle and strong, presented an address on the social question not easily forgotten, and seldom to the present time bettered.

" Lucy Stone, a natural orator, with a silvery voice, a heart warm and glowing with youthful enthusiasm; Antoinette L. Brown, a young minister, met firmly the Scriptural arguments; and Dr. Harriot K. Hunt, earnest for the medical education of woman, gave variety to the discussions of the Convention.

" In this first national meeting the following resolution was passed, which it may be proper here to reiterate, thus showing that our present demand has always been one and the same :

" '*Resolved*, That women are clearly entitled to the right of suffrage, and to be considered eligible to office ; the omission to demand which, on her part, is a palpable recreancy to duty, and a denial of which is a gross usurpation on the part of man, no longer to be endured ; and that every party which claims to represent the humanity, civilization, and progress of the age, is bound to inscribe on its banners, " Equality before the Law, without distinction of Sex or Color." '

" From North to South the press found these reformers wonderfully ridiculous people. The 'hen convention' was served up in every variety of style, till refined women dreaded to look into a newspaper. Hitherto man had assumed to be the conscience of woman, now she indicated the will to think for herself ; hence all this odium. But, however the word was preached, whether for wrath or conscience sake, we rejoiced and thanked God.

" In July, following this Convention, an able and elaborate notice appeared in the *Westminster Review*. This notice, candid in tone and spirit, as it was thorough and able in discussion, successfully vindicated every position we assumed, reaffirmed and established the highest ground taken in principle or policy by our movement. The wide-spread circulation and high authority of this paper told upon the public mind, both in Europe and this country. It was at the time supposed to be by Mr. John Stuart Mill. Later we learned that it was from the pen of his noble wife, to whom be all honor for thus coming to the aid of a struggling cause. I can pay no tribute to her memory so beautiful as the following extract from a letter recently received from her husband:

" ' It gives me the greatest pleasure to know that the service rendered by my dear wife to the cause which was nearer her heart than any other, by her essay in the *Westminster Review*, has had so much effect and is so justly appreciated in the United States. Were it possible in a memoir to have the formation and growth of a mind like hers portrayed, to do so would be as valuable a benefit to mankind as was ever conferred by a biography. But such a psychological history is seldom possible, and in her case the materials for it do not exist. All that could be furnished is her birth-place, parentage, and a few dates, and it seems to me that her memory is more honored by the absence of any attempt at a biographical notice than by the presence of a most meagre one. What she was, I have attempted, though most inadequately, to delineate in the remarks prefaced to her essay, as reprinted with my " Dissertations and Discussions." '

" ' I am very glad to hear of the step in advance made by the Rhode Island Legislature in constituting a Board of Women for some important administrative purposes. Your intended proposal, that women be impaneled on every jury where women are to be tried, seems to me very good, and calculated to place the injustice to which women are at present subjected, by the entire legal system, in a very striking light.

" ' I am, dear madam, yours sincerely,

" ' MRS. PAULINA WRIGHT DAVIS.   J. S. MILL.'

" Immediately after the reports were published, they were sent to various persons in Europe, and before the second Convention was held, letters of cheer were received from Harriet Martineau, Marion Reid, and others.

" Thus encouraged, we felt new zeal to go on with a work which had challenged the understanding and constrained the hearts of the best and soundest thinkers in the nation ; had given an impulse to the women of England and of Sweden—for Frederika Bremer had quoted from our writings and reported our proceedings ; our words had been like an angel's visit to the prisoners of State in France and to the wronged and outraged at home !

" Many letters were received from literary women in this country as well as abroad. If not always ready to be identified with the work, they were appreciative of its good effects, and, like Nicodemus, they came by night to inquire ' how these things could be.' Self-interest showed them the advantages accruing from the recognition of equality—self-ism held them silent before the world till the reproach should be worn away ; but we credit them with a sense of justice and right, which prompts them now to action. The rear guard is as essential in the army as the advance ; each should select the place best adapted to their own powers."

As Mrs. Davis has fallen asleep since writing the above, we have thought best to give what seemed to her the salient points of that period in her own words.

October 23, 1850, a large audience assembled in Brinley Hall, Worcester, Mass. The Convention was called to order by Sarah H. Earle, of Worcester. Nine States were represented. There were Garrison, Phillips, Burleigh, Foster, Pillsbury, leaders in the anti-slavery struggle ; Frederick Douglass and Sojourner Truth representing the enslaved African race. The Channings, Sargents, Parsons, Shaws, from the liberal pulpit and the aristocracy of Boston. From Ohio came Mariana and Oliver Johnson, who had edited the

Anti-Slavery Bugle, that sent forth many a blast against the black laws of that State, and many a stirring call for the woman's conventions. From Ohio, too, came Ellen and Marion Blackwell, sisters of Dr. Elizabeth Blackwell. Pennsylvania sent its Lucretia Mott, its Darlingtons, Plumlys, Hastings, Millers, Hicks, who had all taken part in the exciting divisions among the " Friends," as a sect. On motion of Mariana Johnson, a temporary chairman was chosen, and a nominating committee appointed, which reported the following list of officers adopted by the Convention :

*President—*PAULINA WRIGHT DAVIS, R. I.

*Vice-Presidents—*WILLIAM HENRY CHANNING, Mass. ; SARAH TYNDALE, Pa.

*Secretaries—*HANNAH M. DARLINGTON, Pa. ; JOSEPH C. HATHAWAY, N. Y.

The Call of the Convention was read. It contains so good a digest of the demands then made, in language so calm and choice, in thought so clear and philosophical, that we give it entire, that the women of the future may see how well their mothers understood their rights, and with what modesty and moderation they pressed their wrongs on the consideration of their rulers.

THE CALL.

A Convention will be held at Worcester, Mass., on the 23d and 24th of October next, to consider the question of Woman's Rights, Duties, and Relations. The men and women who feel sufficient interest in the subject to give an earnest thought and effective effort to its rightful adjustment, are invited to meet each other in free conference at the time and place appointed.

The upward tending spirit of the age, busy in an hundred forms of effort for the world's redemption from the sins and sufferings which oppress it, has brought this one, which yields to none in importance and urgency, into distinguished prominence. One-half the race are its immediate objects, and the other half are as deeply involved, by that absolute unity of interest and destiny which Nature has established between them. The neighbor is near enough to involve every human being in a general equality of rights and community of interests ; but men and women in their reciprocities of love and duty, are one flesh and one blood ; mother, sister, wife, and daughter come so near the heart and mind of every man, that they must be either his blessing or his bane. Where there is such mutuality of interests, such an interlinking of life, there can be no real antagonism of position and action. The sexes should not, for any reason or by any chance, take hostile attitudes toward each other, either in the apprehension or amendment of the wrongs which exist in their necessary relations ; but they should harmonize in opinion and co-operate in effort, for the reason that they must unite in the ultimate achievement of the desired reformation.

Of the many points now under discussion, and demanding a just settlement, the general question of woman's rights and relations comprehends these : Her education—literary, scientific, and artistic ; her avocations—industrial, commercial, and professional ; her interests—pecuniary, civil, and political ; in a word, her rights as an individual, and her functions as a citizen.

No one will pretend that all these interests, embracing as they do all that is not merely animal in a human life, are rightly understood, or justly provided for in the existing social order. Nor is it any more true that the constitutional differences of the sexes which should determine, define, and limit the resulting differences of office and duty, are adequately comprehended and practically observed.

Woman has been condemned for her greater delicacy of physical organization, to inferiority of intellectual and moral culture, and to the forfeiture of great social, civil, and religious privileges. In the relation of marriage she has been ideally annihilated and actually enslaved in all that concerns her personal and pecuniary rights, and even in widowed and single life, she is oppressed with such limitation and degradation of labor and avocation, as clearly and cruelly mark the condition of a disabled caste. But by the inspiration of the Almighty, the beneficent spirit of reform is roused to the redress of these wrongs.

The tyranny which degrades and crushes wives and mothers sits no longer lightly on the world's conscience ; the heart's home-worship feels the stain of stooping at a dishonored altar. Manhood begins to feel the shame of muddying the springs from which it draws its highest life, and womanhood is everywhere awakening to assert its divinely chartered rights and to fulfill its noblest duties. It is the spirit of reviving truth and righteousness which has moved upon the great deep of the public heart and aroused its redressing justice, and through it the Providence of God is vindicating the order and appointments of His creation.

The signs are encouraging ; the time is opportune. Come, then, to this Convention. It is your duty, if you are worthy of your age and country. Give the help of your best thought to separate the light from the darkness. Wisely give the protection of your name and the benefit of your efforts to the great work of settling the principles, devising the methods, and achieving the success of this high and holy movement.

This call was signed by eighty-nine leading men and women of six States.*

On taking the chair, Mrs. DAVIS said :

The reformation we propose in its utmost scope is radical and universal. It is not the mere perfecting of a reform already in motion, a detail of some established plan, but it is an epochal movement—the emancipation of a class, the redemption of half the world, and a conforming reorganization of all social, political, and industrial interests and institutions. Moreover, it is a movement without example among the enterprises of associated reformations, for it has

---

* See Appendix.

no purpose of arming the oppressed against the oppressor, or of separating the parties, or of setting up independence, or of severing the relations of either.

Its intended changes are to be wrought in the intimate texture of all societary organizations, without violence or any form of antagonism. It seeks to replace the worn-out with the living and the beautiful, so as to reconstruct without overturning, and to regenerate without destroying.

Our claim must rest on its justice, and conquer by its power of truth. We take the ground that whatever has been achieved for the race belongs to it, and must not be usurped by any class or caste. The rights and liberties of one human being can not be made the property of another, though they were redeemed for him or her by the life of that other; for rights can not be forfeited by way of salvage, and they are, in their nature, unpurchasable and inalienable. We claim for woman a full and generous investiture of all the blessings which the other sex has solely, or by her aid, achieved for itself. We appeal from man's injustice and selfishness to his principles and affectio ns.

It was cheering to find in the very beginning many distinguished men ready to help us to the law, gospel, social ethics, and philosophy involved in our question. A letter from Gerrit Smith to William Lloyd Garrison says :

PETERBORO, N. Y., *Oct.* 16, 1850.

MY DEAR SIR :—I this evening received from my friend H. H. Van Amringe, of Wisconsin, the accompanying argument on woman's rights. It is written by himself. He is, as you are aware, a highly intellectual man. He wishes me to present this argument to the Woman's Convention which is to be held in Worcester. Permit me to do so through yourself.

My excessive business engagements compel me to refuse all invitations to attend public meetings not in my own county. May Heaven's richest blessings rest on the Convention.

Very respectfully and fraternally yours,　　GERRIT SMITH.

Mr. Van Amringe's paper on " Woman's Rights in Church and State " was read and discussed, and a large portion of it printed in the regular report of the proceedings.

The papers read by the women, in style and argument, were in no way inferior to those of the men present.

Letters were read from Elizabeth Cady Stanton, Rev. Samuel J. May, L. A. Hine, Elizur Wright, O. S. Eowler, Esther Ann Lukens, Margaret Chappel Smith, Nancy M. Baird, Jane Cowen, Sophia L. Little, Elizabeth Wilson, Maria L. Varney, and Milfred A. Spaford.*

Mrs. Abby H. Price, of Hopedale, made an address on the injustice of excluding girls from the colleges, the trades and the professions, and the importance of training them to some profitable labor, and thus to protect their virtue, dignity, and self-respect by securing their pecuniary independence.

* See Appendix.

She thought the speediest solution of the vexed problem of prostitution was profitable work for the rising generation of girls. The best legislation on the social vice was in removing the legal disabilities that cripple all their powers. Woman, in order to be equally independent with man, must have a fair and equal chance. He is in nowise restricted from doing, in every department of human exertion, all he is able to do. If he is bold and ambitious, and desires fame, every avenue is open to him. He may blend science and art, producing a competence for his support, until he chains them to the car of his genius, and, with Fulton and Morse, wins a crown of imperishable gratitude If he desires to tread the path of knowledge up to its glorious temple-summit, he can, as he pleases, take either of the learned professions as instruments of pecuniary independence, while he plumes his wings for a higher and higher ascent. Not so with woman. Her rights are not recognized as equal ; her sphere is circumscribed—not by her ability, but by her sex. If, perchance, her taste leads her to excellence, in the way they give her leave to tread, she is worshiped as almost divine ; but if she reaches for laurels they have in view, the wings of her genius are clipped because she is a woman.

Dr. Harriot K. Hunt, of Boston, the first woman who practiced medicine in this country, spoke on the medical education of women.

Sarah Tyndale, a successful merchant in Philadelphia, on the business capacity of woman.

Antoinette L. Brown, a graduate of Oberlin College, and a student in Theology, made a logical argument on woman's position in the Bible, claiming her complete equality with man, the simultaneous creation of the sexes, and their moral responsibilities as individual and imperative.

The debates on the resolutions were spicy, pointed, and logical, and were deeply interesting, continuing with crowded audiences through two entire days. In these debates Lucy Stone, Lucretia Mott, Wendell Phillips, William Henry Channing, Ernestine L. Rose, Frederick Douglass, Martha Mowry, Abby Kelly and Stephen Foster, Elizabeth B. Chase, James N. Buffam, Sojourner Truth, Eliab Capron, and Joseph C. Hathaway, took part. As there was no phonographic reporter present, most of the best speaking, that was extemporaneous, can not be handed down to history.

Among the letters to the Convention, there was one quite novel and interesting from Helene Marie Weber,* a lady of high literary character, who had published numerous tracts on the Rights of Woman. She contended that the physical development of woman was impossible in her present costume, and that her consequent enfeebled condition made her incapable of entering many of the most profitable employments in the world of work. Miss Weber exem-

---

* See Appendix.

plified her teachings by her practice. She usually wore a dress coat and pantaloons of black cloth; on full-dress occasions, a dark blue dress coat, with plain flat gilt buttons, and drab-colored pantaloons. Her waistcoat was of buff cassimere, richly trimmed with plain, flat-surfaced, gold buttons, exquisitely polished; this was an elegant costume, and one she wore to great advantage. Her clothes were all perfect in their fit, and of Paris make; and her figure was singularly well adapted to male attire. No gentleman in Paris made a finer appearance.

One of the grand results of this Convention was the thought roused in England. A good report of the proceedings in the *New York Tribune*, for Europe, of October 29, 1850, was read by the future Mrs. John Stuart Mill, then Mrs. Taylor, and at once called out from her pen an able essay in the *Westminster and Foreign Quarterly Review*, entitled "Enfranchisement of Woman." This attracted the attention of many liberal thinkers, and foremost of these, one of England's greatest philosophers and scholars, the Hon. John Stuart Mill, who became soon after the champion of woman's cause in the British Parliament. The essayist in speaking of this Convention says:

Most of our readers will probably learn, from these pages, for the first time, that there has risen in the United States, and in the most civilized and enlightened portion of them, an organized agitation, on a new question, new not to thinkers, nor to any one by whom the principles of free and popular government are felt, as well as acknowledged; but new, and even unheard of, as a subject for public meetings, and practical political action. This question is the enfranchisement of women, their admission in law, and in fact, to equality in all rights, political, civil, social, with the male citizens of the community.

It will add to the surprise with which many will receive this intelligence, that the agitation which has commenced is not a pleading by male writers and orators *for* women, those who are professedly to be benefited remaining either indifferent, or ostensibly hostile; it is a political movement, practical in its objects, carried on in a form which denotes an intention to persevere. And it is a movement not merely *for* women, but *by* them. . . . .

A succession of public meetings was held, under the name of a "Woman's Rights Convention," of which the President was a woman, and nearly all the chief speakers women; numerously reinforced, however, by men, among whom were some of the most distinguished leaders in the kindred cause of negro emancipation. . . . .

According to the report in the *New York Tribune*, above a thousand persons were present, throughout, and "if a larger place could have been had, many thousands more would have attended."

In regard to the quality of the speaking, the proceedings bear an advantageous comparison with those of any popular movement with which we are acquainted, either in this country or in America. Very rarely in the oratory

15

of public meetings is the part of verbiage and declamation so small, and that of calm good sense and reason so considerable.

The result of the Convention was in every respect encouraging to those by whom it was summoned; and it is probably destined to inaugurate one of the most important of the movements toward political and social reform, which are the best characteristic of the present age. That the promoters of this new agitation take their stand on principles, and do not fear to declare these in their widest extent, without time-serving or compromise, will be seen from the resolutions adopted by the Convention.*

After giving an able argument in favor of all the demands made in the Convention, with a fair criticism of some of the weak things uttered there, she concludes by saying:

There are indications that the example of America will be followed on this side of the Atlantic; and the first step has been taken in that part of England where every serious movement in the direction of political progress has its commencement—the manufacturing districts of the north. On the 13th of February, 1851, a petition of women, agreed to by a public meeting at Sheffield, and claiming the elective franchise, was presented to the House of Lords by the Earl of Carlisle.

William Henry Channing, from the Business Committee, suggested a plan for organization and the principles that should govern the movement. In accordance with his views a National Central Committee was appointed, in which every State was represented.† Paulina Wright Davis, Chairman; Sarah H. Earle, Secretary; Wendell Phillips, Treasurer.

This Convention was a very creditable one in every point of view. The order and perfection of the arrangements, the character of the papers presented, and the sustained enthusiasm, reflect honor on the men and women who conducted the proceedings. The large number of letters addressed to Mrs. Davis show how extensive had been her correspondence, both in the old world and the new. Her wealth, culture, and position gave her much social influence; her beauty, grace, and gentle manners drew around her a large circle of admiring friends. These, with her tall fine figure, her classic head and features, and exquisite taste in dress; her organizing talent and knowledge of the question under consideration, altogether made her so desirable a presiding officer, that she was often chosen for that position.

THE SECOND NATIONAL CONVENTION IN WORCESTER.

In accordance with a call from the Central Committee, the friends of Woman Suffrage assembled again in Brinley Hall, Oct. 15th

---

* See Appendix. † See Appendix.

and 16th, 1851. At an early hour the house was filled, and was called to order by Paulina Wright Davis, who was again chosen permanent President. This Convention was conducted mainly by the same persons who had so successfully managed the proceedings of the previous year. Mrs. Davis, on taking the chair, gave a brief *resumé* of the steps of progress during the year, and at the close of her remarks, letters were read from Ralph Waldo Emerson, Henry Ward Beecher, Horace Mann, Angelina Grimke Weld, Frances D. Gage, Estelle Anna Lewis, Marion Blackwell, Oliver Johnson, and Eliza Barney, all giving a hearty welcome to the new idea. Mrs. Emma R. Coe, of the Business Committee, called upon Wendell Phillips to read the resolutions* prepared for the consideration of the Convention.

On rising Mr. PHILLIPS said :

In drawing up some of these resolutions, I have used very freely the language of a thoughtful and profound article in the *Westminster Review.* It is a review of the proceedings of our Convention, held one year ago, and states with singular clearness and force the leading arguments for our reform, and the grounds of our claim in behalf of woman. I rejoice to see so large an audience gathered to consider this momentous subject, the most magnificent reform that has yet been launched upon the world. It is the first organized protest against the injustice which has brooded over the character and the destiny of one-half of the human race. Nowhere else, under any circumstances, has a demand ever yet been made for the liberties of one whole half of our race. It is fitting that we should pause and consider so remarkable and significant a circumstance ; that we should discuss the questions involved with the seriousness and deliberation suitable to such an enterprise.

It strikes, indeed, a great and vital blow at the whole social fabric of every nation ; but this, to my mind, is no argument against it. . . . . Government commenced in usurpation and oppression ; liberty and civilization at present are nothing else than the fragments of rights which the scaffold and the stake have wrung from the strong hands of the usurpers. Every step of progress the world has made has been from scaffold to scaffold, from stake to stake. . . . . Government began in tyranny and force ; began in the feudalism of the soldier and the bigotry of the priest ; and the ideas of justice and humanity have been fighting their way like a thunderstorm against the organized selfishness of human nature.

And this is the last great protest against the wrong of ages. It is no argument, to my mind, therefore, that the old social fabric of the past is against us. Neither do I feel called upon to show what woman's proper sphere is. In every great reform the majority have always said to the claimant, no matter what he claimed, "You are not fit for such a privilege." Luther asked of the Pope liberty for the masses to read the Bible. The reply was that it would not

---

* See Appendix.

be safe to trust the masses with the word of God. "Let them try," said the great reformer, and the history of three centuries of development and purity proclaims the result.

The lower classes in France claimed their civil rights; the right to vote, and to a direct representation in government, but the rich and lettered classes cried out, "You can not be made fit." The answer was, "Let us try." That France is not as Spain, utterly crushed beneath the weight of a thousand years of mis-government, is the answer to those who doubt the ultimate success of the experiment.

Woman stands now at the same door. She says: "You tell me I have no intellect. Give me a chance." "You tell me I shall only embarrass politics; let me try." The only reply is the same stale argument that said to the Jews of Europe: You are fit only to make money; you are not fit for the ranks of the army, or the halls of Parliament.

How cogent the eloquent appeal of Macaulay: "What right have we to take this question for granted? Throw open the doors of this House of Commons; throw open the ranks of the imperial army, before you deny eloquence to the countrymen of Isaiah, or valor to the descendants of the Maccabees."

It is the same now with us. Throw open the doors of Congress; throw open those court-houses; throw wide open the doors of your colleges, and give to the sisters of the De Staëls and the Martineaus the same opportunity for cult-ure that men have, and let the results prove what their capacity and intellect really are. When woman has enjoyed for as many centuries as we have the aid of books, the discipline of life, and the stimulus of fame, it will be time to be-gin the discussion of these questions: "What is the intellect of woman?" "Is it equal to that of man?" Till then, all such discussion is mere beating of the air. While it is doubtless true, that great minds make a way for themselves, spite of all obstacles, yet who knows how many Miltons have died, "mute and inglorious"? However splendid the natural endowments, the discipline of life, after all, completes the miracle. The ability of Napoleon—what was it? It grew out of the hope to be Cæsar, or Marlborough; out of Austerlitz and Jena—out of his battle-fields, his throne, and all the great scenes of that eventful life.

Open to woman the same scenes, immerse her in the same great interests and pursuits, and if twenty centuries shall not produce a woman Charlemagne, or a Napoleon, fair reason will then allow us to conclude that there is some distinct-ive peculiarity in the intellects of the sexes.

Centuries alone can lay a fair basis for the argument. I believe on this point there is a shrinking consciousness of not being ready for the battle, on the part of some of the stronger sex, as they call themselves; a tacit confession of risk to this imagined superiority, if they consent to meet their sisters in the lecture halls, or the laboratory of science.

My proof of it is this, that the mightiest intellects of the race, from Plato down to the present time, some of the rarest minds of Germany, France, and England, have successively yielded their assent to the fact, that woman is not, perhaps, identically, but equally endowed with man in all intellectual capabili-ties. It is generally the second-rate men who doubt; doubt because, perhaps, they fear a fair field.

Suppose that woman is essentially inferior to man, she still has rights. Grant that Mrs. Norton* never could be Byron; that Elizabeth Barrett never could have written Paradise Lost; that Mrs. Somerville never could be La Place, nor Sirani have painted the Transfiguration. What then? Does that prove they should be deprived of all civil rights?

John Smith will never be, never can be, Daniel Webster. Shall he therefore be put under guardianship, and forbidden to vote? Suppose woman, though equal, does differ essentially in her intellect from man, is that any ground for disfranchising her? Shall the Fultons say to the Raphaels, because you can not make steam engines, therefore you shall not vote? Shall the Napoleons or the Washingtons say to the Wordsworths or the Herschels, because you can not lead armies, and govern States, therefore you shall have no civil rights?

The following interesting letter from Harriet Martineau was then read, which we give in full, that the reader may see how clearly defined was her position at that early day:

CROMER, ENGLAND, *Aug.* 3, 1851.

PAULINA WRIGHT DAVIS:

DEAR MADAM:—I beg to thank you heartily for your kindness in sending me the Report of the Proceedings of your Woman's Rights Convention. I had gathered what I could from the newspapers concerning it, but I was gratified at being able to read, in a collected form, addresses so full of earnestness and sound truth, as I found most of the speeches to be. I hope you are aware of the interest excited in this country by that Convention, the strongest proof of which is the appearance of an article on the subject in *The Westminster Review* (for July), as thorough-going as any of your own addresses, and from the pen (at least as it is understood here) of one of our very first men, Mr. John S. Mill. I am not without hope that this article will materially strengthen your hands, and I am sure it can not but cheer your hearts.

Ever since I became capable of thinking for myself, I have clearly seen, and I have said it till my listeners and readers are probably tired of hearing it, that there can be but one true method in the treatment of each human being, of either sex, of any color, and under any outward circumstances, to ascertain what are the powers of that being, to cultivate them to the utmost, and *then* to see what action they will find for themselves. This has probably never been done for men, unless in some rare individual cases. It has certainly never been done for women, and, till it is done, all debating about what woman's intellect is, all speculation, or laying down the law, as to what is woman's sphere, is a mere beating of the air. *A priori* conceptions have long been worthless in physical science, and nothing was really effected till the experimental method was clearly made out and strictly applied in practice, and the same principle holds most certainly through the whole range of moral science.

Whether we regard the physical fact of what women are able to do, or the moral fact of what women ought to do, it is equally necessary to abstain from making any decision prior to experiment. We see plainly enough the waste of

---

* Mrs. Caroline Norton, a distinguished English author, who separated from her husband because of cruel treatment. He robbed her of all the profits of her books, and of her children, and when she appealed to the Courts, English law sustained the husband in all his violations of natural justice.

time and thought among the men who once talked of Nature abhorring a vacuum, or disputed at great length as to whether angels could go from end to end without passing through the middle; and the day will come when it will appear to be no less absurd to have argued, as men and women are arguing now, about what woman ought to do, before it was ascertained what woman can do.

Let us once see a hundred women educated up to the highest point that education at present reaches; let them be supplied with such knowledge as their faculties are found to crave, and let them be free to use, apply, and increase their knowledge as their faculties shall instigate, and it will presently appear what is the sphere of each of the hundred.

One may be discovering comets, like Miss Herschell; one may be laying open the mathematical structure of the universe, like Mrs. Somerville; another may be analyzing the chemical relations of Nature in the laboratory; another may be penetrating the mysteries of physiology; others may be applying science in the healing of diseases; others may be investigating the laws of social relations, learning the great natural laws under which society, like everything else, proceeds; others, again, may be actively carrying out the social arrangements which have been formed under these laws; and others may be chiefly occupied in family business, in the duties of the wife and mother, and the ruler of the household.

If, among the hundred women, a great diversity of powers should appear (which I have no doubt would be the case), there will always be plenty of scope and material for the greatest amount and variety of power that can be brought out. If not—if it should appear that women fall below men in all but the domestic functions—then it will be well that the experiment has been tried; and the trial better go on forever, that woman's sphere may forever determine itself to the satisfaction of everybody. It is clear that education, to be what I demand on behalf of women, must be intended to issue in active life.

A man's medical education would be worth little, if it was not a preparation for practice. The astronomer and the chemist would put little force into their studies, if it was certain that they must leave off in four or five years, and do nothing for the rest of their lives; and no man could possibly feel much interest in political and social morals, if he knew that he must, all his life long, pay taxes, but neither speak nor move about public affairs.

Women, like men, must be educated with a view to action, or their studies can not be called education, and no judgment can be formed of the scope of their faculties. The pursuit must be life's business, or it will be mere pastime or irksome task. This was always my point of difference with one who carefully cherished a reverence for woman, the late Dr. Channing.

How much we spoke and wrote of the old controversy, Influence *vs.* Office. He would have had any woman study anything that her faculties led her to, whether physical science or law, government and political economy; but he would have her stop at the study. From the moment she entered the hospital as physician and not nurse; from the moment she took her place in a court of justice, in the jury box, and not the witness box; from the moment she brought her mind and her voice into the legislature, instead of discussing the principles of laws at home; from the moment she announced and administered justice instead of looking at it from afar, as a thing with which she had no concern, she would, he feared, lose her influence as an observing intelligence, standing by in a state of purity " unspotted from the world."

My conviction always was, that an intelligence never carried out into action could not be worth much; and that, if all the action of human life was of a character so tainted as to be unfit for women, it could be no better for men, and we ought all to sit down together, to let barbarism overtake us once more.

My own conviction is, that the natural action of the whole human being occasions not only the most strength, but the highest elevation; not only the warmest sympathy, but the deepest purity. The highest and purest beings among women seem now to be those who, far from being idle, find among their restricted opportunities some means of strenuous action; and I can not doubt that, if an active social career were open to all women, with due means of preparation for it, those who are high and holy now, would be high and holy then, and would be joined by an innumerable company of just spirits from among those whose energies are now pining and fretting in enforced idleness, or unworthy frivolity, or brought down into pursuits and aims which are anything but pure and peaceable.

In regard to the old controversy—Influence *vs.* Office—it appears to me that if Influence is good and Office bad for human morals and character, Man's present position is one of such hardship, as it is almost profane to contemplate; and if, on the contrary, Office is good and a life of Influence is bad, Woman has an instant right to claim that her position be amended.

Yours faithfully,   Harriet Martineau.

From her letter, we find, that Miss Martineau shared the common opinion in England that the article in the *Westminster Review* on the "Enfranchisement of Woman" was written by John Stuart Mill. It was certainly very complimentary to Mrs. Taylor, the real author of that paper, who afterward married Mr. Mill, that it should have been supposed to emanate from the pen of that distinguished philosopher. An amusing incident is related of Mr. Mill, for the truth of which we can not vouch, but report says, that after reading this article, he hastened to read it again to Mrs. Taylor, and passing on it the highest praises, to his great surprise she confessed herself the author.

At this Convention Mrs. Elizabeth Oakes Smith made her first appearance on our platform. She was well known in the literary circles of New York as a writer of merit in journals and periodicals. She defended the Convention and its leaders through the columns of the *New York Tribune*, and afterward published a series of articles entitled " Woman and her Needs." She early made her way into the lyceums and some pulpits never before open to woman. Her "Bertha and Lily," a woman's rights novel, and her other writings were influential in moulding popular thought.

Angelina Grimke, familiar with plantation life, spoke eloquently on the parallel between the slave code and the laws for married women.

Mehitable Haskell, of Gloucester, said:

Perhaps, my friends, I ought to apologize for standing here. Perhaps I attach too much importance to my own age. This meeting, as I understand it, was called to discuss Woman's Rights. Well, I do not pretend to know exactly what woman's rights are; but I do know that I have groaned for forty years, yea, for fifty years, under a sense of woman's wrongs. I know that even when a girl, I groaned under the idea that I could not receive as much instruction as my brothers could. I wanted to be what I felt I was capable of becoming, but opportunity was denied me. I rejoice in the progress that has been made. I rejoice that so many women are here; it denotes that they are waking up to some sense of their situation. One of my sisters observed that she had received great kindness as a wife, mother, sister, and daughter. I, too, have brethren in various directions, both those that are natural, and those that are spiritual brethren, as I understand the matter; and I rejoice to say I have found, I say it to the honor of my brothers, I have found more men than women, who were impressed with the wrongs under which our sex labor, and felt the need of reformation. I rejoice in this fact.

Rebecca B. Spring followed with some pertinent remarks. Mrs. Emma R. Coe reviewed in a strain of pungent irony the State Laws in relation to woman. In discussing the resolutions, Charles List, Esq., of Boston, said:

I lately saw a book wherein the author in a very eloquent, but highly wrought sentence, speaks of woman as "the connecting link between man and heaven." I think this asks too much, and I deny the right of woman to assume such a prerogative; all I claim is that woman should be raised by noble aspiration to the loftiest moral elevation, and thus be fitted to train men up to become worthy companions for the pure, high-minded beings which all women should strive to be. A great duty rests on woman, and it becomes you not to lose a moment in securing for yourselves every right and privilege, whereby you may be elevated and so prepared to exert the influence which man so much needs. Women fall far short now of exerting the moral influence intrusted to them as mothers and wives, consequently men are imperfectly developed in their higher nature.

Mrs. NICHOLS rejoined: Woman has been waiting for centuries expecting man to go before and lift her up, but he has failed to meet our expectations, and now comes the call that she should first grasp heaven and pull man up after her.

Mrs. COE said: The signs are truly propitious, when man begins to complain of his wrongs—women not fit to be wives and mothers!

Who placed them in their present position? Who keeps them there? Let woman demand the highest education in our land, and what college, with the exception of Oberlin, will receive her? I have myself lately.

made such a demand and been refused simply on the ground of sex. Yet what is there in the highest range of intellectual pursuits, to which woman may not rightfully aspire? What is there, for instance, in theology, which she should not strive to learn? Give me only that in religion which woman may and should become acquainted with, and the rest may go like chaff before the wind.

LUCY STONE said: I think it is not without reason that men complain of the wives and mothers of to-day. Let us look the fact soberly and fairly in the face, and admit that there *is* occasion to complain of wives and mothers. But while I say this, let me also say that when you can show one woman who is what she ought to be as a wife and a mother, you can show not more than one man who is what he should be as a husband and father. The blame is on both sides. When we add to what woman ought to be for her own sake, this other fact, that woman, by reason of her maternity, must exert a most potent influence over the generations yet to be, there is no language that can speak the magnitude or importance of the subject that has called us together. He is guilty of giving the world a dwarfed humanity, who would seek to hinder this movement for the elevation of woman; for she is as yet a starved and dependent outcast before the law. In government she is outlawed, having neither voice nor part in it. In the household she is either a ceaseless drudge, or a blank. In the department of education, in industry, let woman's sphere be bounded only by her capacity. We desire there should no walls be thrown about it. Let man read his own soul, and turn over the pages of his own Book of Life, and learn that in the human mind there is always capacity for development, and then let him trust woman to that power of growth, no matter who says nay. Laying her hand on the helm, let woman steer straight onward to the fulfillment of her own destiny. Let her ever remember, that in following out the high behests of her own soul will be found her exceeding great reward.

William Henry Channing then gave the report from the committee on the social relations. Those present speak of it as a very able paper on that complex question, but as it was not published with the proceedings, all that can be found is the following meagre abstract from *The Worcester Spy:*

Woman has a natural right to the development of all her faculties, and to all the advantages that insure this result. She has the right not only to civil and legal justice, which lie on the outskirts of social life, but to social justice, which affects the central position of society.

Woman should be as free to marry, or remain single, and as honorable in either relation, as man. There should be no stigma attached to the single woman, impelling her to avoid the possibility of such a position, by crushing her self-respect and individual ambition. A true Christian marriage is a sacred union of soul and sense, and the issues flowing from it are eternal. All obstacles in the way of severing uncongenial marriages should be removed, because such unions are unnatural, and must be evil in their results. Divorce in such cases should be honorable, without subjecting the parties to the shame of exposure in the courts, or in the columns of the daily papers.

Much could be accomplished for the elevation of woman by organizations clustering round a social principle, like those already clustered round a religious principle, such as "Sisters of Mercy," "Sisters of Charity," etc. There should be social orders called "Sisters of Honor," having for their object the interests of unfortunate women. From these would spring up convents, where those who have escaped from false marriages and illegal social relations would find refuge. These organizations might send out missionaries to gather the despised Magdalens into safe retreats, and raise them to the level of true womanhood.

Mr. Channing spoke at length on the civil and political position of woman, eloquently advocating the rightfulness and expediency of woman's co-sovereignty with man, and closed by reading a very eloquent letter from Jeanne Deroine and Pauline Roland, two remarkable French women, then in the prison of St. Lagare, in Paris, for their liberal opinions.

Just as the agitation for woman's rights began in this country, Pauline Roland began in France a vigorous demand for her rights as a citizen. The 27th of February, 1848, she presented herself before the electoral reunion to claim the right of nominating the mayor of the city where she lived. Having been refused, she claimed in April of the same year the right to take part in the elections for the Constituent Assembly, and was again refused. On April 12, 1849, Jeanne Deroine claimed for woman the right of eligibility by presenting herself as a candidate for the Legislative Assembly, and she sustained this right before the preparatory electoral reunions of Paris. On the 3d of October Jeanne Deroine and Pauline Roland, delegates from the fraternal associations, were elected members of the Central Committee of the Associative Unions. This Central Committee was for the fraternal associations what the Constituent Assembly was for the French Republic in 1848.

To the Convention of the Women of America:

DEAR SISTERS:—Your courageous declaration of Woman's Rights has resounded even to our prison, and has filled our souls with inexpressible joy.

In France the reaction has suppressed the cry of liberty of the women of the future. Deprived, like their brothers, of the Democracy, of the right to civil and political equality, and the fiscal laws which trammel the liberty of the press, hinder the propagation of those eternal truths which must regenerate humanity.

They wish the women of France to found a hospitable tribunal, which shall receive the cry of the oppressed and suffering, and vindicate in the name of humanity, solidarity, the social right for both sexes equally; and where woman, the mother of humanity, may claim in the name of her children, mutilated by tyranny, her right to true liberty, to the complete development and free exercise of all her faculties, and reveal that half of truth which is in her, and without which no social work can be complete.

The darkness of reaction has obscured the sun of 1848, which seemed to rise so radiantly. Why ? Because the revolutionary tempest, in over-turning at the same time the throne and the scaffold, in breaking the chain of the black slave, forgot to break the chain of the most oppressed of all of the pariahs of humanity.

"There shall be no more slaves," said our brethren. "We proclaim universal suffrage. All shall have the right to elect the agents who shall carry out the Constitution which should be based on the principles of liberty, equality, and fraternity. Let each one come and deposit his vote; the barrier of privilege is overturned; before the electoral urn there are no more oppressed, no more masters and slaves."

Woman, in listening to this appeal, rises and approaches the liberating urn to exercise her right of suffrage as a member of society. But the barrier of privilege rises also before her. "You must wait," they say. But by this claim alone woman affirms the right, not yet recognized, of the half of humanity—the right of woman to liberty, equality, and fra-ternity. She obliges man to verify the fatal attack which he makes on the integrity of his principles.

Soon, in fact during the wonderful days of June, 1848, liberty glides from her pedestal in the flood of the victims of the reaction; based on the "right of the strongest," she falls, overturned in the name of "the right of the strongest."

The Assembly kept silence in regard to the right of one-half of human-ity, for which only one of its members raised his voice, but in vain. No mention was made of the right of woman in a Constitution framed in the name of Liberty, Equality, and Fraternity.

It is in the name of these principles that woman comes to claim her right to take part in the Legislative Assembly, and to help to form the laws which must govern society, of which she is a member.

She comes to demand of the electors the consecration of the principle of equality by the election of a woman, and by this act she obliges man to prove that the fundamental law which he has formed in the sole name of liberty, equality, and fraternity, is still based upon privilege, and soon privilege triumphs over this phantom of universal suffrage, which, being but half of itself, sinks on the 31st of May, 1850.

But while those selected by the half of the people—by men alone—evoke force to stifle liberty, and forge restrictive laws to establish order by compression, woman, guided by fraternity, foreseeing incessant strug-gles, and in the hope of putting an end to them, makes an appeal to the laborer to found liberty and equality on fraternal solidarity. The par-ticipation of woman gave to this work of enfranchisement an eminently pacific character, and the laborer recognizes the right of woman, his companion in labor.

The delegates of a hundred and four associations, united, without distinction of sex, elected two women, with several of their brethren, to participate equally with them in the administration of the interests of labor, and in the organization of the work of solidarity.

Fraternal associations were formed with the object of enfranchising the laborer from the yoke of spoliage and patronage, but, isolated in the midst of the Old World, their efforts could only produce a feeble amelioration for themselves.

The union of associations based on fraternal solidarity had for its end the organization of labor; that is to say, an equal division of labor, of instruments, and of the products of labor.

The means were, the union of labor, and of credit among the workers of all professions, in order to acquire the instruments of labor and the necessary materials, and to form a mutual guarantee for the education of their children, and to provide for the needs of the old, the sick, and the infirm.

In this organization all the workers, without distinction of sex or profession, having an equal right to election, and being eligible for all functions, and all having equally the initiative and the sovereign decision in the acts of common interests, they laid the foundation of a new society based on liberty, equality, and fraternity.

It is in the name of law framed by man only—by those elected by privilege—that the Old World, wishing to stifle in the germ the holy work of pacific enfranchisement, has shut up within the walls of a prison those who had founded it—those elected by the laborers.

But the impulse has been given, a grand act has been accomplished. The right of woman has been recognized by the laborers, and they have consecrated that right by the election of those who had claimed it in vain for both sexes, before the electoral urn and before the electoral committees. They have received the true civil baptism, were elected by the laborers to accomplish the mission of enfranchisement, and after having shared their rights and their duties, they share to-day their captivity.

It is from the depths of their prison that they address to you the relation of these facts, which contain in themselves high instruction. It is by labor, it is by entering resolutely into the ranks of the working people, that women will conquer the civil and political equality on which depends the happiness of the world. As to moral equality, has she not conquered it by the power of sentiment? It is, therefore, by the sentiment of the love of humanity that the mother of humanity will find power to accomplish her high mission. It is when she shall have well comprehended the holy law of solidarity—which is not an obscure and mysterious dogma, but a living providential fact—that the kingdom of God promised by Jesus, and which is no other than the kingdom of equality and justice, shall be realized on earth.

Sisters of America! your socialist sisters of France are united with you in the vindication of the right of woman to civil and political equality. We have, moreover, the profound conviction that only by the power of association based on solidarity—by the union of the working-classes of both sexes to organize labor—can be acquired, completely and pacifically, the civil and political equality of woman, and the social right for all.

It is in this confidence that, from the depths of the jail which still imprisons our bodies without reaching our hearts, we cry to you, Faith, Love, Hope, and send to you our sisterly salutations.

JEANNE DEROINE,
PAULINE ROLAND.

PARIS, PRISON OF ST. LAGARE, *June* 15, 1851.

Ernestine L. Rose, having known something of European despotism, followed Mr. Channing in a speech of great pathos and power. She said:

After having heard the letter read from our poor incarcerated sisters of France, well might we exclaim, Alas, poor France! where is thy glory? Where the glory of the Revolution of 1848, in which shone forth the pure and magnanimous spirit of an oppressed nation struggling for Freedom? Where the fruits of that victory that gave to the world the motto, "Liberty, Equality, and Fraternity"? A motto destined to hurl the tyranny of kings and priests into the dust, and give freedom to the enslaved millions of the earth. Where, I again ask, is the result of those noble achievements, when woman, ay, one-half of the nation, is deprived of her rights? Has woman then been idle during the contest between "right and might"? Has she been wanting in ardor and enthusiasm? Has she not mingled her blood with that of her husband, son, and sire? Or has she been recreant in hailing the motto of liberty floating on your banners as an omen of justice, peace, and freedom to man, that at the first step she takes practically to claim the recognition of her rights, she is rewarded with the doom of a martyr?

But right has not yet asserted her prerogative, for might rules the day; and as every good cause must have its martyrs, why should woman not be a martyr for her cause? But need we wonder that France, governed as she is by Russian and Austrian despotism, does not recognize the rights of humanity in the recognition of the rights of woman, when even here, in this far-famed land of freedom, under a Republic that has inscribed on its banner the great truth that "all men are created free and equal, and endowed with inalienable rights to life, liberty, and the pursuit of happiness"—a declaration borne, like the vision of hope, on wings of light to the remotest parts of the earth, an omen of freedom to the oppressed and down-trodden children of man—when, even here, in the very face of this eternal truth, woman, the mockingly so-called "better half" of man, has yet to plead for her rights, nay, for her life. For what is life without liberty, and what is liberty without equality of rights? And as for the pursuit of happiness, she is not allowed to choose any line of action that might promote it; she has only thankfully to accept what man in his magnanimity decides as best for her to do, and this is what he does not choose to do himself.

Is she then not included in that declaration? Answer, ye wise men of the nation, and answer truly; add not hypocrisy to oppression! Say that she is not created free and equal, and therefore (for the sequence follows on the premise) that she is not entitled to life, liberty, and the pursuit of happiness. But with all the audacity arising from an assumed superiority, you dare not so libel and insult humanity as to say, that she is not included in that declaration; and if she is, then what right has man, except that of might, to deprive woman of the rights and privileges he claims for himself ? And why, in the name of reason and justice, why should she not have the same rights ? Because she is woman? Humanity recognizes no sex; virtue recognizes no sex; mind recognizes no sex; life and death, pleasure and pain, happiness and misery, recognize no sex. Like man, woman comes involuntarily into existence; like him, she possesses physical and mental and moral powers, on the proper cultivation of which depends her happiness; like him she is subject to all the vicissitudes of life; like him she has to pay the penalty for disobeying nature's laws, and far greater penalties has she to suffer from ignorance of her more complicated nature; like him she enjoys or suffers with her country. Yet she is not recognized as his equal!

In the laws of the land she has no rights; in government she has no voice. And in spite of another principle, recognized in this Republic, namely, that "taxation without representation is tyranny," she is taxed without being represented. Her property may be consumed by taxes to defray the expenses of that unholy, unrighteous custom called war, yet she has no power to give her vote against it. From the cradle to the grave she is subject to the power and control of man. Father, guardian, or husband, one conveys her like some piece of merchandise over to the other.

At marriage she loses her entire identity, and her being is said to have become merged in her husband. Has nature thus merged it ? Has she ceased to exist and feel pleasure and pain ? When she violates the laws of her being, does her husband pay the penalty ? When she breaks the moral laws, does he suffer the punishment ? When he supplies his wants, is it enough to satisfy her nature ? And when at his nightly orgies, in the grog-shop and the oyster-cellar, or at the gaming-table, he squanders the means she helped, by her co-operation and economy, to accumulate, and she awakens to penury and destitution, will it supply the wants of her children to tell them that, owing to the superiority of man she had no redress by law, and that as her being was merged in his, so also ought theirs to be ? What an inconsistency, that from the moment she enters that compact, in which she assumes the high responsibility of wife and mother, she ceases legally to exist, and becomes a purely submissive being. Blind submission in woman is considered a virtue, while submission to wrong is itself wrong, and resistance to wrong is virtue, alike in woman as in man.

But it will be said that the husband provides for the wife, or in other words, he feeds, clothes, and shelters her! I wish I had the power to make every one before me fully realize the degradation contained in that idea. Yes! he *keeps* her, and so he does a favorite horse; by law they are both considered his property. Both may, when the cruelty of the owner compels them to, run away, be brought back by the strong arm of the law, and according to a still extant law of England, both may be led by the halter to the market-place, and sold. This is humiliating indeed, but nevertheless true; and the sooner these things are known and understood, the better for humanity. It is no fancy sketch. I know that some endeavor to throw the mantle of romance over the subject, and treat woman like some ideal existence, not liable to the ills of life. Let those deal in fancy, that have nothing better to deal in; we have to do with sober, sad realities, with stubborn facts.

Again, I shall be told that the law presumes the husband to be kind. affectionate, and ready to provide for and protect his wife. But what right, I ask, has the law to presume at all on the subject? What right has the law to intrust the interest and happiness of one being into the hands of another? And if the merging of the interest of one being into the other is a necessary consequence on marriage, why should woman always remain on the losing side? Turn the tables. Let the identity and interest of the husband be merged in the wife. Think you she would act less generously toward him, than he toward her? Think you she is not capable of as much justice, disinterested devotion, and abiding affection, as he is? Oh, how grossly you misunderstand and wrong her nature! But we desire no such undue power over man; it would be as wrong in her to exercise it as it now is in him. All we claim is an equal legal and social position. We have nothing to do with individual man, be he good or bad, but with the laws that oppress woman. We know that bad and unjust laws must in the nature of things make man so too. If he is kind, affectionate, and consistent, it is because the kindlier feelings, instilled by a mother, kept warm by a sister, and cherished by a wife, will not allow him to carry out these barbarous laws against woman.

But the estimation she is generally held in, is as degrading as it is foolish. Man forgets that woman can not be degraded without its reacting on himself. The impress of her mind is stamped on him by nature, and the early education of the mother, which no after-training can entirely efface; and therefore, the estimation she is held in falls back with double force upon him. Yet, from the force of prejudice against her, he knows it not. Not long ago, I saw an account of two offenders, brought before a Justice of New York. One was charged with stealing a pair of boots, for which offense he was sentenced to six months' imprisonment; the other crime was assault and battery upon his wife: he was let off with a reprimand from the judge! With my principles, I am entirely opposed to punishment, and hold, that to reform the erring and remove the causes of evil is much more efficient, as well as just, than to punish. But the judge showed us the comparative value which he set on these two kinds of *property.* But then you must remember that the boots were taken by a stranger, while the wife was insulted by her legal owner! Here it will be said, that such degrading cases are but few. For the sake of humanity, I hope they are. But as long as woman shall be oppressed by unequal laws, so long will she be degraded by man.

We have hardly an adequate idea how all-powerful law is in forming public opinion, in giving tone and character to the mass of society. To illustrate my point, look at that infamous, detestable law, which was written in human blood, and signed and sealed with life and liberty, that eternal stain on the statute book of this country, the Fugitive Slave Law. Think you that before its passage, you could have found any in the free States—except a few politicians in the market—base enough to desire such a law? No! no! Even those who took no interest in the slave question, would have shrunk from so barbarous a thing. But no sooner was it passed, than the ignorant mass, the rabble of the self-styled Union Safety Committee, found out that we were a law-loving, law-abiding people! Such is the magic power of Law. Hence the necessity to guard against bad ones. Hence also the reason why we call on the nation to remove the legal shackles from woman, and it will have a beneficial effect on that still greater tyrant she has to contend with, Public Opinion.

Carry out the republican principle of universal suffrage, or strike it from your banners and substitute "Freedom and Power, to one half of society, and Submission and Slavery to the other." Give woman the elective franchise. Let married women have the same right to property that their husbands have; for whatever the difference in their respective occupations, the duties of the wife are as indispensable and far more arduous than the husband's. Why then should the wife, at the death of her husband, not be his heir to the same extent that he is heir to her? In this inequality there is involved another wrong. When the wife dies, the husband is left in the undisturbed possession of all there is, and the children are left with him; no change is made, no stranger intrudes on his home and his affliction. But when the husband dies, the widow, at best receives but a mere pittance, while strangers assume authority denied to the wife. The sanctuary of affliction must be desecrated by executors; everything must be ransacked and assessed, lest she should steal something out of her own house; and to cap the climax, the children must be placed under guardians. When the husband dies poor, to be sure, no guardian is required, and the children are left for the mother to care and toil for, as best she may. But when anything is left for their maintenance, then it must be placed in the hands of strangers for safe keeping! The bringing-up and safety of the children are left with the mother, and safe they are in her hands. But a few hundred or thousand dollars can not be intrusted with her!

But, say they, "in case of a second marriage, the children must be protected in their property." Does that reason not hold as good in the case of the husband as in that of the wife? Oh, no! When *he* marries again, he still retains his identity and power to act; but *she* becomes merged once more into a mere nonentity; and therefore the first husband must rob her to prevent the second from doing so! Make the laws regulating property between husband and wife, equal for both, and all these difficulties would be removed.

According to a late act, the wife has a right to the property she brings at marriage, or receives in any way after marriage. Here is some provision for the favored few; but for the laboring many, there is none. The mass of the people commence life with no other capital than the union of heads, hearts, and hands. To the benefit of this best of capital, the wife has no right. If they are unsuccessful in married life, who suffers more the bitter consequences of poverty than the wife? But if successful, she can not call a dollar her own. The husband may will away every dollar of the personal property, and leave her destitute and penniless, and she has no redress by law. And even where real estate is left she receives but a life-interest in a third part of it, and at her death, she can not leave it to any one belonging to her: it falls back even to the remotest of his relatives. This is law, but where is the justice of it? Well might we say that laws were made to prevent, not to promote, the ends of justice.

In case of separation, why should the children be taken from the protecting care of the mother? Who has a better right to them than she? How much do fathers generally do toward bringing them up? When he comes home from business, and the child is in good humor and handsome trim, he takes the little darling on his knee and plays with it. But when the wife, with the care of the whole household on her shoulders, with little or no help, is not able to put them in the best order, how much does he do for them? Oh, no! Fathers like to have children good natured, well-behaved, and comfortable, but how to put them in that desirable condition is out of their philosophy. Children always depend more on the tender, watchful care of the mother, than of the father. Whether from nature, habit, or both, the mother is much more capable of administering to their health and comfort than the father, and therefore she has the best right to them. And where there is property, it ought to be divided equally between them, with an additional provision from the father toward the maintenance and education of the children.

Much is said about the burdens and responsibilities of married men. Responsibilities indeed there are, if they but felt them; but as to burdens, what are they? The sole province of man seems to be centered in that one thing, attending to some business. I grant that owing to the present unjust and unequal reward for labor, many have to work too hard for a subsistence; but whatever his vocation, he has to attend as much to it before as after marriage. Look at your bachelors, and see if they do not strive as much for wealth, and attend as steadily to business, as married men. No! the husband has little or no increase of burden, and every increase of comfort after marriage; while most of the burdens, cares, pains, and penalties of married life fall on the wife. How unjust and cruel, then, to have all the laws in his favor! If any difference should be made by law between husband and wife, reason, justice, and humanity, if their voices were heard, would dictate that it should be in her favor.

No! there is no reason against woman's elevation, but there are deep-rooted, hoary-headed prejudices. The main cause of them is, a pernicious falsehood propagated against her being, namely, that she is inferior by her nature. Inferior in what? What has man ever done, that woman, under the same advantages, could not do? In morals, bad as she is, she is generally considered his superior. In the intellectual sphere, give her

16

a fair chance before you pronounce a verdict against her. Cultivate the frontal portion of her brain as much as that of man is cultivated, and she will stand his equal at least. Even now, where her mind has been called out at all, her intellect is as bright, as capacious, and as powerful as his. Will you tell us, that women have no Newtons, Shakespeares, and Byrons? Greater natural powers than even those possessed may have been destroyed in woman for want of proper culture, a just appreciation, reward for merit as an incentive to exertion, and freedom of action, without which, mind becomes cramped and stifled, for it can not expand under bolts and bars; and yet, amid all blighting, crushing circumstances—confined within the narrowest possible limits, trampled upon by prejudice and injustice, from her education and position forced to occupy herself almost exclusively with the most trivial affairs—in spite of all these difficulties, her intellect is as good as his. The few bright meteors in man's intellectual horizon could well be matched by woman, were she allowed to occupy the same elevated position. There is no need of naming the De Staëls, the Rolands, the Somervilles, the Wollstonecrofts, the Sigourneys, the Wrights, the Martineaus, the Hemanses, the Fullers, Jagellos, and many more of modern as well as ancient times, to prove her mental powers, her patriotism, her self-sacrificing devotion to the cause of humanity, and the eloquence that gushes from her pen, or from her tongue. These things are too well known to require repetition. And do you ask for fortitude, energy, and perseverance? Then look at woman under suffering, reverse of fortune, and affliction, when the strength and power of man have sunk to the lowest ebb, when his mind is overwhelmed by the dark waters of despair. She, like the tender ivy plant bent yet unbroken by the storms of life, not only upholds her own hopeful courage, but clings around the tempest-fallen oak, to speak hope to his faltering spirit, and shelter him from the returning blast of the storm.

In looking over the speeches of Elizabeth Oakes Smith, Abby Kelly Foster, Clarina Howard Nichols, Antoinette Brown, and Lucy Stone, and the well-digested reports by Paulina Wright Davis on Education, Abby Price on Industry, and William Henry Channing on the Social Relations, comprising the whole range of woman's rights and duties, we feel that the report of one of these meetings settles the question of woman's capacity to reason. At every session of this two days' Convention Brinley Hall was so crowded at an early hour that hundreds were unable to gain admittance. Accordingly, the last evening it was proposed to adjourn to the City Hall; and even that spacious auditorium was crowded long before the hour for assembling. It may be said with truth, that in the whole history of the woman suffrage movement there never was at one time more able and eloquent men and women on our platform, and represented by letter there, than in these Worcester Conventions, which called out numerous complimentary comments and editorial notices, notably the following :

[*From the New York Christian Inquirer*, Rev. Henry Bellows, D.D., editor.]

THE WOMAN'S RIGHTS CONVENTION AT WORCESTER.

We have read the report of the proceedings of this Convention with lively interest and general satisfaction. We confess ourselves to be much surprised at the prevailing good sense, propriety, and moral elevation of the meeting. No candid reader can deny the existence of singular ability, honest and pure aims, eloquent and forcible advocacy, and a startling power in the reports and speeches of this Convention. For good, or for evil, it seems to us to be the most important meeting since that held in the cabin of the *Mayflower*. That meeting recognized the social and political equality of one-half the human race; this asserts the social and political equality of the other half, and of the whole. Imagine the difference which it would have made in our Declaration of Independence, to have inserted "and women" in the first clause of the self-evident truths it asserts: "that all men *and women* are created equal." This Convention declares this to be the true interpretation of the Declaration, and at any rate, designs to amend the popular reading of the instrument to this effect. Nor is it a theoretical change which is aimed at. No more practical or tremendous revolution was ever sought in society, than that which this Woman's Rights Convention inaugurates. To emancipate half the human race from its present position of dependence on the other half; to abolish every distinction between the sexes that can be abolished, or which is maintained by statute or conventional usage; to throw open all the employments of society with equal freedom to men and women; to allow no difference whatsoever, in the eye of the law, in their duties or their rights, this, we submit, is a reform, surpassing, in pregnancy of purpose and potential results, any other now upon the platform, if it do not outweigh Magna Charta and our Declaration themselves.

We very well recollect the scorn with which the annual procession of the first Abolitionists was greeted in Boston, some thirty years ago. The children had no conception of the "Bobolition Society," but as of a set of persons making themselves ridiculous for the amusement of the public; but that "Bobolition Society" has shaken the Union to its center, and filled the world with sympathy and concern. The Woman's Rights Convention is in like manner a thing for honest scorn to point its finger at; but a few years may prove that we pointed the finger, not at an illuminated balloon, but at the rising sun.

We have no hesitation in acknowledging ourselves to be among those who have regarded this movement with decided distrust and distaste. If we have been more free than others to express this disgust, we have perhaps rendered some service, by representing a common sentiment with which this reform has to contend. We would be among the first to acknowledge that our objections have not grown out of any deliberate consideration of the principles involved in the question. They have

been founded on instinctive aversion, on an habitual respect for public
sentiment, on an irresistible feeling of the ludicrousness of the proposed
reform in its details. Certainly social instinct has its proper place in
the judgments we pass on the manners of both sexes. What is offensive
to good taste—meaning by good taste, the taste of the most educated
and refined people—has the burden of proof resting upon it when it
claims respect and attention. But we should be the last to assert that
questions of right and rights have no appeal from the bar of conventional taste to that of reason.

And however it may have been at the outset, we think the Woman's
Rights question has now made good its title to be heard in the superior
court. The principles involved in this great question we can not now
discuss; but we have a few thoughts upon the attitude of the reformer
toward society, which we would respectfully commend to attention. If
the female sex is injured in its present position, it is an injury growing
out of universal mistake; an honest error, in which the sexes have conspired, without intentional injustice on one side, or feeling of wrong on
the other. Indeed, we could not admit that there had been thus far
any wrong or mistake at all, except in details. Mankind have hitherto
found the natural functions of the two sexes marking out different
spheres for them. Thus far, as we think, the circumstances of the
world have compelled a marked division of labor, and a marked difference of culture and political position between the sexes.

The facts of superior bodily strength on the masculine side, and of
maternity on the feminine side, small as they are now made to appear,
are very great and decisive facts in themselves, and have necessarily governed the organization of society. It is between the sexes, as between
the races, the strongest rules; and it has hitherto been supposed to be
of service to the common interest of society, that this rule should be legalized and embodied in the social customs of every community. As a
fact, woman, by her bodily weakness and her maternal office, was from
the first, a comparatively private and domestic creature; her education,
from circumstances, was totally different, her interests were different, the
sources of her happiness different from man's, and as a fact, all these things,
though with important modifications, have continued to be so to this day.
The fact has seemed to the world a final one. It has been thought that
in her present position, she was in her best position relative to man,
which her nature or organization admitted of. That she is man's inferior
in respect to all offices and duties requiring great bodily powers, or great
moral courage, or great intellectual effort, has been almost universally
supposed,—honestly thought too, and without the least disposition to
deny her equality, on this account, in the scale of humanity.

For in respect to moral sensibility, affections, manners, tastes, and
the passive virtues, woman has long been honestly felt to be the superior
of man. The political disfranchisement of women, and their seclusion
from publicity, have grown out of sincere convictions that their nature
and happiness demanded from man an exemption from the cares, and a
protection from the perils of the out-of-door world. Mankind, in both
its parts, may have been utterly mistaken in this judgment; but it has

been nearly universal, and thoroughly sincere,—based thus far, we think, upon staring facts and compulsory circumstances.

In starting a radical reform upon this subject, it is expedient that it should be put, not on the basis of old grievances, but upon the ground of new light, of recent and fresh experiences, of change of circumstances. It may be that the relative position of the sexes is so changed by an advancing civilization, that the time has come for questioning the conclusion of the world respecting woman's sphere. All surprise at opposition to this notion, all sense of injury, all complaint of past injustice, ought to cease. Woman's part has been the part which her actual state made necessary. If another and a better future is opening, let us see it and rejoice in it as a new gift of Providence.

And we are not without suspicion that the time for some great change has arrived. At any rate, we confess our surprise at the weight of the reasoning brought forward by the recent Convention, and shall endeavor henceforth to keep our masculine mind,—full, doubtless, of conventional prejudices,—open to the light which is shed upon the theme.

Meanwhile, we must beg the women who are pressing this reform, to consider that the conservatism of instinct and taste, though not infallible, is respectable and worth attention. The opposition they will receive is founded on prejudices that are not selfish, but merely masculine. It springs from no desire to keep women down, but from a desire to keep them up; from a feeling, mistaken it may be, that their strength, and their dignity, and their happiness, lie in their seclusion from the rivalries, strifes, and public duties of life. The strength and depth of the respect and love for woman, as woman, which characterize this age, can not be overstated. But woman insists upon being respected, as a kindred intellect, a free competitor, and a political equal. And we have suspicions that she may surprise the conservative world by making her pretensions good. Only meanwhile let her respect the affectionate and sincere prejudices, if they be prejudices, which adhere to the other view, a view made honorable, if not proved true, by the experiences of all the ages of the past. We hope to give the whole subject more attention in future. Indeed it will force attention. It may be the solution of many social problems, long waiting an answer, is delayed by the neglect to take woman's case into fuller consideration. The success of the present reform would give an entirely new problem to political and social philosophers' At present we endeavor to hold ourselves in a candid suspense.

.' dging Dr. Bellows by the above editorial, he had made some progress in one year. A former article from his pen called out the following criticism from Mrs. Rose :

After last year's Woman's Convention, I saw an article in the *Christian Inquirer,* a Unitarian paper, edited by the Rev. Mr. Bellows, of New York, where, in reply to a correspondent on the subject of Woman's Rights, in which he strenuously opposed her taking part in anything in public, he said: "Place woman unbonneted and unshawled before the public gaze and what becomes of her modesty and her virtue?" In his benighted mind, the modesty and virtue of woman is of so fragile a nature, that when it is in contact with the atmosphere, it evaporates like chloroform. But I refrain to comment on such a sentiment. It carries with it its own deep condemnation. When I read the article, I earnestly wished I had the ladies of the writer's congregation before me, to see whether they could realize the estimation their pastor held them in. Yet I hardly know which sentiment was strongest in me, contempt for such foolish opinions, or pity for a man that has so degrading an opinion of woman— of the being that gave him life, that sustained his helpless infancy with her ever-watchful care, and laid the very foundation for the little mind he may possess—of the being he took to his bosom as the partner of his joys and sorrows—the one whom, when he strove to win her affection, he courted, as all such men court woman, like some divinity. Such a man deserves our pity; for I can not realize that a man purposely and willfully degrades his mother, sister, wife, and daughter. No! my better nature, my best knowledge and conviction forbid me to believe it.

THE UNA.

In February, 1853, Paulina Wright Davis started a woman's paper called *The Una*, published in Providence, Rhode Island, with the following prospectus:

Usage makes it necessary to present our readers with a prospectus setting forth our aims and objects. Our plan is to publish a paper monthly, devoted to the interests of woman. Our purpose is to speak clear, earnest words of truth and soberness in a spirit of kindness. To discuss the rights, duties, sphere, and destiny of woman fully and fearlessly. So far as our voice shall be heard, it will be ever on the side of freedom. We shall not confine ourselves to any locality, sex, sect, class, or caste, for we hold to the solidarity of the race, and believe if one member suffers, all suffer, and the highest made to atone for the lowest. Our mystical name, *The Una*, signifying *Truth*, will be to us a constant suggestion of fidelity to all.

The Una could boast for its correspondents some of the ablest men and women in the nation; such as William H. Channing, Elizabeth Peabody, Thomas Wentworth Higginson, Rev. A. D. Mayo, Dr. William Elder, Ednah D. Cheney, Caroline H. Dall, Fanny Fern, Elizabeth Oakes Smith, Frances D. Gage, Hannah Tracy Cutler, Abby H. Price, Marion Finch, of Liverpool, Hon. John Neal, of Portland, Lucy Stone, and Elizabeth Cady Stanton.

For some time Mrs. Dall assisted in the editorial department. *The Una* was the first pronounced Woman Suffrage paper; it lived three years. Glancing over the bound volumes, one may glean much valuable information of what was said and done during that period. We learn that Lady Grace Vandeleur, in person, canvassed the election of Kilrush, Ireland, and from her ladyship's open carriage, addressed a large assemblage of electors on behalf of her husband, the Conservative candidate. She was enthusiastically greeted by the populace.

The *Maine Age* announces the election of a Miss Rose to the office of Register of Deeds, and remarks : " Before the morning of the twentieth century dawns, women will not simply fill your offices of Register of Deeds, but they will occupy seats in your Legislative Halls, on your judicial benches, and in the executive chair of State and Nation. We deprecate it, yet we perceive its inevitability, and await the shock with firmness and composure."

This same year, *The Una* narrates the following amusing incident that occurred in the town of P——, New Hampshire : It is customary in the country towns for those who choose to do so, to pay their proportion of the highway tax, in actual labor on the roads, at the rate of eight cents an hour, instead of paying money. Two able-bodied and strong-hearted women in P——, who found it very in-convenient to pay the ready cash required of them, determined to avail themselves of this custom. They accordingly presented them-selves to the surveyor of the highway with hoes in their hands, and demanded to be set to work. The good surveyor was sorely puz-zled ; such a thing as women working out their taxes, had never been heard of, and yet the law made no provision against it. He consulted his lawyer, who advised him that he had no power to re-fuse. Accordingly the two brave women worked, and worked well, in spreading sand and gravel, saved their pennies, and no doubt felt all the better for their labor.

In the April Number, 1853, we find the following appeal to the citizens of Massachusetts, on the equal political rights of woman :

FELLOW-CITIZENS :—In May next a Convention will assemble to revise the Constitution of the Commonwealth.

At such a time it is the right and duty of every one to point out what-ever he deems erroneous and imperfect in that instrument, and press its amendment on public attention.

We deem the extension to woman of all civil rights, a measure of vital importance to the welfare and progress of the State. On every principle of natural justice, as well as by the nature of our institutions, she is as fully entitled as man to vote, and to be eligible to office. In govern-ments based on force, it might be pretended with some plausibility, that woman being supposed physically weaker than man, should be excluded from the State. But ours is a government professedly resting on the consent of the governed. Woman is surely as competent to give that consent as man. Our Revolution claimed that taxation and representa-tion should be co-extensive. While the property and labor of women **are** subject to taxation, she is entitled to a voice in fixing the amount of taxes, and the use of them when collected, and is entitled to a voice in the laws that regulate punishments. It would be a disgrace to our schools and civil institutions, for any one to argue that a Massachusetts woman who has enjoyed the full advantage of all their culture, is not as competent to form an opinion on civil matters, as the illiterate foreigner landed but a few years before upon our shores—unable to read or write— by no means free from early prejudices, and little acquainted with our institutions. Yet such men are allowed to vote.

Woman as wife, mother, daughter, and owner of property, has important rights te be protected. The whole history of legislation so unequal between the sexes, shows that she can not safely trust these to the other sex. Neither have her rights as mother, wife, daughter, laborer, ever received full legislative protection. Besides, our institutions are not based on the idea of one class receiving protection from another; but on the well-recognized rule that each class, or sex, is entitled to such civil rights, as will enable it to protect itself. The exercise of civil rights is one of the best means of education. Interest in great questions, and the discussion of them under momentous responsibility, call forth all the faculties and nerve them to their fullest strength. The grant of these rights on the part of society, would quickly lead to the enjoyment by woman, of a share in the higher grades of professional employment. Indeed, without these, mere book study is often but a waste of time. The learning for which no use is found or anticipated, is too frequently forgotten, almost as soon as acquired. The influence of such a share, on the moral condition of society, is still more important. Crowded now into few employments, women starve each other by close competition; and too often vice borrows overwhelming power of temptation from poverty. Open to women a great variety of employments, and her wages in each will rise; the energy and enterprise of the more highly endowed, will find full scope in honest effort, and the frightful vice of our cities will be stopped at its fountain-head. We hint very briefly at these matters. A circular like this will not allow room for more. Some may think it too soon to expect any action from the Convention. Many facts lead us to think that public opinion is more advanced on this question than is generally supposed. Beside, there can be no time so proper to call public attention to a radical change in our civil polity as now, when the whole framework of our government is to be subjected to examination and discussion. It is never too early to begin the discussion of any desired change. To urge our claim on the Convention, is to bring our question before the proper tribunal, and secure at the same time the immediate attention of the general public. Massachusetts, though she has led the way in most other reforms, has in this fallen behind her rivals, consenting to learn, as to the protection of the property of married women, of many younger States. Let us redeem for her the old pre-eminence, and urge her to set a noble example in this the most important of all civil reforms. To this we ask you to join with us* in the accompanying petition to the Constitutional Convention.

---

* Abby May Alcott, Abby Kelly Foster, Lucy Stone, Thomas W. Higginson, Ann Green Phillips, Wendell Phillips, Anna Q. T. Parsons, Theodore Parker, William J. Bow-

In favor of this Appeal Lucy Stone, Theodore Parker, Wendell Phillips, and Thomas Wentworth Higginson, were heard.

We find in *The Una* the following report of Mr. Higginson's speech before the Committee of the Constitutional Convention on the qualification of voters, June 3, 1853, the question being on the petition of Abby May Alcott, and other women of Massachusetts, that they be permitted to vote on the amendments that may be made to the Constitution.

MR. HIGGINSON'S SPEECH.

I need hardly suggest to the Committee the disadvantage under which I appear before them, in coming to glean after three of the most eloquent voices in this community, or any other [Lucy Stone, Wendell Phillips, and Theodore Parker]; in doing this, moreover, without having heard all their arguments, and in a fragment of time at the end of a two hours' sitting. I have also the minor disadvantage of gleaning after myself, having just ventured to submit a more elaborate essay on this subject, in a different form, to the notice of the Convention.

I shall therefore abstain from all debate upon the general question, and confine myself to the specific point now before this Committee. I shall waive all inquiry as to the right of women to equality in education, in occupations, or in the ordinary use of the elective franchise. The question before this Committee is not whether women shall become legal voters—but whether they shall have power to say, once for all, whether they wish to become legal voters. Whether, in one word, they desire to accept this Constitution which the Convention is framing.

It is well that the question should come up in this form, since the one efficient argument against the right of women to vote, in ordinary cases, is the plea that they do not wish to do it. "Their whole nature revolts at it." Very well; these petitioners simply desire an opportunity for Massachusetts women to say whether their nature does revolt at it or no.

The whole object of this Convention, as I heard stated by one of its firmest advocates, is simply this: to "make the Constitution of Massachusetts consistent with its own first principles." This is all these petitioners demand. Give them the premises which are conceded in our existing Bill of Rights, or even its Preamble, and they ask no more. I shall draw my few weapons from this source. I know that this document is not binding upon your Convention; nothing is binding upon you but eternal and absolute justice, and my predecessor has taken care of the claims of that. But the Bill of Rights is still the organic law of this State, and I can quote no better authority for those principles which lie at the foundation of all that we call republicanism.

---

ditch, Samuel E. Sewall, Ellis Gray Loring, Charles K. Whipple, Wm. Lloyd Garrison, Harriot K. Hunt, Thomas T. Stone, John W. Browne, Francis Jackson, Josiah F. Flagg, Mary Flagg, Elizabeth Smith, Eliza Barney, Abby H. Price, William C. Nell, Samuel May, Jr., Robert F. Wallcott, Robert Morris, A. Bronson Alcott.

I. My first citation will be from the Preamble, and will establish as Massachusetts doctrine the principle of the Declaration of Independence, that all government owes its just powers to the consent of the governed.

" The end of the institution, maintenance, and administration of government, is to secure the existence of the body politic. . . . . The body politic is formed by a voluntary association of individuals; it is a social compact, by which the whole people covenants with each citizen and each citizen with the whole people, that all shall be governed by certain laws for the common good. . . . . It is the duty of the people, therefore, in framing a constitution of government, to provide for an equitable mode of making laws, as well as for an impartial interpretation and a faithful execution of them," etc., etc.

Now, women are "individuals"; women are a part of "the people"; women are "citizens," for the Constitution elsewhere distinguishes male citizens. This clause, then, concedes precisely that which your petitioners claim. Observe how explicit it is. The people are not merely to have good laws, well administered; but they must have an equitable mode of making those laws. The reason of this is, that good laws are no permanent security, unless enacted by equitable methods. Your laws may be the best ever devised; yet still they are only given as a temporary favor, not held as a right, unless the whole people are concerned in their enactment. It is the old claim of despots—that their laws are good. When they told Alexander of Russia that his personal character was as good as a constitution for his people, " then," said he, " I am but a lucky accident." Your constitution may be never so benignant to woman, but that is only a lucky accident, unless you concede the claim of these women to have a share in creating it. Nothing else " is an equitable mode of making laws." But it is too late to choose female delegates to your Convention, and the only thing you can do is to allow women to vote on the acceptance of its results. The claim of these petitioners may be unexpected, but is logically irresistible. If you do not wish it to be renewed, you must remember either to alter or abrogate your Bill of Rights; for the petition is based on that.

The last speaker called this movement a novelty. Not entirely so. The novelty is partly the other way. In Europe, women have direct political power; witness Victoria. It is a false democracy which has taken it away. In my more detailed argument, I have cited many instances of these foreign privileges. In monarchical countries the dividing lines are not of sex, but of rank. A plebeian woman has no political power—nor has her husband. Rank gives it to man, and, also, in a degree, to woman. But among us the only rank is of sex. Politically speaking, in Massachusetts all men are patrician, all women plebeian. All men are equal, in having direct political power; and all women are equal, in having none. And women lose by democracy precisely that which men gain. Therefore I say this disfranchisement of woman, as woman, is a novelty. It is a new aristocracy; for, as De Tocqueville says, wherever one class has peculiar powers, as such, there is aristocracy and oligarchy.

We see the result of this in our general mode of speaking of woman. We forget to speak of her as an individual being, only as a thing. A political writer coolly says, that in Massachusetts, "except criminals and paupers, there is no class of persons who do not exercise the elective franchise." Women are not even a "class of persons." And yet, most readers would not notice this extraordinary omission. I talked the other day with a young radical preacher about his new religious organization. "Who votes under it?" said I. "Oh," (he said, triumphantly,) "we go for progress and liberty; anybody and everybody votes." "What!" said I, "women?" "No," said he, rather startled; "I did not think of them when I spoke." Thus quietly do we all talk of "anybody and everybody," and omit half the human race. Indeed, I read in the newspaper, this morning, of some great festivity, that "all the world and his wife" would be there! Women are not a part of the world, but only its "wife." They are not even "the rest of mankind"; they are womankind! All these things show the results of that inconsistency with the first principles of our Constitution of which the friends of this Convention justly complain.

II. So much for the general statement of the Massachusetts Bill of Rights in its Preamble. But one clause is even more explicit. In Section 9, I find the following:

"All the inhabitants of this Commonwealth, having such qualifications as they shall establish by their form of government, have an equal right to elect officers," etc.

As "they" shall establish. Who are *they?* Manifestly, the inhabitants as a whole. No part can have power, except by the consent of the whole, so far as that consent is practicable. Accordingly, you submit your Constitution for ratification—to whom? Not to the inhabitants of the State, not even to a majority of the native adult inhabitants; for it is estimated that at any given moment—in view of the great number of men emigrating to the West, to California, or absent on long voyages—the majority of the population of Massachusetts is female. You disfranchise the majority, then; the greater part of "the inhabitants" have no share in establishing the form of government, or assigning the qualifications of voters. What worse can you say of any oligarchy? True, your aristocracy is a large one—almost a majority, you may say. But so, in several European nations, is nobility almost in a majority, and you almost hire a nobleman to black your shoes; they are as cheap as generals and colonels in New England. But the principle is the same, whether the privileged minority consists of one or one million.

It is said that a tacit consent has been hitherto given by the absence of open protest? The same argument may be used concerning the black majority in South Carolina. Besides, your new Constitution is not yet made, and there has been no opportunity to assent to it. It will not be identical with the old one; but, even if it were, you propose to ask a renewed consent from men, and why not from women? Is it because a lady's "Yes" is always so fixed a certainty, that it never can be transformed to a "No," at a later period?

But I am compelled, by the fixed period of adjournment (10 A.M.), to

cut short my argument; as I have been already compelled to condense
it. I pray your consideration for the points I have urged. Believe me,
it is easier to ridicule the petition of these women than to answer the
arguments which sustain it. And, as the great republic of ancient times
did not blush to claim that laws and governments were first introduced
by Ceres, a woman, so I trust that the representatives of this noblest
of modern commonwealths may not be ashamed to receive legislative
suggestions from even female petitioners.

On Tuesday, August 12, 1853, in Committee of the Whole, the
report that "it is inexpedient to act on the petition" of seve al parties that women may vote, was taken up.

Mr. GREEN, of Brookfield, opposed the report, contending that women
being capable of giving or withholding their assent to the acts of government, should upon every principle of justice and equality, be permitted
to participate in its administration. He denied that men were of right
the guardians or trustees of women, since they had not been appointed,
but had usurped that position. Women had inherent natural rights as
a portion of the people, and they should be permitted to vote in order
to protect those inherent rights.

Mr. KEYES, of Abington, paid a warm tribute to the virtues and abilities of the fairer sex, and was willing to concede that they were to some
extent oppressed and denied their rights; but he did not believe the
granting of the privileges these petitioners claimed would tend to elevate or ameliorate their condition. Woman exerted great power by the
exercise of her feminine graces and virtues, which she would lose the
moment she should step beyond her proper sphere and mingle in the
affairs of State!

Mr. WHITNEY, of Boylston, believed that the same reasoning that would
deny the divine right of kings to govern men without their consent,
would also deny a similar right of men over women. The Committee
had given the best of reasons for granting the prayer of the petitioners,
and then reported that they have leave to withdraw. He expatiated on
the grievances to which women are subjected, and concluded by moving
as an amendment to the report, that the prayer of the petitioners ought
to be granted.

The Committee then rose, and had leave to sit again. Wednesday the
first business of importance was the taking up in Committee of the re-
port "leave to withdraw," relative to giving certain privileges to women.
Question on the amendment of Mr. Whitney to amend the conclusion of
the report, by inserting "that the prayer of the petitioners be granted."
Debate ensued on the subject between Messrs. Marvin, of Winchendon;
Kingman, of West Bridgewater; when the question was taken, and Mr.
Whitney's amendment rejected. Mr. Marvin then moved to substitute
"inexpedient to act" for "leave to withdraw"; which was adopted.
The Committee then rose, and recommended the adoption of the report
as amended, by a vote of 108 to 44.

The prejudices of the 108 outweighed all the able arguments made by those who represented the petitioners, and all the great principles of justice on which a true republic is based.

We find the following comments on the character and duties of the gentlemen who composed the Convention, from the pen of Mr. Higginson, in *The Una* of June, 1853 :

To the members of the Massachusetts Constitutional Convention :

The publication in our newspapers of the list of members of your honorable body, has won the just tribute of men of all parties to the happy result of the selection. Never, it is thought, has Massachusetts witnessed a political assembly of more eminent or accomplished men. And yet there are those to whom the daring thought has occurred, that to convoke such ability and learning, only to decide whether our Legislature shall be hereafter elected by towns or districts, is somewhat like the course of Columbus in assembling the dignitaries of his nation to decide whether an egg could be best poised upon the larger or the smaller end. A question which was necessarily settled, after all, by a compromise, as this will be.

But at that moment, there lay within the brain of the young Genoese a dream, which although denounced by prelates and derided by statesmen, was yet destined to add another half to the visible earth; so there is brooding in the soul of this generation, a vision of the greatest of all political discoveries, which, when accepted, will double the intellectual resources of society, and give a new world, not to Castile and Leon only, but to Massachusetts and the human race.

And lastly, as we owe the labor and the laurels of Columbus only to the liberal statesmanship of a woman, it is surely a noble hope, that the future Isabellas of this Nation may point the way for their oppressed sisters of Europe to a suffrage truly universal, and a political freedom bounded neither by station nor by sex.

Elizabeth Oakes Smith, writing in *The Una*, says of this historical occasion :

The Massachusetts Convention did not deign to notice the prayer of these two thousand women who claimed the privilege of being heard by men who assert that we are represented through them. They decided that " it is inexpedient to act upon said petition." This is no cause for discouragement to those who have the subject at heart. Two thousand signers are quite as many, if not more, than we supposed would be procured. The believers in the rights of woman to entire equality with man in every department involving the question of human justice are entirely in the minority. The majority believe that their wives and mothers are household chattels; believe that they were expressly created for no other purposes than those of maternity in their highest aspect; in their next for purposes of passion, with the long retinue of unhallowed sensualities, debasements, and pollutions which follow in the train of evil indulgence.

With others, women are sewers on of buttons; darners of stockings; makers of puddings; appendages to wash days, bakings, and brewings; echoes and adjectives to men for ever and ever. They are compounds of tears, hysterics, frettings, scoldings, complainings; made up of craftiness and imbecilities, to be wheedled, and coaxed, and coerced like unmanageable children. *The idea of a true, noble womanhood is yet to be created.* It does not live in the public mind. Now, in answer to the petition of these two thousand women, the Committee reply that all just governments exist by the consent of the governed. An old truism. We reply, women have given no such consent, and therefore are not bound to allegiance. But our sapient Legislators say, since there are two hundred thousand women in Massachusetts twenty-one years of age, and only two thousand who sign this petition, therefore it is fair to suppose that the larger part of the women of the State have consented to the present form of government. Now, this is assuredly a willful and unworthy perversion of the truth. These women are simply ignorant, simply supine. They have neither affirmed nor denied. They have not thought at all upon the subject. But there are two thousand women in Massachusetts who think and act, to say nothing of the thousands of intelligent men there who believe in the same doctrine. Now here is a little army in one State alone, and that a conservative one, while through the Middle and Western States are thousands thinking in the same direction. Here is the leaven that must leaven the whole lump. Here is the wise minority which will hereafter become the overwhelming majority of the country. The Committee remark on the fact that while 50,000 women have petitioned for a law to repress the sale of intoxicating liquor, only two thousand petition for the right to vote! While the multitude could readily trace the downfall of father, husband, brother, and son, to the dram-shop, only the thinking few could see the power beyond the law and the lawmaker that protects the traffic, the right to the ballot, with which to strike the most effective blow in the right place.

NEW ENGLAND WOMAN'S RIGHTS CONVENTION.

Boston, Friday, *June* 2, 1854.

This Convention assembled the day on which poor Anthony Burns was consigned to hopeless bondage;* and though many friends of the woman movement remained in the streets to see his surrender, still at an early hour the hall was literally crowded with earnest men and women, whom a deep interest in the cause had drawn together. Sarah H. Earle, of Worcester, was chosen President; Lucy Stone, Chairman of the Business Committee, reported the resolutions, among which we find the following:

Resolved, That the Common Law, which governs the marriage relation, and blots out the legal existence of a wife, denies her right to the product

---

* Anthony Burns, the slave, was a Baptist minister in his Southern home, and had sought freedom in Boston, but was pursued and recaptured.

of her own industry, denies her equal property rights, even denies her right to her children, and the custody of her own person, is grossly unjust to woman, dishonorable to man, and destructive to the harmony of life's holiest relation.

Resolved, That the laws which destroy the legal individuality of woman after her marriage are equally pernicious to man as to woman, and may give to him in marriage a slave, or a tyrant, but never a wife.

William Lloyd Garrison, Emma R. Coe, Josephine S. Griffing, Wendell Phillips, Dr. Harriot K. Hunt, Rev. S. S. Griswold, Sarah Pellet, Abby Kelly Foster, Mrs. Morton, and Lucy Stone took part in the debates. Letters were received from Thomas W. Higginson, Rev. A. D. Mayo, Paulina Wright Davis, Mrs. Nichols, and Sarah Crosby. Francis Jackson,* of Boston, made a contribution of $50. Committees were appointed from each of the New England States to circulate petitions for securing a change in the laws regulating the property of married women, and limiting the right of suffrage to men. All the sessions drew crowded audiences, and the enthusiasm was sustained to the end. The sympathy for Burns intensified the feelings of those present against all forms of oppression. Those who had witnessed the military parade through the streets of Boston to drive the slave—a minister of the Baptist denomination in his southern home—from the land of the Pilgrims where he had sought refuge, were roused to plead with new earnestness and power for equal rights to all without distinction of sex or color.

WOMAN'S RIGHTS CONVENTION IN BOSTON.

Sept. 19 *and* 20, 1855.

This Convention was fully attended through six sessions, and gave great satisfaction to all engaged in it. After its close, its officers received such expressions of interest from persons not previously enlisted in the cause, as to convince them that a lasting impression was made. The attendance was the best that Boston could furnish in intelligence and respectability, and to a greater degree than usual clerical. Mrs. Paulina Wright Davis was again chosen President. Business Committee—Dr. William F. Channing, Caroline H. Dall, Wendell Phillips, and Caroline M. Severance. Among the Vice-Presidents we find the names of Harriot K. Hunt and Thomas Wentworth Higginson. Caroline H. Dall, Ellen M. Tarr, and Paulina Wright Davis presented carefully prepared digests of the laws of several of the New England States. Mrs. Davis said:

---

* A gentleman of wealth, who gave most liberally to all reforms, and in his will bequeathed $5,000 to the cause of woman suffrage.

In 1844 a bill was introduced into the Legislature of this State (Rhode Island) by Hon. Wilkins Updike, securing to married women their property "under certain regulations." The step was a progressive one, and hailed at that time as a bright omen for the future. Other States have followed the example, and the right of woman to some control of her property has been recognized. In 1847 Vermont passed similar enactments; in 1848–'49, Connecticut, New York, and Texas; in 1850–'52, Alabama and Maine; in 1853, New Hampshire, Indiana, Wisconsin, and Iowa followed. But the provisions "under certain regulations" left married women almost as helpless as before.

Mrs. DAVIS further says: If in 1855, from the practical workings of these statutes, we find ourselves compelled to pronounce them despotic in spirit, degrading and tyrannical in effect, we do not the less give honor to the man who was so far in advance of his age as to conceive the idea of raising woman a little in the scale of being.

We have always claimed the honor for New York as being first in this matter, because the Property Bill was presented there in 1836, and when finally passed in 1848, was far more liberal than in any other State ; and step by step her legislation was broadened, until 1860 the revolution was complete, securing to married women their own inheritance absolutely, to use, will, and dispose of as they see fit; to do business in their name, make contracts, sue, and be sued.

The speakers on the first day of this Convention were Wendell Phillips, Thomas W. Higginson, and Lucy Stone ; on the second morning, Caroline H. Dall, Antoinette L. Brown, and Susan B. Anthony. The evening closed with a lecture from Ralph Waldo Emerson, and a poem by Elizabeth Oakes Smith. No report of the debates was preserved.

In a letter to her family Susan B. Anthony, under date of Sept. 27th, says:

I went into Boston on Tuesday, with Lucy Stone, to attend the Convention. We stopped at Francis Jackson's, where we found Antoinette Brown and Ellen Blackwell. A pleasant company in that most hospitable home. The Convention passed off pleasantly, but with none of the enthusiasm we have in our New York meetings. As this was my first visit to Boston, Mr. Jackson took Antoinette and myself round to see the lions; to the House of Correction, the House of Reformation, the Merchant's Exchange, the Custom-House, State House, and Faneuil Hall, and then dined with his daughter, Eliza J. Eddy, in South Boston, returning in the afternoon. Lucy and Antoinette left, one for New York and the other for Brookfield. In the evening, Ellen Blackwell and I attended a reception at Mr. Garrison's, where we met several of the *literati*, and were most heartily welcomed by Mrs. Garrison, a noble, self-sacrificing woman, the loving and the loved, surrounded with healthy, happy children in that model home. Mr. Garrison was omnipresent now talking and introducing guests, now soothing some child to sleep, and now, with his charming wife, looking after the refreshments. There we met Mrs. Dall, Elizabeth Peabody, Mrs. McCready, the Shakespearian reader, Mrs. Severance, Dr. Hunt, Charles F. Hovey, Francis Jackson, Wendell Phillips, Sarah Pugh, of Philadelphia, and others. Having worshiped these distinguished people afar off, it was a great satisfaction to see so many face to face.

On Saturday morning, in company with Mr. and Mrs. Garrison and Sarah Pugh, I visited Mount Auburn. What a magnificent resting-place this is! We could not find Margaret Fuller's monument, which I regretted. I spent Sunday with Charles Lenox Remond; we drove to Lynn with matchless steeds to hear Theodore Parker preach. What a sermon! our souls were filled. We discussed its excellence at James Buffum's, where, with other friends, we dined. Visited the steamer *Africa* next day, in which Ellen Blackwell was soon to sail for Liverpool.

Monday Mr. Garrison escorted me to Charlestown; we stood on the very spot where Warren fell, and mounted the interminable staircase to the top of Bunker Hill Monument, where we had an extensive view of the harbor and surrounding country. Then we called on Theodore Parker; found him up three flights of stairs in his library, covering that whole floor of his house; the room is lined all round with books to the very top—16,000 volumes—and there, at a large table in the center of the apartment, sat the great man himself. It really seemed audacious in me to be ushered into such a presence, and on such a commonplace errand, to ask him to come to Rochester to speak in a course of lectures I am planning. But he received me with such kindness and simplicity, that the awe I felt on entering was soon dissipated. I then called on Wendell Phillips, in his sanctum, for the same purpose. I have invited Ralph Waldo Emerson by letter, and all three have promised to come. In the evening, with Mr. Jackson's son James, the most diffident and sensitive man I ever saw, Miss B—— and I went to the theater to see Dussendoff, the great tragedian, play Hamlet. The theater is new, the scenery beautiful, and, in spite of my Quaker training, I find I enjoy all these worldly amusements intensely.

Returning to Worcester, I attended the Anti-Slavery Bazaar. I suppose there were many beautiful things exhibited, but I was so absorbed in the conversation of Mr. Higginson, Samuel May, Jr., Sarah Earle, Cousin Dr. Seth Rogers, Stephen and Abby Foster, that I really forgot to take a survey of the tables. The next day Charles F. Hovey drove me out to the home of the Fosters, where we had a pleasant call.

Francis Jackson and Charles F. Hovey, though neither speakers nor writers, yet they furnished the " sinews of war." None contributed more generously than they to all the reforms of their times. They were the first men to make a bequest to our movement. To them we are indebted for the money that enabled us to carry on the agitation for years. Beside giving liberally from time to time, Francis Jackson left $5,000 in the hands of Wendell Phillips, which

17

he managed and invested so wisely, that the fund was nearly doubled. Charles F. Hovey left $50,000 to be used in anti-slavery, woman suffrage, and free religion. With the exception of $1,000 from Lydia Maria Child, we have yet to hear of a woman of wealth who has left anything for the enfranchisement of her sex. Almost every daily paper heralds the fact of some large bequest to colleges, churches, and charities by rich women, but it is proverbial that they never remember the Woman Suffrage movement that underlies in importance all others.

HEARING BEFORE THE MASSACHUSETTS LEGISLATURE, MARCH, 1857.

The Boston Traveller says: The Representatives Hall yesterday afternoon was completely filled, galleries and all, to hear the arguments before the Judiciary Committee, to whom was referred the petition of Lucy Stone and others for equal rights for " females " in the administration of government, for the right of suffrage, etc.

Rev. JAMES FREEMAN CLARKE was the first speaker. He said: Gentlemen, the question before you is, Shall the women of Massachusetts have equal rights with the men ? The fundamental principles of the Constitution set forth equal rights to all. A large portion of the property of Massachusetts is owned by women, probably one-third of the whole amount, and yet they are not represented, though compelled to pay taxes. It has been said they are represented by their husbands. So it was said that the American colonies were represented in the British Parliament, but the colonies were not contented with such representation; neither are women contented to be represented by men. As long as we put woman's name on the tax-list we should put it in the ballot-box.

WENDELL PHILLIPS said: Self-government was the foundation of our institutions. July 4, 1776, sent the message round the world that every man can take care of himself better than any one else can do it for him. If you tax me, consult me. If you hang me, first try me by a jury of my own peers. What I ask for myself, I ask for woman. In the banks a woman, as a stockholder, is allowed to vote. In the Bank of England, in the East India Company, in State Street, her power is felt, her voice controls millions.

Three hundred years ago it was said woman had no right to profess any religion, as it would make discord in the family if she differed from her husband. The same conservatism warns us of the danger of allowing her any political opinions.

LUCY STONE said: The argument that the wife, having the right of suffrage, would cause discord in the family, is entirely incorrect. When men wish to procure the vote of a neighbor, do they not approach them with the utmost suavity, and would not the husband who wished to influence the wife's vote be far more gracious than usual ? She instanced the heroic conduct of Mrs. Patton, who navigated her husband's ship into the harbor of San Francisco, as an argument in favor of woman's power of command and of government. The captain and mate lying ill with a fever, she had the absolute control of both vessel and crew. Mrs. Stone's speech was comprehensive and pointed, and called forth frequent applause.

Dr. Harriot K. Hunt, a woman of wealth and position, protested every year against being compelled to pay taxes while not recognized in the government.

DR. HUNT'S PROTEST OF 1852.

To Frederick W. Tracy, Treasurer, and the Assessors, and other Authorities of the city of Boston, and the Citizens generally:

Harriot K. Hunt, physician, a native and permanent resident of the city of Boston, and for many years a taxpayer therein, in making payment of her city taxes for the coming year, begs leave to protest against the injustice and inequality of levying taxes upon women, and at the same time refusing them any voice or vote in the imposition and expenditure of the same. The only classes of male persons required to pay taxes, and not at the same time allowed the privilege of voting, are aliens and minors. The objection in the case of aliens is their supposed want of interest in our institutions and knowledge of them. The objection in the case of minors, is the want of sufficient understanding. These objections can not apply to women, natives of the city, all of whose property interests are here, and who have accumulated, by their own sagacity and industry, the very property on which they are taxed. But this is not all; the alien, by going through the forms of naturalization, the minor on coming of age, obtain the right of voting; and so long as they continue to pay a mere poll-tax of a dollar and a half, they may continue to exercise it, though so ignorant as not to be able to sign their names, or read the very votes they put into the ballot-boxes. Even drunkards, felons, idiots, and lunatics, if men, may still enjoy that right of voting to which no woman, however large the amount of taxes she pays, however respectable her character, or useful her life, can ever attain. Wherein, your remonstrant would inquire, is the justice, equality, or wisdom of this?

That the rights and interests of the female part of the community are sometimes forgotten or disregarded in consequence of their deprivation of political rights, is strikingly evinced, as appears to your remonstrant, in the organization and administration of the city public schools. Though there are open in this State and neighborhood, a great multitude of colleges and professional schools for the education of boys and young men, yet the city has very properly provided two High-Schools of its own, one Latin, the other English, in which the "male graduates" of the Grammar Schools may pursue their education still farther at the public expense. And why is not a like provision made for the girls? Why is their education stopped short, just as they have attained the age best fitted for progress, and the preliminary knowledge necessary to facilitate it, thus giving the advantage of superior culture to sex, not to mind?

The fact that our colleges and professional schools aie closed against females, of which your remonstrant has had personal and painful experience; having been in the year 1847, after twelve years of medical practice in Boston, refused permission to attend the lectures of Harvard Medical College. That fact would seem to furnish an additional reason why the city should provide, at its own expense, those means of superior education which, by supplying our girls with occupation and objects of interest, would not only save them from lives of frivolity and emptiness, but which might open the way to many useful and lucrative pursuits, and so raise them above that degrading dependence, so fruitful a source of female misery.

Reserving a more full exposition of the subject to future occasions, your remonstrant, in paying her tax for the current year, begs leave to protest against the injustice and inequalities above pointed out.

This is respectfully submitted,   HARRIOT K. HUNT,
32 Green Street, Boston, Mass.

Harriot K. Hunt commenced the practice of medicine at the age of thirty, in 1835; twelve years after, was refused admission to Harvard Medical Lectures. She often said that as her love element had all centered in her profession, she intended to celebrate her silver wedding, which she did, in the summer of 1860. Her house was crowded with a large circle of loving friends, who decorated it with flowers and many bridal offerings, thus expressing their esteem and affection for the first woman physician, who had done so much to relieve the sufferings of women and children. The degree of M.D. was conferred on her by " The Woman's Medical College of Pennsylvania," in 1853. Her biographer says she honored the title more than the title could her.

MARRIAGE OF LUCY STONE UNDER PROTEST.

It was my privilege to celebrate May day by officiating at a wedding in a farm-house among the hills of West Brookfield. The bridegroom was a man of tried worth, a leader in the Western Anti-Slavery Movement; and the bride was one whose fair name is known throughout the nation; one whose rare intellectual qualities are excelled by the private beauty of her heart and life.

I never perform the marriage ceremony without a renewed sense of the iniquity of our present system of laws in respect to marriage; a system by which "man and wife are one, and that one is the husband." It was with my hearty concurrence, therefore, that the following protest was read and signed, as a part of the nuptial ceremony; and I send it to you, that others may be induced to do likewise.

Rev. THOMAS WENTWORTH HIGGINSON.

PROTEST.

While acknowledging our mutual affection by publicly assuming the relationship of husband and wife, yet in justice to ourselves and a great principle, we deem it a duty to declare that this act on our part implies no sanction of, nor promise of voluntary obedience to such of the present laws of marriage, as refuse to recognize the wife as an independent, rational being, while they confer upon the husband an injurious and unnatural superiority, investing him with legal powers which no honorable man would exercise, and which no man should possess. We protest especially against the laws which give to the husband:

1. The custody of the wife's person.

2. The exclusive control and guardianship of their children.

3. The sole ownership of her personal, and use of her real estate, unless previously settled upon her, or placed in the hands of trustees, as in the case of minors, lunatics, and idiots.

4. The absolute right to the product of her industry.

5. Also against laws which give to the widower so much larger and more permanent an interest in the property of his deceased wife, than they give to the widow in that of the deceased husband.

6. Finally, against the whole system by which "the legal existence of the wife is suspended during marriage," so that in most States, she neither has a legal part in the choice of her residence, nor can she make a will, nor sue or be sued in her own name, nor inherit property.

We believe that personal independence and equal human rights can never be forfeited, except for crime; that marriage should be an equal and permanent partnership, and so recognized by law; that until it is so recognized, married partners should provide against the radical injustice of present laws, by every means in their power.

We believe that where domestic difficulties arise, no appeal should be made to legal tribunals under existing laws, but that all difficulties should be submitted to the equitable adjustment of arbitrators mutually chosen.

Thus reverencing law, we enter our protest against rules and customs which are unworthy of the name, since they violate justice, the essence of law.

(Signed),	HENRY B. BLACKWELL,
Worcester Spy, 1855.	LUCY STONE.

To the above *The Liberator* appended the following:

We are very sorry (as will be a host of others) to lose Lucy Stone, and certainly no less glad to gain Lucy Blackwell. Our most fervent benediction upon the heads of the parties thus united.

This was a timely protest against the whole idea of the old Blackstone code, which made woman a nonentity in marriage. Lucy Stone took an equally brave step in refusing to take her husband's name, respecting her own individuality and the name that represented it. These protests have called down on Mrs. Stone much ridicule and persecution, but she has firmly maintained her position, although at great inconvenience in the execution of legal documents, and suffering the injustice of having her vote refused as

Lucy Stone, soon after the bill passed in Massachusetts giving all women the right to vote on the school question.

In 1858, Caroline H. Dall, of Boston, gave a series of literary lectures in different parts of the country, on "Woman's Claims to Education," beginning in her native city. Her subjects were:

Nov. 1st.—The ideal standard of education, depressed by public opinion, but developed by the spirit of the age; Egypt and Algiers.

Nov. 8th.—Public opinion, as it is influenced by the study of the Classics and History, by general literature, newspapers, and customs.

Nov. 15th.—Public opinion as modified by individual lives: Mary Wollstonecroft, Anna Jamieson, Charlotte Brontè, and Margaret Fuller.

In June 11th, of this year, Mrs. Dall writes to the *Liberator* of her efforts to circulate the following petition:

To the Honorable, the Senate and House of Representatives of the Commonwealth of Massachusetts, in General Court assembled:

WHEREAS, The women of Massachusetts are disfranchised by its State Constitution solely on account of sex.

We do respectfully demand the right of suffrage, which involves all other rights of citizenship, and one that can not justly be withheld, as the following admitted principles of government show:

1st. "All men are born free and equal."

2d. "Governments derive their just powers from the consent of the governed."

3d. "Taxation and representation are inseparable." We, the undersigned, therefore petition your Honorable Body to take the necessary steps to revise the Constitution so that all citizens may enjoy equal political rights.

NEW ENGLAND CONVENTION.

May 27th, 1859, an enthusiastic Convention was held in Mercantile Hall. Long before the hour announced the aisles, ante-rooms, and lobbies were crowded. At three o'clock Mrs. Caroline H. Dall called the meeting to order. Mrs. Caroline M. Severance was chosen President. On taking the chair, she said:

This movement enrolls itself among the efforts of the age, and the anniversaries of the week as the most radical, and yet in the best sense the most conservative of them all. It bears the same relation, to all the charities of the day, which strive nobly to serve woman, that the Anti-Slavery movement bears to all superficial palliations of slavery. Like that, it goes beneath effects, and seeks to remove causes. After showing in a very lucid manner the difference in the family institution, when the mother is ignorant and enslaved, and when an educated, harmoniously developed equal, she closed by saying: It will be seen then, that instead of confounding the philosophy of the new movement with theories that claim unlimited indulgence for appetite or passion, the world should recognize in this the only radical cure. . . . . No statement could better define this movement than Tennyson's beautiful stanzas:

> The woman's cause is *man's;* they sink or rise
> Together, dwarfed or godlike, bond or free,
> If she be small, slight-natured, miserable,
> How shall man grow?
> The woman is not undeveloped man,
> But diverse.

> Yet in the long years, *liker* must they grow;
> The man be more of woman, she of man :
> *He* gain in sweetness and in moral height—
> *She* mental breadth, nor fail in childward care,
> Nor lose the childlike in the larger mind.

> And so these twain, upon the skirts of Time
> Sit side by side, full-summed in all their powers,
> Self-reverent each, and reverencing each ;
> Distinct in individualities,
> But like each other, as are those who love.

> Then comes the statelier Eden back to man ;
> Then reign the world's great bridals, chaste and calm ;
> Then springs the crowning race of humankind.

And we who are privileged with the poet to foresee this better Eden; we who have

> The Future grand and great,—
> The safe appeal of Truth to Time,—

adopting the victorious cry of the Crusaders, "God wills it!" may listen to hear above the present din and discord, the stern mandate of His laws, bidding the world "Onward! onward!" and catch the rhythmical reply of all its movements, "We advance."

Mrs. Severance then read an appropriate poem from the pen of Mrs. Sarah Nowell, in which she eulogizes Florence Nightingale, Rosa Bonheur, Harriet Hosmer, and asserts the equality of man and woman in the creation.

Dr. Harriot K. Hunt made some pointed remarks on the education of woman.

The Rev. James Freeman Clarke was then introduced. He said :

I understand the cause advocated on this platform to be an unpopular one. It is a feeble cause, a misunderstood cause, a misrepresented cause. Hence, it seems to me, if any one is asked to say anything in behalf of it, and if he really believes it is a good cause, he should speak ; and so I have come.

Certainly any interest which concerns one-half the human race is an important one. Every man, no matter how stern, hard, and unrelenting he may have become in the bitter strife and struggle of the world, every man was once a little infant, cradled on a mother's knee, and taking his life from the sweet fountains of her love. He was a little child, watched by her tender, careful eye, and so secured from ill. He was a little, inquiring boy, with a boundless appetite for information, which only his mother could give. At her knee he found his primary school: it is where we have all found it. He had his sisters—the companions of his childhood; he had the little girls, who were to him the ideals of some wonderful goodness and excellence, some strange grace and beauty, though he could not tell what it was. With these antecedents no man on the face of the round world can refuse to hear woman, when she comes earnestly, but quietly saying, "We are not where we ought to be;" "We do not have what we ought to have." I think their demands are reasonable, all of them. What are they? Occupation, education, and the highest sphere of work of which they are capable. These I understand to be the three demands.

1st. Occupation. When your child steals on a busy hour and asks for "something to do," you feel ashamed that you have nothing for him—that you can not give him the natural occupation which shall develop all the faculties of mind and body. Is it not a reasonable request which women make, when they ask for something to do? They want to be useful in the world. They ask permission to support themselves and those who are dear to them. What can they do now? They can go into factories, a few of them; a few more can be servants in your homes; they can cook your dinner if they have been taught how. If they are women of genius, they can take the pen and write; but how few are there in this world, either *men* or *women* of genius. If they have extraordinary business talent, they can keep a boarding-house. If they have some education they can keep school. After this, there is the point of the needle upon which they may be precipitated—and nothing else.

We see the gloom that must fall on them, on their children, and on all they love, when the male protector is taken away. This demand for more varied occupation is not a new one. Many years ago, one of the wisest and truest men of this country, a philanthropist and reformer—Matthew Carey, of Philadelphia—labored to impress upon the people the fact, that what was wanted for the elevation of woman was to open to her new avenues of business. A very sad book was written a few months ago, "Dr. Sanger's work on Prostitution." It is a very dreadful book; not calculated, I think, to excite any prurient feeling in any one. In that book he says:

First, that the majority of the prostitutes of this country are mere children, between the ages of fifteen and twenty. That the lives of these poor, wretched, degraded creatures, last on an average about four years. Now, when we hear of slaves used up in six years on a sugar plantation, we think it horrible; but here are these poor girls killed in a more dreadful way, in a shorter time. And he adds that the principal cause of their prostitution is that they have no occupation by which they can support themselves. Without support, without resources, they struggle for a while and then are thrown under the feet of the trampling city. Give them occupation and they will take care of themselves: they will rise out of the mire of pollution, out of this filth; for it is not in the nature of woman to remain there. Give them at least a chance; open wide every door; and whenever they are able to get a living by their head or their hands in an honest way, let them do it. This is the first claim; and it seems to me that no one can reasonably object to it.

2d. Education. You say that public schools are open to girls as well as boys. I know that, but what is it that educates? The school has but little to do with it. When the boy goes there you say, "Go there, work with a will, and fit yourself for an occupation whereby you may earn your bread." But you say to the girls, "Go to school, get your education, and then come home, sit still, and do nothing." We must give them every chance to fit themselves for new spheres of duty. If a woman wants to study medicine, let her study it; if she wants to study divinity, let her study it; if she wants to study anything, let her have the opportunity. If she finds faculties within her, let them have a chance to expand. That is the second demand—the whole of it.

And the third claim is for a Sphere of Influence. "That is not it," do you say? "*You* want to take woman *out* of her sphere." Not at all, we wish to give her a sphere, not to take her from any place she likes to fill; to give her a chance to exercise those wonderful, those divine faculties that God has wrapped in the feminine mind, in the woman's heart.

As regards voting, why should not women go to the polls? You think it a very strange desire, I know; but we have thought many things stranger which seem quite natural now. One need not live long to find strange things grow common. Why not vote, then? Is it because they have not as much power to understand what is true and right as man? If you go to the polls, and see the style of men who meet there voting, can you come away, and tell us that the women you meet are not as able to decide what is right as those men? "Ah, it will brush off every feminine grace, if woman goes to the polls." Why? "Because she must meet rude men there." Very well, so she must meet them in the street, and they do not hurt her; nor will I believe that there is not sufficient inventive power in the Yankee intellect to overcome this difficulty. I can conceive of a broader and more generous activity in politics. I can see her drawing out all the harshness and bitterness when she goes to the polls. These three points are all I intended to touch; and I will give way to those who are to follow.

Mrs. CAROLINE H. DALL was then introduced. She said: I have observed that all public orators labor under some embarrassment when they rise to speak. Not to be behind the dignity of my position, I labor under a *double* embarrassment.

The first is the "embarras des richesses." There are so many topics to touch, so many facts to relate, that it is impossible to cover them in one half hour, and the second—perhaps you will think that an embarrassment of riches also; for it is an embarrassment of Clarke and Phillips. The orator needs no common courage who follows the one and precedes the other. It is my duty to speak of the progress of the cause; it is impossible to keep pace with it. You may work day and night, but this thought of God outstrips you, working hourly through the life of man.

Yet we must often feel discouraged. Our war is not without; our work follows us into the heart of the family. We must sustain ourselves in that dear circle against our nearest friends; against the all-pervading law, "Thus far shalt thou come, and no farther."

What have we gained since 1855? Many things, so important, that they can not be worthily treated here. I have often mentioned in my lectures, that in his first report to the French Government, Neckar gave the credit of his retrenchments to his thrifty, order-loving wife. Until this year, that acknowledgment stood alone in history. But now John Stuart Mill, the great philosopher and political economist of England, dedicates his "Essay on Liberty" to the memory of his beloved wife, who has been the *inspiration of all, and the author of much* that was best in his writings for many years past. Still farther, in a pamphlet on "English Political Reform," treating of the extension of the suffrage, he has gone so far as to recommend that all householders, without distinction of sex, be adopted into the constituency, upon proving to the registrar's officer that they have a certain income—say fifty pounds—and "that they can read, write, and calculate."

A great step was taken also in the establishment of the Institution for the Advancement of Social Science. The sexes are equal before it. It has five departments. 1. Jurisprudence, or Law Reform; 2. Education; 3. Punishment and Reformation; 4. Public Health; 5. Social Economy.

The first meeting at Liverpool considered the woman's question; and, while it was debated, Mary Carpenter sat upon the platform, or lifted her voice side by side with Brougham, Lord John Russell, and Stanley. At the second meeting (last October), Lord John Russell was in the chair. The Lord Chancellor of Ireland presided over Law Reform; the Right Hon. W. F. Cooper, over the department of Education; the Earl of Carlyle—personally known to many on this platform—over that which concerns the Reformation of Criminals; the Earl of Shaftesbury over Public Health; and Conolly and Charles Kingsley and Tom Taylor and Rawlinson bore witness side by side with Florence Nightingale. Sir James Stephen presided over Social Economy. Isa Craig, the Burns poetess, is one of its Secretaries.

Ten communications were read at this session by women; among them, Florence Nightingale, Mary Carpenter, Isa Craig, Louisa Twining, and Mrs. Fison. Four were on Popular Education, two upon Punishment and Reformation, three on the Public Health in the Army and elsewhere, one upon Social Economy. Still another proof of progress may be seen in the examination of Florence Nightingale by the Sanitary Commission.

[In the establishment of *The Englishwoman's Journal* with an honorable corps of writers, in the passage of the new Divorce Bill, of the Married Woman's Property Bill in Canada, the cause had gained much; on each of which Mrs. Dall spoke at some length, especially this Property Bill, which some foolish member had shorn of its most precious clause— that which secured her earnings to the working-woman, lest, by tempting her to labor, it should create a divided interest in the family].

Do you ask me why I have dwelt on this Institution for Social Science, cataloguing the noble names that do it honor? To strengthen the timorous hearts at the West End; to suggest to them that a coronet of God's own giving may possibly rest as secure as one of gold and jewels in the United Kingdom. I wish to draw your attention to the social distinction of the men upon that platform. No real nobleness will be imperiled by impartial listening to our plea. Would you rest secure in our respect, first feel secure in your own. If ten Beacon Street ladies would go to work, and take pay for their labor, it would do more good than all the speeches that were ever made, all the conventions that were ever held. I honor women who act. That is the reason that I greet so gladly girls like Harriet Hosmer, Louisa Lander, and Margurèite Foley. Whatever they do, or do not do, for Art, they do a great deal for the cause of Labor. I do not believe any one in this room has any idea of the avenues that are open to women already. Let me read you some of the results of the last census of the United Kingdom. Talk of women not being able to work! Women have been doing hard work ever since the world began. You will see by this that they are doing as much as men now. [Applause].

In 1841, there were engaged in agriculture, 66,329 women. In 1851, 128,418; nearly double the number. Of these, there are 64,000 dairy-women; women who lift enormous tubs, turn heavy cheeses, slap butter by the hundred weight. Then come market-gardeners, bee-mistresses, florists, flax producers and beaters, haymakers, reapers, and hop-pickers.

In natural connection with the soil, we find seven thousand women in the mining interest; not harnessed on all-fours to creep through the shafts, but dressers of ore, and washers and strainers of clay for the potteries. Next largest to the agricultural is one not to be exactly calculated —the fishing interest. The Pilchard fishery employs some thousands of women. The Jersey oyster fishery alone employs one thousand. Then follow the herring, cod, whale, and lobster fisheries.

Apart from the Christie Johnstones—the aristocrats of the trade—the sea nurtures an heroic class like Grace Darling, who stand aghast when society rewards a deed of humanity, and cry out in expostulation, "Why, every girl on the coast would have done as I did!" Then follow the kelp-buṛners, netters, and bathers. The netters make the fisherman's nets; the bathers manage the machines at the watering-places.

And, before quitting this subject, I should like to allude to the French fishwomen; partly as a matter of curiosity, partly to prove that women know how to labor. In the reign of Henry IV., there existed in Paris a privileged monopoly called the United Corporation of Fishmongers and Herringers. In the reign of Louis XIV. this corporation had managed so badly as to become insolvent. The women who had hawked and vended fish took up the business, and managed so well as to become very soon a political power. They became rich, and their children married into good families. You will remember the atrocities generally ascribed to them in the first revolution. It is now known that these were committed by ruffians disguised in their dress.

To return : there are in the United Kingdom 200,000 female servants. Separate from these, brewers, custom-house searchers, matrons of jails, lighthouse-keepers, pew-openers.

I have no time to question; but should not a Christian community offer womanly ministrations to its imprisoned women? Oh, that some brave heart, in a strong body, might go on our behalf to the city jail and Charlestown! Pew-opening has never been a trade in America; but, as there are signs that it may become so in this democratic community, I would advise our women to keep an eye to that. [Laughter].

There are in the United Kingdom 500,000 business women, beer-shop keepers, butcher-wives, milk-women, hack-owners, and shoemakers.

As one item of this list, consider 26,000 butcher-wives—women who do not merely preside over a business, but buy stock, put down meat, drive a cart even if needed—butchers to all intents and purposes. There are 29,000 shop-keepers, but only 1,742 shop-women.

Telegraph reporters are increasing rapidly. Their speed and accuracy are much praised. From the Bright Festival, at Manchester, a young woman reported, at the rate of twenty-nine words a minute, six whole columns, with hardly a mistake, though the whole matter was political, such as she was supposed not to understand!

Phonographic reporters also. A year ago there were but three female phonographers in America; and two of these did not get their bread by the work. Now hundreds are qualifying themselves, all over the land; and two young girls, not out of their teens, are at this moment reporting my words. [Cheers].

I hope the phonographers will take that clapping to themselves. I wish you would make it heartier. [Repeated cheers]. Now let us turn to the American census. I must touch it lightly. Of factory operatives, I will only say, that, in 1845, there were 55,828 men and 75,710 women engaged in textile manufactures. You will be surprised at the preponderance of women: it seems to be as great in other countries. Then follow makers of gloves, makers of glue, workers in gold and silver leaf, hair-weavers, hat and cap makers, hose-weavers, workers in India rubber, lamp-makers, laundresses, leechers, milliners, morocco-workers, nurses, paper-hangers, physicians, picklers and preservers, saddlers and harness-makers, shoemakers, soda-room keepers, snuff and cigar-makers, stock and suspender-makers, truss-makers, typers and stereotypers, umbrella-makers, upholsterers, card-makers.

Cards were invented in 1361. In less than seventy years the German manufacture was in the hands of women—Elizabeth and Margaret, at Nuremberg. Then grinders of watch crystals, 7,000 women in all.

My own observation adds to this list phonographers, house and sign painters, fruit-hawkers, button-makers, tobacco-packers, paper-box makers, embroiderers, and fur-sewers.

Perhaps I should say haymakers and reapers; since, for three or four years, bands of girls have been so employed in Ohio, at sixty-two and a half cents a day.

In New Haven, seven women work with seventy men in a clock factory, at half wages. If the proprietor answered honestly, when asked why he employed them, he would say, "To save money;" but he does answer, "To help our cause."

In Waltham, a watch factory has been established, whose statistics I shall use elsewhere.

In Winchester, Va., a father has lately taken a daughter into partnership; and the firm is "J. Wysong and Daughter." [Applause]. Is it not a shame it should happen first in a slave State?

Then come registers of deeds and postmistresses. We all know that the rural post-office is chiefly in the hands of irresponsible women. Petty politicans obtain the office, take the money, and leave wives and sisters to do the work.

[Here Mrs. Dall read an interesting letter from a female machinist in Delaware; but, as it will be published in another connection, it is here withheld].

Is it easy for women to break the way into new avenues? You know it is not.

[Here Mrs. Dall referred to the opposition shown to the employment of women in watch-making, by Mr. Bennett, in London; to the school at Marlborough House; to the employment of women in printing-offices—substantiating her statements by dates and names].

When I first heard that women were employed in Staffordshire to paint pottery and china—which they do with far more taste than men—I heard, also, that the jealousy of the men refused to allow them the customary hand-rest, and so kept down their wages. I refused to believe anything so contemptible. [Applause]. Now the *Edinburgh Review* confirms the story. Thank God! that could never happen in this country. With us, Labor can not dictate to Capital.

But the great evils which lie at the foundation of depressed wages are:

1st. That want of respect for labor which prevents ladies from engaging in it.

2d. That want of respect for women which prevents men from valuing properly the work they do.

Women themselves must change these facts.

[Mrs. Dall here read some letters to show that wages were at a starving-point in the cities of America as well as in Europe].

I am tired of the folly of the political economist, constantly crying that wages can never rise till the laborers are fewer. You have heard of the old law in hydraulics, that water will always rise to the level of its source; but, if by a forcing-pump, you raise it a thousand feet above, or by some huge syphon drop it a thousand feet below, does that law hold? Very well, the artificial restrictions of society are such a forcing-pump—are such a syphon. Make woman equal before the law with man, and wages will adjust themselves.

But what is the present remedy? A very easy one—for employers to adopt the cash system, and be content with rational profits. In my correspondence during the past year, master-tailors tell me that they pay from eight cents to fifty cents a day for the making of pantaloons, including the heaviest doeskins. Do you suppose they would dare to tell me how they charge that work on their slowly-paying customer's bills? Not they. The eight cents swells to thirty, the fifty to a dollar or a dollar twenty-five. Put an end to this, and master-tailors would no longer vault into Beacon Street over prostrate women's souls; but neither would women be driven to the streets for bread.

If I had time, I would show you, women, how much depends upon yourselves. As it is, we may say with the heroine of "Adam Bede," which you have doubtless all been reading:

"I'm not for denying that the women are foolish. God Almighty made 'em to match the men!" [Laughter].

Do you laugh? It is but a step from the ridiculous to the sublime; and Goethe, who knew women well, was of the same mind when he wrote:

"Wilt thou dare to blame the woman for her seeming sudden changes—
Swaying east and swaying westward, as the breezes shake the tree?
Fool! thy selfish thought misguides thee. Find the man that never ranges.
Woman wavers but to seek him. Is not, then, the fault in thee?"

Mrs. Dall was followed by the Rev. JOHN T. SARGENT, who said:

MADAM PRESIDENT AND FRIENDS:—I appreciate the honor of an invitation to this platform, but my words must be few; first, because the call comes to me within a few hours, and amid the cares and responsibilities of the chair on another platform, and I had no time for preconcerted forms of address; second, because the general principles of this organization, and the subject matters for discussion, are so well sifted and disposed of by previous speakers, that nothing new remains for me to say; and, third, because we are all waiting for the words of one [Wendell Phillips] whose sympathies are never wanting in any cause of truth and justice, whose versatile eloquence never hesitates on any platform where he waves aloft "the sword of the spirit" in behalf of human rights. [Applause].

I may truly say, that this is my maiden speech in behalf of maidens and others [laughter]; and, if it amount to nothing else, I may say, as did my friend Clarke, I feel bound, at least, to take my stand, and show my sympathy for the noble cause. I come here under the pressure of an obligation to testify in behalf of an interest truly Christian, and one of the greatest that can engage the reason or the conscience of a community. I would that you had upon this platform and every other, more women speakers for the upholding and consummation of every righteous cause! And so far am I from being frightened to death or embarrassed, as our friend Mrs. Dall has intimated any one might be, at the prospect of either following James Freeman Clarke or preceding Wendell Phillips, I am much more concerned by the contrast of my speech with such speakers as your President, or Dr. Hunt, or Mrs. Dall herself.

There is one feature of the general question of "Woman's Rights" on which I would say a single word; and it may constitute the specialty of my address, so far as it has any. I mean the bearing of social inequalities particularly upon the poor—the poor of a city—the poor women of a city.

It may not be unknown to most of you, that for nearly two years past, in connection with the so-called "Boston Provident Association," I have been engaged in an agency wherein the peculiar trials of this class have been revealed to me as never before.

Hundreds of poor, desolate, forsaken women, especially in the winter months, have come to that office with the same pitiable tale of poverty, desertion, and tyranny on the part of their worthless and drunken husbands, who had gone off to California, Kansas, or the West, taking away from their wives and children every possible means of support, and leaving them the pauper dependents on a public charity. Now, if this be not the denial of Woman's Rights, I know not what is. Had we time, I might fill the hour with a journal of statistics in painful illustration of these facts. Now, I say, that a system of society which can tolerate such a state of things, and, by sufferance even, allow such men to wrench away the plain rights of their wives and families, needs reforming.

But let us look a little higher in the social scale, to the rights and claims of a class of women not so dependent—a class who, by their education and culture, are competent to fill, or who may be filling, the position of clerks, secretaries, or assistant agents. How inadequate and insufficient, as a general thing, is the compensation they receive!

There was associated with me in the agency and office to which I have referred, as office-clerk and coadjutor, among others, an intelligent and very worthy young woman, whose term of service there has been coeval and coincident with the Association itself, even through the whole seven years or more; and there she still survives, through all the vicissitudes of the General Agency by death or otherwise, with a fidelity of service worthy of more liberal compensation; for she receives, even now, for an amount of service equal to that of any other in the office, only about one-third the salary paid to a male occupant of the same sphere!

Look next at the professional sphere of women, properly so called; and who shall deny her right and claim to that position? A young brother clergyman came to my office one day, wanting his pulpit supplied; and, in the course of conversation, asked very earnestly, " How would it do to invite a woman-preacher into my pulpit?" "Do!" said I (giving him the names of Mrs. Dall, Dr. Hunt, etc., as the most accessible) " of course it'll do." And all I have to say is, if I ever resume again the charge of a pulpit myself, and either of those preachers want an exchange, I shall be honored in the privilege of so exchanging.

Well, my young friend, the brother clergyman referred to, whom I am glad to see in this audience, went and *did* according to my suggestion; and, by the professional service of Mrs. Dall in his pulpit, more than once, I think, ministered no little edification to his people. And, in this connection, let me say : If the argument against woman's preaching be, " Oh! it looks so awkward and singular to see a woman with a gown on in the pulpit " (for that's the whole gist of it), why, then, the same logic might as well disrobe the male priesthood of their silken paraphernalia cassock and bands.

But there are other and better words in waiting, and I yield the floor.

CHARLES G. AMES expressed his gratitude at being permitted to occupy this platform, and identify himself with the cause of those noblest of living women who had dared the world's scorn—had dared to stand alone on the ground of their moral convictions. He thought Rev. Mr. Clarke had spoken but half the truth in saying, "Half the human race are concerned in the Woman's Rights movement."

If the Mohammedan doctrine (that woman has no soul) be true, then the opponents of this cause are justifiable. But concede that she has a rational soul, and you concede the equality of her rights. Concede that she is capable of being a Christian, and you concede that she has a right to help do the Christian's work; and the Christian's work includes all forms of noble activity, as well as the duty of self-development.

But some people are afraid of agitation. You remember the story of the rustic, who fainted away in the car when taking his first railroad ride, and gasped out, on coming to himself, "Has the thing lit?" He belonged, probably, to that large class of people who go into hysterics every time the world begins to move, and who are never relieved from their terror till quiet is restored.

Great alarm prevails lest this agitation should breed a fatal quarrel between man and woman; as though there could be a want of harmony, a collision of rights, between the sexes. Sad visions are conjured up before us of family feuds, mutual hair-pullings, and a general wreck of all domestic bliss. Certainly, there are difficulties about settling some domestic questions. Marriage is a partnership between two; no third person to give the casting vote. Then they must "take turns"; the wife yielding to the husband in those cases where he is best qualified to judge, and the husband yielding to the wife in those matters which most concern her, or concerning which she can best judge. Yet man is the senior partner of the firm: his name comes first. Few women would be pleased to see the firm styled in print as "Mrs. So-and-So and Husband."

Woman wants more self-reliance. Has she not always been taught that it is very proper to faint at the sight of toads and spiders and fresh blood, and whenever a gentleman pops the question? Has she not always been taught that man was the strong, towering oak, and she the graceful, clinging vine, sure to collapse like an empty bag whenever his mighty support was withdrawn? Until all this folly is unlearned, how can she be self-dependent and truly womanly?

Women are afraid to claim their rights; and not timidity only, but laziness—the love of ease—keeps them back from the great duty of self-assertion. True, it is a good deal like work to summon up the soul to such a conflict with an opposing and corrupt public opinion. But woman must do that work for herself, or it will never be done.

Woman's *rights* we talk of. There is a grandeur about these great questions of right, which makes them the glory of our age; and it is the shame of our age, that right and rights in every form get so generally sneered at. What use have I for my conscience, what remains of my noble manhood, if, when half the human race complain that I am doing them a wrong, I only reply with a scoff? A man without a conscience to make him quick and sensitive to right and duty, is neither fit for heaven nor for hell. He is an outsider, a monster!

Conservatism says, "Let the world be as it is"; but Christianity says, "Make it what it should be." No man need call himself a Christian, who admits that a wrong exists, and yet wishes it to continue, or is indifferent to its removal. Let us

"Strike for that which ought to be,
And God will bless the blows."

Paulina W. Davis

The speaker spoke of the abuse and injustice done to the Bible by those who make it the shelter and apologist for all the wrong, vileness, and sneaking meanness that the world bears up; and closed with a testimony against the cowardice of those time-serving ministers who allow their manhood to be suffocated by a white cravat, and who never publicly take sides with what they see to be a good cause, until "popular noises" indicate that the time has come for speaking out their opinions.

The President then introduced to the audience WENDELL PHILLIPS, Esq., of Boston:

MADAM PRESIDENT:—I am exceedingly happy to see that this question calls together so large an audience; and perhaps that circumstance will make me take exception to some representations of the previous speakers as to the unpopularity of this movement. The gentleman who occupied this place before me thought that perhaps he might count the numbers of those that occupied this platform as the real advocates of that question. Oh, no! The number of those who sympathize with us must not be counted so. Our idea penetrates the whole life of the people. The shifting hues of public opinion show like the colors on a dove's neck; you can not tell where one ends, or the other begins. [Cheers]. Everybody that holds to raising human beings above the popular ideas, and not caring for artificial distinctions, is on our side; I think I can show my friend that. Whenever a new reform is started, men seem to think that the world is going to take at once a great stride. The world never takes strides. The moral world is exactly like the natural. The sun comes up minute by minute, ray by ray, till the twilight deepens into dawn, and dawn spreads into noon. So it is with this question. Those who look at our little island of time do not see it; but, a hundred years later, everybody will recognize it.

No one need be at all afraid; there is no disruption, no breaking away from old anchorage—not at all. In the thirteenth and fourteenth centuries, there were two movements—first, the peasants in the town were striving to fortify each man his own house—to set up the towns against the kings; then, in the colleges, the great philosophers were striving each to fortify his own soul to make a revolution against Rome. The peasants branded the collegians as "infidels," and the collegians showed the peasants to be "traitors." Cordially they hated each other; blindly they went down to their graves, thinking they had been fighting each other; but, under the providence of God, they were entwined in the same movement. Now, if I could throw you back to-day into the civilization of Greece and Rome, I could show you the fact that our question is two thousand years old. [Cheers.] In the truest sense, it did not begin in 1848, as my friend Dr. Hunt stated; it began centuries ago. Did you ever hear of the old man who went to the doctor, and asked him to teach him to speak prose? "Why, my dear fellow," was the reply, "you have been speaking prose all your life." But he did not know it. So with some people in regard to the movement for Woman's Rights.

Many think the steps taken since 1850 are shaking this land with a new infidelity. Now, this infidelity is a good deal older than the New Testament. When man began his pilgrimage from the cradle of Asia, woman

18

was not allowed to speak before a court of justice. To kill a woman was just as great a sin as to kill a cow, and no greater. To sell an unlicensed herb in the city of Calcutta, was exactly the same crime as to kill a woman. She did not belong to the human race. Come down thousands of years, and the civilization of Greece said, "Woman has not got enough of truth in her to be trusted in the court of justice;" and, if her husband wants to give her to a brother or friend, he can take her to their door, and say, "Here, I give you this." And so it continues till you reach the feudal ages; when woman, though she might be queen or duchess, was often not competent to testify in a court of justice. She had not soul enough, men believed, to know a truth from a lie. That is the code of the feudal system. But all at once the world has waked up, and thinks a man is not a man because he has a pound of muscle, or because he has a stalwart arm; but because he has thoughts, ideas, purposes: he can commit crime, and he is capable of virtue.

No man is born in a day. A baby is always six months old before he is twenty-one. Our fathers, who first reasoned that God made all men equal, said: "You sha'n't hang a man until you have asked him if he consents to the law." Some meddlesome fanatic, engaged in setting up type, conceived the idea, that he need not pay his tax till he was represented before the law: then why should woman do so? Now, I ask, what possible reason is there that woman, as a mother, as a wife, as a laborer, as a capitalist, as an artist, as a citizen, should be subjected to any laws except such as govern man? What moral reason is there for this, under the American idea? Does not the same interest, the same strong tie, bind the mother to her children, that bind the father? Has she not the same capacity to teach them that the father has? and often more? Now, the law says: "If the father be living, the mother is nothing; but, if the father be dead, the mother is everything." Did she inherit from her husband his great intellect? If she did not, what is the common sense of such a statute? The mother has the same rights, in regard to her children, that the father has: there should be no distinction.

Yours is not a new reform. The gentleman who occupied the platform a few moments ago gave the common representation of this cause: "If a husband doesn't do about right, his wife will pull his hair; and, if you let her have her way, she may vote the Democratic ticket, and he the Republican; and *vice versa*." Well, now, my dear friend, suppose it were just so; it is too late to complain. That point has long been settled; if you will read history a little, you will see it was settled against you. In the time of Luther, it was a question: "Can a woman choose her own creed?" The feudal ages said: "No; she believes as her husband believes, of course." But the reformers said: "She ought to think for herself; her husband is not her God." "But," it was objected, "should there be difference of opinion between man and wife, the husband believing one creed and the wife another, there would be continual discord." But the reply was: "God settled that; God has settled it that every responsible conscience should have a right to his own creed." And Christendom said: "Amen." The reformers of Europe, to this day, have allowed freedom of opinion; and who says that the experience of three centuries has found the husband and wife grappling each other's throats on religious differences? It would be Papal and absurd to deny woman her religious rights. Then why should she not be allowed to choose her party?

We claim the precedents in this matter. It was arranged and agreed upon, in the reform of Europe, that women should have the right to choose their religious creeds. I say, therefore, this is not a new cause; it is an old one. It is as old as the American idea. We are individuals by virtue of our brains, not by virtue of our muscles. "Why do you women meddle in politics?" asked Napoleon of De Staël. "Sire, so long as you will hang us, we must ask the reason," was the answer. The whole political philosophy of the subject is in that. The instant you say, "Woman is not competent to go to the ballot-box," I reply: "She is not competent to go to the gallows or the State prison. If she is competent to go to the State prison, then she is competent to go to the ballot-box, and tell how thieves should be punished." [Applause].

Man is a man because he thinks. Woman has already begun to think. She has touched literature with the wand of her enchantment, and it rises to her level, until woman becomes an author as well as reader. And what is the result? We do not have to expurgate the literature of the nineteenth century before placing it in the hands of youth. Those who write for the lower level sink down to dwell with their kind.

Mr. Sargent and Mr. Clarke expatiated on the wholesome influence of the side-by-side progress of the sexes. There are no women more deserving of your honest approbation than those who dare to work singly for the elevation of their sex. . . . .

Woman's Rights and Negro Rights! What rights have either women or negroes that we have any reason to respect? The world says: "None!"

There has lately been a petition carried into the British Parliament, asking—for what? It asks that the laws of marriage and divorce shall be brought into conformity with the creed and civilization of Great Britain in the middle of the nineteenth century. The state of British law, on the bill of divorce, was a disgrace to the British statute-book. Whose was the intellect and whose the heart to point out, and who had the courage to look in the face of British wealth and conservatism, and claim that the law of divorce was a disgrace to modern civilization? It was the women of Great Britain that first said her statute-book disgraced her. Who could say, that if those women had been voters, they might not have reformed it?

Douglas Jerrold said: "Woman knows she is omnipotent"; and so she is. She may be ignorant, she may not have a dollar, she may have no right given her to testify in the court of justice; she may be a slave, chained by a dozen statutes; but, when her husband loves her, she is his queen and mistress, in spite of them all; and the world knows it. All history bears testimony to this omnipotent influence. What we are here for is to clear up the choked channel; make hidden power confess itself, and feel its responsibility, feel how much rests upon it, and therefore gird itself to its duty. We are to say to the women: "Yours is one-half of the human race. Come to the ballot-box, and feel, when you cast a vote in regard to some great moral question, the dread post you fill, and fit yourself for it." Woman at home controls her son, guides her husband—in reality, makes him vote—but acknowledges no responsibility, and receives no education for such a throne. By her caprices in private life, she often ruins the manhood of her husband, and checks the enthusiastic purposes of her son.

Many a young girl, in her married life, loses her husband, and thus is left a widow with two or three children. Now, who is to educate them and control them? We see, if left to her own resources, the intellect which she possesses, and which has remained in a comparatively dormant state, displayed in its full power. What a depth of heart lay hidden in that woman! She takes her husband's business—guides it as though it were a trifle; she takes her sons, and leads them; sets her daughters an example; like a master-leader, she governs the whole household. That is woman's influence. What made that woman? Responsibility. Call her out from weakness, lay upon her soul the burden of her children's education, and she is no longer a girl, but a woman!

Horace Greeley once said to Margaret Fuller: "If you should ask a woman to carry a ship round Cape Horn, how would she go to work to do it? Let her do this, and I will give up the question." In the fall of 1856, a Boston girl, only twenty years of age, accompanied her husband to California. A brain-fever laid him low. In the presence of mutiny and delirium, she took his vacant post, preserved order, and carried her cargo safe to its destined port. Looking in the face of Mr. Greeley, Miss Fuller said: "Lo! my dear Horace, it is done; now say, what shall woman do next?" [Cheers].

Mrs. CAROLINE H. DALL then dismissed the assembly.*

In *The Liberator* of July 6, 1860, we find a brief mention of what was called Mrs. Dall's "Drawing-room" Convention, in which it was proposed to present the artistic and æsthetic view of the question. The meeting was held June 1st, in the Melodeon. Mrs. Caroline M. Severance presided. Mrs. Dall, Rev. Samuel J. May, R. J. Hinton, Moses (Harriet Tubman), James Freeman Clarke, Dr. Mercy B. Jackson, Elizabeth M. Powell, and Wendell Phillips took part in the discussions.

We close our chapter on Massachusetts, with a few extracts from a sermon by Theodore Parker, to show his position on the most

---

* The Publishing Committee do not willingly print the above report of one of the ablest and most eloquent speeches ever delivered in Boston. Mr. Phillips never writes his speeches. He is now too far distant to be consulted. Two very young girl reporters—after a week's hard practice, and three hours' excessive heat—wrote these heads down, without the most distant idea of publication. All the Committee can do is to rejoice that the accident did not happen to a young speaker, but to one whose reputation is established, and whose immortality is certain.   C. H. D.

momentous question of his day and generation. In March, 1853, he gave two discourses in Music Hall, Boston, one on the domestic, and one on the public function of woman, in which he fully expressed himself on every phase of the question.

THEODORE PARKER—THE PUBLIC FUNCTION OF WOMAN.

If woman is a human being, first, she has the Nature of a human being; next, she has the Right of a human being; third, she has the Duty of a human being. The Nature is the capacity to possess, to use, to develop, and to enjoy every human faculty; the Right is the right to enjoy, develop, and use every human faculty; and the Duty is to make use of the Right, and make her human nature, human history. She is here to develop her human nature, enjoy her human rights, perform her human duty. Womankind is to do this for herself, as much as mankind for himself. A woman has the same human nature that a man has; the same human rights, to life, liberty, and the pursuit of happiness; the same human duties; and they are as inalienable in a woman as in a man.

Each man has the natural right to the normal development of his nature, so far as it is general-human, neither man nor woman, but human. Each woman has the natural right to the normal development of her nature, so far as it is general-human, neither woman nor man. But each man has also a natural and inalienable right to the normal development of his peculiar nature as man, where he differs from woman. Each woman has just the same natural and inalienable right to the normal development of her peculiar nature as woman, and not man. All that is undeniable.

Now see what follows. Woman has the same individual right to determine her aim in life, and to follow it; has the same individual rights of body and of spirit—of mind and conscience, and heart and soul; the same physical rights, the same intellectual, moral, affectional, and religious rights, that man has. That is true of womankind as a whole; it is true of Jane, Ellen, and Sally, and each special woman that can be named.

Every person, man or woman, is an integer, an individual, a whole person; and also a portion of the race, and so a fraction of humankind. Well, the rights of individualism are not to be possessed, developed, used, and enjoyed, by a life in solitude, but by joint action. Accordingly, to complete and perfect the individual man or woman, and give each an opportunity to possess, use, develop, and enjoy these rights, there must be concerted and joint action; else individuality is only a possibility, not a reality. So the individual rights of woman carry with them the same domestic, social, ecclesiastical, and political rights, as those of man.

The Family, Community, Church and State, are four modes of action which have grown out of human nature in its historical development; they are all necessary for the development of mankind; machines which the human race has devised, in order to possess, use, develop, and enjoy their rights as human beings, their rights also as men.

These are just as necessary for the development of woman as of man; and, as she has the same nature, right, and duty, as man, it follows that she has the same right to use, shape, and control these four institutions, for her general human purpose and for her special feminine purpose, that man has to control them for his general human purpose and his special masculine purpose. All that is as undeniable as anything in metaphysics or mathematics.

If woman had been consulted, it seems to me theology would have been in a vastly better state than it is now. I do not think that any woman would ever have preached the damnation of babies new-born; and " hell, paved with the skulls of infants not a span long," would be a region yet to be discovered in theology. A celibate monk—with God's curse writ on his face, which knew no child, no wife, no sister, and blushed that he had a mother—might well dream of such a thing. He had been through the preliminary studies. Consider the ghastly attributes which are commonly put upon God in the popular theology; the idea of infinite wrath, of infinite damnation, and total depravity, and all that. Why, you could not get a woman, that had intellect enough to open her mouth, to preach these things anywhere. Women think they think that they believe them; but they do not. Celibate priests, who never knew marriage, or what paternity was, who thought woman was a " pollution"—they invented these ghastly doctrines; and when I have heard the Athanasian Creed and the Dies Iræ chanted by monks, with the necks of bulls and the lips of donkeys— why, I have understood where the doctrine came from, and have felt the appropriateness of their braying out the damnation hymns; woman could not do it. We shut her out of the choir, out of the priest's house, out of the pulpit; and then the priest, with unnatural vows, came in, and taught these "doctrines of devils." Could you find a woman who would read to a congregation, as words of truth, Jonathan Edwards' sermon on a Future State—"Sinners in the Hands of an Angry God," "The Justice of God in the Damnation of Sinners," "Wrath upon the Wicked to the Uttermost," "The Future Punishment of the Wicked," and other things of that sort? Nay, can you find a worthy woman, of any considerable culture, who will read the fourteenth chapter of Numbers, and declare that a true picture of the God she worships? Only a she-dragon could do it in our day.

The popular theology leaves us nothing feminine in the character of God. How could it be otherwise, when so much of the popular theology is the work of men who thought woman was a "pollution," and barred her out of all the high places of the church? If women had had their place in ecclesiastical teaching, I doubt that the "Athanasian Creed" would ever have been thought a "symbol" of Christianity. The pictures and hymns which describe the last judgment are a protest against the exclusion of woman from teaching in the church. "I suffer not a woman to teach, but to be in silence," said a writer in the New Testament. The sentence has brought manifold evil in its train. So much for the employments of women.

By nature, woman has the same political rights that man has—to vote, to hold office, to make and administer laws. These she has as a matter of right. The strong hand and the great head of man keep her down; nothing more. In America, in Christendom, woman has no political rights, is not a citizen in full; she has no voice in making or administering the laws, none in electing the rulers or administrators thereof. She can hold no office—can not be committee of a primary school, overseer of the poor, or guardian to a public lamp-post. But any man, with conscience enough to keep out of jail, mind enough to escape the poor-house, and body enough to drop his ballot into the box, he is a voter. He may have no character—even no money; that is no matter—he is male. The noblest woman has no voice in the State. Men make laws, disposing of her property, her person, her children; still she must bear it, " with a patient shrug."

Looking at it as a matter of pure right and pure science, I know no reason why woman should not be a voter, or hold office, or make and administer laws. I do not see how I can shut myself into political privileges and shut woman out, and do both in the name of inalienable right. Certainly, every woman has a natural right to have her property represented in the general representation of property, and her person represented in the general representation of persons.

Looking at it as a matter of expediency, see some facts. Suppose woman had a share in the municipal regulation of Boston, and there were as many alderwomen as aldermen, as many common council women as common council men, do you believe that, in defiance of the law of Massachusetts, the city government, last spring, would have licensed every two hundred and forty-fourth person of the population of the city to sell intoxicating drink? would have made every thirty-fifth voter a rum-seller? I do not.

Do you believe the women of Boston would spend ten thousand dollars in one year in a city frolic, or spend two or three thousand every year, on the Fourth of July, for sky-rockets and fire-crackers; would spend four or five thousand dollars to get their Canadian guests drunk in Boston harbor, and then pretend that Boston had not money enough to establish a high-school for girls, to teach the daughters of mechanics and grocers to read French and Latin, and to understand the higher things which rich men's sons are driven to at college? I do not.

Do you believe that the women of Boston, in 1851, would have spent three or four thousand dollars to kidnap a poor man, and have taken all the chains which belonged to the city and put them round the court-house, and have drilled three hundred men, armed with bludgeons and cutlasses, to steal a man and carry him back to slavery? I do not. Do you think, if the women had had the control, "fifteen hundred men of property and standing " would have volunteered to take a poor man, kidnapped in Boston, and conduct him out of the State, with fire and sword? I believe no such thing.

Do you think the women of Boston would take the poorest and most unfortunate children in the town, put them all together into one school, making that the most miserable in the city, where they had not and could not have half the advantages of the other children in different schools, and all that because the unfortunates were dark-colored? Do you think the women of Boston would shut a bright boy out of the High-School or Latin-School, because he was black in the face?

Women are said to be cowardly. When Thomas Sims, out of his dungeon, sent to the churches his petition for their prayers, had women been " the Christian clergy," do you believe they would not have dared to pray?

If women had a voice in the affairs of Massachusetts, do you think they would ever have made laws so that a lazy husband could devour all the substance of his active wife—spite of her wish ; so that a drunken husband could command her bodily presence in his loathly house ; and when an infamous man was divorced from his wife, that he could keep all the children ? I confess I do not.

If the affairs of the nation had been under woman's joint control, I doubt that we should have butchered the Indians with such exterminating savagery, that, in fifty years, we should have spent seven hundred millions of dollars for war, and now, in time of peace, send twenty annual millions more to the same waste. I doubt that we should have spread slavery into nine new States, and made it national. I think the Fugitive Slave bill would never have been an act. Woman has some respect for the natural law of God.

I know men say woman can not manage the great affairs of a nation. Very well. Government is political economy—national housekeeping. Does any respectable woman keep house so badly as the United States? with so much bribery, so much corruption, so much quarrelling in the domestic councils?

But government is also political morality, it is national ethics. Is there any worthy woman who rules her household as wickedly as the nations are ruled? who hires bullies to fight for her? Is there any woman who treats one-sixth part of her household as if they were cattle and not creatures of God, as if they were things and not persons? I know of none such. In government as housekeeping, or government as morality, I think man makes a very poor appearance, when he says woman could not do as well as he has done and is doing.

I doubt that women will ever, as a general thing, take the same interest as men in political affairs, or find therein an abiding satisfaction. But that is for women themselves to determine, not for men.

In order to attain the end—the development of man in body and spirit—human institutions must represent all parts of human nature, both the masculine and the feminine element. For the well-being of the human race, we need the joint action of man and woman, in the family, the community, the Church, and the State. A family without the presence of woman—with no mother, no wife, no sister, no womankind—is a sad thing. I think a community without woman's equal social action, a church without her equal ecclesiastical action, and a State without her equal political action, is almost as bad—is very much what a house would be without a mother, wife, sister, or friend.

You see what prevails in the Christian civilization of the nineteenth century; it is Force—force of body, force of brain. There is little justice, little philanthropy, little piety. Selfishness preponderates everywhere in Christendom—individual, domestic, social, ecclesiastical, national selfishness. It is preached as gospel and enacted as law. It is thought good political economy for a strong people to devour the weak nations; for "Christian" England and America to plunder the "heathen" and annex their land; for a strong class to oppress and ruin the feeble class; for the capitalists of England to pauperize the poor white laborer; for the capitalists of America to enslave the poorer black laborer; for a strong man to oppress the weak men; for the sharper to buy labor too cheap, and sell its product too dear, and so grow rich by making many poor. Hence, nation is arrayed against nation, class against class, man against man. Nay, it is commonly taught that mankind is arrayed against God, and God against man; that the world is a universal discord: that there is no solidarity of man with man, of man with God. I fear we shall never get far beyond this theory and this practice, until woman has her natural rights as the equal of man, and takes her natural place in regulating the affairs of the family, the community, the Church, and the State. It seems to me God has treasured up a reserved power in the nature of woman to correct many of those evils which are Christendom's disgrace to-day.

Circumstances help or hinder our development, and are one of the two forces which determine the actual character of a nation or of mankind, at any special period. Hitherto, amongst men, circumstances have favored the development of only intellectual power, in all its forms—chiefly in its lower forms. At present, mankind, as a whole, has the superiority over womankind, as a whole, in all that pertains to intellect, the higher and the lower. Man has knowledge, has ideas, has administrative skill ; enacts the rules of conduct for the individual, the family, the community, the Church, the State, and the world. He applies these rules of conduct to life, and so controls the great affairs of the human race. You see what a world he has made of it. There is male vigor in this civilization, miscalled " Christian " ; and in its leading nations there are industry and enterprise, which never fail. There is science, literature, legislation, agriculture, manufactures, mining, commerce, such as the world never saw. With the vigor of war, the Anglo-Saxon now works the works of peace. England abounds in wealth—richest of lands ; but look at her poor, her vast army of paupers, two million strong, the Irish whom she drives with the hand of famine across the sea. Martin Luther was right when he said : " The richer the nation, the poorer the poor." Look at the cities of England and America. What riches, what refinement, what culture of man and woman too ! Ay ; but what poverty, what ignorance, what beastliness of man and woman too ! The Christian civilization of the nineteenth century is well summed up in London and New York—the two foci of the Anglo-Saxon tribe, which control the shape of the world's commercial ellipse. Look at the riches and the misery, ; at the " religious enterprise" and the heathen darkness ; at the virtue, the decorum, and the beauty of woman well-born and well bred ; and at the wild sea of prostitution, which swells and breaks and dashes against the bulwarks of society—every ripple was a woman once !

Oh, brother-men, who make these things, is this a pleasant sight ? Does your literature complain of it—of the waste of human life, the slaughter of human souls, the butchery of woman ? British literature begins to wail, in " Nicholas Nickleby " and " Jane Eyre " and " Mary Barton " and " Alton Locke," in many a " Song of the Shirt " ; but the respectable literature of America is deaf as a cent to the outcry of humanity expiring in agonies. It is busy with California, or the Presidency, or extolling iniquity in high places, or flattering the vulgar vanity which buys its dross for gold. It can not even imitate the philanthropy of English letters ; it is " up " for California and a market. Does not the Church speak ?—the English Church, with its millions of money ; the American, with its millions of men—both wont to bay the moon of foreign heathenism ? The Church is a dumb dog, that can not bark, sleeping, lying down, loving to slumber. It is a church without woman, believing in a male and jealous God, and rejoicing in a boundless, endless hell !

Hitherto, with woman, circumstances have hindered the development of intellectual power, in all its forms. She has not knowledge, has not ideas or practical skill to equal the force of man. But circumstances have favored the development of pure and lofty emotion in advance of man. She has moral feeling, affectional feeling, religious feeling, far in advance of man ; her moral, affectional, and religious intuitions are deeper and more trustworthy than his. Here she is eminent, as he is in knowledge, in ideas, in administrative skill.

I think man wil always lead in affairs of intellect—of reason, imagination understanding—he has the bigger brain ; but that woman will always lead in affairs of emotion—moral, affectional, religious—she has the better heart, the truer intuition of the right, the lovely, the holy. The literature of women in this century is juster, more philanthropic, more religious, than that of men. Do you not hear the cry which, in New England, a woman is raising in the world's ears against the foul wrong which America is working in the world ? Do you not hear the echo of that woman's voice come over the Atlantic— returned from European shores in many a tongue—French, German, Italian, Swedish, Danish, Russian, Dutch ? How a woman touches the world's heart ! because she speaks justice, speaks piety, speaks love. What voice is strongest, raised in continental Europe, pleading for the oppressed and down-trodden ? That also is a woman's voice !

Well, we want the excellence of man and woman both united ; intellectual power, knowledge, great ideas—in literature, philosophy, theology, ethics—and practical skill ; but we want something better—the moral, affectional, religious intuition, to put justice into ethics, love into theology, piety into science and letters. Everywhere in the family, the community, the Church, and the State, we want the masculine and feminine element co-operating and conjoined. Woman is to correct man's taste, mend his morals, excite his affections, inspire his religious faculties. Man is to quicken her intellect, to help her will, trans- late her sentiments to ideas, and enact them into righteous laws. Man's moral action, at best, is only a sort of general human providence, aiming at the wel- fare of a part, and satisfied with achieving the "greatest good of the greatest number." Woman's moral action is more like a special human providence, acting without general rules, but caring for each particular case. We need both of these, the general and the special, to make a total human providence.

If man and woman are counted equivalent—equal in rights, though with diverse powers,—shall we not mend the literature of the world, its theology, its science, its laws, and its actions too ? I can not believe that wealth and want are to stand ever side by side as desperate foes ; that culture must ride only on the back of ignorance ; and feminine virtue be guarded by the degra- dation of whole classes of ill-starred men, as in the East, or the degradation of whole classes of ill-starred women, as in the West ; but while we neglect the means of help God puts in our power, why, the present must be like the past— "property" must be theft, "law" the strength of selfish will, and "Christian- ity"—what we see it is, the apology for every powerful wrong.

To every woman let me say—Respect your nature as a human being, your nature as a woman ; then respect your rights, then remember your duty to possess, to use, to develop, and to enjoy every faculty which God has given you, each in its normal way.

And to men let me say—Respect, with the profoundest reverence, respect the mother that bore you, the sisters who bless you, the woman that you love, the woman that you marry. As you seek to possess your own manly rights, seek also, by that great arm, by that powerful brain, seek to vindicate her rights as woman, as your own as man. Then we may see better things in the Church, better things in the State, in the Community, in the Home. Then the green shall show what buds it hid, the buds shall blossom, the flowers bear fruit, and the blessing of God be on us all.

REMINISCENCES OF PAULINA WRIGHT DAVIS.
BY E. C. S.

Hearing that my friend had returned from Europe too ill to leave her room, I hastened to her charming home in the suburbs of Providence, Rhode Island. There in her pleasant chamber, bright with the sunshine of a clear December day,* surrounded with her books and pictures of her own painting, looking out on an extensive lawn, grand old trees, and the busy city in the distance, we passed three happy days together reviewing our own lives, the progress of the reforms we advocated, and in speculations of the unknown world. In my brief sketch of the "Woman's Rights Movement" and its leaders for the "Eminent Women of the Age," I made no mention of Mrs. Davis, being ignorant of the main facts of her life. I waited for her return from Florida, until it was too late, as the work was hurried to press. Hence I was glad of this opportunity to dot down fresh from her own lips some of the incidents and personal experiences of her life.

Paulina Kellogg was born in Bloomfield, New York, the very day Capt. Hall delivered up the fort at Detroit. Her father, Capt. Kellogg, being a volunteer in the army at that time, would often jocosely refer to those two great events on the 7th of August, 1813. Her grandfather Saxton was a colonel in the Revolution, and on Lafayette's staff. Both her father and mother possessed great personal beauty, and were devotedly attached to each other, and were alike conservative in their opinions and associations. When Paulina was four years old her grandfather bought a large tract of land at Cambria, near Niagara Falls, where all his children settled. That trip was the first memory of her childhood. A cavalcade of six army wagons, men, women, children, horses, cattle, dogs, hens, pushed their weary way eleven days through wild woods, cutting their own roads, and fording creeks and rivers. Crossing the Genesee in a scow, one immense cow walked off into the water, others followed and swam ashore. The little girl thinking that everything was going overboard, trembled like an aspen leaf until she felt herself safe on land. The picnics under the trees, the beds in the wagons drawn up in a circle to keep the cattle in, the friendly meetings with the Indians, all charmed her childish fancies. The summer the first bridge was built to Goat Island, her uncle caught her in his arms, ran across the beams, and set her down, saying: "There, you are probably the first white child that ever set foot on Goat Island."

---

* In the year 1875.

When seven years old she was adopted by an aunt, and moved to Le Roy, New York, where she was educated. Her aunt was a strict orthodox Presbyterian, a stern, strong Puritan. Her life in her new home was sad and solitary, and one of constant restraint. In the natural reaction of the human mind, with such early experiences, we can readily account for Paulina's love of freedom, and courage in attacking the wrongs of society. In referring to these early years, she said : " I was not a happy child, nor a happy woman, until in mature life, I outgrew my early religious faith, and felt free to think and act from my own convictions." Having joined the church in extreme youth, and being morbidly conscientious, she suffered constant torment about her own sins, and those of her neighbors. She was a religious enthusiast, and in time of revivals was one of the bright and shining lights in exhortation and prayer.

She was roused to thought on woman's position by a discussion in the church as to whether women should be permitted to speak and pray in promiscuous assemblies. Some of the deacons protested against a practice, in ordinary times, that might be tolerated during seasons of revival. But those who had discovered their gifts in times of excitement were not so easily remanded to silence ; and thus the Church was distracted then as now with the troublesome question of woman's rights. Sometimes a liberal pastor would accord a latitude denied by the elders and deacons, and sometimes one church would be more liberal than others in the same neighborhood, or synod ; hence individuals and congregations were continually persecuted and arraigned for violation of church discipline and God's law, according to man's narrow interpretation. " Thus," she says, " my mind was confused and uncertain with conflicting emotions and opinions in regard to all human relations. And it was many years before I understood the philosophy of life, before I learned that happiness did not depend on outward conditions, but on the harmony within, on the tastes, sentiments, affections, and ambitions of the individual soul."

On leaving school, Paulina had made up her mind to be a missionary to the Sandwich Islands, as that was the Mecca in those days to which all pious young women desired to go. But after five months of ardent courtship, Mr. Francis Wright, a young merchant of wealth and position in Utica, New York, persuaded her that there were heathen enough in Utica to call out all the religious zeal she possessed, to say nothing of himself as the chief of sinners, hence in special need of her ministrations.

So they began life together, worshiped in Bethel church, and devoted themselves to the various reforms that in turn attracted their attention. They took an active part in the arrangements for the first Anti-Slavery Convention, held in Utica, Oct. 21, 1835, a day on which anti-slavery meetings were mobbed and violently dispersed in different parts of the country. It was at this meeting that Gerrit Smith gave in his adhesion to the anti-slavery movement and abandoned the idea of the colonization of slaves to Liberia. As the mob would not permit a meeting to be held in Utica, Mr. Smith invited them to Peterboro, where they adjourned. It was a fearful day for Abolitionists throughout that city, as the mob of roughs was backed by its leading men. Mr. Wright's house was surrounded, piazzas and fences torn down and piled up with wood and hay against it, with the evident intention of burning it down. But several ladies who had come to attend the Convention were staying there, and, as was their custom, they had family prayers that night. The leaders of the mob peeping through the windows, saw a number of women on their knees, and the sight seemed to soften their wrath and change their purpose, for they quietly withdrew their forces, leaving the women in undisturbed possession of the house. The attitude of the Church at this time being strongly pro-slavery, Mr. and Mrs. Wright withdrew, as most Abolitionists did, from all church organizations, and henceforth their religious zeal was concentrated on the anti-slavery, temperance, and woman's rights reforms. Thus passed twelve years of happiness in mutual improvement and co-operation in every good work. Having no children, they devoted themselves unreservedly to one another. But Mr. Wright, being a man of great executive ability, was continually overworking, taxing his powers of mind and body to the uttermost, until his delicate organization gave way and his life prematurely ended.

Having occupied her leisure hours in the study of anatomy and physiology, Mrs. Wright gave a course of lectures to women. As early as 1844 she began this public work. She imported from Paris the first *femme modele* that was ever brought to this country. She tells many amusing anecdotes of the effect of unveiling this manikin in the presence of a class of ladies. Some trembled with fear, the delicacy of others was shocked, but their weaknesses were overcome as their scientific curiosity was awakened. Many of Mrs. Wright's pupils were among the first to enter the colleges, hospitals, and dissecting-rooms, and to become successful practitioners of the healing art.

While lecturing in Baltimore, a " Friend," by the name of Anna

Needles, attended the course. Another " Friend," seeing her frequently pass, hailed her on one occasion, and said, " Anna, where
does thee go every day?" "I go to hear Mrs. Wright lecture."
" What, Anna, does thee go to hear that Fanny Wright?" " Oh,
no! Paulina Wright!" "Ah! I warn thee, do not go near her,
she is of the same species." Many women, now supporting themselves in ease, gratefully acknowledge her influence in directing their
lives to some active pursuits.

Thus passed the four years of her widowed life, lecturing to
women through most of the Eastern and Western States.

In 1849, she was married to the Hon. Thomas Davis, a solid,
noble man of wealth and position, who has since been a member of
the Rhode Island Legislature seven years, and served one term in
Congress. As he is very modest and retiring in his nature, I will
not enumerate his good qualities of head and heart, lest he should be
pained at seeing himself in print ; and perhaps " the highest praise
for a true *man* is never to be spoken of at all." With several successive summers in Newport and winters in Providence, Mrs. Davis
gave more time to fashionable society than she ever had at any
period of her life.

When her husband was elected to Congress, in 1853, she accompanied him to Washington and made many valuable acquaintances.
As she had already called the first National Woman Suffrage
Convention, and started *The Una*, the first distinctively woman's
rights journal ever published, and was supposed to be a fair representative of the odious, strong-minded " Bloomer," the ladies at
their hotel, after some consultation, decided to ignore her, as far
as possible. But a lady of her fine appearance, attractive manners,
and general intelligence, whose society was sought by the most cultivated gentlemen in the house, could not be very long ostracised by
the ladies.

What a writer in the *British Quarterly* for January, says of Mrs.
John Stuart Mill, applies with equal force to Mrs. Davis. " She
seems to have been saved from the coarseness and strenuous tone of
the typical strong-minded woman, although probably some of her
opinions might shock staid people who are innocent alike of philosophy and the doctrines of the new era." Though in fact this typical strong-minded woman of whom we hear so much in England
and America, is after all a " myth "; for the very best specimens of
womanhood in both countries are those who thoroughly respect
themselves, and maintain their political, civil, and social rights.
For nearly three years Mrs. Davis continued *The Una*, publishing

it entirely at her own expense. It took the broadest ground claimed to-day : individual freedom in the State, the Church, and the home ; woman's equality and suffrage a natural right. In 1859, she visited Europe for the first time, and spent a year traveling in France, Italy, Austria, and Germany, giving her leisure hours to picture galleries and the study of art. She made many valuable friends on this trip, regained her health, and returned home to work with renewed zeal for the enfranchisement of woman.

Having decided to celebrate the second decade of the National Woman Suffrage movement, in New York, Mrs. Davis took charge of all the preliminary arrangements, including the foreign correspondence. She gave a good report at the opening session of the Convention, of what had been accomplished in the twenty years, and published the proceedings in pamphlet form, at her own expense. One of Mrs. Davis' favorite ideas was a Woman's Congress in Washington, to meet every year, to consider the national questions demanding popular action ; especially to present them in their moral and humanitarian bearings and relations, while our representatives discussed them, as men usually do, from the material, financial, and statistical points of view. In this way only, said she, " can the complete idea on any question ever be realized. All legislation must necessarily be fragmentary, so long as one-half the race give no thought whatever on the subject."

In 1871, Mrs. Davis, with her niece and adopted daughter, again visited Europe, and pursued her studies of art, spending much time in Julian's life studio, the only one open to women. She took lessons of Carl Marko in Florence. When in Paris she spent hours every day copying in the Louvre and Luxembourg. The walls of her home were decorated with many fine copies, and a few of her own creations. Her enthusiasm for both art and reform may seem to some a singular combination ; but with her view of life, it was a natural one. Believing, as she did, in the realization of the ultimate equality of the human family, and the possibility of the race sometime attaining comparative perfection, when all would be well-fed, clothed, sheltered, and educated ; humanity in its poverty, ignorance, and deformity, were to her but the first rude sketch on the canvas, to be perfected by the skillful hand of the Great Artist. Hence she labored with faith and enthusiasm to realize her ideal alike in both cases.

In Naples she made the acquaintance of Mary Somerville, then in her ninetieth year. She found her quite conversant with American affairs, and she expressed great pleasure in reading Mrs. Davis' history of the suffrage movement in this country. There too she met Mrs. Merrycoyf, a bright, accomplished woman, a sister of Josephine Butler, and like her, engaged in English reforms. She had many discussions with Mrs. Proby, the wife of the English Consul, who thought Mrs. Davis was wasting her efforts for the elevation of woman, as she considered it a hopeless case to make women rational and self-reliant. However, before they parted, Mrs. Davis inspired her with some faith in her own sex. I read a very interesting letter from Mrs. Proby acknowledging the benefit derived from her acquaintance with Mrs. Davis, in giving her new hope for woman. At Rome she received the blessing of the Pope, and met Père Hyacinthe and his charming wife, and attended one of his lectures, but the crowd was so great she could not get in, so she went the Sunday after to hear the prayers for the Pope and the Church against the influence of the dangerous Père. She says: " It was a most impressive occasion, the immense crowd, the grand music swelling through the arches of that vast cathedral, the responses of the ten thousand voices, rolling like the great tidal waves of the mighty ocean, were altogether sublime beyond description." At Paris she met Mrs. Crawford, wife of the corresponding editor of *The London Times*, a woman of fine conversational powers, and a brilliant writer, now the Paris correspondent of *The New York Tribune*. She found her a woman of very liberal opinions. At one of her breakfasts she met Martin, the historian, and several members of the Assembly. She also visited the Countess Delacoste, who sympathized deeply with the republican movement, and had concealed Clusaret three months in her house. There she met several distinguished Russians and Frenchmen. In London she attended one of Mrs. Peter Taylor's receptions, where she met Mrs. Margaret Lucas, sister of John Bright, and other notables. She visited Josephine Butler at her home in Liverpool. Friends sent her tickets of admission to the lady's gallery, in the House of Commons, where she heard Jacob Bright make his opening speech on the woman's disability bill, and Fawcett, the blind member, also on the same bill. And with all these distinguished people, in different countries, speaking different languages, she found the same interest in the progressive ideas that had gladdened and intensified her own life.

On the 29th of May she sailed for America, and reached her home in safety, but the disease that had been threatening her for years (rheumatic gout) began to develop itself, until in the autumn she was confined to her room, and unable at times even to walk. It was thus I found her in a large arm-chair quietly making all her preparations for the sunny land, resigned to stay or to go, to accept the inevitable, whatever that might be.* As she was an enthusiastic spiritualist, the coming journey was not to her an unknown realm, but an inviting home where the friends of her earlier days were waiting with glad hearts to give her the heavenly welcome.

---

* See Appendix.

19

CHAPTER IX.

INDIANA AND WISCONSIN.

Indiana Missionary Station—Gen. Arthur St. Clair—Indian surprises—The terrible war-whoop—One hundred women join the army, and are killed fighting bravely—Prairie schooners—Manufactures in the hands of women—Admitted to the Union in 1816—Robert Dale Owen—Woman Suffrage Conventions—Wisconsin—C. L. Sholes' report.

THE earliest settlement of Indiana was a missionary one, in 1777, though it was not admitted as a Territory until 1800, then including the present States of Michigan and Illinois. A number of Indian wars took place in this part of the country during the twenty-five years between 1780 and 1805. What was known as the Northwest Territory was organized in 1789, and General Arthur St. Clair appointed Governor, an office he held until 1802. In 1790 a war of unusually formidable character broke out among the Indian tribes of the Northwest, and in 1791, St. Clair was created General-in-Chief of the forces against them. Many of the settlers of this portion of the country joined his army, among whom were one hundred women, who accompanied their husbands in preference to being left at home subject to the surprises and tortures of the savages with whom the country was at war. In giving command of these forces to St. Clair, Washington warned him against unexpected assaults from the enemy; but this general who was of foreign birth, a Scotchman, was no match for the cunning of his wily foe, who suddenly fell upon him, November 4th, near the Miami villages (present site of Terra Haute), making great havoc among his forces.

When the terrible war-whoop was heard, the heroism of these hundred women rose equal to the emergency. They did not cling helplessly to their husbands—the women of those early days were made of sterner stuff—but with pale, set faces, they joined in the defense, and the records say, were most of them killed fighting bravely. They died a soldier's death upon the field of battle in defense of home and country. They died that the prairies of the West and the wilderness of the North should at a later period become the peaceful homes of untold millions of men and women. They were the true pioneers of the Northwest, the advance-guard of civilization, giving their lives in battle against a terrible enemy, in order that safety should dwell at the hearth-stones of those who should settle this garden of the continent at a future period. History is very silent upon their record; not a name has been preserved; but we do know that they lived, and how they died, and it is but fitting that a record of woman's work for freedom should embalm their memory in its pages. Many other women defended homes and children against the savage foe, but their deeds of heroism have been forgotten.

There is scarcely a portion of the world so far from civilization as Indiana was at that day. No railroads spanned the continent, making neighbors of people a thousand miles apart; no steamboat sailed upon the Western lakes, nor indeed upon the broad Atlantic; telegraphy, with its annihilation of space, was a marvel as yet unborn; even the lucifer match, which should kindle fire in the twinkling of an eye, lay buried in the dark future. Little was known of these settlements; the Genesee Valley of New York was considered the *far West*, to which people traveled (the Erie Canal was not then in existence) in strong, springless wagons, over which large hoops, covered with white cloth, were securely fastened, thus sheltering the inmates from sun and storm. These wagons, afterward known as "Prairie Schooners," were for weeks and months the traveling homes of many a family of early settlers.

But even in 1816 Indiana could boast her domestic manufactures, for within the State at this time were " two thousand five hundred and twelve looms and two thousand seven hundred spinning-wheels, most of them in private cabins, whose mistresses, by their slow agencies, converted the wool which their own hands had often sheared, and the flax which their own fingers had pulled, into cloth for the family wardrobe."*

Thus in 1816 the manufactures of Indiana were chiefly in the hands of its women. It is upon the industries of the country that a nation thrives. Its manufactures build up its commerce and make its wealth. From this source the Government derives the revenue which is the life-blood circulating in its veins. Its strength and its perpetuity alike depend upon its industries, and when we look upon the work of women through all the years of the Republic, and remember their patriotic self-devotion and self-sacrifice at every important crisis, we are no less amazed at the ingratitude of the country for their services in war than at its non-recognition of their

---

* "The Relation of Woman to Industry in Indiana," by May Wright Sewall.

existence as wealth-producers, the elements which build up and sustain every civilized people.

Viewing its early record, we are not surprised that Indiana claims to have organized the first State Woman's Rights Society, though we are somewhat astonished to know that at the time of the first Convention held in Indianapolis, a husband of position locked his wife within the house in order to prevent her presence thereat, although doubtless, as men have often done before and since, he deemed it not out of the way that he himself should be a listener at a meeting he considered it contrary to family discipline that his wife should attend.

December 11, 1816, Indiana was admitted into the Union. William Henry Harrison, who had been Governor of the Territory, and Brigadier-General in the army, with the command of the Northwest Territory, was afterward President of the United States. He encountered the Indians led by Tecumseh at Tippecanoe, on the Wabash, and after a terrible battle they fled. This was the origin of the song, "Tippecanoe and Tyler too," that was sung with immense effect by the Whigs all over the country in the presidential campaign of 1840, when Harrison and Tyler were the candidates; and when women, for the first time, attended political meetings.

Indiana, though one of the younger States, by her liberal and rational legislation on the questions of marriage and divorce, has always been the land of freedom for fugitives from the bondage and suffering of ill-assorted unions. Many an unhappy wife has found a safe asylum on the soil of that State. Her liberality on this question was no doubt partly due to the influence of Robert Owen, who early settled at New Harmony, and made the experiment of communal life; and later, to his son, the Hon. Robert Dale Owen, who was in the Legislature several years, and in the Constitutional Convention of 1850. The following letter from Mr. Owen gives a few facts worth perusing:

LAKE GEORGE, N. Y., *Sept.* 20, 1876.

DEAR MISS ANTHONY:—I know you will think the reply I am about to make to your favor of September 18th unsatisfactory, but it is the best I can do.

1. As regards Frances Wright: All the particulars regarding her and her noble but unsuccessful experiment at Nashoba, near Memphis, which I thought it important to make public, are contained in an article of mine entitled "An Earnest Sowing of Wild Oats," in the *Atlantic Monthly* for July, 1874.

2. As to Ernestine L. Rose, I think it probable that you know more of her than I do. I remember that she was the daughter of a Polish rabbi;

the wife of William Rose, a silversmith; and that she came with her husband to this country at an early day. She was a great admirer and follower of my father, Robert Owen, and was a skeptic as to any future beyond the grave; greatly opposed to Spiritualism.

3. As to my action in the Indiana Legislature: I was a member of that body during the sessions of 1836–'7, and '8, and in 1851, but I have not the materials here that would enable me to give particulars. In a general way I had the State law so altered that a married woman owned and had the right to manage her own property, both real and personal; and I had the law of descents so changed that a widow, instead of dower, which is a mere tenancy or life interest, now has, in all cases, an *absolute* fee in one-third of her husband's estate; if only one child, then a half; and if no children, I think two-thirds. I also had an additional clause added to the divorce law, making two years' habitual drunkenness imperative cause for divorce.

I took no action in regard to suffrage while in the Legislature. In those days it would have been utterly unavailing.

All this is very meagre, which I the more regret, sympathizing as I do with the object you have in view.

Give my kindest regards to my old friend, Mrs. Stanton, and believe me,

Faithfully your friend,

Miss Anthony.   Robert Dale Owen.

Before 1828, Frances Wright had visited Mr. Owen's colony, and assisted him in the editorial department of the *New Harmony Gazette*, changed afterward to the *Free Enquirer*, published in New York. Such a circle of remarkably intelligent and liberal-minded people, all effective speakers and able writers, was not without influence in moulding the sentiment of that young community. As a glimpse into the domestic life of this remarkable family may be interesting to the reader, we give a pleasing sketch from the pen of Mr. Owen's daughter. No monument of the whitest parian marble could shed such honor on the memory of a venerated father and mother as this tribute from an affectionate, appreciative child:

ROBERT DALE OWEN AND MARY ROBINSON.

BY ROSAMOND DALE OWEN.

Some fifty years ago a large audience was gathered in one of the public halls of New York listening to a lecture. In the sea of faces upturned to him, the speaker read a cold response, the opinions he was expounding being exceedingly unpopular, and rarely expressed in those days. The theme was the equality of the sexes, the right of woman to control person and property in the marriage relation, the right to breathe, to think, to act as an untrammeled citizen, the co-equal of man. His eyes searched tier after tier, seeking in vain for that magnetism of sympathy which is as wine to a man who stands before his people pleading with them that he may save them from their errors.

Suddenly his wandering gaze was arrested by a face, a child's face, with short, clustering curls, but a strong soul steadied the deep eyes, and on the rounded cheek paled and glowed the earnestness of a woman's searching thought. His words grew clear and strong as he looked into the upturned eyes, as he answered the listening face. The speaker was Robert Dale Owen; the hearer, Mary Robinson.

That night when she reached her own room, Mary Robinson flung off bonnet and shawl with a swift gesture, and, slipping into her accustomed seat, gazed at the steady-glowing background of coals, with the blue flames licking in and out like the evil tongues of fire-scourged elves. A strong excitement held her in thrall; she did not seem to see her elder sister's wondering looks; she did not seem to hear the great clocks, far and near, chiming out eleven, and then twelve, with that deep resonance which sounds in the silence of the night like a solemn requiem over lost hours. Presently she became aware that her sister was kneeling beside her, with anxious questioning look; she seemed, this elder sister, in her long, white night-dress, with pale, straight hair pushed back from the clear-tinted, oval face, like a youthful Madonna, and Mary drawing the gentle face close to her own with sudden impulse, said: "I have seen the man I shall marry, I have seen him to-night; he is the homeliest man I have ever known, but if I am married at all, he is to be my husband."

A few months later this prophecy was verified. On the 12th day of April, 1832, Robert Dale Owen and Mary Robinson were joined in those sacred bonds, which, in every true marriage, can be broken only by the shadow hand of Death. The ceremony was simple and unique; it consisted in signing a document written by the bride-groom himself, with a Justice of the Peace and the immediate family as witnesses. The following extracts will show the character of the compact:

NEW YORK, Tuesday, *April* 12, 1832.

This afternoon I enter into a matrimonial engagement with Mary Jane Robinson, a young person whose opinions on all important subjects, whose mode of thinking and feeling, coincide more intimately with my own than do those of any other individual with whom I am acquainted. . . . We have selected the simplest ceremony which the laws of this State recognize. . . . . This ceremony involves not the necessity of making promises regarding that over which we have no control, the state of human affections in the distant future, nor of repeating forms which we deem offensive, inasmuch as they outrage the principles of human liberty and equality, by conferring rights and imposing duties unequally on the sexes. The ceremony consists of a simply written contract in which we agree to take each other as husband and wife according to the laws of the State of New York, our signatures being attested by those friends who are present.

Of the unjust rights which in virtue of this ceremony an iniquitous law tacitly gives me over the person and property of another, I can not legally, but I can morally divest myself. And I hereby distinctly and emphatically declare that I consider myself, and earnestly desire to be considered by others, as utterly divested, now and during the rest of my life, of any such rights, the barbarous relics of a feudal, despotic system, soon destined, in the onward course of improvement, to be wholly swept away; and the existence of which is a tacit insult to the good sense and good feeling of this comparatively civilized age.

I concur in this sentiment,   ROBERT DALE OWEN.
    MARY JANE ROBINSON.

After a wedding tour in Europe, the young couple returning to America, settled in New Harmony, Indiana, a small Western village, where their father, Robert Owen, had been making experiments in Community life.

It was a strange, new world into which these two young creatures were entering. The husband had passed his youth in a well-ordered, wealthy English household; the wife had passed the greater part of her girlhood in Virginia, among slaves. They were now thrown upon the crudities of Western life, and encountered those daily wearing trials which strain the marriage tie to the utmost, even though it be based upon principles of justice. But there was a reserve of energy and endurance in this delicately reared pair; they felt themselves to be pioneers in every sense of the word, and the animus which sustains many a struggling soul seeking to turn a principle into a living reality, sustained these two.

We of a later civilization can scarcely realize the strain upon women in those earlier days. The housekeepers of New Harmony were obliged to buy their groceries in bulk, and have them shipped by slow stages from Cincinnati; meat was bought from the surrounding farmers, a quarter of a beef at a time, to be cut up and disposed of by the housewife; vegetables and most of the small fruits could not be bought at all; stoves were an unknown luxury, all cooking being done in huge fire-places or brick ovens.

For thirty years my father and mother labored with unabated energy; his work leading him into the highways of public affairs, while her way lay through the by-paths of home and village life.

Through these thirty years my father used such influence as he had on the side of the weak and oppressed. In the matter of procuring a more respectful consideration of the property rights of women, he was a pioneer. To attempt a detailed statement of the amelioration of those legal hardships under which women labored, is beyond the scope or purpose of this article. I will only mention, in brief, the more important provisions he was instrumental in passing in the face of ridicule and violent opposition. These amendments were: The abolition of simple dower, giving to widows instead, a fee simple interest; procuring for women the right to their own earnings; abolishing tenancy by courtesy, which, in effect, made the husband the beneficiary of the wife's lands, and in several matters of less radical change rectifying, so far as he could, the injustice of the common law toward widows; always keeping in view, however, the proper heirship of children of a former marriage, and guarding the rights of creditors.

In the matter of the divorce laws of Indiana, my father has not taken as prominent a part as is generally supposed. These laws were referred to him in conjunction with another member of the Legislature for the revision, and they amended them in a single point, namely: by adding to the causes for divorce "habitual drunkenness for two years." My father has expressed himself in full on this point in a discussion between Horace Greeley and himself, first published in the *New York Tribune*.

As early as 1828, my father advocated an equal position for woman, publishing these views through *The Free Enquirer*, a weekly paper edited by Frances Wright and himself in New York.

My father's political life comprised several terms in the Legislature of his own State, being elected in 1850 a member of the Convention which amended the Constitution of Indiana, and chairman of its Revision Committee. The debates in this Convention show the difference in the position of my father and his antagonists.

CONSTITUTIONAL DEBATES.

Mr. OWEN: No subject of greater importance has come up since we met here, as next in estimation to the right of enjoying life and liberty, our Constitution enumerates the right of acquiring, possessing, protecting property. And these sections refer to the latter right, heretofore declared to be natural, inherent, inalienable, yet virtually withheld from one-half the citizens of our State. Women are not represented in our legislative halls; they have no voice in selecting those who make laws and constitutions for them; and one reason given for excluding women from the right of suffrage, is an expression of confident belief that their husbands and fathers will surely guard their interests. I should like, for the honor of my sex, to believe that the legal rights of women are, at all times, as zealously guarded as they would be if women had votes to give to those who watch over their interests.

Suffer me, sir, in defense of my skepticism on this point, to lay before you and this Convention, an item from my legislative recollection.

It will be thirteen years next winter, since I reported from a seat just over the way, a change in the then existing law of descent. At that time the widow of an intestate dying without children, was entitled, under ordinary circumstances, to dower in her husband's real estate, and one-third of his personal property. The change proposed was to give her one-third of the real estate of her husband absolutely, and two-thirds of his personal property—far too little, indeed; but yet as great an innovation as we thought we could carry. This law remained in force until 1841. How stands it now? The widow of an intestate, in case there be no children, and in case there be father, or mother, or brother, or sister of the husband, is heir to no part whatever of her deceased husband's real estate; she is entitled to dower only, of one-third of his estate. I ask you whether your hearts do not revolt at the idea, that when the husband is carried to his long home, his widow shall see snatched from her, by an inhuman law, the very property her watchful care had mainly contributed to increase and keep together?

Yet this idea, revolting as it is, is carried out in all its unmitigated rigor, by the statute to which I have just referred. Out of a yearly rental of a hundred and fifty dollars, the widow of an intestate rarely becomes entitled to more than fifty. The other hundred dollars goes—whither? To the husband's father or mother? Yes, if they survive! But if they are dead, what then? A brother-in-law or a sister-in-law takes it, or the husband's uncle, or his aunt, or his cousin! Do husbands toil through a life-time to support their aunts, and uncles, and cousins? If but a single cousin's child, a babe of six months, survive, to that infant goes a hundred dollars of the rental, and to the widow fifty. Can injustice go beyond this? What think you of a law like that, on the statute book of a civilized and a Christian land? When the husband's sustaining arm is laid in the grave, and the widow left without a husband to cherish, then comes the law more cruel than death, and decrees that poverty shall be added to desolation!

Say, delegates of the people of Indiana, answer and say whether you, whether those who sent you here are guiltless in this thing? Have you done justice? Have you loved mercy?

But let us turn to the question more immediately before us. Let us pass from the case of the widow and look to that of the wife: First, the husband becomes entitled, from the instant of marriage, to all the goods and chattels of his wife. His right is absolute, unconditional. Secondly, the husband acquires, in virtue of the marriage, the rents and profits (in all cases during her life) of his wife's real estate. The flagrant injustice of this has been somewhat modified by a statute barring the marital right to the rent of lands, but this protection does not extend to personal property. Is this as it should be? Are we meting out fair and equal justice? . . . . There is a species of very silly sentimentalism which it is the fashion to put forth in after-dinner toasts and other equally veracious forms, about woman being the only tyrant in a free republic; about the chains she imposes on her willing slaves, etc.; it would be much more to our credit, if we would administer a little less flattery and a little more justice.

From pages upon pages of eloquence delivered in reply, I cull the following extracts, which are a sample of the spirit of the opposition:

"I am of opinion that to adopt the proposition of the gentleman from Posey (Mr. Owen), will not ameliorate the condition of married women."

"I can not see the propriety of establishing for women a distinct and separate interest, the consideration of which would, of necessity, withdraw their attention from that sacred duty which nature has, in its wisdom, assigned to their peculiar care. I think the law which unites in one common bond the pecuniary interests of husband and wife should remain. The sacred ordinance of marriage, and the relations growing out of it, should not be disturbed. The common law does seem to me to afford sufficient protection."

"If the law is changed, I believe that a most essential injury would result to the endearing relations of married life. Controversies would arise, husbands and wives would become armed against each other, to the utter destruction of true felicity in married life."

"To adopt it would be to throw a whole population morally and politically into confusion. Is it necessary to explode a volcano under the foundation of the family union?"

"I object to the gentleman's proposition, because it is in contravention of one of the great fundamental principles of the Christian religion. The common law only embodies the divine law."

"Give to the wife a separate interest in law, and all those high motives to restrain the husband from wrong-doing will be, in a great degree, removed."

"I firmly believe that it would diminish, if it did not totally annihilate woman's influence."

"Woman's power comes through a self-sacrificing spirit, ready to offer up all her hopes upon the shrine of her husband's wishes."

"Sir, we have got along for eighteen hundred years, and shall we change now? Our fathers have for many generations maintained the principle of the common law in this regard, for some good and weighty reasons."

"The immortal Jefferson, writing in reference to the then state of society in France, and the debauched condition thereof, attributes the whole to the effects of the civil law then in force in France, permitting the wife to hold, acquire, and own property, separate and distinct from the husband."

"The females of this State are about as happy and contented with their present position in relation to this right (suffrage), as it is necessary they should be, and I do not favor the proposition (of Woman's Suffrage), which my friend from Posey, Mr. Owen, appears to countenance."

"It is not because I love justice less, but woman more, that I oppose this section."

"This doctrine of separate estate will stifle all the finer feelings, blast the brightest, fairest, happiest hopes of the human family, and go in direct contravention of that law which bears the everlasting impress of the Almighty Hand. Sir, I consider such a scheme not only as wild, but as wicked, if not in its intentions, at least in its results."

It is incredible that men in their sane minds should argue day after day, that if women were allowed to control their own property, it would " strike at the root of Christianity," " ruin the home," and " open wide the door to license and debauchery." And yet these men did so argue through weeks of stormy debate ; the bitterest feeling being shown, not with regard to the proposed change in the law of descent, but with regard to the right of women to "acquire and possess property to their sole use and disposal," during the husband's life-time. It is strange, indeed, that the man who advocated this "most meagre justice," as he truly says, should have been a target, not only for ridicule, but for abuse. I append one extract of the latter description, to illustrate how violent and unreasoning was the prejudice with which my father contended. One gentleman after quoting from the marriage contract of my father and mother, the extract in which he, my father, divests himself of the right to control the " person and property of another," proceeds as follows :

Sir, I would that my principles on this, in contradistinction with those of the gentlemen from Posey, were written in characters of light across the noon-day heavens, that all the world might read them. (Applause). I have in my drawer numerous other extracts from the writings of the gentleman from Posey, but am not allowed to read them ; and, indeed, sir, under the circumstances, decency forbids their use. But if I were permitted to read them, and show their worse than damning influence upon society, in conjunction with this system of separate interests, I venture to aver that gentlemen would turn from them with disgust; aye, sir, they would shun them as they would shun man's worst enemy, and flee from them as from a poisonous reptile. (Page 1161, " Debates in Indiana Convention ").

The section was finally reconsidered and rejected a few days before adjournment (p. 2013). But my father, with his characteristic perseverance, continued his efforts until they were finally crowned with success in the Legislature, after fifteen years of endeavor.

Most of the arguments used by those delegates, if they can be called by so dignified a name, bear a singular resemblance to the arguments used to-day by the opponents of woman's suffrage. May we not then conclude that the fears which have been proved absolutely groundless in the one case, may be equally so in the other?

An enthusiastic public meeting was held in Indianapolis in honor of my father by the women of the State, Mrs. Sarah T. Bolton taking a prominent part. On this occasion a beautiful silver pitcher was presented to him as a token of gratitude for his persevering efforts in behalf of women. This pitcher still holds a place of honor in our family dinings on gala days.

In reply to several slurs in regard to this memorial, my father during the debates in the Convention thus retorted :

Since I have had occasion to allude to the testimonial which it is proposed to offer me on behalf of the women of my adopted State, I will say here, that regarding it as the greatest compliment—if in so grave a connection a word often so lightly used may be properly employed—the greatest compliment I ever received in my life, or ever can receive till I die: it matters little to me what may be said of myself in that connection ; I am accustomed to personal attack, and am proof against ridicule. But if any man, whether he disgrace a chair on this floor, or dishonor by his presence some of the bar-rooms of the city, utter an insinuation, cast a reproach, directly or indirectly, by open assertion, or covert insinuation, against the motives or the character of those courageous women who may have met in Lawrenceburg or elsewhere, to consult regarding rights shamefully denied to them, or those who may have publicly expressed gratitude to the defenders of these rights—if such a man there be, within or without the walls of this capitol, I say here of such a one, let him receive it as he will, that I would give my hand more freely to the inmate of the penitentiary than to him. (Page 1185, " Debates in Indiana Convention ").

In 1843 and 1845 my father was elected to Congress, serving until 1847. In 1853 he was appointed Minister to Naples, remaining there until 1858. During the war his exertions were unremitting. He was the friend of Governor Morton, and was consulted by that energetic statesman in all his more important plans. He wrote several letters on the political crises of the time, which had a wide circulation and influence. Mr. Lincoln said to several of his friends, that a letter addressed to him by Mr. Owen, and a conversation consequent thereon, had done more toward deciding him in favor of the Emancipation Proclamation, than any other influence which had been brought to bear. My father also made strenuous efforts during the winter of 1865–'66 to postpone the enfranchisement of the freedmen ten years, until 1876. (See *Atlantic Monthly*, June, 1875). Subsequent events have shown his judgment to have been correct and far-sighted. He believed the conferring of suffrage upon the negro, dim-visioned in the sudden light of a new liberty, to be a most dangerous experiment; he foresaw that the ballot which the North gave to them as a protection against their arrogant masters, would prove a two-edged sword with a terrible reactionary force in the hands of an untrained race just freed from mental leading-strings; he knew the difficulty to be inherent, a difficulty which the existence of slavery must necessarily have produced. He maintained that although the sword had struck off the outward chains, the white-heat of ire kindled in the hearts of the conquered had not fused the inward shackles of the slave, but had riveted them the firmer, and that the invisible fetters welded by revengeful hate should be broken most carefully.

In the latter years of his life my father gave his entire attention to the study of Modern Spiritualism, or rather to the study of Spiritualism in both its ancient and its modern phases. He published two works on this subject, " Footfalls on the Boundary of Another World," and " The Debatable Land between this World and the Next." In a letter written shortly before his death, he expresses himself as follows : " I hope, my child, that you will never, at any period of your life, be less happy than you now are. If you cultivate your spiritual nature rationally, I feel assured you never will. For one effect of rational Spiritualism is to make one more satisfied the longer one lives, and to make the last scenes of life, hours of pleasant anticipation, instead of a season of dread, or, as with many it has been, of horror." It would be well for non-investigators who maintain that my father's belief in Spiritualism necessarily proves him to have been illogical, to see to it that they are not falling into the inconsequence which they are ascribing to him. Reasoning *a priori*, should we not believe that the man who saw so clearly the dangers which were unperceived by some of our keenest statesmen, could not become, except in a rare instance and for a short time, a misled dupe ? Has any one the right to condemn such a man unproved ?

While my father was exerting his energies for the welfare of the nation, my mother was giving her life to her children. Sons and daughters were welcomed into the Owen homestead, and the wide halls and great rooms of the rambling country house rang with the voices of children. Three of these little ones slipped back to Heaven before the portals had closed. The stricken parents with blinded eyes met only the rayless emptiness of unbelief. May God help the mother, fainting beneath a bereavement greater than she can bear, who cries for help and finds none; who stretches her empty arms upward in an agony of appeal and is answered by the hollow echo of her own cry; may God help her, for she is beyond the help of man. Other children came to fill the vacant places, other voices filled the air, but the hearts of father and mother were not filled until years later, when a sweet faith thrilled the hopeless blank.

The story of these two is the story of many beside. Husband and wife began the long journey side by side with equal talent, hope, energy; his work led him along the high-road, hers lay in a quiet nook; his name became world-known, hers was scarcely heard beyond the precinct of her own village; and yet who can say that his life was the more successful, who can say that the quiet falling rain, with its slow resultant of flower and fruit in each little garden nook, is less important than the mighty ship-laden river bearing its wealth of commerce in triumph to the sea?

George Eliot, in "Middlemarch," says of Dorothea:

Her finely-touched spirit had its fine issues, though they were not widely visible. . . . . The effect of her being on those around her was incalculably diffusive; for the growing good of the world is partly dependent on unhistoric acts; and that things are not so ill with you and me as they might have been, is half owing to the number who lived faithfully a hidden life, and rest in unvisited tombs.

This is true of many Dorotheas; it is true of the Dorothea of whom I am writing. Geographically, Mary Owen's field of labor was narrow; but a small Western village of a thousand souls may hold within its ethical strata all the developments of a continent. Let her who feels that her small limits imprison her, remember that emotions are not registered by the census. Lovers and business men, struggling youths and perplexed mothers, children and veterans, poured their griefs and fears, their hopes and disappointments, into the listening ear of sympathy, knowing that the clear judgment of this little woman could unravel much that seemed to be in hopeless entanglement.

Well do I remember the cheer of this our home. Simple were its duties, simple indeed its pleasures. Well do I remember the busy troop of boys and girls, with the busy mother at their head, directing their exuberant energy with a rare administrative ability. Besides her own children, four of whom reached maturity, she took during her life seven other young people under her protection, so that the great old-fashioned house was always filled to overflowing with fresh young life. Pasture and stable, hennery and dairy, yard and garden, kitchen and parlor, all were under her immediate guidance and control. Well do I remember the pots of golden butter, fresh from her cool hand; the delicious hams cured under her supervision; the succulent vegetables and juicy fruits fresh from her garden—that trim, symmetrical garden, with its well-weeded beds, its well-kept walks! Many a bright summer morning have I seen her resting on a low bench beneath a huge overhanging elm, overlooking the field of our labors. To a stranger the flushed face with its irregular features, might have seemed plain; the earnest, energetic manner might have seemed almost abrupt; but to the children who sat on the grass at her feet looking upward, the face was beautiful. That calm eye had pierced through so many childish intricacies and made them clear; the firm mouth could smile so gently at any youthful shortcoming, and the strong voice rang with a hope which sent fear and doubt skulking away in shamefaced silence. It was the brightest part of the day, this short respite, before mother, marshalling her young army, led them to the study-room. This impromptu lesson-hour was filled with a teaching so trenchant, that oftentimes, in these lonelier days, when perplexed in the intricacies of life's journeyings, a word spoken in some long ago summer morning, floats down the years and rises before my troubled vision a guiding star.

When her children were grown, and the task she had undertaken years before had been well done, our mother turned her attention for a time to public work. She gave much thought to the Woman Question, especially that portion of it pertaining to woman's work, and addressed one or two meetings in New York on this subject. Miss Anthony recently said to me: "Miss Owen, you do not know how great an impression your mother made upon us—a woman who had lived nearly her whole life in a small Western village, absorbed in petty cares, and yet who could stand before us[*] with a calm dignity, telling us searching truths in simple and strong words." The only lecture I heard my mother deliver was in the church of our village. Her subject was the rearing of children. A calm light rested on her silver hair and broad brow; her manner was the earnest manner of a woman who has looked into the heart of life. Blessed is the daughter to whom it is given to reverence a mother as I reverenced mine that night. A quiet, but deep attention was given to her words, for the fathers and mothers who were listening to her

---

[*] The vast audience of women alone, in Apollo Hall, to discuss the McFarland and Richardson tragedy.

knew that she was speaking on a subject to which she had given long years of careful thought and faithful endeavor. It would not be possible in the space allotted me to give a detailed account of my mother's teachings with regard to the rearing of children; but I will state a few of the more prominent theories—theories proved by practice, which I remember.

Self-government was the primary principle, the broad foundation. She held this qualification to be the only guarantee of success in the broadest sense of the word, and that to be effectual and never-failing it must be interwoven into the very fiber of the child. During the earliest years our mother administered punishment, or rather she invented some means by which the child should be made to feel the result of its bad conduct. Injuring another was held to be a cardinal sin. For this misdeed our hands were tied behind us for an interminable length of time ; for running away we were tied to the bed-post ; for eating at irregular hours we were deprived of dainties at the next meal, etc. But as soon as we reached the age of reason, she exerted, not a controlling, but a guiding hand. We were restricted by few rules, for our mother believed in the largest possible liberty, and she held that it was better to pass over the smaller shortcomings unnoticed, than constantly to be finding fault. She maintained that scolding should be indulged in most sparingly, as much of it was detrimental both to the temper of the child and the dignity of the mother. She believed that too little allowance was made for the heedlessness growing out of pure exuberance of spirits. But when a law was once established it was unalterable, and no child ever thought of resisting it. For instance, no one, large or small, was allowed to exhibit a peevish ill-nature, either by word or manner, in the public rooms of the house. My mother merely said, in a quiet tone : "My child, you are either tired or sick ; in either case, it would be better to go to your own room and lie down until you are quite restored." The result of this simple rule was an almost uniform cheerfulness. I have lived in many homes, in many parts of the world, but I have never seen one which equaled my mother's in this respect. I do not remember a single command issued by my mother to her older children; but I can well remember her saying: "I think you had better do so and so"; and I recollect distinctly that when we obstinately followed our own unreasoning will, as we were often inclined to do, we were invariably taught a bitter but wholesome lesson. She believed these lessons to be much more effectual for good than any arbitrary prohibition on her part would have been ; she reserved such prohibition for the cases where the consequences were not confined to ourselves, or were of too serious a nature.

The one mistake made by my mother was in the physical management of her children. Like many mothers whose bodies and minds are kept at the highest tension, she failed to give vital strength to her children. The most promising of these died in early childhood, "by the will of God," as we say in our blindness. One of them especially, the "little king," as he was called, being a magnificent child, both in mental and moral development. Of those who came to maturity, one died at the age of twenty-seven, one has been an invalid for years, one has fair health, and one only rejoices in a vigorous physique. This boy was born in my grandmother's house, near the sea, where my mother had spent, as she expressed it, "the laziest year of her whole life." These children have all had a keen love of study, an energy which carried them far beyond their strength, and she failed sufficiently to curb them. But in other respects, our mother has done to the uttermost. Her children had strong propensities both for good and ill. She has, so far as is possible, strengthened the virtues and repressed the faults of every child given into her keeping.

"The sun shines," is a sentence simple and short, but how infinite is its meaning; myriads of unfolding blossoms flash it back in vivid coloring; myriads of stalwart trees whisper it; myriads of breathing things revel in it; myriads of men thank God for it. So is it with the influence of a good mother. It is not given us to follow each tiny shaft of light in its endless searchings, neither do we note how the riot of the waste places within us is pruned by deft hands into a tenuous symmetry, nor how, in the midst of this life's growth, is laid the foundation of the kingdom of Heaven, by the silent masonry of a mother's constant endeavor.

Mothers, all over this broad land, heavy-laden with the puerile details of daily living, fling off your shrouding cares, and lift your worn faces that you may see with a broad outlook how full-fruited is the vineyard in which you are toiling; the thorns are irritating; the glebe is rough; your spirit faints in the heat of the toilsome day. Look up! the lengthening shadows are falling like dew upon you! tired hearts, look up! purple-red hangs the clustering fruit of your life-long work; the vintage has come, the freest from blight that can ever come—the vintage of a faithful mother!

The name of Mary Owen was not written upon the brains of men, but it is graven upon the hearts of these her children; so long as they live, the blessed memory of that home shall abide with them, a

20

home wherein all that was sweet, and strong, and true, was nurtured by a wise hand, was sunned into blossoming by a loving heart.

A benediction rests upon the brow of him who has given his best work to help this world onward, even though it be but a hair's-breadth; but the mother who has given herself to her children through long years of an unwritten self-abnegation, who has thrilled every fiber of their beings with faith in God and hope in man, a faith and a hope which no canker-worm of worldly experience can ever eat away, she shall be crowned with a sainted halo.

REMINISCENCES BY DR. MARY F. THOMAS AND AMANDA M. WAY.

At an anti-slavery meeting held in Greensboro, Henry Co., in 1851, a resolution was offered by Amanda M. Way, then an active agent in the "Underground Railroad," as follows:

WHEREAS, The women of our land are being oppressed and degraded by the laws and customs of our country, and are in but little better condition than chattel slaves; therefore,

Resolved, That we call a Woman's Rights Convention, and that a committee be now appointed to make the necessary arrangements.

The resolution was adopted. Amanda M. Way, Joel Davis, and Fanny Hiatt were appointed.

The Convention met in October, 1851, in Dublin, Wayne Co., and organized by electing Hannah Hiatt, President; Amanda Way, Vice-President; and Henry Hiatt, Secretary. Miss Way made the opening address, and stated the object of the Convention to be a full, free, and candid discussion of the legal and social position of women. The meetings continued two days. Henry C. Wright addressed large audiences at the evening sessions. A letter was received from Mary F. Thomas, of North Manchester, urging all those who believe in woman's rights to be firm and outspoken. She encouraged young ladies to enter the trades and professions, to fit themselves in some way for pecuniary independence, and adds, "Although a wife, mother, and housekeeper, with all that that means, I am studying medicine, and expect to practice, if I live."

Such a Convention being a novel affair, called out some ridicule and opposition, but the friends were so well pleased with their success, that a committee was appointed to arrange for another the next year, which was held in Richmond, Oct. 15 and 16, 1852. A few of the resolutions* will show the spirit of the leaders at that

---

* See Appendix.

time. A Woman's Rights Society was formed at this Convention, a Constitution and By-laws adopted, and it became one of the permanent organizations of the State. Hannah Hiatt, President; Jane Morrow, Vice-President; Mary B. Birdsall, Secretary; Amanda Way, Treasurer.

Another Convention was held at Richmond October 12, 1853. The President being absent, Lydia W. Vandeburg presided with dignity and ability. Frances D. Gage, Josephine S. Griffing, Emma R. Coe, and Lydia Ann Jenkins were among the prominent speakers. Having heard that Antoinette Brown had been denied admission as a delegate to the "World's Temperance Convention," held in New York, on account of her sex, they passed a resolution condemning this insult offered to all womankind. Thirty-two persons* signed the Constitution in the first Convention, and the movement spread rapidly in the Hoosier State.

The fourth annual meeting convened in Masonic Hall, Indianapolis, October 26, 1854. Frances D. Gage, Caroline M. Severance, and L. A. Hine were the invited speakers, and right well did they sustain the banner of equal rights in the capital of the State. J. W. Gordon, then a young and promising lawyer, and since one of the leading men of the State, avowed himself in favor of woman suffrage, and added much to the success of the Convention. The press, as usual, ridiculed, burlesqued, and misrepresented the proceedings; but the citizens manifested a serious interest, and requested that the next Convention be held at the capital.

About this time the "Maine Liquor Law" was passed in this State. The women took an active part in the temperance campaign, and helped to secure the prohibitory law. This made the suffrage movement more popular, as was shown in the increased attendance at the next Convention in Indianapolis, October 12, 1855, at which Emma B. Swank presided. The prominent speakers were James and Lucretia Mott, Frances D. Gage, Ernestine L. Rose, Joseph Barker, Amanda Way, Henry Hiatt, and J. W. Gordon. With such women as these to declare the gospel of equality, and to enforce it with their pure faces, womanly graces, and noble lives, the people could not fail to give their sympathy, and to be convinced of the rightfulness of our cause. The two leading papers again did their best to make the movement ridiculous. The reporters gave glowing pen sketches of the "masculine women" and "feminine men"; they described the dress and appearance of the women very minutely

* See Appendix.

but said little of the merits of the question, or the arguments of the speakers. Amanda Way was chosen President of the Society; Dr. Mary Thomas, Vice-President; Mary B. Birdsall, Secretary; Abbe Lindley, Treasurer.

The next annual meeting was held in Winchester, October 16 and 17, 1856. In her introductory remarks, the President referred to the great change that had taken place in five years. Women were now often seen on the platform making speeches on many questions, behind the counters as clerks, in the sick-room as physicians. The temperance organization of Good Templars, now spreading rapidly over the State, makes no distinction in its members; women as well as men serve on committees, hold office, and vote on all business matters. Emma B. Swank and Sarah E. Underhill were the principal speakers at this Convention. For logical argument and beauty of style, Miss Swank was said to have few equals. Dr. Mary Thomas was chosen President for the next year.

The annual meeting of 1857 was again held in Winchester, by an invitation from the citizens, and the Methodist Episcopal Church was tendered for their use. On taking the chair, the President, Dr. Mary F. Thomas, said:

This is the first time I have had the pleasure of meeting with this Association, still my heart, my influence, and my prayers have all been with the advocates of this cause. Although I have not enjoyed the privilege of attending the annual meetings, owing to my many cares, I have not been an idler in the vineyard. By my example, as well as my words, I have tried to teach women to be more self-reliant, and to prepare themselves for larger and more varied spheres of activity.

Frances D. Gage, who was always a favorite speaker in Indiana, was again present, and scattered seeds of truth that have produced abundant fruit. On motion of Amanda Way, who said she believed it was time for us to begin to knock at the doors of the Legislature, a committee of three was appointed to prepare a form of petition to be circulated and presented to the next Legislature.

In 1858 the Convention again met in Richmond, Sarah Underhill, President. Adeline T. Swift and Anne D. Cridge, of Ohio, both excellent speakers, were present. The committee appointed to draft a form of petition, reported the following:

To the Honorable Senate and House of Representatives of the State of Indiana:

The undersigned, residents of the State of Indiana, respectfully ask you to grant to women the same rights in property that are enjoyed by men. We also ask you to take the necessary steps to amend the Constitution so as to extend to woman the right of suffrage.

Sarah Underhill, Emma Swank, Mary Birdsall, Agnes Cook, Dr. Mary F. Thomas, and Amanda Way were appointed to present said petition to the Legislature. The interest was so great, and the discussions so animated, for many new speakers from all parts of the State had risen up, that the Convention continued through three days.

On the 19th of January, 1859, the petition was presented to the Legislature by Mary Birdsall, Agnes Cook, and Dr. Mary Thomas. An account of the proceedings was given in *The Lily,* a woman's rights paper, published and edited by Dr. Mary Thomas. The occasion of the presentation of petitions in person by a delegation of the Indiana Woman's Rights Association before the assembled Houses of the Legislature, drew an immense crowd long before the appointed hour. On the arrival of the Committee, they were escorted to the Speaker's stand. The President, J. R. Cravens, introduced them to their Representatives.

Mrs. Agnes Cook, in a few brief remarks, invited a serious and candid consideration of the intrinsic merits of the petition about to be presented, and the arguments of the petitioners.

Dr. Mary Thomas read the petition signed by over one thousand residents of Indiana, and urged the Legislature to pass laws giving equal property rights to married women, and to take the necessary steps to so amend the Constitution of the State as to secure to all women the right of suffrage. She claimed these rights on the ground of absolute justice, as well as the highest expediency, pointing out clearly the evils that flow from class legislation.

Mrs. Birdsall being introduced, read a clear, concise address, occupying about half an hour.

The following resolution, offered by Gen. Steele, was unanimously adopted:

Resolved, That the addresses just read be spread upon the Journal, and that copies be requested for publication in the city papers.

After the Senate adjourned, the Speaker called the House to order, and on the motion of Mr. Murray, it resolved itself into committee of the whole on the memorial just presented. On motion of Mr. Hamilton, the petition was made the special order for Friday, when it was referred to the Committee on " Rights and Privileges," who reported " that legislation on this subject is inexpedient at this time," which report was concurred in by the House.

The ninth annual meeting was held in Good Templars' Hall, Richmond, in October, 1859. It continued but one day, as the time was fully occupied in business plans for future work. Mary B. Birdsall was chosen President of the Association.

The intense excitement of the political campaign of 1860, and the civil war that followed, absorbed every other interest. The women who had so zealously worked for their own rights, were just as ready to help others. Some hastened to the hospitals; others labored in the sanitary movement. Others did double duty at home, tilling the ground and gathering in the harvests, that their fathers, husbands, brothers, and sons might go forth to fight the battles of freedom. No conventions were held for ten years; but public sentiment had taken a long stride during those years of conflict, and when the pioneers of this reform, who had been accustomed to opposition and misrepresentation, again began the work, they were astonished to find themselves in a comparatively popular current.

We find the following letters from Henry C. Wright and Esther Ann Lukens, in *The Liberator:*

DUBLIN, WAYNE CO., Indiana, *Oct.* 14, 1851.

DEAR GARRISON:—I am in a Woman's Rights Convention, the first ever held in this State, called by the women of Indiana to consider the true position of woman. An excellent but short address was made by the President, Hannah Hiatt, on the importance of the movement and the ruinous consequences of dividing the interests of men and women, and making their relations antagonistic in the State, the Church, and the affairs of every-day life. Much was said against woman's taking part in government. It would degrade her to vote and hold office, and destroy her influence as mother, wife, daughter, sister. It was in answer that if voting and holding office would degrade women, they would degrade men also; whatever is injurious to the moral nature, delicacy, and refinement of woman is equally so to man. Moral obligations rest equally on both sexes. Man should be as refined and chaste as woman if we would make our social life pure. Women may as well say to men, "Keep away from the ballot-box and from office, for it degrades you and unfits you to be our companions," as for man to say so to women. Dr. Curtis, a Methodist class-leader, said the Bible had placed the *final appeal* in all disputes in man; that if woman refused obedience, God gave man the right to use force. This "Christian teacher" was the only person in the Convention who appealed to the spirit of rowdyism, whose language was unbecoming the subject and the occasion. He was the only one who appealed to the Bible to justify the subjection of woman. And while he awarded to man the right to use force, he said the only influence the Bible authorized woman to use was moral suasion. Man is to rule woman by violence; woman must rule man by love, kindness, and long-suffering. So says the Bible according to the interpretation of the learned Dr. Curtis. The Convention lasted two days. It was a thrilling meeting.

Yours,   HENRY C. WRIGHT.

NEW GARDEN, Ohio, *Oct.* 2, 1851.

DEAR FRIENDS:—When Goethe was asked if the world would be better if the Golden Age were restored, he answered, "A synod of good women shall decide."

Could his spirit look down upon us he would see those synods, of which he perhaps prophetically spoke, assembling all over the land, not to restore an age of semi-barbarism, but to hasten the advent of a new and far more golden era, when there will be no dangerous pilgrimage of years' duration to win back the Holy Sepulchre, but a far more divine and sacred inheritance shall have been sought and found ; namely, freedom for woman to exercise every right, capacity, and power with which God has endowed her.

If there are any natural rights, then they belong to all by virtue of our humanity, and are not graduated by degrees of superiority. If the privilege of voting had been limited to those men who were strong in mind and morals, we should never have had a Governor's signature to " the black laws of Ohio."

It is perverse and cruel to raise the cry that we make war upon domestic life ; that we would destroy its natural order and attraction by allowing woman to mingle in the coarse and noisy scenes of political life. Is not the aid of man equally important in the family, and would his necessary duties in the home conflict with his duties as a citizen and a patriot ?

Man can not wrong and oppress woman without jeopardizing his own liberty. Cramped and crippled as she may be by inexorable law, she avenges herself, and decides his destiny. So long as woman is outlawed, man pays the penalty in ignorance, poverty, and suffering. Our interests are one, we rise or fall together.

Sisters of Indiana, accept my heartfelt sympathy in the work you have undertaken. It is well for the pioneers of a new country to call down God's blessing on their labors by an early claim to an equality of rights.

Yours, for justice to all,   Esther Ann Lukens.

Having never met the brave women who endured the first shower of ridicule in Indiana, we asked to be introduced to them in some brief pen-sketches, and in the following manner they present themselves :

REV. AMANDA M. WAY

may be truthfully called the mother of " The Woman Suffrage Association " in Indiana organized in 1851, and took an active part in all the Conventions until she became a resident in Kansas in 1872. Miss Way was always an abolitionist, a prohibitionist, and an uncompromising suffragist—the great pioneer of all reforms. It is amusing to hear how many places she has been the first to fill ; yet she has done it all in such a quiet way that no one seemed to feel that she was ever out of place. It was a common remark, " Amanda can do that, but she is not like other people." She was the first woman elected Grand Secretary of the " Indiana Order of Good Templars," in 1856 ; the first State lecturer and organizer ; the first in the world to be elected Grand Worthy Chief Templar ; the first one in her State to be a representative to the national lodge ; the first one admitted as a regular representative to the Grand Division, Sons of Temperance, and the first to be a licensed preacher in the Methodist Episcopal Church. What is better still, she continues in the work she began, gaining power and influence with the experience of years. An editor, speaking of her, said : " There is no woman more widely and favorably known in this State than Amanda Way. Her name is a household word, and in the hearts of the temperance reformers her memory will ever be sacred."

In 1859, she was associated with Mrs. Underhill in editing *The Ladies' Tribune*, and has since been connected with the press much of the time. During the Rebellion, her time and thoughts were given to active labors in the hospitals and the sanitary movement. Many a soldier returned to his home who would have died but for her care. In company with Mrs. Swank she presented a memorial to the Legislature in 1871, asking the elective franchise for women, and made a very effective speech on the occasion.

Her home-life has been equally active and faithful; a widowed mother and a sister's orphaned children, have been her special care, depending on her for support. Once, when asked why she never married, she laughingly replied, " I never had time."

She has been a consistent member of the Methodist Church twenty years, and ten years ago, unsolicited by herself, she was licensed as a minister by the Winchester Quarterly Conference, Rev. Milton Mahin, Presiding Elder. In her travels over the State she preaches almost every Sunday, being invited to fill many pulpits, both in Kansas and this State.

She is a calm, forcible, earnest speaker, and, though quiet and reserved in manner, she is genial and warm in her affections.

She is now fifty-two years old, and though her life has been a constant battle with wrongs, she has not become misanthropic nor despondent. Knowing that progress is the law of life, she has full faith that the moral world, though moving slowly, is still moving in the right direction.

HELEN V. AUSTIN,

Corresponding Secretary of the State Suffrage Association for many years, a position for which she was eminently fitted, being gifted as a writer. Having had a liberal education, and great enthusiasm in our cause, her labors have been valuable and effective. She is a correspondent for several journals and periodicals, is very active in " The State Horticultural Society," and takes a deep interest in all the progressive movements of the day.

LOUISE V. BOYD.

Mrs. Boyd is a lady of fine poetical genius and superior literary attainments. She has been an earnest advocate of woman suffrage for many years, and is herself a living argument of woman's ability to use the rights she asks.

In 1871 she read a very able essay on the " Women of the Bible," before the State Association of the Christian Church. It was the first time a woman's voice had been heard in that religious body. The success of her effort on that occasion opened the way for other women. Mrs. Boyd and her husband (Dr. S. S. Boyd, who is also a zealous friend of our cause), have both been officers of the State W. S. Association for many years, taking an active part in all our Conventions.

REV. MARY T. CLARK.

Mrs. Clark has been an acceptable lecturer and preacher for many years in different parts of the State. She was early a recognized minister among the

Congregational Quakers. More recently she has been ordained in the Universalist Church, and enjoys equal rights and honors with the clergymen of that denomination. She is a woman of education and culture, and of English parentage.

EMMA B. SWANK.

Mrs. Swank is one of the most pleasing speakers of Indiana. She is a graduate of Antioch, and while yet in college she gained quite a reputation by her lecturing on Astronomy. She spent several years lecturing to classes of women on Physiology, Anatomy, and Hygiene. Of late, she has devoted herself to Woman Suffrage and Temperance. She served as president of the State Society one year before the war and one since, and has always done good service to the cause of woman with both pen and tongue.

SARAH E. UNDERHILL.

Mrs. Underhill was first known in Indiana as the editor and proprietor of the *Ladies' Tribune* at Indianapolis in 1857. She associated with her Amanda Way as office editor, that she might devote her entire time to lecturing. Though she remained in the State but three years, she was widely and favorably known as an earnest and effective speaker on Woman Suffrage and Temperance. When the war began, she was among the first to go to the sick and wounded soldiers. A brief account of her work in the hospitals will be found in the " Women of the War."

JANE MORROW.

Miss Morrow was a pioneer in our movement; attended the Second Convention in 1852. She was not a speaker, but a practical business woman, owning and successfully carrying on a dry-goods store in Richmond for many years. By precept and example, she taught the doctrine of woman's independence and self-reliance. She was a kind, genial, sunny-hearted woman, who made all about her bright and happy, though she was what the world calls an " old maid." In 1867, she died suddenly, without a moment's warning or parting word; but " Aunt Jane," as she was familiarly called, will long be remembered in her native town.

MARY B. BIRDSALL

was secretary of the Convention of 1852, and held that position for three years. She purchased *The Lily*, a Woman's Rights paper, of Amelia Bloomer, in 1855, and published it for three years. Her home is in Richmond.

MARY ROBINSON OWEN.

Mrs. Owen, wife of Robert Dale Owen, was not known to the public until after the war. It is said, however, that she suggested and helped prepare the amendments to the laws with reference to woman's property rights, that her husband carried through our Legislature. She had a strong, clear intellect, and her lectures were more argumentative and pointed than rhetorical and finished. She sympathized with and aided her husband in all his reformatory movements, and was his equal in mental power. She was one of the vice-presidents of our Indiana State Woman Suffrage Association at the time of her death, 1871.

MARY F. THOMAS.

Mary F. Thomas, M.D., was born October 28. 1816, in Montgomery County, Maryland. Her parents, Samuel and Mary Myers, were members of the Society of Friends, and resided in their early days in Berks and Chester Counties, in Pennsylvania. Her father was the associate of Benjamin Lundy, in organizing and attending the first anti-slavery meeting held in Washington, at the risk of their lives.

Desiring to place his family beyond the evil influences of slavery, he moved to Columbiana County, Ohio. He purchased a farm there; his daughters assisted him in his outdoor labors in the summer, and studied under his instructions in the winter. While in Washington he frequently took his daughters to the capitol to listen to the debates, which gave them interest in political questions. Mary was early roused to the consideration of woman's wrongs by the unequal wages paid to teachers of her own sex. In 1845 she was much moved in listening to the preaching of Lucretia Mott at a yearly meeting in Salem, Ohio, and resolved that her best efforts should be given to secure justice for woman.

In 1839 she was married to Dr. Owen Thomas. She has three daughters, all well educated, self-reliant women. Her youngest daughter, a graduate of Cornell University, Ithaca, New York, took the Greek prize in the intercollegiate contest in 1874. As Mrs. Thomas' husband was a physician, she studied medicine with him, and graduated at the Penn Medical College of Philadelphia in 1854. She was the first woman to take her place in the State Medical Association as a regularly admitted delegate. She is a member of the Wayne County Medical Association; has been physician for " The Home for Friendless Women " in the city of Richmond for nine years, and has filled the office of City Physician by the appointment of the Commissioners for several years.

Though deeply interested in the woman suffrage reform, owing to her domestic cares and medical studies she could not attend any public meetings until 1857; since that time she has been one of the most responsible standard-bearers, and for several years President of the State Association.

Mrs. Thomas was always a conscientious abolitionist; the poor fugitive from bondage did not knock at her door in vain. The temperance reform, too, has had her warm sympathy and the benefit of her pure example. She is a member of the Grand Lodge of Good Templars, and has held important offices in that Order, having been a faithful disciple in spreading the gospel of temperance over forty years, always a member of some organization.

During the war of the rebellion she gave herself in every way that was open to woman to the loyal service of her country. As assistant physician in hospitals, looking after the sick and wounded, and in sanitary work at home, she manifested as much patriotism as any man did on the battle-field. After her long experience, she comes to the conclusion, that with the ballot in her own hand, with the power to coin her will into law, a woman might do a far more effective work in preventing human misery and crime, than she ever can accomplish by indirect influence, in merely mitigating the evils man perpetuates by law.

(*From the Liberator of May*, 1856).

RIGHTS OF WOMEN IN WISCONSIN.

Minority Report of C. L. Sholes, from the "Committee on Expiration and Re-enactment of Laws," to whom were referred sundry petitions, praying that steps may be taken to confer upon women the right of suffrage in Wisconsin.

The minority of the Committee on Expiration and Re-enactment of Laws, beg leave to report:

The theory of our government, proclaimed some eighty years since, these petitioners ask may be reduced to practice. The undersigned is aware that the opinion has been announced from a high place and high source, that this theory is, in the instrument which contains it, a mere rhetorical flourish, admirable to fill a sentence and round a period, but otherwise useless and meaningless; that so far from all mankind being born free and equal, it is those only who have rights that are entitled to them; those yet out of the pale of that fortunate condition being intended by Providence always to be and remain there. But notwithstanding this opinion has the weight of high authority, and notwithstanding the practice of the American people has thus far been in strict accordance with such opinion, the undersigned believes that the theory proclaimed is not simply a rhetorical flourish, nor meaningless, but that it means just what it says; that it is true, and being true, is susceptible of an application as broad as the truth proclaimed.

All humankind, says the theory, are endowed by their Creator with certain inalienable rights. Other governments proclaim the divine right of kings, and assume that man is the mere creature of the government, deriving all his rights from its concessions, and forever subject to all its impositions, while this government (or at least its theory) elevates all men to an equality with kings, brings every man face to face with the author of his being and the arbiter of his destiny, deriving his rights from that source alone; and makes government his creature instead of his master, instituted by him solely for the better protection and application of his God-given rights. It is important to keep in mind this theory of our government and its difference with the theories of all other governments. Endowed by their Creator with certain inalienable rights, it says, because those rights are necessary to correct relations between each individual of humanity and his Creator. Herein is the whole merit of the American theory of government, and of its practice too, so far as that practice has gone. It is a grand theory, opening as it does to every human being the boundless plains of progress which stretch out to the foot of the eternal throne, and implying as it does such noble powers in humanity, and such noble conditions and uses for those powers. Its effect upon those who have enjoyed the benefit of its application has been in harmony with its own exalted character. Though but a day old, as it were, in the history of nations, the United States, in a great many respects, outstrip all other nations of the earth, and are inferior in few or no particulars to any. The mass of her people are conceded to be the most intelligent people of the world, and manifest, individually and collectively, the fruits of superior intelligence. It will not be denied that our theory of government, viewing as it does every man as a sovereign, opening up to every man all the distinctions, all the honors, and all the wealth which man is capable of desiring, appreciating, or grasping, exercises a powerful, indeed a controlling influence in making our people what they are, and our nation what it is.

These petitions ask only that these rights, enjoyed by one portion of the American people, may be extended to embrace the whole, not less for the abstract but all-sufficient reason, that they have been given to the whole by the Creator, than that by their application to the whole, the more general will be the benefits experienced; and the deeper, broader, more prevailing and more enduring will become those benefits. Manifestly, such must be the case; for as these rights belong to humanity, and produce their exalted and beneficial fruits by their application to and upon humanity, it follows that, wherever humanity is, there they belong, and there they will work out their beneficial results. To exclude woman from the possession of equal political rights with man, it should be shown that she is essentially a different being; that the Creator of man is not her Creator; that she has not the same evil to shun, the same heaven to gain; in short, the same grand, immortal destiny which is supposed to invite to high uses the capacity of man, does not pertain to nor invite her. We say this must be shown; and if it can not be, as certainly it can not, then it follows that to withhold these rights, so beneficial to one portion, is to work an immediate and particular injury to those from whom they are withheld, and, although a more indirect, not a less certain injury to all. Man-masculine is not endowed by his Creator with certain inalienable rights because he is male, but because he is human; and when, in virtue of our strong and superior physical capacity, we deny to man-feminine the rights which are ours only in virtue of our humanity, we exercise the same indefensible tyranny against which *we* felt justified in taking up arms, and perilling life and fortune.

The argument against conceding these rights all are familiar with. They are precisely the same which have been in the mouths of tyrants from the beginning of time, and have been urged against any and every demand for popular liberty. A want of capacity for self-government—freedom will be only licentiousness—and out of the possession of rights will grow only the practice of follies and wrongs. This is the argument, in brief, applied to every step of gradual emancipation on the part of the male, and now by him applied to the female struggling to reach the common platform. Should the American male, in the van of human progress, as the result of this theory of a capacity for self-government, turn round and ignore this divinity, this capacity in another branch of the human family? The theory has worked only good in its application thus far, and it is a most unreasonable, a most unwarrantable distrust to expect it to produce mischief when applied to others in all respects mentally and morally the equals of those who now enjoy it. It neither can nor will do so; but, necessarily, the broader and more universal its application, the broader and more universal its benefits.

The possession of political rights by woman does not necessarily imply that she must or will enter into the practical conduct of all the institutions, proper and improper, now established and maintained by the male portion of the race. These institutions may be right and necessary, or they may not, and the nature of woman may or may not be in harmony with them. It is not proposed to enact a law compelling woman to do certain things, but it is proposed simply to place her side by side with man on a common platform of rights, confident that, in that position, she will not outrage the "higher law" of her nature by descending to a participation in faults, follies, or crimes, for which she has no constitutional predilections. The association of woman with man, in the various relations of life in which such association is permitted, from the first unclosing of his eyes in the imbecility of infancy, till they close finally upon all things earthly, is conceded to be highly beneficial. Indeed, we think it will be found, on scrutiny, that it is only those institutions of society in which women have no part, and from which they are entirely excluded, which are radically wrong, and need either thorough renovation or entire abrogation. And if we have any duties so essentially degrading, or any institution so essentially impure, as to be beyond the renovating influence which woman can bring to bear on them, beyond question they should be abrogated without delay—a result which woman's connection with them would speedily bring about.

Who dares say, then, that such association would not be equally beneficial, if in every sphere of activity opened to man, woman could enter with him and be at his side? Are our politics, in their practice, so exalted, so dignified, so pure, that we need no new associations, no purer and healthier influences, than now connected with them? Is our Government just what we would have it; are our rulers just what we would have them; in short, have we arrived at that happy summit where perfection in these respects is found? Not so. On the con'rary, there is an universal prayer throughout the length and breadth of the land, for reform in these respects; and where, let us ask, could we reasonably look for a more powerful agent to effect this reform, than in the renovating influences of woman? That which has done so much for the fireside and social life generally, neither can nor will lose its potent, beneficial effect when brought to bear upon other relations of life.

To talk of confining woman to her proper sphere by legal disabilities, is an insult to the divinity of her nature, implying, as it does, the absence of instinctive virtue, modesty, and sense on her part. It makes her the creature of law—of our law—from which she is assumed to derive her ability to keep the path of rectitude, and the withdrawal of which would leave her to sink to the depths of folly and vice. Do we really think so badly of our mothers, wives, sisters, daughters? Is it really we only of the race who are instinctively and innately so sensible, so modest, so virtuous, as to be qualified, not only to take care of ourselves, but to dispense all these exalted qualities to the weaker, and, as we assume, inferior half of the race? If it be so, it may be doubted whether Heaven's last gift was its best. Kings, emperors, and dictators confine their subjects, by the interposition of law, to what they consider their proper spheres; and there is certainly as much propriety in it as in the dictation, by one sex, of the sphere of a different sex. In the assumption of our strength, we say woman must not have equal rights with us, because she has a different nature. If so, by what occult power do we understand that different nature to dictate by metes and bounds its wants and spheres? Fair play is a Yankee characteristic; and we submit, if but one-half of the race can have rights at a time because of their different natures, whether it is not about time the proscribed half had its chance in, to assume the reins of Government, and dictate *our* sphere. It is no great compliment to that part of the race to venture the opinion, that the country would be full as well governed as it now is, and our sphere would be bounded with quite as much liberality as now is theirs.

Let every human being occupy a common platform of political rights, and all will irresistibly gravitate exactly to their proper place and sphere, without discord, and with none but the most beneficial results. In this way human energy and capacity will be fully economized and expended for the highest interest of all humanity ; and this result is only to be obtained by opening to all, without restriction, common spheres of activity.

Woman has all the interests on earth that man has—she has all the interest in the future that man has. Man has rights only in virtue of his relations to earth and heaven ; and woman, whose relations are the same, has the same rights. The possession of her rights, on the part of woman, will interfere no more with the duties of life, than their possession by man interferes with his duties ; and as man is presumed to become a better man in all respects by the possession of his rights, such must be the inevitable effect of their possession upon woman.

The history of the race, thus far, has been a history of tyranny by the strong over the weak. Might, not right, has been as yet the fundamental practice of all governments ; and under this order of things, woman, physically weak, from a slave, beaten, bought, and sold in the market, has but become, in the more civilized and favored portions of the earth, the toy of wealth and the drudge of poverty. But we now have at least a new and different theory of government ; and as the aspiration of one age is sure to be the code of the next, and practice is sure at some time to overtake theory, we have reason to expect that principle will take the place of mere brute force, and the truth will be fully realized,

"That men and women have *one* glory and *one* shame ;
Everything that's done inhuman injures all of us the same."

Never, till woman stands side by side with man, his equal in the eye of the law as well as the Creator, will the high destiny of the race be accomplished. She is the mother of the race, and every stain of littleness or inferiority cast upon her by our institutions will soil the offspring she sends into the world, and clip and curtail to that extent his fair proportions. If we would abrogate that littleness of her character which finds a delight in the gewgaws of fashion, and an enjoyment in the narrow sphere of gossipping, social life, or tea-table scandal, so long the ridicule of our sex ; open to her new and more ennobling fields of activity and thought—fields, the exploration of which has filled the American males with great thoughts, and made them the foremost people of the world, and which will place the American females on their level, and make them truly helps meet for them. When we can add to the men of America a race of women educated side by side with them, and enjoying equal advantages with them in all respects, we may expect an offspring of giants in the comprehension and application of the great truths which involve human rights and human happiness.

These petitions ask that the necessary steps may be taken to strike from the Constitution the legal distinction of sex. Your Committee is in favor of the prayer of the petitions ; but, under the most favorable circumstances, that is a result which could not be attained in less than two years. In all probability, it will not be longer than that before the Constitution will come up directly for revision, which will be a proper, appropriate, and favorable time to press the question.

Your Committee, therefore, introduces no bill, and recommends no action at present.

All of which is respectfully submitted.   C. L. SHOLES.

This able report was the result, in a great measure, of the agitation started by Mrs. Nichols and Mrs. Fowler in 1853, and by Lucy Stone's lecturing tour in 1855, thus proving that no true words or brave deeds are ever lost. The experiences of these noble pioneers in their first visits to Wisconsin, though in many respects trying and discouraging, brought their own rich rewards, not only in higher individual development, but in an improved public opinion and more liberal legislation in regard the rights of women in that State.

CHAPTER X.

PENNSYLVANIA.

William Penn—Independence Hall—British troops—Heroism of women—Lydia Darrah—
Who designed the Flag—Anti-slavery movements in Philadelphia—Pennsylvania Hall
destroyed by a mob—David Paul Brown—Fugitives—Millard Fillmore—John Brown
—Angelina Grimké—Abby Kelly—Mary Grew—Temperance in 1848—Hannah Dar-
lington and Ann Preston before the Legislature—Medical College for Women in 1850—
Westchester Woman Rights Convention, 1852—Philadelphia Convention, 1854—Lucre-
tia Mott answers Richard H. Dana—Jane Grey Swisshelm—Sarah Josepha Hale—
Anna McDowell—Rachel Foster searching the records.

In 1680, Charles II., King of England, granted to William Penn a tract of land in consideration of the claims of his father, Admiral Penn, which he named Pennsylvania. The charter for this land is still in existence at Harrisburg, among the archives of the State. The principal condition of the bargain with the Indians was the payment of two beaver skins annually. This was the purchase money for the great State of Pennsylvania.

Penn landed at New Castle October 27, 1682, and in November visited the infant city of Philadelphia, where so many of the eventful scenes of the Revolution transpired. Penn had been already imprisoned in England several times for his Quaker principles, which had so beneficent an influence in his dealings with the Indians, and on the moral character of the religious sect he founded in the colonies.

While yet a student he was expelled from Christ Church, Oxford, because he was converted to Quakerism under the preaching of Thomas Loe. He was imprisoned in Cork for attending a Quaker meeting, and in the Tower of London in 1668 for writing "The Sandy Foundation Shaken," and while there he wrote his great work, "No Cross, No Crown." In 1671, he was again imprisoned for preaching Quakerism, and as he would take no oath on his trial, he was thrown into Newgate, and while there he wrote his other great work on " Toleration."

In 1729 the foundations of Independence Hall, the old State House, were laid, and the building was completed in 1734. Here the first Continental Congress was held in September, 1774 ; a Provincial Convention in January, 1775 ; the Declaration of In dependence proclaimed July 4, 1776, and on the 8th, read to thousands assembled in front of the building. These great events have made Philadelphia the birthplace of freedom, the Mecca of this western world, where the lovers of liberty go up to worship; and made the Keystone State so rich in memories, the brightest star in the republican constellation, where in 1776 freedom was proclaimed, and in 1780 slavery was abolished.

Philadelphia remained the seat of Government until 1800. The British troops occupied the city from September 26, 1777, to June 18, 1778. During this period we find many interesting incidents in regard to the heroism of women. In every way they aided the struggling army, not only in providing food and clothes, ministering to the sick in camp and hospitals, but on active duty as messengers and spies under most difficult and dangerous circumstances. The brave deeds and severe privations the women of this nation endured with cheerfulness would fill volumes, yet no monuments are built to their memory, and only by the right of petition have they as yet the slightest recognition in the Government. A few instances that occurred at Philadelphia will illustrate the patriotism of American women.*

While the American army remained encamped at White Marsh, the British being in possession of Philadelphia, Gen. Howe made some vain attempts to draw Washington into an engagement. The house opposite the headquarters of Gen. Howe, tenanted by William and Lydia Darrah, members of the Society of Friends, was the place selected by the superior officers of the army for private conference, whenever it was necessary to hold consultations.

On the afternoon of the 2d of December, the British Adjutant-General called and informed the mistress that he and some friends were to meet there that evening, and desired that the back room up-stairs might be prepared for their reception. "And be sure, Lydia," he concluded, " that your family are all in bed at an early hour. When our guests are ready to leave the house, I will myself give you notice, that you may let us out and extinguish the candles."

Having delivered this order, the Adjutant-General departed. Lydia betook herself to getting all things in readiness. But she felt curious to know what the business could be that required such secrecy, and resolved on further investigation. Accordingly, in the midst of their conference that night, she quietly approached the door, and listening, heard a plan for the surprise of Washington's forces arranged for the next night. She retreated softly to her room and laid down; soon there was a knocking at her door. She knew well what the signal meant, but took no heed until it was repeated again and again, and then she arose quickly

---

* Mrs. Ellet's " Women of the Revolution."

and opened the door. It was the Adjutant-General who came to inform her they were ready to depart. Lydia let them out, fastened the door, extinguished the fire and lights, and returned to her chamber, but she was uneasy, thinking of the threatened danger.

At the dawn of day she arose, telling her family that she must go to Frankfort to procure some flour. She mounted her horse, and taking the bag, started. The snow was deep and the cold intense, but Lydia's heart did not falter. Leaving the grist at the mill, she started on foot for the camp, determined to apprise Gen. Washington of his danger. On the way she met one of his officers, who exclaimed in astonishment at seeing her, but making her errand known, she hastened home.

Preparations were immediately made to give the enemy a fitting reception. None suspected the grave, demure Quakeress of having snatched from the English their anticipated victory; but after the return of the British troops Gen. Howe summoned Lydia to his apartment, locked the door with an air of mystery, and motioned her to a seat. After a moment of silence, he said: "Were any of your family up, Lydia, on the night when I received my company here?" "No," she replied, "they all *retired* at eight o'clock." "It is very strange," said the officer, and mused a few minutes. "I know you were asleep, for I knocked at your door three times before you heard me; yet it is certain that we were betrayed."

Afterward some one asked Lydia how she could say her family were all in bed while she herself was up; she replied, "Husband and wife are one, and that one is the husband, and my husband was in bed." Thus the wit and wisdom of this Quaker woman saved the American forces at an important crisis, and perhaps turned the fate of the Revolutionary War.

During that dreadful winter, 1780, at Valley Forge, the ladies of Philadelphia combined to furnish clothing for the army. Money and jewels were contributed in profusion. Those who could not give money, gave their services freely. Not less than $7,500 were contributed to an association for this purpose, of which Esther De Berdt Reed was president. Though an English woman, the French Secretary said of her: "She is called to this office as the best patriot, the most zealous and active, and the most attached to the interests of the country."

The archives of the Keystone State prove that she can boast many noble women from the time of that great struggle for the nation's existence, the signal for which was given when the brave old bell rang out from Independence Hall its message of freedom. The very colors then unfurled, and for the first time named the flag of the United States, were the handiwork, and in part the invention of a woman. That to the taste and suggestions of Mrs. Elizabeth Ross, of Philadelphia, we owe the beauty of the Union's flag can not be denied. There are those who would deprive her of all credit in this connection, and assert that the committee appointed to prepare a flag gave her the perfected design; but the evidence is in favor of her having had a large share in the change from the original design to the flag as it now is; the same flag which we have held as a nation since the memorable year of the Declaration of Independence, the flag which now floats on every sea, whose stars and stripes carry hope to all the oppressed nations of the earth; though to woman it is but an *ignis fatuus*, an ever waving signal of the ingratitude of the republic to one-half its citizens.

An anecdote of a female spy is related in the journal of Major Tallmadge. While the Americans were at Valley Forge he was stationed in the vicinity of Philadelphia with a detachment of cavalry to observe the enemy and limit the range of British foraging parties. His duties required the utmost vigilance, his squad seldom remained all night in the same position, and their horses were rarely unsaddled. Hearing that a country girl had gone into the city with eggs; having been sent by one of the American officers to gain information; Tallmadge advanced toward the British lines, and dismounted at a small tavern within view of their outposts. The girl came to the tavern, but while she was communicating her intelligence to the Major, the alarm was given that the British light-horse were approaching. Tallmadge instantly mounted, and as the girl entreated protection, bade her get up behind him. They rode three miles at full speed to Germantown, the damsel showing no fear, though there was some wheeling and charging, and a brisk firing of pistols.

Tradition tells of some women in Philadelphia, whose husbands used to send intelligence from the American army through a market-boy, who came into the city to bring provisions, and carried the dispatches sent in the back of his coat. One morning, when there was some fear that his movements were watched, a young girl undertook to get the papers. In a pretended game of romps, she threw her shawl over his head, and secured the prize. She hastened with the papers to her friends, who read them with deep interest, after the windows were carefully closed. When news came of Burgoyne's surrender, the sprightly girl, not daring to give vent openly to her exultation, put her head up the chimney and hurrahed for Gates.

And not only in the exciting days of the Revolution do we find abundant records of woman's courage and patriotism, but in all the great moral movements that have convulsed the nation, she has taken an active and helpful part. The soil of Pennsylvania is classic with the startling events of the anti-slavery struggle. In the first Anti-Slavery Society, of which Benjamin Franklin was president, women took part, not only as members, but as officers. The name of Lydia Gillingham stands side by side with Jacob M. Ellis as associate secretaries, signing reports of the "Association for the Abolition of Slavery."

The important part women took in the later movement, inaugurated by William Lloyd Garrison, has already passed into history. The interest in this question was intensified in this State, as it was the scene of the continued recapture of fugitives. The heroism of the women, who helped to fight this great battle of freedom, was only surpassed by those who, taking their lives in their hands, escaped from the land of slavery. The same love of liberty that glowed in eloquent words on the lips of Lucretia Mott, Angelina Grimké, and Mary Grew, was echoed in the brave deeds of Margaret Garner, Linda Brent, and Mrs. Stowe's Eliza.

On December 4, 1833, the Abolitionists assembled in Philadelphia to hold a national convention, and to form the American Anti-Slavery Society. During all the sessions of three days, women were constant and attentive listeners. Lucretia Mott, Esther More, Sidney Ann Lewis, and Lydia White, took part in the discussions. The following resolution, passed at the close of the third day, without dissent, or a word to qualify or limit its application, shows that no one then thought it improper for women to speak in public :

Resolved, That the thanks of the Convention be presented to our female friends for the deep interest they have manifested in the cause of anti-slavery, during the long and fatiguing sessions of this Convention.

Samuel J. May, in writing of this occasion many years after, says : " It is one of the proudest recollections of my life that I was a member of the Convention in Philadelphia, in December, 1833, that formed the American Anti-Slavery Society. And I well remember the auspicious sequel to it, the formation of the Philadelphia Female Anti-Slavery Society. Nor shall I ever forget the wise, the impressive, the animating words spoken in our Convention by dear Lucretia Mott and two or three other excellent women who came to that meeting by divine appointment. But with this last recollection will be forever associated the mortifying fact, that we *men* were then so blind, so obtuse, that we did not recognize those women as members of our Convention, and insist upon their subscribing their names to our 'Declaration of Sentiments and Purposes.' "

PHILADELPHIA ANTI-SLAVERY SOCIETY.

No sooner did the National Society adjourn, than the women who had listened to the discussions with such deep interest, assembled to organize themselves for action. A few extracts from Mary Grew's final report of the Philadelphia Female Anti-Slavery Society in 1870 show that—

A meeting convened at the school-room of Catherine McDermott, 12th mo. 9th, 1833, to take into consideration the propriety of forming a Female Anti-Slavery Society; addresses were made by Samuel J. May, of Brooklyn, Conn., and Nathaniel Southard, of Boston, who pointed out the important assistance that might be rendered by our sex in removing the great evil of slavery. After some discussion upon this interesting subject, it was concluded to form a Society, in the belief that our combined efforts would more effectually aid in relieving the oppression of our suffering fellow-creatures. For this purpose a Committee was appointed to draft a Constitution, and to propose such measures as would be likely to promote the Abolition of Slavery, and to elevate the people of color from their present degraded situation to the full enjoyment of their rights, and to increased usefulness in society.

At a meeting held 12th mo. 14th, the Committee appointed on the 9th submitted a form of Constitution, which was read and adopted. After its adoption, the following persons signed their names: Lucretia Mott, Esther Moore, Mary Ann Jackson, Margaretta Forten, Sarah Louisa Forten, Grace Douglass, Mary Sleeper, Rebecca Hitchins, Mary Clement, A. C. Eckstein, Mary Wood, Leah Fell, Sidney Ann Lewis, Catherine McDermott, Susan M. Shaw, Lydia White, Sarah McCrummell, Hetty Burr. The Society then proceeded to the choice of officers for the ensuing year; when the following persons were elected: Esther Moore, Presiding Officer; Margaretta Forten, Recording Secretary; Lucretia Mott, Corresponding Secretary; Anna Bunting, Treasurer; Lydia White, Librarian.

The Annual Reports of the first two years of this Society are not extant; but from its third, we learn that in each of those years the Society memorialized Congress, praying for the abolition of slavery in the District of Columbia and the Territories of the United States. In the second year of its existence, it appointed a Standing Committee for the purpose of visiting the schools for colored children in this city, and aiding them in any practicable way. In the third year it appointed a Committee "to make arrangements for the establishment of a course of scientific lectures, which our colored friends were particularly invited to attend." The phraseology of this statement implies that white persons were not to be excluded from these lectures, and indicates a clear-sighted purpose, on the part of the Society, to bear its testimony against distinctions founded on color. In this year it published an Address to the Women of Pennsylvania, calling their attention to the claims of the slave, and urging them to sign petitions for his emancipation. Mrs. Elizabeth Heyrick's well-known pamphlet, entitled "Immediate, not

Gradual Emancipation," was during the same year republished by the "Anti-Slavery Sewing Society," a body composed of some of the members of this Association, but not identical with it, which met weekly at the house of our Vice-President, Sidney Ann Lewis. Another event, important and far-reaching beyond our power then to foresee, had marked the year. A member of this Society* had received and accepted a commission to labor as an agent of the American Anti-Slavery Society. It is evident, from the language of the Report, that the newly-appointed agent and her fellow-members regarded the mission as one fraught with peculiar trial of patience and faith, and anticipated the opposition which such an innovation on the usages of the times would elicit. Her appointed field of labor was among her own sex, in public or in private; but in the next year's Report it is announced that she had enlarged her sphere. The fact should never be forgotten by us that it was a member of this Society who first broke the soil in that field where so many women have since labored abundantly, and are now reaping so rich a harvest.

The next year, 1837, was made memorable by a still greater innovation upon established usage—the first National Convention of American Anti-Slavery Women. It is interesting and profitable to notice, as the years passed, that new duties and new responsibilities educated woman for larger spheres of action. Each year brought new revelations, presented new aspects of the cause, and made new demands. Our early Reports mention these Conventions of Women, which were held during three consecutive years in New York and this city, as a novel measure, which would, of course, excite opposition; and they also record the fact that "the editorial rebukes, sarcasm, and ridicule" which they elicited, did not exceed the anticipations of the Abolitionists.

The second of these Conventions was held in this city, in the midst of those scenes of riot when infuriated Southern slaveholders and cowardly Northern tradesmen combined for purposes of robbery and arson, and surrounded Pennsylvania Hall with their representatives, the mob which plundered and burnt it, while the City Government looked on consenting to these crimes. That Convention was the last assembly gathered in that Hall, then just dedicated to the service of Freedom. Its fifth session, on the 17th of May, 1838, was held, calmly and deliberately, while the shouts of an infuriated mob rose around the building, mingling with the speakers' voices, and sometimes overwhelming them; while stones and other missiles crashing through the windows imperilled the persons of many of the audience. The presence of an assembly of women was supposed to be a partial protection against the fury of the rioters; and believing that the mob would not fire the building while it was thus filled, a committee of anti-slavery men sent a request to the Convention to remain in session during the usual interval between the afternoon and evening meetings, if, with their knowledge of their perilous surroundings, they felt willing to do so. The President laid the request before the Convention, and asked, Will you remain? A few minutes of

---

* Angelina E. Grimké.

solemn deliberation; a few moments' listening to the loud madness surging against the outer walls; a moment's unvoiced prayer for wisdom and strength, and the answer came: *We will;* and the business of the meeting proceeded. But before the usual hour of adjournment arrived, another message came from the committee, withdrawing their request, and stating that further developments of the spirit pervading the mob and the city, convinced them that it would be unwise for the Convention to attempt to hold possession of the Hall for the evening. The meeting adjourned at the usual hour, and, on the next morning, the burnt and crumbling remains of Pennsylvania Hall told the story of Philadelphia's disgrace, and the temporary triumph of the spirit of slavery.

The experience of that morning is very briefly mentioned in the published "Proceedings," which state that "the Convention met, pursuant to adjournment, at Temperance Hall, but found the doors closed by order of the managers"; that they were offered the use of a school-room, in which they assembled; and there the Convention held its closing session of six hours. But they who made a part of the thrilling history of those times well remember how the women of that Convention walked through the streets of this city, from the Hall on Third Street, closed against them, to the school-room on Cherry Street, hospitably opened to them by Sarah Pugh and Sarah Lewis, and were assailed by the insults of the populace as they went. It was a meeting memorable to those who composed it; and was one of many interesting associations of our early anti-slavery history which cluster around the school-house, which in those days was always open to the advocacy of the slave's cause.*

An incident in connection with the last of these Conventions, shows how readily and hopefully, in the beginning of our work, we turned for help to the churches and religious societies of the land; and how slowly and painfully we learned their real character. It is long since we ceased to expect efficient help from them; but in those first years of our warfare against slavery, we had not learned that the ecclesiastical standard of morals in a nation *can not* be higher than the standard of the populace generally.

A committee of arrangements appointed to obtain a house in which the Convention should be held, reported: "That in compliance with a resolution passed at a meeting of this Society, an application was made to each of the seven Monthly Meetings of Friends, in this city, for one of their meeting-houses, in which to hold the Convention." Two returned respectful answers, declining the application; three refused to hear it read; one appointed two persons to examine it, and then decided "that it should be *returned without being read*," though a few members urged "that it should be treated more respectfully"; and that from one meeting no answer was received.

As to other denominations of professed Christians, similar applications had been frequently refused by them, although there was one exception

---

* This building, the property of Jacob Peirce, was thus imperilled with his free consent.

which should be ever held in honorable remembrance by the Abolitionists of Philadelphia. The use of the church of the Covenanters, in Cherry street, of which Rev. James M. Wilson was for many years the pastor, was never refused for an anti-slavery meeting, even in the most perilous days of our enterprise. Another fact in connection with the Convention of 1839 it is pleasant to remember now, when the faithful friend whose name it recalls has gone from among us. The Committee of Arrangements reported that their difficulties and perplexities "were relieved by a voluntary offer from that devoted friend of the slave, John H. Cavender, who, with kindness at once unexpected and gratifying, offered the use of a large unfurnished building in Filbert Street, which had been used as a riding school; which was satisfactorily and gratefully occupied by the Convention."

In the year 1840, our Society sent delegates to the assembly called "The World's Anti-Slavery Convention," which was held in London, in the month of May of that year. As is well known, that body refused to admit any delegates excepting those of the male sex, though the invitation was not thus limited; consequently, this Society was not represented there.

The year 1850 was an epoch in the history of the anti-slavery cause. The guilt and disgrace of the nation was then intensified by that infamous statute known by the name of "The Fugitive Slave Law." Its enactment by the Thirty-first Congress, and its ratification by Millard Fillmore's signature, was the signal for an extensive and cruel raid upon the colored people of the North. Probably no statute was ever written, in the code of a civilized nation, so carefully and cunningly devised for the purpose of depriving men of liberty. It put in imminent peril the personal freedom of every colored man and woman in the land. It furnished the kidnapper all possible facilities, and bribed the judge on the bench to aid him in his infamous work. The terrible scenes that followed; the cruel apathy of the popular heart and conscience; the degradation of the pulpit, which sealed the deed with its loud Amen! the mortal terror of a helpless and innocent race; the fierce assaults on peaceful homes; the stealthy capture, by day and by night, of unsuspecting free-born people; the blood shed on Northern soil; the mockeries of justice acted in United States courts; are they not all written in our country's history, and indelibly engraven on the memories of Abolitionists?

The case of Adam Gibson, captured in this city by the notorious kidnapper, Alberti, and tried before the scarcely less notorious Ingraham, in the year 1850, and which was succeeded in the next year by the Christiana tragedy, are instances of many similar outrages committed in Pennsylvania. No pen can record, no human power can estimate, the aggregate of woe and guilt which was the legitimate result of that Fugitive Slave Bill.

The year 1855 was marked by a series of events unique in our history. A citizen of Philadelphia, whose name will always be associated with the cause of American liberty, in the legal performance of his duty, quietly informed three slaves who had been brought into this State by their master, a Virginia slaveholder, that by the laws of Pennsylvania they were free. The legally emancipated mother, Jane Johnson, availing herself of this knowledge, took possession of her own person and her own children; and their astonished master suddenly discovered that his power to hold them was gone forever. No judge, commissioner, or lawyer, however willing, could help him to recapture his prey. But a judge of the United States District Court could assist him in obtaining a mean revenge upon the brave man who had enlightened an ignorant woman respecting her legal right to freedom. Judge Kane, usurping jurisdiction in the case, and exercising great ingenuity to frame a charge of contempt of Court, succeeded in his purpose of imprisoning Passmore Williamson in our County jail. The baffled slaveholder also found sympathizers in the Grand Jury, who enabled him to indict for riot and assault and battery, Passmore Williamson, William Still, and five other persons. During the trial which ensued, the prosecutor and his allies were confounded by the sudden appearance of a witness whose testimony that she was not forcibly taken from her master's custody, but had left him freely, disconcerted all their schemes, and defeated the prosecution. The presence of Jane Johnson in that court room jeoparded her newly-acquired freedom; for though Pennsylvania was pledged to her protection, it was questionable whether the slave power, in the person of United States officers and their ever ready minions, would not forcibly overpower State authority and obtain possession of the woman. It was an intensely trying hour for her and for all who sympathized with her. Among those who attended her through that perilous scene, were the president of this Society, Sarah Pugh, and several of its members. All those ladies will testify to the calm bearing and firm courage of this emancipated slave-mother, in the hour of jeopardy to her newly-found freedom. Protected by the energy and skill of the presiding Judge, William D. Kelley, and of the State officers, her safe egress from the court-room was accomplished; and she was soon placed beyond the reach of her pursuers.

In 1859 we reaped a rich harvest from long years of sowing, in the result of the trial of the alleged fugitive slave, Daniel Webster. This trial will never be forgotten by those of us who witnessed it. The arrest was made in Harrisburg, in the month of April, and the trial was in this city before United States Commissioner John C. Longstreth. We do not, at this distance of time, need the records of that year, to remind us that "it was with heavy and hopeless hearts that the Abolitionists of this city gathered around that innocent and outraged man, and attended him through the solemn hours of his trial." The night which many of the members of this Society passed in that court, keeping vigils with the unhappy man whose fate hung tremulous on the decision of the young commissioner, was dark with despair; and the dawn of morning brought no hope to our souls. We confidently expected to witness again, as we had often witnessed before, the triumph of the kidnapper and his legal allies over law and justice and human liberty. In the afternoon of that day we re-assembled to hear the judicial decision which should consign the wretched man to slavery, and add another page to the record of Pennsylvania's disgrace. But a far different experience awaited us. Commissioner Longstreth obeyed the moral sentiment around him, and, doubtless the voice of his conscience, and pronounced the captive free. "The closing scenes of this trial; the breathless silence with which the crowded assembly in the court-room waited to hear the death-knell of the innocent prisoner; the painfully sudden transition from despair to hope and thence to certainty of joy; the burst of deep emotion; the fervent thanksgiving, wherein was revealed that sense of the brotherhood of man which God has made a part of every human soul; the exultant shout which went up from the multitude who thronged the streets waiting for the decision"; these no language can portray, but they are life-long memories for those who shared in them. This event proved the great change wrought in the popular feeling, the result of twenty-five years of earnest effort to impress upon the heart of this community anti-slavery doctrines and sentiments. Then for the first time the Abolitionists of Philadelphia found their right of free speech protected by city authorities. Alexander Henry was the first Mayor of this city who ever quelled a pro-slavery mob.

Our last record of a victim sacrificed to this statute, is of the case of Moses Horner, who was kidnapped near Harrisburg in March, 1860, and doomed to slavery by United States Judge John Cadwallader, in this city. One more effort was made a few months later to capture in open day in the heart of this city a man alleged to be a fugitive slave, but it failed of ultimate success. The next year South Carolina's guns thundered forth the doom of the slave power. She aimed them at Fort Sumter and the United States Government. God guided their fiery death to the very heart of American slavery.

If the history of this Society were fully written, one of its most interesting chapters would be a faithful record of its series of annual fairs. Beginning in the year 1836, the series continued during twenty-six years, the last fair being held in December, 1861. The social attraction of these assemblies induced many young persons to mingle in them, besides those who labored from love of the cause. Brought thus within the circle of anti-slavery influence, many were naturally converted to our principles, and became earnest laborers in the enterprise which had so greatly enriched their own souls. The week of the fair was the annual Social Festival of the Abolitionists of the State. Though held under the immediate direction of this Society, it soon became a Pennsylvania institution. Hither our tribes came up to take counsel together, to recount our victories won, to be refreshed by social communion, and to renew our pledges of fidelity to the slave. There were years when these were very solemn festivals, when our skies were dark with gathering storms, and we knew not what peril the night or the morning might bring. But they were always seasons from which we derived strength and encouragement for future toil and endurance, and their value to our cause is beyond our power to estimate.

The pro-slavery spirit which always pervaded our city, and which sometimes manifested itself in the violence of mobs, never seriously disturbed our fair excepting in one instance. In the year 1859 our whole Southern country quaked with mortal fear in the presence of John Brown's great deed for Freedom. The coward North trembled in its turn lest its Southern trade should be imperilled, and in all its cities there went up a frantic cry that the Union must be saved and the Abolitionists suppressed. The usual time for holding our fair was at hand. Before it was opened a daily newspaper of this city informed its readers that notwithstanding the rebuke which the Abolitionists had received from a recent meeting of Union-savers, they had audaciously announced their intention of holding another fair, the avowed purpose of which was the dissemination of anti-slavery principles. The indignant journalist asked if Philadelphia would suffer such a fair to be held. This was doubtless intended as a summons to a mob, and a most deadly mob responded to the call. It did not expend its violence upon our fair, but against an assembly in National Hall, gathered to listen to a lecture by George W. Curtis, upon the Present Aspect of the Country.

The High Constable, Mayor, and Sheriff were the agents employed by the slave power to take and hold possession of Concert Hall, and in its behalf, if not in its name, to eject us and our property. The work was commenced by the Mayor, who sent the High Constable with an order that our flag should be removed from the street. Its offensiveness consisted in the fact that it presented to the view of all passers-by a picture of the Liberty Bell in Independence Hall, inscribed with the words, "Proclaim liberty throughout all the land, to all the inhabitants thereof." The next step was an attempt to induce the lessee to eject us from the hall. On his refusal to violate his contract with us, the trustees obtained legal authority to dispossess us on the plea that the hall had been rented for a purpose which tended to excite popular commotion. The sheriff entered, took possession, and informed the managers that our property must be removed within three hours. Then were the doors of this hall,* where we are now assembled, opened to us, and here our fair was held, with great success, during the remainder of the week. In the stormiest seasons of our enterprise these saloons have never been closed against anti-slavery meetings; and our fair of 1860 was welcomed to them amidst the loud threatenings of a mob which were seeking to appease the angry South, then just rising in open rebellion against the United States Government. The experience of those four days of December spent in these rooms will never be forgotten by us. It was a season of trial, of rejoicing, and of victory. The veterans of our cause, long accustomed to the threats and the presence of mobs, found reason for rejoicing in the courage and serenity with which the young recruits in our ranks faced the peril of scenes so new to them, and proved their faith in the principles of our cause and their devotion to the right. Our victory was complete, our right of peaceful assemblage maintained, without any active demonstration of hostility from the indignant citizens who had fiercely resolved that the Anti-Slavery Fair should be suppressed. Such demonstrations were, doubtless, restrained by a knowledge of the fact that they would be met by vigorous and effectual opposition by the Mayor of the city, who,

---

* The Assembly Buildings, opened to us by the kindness of the lessee, Mr. John Toy.

upon that occasion, as upon many other similar ones, was faithful to the responsibility of his office.

* In the year 1862 the nation was convulsed with the war consequent upon the Southern Rebellion; our soldiers, wounded and dying in hospitals and on battle-fields; claimed all possible aid from the community; anti-slavery sentiments were spreading widely through the North, and it was believed to be feasible and expedient to obtain the funds needful for our enterprise by direct appeal to the old and new friends of the cause. Therefore, our series of fairs closed with the twenty-sixth, in December, 1861.

The money raised by this Society in various ways amounted to about $35,000. Nearly the whole of this revenue has been expended in disseminating the principles of our cause, by means of printed documents and public lectures and discussions. In the earlier years of this Society, a school for colored children, established and taught by Sarah M. Douglass, was partially sustained from our treasury. We occasionally contributed, from our treasury, small sums for the use of the Vigilance Committees, organized to assist fugitive slaves who passed through this State on their way to a land where their right to liberty would be protected. But these enterprises were always regarded as of secondary importance to our great work of direct appeal to the conscience of the nation, in behalf of the slave's claim to immediate, unconditional emancipation. To this end a large number of tracts and pamphlets have been circulated by this Society; but its chief agencies have been the anti-slavery newspapers of the country. Regarding these as the most powerful instrumentalities in the creation of that public sentiment which was essential to the overthrow of slavery, we expended a considerable portion of our funds in the direct circulation of *The Liberator, The Pennsylvania Freeman,* and *The National Anti-Slavery Standard,* and a small amount in the circulation of other anti-slavery papers. Our largest appropriations of money have been made to the Pennsylvania and American Anti-Slavery Societies, and by those Societies to the support of their organs and lecturing agents.

The financial statistics of this Society are easily recorded. Certain great and thrilling events which marked its history are easily told and written. But the life which it lived through all its thirty-six years; the influence which flowed from it, directly and indirectly, to the nation's heart; the work quietly done by its members, individually, through the word spoken in season, the brave, self-sacrificing deed, the example of fidelity in a critical hour, the calm endurance unto the end; these can be written in no earthly book of remembrance. Its life is lived ; its work is done; its memorial is sealed. It assembles to-day to take one parting look across its years; to breathe in silence its unutterable thanksgiving; to disband its membership, and cease to be. Reviewing its experience of labor and endurance, the united voices of its members testify that it has been a service whose reward was in itself; and contemplating the grandeur of the work accomplished (in which it has been permitted to bear a humble part), the overthrow of American slavery, the uplifting from chattelhood to citizenship of four millions of human souls; with one heart and one voice we cry, "Not unto us, O Lord! not unto us, but unto Thy name " be the glory; for Thy right hand and Thy holy arm " hath gotten the victory."

In 1838, Philadelphia was the scene of one of the most disgraceful mobs that marked those eventful days. The lovers of free speech had found great difficulty in procuring churches or halls in which to preach the anti-slavery gospel. Accordingly, a number of individuals of all sects and no sect, of all parties and no party, erected a building wherein the principles of Liberty and Equality could be freely discussed.

David Paul Brown, one of Pennsylvania's most distinguished lawyers, was invited to give the oration dedicating this hall to "Freedom and the Rights of Man." In accepting the invitation, he said:

For some time past I have invariably declined applications that might be calculated to take any portion of my time from my profession. But I always said, and now say again, that I will fight the battle of liberty as long as I have a shot in the locker. Of course, I will do what you require.

Yours truly,   DAVID PAUL BROWN.
S. WEBB and WM. H. SCOTT, Esqs.

Whenever fugitives were arrested on the soil of Pennsylvania, this lawyer stood ready, free of charge, to use in their behalf his skill and every fair interpretation of the letter and spirit of the law, and availing himself of every quirk for postponements, thus adding to the expense and anxiety of the pursuer, and giving the engineers of the underground railroad added opportunities to run the fugitive to Canada.

Pennsylvania Hall was one of the most commodious and splendid buildings in the city, scientifically ventilated and brilliantly lighted with gas. It cost upward of $40,000. Over the forum, in large gold letters, was the motto, "Virtue, Liberty, Independence." On the platform were superb chairs, sofas, and desk covered with blue silk damask; everything throughout the hall was artistic and complete. Abolitionists from all parts of the country hastened to be present at the dedication; and among the rest came representatives of the Woman's National Convention, held in New York one year before.

Notices had been posted about the city threatening the speedy destruction of this temple of liberty. During this three days' Convention, the enemy was slowly organizing the destructive mob that finally burned that grand edifice to the ground. There were a large number of strangers in the city from the South, and many Southern students attending the medical college, who were all active in the riot. The crowds of women and colored people who had attended the Convention intensified the exasperation of the mob. Black men and white women walking side by side in and out of the hall, was too much for the foreign plebeian and the Southern patrician.

As it was announced that on the evening of the third day some ladies were to speak, a howling mob surrounded the building. In the midst of the tumult Mr. Garrison introduced Maria Chapman,* of Boston, who rose, and waving her hand to the audience to become quiet, tried in a few eloquent and appropriate remarks to bespeak a hearing for Angelina E. Grimké, the gifted orator from South Carolina, who, having lived in the midst of slavery all her life, could faithfully describe its cruelties and abominations. But the indescribable uproar outside, cries of fire, and yells of defiance, were a constant interruption, and stones thrown against the windows a warning of coming danger. But through it all this brave Southern woman stood unmoved, except by the intense earnestness of her own great theme.

ANGELINA GRIMKÉ'S ADDRESS.

Do you ask, "What has the North to do with slavery?" Hear it, hear it! Those voices without tell us that the spirit of slavery is *here*, and has been roused to wrath by our Conventions; for surely liberty would not foam and tear herself with rage, because her friends are multiplied daily, and meetings are held in quick succession to set forth her virtues and extend her peaceful kingdom. This opposition shows that slavery has done its deadliest work in the hearts of our citizens. Do you ask, then, "What has the North to do?" I answer, cast out first the spirit of slavery from your own hearts, and then lend your aid to convert the South. Each one present has a work to do, be his or her situation what it may, however limited their means or insignificant their supposed influence. The great men of this country will not do this work; the Church will never do it. A desire to please the world, to keep the favor of all parties and of all conditions, makes them dumb on this and every other unpopular subject.

As a Southerner, I feel that it is my duty to stand up here to-night and bear testimony against slavery. I have seen it! I have seen it! I know it has horrors that can never be described. I was brought up under its wing. I witnessed for many years its demoralizing influences and its destructiveness to human happiness. I have never seen a happy slave. I have seen him dance in his chains, it is true, but he was not happy. There is a wide difference between happiness and mirth. Man can not enjoy happiness while his manhood is destroyed. Slaves, however, may be, and sometimes are mirthful. When hope is extinguished, they say,

---

* She was the positive power of so much anti-slavery work, that James Russell Lowell spoke of her as "the coiled-up mainspring of the movement."

"Let us eat and drink, for to-morrow we die." [Here stones were thrown at the windows—a great noise without and commotion within].

What is a mob ? what would the breaking of every window be ? What would the levelling of this hall be ? Any evidence that we are wrong, or that slavery is a good and wholesome institution ? What if the mob should now burst in upon us, break up our meeting, and commit violence upon our persons, would that be anything compared with what the slaves endure ? No, no; and we do not remember them, "as bound with them," if we shrink in the time of peril, or feel unwilling to sacrifice ourselves, if need be, for their sake. [Great noise]. I thank the Lord that there is yet life enough left to feel the truth, even though it rages at it; that conscience is not so completely seared as to be unmoved by the truth of the living God. [Another outbreak of the mob and confusion in the house].

How wonderfully constituted is the human mind! How it resists, as long as it can, all efforts to reclaim it from error! I feel that all this disturbance is but an evidence that our efforts are the best that could have been adopted, or else the friends of slavery would not care for what we say and do. The South know what we do. I am thankful that they are reached by our efforts. Many times have I wept in the land of my birth over the system of slavery. I knew of none who sympathized in my feelings; I was unaware that any efforts were made to deliver the oppressed; no voice in the wilderness was heard calling on the people to repent and do works meet for repentance, and my heart sickened within me. Oh, how should I have rejoiced to know that such efforts as these were being made. I only wonder that I had such feelings. But in the midst of temptation I was preserved, and my sympathy grew warmer, and my hatred of slavery more inveterate, until at last I have exiled myself from my native land, because I could no longer endure to hear the wailing of the slave.

I fled to the land of Penn; for here, thought I, sympathy for the slave will surely be found. But I found it not. The people were kind and hospitable, but the slave had no place in their thoughts. I therefore shut up my grief in my own heart. I remembered that I was a Carolinian, from a State which framed this iniquity by law. Every Southern breeze wafted to me the discordant tones of weeping and wailing, shrieks and groans, mingled with prayers and blasphemous curses. My heart sank within me at the abominations in the midst of which I had been born and educated. What will it avail, cried I, in bitterness of spirit, to expose to the gaze of strangers the horrors and pollutions of slavery, when there is no ear to hear nor heart to feel and pray for the slave ? But how different do I feel now! Animated with hope, nay, with an assurance of the triumph of liberty and good-will to man, I will lift up my voice like a trumpet, and show this people what they can do to influence the Southern mind and overthrow slavery. [Shouting, and stones against the windows].

We often hear the question asked, "What shall we do ?" Here is an opportunity. Every man and every woman present may do something, by showing that we fear not a mob, and in the midst of revilings and threatenings, pleading the cause of those who are ready to perish. Let me urge every one to buy the books written on this subject; read them, and lend them to your neighbors. Give your money no longer for things which pander to pride and lust, but aid in scattering " the living coals of truth upon the naked heart of the nation "; in circulating appeals to the sympathies of Christians in behalf of the outraged slave.

But it is said by some, our "books and papers do not speak the truth"; why, then, do they not contradict what we say ? They can not. Moreover, the South has entreated, nay, commanded us, to be silent; and what greater evidence of the truth of our publications could be desired ?

Women of Philadelphia! allow me as a Southern woman, with much attachment to the land of my birth, to entreat you to come up to this work. Especially, let me urge you to petition. Men may settle this and other questions at the ballot-box, but you have no such right. It is only through petitions that you can reach the Legislature. It is, therefore, peculiarly your duty to petition. Do you say, " It does no good ! " The South already turns pale at the number sent. They have read the reports of the proceedings of Congress, and there have seen that among other petitions were very many from the women of the North on the subject of slavery. Men who hold the rod over slaves rule in the councils of the nation; and they deny our right to petition and remonstrate against abuses of our sex and our kind. We have these rights, however, from our God. Only let us exercise them, and, though often turned away unanswered, let us remember the influence of importunity upon the unjust judge, and act accordingly. The fact that the South looks jealously upon our measures shows that they are effectual. There is, therefore, no cause for doubting or despair.

It was remarked in England that women did much to abolish slavery in her colonies. Nor are they now idle. Numerous petitions from them have recently been presented to the Queen to abolish apprenticeship, with its cruelties, nearly equal to those of the system whose place it supplies. One petition, two miles and a quarter long, has been presented. And do you think these labors will be in vain ? Let the history of the past answer. When the women of these States send up to Congress such a petition our legislators will arise, as did those of England, and say: " When all the maids and matrons of the land are knocking at our doors we must legislate." Let the zeal and love, the faith and works of our English sisters quicken ours; that while the slaves continue to suffer, and when they shout for deliverance, we may feel the satisfaction of " having done what we could."

ABBY KELLY, of Lynn, Massachusetts, rose, and said: I ask permission to say a few words. I have never before addressed a promiscuous assembly; nor is it now the maddening rush of those voices, which is the indication of a moral whirlwind; nor is it the crashing of those windows, which is the indication of a moral earthquake, that calls me before you. No, these pass unheeded by me. But it is the " still small voice within," which may not be withstood, that bids me open my mouth for the dumb· that bids me plead the cause of God's perishing poor; aye, *God's* poor.

The parable of Lazarus and the rich man we may well bring home to ourselves. The North is that rich man. How he is clothed in purple and fine linen, and fares sumptuously! *Yonder,* YONDER, at a little distance, is the gate where lies the Lazarus of the South, full of sores and desiring to be fed with the crumbs that fall from our luxurious table. Look! see him there! even the dogs are more merciful than we. Oh, see him where he lies! We have long, very long, passed by with averted eyes. Ought not we to raise him up; and is there one in this Hall who sees nothing for himself to do ?

LUCRETIA MOTT, of Philadelphia, then stated that the present was not a meeting of the Anti-Slavery Convention of American women, as was supposed by some, and explained the reason why their meetings were confined to females; namely, that many of the members considered it improper for women to address promiscuous assemblies. She hoped that such false notions of delicacy and propriety would not long obtain in this enlightened country.

While the large Hall was filled with a promiscuous audience, and packed through all its sessions with full three thousand people, the women held their Convention in one of the committee-rooms. As they had been through terrible mobs already in Boston and New York, they had learned self-control, and with their coolness and consecration to the principles they advocated, they were a constant inspiration to the men by their side.

The Second National Anti-Slavery Convention of American Women assembled in the lecture-room of Pennsylvania Hall in Philadelphia, May 15, 1838, at ten o'clock A.M. The following officers were appointed :

PRESIDENT—Mary L. Parker, of Boston.

VICE-PRESIDENTS—Maria Weston Chapman, Catharine M. Sullivan, Susan Paul, of Boston, Mass.; Mariana Johnson, Providence, R. I.; Margaret Prior, Sarah T. Smith, of New York; Martha W. Storrs, of Utica, N. Y.; Lucretia Mott, of Philadelphia; Mary W. Magill, of Buckingham, Pa.; Sarah Moore Grimké, of Charleston, S. C.

SECRETARIES—Anne W. Weston, Martha V. Ball, of Boston; Juliana A. Tappan, of New York; Sarah Lewis, of Philadelphia.

TREASURER—Sarah M. Douglass, of Philadelphia.

BUSINESS COMMITTEE—Sarah T. Smith, Sarah R. Ingraham, Margaret Dye, Juliana A. Tappan, Martha W. Storrs, New York; Miriam Hussey, Maine; Louisa Whipple, New Hampshire; Lucy N. Dodge, Miriam B. Johnson, Maria Truesdell, Waity A. Spencer, Rebecca Pittman, Rhode Island; Lucretia Mott, Mary Grew, Sarah M. Douglass, Hetty Burr, Martha Smith, Pennsylvania; Angelina Grimké Weld, South Carolina.

On motion of SARAH PUGH, Elizabeth M. Southard, Mary G. Chapman, and Abby Kelly were appointed a committee to confer with other associations and the managers of Pennsylvania Hall to arrange for meetings during the week.

SARAH T. SMITH, from the Business Committee, presented letters from

22

the Female Anti-Slavery Societies of Salem and Cambridgeport, Massachusetts, signed by their respective secretaries, Mary Spencer and L. Williams.

At this time, even the one and only right of woman, that of petition, had been trampled under the heel of slavery on the floor of Congress, which roused those noble women to a just indignation, as will be seen in their resolutions on the subject, presented by Juliana A. Tappan:

Resolved, That whatever may be the sacrifice, and whatever other rights may be yielded or denied, we will maintain practically the right of petition until the slave shall go free, or our energies, like Lovejoy's, are paralyzed in death.

Resolved, That for every petition rejected by the National Legislature during their last session, we will endeavor to send *five* the present year; and that we will not cease our efforts until the prayers of every woman within the sphere of our influence shall be heard in the halls of Congress on this subject.

Mary Grew offered the following resolution, which was adopted:

Whereas, The disciples of Christ are commanded to have no fellowship with the "unfruitful works of darkness"; and

Whereas, Union in His Church is the strongest expression of fellowship between men; therefore

Resolved, That it is our duty to keep ourselves separate from those churches which receive to their pulpits and their communion tables those who buy, or sell, or hold as property, the image of the living God.

This resolution was supported by Miss Grew, Lucretia Mott, Abby Kelly, Maria W. Chapman, Anne W. Weston, Sarah T. Smith, and Sarah Lewis; and opposed by Margaret Dye, Margaret Prior, Henrietta Wilcox, Martha W. Storrs, Juliana A. Tappan, Elizabeth M. Southard, and Charlotte Woolsey. Those who voted in the negative stated that they fully concurred with their sisters in the belief that slaveholders and their apologists were guilty before God, and that with the former, Northern Christians should hold no fellowship; but that, as it was their full belief that there was moral power sufficient in the Church, if rightly applied, to purify it, they could not feel it their duty to withdraw until the utter inefficiency of the means used should constrain them to believe the Church totally corrupt. And as an expression of their views, Margaret Dye moved the following resolution:

Resolved, That the system of American slavery is contrary to the laws of God and the spirit of true religion, and that the Church is deeply implicated in this sin, and that it therefore becomes the imperative duty of her members to petition their ecclesiastical bodies to enter their decided protests against it, and exclude slaveholders from their pulpits and communion tables.

The last session was opened by the reading of the sixth chapter of 2 Corinthians, and prayer by Sarah M. Grimké. An Address to Anti-Slavery Societies was read by Sarah T. Smith, and adopted. We copy from it the plea and argument for woman's right and duty to be interested in all questions of public welfare :

ADDRESS TO ANTI-SLAVERY SOCIETIES.

DEAR FRIENDS:—In that love for our cause which knows not the fear of man, we address you in confidence that our motives will be understood and regarded. We fear not censure from you for going beyond the circle which has been drawn around us by physical force, by mental usurpation, by the usages of ages; not any one of which can we admit gives the right to prescribe it; else might the monarchs of the old world sit firmly on their thrones, the nobility of Europe lord it over the man of low degree, and the chains we are now seeking to break, continue riveted on the neck of the slave. Our faith goes not back to the wigwam of the savage, or the castle of the feudal chief, but would rather soar with hope to that period when "right alone shall make might"; when the truncheon and the sword shall lie useless; when the intellect and heart shall speak and be obeyed; when "He alone whose right it is shall rule and reign in the hearts of the children of men."

We are told that it is not within "the province of woman" to discuss the subject of slavery; that it is a "political question," and that we are "stepping out of our sphere" when we take part in its discussion. It is not true that it is merely a political question; it is likewise a question of justice, of humanity, of morality, of religion; a question which, while it involves considerations of immense importance to the welfare and prosperity of our country, enters deeply into the home—concerns the every-day feelings of millions of our fellow beings. Whether the laborer shall receive the reward of his labor, or be driven daily to unrequited toil; whether he shall walk erect in the dignity of conscious manhood, or be reckoned among the beasts which perish; whether his bones and sinews shall be his own, or another's; whether his child shall receive the protection of its natural guardian, or be ranked among the live-stock of the estate, to be disposed of as the caprice or interest of the master may dictate; whether the sun of knowledge shall irradiate the hut of the peasant, or the murky cloud of ignorance brood darkly over it; whether "every one shall have the liberty to worship God according to the dictates of his own conscience," or man assume the prerogative of Jehovah and impiously seek to plant himself upon the throne of the Almighty. These considerations are all involved in the question of liberty or slavery.

And is a subject comprehending interests of such magnitude, merely a "political question," and one in which woman "can take no part without losing something of the modesty and gentleness which are her most appropriate ornaments" ? May not the "ornament of a meek and quiet spirit" exist with an upright mind and enlightened intellect? Must woman necessarily be less gentle because her heart is open to the claims of humanity, or less modest because she feels for the degradation of her enslaved sisters, and would stretch forth her hand for their rescue?

By the Constitution of the United States, the whole physical power of the North is pledged for the suppression of domestic insurrections; and should the slaves maddened by oppression endeavor to shake off the yoke of the task-master, the men of the North are bound to make common cause with the tyrant, to put down at the point of the bayonet every effort on the part of the slave for the attainment of his freedom. And when the father, husband, son, and brother shall have left their homes to mingle in the unholy warfare; "to become the executioners of their brethren, or to fall themselves by their hands," will the mother, wife, daughter, and sister feel that they have no interest in this subject? Will it be easy to convince them that it is no concern of theirs, that their homes are rendered desolate and their habitations the abodes of wretchedness? Surely this consideration is of itself sufficient to arouse the slumbering energies of woman, for the overthrow of a system which thus threatens to lay in ruins the fabric of her domestic happiness; and she will not be deterred from the performance of her duty to herself, her family, and her country, by the cry of "political question."

But, admitting it to be a political question, have we no interest in the welfare of our country? May we not permit a thought to stray beyond the narrow limits of our own family circle and of the present hour? May we not breathe a sigh over the miseries of our countrywomen nor utter a word of remonstrance against the unjust laws that are crushing them to the earth? Must we witness "the headlong rage of heedless folly" with which our nation is rushing onward to destruction, and not seek to arrest its downward course? Shall we silently behold the land which we love with all the heart-warm affection of children, rendered a hissing and a reproach throughout the world by the system which is already "tolling the death-knell of her decease among the nations" ?

No; the events of the last two years have "cast their dark shadows before," overclouding the bright prospects of the future, and shrouding our country in more than midnight gloom; and we can not remain inactive. Our country is as dear to us as to the proudest statesman; and the more closely our hearts cling to "our altars and our homes," the more fervent are our aspirations, that every inhabitant of our land may be protected in his fireside enjoyments by just and equal laws; that the foot of the tyrant may no longer invade the domestic sanctuary, nor his hand tear asunder those whom God himself has united by the most holy ties.

Let our course then still be onward! Justice, humanity, patriotism; every high and every holy motive urge us forward, and we dare not refuse to obey. The way of duty lies open before us, and though no pillar of fire be visible to the outward sense, yet an unerring light shall illumine our pathway, guiding us through the sea of persecution and the wilderness of prejudice and error, to the promised land of freedom, where "every man shall sit under his own vine and fig-tree, and none shall make him afraid."

THANKFUL SOUTHWICK* moved the following:

Resolved, That it is the duty of all those who call themselves Abolitionists, to make the most vigorous efforts to procure for the use of their families the products of FREE LABOR, so that their hands may be clean in this particular when inquisition is made for blood.

ESTHER MOORE made remarks upon the importance of carrying into effect the resolutions that had been passed.

This was the last meeting held in Pennsylvania Hall! Business connected with the safety of the building made it necessary for members of the board of managers to pass several times through the saloon, when this Convention was in session, and they said they never saw a more dignified, calm, and intrepid body of persons assembled. Although the building was surrounded all day by the mob who crowded about the doors, and at times even attempted to enter the saloon, yet the women were perfectly collected, unmoved by the threat-

---

* In speaking of her, Lydia Maria Child said in her obituary notice in the *National Anti-Slavery Standard* of May 11, 1867: "All survivors of the old Abolition band will remember Thankful Southwick as one of the very earliest, the noblest, and the most faithful of that small army of moral combatants who fought so bravely and so perseveringly for the deliverance of the down-trodden. Mrs. Southwick was born and educated in the Society of Friends, and to their calmness of demeanor she added their indomitable persistence in the path of duty. One of the most exciting affairs that ever occurred in Boston was known as the 'Baltimore Slave Case.' Two girls had escaped in a Boston vessel, and when about to be carried back, were brought out on a writ of '*habeas corpus.*' All Boston was in a ferment for and against the fugitives. The commercial world were determined that this Southern property should be restored to the white claimants, and the Abolitionists were determined that it should remain in the possession of the original owners until a bill of sale from the Almighty could be produced. By the vigilance and ingenious arrangements of 'Father Snowden' and Thankful Southwick, at a given signal the slaves were spirited away from the crowded court-room, and out of the city. The agent of the slaveholders standing near Mrs. Southwick, and gazing with astonishment at the empty space, where an instant before the slaves stood, she turned her large gray eyes upon him and said, 'Thy prey hath escaped thee.' Wherever working or thinking was to be done for our righteous cause, there was Thankful Southwick ever ready with wise counsel and energetic action. She and her excellent husband were among the very first to sustain Garrison in his unequal contest with the strong Goliath of slavery. At that time they were in affluent circumstances, and their money was poured forth freely for the unpopular cause which had as yet found no adherents among the rich. Their commodious house was a caravansary for fugitive slaves, and for anti-slavery pilgrims from all parts of the country. At the anniversary meetings when most of the Abolitionists were desirous to have for their guests, Friend Whittier, the Hon. James G. Birney, George Thompson, Theodore, or Angelia Weld, Joseph and Thankful Southwick were quietly looking about for such of the anti-slavery brothers and sisters as were too little known to be likely to receive invitations. Always kindly unpretending, clear-sighted to perceive the right, and faithful in following it wherever it might lead. They were upright in all their dealings with the world, tender and true in the relations of private life and the memory they have left is a benediction."

ening tempest. The cause which they were assembled to promote is one that nerves the soul to deeds of noble daring. The Convention had already adjourned late in the afternoon, when the mob which destroyed the building began to assemble. The doors were blocked up by the crowd, and the streets almost impassable from the multitude of "fellows of the baser sort." But these "American Women" passed through the whole without manifesting any sign of fear, as if conscious of their own greatness and of the protecting care of the God of the oppressed.

We give our readers these interesting pages of anti-slavery history because they were the initiative steps to organized public action and the Woman Suffrage Movement *per se*, and to show how much more enthusiasm women manifested in securing freedom for the slaves, than they ever have in demanding justice and equality for themselves. Where are the societies to rescue unfortunate women from the bondage they suffer under unjust law? Where are the loving friends who keep midnight vigils with young girls arraigned in the courts for infanticide? Where are the underground rail-roads and watchful friends at every point to help fugitive wives from brutal husbands? The most intelligent, educated women seem utterly oblivious to the wrongs of their own sex; even those who so bravely fought the anti-slavery battle have never struck as stout blows against the tyranny suffered by women.

Take, for example, the resolution presented by Mary Grew, and passed in the Woman's Anti-Slavery Convention forty-three years ago, declaring that it was the Christian duty of every woman to withdraw from all churches that fellowshiped with slavery, which was a sin against God and man. Compare the conscience and religious earnestness for a principle implied in such a resolution with the apathy and supineness of the women of to-day. No such resolution has ever yet passed a woman's rights convention. And yet is injustice to a colored man a greater sin than to a woman? Is liberty and equality more sweet to him than to her? Is the declaration by the Church that woman may not be ordained or licensed to preach the Gospel, no matter how well fitted, how learned or devout, because of her sex, less insulting and degrading than the old custom of the negro pew?

The attitude of the Church to-day is more hostile and insulting to American womanhood than it ever was to the black man, by just so much as women are nearer the equals of priests and bishops than were the unlettered slaves. When women refuse to enter churches that do not recognize them as equal candidates for the joys of earth and heaven, equal in the sight of man and

God, we shall have a glorious revival of liberty and justice everywhere.

How fully these pages of history illustrate the equal share woman has had in the trials and triumphs of all the political and moral revolutions through which we have passed, from feeble colonies to an independent nation ; suffering with man the miseries of poverty and war, all the evils of bad government, and enjoying with him the blessings of luxury and peace, and a wise administration of law. The experience of the heroines of anti-slavery show that no fine-spun sentimentalism in regard to woman's position in the clouds ever exempt her from the duties or penalties of a citizen. Neither State officers, nor mobs in the whirlwind of passion, tempered their violence for her safety or benefit.

When women proposed to hold a fair in Concert Hall, their flag was torn down from the street, while they and their property were ejected by the high constable. When women were speaking in Pennsylvania Hall, brickbats were hurled at them through the windows. When women searched Philadelphia through for a place where they might meet to speak and pray for the slave-mother and her child (the most miserable of human beings), halls and churches were closed against them. And who were these women ? Eloquent speakers, able writers, dignified wives and mothers, the most moral, religious, refined, cultured, intelligent citizens that Massachusetts, New York, South Carolina, and Pennsylvania could boast. There never was a queen on any European throne possessed of more personal beauty, grace, and dignity than Maria Weston Chapman.* The calmness and impassioned earnestness of Angelina Grimké, speaking nearly an hour 'mid that howling mob, was not surpassed in courage and consecration even by Paul among the wild beasts at Ephesus. Here she made her last public speech, and as the glowing words died upon her lips, a new voice was heard, rich, deep, and clear upon the troubled air ; and the mantle of self-sacrifice, so faithfully worn by South Carolina's brave daughter, henceforth rested on the shoulders of an equally brave and eloquent Quaker girl from

---

* On a recent visit at the home of Robert Purvis, of Philadelphia, in talking over those eventful days one evening in company with Daniel Neale, it was amusing and gratifying to hear those gentlemen dilate on the grandeur of her bearing through those mobs in Pennsylvania Hall. It seems on that occasion she had a beautiful crimson shawl thrown gracefully over her shoulders. One of these gentlemen remarked, " I kept my eye on that shawl, which could be seen now here, now there, its wearer consulting with one, cheering another; and I made up my mind that until that shawl disappeared, every man must stand by his guns."

Massachusetts,* who for many years afterward preached the same glad tidings of justice, equality, and liberty for all.

TEMPERANCE.

In this reform, also, the women of Pennsylvania took an equally active part. We are indebted to Hannah Darlington, of Kennett Square, Chester Co., for the following record of the temperance work in this State:

KENNETT SQUARE, 2 mo., 6, 1881.

DEAR MRS. STANTON:—I did not think our early temperance work of sufficient account to preserve the reports, hence with considerable research am able to send you but very little. Many mixed meetings were held through the county before 1847. Woods-meetings, with decorated stands, were fashionable in Chester in warm weather, for several years before we branched off with a call for a public meeting. That brought quite a number together in Friends' Meeting-house at Kennett Square, where we discussed plans for work and appointed committees to carry them out.

Sidney Peirce, Ann Preston, and myself, each prepared addresses to read at meetings called in such places as the Committee arranged; and with Chandler Darlington to drive us from place to place, we addressed many large audiences, some in the day-time and some in the evening; scattered appeals and tracts, and collected names to petitions asking for a law against licensing liquor-stands.

In 1848, we went to Harrisburg, taking an address to the Legislature written by Ann Preston, and sanctioned by the meeting that appointed us. The address, with our credentials and petitions, was presented to the two Houses, read in our presence, and referred to the Committee on "Vice and Immorality," which called a meeting and invited us to give our address. Sidney Peirce, who was a good reader, gave it with effect to a large roomful of the Committee and legislators. It was listened to with profound attention, complimented highly, and I think aroused a disposition among the best members to give the cause of temperance more careful consideration. The Local Option Law was passed by that Legislature.

We also aided the mixed meetings by our presence and addresses, and by circulating petitions, and publishing appeals in the county papers; helping in every way to arouse discussion and prepare the people to sustain the new law. But the Supreme Court of the State, through the liquor influence, declared the law unconstitutional, after a few months' successful trial. Drinking, however, has not been as respectable since that time. We continued active work in our association until the inauguration of the Good Templars movement, in which men and women worked together on terms of equality.

Respectfully yours,   HANNAH M. DARLINGTON.

---

* Abby Kelly.

TEMPERANCE CONVENTION.

A Temperance Convention of Women of Chester County, met at Marlborough Friends' Meeting-house, on Saturday, the 30th of December, 1848, and was organized by the appointment of MARTHA HAYHURST, President; SIDNEY PEIRCE and HANNAH PENNOCK, Secretaries.

Letters received by a Committee of Correspondence, appointed at a Convention last winter, were read; one, from Pope Bushnell, Chairman of the Committee on Vice and Immorality, to which temperance petitions were referred; and also from our Representatives in the Legislature, pledging themselves to use all their influence to obtain the passage of a law to prohibit the sale of intoxicating liquors as a beverage amongst us. The Business Committee reported addresses to the men and women of Chester County, which were considered, amended, and adopted, as follows:

To the Women of Chester County :

DEAR SISTERS:—Again we would urge upon you the duty and necessity of action in the temperance cause. Notwithstanding the exertions that have been made, intoxicating liquors continue to be sold and drank in our midst. Still, night after night, the miserable drunkard reels to that home he has made desolate. Still. wives and sisters weep in anguish as they look on those dearer to them than life, and see, trace by trace, their delicacy and purity of soul vanishing beneath the destroying libations that tempt them when they pass the domestic threshold.

We need not depict to you the poverty and crime and unutterable woe that result from intemperance. nor need you go far to be reminded of the revolting fact, that under the sanction of laws, men still make it a deliberate business to deal out that terrible agent, the only effect of which is to darken the God-like in the human soul, and to foster in its place the appetites of demons. The law passed the 7th of April, 1846, under which the sale of intoxicating drinks was prohibited by vote of the people in most of the townships in Chester County, has been decided by the Supreme Court to be unconstitutional;, and this decision, by inspiring confidence in the dealers and consumers of the fatal poison, seems to have given a new impetus to this diabolical traffic. Wider and deeper its ravages threaten to extend themselves; and to every benevolent mind comes the earnest question, What must now be done ? It is too late for women to excuse themselves from exertion in this cause, on the ground that it would be indelicate to leave the sheltered retirement of home. Alas! where is the home-shelter that guards the delicacy of the drunkard's wife and daughter ? We all recognize the divine obligation to relieve suffering and to cherish virtue as binding alike on man and woman. Our hearts thrill at the mention of those women who were "last at the cross and earliest at the grave" of the crucified Nazarine. We commend her whose prayers and entreaties once saved her native Rome from pillage. We admire the heroism of a Joan of Arc, as it is embalmed in history and song. We boast of virgin martyrs to the faith of their convictions, and we dare not now put forth the despicable plea of feminine propriety to excuse our supineness, when fathers, sons, and brothers are falling around us, degraded, bestialized, thrice murdered by this foe at our doors. No! we have solemn obligations resting upon us, and we should be unfaithful to the holiest call of duty, false to the instincts of womanhood and the pleading voice of love, if we should sit quietly down in careless ease while vice is thus spreading around us, and human souls are falling into the fell snare of the destroyer.

By meeting together and taking counsel one with another, we will become more alive to our duty in relation to this momentous subject. The more we prize the sweet privacy of happy homes, the more strong is the appeal to us to labor to make sacred and joyful the hearth-stones of others. If *men* will remain comparatively supine we must the more energetically sound the alarm, and point them to the danger. If rulers will devise wickedness by law, we must give them no rest, till, like the unjust judge, they yield to our very importunity, and repeal their iniquitous statutes. The temporal and spiritual welfare of many an immortal being is at stake, and we should esteem it a high privilege to labor in this holy cause with an earnest and, if need be, a life-long consecration. Let us, then, apply ourselves devotedly to the work, and a fresh and resistless impulse will be given to the temperance reformation. The electrical fervor of earnest spirits ever communicates itself to others, and the Legislature itself can not long resist our united efforts. In such a cause "we have great allies." God and humanity are on our side, our own souls will be strengthened and elevated by the work; "failure" is a word that belongs not to us, since our efforts are in a righteous cause. ·

To the Men of Chester County :

Permit us once more to plead with you on behalf of temperance. We know that to some of you this may seem an old and wearisome subject, but we know also that the sorrow and crime caused by intemperance are *not* old; new, fresh cases are around us now. Its ravages are repeated every day, and we must beseech you to "hear us for our cause." We can not be silent while the grog-shop stands like the poisonous upas amongst us, and men openly deal out crime and wretchedness in the form of intoxicating drinks.

We need not in this place enlarge upon the danger ever attendant upon the use of those stimulants, nor will we now stop long to dwell upon the solemn fact, that whoever, at the demand of appetite, drinks even the sweet cider, weakens his own moral strength, becomes a tempter to the weak, and casts away the pure influence of an unsullied example. Reckless and guilty indeed is that man who, in the light of this day, dares to insult humanity and defy heaven by publicly putting the glass to his lips.

Men of Chester County! you possess the power to put a stop to the traffic in liquors, and we conjure you by the sacred obligations of virtue and humanity, as you hope to stand acquitted before the just tribunal of God, to arise in your might and banish it from the community; think, we beseech you, of the depths of pollution to which intemperance leads, of the bestial appetites it fosters, of all the unnameable impurities that revel in its abodes; think of the hearth-stones desolated, of the mothers and daughters whose earthly hopes and joys have been destroyed by that charnel-house, the tavern. The incendiary who applies the midnight torch to peaceful dwellings, the robber who commits murder to secure his prey, is not an enemy to society half so dangerous, as he who inflames all evil passions and scatters wretchedness through a community, by dispensing alcoholic poison. Oh! are there not sorrows enough in our best condition? have we not temptations strong enough within and without? Shall men progress too fast in the "onward and upward" road of virtue and happiness, that you leave before them these sinks of pollution, these trap-doors of ruin, these fatal sirens, enticing the unwary listener to destruction? Call us not fanatical. Indifference is crime; silence is fatal here. When the midnight cry of fire is sounded, you rush from your slumbers, and, heedless of danger, hasten to extinguish the flames; but here is a devouring element, burning on from year to year, consuming not mere shingles and rafters, but the priceless hopes and aspirations of immortal souls, leaving blackened ruins in the place of beauty; and we must continue to cry "Fire! fire!" until you hasten to stop the fearful conflagration. Tell us not of liberty and natural right, as a plea for this traffic. It is the liberty to rob innocent families and reduce them to pauperism; the right to break hearts and hopes, to reduce men to demons, to scatter vice and anguish and desolation around the land. Well may we exclaim with Madame Roland, when she was taken along the bloody streets of Paris, about to be murdered in the abused name of freedom, "Oh, Liberty, what crimes are committed in thy name!"

Fathers and brothers, shall woman in her agony, and man in his degradation, appeal to you in vain? Too long has this evil been borne, too long have minor points of public good taken precedence of this reform. It must not be that you will be content to dwell in quiet indifference, in the midst of a rum-selling community, and die, leaving your children exposed to the tempter's snare. It must not be endured that this infernal traffic, this shame to civilization, this slur on Christianity, shall continue amongst us. It must not be endured that men shall be clothed with the monstrous authority to demoralize neighborhoods and scatter the fire-brands of death and destruction. The power to arrest this horrible work is in your hands. Be vigilant, be active. There is resistless might in the energy of earnest wills devoted to a noble cause. Petition, remonstrate, work while yet it is day. Say not that we can gain nothing by petitioning. Was it not through this means, we obtained the law under which a vote of the majority excluded the sale of itoxicating liquors amongst us? Did not our petitions last winter cause a bill for its prohibition to be reported in the Legislature, which was lost in the House by a small majority? True, the law we desire may not entirely prevent drunkenness, but it will certainly act as a restraint. It will make drinking less reputable, and thus prevent drunkard-making. It will have the moral influence of a State verdict against the practice. The dread responsibility of this traffic must rest upon you, if, through silent acquiescence, you permit its ravages. Do what you can, and peace and prosperity will soon sit where the blackness of ruin has brooded, and the sweet reward of approving consciences and the blessings of joyful hearts will gladden your pathway.

The following resolutions were adopted:

Resolved, That petitioning the Legislature is the most definite and efficient means at our command, whereby to obtain a law to abolish the sale of intoxicating drinks, as a beverage amongst us.

Resolved, That the following persons be appointed to obtain names in their respective neighborhoods, to the petition referred to: Sarah Evans, Grace Anna Lewis, Jane Kimber, H. A. Pennypacker, Catherine Hawley, Deborah Way, Sarah Wood, M. B. Thomas, Anna Parke, Margaret Lea, Susannah Cox, Elizabeth Evans, E. Garrett, M. Darlington, Eliza Agnew, M. P. Wilson, Eliza Pyle, Mary Chambers, H. M. Barnard, Mrs. Jefferis, Alice Speakman, Sarah S. Barnard, Susan Fulton, Mary W. Coates, Millicent Stern, Mrs. Ramsey, Mrs. Hamilton, A. E. Valentine, Ruth Ann Seal, R. W. Taylor, M. K. Darlington, Lydia Agnew, M. Taylor, Alice Lewis, Ann Barnard, Rebecca Pugh, Lydia Jacobs, Margaret Ross, Rachel Leake, Ann Preston, M. W. Cox, Ann Coates, Rachel Good, Esther Jane Kent, Ellen Wilkinson, Mary Pugh, Sarah Ann Cunningham, Eliza Lysle, Beulah Hughes, Sarah Ann Conard.

Resolved, That we urgently solicit those having care of petitions, to make use of every opportunity to obtain men's and women's names in different columns, or on separate petitions, and thus aid the Chester County Temperance Society in procuring the names of those favorable to obtaining a probibitory law.

Resolved, That Hannah Cox, Sidney Peirce, Ann Preston, Mary Cox, Mary Ann Fulton, Dinah Mendenhall, Mary K. Darlington, Mary S. Agnew, and Hannah M. Darlington, be a committee to call meetings of the people in different neighborhoods, at which to read the addresses to men and women, obtain signatures to petitions, etc.

Resolved, That we offer the proceedings of this meeting for publication in the County papers and *Temperance Standard*.

Resolved, That we adjourn to meet in Kennett Square, on Saturday, the 3d of February, 1849.

MARTHA HAYHURST, *President.*

SIDNEY PEIRCE, } *Secretaries.*
HANNAH PENNOCK, }

At their next Convention in Kennett Square, another stirring appeal was issued, and the following resolutions adopted:

WHEREAS, The peace of our homes, the security of our property, and our inalienable right to life, liberty, and the pursuit of happiness, are all jeoparded by intemperance; and whereas, this monstrous vice, with all its attendant train of evils, will continue to spread its ravages over our fair country so long as the traffic in intoxicating drinks is supported and sanctioned by law; and,

WHEREAS, The people have the same right to be protected from the desolations of this vice, that they have to be protected from the depredations of the incendiary, the robber, and the murderer, whose deeds are but too often instigated by it; therefore,

Resolved, That we demand of the Representatives of the people, at the next session, a law for the total prohibition of the traffic in intoxicating drinks as a beverage, within the limits of Chester County.

Resolved, That we see neither reason nor consistency in the conduct of our law-makers in restraining the thief, the burglar, the counterfeiter, and the robber, while they let loose upon society the legalized rum-seller.

> " Will they the felon fox restrain,
> And yet take off the tiger's chain ? "

Resolved, That we hail with joy the appearance of a recent pastoral letter issued by the Synod of the Free Church of Cincinnati, containing sentiments in regard to the advancement of this reform, which meet our hearty approval, and which, if adopted by all religious bodies, would insure the speedy triumph of temperance, with all the blessings that follow in its train.

Resolved, That we adjourn to meet at Old Kennett, on Saturday, the 8th of December, 1849.

HANNAH M. DARLINGTON, *President.*

ALICE LEWIS, } *Secretaries.*
MARY S. AGNEW, }

NORTH AMERICAN AND UNITED STATES GAZETTE, FEB. 6, 1852.

The ladies of the City and County of Philadelphia, and all other persons who feel impressed with the importance of PETITIONING THE LEGISTURE TO ENACT A LAW PROHIBITING THE USE OF ALL INTOXICATING DRINKS AS A BEVERAGE, are earnestly requested to attend a meeting to be held at the CHINESE MUSEUM, corner of NINTH and GEORGE STREETS, on SATURDAY EVENING, Feb. 7th, at 7½ o'clock.

The meeting will be addressed by the REV. ALBERT BARNES, REV. JOHN CHAMBERS, JUDGE KELLEY, DR. JAS. BRYAN, and WM. J. MULLEN. JUDGE ALLISON will preside. The LADIES' TEMPERANCE UNION is particularly invited to attend. Admittance five cents, to defray expenses.

Two weeks after this, Feb. 21st, a Woman's Temperance Mass Meeting was held in Philadelphia; an immense assemblage of both sexes.

The Pennsylvania Freeman of March 4, 1852, says: "A large number of petitions from various parts of the State, most of them numerously signed, asking for the passage of the Maine Anti-Liquor Law, have been presented in both Houses. On Tuesday, in the Senate, one was presented from this city signed by 15,580 ladies; and another in the House, signed by 14,241 ladies. What the Legislature will do we shall not venture to predict."

It is interesting to note the same successive steps in every State, and how naturally, in laboring for anti-slavery and temperance, women have at last in each case demanded freedom for themselves. In the anti-slavery school, 'mid violence and persecution they learned the a, b, c of individual rights; in the temperance struggle they learned that the ultimate power in moral movements is found in wise legislation, and in graduating on the woman suffrage platform, they have learned that prayers and tears are worth little until coined into law, and that to command the attention of legislators, petitioners must represent votes.

A moral power that has no direct influence on the legislation of a nation, is an abstraction, and might as well be expended in the clouds as outside of codes and constitutions, and this has too long been the realm where women have spent their energies fighting shadows. The power that makes laws, and baptizes them as divine at every church altar, is the power for woman to demand now and forever.

WESTCHESTER CONVENTION.
June 2, 1852.

The first Woman's Rights Convention held in Pennsylvania was called in the leafy month of June, in the quiet Quaker town of West Chester, in one of the loveliest regions of that State. Chester County had long been noted for its reform movements and flourishing schools, in which the women generally took a deep interest.

It was among these beautiful hills that Bayard Taylor lived and wrote his " Hannah Thurston," a most contemptible burlesque of his own neighbors and the reforms they advocated.

Kennett Square and Longwood have for years been noted for their liberal religious meetings, in which the leading reformers of the nation have in turn been annually represented. In those gatherings of the Progressive Friends, all the questions of the hour were freely discussed, and their printed testimonies *sent* forth to enlighten the people.

The Convention assembled at ten o'clock in Horticultural Hall, and was called to order by Lucretia Mott, and the following officers chosen :

PRESIDENT.—Mariana Johnson.

VICE - PRESIDENTS.—Mary Ann Fulton, William Jackson, Chandler Darlington.

SECRETARIES.—Sarah L. Miller, Hannah Darlington, Sidney Peirce, Edward Webb.

BUSINESS COMMITTEE. — James Mott, Ann Preston, Lucretia Mott, Frances D. Gage, Sarah D. Barnard, Dr. Harriot K. Hunt, Joseph A. Dugdale, Margaret Jones. Ernestine L. Rose, Alice Jackson, Jacob Painter, Phebe Goodwin.

FINANCE COMMITTEE, appointed by the Chair.—Hannah Darlington, Jacob Painter, Isaac Mendenhall, Elizabeth Miller.

Mrs. Mott read the following call:

The friends of Justice and Equal Rights are earnestly invited to assemble in Convention, to consider and discuss the present position of Woman in Society, her Natural Rights and Relative Duties.

The reasons for such a Convention are obvious. With few exceptions, both the radical and conservative portions of the community agree that woman, even in this progressive age and country, suffers under legal, educational, and vocational disabilities which ought to be removed. To examine the nature of these disabilities, to inquire into their extent, and to consider the most feasible and proper mode of removing them, will be the aim of the Convention which it is proposed to hold.

If it shall promote in any degree freedom of thought and action among women; if it shall assist in opening to them any avenues to honorable and lucrative employment (now unjustly and unwisely closed); if it shall aid in securing to them more thorough intellectual and moral culture; if it shall excite higher aspirations; if it shall advance by a few steps just and wise public sentiment, it will not have been held in vain.

The elevation of woman is the elevation of the human race. Her interests can not be promoted or injured without advantage or injury to the whole race. The call for such a Convention is therefore addressed to those who desire the physical, intellectual, and moral improvement of mankind. All persons interested in its objects are respectfully requested to be present at its sessions and participate in its deliberations.

THE PRESIDENT'S ADDRESS.

The position in which woman has been placed is an anomaly. On the one hand she is constantly reminded of duties and responsibilities from which an angel might shrink. The world is to be saved by her prayers, her quiet and gentle efforts. Man, she is told, is ruled by her smiles; his whole nature subdued by the potency of her tears. Priests, politicians, and poets assure her with flattering tongue, that on her depend the progress and destiny of the race. On the other hand, she is told that she must lovingly confide in the strength and skill of man, who has been endowed with superior intellectual powers; that she must count it her highest honor to reflect upon the world the light of his intelligence and wisdom, as the moon reflects the light of the sun!

We may congratulate one another on this occasion in view of the cheering indications so manifest on every hand that the ignorance and darkness which have so long brooded over the prospects of woman, are beginning to give place to the light of truth. In the summer of 1848, in the village of Seneca Falls, a small number of women, disregarding alike the sneers of the ignorant and the frowns of the learned, assembled in Convention and boldly claimed for themselves, and for their sex, the rights conferred by God and so long withheld by man. Their courageous words were the expression of sentiments which others had felt as deeply as themselves, but which the restraints imposed by long-established custom had taught them to suppress. But now the hour had come, and the world stood prepared for the reception of a new thought, which is destined to work a revolution in human society, more beneficent than any that has preceded it. The seeds of truth which that Convention planted in faith and hope were not left to perish. In many thoughtful minds they germinated apace and brought forth fruit. That fruit was seen in the large Convention held in Ohio in the spring of 1850, in that held in Massachusetts in the autumn of the same year, and in those which have followed since in New England and the West.

Woman at length is awaking from the slumber of ages. Many of the sex already perceive that knowledge, sound judgment, and perfect freedom of thought and action are quite as important for the mothers as for the fathers of the race. They weary of the senseless talk of " woman's sphere," when that sphere is so circumscribed that they may not exert their full influence and power to save their country from war, intemperance, slavery, licentiousness, ignorance, poverty, and crime, which man, in the mad pursuit of his ambitious schemes, unchecked by their presence and counsel, permits to desolate and destroy all that is fair and beautiful in life and fill the world with weeping, lamentation, and woe. Woman begins to grow weary of her helpless and dependent position, and of being treated as if she were formed only to cultivate her affections, that they may flow in strong and deep currents merely to gratify the self-love of man.

She does not listen with delight, as she once did, when she hears her relations to her equal brother represented by the poetical figure of the trellis and creeping tendril, or of the oak and the gracefully clinging vine. No, she feels that she is, like him, an accountable being—that the Infinite Father has laid responsibilities upon her which may not be innocently transferred to another, but which, in her present ignorance, she is not prepared to meet. She is becoming rapidly imbued with the spirit of progress, and will not longer submit, without remonstrance, to the bondage of ancient dogmas and customs. In the retirement and seclusion of life, the stirring impulse of the times has reached even the heart of woman, and she feels the necessity of a more thorough culture and a wider field of usefulness. She sees the glaring injustice by which she has long been deprived of all fair opportunity to earn an independent livelihood, and thus, in too many instances, constrained to enter the marriage relation, as a choice of evils, to secure herself against the ills of impending poverty. The wrong she so deeply feels she is at length arousing herself to redress.

What, then, is the substance of our demand? I answer, we demand for woman equal freedom with her brother to raise her voice and exert her influence directly for the removal of all the evils that afflict the race; and that she be permitted to do this in the manner dictated by her own sense of propriety and justice. We ask for her educational advantages equal to those enjoyed by the other sex; that the richly endowed institutions which she has been taxed to establish and support, may be open alike to all her children. We claim for her the right to follow any honorable calling or profession for which she may be fitted by her intellectual training and capacity. We claim for her a fair opportunity to attain a position of pecuniary independence, and to this end that she receive for her labor a compensation equivalent to its recognized value when performed by the other sex.

These demands, we think, must be admitted to be essentially wise and just. We make them in no spirit of selfish antagonism to the other sex, but under a deep conviction that they are prompted by an enlightened regard for the highest welfare of the race. Some one has justly said that God has so linked the human family together that any violence done at one end of the chain is felt throughout its length. The true interests of the sexes are not antagonistic, but harmonious. There can be no just conflict between their respective rights and duties. For the coming of the day when this great truth shall be universally received, we must work and pray as we have opportunity. When that day shall arrive, it will be clearly perceived that in the true Harmonic Order "woman and her brother are pillars in the same temple and priests of the same worship."

The Secretary, SIDNEY PEIRCE, read the following letter from

SARAH M. GRIMKÉ.

When an insect emerges with struggles from its chrysalis state, how feeble are all its movements, how its wings hang powerless until the genial air has dried and strengthened them, how patiently the insect tries again and again to spread them, and visit the flowers which bloom around, till at last it enjoys the recompense of its labors in the nectar and the fragrance of the garden.

This illustrates the present condition of Woman. She is just emerging from the darkness and ignorance by which she has been shrouded. She looks forth from her chrysalis and sees the natural and intellectual world lying around her clothed in radiant beauty, and inviting her to enter and possess this magnificent inheritance. How came I, she asks, to be excluded from all these precious privileges? I will arise and go to my Father and say, "Father, permit me to share the labors of my brethren and partake of the fruits which they enjoy." "Go, my daughter," is the paternal response. "Be unto man, in an infinitely higher sense than heretofore, a help-meet." How is woman fulfilling her divine mission? Is she looking on the benefits she is commissioned to bestow on the human race, or is she keeping her eye on her own interests and seeking her own elevation, with little of that expansive benevolence, that philosophical foresight which seeks the development of all?

Woman is now in the transition state, a glorious mission is before her, a glorious destiny awaits her. To fulfill that mission, to be worthy of that destiny, she must patiently wait and quietly hope, blessing those who scorn and deride her feeble and often unsuccessful efforts, to free herself from her entanglements. She must expect many failures in her attempts to emancipate herself from the thralldom of public opinion. Those who have long held the reins of power and the rank of superiority, naturally look with distrust on a movement which threatens to overturn long established customs and transform the baby and the toy into an intellectual being, desiring equal rights with themselves and asserting her claim to all the immunities they enjoy. Woman must be willing

23

to see herself as she is, the slave of fashion, assuming all the Proteus forms she invents, without reference to health or convenience. She must remember how few of us give evidence of sufficient development to warrant our claims; and whilst we feel a divine impulse to proceed in achieving the enlargement of woman, whilst we hear a voice saying, "Ye have compassed this mountain long enough; speak to the people that they go forward," let us not be dismayed at the hindrances we shall encounter from those whom we are laboring to release from the swaddling bands of infancy, or the grave-clothes of superstition, time-honored opinion and crushing circumstances. We are now in a perilous and difficult position. We feel all the inconveniences of our past condition, all the disadvantages and uneasiness of the one we are constrained to occupy, and see in bold relief all the advantages which a change will yield us. But let us remember that our transition state, although replete with temptations and suffering, is necessary to our improvement; we need it to strengthen us and enable us to bear hardships as good soldiers of truth.

To regard any state of society as fixed, is to regard it as the ultimate good, as the best condition to which we can attain. But when man has progressed, when his morality and his religion have assumed a higher tone, it is impossible to perpetuate his childhood, or to give permanence to institutions and opinions whose days are numbered. When reform has truth for its basis and is instinct with the life of progression, no power can dress it in the habiliments of the grave, and bury it out of sight, either in the Potter's-field or under the magnificent mausoleum. There is nothing so precious to man as progress; he has defended it with his heart's best blood, and according to his development has aided it, although sometimes in his blindness he has scattered fire and sword, destruction and misery around, in endeavoring to force mankind to adopt the truths he thought essential to progress. "Woman has come on the stage," says Horace Mann, "6,000 years after man, to profit by his misdeeds and correct his errors." Until now, the world was not prepared to receive, in full measure, the hallowed influence which woman is designed to shed. Her holy mission is to bring peace on earth and goodwill to man. She does not ask for irresponsible power; she has seen that from the earliest records of the human race the possession of such power is fraught with danger, that it has always made tyrants. She feels Divinity stirring within her, and its irrepressible aspirings can not, should not be controlled. Mankind have always rejected the means appointed by Infinite Wisdom to assist their upward flight. Let us then go calmly forward, alike regardless of the scorn and ridicule of the shallow, the grave denunciations of the bigot, or the weighty counsel of the narrow-minded and selfish, who would point out the exact position fitted for us to occupy, and with seeming condescension invite us to fill some posts of honor and profit, while they undertake to confine us within their bounds, leaving nothing to our good sense, intelligence, intuitive desires, and aspiring hopes. The truth is, "It is not in man that walketh to direct his steps." God alone is competent to do this, and in the present movement His power, wisdom, and will, are so conspicuous, that it will be well to set no bounds to His work, but let it have free course, expecting that contradictions and inconsistencies will mar it, but believing that those contradictions will cease, those inconsistencies disappear, and the perfected human being be developed.

If we adopt as our watchword the language of Margaret Fuller, we can not but overcome all obstacles, outlive all opposition : " Give me Truth. Cheat me by no illusion. Oh, the granting of this prayer is sometimes terrible; I walk over the burning plowshares and they sear my feet—yet nothing but Truth will do."   Sarah M. Grimké.

Lucretia Mott addressed the Convention, briefly referring to the importance of the movement and expressing her gratification on seeing the response given to the call, by the great number of persons assembled. She saw before her not only a large delegation from the immediate vicinity, but a goodly number from other and distant States.

The movement for the enfranchisement of woman is indeed making rapid progress. Since the first Convention held at Seneca Falls, in 1848, where a few women assembled, and notwithstanding their ignorance of the parliamentary modes of conducting business, promulgated these principles, which took deep root, and are already producing important results. Other large Conventions have been held in different places, which have done much toward disseminating the great principles of equality between the sexes; and a spirit of earnest inquiry has been aroused. She referred to the fact that the agitation commenced in those States most distinguished for intellectual and moral culture, while we in Pennsylvania are ready to embrace their views on this subject; and trusted that the Convention now assembled, would be neither less interesting nor less efficient than those that have been already held.

Mrs. Clarina Howard Nichols, of Brattleboro, Vermont, spoke briefly on the absurdity of the popular idea of woman's sphere. She thought the sphere of sex could only be determined by capacity and moral obligation. She had once thought politics necessarily too degrading for woman, but she had changed her views. The science of government, it is said, is of divine origin; a participation in its administration can not then necessarily involve anything to deteriorate from the true dignity of woman. The world's interests have never yet been fully represented. The propriety of woman voting had been to her a stumbling-block; the idea was repelling. She was not yet allowed to vote, but she had ceased to consent to the arrangement which deprived her of that right, and therefore experienced a freedom of spirit which she had not known before. The idea that woman could not go to the ballot-box without a sacrifice of her delicacy was absurd. Women were allowed to vote in church matters unquestioned. They can hold railroad stock, bank stock, and stock of other corporations, where their influence is in proportion to the amount held.

But we are not called upon to maintain the position of the propriety or expediency of women voting. The question is, Shall they have the right so to do?—the propriety should be left to themselves. Woman can now travel alone securely, where formerly it was considered a risk. She can deposit her vote with men, with as much propriety as she can ride with them in railroad cars, on steamboats, etc. She came all the way from the Green Mountains without any male attendant; she traveled with members of Congress and delegates to the Baltimore Convention, and not a "bear",among them offered her the least indignity.

ERNESTINE L. ROSE quoted the testimony of Horace Mann,* that our Legislatures were "bear gardens, our representatives too rude and rough for woman's association, hence the impropriety and indelicacy of her mingling in politics." But we are told it is woman's province to soothe the angry passions and calm the belligerent feelings of man, and if what Horace Mann says is true, where can we find a riper harvest awaiting us than in the halls of legislation!

Harriot K. Hunt then read an address upon the medical education of women; on concluding, she offered the following resolutions :

1st. *Resolved*, That the present position of medical organizations, precluding women from the same educational advantages with men, under pretext of delicacy, virtually acknowledges the impropriety of his being her medical attendant.

2d. *Resolved*, That we will do all in our power to sustain those women who, from a conviction of duty, enter the medical profession, in their efforts to overcome the evils that have accumulated in their path, and in attacking the strongholds of vice.

3d. *Resolved*, That the past actions and present indications of our medical schools should not affect us at all; and notwithstanding Geneva and Cleveland Medical Colleges closed their doors after graduating one woman each, and Harvard, through the false delicacy of the students, declared it inexpedient to receive one who had been in successful practice many years, we would still earnestly follow in peace and love where duty points, and leave the verdict to an enlightened public sentiment.

The address of Dr. Hunt called out a discussion on the importance of a thorough medical training for women in all departments of science belonging to that profession.

Mrs. NICHOLS spoke earnestly of the imperfect education of woman. With no knowledge of the laws of health, she has no means of obtaining the required information. Men hold the purse even when it is filled by the labor of both. They close the college doors, though we have helped to build and endow them. And at what a fearful cost of life and health are we thus wronged. Does it cost too much to educate the future mothers of this nation in the science of life ? Who can estimate how

* Just previous to this Convention Horace Mann, President of Antioch College, had been giving a lecture through the country, and made many severe strictures on the false philosophy of the woman suffrage movement, or rather what he supposed it to be. This was considered the more damaging because Mr. Mann so strongly favored co-education. It was as if one in our own camp had suddenly turned traitor. Among other things he said that our legislative halls were such bear gardens that they were not fit for women to enter. It is to this remark reference is made in the debates.

much greater are the expenses incurred by our ignorant violation of the laws of health ?

FRANCES DANA GAGE, of Ohio, spoke of the high scholarship and very successful examinations of those women who had been admitted into the medical colleges, far surpassing the young men in their recitations and general intelligence. So long as the lives of children are conceded to be in the hands of their mothers, it is of vital consequence to the race that women be thoroughly educated for the medical profession.

Mrs. ROSE said: These are mighty questions. When our little ones are removed by death from our care and affection, we feel most keenly our ignorance, and long to know something of those immutable laws of life and health we have so long violated. Woman should at least know enough to be physician to herself and children, but she is denied the advantages granted to man for obtaining knowledge of these things more necessary if possible to her than to him.

The idea of a female doctor is ridiculed. But what is she worth as a nurse of the sick without a knowledge of the art of healing ? Why am I in the prime of life in such feeble health ? In my country, the laws of life are, comparatively speaking, kept in a nutshell. The girl must not exercise ; it is not fashionable. She must not be seen in active life; it is not feminine. The boy may run, the girl must creep. It is to discuss all these grave inequalities that we have assembled here, and I trust the influence of this Convention may be felt in opening to woman all honest and honorable means of self-support and self-development, and in removing all the legal shackles that block her pathway through life.

EVA PUGH said: The degradation of one sex is the degradation of the other. This question is universal, affecting all alike. No fact is better established than that the character of the parent is inherited by the child. Can noble men be born of infirm women ? Who are the mothers of great men ? Women of mind, of thought, of independence ; not women degraded by man's tyranny, laboring in prescribed limits, thinking other people's thoughts, and echoing their opinions. This question of woman's rights affects the whole human race. We know from sad experience that man can not rise while woman is degraded.

Mrs. MOTT spoke of the great change in public sentiment within her recollection in regard to the so-called sphere of woman. Twenty years ago people wondered how a modest girl could attend lectures on Botany; but modest girls did attend them and other places frequented only by men, and the result was not a loss of delicacy, but a higher and nobler development; a true modesty.

JOSEPH A. DUGDALE made a few remarks on the injustice of the laws by which happy households are often broken up on the death of the husband and father. He said there remained one way in which this great evil could be avoided even while the law remains unchanged, and that was by a will of the husband conveying the whole property of their joint industry and economy to the wife, in the event of his death. He urged this as the duty of every husband and father. He closed his remarks with the following extract from the will of Martin Luther, proving that other errors than those of the Church, were deemed by the great reformer of sufficient magnitude to awaken his earnest opposition:

MARTIN LUTHER'S WILL.

"This is all I am worth, and I give it all to my wife for the following reasons:

"1. Because she has always conducted herself toward me lovingly, worthily, and beautifully, like a pious, faithful, and noble wife; and by the rich blessings of God, she has borne and brought up five living children, who yet live, and God grant they may long live.

"2. Because she will take upon herself and pay the debts which I owe and may not be able to pay during my life, which, so far as I can estimate, may amount to about 450 florins, or perhaps a little more.

"3. But most of all, because I will not have her dependent on the children, but the children on her; that they may hold her in honor, and submit themselves to her as God has commanded. For I see well and observe, how the devil, by wicked and envious mouths, heats and excites children, even though they be pious, against this command; especially when the mothers are widows, and the sons get wives, and the daughters get husbands, and again *socrus murum, nurus socrum.* For I hold that the mother will be the best guardian for her own children, and will use what little property and goods she may have, not for their disadvantage and injury, but for their good and improvement, since they are her own flesh and blood, and she carried them under her heart.

"And if, after my death, she should find it necessary or desirable to marry again (for I can not pretend to set limits to the will or providence of God), yet I trust and herewith express my confidence that she will conduct herself toward our mutual children as becometh a mother, and will faithfully impart to them property, and do whatever else is right.

"And herewith I humbly pray my most gracious lord, his grace Duke John Frederick, elector of Saxony, graciously to guard and protect the above-named gifts and property.

"I also entreat all my good friends to be witnesses for my dear Catey, and help to defend her should any good-for-nothing mouth reprove and slander her, as if she had secretly some personal property of which she would defraud the poor children. For I testify there is no personal property except the plate and jewelry enumerated above.

"Finally, I beg, since in this will or testament I have not used legal forms or words (and thereto I have my reasons), that every one may let me be the person that I am in truth, namely, openly and known both in heaven and earth, and in hell, and let me have respect and authority enough so that I may be trusted and believed more than any lawyer. For so God the Father of all mercies hath entrusted to me, a poor, miserable, condemned sinner, the Gospel of His dear Son, and therein thus far I have behaved and conducted myself truly and faithfully, and it has made much progress in the world through me, and I am honored as a teacher of truth, notwithstanding the curse of the Pope and the wrath of emperors, kings, princes, priests, and all kinds of devils ; much rather then let me be believed in this little matter, especially as here in my hand which is very well known; and I hope it may be enough, when it can be said and proved that this is the serious and deliberate desire of

Dr. Martin Luther (who is God's lawyer and witness of His Gospel) to be proved by his own hand and seal, Sept. 16, 1542."

LUCRETIA MOTT (see 8th resolution) thought it important that we should not disclaim the antagonism that woman's present position rendered it necessary she should assume. Too long had wrongs and oppressions existed without an acknowledged wrong-doer and oppressor. It was not until the slaveholder was told, "thou art the man," that a healthful agitation was brought about. Woman is told that the fault is in herself, in too willingly submitting to her inferior condition; but, like the slave, she is pressed down by laws in the making of which she has had no voice, and crushed by customs that have grown out of such laws. She can not rise, therefore, while thus trampled in the dust. The oppressor does not see himself in that light until the oppressed cry for deliverance.

In commenting on the will just read, she further said :

The extract from Luther's will which has been read, while it gives evidence of the appreciation of the services of his wife, to a certain extent, and manifests a generous disposition to reward her as a faithful wife, still only proves the degrading relation she bore to her husband. There is no recognition of ·her equal right to their joint earnings. While the wife is obliged to accept as a gift that which in justice belongs to her, however generous the boon, she is but an inferior dependent.

The law of our State and of New York, has within a few years been so amended that the wife has some control over a part of her property. Much yet remains to be done; and if woman "contend earnestly" for the right, man will co-operate with her in adjusting all her claims. We have only to look back a few years, to satisfy ourselves that the demands already made are met in a disposition to redress the grievances. When a delegation of women to the World's Anti-Slavery Convention in 1840, could find no favor in London, what were the reasons assigned for the exclusion ? Not that the right of representation was not as much woman's as man's, but that "they would be ridiculed in the morning papers."

Daniel O'Connell felt the injustice done to those delegates, and in a letter on the subject to me, expressed his deep regret, that owing to business engagements, he was not able to attend the Convention and take part in the discussion.*

Dr. Bowring advocated the admission of the delegates at that time; and afterward in a letter to this country, said: "How often have I regretted that the woman's question, to me of singular interest, was launched with so little preparation, so little knowledge of the manner in which it had been entangled, by the fears of some and the follies of others! But, bear up! for the coming of those women will form an era in the future history of philanthropic daring. They made a deep, if not a wide impression; and have created apostles, if as yet they have not multitudes of followers. The experiment was well worth making. It honored America—it will instruct England. If in some matters of high civ-

* This letter will be found in "Reminiscences of Lucretia Mott," at the close of this chapter.

ilization you are behind us, in this matter of courageous benevolence how far are you before us!"

Since that time women have fairly entered the field as students of medicine and as physicians, as editors and lecturers, engaged in schools of design, and in the taking of daguerres, as well as in some other works of art, and in holding Conventions in several of the States of our Union for the advocacy of our entire claims. A National Society has been formed; and the proceedings of these Conventions and Society meetings have been fairly reported, and have received favorable notices in many of the papers of this country, as well as in the *Westminster Review* in England.

FRANCES D. GAGE said that allusion had been made in the address to the popular sentiment, that men are what their mothers made them. She repelled this sentiment as an indignity to her sex. What mother, she asked, ever taught her son to drink rum, gamble, swear, smoke, and chew tobacco? The truth was, that the boy was virtually taught to regard his mother as inferior, and that it was not manly to follow her instructions. When he left the hearth-stone he was beyond her reach. He found men, and those, too, in elevated stations, addicted to vulgar and vicious practices, and he was liable, in forgetfulness of all that his mother had taught him, to fall into such habits himself. Men allowed grog-shops to be set up on the street corners, and permitted gambling-houses to exist, to tempt the boy from the path of virtue; and when the mothers asked for the abatement of these evils, they were told to keep in their sphere. In the town where she resided (McConnellsville, Morgan Co., Ohio), the women sent a large petition to the court asking that grog-shops might not be licensed. The judge thereupon remarked that "woman's place was in the nursery and the parlor, and that when she interfered with public affairs, or set herself up as an instructor of the courts, she was out of her sphere." Thus men perpetuate institutions which undermine the influence of the mothers, and corrupt the morals of the sons. The boys were, therefore, in many cases, what men made them. True, there were some cases in which the mother, by superior power, shaped the destiny of her sons, in spite of adverse influences. Such cases were not the rule, but the exception. Mothers, generally, could not exert their full influence over their sons, unless they were permitted to stand by them as the equals of their fathers in all relations of life.

The following address, written by Ann Preston, and adopted as an exposition of the principles and purposes of the Convention, was impressively read by the author:

ANN PRESTON'S ADDRESS.

The question is repeatedly asked by those who have thought but little upon the subject of woman's position in society, "What does woman want more than she possesses already? Is she not beloved, honored, guarded, cherished? Wherein are her rights infringed, or her liberties curtailed?"

Glowing pictures have been drawn of the fitness of the present relations of society, and of the beauty of woman's dependence upon the pro-tecting love of man, and frightful visions have been evoked of the confusion and perversion of nature which would occur if the doctrine of the equal rights of man and woman was once admitted.

The idea seems to prevail that movements for the elevation of woman arise, not from the legitimate wants of society, but from the vague restlessness of unquiet spirits; not from the serene dictates of wisdom, but from the headlong impulses of fanaticism.

We came not here to argue the question of the relative strength of intellect in man and woman; for the reform which we advocate depends not upon its settlement. We place not the interests of woman in antagonism to those of her brother, for

> "The woman's cause is man's :
> They rise or sink together,
> Dwarfed or God-like, bond or free."

We maintain not that woman should lose any of that refinement and delicacy of spirit which, as a celestial halo, ever encircles the pure in heart. We contend not that she shall become noisy and dictatorial, and abjure the quiet graces of life. We claim not that she, any more than her brother, should engage in any vocation or appear in any situation to which her nature and abilities are not fitted. But we ask for her, as for man, equality before the law, and freedom to exercise all her powers and faculties under the direction of her own judgment and volition.

When a woman dies, leaving behind her a husband and children, no appraisers come into the desolated home to examine the effects; the father is the guardian of his offspring; the family relation is not invaded by law. But when a man dies the case is entirely different; in the hour of the widow's deep distress strangers come into the house to take an inventory of the effects, strangers are appointed to be the guardians of her children, and she, their natural care-taker, thenceforth has no legal direction of their interests; strangers decide upon the propriety of the sale of the property—earned, perhaps, by her own and her husband's mutual efforts—and her interest in the estate is coolly designated as the "widow's incumbrance!" In the extremity of her bereavement there is piled upon her, not only the dread of separation from her children, but that of being sent homeless from the spot where every object has been consecrated by her tenderest affections.

Nor is the practical working of this law better than its theory; all over the country there are widows who have been made doubly desolate by its provisions—widows separated from their children, who, if they had had the disposal of their own and their husbands' mutual property, might have retrieved their circumstances, and kept the household band together. We ask for such change in public sentiment as shall procure the repeal of this oppressive law.

We ask that woman shall have free access to vocations of profit and honor, the means of earning a livelihood and independence for herself! As a general rule, profitable employments are not considered open to woman, nor are her business capabilities encouraged and developed by systematic training. Gloomy must be the feelings of the father of a family of young daughters, when he is about to bid farewell to the world, if he is leaving them without the means of pecuniary support. Their brothers may go out into society and gain position and competency; but for them there is but little choice of employment, and, too often, they are left with repressed and crippled energies to pine and chafe under the bitter sense of poverty and dependence.

Their pursuits are to be determined, not by their inclination, judgment, and ability, as are those of man, but by the popular estimate of what is proper and becoming. In Turkey public delicacy is outraged if a woman appears unveiled beyond the walls of the harem; in America a sentiment no less arbitrary presumes to mark out for her the precise boundaries of womanly propriety; and she who ventures to step beyond them, must do it at the peril of encountering low sneers, coarse allusions, and the withering imputation of want of feminine delicacy.

Even for the same services woman generally receives less than man. The whole tendency of our customs, habits, and teaching, is to make her dependent—dependent in outward circumstances, dependent in spirit.

As a consequence of her fewer resources, marriage has been to her the great means of securing position in society. Thus it is that this relation —which should ever be a "holy sacrament," the unbiased and generous election of the free and self-sustained being—too often is degraded into a mean acceptance of a shelter from neglect and poverty! We ask that woman shall be trained to unfold her whole nature; to exercise all her powers and faculties.

It is said that the domestic circle is the peculiar province of woman; that "men are what mothers make them." But how can that woman who does not live for self-culture and self-development, who has herself no exalted objects in life, imbue her children with lofty aspirations, or train her sons to a free and glorious manhood? She best can fulfill the duties of wife and mother, who is fitted for other and varied usefulness.

The being who lives for one relation only can not possess the power and scope which are required for the highest excellence even in that one. If the whole body is left without exercise, one arm does not become strong; if the tree is stunted in its growth, one branch does not shoot into surpassing luxuriance.

That woman whose habits and mental training enable her to assist and sustain her husband in seasons of difficulty, and whose children rely on her as a wise counselor, commands a life-long reverence far deeper and dearer than can be secured by transient accomplishments, or the most refined and delicate imbecility! All women are not wives and mothers, but all have spirits needing development, powers that grow with their exercise.

Those who are best acquainted with the state of society know that there is, at this time, a vast amount of unhappiness among women for want of free outlets to their powers; that thousands are yearning for fuller development, and a wider field of usefulness. The same energies which in man find vent in the professions, and in the thousand forms of

business and study, must find an ennobling channel in woman, else they
will be frittered away in trifles, or turned into instruments to prey upon
their possessor.

To follow the empty round of fashion, to retail gossip and scandal, to
be an ornament in the parlor or a mere drudge in the kitchen, to live as
an appendage to any human being, does not fill up nor satisfy the capacities of a soul awakened to a sense of its true wants, and the far-reaching
and mighty interests which cluster around its existence.

We protest against the tyranny of that public sentiment which assigns
any arbitrary sphere to woman. God has made the happiness and development of His creatures to depend upon the free exercise of their
powers and faculties. Freedom is the law of beauty, written by His
fingers upon the human mind, and the only condition upon which it can
attain to its full stature, and expand in its natural and beautiful proportions.

It is recognized, in reference to man, that his judgment, opportunities,
and abilities are the proper measure of his sphere. "The tools to him
who can use them." But the same principles are not trusted in their
application to woman, lest, forsooth, she should lose her feminine characteristics, and, like the lost Pleiad, forsake her native sphere!

It seems to be forgotten that the laws of nature will not be suspended;
that the human mind, when released from pressure, like water, must
find its own level; that woman can not, if she would, cast away her nature and instincts; that it is only when we are left free to obey the inward attractions of our being that we fall into our natural places, and
move in our God-appointed orbits.

We ask that none shall dare to come in between woman and her
Maker, and with unhallowed hands attempt to plant their shallow posts
and draw their flimsy cords around the Heaven-wide sphere of an immortal spirit! We maintain that God has not so failed in His adapta-
tions as to give powers to be wasted, talents to be wrapped in a napkin;
and that the possession of faculties and capabilities is the warrant of
nature, the command of the All-Wise for their culture and exercise.

We believe that the woman who is obeying the convictions of her own
soul, and whose ability is commensurate with her employment, is ever
in her own true sphere; whether in her quiet home she is training her
children to nobleness and virtue, or is standing as a physician by the
bed of sickness and sorrow; whether, with Elizabeth Fry, she is preaching the gospel of glad tidings to the sad dwellers in prison, or like the
Italian, Lauri Bassi, is filling a professor's chair and expounding philosophy to admiring and instructed listeners.

While we demand for woman a more complete physical, intellectual,
and moral education, as the means of strengthening and beautifying her
own nature, and of ennobling the whole race, we also ask for a more
elevated standard of excellence and moral purity in man; and we maintain that if there is any place of resort or employment in society, which
necessarily would sully the delicacy of woman's spirit, in that, man also
must be contaminated and degraded. Woman indeed should wear about
her, wherever she moves, the protecting investment of innocence and

purity; but not less is it requisite that he, who is the companion of her life, should guard his spirit with the same sacred and beautiful covering.

We believe that woman, as an accountable being, can not innocently merge her individuality in that of her brother, or accept from him the limitations of her sphere. In all life's great extremities she also is thrown upon her inward resources, and stands alone. Man can not step in between her and the "accusing angel" of her own conscience; alone in the solitude of her spirit she must wrestle with her own sorrows; none can walk for her "the valley of the shadow of death!" When her brother shall be able to settle for her accountabilities, and "give to God a ransom for her soul," then, and not till then, may she rightly commit to him the direction of her powers and activities.

We ask, in fine, for the application of the fundamental principles of Christianity and republicanism to this, as to all other questions of vital importance; and appealing to all who desire the progression and happiness of the whole race, we ask them, as magnanimous men and true women, to examine this subject in the spirit of a generous and candid investigation.

RUSH PLUMLY said: Although institutions which recognize all the rights of all classes of the people, and allow scope for the growth and activity of every faculty, must, in their very nature, increase in power and permanence; yet, compared with the duration of things, the oldest nations and the best founded governments have had but an ephemeral existence, appearing, maturing, and decaying with startling rapidity and endless succession.

No form has been exempt from this national mortality. Theocracies, oligarchies, monarchies, despotisms, republics, have arisen, flourished, and vanished into history or tradition. So inevitable does the successive ruin appear, that we have incorporated into our religious faith the idea that limitation, conflict, and decay, rather than expansion, permanence, and peace, are inherent in all human governments, and, in despair man postpones his hope of national, as well as of individual stability and happiness, to some future existence.

For results so certain and so universal among all people, in every age, there must be some profound and radical cause which religion and philosophy have not discovered, or for which they have proposed no remedy. It is not sufficient to say that these are consequences of human imperfection; that we know; but whence arises the imperfection? It does not satisfy us to assert that they proceed from the depravity of man; how came he depraved? Nor is it more consoling to declare that all human institutions must change and perish. Why must they? Human institutions, if founded upon eternal principles, become divine, and may be immortal; it is not the human, but the inhuman institutions which perish; not humanity, but inhumanity which fills the earth with strife and blood.

No! there is behind and below all these imaginary causes, a real cause for the degeneracy of the race. It may be traced to the long continued disregard of the laws of God in relation to woman, and the retribution is worked out physiologically upon the whole nature of man, reaching every tissue of his body and every faculty of his mind.

It is a law of God, well understood, that whenever and wherever any community forcibly depresses any class of its people below the general level, it not only injures and degrades that class, but is itself injured, degraded, and deranged in exact proportion to the wrong it perpetrates. Whenever we crowd any portion of our fellow-beings into an abyss of ignorance and servitude, we are drawn irresistibly, by their weight, to the brink of the same gulf.

If this be the inevitable result of the oppression of an individual, or a class, how much more forcibly must it apply when one-half the world, the " mothers of the living," are made subject to systematic deprivation of rights and tyrannous restriction in the exercise of high and noble faculties.

I do not propose to detail the disabilities under which woman suffers. They have been ably depicted by women in this meeting. But I wish to indicate the breadth and basis of this reform, for the consideration of those people who suppose it to be a fractional and transient movement.

Whatever suffering or degradation woman is subjected to, by the depression of the whole sex below the level of society, reacts with frightful force upon man; who is thus compelled to compensate for the cruel and mistaken policy, which, in all time, has denied to her equal opportunities of education and development, closed to her those avenues to profit and progress open to him, ignored her in the Church and State as feeble and inferior, rejected her counsels, and derided her authority in the creation of those institutions of society to which not only she, but her children are to be subject; although, if there be any induction more striking than another it is this, that a child, who is the offspring of the physical union of man and woman, can only be truly educated and nurtured by institutions springing from the unity of mental and moral elements in the father and mother.

This universal ignoring of the feminine element pervades not only the politics, but the religion of every country on earth. Men worship, as their supreme God, only an embodiment of the masculine element— " Power," whether in Jove or Jehovah; and ever in the Christian Trinity or Unity, the same masculine ideal is maintained. Jesus did, indeed, recognize the feminine element in His emphatic declaration that " God is Love," but His professed followers have " not so learned Him," for they not only declare God to be a triune masculinity, but they have driven woman from the pulpit, and would dispute with her the place at the cross and the sepulchre.

The religions of antiquity permitted woman to be a priestess at the expense of wifehood and maternity, but our Christian Protestantism denies to her the mission of minister, even with that penalty. It is true the Catholic Church does recognize women among its divinities, and it might be a curious and instructive inquiry, how far that Church owes its perpetuity, despite its gigantic crimes and crushing despotism, to the recognition of "Mary the mother of God." In its effort to perpetuate the servitude of woman, as in other attempts to defend oppression and falsehood, society has suborned the handmaids of progress, Religion and Science, to justify its wickedness; the one to prove inferiority from her organism, the other to add the weight of its anathema against any effort at equality.

But Nature vindicates herself against the first, by presenting De Staël, Margaret Fuller, and others; and to the cavilling bigot it may be said that whoever declared that "man is the head of the woman," if he designed to justify the present interpretation of that expression, has forfeited all claim to the apostleship of a religion whose highest merit it is to equalize the people by elevating the oppressed. But Paul taught no such doctrine.

The result of all this circumscription of woman has been to enfeeble and misdirect her faculties, to weaken the influence of her nature upon society and especially upon her offspring. Driven from the thousand avenues to wealth and position open to man, denied access to the best institutions of learning, permitted to acquire only superficial accomplishments, she is ushered into society at an age when her brothers are preparing to enter colleges and halls of learning from which she is excluded, and thus undeveloped and comparatively helpless, her instincts vitiated and no freedom for her affinities, she is turned adrift to encounter obstacles for which she is unprepared, and in' the severe conflict to barter her honor for subsistence; or if she escape that horrible contingency, to exchange her beauty or her services for a matrimonial establishment, and thus prepare to perpetuate human degeneracy.

There are many exceptions to this statement, but the statement is the rule. From these unequal and discordant relations, and the feeble and restricted influence of the mother, spring generations of children who are born constitutionally defective in the feminine qualities of gentleness, purity, and love; and the utter rejection of that element in the societary arrangements under which they grow to manhood, aggravates their inherited tendencies, until whole nations of warriors founding governments of blood have filled the earth, and war and rapine have not only become the occupation and the pastime of man, but have grown into his religion and become incarnate in the Deities he worships.

It is thus that the seeds of violence and vice are sown with the germs of the generations, and they spring to a frightful harvest in each succeeding growth of the race. Millions of human beings issue into life, pre-ordained—not in the theological, but in the physiological sense—to violence and crime, and they go forth to make their calling and election sure. From these the world recruits its armies, renews its tyrants, refills its slave-pens and its brothels, populates its prisons, alms-houses, and asylums. It is in vain to hope for other results while woman, upon whom, as "mother of the living," depends the progress of man, is denied any other than a limited and indirect influence in the fabric of society.

We may abolish slavery, remove intemperance, banish war and licentiousness, but they will have frightful reproduction in the elemental discord of our natures; for that which is "in us will be revealed." Man indicates his condition by the institutions he creates; they are the issues of the life he lives at the time, the outward sign of his inward state.

To improve that inward condition, and arrest at their origin these causes of human degeneracy, is the object of this reform. It proposes, as before stated, not only to cure, but to prevent the diseases of the body politic; to place man and woman in such natural and true relations of equal and mutual development, and to so sanctify marriage that from their union under the highest auspices, a regenerate humanity shall not only cease to be violent and vicious, but shall outgrow the dispositions to violence and vice.

We know that this is a work for whole generations, but as we believe it to be radical and effectual, it should be at once begun. We think the first great step is to clear away the rubbish of ages from the pathway of woman, to abolish the onerous restrictions which environ her in every direction, to open to her the temples of religion, the halls of science and of art, and the marts of commerce, affording her the same opportunity for education and occupation now enjoyed by man; no longer, by corrupt public sentiment and partial legislation, to limit her to a few and poorly paid pursuits to obtain subsistence and thus increase her dependence upon the charity of man, nor to deny her admission to any institution of learning, whose richly endowed professorships and vast advantages she by her labor has contributed to create, only to see them monopolized by man. I know that in answer to this it is urged that she has organic limits intellectually which deny to her such attainments. It is sufficient to reply, that under all the disabilities to which she is subject, her sex has produced De Staël and Margaret Fuller.

Letters were read from Mary Mott, of Auburn, De Kalb County, Indiana; Paulina Wright Davis, Dr. Elizabeth Blackwell, William and Mary Johnson, and a series of resolutions passed.* Oliver Johnson took an active part in the discussions, and at the close of the Convention, moved a resolution of thanks to the friends who had come from a distance, and contributed so much to the success of the meeting. The Convention then adjourned *sine die*.

In 1849, Richard H. Dana, of Boston, well known as a man of rare literary culture, delivered a lecture on womanhood throughout the country. He ridiculed the new demand of American women for civil and political rights, and for a larger sphere of action, and eulogized Shakespeare's women, especially Desdemona, Ophelia, and Juliet, and recommended them to his dissatisfied countrywomen as models of innocence, tenderness, and confiding love in man, for their study and imitation.

He gave this lecture in Philadelphia, and Lucretia Mott was in the audience. At the close she asked an introduction, and told him that while she had been much interested in his lecture, and profited by the information it contained, she could not respond to his idea

---

* See Appendix.

of woman's true character and destiny. "I am very sorry," he replied quickly, at the first word of criticism, and rushed out of the house, leaving Mrs. Mott, who had hoped to modify his views, somewhat transfixed with surprise. In describing the scene to some friends afterward, she remarked that she had never been treated with more rudeness by one supposed to understand the rules of etiquette that should always govern the behavior of a gentleman.

Soon after this, she delivered the following discourse in the Assembly buildings in Philadelphia. After giving the Bible view of woman's position as an equal,

LUCRETIA MOTT said: I have not come here with a view of answering any particular parts of the lecture alluded to, in order to point out the fallacy of its reasoning. The speaker, however, did not profess to offer anything like argument on that occasion, but rather a sentiment. I have no prepared address to deliver to you, being unaccustomed to speak in that way; but I felt a wish to offer some views for your consideration, though in a desultory manner, which may lead to such reflection and discussion as will present the subject in a true light.

Why should not woman seek to be a reformer? If she is to shrink from being such an iconoclast as shall "break the image of man's lower worship," as so long held up to view; if she is to fear to exercise her reason, and her noblest powers, lest she should be thought to "attempt to act the man," and not "acknowledge his supremacy"; if she is to be satisfied with the narrow sphere assigned her by man, nor aspire to a higher, lest she should transcend the bounds of female delicacy; truly it is a mournful prospect for woman. We would admit all the difference, that our great and beneficent Creator has made, in the relation of man and woman, nor would we seek to disturb this relation; but we deny that the present position of woman is her true sphere of usefulness; nor will she attain to this sphere, until the disabilities and disadvantages, religious, civil, and social, which impede her progress, are removed out of her way. These restrictions have enervated her mind and paralyzed her powers. While man assumes that the present is the original state designed for woman, that the existing "differences are not arbitrary nor the result of accident," but grounded in nature; she will not make the necessary effort to obtain her just rights, lest it should subject her to the kind of scorn and contemptuous manner in which she has been spoken of.

So far from her "ambition leading her to attempt to act the man," she needs all the encouragement she can receive, by the removal of obstacles from her path, in order that she may become the "true woman." As it is desirable that man should act a manly and generous part, not "mannish," so let woman be urged to exercise a dignified and womanly bearing, not womanish. Let her cultivate all the graces and proper accomplishments of her sex, but let not these degenerate into a kind of effeminacy, in which she is satisfied to be the mere plaything or toy of so-

affec'y. thine
Lucretia Mott

ciety, content with her outward adornings, and the flattery and fulsome adulation too often addressed to her.

Did Elizabeth Fry lose any of her feminine qualities by the public walk into which she was called ? Having performed the duties of a mother to a large family, feeling that she owed a labor of love to the poor prisoner, she was empowered by Him who sent her forth, to go to kings and crowned heads of the earth, and ask audience of these, and it was granted her. Did she lose the delicacy of woman by her acts ? No. Her retiring modesty was characteristic of her to the latest period of her life. It was my privilege to enjoy her society some years ago, and I found all that belonged to the feminine in woman—to true nobility, in a refined and purified moral nature. Is Dorothea Dix throwing off her womanly nature and appearance in the course she is pursuing ? In finding duties abroad, has any "refined man felt that something of beauty has gone forth from her"? To use the contemptuous word applied in the lecture alluded to, is she becoming "mannish"? Is she compromising her womanly dignity in going forth to seek to better the condition of the insane and afflicted ? Is not a beautiful mind and a retiring modesty still conspicuous in her ?

Indeed, I would ask, if this modesty is not attractive also, when manifested in the other sex ? It was strikingly marked in Horace Mann, when presiding over the late National Educational Convention in this city. The retiring modesty of William Ellery Channing was beautiful, as well as of many others who have filled elevated stations in society. These virtues, differing as they may in degree in man and woman, are of the same nature, and call forth our admiration wherever manifested.

The noble courage of Grace Darling is justly honored for risking her own life on the coast of England, during the raging storm, in order to rescue the poor, suffering, shipwrecked mariner.

Woman was not wanting in courage in the early ages. In war and bloodshed this trait was often displayed. Grecian and Roman history have lauded and honored her in this character. English history records her courageous women too, for unhappily we have little but the records of war handed down to us. The courage of Joan of Arc was made the subject of a popular lecture not long ago by one of our intelligent citizens. But more noble, moral daring is marking the female character at the present time, and better worthy of imitation. As these characteristics come to be appreciated in man too, his warlike acts with all the miseries and horrors of the battle-ground will sink into their merited oblivion, or be remembered only to be condemned. The heroism displayed in the tented field must yield to the moral and Christian heroism which is shadowed in the signs of our times.

The lecturer regarded the announcement of woman's achievements, and the offering of appropriate praise through the press, as a gross innovation upon the obscurity of female life—he complained that the exhibition of attainments of girls in schools was now equal to that of boys, and the newspapers announce that "Miss Brown received the first prize for English grammar," etc. If he objected to so much excitement of emulation in schools, it would be well; for the most enlightened teachers discoun-

24

tenance these appeals to love of approbation and self-esteem.   But while
prizes continue to be awarded, can any good reason be given why the name
of the girl should not be published as well as that of the boy ?   He spoke
with scorn, that "we hear of Mrs. President so and so; and committees
and secretaries of the same sex."   But if women can conduct their own
business, by means of presidents and secretaries of their own sex, can he
tell us why they should not ?   They will never make much progress in any
moral movement while they depend upon men to act for them.   Do we
shrink from reading the announcement that Mrs. Somerville is made an
honorary member of a scientific association ?   That Miss Herschel has
made some discoveries, and is prepared to take her equal part in science ?
Or that Miss Mitchell, of Nantucket, has lately discovered a planet, long
looked for ?   I can not conceive why "honor to whom honor is due"
should not be rendered to woman as well as man; nor will it necessarily
exalt her, or foster feminine pride.   This propensity is found alike in
male and female, and it should not be ministered to improperly in either
sex.

In treating upon the affections, the lecturer held out the idea that as
manifested in the sexes they were opposite if not somewhat antagonistic,
and required a union as in chemistry to form a perfect whole.   The simile
appeared to me far from a correct illustration of the true union.   Minds that
can assimilate, spirits that are congenial, attract one another.   It is the
union of similar, not of opposite affections, which is necessary for the
perfection of the marriage bond.   There seemed a want of proper delicacy in his representing man as being bold in the demonstration of the
pure affection of love.   In persons of refinement, true love seeks concealment in man as well as in woman.   I will not enlarge upon the subject,
although it formed so great a part of his lecture.   The contrast drawn
seemed a fallacy, as has much, very much, that has been presented in the
sickly sentimental strains of the poet from age to age.

The question is often asked, "What does woman want, more than she
enjoys ?   What is she seeking to obtain ?   Of what rights is she deprived ?
What privileges are withheld from her ?"   I answer, she asks nothing as
favor, but as right; she wants to be acknowledged a moral, responsible
being.   She is seeking not to be governed by laws in the making of which
she has no voice.   She is deprived of almost every right in civil society,
and is a cipher in the nation, except in the right of presenting a petition.
In religious society her disabilities have greatly retarded her progress.
Her exclusion from the pulpit or ministry, her duties marked out for
her by her equal brother man, subject to creeds, rules, and disciplines
made for her by him, is unworthy her true dignity.

In marriage there is assumed superiority on the part of the husband, and
admitted inferiority with a promise of obedience on the part of the wife.
This subject calls loudly for examination in order that the wrong may be
redressed.   Customs suited to darker ages in Eastern countries are not
binding upon enlightened society.   The solemn covenant of marriage
may be entered into without these lordly assumptions and humiliating
concessions and promises.

There are large Christian denominations who do not recognize such degrading relations of husband and wife. They ask no aid from magistrate or clergyman to legalize or sanctify this union. But acknowledging themselves in the presence of the Highest and invoking His assistance, they come under reciprocal obligations of fidelity and affection, before suitable witnesses. Experience and observation go to prove that there may be as much harmony, to say the least, in such a union, and as great purity and permanence of affection, as can exist where the common ceremony is observed.

The distinctive relations of husband and wife, of father and mother of a family, are sacredly preserved, without the assumption of authority on the one part, or the promise of obedience on the other. There is nothing in such a marriage degrading to woman. She does not compromise her dignity or self-respect; but enters married life upon equal ground, by the side of her husband. By proper education, she understands her duties, physical, intellectual, and moral; and fulfilling these, she is a helpmeet in the true sense of the word.

I tread upon delicate ground in alluding to the institutions of religious associations; but the subject is of so much importance that all which relates to the position of woman should be examined apart from the undue veneration which ancient usage receives.

> "Such dupes are men to custom, and so prone
> To reverence what is ancient, and can plead \
> A course of long observance for its use,
> That even servitude, the worst of ills,
> Because delivered down from sire to son,
> Is kept and guarded as a sacred thing."

So with woman. She has so long been subject to the disabilities and restrictions with which her progress has been embarrassed, that she has become enervated, her mind to some extent paralyzed; and like those still more degraded by personal bondage, she hugs her chains. Liberty is often presented in its true light, but it is liberty for man. I would not go so far, either as regards the abject slave or woman; for in both cases they may be so degraded by the crushing influences around them, that they may not be sensible of the blessings of freedom. Liberty is not less a blessing, because oppression has so long darkened the mind that it can not appreciate it. I would, therefore, urge that woman be placed in such a situation in society, by the recognition of her rights, and have such opportunities for growth and development, as shall raise her from this low, enervated, and paralyzed condition, to a full appreciation of the blessing of entire freedom of mind.

It is with reluctance that I make the demand for the political rights of women, because this claim is so distasteful to the age. Woman shrinks, in the present state of society, from taking any interest in politics. The events of the French Revolution, and the claim for woman's rights, are held up to her as a warning. Let us not look at the excesses of women alone, at that period; but remember that the age was marked with extravagances and wickedness in men as well as women. Political life abounds with these excesses and with shameful outrage. Who knows but that if woman acted her part in governmental affairs, there might be an entire change in the turmoil of political life? It becomes man to speak modestly of his ability to act without her. If woman's judgment were exercised, why might she not aid in making the laws by which she is governed? Lord Brougham remarked that the works of Harriet Martineau upon Political Economy were not excelled by those of any political writer of the present time. The first few chapters of her "Society in America," her views of a Republic, and of government generally, furnish evidence of woman's capacity to embrace subjects of universal interest.

Far be it from me to encourage women to vote, or to take an active part in politics in the present state of our government. Her right to the elective franchise, however, is the same, and should be yielded to her, whether she exercise that right or not. Would that man, too, would have no participation in a government recognizing the life-taking principle; retaliation and the sword. It is unworthy a Christian nation. But when in the diffusion of light and intelligence a Convention shall be called to make regulations for self-government on Christian principles, I can see no good reason why women should not participate in such an assemblage, taking part equally with man.

Professor Walker, of Cincinnati, in his "Introduction to American Law," says: "With regard to political rights, females form a positive exception to the general doctrine of equality. They have no part or lot in the formation or administration of government. They cannot vote or hold office. We require them to contribute their share in the way of taxes to the support of government, but allow them no voice in its direction. We hold them amenable to the laws when made, but allow them no share in making them. This language applied to males would be the exact definition of political slavery; applied to females custom does not teach us so to regard it." Woman, however, is beginning so to regard it.

He further says: "The law of husband and wife, as you gather it from the books, is a disgrace to any civilized nation. The theory of the law degrades the wife almost to the level of slaves. When a woman marries, we call her condition coverture, and speak of her as a *femme covert*. The old writers call the husband baron, and sometimes in plain English, lord. . . . . The merging of her name in that of her husband is emblematic of the fate of all her legal rights. The torch of Hymen serves but to light the pile on which these rights are offered up. The legal theory is, that marriage makes the husband and wife one person, and that person is the husband. On this subject, reform is loudly called for. There is no foundation in reason or expediency for the absolute and slavish subjection of the wife to the husband, which forms the foundation of the present legal relations. Were woman, in point of fact, the abject thing which the law in theory considers her to be when married, she would not be worthy the companionship of man."

I would ask if such a code of laws does not require change? If such a condition of the wife in society does not claim redress? On no good ground can reform be delayed. Blackstone says: "The very being and legal existence of woman is suspended during marriage; incorporated or consolidated into that of her husband under whose protection and cover she performs everything." Hurlbut, in his Essay upon Human Rights, says: "The laws touching the rights of women are at variance with the laws of the Creator. Rights are human rights, and pertain to human beings without distinction of sex. Laws should not be made for man or for woman, but for mankind. Man was not born to command, nor woman to obey. . . . . The law of France, Spain, and Holland, and one of our own States, Louisiana, recognizes the wife's right to property, more than the common law of England. . . . . The laws depriving woman of the right of property are handed down to us from dark and feudal times, and are not consistent with the wiser, better, purer spirit of the age. The wife is a mere pensioner on the bounty of her husband. Her lost rights are appropriated to himself. But justice and benevolence are abroad in our land awakening the spirit of inquiry and innovation; and the Gothic fabric of the British law will fall before it, save where it is based upon the foundation of truth and justice."

May these statements lead you to reflect upon this subject, that you may know what woman's condition is in society, what her restrictions are, and seek to remove them. In how many cases in our country the husband and wife begin life together, and by equal industry and united effort accumulate to themselves a comfortable home. In the event of the death of the wife the household remains undisturbed, his farm or his workshop is not broken up or in any way molested. But when the husband dies he either gives his wife a portion of their joint accumulation, or the law apportions to her a share; the homestead is broken up, and she is dipossessed of that which she earned equally with him; for what she lacked in physical strength she made up in constancy of labor and toil, day and evening. The sons then coming into possession of the property, as has been the custom until of later time, speak of having to keep their mother, when she in reality is aiding to keep them. Where is the justice of this state of things? The change in the law of this State and of New York in relation to the property of the wife, goes to a limited extent toward the redress of these wrongs which are far more extensive and involve much more than I have time this evening to point out.

On no good ground can the legal existence of the wife be suspended during marriage, and her property surrendered to her husband. In the intelligent ranks of society the wife may not in point of fact be so degraded as the law would degrade her; because public sentiment is above the law. Still, while the law stands, she is liable to the disabilities which it imposes. Among the ignorant classes of society, woman is made to bear heavy burdens, and is degraded almost to the level of the slave. There are many instances now in our city, where the wife suffers much from the power of the husband to claim all that she can earn with her own hands. In my intercourse with the poorer class of people, I have known cases of extreme cruelty from the hard earnings of the wife being thus robbed by the husband, and no redress at law.

An article in one of the daily papers lately presented the condition of needle-women in England. There might be a presentation of this class in our own country which would make the heart bleed. Public attention should be turned to this subject in order that avenues of more profitable employment may be opened to women. There are many kinds of business which women, equally with men, may follow with respectability and success. Their talents and energies should be called forth, and their powers brought into the highest exercise. The efforts of women in France are sometimes pointed to in ridicule and sarcasm, but depend upon it, the opening of profitable employment to women in that country is doing much for the enfranchisement of the sex.

In England and America it is not an uncommon thing for a wife to take up the business of her deceased husband and carry it on with success.

Our respected British Consul stated to me a circumstance which occurred some years ago, of an editor of a political paper having died in England; it was proposed to his wife, an able writer, to take the editorial chair. She accepted. The patronage of the paper was greatly increased, and she a short time since retired from her labors with a handsome fortune. In that country, however, the opportunities are by no means general for woman's elevation.

In visiting the public school in London a few years since, I noticed that the boys were employed in linear drawing, and instructed upon the black-board in the higher branches of arithmetic and mathematics; while the girls, after a short exercise in the mere elements of arithmetic, were seated during the bright hours of the morning, stitching wristbands. I asked why there should be this difference made; why the girls too should not have the black-board? The answer was, that they would not probably fill any station in society requiring such knowledge.

The demand for a more extended education will not cease until girls and boys have equal instruction in all the departments of useful knowledge. We have as yet no high-school in this State. The normal school may be a preparation for such an establishment. In the late convention for general education, it was cheering to hear the testimony borne to woman's capabilities for head teachers of the public schools. A resolution there offered for equal salaries to male and female teachers when equally qualified, as practiced in Louisiana, I regret to say, was checked in its passage by Bishop Potter; by him who has done so much for the encouragement of education, and who gave his countenance and influence to that Convention. Still, the fact of such a resolution being offered, augurs a time coming for woman which she may well hail. At the last examination of the public schools in this city, one of the alumni delivered an address on Woman, not as is too common in eulogistic strains, but directing the attention to the injustice done to woman in her position in society in a variety of ways, the unequal wages she receives for her constant toil, etc., presenting facts calculated to arouse attention to the subject.

Women's property has been taxed equally with that of men's to sustain colleges endowed by the States; but they have not been permitted to enter those high seminaries of learning. Within a few years, however, some colleges have been instituted where young women are admitted upon nearly equal terms with young men; and numbers are availing themselves of their long denied rights. This is among the signs of the times, indicative of an advance for women. The book of knowledge is not opened to her in vain. Already is she aiming to occupy important posts of honor and profit in our country. We have three females editors in our State, and some in other States of the Union. Numbers are entering the medical profession; one received a diploma last year; others are preparing for a like result.

Let woman then go on, not asking favors, but claiming as right, the removal of all hindrances to her elevation in the scale of being; let her receive encouragement for the proper cultivation of all her powers, so that she may enter profitably into the active business of life; employing her own hands in ministering to her necessities, strengthening her physical being by proper exercise and observance of the laws of health. Let her not be ambitious to display a fair hand

and to promenade the fashionable streets of our city, but rather, coveting earnestly the best gifts, let her strive to occupy such walks in society as will befit her true dignity in all the relations of life. No fear that she will then transcend the proper limits of female delicacy. True modesty will be as fully preserved in acting out those important vocations, as in the nursery or at the fireside ministering to man's self-indulgence. Then in the marriage union, the independence of the husband and wife will be equal, their dependence mutual, and their obligations reciprocal.

In conclusion, let me say, with Nathaniel P. Willis: "Credit not the old-fashioned absurdity that woman's is a secondary lot, ministering to the necessities of her lord and master! It is a higher destiny I would award you. If your immortality is as complete, and your gift of mind as capable as ours of increase and elevation, I would put no wisdom of mine against God's evident allotment. I would charge you to water the undying bud, and give it healthy culture, and open its beauty to the sun; and then you may hope that when your life is bound up with another, you will go on equally and in a fellowship that shall pervade every earthly interest."

NATIONAL CONVENTION IN PHILADELPHIA.

October 18, 1854, the Fifth National Convention was held in Sansom Street Hall, where a large audience, chiefly of ladies, assembled at an early hour.

At half-past ten o'clock Lucretia Mott made her appearance on the platform, accompanied by several ladies and gentlemen, notably Lucy Stone in Bloomer costume. She was the observed of all observers; the neatness of her attire, and the grace with which she wore it, did much to commend it to public approval. The press remarked that the officers of the Convention were all without bonnets, and that many ladies in the audience had their knitting-work. " A casual visitor," says *The Bulletin*, " would have been impressed with the number and character of this assembly, both among the actors and spectators. Every variety of age, sex, race, color, and costume were here represented. Bloomers were side by side with the mouse-colored gowns and white shawls of the wealthy Quaker dames, and genteelly dressed ladies of the latest Paris fashion."

The house was crowded, and on the steps ascending the platform were seated William Lloyd Garrison and James Mott, side by side with men of the darkest hue. The colored people scattered through the audience seemed quite at their ease, and were evidently received on grounds of perfect equality, which was the subject of much comment by outsiders.

Mrs. Frances D. Gage, President of the last Convention at Cleveland, called the assembly to order, and read

THE CALL.

In accordance with a vote passed at the adjournment of the Woman's Rights Convention held in Cleveland, Ohio, in October, 1853, the Fifth National Convention will be held in Philadelphia, October 18th, to continue three days. The subjects for consideration will be the Equal Right of Woman to all the advantages of education, literary, scientific, artistic; to full equality in all business avocations, industrial, commercial, professional; briefly, all the rights that belong to her as a citizen.

This wide range of subjects for discussion can not fail to awaken the attention of all classes; hence we invite all persons irrespective of sex or color to take part in the deliberations of the Convention, and thus contribute to the progress of truth and the redemption of humanity.

On behalf of the Central Committee,

PAULINA WRIGHT DAVIS, *President.*
ANTOINETTE L. BROWN, *Secretary.*

The following officers were chosen for the Convention:

PRESIDENT.—Ernestine L. Rose, of New York.

VICE-PRESIDENTS.—Lucretia Mott, Philadelphia; Frances D. Gage, Missouri; Thomas Wentworth Higginson, Massachusetts; Martha C. Wright, New York; Thomas Garrett, Delaware; Hannah Tracy Cutler, Illinois; Robert Purvis; Pennsylvania; John O. Wattles, Indiana; Marenda B. Randall, Vermont; George Sunter, Canada.

SECRETARIES.—Joseph A. Dugdale, Abby Kimber, Hannah M. Darlington.

BUSINESS COMMITTEE.—Lucy Stone, William Lloyd Garrison, Myra Townsend, Mary P. Wilson, Sarah Pugh, Lydia Mott, Mary Grew.

FINANCE COMMITTEE.—Susan B. Anthony, James Mott, Ruth Dugdale, Rebecca Plumbly.

Mrs. ROSE, on taking the chair, said:

There is one argument which in my estimation is the argument of arguments, why woman should have her rights; not on account of expediency, not on account of policy, though these too show the reasons why she should have her rights; but we claim—I for one claim, and I presume all our friends claim—our rights on the broad ground of human rights; and I for one again will say, I promise not how we shall use them. I will no more promise how we shall use our rights than man has promised before he obtained them, how he would use them. We all know that rights are often abused; and above all things have human rights in this country been abused, from the very fact that they have been withheld from half of the community.

By human rights we mean natural rights, and upon that ground we claim our rights, and upon that ground they have already been conceded by the Declaration of Independence, in that first great and immutable truth which is proclaimed in that instrument, " that all men are created equal," and that therefore all are entitled to " certain inalienable rights, among which are life, liberty, and the pursuit of happiness." Our claims are based upon that great and immutable truth, the rights of all humanity. For is woman not included in that phrase, "all men are created free and equal"? Is she not included in that expression? Tell us, ye men of the nation, ay, ye wise law-makers and law-breakers of the nation, whether woman is not included in that great Declaration of Independence? And if she is, what right has man to deprive her of her natural and inalienable rights? It is natural, it is inherent, it is inborn, it is a thing of which no one can justly deprive her. Upon that just and eternal basis do we found our claims for our rights; political, civil, legal, social, religious, and every other.

But, at the outset, we claim our equal political rights with man, not only from that portion of the Declaration of Independence, but from another, equally well-established principle in this country, that "taxation and representation are inseparable." Woman, everybody knows, is taxed; and if she is taxed, she ought to be represented.

I will simply here throw out a statement of these principles upon which our claims are based; and I trust each separate resolution will be taken up by this Convention, fully canvassed and commented upon, so as to show it not only an abstract right, but a right which can be wisely made practical.

Again, it is acknowledged in this country, and it is eternally true, that "all the just powers of government are derived from the consent of the governed." If so, then, as woman is a subject of government, she ought to have a voice in enacting the laws. If her property is taxed to maintain government, she ought to have a voice in forming that government. If she has to pay taxes to maintain government, she ought to have a voice in saying how those taxes shall be applied.

On these grounds we make our claims, on natural, humane, eternal, and well-recognized laws and principles of this republic. On these grounds we ask man to meet us, and meet us in the spirit of inquiry, in the spirit of candor and honesty, as rational human beings ought to meet each other, face to face, and adduce arguments, if they can, to convince us that we are not included in that great Declaration of Independence; that although it is a right principle that taxation and representation are inseparable, yet woman ought to be taxed, and ought not to be represented; and that although it is an acknowledged principle that all just power of government is derived from the consent of the governed, yet woman should be governed without her consent. Let them meet us fairly and openly; let them meet us like rational men, men who appreciate their own freedom, and we will hear them. If they can convince us that we are wrong, we will give up our claims; but if we can convince them that we are right in claiming our rights, as they are in claiming theirs, then we expect them in a spirit of candor and honesty to acknowledge it.

Joseph Dugdale read several letters, which, as usual, seemed to be something of a bore to the audience. When he finished, Lucretia Mott suggested that if there were any more lengthy epistles to be read, it would be well for the secretaries to look them over, and omit all that in their wisdom might not be worth reading.

Lucy Stone, from the Business Committee, read a series of resolutions,* and as some one from the audience called. "Louder!" she re-

---

* See Appendix.

marked that if ladies would keep their bonnets tied down over their ears, they must not ask others to find lungs of sufficient power to penetrate the heavy pasteboard and millinery over them. She spoke briefly on the resolutions, and the steadily increasing interest in the subject of woman's rights.

Hannah Tracy Cutler gave a report of Illinois, Frances Dana Gage of Missouri, and Susan B. Anthony of New York.

Thomas Wentworth Higginson, of Massachusetts, said he had a matter of business to present. Mrs. Paulina Wright Davis being too ill to attend the Convention, Mr. Higginson read a letter from her sister, Mary K. Spaulding, suggesting the establishment of a newspaper in the city of New York as " the national organ " of the Woman's Rights movement. He doubted the wisdom of such a step, and after setting forth the expense of a central organ and the great danger of its creating a schism, he offered the following resolutions :

Resolved, That in the opinion of this Convention it is not expedient, at present, to establish a newspaper as The National Organ of the Woman's Rights Movement.

Resolved, That it is expedient to appoint a Committee who shall provide for the preparation and publication, in widely circulated journals, facts and arguments relating to the cause.

Mrs. Mott approved of the resolutions, and said they had arrived at a similar conclusion in the Syracuse Convention ; she fully concurred in the views of Mr. Higginson.

William Lloyd Garrison replied, that if organization for any good cause be right, it was right for this. Every reform movement needs an organ of its own. And this cause needs a paper of the most radical character ; that shall make no compromises with popular prejudices ; far above the paralyzing influences of Church and State.

Mrs. Mott said she did not oppose organization, but was in favor of individual freedom and responsibility. *The Liberator*, Mr. Garrison's paper, has done far more good than *The Anti-Slavery Standard*, the organ of the Anti-Slavery movement.

Mr. Garrison said *The Liberator* was not simply an anti-slavery paper, but an advocate of general reform.

Remarks were made on this point by Elizabeth Paxton, Susan H. Cox, George P. Davis, and George Sunter, of Canada.

Lucy Stone advocated the resolutions; her experience in the anti-slavery cause had taught her a lesson of wisdom for this movement. We are rich in principle and enthusiasm, but not in silver and gold, and therefore should avoid taking on our shoulders a national organ. Widely circulated journals are now open to us, in which we can express our opinions with freedom and without expense. There is nothing so strong as individual purpose and freedom to carry it out. The papers established by Mrs. Davis and Mrs. Bloomer are good, and she hoped the friends would give generously to their support.

The resolutions were unanimously adopted, and Elizabeth Cady Stanton, of New York; Paulina Wright Davis, of Rhode Island; Thomas Wentworth Higginson and Lucy Stone, of Massachusetts; and Oliver Johnson, of New York, were appointed as the Committee to superintend the work.

Lucy Stone said she had a new item of business to propose. She knew that those who came to these Conventions went away feeling stronger and better. She held in her hand a pamphlet containing five tracts; one from Wendell Phillips, one from Theodore Parker, one from *The Westminster Review*, by Mrs. John Stuart Mill, one from Mr. Higginson, and last, but not least, one from Mrs. C. I. H. Nichols, which should be distributed. They were able papers, and all interested in the movement should exert themselves to circulate them. The people only wanted light.

Another mode of disseminating the principles was by stories illustrating the wrongs of women under the present laws. The right of a woman to what she earns; to the custody of her person; to the guardianship of her children, and all of her other rights, should be illustrated in fiction. Prizes should be offered for the best stories upon these subjects. She pledged herself to raise $500 for the purpose. She pointed to " Uncle Tom's Cabin " to show what fiction could accomplish, and trusted that action would be taken upon the subject before the Convention adjourned.

Mr. Garrison arose to say " ditto to Lucy Stone." In regard to " Uncle Tom's Cabin," it was known that Mrs. Stowe was induced to write it from a request of Dr. Bailey, of *The National Era*, to write a story for his paper. And he thought that such an offer might now call forth something to aid the cause of woman. He praised the tracts to which Miss Stone alluded.

The President appointed Wendell Phillips, Elizabeth Cady Stanton, and Mary Channing Higginson, the Committee on prize tracts.*

Mrs. Tracy Cutler read an invitation from the Female Medical College for the members of the Convention to visit that institution and attend its lectures, and took the opportunity to compliment Philadelphia as being the first city, not only in the United States, but in the world, to establish a Medical College for Women.

Dr. Ann Preston gave an interesting report of The Woman's Medical College; of all the persecutions women had encountered in securing a medical education and entering that profession. She noted the signs of a growing liberality with satisfaction.

The Rev. Henry Grew, of Philadelphia, then appeared upon the platform, and said he was sorry to differ from the general tone of the speakers present, but he felt it to be his duty to give his views on the questions under consideration. His opinions as to woman's rights and duties were based on the Scriptures.

---

* In accordance with this plan Matilda Joslyn Gage prepared a story, entitled " The Household," treating different phases of woman's wrongs, and presented it to the Committee. But as nothing was ever done to carry out the proposition, the manuscript was returned to the author, and slumbers in her garret with other rejected manuscripts.

He quoted numerous texts to show that it was clearly the will of God that man should be superior in power and authority to woman; and asserted that no lesson is more plainly and frequently taught in the Bible, than woman's subjection.

Mrs. CUTLER replied at length, and skillfully turned every text he had quoted directly against the reverend gentleman, to the great amusement of the audience. She showed that man and woman were a simultaneous creation, with equal power and glory on their heads, and that dominion over the fowl of the air, the fish of the sea, and every creeping thing on the earth was given to *them*, and not to man alone. The time has come for woman to read and interpret Scripture for herself; too long have we learned God's will from the lips of man and closed our eyes on the great book of nature, and the safer teaching of our own souls. It is a pity that those who would recommend the Bible as the revealed will of the all-wise and benevolent Creator, should uniformly quote it on the side of tyranny and oppression. I think we owe it to our religion and ourselves to wrest it from such hands, and proclaim the beautiful spirit breathed through all its commands and precepts, instead of dwelling so much on isolated texts that have no application to our day and generation.

Mrs. MOTT said: It is not Christianity, but priestcraft that has subjected woman as we find her. The Church and State have been united, and it is well for us to see it so. We have had to bear the denunciations of these reverend (irreverend) clergymen, as in New York, of late. But if we look to their authority to see how they expound the text, quite likely we shall find a new reading. Why, when John Chambers returned to Philadelphia from the World's Temperance Convention at New York, he gave notice that he would give an address, and state the rights of woman as defined by the Bible. Great allowance has been made by some of the speakers in this Convention, on account of his ignorance, and certainly this was charitable. But I heard this discourse. I heard him bring up what is called the Apostolic prohibition, and the old Eastern idea of the subjection of wives; but he kept out of view some of the best ideas in the Scriptures.

Blame is often attached to the position in which woman is found. I blame her not so much as I pity her. So circumscribed have been her limits that she does not realize the misery of her condition. Such dupes are men to custom that even servitude, the worst of ills, comes to be thought a good, till down from sire to son it is kept and guarded as a sacred thing. Woman's existence is maintained by sufferance. The veneration of man has been misdirected, the pulpit has been prostituted, the Bible has been ill-used. It has been turned over and over as in every reform. The temperance people have had to feel its supposed denunciations. Then the anti-slavery, and now this reform has met, and still continues to meet, passage after passage of the Bible, never intended to be so used. Instead of taking the truths of the Bible in corroboration of the right, the practice has been, to turn over its pages to find example and authority for the wrong, for the existing abuses of society. For the usage of drinking wine, the example of the sensualist Solomon, is always appealed to. In reference to our reform, even admitting that Paul did mean preach, when he used that term, he did not say that the recommendation of that time was to be applicable to the churches of all after-time. We have been so long pinning our faith on other people's sleeves that we ought to begin examining these things daily ourselves, to see whether they are so; and we should find on comparing text with text, that a very different construction might be put upon them. Some of our early Quakers not seeing how far they were to be carried, became Greek and Hebrew scholars, and they found that the text would bear other translations as well as other constructions. All Bible commentators agree that the Church of Corinth, when the apostle wrote, was in a state of great confusion. They fell into discussion and controversy; and in order to quiet this state of things and bring the Church to greater propriety, the command was given out that women should keep silence, and it was not permitted them to speak, except by asking questions at home. In the same epistle to the same Church, Paul gave express directions how women shall prophesy, which he defines to be preaching, "speaking to men," for "exhortation and comfort." He recognized them in prophesying and praying. The word translated servant, is applied to a man in one part of the Scripture, and in another it is translated minister. Now that same word you will find might be applied to Phebe, a deaconess. That text was quoted in the sermon of John Chambers, and he interlarded it with a good many of his ideas, that women should not be goers abroad, and read among other things " that their wives were to be teachers." But properly translated would be " deaconesses."

It is not so Apostolic to make the wife subject to the husband as many have supposed. It has been done by law and public opinion since that time. There has been a great deal said about sending missionaries over to the East to convert women who are immolating themselves on the funeral pile of their husbands. I know this may be a very good work, but I would ask you to look at it. How many women are there now immolated upon the shrine of superstition and priestcraft, in our very midst, in the assumption that man only has a right to the pulpit, and that if a woman enters it she disobeys God; making woman believe in the misdirection of her vocation, and that it is of divine authority that she should be thus bound. Believe it not, my sisters. In this same epistle the word "prophesying" should be "preaching"—"preaching godliness," etc. On the occasion of the first miracle which it is said Christ wrought, a woman went before Him and said, "Whatsoever he biddeth you do, that do." The woman of Samaria said, " Come and see the man who told me all the things that ever I did."

These things are worthy of note. I do not want to dwell too much upon Scripture authority. We too often bind ourselves by authorities rather than by the truth. We are infidel to truth in seeking examples to overthrow it. The very first act of note that is mentioned when the disciples and apostles went forth after Jesus was removed from them, was the bringing up of an ancient prophecy to prove that they were right in the position they assumed on that occasion, when men and women were gathered together on the holy day of Pentecost, when every man heard and saw those wonderful works which are recorded. Then Peter stood forth—some one has said that Peter made a great mistake in quoting the prophet Joel—but he stated that " the time is come, this day is fulfilled the prophecy, when it is said, I will pour out my spirit upon all flesh, and your sons and your daughters shall prophesy,'' etc.—the language of the Bible is beautiful in its repetition—" upon my servants and my handmaidens I will pour out my spirit and they shall prophesy." Now can anything be clearer than that?

Rev. HENRY GREW again quoed Scripture in reply to Mrs. Mott, and said the coming of Christ into the world did not restore man and woman to the original condition of our first parents. If the position assumed by the women be true, then must the Divine Word from Genesis to Revelation be set aside as untrue, that woman may be relieved from the, perhaps, unfortunate limitations that hold her back in this age of progress.

Mr. HIGGINSON related a story of an old Methodist clergyman who by chance stepped into a Quaker meeting where he heard a woman speaking, which so shocked him that he thought Anti-Christ was now bound to rule. He went home sad. He had four daughters, one of whom, at the age of sixteen, in a few minutes opened the eyes of his understanding after he had groped in darkness a long time, by showing him a passage in the Testament describing a friend of Paul's at Phillippi, who had four daughters that prophesied. This girl referred her father to the Greek Testament, and showed him that the original word, properly translated, means to preach instead of to prophesy. Before we resort to Scriptural texts we should be careful to ascertain that they are right, or all arguments founded on them must fall.

Mr. GREW did not consider that the story of the four daughters invalidated his position.

Mr. GARRISON said: Consulting the Bible for opinions as to woman's rights, is of little importance to the majority of this Convention. We have gone over the whole ground, and placed our cause upon the decrees of nature. We *know* that man and woman are equal in the sight of God. We know that texts and books are of no importance, and have no taste for the discussion of dry doctrinal points.

But with the American people the case is different. The masses believe the Bible directly from God; that it decrees the inequality of the sexes; and that settles the question. There is no doubt that there are many persons connected with the Protestant churches who would be with the movement were it not for the supposed Bible difficulty. They shudder at anything they think against the Bible, as against the will of God. Take away this incubus, and these persons would experience a change in their views; they would be with us.

In regard to Mr. Grew, Mr. G. said he had long known him and loved him. He was a man of purity and charity, and he was glad he had given his views. Yet this kindly man did not stand upon a solid foundation.

Why go to the Bible to settle this question? As a nation, we have practically ignored the Bible. The assertion of the equality and inalienability of the rights of man, in the Declaration of Independence, includes the whole of the human race. He would never attempt to prove to an American the right of any man to liberty. He asserted the fact; and considered that in holding slaves while they proclaimed liberty to all men, the American people were hypocrites and tyrants. Mr. Grew goes to St. Paul to prove that woman is not equal to man. Why go to the Bible? What question was ever settled by the Bible? What question of theology or any other department? None that I ever heard of! With this same version of the Bible, and the same ability to read it, we find that it has filled all Christendom with theological confusion. All are Ishmaelites; each man's hand against his neighbor.

The human mind is greater than any book. The mind sits in judgment on every book. If there be truth in the book, we take it; if error, we discard it. Why refer this to the Bible? In this country, the Bible has been used to support slavery and capital punishment; while in the old countries, it has been quoted to sustain all manner of tyranny and persecution. All reforms are anti-Bible. We must look at all things rationally. We find women endowed with certain capacities, and it is of no importance if any book denies her such capacities. Would Mr. Grew say that woman can not preach, in the face of such a preacher as LUCRETIA MOTT ?

Mrs. MOTT begged leave to substitute friend Grew's own daughter, Mary Grew, who has already spoken on this platform !! and said, Mr. Grew himself does not take all the Bible as inspiration, in which most of the speakers concurred. She expressed her attachment to the Scriptures, and said many excellent lessons could be learned from them. She showed the misinterpretations of the texts quoted by Mr. Grew and others against the equality of the sexes. Mr. Grew does not take the Bible for his guide, altogether. Mrs. Mott then quoted St. Paul in regard to marriage, and said : Why in opposition to that text has Mr. Grew married a second time? It was because he did not really believe that the Scriptures were entirely inspired.

EMMA R. COE made a few remarks on the position of the clergy generally toward this reform, the most beneficent in its results of any, man has ever yet been called upon to consider. We often hear it remarked that woman owes so much to Christianity. It can not be the Christianity that the clergy have proclaimed on our platform. From them we hear only of woman's degradation and subjection. We have certainly nothing to be thankful for if such are the principles Christ came into the world to declare; the subjection of one-half of the race to the other half, as far as we are concerned, is no improvement upon the religions of all nations and ages.

At the close of this protracted discussion on the Bible position of woman, the following resolutions, presented by Mr. Garrison, were unanimously adopted :

Resolved, That while remembering and gladly acknowledging the exceptional cases which exist to the contrary, we feel it a duty to declare in regard to the sacred cause which has brought us together, that the most determined opposition it encounters is from the clergy generally, whose teachings of the Bible are intensely inimical to the equality of woman with man.

Resolved, That whatever any book may teach, the rights of no human being are dependent upon or modified thereby, but are equal, absolute, essential, inalienable in the person of every member of the human family, without regard to sex, race, or clime.

JOHN SIDNEY JONES made a few remarks on the monoply of the pulpit.

SUSAN B. ANTHONY wished to remind the friends, before separating, of one practical measure to be considered in the advancement of our noble enterprise. For the purpose of holding Conventions, circulating tracts and petitions, giving prizes for good stories, supporting newspapers and agents, the first great requisite is money, and I hope every one present will contribute generously to help us carry on this grand reform.

Mr. GARRISON seconded Miss Anthony's demand for " the sinews of war." He said we Americans are a theoretical people, and we are also a practical peo ple. If the women intend to kn ck at the door of every State house to demand their rights, the question must be argued in a practical way with facts and statistics.

When I undertook to have the gallows abolished in Massachusetts, I asked the Committee of the Legislature if they wanted a certain number of Bible-texts quoted on each side of the question, they said, "No, we want facts and statistics; we do not ask the opinions of Moses and Aaron on this point, but the result of human experience in the punishment of crime." So in this case; Legislatures will not ask for nor appreciate Bible arguments; they will ask for facts as to woman's achievements in education, industry, and practical usefulness.

JOSEPH DUGDALE, whose special concern always seemed to be the action of dead men on this question, said it had been his fortune to be present at the making of the last wills and testaments of many men, and he never knew of a case where a dying husband would practically admit that his wife was his equal. He stated a case in which a husband of his acquaintance proposed to leave a large property, the inheritance and accumulation of his wife's labors, to *her* as long as she remained his widow, and then to divide it among *his* family relatives. And yet this husband claimed to have great admiration and affection for this woman whom he would deliberately rob of her inheritance from her own father. The magnanimity of man passes all understanding!

Mrs. PRINCE, a colored woman, invoked the blessing of God upon the noble women engaged in this enterprise, and said she understood woman's wrongs better than woman's rights, and gave some of her own experiences to illustrate the degradation of her sex in slavery. On a voyage to the West Indies the vessel was wrecked, and she was picked up and taken to New Orleans. Going up the Mississippi she saw the terrible suffering of a cargo of slaves on board and on the plantations along the shores. On her return voyage, attached to the steamboat was a brig containing several hundred slaves, among them a large number of young quadroon girls with infants in their arms as fair as any lady in this room.

MATILDA JOSLYN GAGE spoke at length of the brilliant record of women in the past in every department of human activity—in art, science, literature, invention; of their heroism and patriotism in time of war, and their industry and endurance in many equally trying emergencies in time of peace. Woman has so fully proved her equality with man in every position she has filled, that it is too late now for clergymen on our platform to remand us to the subjection of the women of Corinth centuries ago. We have learned too well the lessons of liberty taught in our revolution to accept now the position of slaves.

Mrs. TRACY CUTLER: It would appear, after all, that we women are placed pretty much in the condition of the veriest slave. We must prove our own humanity by exhibiting our skill in work. We must bring forth our own samples; put them, as it were, on the auction-block, and thus make our claim to equality of rights a matter of dollars and cents. Is it here only that woman can touch man's sympathy? She then described the degraded condition of women in Europe, and particularly in London, where poverty and the tyranny of man have driven women to despair, until they were forced to prostitute their own bodies to procure bread. This vice, horribly revolting as it is, seems to go hand in hand with intemperance. She did not wish women to go into the field to be yoked with mules, or to turn scavenger, to pick up rags and crusts in tne streets to carry home in their aprons. Men bring the elements to their aid, and we wish women to do the same. She then adverted to the difference in the labor of the kitchen and other pursuits open to women. Let the printer advertise for two girls to set type, and a hundred applications will be made, while women for the kitchen are very scarce. The reason for this is, that all other kinds of work are better paid. When woman's labor is justly remunerated and equally respected in all departments of industry, there will be no such difference in the supply of help for the factory, shop, and kitchen.

FRANCES D. GAGE said: The reason why the work of the kitchen is looked upon as degrading, is because the girl is never taken by the hand. Where are your philanthropic ladies who assist her? Where is she to go when her work is done? Does she sit in the same room with you? Does she eat at the same table? No, to your shame, she is confined to the basement and the garret. It is not so much because the pay for kitchen labor is not so good, as it is chiefly because of the public opinion that they are employed to *serve.* It is true that there are many who will take a quarter off the wages of a girl to put a new bow on their own bonnets. The men are not to be blamed for this; they have enough sins to answer for.

Mrs. COE said: It would afford women great pleasure to be able to pay their own expenses on pleasure excursions and to the concert-room, instead of being always compelled to allow the gentlemen to foot the bills for them. Women must have equal pay for equal work. Among the Quakers the sexes stand on an equality, and everything moves on smoothly and happily.

SUSAN B. ANTHONY, after relating several instances of the injustice of the laws that made the wife subject to the husband, said: And all these wrongs are to be redressed by appeals to the State Legislatures. In New York and Ohio the women had already commenced with every prospect of success. Thousands of petitions had been sent into both Legislatures asking for suffrage and equal property rights, and their Committees had granted hearings to our representatives—Caroline M. Severance, in Ohio; Ernestine L. Rose, Rev. William Henry Channing, Elizabeth Cady Stanton, Rev. Antoinette L. Brown, and herself, in New York. And closed with an earnest appeal to the women of every State to petition, PETITION, remembering that "what is worth having is worth asking for," and that "who would be free must themselves strike the blow."

Frances D. Gage moved that the next National Convention be held at Cincinnati, Ohio. A gentlemen suggested Washington, to which Mr. Garrison replied, "We shall go there by and by."* After discussion by Mrs. Mott, Mrs. Rose, and others, the motion was unanimously adopted. Mrs. Gage then spoke of the Press of the city; its faithful reports of the proceedings of the Convention, and moved a vote of thanks. Edward M. Davis begged Mrs. Gage to accept as a substitute the following resolutions:

Resolved, That the thanks of this Convention are due, and are hereby conveyed, to Mrs. Ernestine L. Rose, of New York, for the courtesy, impartiality, and dignity with which she has presided over its proceedings.

---

* The first National Convention held in Washington was in January, 1869.

25

Resolved, That in the crowded and intelligent audiences which have attended the sessions of this Convention; in the earnest attention given to its proceedings from the commencement to its close; in the fair reports of the Press of the city, and in the spirit of harmony and fraternity which has prevailed amongst its members, we see evidence of the rapid progress of our cause, and find incitement to renewed and more earnest efforts in its behalf.

Thus closed another most successful Convention. Notwithstanding an admission fee of ten cents during the day and twenty-five at night, the audiences grew larger every session, until the last evening the spacious hall, aisles, stairs, and all available standing-room, was densely packed, and hundreds went away unable to get in.

Let us remember that behind the chief actors in these Conventions, there stands in each State, a group of women of stern moral principle, large experience, refinement and cultivation, filling with honor the more private walks of life, who, by their sympathy, hospitality, and generous contributions, are the great sources of support and inspiration to those on the platform, who represent the ideas they hold sacred, whose tongues and pens proclaim their thoughts. Among such in Pennsylvania, let us ever remember Sarah Pugh, Mary Ann McClintock, Elizabeth Phillips, Anna and Adeline Thomson, Abby and Gertrude Kimber, Margaretta Forten, Harriet Forten Purvis, Hannah M. Darlington, Dinah Mendenhall, Sarah Pierce, Elizabeth and Sarah Miller, and Ruth Dugdale. When success shall at last crown our efforts, in according due praise to those who have achieved the victory, such names as these must not be forgotten.

Alice Bradley Neal, of Philadelphia, ridiculed this Woman's Rights Convention in her husband's* paper, and Jane Grey Swisshelm indignantly replied in her *Pittsburgh Saturday Visitor* as follows:

Mrs. Neal can not be ignorant that the principal object of the Convention, and all the agitation about woman's rights, is to secure to the toiling millions of her own sex a just reward for their labor; to save them from the alternative of prostitution, starvation, or incessant life-destroying toil; and yet the whole subject furnishes her with material for scorn and merriment! Tell it not in Gath! Publish it not in the streets of Askelon, lest the sons of the Phillistines rejoice that one of the daughters of Eve, beautiful and gentle, throws down her knitting-pins, and tries her strength to wield the hammer of old Vulcan to aid them in forging fetters for the wrists of her unfortunate sisters. We would that it had been some one else than the gentle Alice Neal who had volunteered to soil her white hands and sweat her fair face, laboring in such a blacksmith-shop.

---

* Joseph C. Neal.

While ever and anon during the last forty years Mrs. Swisshelm has seized some of these *dilettante* literary women with her metaphysical tweezers, and held them up to scorn for their ridicule of the woman suffrage conventions, yet in her own recently published work in her mature years, she vouchsafes no words of approval for those who have inaugurated the greatest movement of the centuries. She complains that in some of the woman suffrage conventions she attended, there was not a strict observance of parliamentary rules, and that the resolutions and speeches were unworthy the occasion. Yet the only time Mrs. Swisshelm ever honored our platform at a National Convention, her speech was far below the level of most of the others, and the resolutions she offered were so verbose and irrevelant, that the Committee declined to present them to the Convention.

It is quite evident from her last pronunciamento that she has no just appreciation of the importance and dignity of our demand for justice and equality. A soldier without a leg is a fact so much more readily understood, than all women without ballots, and his loss so much more readily comprehended and supplied, that we can hardly blame any one for doing the work of the hour, rather than struggling a life-time for an idea. Hence it is not a matter of surprise that most women are more readily enlisted in the suppression of evils in the concrete, than in advocating the principles that underlie them in the abstract, and thus ultimately doing the broader and more lasting work. On this ground we can excuse the author of "Half a Century" for giving the reader one hundred and twenty-five pages of her own work in hospitals and three to the Woman Suffrage movement, but considering the tone of the three pages, the advocates of the measure should be thankful she gave no more.

Mrs. Swisshelm's contempt is only surpassed by Mrs. Hale's "Jeremiad" over the infidelity of the noble leader of our movement. For a woman so thoroughly politic and time-serving, who, unlike the great master she professed to follow, never identified herself with one of the unpopular reforms of her day, whose pen never by any chance slipped outside the prescribed literary line of safety, to cheer the martyrs to truth in her own generation; lamentations from such a source over Lucretia Mott, are presumptuous and profane. If such a life of self-sacrifice and devotion to the best interests of humanity; such courage to stand alone, to do and say the right, 'mid persecution, violence and mobs; such charity and faithfulness in every relation of life, as daughter, sister, wife, mother, and friend; such calm declining years and peaceful death could all be realized without a

belief in the creed of Sarah Josepha Hale ; the philosophical conclusion is that there may be some Divine light and love outside of
Mrs. Hale's horizon ; that her shibboleth may after all not be the
true measure for the highest Christian graces.

Sarah J. Hale, shuddering over the graves of such women as Harriet Martineau, Frances Wright, Mary Wollstonecroft, George Sand,
George Eliot and Lucretia Mott, might furnish a subject for an
artist to represent as "bigotry weeping over the triumphs of
truth."

Nevertheless, as Mrs. Hale lived in Pennsylvania forty years, the
women of that State may rejoice in the fact that in her great work,
"Woman's Record," she has given "Sketches of all the distinguished
women from the Creation to A.D. 1868"; a labor for which our
sex owe her a debt of gratitude. To exhume nearly seventeen hundred women from oblivion, classify them, and set forth their distinguished traits of character, was indeed an herculean labor. This
is a valuable book of reference for the girls of to-day. When our
opponents depreciate the achievements of woman they can turn to
the "Woman's Record" and find grand examples of all the cardinal
virtues, of success in art, science, literature, and government.

In Jane Grey Swisshelm, Pennsylvania can boast a successful
editor of a liberal political newspaper during the eventful years of
our anti-slavery struggle. *The Pittsburgh Saturday Visitor* was
established Jan. 20, 1848. It was owned and edited by Mrs. Swisshelm for some years; merged into *The Family Journal and Visitor*
in 1852, in which she was co-editor until 1857, when she removed
to Minnesota. In spite of a few idiosyncrasies, Mrs. Swisshelm is a
noble woman, and her influence has been for good in her day and
generation. However much we may differ from her in some points,
we must concede that she is a strong, pointed writer.

Among the editors of Pennsylvania, Anna E. McDowell deserves mention. In *The Una* of January, 1855, we find the following :

THE WOMAN'S ADVOCATE.

We have received the first number of a paper bearing the above name.
It is a fair, handsome sheet, seven columns in width, edited by Miss
Anna E. McDowell, in Philadelphia. It claims to be an independent
paper. Its design is not to press woman's right to suffrage, but to present her wrongs, and plead for their redress. It is owned by a joint
stock company of women, and is printed and all the work done by
women. We most heartily bid it God-speed, for the great need of woman
now is work, work, that she may eat honest bread.

Miss McDowell continued her paper se/eral years, and has ever since been a faithful correspondent in many journals, and now edits a " Woman's Department " in *The Philadelphia Sunday Republic.* She pleads eloquently for the redress of all the wrongs of humanity. Jails, prisons, charitable institutions, the oppression of women and children, the laborer, the Indian, have all in turn been subjects of her impartial pen.

Philadelphia was the first city in this country to open her retail stores to girls as clerks, and among the first to welcome them as type-setters in the printing offices.

In the city press, from 1849 to 1854, we find the following announcements, which show the general agitation on woman's position :

The Pennsylvania Freeman : " A Discourse on Woman," to be delivered by Lucretia Mott, at the Assembly Buildings, December 17, 1849.

Lectures by Elizabeth Oakes Smith, April 6, 8, and 10, 1853, on " Manhood," " Womanhood," " Humanity."

North American and United States Gazette : Lucretia Mott will deliver a lecture on the " Medical Education of Woman," February 2, 1853.

Horace Mann will lecture on " Woman," February 3, 1853.

Philadelphia Public Ledger, January 20, 1854: Lucy Stone will deliver a lecture on " Woman's Rights," at Musical Fund Hall, Saturday evening, January 21.

April 12, 1854: Mrs. Ernestine L. Rose will lecture on Thursday evening, April 13, at Spring Garden Institute, on " The Education and Influence of Woman " ; and on Friday evening, April 14th, at Sansom Street Hall, on " The Legal Disabilities of Woman." Tickets, 25 cents.

WOMAN'S MEDICAL COLLEGE OF PENNSYLVANIA.

In September, 1850, in a rented building, No. 229 Arch Street, Philadelphia, the College began its first session with six pupils; others were added before the class graduated, so that it then numbered eight:—Hannah E. Longshore, Ann Preston, Phebe W. May, Susanna H. Ellis, Anna M. Longshore, Pennsylvania ; Martha M. Laurin, Massachusetts ; Angonette A. Hunt, New York ; Frances G. Mitchell, England. Since its foundation, the " Woman's Medical College of Pennsylvania " has prospered, and on its lists of graduates we see, among other familiar names, those of Dr. Laura Ross Wolcott (1856), Dr. Mary J. Scarlett Dixon (1857), and Dr. Emeline H. Cleveland (1855).

Chief among those interested in placing the medical education of woman on a sound foundation was Ann Preston. The " Woman's

Medical College of Pennsylvania " was the first ever chartered for this purpose, and Dr. Preston early became identified with its interests. She was one of its first students, and a graduate at its first commencement. After the didactic teaching of the regular college course was well established, each year showed to her more clearly the necessity for clinical and hospital instruction, since its students were denied such advantages in other places; and to Dr. Preston's thorough appreciation of this need may be traced the very origin of the Woman's Hospital in Philadelphia. Speaking of her efforts in this direction, she says: " I went to every one who I thought would give me either money or influence." She was liberally assisted by many noble and true-hearted men and women, and at last raised sufficient funds, obtained the charter, found competent men and women willing to serve as Managers, and skillful physicians who would act on a Consulting Board; and, when the Hospital was opened, was herself appointed one of the Managers, Corresponding Secretary, and Consulting Physician—offices which she held till her death, April 18, 1872.

At the same time, she was serving with equal fidelity and ability the College whose advancement had so long been one of the chief interests of her life. For nineteen years she had been one of its Professors, for six years Dean of the Faculty, and for four years a member of its Board of Corporators. She lived long enough to see the fruits of her labors, and to foresee to some extent the position which both College and Hospital would hold in the medical world. And when, after her death, her will was published, the friends of the College and Hospital found that both institutions had been remembered by endowments.

Almost contemporary in length of days with the Medical College is another useful institution, The Philadelphia School of Design for Women, which began its corporate existence the first Monday of November, 1853. There had previously been a class for women in connection with the Franklin Institute, and this school was its further development. It was mainly supported by contributions, the scholars' fees paying merely for the coal, gas, and other necessaries of the house. The management of the institution was vested in a Board of twelve Directors, elected annually, and a Board of twelve Lady Managers, elected by the Board of Directors at the first stated meeting after the election; these ladies disburse the money received at the school, and also that appropriated monthly by the Directors. It is noticeable in the first report of the School of Design for Women, that men held the leading positions and received the highest salaries, but that has since been changed.

That there was no organized action in this State, no woman suffrage association formed, until after the war, was undoubtedly due to the fact that the same women were prominent in both the antislavery and woman's rights movements. And as Pennsylvania bordered on three slave States, the escape of fugitives and their innumerable trials in the courts, just as the whole system was on the eve of dissolution, compelled the Philadelphia friends to incessant vigilance in the care and concealment of the unhappy victims. Thus their hands and thoughts were wholly occupied until the first gun at Sumter proclaimed freedom in the United States.

For collecting many of the facts contained in this chapter we are indebted to Julia and Rachel Foster, daughters of Heron Foster, who founded *The Pittsburgh Dispatch.* What an inspiring vision it would have been to the earnest women sitting in that Convention in 1854, could they in imagination have stretched forward to the bright winter days of 1881, and seen these two young girls tastefully attired, enthusiastic in the cause of woman's suffrage, tripping through the streets of Philadelphia, paper and pencil in hand, intent on some important errand, now here, now there, climbing up long flights of stairs into the offices of the various journals, to find out from the records what Lucretia Mott, Frances Dana Gage, and Ernestine L. Rose had said over a quarter of a century before, about the rights and wrongs of women. Turning over the dusty journals hour after hour as they copied page by page, it would have been a pleasing study to watch their earnest faces, now sad, now pleased, reflecting with every changing sentiment they read the feelings of their souls, just as their diamonds paled and glowed in the changing light.

Could the satisfaction of these girls in reading Garrison's stern logic, Mrs. Mott's repartee and earnest appeal, and all the arguments by which their opponents had been fairly vanquished; could the new-born dignity they realized in the conscious possession of rights and liberties once unknown, confident that full equality could not be long deferred; could all this have been pre-visioned by the actors in those scenes, they would have felt themselves fully compensated for the persecution and ridicule they had endured. And thus the great work of life goes on; the toils of one generation are the joys of the next. We have reaped what other hands have planted; let us then in turn sow bountifully for those who shall follow us, that our children may enter into a broader inheritance than any legal parchment can bequeath.

ANGELINA GRIMKÉ.

Reminiscences by E. C. S.

My first introduction to Mrs. Weld was two years after her marriage, when she and her husband had retired from the stormy scenes of the anti-slavery conflict, and in their own home found a harbor of rest, for quiet though useful occupation. In company with my husband and Charles Stuart, a Scotch Abolitionist, we took one of those long closely-covered stages peculiar to New Jersey, for a twelve miles drive to Belleville, where at the door of an old Dutch-built stone house, Theodore Weld and the famous daughters of South Carolina gave us a welcome. There was nothing attractive at first sight in those plain, frail women, except their rich voices, fluent language, and Angelina's fine dark eyes. The house with its wide hall, spacious apartments, deep windows, and small panes of glass was severely destitute of all tasteful, womanly touches, and though neat and orderly, had a cheerless atmosphere. Neither was there one touch of the artistic in the arrangement of the ladies' hair and dresses. They were just then in the Graham dispensation, and the peculiar table arrangements, with no tray to mark the charmed circle whence the usual beverages were dispensed, the cold dishes without a whiff of heat, or steam, gave one a feeling of strangeness; all those delightful associations gathering round a covered dish and hot beefsteak, the tea-pot and china cups and saucers, were missing. A cool evening in the month of May, after a long drive had left us in a condition peculiarly susceptible to the attractions of something hot and stimulating; but they came not. There was no catering in this household to the weaknesses of those who were not yet weaned from the flesh-pots of Egypt. The sharp edge of our appetite somewhat dulled with the simple fare, we were thrown on our own resources, and memories of tea and coffee for stimulus.

After our repast, the high discourse was slightly interrupted by the appearance of the infant, Charles Stuart Weld, and his formal presentation to the distinguished gentleman after whom he was named. And when Mr. Weld told us how near the boy, in the initiative steps of his existence, came to being sacrificed to a theory, the old stone walls rang with bursts of laughter.* But the chilling

---

* It seems these inexperienced parents had armed themselves with the most approved works on the construction and capacities of infants, in one of which they found the statement that the stomach of a new-born child could hold only one tablespoonful of milk. Accordingly the boy was restricted to that amount, once an hour. Although he protested against this limited supply by constant wailing, and shrivelled from day to day into a miniature mummy, the system was pursued, until at last "Sister Sarah," who had

environments of these noble people were modified by the sincere hospitality with which we were received. My husband and Mr. Weld had been classmates in Lane Seminary, and were among the students who left that institution when the discussion of the slavery question was forbidden by the President, Dr. Lyman Beecher. They talked with zest of those early days until a late hour. As Charles Stuart and the two sisters were also good conversationalists, I listened with pleasure and profit, and during the three days under that roof obtained much general knowledge of anti-slavery and church history; volumes of information were condensed in those familiar talks, of lasting benefit to me, who then knew so little of reforms.

How changed was the atmosphere of that home to me next day. True, there were still no pictures on the walls, but the beautiful boy in his bath, the sunlight on his golden hair, with some new grace or trick each day, surpassed what any brush could trace. No statues graced the corners; but the well-built Northern hero of many slavery battles, bound with the silken cords of love and friendship to those brave women from the South, together sacrificing wealth and fame and ease for a great principle, formed a group worthy the genius of a Rogers to portray.

It has been my good fortune to meet these noble friends occasionally in the course of our busy lives, sometimes under their roof, sometimes under mine, and as, day by day, the nobility, the transparency, the unselfishness of their characters have grown upon me, the memories of the old stone house and its care-worn inmates, have stood transfigured before me, with almost a celestial radiance. In grouping the main facts of this eventful life, and analyzing the impelling motives that made Angelina Grimké the heroic woman she was, I can not serve her memory better than in giving the beautiful tributes of loving friends at the close of her life.

Angelina, the youngest daughter of Judge Grimké, of the Supreme Court of South Carolina, was born in Charleston, S. C., February 20, 1805. From her earliest years, her sympathies were with the cruelly treated race around her; and when a child, she had her little bottle of oil, and other simple medicaments, with which in the darkness she would steal out of the house to some wretched

---

had suspicions for some time that the child's capacity was underrated, thought she would assume the responsibility of giving him for once all the milk he could take. What he did do, so far outmeasured what the doctrinaire said he could do, that the child was happily permitted ever after to decide for himself. The faith of the trusting parents was thus visibly shaken in one theory, and I am happy to add, in due time in many others, regarding the Graham system of dietetics.

creature who had been terribly whipped, and do what she could to assuage his sufferings. At the age of fourteen, she was asked by the rector of the Episcopal church to which her family belonged, to be confirmed—a form, she was told, which all her companions went through as a matter of course. But she insisted on knowing the meaning of this form, and, on reading it in the Prayer-Book, she said she could not promise what was there required. "But it is only a form," she was told. "If with my feelings and views as they now are, I should go through that form, it would be a lie. I can not do it." This single-hearted truthfulness, without regard to personal consequences to herself, was the key to all her conduct.

Some years afterward, under the influence of an eloquent Presbyterian preacher, her religious sensibilities were awakened. Her eyes were opened to a new world. Through deeper and more vital spiritual experiences, she entered into a new life, which took entire possession of all her faculties. She joined the Presbyterian church, and carried into it the fervor and strength of a regenerated nature. She became a teacher in its Sunday-school, and after a lapse of fifty years, there came a letter from one of her first Sunday-school scholars, living in Georgia, to express thanks for the benefits which her instructions had been to her. Angelina soon endeavored to impress upon the officers of the church a sense of what they should do for the slaves, but her pleadings for them found no response. "Could it then," said she, "be a Church of Christ?"

There was in Charleston at that time a Friends' Meeting-house, where there were only two worshipers, and they agreed with her in regard to slavery. For a year she worshiped there in silence. No word was spoken. The two aged men, and this young, accomplished, attractive woman, sat there under a canopy of divine silence, sanctified and blessed to her. At length she felt that her mission there was ended. Her elder sister, Sarah, had united with the Friends in Philadelphia; and she joined her in 1830, giving up in agony of heart all the dear ties that bound her to her home. But even in the Friends' Meeting-house, her eye was quick to see negro seats where women of the despised race were still publicly humiliated. She and her sister seated themselves with them. The Friends were grieved by their conduct, and called them to account. The sisters replied: "While you put this badge of degradation on our sisters, we feel that it is our duty to share it with them."

In 1833, they attached themselves to the American Anti-Slavery Society, and lent their powerful aid to the work which it was doing. There was no more effective or eloquent speaker in the cause than

Angelina Grimké. She had not thought at first of speaking in public; but wherever she was, among friends and neighbors, she sought relief to her burdened spirit by testifying to the cruel and fatal influences of slavery. A few women at first came together to meet her and her sister Sarah. The numbers and the interest increased till she became widely known. She and her sister talked to them about slavery in their own parlors. Soon no parlors could hold the throngs that gathered to hear her. The small vestry of a church was given to her, then a large vestry. But this was too small, and the body of the church was opened to the crowd which had been attracted by her. There, on a platform beneath the pulpit, for the first time she stood and spoke at what might be called a public meeting, though she spoke only to women. In the spring of 1837, the sisters went through a similar experience in Boston, speaking to women only. She went to Lynn to address the women, and there men crowded in with their wives and daughters. That was the beginning of women's speaking to promiscuous assemblies in Massachusetts.

" Hers was the eloquence of a broken heart. As she gave way to the deep yearnings of affection for the mother that bore her, still a slaveholder, for her brothers and sisters, a large family circle, and for all who had been most closely bound to her by ties of kindred and neighborhood, she must have felt the desolation of a soul disappointed and broken in its dearest earthly hopes and love. All the sweet and tender affections which intertwine themselves so inseparably with the thought of home had been turned into instruments of torture. As she thought of her native city, and spoke out her feelings toward it, her language might well remind one of the lamentations of the ancient prophets, ' O Jerusalem, Jerusalem, thou that killest the prophets, and stonest them that are sent unto thee ! ' But this broken heart had a higher life and a mightier voice than can be given or taken away by any earthly affection. While therefore she often spoke with a pathos which melted and subdued those who listened to her, she also rose into a loftier strain, and spoke with the mingled love and sternness of a messenger from God."

Passages like the following may give some idea of the solemnity and power with which she, who had left all and taken up her cross in defence of a poor and friendless race, could appeal to assembled multitudes :

The sufferings of the slaves are not only innumerable, but they are indescribable. I may paint the agony of kindred torn from each other's arms, to meet no more in time; I may depict the inflictions of the blood-stained lash; but I can not describe the daily, hourly, ceaseless torture, endured by the heart that is constantly trampled under the foot of arbitrary power. This is a part of the horrors of slavery which, I believe, no one has ever attempted to delineate. I wonder not at it; it mocks all power of language. Who can describe the anguish of that mind which feels itself impaled upon the iron of arbitrary power—its living, writhing, helpless victim! every human susceptibility tortured, its sympathies torn, and stung, and bleeding—always feeling the death weapon in its heart, and yet not so deep as to kill that humanity which is made the curse of its existence?

No one who has not been an integral part of a slaveholding community can have any idea of its abominations. It is a whited sepulchre, full of dead men's bones and all uncleanness. Blessed be God, the angel of truth has descended, and rolled away the stone from the mouth of the sepulchre, and sits upon it. The abominations so long hidden are now brought forth before all Israel and the sun. Yes, the angel of truth sits upon this stone, and it can never be rolled back again.

There is a spirit abroad in this country which will not consent to barter principle for an unholy peace—a spirit which will not hide God's eternal principles of right and wrong, but will stand erect in the storm of human passion, prejudice, and interest, holding forth the light of truth in the midst of a crooked and perverse generation; a spirit which will never slumber nor sleep till man ceases to hold dominion over his fellow-creatures, and the trump of universal liberty rings in every forest, and is re-echoed by every mountain and rock.

" She who spoke in tones like these never lost one of her purely feminine qualities. Graceful, gentle, retiring, taking upon herself the lowliest duties as if she had been born to them, this woman, who stood up that her light might shine on all, and reveal to them the terrible atrocities of slavery, was like Jeremy Taylor's taper, which cast ever a modest shadow round itself. She had a very lofty idea of what a woman should be. ' Whatever it is morally right for a man to do, it is morally right for a woman to do. I recognize no rights but human rights. I know nothing of men's rights and women's rights; for in Christ Jesus there is neither male nor female.' ' Sure I am that woman is not to be, as she has been, a mere " second-hand agent " in the regeneration of a fallen world, but the acknowledged equal and co-worker with man in this glorious work. . . . . Just in proportion as her moral and intellectual capacities become enlarged, she will rise higher and higher in the scroll of creation, until she reaches that elevation prepared for her by her Maker, and upon whose summit she was originally stationed, only ' a little lower than the angels.' "

In the darkest hours of that fearful conflict with slavery in which she was engaged, when its advocates were everywhere met with violence, and threatened with death, she wrote to William Lloyd Garrison as follows:

I can hardly express to thee the deep and solemn interest with which I have viewed the violent proceedings of the last few weeks. Although I expected opposition, yet I was not prepared for it so soon; it took me by surprise, and I greatly feared the Abolitionists would be driven back in the first onset and thrown into confusion. I was afraid of even opening one of thy papers lest I should see some indications of a compromise, some surrender, some palliation. But I read thy appeal to the citizens of Boston, and found my fears were utterly groundless, and that thou stoodest firm in the midst of the storm, determined to suffer and to die rather than yield one inch!

Religious persecution always begins with mobs; it is always unprecedented in any age or country in which it commences, and therefore there are no laws by which reformers can be punished; consequently, a lawless band of unprincipled men determine to take the matter into their hands, and act out in mobs what they know are the principles of a large majority of those who are too high in Church and State to condescend to mingle with them, though they secretly approve and rejoice over their violent measures. The first martyr who ever died was stoned by a lawless mob; and, if we look at the rise of various sects—Methodists, Friends, etc.—we shall find that mobs began the persecution against them; and it was not until after the people had thus spoken out their wishes that laws were framed to fine, imprison, or destroy them. Let us, then, be prepared for the enactment of laws, even in our free States, against Abolitionists. And how ardently has the prayer been breathed that God would fit us for all He is preparing for us!

My mind has been especially turned toward those who are standing in the fore-front of the battle; and the prayer has gone up for their preservation, not the preservation of their lives, but the preservation of their minds in humility and patience, faith, hope, and charity, that charity which is the bond of perfectness. If persecution is the means which God has ordained for the accomplishment of this great end—emancipation—then, in dependence upon Him for strength to bear it, I feel as if I could say, let it come; for it is my deep, solemn conviction that this is a cause worth dying for. At one time, I thought this system would be overthrown in blood, with the confused noise of the warrior; but a hope gleams across my mind that our blood will be spilt instead of the slaveholders'; that our lives will be taken, and theirs spared. I say a hope; for of all things I desire to be spared the anguish of seeing our beloved country desolated with the horrors of a servile war.

" These words were written by one who was standing not apart in a place of safety, but in the foremost post of danger, and who knew that she was as likely as any one to share in the martyrdom which she foresaw. The spirit which dictated these sentences went through her whole life as its ruling influence.

" There is the courage of the mariner who buffets the angry waves. There is the courage of the warrior who marches up to the cannon's mouth, coolly pressing forward amidst engines of destruc-

tion on every side. But hers was a courage greater than theirs.
She not only faced death at the hands of stealthy assassins and
howling mobs in her loyalty to truth, duty, and humanity, but she
encountered unflinchingly the awful frowns of the mighty consecrated leaders of society, the scoffs and sneers of the multitude, the
outstretched finger of scorn, and the whispered mockery of pity,
standing up for the lowest of the low. Nurtured in the very bosom
of slavery, by her own observation and thought, of one thing she became certain, that it was a false, cruel, accursed relation between
human beings. And to this conviction, from the very budding of
her womanhood, she was true."

"Well do I remember," said one, "when, after the American
Anti-Slavery Society, founded in 1833, had battled for a year or two
with the combined forces of the mob, the press, and the commercial,
political, and ecclesiastical authorities, and it was said in the highest
quarters that we had only exasperated the slaveholders, and made all
the North sympathize with them, when the storm of public indignation, gathering over the whole heavens, was black upon us, and we
were comparatively only a handful, there appeared in the *Anti-
Slavery* office in New York this mild, modest, soft-speaking woman,
then in the prime of her beauty, delicate as the lily-of-the-valley.
She placed in my hands a roll of manuscript, beautifully written. It
was her ' Appeal to the Christian Women of the South.' It was like
a patch of blue sky breaking through that storm cloud." The manuscript was passed round among the members of our Executive
Committee, and read with wet eyes. The Society printed it in
a pamphlet of thirty-six pages, and circulated it widely. It made its
author a forced exile from her native State, but it touched hearts
that had been proof against everything else. I remember that the
Quarterly Anti-Slavery Magazine for October, 1836, said of it
something to this effect:

This eloquent pamphlet is from the pen of a sister of the late Thomas S.
Grimké, of Charleston, S. C. We need hardly say more of it than that it is
written with that peculiar felicity and unction which characterized the works
of her lamented brother. Among anti-slavery writings there are two classes,
one specially adapted to make new converts, the other to strengthen the old. We
can not exclude Miss Grimké's Appeal from either class. It belongs pre-eminently to the former. The converts that will be made by it, we have no doubt,
will be not only numerous, but thorough-going.

"Many of us remember," said another, "with what awakening power
such God-inspired souls have roused us from the apathy of our lives.

Some great wrong, like slavery, over which the world had slept for ages, becomes thus revealed to the clearer vision. Slavery, war, intemperance, licentiousness, injustice to woman, have thus one after another been brought to the light, as violations of God's eternal laws. The soul of Angelina Grimké, and that of her sister Sarah, were in vital sympathy with all attempts to reform these great wrongs; but the one which then had pre-eminence above all was human slavery. All of us who are advanced in years can recall with what almost overwhelming effect the appeals of our beloved and lamented Garrison first came to our minds. The conscience of the community was slumbering over this sin: his utterances stung it to frenzy. In the midst of it, and in the heartiest response to his appeals, came the gentle, calm voices of Sarah and Angelina Grimké, enforcing those appeals by facts of their own observation and experience. I have said that their nature was full of tenderness and compassion; but, in addition to this, Angelina, especially, possessed a rare gift of eloquence, a calm power of persuasion, a magnetic influence over those that listened to her, which carried conviction to hearts that nothing before had reached." "I shall never forget the wonderful manifestation of this power during six successive evenings in what was then called the Odeon, at the corner of Franklin and Federal Streets. It was the old Boston Theater, which had been converted into a music hall, the four galleries rising above the auditorium all crowded with a silent audience, carried away with the calm, simple eloquence which narrated what she and her sister had seen from their earliest days. And yet this Odeon scene, the audience so quiet and intensely absorbed, occurred at the most enflamed period of the anti-slavery contest. The effective agent in this phenomenon was Angelina's serene, commanding eloquence, a wonderful gift, which enchained attention, disarmed prejudice, and carried her hearers with her."

WENDELL PHILLIPS said:

Friends, this life carries us back to the first chapter of that great movement with which the name of Angelina Grimké is associated— when our cities roared with riot, when William Lloyd Garrison was dragged through the streets, when Dresser was mobbed in Nashville, and Mackintosh burned in St. Louis. At that time, the hatred toward Abolitionists was so bitter and merciless that the friends of Lovejoy left his grave a long time unmarked; and at last ventured to put, with his name, on his tombstone, only this piteous entreaty: *Jam parce sepulto*, "Spare him now in his grave."

We were but a handful then, and our words beat against the stony public as powerless as if against the north wind. We got no sym- pathy from most Northern men : their consciences were seared as with a hot iron. At this time, a young girl came from the proudest State in the slave-holding section. She come to lay on the altar of this despised cause, this seemingly hopeless crusade, both family and friends, the best social position, a high place in the church, genius, and many gifts. No man at this day can know the gratitude we felt for this help from such an unexpected source. After this came James G. Birney from the South, and many able and influential men and women joined us. At last John Brown laid his life, the crowning sacrifice, on the altar of the cause. But no man who re- members 1837 and its lowering clouds will deny that there was hardly any contribution to the anti-slavery movement greater or more impressive than the crusade of these Grimké sisters from South Carolina through the New England States.

Gifted with rare eloquence, she swept the chords of the human heart with a power that has never been surpassed, and rarely equal- ed. I well remember, evening after evening, listening to eloquence such as never then had been heard from a woman. Her own hard experience, the long, lonely, intellectual and moral struggle from which she came out conqueror, had ripened her power, and her wondrous faculty of laying bare her own heart to reach the hearts of others, shone forth till she carried us all captive. She was the first woman to whom the halls of the Massachusetts Legislature were opened. My friend, James C. Alvord, was the courageous chairman who broke that door open for the anti-slavery women. It gave Miss Grimké the opportunity to speak to the best culture and character of Massachusetts ; and the profound impression then made on a class not often in our meetings was never wholly lost. It was not only the testimony of one most competent to speak, but it was the profound religious experience of one who had broken out of the charmed circle, and whose intense earnestness melted all opposition. The converts she made needed no after- training. It was when you saw she was opening some secret record of her own experience, that the painful silence and breathless inter- est told the deep effect and lasting impression her words were mak- ing on minds, that afterward never rested in their work.

In 1840, '41, this anti-slavery movement was broken in halves by the woman question. The people believed in the silence of women. But, when the Grimkés went through New England, such was the overpowering influence with which they swept the churches that men did not remember this dogma till after they had gone. When they left, and the spell weakened, some woke to the idea that it was wrong for a woman to speak to a public assembly. The wakening of old prejudice to its combat with new convictions was a fearful storm. But she bore it, when it broke at last, with the intrepidity with which she surmounted every obstacle. By the instinctive keenness of her conscience, she only needed to see truth to recognize it, as the flower turns to the sun. God had touched that soul so that it needed no special circumstance, no word of warning or instruction from those about her; for she was ever self-poised.

When I think of her, there comes to me the picture of the spotless dove in the tempest, as she battles with the storm, seeking for some place to rest her foot. She reminds me of innocence personified in Spencer's poem. In her girlhood, alone, heart-led, she comforts the slave in his quarters; mentally struggling with the problems his position wakes her to. Alone, not confused, but seeking something to lean on, she grasps the Church, which proves a broken reed. No whit disheartened, she turns from one sect to another, trying each by the infallible touchstone of that clear, childlike conscience. The two old lonely Quakers in their innocence rest her foot awhile. But the eager soul must work, not rest in testimony. Coming North, at last, she makes her own religion,—one of sacrifice and toil. Breaking away from, rising above all forms, the dove floats at last in the blue sky where no clouds reach.

And thus exiled from her native city, she goes forth with her sister to seek the spot where she can most effectually strike at the institution. Were I to single out the moral and intellectual trait which most won me, it was her serene indifference to the judgment of those about her. Self-poised, she seemed morally sufficient to herself. Her instincts were all so clear and right she could trust their lesson. But a clear, wide, patient submission to all suggestion and influence preceded opinion, and her public addresses were remarkable for the fullness and clearness of the arguments they urged. She herself felt truths, but patiently argued them to others.

The testimony she gave touching slavery was, as she termed it, " the wail of a broken-hearted child." It was known to a few that the pictures she drew were of her own fireside. That loving heart! how stern a sense of duty must have wrung it before she was willing to open that record! But with sublime fidelity, with entire self-sacrifice, she gave all she could to the great argument that was to wake a nation to duty. Listen to the fearful indictment she records against the system. And this was not slavery in its most brutal, repulsive form. It was slavery hid in luxury, when refinement seemed to temper some of its worst elements. But, with keen sense of right, even a child of a dozen years saw through the veil, saw the system in its inherent vileness, saw the real curse of slavery in the hardened heart of the slave-holder.

A few years of active life, extensive and most influential labor, many sheaves and a rich harvest, God's blessing on her service, then illness barring her from the platform. How serenely she took up the cross! So specially endowed; men bowing low so readily to the power and magic of her words; she could not but have seen the grand possibilities that were opening before her. How peacefully she accepted the bond, and set herself to training others for the work against which her own door was shut! East, West, North, and South, come up to give testimony that these later years bore ample fruit. How many souls have cause to thank that enforced silence! I have listened to such testimonies, spoken sometimes in tears, on the shores of the Great Lakes and beyond the Mississippi."

From the following facts and anecdotes told by her husband, we see that Angelina united with the highest moral heroism, the physical courage and coolness in the hour of danger that but few men can boast. Theodore D. Weld, in his published sketch, says:

Though high physical courage is also fairly inferrable from her anti-slavery career, yet only those most with her in life's practical affairs can appreciate her self-poise in danger. Peril was to her a sedative; it calmed and girded her, bringing out every resource, and making self-command absolute. She knew nothing of that flutter which confuses. Great danger instantly brought thought and feeling to a focus, and held them there. Several perilous emergencies in her life are vividly recalled—such as being overturned while in a carriage with a child in her arms, the horse meanwhile floundering amid the *débris,* a shaft broken, and dash-board kicked into splinters. At another time, shots at the road-side set off the horses in a run. Seeing her husband, in his struggle to rein them in, jerked up from his seat and held thus braced and half-standing, she caught him round the waist, adding her weight to his, and thus enabled him to pull the harder, till the steady, silent tug upon the reins tamed down the steeds. Her residence at Belleville, N. J., had no near neighbors, stood back from the road, and was nearly hidden by trees and shrubbery. The old stone structure, dating back to 1700, was known as the "haunted house." Being very large, with barn, sheds, and several out-houses, it was specially attractive to stragglers and burglars. Stories had been long afloat of outrages perpetrated there, among which was a murder a century before, with a burglary and robbery more recent. We had not been long there, when one night Angelina, waked by suspicious noises, listened, till certain that a burglar must be in the house. Then, stealing softly from the room, she struck a light, and explored from cellar to attic, looking into closets, behind doors, and under beds. For a slight, weak woman, hardly able to lift an empty tea-kettle, thus to dare, shows, whether we call it courage or presumption, at least the absence of all fear. None of the family knew of this fact, until an accident long after revealed it.

Some years after this, when visiting in a friend's family in the absence of the parents, she often took the children to ride. Upon returning one day, she said to the cook, " Maggie, jump in, and I'll give you a ride." So away they went. Soon a by-road struck off from the main one. Turning in to explore it, she found that it ran a long way parallel to the railroad. Suddenly Maggie screamed : " O missus ! I forgot. This is just the time for the express, and this is the horse that's awful afraid of the cars, and nobody can hold him. Oh, dear, dear ! " Seeing Maggie's fright, she instantly turned back, saying, " Now, Maggie, if the train should come before we get back to the turn, do just what I tell you, and I'll bring you out safe." " Oh, yes, missus ! I will ! I will ! " " Mark, now. Don't scream ; don't touch the reins ; don't jump out : 'twill kill you dead if you do. Listen, and, as soon as you hear the cars coming, drop down on the bottom of the wagon. Don't look out ; keep your eyes and mouth shut tight. I'll take care of you." Down flat dropped Maggie on the bottom, without waiting to hear the train. Soon the steam-whistle screamed in front, instead of rear, as expected ! Short about she turned the horse, and away he sprang, the express thundering in the rear. For a mile the road was a straight, dead level, and right along the track. At utmost speed the frantic animal strained on. On plunged the train behind. Neither gained nor lost. No sound came but the rushing of steed and train. It was a race for life, and the blood horse won. Then, as the road turned from the track up a long slope, the train shot by, taming the horse's fright ; but, as his blood was up, she kept him hard pushed to the crest of the slope, then slacked his pace, and headed him homeward. Faithful Maggie stuck fast to her promise and to the wagon-bottom, until told, " It's all over," when she broke silence with her wonderments. When she got home the kitchen rang with exclamations. That race was long her standing topic, she always insisting that she wasn't scared a bit, not she, because she " knew the missus wasn't."

While living in New Jersey, word came that a colored man and his wife, who had just come to the township, were lying sick of malignant small-pox, and that none of their neighbors dared go to them. She immediately sought them out, and found them in a deplorable plight, neither able to do anything for the other, and at once became to them eyes, hands, feet, nurse, care-taker and servant in all needed offices ; and thus, relieved in nursing and watching by a friend, her patients were able, after three days, to minister in part to each other. Meanwhile, no neighbor approached them.

Some striking traits were scarcely known, except by her special intimates ; and they were never many. Her fidelity in friendship was imperishable. Friends might break with her ; she never broke with them, whatever the wrong they had done her. She never stood upon dignity, nor exacted apology, nor resented an unkindness, though keenly feeling it ; and, if falsely accused, answered nothing. She never spoke disparagingly of others, unless clearest duty exacted it. Gossips, tattlers, and backbiters were her trinity of horrors. Her absolute truthfulness was shown in the smallest things. With a severe sincerity, it was applied to all those customs looked upon as mere forms involving no principle—customs exacting the utterance of what is not meant, of wishes unfelt, sheer deceptions. She never invited a visit or call not desired.

If she said, "Stay longer," the words voiced a wish felt. She could not be brought under bondage to any usage or custom, any party watch-word, or shibboleth of a speculative creed, or any mode of dress or address. In Charleston, she was exact in her Quaker costume, because, to the last punctilio, it was an anti-slavery document; and for that she would gladly make any sacrifice of personal comfort. But, among the "Friends" in Philadelphia, she would not wear an article of dress which caused her physical inconvenience, though it might be dictated by the universal usage of "Friends." Upon first exchanging the warmth of a Carolina winter for the zero of a Northern one, she found the "regulation" bonnet of the "Friends" a very slight protection from the cold. So she ordered one made of fur, large enough to protect both head and face. For this departure from usage, she was admonished, "It was a grief to 'Friends,'" "It looked like pride and self-will," "It was an evil example," etc. While adhering strictly to the principles of "Friends," neither she nor her sister Sarah could conform to all their distinctive usages, nor accept all their rules. Consequently, their examples were regarded as quiet protests against some of the settled customs of the Society. Such they felt bound to make them in word and act. Thus they protested against the negro-seat in their meeting-house, by making it their seat. They also felt constrained to testify against a rule requiring that no Friend should publish a book without the sanction of the "Meeting for Sufferings"; so, also, the rule that any one who should marry out of the Society should, unless penitent, be disowned. Consequently, when Angelina thus married, she was disowned, as was Sarah for sanctioning the marriage by her presence. The committee who "dealt" with them for those violations of the rule, said that if they would "express regret," they would relieve the meeting from the painful necessity of disowning them. The sisters replied that, feeling no regret, they could express none; adding that, as they had always openly declared their disapproval of the rule, they could neither regret their violation of it, nor neglect so fit an occasion for thus emphasizing their convictions by their acts; adding that they honored the "Friends" all the more for that fidelity which constrained them to do, however painful, what they believed to be their duty.

Angelina's "Appeal to the Christian Women of the South" "made her a forced exile from her native State." As she never voluntarily spoke of what she had done or suffered, few, if any, of the Abolitionists, either knew then, or know now, that she was really exiled by an Act of the Charleston city government. When her "Appeal" came out, a large number of copies were sent by mail to South Carolina. Most of them were publicly burned by postmasters. Not long after this, the city authorities learned that Miss Grimké was intending to visit her mother and sisters, and pass the winter with them. Thereupon the mayor of Charleston called upon Mrs. Grimké, and desired her to inform her daughter that the police had been instructed to prevent her landing while the steamer remained in port, and to see to it that she should not communicate, by letter or otherwise, with any persons in the city; and, further, that if she should elude their vigilance, and go on shore, she would be arrested and imprisoned, until the return of the steamer. Her Charleston friends at once conveyed to her the message of the mayor, and added that the people of Charleston were so incensed against her, that if she should go there, despite the mayor's threat of pains and penalties, she could not escape personal violence at the hands of the mob. She replied to the letter, that her going would doubtless compromise her family; not only distress them, but put them in peril, which she had neither heart nor right to do; but for that fact, she would certainly exercise her constitutional right as an American citizen, and go to Charleston to visit her relatives, and, if for that the authorities should inflict upon her pains and penalities, she would willingly bear them, assured that such an outrage would help to reveal to the free States the fact that slavery defies and tramples alike constitutions and laws, and thus outlaws itself.

When the American Anti-Slavery Society wrote to Miss Grimké, inviting her to visit New York city, and hold meetings in private parlors with Christian women, on the subject of slavery, upon reading their letter, she handed it to her sister Sarah, saying, "I feel this to be God's call. I can not decline it." A long conversation followed, the details of which I received from Sarah not long after; and, as they present vividly the marked characteristics of both sisters, I give in substance such as I can recall.

S.—But you know that you are constitutionally retiring, self-distrustful, easily embarrassed. You have a morbid shrinking from whatever would make you conspicuous.

A.—Yes, you have drawn me to the life. I confess that I have all that, and yet at times I have nothing of it. I know that I am diffident about assuming responsibilities; but when I feel that anything is mine to do, no matter what, then I have no fear.

S.—You are going among strangers, you wear strange garments, speak in a strange language, will be in circumstances wholly novel, and about a work that you never attempted, and most of those who will listen to you have prejudices against Abolitionists, and also against a woman's speaking to any audience. Now in all there embarrassing circumstances, and in your lack of self-confidence when you come to face an unsympathizing audience, does not it seem likely that you will find it impossible to speak to edification, and thus will be forced to give it up altogether?

A.—Yes, it seems presumptuous for me to undertake it; but yet I can not refuse to do it. The conviction is a part of me. I can not absolve myself from it. The responsibility is thrust upon me. I can not thrust it off.

S.—I know you will not and can not. My only desire is for you deliberately to look at all things just as they are, and give each its due weight. If, after that, your conviction is unchanged, with my whole heart I'll help you to carry it out. There is but one thing more that I think of. If you were to go upon this mission without the sanction of the "Meeting for Sufferings," it would be regarded as disorderly, a violation of the established usage of the Society, and they would probably feel compelled to disown you. [This was prior to the disownment that followed the marriage].

A.—As my mind is made up absolutely to go, I can not ask their leave to go. For their fidelity to their views of duty, I honor them. It is a grief to me to grieve them, but I have no alternative. Very unpleasant it will be to be disowned, but misery to be self-disowned.

S.—I have presented these considerations, that you might carefully traverse the whole question and count all the costs. I dare not say a word against your decision. I see that it is final, and that you can make no other. To me, it is sacred. While we have been talking, I, too, have made my decision. It is this: where you go, I will go; what you do, I will to my utmost help you in doing. We have always thought and wept and prayed together over this horrible wrong, and now we will go and work together. There will be a deal to be done in private also; that I can help you about, and thus you will have the more strength to give to the meetings.

So Miss Grimké wrote at once to the committee, accepting their invitation, thanking them for the salary offered, but declining to receive any; informing them that her sister would accompany her, and that they should both go exclusively at their own expense.

In 1864, Mr. and Mrs. Weld removed to Hyde Park, where the sisters spent the rest of their days. No one who met Angelina there would have any suspicion of the great work which she had done: she was interested in her household duties, and the little charities of the neighborhood. Once, during the war, she was persuaded to go out of her daily routine, and to attend a small meeting called for the purpose of assisting the Southern people—freedmen, and those who had formerly held them in slavery. Very simply and modestly, but very clearly and impressively, she spoke of the condition of things at the South, of her friends there, and how we could best help them—all in the most loving and tender spirit, as if she had only grateful memories of what they had been, and as if no thought of herself mingled with the thought of them. The simplicity, directness, and practical good sense of her speech then, its kindliness toward those who had done her the greatest wrong, and the entire absence of self-consciousness, made those who heard her feel that a woman might speak in public without violating any of the proprieties or prejudices of social traditions and customs. There was a refinement and dignity about her, an atmosphere of gentleness and sweetness and strength, which won their way to the heart. To those who knew her history, there was something very affecting, sublime, in her absolute self-forgetfulness. As one who knew her most intimately said, "She seems to have been born in that mood of mind which made vanity or display impossible. She was the only person I have ever known who was absolutely free from all ambition."

Space prevents a fitting record of the noble words and deeds of Sarah Moore Grimké. She published in 1838, a volume of "Letters on the Equality of the Sexes," which called out much discussion on woman's position in both State and Church. The last time Angelina spoke in public was at the Loyal League Convention in New York in 1863. She took an active part in the discussion of resolutions, speaking clearly and concisely on every point, and read a beautiful address she had prepared—"To the Soldiers of our Second Revolution." All through the years that Angelina was illustrating woman's capacity on the platform by holding her audiences spellbound, Sarah was defending woman's right to be there with her pen.

CHAPTER XI.

LUCRETIA MOTT.

Eulogy at the Memorial Services* held in Washington by the National Woman Suffrage Association, January 19, 1881. By Elizabeth Cady Stanton.

On the 3d of January, 1793, the little island of Nantucket, fifteen miles by three and a half, lying far out into the sea on the coast of Massachusetts, welcomed to its solitude a child destined to be one of America's most famous women. This was a fitting birthplace for Lucretia Mott; as the religion and commerce of the island (named for a woman) had been guided by a woman's brain. In 1708 Mary Starbuck, known as "The Great Merchant," a woman of remarkable breadth of intellect, as well as great executive ability, converted the colony to Quakerism, and vindicated woman's right to interest herself in the commerce of the world. Perhaps she, like the good genii of old, brought her gifts to that cradle and breathed into the new life the lofty inspiration that made this woman the prophet and seer she was. Here were the descendants of John Wolman, William Rotch, George Fox, the Macys, the Franklins, the Folgers; and in this pure atmosphere, and from these distinguished ancestors, Lucretia Mott received her inheritance. Her father was an honest, sea-faring Quaker. Her mother belonged to the Folger family, whose culture, genius, common-sense, and thrift culminated in Benjamin Franklin, and later, in Lucretia Mott. The resemblance between her head and that of the philosopher and statesman, was apparent to the most casual observer.

Mrs. Mott says in her diary: "I always loved the good in childhood, and desired to do the right. In those early years I was actively useful to my mother, who, in the absence of my father on his long voyages, was engaged in mercantile business, often going to Boston to purchase goods in exchange for oil and candles, the staple of the island. The exercise of women's talents in this line, as well as the general care which devolved upon them, in the absence of

---

* In the midst of our first volume the announcement of the death of Lucretia Mott, Nov. 11th, 1880, reached us. As she was identified with so many of the historical events of Pennsylvania, where nearly seventy years of her life were passed, it is fitting that this sketch should follow the State in which she resided for so long a period.

their husbands, tended to develop and strengthen them mentally and physically.

" In 1804 my father's family removed to Boston, and in the public and private schools of that city I mingled with all classes without distinction. It was the custom then to send the children of such families to select schools; but my parents feared that would minister to a feeling of class pride, which they felt was sinful to cultivate in their children. And this I am glad to remember, because it gave me a feeling of sympathy for the patient and struggling poor, which but for this experience I might never have known." Under such humane influences, with such ancestors and associations, in the public schools, in the Friends' meeting, on the adventurous island, and in the suburbs of Boston, the child passed into girlhood, with lessons of industry and self-denial well learned, and with her life all before. She lived in a period when women of genius had vindicated their right to be recognized in art, science, literature, and government, and through many of the great events that have made the United States a Nation. It was such a combination of influences that developed Lucretia Mott into the exceptional woman she was.

In an unlucky hour her father endorsed for a friend, and to save his honor, was compelled to lose his property. It was a blow from which he did not recover, and henceforward much of the support of the family devolved upon the mother, who had remarkable tact, energy, and courage. Both parents were ambitious for their children, and did all they could for their education; that was one thing about which all Quakers were tenacious. In her fourteenth year Lucretia and her elder sister were sent to " The Nine Partners," a Friends boarding-school in Dutchess County, New York, and there pursuing her studies with patient zeal, she remained two years without once going home for a holiday vacation. At fifteen, a teacher having left, Lucretia was made an assistant, and at the end of the second year, was tendered the place of teacher, with the inducement beside, that her services would entitle a younger sister to her education.

Her well-balanced character enabled her to meet with calmness, all life's varied trials, of which she had her full share. As one of eight children in her father's house, with his financial embarrassments, and sudden death: and afterward with five children of her own, and her husband's reverses; Lucretia's heroism and strength of mind were fairly tested. In both of these financial emergencies, she opened a school, and by her success as a teacher, bridged over the chasm.

In her eighteenth year, Lucretia Coffin and James Mott, according to Quaker ceremony, became husband and wife, the result of an attachment formed at boardiug-school, which proved to be an exceptionally happy union, and through their long wedded life, of over half a century, they remained ever loyal to one another. James Mott, though a Quaker, was in all personal qualities the very opposite of his wife. He had the cool judgment, she the enkindling enthusiasm. He had the slow, sure movement; she the quick, impulsive energy. He enjoyed nothing more than silence; she nothing more than talking. The one was completely the complement of the other. She possessed a delicate love of fun, and was full of dry humor. Once during a visit from her husband's brother, Richard Mott, of Toledo, Ohio, who like James was a very silent man, she became suddenly aware of their absence and started to look for them. Finding them seated on either side of a large wood fire in the drawing-room, she said, " Oh, I thought you must both be here it was so quiet."

In speaking of them, Robert Collyer says: " If James and Lucretia had gone around the world in search of a mate, I think they would have made the choice which heaven made for them. They had lived together more than forty years when I first knew them. I thought then, as I think now, that it was the most perfect wedded life to be found on earth. They were both of a most beautiful presence. He, large, fair, with kindly blue eyes, and regular features. She, slight, with dark eyes and hair. Both, of the sunniest spirit; both, free to take their own way, as such fine souls always are, and yet their lives were so perfectly one that neither of them led or followed the other, so far as one could observe, by the breadth of a line. He could speak well, in a slow, wise way, when the spirit moved him, and the words were all the choicer because they were so few. But his greatness, for he was a great man, lay still in that fine, silent manhood, which would only break into fluent speech as you sat with him by the bright wood fire in winter, while the good wife went on with her knitting, putting it swiftly dówn a score of times in an hour, to pound a vagrant spark which had snapped on the carpet, oi as we sat under the trees in the summer twilight. Then James Mott would open his heart to those he loved, and touch you with wonder at the depth and beauty of his thoughts; or tell you stories of the city where when a young man he lived, or of the choice humors of ancient Quakers, who went through the world esteeming laughter vain, and yet set the whole world which knew them laughing at their quaint ways and curious fancies."

In his young days, James Mott was a teacher; later on he engaged in the cotton business, but abandoned it when it was becoming re-munerative, because of its connection with slave labor. He finally took up the wool business, and retired with a competency some years before his death, which enabled them to take a trip to Europe, and afterward live the life of leisure they desired, indulging their literary tastes. James Mott wrote a very creditable book of their travels, and Lucretia carried enough observations of foreign life in her head to fill folios.

Mrs. Mott was a housekeeper of the old school, in so far as every-thing from garret to cellar passed under her supervision. She took the entire care of her children, and although with remarkable economy supplying the wants and guarding against the wastes of a large family, she did not allow these necessary cares to absorb all her time and thought, but cultivated the talents entrusted to her in broader inter-ests than family life. She felt she had duties in the Church and the State as well as the home. The time most wives and mothers spend in gaiety and embroidery, she spent in reading and committing to memory choice thoughts in poetry and prose. The money others spent in filling their homes with bric-a-brac she spent in books, and the result proves the superior wisdom of her course.

When conventions were held in Philadelphia, her house was al-ways filled with guests. As presiding officer in a woman's conven-tion nothing escaped her notice. She felt responsible that every-thing should be done in good taste and order. Her opinions on woman's nature, sphere, destiny, were thoroughly digested, and any speaker that did not come up to her exact ideal, was taken delicately to task when her turn came to speak. As some one remarks, " she had a playful way of tapping a speaker in a public meeting, as a skillful driver touches his horses with the tip end of his whip." Once, says Wendell Phillips, she tried the experiment on me when I had ventured to say that one of the drawbacks to the move-ment, was the indifference of women themselves. Other speakers too expressed sentiments on which Mrs. Mott differed from them. When she arose she touched them all round with her gentle raillery, offending no one, just pronounced enough in her speech to be effect-ive, and in no way compromising herself. Glancing at the platform on one occasion in Philadelphia, the central figure is Lucretia Mott in Quaker costume, in the zenith of her refined beauty; around her are grouped James Mott, William Lloyd Garrison, Wendell Phillips, Thomas Wentworth Higginson, Robert Purvis, Charles Burleigh, Ernestine L. Rose, Frances Dana Gage, Hannah Tracy Cutler, Lydia Mott, Martha C. Wright, Ann Preston, Sarah Pugh, Hannah

Darlington, Mary Grew, Matilda Joslyn Gage, Susan B. Anthony, and Lucy Stone, as refined and remarkable an assembly of men and women as could be found in any European court. Yet these were the people so hated and ridiculed by the press and the pulpit, whose grand utterances and spicy debates were stigmatized as " the maudlin sentimentalisms of unsexed men and women."

But let us follow these friends to the home of Lucretia Mott. A large house on Arch Street, like all buildings in the city of brotherly love, with white shutters, marble cappings and steps, and dining-room on the second floor of the rear building. There are our stern reformers, round the social board, as genial a group of martyrs as one could find. Without the shadow of a doubt as to the rightfulness of their own position, and knowing too that the common sense of the nation was on their side, they made merry over the bigotry of the Church, popular prejudices, conservative fears, absurd laws and customs hoary with age. How they did hold up in their metaphysical tweezers the representatives of the dead past that ever and anon ventured upon our platform. With what peals of laughter their assumptions and contradictions were chopped into mince meat. On this occasion, William Lloyd Garrison occupied the seat of honor at Mrs. Mott's right hand, and led the conversation which the hostess always skillfuly managed to make general. When seated around her board, no two-and-two side talk in monotone was ever permissible; she insisted that the good things said should be enjoyed by all. At the close of the meal, while the conversation went briskly on, with a neat little tray and snowy towel, she washed up the silver and china as she uttered some of her happiest thoughts. James Mott at the head of the table maintained the dignity of his position, ever ready to throw in a qualifying word, when these fiery reformers became too intense.

Theirs was the ideal home, perfect in its appointments, and where discussion on all subjects took the widest range. Being alike in search of truth, one felt no fear of shocking them. Those accustomed to see priests and bigots, whenever a doubt was expressed as to any of their cherished opinions, rise and leave the room with a deeply wounded expression, were surprised to see James and Lucretia Mott calmly discussing with guests, their own most cherished creeds, and questioning the wisdom of others in turn. Freedom was not a deity in their home to be worshiped afar off, but the patron saint of the household, influencing all who entered there, giving her benedictions to each at every feast.

Their home was the castle of safety for runaway slaves, and the paradise of the unfortunate. All knew that if the mistress met them empty handed, she would cheer their lonely hearts with kind words, recognizing their humanity, and with sure promise of some future consideration. Her house was a resort too for people of distinction. When Frederika Bremer, Harriet Martineau, Lord Morpeth, Lord and Lady Amberley, visited this country, the reformers were the people they desired to see, and chief among them Lucretia Mott, after whom Lady Amberley named her first daughter. Thus titled foreigners, scholars, and politicians often met at her fireside. I have frequently heard Gerrit Smith describe a call he once made there. In a conversation of an hour, she was interrupted half a dozen times with applications for charity. At last, in came the glorious Fanny Kemble, meeting Mrs. Mott in a manner that clearly showed they were warm and well-known friends; and soon came Frederick Douglass. There sat the millionaire philanthropist, the world-renowned actor, the grandest representative of slavery, and the fearless disciple of Elias Hicks. I doubt if the Quaker City ever unveiled so magnificent a tableaux for the pen of an artist.

In her diary Mrs. Mott says: "At twenty-five years of age, surrounded with a family and many cares, I felt called to a more public life of devotion to duty, and engaged in the ministry in the 'Society of Friends,' receiving every encouragement from those in authority until the separation amongst us in 1827, when my convictions led me to adhere to those who believed in the sufficiency of the light within, resting on 'truth for authority rather than authority for truth.' The popular doctrine of original sin never commended itself to my reason or conscience, except on the theory of original holiness also. I searched the Scriptures daily, ofttimes finding a construction of the text wholly different from that which had been pressed on our acceptance. The highest evidence of a sound faith being the practical life of the Christian, I have felt a far greater interest in the moral movements of the age than in any theological discussion."

In 1818 she began to preach in "Friends' Meeting," and through New England, Pennsylvania, Maryland, and Virginia, she spoke at an early day on the tenets of her sect. She affiliated with the branch called "Hicksite," or "Unitarian Quakers." As Mrs. Mott was a disciple of Elias Hicks, we can get some insight as to her religious faith by a few extracts from different points in his creed as stated by himself. In one of his sermons he says:

As many as are led by the Spirit of God they are the sons of God. What is the Spirit of God? It is the light and life in the soul of man. All that men and books can do is to point us to this great principle which is only to be known in our own souls. The way to arrive at a knowledge of this divine love and divine light, and to fulfill the whole law, is to love all the creation of God, and do right to all men and beasts.

Again he speaks of the divine love and divine light which he says are one, indivisibly one. The Lord is love, and love may be considered as comprehending all His power and all His wisdom; but goodness is the most proper term that we can apply. Every one, he says, is enlightened by the same divine light that enlightened Jesus, and we receive it from the same source. He had the fullness of it as we have our several allotments. All the varied names given in Scripture to this divine light and life such as, "Emmanuel," "Jesus," "Sent of God," "Great Prophet," "Christ our Lord," "Grace," "Unction," "Anointed," mean one and the same thing, and are nothing less nor more than the spirit and power of God in the soul of man as his Creator, Preserver, Condemner, Redeemer, Saviour, Sanctifier, and Justifier.

The Hicksites differed from the other Friends in that they placed the light within above all external authority, while the Orthodox Friends make the Scriptures the surer guide, though some make the written word and inner light of equal authority. In a letter to John C. Sanders, in 1828, Elias Hicks says:

Not all the books ever written, nor all the miracles recorded in the Scriptures, nor all other external evidence of what kind soever, has ever revealed God (who is an eternal invisible Spirit) to any one of the children of men. Heaven is not a fixed place above, nor hell below, but both are states of the soul. The blood of Christ shed upon the cross has no more power to cleanse us from sin than the blood of bullocks and rams poured out on Jewish altars could cleanse that people from their sins. We must know Christ within us to save us from sin; men depend so much on the crucifixion that they heed not the light within.

This wonderful prophet and seer was seventy-nine years old when the separation began in Philadelphia. The division in this country created great excitement among the Quakers in England, who were very active in their hostility to Elias Hicks and his doctrines. Some of them came to America to bear their testimony. Among others, Annie Braithwaite traveled extensively and addressed Friends' meetings. Mrs. Mott states that on one occasion when she was present, the English Quakeress, in preaching salvation by the blood of Christ, had spoken with more than usual unction and enthusiasm. As soon as she finished a profound silence reigned. Elias Hicks, slowly rising and removing his hat, said in deep inspired tones: "Friends, to the Christ that never was crucified; to the Christ that never was slain; to the Christ that can not die, I commend you."

Many of the professed followers of Elias Hicks lacked the courage and conscience to maintain his principles when the magnetism of his direct influence was withdrawn by his death. Hence even in that division of the Friends to which she belonged, Mrs. Mott encountered much opposition, especially for her public identification with unpopular reforms. Many would have gladly seen her withdraw from their membership, and others were desirous that she should be disowned. But she understood her own rights and Friends Discipline too well to violate a single rule. Although her enemies kept close watch, they never caught her off her guard. At the time of the division, she remarked to an acquaintance: " It seemed to me almost like death at first to be shut out of the Friends Meeting where I had loved to go for religious communion, to see the cold averted looks from those whose confidence I once enjoyed, to be shunned as unworthy of notice; all this was hard to endure, but it was the price I paid for being true to the convictions of my own soul."

Her spiritual life was deep and earnest, but entirely her own. It was intuitional, not emotional. It was expressed in her love for man in God, and not God in creeds and ceremonies. She prized the free sentiments of William Ellery Channing, read his works with avidity, and always had some volume of his at hand. The Life of Rev. Joseph Blanco White, a rare book, was for years one of the companions of her solitude. It was thoroughly worn, and the margin covered with her notes and marks of approval. Dean Stanley and Buckle's " History of Civilization " were favorites with her also. Cowper's " Task " and Young's " Night Thoughts," which had been her text-books at " Nine Partners," never lost their charm for her. She could repeat pages of them. In her last days she read " The Light of Asia " with intense pleasure. When she had already passed her eighty-seventh year, Susan B. Anthony visiting her, says: " She read aloud to us from that charming poem until after eleven o'clock at night." Her conversation, as well as her public addresses, were sprinkled with beautiful and apt citations from her favorite authors, as it was the habit of her life to commit to memory sentiments she most valued in poetry and prose.

It was not possible that a woman like Lucretia Mott should keep silence in the churches, no matter what Paul might say to the contrary, because that great brain was created to think, that noble heart to beat through making and moulding speech, and those fine gray eyes to see what the prophets in all times have seen. I can not imagine her as one of the silent sisters who though having something to say, dare not say it though to save her own soul or the souls of those about her.

An old friend in Lancaster County, says Robert Collyer, told me of his first hearing her in the early days when as yet she was almost unknown. It had been a dreary time among Friends up there, and being a man who did not care for the traditions of " first day " and " fourth day," he was getting tired of silence. One " first day " he went to his meeting expecting nothing as usual, and pretty sure he would not be disappointed. Nor was he for a time. But presently a young woman arose in the high seat he had never seen before, whose presence touched him with strange new expectations. She looked, he said, as one whc had no great hold on life, and began to speak in low tones, with just a touch of hesitation as of one feeling after her thought, and there was a tremor in her voice as if she felt the burden of the spirit. But she soon found her way out of this, and then he said he began to hold his breath. He had never heard such speaking in all his life, so born of conviction, so radiant with that inward light for which he had been waiting, that he went home feeling as he supposed they must have felt in the olden time who thought they had heard an angel.

I once heard such an outpouring. It was at a woods-meeting up among the hills where quite a number of us had our say, and then my friend's turn came. She was well on in years then, but the old fire still burned clear, and God's breath touched her out of heaven and she prophesied. I suppose she spoke for two hours, but after the first moment she never faltered or failed to hold the multitude spell-bound, and waiting on her words. Yet there was not the least hint of premeditation, while there was boundless wealth of meditation in her deep, pregnant thoughts. I have said she prophesied, no other term would answer to her speech. Her eyes had seen the coming glory of the Lord, and she testified that she had seen ; and this was all the more wonderful to me, because it was the habit of her mind in later years to reason, as President McCosh does, from premise to conclusion. But she had seen a vision there sitting in the August splendor with the voice of God's presence whispering in the trees, and the vision had set the heart high above the brain. These were care-worn and work-worn folks she saw about her with knotted hands resting on the staff, or folded quietly on the lap. They had nearly done the good day's work, and now preacher and prophet were needed to tell them what that day's work meant, where they keep the books for us, and so it was not a speech, but a psalm of life.

Mrs. Mott was safe at all points in taking Elias Hicks for a teacher of morals, as he was pronounced on every reform. On the question of woman's rights, he says :

If Paul said of women preachers what we find in Corinthians and Timothy, I judge that he had no allusion at all to their preaching or prophesying in the churches ; and if he had, we have no right to admit it as sound doctrine, as it contradicts a number of his own declarations (and the general testimony of Scripture), which are more rational and clear, as in the fourteenth chapter of Romans ; and in Philippians where he speaks of the women who labored with him in the Gospel ; and in 1st Corinthians where he speaks of women praying and prophesying ; and Paul assures us that male and female are one in Christ. Also under the law there were prophetesses as well as prophets, and the effusion of the Spirit in the latter days as prophesied by Joel was to be equally on sons and daughters, servants and handmaids. To believe otherwise is irrational and in-consistent with the divine attributes, and would charge the Almighty with par-tiality and injustice to one-half of His rational creation. Therefore I believe it would be wrong to admit it, although asserted in the most plain and positive manner by men or angels.

In our last conflict with Great Britain, Elias Hicks called the attention of "Friends" to a faithful support of their testimony against war and injustice, desiring them to maintain their Christian liberties against encroachment of the secular powers, laws having been enacted levying taxes for the support of the war. At one meeting there was considerable altercation; as some Friends who refused payment had been distrained some three or four fold more than the tax demanded, while others complied, paid the tax, and justified themselves in so doing. On this point his mind was deeply exercised and he labored to encourage Friends to faithfulness to exalt their testimonies for the Prince of Peace.

Elias Hicks preached against slavery both in Maryland and Virginia. He says of a meeting in Baltimore that he especially addressed slave-holders. Further, he opposed the use of slave-grown goods. At a meeting in Providence, R. I., he said he was moved to show the great and essential difference there is between the righteousness of man comprehended in his laws, customs, and traditions, and the righteousness of God which is comprehended in pure, impartial, unchangeable justice. They who continue this traffic, and enrich themselves, by the labor of these deeply oppressed Africans, violate these plain principles of justice, and no cunning sophistical reasoning in the wisdom of this world can justify them, or silence the convictions of conscience.

Some other Friends were much opposed to the use of slave products, but the Society in general "had no concern" on this point. Lucretia Mott used "free goods," and thought that Elias' preaching such extreme doctrines on all these practical reforms, had their effect in the division. To refuse to pay taxes, or to use any "slave produce," involved more immediate and serious difficulties, than any theoretical views of the hereafter, and even Friends may be pardoned for feeling some interest in their own pecuniary independence. To see their furniture, cattle, houses, lands, all swept away for exorbitant taxes, seemed worse than paying a moderate one to start with. From these quotations from the great reformer and religious leader, we see how fully Mrs. Mott accepted his principles; not because they were his principles, for she called no man master, but because she felt them to be true. In her diary she says:

My sympathy was early enlisted for the poor slave by the class-books read in our schools, and the pictures of the slave-ship, as published by Clarkson. The ministry of Elias Hicks and others on the subject of the unrequited labor of slaves, and their example in refusing the products of slave labor, all had effect in awakening a strong feeling in their behalf.

The unequal condition of woman in society, also early impressed my mind. Learning while at school that the charge for the education of girls was the same as that for boys, and that when they became teachers women received but half as much as men for their services, the injustice of this was so apparent, that I early resolved to claim for my sex all that an impartial Creator has bestowed.

The Temperance reform too engaged my attention; and for more than forty years I have practiced total abstinence from all intoxicating drinks.

The cause of Peace has had a share of my efforts; leading to the ultra non-resistance ground; that no Christian can consistently uphold a government based on the sword, or relying on that as an ultimate resort.

The oppression of the working classes by existing monopolies, and the lowness of wages often engaged my attention; and I have held many meetings with them, and heard their appeals with compassion, and a great desire for a radical change in the system which makes the rich richer, and the poor poorer. The various associations and communities, tending to greater equality of condition, have had from me a hearty God-speed.

But the millions of down-trodden slaves in our land being the most oppressed class, I have felt bound to plead their cause, in season and out of season, to endeavor to put my soul in their souls' stead, and to aid in every right effort for their immediate emancipation. This duty was impressed upon me at the time I consecrated myself to that Gospel which anoints to "preach deliverance to the captive," to "set at liberty them that are bruised." From that time the duty of abstinence, as far as practicable, from slave-grown products was so clear that I resolved to make the effort "to provide things honest" in this respect. Since then, our family has been supplied with free labor, groceries, and to some extent, with cotton goods unstained by slavery.

The labors of the devoted Benjamin Lundy, and his "Genius of Universal Emancipation," published in Baltimore, added to the untiring exertions of Clarkson, Wilberforce, and others in England, including Elizabeth Heyrick, whose work on slavery aroused them to a change in their mode of action; and of William Lloyd Garrison, in Boston, prepared the way for a Convention in Philadelphia, to take the ground of immediate, not gradual emancipation, and to impress the duty of unconditional liberty without expatriation.

December 3, 1833, the American Anti-Slavery Society was formed in Philadelphia. Among the sixty-two people present were Lucretia Mott, Lydia White, and Esther Moore, Rev. Beriah Green in the chair. In reading and discussing their Declaration of Sentiments, Mrs. Mott wishing to make some suggestions, asked the chairman in her modest way if she might speak. Mr. Green promptly and enthusiastically responded, "Certainly, certainly, say all you are moved to say." She at once proposed to strike out two words from one sentence in the Declaration, "We may be personally defeated, but our principles never (can be)." One readily sees how much stronger the sentence is made by striking out the last two words. The quickness of Mrs. Mott in grasping the sentiment and phraseology of a resolution or appeal was always remarkable in our conventions. Mr. Garrison, who wrote the anti-slavery Declaration, readily accepted her amendment. When the members were asked for their signatures, as James Mott pen in hand stood near the desk,

27

Thomas Shipley said that before signing it would be well to consider, as it would bring down on their heads terrible persecutions and great losses in their business relations. He said he should sign it himself, but he would advise James Mott and others to pause. The moment Mr. Shipley ceased speaking, Lucretia, in a brave inspiring tone said, "James, put down thy name," which he quickly did, joining in the general smile of satisfaction.

Soon after the burning of Pennsylvania Hall, at a social gathering one evening, Dr. Moore in conversation with Mrs. Mott strongly condemned the fanaticism and impolicy of the Abolitionists, and especially the women; he said they should do all their reform work through the Friends' meeting. Being much excited, in the course of his remarks, he became very insulting. Mrs. Mott patiently reasoned with him for awhile; at last becoming very indignant, she arose, and leaving him remarked: "All I have to say to thee in parting is, 'Get thee behind me, Satan.'" He immediately took his hat and in silence left the house. Lucretia Mott ante-dated even Mr. Garrison in her protests against slavery. Robert Purvis, of Philadelphia, says he heard her as early as 1829 preach against slavery, on several occasions in the colored church.

In 1833, says Mrs. Mott, the Philadelphia Female Anti-Slavery Society was formed, and being actively associated in the efforts for the slaves' redemption, I have traveled thousands of miles in this country, holding meetings in some of the slave States, have been in the midst of mobs and violence, and have shared abundantly in the odium attached to the name of an uncompromising modern Abolitionist, as well as partaken richly of the sweet return of peace, attendant on those who would "undo the heavy burdens and let the oppressed go free; and break every yoke."

In 1840, a World's Anti-Slavery Convention was called in London. Women from Boston, New York, and Philadelphia, were delegates to that Convention. I was one of the number; but, on our arrival in England, our credentials were not accepted, because we were women. We were, however, treated with the greatest courtesy and attention, as strangers, and were admitted to chosen seats as spectators and listeners, while our right of membership was denied. This brought the woman question more into view, and an increase of interest on the subject has been the result. In this work, too, I have engaged heart and hand; as my labors, travels, and public discourses evince. The misrepresentation, ridicule, and abuse heaped upon this, as well as other reforms, do not in the least deter me from my duty. To those whose name is cast out as evil for the truth's sake, it is a small thing to be judged of man's judgment.

This imperfect sketch may give some idea of the mode of life of one who has found it "good to be always zealously affected in a good thing."

When, as an enthusiastic Abolitionist, Mrs. Mott crossed the ocean to take part in the deliberations of the World's Anti-Slavery

Convention, the last drop in her cup of sorrow was the humiliation she was called to suffer on account of sex. The vote by which this injustice was perpetrated, was due to the overwhelming majority of the clergy, who, with Bible in hand, swept all before them. No man can fathom the depths of rebellion in woman's soul when insult is heaped upon her sex, and this is intensified when done under the hypocritical assumption of divine authority. This fresh baptism into woman's degradation impelled the current of her thoughts into a new channel, and returning home, she, with a few friends as rebellious as herself, called the first Woman's Rights Convention. To this cause she brought a zeal unknown before, as here she could see the wrongs of a class from a purely subjective point of view.

There are often periods in the lives of earnest, imaginative beings, when some new book or acquaintance comes to them like an added sun in the heavens, lighting the darkest recesses and chasing every shadow away. Thus came Lucretia Mott to me, at a period in my young days when all life's problems seemed inextricably tangled; when, like Noah's dove on the waters, my soul found no solid resting-place in the whole world of thought. The misery of the multitude was too boundless for comprehension, too hopeless for tender feeling; despair supplanted all other emotions, and the appalling views of the future threw their dark shadows over the sweetest and most innocent pleasures of life. Before meeting Mrs. Mott, I had heard a few men of liberal opinions discuss various political, religious, and social theories, but with my first doubt of my father's absolute wisdom, came a distrust of all men's opinions on the character and sphere of woman; and I naturally inferred that if their judgments were unsound on a question I was sure I did understand, they were quite likely to be so on those I did not. Hence, I often longed to meet some woman who had sufficient confidence in herself to frame and hold an opinion in the face of opposition, a woman who understood the deep significance of life to whom I could talk freely; my longings were answered at last.

In June, 1840, I met Mrs. Mott for the first time, in London. Crossing the Atlantic in company with James G. Birney, then the Liberty Party candidate for President, soon after the bitter schism in the anti-slavery ranks, he described to me as we walked the deck day after day, the women who had fanned the flames of dissension, and had completely demoralized the anti-slavery ranks. As my first view of Mrs. Mott was through his prejudices, no prepossessions in her favor biased my judgment. When first introduced to her at our hotel in Great Queen Street, with the other ladies from Boston and

Philadelphia who were delegates to the World's Convention, I felt somewhat embarrassed, as I was the only lady present who represented the "Birney faction," though I really knew nothing of the merits of the division, having been outside the world of reforms. Still, as my husband and my cousin, Gerrit Smith, were on that side, I supposed they would all have a feeling of hostility toward me. However, Mrs. Mott, in her sweet, gentle way, received me with great cordiality and courtesy, and I was seated by her side at dinner.

No sooner were the viands fairly dispensed, than several Baptist ministers began to rally the ladies on having set the Abolitionists all by the ears in America, and now proposing to do the same thing in England. I soon found that the pending battle was on woman's rights, and that unwittingly I was by marriage on the wrong side. As I had thought much on this question in regard to the laws, Church action, and social usages, I found myself in full accord with the other ladies, combating most of the gentlemen at the table ; our only champion, George Bradburn, was too deaf to hear a word that was said. In spite of constant gentle nudgings by my husband under the table, and frowns from Mr. Birney opposite, the tantalizing tone of the conversation was too much for me to maintain silence. Calmly and skillfully Mrs. Mott parried all their attacks, now by her quiet humor turning the laugh on them, and then by her earnestness and dignity silencing their ridicule and sneers. I shall never forget the look of recognition she gave me when she saw by my remarks that I fully comprehended the problem of woman's rights and wrongs. How beautiful she looked to me that day.

I had always regarded a Quaker woman, as one does a Sister of Charity, a being above ordinary mortals, ready to be translated at any moment. I had never spoken to one before, nor been near enough to touch the hem of a garment. Mrs. Mott was to me an entire new revelation of womanhood. I sought every opportunity to be at her side, and continually plied her with questions, and I shall never cease to be grateful for the patience and seeming pleasure with which she fed my hungering soul. Seeing the lions in London together, on one occasion with a large party we visited the British Museum, where it is supposed all people go to see the wonders of the world. On entering, Mrs. Mott and myself sat down near the door to rest for a few moments, telling the party to go on, that we would follow. They accordingly explored all the departments of curiosities, supposing we were slowly following at a distance ; but when they returned, after an absence of three hours, there we sat in the same spot, having seen nothing but each other, wholly absorbed in questions of theology and social life. She had told me of the doctrines and divisions among " Friends," of the inward light, of Elias Hicks, of Channing, of a religion of practical life, of Mary Wollstonecroft, her social theories, and her demands of equality for women. I had been reading Combe's " Constitution of Man " and " Moral Philosophy," Channing's works, and Mary Wollstonecroft, though all tabooed by orthodox teachers, but I had never heard a woman talk what, as a Scotch Presbyterian, I had scarcely dared to think.

On the following Sunday I went to hear Mrs. Mott preach in a Unitarian church. Though I had never heard a woman speak, yet I had long believed she had the right to do so, and had often expressed the idea in private circles ; but when at last I saw a woman rise up in the pulpit and preach as earnestly and impressively as Mrs. Mott always did, it seemed to me like the realization of an oft-repeated happy dream. The day we visited the Zoological Gardens, as we were admiring the gorgeous plumage of some beautiful birds, one of our gentlemen opponents remarked, " You see, Mrs. Mott, our Heavenly Father believes in bright colors. How much it would take from our pleasure if all the birds were dressed in drab." " Yes," said she, " but immortal beings do not depend on their feathers for their attractions. With the infinite variety of the human face and form, of thought, feeling, and affection, we do not need gorgeous apparel to distinguish us. Moreover, if it is fitting that woman should dress in every color of the rainbow, why not man also? Clergymen, with their black clothes and white cravats, are quite as monotonous as the Quakers."

I remember on one occasion the entire American delegation were invited to dine with Samuel Gurney, a rich Quaker banker. He had an elegant place, a little out of London. The Duchess of Sutherland and Lord Morpeth, who had watched our anti-slavery struggle in this country with great interest, were quite desirous of meeting the American Abolitionists, and had expressed the wish to call on them at this time. Standing near Mrs. Mott when the coach and four gray horses with the six out-riders drove up, Mr. Gurney, in great trepidation, said, " What shall I do with the Duchess ? " " Give her your arm," said Mrs. Mott, " and introduce her to each member of the delegation." A suggestion no commoner in England would have presumed to follow. When the Duchess was presented to Mrs. Mott, her gracious ease was fully equaled by that of the simple Quaker woman. Oblivious to all distinctions of rank, she talked freely and wisely on many topics, and proved herself in manner and conversation the peer of the first woman in En gland. Mrs. Mott did not manifest the slightest restraint or embarrassment during that marked social occasion. No fictitious superiority ever oppressed her, neither did she descend in familiar surroundings from her natural dignity, but always maintained the perfect equilibrium of respect for herself and others.

I found in this new friend a woman emancipated from all faith in man-made creeds, from all fear of his denunciations. Nothing was too sacred for her to question, as to its rightfulness in principle and practice. " Truth for authority, not authority for truth," was not only the motto of her life, but it was the fixed mental habit in which she most rigidly held herself. It seemed to me like meeting a being from some larger planet, to find a woman who dared to question the opinions of Popes, Kings, Synods, Parliaments, with the same freedom that she would criticise an editorial in the *London Times*, recognizing no higher authority than the judgment of a pure-minded, educated woman. When I first heard from the lips of Lucretia Mott that I had the same right to think for myself that Luther, Calvin, and John Knox had, and the same right to be guided by my own convictions, and would no doubt live a higher, happier life than if guided by theirs, I felt at once a new-born sense of dignity and freedom ; it was like suddenly coming into the rays of the noon-day sun, after wandering with a rushlight in the caves of the earth. When I confessed to her my great enjoyment in works of fiction, dramatic performances, and dancing, and feared from underneath that Quaker bonnet (I now loved so well) would come some platitudes on the demoralizing influence of such frivolities, she smiled, and said, " I regard dancing a very harmless amusement "; and added, " the Evangelical Alliance that so readily passed a resolution declaring dancing a sin for a church member, tabled a resolution declaring slavery a sin for a bishop."

Sitting alone one day, as we were about to separate in London, I expressed to her my great satisfaction in her acquaintance, and thanked her for the many religious doubts and fears she had banished from my mind. She said, " There is a broad distinction between religion and theology. The one is a natural, human experience common to all well-organized minds. The other is a system of speculations about the unseen and the unknowable, which the human mind has no power to grasp or explain, and these speculations vary with every sect, age, and type of civilization. No one knows any more of what lies beyond our sphere of action than thou and I, and we know nothing." Everything she said seemed to me so true and rational, that I accepted her words of wisdom with the same confiding satisfaction that did the faithful Crito those of his beloved Socrates. And yet this pure, grand woman was shunned and feared by the Orthodox Friends throughout England. While in London a rich young Quaker of bigoted tendencies, who made several breakfast and tea parties for the American delegates, always omitted to invite Mrs. Mott. He very politely said to her on one occasion when he was inviting others in her presence, " Thou must excuse me, Lucretia, for not inviting thee with the rest, but I fear thy influence on my children ! ! "

On several occasions when we all met at social gatherings in London, Elizabeth Fry studiously avoided being in the same apartment with Lucretia Mott. If Mrs. Mott was conversing with a circle of friends on the lawn, Mrs. Fry would glide into the house. If Mrs. Mott entered at one door, Mrs. Fry walked out the other. She really seemed afraid to breathe the same atmosphere. On another occasion, at William Ball's, at Tottenham, when more circumscribed quarters made escape impossible, it was announced that Mrs. Fry felt a concern to say something to those present. When all was silent she knelt and prayed, pouring forth a solemn Jeremiad against the apostasy and infidelity of the day in language so pointed and personal, that we all felt that Mrs. Mott was the special subject of her petition. She accepted the intercession with all due humility, and fortunately for the harmony of the occasion was not moved to pray for Mrs. Fry, that she might have more love and charity for those who honestly differed with her on unimportant points of theology. How hateful such bigotry looks to those capable of getting outside their own educational prejudices. How pitiable, that even good people should thus allow themselves to ostracise and persecute those who hold different opinions from their own. Elizabeth Fry was not afraid to mingle in Newgate prison with the scum of the earth, but she was afraid to touch the hem of Lucretia Mott's garment. If Mrs. Fry felt that she had a higher truth, how did she know that she might not influence Mrs. Mott for good? Lucretia was never afraid of anybody. Nothing would have pleased her better than to compare her pearls of thought and faith with Elizabeth Fry.

Visiting in many Quaker families during our travels in England, I was amazed to hear Mrs. Mott spoken of as a most dangerous woman. Again and again I was warned against her influence. She was spoken of as an infidel, a heretic, a disturber, who had destroyed the peace in the Friends Society in Pennsylvania, and thrown a firebrand into the World's Convention, and that in a recent speech in London she quoted sentiments from Mary Wollstonecroft and Thomas Paine. Having just learned to worship Lucretia Mott as the embodiment of all that was noble and charming in womanhood, the terrible fear that she inspired among English "Friends" filled me with sorrow and surprise. I never ventured to mention her name in their homes unless they first introduced it.

Sitting in the World's Convention one day after half the world had been voted out, when Joseph Sturge, a wealthy Quaker, occupied the chair, I suggested to Mrs. Mott a dangerous contingency. Said I, " Suppose in spite of the vote of excommunication the Spirit should move you to speak, what could the chairman do, and which would you obey? the Spirit or the Convention?" She promptly replied, "Where the Spirit of God is, there is liberty."

Many anecdotes are told of Mrs. Mott's rigid economy, such as sewing together the smallest rags to be woven into carpets, and writing letters on infinitesimal bits of paper; but it must not be inferred from this peculiarity that she was penurious, as she was generous in her charities, and in the support of every good cause. Considering her means and the self-denial she practiced in her personal expenses, her gifts were lavish. Alfred Love, President of the Peace Society, who frequently received letters from Mrs. Mott, says : " The one before me is two and a half inches wide by two and a quarter inches long, written on both sides, and contains one hundred and forty-one words, and treats of seven distinct matters, and disposes of them in good order, apologizing for her apparent economy of paper, and enclosing a contribution of five dollars for a benevolent object." Though she always dressed in Quaker costume, she attached no special significance to it as a means of grace. One Sunday morning at a religious meeting, she was in her accustomed seat in the gallery, when a young man, a stranger to many, spoke in behalf of Peace. At the close of the meeting some one who could not see the speaker asked Lucretia Mott his name, and added : " Does he wear a standing collar and dress plain?" She replied in her happy, cheerful manner, " Well, really I did not look to see, I was too much interested in what he said to look at the cut of his coat."

'Mid all the differences, dissensions, and personal antagonisms, through the years we have labored together in the Woman's Rights movement, I can not recall one word or occasion in which Mrs. Mott's influence has not been for harmony, good-will, and the broadest charity. She endured too much persecution herself ever to join in persecuting others. In every reform she stood in the forefront of the battle. Wherever there was a trying emergency to be met, there you could rely on Lucretia Mott. She never dodged responsibility nor disagreeable occasions. At one time when excitement on the divorce question ran high in New York, and there was a great hue and cry about free love on our platform, I was invited to speak before the Legislature on the bill then pending asking " divorce for drunkenness." We chose the time at the close of one of our Conventions, that Mrs. Mott might be present, which she readily consented to do, and promised to speak if she felt moved. She charged Ernestine Rose and myself not to take too radical ground, in view of the hostility to the bill, but to keep closely to the merits of the main question. I told her she might feel sure of me, as I had my speech written, and I would read it to her, which I did, and received her approval.

The time arrived for the hearing, and a magnificent audience greeted us at the Capitol. The bill was read, I made the opening speech, Mrs. Rose followed. We had asked for the modification of certain statutes and the passage of others making the laws more equal for man and woman. Mrs. Mott having listened attentively to all that was said, and coming to the conclusion that with eighteen different causes for divorce in the different States, there might as well be no laws at all on the question, she arose and said, that " she had not thought profoundly on this subject, but it seemed to her that no laws whatever on this relation would be better than such as bound pure, innocent women in bondage to dissipated, unprincipled men. With such various laws in the different States, and fugitives from the marriage bond fleeing from one to another, would it not be better to place all the States on the same basis, and thus make our national laws homogeneous?" She was surprised on returning to the residence of Lydia Mott, to hear that her speech was altogether the most radical of the three. The bold statement of " no laws," however, was so sugar-coated with eulogies on good men and the sacredness of the marriage relation, that the press complimented the moderation of Mrs. Mott at our expense. We have had many a laugh over that occasion.

An amusing incident occurred the first year, 1869, we held a Convention in Washington. Chaplain Gray, of the Senate, was invited to open the Convention with prayer. Mrs. Mott and I were sitting close together, with our heads bowed and eyes closed, listening to the invocation. As the chaplain proceeded, he touched the garden scene in Paradise, and spoke of woman as a secondary creation, called into being for the especial benefit of man, an afterthought with the Creator. Straightening up, Mrs. Mott whispered to me, "I can not bow my head to such absurdities." Edward M. Davis, in the audience, noticed his mother's movements, and knowing that what had struck his mind had no doubt disturbed hers also, he immediately left the hall, returning shortly after Bible in hand, that he might confound the chaplain with the very book he had quoted. He ascended the platform just as Mr. Gray said "amen," and read from the opening chapter of Genesis, the account of the simultaneous creation of man and woman, in which dominion was given to both alike over every living thing. After Mr. Davis made a few pertinent remarks on the allegorical character of the second chapter of Genesis, Mrs. Mott followed with a critical analysis of the prayer, and the portion of the Scripture read by her son, showing the eternal oneness and equality of man and woman, the union of the masculine and feminine elements, like the positive and negative magnetism, the centripetal and centrifugal forces in nature, pervading the animal, vegetable, and mineral kingdoms, the whole world of thought and action, as there could have been no perpetuation of creation without these elements equal and eternal in the Godhead. The press commented on the novelty of reviewing an address to the throne of grace, particularly when uttered by the chaplain of Congress. Mrs. Mott remarked on these criticisms, "If we can teach clergymen to be as careful what they say to God as to man, our Conventions at the capital will be of great service to our representatives."

As a writer Mrs. Mott was clear and concise; her few published sermons, her charming private letters and diary, with what those who knew her best can remember, are all of her thoughts bequeathed to posterity. As a speaker she was calm, clear, and unimpassioned; indulged but little in wit, humor, or pathos, but by her good common sense and liberality on all questions, by her earnestness and simplicity, she held the most respectful attention of her audiences. Hence an occasional touch of humor or sarcasm, or an outburst of eloquent indignation came from her with great power. She had what the Friends call unction; that made the most radical utterances from her lips acceptable. In her conversation she was original and brilliant, earnest and playful. Such was her persuasiveness of voice and manner that opinions received with hisses from another speaker, were applauded when uttered by Mrs. Mott.

Some one has said that "sagacity, a mental quick-wittedness for meeting an emergency, a sagacity that might have been called shrewdness, had it not been for a pervading heart quality that went with it, was one of her prominent traits." Perhaps a wise diplomacy might express this quality more nearly. No one knew better than she how to avoid the sharp angles of a character or an occasion, as the many anecdotes told of her so fully illustrate.

Returning from England in 1840, in a merchant vessel, a large number of Irish emigrants were on board in the steerage. On the voyage Mrs. Mott was moved to hold a religious meeting among them, but the matter being broached to them, their Catholic prejudices objected. They would not hear a woman preach, for women priest were not allowed in their Church. But the spirit that was pressing upon the "woman preacher" for utterance was not to be prevented from delivering its message without a more strenuous effort to remove the obstacle. She asked that the emigrants might be invited to come together to consider with her whether they would have a meeting. This was but fair and right, and they came. She then explained how different her idea of a meeting was from a church service to which they were accustomed; that she had no thought of saying anything derogatory of that service nor of the priests who ministered to them; that her heart had been drawn to them in sympathy, as they were leaving their old homes for new ones in America; and that she had wanted to address them as to their habits and aims in their every-day life in such a way as to help them in the land of strangers to which they were going. And then asking if they would listen (and they were already listening because her gracious voice and words so entranced them they could not help it), she said she would give an outline of what she had wanted to say at the meeting, and so she was drawn on by the silent sympathy she had secured until the Spirit's message was delivered; and only the keenest witted of her Catholic hearers waked up to the fact, as they were going out, that they had got the preachment from the woman priest after all.

Presiding at a woman's convention on one occasion, a speaker painted a very vivid picture in the darkest colors of this nation's injustice to oppressed classes, and from the experience of other nations not based upon principle, he foretold the certain downfall of our republic. On rising, he had said that "he feared he should not be able to do his theme justice, as he had just risen from a bed of sickness," but warming up with his subject he rivaled Isaiah in his Jeremiad, and left his audience in gloom and despair, the president sharing in the general feeling, for the appeal had been thrilling and terrible. In a moment, however, Mrs. Mott arose, saying: "I trust our future is not as hopeless as our faithful friend, Parker Pillsbury, has just pictured. We must remember he told us in starting that he had just risen from a bed of sickness, and that may in a measure account for his gloomy forebodings." The audience burst forth into a roar of applause and laughter, and the president introduced the next speaker, seemingly unconscious that she had stabbed the prophet through and through, and dissipated the effect of his warnings.

Mrs. Mott was frequently chosen the presiding officer of the early conventions. Though she seldom regarded Cushing's Manual in her rulings, she maintained order and good feeling by the persuasiveness and serenity of her voice and manner. Emerson says: " It is not what the man says, but it is the spirit behind it which makes the impression." It was this subtle magnetism of the true, grand woman, ever faithful to her highest convictions of truth, that made her always respected in every position she occupied. Hers was pure moral power, for in that frail organization there could be but little of what is called physical magnetism. Her placid face showed that she was at peace with herself, the first requisite in a successful leader of reform. That Mrs. Mott could have maintained her sweetness and charity to the end, is a marvel in view of the varied and protracted persecutions she endured.

Rarely have so many different and superior qualities been combined in one woman. She had great personal beauty; her brow and eye were remarkable. Although small in stature, it is said of her as it was of Channing, he too being of diminutive size, that she made you think she was larger than she was. She had a look of command. The amount of will force and intelligent power in her small body was enough to direct the universe; yet she was modest and unassuming and had none of the personal airs of leadership. Her manners were gentle and self-possessed under all circumstances. Her conversation, though generally serious, earnest and logical, was sometimes playful and always good humored. Her attitude of mind was receptive. She never seemed to think even in her latest years that she had explored all truth. Though she had very clearly defined opinions on every subject that came under her consideration, she never dogmatized.

It was this healthy balance of good qualities that made her great among other women of genius; and the multiplicity of her interests in human affairs that kept her fresh and young to the last. The thinkers, the scholars, the broadest intellects are often the octogenarians, while the narrow selfish souls dry up in their own channels One of her noble sisters in reform has truly said, " Birth made Victoria a queen, but her own pure, sweet life made Lucretia Mott a queen; queen of a realm on which the sun never sets, the realm of humanity. If ever any one inherited the earth it was this blessed Quaker woman."

Space fails me to tell of all the pleasant memories of our forty years friendship, of the inspiration she has been to those on our platform, of the bond of union to hold us together, of the innumerable conventions over which she has presided, of the many long journeys both North and South to carry the glad tidings of justice, liberty, and equality to all. A missionary who always traveled at her own expense, giving her best thoughts freely, asking nothing in return, neither money, praise, nor honor; for misrepresentation and cruel persecution were the only return she had for years. Both in religion and reform hers was a free gospel to the multitude.

As division has been the law in politics, religion, and reform, woman suffrage proved no exception. But Lucretia Mott and her noble sister, Martha C. Wright, remained steadfast with those who had taken the initiative steps in calling the first Convention, and with the larger and more radical division their sympathies remained, both being prominent officers of the National Woman Suffrage Association at the time of their death. They fully endorsed the great lesson of the war, National protection for United States citizens, applied to woman as well as to the African race, the doctrine the association to which they belonged has so successfully advocated at Washington for twelve years.

Reading the numerous complimentary obituary notices of our long loved friend, so fair, so tender, so full of praise, we have exclaimed, what changes the passing years have wrought in the popular estimate of a woman once considered so dangerous an innovator in the social and religious world; and yet the Lucretia Mott of to-day is only the perfected, well-rounded character of half a century ago. But the slowly moving masses that feared her then as an infidel, a fanatic, an unsexed woman, have followed her footsteps until a broader outlook has expanded their moral vision. The "vagaries" of the anti-slavery struggle, in which she took a leading part, have been coined into law; and the "wild fantasies" of the Abolitionists are now the XIII., XIV., and XV. Amendments to the National Constitution. The prolonged and bitter schisms in the Society of Friends have shed new light on the tyranny of creeds and scriptures. The infidel Hicksite principles that shocked Christendom, are now the corner-stones of the liberal religious movement in this country. The demand for woman's social, civil, and political equality—in which she was foremost—laughed at from the Atlantic to the Pacific, has been recognized in a measure by courts and legislatures, in Great Britain and the United States. The old Blackstone code for woman has received its death-blow, and the colleges, trades, and professions have been opened for her admission.

The name of Lucretia Mott represents more fully than any other in the nineteenth century, the sum of all womanly virtues. As wife, mother, friend, she was marked for her delicate sentiments, warm affections, and steadfast loyalty; as housekeeper, for her rigid economy, cleanliness, order, and exhaustless patience with servants and children; as neighbor, for justice and honor in all her dealings; as teacher, even at the early age of fifteen, for her skill and faithfulness.

One who has lived eighty-eight years 'mid a young, impressible people like ours, ever reflecting the exalted virtues of the true woman, the earnest reformer, the religious teacher, must have left her impress for good in every relation of life. When we remember that every word we utter, every act we perform, the individual atmosphere we create have their effect, not only on all who come within the circle of our daily life, but through them are wafted to innumerable other circles beyond, we can in a measure appreciate the far-reaching influence of one grand life. Great as has been the acknowledged moral power of Lucretia Mott, it would have been vastly greater, had her opinions been legitimately recognized in the laws and constitutions of the nation; and could she have enjoyed the consciousness of exerting this direct influence, it would have intensified the holy purpose of her life. "The highest earthly desire of a ripened mind," says Thomas Arnold, "is the desire of taking an active share in the great work of government." Those only who are capable of appreciating this dignity can measure the extent to which this noble woman has been defrauded as a citizen of this great Republic. Neither can they measure the loss to the councils of the nation, of the wisdom of such a representative woman.

In the manifold tributes to the memory of our beloved friend, we have yet to see the first mention of her political degradation, which she so keenly felt and so often deplored on our platform. Why are the press and the pulpit, with all their eulogiums of her virtues, so oblivious to the humiliating fact of her disfranchisement? Are political disabilities, accounted such grievous wrongs to the Southern aristocrat, to the emancipated slave, to the proud Anglo-Saxon man in every latitude, of so little value to woman that when a nation mourns the loss of the grandest representative of our sex, no tear is shed, no regret expressed, no mention even made of her political degradation?

We might ask the question why this universal outpouring of tributes to our venerated friend, exceeding all honors hitherto paid to the great women of our nation, who, one by one, have passed away

It is because Lucretia Mott was a philanthropist ; her life was dedicated to the rights of humanity. When the poet, the novelist, the philosopher, and the metaphysican have been forgotten, the memory of the true reformer will remain engraven on the hearts of the multitude. Behold ! the beauty of yonder fountain, after its upward flight, is where it turns again to earth, so is the life of one morally beautiful, ever drawn by a law of its being from the clouds of speculation to the common interests of humanity.

The question is often asked of us on this platform, will the children of these reformers take up the work that falls from their hands ? It is more than probable they will not. It is with reformers' children as others, they seldom follow in the footsteps of their parents. As a general thing the son of a farmer hates the plow, the son of a lawyer is not attracted to the bar, nor the son of a clergyman to the pulpit. The daughter of the pattern housekeeper turns to literature or art, and the child of the reformer has no heart for martyrdom. It is philosophical that our sons and daughters should not be here. To a certain extent they have shared the odium and persecution we have provoked, they have been ostracised and ignored for heresies they have never accepted. The humiliation of our children has been the bitterest drop in the cup of reformers. Look around our platform, not one representative of the brave band of women who inaugurated this movement is here! Not one of our kindred has ever yet in these conventions echoed our demands. Nevertheless we are, and shall be represented ! We see bright new faces; we hear eloquent new voices; brave young women are gathering round us, to plead our cause in more august assemblies, and to celebrate the victory at last. These are our kindred, by holier ties than blood. As their way through life will be smoother for all our noble friend has dared and suffered, may they by the same courage and conscientious devotion to principle, shed new light on the path of those who follow their footsteps. This is the great moral lesson the life of our dear friend should impress on the coming generation.

Having known Lucretia Mott, not only in the flush of life, when all her faculties were at their zenith, but in the repose of advanced age, her withdrawal from our midst seems as natural and as beautiful as the changing foliage of some grand oak from the spring-time to the autumn.

ENGLISH CORRESPONDENCE.

The following interesting correspondence in regard to the exclusion of women from the World's Convention, reveals the fact that the action was the result, after all, of religious bigotry more than prejudice against sex.   And this opinion is further confirmed by the decided opposition promptly manifested to Lucretia Mott's proposal to have a series of meetings for women alone.   Some of the Orthodox Friends said they were afraid, that under the plea of discussing emancipation for the slave, other subjects might be introduced. Mrs. Mott, desiring to know what Daniel O'Connell thought of the action of the Convention, wrote him as follows :

To Daniel O'Connell, M.P. :

The rejected delegates from America to the "General Anti-Slavery Conference," are desirous to have the opinion of one of the most distinguished advocates of universal liberty, as to the reasons urged by the majority for their rejection, viz: that the admission of women being contrary to English usage would subject them to ridicule, and that such recognition of their acknowledged principles would prejudice the cause of human freedom.

Permit me, then, on behalf of the delegation, to ask Daniel O'Connell the favor of his sentiments as incidentally expressed in the meeting on the morning of the 13th inst., and oblige his sincere friend,

LUCRETIA MOTT.

LONDON, *sixth mo.*, 17, 1840.

16 PALL MALL, *20th June*, 1840.

MADAM:—Taking the liberty of protesting against being supposed to adopt any of the complimentary phrases in your letter as being applicable to me, I readily comply with your request to give my opinion as to the propriety of the admission of the female delegates into the Convention.

I should premise by avowing that my first impression was strong against that admission; and I believe I declared that opinion in private conversation.   But when I was called on by you to give my personal decision on the subject, I felt it my duty to investigate the grounds of the opinion I had formed; and upon that investigation I easily discovered that it was founded on no better grounds than an apprehension of the ridicule it might excite if the Convention were to do what is so unusual in England—admit women to an equal share and right of the discussion. I also without difficulty recognized that this was an unworthy, and, indeed, a cowardly motive, and I easily overcame its influence.

My mature consideration of the entire subject convinces me of the right of the female delegates to take their seats in the Convention, and of the injustice of excluding them.   I do not care to add that I deem it also impolitic; because, that exclusion being unjust, it ought not to have taken place even if it could also be politic.   My reasons are:

First. That as it has been the practice in America for females to act as delegates and office-bearers, as well as in common capacity of members of Anti-Slavery Societies, the persons who called this Convention ought to have warned the American Anti-Slavery Societies to confine their choice to males, and for want of this caution many female delegates have made long journeys by land and crossed the ocean to enjoy a right which they had no reason to fear would be withheld from them at the end of their tedious voyage.

Secondly. The cause which is so intimately interwoven with every good feeling of humanity and with the highest and most sacred principles of Christianity—the Anti-Slavery cause in America—is under the greatest, the deepest, the most heart-binding obligations to the females who have joined the Anti-Slavery Societies in the United States. They have shown a passive but permanent courage, which ought to put many of the male advocates to the blush. The American ladies have persevered in our holy cause amidst difficulties and dangers, with the zeal of confessors and the firmness of martyrs; and, therefore, emphatically they should not be disparaged or discouraged by any slight or contumely offered to their rights. Neither are this slight and contumely much diminished by the fact that it was not intended to offer any slight or to convey any contumely. Both results inevitably follow from the fact of rejection. This OUGHT NOT to be.

Thirdly. Even in England, with all our fastidiousness, women vote upon the great regulation of the Bank of England; in the nomination of its directors and governors, and in all other details equally with men; that is, they assist in the most awfully important business—the regulation of the currency of this mighty Empire—influencing the fortunes of all commercial nations.

Fourthly. Our women in like manner vote at the India House; that is, in the regulation of the government of more than one hundred millions of human beings.

Fifthly. Mind has no sex; and in the peaceable struggle to abolish slavery all over the world, it is the basis of the present Convention to seek success by peaceable, moral, and intellectual means alone, to the utter exclusion of armed violence. We are engaged in a strife not of strength, but of argument. Our warfare is not military; it is Christian. We wield not the weapons of destruction or injury to our adversaries. We rely entirely on reason and persuasion common to both sexes, and on the emotions of benevolence and charity, which are more lovely and permanent amongst women than amongst men.

In the Church to which I belong the female sex are devoted by as strict rules and with as much, if not more, unceasing austerity to the performance (and that to the exclusion of all worldly or temporal joys and pleasures) of all works of humanity, of education, of benevolence, and of charity, in all its holy and sacred branches, as the men. The great work in which we are now engaged embraces all these charitable categories; and the women have the same duties, and should, therefore, enjoy the same rights with men in the performance of their duties.

I have a consciousness that I have not done *my* duty in not sooner

28

urging these considerations on the Convention. My excuse is that I was unavoidably absent during the discussion on the subject.

I have the honor to be, very respectfully, madam,

Your obedient servant,

LUCRETIA MOTT.   DANIEL O'CONNELL.

The following earnest and friendly letter from William Howitt, was highly prized by Mrs. Mott:

LONDON, *June* 27, 1840.

DEAR FRIEND:—. . . . I regret that I was prevented from making a part of the Convention, as nothing should have hindered me from stating there in the plainest terms my opinion of the *real grounds* on which you were rejected. It is a pity that you were excluded on the plea of being women; but it is disgusting that under that plea you were actually excluded as heretics. That is the real ground, and it ought to have been at once proclaimed and exposed by the liberal members of the Convention; but I believe they were not aware of the fact. I heard of the circumstance of your exclusion at a distance, and immediately said: "Excluded on the ground that they are women?" No, that is not the real cause; there is something behind. And what are these female delegates? Are they orthodox in religion? The answer was "No, they are considered to be of the Hicksite party of Friends." My reply was, "That is enough; *there* lies the real cause, and th3re needs no other. The influential Friends in the Convention would never for a moment tolerate their presence there if they could prevent it. They hate them because they have dared to call in question their sectarian dogmas and assumed authority; and they have taken care to brand them in the eyes of the Calvinistic Dissenters, who form another large and influential portion of the Convention, as Unitarians; in their eyes the most odious of heretics."

But what a miserable spectacle is this! The "World's Convention" converting itself into the fag-end of the Yearly Meeting of the Society of Friends! That Convention met from various countries and climates to consider how it shall best advance the sacred cause of humanity; of the freedom of the race, independent of caste or color, immediately falls the victim of bigotry; and one of its first acts is to establish a caste of sectarian opinion, and to introduce color into the very soul! Had I not seen of late years a good deal of the spirit which now rules the Society of Friends, my surprise would have been unbounded at seeing *them* argue for the exclusion of women from a public assembly, *as women*. But nothing which they do now surprises me. They have in this case to gratify their wretched spirit of intolerance, at once abandoned one of the most noble and most philosophical of the established principles of their own Society.

That Society claims, and claims justly, to be the first Christian party which has recognized the great Christian doctrine that THERE IS NO SEX IN SOULS; that male and female are one in Christ Jesus. There were Fox and Penn and the first giants of the Society who dared in the face of the world's prejudices to place woman in her first rank; to recognize and maintain her moral and intellectual equality. It was this Society which thus gave to woman her inalienable rights, her true liberty; which restored to her the exercise of mind, and the capacity to exhibit before her assumed ancient lord and master, the highest qualities of the human heart and understanding; discretion, sound counsel, sure sagacity, mingled with feminine delicacy, and that beautiful innate modesty which avails more to restrain its possessor within the bounds of prudence and usefulness than all the laws of corrupt society. It was this Society which, at once fearless in its confidence in woman's goodness and sense of propriety, gave its female portion its own meetings of discipline, meetings of civil discussion and transaction of actual and various business. It was this Society which did more; which permitted its women in the face of a great apostolic injunction to stand forth in its churches and preach the Gospel. It has, in fact, sent them out armed with the authority of its certificates to the very ends of the earth to preach in public; to visit and persuade in private.

And what has been the consequence ? Have the women put their faith and philosophy to shame ? Have they disgraced themselves or the Society which has confided in them ? Have they proved by their follies, their extravagances, their unwomanly boldness and want of a just sense of decorum that these great men were wrong ? On the contrary, I will venture to say, and I have seen something of all classes, that there is not in the whole civilized world a body of women to be found of the same numbers, who exhibit more modesty of manner and delicacy of mind than the ladies of the Society of Friends; and few who equal them in sound sense and dignity of character. There can be no question that the recognition of the moral and intellectual equality of the most lovely and interesting portion of our Society has tended, and that very materially, to raise them greatly in value as wives, as bosom friends and domestic counselors, whose inestimable worth is only discovered in times of trial and perplexity.

And here have gone the little men of the present day, and have knocked down in the face of the world all that their ancestors, in this respect, had built up ! If they are at all consistent they must carry out their new principle and sweep it through the ancient constitution of their own Society. They must at once put down meetings of discipline among their women; they must call home such as are in distant countries, or are traversing this, preaching and visiting families. There must be no appointments of women to meet committees of men to deliberate on matters of great importance to the Society. But the fact is, my dear friend, that bigotry is never consistent except that is always narrow, always ungracious, and always under plea of uniting God's people, scattering them one from another, and rendering them weak as water.

I want to know what religious opinions have to do with a "World's Convention." Did you meet to settle doctrines, or to conspire against slavery ? Many an august council has attempted to settle doctrines, and in vain; and you had before you a subject so vast, so pressing, so momentous, that in presence of its sublimity, any petty jealousy and fancied idea of superiority ought to have fallen as dust from the boughs of a cedar. You as delegates, had to meet this awful fact in the face, and to consider how it should be grappled with; how the united power of civilized nations should be brought to bear upon it ! The fact that after nearly a century of gradually growing and accumulating efforts to put down slavery and the slave trade, little has been done; that there are now more slaves in the world than ever, and that the slave trade is far more extensive and monstrous than it was when Clarkson raised his voice against its extinction; that is a fact which, if the men who now take the lead in warring on the evil were truly great men, it would silence in them every other feeling than that of its enormity, and the godlike resolve that all hands and all hearts should be raised before Heaven and united in its spirit to chase this spreading villainy from the earth speedily and forever. But men, however benevolent, can not be great men if they are bigots. Bigots are like the peasants who build their cabins in the mighty palaces of the ancient Cæsars. The Cæsars who raised the past fabrics are gone, and the power in which they raised them is gone with them. Poor and little men raise their huts within those august palace walls, and fancy themselves the inhabitants of the palaces themselves. So in the mighty fane of Christianity, bigots and sectarians are continually rearing their little cabins of sects and parties, and would fain persuade us, while they fill their own narrow tenements, that they fill the glorious greatness of Christianity itself !

It is surely high time that after eighteen hundred years of Christ's reign we should be prepared to allow each other to hold an opinion on the most important of all subjects to ourselves ! It is surely time that we opened our eyes sufficiently to see what is so plain in the Gospel: the sublime difference between the Spirit of Christ and the spirit of His disciples when they fain would have made a bigot of Him. "We saw men doing miracles in thy name; and we forbade them." "Forbid them not, for they who are not against us are for us." It is not by *doctrines* that Christ said His disciples should be known, but by their fruits; and by the greatest of all fruits—love.

You, dear friend, and those noble women to whom I address myself when addressing you, have shown in your own country the grand Christian testimonial of love to mankind in the highest degree. You have put your lives in your hands for the sake of man's freedom from caste, color, and mammon; and the greatest disgrace that has of late years befallen this country is, that you have been refused admittance as delegates to the Convention met ostensibly to work that very work for which you have so generously labored and freely suffered. The Convention has not merely insulted you, but those who sent you. It has testified that the men of America are at least far ahead of us in their opinion of the discretion and usefulness of women. But above all, this act of exclusion has shown how far the Society of Friends is fallen from its ancient state of greatness and catholic nobleness of spirit.

But my time is gone. I have not said one-half, one-tenth, one-hundredth part of what I could say to you and to your companions on this subject; but of this be assured, time and your own delegators will do you justice. The true Christians in all ages were the heretics of the time; and this I say not because I believe exactly as you do, for in truth I neither know nor desire to know exactly how far we think alike. All that I know or want to know is, that you have shown the grand mark of Christian truth—love to mankind.

I have heard the noble Garrison blamed that he had not taken his place in the Convention because you and your fellow-delegates were excluded. I, on the contrary, honor him for his conduct. In mere worldly wisdom he might have entered the Convention and there made his protest against the decision; but in at once refusing to enter where you, his fellow-delegates, were shut out, he has made a far nobler protest; not in the mere Convention, but in the world at large. I honor the lofty principle of that true champion of humanity, and shall always recollect with delight, the day Mary and I spent with you and him.

I must apologize for this most hasty and I fear illegible scrawl, and with our kind regards and best wishes for your safe return to your native country, and for many years of honorable labor there for the truth and freedom, I beg to subscribe myself,

Most sincerely your friend,

WILLIAM HOWITT.

Harriet Martineau, who had visited Mrs. Mott when in America, and was prevented from attending the Convention by illness, wrote as follows:

I can not be satisfied without sending you a line of love and sympathy. I think much of you amidst your present trials, and much indeed have I thought of you and your cause since we parted. May God strengthen you. It is a comfort to me that two of my best friends, Mrs. Reid and Julia Smith, are there to look upon you with eyes of love. I hear of you from them, for busy as they are, they remember me from day to day, and make me a partaker of your proceedings. . . . . I can not but grieve for you in the heart-sickness which you have experienced this last week. We must trust that the spirit of Christ will in time enlarge the hearts of those who claim his name, that the whites as well as the blacks will in time be free.

After the Convention, Mrs. Mott visited Miss Martineau, who was an invalid, staying at Tynemouth, for the benefit of sea air. And on her return to London, she received another letter, from which we extract the following:

I felt hardly as if I knew what I was about that morning, but I was very happy, and I find that I remember every look and word. I did not make all the use I might of the opportunity; but when are we ever wise enough to do it? I do not think we shall ever meet again in this world, and I believe that was in your mind when you said farewell. I feel that I have derived somewhat from my intercourse with you that will never die, and I am thankful that we have been permitted to meet. You will tell the Furnesses (Rev. Wm. H.) where and how you found me. Tell them of my cheerful room and fine down and sea. I wish my friends would suffer for me no more than I do for myself. I hope you have yet many years of activity and enjoyment before you. My heart will ever be in your cause and my love with yourself.

In James Mott's published volume, " Three months in Great Britain," he speaks of many distinguished persons who extended to them most gracious hospitalities, for although Mrs. Mott had been ostracised by some of the more bigoted " Friends," others were correspondingly marked in their attentions. Among such was that noble-hearted young woman, Elizabeth Pease, of Darlington, who was one of the first to call upon them on their arrival in London, and the last to bid them farewell on the morning they sailed from Liverpool ; having in company with her father gone from Manchester for that purpose. Her cultivated mind and fine talents were devoted to subjects of reform, with an energy and perseverance rarely equaled.

Ann Knight, another sincere friend and advocate of human rights, was quite indignant, that a Convention called for such liberal measures should reject women on the flimsy plea, " that it being contrary to English usage, it would subject them to ridicule and prejudice their cause." She was unremitting in her attentions to the American women, doing many things to make their visit pleasant while in London, and afterward, entertaining several as guests in her own " quiet home." Amelia Opie, with her happy face and genial manners, was in constant attendance at the Convention. On entering one of the sessions, she accosted Mrs. Mott, saying, "though in one sense the women delegates were rejected, yet they were held in high esteem, and their coming would have immense influence on the action of future assemblies."

At the " Crown and Anchor," one evening, the members of the Convention took a parting cup of tea ; nearly five hundred persons were present. As the resolution excluding women did not extend to this company, Mrs. Mott gave her views on the use of slave products, which were well received. In the course of her remarks she referred to the example and faithfulness of the " Society of Friends," in using as far as possible the produce of free labor in their families. Josiah Forster, ever vigilant on the battlements of bigotry, could not allow this allusion to pass unnoticed, and when Mrs. Mott sat down, he arose and said he " could not conscientiously refrain from informing the company, that Mrs. Mott did not represent the Society of Friends. He did so with no other than feelings of kindness, but,"—when he had proceeded thus far it was evident he was

about to disclaim religious fellowship with her, and a general burst
of disapprobation was manifested by cries of " down, down ! order,
order ! shame, shame ! "—but he finished his disavowal amidst the
confusion, though few heard what he said, neither did they wish to
hear his expressions of intolerance. As soon as he had finished his
speech he left the room, probably displeased that his feelings met
with so little sympathy, or at the manifestation of dissatisfaction
with his remarks.

At a dinner party, at Elizabeth J. Reid's, a few days after, Lady
Byron was one of the company; with whom Mr. and Mrs. Mott
had a previous acquaintance, through a letter of introduction from
George Combe. As Colonel Miller, one of the American delegation, had been in the Greek war with Lord Byron, and knew him
well, several interesting interviews with the wife and daughter
grew out of that acquaintance. They also visited Dr. Bowring and
his interesting family several times, and on one occasion met there
Charles Pelham Villiers, the leading advocate in Parliament for
the modification of their corn laws. Dr. Bowring was a near neighbor and great admirer of Jeremy Bentham, and entertained them
with many anecdotes of his original friend. William H. Ashurst,
a lawyer of eminence in London, gave them a cordial welcome to
his family circle, where they met William and Mary Howitt, and
Robert Owen, the philanthropist. Mr. Ashurst took an active part
in favor of reducing the postage on letters and papers.

At Birmingham, they passed a few days with their liberal
" Friend," William Boultbee, and visited several of the great manufacturing establishments. Here they made the acquaintance of a
Catholic priest, Thomas M. McDonald, a man of broad views and
marked liberality. He tendered Mrs. Mott the use of a large room
at his disposal, and urged her to hold a meeting. At Liverpool,
they were the guests of William Rathbone and family. In Dublin,
they met James Houghton, Richard Allen, Richard Webb, and the
Huttons, who entertained them most hospitably and gave them
many charming drives in and about the city. At Edinburgh, they
joined Sarah Pugh and Abby Kimber, who had just returned from
the Continent, and had a cordial reception at the home of George
Thompson. They passed two days with George Combe, the great
phrenologist, who examined and complimented Mrs. Mott's head,
as indicating a strong symmetrical character. They took tea with his
brother, Andrew Combe, the author of that admirable work on " Infancy," which has proved a real blessing to many young mothers.

At a meeting in Glasgow, to hear George Thompson on the subject of British India, Mrs. Mott asked the chairman for the liberty of addressing the audience for a few minutes, but was denied, though a colored man, Charles Lenox Remond, of Salem, Massachusetts, was listened to with attention, as he had been in London and other places, showing that the unholy prejudice against color was not so bitter in. England as that against sex. George Harris, the minister of the Unitarian Chapel in Glasgow, cordially extended to Mrs. Mott the use of his church for a lecture on slavery, which was gladly accepted. The house was crowded, and there was abundant reason to believe the people were well pleased. But the small handful of " Friends " in that city did not suffer so good an opportunity of disclaiming them to pass, and accordingly had the following communication published in the papers :

To the Editor of the Glasgow Gazette :

RESPECTED FRIEND:—Intimation having been given on the 8th, current, by means of placards extensively posted throughout the city, that " On Sabbath first, the 9th instant, Mrs. Lucretia Mott, a minister of the Society of Friends, Philadelphia, would hold a meeting in the Christian Unitarian Chapel"; and that the meeting was held and numerously attended by our fellow-citizens, we deem it right on behalf of the Society of Friends residing in Glasgow, to inform the public that we hold no religious fellowship with Lucretia Mott, nor with the body in the United States called Hicksites, to which she belongs, they not being recognized by the Society of Friends in the United Kingdom, nor by those "Friends" with whom we are in connection in America ; and that we do not wish to be in any way identified with, or considered responsible for any sentiments that Lucretia Mott may have uttered at the meeting above referred to.

We are, respectfully, thy friends,

WILLIAM SMEAL, WILLIAM WHITE, JOHN MAXWELL,
JAMES SMEAL, EDWARD WHITE.
GLASGOW, 12*th of* 8*th mo.*, 1840.

To us who knew, loved, and honored Lucretia Mott for her many virtues, these manifestations of bigotry, so narrowing and embittering in their effect on the mind, should be an added warning against that evil spirit of persecution that has brought such sorrow to mankind. We sincerely hope these few examples we have endeavored to place in their true light, may awaken thought in the minds of our readers, and incline them to renewed charity and a wiser appreciation of what is and what is not vital in religion. Surely life must ever stand for more than faith.

CHAPTER XII.

NEW JERSEY.

In 1682, William Penn purchased Eastern Jersey, and under a Governor of his choosing, Robert Barclay, the colony became a refuge for the persecuted "Friends." It was no doubt due to the peaceful measures of William Penn in his dealings with the Indians, that this colony was free from all troubles with them. The last loyal Governor of New Jersey—1763—was William Franklin, a natural son of Benjamin Franklin, and a bitter Tory.

The struggle for independence was at this time interesting and exciting, and behind the Governor was a strong party for reconciliation with Great Britain. Besides the Governor's instructions against independence, the Assembly had resolved on a separate petition to the King.

Aware of this feeling in New Jersey, Congress sent that illustrious trio, John Dickinson, John Jay, and George Wythe, to procure a reversal of their determination. They were courteously received on the floor, and urged in their addresses that nothing but unity and bravery in the Colonies would bring Great Britain to terms ; that she wanted to procure separate petitions, but that such a course would break the union, when the Colonies would be like a rope of sand. The Assembly yielded to their entreaties, and on the 25th of June, 1776, Governor Franklin, who opposed the action of Congress, was deposed,* and William Livingston, a true patriot, was elected Governor, and re-elected for fourteen years.

---

* The *New York Tribune*, Feb. 19, 1881, gives the following interesting facts : " William Franklin, the illegitimate son of Benjamin, who was long a resident of New York and hereabout, conducted in person his father's postal system. At Amboy, or Perth Amboy, a little town of once high aristocratic standing, which dozes on the edge of the Jersey hills and overlooks the oyster groves of Prince's Bay, began the Post-Office of North America under John Hamilton in 1694. It was a private patent, and he sold it to the Government. Many years afterward William Franklin settled at the same place, where once his father passed in Hamilton's day a footsore vagrant pressing from Boston to Philadelphia to get bread. There the younger Franklin reared a ' palace,' and lived in it as Governor of New Jersey till his adherence to the Crown, that had done better for

(441)

The intense excitement of this period in New Jersey roused many women loyal to freedom and the independence of the Colonies to persistent action. Among these was Hannah Arnett, of Elizabethtown, whose story was first made public one hundred years after the date of its occurrence.* The latter part of the year 1776 was a period of doubt and despondency to the patriot troops. Although the Colonies had declared their independence several months before, the American forces had since suffered many severe defeats, and it seemed not unlikely that Great Britain would be victorious in her struggle with the new-born republic. On the 30th of November, Gen. Howe had issued his celebrated proclamation offering amnesty and protection to all who, within sixty days, should declare themselves peaceable British subjects, and bind themselves to neither take up arms nor encourage others to do so.

After his victory at Fort Lee, Lord Cornwallis marched his army to New Jersey, encamping at Elizabethtown. His presence on New Jersey soil so soon after Gen. Howe's proclamation, and the many defeats of the patriot army, had a very depressing effect. Of this period Dr. Ashbel Green wrote: " I heard a man of some shrewdness once say, that when the British troops overran the State of New Jersey, in the closing part of the year 1776, the whole population could have been bought for eighteen pence a head."

But however true this statement may have been of the men of New Jersey, it could not be justly made in regard to its women, one of whom, at least, did much to stem the tide of panic so strong at this point where Cornwallis was encamped. A number of men of Elizabeth assembled one evening in one of the spacious mansions for which this place was rather famous, to discuss the advisability of accepting the proposed amnesty. The question was a momentous one, and the discussion was earnest and protracted. Some were for accepting this proffer at once ; others hesitated ; they canvassed the subject from various points, but finally decided that submission was all that remained to them. Their hope was gone, and their courage with it ; every remnant of patriotic spirit seemed swept away in the darkness of the hour. But there was a listener of whom they were ignorant ; a woman, Hannah Arnett, the wife of the host, sitting at her work in an adjoining room. The discussion had reached

---

him than his father—made him an exile and a captive. He was sent under guard to East Windsor, Conn., and his jail was made in the house of Captain Ebenezer Grant there, of the family of President Grant's ancestors, and he was prohibited the use of pen, ink, and paper—a needless punishment to a man who had delivered so many letters to others."

* In the *New York Observer*, 1876.

her ears, rousing her intense indignation. She listened until she could sit still no longer; springing to her feet she pushed open the parlor door, confronting the amazed men. The writer from whom we glean these facts, says: "Can you fancy the scene? A large, low room, with the dark, heavy furniture of the period, dimly lighted by the tall wax candles and the wood fire which blazed on the hearth. Around the table the group of men, pallid, gloomy, dejected, disheartened. In the door-way the figure of the woman in in antique costume, with which in these Centennial days we have become so familiar. Can you not fancy the proud poise of her head, the indignant light of her blue eyes, the crisp, clear tones of her voice, the majesty, and defiance, and scorn, which clothed her as with a garment?"

The men were appalled and started at the sight. She seemed like some avenging angel about to bring them to judgment for the words they had spoken; and, indeed, such she proved. It was strange to see a woman thus enter the secret councils of men, and her husband hastily approaching her, whispered: "Hannah, Hannah, this is no place for you, we do not want you here just now;" and he tried to take her hand to lead her from the room. But she pushed him gently back, saying to the startled group: "Have you made your decision, gentlemen? Have you chosen the part of men, or traitors?"

They stammered and blundered as they tried to find answer. Things appeared to them in a new light as this woman so pointedly questioned them. Their answers were a mixture of excuses and explanations. They declared the country to be in a hopeless condition; the army starving, half-clothed, undisciplined, the country poor, while England's trained troops were backed by the wealth of a thousand years.

Hannah Arnett listened in silence until the last abject word was spoken, when she rapidly inquired: "But what if we should live after all?" The men looked at each other, but not a word was spoken. "Hannah, Hannah," cried her husband, "do you not see these are no questions for you? We are discussing what is best for us all. Women do not understand these things; go to your spinning-wheel and leave us to discuss these topics. Do you not see that you are making yourself ridiculous?"

But Mrs. Arnett paid no heed. Speaking to the men in a strangely quiet voice, she said: "Can you not tell me? If, after all, God does not let the right perish; if America should win in the conflict, after you have thrown yourselves upon British clemency, where will you be then?" "Then?" spoke a hesitating voice, "why then, if it ever could be so, we should be ruined. We must then leave home and country forever. But the struggle is an entirely hopeless one. We have no men, no money, no arms, no food, and England has everything."

"No," said Mrs. Arnett, "you have forgotten one thing which England has not, and which we have—one thing which outweighs all England's treasures, and that is the right. God is on our side; and every volley from our muskets is an echo of His voice. We are poor and weak and few, but God is fighting for us. We counted the cost before we began; we knew the price and were willing to pay; and now, because for the time the day is going against us, you would give up all and sneak back like cravens, to kiss the feet that have trampled upon us! And you call yourselves men; the sons of those who gave up homes and fortune and fatherland to make for themselves and for dear liberty a resting-place in the wilderness! Oh, shame upon you, cowards!"

The words had rushed out in a fiery flood which her husband had vainly striven to check. Turning to the gentlemen present, Mr. Arnett said: "I beg you will excuse this most unseemly interruption to our council. My wife is beside herself, I think. You all know her, and that it is not her custom to meddle with politics. To-morrow she will see her folly; but now I beg your patience."

But her words had roused the slumbering manhood of her hearers. Each began to look upon himself as a craven, and to withdraw from the position he had taken. No one replied to her husband, and Mrs. Arnett continued. "Take your protection if you will. Proclaim yourselves traitors and cowards, false to your country and your God, but horrible will be the judgment upon your heads and the heads of those that love you. I tell you that England will never conquer. I know it and feel it in every fiber of my heart. Has God led us thus far to desert us now? Will He who led our fathers across the stormy winter seas forsake their children who have put their trust in Him? For me, I stay with my country, and my hand shall never touch the hand, nor my heart cleave to the heart of him who shames her"; and she turned a glance upon her husband; "Isaac, we have lived together for twenty years, and for all of them I have been a true and loving wife to you. But I am the child of God and of my Country, and if you do this shameful thing, I will never again own you for my husband."

"My dear wife!" he cried, aghast, "you do not know what you are saying. Leave me for such a thing as this?" "For such a thing as this!" she cried, scornfully. "What greater cause could there be ? I married a good man and true, a faithful friend, and it needs no divorce to sever me from a traitor and a coward. If you take your amnesty you lose your wife, and I—I lose my husband and my home!"

With the last words her voice broke into a pathetic fall, and a mist gathered before her eyes. The men were deeply moved; the words of Mrs. Arnett had touched every soul. Gradually the drooping heads were raised, and eyes grew bright with manliness and resolution. Before they left the house that night they had sworn a solemn oath to stand by the cause they had adopted, and the land of their birth through good or evil, and to spurn as deadliest insult the proffered amnesty of their tyrannical foe.

Some of the men who met in this secret council afterward fought nobly, and died upon the field of battle for their country. Others lived to rejoice when the day of triumph came; but the name of this woman was found upon no heroic roll, nor is it on the page of any history that men have since written, although she made heroes of cowards, and helped to stay the wave of desolation which, in the dark days of '76, threatened to overwhelm the land.

At one time some British officers quartered themselves at the house of Mrs. Dissosway, situated at the western end of Staten Island, opposite Amboy. Her husband was a prisoner; but her brother, Captain Nat. Randolph, was in the American army, and gave much annoyance to the tories by his frequent incursions. A tory colonel promised Mrs. Dissosway to procure the release of her husband on condition of her prevailing on her brother to stay quietly at home. " And if I could," she replied, with a look of scorn, drawing up her tall figure to its utmost height, " if I could act so dastardly a part, think you General Washington has but one Captain Randolph in his army ?"

At a period when American prospects were most clouded, and New Jersey overrun by the British, an officer stationed at Bordentown (said to be Lord Cornwallis) endeavored to intimidate Mrs. Borden into using her influence over her husband and son, who were absent in the American army. The officer promised her that if she would induce them to quit the standard they followed and join the royalists, her property should be protected; while in case of refusal, her estate would be ravaged and her elegant mansion destroyed. Mrs. Borden answered, " Begin your threatened havoc then ; the sight of my house in flames would be a treat to me ; for I have seen enough to know that you never injure what you have power to keep and enjoy. The application of a torch to my dwelling I should regard as a signal for your departure." The house was burned in fulfillment of the threat, and the estate laid waste ; but, as Mrs. Borden predicted, the retreat of the spoiler quickly followed.

During the battle of Monmouth a gunner named Pitcher was killed, and the call was made for some one to take his place; his wife, who had followed him to the camp and thence to the field of conflict, unhesitatingly stepped forward and offered her services. The gun was so well managed as to draw the attention of General Washington to the circumstance, and to call forth an expression of his admiration of her bravery and fidelity to her country. To show his appreciation of her virtues and her highly valuable services, he conferred on her a lieutenant's commission. She afterward went by the name of " Captain Molly."

As early as 1706, Thomas Chalkley, visiting the Conestogae Indians, near Susquehannah, says : " We treated about having a meeting with them in a religious way, upon which they called a council, in which they were very grave, and spoke one after another without any heat or jarring (and some of the most esteemed of their women do sometimes speak in their councils). I asked our interpreter why they suffered or permitted the women to speak ; he answered : 'Some women are wiser than some men.' Our interpreter told me that they had not done anything for many years without the counsel of an ancient, grave woman, who, I observed, spoke much in their councils, for I was permitted to be present, and asked what she said. He replied that she was an empress, and that they gave much heed to what she said amongst them ; that she then said to them that she looked upon our coming to be more than natural, because we did not come to buy nor sell nor get gain, but came in love and respect to them, and desired their well doing both here and hereafter ; and that our meeting among them might be very beneficial to their young people. She related a dream she had three days before, and interpreted it, advising them to hear us and entertain us kindly, etc., which they did.

Chief Justice Green, in behalf of Miss Leake, of Trenton, presented to the New Jersey Historical Society copies of the correspondence between Colonel Mawhood of the British forces, and Colonel Hand of the American army, proposing to the latter to surrender, and each man to go to his home, etc., dated Salem County, March, 1778. The New Jersey Historical Society has a photographic copy of a print, contemporary with the event, representing the triumphal arch erected by the ladies of Trenton in honor of Washington, on his passage through the place in April, 1779, and a photographic copy of the following original note (now in possession of the lady who received it), which was written by Washington at the time:

General Washington can not leave this place without expressing his acknowledgements to the Matrons and Young Ladies who received him in so novel and grateful a manner at the Triumphal Arch in Trenton, for the exquisite sensations he experienced in that affecting scene. The astonishing contrast between his former and actual situation at the same spot, the elegant taste with which it was adorned for the present occasion, and the innocent appearance of the *white-robed choir*, who met him with the gratulatory song, have made such an impression on his remembrance as he assures them will never be effaced.

TRENTON, *April* 21, 1789.

THE ORIGIN, PRACTICE, AND PROHIBITION OF FEMALE SUFFRAGE IN NEW JERSEY.

William A. Whitehead, Corresponding Secretary of the New Jersey Historical Society, read the following paper at their annual meeting, January 21, 1858:

By the Proprietary laws, the right of suffrage in New Jersey was expressly to the *free men* of the province; and in equally explicit terms a law passed in 1709 prescribing the qualifications of electors, confined the privilege to male freeholders having one hundred acres of land in their own right, or worth fifty pounds, current money of the province, in real and personal estate, and during the whole of the colonial period these qualifications remained unaltered.

By the Constitution adopted July 2, 1776, the elective franchise was conferred upon all inhabitants of this colony, of full age, who are worth fifty pounds, proclamation money, clear estate in the same, and have resided within the county in which they claim a vote for twelve months immediately preceding the election; and the same, or similar language, was used in the different acts regulating elections until 1790; but I have not discovered any instance of the exercise of the right by females, under an interpretation which the full import of the words, " all inhabitants," was subsequently thought to sanction, during the whole of this period.

In 1790, however, a revision of the election law then in force was proposed, and upon the committee of the Legislature to whom the subject was referred was Mr. Joseph Cooper, of West Jersey, a prominent member of the Society of Friends. As the regulations of that society authorized females to vote in matters relating thereto, Mr. Cooper claimed for them the like privilege in matters connected with the State, and to support his views, quoted the provisions of the Constitution as sanctioning such a course. It was therefore to satisfy him that the committee consented to report a bill in which the expression, " he or she," applied to the voter, was introduced into the section specifying the necessary qualifications; thus giving a legislative endorsement of the alleged meaning of the Constitution. Still, no cases of females voting by virtue of this more definite provision are on record, and we are warranted in believing that the women of New Jersey then, as now, were not apt to overstep the bounds of decorum, or intrude where their characteristic modesty and self-respect might be wounded.

This law and its supplements were repealed in 1797, and it is some proof that the peculiar provision under review had not been availed of to any extent, if at all (as its evil consequences would otherwise have become apparent), that we find similar phraseology introduced into the new act. The right of suffrage was conferred upon "all free inhabitants of this State of full age," etc., thus adopting the language of the Constitution with the addition of the word "free," and "no person shall be entitled to vote in any other township or precinct than that in which he or she doth actually reside," etc., and in two other places is the possible difference in the sex of the voters recognized.

The first occasion on which females voted, of which any precise information has been obtained, was at an election held this year (1797) at Elizabethtown, Essex County, for members of the Legislature. The candidates between whom the greatest rivalry existed, were John Condit and William Crane, the heads of what were known a year or two later as the "Federal Republican" and "Federal Aristocratic" parties, the former the candidate of Newark and the northern portions of the county, and the latter the candidate of Elizabethtown and the adjoining country, for the Council. Under the impression that the candidates would poll nearly the same number of votes, the Elizabethtown leaders thought that by a bold *coup 'd'etat* they might secure the success of Mr. Crane. At a late hour of the day, and, as I have been informed, just before the close of the poll, a number of females were brought up, and under the provisions of the existing laws, allowed to vote; but the manœuvre was unsuccessful, the majority for Mr. Condit, in the county, being ninety-three, notwithstanding. These proceedings were made the topic of two or three brief articles in the *Newark Sentinel,* in one of which the fact that "no less than seventy-five women were polled at the late election in a neighboring borough," was used as a pretended argument for the admission of females to office, and to service in the diplomatic corps; while another ironically asserts that "too much credit can not be given to the Federal leaders of Elizabethtown for the heroic virtue displayed in advancing in a body to the poll to support their favorite candidates."

So discreditable was this occurrence thought, that although another closely contested election took place the following year, we do not find any other than male votes deposited then, in Essex County, or elsewhere, until the Presidential election of 1800, between Mr. Adams and Mr. Jefferson, at which females voted very generally throughout the State; and such continued to be the practice until the passage of the act positively excluding them from the polls. At first the law had been so construed as to admit single women only, but as the practice extended, the construction of the privilege became broader and was made to include females eighteen years old, married or single; and even women of color. At a contested election in Hunterdon County, in 1802, the votes of two or

Engraved by J.C.Buttre.

Antoinette L. Brown.

three such, actually electing a member of the Legislature. It is remarkable that these proceedings did not sooner bring about a repeal of the laws which were thought to sanction them; but that event did not occur until 1807, and it is noticeable that, as the practice originated in Essex County, so the flagrant abuses which resulted from it reached their maximum in that county, and brought about its prohibition.

The circumstances attendant upon this event afford abundant matter for a most interesting chapter of local history, which I am happy to say has been written by a member of the Society (Mr. James Ross),* and will be communicated before long, I trust, for insertion in our Proceedings. But the scope of this paper merely calls for a statement of facts. These are as follows:

In the year 1806 a new Court House and Jail were to be erected in the county of Essex. Strenuous exertions were made to have them located elsewhere than at Newark, which had been the county town from a very early period. Sufficient influence was brought to bear upon the Legislature to secure the passage of an act (approved November 5th of that year) authorizing a special election, at which "the inhabitants" of the county, "qualified to vote in elections for members of the State Legislature," etc., were described as the qualified electors to determine by their votes where the buildings should be located. The contest caused a great excitement throughout the county, and, under the existing laws, when the election was held in February, 1807, women of "full age," whether single or married, possessing the required property qualification, were permitted by the judges of election to vote. But as the conflict proceeded, and the blood of the combatants waxed warmer, the number of female voters increased, and it was soon found that every single and every married woman in the county was not only of "full age," but also "worth fifty pounds proclamation money, clear estate," and as such entitled to vote if they chose. And not only once, but as often as by change of dress or complicity of the inspectors, they might be able to repeat the process.

This was not confined to any one precinct, but was more or less the case in all, and so apparent were these and many other frauds that the Legislature at the ensuing session did not hesitate to set it aside as having been illegally conducted; and, by repealing the act authorizing it, left the buildings to be erected in Newark, to which they legitimately belonged. And, in order that no future occurrence of the kind should take place, an act was passed (approved November ,16, 1807), the preamble to which is as follows:

"Whereas, doubts have been raised and great diversities in practice obtained throughout the State in regard to the admission of aliens, females, and persons of color or negroes to vote in elections, as also in regard to the mode of ascertaining the qualifications of voters in respect to estate; and whereas, it is highly necessary to the safety, quiet good order and dignity of the State to clear up the said doubts by an act of the repre-

---

* After a diligent search for Mr. James Ross and his promised "interesting chapter of local history," we learned that the author was in his grave, and that from his posthumous papers this valuable document had not yet been exhumed by his literary executor.

sentatives of the people declaratory of the true sense and meaning of the Constitution, and to ensure its just execution in these particulars according to the intent of the framers thereof: Therefore," etc., etc.

This act confined the right of suffrage to free white male citizens twenty-one years of age, worth fifty pounds proclamation money, clear estate; and disposed of the property qualification by declaring that every person otherwise entitled to vote whose name should be enrolled on the last tax-lists for the State or County should be considered as worth the fifty pounds, thus by legislative enactment determining the meaning of the Constitution and settling the difficulty. The law remained unchanged until the adoption of the new Constitution a few years since, which instrument is equally restrictive as to persons who shall vote, and removes the property qualification altogether.

Very recently a refusal to respond to a demand for taxes legally imposed, was received from a distinguished advocate of "Woman's Rights" in one of the northern counties; who gave as her reasons "that women suffer taxation, and yet have no representation, which is not only unjust to one-half of the adult population, but is contrary to our Theory of Government"—and that when the attention of men is called to the wide difference between their theory of government and its practice in this particular, that they can not fail to see the mistake they now make, by imposing taxes on women when they refuse them the right of suffrage.*

Similar arguments were advanced by a sister of Richard Henry Lee, in 1778,† when, if ever, they were calculated to receive due consideration, yet the distinguished Virginian did not hesitate to show the unreasonableness of the demand; in the course of his able answer remarking that (setting aside other motive for restricting the power to males) " perhaps 'twas thought rather out of character for women to press into those tumultuous assemblages of men where the business of choosing representatives is conducted ! " And as it is very evident that when in times past the right was, not only claimed, but exercised in New Jersey, it never accorded with public sentiment; so it may be safely predicted that, as

---

* The following letter contains the sentiments referred to in the text:

ORANGE, N. J., *Dec.* 18, 1858.

MR. MANDEVILLE, TAX COLLECTOR, SIR :—Enclosed I return my tax bill, without paying it. My reason for doing so is, that women suffer taxation, and yet have no representation, which is not only unjust to one-half the adult population, but is contrary to our theory of government. For years some women have been paying their taxes under protest, but still taxes are imposed, and representation is not granted. The only course now left us is to refuse to pay the tax. We know well what the immediate result of this refusal must be.

But we believe that when the attention of men is called to the wide difference between their theory of government and its practice, in this particular, they can not fail to see the mistake they now make, by imposing taxes on women, while they refuse them the right of suffrage, and that the sense of justice which is in all good men, will lead them to correct it. Then we shall cheerfully pay our taxes—not till then.

Respectfully,   LUCY STONE.

† See *Washington National Intelligencer* for Oct. 15, 1857, and *Historical Magazine*, Vol. I., page 360.

was the case in 1807, "the safety, quiet, good order, and dignity of the State," will ever call for its explicit disavowal in times to come.

In his speech at the Woman's Rights Convention, 1853, in New York, Rev. John Pierpont said : "I can go back forty years ; and forty years ago, when most of my present audience were not in, but behind, their cradles, passing a stranger, through the neighboring State of New Jersey, and stopping for dinner at an inn, where the coach stopped, I saw at the bar where I went to pay, a list of the voters of the town stuck up. My eye ran over it, and I read to my astonishment the names of several women. 'What!' I said, 'do women vote here?' 'Certainly,' was the answer, 'when they have real estate.' Then the question arose in my mind, why should not women vote : Laws are made regulating the tenure of real estate, and the essence of all republicanism is, that they who feel the pressure of the law should have a voice in its enactment."

DEFECTS IN THE CONSTITUTION OF NEW JERSEY.

In a very singular pamphlet published in Trenton, 1779, called " Eumenes : A collection of papers on the Errors and Omissions of the Constitution of New Jersey," the writer is very severe upon the fact that women were allowed to exercise the same right as the sterner sex ; observing that " Nothing can be a greater mockery of this inalienable right, than to suffer it to be exercised by persons who do not pretend any judgment on the subject."*

Extract from " Eumenes," page 31, No. 8 : " Defects of the Constitution respecting the Qualification of Electors and Elected " :

It will not be denied that a Constitution ought to point out what persons may elect and who may be elected; and that it should as distinctly prescribe their several qualifications, and render those qualifications conformable to justice and the public welfare. Indeed, on the proper adjustment of the elective franchise depends, in a great measure, the liberty of the citizen and the safety of the Government. Upon examination it will be found that the Constitution requires amendment upon this head in several particulars.

It has ever been a matter of dispute upon the Constitution, whether females, as well as males, are entitled to elect officers of Government. If we were to be guided by the *letter* of the charter, it would seem to place them on the same footing. in this particular ; and yet, recurring to *political right* and the nature of things, a very forcible construction has been raised against the admission of *women* to participate in the public suffrage.

The 4th Article of the Constitution declares that " *all the inhabitants*

---

* *Frank Leslie's Magazine*, Feb., 1877.

of this colony of full age who are worth fifty pounds, shall be entitled to vote for representatives."

Those who support the rights of women say, that "all inhabitants" must mean "*all women*" inhabitants as well as "*all men*." Whereas, it is urged on the other side that the makers must have meant "all *male* inhabitants," and that the expression is to be restrained so as to arrive at the *intent* of the framers of the instrument.

This difference of sentiment has given rise to diversity of *practice* on this head, and furnished a pretence from which many an electioneering trick has resulted. I could refer to instances which would prove what is advanced, but the people want no proofs. It is well known that women are admitted or rejected, just as may suit the views of the persons in direction. The thing should be rectified. If women are fit persons to take part in this important franchise, though excluded from other public functions, it should be expressed in the Constitution. They would then know their rights, and those rights could not be sported with to serve the wretched purposes of a party election.

To my mind, without going into an historical or philosophical deduction of particulars on the subject, it is evident that women, generally, are neither by nature, nor habit, nor education, nor by their necessary condition in society, fitted to perform this duty with credit to themselves or advantage to the public. In a note the author adds: It is perfectly disgusting to witness the manner in which women are polled at our elections. Nothing can be greater mockery of this invaluable and sacred right, than to suffer it to be exercised by persons who do not even pretend to any judgment on the subject. The great practical mischief, however, resulting from their admission under our present form of government, is that the towns and populous villages gain an unfair advantage over the country, by the greater facility they enjoy over the latter in drawing out their women to the elections. Many important election contests have been terminated at last by these auxiliaries in favor of candidates supported by town interests.

I believe that the Convention which framed the Constitution had no view to the admission of females, either single women or widows, to elect the public officers. But such is the phraseology of the Constitution that it seems a violation of it not to admit their votes. The best constitutions have guarded against mistakes on this head. Those of Massachusetts, New York, Pennsylvania, Maryland, Vermont, etc., do not admit of female electors. Whether this be right or wrong, the objection to our Constitution is, that it does not settle the point one way or the other with an absolute certainty. The practice is variable. The generally received opinion, however, is that the Constitution permits it. In this state of the matter it is not competent for the Legislature to interfere. Nothing short of a constitutional declaration can decide the question; which is, in fact, an important one, and is growing more and more so to the country in proportion as the towns and villages increase in numbers and population. For, independent of the theoretic question, it is evident that the admission of these votes gives a vast advantage to the thickly settled places over the more dispersed population of the country.

In another note the author says: "Mr. Fox in his late harangue in the British House of Commons, in favor of more *equal* suffrage, concedes the unfitness of *females* to share in elections. He says no instance of their participation of public suffrage in any government can be shown; and that this right (which many of his party hold to be a natural one, though he affects to stop short of that) is properly denied to the fairest productions of nature. Of widows and spinsters above twenty-one, there can not, I imagine, be fewer than 10,000. It is certainly not unimportant to leave doubtful the rights of so great a number of people."

Mr. Whitehead's report clearly shows three unjust inferences from the facts stated:

First. That all the corruptions of that special election in Essex County could be traced to the women.

Second. That the quiet, good order, and dignity of the State could be secured only by the restriction of the suffrage to "free white male citizens worth fifty pounds."

Third. "The unreasonableness of the demand" for representation by women tax-payers.

1st. Tradition shows that the voting early and often in varied feminine costume, was done by men five feet four, "picked men," not for their bravery, but for their inferiority. Depriving women of their right to vote, because the men abused their privilege, under cover of sex, in 1807, was, however, on the same principle that politicians in 1881 propose to disfranchise the women of Utah, because of their polygamous relations. That is, punish the women who claim a right to only one-sixth part of a man's time and affections, because the men claim six wives apiece. The question naturally suggests itself to any fair mind, why not deprive the men of the suffrage, and let the women vote themselves each one husband? Who doubts the fate of the system under such legislation? Every woman in her normal condition, unless wholly perverted by the religious dogma of self-sacrifice and self-crucifixion, desires to own the man she loves as absolutely and completely, as every man desires to consecrate to himself alone the woman he loves. So to deprive the women of Essex of their right to vote to have the county buildings in Elizabeth, because of the undue excitement and dishonesty of the men, was to punish the best class of citizens for the crimes of the worst.

2d. The assumption that "free white male citizens worth fifty pounds," could legislate for "aliens, women, and negroes," better than those classes could for themselves, is to deny the fundamental principle of republicanism; Governments derive their just powers from the consent of the governed; and to reassert the despotic ideas of the old world: that national safety depends on the wisdom of privileged orders—nobles, kings, and czars. The experiment in Wyoming has fully proved that when "free white male citizens" reigned supreme, the polls there were scenes of drunkenness, violence, and death; men knocking each other down and putting bullets through each other's brains were of annual occurrence. But when the suffrage was extended, and women admitted to the polling booths, quiet, good order, and dignity were inaugurated.

3d. "Taxation without representation is tyranny." James Otis said: "To tax a man's property without his consent, is in effect disfranchising him of every civil right. For what one civil right is worth a rush, after a man's property is subject to be taken from him at the pleasure of another?" Is not such injustice as grievous to woman as man? Does the accident of sex place woman outside of all ordinary principles of law and justice? It is the essence of cruelty and tyranny to take her hard earnings without her consent, blocked as her way is to wealth and independence, to make sidewalks, highways, and bridges; to build jails, prisons, and alms-houses, the legitimate outgrowth of the whisky traffic, which she abhors. On what principle of republican government is one class of taxpayers thus defrauded of one of the most sacred rights of citizenship? What logical argument can be made to prove "the unreasonableness of this demand," for one class above all others? Principles of justice, to have any value or significance, must be universal in their application to all humanity.

4th. As to the point made by "Eumenes," "that women are not fit persons to take part in government," "that they do not even pretend to any judgment on the subject," we have simply to say that the writer's prejudices contradict all the facts of our common experience. Women are so pre-eminently fitted for government, that the one fear in all ages among men has been lest by some chance they should be governed by women; and the smaller the man the greater the fear.

Blackstone says "the elements of sovereignty are three: 'Wisdom, Goodness, and Power.'" Admitting for the sake of argument that "Power" in this connection means physical force, the distinctive point of male superiority, and not moral power, which may be equal in both sexes, all must concede the remaining necessary elements to woman as well as man. Who so bold, or blind, as to deny wisdom and goodness, the chief elements of beneficent government, to woman, with the long record of illustrious and saintly characters gilding every page of history before him?

Whatever doubts the women known to the author of "Eumenes" might have had as to their own capacities; the women of to-day do assume to know that they are more capable of self-government than men are, and that they understand the principles that underlie a republic far better than the vast majority of foreigners now crowding our shores, the Right Honorable James Charles Fox to the contrary notwithstanding. Yea, without danger of contradiction, we may say there are women in this nation even now, who understand the political issues of this hour quite as well as those who stand at the head of our government.

We are very apt to accept popular assertions ofttimes repeated as truisms, and in this way man's superiority has passed into a proverb, and the sex in general believe it. When Milton penned the line, " God, thy will, thou mine," and made his Eve thus reverently submissive to her Adam, he little thought of bright girls in the nineteenth century, well versed in science, philosophy, and the languages, sitting in the senior class of a college of the American republic, laughing his male conceit to scorn.

CHAPTER XIII.

REMINISCENCES.

BY E. C. S.

The reports of the Conventions held in Seneca Falls and Rochester, N. Y., in 1848, attracted the attention of one destined to take a most important part in the new movement—Susan B. Anthony, who for her courage and executive ability was facetiously called by William Henry Channing, the Napoleon of our struggle. At this time she was teaching in the Academy at Canajoharie, a little village in the beautiful valley of the Mohawk.

"The Woman's Declaration of Independence" issued from those conventions, startled and amused her, and she laughed heartily at the novelty and presumption of the demand. But on returning home to spend her vacation, she was surprised to find that her sober Quaker parents and sisters having attended the Rochester meetings, regarded them as very profitable and interesting, and the demands made as proper and reasonable. She was already interested in the anti-slavery and temperance reforms, and was an active member of an organization called "The Daughters of Temperance," and had spoken a few times in their public meetings. But the new gospel of "Woman's Rights," found a ready response in her mind, and from that time her best efforts have been given to the enfranchisement of woman.

It was in the month of May, of 1851, that I first met Miss Anthony. That was to both of us an eventful meeting, that in a measure henceforth shaped our lives. As our own estimate of ourselves and our friendship may differ somewhat from that taken from an objective point of view, I will give an extract from what a mutual friend wrote of us some years ago:

Miss Susan B. Anthony, a well-known, indefatigable and life-long advocate of temperance, anti-slavery, and woman's rights, has been, since 1851, Mrs. Stanton's intimate associate in reformatory labors. These celebrated women are of about equal ages, but of the most opposite characteristics, and illustrate the theory of counterparts in affection by entertaining for each other a friendship of extraordinary strength.

Mrs. Stanton is a fine writer, but a poor executant; Miss Anthony is a thorough manager, but a poor writer. Both have large brains and great

(456)

hearts; neither has any selfish ambition for celebrity; but each vies with the other in a noble enthusiasm for the cause to which they are devoting their lives.

Nevertheless, to describe them critically, I ought to say that opposites though they be, each does not so much supplement the other's difficiencies as augment the other's eccentricities. Thus they often stimulate each other's aggressiveness, and at the same time diminish each other's discretion.

But whatever may be the imprudent utterances of the one, or the impolitic methods of the other, the animating motives of both are evermore as white as the light. The good that they do is by design; the harm by accident. These two women sitting together in their parlors, have for the last thirty years been diligent forgers of all manner of projectiles, from fire works to thunderbolts, and have hurled them with unexpected explosion into the midst of all manner of educational, reformatory, religious, and political assemblies, sometimes to the pleasant surprise and half welcome of the members, more often to the bewilderment and prostration of numerous victims; and in a few signal instances, to the gnashing of angry men's teeth. I know of no two more pertinacious incendiaries in the whole country! Nor will they themselves deny the charge. In fact this noise-making twain are the two sticks of a drum for keeping up what Daniel Webster called "the rub-a-dub of agitation."

How well I remember the day I first met my life-long friend. George Thompson and William Lloyd Garrison having announced an anti-slavery meeting in Seneca Falls, Miss Anthony came to attend it. These gentlemen were my guests. Walking home after the adjournment, we met Mrs. Bloomer and Miss Anthony on the corner of the street waiting to greet us. There she stood with her good earnest face and genial smile, dressed in gray silk, hat and all the same color, relieved with pale blue ribbons, the perfection of neatness and sobriety. I liked her thoroughly, and why I did not at once invite her home with me to dinner, I do not know. She accuses me of that neglect and never has forgiven me, as she wished to see and hear all she could of our noble friends. I suppose my mind was full of what I had heard, or my coming dinner, or the probable behavior of three mischievous boys who had been busily exploring the premises while I was at the meeting. That I had abundant cause for anxiety in regard to the philosophical experiments these young savages might try, the reader will admit when informed of some of their performances.*

---

* One imagined himself possessed of rare powers of invention (an ancestral weakness for generations), and had just made a life-preserver of corks, and tested its virtues on a brother about eighteen months old. Accompanied by a troop of expectant boys, the baby was drawn in his carriage to the banks of the Seneca, stripped, the string of corks tied

It is often said by those who know Miss Anthony best, that she has been my good angel, always pushing and guiding me to work, that but for her pertinacity I should never have accomplished the little I have; and on the other hand, it has been said that I forged the thunderbolts and she fired them. Perhaps all this is in a measure true. With the cares of a large family, I might in time, like too many women, have become wholly absorbed in a narrow family selfishness, had not my friend been continually exploring new fields for missionary labors. Her description of a body of men on any platform, complacently deciding questions in which women had an equal interest, without an equal voice, readily roused me to a determination to throw a firebrand in the midst of their assembly.

Thus, whenever I saw that stately Quaker girl coming across my lawn, I knew that some happy convocation of the sons of Adam were to be set by the ears, by one of our appeals or resolutions. The little portmanteau stuffed with facts was opened, and there we had what the Rev. John Smith and the Hon. Richard Roe had said, false interpretations of Bible texts, the statistics of women robbed of their property, shut out of some college, half paid for their work, the reports of some disgraceful trial, injustice enough to turn any woman's thoughts from stockings and puddings. Then we would get out our pens and write articles for papers, or a petition to the Legislature, letters to the faithful here and there, stir up the women in Ohio, Pennsylvania, or Massachusetts, call on *The Lily,*

---

under his arms, and set afloat in the river, the philosopher and his satellites in a row-boat, watching the experiment. The child, accustomed to a morning bath in a large tub, splashed about joyfully, keeping his head above water. He was as blue as indigo, and as cold as a frog when rescued by his anxious mother. The next day, the same victim-ized infant was seen by a passing friend, seated on the chimney, on the highest peak of the house. Without alarming any one, the friend hurried up to the house-top, and res-cued the child from the arms of the philosopher. Another time, three elder brothers entered into a conspiracy, and locked up the fourth in the smoke-house. Fortunately, he sounded the alarm loud and clear, and was set free in safety, whereupon the three were imprisoned in a garret with two barred windows. They summarily kicked out the bars, and sliding down on the lightning-rod betook themselves to the barn for liberty. The youngest boy, then only five years old, skinned his hands in the descent. This is a fair sample of the quiet happiness I enjoyed in the first years of motherhood. It was 'mid such exhilarating scenes that Miss Anthony and I wrote addresses for temperance, anti-slavery, educational and woman's rights conventions. Here we forged resolutions, protests, appeals, petitions, agricultural reports, and constitutional arguments, for we made it a matter of conscience to accept every invitation to speak on every question, in order to maintain woman's right to do so. To this end, we took turns on the domestic watch-towers, directing amusements, settling disputes, protecting the weak against the strong, and trying to secure equal rights to all in the home as well as the nation. I can recall many a stern encounter between my friend and the young experimenter. It is pleasant to remember that he never seriously injured any of his victims, and only once came near shooting himself with a pistol. The ball went through his hand; happily a brass button prevented it from penetrating his heart.

The Una, *The Liberator*, and *The Standard*, to remember our wrongs as well as those of the slave. We never met without issuing a pronunciamento on some question.

We were at once fast friends, in thought and sympathy we were one, and in the division of labor we exactly complemented each other. In writing we did better work together than either could alone. While she is slow and analytical in composition, I am rapid and synthetic. I am the better writer, she the better critic. She supplied the facts and statistics, I the philosophy and rhetoric, and together we have made arguments that have stood unshaken by the storms of thirty long years : arguments that no man has answered. Our speeches may be considered the united product of our two brains.

So entirely one are we, that in all our associations, ever side by side on the same platform, not one feeling of jealousy or envy has ever shadowed our lives. We have indulged freely in criticism of each other when alone, and hotly contended whenever we have differed, but in our friendship of thirty years there has never been a break of one hour. To the world we always seem to agree and uniformly reflect each other. Like husband and wife, each has the feeling that we must have no differences in public. Thus united, at an early day we began to survey the State and nation, the future field of our labors. We read with critical eyes the proceedings of Congress and Legislatures, of General Assemblies and Synods, of Conferences and Conventions, and discovered that in all alike the existence of woman was entirely ignored.

Night after night by an old-fashioned fireplace we plotted and planned the coming agitation, how, when, and where each entering wedge could be driven, by which woman might be recognized, and her rights secured. Speedily the State was aflame with disturbances in temperance and teachers' conventions, and the press heralded the news far and near that women delegates had suddenly appeared demanding admission in men's conventions ; that their rights had been hotly contended session after session, by liberal men on the one side ; the clergy and learned professors on the other ; an overwhelming majority rejecting the women with terrible anathemas and denunciations. Such battles were fought over and over in the chief cities of many of the Northern States, until the bigotry of men in all the reforms and professions was thoroughly tested. Every right achieved : to enter a college ; to study a profession ; to labor in some new industry, or to advocate a reform measure, was contended for inch by inch.

Many of those enjoying all these blessings, now complacently say, "If these pioneers in reform, had only pressed their measures more judiciously; in a more ladylike manner; in more choice language; in a more deferential attitude, the gentlemen could not have behaved so rudely." We give in these pages enough of the characteristics of these women, of the sentiments they expressed, of their education, ancestry, and position, to show that no power could have met the prejudice and bigotry of that period more successfully than they did, who so bravely and persistently fought and conquered them.

True, those gentlemen were all quite willing that women should join their societies and churches, to do the drudgery, to work up the enthusiasm in fairs and revivals, conventions and flag presentations, to pay a dollar apiece into their treasury for the honor of being members of their various organizations, to beg money for the church, circulate petitions from door to door, to visit saloons, to pray with or defy rum-sellers, to teach school at half-price, and sit round the outskirts of a hall like so many wall flowers in teachers' State Conventions; but they would not allow them to sit on the platform, address the assembly, nor vote for men and measures.

Those who had learned the first lessons of human rights from the lips of Beriah Green, Samuel J. May, and Gerrit Smith, would not accept any such position. When women abandoned the temperance reform, all interest in the question gradually died out in the State, and practically nothing was done in New York for nearly twenty years. Gerrit Smith made one or two attempts toward an "anti-dram-shop party," but as women could not vote they felt no interest in the measure, and failure was the result.

I soon convinced my new friend that the ballot was the key to the situation, that when we had a voice in the laws we should be welcomed to any platform. In turning the intense earnestness and religious enthusiasm of this great-souled woman into this one channel, I soon felt the power of my convert in goading me forever forward to more untiring work. Soon fastened heart to heart with hooks of steel in a friendship that thirty years of confidence and affection have steadily strengthened, we have labored faithfully together.

After twelve added years of agitation, from the passage of the property bill, New York conceded other civil rights to married women. Pending the discussion of these various bills, Susan B. Anthony circulated petitions both for the civil and political rights of woman throughout the State, traveling in stage coaches and open wagons and sleighs in all seasons, and on foot from door to door through towns and cities, doing her uttermost to rouse women to some sense of their natural rights as human beings, to their civil and political rights as citizens of a republic; and while expending her time, strength, and money to secure these blessings for the women of the State, they would gruffly tell her they had all the rights they wanted, or rudely shut the door in her face, leaving her to stand outside, petition in hand, with as much contempt as if she were asking alms for herself. None but those who did that petition work in the early days for the slaves and the women, can ever know the hardships and humiliations that were endured. But it was done because it was only through petitions, a power seemingly so inefficient, that disfranchised classes could be heard in the national councils, hence their importance.

The frivolous objections some women made to our appeals were as exasperating as ridiculous. To reply to them politely at all times, required a divine patience. On one occasion, after addressing the Legislature, some of the ladies in congratulating me, inquired in a deprecating tone, "What do you do with your children?" "Ladies," I said, "it takes me no longer to speak than you to listen; what have you done with your children the two hours you have been sitting here? But to answer your questions. I never leave my children to go to Saratoga, Washington, Newport, or Europe, nor even to come here. They are at this moment with a faithful nurse at the Delavan House, and having accomplished my mission, we shall all return home together."

Miss Anthony, who was a frequent guest at my home, sometimes stood guard on such occasions.* The children of our household say that among their earliest recollections is the tableau of "Mother and Susan," seated by a large table covered with books and papers,

---

* When the flock reached the magic number of seven, my good angel would sometimes take one or two to her own quiet home just out of Rochester, where on a well-cultivated little farm, one could enjoy uninterrupted rest and the choicest fruits of the season. That was always a safe harbor for my friend, as her family sympathized fully in the reforms to which she gave her life. I have many pleasant memories of my own flying visits to that hospitable Quaker home and the broad catholic spirit of Daniel and Lucy Anthony. Whatever opposition and ridicule their daughter endured elsewhere, she enjoyed the steadfast sympathy and confidence of her own home circle. Her faithful sister Mary, a most successful principal in the public schools of Rochester for a quarter of a century, and a good financier, who with her patrimony and salary has laid by a competence, took on her shoulders double duty at home in cheering the declining years of her parents, that Susan might do the public work in these reforms, in which the sisters were equally interested. At one time when Susan had expended her last dollar in the publication of her paper, *The Revolution*, and also $5,000 given her by a wealthy cousin, Anson Lapham, Mary generously advanced another five thousand, and thus bridged the last chasm. And now with life's earnest work nearly accomplished, the sisters are living happily together, illustrating another of the many charming homes of single women so rapidly multiplying in later years.

always writing and talking about the Constitution, interrupted with occasional visits from others of the faithful. Hither came Elizabeth Oakes Smith, Paulina Wright Davis, Frances Dana Gage, Dr. Harriot Hunt, Antoinette Brown, Lucy Stone, Abby Kelly, by turn, until all these names were as familiar as household words to the children.

Martha C. Wright, of Auburn, was a frequent visitor at the center of the rebellion, as my sequestered cottage on Locust Hill was facetiously called. She brought to these councils of war not only her own individual wisdom, but that of the wife and sister of William H. Seward, and sometimes encouraging suggestions from the great statesman himself, from whose writings we often gleaned grand and radical sentiments. Lucretia Mott, too, being an occasional guest at her sister's in Auburn, added the dignity of her presence at many of these important consultations. She was uniformly in favor of toning down our fiery pronunciamentoes. For Miss Anthony and myself, the English language had no words strong enough to express the indignation we felt in view of the prolonged injustice to woman. We found, however, that after expressing ourselves in the most vehement manner, and thus in a measure giving our feelings an outlet, we were reconciled to issue the documents at last in milder terms. If the men of the State could have known the stern rebukes, the denunciations, the wit, the irony, the sarcasm that were garnered there, and then judiciously pigeon-holed, and milder and more persuasive appeals substituted, they would have been truly thankful that they fared no worse.

Mr. Seward, in the brief intervals in his Washington life, made frequent visits in our neighborhood at the house of Judge G. V. Sackett, a man of wealth and some political influence. One of the Senator's standing anecdotes at dinner to illustrate the purifying influence of woman at the polls, which he always told with great zest for my special benefit, was in regard to the manner his wife's sister exercised the right of suffrage.

" Mrs. Worden having the supervision of a farm near Auburn, was obliged to hire two or three men for its cultivation. It was her custom, having examined them as to their capacity to perform the required labor, their knowledge of tools, horses, cattle, gardening, and horticulture, to inquire as to their politics. She informed them that being a woman and a widow, and having no one to represent her, she must have Republicans to do her voting, to represent her political opinions, and it always so happened that the men who offered their services belonged to the Republican party.

"Some one remarked to her one day, 'Are you sure your men vote as they promise?' 'Yes,' she replied, 'I trust nothing to their discretion. I take them in my carriage within sight of the polls, put them in charge of some Republican who can be trusted. I see they have the right tickets, then I feel sure I am faithfully represented, and I know I am right in so doing. I have neither husband, father, nor son; am responsible for my own taxes; am amenable to all the laws of the State; must pay the penalty of my own crimes if I commit any; hence I have the right, according to the principles of our government, to representation, and so long as I am not permitted to vote in person, I have a right to do so by proxy, hence I hire men to vote my principles.'" Thus she disposed of the statesman and his serio-comic morality.

These two sisters, daughters of Judge Miller, an influential man of wealth and position, were women of culture and remarkable natural intelligence, and interested in all progressive ideas. They had rare common-sense and independence of character, great simplicity of manner, and were wholly indifferent to the little arts of the toilet.

I was often told by fashionable women that one great objection to the woman's rights movement was the publicity of the conventions; the immodesty of speaking from a platform; and the trial of seeing one's name in the papers. Several ladies made such remarks to me one day as a bevy of us were sitting together in one of the fashionable hotels in Newport. We were holding a Convention there at that time, and some of them had been present at one of the sessions. "Really," said I, "ladies, you surprise me; our Conventions are not as public as the ball-room where I saw you all dancing last night. As to modesty, it may be a question in many minds whether it is less modest to speak words of soberness and truth, plainly dressed with one's person decently covered on a platform, than gorgeously arrayed with bare arms and shoulders, to waltz in the arms of strange gentlemen.

"And as to the press, I noticed you all reading with evident satisfaction the personal compliments and full descriptions of your dresses at the last ball, in this morning's papers. I presume that any one of you would have felt slighted if your name had not been mentioned in the general description. When my name is mentioned, it is in connection with some great moral movement, as making a speech, or reading a resolution. Thus we all suffer or enjoy the same publicity, we are all alike ridiculed, wise men pity and ridicule you, fops and fools pity and ridicule me, you as the victims of folly and fashion, me as the representative of many of the disagreeable 'isms' of the age, as they choose to distinguish liberal opinions. It is amusing in analyzing prejudices to see on what slender foundations they rest," and the ladies around me were so completely cornered that no one attempted an answer.

I remember being at a party at Gov. Seward's one evening, when Mr. Burlingame and his Chinese delegation were among the guests. As soon as the dancing commenced, and young ladies and gentlemen locked in each other's arms, began to whirl in the giddy waltz, these Chinese gentlemen were so shocked that they covered their faces with their fans, occasionally peeping out each side and expressing their surprise to each other. They thought us the most immodest women on the face of the earth. Modesty and good taste are questions of latitude and education; the more people know, the more their ideas are expanded, by travel, experience, and observation; the less easily they are shocked. The narrowness and bigotry of women, are the result of their circumscribed sphere of thought and action.

Soon after Judge Hurlbut had published his work on "Human Rights," and I had addressed the Legislature the first time, we met at a dinner party in Albany; Mr. and Mrs. Seward were there. The Senator was very merry on that occasion, and made Judge Hurlbut and myself the target for all his ridicule on the woman's rights question, in which most of the company joined, so that we stood quite alone. Sure that we had the right on our side, and the arguments clearly defined in our own minds, and both being cool and self-possessed, and with wit and sarcasm quite equal to any of them, we fought the Senator inch by inch until he had a very narrow platform to stand on. Mrs. Seward maintained an unbroken silence, while those ladies who did open their lips were with the opposition, supposing, no doubt, that Mr. Seward represented his wife's opinions.

When the ladies withdrew from the table, my embarrassment may be easily imagined. Separated from the Judge, I should now be an hour with a bevy of ladies who evidently felt a repulsion to all my most cherished opinions. It was the first time I had met Mrs. Seward, and I did not then know the broad liberal tendencies of her mind. What a tide of disagreeable thoughts rushed through me in that short passage from the dining-room to the parlor; how gladly I would have glided out the front door, but that was impossible, so I made up my mind to stroll round as if self-absorbed and look at the books and paintings until the Judge appeared, as I took it for granted that after all I said at the table on the political,

religious, and social equality of woman, not a lady would have anything to say to me.

Imagine then my surprise when the moment the parlor door was
closed upon us, Mrs. Seward, approaching me most affectionately
said, "Let me thank you for all the brave words you uttered at the
dinner-table, and for your speech before the Legislature, that thrilled
my soul as I read it over and over." I was filled with joy and astonishment. Recovering myself, I said, "Is it possible, Mrs. Seward, that you agree with me? Then why, when I was so hard
pressed with foes on every side, did you not come to the defence?
I supposed that all you ladies were hostile to every one of my
ideas on this question!" "No, no!" said she, "I am with you
thoroughly, but I am a born coward; there is nothing I dread more
than Mr. Seward's ridicule. I would rather walk up to the cannon's
mouth than encounter it." "I too am with you," "And I," said
two or three others who had been silent at the table. I never had
a more serious, heartfelt conversation than with these ladies. Mrs.
Seward's spontaneity and earnestness had moved them all deeply,
and when the Senator appeared the first word he said was, "Before
we part I must confess that I was fairly vanquished by you and the
Judge, on my own principles (for we had quoted some of his most
radical utterances). You have the argument, but custom and prejudice are against you, and they are stronger than truth and logic."

We had quite a magnetic circle of reformers in Central New
York, that kept the missives flying. At Rochester, were William
H. Channing, Frederick Douglass, the Anthonys, the Posts, the
Hallowells, the Stebbins, some grand Quaker families in Farming-
ton, and Waterloo; Mrs. Bloomer and her sprightly weekly called
The Lily, at Seneca Falls; Mrs. Wright, Mrs. Worden, Mrs. Seward, at Auburn; Gerrit Smith's family at Peterboro; Beriah Green's
at Whitesboro, with the Sedgwicks and Mays, and Matilda Joslyn
Gage at Syracuse. Although Mrs. Gage was surrounded with a
family of small children for years, yet she was always a student,
an omnivorous reader and liberal thinker, and her pen was ever at
work answering the attacks on the woman movement in the county
and State journals. In the village of Manlius, where she lived some
time after her marriage, she was the sole representative of this unpopular reform. When walking the street she would often hear
some boy, shielded by a dry-goods box or a fence, cry out "woman's
rights."

On one occasion, at a large evening party at Mr. Van Schaick's,
the host read aloud a poem called Rufus Chubb, a burlesque on

30

" strong-minded " women, ridiculing careers and conventions, and the many claims being made for larger freedom. Mrs. Gage, then quite young, was surprised and embarrassed. Every eye was fixed on her, as evidently the type of womanhood the author was portraying. As soon as the reader's voice died away, Mrs Gage, with marked coolness and grace, approached him, and with an imaginary wreath crowned him the poet-laureate of the occasion, and introduced him to the company as " the immortal Rufus Chubb." The expressive gesture and the few brief words conferring the honor, turned the laugh on Mr. Van Schaick so completely, that he was the target for all the merriment of the evening.

Mrs. Gage was the only daughter of Dr. Hezekiah Joslyn, a man of learning and philanthropic tendencies. He gave much attention to the direction of his daughter's thought and reading. She always had a knack of rummaging through old libraries, bringing more startling facts to light than any woman I ever knew.*

In the winter of 1861, just after the election of Lincoln, the Abolitionists decided to hold a series of Conventions in the chief cities of the North. All their available speakers were pledged for active service. The Republican party, having absorbed the political Abolitionists within its ranks by its declared hostility to the extension of slavery, had come into power with overwhelming majorities; hence the Garrisonian Abolitionists, opposed to all compromises, felt this was the opportune moment to rouse the people to the neces-

---

* Mrs. Gage received a somewhat remarkable early training. Not only was her father a man of profound thought, a reformer thoroughly studying all the new questions coming up, but his house was a station on the underground railroad, the home of anti-slavery speakers upon every subject, as well as that of a large number of clergymen, who yearly held " protracted meetings " in the place. Sitting up until midnight listening to the discussions of those reverend gentlemen upon baptism, original sin, predestination, and other doctrinal points, her thought was early turned to religious questions. She read the Bible through before she was nine years old, and became a church member at the early age of eleven, her parents, in accordance with their habits, not attempting to influence her mind for or against this step.

Dr. Joslyn paid great attention to his daughter's education. From her earliest years it was a law of the household that her childish questions should not be put off with an idle reply, but must be reasonably answered ; and when she was older, he himself instructed her in mathematics, Greek, and physiology. But that for which she feels most indebted to him, as she often says—the grandest training given her—was to think for herself. She was taught to accept no opinion because of its authority, but to question the truth of all things. Thus was laid the foundation of Mrs. Gage's reform tendencies and of her non-acceptance of masculine authority in matters of religion and politics. Nor was she, in a certain way, less indebted to her mother, a Scotch lady, belonging to the noble, old, and influential family of Leslie, a woman of refined and elevated tastes, universally respected and beloved. From this side Mrs. Gage inherited her antiquarian tastes and habits of delving into old histories, from which she has unearthed so many facts bearing upon woman's degradation.

sity of holding that party to its declared principles, and pushing it, if possible, a step or two forward.

I was invited to accompany Miss Anthony and Beriah Green to a few points in Central New York. But we soon found, by the concerted action of Republicans all over the country, the Conventions were broken up at every point. This furnished one occasion on which Republicans and Democrats could work harmoniously together, and they made common cause against the Abolitionists. The John Brown raid the year before had intimidated Northern politicians as much as Southern slaveholders, and the general feeling was that the discussion of the question at the North should be altogether suppressed.

From Buffalo to Albany our experience was the same, varied only by the fertile resources of the actors and their surroundings. Thirty years of education had somewhat changed the character of Northern mobs. They no longer dragged men through the streets with ropes round their necks, nor broke up women's prayer-meetings; they no longer threw eggs and brickbats at the apostles of reform, nor dipped them in barrels of tar and feathers; they simply crowded the halls, and with laughing, groaning, clapping, and cheering, effectually interrupted the proceedings.

Thus we passed the two days we had advertised for a Convention in St. James' Hall, Buffalo. As we paid for the Hall, the mob enjoyed themselves at our expense in more ways than one. At the appointed time every session we took our places on the platform, making at various intervals of silence renewed efforts to speak. Not succeeding, we sat and conversed with each other and many friends who crowded the platform and ante-rooms. Thus among ourselves we had a pleasant reception and a discussion of many phases of the question that brought us together. The mob not only vouchsafed to us the privilege of talking to our friends without interruption, but delegations of their own came behind the scenes from time to time, to discuss with us the right of free speech and the constitutionality of slavery.

These Buffalo rowdies were headed by ex-Justice Hinson, aided by younger members of the Fillmore and Seymour families and the Chief of Police and fifty subordinates, who were admitted to the hall free for the express purpose of protecting our right of free speech, which in defiance of the Mayor's orders, they did not make the slightest effort to do. At Lockport there was a feeble attempt in the same direction. At Albion neither hall, church, nor school-house could be obtained, so we held small meetings in the dining-room of the hotel.

At Rochester, Corinthian Hall was packed long before the hour advertised. This was a delicately appreciative jocose mob. At this point Aaron Powell joined us. As he had just risen from a bed of sickness, looking pale and emaciated, he slowly mounted the platform. The mob at once took in his look of exhaustion, and as he seated himself they gave an audible, simultaneous sigh, as if to say, What a relief it is to be seated! So completely did the tender manifestation reflect Mr. Powell's apparent condition, that the whole audience burst into a roar of laughter. Here, too, all attempts to speak were futile.

At Port Byron a generous sprinkling of cayenne pepper on the stove, soon cut short all constitutional arguments and pæans to liberty. And so it was all the way to Albany. The whole State was aflame with the mob spirit, and from Boston and various points in other States, the same news reached us. As the Legislature was in session, and we were advertised in Albany, a radical member sarcastically moved " that as Mrs. Stanton and Miss Anthony were about to move on Albany, the militia be ordered out for the protection of the city."

Happily, Albany could then boast a democratic Mayor, a man of courage and conscience, who said the right of free speech should never be trodden underfoot where he had the power to prevent it. And grandly did that one determined man maintain order in his jurisdiction. Through all the sessions of the Convention Mayor Thatcher sat on the platform, his police stationed in different parts of the Hall and outside the building, to disperse the crowd as fast as collected. If a man or boy hissed or made the slightest interruption, he was immediately ejected. And not only did the Mayor preserve order in the meetings, but with a company of armed police, he escorted us every time to and from the Delavan House. The last night Gerrit Smith addressed the mob from the steps of the hotel, after which they gave him three cheers, and dispersed in good order.

When proposing for the Mayor a vote of thanks at the close of the Convention, Mr. Smith expressed his fears that it had been a severe ordeal for him to listen to these prolonged anti-slavery discussions, he smiled, and said : " I have really been deeply interested and instructed. I rather congratulate myself that a Convention of this character has at last come in the line of my business, otherwise I should have probably remained in ignorance of many important facts and opinions I now understand and appreciate."

Whilst all this was going on publicly, we had an equally trying experience progressing day by day behind the scenes. Miss Anthony had been instrumental in helping a fugitive mother with her child, escape from a husband who had immured her in an insane asylum. The wife, belonging to one of the first families of New York, her brother a United States Senator, and the husband a man of position, a large circle of friends and acquaintances were interested in the result. Though she was incarcerated in an insane asylum for eighteen months, yet members of her own family again and again testified that she was not insane. Miss Anthony knowing that she was not, and believing fully that the unhappy mother was the victim of a conspiracy, would not reveal her hiding-place.

Knowing the confidence Miss Anthony felt in the wisdom of Mr. Garrison and Mr. Phillips, they were implored to use their influence with her to give up the fugitives. Letters and telegrams, persuasions, arguments, warnings, from Mr. Garrison, Mr. Phillips, the Senator, on the one side, and from Lydia Mott, Mrs. Elizabeth F. Ellet, Abby Hopper Gibbons, on the other, poured in upon her day after day, but Miss Anthony remained immovable, although she knew she was defying authority and violating law, and that she might be arrested any moment on the platform. We had known so many aggravated cases of this kind, that in daily counsel we resolved that this woman should not be recaptured if it was possible to prevent it. To us it looked as imperative a duty to shield a sane mother who had been torn from a family of little children and doomed to the companionship of lunatics, and to aid her in fleeing to a place of safety, as to help a fugitive from slavery to Canada. In both cases an unjust law was violated; in both cases the supposed owners of the victims were defied, hence, in point of law and morals, the act was the same in both cases. The result proved the wisdom of Miss Anthony's decision, as all with whom Mrs. P. came in contact for years afterward, expressed the opinion that she was perfectly sane and always had been. Could the dark secrets of these insane asylums be brought to light, we should be shocked to know the countless number of rebellious wives, sisters, and daughters that are thus annually sacrificed to false customs and conventionalisms, and barbarous laws made by men for women.

Quite an agitation occurred in 1852, on woman's costume. In demanding a place in the world of work, the unfitness of her dress seemed to some, an insurmountable obstacle. How can you, it was said, ever compete with man for equal place and pay, with garments of such frail fabrics and so cumbrously fashioned, and how can you ever hope to enjoy the same health and vigor with man, so long as the waist is pressed into the smallest compass, pounds of clothing hung on the hips, the limbs cramped with skirts, and with high heels the whole woman thrown out of her true equilibrium. Wise men, physicians, and sensible women, made their appeals, year after year; physiologists lectured on the subject; the press commented, until it seemed as if there were a serious demand for some decided steps, in the direction of a rational costume for women. The most casual observer could see how many pleasures young girls were continually sacrificing to their dress: In walking, running, rowing, skating, dancing, going up and down stairs, climbing trees and fences, the airy fabrics and flowing skirts were a continual impediment and vexation. We can not estimate how large a share of the ill-health and temper among women is the result of the crippling, cribbing influence of her costume. Fathers, husbands, and brothers, all joined in protest against the small waist, and stiff distended petticoats, which were always themes for unbounded ridicule. But no sooner did a few brave conscientious women adopt the bifurcated costume, an imitation in part of the Turkish style, than the press at once turned its guns on "The Bloomer," and the same fathers, husbands, and brothers, with streaming eyes and pathetic tones, conjured the women of their households to cling to the prevailing fashions.* The object of those who donned the new attire, was primarily health and freedom ; but as the daughter of Gerrit Smith introduced it just at the time of the early conventions, it was supposed to be an inherent element in the demand for political equality. As some of those who advocated the right of suffrage, wore the dress, and had been identified with all the unpopular reforms, in the reports of our conventions, the press rung the changes on "strong-minded," "Bloomer," "free love," "easy divorce," "amalgamation." I wore the dress two years and found it a great blessing. What a sense of liberty I felt, in running up and down stairs with my hands free to carry whatsoever I would, to trip through the rain or snow with no skirts to hold or brush, ready at any moment to climb a hill-top to see the sun go down, or the moon rise, with no ruffles or trails to be limped by the dew, or soiled by the grass. What an emancipation from little petty vexatious trammels and annoyances every hour of the day. Yet such is the tyranny of custom, that to escape constant observation, criticism, ridicule, per-

---

* See Appendix.

secution, mobs,* one after another gladly went back to the old slavery and sacrificed freedom to repose. I have never wondered since that the Chinese women allow their daughters' feet to be encased in iron shoes, nor that the Hindoo widows walk calmly to the funeral pyre. I suppose no act of my life ever gave my cousin, Gerrit Smith, such deep sorrow, as my abandonment of the "Bloomer costume." He published an open letter* to me on the subject, and when his daughter, Mrs. Miller, three years after, followed my example, he felt that women had so little courage and persistence, that for a time he almost despaired of the success of the suffrage movement; of such vital consequence in woman's mental and physical development did he feel the dress to be.

Gerrit Smith † Samuel J. May, J. C. Jackson, C. D. Miller and D. C. Bloomer, sustained the women who lead in this reform, unflinchingly, during the trying experiment. Let the names of those who made this protest be remembered. We knew the Bloomer costume never could be generally becoming, as it required a perfection of form, limbs, and feet, such as few possessed, and we who wore it also knew that it was not artistic. Though the martyrdom proved too much for us who had so many other measures to press on the public conscience, yet no experiment is lost, however evanescent, that rouses thought to the injurious consequences of the present style of dress, sacrificing to its absurdities so many of the most promising girls of this generation.

---

* See Appendix.

† Gerrit Smith's home was ever a charming resort for lovers of liberty as well as lovers of Eve's daughters. In his leisure hours my cousin had a turn for match-making, and his chief delight in this direction was to promote unions between good Abolitionists and the sons and daughters of conservative families. Here James G. Birney, among others, wooed and won his wife. Here one would meet the first families in the State, with Indians, Africans, slaveholders, religionists of all sects, and representatives of all shades of humanity, each class alike welcomed and honored, feasting, fêting, dancing—joining in all kinds of amusements and religious worship together (the Indians excepted, as they generally came for provisions, which, having secured, they departed). His house was one of the depots of the underground railroad. One day Mr. Smith summoned all the young girls then visiting there, saying he had a great secret to tell them if they would sacredly pledge themselves not to divulge it. Having done so, he led the way to the third story, ushered us into a large room, and there stood a beautiful quadroon girl to receive us. "Harriet," said Mr. Smith, "I want you to make good Abolitionists of these girls by describing to them all you have suffered in slavery." He then left the room, locking us in. Her narrative held us spell-bound until the lengthening shadows of the twilight hour made her departure safe for Canada. One remark she made impressed me deeply. I told her of the laws for women such as we then lived under, and remarked on the parallel condition of slaves and women. "Yes," said she, "but I am both. I am doubly damned in sex and color. Yea, in class too, for I am poor and ignorant; none of you can ever touch the depth of misery where I stand to-day." We had the satisfaction to see Harriet dressed in Quaker costume, closely veiled, drive off in the moonlight that evening, to find the liberty she could not enjoy in this Republic, under the shadow of a monarch's throne

CHAPTER XIV.

NEW YORK.

First Steps in New York—Woman's Temperance Convention, Albany, January, 1852—
New York Woman's State Temperance Society, Rochester, April, 1852—Women be-
fore the Legislature pleading for a Maine Law—Women rejected as Delegates to
Men's State Conventions at Albany and Syracuse, 1852 ; at the Brick Church Meeting
and World's Temperance Convention in New York, 1853—Horace Greeley defends the
Rights of Women in *The York Tribune*—The Teachers' State Conventions—The Syracuse
National Woman's Rights Convention, 1852—Mob in the Broadway Tabernacle Wom-
an's Rights Convention through two days, 1853—State Woman's Rights Convention at
Rochester, December, 1853—Albany Convention, February, 1854, and Hearing before
the Legislature demanding the Right of Suffrage—A State Committee Appointed—
Susan B. Anthony General Agent—Conventions at Saratoga Springs, 1854, '55, '59—
Annual State Conventions with Legislative Hearings and Reports of Committees, until the War—Married Women's Property Law, 1860—Bill before the Legislature Granting Divorce for Drunkenness—Horace Greeley and Thurlow Weed oppose it—Ernestine L. Rose, Lucretia Mott, and Elizabeth Cady Stanton Address the Legislature in
favor of the Bill—Robert Dale Owen defends the Measure in *The New York Tribune*—
National Woman's Rights Conventions in New York City, 1856, '58, '59, '60—Status of
the Woman's Rights Movement at the Opening of the War, 1861.

A FULL report of the woman's rights agitation in the State of
New York, would in a measure be the history of the movement.
In this State, the preliminary battles in the anti-slavery, temperance,
educational, and religious societies were fought; the first Governmental aid given to the higher education of woman, and her voice
first heard in teachers' associations. Here the first Woman's Rights
Convention was held, the first demand made for suffrage, the first
society formed for this purpose, and the first legislative efforts made
to secure the civil and political rights of women ; commanding the
attention of leading members of the bar ; of Savage, Spencer, Hertell,
and Hurlbut. Here too the pulpit made the first demand for the
political rights of woman. Here was the first temperance society
formed by women, the first medical college opened to them, and
woman first ordained for the ministry.

In 1850, in the city of Buffalo, 1,500 women petitioned the Common Council not to license the sale of intoxicating drinks; and the following year, they sent a petition to the Legislature, signed by 2,200, asking for an act authorizing some official body to take into custody, and provide for the swarms of vagrant children, growing up in ignorance and vice. This may be considered the initiative step to a Board of Charities. In the same year, a number of spirited women in Fulton, Oswego Co., disgusted with the inefficient action of the temperance men, entered complaint against the liquor dealers, for the violation of the license laws, and some of them attended the trials in person. In 1851, the ladies of Cardiff, Onondaga Co., appeared before the Grand Jury, and made complaint against the liquor dealers and overseers of the poor, the one for violating the law, the other for neglecting to prosecute the violators on their complaint, and they succeeded in getting both indicted. In 1851, a petition was sent from Ontario County, praying the Legislature to exempt women from taxation.

September 15, 1853, Antoinette L. Brown was ordained as pastor of a church in South Butler, and November 15, performed the ceremony at the marriage of a daughter of Rhoda de Garmo, of Rochester. In this year, at a large Convention of liberal people, to promote Christian Union, held in Syracuse, she made an address. All denominations took part on the occasion and listened to her with respectful attention. In New York, woman's voice was first heard on the Nation's great festal day. In 1853, Mary Vaughan gave the fourth of July oration at Speedsville, Emily Clarke at Watkins, Amelia Bloomer at Hartford, and Antoinette Brown at South Butler. Everything on these occasions was conducted as usual: the grand procession to the grove, or town hall, the military escort, reading the Declaration, martial music, cannon, fire-crackers, torpedoes, roast pig, and green peas; none of the usual accompaniments were omitted. In the same year, Antoinette Brown and Lucy Stone canvassed the twenty-second district, to secure the election of the Hon. Gerrit Smith for Congress, and were successful in their efforts.

In April, 1854, the Daughters of Temperance at Johnson's Creek, sent thirty pieces of silver to Gov. Seymour, for vetoing a bill for a prohibitory law, and thus betraying the friends of temperance. In New York, the first anti-tax association, the first woman's club and Loyal League were formed. Here, too, a woman, Mrs. Josephine Shaw Lowell, was appointed State Commissioner of Charities, by Gov. Samuel J. Tilden. Whether the Governor of any other State had preceded him in a more profitable or honorable appointment, has not yet been discovered. Lest women should feel too deep a sense of gratitude, they should understand that this office involves arduous labors, but no pecuniary recompense. This may be a reason that such positions are being gradually assigned to women.

At the time of this general uprising, New York was thoroughly stirred with temperance and anti-slavery excitement. George Thompson, the great English reformer and orator, who had been mobbed in all the chief cities of the North, accompanied by William Lloyd Garrison, was holding a series of conventions through the State. And as these conventions were held in the midst of the " Jerry rescue trials,"* the apostles of freedom spoke with terrible vehemence and denunciation. Popular orators, too, were rushing here and there in the furor of a Presidential campaign, and as all these reforms were thrown into the governmental cauldron for discussion, the whole people seemed to be on the watch towers of politics and philanthropy. Women shared in the general unrest, and began to take many steps before unknown. Since 1840, they had generally attended political meetings, as with the introduction of moral questions into legislation, they had manifested an increasing interest in government.

The repeal of the License Law of 1846, filled the temperance hosts throughout the State with alarm, and roused many women to the assertion of their rights. Impoverished, broken-hearted wives and mothers, were for the first time looking to the State for some protection against the cruelties and humiliations they endured at the hands of liquor dealers, when suddenly the beneficent law was repealed, and their reviving hopes crushed. The burning indignation of women, who had witnessed the protracted outrages on helpless wives and children in the drunkard's home, roused many to public speech, and gave rise to the secret organizations called " Daughters of Temperance." Others finding there was no law nor gospel in the land for their protection, took the power in their own hands, visiting saloons, breaking windows, glasses, bottles, and

---

* Jerry McHenry was an athletic mulatto, a cooper by trade, who had been living in Syracuse for many years, since his escape from slavery. On the 12th of October, 1850, there was an attempt to kidnap him, but the Abolitionists, with such men as Samuel J. May and Gerrit Smith at their head, succeeded in rescuing him by a *coup d'état*, from the officers of the law, which involved several trials in Auburn, Canandaigua, Buffalo, and Albany. As this occurred soon after the passage of the Fugitive Slave Law, the leading Abolitionists were determined to test its constitutionality in the courts. It was so systematically and universally violated, that it soon became a dead letter.

emptying demijohns and barrels into the streets. Coming like whirlwinds of vengeance, drunkards and rum-sellers stood paralyzed before them. Though women were sometimes arrested for these high-handed proceedings, a strong public sentiment justified their acts, and forced the liquor dealers to withdraw their complaints.*

There is nothing more terrible than the reckless courage of despairing women, who, though knowing they have eternal truth and justice on their side, know also their helplessness against the tide of

---

* A HEROIC WOMAN.—Mrs. Margaret Freeland, of Syracuse, was recently arrested upon a warrant issued on complaint of Emanuel Rosendale, a rum-seller, charging her with forcing an entrance to his house, and with stones and clubs smashing his doors and windows, breaking his tumblers and bottles, and turning over his whisky barrels and spilling their contents. Great excitement was produced by this novel case. It seems that the husband of Mrs. Freeland was a drunkard—that he was in the habit of abusing his wife, turning her out of doors, etc., and this was carried so far that the police frequently found it necessary to interfere to put a stop to his ill-treatment of his family. Rosendale, the complainant, furnished Freeland with the liquor which turned him into a demon. Mrs. Freeland had frequently told him of her sufferings and besought him to refrain from giving her husband the poison. But alas! she appealed to a heart of stone. He disregarded her entreaties and spurned her from his door. Driven to desperation she armed herself, broke into the house, drove out the base-hearted landlord and proceeded upon the work of destruction.

She was brought before the court and demanded a trial. The citizens employed Charles B. Sedgwick, Esq., as her counsel, and prepared to justify her assault upon legal grounds. Rosendale, being at once arrested on complaint of Thomas L. Carson for selling liquor unlawfully, and feeling the force of the storm that was gathering over his head, appeared before the Justice, withdrew his complaint against Mrs. Freeland, paid the costs, and gave bail on the complaint of Mr. Carson, to appear at the General Sessions, and answer to an indictment should there be one found.

Mrs. Freeland is said to be " the pious mother of a fine family of children, and a highly respectable member of the Episcopal Church."

The *Carson League* commenting on this affair says :

" The rum-seller cowered in the face of public feeling. This case shows that public feeling will justify a woman whose person or family is outraged by a rum-seller, for entering his grocery or tavern and destroying his liquor. If the law lets loose a tiger upon her, she may destroy it. She has no other resort but force to save herself and her children. Were the women of this city to proceed in a body and destroy all the liquor of all the taverns and groceries, they would be justified by law and public opinion. Women should take this war into their hands, when men take side with the murderers of their peace.

" A tavern or grocery which makes the neighbors drunken and insane is a public nuisance, and may be pulled down and destroyed by the neighbors who are injured by it. It is worse than the plague. And if men will not put hands on it, then should the women do it. Tell us not it is property. It ceases to be property when it is employed to destroy the people. If a man lights his torch and sets about putting fire to the houses about him, any person may seize the torch and destroy it. So if a man takes a pistol and passes through the streets shooting the people, the pistol ceases to be property and may be taken from him by force and destroyed by any person who can do it. We sincerely hope that the women of the State will profit by this example, and go to destroying the liquor vessels and their contents." To all of which we respond AMEN.

The Lily, June, 1853.

misery engulphing the drunkard's home. Women were applauded for these acts of heroism by the press and temperance leagues; they were welcomed too as speakers sometimes on their platforms, just as slaves were in the olden days, to move an audience with their tales of woe. But when they organized themselves into associations, adopted constitutions, passed resolutions, and sent their delegates to men's conventions, asking to be recognized as equals, then began the battle in the temperance ranks, vindictive and protracted for years. The clergy were the most bitter opponents of the public action of women; but throughout the conflict they were sustained by the purest men in the nation, such as Horace Greeley, Joshua R. Giddings, Rev. E. H. Chapin, Rev. Samuel J. May, Thomas W. Higginson, William H. Channing, Gerrit Smith, Wendell Phillips, William Lloyd Garrison, and others. All this persecution on the ground of sex, intensified the love of liberty in woman's soul, and deepened the oft repeated lesson of individual rights.

On January 28, 1852, "The Daughters of Temperance" assembled in Albany to take part in a mass meeting of all the "Divisions" in the State. Among the delegates present were Susan B. Anthony, Mary C. Vaughan, and Lydia Fowler, who were received as members of the Convention. But at the first attempt by Miss Anthony to speak, they were informed that the ladies were invited to listen, and not to take part in the proceedings. Those women present who were not satisfied with such a position withdrew, announcing that they would hold a meeting that evening in which men and women would stand on equal ground.

At the appointed time they assembled in the vestry-room of the Presbyterian church on Hudson Street. Samuel J. May, who was in Albany attending one of the "Jerrey Rescue Trials," was present, and opened the meeting with prayer. Mrs. Vaughan was chosen President,* and on taking the chair, said:

We have met to consider what we, as women, can do and may do, to forward the temperance reform. We have met, because, as members of the human family, we share in all the sufferings which error and crime bring upon the race, and because we are learning that our part in the drama of life is something beside inactive suffering and passive endurance. We would act as well as endure; and we meet here to-day because

---

* Mrs. Thompson, of Albany; Mrs. Cushman, of New York, *Vice-Presidents*. Mrs. Fowler and Miss Anthony, *Secretaries*. Lydia Mott, of Albany; Phebe Hoag Jones, of Troy; Eliza Hoxie Shove, of Easton; and Elizabeth Van Alstine, of Canajoharie, *Business Committee*.

many of us have been trying to act, and we would combine our individual experiences, and together devise plans for the future, out of which shall arise well-based hopes of good results to humanity. We are aware that this proceeding of ours, this calling together of a body of women to deliberate publicly upon plans to carry out a specified reform, will rub rather harshly upon the mould of prejudice, which has gathered thick upon the common mind.

. . . . There are plenty of women, as well as men, who can labor for reforms without neglecting business or duty. It is an error that clings most tenaciously to the public mind, that because a part of the sex are wives and mothers and have absorbing duties, that all the sex should be denied any other sphere of effort. To deprive every unmarried woman, spinster, or widow, or every childless wife, of the power of exercising her warm sympathies for the good of others, is to deprive her of the greatest happiness of which she is capable; to rob her highest faculties of their legitimate operation and reward; to belittle and narrow her mind; to dwarf her affections; to turn the harmonies of her nature to discord; and, as the human mind must be active, to compel her to employ hers with low and grovelling thoughts, which lead to contemptible actions.

There is no reform in which woman can act better or more appropriately than temperance. I know not how she can resist or turn aside from the duty of acting in this; its effects fall so crushingly upon her and those whose interests are identical with her own; she has so often seen its slow, insidious, but not the less surely fatal advances, gaining upon its victim; she has seen the intellect which was her dearest pride, debased; the affections which were her life-giving springs of action, estranged; the children once loved, abused, disgraced and impoverished; the home once an earthly paradise, rendered a fit abode for lost spirits; has felt in her own person all the misery, degradation, and woe of the drunkard's wife; has shrunk from revilings and cowered beneath blows; has labored and toiled to have her poor earnings transferred to the rumseller's ill-gotten hoard; while her children, ragged, fireless, poor, starving, gathered shivering about her. and with hollow eyes, from which all smiles had fled, begged vainly for the bread she had not to bestow. Oh! the misery, the utter, hopeless misery of the drunkard's wife!

. . . . We account it no reason why we should desist, when conscience, an awakened sense of duty, and aroused heart-sympathies, would lead us to show ourselves something different than an impersonation of the vague ideal which has been named, Woman, and with which woman has long striven to identify herself. A creature all softness and sensibility, who must necessarily enjoy and suffer in the extreme, while sharing with man the pleasures and the ills of life; bearing happiness meekly, and sorrow with fortitude; gentle, mild, submissive, forbearing under all circumstances; a softened reflex of the opinions and ideas of the masculines who, by relationship, hold mastery over her; without individualism, a mere adjunct of man, the chief object of whose creation was to adorn and beautify his existence, or to minister to some form of his selfishness. This is nearly the masculine idea of womanhood, and poor womanhood strives to personify it. But not all women.

This is an age of iconoclasms; and daring hands are raised to sweep from its pedestal, and dash to fragments, this false image of woman. We care not how soon, if the true woman but take its place. This is also, and most emphatically, an age of progress. One old idea, one mouldering form of prejudice after another, is rapidly swept away. Thought, written and spoken, acts upon the mass of mind in this day of railroads and telegraphs, with a thousandfold more celerity than in the days of pillions and slow coaches. Scarce have the lips that uttered great thoughts ceased to move, or the pen which wrote them dropped from the weary hand, ere they vibrate through the inmost recesses of a thousand hearts, and awaken deep and true responses in a thousand living, truthful souls. Thence they grow, expand, fructify, and the result is Progress.

Mrs. Lydia F. Fowler then gave several very touching recitals of the evils of intemperance in family circles within her own observation. Her lectures on Hygiene and Physiology through the State, illustrating as she did the effect of alcohol on the system, and pointing out to mothers what they could do to promote the health of their children, and thus ensure temperance and morality, were most effective in their bearings on this question. Letters were read from Elizabeth Cady Stanton, Clarina Howard Nichols, and Amelia Bloomer.

Mr. MAY, on rising, said: The sudden and unjustifiable repeal of the License Law of 1846, changed the face of the community, which had everywhere brightened with new hope under the brief but salutary operation of that law. That repeal, which it was indecorous if not presumptuous in the representatives of the people to make, seeing the law had been enacted directly by the people in their primary assemblies; that repeal brought back all the evils of intemperance aggravated by the successful efforts which had been openly and covertly made to break down the barriers which the law of 1846 had set up. The flood-gates of this loathsome vice were slammed open, as if never to be shut again. What I have seen and heard since I came to the capital, has encouraged me not a little. I have met with gentlemen from all parts of the State, who seem to be convinced that the people are ready for the passage of a stringent law similar to that which has recently gone into operation in Maine.

But I am particularly encouraged that the women of the State have made an especial and somewhat novel movement in this behalf. It has in all ages of the world been ominous when the women of a country have come out of the retirement they generally choose, to take a public part in the affairs of the State. What if this Convention be not a large one, it is significant nevertheless. I could cite you to a reform in our own country which commenced with less than twelve individuals twenty years ago, and now that reform has drawn into its vortex all the living spirits in the land, and has created an agitation of the public mind that will never be quelled until Slavery is buried out of sight forever. If the women of New York will act up to the noble sentiments that have been expressed in the addresses and letters written by women to this Convention, great and glorious results must follow. And there are especial reasons why women should be earnest in this cause. Their sex, though not so much addicted as ours to the use of intoxicating drinks, suffers more from the effects of the evil. To them it is the destruction of all domestic peace, the wreck of all conjugal and maternal hopes; it is ignorance, poverty, misery, for themselves and children. My own attention was first called to this reform by the sufferings of women. (Mr. May here related several touching anecdotes of most estimable women he had known, devoted wives, mothers, sisters, daughters, who had been utterly despoiled of all earthly comfort by the intemperance of those they loved).

At one time I thought this evil might be repressed by man alone; but I have learned that humanity is dual. God made man male and female. The sexes are equally concerned in the welfare of the race. What God has joined together must not be put asunder. Women are constituent parts of the State and the Church, as well as of the home; and their influence is as indispensable to the well-being of the former as the latter. A State or Church that excludes woman from its councils, is like a family without a mother, in a condition of half orphanage.

In the days of our Revolution women made as many sacrifices and endured as great sufferings for independence, as did the men. It is most ungrateful when we are speaking of that event, and the actors in it, not to make mention of our Revolutionary Mothers. In the French Revolution women were conspicuous actors. If Madame Roland and her coadjutors had been allowed to sway the public councils, the results would have been far happier for France.

In moral revolutions women have ever signalized themselves. It was a woman, Elizabeth Fry, who in England commenced the reform in the discipline of prisons, and prosecuted it in person for years, until she had proven her plans feasible, and inspired others with a faith like her own. It was Dorothea Dix (a very delicately organized woman), who first in this country recognized the claims and acknowledged the rights of the insane. She found these poor victims of man's ignorance everywhere suffering terrible hardships. They were dreaded by all, and abhorred by many who had charge of them, and believed to be incapable of suffering as sane people suffer, and to be beyond the reach of those kindly influences which more than all others control those who are in their right minds. Miss Dix penetrated their cheerless, dark, damp abodes. She brought to light the wrongs that were inflicted upon them. She exposed the folly of the fears which were entertained of them. She showed by her own courageous experiments that even furious maniacs could be controlled by the spirit of Christian love. The asylums in many of our States to-day are noble monuments to the inestimable value of her services.

When Miss Dix first visited the insane department of the jail in Cambridge, to look after one miserable human being she had chanced to hear was immured there, she little thought of the career of benevolent effort and of high distinction as a philanthropist that was opening before her. She went only to give relief to a solitary sufferer. But the dejected, helpless and wretched condition in which she found the insane there, raised the inquiry in her mind whether it could be that the same class of unfortunates were treated in this wise elsewhere. Such an inquiry could not be suppressed in a heart like hers; it urged her on to further investigation. It led to new developments of the methods that philanthropists and scientists were advocating in France. She came at last to feel that she had a mission to that class of " the lost ones," and she has fulfilled it gloriously. She has been the angel of the Lord to the insane in almost all the States of the Union.

The Anti-Slavery cause in both England and America, owes as much to woman as to man. If in Great Britain the suppression of the African slave trade was commenced by men, the abolition of West India slavery was begun by women; and it is acknowledged that they did more than the men to accomplish the overthrow of that system of all imaginable wickedness, which, while it endured, stimulated the cupidity of the slave-trader, so that he prosecuted his accursed traffic as much as ever, notwithstanding the acts of the American Congress and the British Parliament. In our country the most efficient, untiring laborers in the anti-slavery cause, have from the beginning been women. Lydia Maria Child, a lady highly distinguished among the authors of America, was the first to publish a sizable book upon slavery. Its very title was a pregnant one, viz, " An Appeal in behalf of that Class of Americans called Africans." Its contents were of great and permanent value. The publication of that volume was to her a costly sacrifice of popularity as an author. At a very early period of the enterprise, Elizabeth M. Chandler published many essays and poems that will live forever. The bravery and persistence of Prudence Crandall in maintaining a school for colored girls in Connecticut, in the face of terrible persecution, is beyond praise. Maria Weston Chapman, since 1834, has been among the leaders of the anti-slavery host, directing their movements and stimulating them to effort. Lucretia Mott, Sarah Pugh, Eliza Lee Follen, Abby Kelly, Mary Grew, are all worthy of mention—there is no end to the names of excellent, wise, courageous women who have contended nobly for the anti-slavery faith and practice. They have been traduced, reviled, persecuted, but nothing has deterred them from advocating the rights of humanity.

NEW YORK STATE TEMPERANCE CONVENTION,
ROCHESTER, N. Y., *April* 20 *and* 21, 1852.

At ten o'clock a large audience assembled in Corinthian Hall. The morning session was composed entirely of women; more than five hundred being present. The meeting was called to order by

Susan B. Anthony, who read the following call that had been extensively circulated throughout the State:

The women of the State of New York who desire to aid in advancing the cause of Temperance, and are willing to labor earnestly and truthfully for its success, are respectfully invited to meet at Corinthian Hall in the city of Rochester on the 20th of April, for the purpose of devising, maturing, and recommending such a course of associated action as shall best subserve for the protection of their interests and of society at large, too long invaded and destroyed by legalized intemperance. Feeling that woman has hitherto been greatly responsible for the continuance of this vice by encouraging social drinking, and by not sufficiently exerting her influence for its overthrow, and realizing that upon her rest the heaviest burthens which follow in its train, the Committee are convinced that they will be sustained by all good men and women in urging upon the sex such noble and energetic action as shall tend to the downfall of the traffic in intoxicating drinks.

Arrangements have been made to render the occasion one of interest to all friends of the cause. Addresses and communications from both ladies and gentlemen of known ability will be presented, and a general and comprehensive plan of operation proposed, whereby woman may aid in the promotion of a cause which appeals to her sympathy through the avenue of every relation which binds her to the race.

It is earnestly hoped that this meeting will be numerously attended.*

SUSAN B. ANTHONY, H. ATTILIA ALBRO, and MARY C. VAUGHAN,
Central Committee.

The officers of the Convention were then chosen. Elizabeth Cady Stanton, President,† who on rising said:

I fully appreciate, ladies, the compliment intended, in choosing me to fill this place on an occasion of such interest and importance. If a sincere love for the principles of temperance, a fervent zeal in the welfare of woman, and an unwavering faith in the final triumph of truth, fits one for this post of honor, then am I not unworthy, though I must confess myself, from the novelty of the position, ignorant alike of the rights and duties of the office of President. I shall deeply regret if in any omissions or commissions of duty I fail to reflect back on this Convention a full share of the honor now conferred upon me.

How my heart throbs to see women assembling in convention to inquire what part they have in the great moral struggles of humanity!

---

* The following citizens of Rochester concur in the above call: Samuel Richardson, Rev. Wm. H. Goodwin, Samuel Chipman, Geo. A. Avery, James P. Fogg, J. O. Bloss, Wm. R. Hallowell, James Vick, Jr., E. C. Williams, Daniel Anthony.

† *Vice-Presidents.*—Mary C. Vaughan, Olivia Fraser, Frances Stanton Avery, Rhoda De Garmo, Sarah D. Fish, and Mrs. D. C. Alling.

Secretaries.—Amelia Bloomer and Susan B. Anthony.

Resolutions.—Amy Post, Elizabeth Monroe, Rachel Van Lew.

Finance.—Susan B. Anthony, Mary H. Hallowell, H. Attilia Albro.

31

Verily a new era is dawning upon the world, when woman, hitherto the mere dependent of man, the passive recipient alike of truth and error, at length shakes off her lethargy, the shackles of a false education, customs and habits, and stands upright in the dignity of a moral being, and not only proclaims her own freedom, but demands what she shall do to save man from the slavery of his own low appetites. We have come together at this time to consult each other as to what woman may do in banishing the vice of intemperance from the land. We can do much by years of preparation and education of ourselves, for a great moral revolution will burst forth with the regeneration of woman. We shall do much when the pulpit, the forum, the professor's chair, and the ballot-box are ours; but the question is, what can we do to-day, under existing circumstances, under all the adverse influences that surround us ? I will briefly mention several points for your consideration that have suggested themselves to my mind.

1. Let no woman remain in the relation of wife with the confirmed drunkard. Let no drunkard be the father of her children. Let no woman form an alliance with any man who has been suspected even of the vice of intemperance; for the taste once acquired can never, never be eradicated. Be not misled by any pledges, resolves, promises, prayers, or tears. You can not rely on the word of a man who is, or has been, the victim of such an overpowering appetite.

2. Let us petition our State governments so to modify the laws affecting marriage, and the custody of children, that the drunkard shall have no claims on either wife or child.

3. Let us touch not, taste not, handle not, the unclean thing in any combination. Let us eschew it in all culinary purposes, and refuse it in all its most tempting and refined forms.

4. With an efficient organization, lectures, tracts, newspapers, and discussion, we shall accomplish much. I would give more for the agitation of any question on sound principles, thus enlightening and convincing the public mind, than for all the laws that could be written or passed in a century. By the foolishness of preaching, must all moral revolutions be achieved; but remember the truth, the whole truth must be faithfully preached.

5. We must raise the standard of temperance in all things. The man who over-eats takes a little wine to aid digestion, and he who exhausts himself by licentious indulgence takes a little as a stimulus ; thus one vice induces another, and all go hand in hand together.

6. Let us endeavor to make labor honorable in all. Work is worship, says Emerson. Let us honor the hard hand and sun-burnt brow. Remember idleness is the parent of vice; and there is no surer way to banish vice from our land, than to see that the young just coming on the stage of life are wisely and fully employed.

And lastly, inasmuch as charity begins at home, let us withdraw our mite from all associations for sending the Gospel to the heathen across the ocean, for the education of young men for the ministry, for the building up of a theological aristocracy and gorgeous temples to the unknown God, and devote ourselves to the poor and suffering about us. Let us feed and clothe the hungry and naked, gather children into schools, and provide reading-rooms and decent homes for young men and women thrown alone upon the world. Good schools and homes where the young could ever be surrounded by an atmosphere of purity and virtue, would do much more to prevent immorality and crime in our cities than all the churches in the land could ever possibly do toward the regeneration of the multitude sunk in poverty, ignorance, and vice.

Susan B. Anthony, Chairman of the Central Committee, addressed the meeting in a clear, forcible manner, alluding to the indifference manifested by many women on the subject of temperance, and stated the object of calling the women of the State together at this time. She read letters* from Frances Dana Gage, Clarina Howard Nichols, Elizabeth Oakes Smith, Abby Kelly Foster, and Horace Greeley. In the discussion of the resolutions* during the different sessions, Giles B. Stebbins, Benjamin Fish, William Barnes, Amy Post, Mrs. Albro, Mrs. Vaughan, William C. Bloss, George W. Clark, and the Rev. Mr. Goodwin, all took part. One resolution denouncing Mr. Gale, a State Senator, for his insulting epithets in regard to the women who had petitioned for a Maine law, called down on that gentleman some well-deserved reprimands. The Rev. Mr. Goodwin expressed his indignation and shame, that any man of education and position should use such language in speaking of women who were so faithfully laboring in all the great reforms of the day. Mrs. Bloomer in the course of her remarks also criticised Mr. Gale for saying in a sneering way "that representatives were not accustomed to listen to the voice of woman in legislating upon great public questions; that the constitution of the female mind was such as to render woman incapable of correctly deciding upon the points involved in the passage of the proposed bill." After rousing the attention of the people of the State by large and enthusiastic meetings in all the chief cities, and sending into the Legislature a mammoth petition for a Maine law, this was woman's answer. On the Divorce resolution,

Mrs. BLOOMER said: We believe the teachings which have been given to the drunkard's wife touching her duty—the commendable examples of angelic wives which she has been exhorted to follow, have done much to continue and aggravate the vices and crimes of society growing out of intemperance. Drunkenness is good ground for divorce, and every woman who is tied to a confirmed drunkard should sunder the ties; and if she do it not otherwise the law should compel it—especially if she have children.

---

* See Appendix.

We are told that such sentiments are "exceptional," "abhorrent," that the moral sense of society is shocked and outraged by their promulgation. Can it be possible that the moral sense of a people is more shocked at the idea of a pure-minded, gentle woman sundering the ties which bind her to a loathsome mass of corruption, than it is to see her dragging out her days in misery, tied to his besotted and filthy carcass ? Are the morals of society less endangered by the drunkard's wife continuing to live in companionship with him, giving birth to a large family of children who inherit naught but poverty and disgrace, and who will grow up criminal and vicious, filling our prisons and penitentiaries and corrupting and endangering the purity and peace of community, than they would be, should she separate from him and strive to win for herself and the children she may have, comfort and respectability ? The statistics of our prisons, poor-houses, and lunatic asylums, teach us a fearful lesson on this subject of morals.

The idea of living with a drunkard is so abhorrent, so revolting to all the finer feelings of our nature, that a woman must fall very low before she can endure such companionship. Every pure-minded woman must look with loathing and disgust upon such a union of virtue and vice; and he who would compel her to it, or dissuade the drunkard's wife from separating herself from such wretchedness and degradation, is doing much to perpetuate drunkenness and crime, and is wanting in the noblest feelings of human nature. Thanks to our Legislature, if they have not given us the Maine law, they are deliberating upon the propriety of giving to the wives of drunkards and tyrants a loop-hole of escape from the brutal cruelty of their self-styled lords and masters. A bill of this kind has passed the House, but may be lost in the Senate. Should it not pass now, it will be brought up again, and passed at no distant day. Then if women have any spirit, they will free themselves from much of the oppression and wrong which they have hitherto of necessity borne.

A brief address was read by Mrs. Robinson, of Darien. This woman had been for many years the wife of a drunkard; she had overcome many obstacles to attend this Convention for the purpose of relating her experience, and offering words of encouragement. Her narration of the trials and sufferings she had endured was very affecting. She fully endorsed the tenth resolution, " That the woman who consents to live in the relation of wife with a confirmed drunkard, is, in so doing, recreant to the cause of humanity, and to the dignity of a true womanhood."

An organization was effected called " The Woman's New York State Temperance Society "; large numbers of the members of the Convention signed the Constitution, and elected Elizabeth Cady Stanton President.* A vote of thanks was passed to Horace

---

* *Vice-Presidents*—Mrs. Gerrit Smith, Peterboro ; Mrs. E. C. Delevan, Ballston Spa ; Mrs. D. C. Alling, Rochester ; Lydia F. Fowler, Mrs. J. T. Coachman, Mary S. Rich,

Greeley for the kind manner in which he had uniformly sustained the women in their temperance efforts in *The New York Tribune,* and after six long sessions, the Convention adjourned.

As President of "The Woman's State Temperance Society," Mrs. Stanton issued a plain, strong appeal to the women of the State in which it was said woman's rights predominated over temperance. The strong point she uniformly pressed on the temperance question was the right and duty of divorce for drunkenness. A letter of hers to the Convention in Albany on this point, was so radical, that the friends feared to read it; however, after much discussion, Susan B. Anthony took the responsibility. It was read to the Convention, and published in *The Lily* and other papers, and called out many condemnatory notices by the press. *The Troy Journal* was much excited at the idea of "a virtuous woman severing the tie that bound her to a confirmed drunkard," and spoke of such a union of virtue and vice as a "divine institution," sacred in the eye of the "divine author," and declared Mrs. Stanton's teachings "reviling Christianity."

However, these bold utterances roused the consciences of many women to the sinfulness of such relations, and encouraged them in sundering such unholy ties.

At the Rochester Convention, Gerrit Smith, Susan B. Anthony, and Amelia Bloomer were appointed delegates to "The Men's State Temperance Society," to be held in June, at Syracuse. The call for the meeting contained these words, "Temperance associations of every name are invited to send delegates." Hence the Woman's State Society being earnestly enlisted in the good work, responded to this invitation. Miss Anthony and Mrs. Bloomer accepted the appointment, and on arriving at Syracuse, found many of the delegates already there, and everything indicating a large Convention. The next morning, while preparing to go to the hall, a gentleman was announced, who wished to see them in the parlor. On descending thither, they were happy to meet Samuel J. May. He came to inform them that their arrival had created great excitement among some of the clergy, who were

New York; Julia Clark Lewis, Oswego; Olivia Fraser, Elmira; Emily Clark, Le Roy; Mrs. A. N. Cole, Belfast; Betsy Hawks, Bethany Centre; Antoinette L. Brown, Henrietta.

Recording Secretaries—Susan B. Anthony, Rochester; Mary C. Vaughan, Oswego.

Corresponding Secretary—Amelia Bloomer, Seneca Falls.

Treasurer—Elvira Marsh, Rochester.

Executive Committee—Sarah T. Gould, Mary H. Hallowell, and Mrs. Samuel Richardson, Rochester.

shocked at the idea of women delegates to the Convention, and
threatened if they were admitted, to withdraw. This had alarmed
others who were not quite so conservative, but who feared to have
anything occur to create disturbance. They had persuaded Mr.
May to wait upon the ladies and urge them quietly to withdraw.
Mr. May performed his part well, merely stating the facts of the
case, and leaving them to act upon their own judgment. But when
they decided to present their credentials and demand their rights as
members of the Convention, his face beamed with joy, as he said to
them, " You are right." At the appointed time they were seated
with other ladies in attendance at the side of the platform. Presently Rev. Dr. Mandeville, of Albany, arose, turned his chair facing
them, his back to the audience, and stared at them with all the impudence of a boor, as if to wither them with his piercing glance.

WILLIAM H. BURLEIGH, says *The Lily*,* read the annual report, which,
among other things, "hailed the formation of the Woman's State Society
as a valuable auxiliary in the cause of temperance." Rev. J. Marsh
moved that the report be accepted and adopted.

Dr. MANDEVILLE objected in a speech of some length, characterized by
more venom and vulgarity than it had ever before been our fortune to
hear; and such as the most foul-mouthed politician or bar-room orator
would have hesitated to utter before respectable audiences. He denounced the Woman's State Temperance Society, and all women who
took an active public part in promoting the cause. Spoke contemptuously of woman going from home to attend a temperance convention,
and characterized such as a sort of "hybrid species, half man and half
woman, belonging to neither sex." The short dress and woman's rights
questions were "handled without gloves." These movements must be
put down; cut up root and branch, etc., etc., and finally his Reverence
wound up with a threat that if the report was adopted without striking
out the offensive sentence he would dissolve his connection with the
Society. Having thus discharged his venom, and issued his commands,
he took his hat and with a pompous air left the house and did not again
show himself at the meetings.

A warm discussion followed the motion for striking out, which it would
be impossible to describe. Mr. Havens, of New York, offered an amendment—substituting a sort of unmeaning compliment to the ladies, and
asking their influence in their proper sphere—the domestic circle. The
discussion was kept up, but amid the confusion of "Mr. President!"
"Mr. President!" "Order!" "Order!" "I have the floor!" "I will

---

* *The Lily* was a temperance paper started in Seneca Falls, N. Y., in 1849. It was owned
and edited by Mrs. Amelia Bloomer. Though starting as the organ of a society, it
soon became her individual property. She carried it successfully six years, her subscrip-
tion list reaching 4,000. It was pronounced on woman's rights as temperance, and did
good service in both reforms. We are indebted to *The Lily* for most of our facts on the
temperance movement in New York.

speak, right or wrong !" from at least half a dozen voices, until all lost sight of both motion and amendment.

Miss Anthony arose and addressed the Chair, but was at once called to order by Rev. Fowler, of Utica. He denied woman's right to speak in that meeting. Here the confusion again began. "Mr. President !" "Mr. President !" "Order !" "Order !" "Hear the lady !" "Hear the lady !" "Let her speak !" "Let her speak !" "Go on, go on !" "Order ! order !" in the midst of which the president left the chair, and said if there was any gentleman present who could keep order he would thank him to take the chair; he could hear nothing when so many were talking at once, and if order was not preserved he would not attempt to preside. A moment's quiet followed, and then all was confusion again. The conservatives were determined to have their way, and nearly every attempt on the part of the liberals to make themselves heard was frustrated.

A. N. COLE, of Belfast, succeeded in keeping the floor a few moments, and spoke ably in defence of woman and of her right to be heard. He declared that man had no more right to prescribe woman's sphere and mark out a course of action for her, than she had to prescribe man's sphere and dictate his course of action. Woman had ever been untiring and earnest in her labors in this cause, and he was ready at all times and everywhere to acknowledge her aid, and hail her as a co-worker. He insisted that woman had a right to be heard on that floor; that she was there on the invitation of the Society, and they could not refuse her a voice in the proceedings.

But points of order were raised, and a determination manifested not to permit a fair discussion of the subject. The Chair was at length appealed to for a decision. He decided that the letter of the Constitution of the State Society, and also the call for this meeting would admit woman to an equal participation in the proceedings, and allow her a vote; but as there were no female societies in existence five years ago when this Society was organized, such a thing was not contemplated at that time; he therefore considered her inadmissible. "The letter of the Constitution and call would admit her, but the spirit would not."

Mr. Camp must have been very ignorant not to know that ten years before there were efficient woman's temperance societies all over the State. He was doubtless right in saying that such a thing as a woman presuming to speak or vote in the meetings of that Society was not contemplated by its founders, but he greatly erred in giving a reason for their short-sightedness.

The decision of the Chair was appealed from, and the excitement continued. All tried to talk at the same time, but those possessing more firmness than others succeeded in having their say : while the opponents of woman were allowed to express their sentiments freely, those in favor were called to order and forced to yield the floor. The decision of the Chair was finally sustained by two votes. As the delegates had not been required to make themselves known, it was not ascertained how many were present, or who they were; nor how many persons in the crowd voted who had no right to do so. All men were permitted to vote, without its even being known whether they were temperance men or not.

And so, after spending the whole afternoon in hot discussion of the woman's rights question, the disgraceful affair terminated by refusing woman the right of uttering her sentiments on a subject in which she was deeply interested, and of pleading in behalf of the poor crushed victims of man's injustice and cruelty.

Rev. Luther Lee offered his church just before the adjournment, and Mr. May announced that Miss Anthony and Mrs. Bloomer would speak there in the evening. They had a crowded house, while the conservatives had scarce fifty people. The general feeling was hostile to the action of the Convention. This same battle on the temperance platform was fought over and over in various parts of the State, and the most deadly opposition uniformly came from the clergy, though a few noble men in that profession ever remained true to principle through all the conflicts of those days, in the anti-slavery, temperance, and woman's rights movements.

SUSAN B. ANTHONY'S LETTER, FROM THE "CARSON LEAGUE."

BUFFALO, *July* 28, 1852.

DEAR LEAGUE:—Permit me to say a few words to your readers, relative to the plan of action, recommended by the "Women's New York State Temperance Society." We have now three agents lecturing, who are endeavoring, by a novel application of woman's "marvelous gift of tongue." to rouse their sisters of Western New York, to render active service in aid of the Temperance cause. Woman has so long been accustomed to "non-intervention" with the business of law-making—so long considered it men's business to regulate the Liquor Traffic, that it is with much cautiousness that she receives the new doctrine which we preach; the doctrine that it is her right and her duty to speak out against the liquor traffic and all men and institutions that in any way sanction, sustain, or countenance it; and since she can not vote, to duly instruct her husband, father, or brother how she would have him vote, and if he longer continue to misrepresent her, take the right to march to the ballot-box, with firm, unwavering tread, and deposit a vote indicative of her highest ideas of practical temperance. For women longer to submit to be ruled by men and legislators who sanction license laws, is to act the part of slaves and cowards. Men are just beginning to see that they must carry this temperance question into politics, but can see no farther than to vote for a rum-drinking President, Vice-President, and Congressmen. If they can place temperance men in those offices which directly control the license system of our own State, they seem to think they need look to, nor care for, the habits and principles of the men who fill the National offices. And it is for woman now, in the present Presidential campaign, to say to her husband, father, or brother, if you vote for any candidate for any office whatever, who is not pledged to total abstinence and the Maine law, we shall hold you alike guilty with the rum-seller. He who loves not humanity better than his whig or loco partyism, is not worthy the name of man nor the love and respect of woman. But to our Society.

We recommend that women form temperance societies in their respective cities, towns, and villages, which shall be auxiliary to the State Association. The work which we propose to do is a missionary one. We therefore suggest the name "Temperance Home Missionary Society," whose object shall be to raise funds, by means of an admission fee and donations, to be expended in subscribing for temperance newspapers, for gratuitous distribution among all families, both rich and poor, who do not furnish themselves with such reading. During the last two weeks I have visited several villages in Genesee and Erie Counties, have found the women ready for work, and now and then a temperance man who had taken in the whole idea of political action.

Home Missionary Societies are formed in all of the places visited except two, and will doubtless soon be in those. I recommend them to take *The Lily* and *Carson League*. *The Lily*, because it is particularly devoted to woman's interest in temperance and kindred reforms, and because it is their duty to sustain the only paper in the State owned and edited by a woman. *The Carson League*, because it presents and advocates a definite plan for temperance political action. It is to be hoped that the State Alliance, at its session at Rochester, the 18th of August, will make converts not only of all the professed temperance men of Western New York, but of all the temperance newspapers. Alliances must be formed in every county and town of the State. An additional clause must be appended to the pledge, "that no member of the Society shall vote for any officer who is not an open and avowed total abstinence man, and pledged to use his influence to secure the enactment of the Maine law." There must be concert of action; every man must know exactly how and for whom all other men of the State are going to vote. Let there be combined political action and the Maine law is ours.

Yours for Temperance Politics,   S. B. A.

During this year the Society was active, its agents visiting nearly every county, forming auxiliary societies, circulating tracts and petitions, and rolling up subscribers to *The Lily*.

In January, 1853, a great mass-meeting of all the temperance organizations of the State was held in Albany. Nearly every hall and church in the city was occupied, with different associations of men and women. "The Woman's Society" met in the Baptist church in State Street, which was crowded at every session. Susan B. Anthony presided. Emily Clark, Mrs. Bloomer, Mrs. Vaughan and Mrs. Albro were appointed a committee to present to the Legislature a petition signed by 28,000 women for a prohibitory law. On motion of S. M. Burroughs, of Orleans, the rules of the House were suspended and the ladies invited to the Speaker's desk. In a brief and dignified speech, Miss Clark presented the petition, after which they returned to the Convention, and reported the success of their mission, in full confidence that their prayers would be answered. But alas! they forgot that women were a disfranchised class, and that legislators give no heed to the claims of such for protection.

In the evening, the ladies had two immense meetings, one in the church, and one in the Assembly Chamber of the Capitol. At the latter, Susan B. Anthony read Mrs. Stanton's " Appeal to the Legislature," and addresses were made by Mary C. Vaughan and Antoinette Brown ; the galleries as well as the floor of the house being literally packed ; while at the former, Mrs. Bloomer, Mrs. Fowler, Mrs. Albro, and Miss Clark addressed an equally crowded audience.

Following this Convention, Mrs. Bloomer, Miss Brown, and Miss Anthony went to New York, on the invitation of S. P. Townsend, and addressed 3,000 people in Metropolitan Hall ; Lydia F. Fowler presided ; Mr. and Mrs. Horace Greeley, Abby Hopper Gibbons, and other prominent gentlemen and ladies sat on the platform. They also addressed large audiences in the Broadway Tabernacle and Knickerbocker Hall, and in Brooklyn. And during March and April made a most successful tour through the State, speaking at Sing Sing, Poughkeepsie, Hudson, Troy, Cohoes, Utica, Syracuse, Rochester, Lockport, Buffalo, and many of the smaller cities, and were greeted everywhere with large audiences and the most respectful attention from both press and people.

The New York Tribune, under the heading of GREAT GATHERING OF THE WOMEN OF NEW YORK, said of their Metropolitan meeting: The Women's Grand Temperance Demonstration at Metropolitan Hall last evening, was a most brilliant and successful affair. The audience which assembled on that occasion to welcome Mrs. Bloomer and her assistants in the cause of Temperance, was almost as large and fully as respectable as the audiences that nightly greeted Jenny Lind and Catharine Hays during their engagement in that hall. Good order was observed throughout the evening, and earnest and hearty applause was frequent. The only hissing evidently intended for the speakers was when Mrs. Bloomer reviewed the sentiments of Hon. Horace Mann relative to woman ; and then the plaudits came to her rescue and triumphantly sustained the speaker. The audience was a smiling one ; some smiled at the novelty of the occasion ; others with admiration ; the latter, judging from the twinkling of eyes and clapping of hands, were in the majority. While some evidently writhed under the application of the lash for their disregard of the principles of temperance ; others enjoyed the rigor of the infliction and manifested their satisfaction by applause.

The *New York Evening Post* said: The first meeting of the Women's Temperance Society was held last evening in Metropolitan Hall. There were about three thousand persons present, a large proportion of whom were ladies.. It was the first time that an audience in this hall was to bo addressed by women, and the novelty of the occasion doubtless attracted a large number who would otherwise have been absent. The proceedings, however, were conducted in the most orderly manner, and the speakers apparently felt themselves as much at home with their hearers, as if they were merely a private company. They were listened to with much attention and frequently applauded. Altogether, the meeting was very successful and would compare most favorably with any that has ever been held in the same building.

The proceedings were commenced by Mrs. Lydia F. Fowler being appointed President, and Miss Mary S. Rich Secretary. Prayer was offered by Rev. Antoinette L. Brown, after which Mrs. Amelia Bloomer was introduced amid warm applause. She was dressed in the peculiar costume to which her name is given. Her speech, which occupied more than an hour in its delivery, was an able exposition of the reasons why women should be amongst the foremost of the advocates of the temperance reformation. Her remarks on the position of woman under the law, and the subordinate part she was compelled to play in all the relations of life, were listened to with much attention, and though sometimes very caustic and severe upon the other sex, they were received not only with forbearance, but were frequently applauded. Rev. Antoinette L. Brown made a very effective and eloquent address, urging the necessity for legislative action against the evils of intemperance, and recommended the passage of the Maine Law in our Legislature. Addresses were also made by Susan B. Anthony, and Horace Greeley.

The Tribune, under the heading of "Grand Temperance Rally," said: Last evening an exceedingly numerous and enthusiastic meeting was convened in the Tabernacle, under the auspices of the "Fifth Ward Temperance Alliance," it then gave a full report of the addresses of the four ladies, and closed with:

Horace Greeley then came forward in response to numerous and repeated calls, and said that within his immediate recolletion the Temperance cause had been utterly ruined (as it was said) three distinct times; first when the pledge of total abstinence was introduced; again when the Washingtonian movement was set on feet, and then when the Maine Liquor Law came out, every rum-drinker in the country mourned the cause as irrevocably ruined. But now, however, it was gone entirely, because some women came forward to speak for temperance. He had spoken so often on the subject that he had nothing new to say; but he rejoiced to see that there was another army coming up who could speak, as they had heard them that evening and on other occasions. There was something of freshness in them; and if they did not advance new truth, we, at least, heard truth from a new point of view. He had often heard of the fascinating influence of woman, and he was glad if she had such that it should be put forth for temperance. He was happy to hear her explain the wants of the poor mother, or sister, or wife of the unfortunate drunkard; he would not object to her saying if her home had become intolerable that she should be allowed a separation, and permitted to earn a living for herself, seeing that her brute of a husband was unwilling or unable to give her a support. The great cause would be advanced, he thought, by the advocacy of it by women. He considered that the people would be called upon to vote for the Maine Liquor Law one way or the other within a year, for the politicians were becoming tired of this mischievous element. It was one on which they could not calculate, and would be glad to get it out of the way by submitting it to the people for their disposition. The friends of the cause should be rejoiced if women who could speak on this subject did come forward and speak until the law was passed. He would feel their advocacy an additional assurance of success.

The women of New York brought to this work a religious earnestness and intense enthusiasm, that seemed determined to override every obstacle that blocked the way to family purity and peace. Every phase of the question, without a thought of policy or conciliation, was freely discussed. Seeing the evils in social life, in the destruction of all domestic harmony, they demanded divorce for drunkenness. Seeing wine on the tables of clergymen and bishops, liquor-dealers and wine-bibbers dignified and honored as elders and deacons in churches, they called on the women to leave all such unholy organizations. Thus besieging legislators for a " Maine Law," demanding purity at the family altar, denouncing the Church for its apathy, and the clergy for their hostility to the public action of woman, this State Temperance Society roused the enmity of many classes, and was the target for varied criticism.

Politicians said such radical measures as the women proposed would destroy the Whig party, if carried into legislation. Churchmen said such infidel measures would undermine the influence of the clergy and the foundations of the Church. Conservatives said the divorce measures proposed would upheave the whole social fabric. Thus a general disintegration of society was threatened, if freedom was granted to woman. Not being allowed to vote themselves, they used their influence both in the anti-slavery and temperance reforms, to strengthen many men in their determination not to vote for any man who was in favor of slavery and license ; hence there had been a steadily increasing defection in the Whig ranks, that cost Clay his election in 1844, and Scott in 1852.

Mr. Pierce's administration, beginning in 1853, was a period of great political overturning. Innumerable small office-holders being thrown out of employment, and feeling hostile to all " isms," as the opposition designated the reforms of the day, they became a troublesome element in our Conventions.

To avoid this class in organizing " The Woman's Temperance Society," it was decided to enroll men as members, but not to allow them to vote and hold office. They were permitted to attend the meetings, talk, and contribute money, but they were to have no direct power. On this basis the Society was formed, and maintained its integrity one year. However, as the justice of such discrimination on the ground of sex was questionable, and some wom en and many men refused to unite with a Society thus proscriptive, the Constitution was amended, and men admitted to full membership.

FIRST ANNUAL MEETING OF THE WOMAN'S STATE TEMPERANCE SOCIETY.

ROCHESTER, JUNE 1 AND 2, 1853.

The Rochester Advertiser gives the following report: In Corinthian Hall yesterday, at ten o'clock, a large audience assembled. The Society was called to order by Mrs. E. C. Stanton, who said if any one present desired to offer vocal prayer, there was now an opportunity. Prayer was then offered by a young man in one of the side seats. The platform was occupied by Mrs. Stanton, Emily Clark, Lucy Stone, Mrs. Vaughan, Dr. Harriot Hunt, Mrs. Nichols, Mrs. Fish, Mrs. Albro, Mrs. Alling, Elizabeth C. Wright, and Mrs. Lydia F. Fowler.

The attendance at this opening session is much larger this year than last, and a more hopeful spirit prevails. There are several of the notabilities of the Woman's Rights cause present, and a fair sprinkling of Bloomers is scattered through the audience. There were many out, attracted by curiosity, though probably the most are earnest friends of the Society. The proceedings were of a deeply interesting character, both from their novelty and their importance. After the prayer was concluded, Mrs. Stanton gave her opening address, as follows:

MRS. STANTON'S ADDRESS.

A little more than one year ago, in this same hall, we formed the first Woman's State Temperance Society. We believed that the time had come for woman to speak on this question, and to insist on her right to be heard in the councils of Church and State. It was proposed at that time that we, instead of forming a society, should go *en masse* into the Men's State Temperance Society. We were assured that in becoming members by paying the sum of $1, we should thereby secure the right to speak and vote in their meetings.

We who had watched the jealousy with which man had ever eyed the slow aggressions of woman, warned you against the insidious proposition made by agents from that Society. We told you they would no doubt gladly receive the dollar, but that you would never be allowed to speak or vote in their meetings. Many of you thought us suspicious and unjust toward the temperance men of the Empire State. The fact that Abby Kelly had been permitted to speak in one of their public meetings, was brought up as an argument by some agent of that Society to prove our fears unfounded. We suggested that she spoke by favor and not right, and our right there as equals to speak and vote, we well knew would never be acknowledged. A long debate saved you from that false step, and our predictions have been fully realized in the treatment our delegates received at the annual meeting held at Syracuse last July, and at the recent Brick Church meeting in New York.

In forming our Society, the mass of us being radical and liberal, we left our platform free; we are no respecters of persons, all are alike welcome here without regard to sect, sex, color, or caste. There have been, however, many objections made to one feature in our Constitution, and that is, that although we admit men as members with equal right to speak in our meetings, we claim the offices for women alone. We felt, in starting, the necessity of throwing all the responsibility on woman, which we knew she never would take, if there were any men at hand to think, act, and plan for her. The result has shown the wisdom of what seemed so objectionable to many. It was, however, a temporary expedient, and as that seeming violation of man's rights prevents some true friends of the cause from becoming members of our Society, and as the officers are now well skilled in the practical business of getting up meetings, raising funds, etc., and have fairly learned how to stand and walk alone, it may perhaps be safe to raise man to an entire equality with ourselves, hoping, however, that he will modestly permit the women to continue the work they have so successfully begun. I would suggest, therefore, that after the business of the past year be disposed of, this objectionable feature of our Constitution be brought under consideration.

Our experience thus far as a Society has been most encouraging. We number over two thousand members. We have four agents who have traveled in various parts of the State, and I need not say what is well known to all present, that their labors thus far have given entire satisfaction to the Society and the public. I was surprised and rejoiced to find that women, without the least preparation or experience, who had never raised their voices in public one year ago, should with so much self-reliance, dignity, and force, enter at once such a field of labor, and so ably perform the work. In the metropolis of our country, in the capital of our State, before our Legislature, and in the country schoolhouse, they have been alike earnest and faithful to the truth. In behalf of our Society, I thank you for your unwearied labors during the past year. In the name of humanity, I bid you go on and devote yourselves humbly to the cause you have espoused. The noble of your sex everywhere rejoice in your success, and feel in themselves a new impulse to struggle upward and onward; and the deep, though silent gratitude that ascends to Heaven from the wretched outcast, the wives, the mothers, and the daughters of brutal drunkards, is well known to all who have listened to their tales of woe, their bitter experience, the dark, sad passages of their tragic lives.

I hope this, our first year, is prophetic of a happy future of strong, united, and energetic action among the women of our State. If we are sincere and earnest in our love of this cause, in our devotion to truth, in our desire for the happiness of the race, we shall ever lose sight of self; each soul will, in a measure, forget its own individual interests in proclaiming great principles of justice and right. It is only a true, a deep, and abiding love of truth, that can swallow up all petty jealousies, envies, discords, and dissensions, and make us truly magnanimous and self-sacrificing. We have every reason to think, from reports we hear on all sides, that our Society has given this cause a new impulse, and if the condition of our treasury is a test, we have abundant reason to believe that in the hearts of the people we are approved, and that by their purses we shall be sustained.

It has been objected to our Society that we do not confine ourselves to the subject of temperance, but talk too much about woman's rights, divorce, and the Church. It could be easily shown how the consideration of this great question carries us legitimately into the discussion of these various subjects. One class of minds would deal with effects alone; another would inquire into causes; the work of the former is easily perceived and quickly done; that of the latter requires deep thought, great patience, much time, and a wise self-denial. Our physicians of the present day are a good type of the mass of our reformers. They take out cancers, cut off tonsils, drive the poison which nature has wisely thrown to the surface, back again, quiet unsteady nerves with valerian, and by means of ether infuse an artificial courage into a patient that he may bravely endure some painful operation. It requires but little thought to feel that the wise physician who shall trace out the true causes of suffering; who shall teach us the great, immutable laws of life and health; who shall show us how and where in our every-day life, we are violating these laws, and the true point to begin the reform, is doing a much higher, broader, and deeper work than he who shall bend all his energies to the temporary relief of suffering. Those temperance men or women whose whole work consists in denouncing rum-sellers, appealing to legislatures, eulogizing Neal Dow, and shouting Maine Law, are superficial reformers, mere surface-workers. True, this outside work is well, and must be done; let those who see no other do this, but let them lay no hindrances in the way of that class of mind, who, seeing in our present false social relations the causes of the moral deformities of the race, would fain declare the immutable laws that govern mind as well as matter, and point out the true causes of the evils we see about us, whether lurking under the shadow of the altar, the sacredness of the marriage institution, or the assumed superiority of man.

1. We have been obliged to preach woman's rights, because many, instead of listening to what we had to say on temperance, have questioned the right of a woman to speak on any subject. In courts of justice and legislative assemblies, if the right of the speaker to be there is questioned, all business waits until that point is settled. Now, it is not settled in the mass of minds that woman has any rights on this footstool, and much less a right to stand on an even pedestal with man, look him in the face as an equal, and rebuke the sins of her day and generation. Let it be clearly understood, then, that we are a woman's rights Society; that we believe it is woman's duty to speak whenever she feels the impression to do so; that it is her right to be present in all the councils of

Church and State. The fact that our agents are women, settles the question of our character on this point.

Again, in discussing the question of temperance, all lecturers, from the beginning, have made mention of the drunkards' wives and children, of widows' groans and orphans' tears; shall these classes of sufferers be introduced but as themes for rhetorical flourish, as pathetic touches of the speaker's eloquence; shall we passively shed tears over their condition, or by giving them their rights, bravely open to them the doors of escape from a wretched and degraded life ? Is it not legitimate in this to discuss the social degradation, the legal disabilities of the drunkard's wife ? If in showing her wrongs, we prove the right of all womankind to the elective franchise; to a fair representation in the government; to the right in criminal cases to be tried by peers of her own choosing, shall it be said that we transcend the bounds of our subject ? If in pointing out her social degradation, we show you how the present laws outrage the sacredness of the marriage institution; if in proving to you that justice and mercy demand a legal separation from drunkards, we grasp the higher idea that a unity of soul alone constitutes and sanctifies true marriage, and that any law or public sentiment that forces two immortal, high-born souls to live together as husband and wife, unless held there by love, is false to God and humanity; who shall say that the discussion of this question does not lead us legitimately into the consideration of the important subject of divorce?

But why attack the Church ? We do not attack the Church; we defend ourselves merely against its attacks. It is true that the Church and reformers have always been in an antagonistic position from the time of Luther down to our own day, and will continue to be until the devotional and practical types of Christianity shall be united in one harmonious whole. To those who see the philosophy of this position, there seems to be no cause for fearful forebodings or helpless regret. By the light of reason and truth, in good time, all these seeming differences will pass away. I have no special fault to find with that part of humanity that gathers into our churches; to me, human nature seems to manifest itself in very much the same way in the Church and out of it. Go through any community you please—into the nursery, kitchen, the parlor, the places of merchandise, the market-place, and exchange, and who can tell the church member from the outsider ? I see no reason why we should expect more of them than other men. Why, say you, they lay claim to greater holiness; to more rigid creeds; to a belief in a sterner God; to a closer observance of forms. The Bible, with them, is the rule of life, the foundation of faith, and why should we not look to them for patterns of purity, goodness, and truth above all other men ? I deny the assumption. Reformers on all sides claim for themselves a higher position than the Church. Our God is a God of justice, mercy, and truth. Their God sanctions violence, oppression, and wine-bibbing, and winks at gross moral delinquencies. Our Bible commands us to love our enemies; to resist not evil; to break every yoke and let the oppressed go free; and makes a noble life of more importance than a stern faith. Their Bible permits war, slavery, capital punishment, and makes salvation depend

Amelia Bloomer

on faith and ordinances. In their creed it is a sin to dance, to pick up sticks on the Sabbath day, to go to the theater, or large parties during Lent, to read a notice of any reform meeting from the altar, or permit a woman to speak in the church. In our creed it is a sin to hold a slave; to hang a man on the gallows; to make war on defenseless nations, or to sell rum to a weak brother, and rob the widow and the orphan of a protector and a home. Thus may we write out some of our differences, but from the similarity in the conduct of the human family, it is fair to infer that our differences are more intellectual than spiritual, and the great truths we hear so clearly uttered on all sides, have been incorporated as vital principles into the inner life of but few indeed.

We must not expect the Church to leap *en masse* to a higher position. She sends forth her missionaries of truth one by one. All of our reformers have, in a measure, been developed in the Church, and all our reforms have started there. The advocates and opposers of the reforms of our day, have grown up side by side, partaking of the same ordinances and officiating at the same altars; but one, by applying more fully his Christian principles to life, and pursuing an admitted truth to its legitimate results, has unwittingly found himself in antagonism with his brother.

Belief is not voluntary, and change is the natural result of growth and development. We would fain have all church members sons and daughters of temperance; but if the Church, in her wisdom, has made her platform so broad that wine-bibbers and rum-sellers may repose in ease thereon, we who are always preaching liberality ought to be the last to complain. Having thus briefly noticed some of the objections to our movement, I will not detain the audience longer at this time.

An able report of the Executive Committee was then read by Mrs. Vaughan.

The President, on motion, appointed the various Committees,* and read a letter from Gerrit Smith to Susan B. Anthony:

PETERBORO, *May* 7, 1853.

DEAR MADAM:—I thank you for your letter. So constantly am I employed in my extensive private concerns, that I can attend none of the anniversaries this spring. I should be especially happy to attend yours; and to testify by my presence, if not by my words, that woman is in her place when she is laboring to redeem the world from the curse of drunkenness.

I know not why it is not as much the duty of your sex, as it is of mine, to establish newspapers, write books, and hold public meetings for the promotion of the cause of temperance. The current idea, that modesty should hold women back from such services, is all resolvable into non-

---

* *Nomination*—Lemira Kedzie, Lydia F. Fowler, Amy Post, Mary H. Hallowell, Frederick Douglass, Lydia Jenkins.

Business Committee—Emily Clark, W. H. Channing, Mary H. Hallowell, Rev. S. J. May, Mrs. Robie, Mrs. C. I. H. Nichols.

Finance—Susan B. Anthony, Mrs. Bloomer, H. Attilia Albro. Also, on motion, the President was added to the Business Committee.

32

sense and wickedness. Female modesty! female delicacy! I would that I might never again hear such phrases. There is but one standard of modesty and delicacy for both men and women; and so long as different standards are tolerated, both sexes will be perverse and corrupt. It is my duty to be as modest and delicate as you are; and if your modesty and delicacy may excuse you from making a public speech, then may mine excuse me from making one.

The Quakers are the best people I have ever known—the most serious and chaste, and yet the most brave and resisting. But there is no other people who are so little concerned, lest man get out of his sphere, or lest woman get out of hers. No people make so little difference as they do, between man and woman. Others appear to think that the happiness and safety of the world consist in magnifying the difference. But when reason and religion shall rule the world, there will be felt to be no other difference between man and woman, than that of their physical constitutions. None will then be acknowledged in respect to the intellect, the heart, or the manners.

Very respectfully, your friend,   GERRIT SMITH.

The attendance at this Convention was larger than the year previous, and the debates more interesting, as Mrs. Nichols, William Henry Channing, Lucy Stone, Antoinette Brown, and Frederick Douglass all took an active part in the proceedings. During one of the sessions quite a heated discussion took place on the subject of Divorce, Mrs. Stanton and Lucy Stone taking the ground that it was not only woman's right, but her duty, to withdraw from all such unholy relations, Mrs. Nichols and Miss Brown taking the opposite position.

As it was decided at this second convention to admit gentlemen, a schism was the immediate result. By their party tactics, in which they were well versed, they took the initiative steps to scatter the forces so successfully gathered. The Society, with its guns silenced on the popular foes, lingered a year or two, and was heard of no more. It was the policy of these worldly wise men to restrict the debate on temperance within such narrow limits as to disturb none of the existing conditions of society. They said, treat it as a purely moral and religious question; "pray over it," it being too knotty a problem to be solved on earth, they proposed to have the whole case adjusted in the courts of Heaven: very much as the wise men to-day think best to dispose of the temperance reform.

Thus these politic gentlemen manipulated the association, eliminated the woman's rights element *per se*, which, having been educated in the anti-slavery school of morals, could not be blinded with any male sophistries or considerations of policy. It was the universal plea then as now, in advocating reforms, "Sacrifice principle to numbers, if you would secure victory," forgetting that one company of brave men could clear their path to the enemy quicker than a battalion of cowards. A multitude of timid, undeveloped men and women, afraid of priests and politicians, are a hindrance rather than help in any reform. When Garrison's forces had been thoroughly sifted, and only the picked men and women remained, he soon made political parties and church organizations feel the power of his burning words. The temperance cause has had no organized body of fearless leaders. Psalm singing and prayer it was supposed would accomplish what only could be done by just laws, enlightened public sentiment, and pure religion, applied to the practical interests of mankind. When abolitionists left parties and churches, because of their pro-slavery codes and creeds, they began alike to purify their organizations in order to win back that noble army of patriots. Women were urged to enroll themselves as members of men's associations, pay their initiation fee of one dollar, gather petitions, do all in their power to rouse enthusiasm; but they must not presume to sit on the platform, nor speak, nor vote in the meetings. Those women who had no proper self-respect accepted the conditions; those who had, tested their status on the platform, and not being received as equals, abandoned all temperance organizations, as the same proper pride that forbade them to accept the conditions of a proscribed class in men's conventions, also prevented their affiliation with women who would tolerate such insults to the sex. The long, persistent struggle at last culminated in the World's Temperance Convention, which may be called our Waterloo in that reform.

BRICK CHURCH MEETING.

May 12th, 1853, the friends of temperance assembled in New York to make arrangements for a World's Temperance Convention. The meeting was held in Dr. Spring's old Brick Church, on Franklin Square, where the *New York Times* building now stands. It was organized by nominating the Hon. A. C. Barstow, of Rhode Island, chairman; the Rev. R. C. Crampton, of New York, and the Rev. George Duffield, of Pennsylvania, secretaries. The meeting opened with prayer, "asking God's blessing on the proceedings."* A motion was made that all gentlemen present be

---

* Throughout this protracted, disgraceful assault on American womanhood, the clergy baptized each new insult and act of injustice in the name of the Christian religion, and uniformly asked God's blessing on proceedings that would have put to shame an assembly of Hottentots.

admitted as delegates. Dr. Trall, of New York, moved an amendment that the word "ladies" be inserted, as there were delegates present from the Woman's State Temperance Society. The motion was carried, and credentials received, and every man and woman became members of the convention. A business committee of one from each State was appointed. A motion was made that Susan B. Anthony, Secretary of the Woman's State Temperance Society, be added to the business committee. Then the war commenced in earnest. D.D.'s, M.D.'s, and Honorables were horrified. Speech followed speech in rapid succession, with angry vehemence. As the committee was already full, the motion was ruled out of order. Thomas Wentworth Higginson asked that he be excused from serving on the committee, and moved that Lucy Stone be added in his place. Then the confusion was increased. Abby Kelly Foster arose and tried to explain, but shouts of "order" drowned her voice, and after persisting in her attempt to speak for ten minutes the uproar was frightful, and she was compelled to sit down. Emily Clark made a similar attempt, with the same result.

Hon. Bradford R. Wood, of Albany, then moved, that as there was a party present determined to introduce the question of woman's rights, and to run it into the ground, that this convention adjourn *sine die ;* but on request he withdrew it, and moved that a committee on credentials be appointed to decide who were members of the convention. This committee, consisting of Rev. John Chambers, of Philadelphia, Hon. B. R. Wood, of Albany, and Dr. Condit, of New Jersey, were absent fifteen minutes, and then reported that, as in their opinion, the call for this meeting was not intended to include female delegates, and custom had not sanctioned the public action of women in similar situations, the credentials of the ladies should be rejected. The report was received, and after a disgraceful contest on the part of those from whom we look for honor, truth, and nobleness, and every Christian virtue, on account of their sacred calling and high position, it was adopted by a vote of 34 to 32, ten of those voting in the negative being women. During the progress of the discussion— if discussion it could be called, where all the women who attempted to speak were silenced, and the men who attempted to speak for them were almost as rudely treated — Mayor Barstow twice requested the appointment of another chairman in his stead, stating that he would not preside over a meeting where woman's rights were introduced, or women allowed to speak. Having finally silenced them, he was henceforward content to wear the honors of his temporary office.

Mr. Higginson protested against the action of the meeting as disgraceful to the leaders, and tendered his resignation as one of the business committee. He then stated that all persons favorable to calling a *whole* world's temperance convention were invited to meet at Dr. Trall's office at 2 o'clock. The ladies present, and the gentlemen who had contended for their admission as delegates, then withdrew. Another disgraceful scene occurred on a protest from Dr. Townsend against the action of the convention, and a motion to pay the expenses of the ladies who had come some distance as delegates and been excluded. The motion was seconded. Again shouts of "order," "order," arose, and the confusion was worse than ever. Dr. T. finally withdrew his motion, on being told that the ladies would accept no such favor at the hands of a convention of rowdies.

Several speeches then followed, mostly from clergymen; all condemning the public action of women in any reforms, and defending the position of the convention, quoting Scripture and the Divine Will to sanction their injustice. One Rev. gentleman stated that he would have nothing to do with the women. Rev. John Chambers said, for one, he rejoiced that the women were gone; they were now rid of the scum of the convention!! Other clergymen spoke in the same strain. A motion was made by Dr. Snodgrass that the committee assign some part of the work of the World's Convention to women, which called out from Mr. Barstow some remarks too indecent for repetition. The motion was withdrawn. The gall and bitterness, the ridicule and vulgarity of the Rev. D.D.'s being expended on some of the grandest women our nation could boast, they adjourned, after deciding to hold a four days' convention, beginning the 6th of September. The other wing of the temperance army decided to do the same, and held a meeting of protest a few days after in the Tabernacle.

The *New York Tribune* says of the meeting of protest, Saturday evening, May 14, 1852: A grand Temperance demonstration was held in the Broadway Tabernacle Saturday evening. There could not have been less than 3,000 persons present. The floor of the house, the aisles, the galleries, every inch of sitting and standing room was literally packed. The greatest enthusiasm prevailed throughout. The officers of the meeting were:

PRESIDENT—Susan B. Anthony.*

LUCY STONE, in a letter to *The Una*, says: Last week, at New York,

* *Vice-Presidents*—Dr. Harriot K. Hunt, Mass.; Charles C. Burliegh, Ct.; Edward M. Davis, Pa.; Frances Dana Gage, Mo.; Ashby Pierce, Oregon; Rowland T. Robinson, Vt.; Melissa J. Driggs, Ind.; Thomas Garrett, Del.; Angelina Grimké Weld, N. J.; Hannah Tracy Cutler, Ill.

we had a foretaste of what woman is to expect when she attempts to exercise her equal rights as a human being. In conformity with a resolution adopted by the Mass Convention recently held in Boston, a call was issued, inviting "the *friends of temperance*" to meet in New York, May 11th, and prepare for a "World's Convention." Under that call, the Woman's State Society of New York, an active and efficient body, sent delegates; but though regularly elected, their credentials were rejected with scorn. The chairman of the committee reported that those who called the meeting never intended to include women. Think of it, a *World's* Convention, in which woman is voted not of the world!!

Rev. Dr. Hewitt affirmed it a burning shame for women to be there; and though it was entirely out of order, he discussed the question of "Woman's Rights," taking the ground that women should be nowhere but at home. Rev. E. M. Jackson, gave it as his opinion, that "the women came there expressly to disturb." The Rev. Mr. Fowler, of Utica, showed the same contempt for woman that he did last year, at the N. Y. State Temperance Society, at Syracuse. Rev. Mr. Chambers was particularly bitter.

It would have been well for those women who accept the foolish flattery of men, to have been present to see the real estimate in which woman is held by these men who surely represent a large class. The President of the meeting, Mayor Barstow, of your city, indignantly refused to put the motion made—that Susan B. Anthony should be on a committee, declaring "that he would resign rather than do it." He said it "was not fit that a woman should be in such places." After we left, if the papers reported him correctly, he used language which proved that he was not fit to be where decent people are. It was next to impossible for us or our friends to get a hearing. The "previous question" was called, or we were voted out of order, or half a dozen of the opposing party talked at once to keep us silent. Rev. T. W. Higginson declined serving on a committee from which women were excluded, and when it became apparent that only half of the world could be represented, he entered his protest, and invited those who were in favor of a *Whole* World's Temperance Convention to meet that afternoon at Dr. Trall's. A large minority withdrew, including several ministers, and arranged for a Convention that shall know "neither male nor female," to be held in New York sometime during The World's Fair.

A large and enthusiastic meeting was held at the Broadway Tabernacle, to protest against the above proceedings, and although twelve and a half cents were charged at the door, every seat was occupied, and much of the "standing room" also.

The same gentlemen! who excluded us, held a meeting subsequently in Metropolitan Hall. There your Major Barstow said: "God has placed woman in the moral world where he has the sun in the physical, to regulate, enlighten, and cheer." C. C. Burleigh, alluding to this remark, in our meeting at the Tabernacle, said: "Thus he calls his Convention, in which Mars, Jupiter, Saturn, Mercury, and Neptune are appointed a committee of arrangements, and says the Sun shall be excluded."

At this meeting, *ladies* were especially invited to vote, as though they had a heart in it, and were urged also to give their money to aid these very men by whom every soul of us had been insulted. I am sorry to say some gave. But taught such lessons, by such masters, woman will one day be wiser. Yours, for humanity, without distinction of sex,

LUCY STONE.

After the Brick Church meeting was over, some of the actors being ashamed of themselves, the Rev. John Marsh tried to defend himself and his coadjutors, but Mr. Greeley very summarily brushed his sophistry aside, and placed all the actors in that disgraceful farce in their true colors.

The New York Daily Tribune, Wednesday, May 18, 1853.

THE WORLD'S TEMPERANCE CONVENTION.

To the Editor of the New York Tribune:

SIR :—Your "Inquirer," it appears to me, is bent on throwing firebrands into the temperance ranks, and the worst kind of firebrands, those of vile sectarianism. Will you permit me to answer and remark upon a few of his inquiries?

1. "Are there to be *two* World's Conventions?"

Answer. That will be, I suppose, as people please. There may be a dozen; and I know not that any harm will be done.

2. "Did Mayor Barstow occasion the schism in the temperance ranks, by refusing to recognize the feminine element in the movement?"

Ans. No. The schism, such as there was, was caused by a proposal of Rev. Mr. Higginson, and a persistence in it, that a representative of the Women's State Society should be added to the Business Committee of one from each State; and this after the Committee was full. With as good reason, it was said, might one be pressed from the *Men's* State Society or State Alliance. Mr. Higginson pertinaciously pressed the matter; and because he could not have his own way and rule the Convention, he refused to serve on the Committee; and hence arose all the disturbance and the schism.

3. "Did Dr. Hewitt rule out from office Mr. Barnum on the ground that he (Mr. Barnum) was an infidel?"

Ans. No. I am confident he used no such phraseology; and "Inquirer" has no more right to ask such a question, than he has to ask if Dr. Hewitt did not rule him out on the ground that Mr. Barnum was a horse thief. The very question amounts to an assertion (as is announced in the next inquiry) that he *did* say it; which, if he did not, is calumny. Dr. H. *did* object to Mr. Barnum, as he had a perfect right to do, as one of the Appointing Committee. It was desirable to find the best men to get up to the World's Convention. I proposed Mr. Barnum as one, knowing his amazing efficiency. Dr. H. objected, on the ground that he (Barnum) was a very exceptionable man in his part of Connecticut, and would do injury to the Convention; and, as harmony was desirable, and unexceptionable men should be put upon the Committee, his name was withdrawn. It was agreed that what was said in Committee should not go abroad.

4. "Does Mr. Barnum's infidelity consist in his attending another church in Bridgeport from Dr. Hewitt's?"

Here appears the cloven foot of sectarianism. One sect is to be held up as persecuted. Here the writer assumes that Dr. Hewitt did say that Mr. B. was an infidel; and, assuming it and knowing it, why does he hypocritically ask whether Dr. H. *did* say it?

5. "Is it true that Dr. H. refused his pulpit for a temperance lecture by Rev. E. H. Chapin, on the ground that he was a Universalist?"

Sectarianism again! What has all this to do with the meeting at the Brick Chapel? Why is it brought here but to kindle up sectarian fires? A pastor of a church has everywhere conceded to him the control of his pulpit, and no one may contend with him in this matter. Whether that was so or not, I know not, nor is it any concern of mine, nor of the public. Such a rule the world knows does not govern us in selecting temperance speakers. We will not invite speakers to speak at temperance meetings who have something else more at heart than temperance, which they will most offensively thrust in their speech upon the meeting. But we, without hesitation, invite men of all sorts to speak at temperance meetings, who will speak to the point, and do us good and not hurt. Rev. Mr. Chapin, we all know, is of this character, and, without hesitation, I invited him to speak at the late Anniversary of the American Temperance Union (as I did Rev. Mr. Higginson, who differs from me perhaps as much in religious belief), and he (Mr. C.) would have spoken, but was to be out of the city.

6. "How can the proposed Convention be a *World's* Convention, if women and all who do not belong to a particular Church are to be excluded?"

Sectarianism again! Who has said a word about Church but this writer, and about excluding women from the Convention and all its entertainments? No one. The basis of the Convention has not been settled. It probably will be as broad as the world. The last query I think unworthy an answer. And I must be permitted to say the whole inquiry manifests a very bad spirit, and is calculated to promote evils which the public press should suppress rather than foster.

As I sent you an anonymous communication explaining some of these matters last Saturday, which you declined publishing, because, I suppose, it was anonymous, I feel constrained, though reluctantly, to give this my name.

Yours, etc.,   John Marsh,

Office of Am. Temp. Union, No. 149 *Nassau St.*

HORACE GREELEY'S REPLY.

Rev. John! we have allowed you to be heard at full length; now you and your set will be silent and hear us.

Very palpably your palaver about Mr. Higginson's motion is a dodge, a quirk, a most contemptible quibble, reluctant as we are to speak thus irreverently of the solemn utterances of a Doctor of Divinity. Right well do you know, reverend sir, that the particular form, or time, or fashion in which the question came up is utterly immaterial, and you interpose it only to throw dust in the eyes of the public. Suppose a woman had been nominated at the right time, and in the right way, according to your understanding of punctilios, wouldn't the same resistance have been made and the same row got up? You know right well that there would. Then what is all your pettifogging about technicalities worth? The only question that anybody cares a button about is this, Shall woman be allowed to participate in your World's Temperance Convention on a footing of perfect equality with man? If yea, the whole dispute turns on nothing, and isn't worth six lines in *The Tribune*. But if it was and is the purpose of those for whom you pettifog to keep woman off the platform of that Convention, and deny her any part in its proceedings except as a spectator, what does all your talk about Higginson's untimeliness and the Committees being full amount to? Why not treat the subject with some show of honesty?

Now as to Barnum and Hewitt: it is eminently proper that the public should know exactly on what ground H. ruled B. off the Business Committee, and it is self-criminating to plead that a mantle of secrecy was spread over the doings in Committee. If Hewitt protested against Barnum on the assumption that the latter is a sinner, while this is to be a Convention of saints, let that fact be known, so that sinners may keep away from the Convention. If on the assumption that Mr. Barnum is an infidel or a heretic, let that fact come squarely out, so that we may know that infidels or heretics, either or both, are to be proscribed at the Hewitt-Marsh Convention. For if there is to be really and truly a World's Temperance Convention, according to any fair meaning of the phrase, then we say women, as well as men, youth, as well as adults, colored, as well as white, heretic, as well as orthodox, sinners, as well as saints—so that they be earnest and undoubted upholders of total abstinence—should be invited to send delegates, who should be equally welcome to its platform and eligible to its offices. An Orthodox White Male Adult Saints' Convention may be very proper and very useful, but it should be called distinctly as such, and not unqualifiedly as a World's Convention.

Dr. Marsh thinks it nobody's business whether Dr. Hewitt did or did not refuse the use of his church for a temperance-meeting at which Mr. Chapin was to speak, because he (Mr. C.) was a Universalist. Yes, reverend sir, it is a good many people's business if the public are purposely left in doubt as to the character of the World's Convention that is to issue from the Brick Church meeting. For if Dr. Hewitt shut his pulpit against so unexceptionable, assiduous, effective an advocate of temperance as Mr. Chapin confessedly is (see Marsh, above), then we have a cue to his objection to Barnum and to the general bearings of the "World's Convention" to be incubated under his auspices. That single incident of the pulpit-shutting will have a great deal of significance to many other people; wherefore the fact that it has none to Marsh is overruled.

Whenever a real "World's Temperance Convention" shall assemble, an inquiry may be found necessary as to what Dr. Hewitt has done and sacrificed for temperance these five years that should authorize him to rule P. T. Barnum off a temperance committee; also, whether men who live by Temperance, like Dr. Marsh, are in the right position to judge those, like Barnum, who labor and spend money for it. For the present, however, we will leave these inquiries on the General Orders.

One word as to Sectarianism. If "Inquirer," or Mr. Barnum, or Mr. Chapin has proposed or intrigued to keep any one out of office, or otherwise overslaughed in the Brick Church Meeting, or any of its meetings, because of said body's religious opinions or associations, then said intriguer has been guilty of a very faulty and culpable sectarian dodge, which can not be too severely reproached. But if it be in fact t'other fellow's bull that has gored this one's ox, then the facts should come out, and the culprit can not escape censure by raising the stop-thief cry of "Sectarianism." "*Thou* art the man!"

Let the women of this nation ponder Horace Greeley's arraignment of the reverend gentlemen who were the chief actors in this farce, and remember that in all ages of the world the priesthood have found their pliant tools and most degraded victims in the women of their respective sects. In all of these meetings there were intelligent, sincere women, so blinded by the sophistry and hypocrisy of Marsh, Chambers, Hewitt, *et al.*, that they gave them their countenance and support throughout this disgraceful mob, so shocking and revolting to the best men of that day and generation.

In consequence of the action in the Brick Church two temperance conventions were called, to meet in New York the first week in September. One designated "The Whole World's Convention," including men and women, black and white, orthodox and heretic; the other the "Half World's Convention," restricted to the "simon pure, white (male) orthodox saints"; which for ribaldry of speech and rudeness of action surpassed in its proceedings the outside mob, that raged and raved through an entire week, making pandemonium of our metropolis.

A GRAND GATHERING — ANTI-SLAVERY — WOMAN'S RIGHTS— TEMPERANCE—THE WORLD'S FAIR, SEPTEMBER, 1853.

The opening days of the autumn of this year were days of intense excitement in the city of New York. Added to the numbers attracted by the World's Fair was the announcement of the Anti-Slavery, Woman's Rights, and two Temperance Conventions. The reformers from every part of the country assembled in force, each to hold their separate meetings, though the leaders were to take a conspicuous part in all. The anti-slavery meetings began on Sunday, and every day two or three of these conventions were in session, all drawing crowds to listen or to disturb. William Henry Channing, William Lloyd Garrison, Wendell Phillips and Thomas Wentworth Higginson eloquently pleading for the black man's freedom on the anti-slavery platform, and for the equality of their mothers, wives, and daughters on the woman's rights platform, and for both the woman and the black man on the temperance platform; now face to face with Rynders and his mob, and then with the Rev. John Chambers, Marsh and Hewitt and their mob, the viler of the two.

THE HALF WORLD'S TEMPERANCE CONVENTION,

led by Chambers, Hewitt, and Marsh, was in session in Metropolitan Hall several days. As it was simply an organized mob, we find in the journals of the day no speeches or resolutions on the great question on which they nominally assembled.

In trying to get rid of Antoinette L. Brown, who had been sent as a delegate from two respectable and influential societies, and of James McCune Smith, a colored delegate, they quarrelled through most of the allotted time for the convention over what class of persons could be admitted. In summing up the proceedings of these meetings

HORACE GREELEY says, in the *Tribune*, September 7, 1853 : " This convention has completed three of its four business sessions, and the results may be summed up as follows :

" *First Day*—Crowding a woman off the platform.

" *Second Day*—Gagging her.

" *Third Day*—Voting that she shall stay gagged. Having thus disposed of the main question, we presume the incidentals will be finished this morning."

Antoinette Brown was asked why she went to that Convention, knowing, as she must, that she would be rejected.

"I went there," she said, " to assert a principle—a principle relevant to the circumstances of that convention, and one which would promote *all* good causes and retard *all* bad ones. I went there, as an item of the world, to contend that the sons and daughters of the race, without distinction of sex, sect, class or color, should be recognized as belonging to the world, and I planted my feet upon the simple *rights of a delegate.* I asked no favor as a woman, or in behalf of woman; no favor as a woman advocating temperance; no recognition of the cause of woman above the cause of humanity ; the indorsement of no 'ism' and of no measure; but I claimed, in the name of the world, the rights of a delegate in a world's convention.

" Is it asked, Why did you make that issue at that time ? I answer, I have made it at all times and in all places, whenever and wherever Providence has given me the opportunity, and in whatever way it could be made to appear most prominent. Last spring, when woman claimed the supremacy—the right to hold all the offices in the Woman's State Temperance Society—I contended, from this platform, for the equality of man; the equal rights of all the members of this society. I have claimed everywhere the equality of humanity in Church and in State; God helping me, I here pledge myself anew to Him, and to you all, to be true everywhere to the central principle—the soul of the Divine commandment, 'Thou shalt love thy neighbor as thyself.' The temperance cause was not injured by our course at that Convention. We went there with thoughtful hearts. Said Wendell Phillips : 'Take courage, and remember that whether you are received or rejected, you are going to make the most effectual speech for temperance, for woman, and humanity that you have ever made in your life.' 'God bless you,' were the fervent words of Mr. Channing, in a moment when there was most need of Divine assistance ; and when I stood on the platform for an hour and a half, waiting to be heard, I could read in the faces of men such as these, and in the faces, too, of our opposers, the calm assurance, 'You are making the most effectual speech for temperance, for woman, and humanity, that you have ever made in your life.' I believed it then ; I believe it now." *

* See page 152—Cleveland Convention—for the full description of this mob by Miss Brown herself.

Rev. William Henry Channing, in giving his report of the World's Temperance Convention to the Toronto Division of Sons of Temperance of the City of Rochester, said:

And now it becomes my disagreeable duty, as one of your delegates, to report to the Toronto Division how my highly honored fellow-delegate was treated. Her credentials were received without dissent; she was, of course, then entitled, *equally* with every other delegate, to take part in all the proceedings of the Conventions. At a suitable time and in a perfectly orderly manner she rose to speak; the floor was adjudged to her by Hon. Neal Dow, the President, but her right to the platform was questioned. Again and again the President declared your delegate to be in order; again and again appeal was made to the Convention and the decision of the President sustained; but a factious minority succeeded in silencing her voice, and so ended the first session in storm.

On the second morning your delegate wisely waited until the resolutions offered to the convention by the Business Committee were opened for discussion. When the first resolution, declaring the *religious character* of the Temperance Movement, was submitted to the meeting, Miss Brown rose to speak. She rose calmly in the body of the house; she was a minister of religion, an advocate of temperance; she had it in her heart to press this reformation onward in a religious spirit; she had avoided all disputes on petty points of order, and now wished to address herself earnestly to the momentous theme. Had she not a perfect right to do so? And what fitter occasion could occur? The very topic was of a kind to banish personalities and hush low passions. Your delegate was invited by the President to take the platform; she did so with quiet dignity, but scarcely had she reached the stand when all around her on the platform itself, and among the officers of the Convention, began that disgraceful row, which led an onlooker in the gallery to cry out, "Are those men drunk?" I have no wish to dwell upon that cowardly transaction, but this remark I am bound in honor to make: If any man says that Antoinette Brown forced the subject of "Woman's Rights" on that Temperance Convention, in plain Saxon speech, *He Lies*. She never dreamed of asking any *privilege* as a woman; she stood there in her *right* as a delegate; her aim was to urge forward the Temperance Reform. No! the whole uproar on "Woman's Rights" came from the professed friends of Temperance, and began with the insulting cry—from a man on the platform—of, "Shame on the woman!" That man I need hardly tell you was the notorious John Chambers, of Philadelphia—the so-called Rev. John Chambers!—he it was who, with brazen face and clanging tongue, stood stamping until he raised a cloud of dust around him, pointing with coarse finger and rudely shouting "shame on the woman," until he even stood abashed before the indignant cry from the Convention of "shame on John Chambers."

The Reverend John Chambers! *Reverend* for what? For his piety; manifested in the fact that he, a professed minister of the gospel, could by rowdy tumult drown the voice of another minister of the gospel while she was asserting the religious character of the Temperance Reform! *Reverend* for what? For his charity; manifested by low cries and insulting gestures to a gentlewoman who stood there firm yet meek, before him! Strange that he, of all, should thus seek a bad eminence in outraging the decencies of social life; for unless report is false, John Chambers owes whatever position he may have to woman. It is said—I beleive on good authority—that he was educated for the ministry by the contributions of women; that he preaches in a church built and endowed by a woman: that his salary is chiefly paid by hard-working needle-women; finally, that he married a rich wife! Now what a sight was there! A man, whose brain had been fed with books by woman, whose body had been fattened with bread by woman, every fragment and stitch of whose ministerial garb, from his collar to his boot-heels, had been paid for by woman, whose very traveling ticket to that convention had been bought by woman, could find no better way to discharge his mission as minister of the gospel than to point his finger and shout, " Shame on the woman ! "

Mr. Channing then bore his testimony to the admirable combination of energy and mildness, by which Miss Brown's whole air and manner were distinguished amid these hours of tumult. He said: " Such serene strength comes only from religious principle and life. I know not how it may have been with nerves and pulses—there was no apparent tremor. But of this I am assured, whatever disturbance there was in the outer court of the Temple, in the Holy of Holies was the heart of peace, and the dove of the Spirit brooded in light on the tabernacle of conscience."

In an editorial of *The Una*, headed " Rev. John Chambers Recommended to Mercy," Mrs. Davis says : " We publish the letter of Rev. Wm. Henry Channing because it is a noble defence of woman and a part of the history of the movement. We do not give Mr. Chambers' reply, 1st, Because we find in it no evidence of penitence nor any testimony as to who was the guilty party—if he was not ; and 2d, Because the tone and language of the letter is of a character we trust will never sully the pages of *The Una*. Mr. Channing's rebuke is severe, but we believe it to have been richly deserved and given in true Christian love."

ROCHESTER, N. Y., Oct. 18, 1853.

EDITORS SUNDAY MERCURY:—You ask for proof that Rev. John Chambers took part in the brutal insult offered to a Christian gentlewoman at the late " World's Temperance Convention." I *was witness* of the conduct of that man and his abettors during that *cowardly transaction*, and I hereby charge him with being a ringleader in that platform row.

When my honored friend and fellow-delegate, the Rev. Antoinette L. Brown, was standing calm, yet firm, amidst those rude scoffers, the words of the Psalmist kept sounding in my ear : " Strong bulls of Bashan have beset me round about, gaping upon me with their mouths." I marked the *biggest* of the herd with the purpose, at the first suitable season, of laying on one blow of the lash with such a will that it should cut through any hide, however callous. That season came when, as a delegate, I was called upon to report to the " Toronto Division of the Sons of Temperance " how my fellow-delegate had been treated.

But having thus *indicted the bully* and put him on trial in open court, I merely record my testimony and leave him to go to judgment; the public will render a verdict, pass sentence, and inflict the *penalty* in the pillory where he has placed himself; may their justice be tempered with mercy. It was necessary, in order to *protect women* in future from the *insolence of tyrants,* to make this example; yet let him be cordially pardoned as soon as he gives sincere proof of penitence.

WILLIAM HENRY CHANNING.

Another letter of Mr. Channing's of same date to the editor of *The Daily Register:*

SIR:—Respect for yourself, your readers, and your paper, prompts me to reply at once to your article headed, "Answer," etc., by Rev. John Chambers, which, through the courtesy of some friend, reached me last evening. I must be frank, but will aim to be brief.

And first, Mr. Birney, a word to yourself. You knew me in "former days as mild," etc., and were not prepared for such a speech; you charitably suggest that its "vindictiveness" may be owing to a substitution of the reporter's language for my own, and "are not without hope of seeing a disclaimer." Now, far from wishing to disclaim the *one real accusation* made in my remarks, I am ready, anywhere and everywhere, to reiterate that charge. Yet there is no "vindictiveness" in my heart toward the criminal whom I thus arraign, and no emotion which I should not honor any man for feeling toward myself, if I was consciously guilty of having played so base a part. You were not wrong in thinking me "mild in former days"; I trust I am milder now than then. But my mildness never was, and never will be, of that mean quality, which can tamely see a sister insulted, whether by a pugilist from the ring, or by a *rowdy from the pulpit.* My principle is peace, but I remember the saying, "You can not become an angel till you are first a man." . . . . Womanhood, as such, claims honorable courtesy of every manly heart; and he is unmanly who does not rejoice to testify this respect. The man who can be rude to even a poor prostitute in the street, will be rude to wife or daughter at his own fireside; while he who is a *gentle*man to any woman, will be a *gentle*man to all women. *His spirit is brutal,* who could ever dream of applying the slang phrase "creature" to any woman under any conceivable conditions. What shall be thought then of the moral grade of him who chose as the mark for his missiles of "contempt," a young lady of rare refinement in her whole presence and manner, of spotless delicacy and gentlest dignity, of commanding talent and philanthropic earnestness, and who stood there before him, serene amid the tumult, clad, even then, in the bright robe of heavenly peace?

And now one word in closing. Let Mr. Chambers, and all of like spirit, be assured, that I am but a representative of a large, rapidly growing, and influential body in every community throughout our land, who are resolved, that women shall no longer be insulted in public assemblies with impunity.

WM. HENRY CHANNING.

Through this fierce conflict Horace Greeley, with his personal presence on the platform, and his brave editorials in the *New York Tribune*, fought a great battle for free speech and human equality. Speaking of the *Whole* World's Convention, he said:

New York Tribune, September 3, 1853.

This has been the most spirited and able Convention on behalf of temperance that was ever held. It has already done good, and can not fail to do more. The scarcity of white neck-ties on the platform so fully atoned for by the presence of such champions of reform and humanity as Antoinette L. Brown, Lucy Stone, and Mrs. Jackson, of England, Mrs. C. I. H. Nichols, Mrs. Frances D. Gage, etc., that like the absence of wine from our festive board when it is graced by women, it was the theme of no general or very pointed regret. It was a great occasion, and we know truth was there uttered which will bear fruit through coming years.

Tribune, September 7, 1853.

When the call of the World's Temperance Convention was issued, we were appealed to by valued friends, whom we know as devoted to the temperance cause, to discountenance all efforts to get up a rival Convention. "The call is unexceptionably broad," we were reminded, "it invites all and excludes nobody, then why not accept it and hold but one Convention?" The question was fair and forcible, and had there been no antecedents we should have acceded to its object. But we could not forget the preliminary meeting at the Brick Church Chapel, and we could not take the hazard of having many whom we knew as among the most efficient and faithful laborers in the Temperance cause shut out of a World's Convention of its advocates; so we cast our lot with them about whose catholicity of sentiment and action there could be no dispute, and yesterday's doings at the Metropolitan Convention maintained the conviction created by the whole World's Convention that our decision was right.

We ask especial attention to the proceedings of the World's Convention yesterday morning, particularly with reference to Antoinette Brown, who had been chosen by two separate temperance organizations of men to represent them at this Convention. How she was received, how treated, and how virtually crowded off the platform, our report most faithfully exhibits. They who are sure that the Age of Chivalry is not gone, are urged to ponder this treatment of a pure and high-souled woman, a teacher of Christian truth, an ornament of her sex, and an example to all, by a Convention of Reformers and Gentlemen, many of them from that section of the Union where the defence of woman from insult has been deemed a manly grace, if not a manly duty. We presume the matter will be further considered to-day.

Of the *Whole* World's Temperance Convention a correspondent of *The Una* says: "Throughout, the meeting has been one of intense interest; not a moment's flagging, not a poor or unworthy speech made by either man or woman. Again and again, as we passed into the large hall, filled with eager listeners, we felt it to be one of the most sublime scenes we had ever looked upon. There the audience remained, hour after hour, patient, earnest, full of enthusiasm, and yet hundreds could scarcely hear a single connected sentence. The majority were women, but the larger number of the speakers were men. The right and equality being recognized, there was no longer a necessity for controversy to maintain principle, hence no woman attempted to speak except she had something to say. Mrs. Jackson, of England, Mrs. Nichols, Mrs. Vaughan, Miss Stone, Rev. A. L. Brown, Lucretia Mott, and Mrs. F. D. Gage addressed the Convention during the different sessions."

The same correspondent says of the *World's* Temperance Convention : "There was one feature more anomalous than the rejection and gagging of Miss Brown, darker and far more cruel, for it has not the excuse of custom, nor can the Bible be tortured into any justification of it. This was the exclusion of Dr. James McCune Smith, a gentleman, a graduate of the Edinburgh University, a member of a long-established temperance society, and a regularly appointed delegate. And wherefore? simply for the reason that nature had bestowed on his complexion a darker, richer tint than upon some of the sycophants who gathered there; it appears to have been simply to pander to a bigoted priesthood and a corrupt populace."

In deciding the action of the Convention to be worse in its treatment toward Mr. Smith than toward Miss Brown, we think *The Una* correspondent makes a grave mistake.

In point of courtesy the treatment of a lady of culture and refinement, the peer of any man in that assembly, with the unpardonable rudeness they did, was infinitely worse than to have done the same thing to any man, white or black, because by every code of honor or chivalry all men are bound to defend woman. Again, as a question of morals, custom, and prejudice, they occupied the same position in the State and the Church. The "white male" in the Constitutions placed women and black men on the same platform as citizens. The popular interpretation of Scripture sanctioned the same injustice in both cases. In the mouths of the false prophets, "Servants, obey your masters," was used for the same purpose, and with equal effect, as "Wives, be in subjection to your own husbands." "Servant of servants shall he be" has been used with the same prophetic force as the more cruel curse pronounced on woman. The white man's Bible has been uniformly used to show that the degradation of the woman and the black man was in harmony with God's will. On what principle is proscription on account of color more cruel than on account of sex?

Most of the liberal men and women now withdrew from all temperance organizations, leaving the movement in the hands of timeserving priests and politicians, who, being in the majority, effectually blocked the progress of the reform for the time—destroying, as they did, the enthusiasm of the women in trying to press it as a moral principle, and the hope of the men, who intended to carry it as a political measure. Henceforward women took no active part in temperance until the Ohio crusade revived them again all over the nation, and gathered the scattered forces into " The Woman's National Christian Temperance Union," of which Miss Frances E. Willard is president. As now, so in 1853, intelligent women saw that the most direct way to effect any reform was to have a voice in the laws and lawmakers. Hence they turned their attention to rolling up petitions for the civil and political rights of women, to hearings before legislatures and constitutional conventions, giving their most persistent efforts to the reform technically called " Woman's Rights."

Susan B. Anthony had a similar battle to fight in the educational conventions. Having been a successful teacher in the State of New York fifteen years of her life, she had seen the need of many improvements in the mode of teaching and in the sanitary arrangements of school buildings ; and more than all, the injustice to women in their half-pay as teachers. Her interest in educational conventions was first roused by listening to a tedious discussion at Elmira on the " Divine ordinance " of flogging children, in which Charles Anthony, principal of the Albany Academy, quoted Solomon's injunction, " Spare the rod, and spoil the child."

In 1853, the annual convention being held in Rochester, her place of residence, Miss Anthony conscientiously attended all the sessions through three entire days. After having listened for hours to a discussion as to the reason why the profession of teacher was not as much respected as that of the lawyer, minister, or doctor, without once, as she thought, touching the kernel of the question, she arose to untie for them the Gordian knot, and said, " Mr. President." If all the witches that had been drowned, burned, and hung in the Old World and the New had suddenly appeared on the platform, threatening vengeance for their wrongs, the officers of that convention could not have been thrown into greater consternation.

There stood that Quaker girl, calm and self-possessed, while with hasty consultations, running to and fro, those frightened men could not decide what to do ; how to receive this audacious invader of their sphere of action. At length President Davies, of West Point, in full dress, buff vest, blue coat, gilt buttons, stepped to the front, and said, in a tremulous, mocking tone, " What will the lady have ? " " I wish, sir, to speak to the question under discussion," Miss Anthony replied. The Professor, more perplexed than before, said : " What is the pleasure of the Convention ? " A gentleman moved

33

that she should be heard ; another seconded the motion ; whereupon a discussion pro and con followed, lasting full half an hour, when a vote of the men only was taken, and permission granted by a small majority ; and lucky for her, too, was it, that the thousand women crowding that hall could not vote on the question, for they would have given a solid " no." The president then announced the vote, and said : " The lady can speak."

We can easily imagine the embarrassment under which Miss Anthony arose after that half hour of suspense, and the bitter hostility she noted on every side. However, with a clear, distinct voice, which filled the hall, she said : " It seems to me, gentlemen, that none of you quite comprehend the cause of the disrespect of which you complain. Do you not see that so long as society says a woman is incompetent to be a lawyer, minister, or doctor, but has ample ability to be a teacher, that every man of you who chooses this profession tacitly acknowledges that he has no more brains than a woman ? And this, too, is the reason that teaching is a less lucrative profession, as here men must compete with the cheap labor of woman. Would you exalt your profession, exalt those who labor with you. Would you make it more lucrative, increase the salaries of the women engaged in the noble work of educating our future Presidents, Senators, and Congressmen."

This said, Miss Anthony took her seat, amid the profoundest silence, broken at last by three gentlemen, Messrs. Cruttenden, Coburn, and Fanning, walking down the broad aisle to congratulate the speaker on her pluck and perseverance, and the pertinency of her remarks. The editor of *The Rochester Democrat* said the next morning, that " whatever the schoolmasters might think of Miss Anthony, it was evident that she hit the nail on the head."

To give the women of to-day some idea of what it cost those who first thrust themselves into these conventions, at the close of the session Miss A. heard women remarking : " Did you ever see anything like this performance ? " " I was actually ashamed of my sex." " I felt so mortified I really wished the floor would open and swallow me up." " Who can that creature be ? " " She must be a dreadful woman to get up that way and speak in public." " I was so mad at those three men making such a parade to shake hands with her ; that will just encourage her to speak again." These ladies had probably all been to theatres, concerts, operas, and gone into ecstasies over Fanny Kemble, Rachel, and Jenny Lind ; and Fanny Elsler, balanced on one toe, the other foot in the air, without having their delicacy shocked in the least. But a simple Quaker girl rising in a teachers' convention to make a common-sense remark modestly, dressed, making no display of her neck, or arms, or legs, so tried their delicate sensibilities that they were almost afraid to attend the next session.

At the opening of the next morning's session, after Miss Anthony's début, Professor Davies, in all his majesty and pomposity, with his thumbs in the arm-holes of his regulation buff vest, called the Convention to order, and said: "I have been asked by several persons, why no provisions have been made for women to speak, and vote, and act on committees, in these assemblies?" My answer is, "Behold yonder beautiful pilaster of this superb hall! contemplate its pedestal, its shaft, its rich entablature, the crowning glory of the whole. Each and all the parts in their appropriate place contribute to the strength, symmetry, and beauty of the whole. Could I aid in taking down that magnificent entablature from its proud elevation, and placing it in the dust and dirt that surround the pedestal? Neither could I drag down the mother, wife, and daughter, whom we worship as beings of a higher order, on the common plane of life with ourselves."

If all men were pedestals and shafts capable of holding the women of their households above the dirt and dust of common life, in a serene atmosphere of peace and plenty, the good professor's remarks would have had some significance; but as the burdens of existence rest equally on the shoulders of men and women, and we must ever struggle together on a common plane for bread, his metaphor has no foundation. Miss Anthony attended these teachers' conventions from year to year, at Oswego, Utica, Poughkeepsie, Lockport, Syracuse, making the same demands for equal place and pay, until she had the satisfaction to 'see every right conceded. Women speaking and voting on all questions; appointed on committees, and to prepare reports and addresses, elected officers of the Association, and seated on the platforms. In 1856, she was chairman of a committee herself, to report on the question of co-education; and at Troy, before a magnificent audience of the most intelligent men and women of the State, she read her report, which the press pronounced able and conclusive. The President, Mr. Hazeltine, of New York, congratulating Miss Anthony on her address, said: "As much as I am compelled to admire your rhetoric and logic, the matter and manner of your address and its delivery, I would rather follow a daughter of mine to her grave, than to have her deliver such an address before such an assembly." Superintendent Randall, overhearing the President, added: "I should be proud, Madam, if

I had a daughter capable of making such an eloquent and finished argument, before this or any assembly of men and women. I congratulate you on your triumphant success."

In 1857, at Binghamton, Professor Fowler, of Rochester, took up the gauntlet thrown down by Miss Anthony, and presented the other side of the question, taking the ground that boys and girls should not be educated together, and that women should not be paid equal wages even for equally good work. The gentlemen who sustained the side demanding equal rights for women in these conventions, were Randall, Rice, Cruttenden, Cavert, Fanning, Johonett, Coburn, Wilder, and Farnham. The opposition was led by Davies, Valentine, Buckley, Anthony (not S. B. A.), Ross, an old bachelor, the butt of ridicule, the clown of the Convention; and McElligott, the latter hardly ranking with the rest, for though opposed, he was always a gentleman, the others being ofttimes so coarse in their sneers and innuendoes, that they disgraced the positions they occupied, as the educators of the youth of the State. In the discussion at Binghamton, where Miss Anthony introduced a resolution in favor of co-education, Mr. McElligott said "he was in favor of allowing her full and equal opportunity with any other member to present resolutions, or to call them up for discussion. Standing up as she does before large audiences, to advocate what she conscientiously considers the rights and privileges of her sex, gives a touch of moral sublimity to our proceedings worthy the admiration of all."

Professor Davies denounced the resolutions in the strongest terms. "He had for four years been trying to escape this discussion; but if the question must come, let it be boldly met and disposed of. These resolutions involve a great social rather than an educational question, calculated to introduce a vast social evil; they are the first step in that school which seeks to abolish marriage, and behind the picture presented by them, I see a monster of deformity."*

In view of the grand experiment of co-education, so successful in every part of our country, the fears of those timid men thirty years ago provoke nothing now but a passing smile. How few of them with a sober face could at this time defend their old positions. It is creditable to the stronger sex that so many men in all those

---

* The *Binghamton Daily Republican* said: Miss Anthony vindicated her resolutions with great eloquence, spirit, and dignity, and showed herself a match, at least, in debate, for any member of the Convention. She was *equal* if not *identical*. Whatever may be thought of her notions, or sense of propriety in her bold and conspicuous positions, personally, intellectually, and socially speaking, there can be but one opinion as to her superior ability, energy, and moral courage; and she may well be regarded as an evangel and heroine by her sex; especially by the "Strong Minded" portion of them.

encounters, took no counsel with their fears nor prejudices, but seeing the principle steadfastly maintained it.

But the temperance and educational conventions, the clergy and
the pedagogues, were alike abandoned now for the legislators. All
this escapading of Miss Anthony's was mere child's play, compared
with the steady bombardment kept up until the war on the legislators of the Empire State. Calls, appeals, petitions to rouse the
women, fell like snow-flakes in every county, asking for the civil
and political rights of woman ; they were carried into the Legislature, frequent hearings secured, the members debating the question as hotly there as it had already been discussed in popular conventions. As New York could boast a larger number of strong-
minded women than any other State, whose continuity of purpose
knew no variableness nor shadow of turning, the agitation was persistently continued in all directions.

THE SYRACUSE NATIONAL CONVENTION,
September 8, 9, *and* 10, 1852.

This Convention, lasting three days, was in many respects remarkable, even for that " City of Conventions." It called out immense
audiences, attracted many eminent persons from different points of
the State, and was most favorably noticed by the press ; the debates
were unusually earnest and brilliant, and the proceedings orderly and
harmonious throughout. Notwithstanding an admission fee of one
shilling, the City Hall was densely packed at every session, and at
the hour of adjournment it was with difficulty that the audience
could gain the street. The preliminary * editorials of the city papers
reflected their own conservative or progressive tendencies.

In no one respect were the participants in these early Conventions
more unsparingly ridiculed, and more maliciously falsified, than in
their personal appearance ; it may therefore be wise to say that in
dignity and grace of manner and style of dress, the majority of these
ladies were superior to the mass of women ; while the neat and
unadorned Quaker costume was worn by some, many others were
elegantly and fashionably attired ; two of them in such extreme style

---

* *The Daily Standard*, Sept. 8th, 1852, said : The Woman's Rights Convention will assemble at the City Hall this morning. Some of the most able women of the country
will be present, and the discussion can not fail to be particularly interesting.

The Daily Star, a pro-slavery paper of the most pronounced and reckless character, said :
The women are coming ! They flock in upon us from every quarter, all to hear and talk
about Woman's Rights. The blue stockings are as thick as grasshoppers in hay-time,
and mighty will be the force of " jaw-logic " and " broom-stick ethics " preached by the
females of both sexes.

as to call forth much criticism from the majority, to whom a happy medium seemed desirable.

The Convention was called to order by Paulina Wright Davis, chairman of the Central Committee, and prayer offered by the Rev Samuel J. May, pastor of the Unitarian Church in Syracuse.

Although this was the first Woman's Rights Convention at which Mr. May was ever present, he had been represented in nearly all by letter, and as early as 1845 had preached an able sermon advocating the social, civil, and political rights of woman. He had been an early convert to this doctrine, and enjoyed telling the manner of his conversion. Speaking once in Providence on the question of slavery, he was attracted by the earnest attention he received from an intelligent-looking woman. At the close of the meeting, she said to him: "I have listened to you with an interest that only a woman can feel. I doubt whether you see how much of your description of the helpless dependence of slaves applies equally to all women." She ran the parallel rapidly, quoting law and custom, maintaining her assertion so perfectly that Mr. May's eyes were opened at once, and he promised the lady to give the subject his immediate consideration.

Lucy Stone read the call * and expressed the wish that every one present, even if averse to the new demands by women, would take part in the debates, as it was the truth on this question its advocates were seeking. Among the most noticeable features of these early Conventions was the welcome given to opposing arguments.

---

* THE NATIONAL WOMAN'S RIGHTS CONVENTION.

The friends of equality, justice, and truth are earnestly invited to meet in Syracuse, N. Y., Sept. 8th, 9th, and 10th, 1852, to discuss the important question of " Woman's Rights." We propose to review not only the past and consider the present, but to mark out new and broader paths for the future.

The time has come for the discussion of woman's social, civil, and religious rights, and also for a thorough and efficient organization ; a well-digested plan of operation whereby these social rights, for which our fathers fought, bled, and died, may be secured by us. Let woman no longer supinely endure the evils she may escape, but with her own right hand carve out for herself a higher, nobler destiny than has heretofore been hers. Inasmuch as through the folly and imbecility of woman, the race is what it is, dwarfed in mind and body ; and as through her alone it can yet be redeemed, all are equally interested in the objects of this Convention.

We therefore solemnly urge those men and women who desire the elevation of humanity, to be present at the coming Convention, and aid us by their wisdom. Our platform will be free to all who are capable of discussing the subject with candor and truth. On behalf of the Central Committee,

ELIZABETH CADY STANTON,
PAULINA WRIGHT DAVIS,
WILLIAM HENRY CHANNING,
LUCY STONE,
SAMUEL J. MAY.

The Nominating Committee reported the list of officers,* with Lucretia Mott as permanent President. She asked that the vote be taken separately, as there might be objections to her appointment. The entire audience (except her husband, who gave an emphatic " No! ") voted in her favor. The very fact that Mrs. Mott consented, under any circumstances, to preside over a promiscuous assemblage, was proof of the progress of liberal ideas, as four years previously she had strenuously opposed placing a woman in that position, and as a member of the Society of Friends, by presiding over a meeting to which there was an admission fee, she rendered herself liable to expulsion. The vote being taken, Mrs. Mott, who sat far back in the audience, walked forward to the platform, her sweet face and placid manners at once winning the confidence of the audience. This impression was further deepened by her opening remarks. She said she was unpracticed in parliamentary proceedings, and felt herself incompetent to fulfill the duties of the position now pressed upon her, and was quite unprepared to make a suitable speech. She asked the serious and respectful attention of the Convention to the business before them, referred to the success that had thus far attended the movement, the respect shown by the press, and the favor with which the public generally had received these new demands, and closed by inviting the cordial co-operation of all present.

In commenting upon Mrs. Mott's opening address, the press of the city declared it to have been " better expressed and far more appropriate than those heard on similar occasions in political and legislative assemblages." The choice of Mrs. Mott as President was pre-eminently wise; of mature years, a member of the Society of Friends, in which woman was held as an equal, with undoubted right to speak in public, and the still broader experience of the Anti-Slavery

---

* *President.*—Lucretia Mott, Philadelphia.

Vice-Presidents.—Paulina Wright Davis, Rhode Island; Caroline M. Severance, Ohio; Elizabeth Oakes Smith, New York; Clarina I. H. Nichols, Vermont; Gerrit Smith, Peterboro; Sarah L. Miller, Pennsylvania.

Secretaries.—Susan B. Anthony, Martha C. Wright, Samuel J. May, Lydia F. Fowler.

Business Committee.—Elizabeth Oakes Smith, Lucy Stone, Caroline M. Severance, Harriot K. Hunt, Jane Elizabeth Jones, James Mott, Ernestine L. Rose, Elizabeth W. Phillips, Pliny Sexton, Benjamin S. Jones.

Committee on Finance.—Rosa Smith, Joseph Savage, Caroline M. Severance.

Many earnest friends beside the officers were present and took part in the discussions; among them Amy Post, Mary and Sarah Hallowell, Catharine A. F. Stebbins, Thomas and Mary Ann McClintock, Elizabeth Smith Miller, Rev. Lydia Ann Jenkins, Rev. Antoinette L. Brown, Lydia Mott, Phebe H. Jones, Mary A. Springstead, Abby H. Price, Rev. Abraham Pryne, Eliza A. Aldrich, editor *Genius of Liberty;* Dr. Cutcheon, of McGrawville College; Matilda Joslyn Gage, Lydia P. Savage, Sarah Hallock, Griffith M. Cooper.

platform, she was well fitted to guide the proceedings and encourage the expression of opinions from those to whom public speaking was an untried experiment. "It was a singular spectacle," said the *Syracuse Standard*, "to see this gray-haired matron presiding over a Convention with an ease, dignity, and grace that might be envied by the most experienced legislator in the country."

Delegates were present from Canada and eight different States. Letters were received from Mrs. Marion Reid, of England, author of an able work upon woman; from John Neal, of Maine, the veteran temperance reformer; from William Lloyd Garrison, Rev. William Henry Channing, Rev. A. D. Mayo, Margaret H. Andrews, Sarah D. Fish, Angelina Grimké Weld, Elizabeth Cady Stanton, from G. W. Johnson, chairman of the State Committee of the Liberty party, and Horace Greeley, the world-renowned editor of the *Tribune*. Mr. Johnson's letter enclosed ten dollars and the following sentiments: 1. Woman has, equally with man, the inalienable right to education, suffrage, office, property, professions, titles, and honors—to life, liberty, and the pursuit of happiness. 2. False to our sex, as well as her own, and false to herself and to God, is the woman who approves, or who submits without resistance or protest, to the social and political wrongs imposed upon her in common with the rest of her sex throughout the world.

Mrs. Stanton's letter * presented three suggestions for the consideration of the Convention, viz.: That all women owning property should refuse to pay taxes as long as unrepresented; that man and woman should be educated together, and the abuse of the religious element in woman. This letter created much discussion, accompanied as it was by a series of resolutions of the most radical character, which were finally, with one exception, adopted. Thus at that early day was the action of those women, who have since refused to pay taxes, prefigured and suggested. One of the remarkable aspects of this reform, is the fact that from the first its full significance was seen by many of the women who inaugurated it.

HORACE GREELEY'S LETTER.

NEW YORK, *Sept.* 1, 1852.

My Friend:—I have once or twice been urged to attend a Convention of the advocates of woman's rights; and though compliance has never been within my power, I have a right to infer that some friends of the cause desire suggestions from me with regard to the best means of advancing it. I therefore venture to submit some thoughts on that sub-

---

* See Appendix.

ject. To my mind the BREAD problem lies at the base of all the desirable and practical reforms which our age meditates. Not that bread is intrinsically more important to man than Temperance, Intelligence, Morality, and Religion, but that it is essential to the just appreciation of all these. Vainly do we preach the blessings of temperance to human beings cradled in hunger, and suffering at intervals the agonies of famine; idly do we commend intellectual culture to those whose minds are daily racked with the dark problem, "How shall we procure food for the morrow?" Morality, religion, are but words to him who fishes in the gutters for the means of sustaining life, and crouches behind barrels in the street for shelter from the cutting blasts of a winter's night.

Before all questions of intellectual training or political franchises for women, not to speak of such a trifle as costume, do I place the question of enlarged opportunities for work; of a more extended and diversified field of employment. The silk culture and manufacture firmly established and thriftily prosecuted to the extent of our home demand for silk, would be worth everything to American women. Our now feeble and infantile schools of design should be encouraged with the same view. A wider and more prosperous development of our Manufacturing Industry will increase the demand for female labor, thus enhancing its average reward and elevating the social position of woman. I trust the future has, therefore, much good in store for the less muscular half of the human race.

But the reform here anticipated should be inaugurated in our own households. I know how idle is the expectation of any general and permanent enhancement of the wages of any class or condition above the level of equation of Supply and Demand; yet it seems to me that the friends of woman's rights may wisely and worthily set the example of paying juster prices for female assistance in their households than those now current. If they would but resolve never to pay a capable, efficient woman less than two-thirds the wages paid to a vigorous, effective man employed in some corresponding vocation, they would very essentially aid the movement now in progress for the general recognition and conception of Equal Rights to Woman.

Society is clearly unjust to woman in according her but four to eight dollars per month for labor equally repugnant with, and more protracted than that of men of equal intelligence and relative efficiency, whose services command from ten to twenty dollars per month. If, then, the friends of Woman's Rights could set the world an example of paying for female service, not the lowest pittance which stern Necessity may compel the defenceless to accept, but as approximately fair and liberal compensation for the work actually done, as determined by a careful comparison with the recompense of other labor, I believe they would give their cause an impulse which could not be permanently resisted.

With profound esteem, yours,   HORACE GREELEY.

MRS. PAULINA W. DAVIS, Providence, R. I.

Mr. Greeley's letter bore two remarkable aspects. First, he recognized the poverty of woman as closely connected with her degradation. One of the brightest anti-slavery orators was at that time in the habit of saying, " It is not the press, nor the pulpit, which rules the country, but the counting-room "; proving his assertion by show-ing the greater power of commerce and money, than of intellect and morality. So Mr. Greeley saw the purse to be woman's first need ; that she must control money in order to help herself to freedom.

Second, ignoring woman's pauperized condition just admitted, he suggested that women engaged in this reform should pay those em-ployed in the household larger wages than was customary, although these very women were dependent upon others for their shelter, food, and clothes ; so impossible is it for a governing class to under-stand the helplessness of dependents, and to fully comprehend the disabilities of a subject class.

The declaration of sentiments* adopted at the Westchester Con-vention was read by Martha C. Wright, and commented upon as follows by

CLARINA HOWARD NICHOLS: There *is* no limit to personal responsi-bility. Our duties are as wide as the world, and as far-reaching as the bounds of human endeavor. Woman and man must act together; she, *his* helper. She has no sphere peculiar to herself, because she could not then be his helper. It is only since I have met the varied responsibilities of life, that I have comprehended woman's sphere; and I have come to re-gard it as lying within the whole circumference of humanity. If, as is claimed by the most ultra opponents of the wife's legal individuality, the *interests of the parties are identical,* then I claim as a legitimate conclu-sion that their spheres are also identical. For interests determine duties, and duties are the land-marks of spheres. The dependence of the sexes is mutual.

It is in behalf of our sons, the future men of the Republic, as well as of our daughters, its future mothers, that we claim the full development of our energies by education, and legal protection in the control of all the issues and profits of our lives called *property.* Woman must seek in-fluence, independence, representation, that she may have power to aid in the elevation of the human race. When men kindly set aside woman from the National Councils, they say the moral field belongs to her; and the strongest reason why woman should seek a more elevated position, is because her moral susceptibilities are greater than those of man.

Mrs. MOTT thought differently from Mrs. Nichols; she did not believe that woman's moral feelings were more elevated than man's; but that with the same opportunities for development, with the same restrictions and penalties, there would probably be about an equal manifestation of virtue.

ELIZABETH OAKES SMITH: My friends, do we realize for what purpose we are convened ? Do we fully understand that we aim at nothing less

---

* See Pennsylvania Chapter, page 360.

than an entire subversion of the present order of society, a dissolution of the whole existing social compact ? Do we see that it is not an error of to-day, nor of yesterday, against which we are lifting up the voice of dissent, but that it is against the hoary-headed error of all times—error borne onward from the foot-prints of the first pair ejected from Paradise, down to our own time ? In view of all this, it does seem to me that we should each and all feel as if anointed, sanctified, set apart as to a great mission. It seems to me that we who struggle to restore the divine order to the world, should feel as if under the very eye of the Eternal Searcher of all hearts, who will reject any sacrifice other than a pure offering.

We are said to be a " few disaffected, embittered women, met for the purpose of giving vent to petty personal spleen and domestic discontent." I repel the charge; and I call upon every woman here to repel the charge. If we have personal wrongs, here is not the place for redress. If we have private griefs (and what human heart, in a large sense, is without them ?), we do not come here to recount them. The grave will lay its cold honors over the hearts of all here present, before the good we ask for our kind will be realized to the world. We shall pass onward to other spheres of existence, but I trust the seed we shall here plant will ripen to a glorious harvest. We " see the end from the beginning," and rejoice in spirit. We care not that we shall not reach the fruits of our toil, for we know in times to come it will be seen to be a glorious work.

Bitterness is the child of wrong; if any one of our number has become embittered (which, God forbid!), it is because social wrong has so penetrated to the inner life that we are crucified thereby, and taste the gall and vinegar with the Divine Master. All who take their stand against false institutions, are in some sense embittered. The conviction of wrong has wrought mightily in them. Their large hearts took in the whole sense of human woe, and bled for those who had become brutalized by its weight, and they spoke as never man spoke in his own individualism, but as the embodied race will speak, when the full time shall come Thus Huss and Wickliffe and Luther spoke, and the men of '76.

No woman has come here to talk over private griefs, and detail the small coin of personal anecdote; and yet did woman speak of the wrongs which unjust legislation; the wrongs which corrupt public opinion; the wrongs which false social aspects have fastened upon us; wrongs which she hides beneath smiles, and conceals with womanly endurance; did she give voice to all this, her smiles would seem hollow and her endurance pitiable.

I hope this Convention will be an acting Convention. Let us pledge ourselves to the support of a paper in which our views shall be fairly presented to the world. At our last Convention in Worcester, I presented a prospectus for such a paper, which I will request hereafter to be read here. We can do little or nothing without such an organ. We have no opportunity now to repel slander, and are restricted in disseminating truth, from the want of such an organ. *The Tribune*, and some other papers in the country, have treated us generously; but a paper to represent us must be sustained by ourselves. We must look to our own resources. We must work out our own salvation, and God grant it be not in fear and trembling! Woman must henceforth be the redeemer, the regenerator of the world. We plead not for ourselves alone, but for Humanity. We must place woman on a higher platform, and she will raise the race to her side. We should have a literature of our own, a printing-press and a publishing-house, and tract writers and distributors, as well as lectures and conventions; and yet I say this to a race of beggars, for women have no pecuniary resources.

Well, then, we must work, we must hold property, and claim the consequent right to representation, or refuse to be taxed. Our aim is nothing less than an overthrow of our present partial legislation, that every American citizen, whether man or woman, may have a voice in the laws by which we are governed. We do not aim at idle distinction, but while we would pull down our present worn-out and imperfect human institutions, we would help to reconstruct them upon a new and broader foundation.

LUCY STONE: It seems to me that the claims we make at these Conventions are self-evident truths. The second resolution affirms the right of human beings to their persons and earnings. Is not that self-evident? Yet the common law which regulates the relation of husband and wife, and which is modified only in a very few instances where there are statutes to the contrary, gives the "custody" of the wife's person to her husband, so that he has a right to her even against herself. It gives him her earnings, no matter with what weariness they have been acquired, or how greatly she may need them for herself or her children. It gives him a right to her personal property, which he may will entirely from her, also the use of her real estate; and in some of the States, married women, insane persons, and idiots are ranked together as not fit to make a will. So that she is left with only one right, which she enjoys in common with the pauper, viz.: the right of maintenance. Indeed when she has taken the sacred marriage vow, her legal existence ceases.

And what is our position politically? Why, the foreigner who can't speak his mother tongue correctly; the negro, who to our own shame, we regard as fit only for a boot-black (whose dead even we bury by themselves), and the drunkard, all are entrusted with the ballot, all placed by men politically higher than their own mothers, sisters, wives, and daughters. The woman who, seeing and feeling this, dare not maintain her rights, is the woman to hang her head and blush. We ask only for justice and equal rights—the right to vote, the right to our own earnings, equality before the law—these are the Gibraltar of our cause.

REV. ANTOINETTE L. BROWN: Man can not represent woman. They differ in their nature and relations. The law is wholly masculine; it is created and executed by man. The framers of all legal compacts are restricted to the masculine stand-point of observation, to the thought, feelings, and biases of man. The law then could give us no representation as woman, and therefore no impartial justice even if the present lawmakers were honestly intent upon this; for we can be represented only by our peers. It is expected then under the present administration, that woman should be the legal subject of man, legally reduced to pecuniary dependence upon him; that the mother should have lower legal claims upon the children than the father, and that, in short, woman should be in all respects the legal inferior of man, though entitled to full equality.

Here is the fact and its cause. When woman is tried for crime, her jury, her judges, her advocates, are all men; and yet there may have been temptations and various palliating circumstances connected with her peculiar nature as woman, such as man can not appreciate. Common justice demands that a part of the law-makers and law executors should be of her own sex. In questions of marriage and divorce, affecting interests dearer than life, both parties in the compact are entitled to an equal voice. Then the influences which arise from the relations of the sexes, when left to be exerted in our halls of justice, would at least cause decency and propriety of conduct to be maintained there; but now. low-minded men are encouraged to jest openly in court over the most sacred and most delicate subjects. From the nature of things, the guilty woman can not now have justice done her before the professed tribunals of justice; and the innocent but wronged woman is constrained to suffer on in silence rather than ask for redress.

CLARINA HOWARD NICHOLS said: There is one peculiarity in the laws affecting woman's property rights, which as it has not to my knowledge been presented for the consideration of the public, except by myself to a limited extent in private conversation and otherwise, I wish to speak of here. It is the unconstitutionality of laws cutting off the wife's right of dower. It is a provision of our National and State Constitutions, that property rights shall not be confiscated for political or other offences against the laws. Yet in all the States, if I am rightly informed, the wife forfeits her right of dower in case of divorce for infidelity to the marriage vow. In Massachusetts and several other States, if the wife desert her husband for any cause, and he procure a divorce on the ground of her desertion, she forfeits her right of dower. But it is worthy of remark that in no case is the right of the husband to possess and control the estate which is their joint accumulation, set aside; no, not even when the wife procures a divorce for the most aggravated abuse and infidelity combined. She, the innocent party, goes out childless and portionless, by decree of law; and he, the criminal, retains the home and the children, by the favor of the same law. I claim, friends, that the laws which cut off the wife's right of dower, in any case do confiscate property rights, and hence are *unconstitutional.* The property laws compel the wife to seek divorce in order to protect her earnings for the support of her children. A rum-drinker took his wife's clothing to pay his rum bill, and the justice decided that the clothing could be held, because the wife belonged to him.

Only under the Common Law of England has woman been deprived of her natural rights. Instances are frequent where the husband's aged parents are supported by the wife's earnings, and the wife's parents left paupers.

Mrs. Nichols here offered the following resolution:

Resolved, That equally involved as they are in all the Natural Relations which lie at the base of society, the sexes are equally entitled to all the rights necessary to the discharge of the duties of those relations.

ELIZABETH OAKES SMITH presented the following resolution offered by Lucretia Mott:

Resolved, That as the imbruted slave, who is content with his own lot, and would not be free if he could, if any such there be, only gives evidence of the depth of his degradation; so the woman who is satisfied with her inferior condition, avering that she has all the rights she wants, does but exhibit the enervating effects of the wrongs to which she is subjected.

Susan B. Anthony read the resolutions.* The audience called upon Hon. Gerrit Smith for a speech. His rising was received with cheers. This was Mr. Smith's first appearance upon our platform, although in letters to different Conventions he had already expressed his sympathy. His commanding presence, his benevolent countenance, and deep rich voice, made a profound impression, and intensified the power of his glowing words. Being well known in Syracuse for his philanthropy, his presence added dignity and influence to the assembly.†

Mr. SMITH said: The women who are engaged in this movement are ridiculed for aspiring to be doctors, lawyers, clergymen, sea captains, generals, presidents. For the sake of argument admitting this to be true, what then ? Shall we block the way to any individual aspiration ? But women are totally unfit for these places. Let them try, and their failure will settle the matter to their own satisfaction. There is not the slightest danger of a human being holding any position that he is incapable of attaining. We can not lay down a rule for all women. Because all women are not born with a genius for navigation, shall we say that one who is by skill and education able to take observations, who understands the chart and compass, the dangerous shores, currents, and latitudes, shall not, if she chooses, be a sea captain ? Suppose we apply that rule to man. Because I can not stand on my head, shall we deny that right to all acrobats in our circuses ? Because I can not make a steam engine, shall all other men be denied that right ? Because all men can not stand on a platform and make a speech, shall I be denied the exercise of that right ? Each individual has a sphere, and that sphere is the largest place that he or she can fill.

These women complain that they have been robbed of great and essential rights. They do not ask favors; they demand rights, the right to do whatever they have the capacity to accomplish, the right to dictate their

---

* *The Syracuse Journal* said : "Miss Anthony has a capital voice and deserves to be made clerk of the Assembly."

† When Gerrit Smith was in Congress, elected on account of his anti-slavery principles, his power to make friends even among foes was fully illustrated. At his elegant dinners distinguished Southerners were frequent guests. Hence it was said of him that he dined with slaveholders, and would have wined with them but for his temperance principles.

own sphere of action, and to have a voice in the laws and rulers under which they live. Suppose I should go to vote, and some man should push me back and say, "You want to be Governor, don't you ?" "No," I reply, "I want to exercise my God-given right to vote." Such a taunt as this would be no more insulting than those now cast at women, when they demand rights so unjustly denied.

I make no claim that woman is fit to be a member of Congress or President; all I ask for her is what I ask for the negro, a fair field. All will admit that woman has a right to herself, to her own powers of locomotion, to her own earnings, but how few are prepared to admit her right to the ballot. But all rights are held by a precarious tenure, if this one be denied. When women are the constituents of men who make and administer the laws, they will pay due consideration to their interests and not before. The right of suffrage is the great right that guarantees all others.

Mr. Smith set forth the education, the dignity, the power of self-government, and took his seat amid great applause.

Lucy Stone said: It is the duty of woman to resist taxation as long as she is not represented. It may involve the loss of friends as it surely will the loss of property. But let them all go; friends, house, garden spot, and all. The principle at issue requires the sacrifice. Resist, let the case be tried in the courts; be your own lawyers; base your cause on the admitted self-evident truth, that taxation and representation are inseparable. One such resistance, by the agitation that will grow out of it, will do more to set this question right than all the conventions in the world. There are $15,000,000 of taxable property owned by women of Boston who have no voice either in the use or imposition of the tax.

J. B. Brigham, a school teacher, said: That the natures of men and women showed that their spheres were not the same, and woman was only truly lovely and happy when in her own element. He wished woman to recognize the feminine element in her being, for if she understood this, it would guide her in everything. In the domestic animals even this difference was manifest. Women should be keepers at home, and mind domestic concerns. The true object of this Convention is, I fear, not so much to acquire any real or supposed rights, as to make the speakers and actors conspicuous. I urge those engaged in this movement to claim nothing masculine for woman.

Mrs. Nichols said: Mr. Brigham's allusion to the animal world is not a happy one, as no animal has been discovered which legislated away the rights of the female.

Gerrit Smith said: He would hand his esteemed friend over to Lucretia Mott, that he might be slain like Abimelech of old, by the hand of a woman; as evidently from his estimate of the sex, that would be the most humiliating death he could suffer. I trust no gentleman on this platform will consent to play the part of the armor-bearer in his behalf, and rescue him from his impending fate.

Lucretia Mott said: It was impossible for one man to have arbitrary power over another without becoming despotic. She did not expect man to see how woman is robbed. Slaveholders did not see that they were oppressors, but slaves did. Gerrit Smith alluded to one woman that he intends me to personify, whom our friend would consider far out of her sphere. Yet if he believes his Bible, he must acknowledge that Deborah, a mother in Israel, arose by divine command, and led the armies of Israel,—the wife of Heber the Kenite, who drove the nail into the head of the Canaanite General, and her praises were chanted in the songs of Israel. The preaching of women, too, is approved in the Bible. Paul gives special directions to women how to preach, and he exhorts them to qualify themselves for this function and not to pin their faith on the sleeves of the clergy. I would advise Mr. Bingham not to set up his wisdom against the plain decrees of the Almighty. As to woman's voice being too weak to be heard as a public speaker, did Mr. Brigham send a protest to England against Victoria's proroguing Parliament?

Mr. MAY moved that Mrs. Stephen Smith be placed on a Committee in his stead.

The PRESIDENT quickly replied: Woman's Rights' women do not like to be called by their husbands' names, but by their own.

Mr. MAY corrected himself and said—*Rosa Smith.*

Matilda Joslyn Gage made her first public appearance in an address to this Convention. She pressed the adoption of some settled plan for the future—brought up many notable examples of woman's intellectual ability, and urged that girls be trained to self-reliance. Although Mrs. Gage, whose residence was Onondaga County, had not before taken part in a Convention, yet from the moment she read of an organized effort for the rights of woman, she had united in it heart and soul, merely waiting a convenient opportunity to publicly identify herself with this reform; an opportunity given by the Syracuse Convention. Personally acquainted with none of the leaders except Mr. May, it was quite a test of moral courage for Mrs. Gage, then quite a young woman, in fact the youngest person who took part in that Convention, to speak upon this occasion. She consulted no one as to time or opportunity, but when her courage had reached a sufficiently high point, with palpitating heart she ascended the platform, where she was cordially given place by Mrs. Mott, whose kindness to her at this supreme moment of her life was never forgotten.

Mrs. GAGE said: This Convention has assembled to discuss the subject of Woman's Rights, and form some settled plan of action for the future. While so much is said of the inferior intellect of woman, it is by a strange absurdity conceded that very many eminent men owe their station in life to their mothers. Women are now in the situation of the mass of mankind a few years since, when science and learning were in the hands of the priests, and property was held by vassalage. The Pope and the priests claimed to be not only the teach ers, but the guides of the people; the laity were not permitted to examine for themselves; education was held to be unfit for the masses, while the tenure of their landed property was such as kept them in a continual state of dependence on their feudal lords.

It was but a short time since the most common rudiments of education were deemed sufficient for any woman ; could she but read tolerably and write her own name it was enough. Trammeled as women have been by might and custom, there are still many shining examples, which serve as beacon lights to show what may be attained by genius, labor, energy, and perseverance combined. "The longer I live in the world," says Göethe, "the more I am certain that the difference between the great and the insignificant, is energy, invincible determination, an honest purpose once fixed, and then victory."

Although so much has been said of woman's unfitness for public life, it can be seen, from Semiramis to Victoria, that she has a peculiar fitness for governing. In poetry, Sappho was honored with the title of the Tenth Muse. Helena Lucretia Corano, in the seventeenth century, was of such rare scientific attainments, that the most illustrious persons in passing through Venice, were more anxious to see her than all the curiosities of the city; she was made a doctor, receiving the title of Unalterable. Mary Cunity, of Silesia, in the sixteenth century, was one of the most able astronomers of her time, forming astronomical tables that acquired for her a great reputation. Anna Maria Schureman was a sculptor, engraver, musician, and painter; she especially excelled in miniature painting. Constantina Grierson, an Irish girl, of humble parentage, was celebrated for her literary acquirements, though dying at the early age of twenty-seven.

With the learning, energy, and perseverance of Lady Jane Grey, Mary and Elizabeth, all are familiar. Mrs. Cowper was spoken of by Montague as standing at the head of all that is called learned, and that every critic veiled his bonnet at her superior judgment. Joanna Baillie has been termed the woman Shakespeare. Caroline Herschell shares the fame of her brother as an astronomer. The greatest triumphs of the present age in the drama, music, and literature have been achieved by women, among whom may be mentioned, Charlotte Cushman, Jenny Lind, the Misses Carey, Mrs. Stowe, and Margaret Fuller. Mrs. Somerville's renown has long been spread over both continents as one of the first mathematicians of the present age.

Self-reliance is one of the first lessons to be taught our daughters; they should be educated with our sons, and equally with them, taught to look forward to some independent means of support, either to one of the professions or the business best fitted to exercise their talents. Being placed in a position compelling them to act, has caused many persons to discover talents in themselves they were before unaware of possessing. Great emergencies produce great leaders, by arousing hitherto dormant energies.

Let us look at the rights it is boasted women now possess. After marriage the husband and wife are considered as one person in law, which I hold to be false from the very laws applicable to married parties. Were it so, the act of one would be as binding as the act of the other, and wise legislators would not need to enact statutes defining the peculiar rights of each ; were it so, a woman could not legally be a man's inferior. Such a thing would be a veritable impossibility. One-half of a person can not be made the protection or direction

34

of the other half. Blackstone says "a woman may indeed be attorney for her husband, for that implies no separation from, but rather a representation of, her lord. And a husband may also bequeath anything to his wife by will; for it can not take effect till the coverture is determined by his death." After stating at considerable length, the reasons showing their unity, the learned commentator proceeds to cut the knot, and show they are not one, but are considered as two persons, one superior, the one inferior, and not only so, but the inferior in the eye of the law as acting from compulsion.

J. ELIZABETH JONES of Ohio: This is a time of progress; and man may sooner arrest the progress of the lightning, or the clouds, or stay the waves of the sea, than the onward march of Truth with her hand on her sword and her banner unfurled. I am not in the habit of talking much about rights; I am one of those who take them. I have occupied pulpits all over the country five days out of seven, in lecturing on science, and have found no objection.

I do not know what all the women want, but I do know what I want myself, and that is, what men are most unwilling to grant; the right to vote. That includes all other rights. I want to go into the Legislative Hall, sit on the Judicial Bench, and fill the Executive Chair. Now do you understand me? This I claim on the ground of humanity; and on the ground that taxation and representation go together. The whole question resolves itself into this; there has been no attempt to dispute this. No man will venture to deny the right of woman to vote. He may urge many objections against the expediency of her exercising it, but the right is hers.

But though women are deprived of political rights, there are other rights which no law prevents. We can take our rights as merchants and in other avocations, by investing our capital in them; but we stand back and wait till it is popular for us to become merchants, doctors, lecturers, or practitioners of the mechanic arts. I know girls who have mechanical genius sufficient to become Arkwrights and Fultons, but their mothers would not apprentice them. Which of the women of this Convention have sent their daughters as apprentices to a watchmaker? There is no law against this!!

Mrs. MOTT: The Church and public opinion are stronger than law.

LYDIA JENKINS: Is there any law to prevent women voting in this State? The Constitution says "white male citizens" may vote, but does not say that white female citizens may not.

Mrs. JONES said: I do not understand that point sufficiently well to explain, but whether the statute book is in favor or opposed, every citizen in a republic (and a woman is a citizen) has a natural right to vote which no human laws can abrogate; the right to vote is the right of self-government.

ANTOINETTE BROWN said: I know instances of colored persons voting under the same circumstances, and their votes being allowed by the legal authorities; but John A. Dix declared the proceedings of a school meeting void because two women voted at it.

BENJAMIN S. JONES said, in Ohio where there is much splitting of hairs between white and black blood, the judges decided in favor of a certain colored man's right to vote, because there was 50 per cent. of white blood in the person in question.

Mrs. DAVIS: The first draft of the Rhode Island Constitution said "all citizens," but as soon as some one suggested that the door was thus left open for women to vote, the word "male" was promptly inserted.

Mrs. Davis read an interesting letter from the Rev. A. D. Mayo.*
Samuel J. May read letters from William Lloyd Garrison, of Boston,
and Margaret H. Andrews, of Newburyport, Massachusetts.

NEWBURYPORT, Mass., *September* 4, 1852.

REV. SAMUEL J. MAY.

DEAR FRIEND—I wish to express my deep sympathy with those brave women
who are struggling against ancient prejudices and modern folly, and who will
eventually elevate our sex to a position which will command the respect of
those who now regard them with derision and contempt, and my gratitude to
the noble-minded men who are extending a helping hand to those who have
hitherto been considered the weak and dependent portion of society, and are
endeavoring to raise them to *their* level, instead of trying to establish their
superiority over them. Such conduct shows true greatness and dignity of
character. I wish to bear my share of the reproach and contumely which will be
liberally bestowed upon this movement by many who ought to know and to
do better; this is indeed the actuating motive which impels me to write.

With regard to the counsel which has been requested, I have little to say.
If there be any one subject which has not been sufficiently insisted on, it is the
aimless life which young women generally lead after they have left school. A
large portion are occupied in forming matrimonial plans when they are wholly
unfit to enter into that sacred state. Dr. Johnson makes his Nekayah say
of young ladies with whom she associated, "Some imagined they were in
love, when they were only idle." If young ladies directed their attention
to some definite employment, this evil would be remedied.

I am, dear sir,

Very truly yours,

MARGARET H. ANDREWS.

LUCY STONE said: Mrs. Jones' idea of taking our rights is inspiring, but it
can not be done. In Massachusetts some women apprenticed themselves as
printers, but were expelled because men would not set type beside them. Dr.
Harriot K. Hunt asked permission to attend medical lectures at Harvard, but
the students declared that if she were admitted they would leave, and so she
was sacrificed.

HARRIOT K. HUNT: No; I am here.

LUCY STONE: Mrs. Mott says she was only suspended. So, too, when the
Grimké sisters and Abby Kelley began publicly to plead the cause of the slave,
they were assailed both by pulpit and press, and every species of abuse was
heaped upon them; but they persevered and proved their capacity to do it, and
now we meet in quietness, and our right to speak in public is not questioned.
The woman who first departs from the routine in which society allows her to
move must suffer. Let us bravely bear ridicule and persecution for the sake of
the good that will result, and when the world sees that we can accomplish what
we undertake, it will acknowledge our right. We must be true to each other.

---

* See Appendix.

We must stand by the woman whose work of hand or brain removes her from the customary sphere. Employ the woman physician, dentist, and artist rather than a man of the same calling, and in time all professions and trades will be as free to us as to our brothers.

ABBY PRICE, of Hopedale, said: I shall briefly consider woman's religious position, her relation to the Church, and show that by its restrictions she has suffered great injustice; that alike under all forms of religion she has been degraded and oppressed, the Church has proscribed her, and denied the exercise of her inalienable rights, and in this the Church is false to the plainest principles of Christianity. "There is neither Jew nor Greek; there is neither bond nor free; there is neither male nor female; for ye all are one in Christ Jesus." Gal., chap. iii., v. 28. "So God created man in His *own* image; in the image of God created He him; male and *female* created He *them*, and said unto *them*: have dominion over the fish of the sea, and over the fowl of the air; over every living thing that moveth upon the earth." Genesis i., v. 27, 28. Notwithstanding these explicit declarations of equality, even in the Godhead, the Church claiming to be "Christian" denies woman's right of free speech. The priesthood, from Paul down, say gravely: "It is not permitted for woman to speak in the churches." Some denominations have gravely debated whether she should be allowed in the service, or chants, to respond Amen!

The whole arrangement of Nature in her beautiful and wise manifestations to us evinces that the Divine order is for the sexes to mingle their different and peculiar characteristics in every relation of life. In Jesus the masculine and feminine elements of humanity were blended harmoniously. These different characteristics in His own person were distinctly and plainly seen. The masculine, when He fixed His eye in stern rebuke, and made the hypocrite and the Pharisee tremble; and the feminine gleamed often through His tears of affection and pity, and shone ever a glorious halo of patience and love around Him in the midst of suffering the most wasting and intense. The Church, as His Representative, should also exhibit these peculiarities in as full and glorious harmony.

Yet very few of the sects allow woman to assume the responsibility as religious teacher. However great she may feel the duty to be upon her, and however well qualified she may be, all ecclesiastical authorities, with one accord, begin to make excuses whenever a woman presents herself to be properly authorized, according to the popular usage of that Church, to preach the Gospel to a people, one-half of whom are her own sex.

Again, *woman is denied* a representation in all *Ecclesiastical Assemblies.*

The male portion of the Church assemble in delegation from the different bodies with which they are connected to legislate in behalf of the churches, but woman has no representation in these councils. Her opinion of what is best to promote the interests of religion is not respected; her right to representation being denied, her claim to just recognition is solemnly mocked. The Church places its hands on woman's lips, and says to her, "You shall not *speak;* you shall not be represented; you are not eligible to office because *you are a woman!*" Is not this crucifying with a strange presumption the soul of Christ? —treating with contempt the purity of the Christian character?—trampling upon *Human Rights?* And yet woman patiently bears this contumely and scorn. The poor young men that she often educates by toil early and late, labor, arduous and half paid, teach her, when properly prepared, that this absurd tyranny is supported by the word of God!

Woman may speak when the thoughtless crowd the halls of fashion, with no aim but amusement. in the theatre, opera, or concert hall; she may meet with ministers in revivals, camp meetings, and sociables, and reply with smile and bow to the hollow compliments addressed to her vanity, but she must keep silence in the churches and all religious meetings; if there are only six persons present woman may not ask God's blessing to rest there, nor presume, should one man be present, to give utterance to her religious aspiration.

Every class of society, and especially each sex, need religious teachers of their own class and sex with themselves, having the same experience, the same hopes, aims, and relations. Human minds are so constituted as to need not merely intellectual instruction, but the strength imparted by an earnest sympathy born of a like experience. In order rightly to appreciate the wants of others, we must know and realize the trials of their situation, the struggles they may encounter, the burthens, the toils, the temptations that beset their different relations. These should be apprehended to some extent, and the more the better by the person qualified to speak to the spiritual wants of all. Each relation, therefore, needs its teacher—its peculiar ministry. No one can demonstrate by college lore the weight of a mother's responsibility.

No man—not even the kindest father—can fully apprehend the wearisome cares and anxious solicitude for children of her who bore them. The tremblings of a mother's soul none save a mother can feel. Man may prepare sound and logical discourses; he may clearly define a mother's duty; he may talk eloquently about her responsibility; he may urge upon her strong motives to faithfulness in the discharge of her maternal duties; he may tell her what her children should be in all life's varied aspects. She hears the good instruction and advice with more or less of the feeling, " *You* cannot *know* of what you are talking." . . . .

The Church needs a varied ministry. Not alone is the power of mind needed, but the zeal and the inspiration of the inner life; the unction of love and faith and courage produced by a struggle amid life's realities. Not the dreamer, but the toiler can best affect the lives of others through their hearts. In this ministry the sexes must blend harmoniously their ministrations to others from their own lives and experiences. This must be the Divine order. Reason teaches it to the calm observer. Our souls respond to this truth from their deepest chambers.

. . . . Doom woman no longer to banishment from the hallowed ground of Church and State. She has too long been but as the Pariah of the desert. Welcome her ministrations reverently to her human nature, kindly to her present weakness, encouragingly to her hopes; receive her counsels with respect and confidence, so far as they are worthy, and be assured that a better day will begin to dawn. The birth of a new spiritual life will be given in this new marriage, and melody as from the harps of angels will be breathed from the circles of earth.

PAULINA WRIGHT DAVIS: . . . . We commence life where our fathers left it. We have their mistakes and their achievements. We attempt to walk in the paths they trod, and wear the garments left by them; but they are all too short and narrow for us; they deform and cramp our energies; for they demand the

Procrustean process to conform the enlarged natures of the present to the past. While the human soul, like the infinite in wisdom and love, is ever governed by the eternal law of progress, creeds and codes are always changing. All things founded in immutable truth grow only the stronger by every trial.

. . . . The sacred traditions of both Jew and Gentile agree in ascribing to woman a primary agency in the introduction of human evils. In the Greek Mythology, she is indeed not the first offender; but she is the bearer of the box that contained all the crimes and diseases which have punished our world for the abuse of liberty. It is worthy of remark that Pandora, who is the Eve of the Grecian system, being like her Hebrew correspondent, created for special purposes, was the joint work of all the gods. Venus gave her beauty, Minerva wisdom, Apollo the art of music, Mercury eloquence, and the rest the perfection and completeness of all her divine accomplishments. Her name signifies gifts from all.

> "A combination and a form indeed
> Where every god did seem to set his seal,
> To give the world assurance of a paragon."

Prometheus made the first man of clay and animated him with fire stolen from Heaven. Jupiter is represented as attaching the terrible consequences of a rational and responsible vitality, thus conferred upon a creation of earth, by sending this wonderfully gifted Pandora into the world loaded with all the evils which it was fated to endure. It was her destiny to be the occasion of the fall, the instrument of doom; but her fortunes are linked to the resurrection and life, as well as the suffering and death of the race. Among the gifts of Pandora which had otherwise been fatal, she brought hope which lay concealed after all the others had flown abroad on their missions of mischief. In our Sacred Story this point in the parable has a clear explanation: "The seed of the woman shall bruise the serpent's head." If she brought death into the wrold, she brought forth a Son who "taketh away the sins of the world." . . . . These myths, whether received as simple facts, or poetic fiction, whose oracles always reveal the deepest signification of facts, alike indicate the eminent agency of woman in the fall and rising again of the human image of the divine upon earth.

. . . . From the marriage hour woman is presented only in a series of dissolving views. First. She stands beside her husband radiant in girlish beauty. She worships. One side of the lesson is well learned, that of entire dependence. Not once has she dreamed that there must be mutual dependence and separate fountains of reciprocal life. . . . . In the next scene the child wife appears withering away from life as from the heart she is not large or noble enough to fill— pining in the darkness of her home-life, made only the deeper by her inactivity, ignorance, and despair. . . . . In another view she has passed the season of despair, and appears as the heartless votary of fashion, a flirt, or that most to be dreaded, most to be despised being, a married coquette; at once seductive, heartless, and basely unprincipled; or as beauty of person has faded away, she may be found turning from these lighter styles of toys to a quiet kind of handmaiden piety and philanthropy.

. . . . Marriage as it now exists is only a name, a form without a soul, a bondage, legal and therefore honorable. Only equals can make this relation. True marriage is a union of soul with soul, a blending of two in one, without mastership or helpless dependence. The true family is the central and supreme institution among human societies. All other organizations, whether of Church or State, depend upon it for their character and action. Its evils are the source of all evils; its good the fountain of all good. The correction of its abuses is the starting-point of all the reforms which the world needs.

Dr. Harriot K. Hunt attracted much attention from the fact of her yearly protest against taxation. In the course of her remarks she said, " Unseen spirits have been with us in this Convention; the spirits of our Shaker sisters whom untold sorrows have driven into those communal societies, the convents of our civilization."

After quite a brilliant discussion, in which Mr. Brigham made himself a target for Lucy Stone, Martha C. Wright, Eliza Aldrich, Clarina Howard Nichols, Harriot K. Hunt, and Mrs. Palmer to shoot at, Antoinette L. Brown offered the following resolution, and made a few good points on the Bible argument :

Resolved, That the Bible recognizes the rights, duties, and privileges of woman as a public teacher, as every way equal with those of man; that it enjoins upon her no subjection that is not enjoined upon him; and that it truly and practically recognizes neither male nor female in Christ Jesus.

God created the first human pair equal in rights, possessions, and authority. He bequeathed the earth to them as a joint inheritance; gave them joint dominion over the irrational creation; but none over each other. (Gen. i. 28). They sinned. God announced to them the results of sin. One of these results was the rule which man would exercise over woman. (Gen. iii. 16). This rule was no more approved, endorsed, or sanctioned by God, than was the twin-born prophecy, "thou (Satan) shalt bruise his (Christ's) heel." God could not, from His nature, command Satan to injure Christ, or any other of the seed of woman. What particle of evidence is there then for supposing that in the parallel announcement He commanded man to rule over woman? Both passages should have been translated will, instead of shall. Either auxiliary is used indifferently according to the sense, in rendering that form of the Hebrew verb into English.

Because thou hast done this, is God's preface to the announcement. The results are the effects of sin. Can woman then receive evil from this rule, and man receive good? Man should be blessed in exercising this power, if he is divinely appointed to do so; but the two who are one flesh have an identity of interests, therefore if it is a curse or evil to woman, it must be so to man also. We mock God, when we make Him approve of man's thus cursing himself and woman.

The submission enjoined upon the wife in the New Testament, is not the unrighteous rule predicted in the Old. It is a Christian submission due from man towards man, and from man towards woman: " Yea, all of you be subject one to another " (1 Pet. v. 5; Eph. v. 21; Rom. xii. 10, etc.) In 1 Cor. xvi. 16, the disciples are besought to submit themselves " to every one that helpeth with us and laboreth." The same apostle says, " help those women which labored with me in the Gospel, with Clement also, and with other of my fellow-laborers."

Man is the head of the woman. True, but only in the sense in which Christ is represented as head of His body, the Church. In a different sense He is head of all things—of wicked men and devils. If man is woman's head in this sense, he may exercise over her all the prerogatives of God Himself. This would be blasphemous. The mystical Head and Body, or Christ and His Church, symbolize oneness, union. Christ so loved the Church He gave Himself for it, made it His own body, part and parcel of Himself. So ought men to love their wives. Then the rule which grew out of sin, will cease with the sin.

It is said woman is commanded not to teach in the Church. There is no such command in the Bible. It is said (1 Cor. xiv. 34), " Let your women keep silence in the churches ; for it is not permitted unto them to speak." This injunction, taken out of its connection, forbids singing also ; interpreted by its context, woman is merely told not to talk unless she does teach. On the same principle, one who has the gift of tongues is told not to use it in the Church, unless there is an interpreter. The rule enforced from the beginning to the end of the chapter is, " Let all things be done unto edifying." Their women, who had not been previously instructed like the men, were very naturally guilty of asking questions which did not edify the assembly. It was better that they should wait till they got home for the desired information, rather than put an individual good before the good of the Church. Nothing else is forbidden. There is not a word here against woman's teaching. The apostle says to the whole Church, woman included, " Ye may all prophesy, one by one."

In 1 Tim. ii. 12, the writer forbids woman's teaching over man, or usurping authority over him ; that is, he prohibits dogmatizing, tutoring, teaching in a dictatorial spirit. This is prohibited both in public and private ; but a proper kind of teaching is not prohibited. Verse 14—a reference to Eve, who, though created last, sinned first, is merely such a suggestion as we would make to a daughter whose mother had been in fault. The daughters are not blamed for the mother's sin, merely warned by it ; and cautioned against self-confidence, which could make them presume to teach over man. The Bible tells us of many prophetesses approved of God. The Bible is truly democratic. Do as you would be done by, is its golden commandment, recognizing neither male nor female in Christ Jesus.

ERNESTINE L. ROSE : If the able theologian who has just spoken had been in Indiana when the Constitution was revised, she might have had a chance to give her definitions on the Bible argument to some effect. At that Convention Robert Dale Owen introduced a clause to give a married woman the right to her property. The clause had passed, but by the influence of a minister was recalled ; and by his appealing to the superstition of the members, and bringing the whole force of Bible argument to bear against the right of woman to her property, it was lost. Had Miss Brown been there, she might have beaten him with his own weapons. For my part, I see no need to appeal to any written authority, particularly when it is so obscure and indefinite as to admit of different interpretations. When the inhabitants of Boston converted their harbor into a teapot rather than submit to unjust taxes, they did not go to the Bible for their authority; for if they had, they would have been told from the same authority to " give unto Cæsar what belonged to Cæsar." Had the people, when they rose in the might of their right to throw off the British yoke, appealed to the Bible for authority, it would have answered them, "Submit to the powers that be, for they are from God." No! on Human Rights and Freedom, on a subject that is as self-evident as that two and two make four, there is no need of any written authority. But this is not what I intended to speak upon. I wish to introduce a resolution, and leave it to the action of the Convention :

Resolved, That we ask not for our rights as a gift of charity, but as an act of justice. For it is in accordance with the principles of republicanism that, as woman has to pay taxes to maintain government, she has a right to participate in the formation and administration of it. That as she is amenable to the laws of her country, she is entitled to a voice in their enactment, and to all the protective advantages they can bestow; and as she is as liable as man to all the vicissitudes of life, she ought to enjoy the same social rights and privileges. And any difference, therefore, in political, civil, and social rights, on account of sex, is in direct violation of the principles of justice and humanity, and as such ought to be held up to the contempt and derision of every lover of human freedom.

. . . . But we call upon the law-makers and law-breakers of the nation, to defend themselves for violating the fundamental principles of the Republic, or disprove their validity. Yes! they stand arrayed before the bar, not only of injured womanhood, but before the bar of moral consistency; for this question is awakening an interest abroad, as well as at home. Whatever human rights are claimed for man, moral consistency points to the equal rights of woman ; but statesmen dare not openly face the subject, knowing well they can not confute it, and they have not moral courage enough to admit it; and hence, all they can do is to shelter themselves under a subterfuge which, though solidified by age, ignorance, and prejudice, is transparent enough for the most benighted vision to penetrate. A strong evidence of this, is given in a reply of Mr. Roebuck, member of Parliament, at a meeting of electors in Sheffield, England. Mr. R., who advocated the extension of the franchise to the occupants of five-pound tenements, was asked whether he would favor the extension of the same to women who pay an equal amount of rent? That was a simple, straight-forward question of justice ; one worthy to be asked even in our republican legislative halls. But what was the honorable gentleman's reply? Did he meet it openly and fairly? Oh, no! but hear him, and I hope the ladies will pay particular attention, for the greater part of the reply contains the draught poor, deluded woman has been accustomed to swallow—Flattery :

"There is no man who owes more than I do to woman. My education was formed by one whose very recollections at this moment make me tremble. There is nothing which, for the honor of the sex, I would not do ; the happiness of my life is bound up with it; mother, wife, daughter, woman, to me have been the oasis of the desert of life, and, I have to ask myself, would it conduce to the happiness of society to bring woman more distinctly than she now is brought, into the arena of politics? Honestly I confess to you I believe not. I will tell you why. All their influences, if I may so term it, are gentle influences. In the rude battle and business of life, we come home to find a nook and shelter of quiet comfort after the hard and severe, and, I may say, the sharp ire and the disputes of the House of Commons. I hie me home, knowing that I shall there find personal solicitude and anxiety. My head rests upon a bosom throbbing with emotion for me and our child; and I feel a more hearty man in the cause of my country, the next day, because of the perfect, soothing, gentle peace which a mind sullied by politics is unable to feel. Oh! I can not rob myself of that inexpressible benefit, and therefore I say, No."

Well, this is certainly a nice little romantic bit of parliamentary declamation. What a pity that he should give up all these enjoyments to give woman a vote! Poor man! his happiness must be balanced on the very verge of a precipice, when the simple act of depositing a vote by the hand of woman, would overthrow and destroy it forever. I don't doubt the honorable gentleman meant what he said, particularly the last part of it, for such are the views of the unthinking, unreflecting mass of the public, here as well as there. But like a true politician, he commenced very patriotically, for the happiness of society, and finished by describing his own individual interests. His reply is a curious mixture of truth, political sophistry, false assumption, and blind selfishness. But he was placed in a dilemma, and got himself out as he could. In advocating the franchise to five-pound tenement-holders, it did not occur to him that woman may possess the same qualification that man has, and in justice, therefore, ought to have the same rights; and when the simple question was put to him (simple questions are very troublesome to statesmen), having too much sense not to see the justness of it, and too little moral courage to admit it, he entered into quite an interesting account of what a delightful little creature woman is, provided only she is kept quietly at home, waiting for the arrival of her lord and master, ready to administer a dose of purification, " which his politically sullied mind is unable to feel." Well! I have no desire to dispute the necessity of it, nor that he owes to woman all that makes life desirable— comforts, happiness, aye, and common sense too, for it's a well-known fact that smart mothers always have smart sons, unless they take after their father. But what of that? Are the benefits woman is capable of bestowing on man, reasons why she must pay the same amount of rent and taxes, without enjoying the same rights that man does?

But the justice of the case was not considered. The honorable gentleman was only concerned about the " happiness of society." Society! what does the term mean? As a foreigner, I understand by it a collection or union of human beings—men, women, and children, under one general government, and for mutual interest. But Mr. Roebuck, being a native Briton and a member of Parliament, gave us a parliamentary definition, namely; society means the male sex only; for in his solicitude to consult " the happiness of society," he enumerated the benefits man enjoys from keeping woman from her rights, without even dreaming that woman was at all considered in it; and this is the true parliamentary definition, for statesmen never include woman in their solicitude for the happiness of society. Oh, no! she is not yet recognized as belonging to the honorable body, unless taxes are required for its benefit, or the penalties of the law have to be enforced for its security.

Thus, being either unwilling or afraid to do woman justice, he first flattered her, then, in his ignorance of her true nature, he assumed that if she has her rights equal with man, she would cease to be woman—forsake the partner of her existence, the child of her bosom, dry up her sympathies, stifle her affections, turn recreant to her own nature. Then his blind selfishness took the alarm, lest, if woman were more independent, she might not be willing to be the obedient, servile tool, implicitly to obey and minister to the passions and follies of man; "and as he could not rob himself of these inexpressible benefits, therefore he said, No."

The speech of Antoinette Brown, and the resolution she presented opened the question of authority as against individual judgment, and roused a prolonged and somewhat bitter discussion, to which Mrs. Stanton's letter,* read in a most emphatic manner by Susan B. Anthony, added intensity. It continued at intervals for two days, calling out great diversity of sentiment. Rev. Junius Hatch, a Congregational minister from Massachusetts, questioned the officers of the Convention as to their belief in the paramount authority of the Bible, saying the impression had gone abroad that the Convention was infidel in character. The President ruled that question not before the Convention.

Thomas McClintock † said, to go back to a particular era for a standard of religion and morality, is to adopt an imperfect standard and impede the progress of truth. The best minds of to-day surely understand the vital issues of this hour better than those possibly could who have slumbered in their graves for centuries. Mrs. Nichols, whom the city press spoke of as wielding a trenchant blade, announced herself as having been a member of a Baptist church since the age of eight years, thus sufficiently proving her orthodoxy. Mrs. Rose, expressing the conviction that belief does not depend upon voluntary inclination, deemed it right to interpret the Bible as he or she thought best, but objected to any such interpretation going forth as the doctrine of the Convention, as, at best, it was but mere opinion and not authority.

The debate upon Miss Brown's resolution was renewed in the afternoon, during which the Rev. Junius Hatch made so coarse a speech that the President was obliged to call him to order. ‡ Paying

---

* See Appendix.

† This noble man was among the first to append his name to the declaration of rights issued at Seneca Falls, and he did not withdraw it when the press began to ridicule the proceedings of the Convention.

‡ Rev. Mr. Hatch gave his idea of female loveliness. It consisted in that shrinking delicacy which, like the modest violet, hid itself until sought; that modesty which led women to blush, to cast down their eyes when meeting men, or walking up the aisle of a church to drop the veil; to wear long skirts, instead of imitating the sun-flower, which lifted up its head, seeming to say: "Come and admire me." He repeated the remarks made near the door on some of the speakers. The President hoped he would keep in order, and not relate the vulgar conversation of his associates. He went on in a similar strain until the indignation of the audience became universal, when he was summarily stopped.

In the midst of his remarks Miss Anthony suggested that the Reverend gentleman doubtless belonged to the pin-cushion ministry, educated by women's sewing societies! which, on inquiry, proved true. It was almost always the case that the "poor but pious" young man, who had studied his profession at the expense of women, proved most narrow and bigoted in his teachings.

no heed to this reprimand he continued in a strain so derogatory to his own dignity and so insulting to the Convention, that the audience called out, "Sit down! Sit down! Shut up!" forcing the Reverend gentleman to his seat. The discussion still continued between the members of the Convention; Miss Brown sustaining her resoultion, Mrs. Rose opposing it.

Mrs. MOTT, vacating the chair, spoke in opposition to the resolution, and related her anti-slavery experience upon the Bible question; one party taking great pains to show that the Bible was opposed to slavery, while the other side quoted texts to prove it of divine origin, thus wasting their time by bandying Scripture texts, and interfering with the business of their meetings. The advocates of emancipation soon learned to adhere to their own great work—that of declaring the inherent right of man to himself and his earnings—and that self-evident truths needed no argument or outward authority. We already see the disadvantage of such discussions here. It is not to be supposed that all the advice given by the apostles to the women of their day is applicable to our more intelligent age; nor is there any passage of Scripture making those texts binding upon us.

A GENTLEMAN said: "All Scripture is given by inspiration of God, and profitable, etc." Does not this apply to the latest period?

LUCRETIA MOTT: If the speaker will turn to the passage he will find that the word "*is,*" being in italics, was inserted by the translators. She accepted it as in the original, "All Scriptures *given* by inspiration of God, is profitable, etc." She was somewhat familar with the Scriptures, and at a suitable time would have no objection to discuss the question. She concluded by moving that the resolution be laid on the table, which was unanimously carried.

On the morning of the last day the President stated that the subject of organizing a National Society was to be discussed, and at her suggestion Mr. May read a long and interesting letter from Angelina Grimké Weld, from which we give the salient points:

"Organization is two-fold—natural and artificial, divine and human. Natural organizations are based on the principle of progression; the eternal law of change. But human or artificial organizations are built upon the principle of crystallization; they *fix* the conditions of society; they seek to daguerreotype themselves, not on the present age only, but on future generations; hence, they fetter and distort the expanding mind. Organizations do not protect the sacredness of the individual; their tendency is to sink the individual in the mass, to sacrifice his rights, and immolate him on the altar of some fancied good.

It is not to organization that I object, but to an *artificial society* that must prove a burden, a clog, an incumbrance, rather than a help. Such an organization as now actually exists among the women of America I hail with heartfelt joy. We are bound together by the natural ties of spiritual affinity; we are drawn to each other because we are attracted toward one common center—the good of humanity. We need no external bonds to bind us together, no cumbrous machinery to keep our minds and hearts in unity of purpose and effort ·

we are not the lifeless staves of a barrel which can be held together only by the iron hoops of an artificial organization.

The present aspect of organizations, whether in Church, or State, or society at large, foretokens dissolution. The wrinkles and totterings of age are on them. The power of organization has been deemed necessary only because the power of Truth has not been appreciated, and just in proportion as we reverence the individual, and trust the unaided potency of Truth, we shall find it useless. What organization in the world's history has not encumbered the unfettered action of those who created it? Indeed, has not been used as an engine of oppression.

The importance of this question can hardly be duly magnified. How few organizations have ever had the power which this is destined to wield! The prayers and sympathies of the ripest and richest minds will be ours. Vast is the influence which true-hearted women will exert in the coming age. It is a beautiful coincidence, that just as the old epochs of despotism and slavery, Priestcraft and Political intrigue are dying out, just as the spiritual part of man is rising into the ascendency, Woman's Rights are being canvassed and conceded, so that when she becomes his partner in office, higher and holier principles of action will form the basis of Governmental administration.

ANGELINA GRIMKÉ WELD.

The reading of Mrs. Weld's letter was followed by a spirited discussion, resulting in the continuance of the Central Committee, composed of representative men and women of the several States, which was the only form of National Organization until after the war.

MARY SPRINGSTEAD moved that the Convention proceed to organize a National Woman's Rights Society.

Mrs. SMITH and Mrs. DAVIS did not like to be bound by a Constitution longer than during the sessions of the Convention. Both recommended the formation of State Societies.

Dr. HARRIOT K. HUNT spoke as a physician in deeming spontaneity as a law of nature.

ERNESTINE L. ROSE declared organizations to be like Chinese bandages. In political, moral, and religious bodies they hindered the growth of men; they were incubi; she herself had cut loose from an organization into which she had been born;[*] she knew what it had cost her, and having bought that little freedom for what was dearer to her than life itself, she prized it too highly to ever put herself in the same shackles again.

LUCY STONE said, that like a burnt child that dreads the fire, they had all been in permanent organizations, and therefore dread them. She herself had had enough of thumb-screws and soul screws ever to wish to be placed under them again. The present duty is agitation.

Rev. SAMUEL J. MAY deemed a system of action and co-operation all that was needed. There is probably not one woman in a thousand, not one in ten thousand who has well considered the disabilities, literary, pecuniary, social, politi-

---

* The Jewish.

cal, under which she labors. Ample provision must be made for woman's education, as liberal and thorough as that provided for the other sex.

Mrs. C. I. H. NICHOLS favored organization as a means to collect and render operative the fragmentary elements now favoring the cause.

Rev. ABRAM PRYNE, in an able speech, favored National and State organization.

The discussion was closed by the adoption of the following resolution, introduced by Paulina Wright Davis:

Resolved, That this National Convention earnestly recommends to those who are members of it from several States, and to those persons in any or all of our States, who are interested in this great reform, that they call meetings of the States or the counties in which they live, certainly as often as once a year, to consider the principles of this reform, and devise measures for their promulgation, and thus co-operate with all throughout the nation and the world, for the elevation of woman to a proper place in the mental, moral, social, religious, and political world.

It is impossible to more than give the spirit of the Convention, though glimpses of it and its participants may be caught in the brief sketch of its proceedings. In accordance with the call, woman's social, civil, and religious rights were all discussed. Lucy Stone made a brilliant closing address, the doxology was sung to " Old Hundred," and the Convention adjourned.

The character and influence of this Convention can best be shown by the reports of the city press.*

The Standard, September 13, 1852.

THE WOMAN'S RIGHTS CONVENTION was in session during three days of last week in this city, and was attended by a large number of persons, not less, probably, than 2,000. Such a Convention, even in this city of conventions, was something new under the sun. . . . . The discussions were characterized by a degree of ability that would do credit to any deliberative body in the country. . . . . Some able letters were read to the Convention. Among the most noteworthy was that of Mrs. Stanton. . . . . Mrs. Mott presided over the Convention with much dignity and ability. . . . . If any of the natural rights belonging to women are withheld from them by the laws and customs of society, it is due to them that a remedy should be applied; . . . . those among them who are aggrieved should have an opportunity to give free expression to their opinions. This will hurt nobody, and those who profess to be alarmed at the result, should dismiss their fears.

The Daily Journal (Whig), September 13, 1852.

THE NATIONAL WOMAN'S RIGHTS CONVENTION.—After a duration of three mortal days this august Convention came to a " happy and peaceful end " Friday evening. . . . . All who attended any portion of the Convention, or the whole, will unite with us in pronouncing it the most dignified, orderly, and interesting deliberative body ever convened in this city. The officers, and most

---

* See Appendix for comments of *Syracuse Star* and *New York Herald.*

especially the distinguished woman who occupied the president's chair, evinced a thorough acquaintance with the duties of their station, and performed them in an admirable manner. . . . . No person acquainted with the doings of the assembly and capable of passing judgment in the matter, will deny there was a greater amount of talent in the Woman's Rights Convention than has characterized any public gathering in this State during ten years past, and probably a longer period, if ever. . . . . For compact logic, eloquent and correct expression, and the making of plain and frequent points, we have never met the equal of two or three of the number. The appearance of all before the audience was modest and unassuming, though prompt, energetic, and confident.

Business was brought forward, calmly deliberated upon, and discussed with unanimity, and in a spirit becoming true woman, and which would add an unknown dignity and consequent influence to the transactions of public associations of the "lords." . . . . The appearance of the platform was pleasing and really imposing in the extreme. The galaxy of bold women—for they were really bold, indeed they are daring women—presented a spectacle the like of which we never before witnessed. A glance at the "good old lady" who presided with so much dignity and propriety, and through the list to the youngest engaged in the cause, was enough to impress the unprejudiced beholder with the idea that there must be *something* in the movement. . . . . The audience was large and more impressive than has marked any convention ever held here. . . . . We feel in a mood to dip lightly into a discussion of the Woman's Rights question. . . . . Our sober second thought dictates that a three days' enlightenment at the intellectual feast spread by Beauty and Genius, may have turned our brains, and consequently we desist.

The discussions of this Convention did not end with its adjournment; its *sine die* had effect only upon the assembled body; for months afterward controversies and discussions, both public and private, took place. Clergymen of Syracuse and adjoining cities kept the interest glowing by their efforts to destroy the influence of the Convention by the cry of "infidel." A clergyman of Auburn not only preached against the Convention as "infidel," but as one holding authority over the consciences of his flock, boldly asserted that "no member of his congregation was tainted with the unholy doctrine of woman's rights."

Rev. Byron Sunderland, pastor of the Plymouth Congregational Church of Syracuse (since Chaplain of the United States Senate), characterized it in his sermon* as a "Bloomer Convention," taking for his text Deut. xxii. 5:

The woman shall not wear that which pertaineth unto man; neither shall a man put on a woman's garment; for all that do so are an abomination to the Lord thy God.

---

* This sermon was reviewed by Matilda Joslyn Gage, and a newspaper controversy between Mr. Sunderland, Mrs. Gage, and others inaugurated. For several months the press of the city was enlivened by these supplementary debates.

Mrs. Gage's reply, in the absence of the editor, appeared in *The Star*, in whose columns Rev. Mr. Sunderland's sermon had been given the public, calling forth the following letter :

WASHINGTON, *Nov.* 20, 1852.

The readers of *The Star* are aware that the editor does not sanction the ridiculous stuff which appeared in the issues of the 17th and 18th insts. over the signature of "M" upon the subject of "Woman's Rights," nor does he approve of its admission in the columns of the paper, and hereby disclaims having authorized the publication of any such emanations from the pit during his absence from home. When at his post he sometimes gives publicity to such communications for the purpose of showing up the fallacy of the positions taken, but never does he intend, so long as he has control of its columns, to allow *The Star* to become the medium of disseminating corrupt and unwholesome doctrines. Such doctrines have found and will continue to find means enough with which to do their duty in Syracuse without the aid of a *reputable* newspaper in their behalf; and the editor indeed is greatly surprised that those who temporarily fill his place, should lend *The Star* to so base purposes. We trust that these words (if discretion does not) will prevent further encroachment upon our good nature.

The Carson League, quoting the above editorial, says :

It is the first paragraph of the above letter that is noticeable. *The Star* is the organ of a certain class of ministers. Messrs. Sunderland and Ashley and *The Star* nestle in a common sympathy. It is significant of the character of their published sermons, that *The Star* stands alone in their defence. More significant still that *The Star* negates all replies to them, even by a lady. "*Put out the light,*" says the thief. "*Put out the light,*" says the assassin. "*Put out the light,*" says *The Star;* and verily if these gentlemen had their way, the light would go out in Egyptian darkness. It is wholesome doctrine, in the opinion of *The Star,* to deny woman's rights and negro's rights and the right of free discussion, to maintain them is to countenance "corrupt and unwholesome doctrines."

The subject of woman's rights somehow is attracting general attention. Rev. Mr. Sunderland, of this city, in a published sermon, sought to bring the whole matter into contempt, under cover of the ridicule of the Bloomer dress. His position is, that if God made man a little lower than the angels, He made woman a little lower still. His sermon we gave last week. This week we give a woman's reply to it. Nobly has she shown him up. We like her review. She treats his argument gravely, and answers it logically. She has touched the tender in him. He will begin to think women are somebody after all. We think he should have measured his *calibre* before making such a tilt. . . . . Regarding his condition as rather awkward, and finding it difficult to be quiet, he appears in the Friday *Star* with the following equivocal communication :

The Woman's Rights Question.—Mr. Editor: The last two numbers of *The Star* contain an article purporting to review my Sermon from Deut. xxii. 5, but the author does not appear. The article in question contains inaccuracies which should be noticed for the author's future benefit. If the author should turn out to be a man, I should have no objection to point out those inaccuracies through your columns. But if the writer is a lady, why, I really don't know yet what I shall do. If I thought she would consent to a personal interview, I should like to see her. Very truly,

Syracuse, Nov. 18. B. SUNDERLAND.

Some other person, under the head of " A Reader," addressed the following to *The Star*, which, in the editor's absence, was published :

How is this, Mr. Editor ? A few days since I read in your papers a sermon on woman's rights by Rev. Byron Sunderland. In your numbers of Wednesday and Thursday I found an able and respectful Review of that discourse—a Review which, in some points, is unanswerable, especially in the matter of Scripture and female dress. The dominie appealed to Scripture, and the reviewer " has him fast." I have heard it more than once intimated that the writer of this able, and in some instances most eloquent, review, is a lady of this city. Are we to understand that it is an article in the code of anti-progressive ethics, that the same article written by a man, will be answered by Mr. Sunderland, but if written by a woman, will not be answered ? I may have misunderstood Mr. Sunderland's note in this morning's *Star*, but I so understood it. If correctly understood no comment is necessary. A READER.

November 19, 1852.

Upon the expression of Mr. Sunderland's desire to meet the reviewer of his sermon, if a lady, and his willingness to continue the controversy, *The Star* finally opened its columns to Mrs. Gage, although delaying the publication of her articles, sometimes for weeks, to suit the dominie's convenience, and allowing his reply to appear in the same issue of the paper with her answer to his preceding article. Mr. Sunderland's reply to " A Reader " was characteristic of the spirit of the clergy, not only of their intolerance, but of their patronizing and insulting manner toward all persons who presumed to question either their authority or learning.

The impertinence of " A Reader " is quite characteristic. That individual probably knows as much about the Bible as a wild ass' colt, and is requested at this time to keep a proper distance. When a body is trying to find out and pay attention to a lady, it is not good manners for " A Reader " to be thrust in between us.

Rev. Mr. Ashley, rector of St. Paul's, the first Episcopal Church of Syracuse, also preached a sermon against woman, which was published in pamphlet form, and scattered over the State. This sermon was reviewed by a committee of ladies appointed by the Ladies' Lyceum. It was an able and lengthy document from the pen of the chairman of the committee, a member of the Episcopal Church, and was a significant sign of woman's growing independence of clerical authority. This sermon and its reply was also published by the city

35

press; the Church, the press, and the fireside all aiding in the contin
ued dissemination of the woman's rights discussion.

The publication of the proceedings of the Convention in pamphlet
form gave *The Star* occasion for a new fulmination which not only
farther showed the base character of this sheet, but which shocked
all devout minds by its patronizing tone toward the Deity. Both in
the Convention and its following debate, Syracuse well maintained
its character for radicalism.

MOB CONVENTION IN NEW YORK.

BROADWAY TABERNACLE, *Sept. 6 and 7,* 1853.

This week as already stated was one of unusual excitement in the
city of New York, as representatives of all the unpopular reforms
were holding their several conventions. The fact that the Anti-
Slavery Society held a meeting on Sunday morning, and Antoinette
Brown preached to five thousand people the same evening, called
out the denunciations of the religious press, which intensified the
mob spirit, culminating at last in the Woman's Rights Convention.
That portion of the secular press which had shown the most bitter
opposition to the anti-slavery cause, now manifested the same spirit
toward the enfranchisement of woman.

The leading papers in the United States were *The Tribune, The
Herald, The Times, The Evening Post,* and *The Express,* which
gave tone to the entire press of the country. All these journals
were edited by men of marked ability, each representing a different
class of thought in the community. *The Tribune* was independent,
and fearless in the expression of opinions on unpopular reforms; its
editor, Horace Greeley, ever ready for the consideration of new ideas,
was on many points the leader of liberal thought.

The Herald was recognized by reformers as at the head of the
opposition, and its diatribes were considered "Satanic." Its editor,
James Gordon Bennett, pandered to the lowest tastes in the community, not merely deriding reforms, but holding their advocates up
to the ridicule of a class too degraded to understand the meaning of
reform.

The Times held a middle position; established at a much later
date, its influence was not so great nor extended as either *The Tribune* or *The Herald.* It represented that large conservative class
that fears all change, and accepts the conditions of its own day and
generation, knowing that in all upheavals the wealthy class is the first
and greatest loser. From this source the mob spirit draws its in-

spiration. Violence being the outgrowth of superstition and despotism; the false morality and philosophy taught by the press and the pulpit are illustrated by the lower orders in hisses, groans, and brickbats. Although far below Horace Greeley in sagacity, intelligence, and conscience, Henry J. Raymond claimed for his paper a position superior in respectability. Having originated the present system of reporting, and thereby acquired his first reputation, Mr. Raymond prided himself upon reportorial sharpness, even at the expense of veracity and common self-respect. That woman so long degraded should dare to speak of injustice, so long defrauded of her social, civil, and political rights, should dare to demand some restitution, was to Mr. Raymond so fit a subject for ridicule that he could not refrain from making even such women as Lucretia Mott and Ernestine L. Rose targets for his irony.

The Express, an organ of the Democratic party, was in its debasement on a par with *The Herald* and *Times*, though each had different styles, more or less refined, of doing the same thing. Encouraged by these three papers, the mob element held high carnival through that eventful week. Starting in the anti-slavery and temperance meetings, they assembled at every session in the Woman's Rights Convention. Gentlemen and ladies alike who attempted to speak were interrupted by shouts, hisses, stamping, and cheers, rude remarks, and all manner of noisy demonstrations. The clergy, the press, and the rowdies combined to make those September days a disgrace to the metropolis, days never to be forgotten by those who endured the ridicule and persecution.

Although the Mayor with a large police force at his command made no show even of protecting the right of free speech, the editor of *The Tribune* sent forth his grand fulminations against bigotry, hypocrisy, and vulgarity in every issue of his journal. William Cullen Bryant, editor of *The Post*, one of the purest men that ever stood at the head of a daily paper, also spoke out grandly against mob law, and for the rights of woman. We have made this brief episode on the press, that our readers may see how characteristic are the comments of each paper that we give here and there in this chapter.

This Convention, interrupted throughout by the mob, has an unique and historic value of its own. It was the first overt exhibition of that public sentiment woman was then combating. The mob represented more than itself; it evidenced that general masculine opinion of woman, which condensed into law, forges the chains which enslave her. Owing to the turmoil we have no fair report of the proceedings; it was impossible for the representatives of the press to catch what was said, hence their reports, as well as the one issued by our Central Committee, are alike fragmentary. And yet with such a brilliant array of speakers of both men and women, it should have been one of our most interesting and successful Conventions. The Tabernacle, holding three thousand persons, was packed long before the hour announced. At ten o'clock Lucy Stone called the Convention to order, and presented a list of officers* nominated at a preliminary meeting, which was adopted. In this list we find England, Germany, and eleven States represented. The Rev. William Henry Channing opened the meeting with prayer. After which Mrs. Mott made a few appropriate remarks. Lucy Stone read a series of resolutions† which were accepted and laid on the table for discussion.

Charles Burleigh and Lydia A. Jenkins spoke briefly on the many grounds of opposition to this movement, which in all respects commends itself as one of the greatest reforms of the age.

Mr. GARRISON said: The first pertinent question is, what has brought us together ? Why have we come from the East and from the West, and from the North ? I was about to add, and from the South; but the South, alas ! is so cursed by the spirit of slavery, that there seems to be no vitality left there in regard to any enterprise, however good; hence the South is not represented on an occasion like this. It is because justice is outraged. We have met to protest against proud, rapacious, inexorable usurpation. What is this usurpation ? What is this oppression of which we complain ? Is it local ? Does it pertain to the city of New York, or to the Empire State ? No ! It is universal—broader than the Empire State—broader than our national domains—wide as the whole world, weighing on the entire human race. How old is the oppression which we have met to look in the face ? Is it of to-day ? Is it young in years, or is it as old as the world itself ? In all ages men have regarded women as inferior to themselves, and have robbed them of their co-equal rights. We are, therefore, contesting hoary tyranny—universal tyranny. And what follows, as a natural result ?

---

* *President.*—Lucretia Mott.

Vice-Presidents.—Ernestine L. Rose, New York; Paulina W. Davis, Rhode Island ; Clarina I. H. Nichols, Vermont ; Mary Jackson, England ; Caroline M. Severance, Ohio ; S. M. Booth, Wisconsin ; Wm. Lloyd Garrison, Massachusetts ; Mrs. J. B. Chapman, Indiana ; Charlotte Hubbard, Illinois ; Ruth Dugdale, Pennsylvania ; C. C. Burleigh, Connecticut ; Angelina G. Weld, New Jersey ; Mathilde Franceska Anneké, Germany.

Secretaries.—Lydia F. Fowler, Sidney Peirce, Oliver Johnson.

Business Committee.—Lucy Stone, Antoinette L. Brown, James Mott, Harriot K. Hunt, Mariana Johnson, Lydia Mott, Wendell Phillips, Sarah Hallock, Wm. H. Channing, Ruth Dugdale, Martha J. Tilden, Ernestine L. Rose, Elizabeth Oakes Smith.

Finance Committee.—Susan B. Anthony, Lydia A. Jenkins, Edward A. Stansbury.

† See Appendix.

That the land is beginning to be convulsed. The opposition to the movement is assuming a malignant, desperate, and satanic character; every missile of wickedness that can be hurled against it is used. The pulpit is excited, the press is aroused; Church and State are in arms to put down a movement on behalf of justice to one-half of the whole human race. (Laughter and cheers). The Bible, revered in our land as the inspired Word of God, is, by pulpit interpreters, made directly hostile to what we are endeavoring to obtain as a measure of right and justice; and the cry of infidelity is heard on the right hand and on the left, in order to combine public opinion so as to extinguish the movement.

Now, beloved, let us not imagine that any strange thing has happened to us. We are but passing through one of the world's great crises; we, too, in our day, are permitted to contend with spiritual wickedness in high places—with principalities and powers. What reform was ever yet begun and carried on with any reputation in the day thereof ? What reform, however glorious and divine, was ever advocated at the outset with rejoicing ? And if they have called the Master of the house Beelzebub, how much more them of his household ? (Cheers and stamping).

I have been derisively called a *"Woman's Rights Man."* I know no such distinction. I claim to be a HUMAN RIGHTS MAN, and wherever there is a human being, I see God-given rights inherent in that being whatever may be the sex or complexion.

To the excellence of the movement God has given witnesses in abundance, on the right hand and on the left. Show me a cause anathematized by the chief priests, the scribes, and the pharisees; which politicians and demagogues endeavor to crush, which reptiles and serpents in human flesh try to spread their slime over, and hiss down, and I will show you a cause which God loves, and angels contemplate with admiration. Such is our movement. Do you want the compliments of the satanic press, *The New York Times, Express,* and *Herald ?* (Roars of laughter). If you want the compliments of such journals, you will be bad enough to take a place among the very vilest and lowest of the human race. They are animated by a brutal, cowardly, and devilish spirit. Let us rejoice at the manifestation ! Not for the wickedness, but at the evidence thus afforded by God, that our cause is of Heaven, and therefore has on its side all the power and might of God, and in due season is destined to have a glorious triumph !

CHARLES C. BURLEIGH said: There is a feeling to-day that woman has some rights, that she has some reason to complain of the present relation in which she is placed. In this country we congratulate ourselves that woman occupies a higher position than elsewhere, although some think it would be a calamity to improve her condition still further, and mere fanaticism to raise her still higher.

The cry is—"unnatural !" The aspiration of woman for a better lot, say her oppressors, is not natural, it is abnormal ! So they say; but why not hear her on the matter ? Is she, the most interested party, to have no voice in the solution of a question which is to her of such overwhelming interest ? I ask, did God give woman aspirations which it is a sin for her to gratify ? Abnormal ! No, it is to be found everywhere. The man whose soul is so callous that he can hold his fellow-man as a slave, cries out (as in excuse) that the slave is contented. The autocrat exclaims that it is only a turbulent Kossuth or a factious Mazzini who feels that uneasy discontent which preys not on the hearts of his millions of legal slaves. Will that be, to us, an argument that the tyrant is in the right ? No ! the aspirations to liberty and justice are universal, and ever though the volcanic blaze breaks into the air only through the loftiest mountain peaks, the volcano is in itself an index to the ocean of molten fire that boils inaudibly beneath it. And so the deep discontent of humble millions breaks through the mountain-minds of their great leaders. Woman is a part of the human commonwealth; why deprive her of a voice in its government ? Woman herself, a component part of the community, must be called into the councils which direct it, else a wrong is done her, the responsibility of which lies heavily on those who do it. We ask rights for woman, because she has a human nature, and it is not only ungenerous and unmanly, but in the highest degree unjust to banish her from the discussion of questions which so nearly and dearly concern her, and in which nature, reason, and God have announced that she should have a voice.

Either there is a distinction between the sphere of man and that of woman, or there is not. If there is, it is unfair to have one determine both; if there is not, why does tyrannous custom separate her ? The dilemma is clear, and can not be escaped. Both should be called into counsel, every note in the scale of harmony should be sounded; and to say that hers, because an octave higher, should not be heard, is downright nonsense. (Rousing cheers and laughter). We claim for woman simply the right to decide her own sphere, or, in conjunction with man, to determine what should be the relative position of both.

W. H. CHANNING said: When I was returning from the first Woman's Rights Meeting, at Worcester, a friend said to me, "I intend getting up a Man's Rights Society; you misunderstand the matter; all the efforts of society are for the elevation of woman, and man has to perform the drudgery. The consequence is, the women are far better educated than the men." The answer was obvious. "If women are, according to your admission, fitted for the higher plane, why keep them on the lower ?" My friend then went on to say, that the whole of this scheme was considered to be of the most morally visionary character, and the proof of this feeling was the slight opposition it met, "for," said he "if it were looked on by society as serious, it would be at once, and forcibly, opposed in the church, by the press, in all public assemblies and private circles." Now, the object of this, and all such conventions, is to prove that we have made up our minds as regards operation and method; that we have looked clearly into the future; and that we have at heart this movement, as we have no other of the day, believing that out of this central agitation of society will come healthful issues of life. The inhabitants of Eastern India speak of a process for gaining immortality, namely, churning together the sea and the earth. They say the gods had the serpent by the head, and the devils had it by the tail, and out of the churning of the foam came the waters of immortality. The movement we are engaged in, may be typified by the Indian allegory; and out of the commotion we make shall be drawn a new principle which shall be one of immortal growth to all society. (Stamping, cheers, and laughter).

As regards the differences between men and women, we say that out of them grows union, not separation. Every organ of the body is double; in the pulsations of the heart a double machinery is used, there is a double auricle and a double ventricle. It is so in the inspirations which flow from God to society; they must pass twice, once through the heart of man, once through the heart of woman; they must stream through the reforming and through the conservative organ; and thus, out of the very difference which exists between man and woman, arises the necessity for their co-operation. It has never been asserted that man and woman are alike; if they were, where would be the necessity for urging the claims of the one ? No; they differ, and for that very reason it is, that only through the action of both, can the fullness of their being find development and expression. We know that woman exerts an influence on man, as man does on woman, to call forth his latent resources. In the difference, we find a call for union. And to this union we perceive no limit; on the contrary, whatever necessity there is for the combination in the private, there is the same necessity for it in the public sphere. (Long continued stamping and cheers).

And now I will meet the two great objections made. It is not objectionable, it is said, that woman, in some spheres of life, should give an expression of her intellect; but, on the platform, she loses her character of woman, and becomes incidentally masculine. Just observe the practical absurdities of which society is guilty. The largest assemblies greet with clamors Jenny Lind, when she enchains the ear and exalts the soul with the sublime strain, "I know that my Redeemer liveth"; but when Mrs. Mott or Miss Brown stands with a simple voice, and in the spirit of truth, to make manifest the honor due to our Redeemer, rowdies hiss, and respectable Christians veil their faces ! So, woman can sing, but not speak, that "our Redeemer liveth." Again, the great men of our land do not consider it unworthy of their character to take from Fanny Ellsler what she makes by the movement of her limbs, by a mere mechanical action,* to aid in erecting a column to commemorate our struggles for liberty. The dollars are received and built into the column; but when Mrs. Rose or Mrs. Foster, who feels the spirit of justice within her, and who has felt the injustice of the laws, stands up to show truth and justice, and build a spiritual column, she is out of her sphere ! and the honorable men turn aside, and leave her to be the victim of rowdyism, disorder, and lawlessness ! It is not out of character that Fanny Kemble should read Shakespeare on the stage, to large circles. The exercise of the voice on the stage is womanly, while she gives out the thoughts of another; but suppose (and it is not unsupposable) a living female Shakespeare to appear on a platform, and utter her inspirations, delicacy is shocked, decency is outraged, and society turns away in disgust ! Such are the consistencies of the nineteenth century ! (Great uproar).

---

* Fanny Ellsler danced for the Bunker Hill monument.

This is simply and merely prejudice, and it reminds me of the proverb, "If you would behold the stars aright, blow out your own taper." I say there is a special reason why woman should come forward as a speaker; because she has a power of eloquence which man has not, arising from the fineness of her organization and the intuitive power of her soul; and I charge any man with arrogance, if he pretend to match himself in this respect with many women here, and thousands throughout our country. (Hissing). I take it, the hissing comes from men who never had a mother to love and honor, a sister to protect, and who never knew the worth of a wife. Woman's power to cut to the quick and touch the conscience, is beautifully accompanied by her unmatched adaptation to pour balm into the wound; and though the flame she applies may burn into the soul, it also affords a light to the conscience which never can be dimmed.

There is an exquisite picture by Retsch, which represents angels showering roses on devils; to the angels they are roses, but the devils writhe under them as under fire. On sinful souls the words of women fall as coals from the altar of God. And here let me offer my humble gratitude to the women who have borne the brunt of the test with the calm courage which women alone can exhibit; to the women who have taught us that, as daughters of God, they are the equals of His children everywhere on earth. (Cheers and stamping).

Let me add another word upon this interference, or, rather, entrance of woman into the sphere of politics. As a spiritual being, her duties are like those of man; but, inasmuch as she is different from man, man can not discharge them; and if there be any truth in holding (as our institutions do), that the voice of the whole is the nearest approach we can make to eternal truth, we, of course, can not arrive at it till woman, as well as man, is heard in the search for it. God, not man, nor herself, made her woman; there is nothing arbitrary in the distinction; and let the true woman go where she may, she will retain her womanhood. We wish to see her enter into politics, not to degrade herself, but to bring them up to her own level of simple-heartedness and purity of soul. Can man ever raise them to that lofty height? Never! woman alone can do it; it is a work reserved for her, and by her and her alone will it be done. (Roars of laughter).

Whose exploits leave the brightest lines of moral courage on the historic page? Those of woman! When the French had broken through the barriers, the maid of Saragossa rushed to the breach. The demand of the invader came to Palafox, and he trembled; but what the heart of man was unequal to, the courage of woman could perform, and the answer of the heroic maiden was, "War to the knife!" And so, always when man has faltered, woman, earnest and simple-hearted, has answered, War to the knife with evil! (A frightful yell from the gallery.) I perceive my friend is anxious to hear a woman speak to him as only a woman can. I will soon give way and let him be gratified; but, first, I will tell him an anecdote. A woman once told me she never saw a horse so wild that she could not tame him. I asked her how, and she answered, "Simply by whispering in his ear." Our wild friend in the gallery will probably receive some benefit listening to the voice of a woman, if his ears be only long enough to hear her. (Prolonged cheers).

ANTOINETTE BROWN said: Our cause is progressing triumphantly; and yet it is not without some to oppose it. Who are they? Persons utterly ignorant of the claims which its advocates advance, ignorant alike of the wrongs existing and of the remedy proposed. They suppose that a few mad-cap reformers are endeavoring to overthrow dame Nature, to invert society, to play the part of merciless innovators to imperil religion, to place all civil and religious freedom in jeopardy; that if our ends were accomplished all the public and private virtues would be melted as in a crucible and thrown upon the ground, thence to cry aloud to heaven like the blood of righteous Abel. Were it not that curiosity is largely developed in this class, they would go down to their graves wholly uninformed of our true principles, motives, and aims. They look upon us as black beetles or death's-heads, to be turned away from with horror; but their curiosity overcomes their repugnance, and they would investigate some of our properties, as a naturalist does those of a noxious animal. (Cheers and laughter).

There is another class, that of genuine bigots, with hearts so ossified that no room can be found for one noble and expansive principle within those little stony cells. Many of this class may be persons of excellent intentions; they would do us good if they could, but they approach us with somewhat of the feeling with which Miss Ophelia regarded Topsy, the abhorrence that is experienced on drawing near a large black spider. They try to show us our errors, but if we attempt to justify by argument the ground we have taken, they cry aloud that we are obstinate and unreasonable, especially when we quote text for text, as Christ did when talking with a certain person of old.

But the most hopeless and spiteful of our opponents is that large class of women whose merits are not their own; who have acquired some influence in society, not by any noble thoughts they have framed and uttered, not by any great deed they have done, but by the accident of having fathers, brothers, or husbands whose wealth elevates them to the highest wave of fashion, and there enables them to roll in luxurious and indolent pomp, like Venus newly risen from the ocean. They feel how much easier it is to receive the incense of honor and respect (however insincerely paid to them) without any effort of their own, than to undergo the patient toil after excellence which wrings from the heart of all that homage of true honor which can not be denied to it. They, unused to any noble labor (as all labor is), either physical or mental, will be careful, to a degree of splenetic antagonism, how they will allow the introduction, into the acknowledged rights and duties of their sex, of a new element which may establish the necessity of their being themselves energetic and efficient. We need never hope to find any of this class change, until compelled to do so by public sentiment. The opposition here is really rabid. Intellectual women! oh, they are monsters! As soon allow wild beasts to roam at large as these to be let loose on society. Like lions and tigers, keep them in their menagerie; perhaps they needn't be actually chained, but see that they are well secured in their cages! (Stamping, groans, and laughter).

These are far more bitterly hostile than the men of small proportions, who are willing to have a great woman tower above them from time to time—as a Madame de Stael. Such a case, however, they would rank as an exception, not admit as a rule. To allow women to stand every day in the foremost lines of intellect and ability, is a thought altogether too expansive to be entertained by them.

Such are the oppositions we meet; but they are all melting down like frost-work before the morning sun. The day is dawning when the intellect of woman shall be recognized as well as that of man, and when her rights shall meet an equal and cordial acknowledgment. The greatest wrong and injustice ever done to woman is that done to her intellectual nature. This, like Goliath among the Philistines, overtops all the rest. Drones are but the robbers of the hive; ladies educated to no purpose are but surfeited to a dronish condition on the sweets of literature. Such minds are not developed, but molded in a fashionable pattern.

LUCY STONE said: It has been stated that we women were not fit for anything but to stay in the house! I look over the events of the last five years, and almost smile at the confutation of this statement which they supply. Let it not be supposed that I wish to depreciate the value of house-duties, or the worth of the woman who fitly discharges them. No! I think that any woman who stands on the throne of her own house, dispensing there the virtues of love, charity, and peace, and sends out of it into the world good men, who may help to make the world better, occupies a higher position than any crowned head. However, we said women could do more; they could enter the professions, and there serve society and do themselves honor. We said that women could be doctors of medicine. Well, we can now prove the statement by fact. Harriot K. Hunt is among us to-day, who, by recognized attainment and successful practice, has shown that women can be physicians, and good ones. You have in your city two women who are good physicians; there are female medical colleges, with their classes, as well ordered, and showing as good a proficiency as any classes of men. Thus that point is gained. It was said women could not be merchants. We thought they could; we saw nothing to prevent women from using the power of calculation, the knowledge of goods, and the industry necessary to make a successful trader. Here, again, we have abundant examples. Many women could be pointed to whose energy and ability for business have repaired the losses of their less competent husbands. I will mention a particular case. Mrs. Tyndal, of Lowell, Mass., has for years carried on business in a quiet way; she has made herself rich by conducting a ladies' shoe store in Lowell. She said to herself: "What is to hinder me from going into this business? I should know ladies' shoes, whether they were good or bad, and what price they can bring. The ladies should support me." And so they did, and that woman has given a proof that her sex does not incapacitate for successful mercantile operations.

It is said women could not be ministers of religion. Last Sunday, at Metropolitan Hall, Antoinette L. Brown conducted divine service, and was joined in it by the largest congregation assembled within the walls of any building in this city. (Hisses). Some men hiss who had no mothers to teach them better. But I tell you that some men in New York, knowing that they can hear the word of God from a woman, as well as from a man, have called her to be their pastor, and she is to be ordained in this month. Some of you reporters said she was a Unitarian, but it is not so; she is among the most orthodox, and so is her church.

We have caused woman's right to address an audience to be more fully recognized than before. I once addressed an assemblage of men, and did so without giving previous notice, because I feared the opposition of prejudice. A lady who was among the audience said to me afterward, "How could you do it ? My blood ran cold when I saw you up there among those men!" "Why," I asked, "are they bad men ?" "Oh, no! my own husband is one of them; but to see a woman mixing among men in promiscuous meetings, it was horrible!" That was six or seven years ago last fall; and that self-same woman, in Columbus, Ohio, was chosen to preside over a temperance meeting of men and women; yes, and she took the chair without the least objection! In Chicago, a woman is cashier of a bank; and the men gave her a majority of three hundred votes over her man-competitor. In another State, a woman is register of deeds. Women can be editors; two sit behind me, Paulina W. Davis and Mrs. Nichols. Thus we have an accumulation of *facts* to support our claims and our arguments.

Daily Tribune, Sept. 7, 1853.

The Woman's Rights Convention was somewhat disturbed last evening by persons whose ideas of the rights of free speech are these: two thousand people assemble to hear a given public question discussed under distinct announcement that certain persons whose general views are well known, are to speak throughout the evening. At least nineteen-twentieths come to hear those announced speakers, and will be bitterly disappointed if the opportunity be not afforded them. But one-twentieth have bought tickets and taken seats on purpose to prevent the hearing of those speakers, by hissing, yelling, and stamping, and all manner of unseemly interruptions. Under such circumstances, which should prevail; the right of the speakers to be heard and the great body of the audience to hear them according to the announcement, or the will of the disturbers who choose to say that nineteen out of twenty shall not have what they have paid for, and what the promised speakers are most willing to give them ?

To state the case exactly as it is, precludes the necessity of arguing it. We rejoice to say that the will of the great majority prevailed, and that the discussion which was marked in its earlier days by occasional tumult was closed in good order, and amid hushed and gratified attention. We ought, perhaps, to return thanks to the disturbers for so stirring the souls of the speakers that their words came gushing forth from their lips with exceeding fluency and power. We certainly never before heard Antoinette Brown, Mrs. Rose, and Lucy Stone speak with such power and unction as *last night.* It was never before so transparent that a hiss or a blackguard yell was the only answer that the case admitted of, and when Lucy Stone closed the discussion with some pungent, yet pathetic remarks on the sort of opposition that had been manifest, it was evident that if any of the rowdies had an ant-hole in the bottom of his boot, he would inevitably have sunk through it and disappeared forever.

Herald, Sept. 7, 1853.

THE LAST VAGARY OF THE GREELEY CLIQUE—THE WOMEN, THEIR RIGHTS, AND THEIR CHAMPIONS.

The assemblage of rampant women which convened at the Tabernacle yesterday was an interesting phase in the comic history of the nineteenth century.

We saw, in broad daylight, in a public hall in the city of New York, a gathering of unsexed women—unsexed in mind all of them, and many in habiliments—publicly propounding the doctrine that they should be allowed to step out of their appropriate sphere, and mingle in the busy walks of every-day life, to the neglect of those duties which both human and divine law have assigned to them. We do not stop to argue against so ridiculous a set of ideas. We will only inquire who are to perform those duties which we and our fathers before us have imagined belonged solely to women. Is the world to be depopulated? Are there to be no more children? Or are we to adopt the French mode, which is too well known to need explanation?

Another reason why we will not answer the logic which is poured out from the lips of such persons as Lucy Stone, Mrs. Mott, Mrs. Amelia Bloomer, and their male coadjutors, Greeley, Garrison, Oliver, Johnson, Burleigh, and others, is because they themselves do not believe in the truth or feasibility of the doctrines they utter. In some cases eccentricity is a harmless disease; but the idiosyncrasies of these people spring from another source. They admit the principle that fame and infamy are synonymous terms. Disappointed in their struggle for the first, they grasp the last, and at the same time pocket all the money they can wring from the " barren fools " who can be found in any community eager to grasp at any doctrine which is novel, no matter how outrageous it may be. They are continually advertising from their platforms some "Thrilling Narrative," or "Account of the Adventures of a Fugitive," which may be had at the low price of one shilling each, or eight dollars per hundred. Recently they have discovered that the great body of their audiences came only to be amused, and they have therefore imposed an admission fee. Lucy Stone, who is a shrewd Yankee, has gone a step further, and in her management of the business of the " Woman's Rights Convention," has provided for season tickets, to be had at "the extremely low price of two shillings."

It is almost needless for us to say that these women are entirely devoid of personal attractions. They are generally thin maiden ladies, or women who perhaps have been disappointed in their endeavors to appropriate the breeches and the rights of their unlucky lords; the first class having found it utterly impossible to induce any young or old man into the matrimonial noose, have turned out upon the world, and are now endeavoring to revenge themselves upon the sex who have slighted them. The second, having been dethroned from their empire over the hearts of their husbands, for reasons which may easily be imagined, go vagabond izing over the country, boring unfortunate audiences with long essays lacking point or meaning, and amusing only from the impudence displayed by the speakers in putting them forth in a civilized country. They violate the rules of decency and taste by attiring themselves in eccentric habiliments, which hang loosely and inelegantly upon their forms, making that which we have been educated to respect, to love, and to admire, only an object of aversion and disgust. A few of these unfortunate women have awoke from their momentary trance, and quickly returned to the dress of decent society; but we saw yesterday many disciples of the Bloomer school at the Tabernacle. There was yesterday, and there will be to-day, a wide field for all such at the Tabernacle.

The "compliments" showered upon *The Herald* by the wretched Garrison yesterday afternoon, at the Woman's Wrong Convention, fully show that he and his coadjutors, Greeley and the rest, are beginning to feel the truth of our remarks during the time they have been amusing our citizens. His insane attack shows that our course has been the true one.

To the credit of Mr. Greeley, he made an effort to suppress the disturbance. Raymond, of *The Times*, gave the following report:

Times, September 8, 1853.

(Evening of the first day, Mrs. Rose speaking).

Mr. Greeley was among the audience, and in passing through the gallery, it was supposed he remonstrated with the sibillating gentlemen, and a great rumpus was raised. Some cheered the peace-maker, others hissed, the rush collected about the scene of the disturbance, and all proceedings were interrupted. Mrs. Rose suspended her remarks for a few moments, but presently said : "Friends, be seated, and I will continue." The audience would not listen, however. The uproar still continued. Cries of "Order," "Mrs. President," "Put him out," "Hurrah !" hisses, groans, and cheers. Mr. Greeley and a policeman presently succeeded in stilling the tumult, the officer collaring several men and compelling them to keep quiet. Mrs. Rose resumed and continued her remarks.

SECOND DAY, MORNING SESSION, Opened at 10 A.M.

MRS. MOTT: The uproar and confusion which attended the close of our proceedings of last night, although much to be regretted, as indicating an unreasonable and unreasoning disposition on the part of some, to close their ears against the truth, or rather, to drown its voice by vulgar clamor, yet, when viewed aright, and in some phases, present to us matter of congratulation. I do suppose that never, at any meeting, was public propriety more outraged, than at ours of last evening. I suppose no transactions of a body assembled to deliberate, were ever more outrageously invaded by an attempt to turn them into a mere tumult; yet, though voices were loud and angry, and the evil passions exhibited themselves with much of that quality to affright, which usually, if not always, attends their exhibition, not a scream was heard from any woman, nor did any of the "weaker sex" exhibit the slightest terror, or even alarm at the violent manifestations which invaded the peace of our assemblage.

I felicitate the women on this exhibition of fortitude; of calm moral courage. Should not our opponents, if they have any reason among them, reflect that these exhibitions are, in reality, some of the strongest arguments that can be offered to support the claims which we stand here to advocate? Do they not show, on the one hand, that men, by whom such an overpowering superiority is arrogated, can betimes demean themselves in such a way as to show that they are wholly unfit for the lofty functions which they demand as their exclusive right? And, on the other hand, do they not conclusively show, that women are possessed of, at least, some of those qualities which assist in calmness of deliberation during times of excitement and even danger? I think it was really a beautiful sight to see how calm the women remained during last evening's excitement; their self-possession I consider something truly admirable. I know that in the tumult and noise it would have been vain for any woman to raise her voice in an attempt to check it. Indeed, I am satisfied the outrage was predetermined, and I regret that the aid of the police had to be called in to quell it. Had there been here a company of women who were taught to rely upon others, they would, doubtless, have felt bound to scream for "their protectors"; but the self-reliance displayed, which must have its basis in a consciousness of the truth and justice of our cause, and which kept the members of the Convention unmoved, amid all the prevailing confusion, gives us matter of real congratulation. Let us rejoice in this, my friends; and let us remember, that when we have a true cause—while our cause rests on the basis of right—we have nothing to fear, but may go on unmoved by all these petty circumstances, by which we may be surrounded.

Mr. BURLEIGH said: A request was made last night by some person, I don't know who, or rather a challenge was offered, that three good reasons should be given why women should vote. Perhaps, had the person making this demand had this question put to him, namely: "What reasons are there why men should vote?" he would have considered them so self-evident as to make any answer superfluous. Yet it would be found difficult, I apprehend, to assign any reason why men should vote, which would not be found to be an equally good one for extending the elective franchise to women. He asked, however, why women should be allowed to take a part in the civil government of the country. This question will, I doubt not, be answered to-day by some one more able than myself; and if the person who asked it be present, and open to conviction, he will hear reasons sufficient to convince him.

Why should women vote? She should vote, first, because she has to bear her portion of the burdens imposed by the government which the voting makes. Is not this one reason amply sufficient for any honest-minded man? Taxation and representation go hand in hand, says a principle of our body politic. Is woman represented? No. Is woman taxed? Yes. How is that? Is it consistent with the profession; and, if there were no profession, is it right, is it just? The burden falls equally on woman and her brother; but he has all the power of applying it; she must bear it to the end of the journey, and then know nothing, say nothing, as to how it is to be disposed of. What kind of justice is that? Were woman exempted from those burdens, why, then, the exemption would so far be an argument on the other side; although even that would fail on investigation, because other equally immutable principles show that neither exemption nor representation is the condition in which any portion of the political body should be allowed to remain. But where there is no exemption, but a full apportionment of the burden, and, at the same time, no representation, the absurdity of injustice has reached its climax. (Laughter and cheers).

In the second place, woman should vote, because she ought to be a sharer in those benefits which government is formed to confer upon the governed. She has property which the government must protect, a person which it must defend, and rights which it is bound to secure. Were the millennium arrived, were there no such thing as selfishness on earth; were simple truth and justice the prominent elements in all men's minds, and the guiding spirit of all men's actions, then indeed might woman confide herself to man; then might she rely on him to secure those governmental benefits which are her due, as a portion of the general community. But is this the state of things? Alas! not yet; and, until it is, the horrible injustice of the laws which exclude woman from a share in making them, while they are her only security for the advantages she ought to enjoy, will never cease crying aloud to all men for purification. One of the great aims of all government, one of the strong considerations which alone makes its restrictions endurable, is the assurance which it gives the governed, that the sum of their happiness, and even of their liberty, shall, by individual restraints, become greater on the whole. It holds out a bonus to society, or rather, to its individual members, "Give me this little, and I will give you in exchange this much." Thus each individual puts a stake into the common fund, has an interest in the common weal, which demands careful watching. Can woman watch the large, the all-absorbing interest she has at stake? She, above all, the most tender, the most sensitive of beings, the most keenly alive to wrong, to insult, to oppression, to aught that bruises her womanly nature, can she give a careful eye to the disposal of those important questions which touch the very core of her heart? Why, when reduced to these, its naked dimensions, the injustice seems so horrible, as not to be credible, and did we not know the facts, we would find it hard to believe that man, made in the image of his Maker, could violate justice so barbarously. Surely woman lies under no moral obligation to any laws which, wanting her assent, yet assume to control her every action, word, and even thought. Her property, her person, all her rights, her most sacred affections, come within the province of those enactments; yet she can have no voice, no weight in determining what those enactments shall be. (Stamping and groans).

In the third place, woman is entitled to vote, because she is liable to all the penalties imposed by government. Not only is it that she confides, or rather, that government compels her to confide to it, the custody of person, property, rights, and all dearest interests, but it goes a step further, and thus adds another link (though quite a superfluous one) to the adamantine chain of argument which it supplies to bind down its own injustice. It stands not merely in a passive or receiving relation to woman, it becomes the active arbiter of her doom; it declares itself competent to lay hands on her, to shut her up in prison, to take away her life, the life of one who has made with it no compact—giving such awful power—the life of one who never consented to the laws which assert over her so terrible a supremacy! All the principles already applied come in here with perhaps renewed force, as being the arbiters of a question which may be regarded by some as of a still more absorbing interest, although to woman it may not be so, for when did she value life more highly than tenderness, domestic confidence, and affection? (Prolonged laughter).

Dr. H. K. ROOT, of New York, rose in his place among the audience and declared his intention of arguing against the principles and demands of the Convention. Being requested to take the rostrum, he did so, and spoke thus:

Mrs. President and Ladies: I do not come here with the slightest intention of offering to the ladies any opposition for mere opposition's sake. If they are proved to have more knowledge and intelligence than men, let them govern! My purpose, ladies, is to try and attain truth, which, I think, will not be found favorable to the views you express. I come, rather, as a matter of intelligence than opposition. I do not come here for the purpose of opposing the ladies too much; but as the question was not only open yesterday, but still is for discussion, I maintain that if the ladies have more intelligence, and more energy, and science than the male sex, they should rule. I think I can give three reasons why men should vote, and one why woman should not vote. (Cheers).

My first reason is, because there was an original command from God that man should rule. It may be supposed that we are in the garden of Eden now, as in the days of Adam and Eve. Now, it will be remembered, when Adam and Eve fell, Adam, because Eve tempted him, was placed in the garden as its keeper, and it was necessary in those days, as it is now, that woman should be a helpmeet for him; but you recollect that by the eating of the forbidden fruit, original sin came into the world. What was the expression of God to Adam? He says in the third chapter of Genesis, 17th verse: "Because thou hast hearkened unto the voice of thy wife, and hast eaten of the tree of which I commanded thee, saying, thou shalt not eat of it: cursed is the ground for thy sake; in sorrow shalt thou eat of it all the days of thy life." Now, permit us to be in the relation that Adam and Eve were originally. It behooves the male sex to answer the objections of the female sex—not that we wish to combat them in public; but it behooves us, as a matter of justice, to put the question on a right foundation. It may be necessary, in ninety-nine cases out of a hundred, that the ladies should be here, but in the hundredth it may be necessary that man should say, "Thus far shalt thou go, and no farther." You see the original cause of sin was because man, being placed in the garden, gave way to woman, and the curse fell upon him; the original cause of sin was because man gave up his judgment to woman; and it may be, if we now give up our rights to woman, some great calamity may fall upon us. Had woman only sinned, perhaps we might still have been in Eden. (Great applause).

My second reason why man should vote is the law of physical force over the woman—because man's strength is greater than woman's.

The third reason is, because if women enter the field of competition with men, it may lead not only to domestic unhappiness, but a great many other ill feelings. And I will give another reason why men should be dictators. If woman says she shall vote, and man says she sha'n't, he is in duty bound to maintain what he says. If he says she sha'n't, that is reason enough why she should not." (Cheers and laughter).

ALEXANDER PARKER, of Philadelphia, rose in his place, and on being invited to the platform, spoke thus:

Adam was the first gardener in the world; he belonged to my business, for I am a gardener—a business I took up myself, so I should have something to say about the garden of Eden. Well, I have often thought about the fall, and I have often pictured it in this manner: the very moment the charge was given not to do such a thing, that was just the time they wanted to do it. (Prolonged cheers).

It is often said that woman has a great deal of curiosity, and no doubt it was whispered into her ear, that the moment she ate of the forbidden fruit she should become a god. Now, I have seen more reason this morning why women should vote than I have ever seen before. In Pennsylvania a man has got but one vote, while a woman has three—her husband's and her two sons'. Eve tried to get over the temptation, but she could not; and so, after many efforts, she clutched the apple she looked at so, and so, and she reached out to it; afraid at first, but at last she laid hold of it, and, seeing that her fear was over, she kissed its lovely cheek. Then she ran to Adam, and said it was good, and he ate of it. Then his eyes were opened and he saw he was naked, and ran and hid himself. He tried to hide himself among the bushes, but he could not deny the eating of it, because the core was sticking in his throat, and it is sticking there still; but woman has not got the core sticking in her throat. Well, Adam pretended to be innocent, like all the rest of mankind, and said it was not he, but the woman that did it. No, no; it was not his fault, it was the woman who gave it to him. Oh, yes! he was not to blame, no more than any lord of creation. Well, then, there was a curse upon him; but there was a promise to woman that her seed should bruise the head of the serpent with her heel. (Shouts of laughter).

Mrs. NICHOLS: As to the text which says that woman must obey her husband, surely that is no reason why she should obey all the bachelors and other women's husbands in the community. My husband would have me advocate the claims I do, therefore by the logic of our cause my husband wishes me to vote, and, according to the Scripture, the gentleman must, even in his own reasoning, allow me the right to vote. In one place the gentleman said that woman had already turned the world over; and that man must be cautious not to allow her to do so again. Perhaps, if he reconsidered these statements he might be willing to retract the latter; because, if she turned the world over once and put the wrong side up, he ought now to allow her to turn it back, that she may bring the right side up again.

Mrs. ROSE said: As to the personal property, after all debts and liabilities are discharged, the widow receives one-half of it; and, in addition, the law kindly allows her her own wearing apparel, her own ornaments, proper to her station, one bed, with appurtenances for the same; a stove, the Bible, family pictures, and all the school-books; also, all spinning-wheels and weaving-looms, one table, six chairs, tea cups and saucers, one tea-pot, one sugar dish, and six spoons. (Much laughter). But the law does not inform us whether they are to be tea or table spoons; nor does the law make any provision for kettles, sauce-pans, and all such necessary things. But the presumption seems to be that the spoons meant are teaspoons; for, as ladies are generally considered very delicate, the law presumed that a widow might live on tea only; but spinning-wheels and weaving-looms are very necessary articles for ladies nowadays. (Hissing and great confusion). Why, you need not hiss, for I am expounding the law. These wise law-makers, who seem to have lived somewhere about the time of the flood, did not dream of spinning and weaving by steam-power. When our great-great-grandmothers had to weave every article of apparel worn

36

by the family, it was, no doubt, considered a very good law to allow the widow the possession of the spinning-wheels and the weaving-looms. But, unfortunately for some laws, man is a progressive being; his belief, opinions, habits, manners, and customs change, and so do spinning-wheels and weaving-looms; and, with men and things, law must change too, for what is the value of a law when man has outgrown it? As well might you bring him to the use of his baby clothes, because they once fitted him, as to keep him to such a law. No. Laws, when man has outgrown them, are fit only to be cast aside among the things that were.

But I must not forget, the law allows the widow something more. She is allowed one cow, all sheep to the number of ten, with the fleeces and the cloth from the same, two swine, and the pork therefrom. (Great laughter). My friends, do not say that I stand here to make these laws ridiculous. No; if you laugh, it is at their own inherent ludicrousness; for I state them simply and truly as they are; for they are so ridiculous in themselves, that it is impossible to make them more so.

Mrs. NICHOLS said: As widow, too, the law bears heavily on woman. If her children have property, she is adjudged unworthy of their guardianship; and although the decree of God has made her the true and natural guardian of her children, she is obliged to pay from her scanty means to be constituted so by law.

I have conversed with judges and legislators, and tried to learn a reason for these things, but failed to find it. A noble man once gave me what he probably thought was a good one. " Women," he said to me, " can not earn as much as men!" We say they should be allowed to earn as much. They have the ability, and the means should not be shut out from them. I have heard of another man who held woman's industrial ability at a low rate. "His wife," he said, "had never been able to do anything but attend to her children." "How many have you?" he was asked; and the answer was, "Nine." Nine children to attend to! nine children cared for! and she could do nothing more, the wife of this most reasonable man. Now, which is of more importance to the community, the property which that reasonable husband made, or the nine children whom that mother brought, with affectionate and tender toil, through the perils of infancy and youth, until they were men and women? Which was of more importance to this land, the property which the father of George Washington amassed, or the George Washington whom a noble mother gave to his country? The name of Washington, his glorious deeds, and the enduring benefits he secured for us, still remain, and will long after the estates of Washington have passed from his name forever!

In the State of Vermont, a wife sought a divorce from her husband on the ground of his intemperance. They were persons moving among our highest circles—wealthy people; and the wife knew that she could, through the aid of her friends and relations, with the influence and sympathy of the community, obtain a divorce and a support for her children. That father carried away into Canada one child, a little girl, and paid three hundred dollars to a low, vile Frenchman, that he might keep her from her mother and friends. Three times her almost heart-broken mother went in search of her; twice in vain, but the third time she was found. So badly had the poor child been treated in the vile hands in which her father had placed her, that, when recovered, she was almost insensible; and when, by her mother's nursing care, her intelligence was at length restored, her joy at seeing her mother was so violent, that it was feared its excess might prove fatal. The case came into court, and the judge decided that the two daughters should be given to their mother, but that the custody of the son should be given to the father. She was acquitted of the least impropriety or indiscretion; yet, though the obscenity and profanity of her husband in his own family was shocking, and it was in the last degree painful to that high-minded woman to see her son brought up under the charge of such a man, the law decided that the unworthy father was the more proper guardian for the boy!

In the Green Mountain State a great many sermons have lately been preached on the text, "Wives, submit yourselves to your husbands." The remaining words, "in the Lord," are generally omitted; so that the text is made to appear like an injunction that the wives should submit to their husbands, whether they were in the Lord or in the devil. And the best of all is, that we are told that if we would be submissive, we could change our husbands from devils into angels.

Mrs. MOTT: I now introduce to the Convention Frances Dana Gage, of St. Louis, Mo., better known as "Aunt Fanny," the poet.

Mrs. GAGE said: This morning, when I was leaving my boarding-house, some one said to me, "So you are ready armed and equipped to go and fight the men." I was sorry, truly sorry, to hear the words—they fell heavily on my heart. I have no fight with men. I am a daughter, a sister, a wife, and a mother, and in all these relations I live in harmony with man. Neither I, nor any of the sisters with whom I am united in this movement, have any quarrel with men. What is it that we oppose? What do we seek to overturn? The bad laws and customs of society. These are our only enemies, and against these alone is our hostility directed; although they be " hallowed by time," we seek to eradicate them, because the day for which they were suited, if such ever existed, is long since gone by. The men, we may suppose, are above and beyond the laws, and we assail the laws only.

There is one law which I do not remember having heard any of my sisters touch upon, that is the Law of Wills, as far as it relates to married women, and as far as it allows a husband (which it fully does), along with his power to determine the lot of his wife while he is alive, also to control her when he is dead. Would any gentleman like to have that law reversed? Let me read to you a will after that odd fashion. It will fall on your ears, gentlemen, with as loud a tone of injustice as it does on mine:

WILL OF BRIDGET SMITH.—In the name of God, amen. I, Bridget Smith, being weak in body, though sound in mind, blessed be God for the same, do make and declare this my last will and testament. Item first: I give my soul to God, and my body to the earth, from which it came. Item second: I give to my beloved husband, John Smith, Sen., my Bible, and forty acres of wild land which I own in Bear Marsh, Ill., for the term of his natural life, when it shall descend to our son, John Smith, Jr. Item third: I give and bequeath to my daughter, Tabitha, my farm, house, outhouse, barns, and all the stock on said farm, situated in Pleasant Valley, and which said farm consists of 160 acres. I also give to my said daughter Tabitha, the wagons, carriages, harnesses, carts, plows, and all other property that shall be on said farm at the time of my death. Item fourth : I give to my son, John Smith, Jr., my family horse, my buggy, harness, and saddle, and also eighty acres of wild land which I own in the State of Iowa, for which I have a patent. Item fifth : I give to my beloved husband, John Smith, Sen., the use of the house in which we live, together with my bed, so long as he shall live, or remain my widower; but in case he shall die, or get married, then it is my will that my house and bed shall descend to my said daughter, Tabitha. Recommending my said husband to her care, whom I make the sole executrix of this my last will and testament, hereby revoking all others.

Signed, sealed, and proclaimed this —— day of ——, 1853, in the presence of John Doe and Richard Roe.

BRIDGET SMITH.

Would any of you like such power as that to be placed in our hands? Yet, is it not as fair that married women should dispose of their property, as that married men should dispose of theirs? It is true, the power thus given to husbands is not always used to the detriment of women, and this is frequently urged in support of the law. But I reply, that law is made for extreme cases; and while any such statutes remain on the books, no good man will cease to exert himself for their removal. I ask the right to vote, not because it would create antagonism, but because it would create harmony. I want to do away with antagonism by removing oppression, for where oppression exists, there antagonism must exist also.

ERNESTINE L. ROSE: In allusion to the law respecting wills, I wish to say that, according to the Revised Statutes of our State, a married woman has not a right to make a will. The law says that wills may be made by all persons, except idiots, persons of unsound mind, married women, and infants. Mark well, all but idiots, lunatics, married women, and infants. Male infants ought to consider it quite an insult to be placed in the same category with married women. No, a married woman has no right to bequeath a dollar of the property, no matter how much she may have brought into the marriage, or accumulated in it. Not a dollar to a friend, a relative, or even to her own child, to keep him from starving. And this is the law in the nineteenth century, in the enlightened United States, under a Republic that declares all men to be free and equal.

LUCY STONE: Just one word. I think Mrs. Rose is a little mistaken ; I wish to correct her by saying that of some States in—

Mrs. ROSE : I did not say this was the universal law ; I said it was the law in the State of New York.

LUCY STONE : I was not paying close attention, and must have been mistaken. In Massachusetts the law makes a married woman's will valid in two cases: the first is, where the consent of her husband is written on the will ; the second, where she wills all she has to her husband, in which case his written consent is not deemed requisite.

Dr. HARRIOT K. HUNT spoke on the fruitful theme of taxation without representation! and read her annual protest* to the authorities of Boston

---

* See p. 259.

against being compelled to submit to that injustice. She said: I wish to vote, that women may have, by law, an equal right with men in property. In October, 1851, I went to pay my taxes in Boston. Going into the Assessor's office, I saw a tall, thin, weak, stupid-looking Irish boy. It was near election time, and I looked at him scrutinizingly. He held in his hand a document, which, I found on inquiry, was one of naturalization; and this hopeful son of Erin was made a citizen of the United States, and he could have a voice in determining the destinies of this mighty nation, while thousands of intellectual women, daughters of the soil, no matter how intelligent, how respectable, or what amount of taxes they paid, were forced to be dumb!

Now, I am glad to pay my taxes, am glad that my profession enables me to pay them; but I would like very much to have a voice in directing what is to be done with the money I pay. I meditated on what I had seen, and, in 1852, when paying my taxes, I took to the Treasurer's office my protest.

The case of the Hon. Mrs. Norton before the English courts, then attracting much attention, was a fair exemplification of the injustice of the law to married women.

LUCY STONE said: I have before me, in a newspaper, a case which shows strongly the necessity for woman's legislating for herself. I mean the case of the Hon. Mrs. Norton, which lately transpired in a court in London, and which fully proves that it is never right for one class to legislate for another. There are, probably, few here who have not been made better and wiser by the beautiful things which have fallen from the pen of that lady. In 1836 her husband obtained a separation from her on the charge of infidelity. Eighteen years of a blameless life since, and the conviction every pure mind must feel, that nothing impure could ever dwell in a mind such as her productions show hers to be, will fully relieve her of any suspicion that she ever was guilty of acts justifying that charge. She was a woman of transcendent abilities; and her works brought her in £1,000 a year—sometimes more, sometimes less. This her husband procured to be paid over to himself, by securing the profits of her copyrights; and this husband allowed her only £400 a year! and, at last, refused to pay her even this sum; so that, for her necessary expenses, she was obliged to go into debt, and her debtors brought a suit against her husband, which was taken into court. In the court she stood before her husband's lawyer, and said to him: "If you are afraid of what I may say, beware how you ask me questions!" Wealth and power were against her, and the lawyer *did* ask questions which wrung from her what she had concealed for seventeen long years, and the world at last knew how her husband had kept the money she earned by her pen. She stood in court, and said: "I do not ask for rights; I have no rights, I have only wrongs. I will go abroad, and live with my son." Her husband had proposed to take her children from her, but she said: "I would rather starve than give them up." And for a time she did starve. I will read for you her poem of "Twilight," and you will all see what kind of woman has been so wronged, and has so suffered.

That woman, gifted, noble, and wealthy, with such great yearnings in her soul, whose heart was so bound up in her children, was thus robbed not only of her own rights, but also of theirs. Men! we can not trust you! You have deceived us too long! Since this movement began, *some* laws have been passed, securing to woman her personal property, but they are as nothing in the great reform that is needed. I can tell you a case. A woman married a man, whom she did not love, because he had a fortune. He died, and she married the man whom she loved before her first marriage. He died, too, and the fortune which was hers through her first husband was seized on by the relatives of the second, and she was left penniless in the wide world. Here, as in England, women earn large sums by their literary fame and talents; and I know a *man* who watches the post-office, and, because the Law gives him the power, secures the letters which contain the wages of his wife's intellectual toil, and pockets them for his own use.

I will conclude by reading a letter from an esteemed friend, Mr. Higginson. It proposes certain questions which I should wish to hear our enemies answer.

WORCESTER, *Sept.* 4, 1853.

DEAR FRIEND:—You are aware that domestic duties alone prevent my prolonging my stay in New York during the session of the Woman's Rights Convention. But you know, also, that all my sympathies are there. I hope you will have a large representation of the friends of the great movement—the most important of the century ; and that you will also assemble a good many of the opposition during the discussion. Perhaps from such opponents I might obtain answers to certain questions which have harassed my mind, and are the following:

If there be a woman's sphere, as a man's sphere, why has not woman an equal voice in fixing the limits ? If it be unwomanly for a girl to have a whole education, why is it not unwomanly for her to have even a half one ? Should she not be left where the Turkish women are left ? If women have sufficient political influence through their husbands and brothers, how is it that the worst laws are confessedly those relating to female property ? If politics are necessarily corrupting, ought not good men, as well as good women, to be exhorted to quit voting ?

If, however, man's theory be correct—that none should be appointed jurors but those whose occupations fit them to understand the matters in dispute—where is the propriety of empanneling a jury of men to decide on the right of a divorced mother to her child ? If it be proper for a woman to open her lips in jubilee to sing nonsense, how can it be improper for her to open them and speak sense ? These afford a sample of the questions to which I have been trying in vain to find an answer. If the reasonings of men on this subject are a fair specimen of the masculine intellect of the nineteenth century, I think it is certainly quite time to call in women to do the thinking.

Yours, respectfully and cordially,   T. W. HIGGINSON.

Miss LUCY STONE.

MATILDA JOSLYN GAGE cited the Convention to a case recently tried before the Court of Common Pleas of New York, as illustrating the husband's ownership of the wife, the Court deciding that the friends of a woman who hàd "harbored" and detained her from her husband, though with her own consent and desire, should pay him $10,000. He recovered this sum on the principle of ownership; the wife's services were due him, and he recovered their value.

Mrs. Gage also commented on the divorce laws, which she declared were less just in Christian than in Mohammedan countries. In those countries if the husband sues for a divorce he is obliged to restore the dower, but in Christian America the husband not only retains all the property in case he sues for a divorce, but where the wife, being the innocent party, sues, she even then receives neither property nor children, unless by an express decree of the court. She is alike punished, whether innocent or guilty. Mrs. Gage also discussed the question so often put, "What has woman to do with politics?" She said the country must look to women for its salvation.

Sojourner Truth, a tall colored woman, well known in anti-slavery circles, and called the Lybian Sybil, made her appearance on the platform. This was the signal for a fresh outburst from the mob; for at every session every man of them was promptly in his place, at twenty-five cents a head. And this was the one redeeming feature of this mob—it paid all expenses, and left a surplus in the treasury. Sojourner combined in herself, as an individual, the two most hated elements of humanity. She was black, and she was a woman, and all the insults that could be cast upon color and sex were together hurled at her; but there she stood, calm and dignified, a grand, wise woman, who could neither read nor write, and yet with deep insight could penetrate the very soul of the universe about her. As soon as the terrible turmoil was in a measure quelled

SHE SAID: Is it not good for me to come and draw forth a spirit, to see what kind of spirit people are of? I see that some of you have got the spirit of a goose, and some have got the spirit of a snake. I feel at home here. I come to you, citizens of New York, as I suppose you ought to be. I am a citizen of the State of New York; I was born in it, and I was a slave in the State of New York; and now I am a good citizen of this State. I was born here, and I can tell you I feel at home here. I've been lookin' round and watchin' things, and I know a little mite 'bout Woman's Rights, too. I come forth to speak 'bout Woman's Rights, and want to throw in my little mite, to keep the scales a-movin'. I know that it feels a kind o' hissin' and ticklin' like to see a colored woman get up and tell you about things, and Woman's Rights. We have all been thrown down so low that nobody thought we'd ever get up again; but we have been long enough trodden now; we will come up again, and now I am here.

I was a-thinkin', when I see women contendin' for their rights, I was a-thinkin' what a difference there is now, and what there was in old times. I have only a few minutes to speak; but in the old times the kings of the earth would hear a woman. There was a king in the Scriptures; and then it was the kings of the earth would kill a woman if she come into their presence ; but Queen Esther come forth, for she was oppressed, and felt there was a great wrong, and she said I will die or I will bring my complaint before the king. Should the king of the United States be greater, or more crueler, or more harder? But the king, he raised up his sceptre and said: "Thy request shall be granted unto thee—to the half of my kingdom will I grant it to thee!" Then he said he would hang Haman on the gallows he had made up high. But that is not what women come forward to contend. The women want their rights as Esther. She only wanted to explain her rights. And he was so liberal that he said, "the half of my kingdom shall be granted to thee," and he did not wait for her to ask, he was so liberal with her.

Now, women do not ask half of a kingdom, but their rights, and they don't get 'em. When she comes to demand 'em, don't you hear how sons hiss their mothers like snakes, because they ask for their rights; and can they ask for anything less ? The king ordered Haman to be hung on the gallows which he prepared to hang others; but I do not want any man to be killed, but I am sorry to see them so short-minded. But we'll have our rights; see if we don't; and you can't stop us from them ; see if you can. You may hiss as much as you like, but it is comin'. Women don't get half as much rights as they ought to; we want more, and we will have it. Jesus says: "What I say to one, I say to all—watch!" I'm a-watchin'. God says: "Honor your father and your mother." Sons and daughters ought to behave themselves before their mothers, but they do not. I can see them a-laughin', and pointin' at their mothers up here on the stage. They hiss when an aged woman comes forth. If they'd been brought up proper they'd have known better than hissing like snakes and geese. I'm 'round watchin' these things, and I wanted to come up and say these few things to you, and I'm glad of the hearin' you give me. I wanted to tell you a mite about Woman's Rights, and so I came out and said so. I am sittin' among you to watch; and every once and awhile I will come out and tell you what time of night it is.

The Times next day commented as follows :

The New York Times, Sept. 9, 1853.

THE ROW OF YESTERDAY.—Row No. 3 was a very jolly affair, a regular break-down, at the Woman's Convention. The women had their rights, and more beside. The cause was simply that the rowdyish diathesis is just now prevalent. True, a colored woman made a speech, but there was nothing in that to excite a multitude; she did not speak too low to be heard; she did not insult them with improper language; nor did the audience respond at all insultingly. They did not curse, they only called for "half a dozen on the shell." They did not swear, they only "hurried up that stew." They did wrong, however.

If we had our own way every rascally rowdy among them should have Bloomers of all colors preaching at them by the year—a year for every naughty word they uttered, a score of them for every hiss. Out upon the villains who go to any meeting to disturb it. Let anybody who can hire a house and pay for it have his way, and let none be disturbed; the opposers can stay away. But for us, let us be thankful that in such hot weather there is something to amuse us, something to season our insipid dishes, something to spice our dull days with. *Mem.* It was cooler in the evening.

CAROLINE M. SEVERANCE, of Ohio, presented an argument and appeal based upon the following propositions: That as the manifest dissimilarities which cause the *nations* of the earth to differ, physically, and in degree of mental and moral development and cultivation, are not found justly to invalidate their claim to a place in the vast brotherhood of man —to fullness of family communion and rights; so there are no radical differences of *the sexes* in these respects, which can at all impair the integrity of an equal humanity—no sufficient basis for a distinction in so comprehensive a classification.

The fundamental facts and faculties—the higher and more essential attributes which make up the accepted definition of humanity in our day, are identical in both—are no more confined or unduly allotted to one sex than to one nation.

On the broad basis of this philosophy, on the ground of woman's undeniable and equal humanity, proven by the possession of identical human faculties, and equal human needs, we claim for her the recognition of that humanity and its rights—for the freedom, protection, development, and use of those faculties, and the supply of those needs. And we maintain that no accident of sex, no prejudged or proven dissimilarity *in degree* of physical, mental, or moral endowment, or development, can at all stand in the way of the admission of such just claim; and no denial of such claim but must necessarily be fraught with evil, as subversive of the Creator's economy and design. [Shouts and laughter.]

Rev. JOHN PIERPONT, who, for the first time, took part in a Woman's Rights Convention, said: Ladies and gentlemen, a woman, at this hour, occupies the throne of the mightiest kingdom of the globe. Under her sway there are some hundred and fifty millions of the human race. Has she a right to sit there? [Several voices, "No!"] The vote here is—no; but a hundred and fifty millions vote the contrary. If a woman can thus have the highest right conceded to her, why should not woman have a lower? Therefore, some women have some rights. Is not the question a fair one,—how many women have any rights? And, also, how many rights has any woman? Are not these fair subjects for discussion? I do not come here to advocate any specific right for women; I come merely for the consideration of the question, what right she has. What are the rights which can not rightfully be denied her? Surely, some belong to the sex at large, as part of the great family of man. We lay it down as the foundation of our civil theory, that man, as man, has, and by nature is endowed with certain natural, inviolable, indefeasible rights; not that men who have attained the age of majority alone possess those rights; not that the older, the young, the fair, or the dark, are alone endowed with them; but that they belong to *all*. The rights are not of man's giving;

God gave them; and if you deny or withhold them, you place yourself in antagonism with your Creator. The more humble and despised is the human being claiming those rights, the more prompt should be the feeling of every manly bosom to stand by that humble creature of God, and see that its right is not withheld from it! Is it a new thing in this country to allow civil rights to a woman?

Susan B. Anthony, who had been a teacher for fifteen years, gave an amusing description of her recent experience in attempting to speak at a teachers' convention. Paulina Wright Davis offered the following resolution:

Resolved, That inasmuch as this great movement is intended to meet the wants, not of America only, but of the whole world, a committee be appointed to prepare an address from this Convention to the women of Great Britain and the continent of Europe, setting forth our objects, and inviting their co-operation in the same.*

WM. LLOYD GARRISON: I second the resolution, because it shows the universality of our enterprise. I second it heartily, for it manifests the grandeur of the object we are pursuing. There never yet was a struggle for liberty which was not universal, though, for the time, it might have appeared to be no more than local. If the women of this country have to obtain rights which have been denied them, the women of England, of France, of the world, have to obtain the same; and I regard this as a struggle for the race, sublime as the world itself. It is right that this Convention should address the women of the whole world, in order that they should announce precisely how they regard their own position in the universe of God. What rights they claim are God-given; what rights they possess, and what rights they have still to achieve. It is time that the women of America should ask the women beyond the Atlantic to consider their own condition, and to co-operate with them in the same glorious struggle. There is not an argument that God ever permitted a human being to frame, that can be brought against this cause. This is a free Convention, and we are willing that any man or woman who has aught against its principles, should come here and freely urge it. And yet, with a free platform, where is the human being who cares to argue the question? Where is the man who presents himself decently, and proffers a word of reasonable argument against our cause? I have yet to see that man. Instead, we have blackguardism, defamation, rowdyism, profanity; we have all the indications that hell from beneath is stirred up against this divine Convention, for it is divine—it takes hold of heaven and the throne of God! (Hisses). Hiss, ye serpents! ye have nothing else to offer. There is not one of you to whom God has given a brain to fashion an argument. But it goes on record, and all the journals of this city will themselves bear testimony, that no one takes the platform, like

---

* The Committee were: Lucretia Mott, Ernestine L. Rose, Marion C. Houghton, Lucy Stone, Caroline H. Dall, Paulina Wright Davis, Dr. Harriot K. Hunt, Mathilde Franceska Anneké, Dr. Elizabeth Blackwell.

an honest and honorable man, to argue this cause down. Therefore, the whole ground is won, and we stand, as we have stood from the beginning, on the rock of victory.

It was rather singular that in this Convention, so entirely under the control of a mob, that there should be found one man who dared to stand upon the platform and announce that he had been an opponent for ten years, and was connected with a journal which had initiated this mob; and now he desired to give in his adhesion, and to confess his conversion. This was one of the remarkable incidents of the occasion.

Isaac C. Pray said: Until within two years I have been an incessant opponent of the persons on this platform, in a leading journal in this city, which gives the cue to the hisses in that gallery. I have myself given— (applause). Pray spare your plaudits; I do not wish for them. In November, 1851, I retired from that journal, and I have since applied myself to study. This movement, among others, has come under my notice, and I have given it much attention. The result is, that I have entirely changed my opinion with regard to it. I know, not only that my former opinion was wrong, but that this movement is one which you can not stop; it emanates from the Deity himself, whose influence urges man forward on the path of progress. I say to the clergy, if they ignore this movement, they ignore that accountability to the Almighty which they preach. I do not mean to enter into any argument on this subject, but merely wish to say, as each one is accountable for his energies to God, you must go on in this good and holy cause; also, I wish to show that there is such a thing as a man's changing his opinion. This cause has been the butt of all the ridicule I could command. I scoffed at it, in season and out of season. There is not a lady on this platform whom my pen has not assailed; and now I come to make all the reparation in my power, by thus raising my voice on behalf of them and the cause committed to their hands. (Cheers and stamping).

As it was inconsistent with Mrs. Mott's Quaker principles to call upon the police for the forcible suppression of the mob, she vacated the chair, inviting Ernestine L. Rose to take her place. The last evening session opened with a song by G. W. Clark; but the music did not soothe the mob soul; he was greeted with screeches, which his voice only at brief intervals could drown.

The President then introduced a German lady, Madame Mathilde Francesca Anneké, editor of a liberal woman's rights newspaper which had been suppressed in Germany. She had but recently landed in our country, and hastened to the Convention to enjoy the blessings of free speech in a republic. She had heard so much of freedom in America, that she could hardly express her astonishment at what she witnessed. After many attempts, and with great difficulty, owing to the tumult and interruption by impertinent noises, she spoke as follows, in German, Mrs. Rose translating her remarks into English:

I wish to say only a few words. On the other side of the Atlantic there is no freedom of any kind, and we have not even the right to claim freedom of speech. But can it be that here, too, there are tyrants who violate the individual right to express opinions on any subject? And do you call yourselves republicans? No; there is no republic without freedom of speech. (The tumult showing no signs of abatement),

WENDELL PHILLIPS came forward, and said: Allow me to say one word, purely as a matter of the self-respect which you owe to yourselves. We are citizens of a great country, which, from Maine to Georgia, has extended a welcome to Kossuth, and this New York audience is now looking upon a noble woman who stood by his side in the battle-fields of Hungary; one who has faced the cannon of Francis Joseph of Austria, for the rights of the people. Is this the welcome you give her to the shores of republican America? A woman who has proved her gallantry and attachment to principles, wishes to say five words to you of the feelings with which she is impressed toward this cause. I know, fellow-citizens, that you will hear her.

The audience showing a better disposition to hear Madame Anneké, she proceeded thus:

I saw this morning, in a paper, that the women of America have met in convention to claim their rights. I rejoiced when I saw that they recognized their equality; and I rejoiced when I saw that they have not forgotten their sisters in Germany. I wished to be here with my American sisters, to tell them that I sympathize in their efforts; but I was too sick to come, and would probably not have been here but that another German woman, a friend of this movement, came to Newark and took me out of my sick bed. But it was the want of a knowledge of the English language which kept me away, more than sickness.

Before I came here, I knew the tyranny and oppression of kings; I felt it in my own person, and friends, and country; and when I came here I expected to find that freedom which is denied us at home. Our sisters in Germany have long desired freedom, but there the desire is repressed as well in man as in woman. There is no freedom there, even to claim human rights. Here they expect to find freedom of speech; here, for if we can not claim it here, where should we go for it? Here, at least, we ought to be able to express our opinions on all subjects; and yet, it would appear, there is no freedom even here to claim human rights, although the only hope in our country for freedom of speech and action, is directed to this country for illustration and example. That freedom I claim. The women of my country look to this for encouragement and sympathy; and they, also, sympathize with this cause. We hope it will go on and prosper; and many hearts across the ocean in Germany are beating in unison with those here.

Madame Anneké retired amid a great uproar, which increased when Mr. Phillips presented himself again. He persisted against frequent clamorous interruptions in his purpose to speak, and addressed the meeting as follows :

Mr. Phillips: I am not surprised at the reception I meet. (Interruption).

Mrs. Rose: As presiding officer for this evening, I call upon the police. The mayor, too, promised to see that our meetings should not be disturbed, and I now call upon him to preserve order. As citizens of New York, we have a right to this protection, for we pay our money for it. My friends, keep order, and then we shall know who the disturbers are.

Mr. Phillips: You are making a better speech than I can, by your conduct. This is proof positive of the necessity of this Convention. The time has been when other Conventions have been met like this— with hisses. (Renewed hisses). Go on with your hisses; geese have hissed before now. If it be your pleasure to argue the question for us, by proving that the men here, at least, are not fit for exercising political rights. (Great uproar).

Mrs. Rose: I regret that I have again to call upon the police to keep order; and if they are not able to do it, I call upon the meeting to help them.

Mr. Phillips: You prove one thing to-night, that the men of New York do not understand the meaning of civil liberty and free discussion.

Antoinette Brown made an attempt to speak, but soon ceased amidst the most indescribable uproar. Mr. Elliott then jumped upon the platform, and harangued the audience as a representative of the rowdies, though he claimed for himself great fairness and respectability. He said :

If taxation without representation be robbery, then robbery is right, and I am willing to be robbed. For twelve years I have paid taxes; and here and in other countries I have, in return, got protection. Robbery is, to take away property forcibly without giving an equivalent for it; but a good equivalent is given for taxation. In this and other countries, the property of individuals is taken from them, as when an owner of land is deprived of it by the State to make a railroad through it; that is no robbery; an equivalent is given, and the owner is fairly dealt by. We have heard many instances of the tyranny inflicted on women; but is that a reason that they should vote ? If it be, minors, who are under a double tyranny, that of father and mother—

Here the audience seemed to have lost all patience, and Mr. Elliott's voice was completely drowned in the uproar. He retired, repeating that he had proved the rowdies were not all on one side. The confusion now reached its climax. A terrific uproar, shouting, yelling, screaming, bellowing, laughing, stamping, cries of

" Burleigh," " Root," " Truth," " Shut up," " Take a drink," " Greeley," etc., prevented anything orderly being heard, and the Convention, on the motion of Mrs. Rose, was adjourned *sine die ;* the following resolution having first been read by Dr. Harriot K. Hunt,
and passed without dissent :

> *Resolved,* That the members of this Convention, and the audience
> assembled, tender their thanks to Lucretia Mott for the grace, firmness,
> ability, and courtesy with which she has discharged her important and
> often arduous duties.

Daily Tribune, Sept. 8, 1853.

WOMAN'S RIGHTS CONVENTION:—Meeting at the Tabernacle.

Evening Session.—Tremendous uproar—close of the Convention.

Yesterday evening being the last sitting of this Convention, the approach to the Tabernacle was thronged long before the hour for opening
the doors, and considerable excitement seemed to prevail. At about
seven o'clock the Tabernacle doors were thrown open, and the rush for
tickets and admission to the anxious throng could only be equalled by
that of a Jenny Lind night. The building, capable of holding some 2,000
persons, was immediately filled to excess, and the principal promoters of
the movement took their places on the platform. . . . . Mr. George W.
Clark, who had been requested to sing a song on " Freedom of Thought,"
did so in a style apparently not much approved by the audience, who at
a very early stage began to give vent to all kinds of groans and ironical
cheers.

Mrs. Martin, of this State, was then introduced, and with considerable
difficulty began her address.

(Cries—" No! no! " and tremendous yells and laughter). " Time's up,"
" That'll do." (Loud hisses, groans, laughter, tigers, and demoniac sounds
from the galleries). Cries of " Phillips! Phillips." (Hisses and yells).

Tribune, Sept. 9, 1853.

We do not know whether any of the *gentlemen* who have succeeded in
breaking up the Woman's Rights Convention, or of the other *gentlemen*
who have succeeded in three sessions at Metropolitan Hall in silencing a
regularly appointed and admitted delegate, will ever be ashamed of their
passion and hostility, but we have little doubt that some of them will
live to understand their own folly. At any rate, they have accomplished
a very different thing from what they now suppose. For if it had been
their earnest desire to strengthen the cause of Woman's Rights, they
could not have done the work half so effectively. Nothing is so good for a
weak and unpopular movement as this sort of opposition. Had Antoinette Brown been allowed to speak at Metropolitan Hall, her observations
would certainly have occupied but a fraction of the time now wasted,
and would have had just the weight proper to their sense and appropriateness, and no more. But instead of this the World's Convention was
disturbed and its orators silenced. The consequences will be the mass
of people throughout the country who might otherwise not know of its

existence, will have their attention called and their sympathies enlisted in its behalf. So, too, when Antoinette Brown is put down by Rev. John Chambers and his colleagues, and denied what is her clear right as a member of the Temperance Convention by a vociferous mob, composed, we are sorry to say, very largely of clergymen, every impartial person sees that she is surrounded with a prestige and importance which, whatever her talents as a speaker, she could hardly hope to have attained. Many who question the propriety of woman's appearing in public, will revolt at the gagging of one who had a right to speak and claimed simply to use it on a proper occasion. There is in the public mind of this country an intuitive love of fair play and free speech, and those who outrage it for any purpose of their own merely reinforce their opponents, and bestow a mighty power on the ideas they hate and fain would suppress.

Tribune, Sept. 12, 1853.

Arguments *pro* and *con.* The meetings at the Tabernacle Tuesday and Wednesday last, exhibited some features not often paralleled in the progress of any public agitation for the redress of grievances, or the vindication of rights. The advocates of an enlargement of the allotted sphere of woman, had hired the house, paid the advertising and other expenses, gathered at their own expense from their distant homes, and taken all the responsibilities of the outlay, yet they offered and desired throughout to surrender their own platform for one-half of the time, to any respectable and capable antagonists who should see fit to appear and attempt to show why their demands were not just and their grievances real. Consequently, though they are engaged in a struggle, not only against numbers and power, and fashion and immemorial custom, but with the Pulpit and the Press actively and bitterly leading and spurring on their antagonists, and with no access to the public ear but from the public platform, we consider this proposition more than liberal—it was chivalric and generous. We listened with interest to some of the arguments *pro* and *con,* and propose here to recapitulate their substance, that our readers may see at a glance the present position and bearing of the controversy. We will begin with the first speech we heard, that of

Rev. WM. H. CHANNING: They say the public platform is not in woman's sphere; but let us understand why. Jenny Lind stands on that platform before thousands of men and women, and sings, "I know that my Redeemer liveth," with all hearts approving, all voices applauding, and nobody lisps a word that she is out of her sphere. Well, Antoinette Brown believes the sentiment so sang to be the hope of a lost world, and feels herself called to bear witness in behalf of that religion, and to commend His salvation to the understanding and hearts of all who will hear her. Why may she not obey this impulse, and bear the tidings of a world's salvation to those perishing in darkness and sin ? What is there unfeminine or revolting in her preaching the truth which Jenny Lind may sing without objection and amid universal applause ?

Answer by things " in male costumes." Hiss-s-s.

Mrs. ERNESTINE L. ROSE: The law declares husband and wife one; and such we all feel that they should be, and must be when the marriage is a true one. Now, why should that same law base their union or oneness on inequality or subjugation ? The wife dies and the husband inherits all her property, as is right; but let the husband die, and the greater part of the property is taken from the wife and given to others, even though all that property was earned or inherited by the wife. She may be turned out of the house she was born in and which was hers until marriage, and see it given to her husband's brothers or other kindred who are strangers to her. I insist that the wife should own and inherit the property of the husband just to the same extent that the husband inherits that of the wife—why not ?

Answer to the aforesaid—Hiss-s-s-s! Bow-ow-ow!

HARRIOT K. HUNT: I plant myself on the basis of the Declaration of Independence and insist, with our Revolutionary sires, that taxation without representation is tyranny. Well; here am I, an independent American woman, educated for and living by the practice of medicine. I own property, and pay taxes on that property. I demand of the Government that taxes me that it should allow me an equal voice with the other tax-payers in the disposal of the public money. I am certainly not less intelligent than thousands who, though scarcely able to read their ballots, are entitled to vote. I am allowed to vote in any bank or insurance company when I choose to be a stockholder; why ought I not to vote in the disposition of public money raised by tax, as well as those men who do not pay taxes, or those who do either ?

Answer of the aforesaid—Yah! wow! Hiss-s-s-s!

LUCY STONE: I plead for the right of woman to the control of her own person as a moral, intelligent, accountable being. I know a wife who has not set foot outside of her husband's house for three years, because her husband forbids her doing so when he is present, and locks her up when he is absent. That wife is gray with sorrow and despair though now in middle life, but there is no redress for her wrongs because the law makes her husband her master, and there is no proof that he beats or bruises her; there is nothing in his treatment of her that the law does not allow. I protest against such a law and demand its overthrow; and I protest against any law which limits the sphere of woman, as a bar to her intellectual development. You say she *can not* do this and that, but if so, what need of a law to prevent her ? You say her intellectual achievements have not equaled those of man; but I answer, that she has had no motive, no opportunity for such achievement. Close all the avenues, take away all the incitement for man's ambition, and he would do no more than woman does. Grant her freedom, education, and opportunity, and she will do what God intended she should do, no less, no more. Men! you dwarf, you wrong yourselves in restraining and fettering the intellectual development of woman! I ask for her liberty to do whatever moral and useful deed she proves able to do—why should I ask in vain ?

Answer by time-serving Press: Men, Women, and Bloomers! Faugh! Bah!

ANTOINETTE BROWN: I plead that the mother may not be legally robbed of her children. I know a mother who was left a widow with

Eng⁴ by G.E.Perine &c⁰ N.Y.

Susan B. Anthony

three young children. She was able, and most willing to support them in humble independence; but her husband before he died, had secretly given two of them to his relatives, and the law tore them from the mother's bosom, and left her but the youngest, who was soon taken from her by death. That mother lived to see her two surviving children grow up, the one to be a drunkard and the other a felon, all through neglect and the want of that care and guardianship which none so well as a parent can be relied on to afford. I plead for woman as a mother, that her right to her children be recognized as at least equal to that of the father, and that he, being dead, no other can have a right to their guardianship paramount or even equal to hers.

Pantalooned mob as aforesaid: Oh, dry up! Bow-ow! Waugh! Hiss-s-s! Get out!

The case is still on.

WOMAN'S RIGHTS STATE CONVENTION,

ROCHESTER, N. Y., NOVEMBER 30 AND DECEMBER 1, 1853.

As William Henry Channing resided at Rochester, and felt that the time had come for some more active measures, he was invited to prepare the call and resolutions for the Convention. The following was issued and extensively circulated, and signed by many of the leading men and women of the State:

THE JUST AND EQUAL RIGHTS OF WOMEN.

To the Men and Women of New York:

The "Woman's Rights" Movement is a practical one, demanding prompt and efficient action for the relief of oppressive wrongs; and, as the Conventions held for several years past in different States, have answered their end of arousing earnest public attention, the time has come for calling upon the people to reform the evils from which women suffer, by their Representatives in Legislative Assemblies.

The wise and humane of all classes in society, however much they may differ upon speculative points as to woman's nature and function, agree that there are actual abuses of women, tolerated by custom and authorized by law, which are condemned alike by the genius of republican institutions and the spirit of the Christian religion. Conscience and common sense, then, unite to sanction their immediate redress. Thousands of the best men and women, in all our communities, are asking such questions as these:

1. Why should not woman's work be paid for according to the quality of the work done, and not the sex of the worker?

2. How shall we open for woman's energies new spheres of well remunerated industry?

3. Why should not wives, equally with husbands, be entitled to their own earnings?

4. Why should not widows, equally with widowers, become by law the legal guardians, as they certainly are by nature the natural guardians, of their own children?

37

5. On what just ground do the laws make a distinction between men and women, in regard to the ownership of property, inheritance, and the administration of estates ?

6. Why should women, any more than men, be taxed without representation ?

7. Why may not women claim to be tried by a jury of their peers, with exactly the same right as men claim to be and actually are ?

8. If women need the protection of the laws, and are subject to the penalties of the laws equally with men, why should they not have an equal influence in making the laws, and appointing Legislatures, the Judiciary, and Executive ?

And, finally, if governments—according to our National Declaration of Independence—" derive their just powers from the consent of the governed," why should women, any more than men, be governed without their own consent; and why, therefore, is not woman's right to suffrage precisely equal to man's ?

For the end of finding out practical answers to these and similar questions, and making suitable arrangements to bring the existing wrongs of women, in the State of New York, before the Legislature at its next session, we, the undersigned, do urgently request the men and women of the Commonwealth to assemble in Convention, in the city of Rochester, on Wednesday, November 30th, and Thursday, December 1, 1853.*

The Convention assembled at Corinthian Hall at 10 o'clock. Rev. Samuel J. May, of Syracuse, in the chair.† After thanking

* Elizabeth Cady Stanton, Seneca Falls ; Mary Cheney Greeley, New York ; Ernestine L. Rose, New York ; Samuel J. May, Syracuse ; George W. Jonson, Buffalo ; Antoinette L. Brown, South Butler ; Frederick Douglass, Rochester ; Hiram Corliss, Greenwich ; Lydia A. Jenkins, Geneva ; William H. Channing, Rochester ; William Hay, Saratoga Springs ; Amy Post, Rochester ; Mary H. Hallowell, Rochester ; Susan B. Anthony, Rochester ; William R. Hallowell, Rochester ; Isaac Post, Rochester ; Mary B. F. Curtis, Rochester ; Lemira Kedzie, Rochester ; James M'Cune Smith, New York ; S. G. Love, Randolph ; Mary F. Love, Randolph ; C. M. Crowley, Randolph ; R. T. Trall, New York ; Emily S. Trall, New York ; Oliver Johnson, New York ; Mariana W. Johnson, New York ; Sydney Howard Gay, New York : Catharine E. Welling, Elmira ; Mrs. Holbrook, Elmira ; H. A. Zoller, Little Falls ; Stephen Haight, Dutchess County ; Sarah A. Burtis, Rochester ; Lydia P. Savage, Syracuse ; Lydia Mott, Albany ; J. B. Sands, Canandaigua ; Catharine H. Sands, Canandaigua.

† *Vice-Presidents.*—Ernestine L. Rose, New York ; S. C. Cuyler, Wayne ; Amy Post, Rochester ; Mary F. Love, Randolph ; Amelia Bloomer, Seneca Falls ; Caroline Keese, Cayuga ; Griffith M. Cooper, Wayne ; Rev. Antoinette L. Brown, South Butler ; Matilda Joslyn Gage, Manlius ; Rev. J. W. Loguin, Syracuse ; Sarah A. Burtis, Rochester ; Emma R. Coe, Buffalo.

Secretaries.—Susan B. Anthony, Sarah Pellet, Wm. J. Watkins, and Sarah Willis.

Finance Committee.—Mary S. Anthony, Mary H. Hallowell, E. J. Jenkins, Lucy Colman, and Mary Cooper.

Business Committee.—Ernestine L. Rose, William Henry Channing, Antoinette L. Brown, Frederick Douglass, Amy Post, and Samuel J. Love.

the Convention for the honor conferred, he ran the parallel between the laws for married women and the slaves on the Southern plantation, and then introduced Ernestine L. Rose, to paint in more vivid colors the picture he had outlined.

Mrs. ROSE said: The remarks of the president have impressed us to do our duty with all the earnestness in our power. This is termed a woman's rights movement. Alas! that the painful necessity should exist, for woman's calling a Convention to claim her rights from those who have been created to go hand in hand, and heart in heart with her; whose interests can not be divided from hers. Why does she claim them? Because every human being has a right to all the advantages society has to bestow, if his having them does not injure the rights of others. Life is valueless without liberty, and shall we not claim that which is dearer than life? In savage life, liberty is synonymous with aggression. In civilized countries it is founded on equality of rights. Oppression always produces suffering through the whole of the society where it exists; this movement ought, therefore, to be called a human rights movement. The wrongs of woman are so many (indeed there is scarcely anything else but wrongs) that there is not time to mention them all in one convention. She would speak at present of legal wrongs, and leave it to her hearers, if all are not—men, perhaps, more than women—sufferers by these wrongs. How can woman have a right to her children when the right to herself is taken away? At the marriage altar the husband says in effect, "All this is mine, all mine is my own." She ceases to exist legally, except when she violates the laws; then she assumes her identity just long enough to receive the penalty. When the husband dies poor, leaving the widow with small children (here the speaker pictured thrillingly the suffering of a poor, weak-minded, helpless woman, with small children dependent on her), she is then acknowledged the guardian of her children. But any property left them takes away her right of control. If there is property the law steps in as guardian of it and therefore of the children. The widowed mother is their guardian, only on condition that the husband has made her so by will. Can any human being be benefited by such gross violations of humanity?

MATILDA JOSLYN GAGE said: The legal disabilities of woman are many, as not only known to those who bear them, but they are acknowledged by Kent, Story, and many other legal authorities. A wife has no management in the joint earnings of herself and her husband; they are entirely under control of the husband, who is obliged to furnish the wife merely the common necessaries of life; all that she receives beyond these is looked upon by the law as a favor, and not held as her right. A mother is denied the custody of her own child; a most barbarous and unjust law, which robs her of the child placed in her care by the great Creator himself. A widow is allowed the use merely of one-third of the real estate left at the husband's death; and when her minor children have grown up she must surrender the personal property, even to the family Bible, and the pictures of her dear children. In view of such laws the women engaged in this movement ask that the wife shall be made heir to the husband to the same extent that he is now her heir.

Taxation without representation is another of the wrongs that woman endures. In this she is held below the negro in the political scale; for the black man, when not possessing property to the extent of two hundred and fifty dollars, is not allowed to vote, but neither is he taxed. The present law of divorce is very unjust; the husband, whether the innocent or the guilty party, retaining all the wife's property, as also the control of the children unless by special decree of the court they are assigned to the mother.

Rev. ANTOINETTE BROWN said: The wife owes service and labor to her husband as much and as absolutely as the slave does to his master. This grates harshly upon the ears of Christendom; but it is made palpably and practically true all through our statute books, despite the poetic fancy which views woman as elevated in the social estate; but a little lower than the angels.

Letters were read from Paulina Wright Davis, Dr. Trall, Mary C. Vaughan, and Hon. William Hay. A series of fourteen resolutions were presented by Mr. Channing, and discussed, which suggested the appointment of various committees. One to prepare an address to the Legislature, and to ask a special hearing before a joint committee to consider the whole subject of the just and equal rights of woman; another to prepare an address to the capitalists and industrialists of New York on the best modes of employing and remunerating women.

Resolved, That the movement, now in progress throughout the United States, for securing the just and equal rights of women, in education, industry, law, politics, religion, and social life, is timely, wise, and practical; that it is authorized by all the essential principles of Republican institutions, and sanctioned by the spirit of the Christian religion; and finally that it is but a carrying on to completeness of a reform, already begun, by legal provisions, in the most advanced States of the Union.

Resolved, That the design of all true legislation should be the elevation of every member of the community—and that the violation of this legitimate design, in depriving woman of her just and equal rights, is not only highly injurious to her, but by reason of the equilibrium which pervades all existence, that man, too, is impeded in his progress by the very chains which bind woman to the lifeless skeleton of feudal civilization.

Resolved, That we do not ask for woman's political, civil, industrial, and social equality with man, in the spirit of antagonism, or with a wish to produce separate and conflicting interests between the sexes, but because the onward progress of society and the highest aspirations of the human race, demand that woman should everywhere be recognized as the co-equal and co-sovereign of man.

Resolved, That women justly claim an equally free access with men, to the highest means of mental, moral, and physical culture, provided in seminaries, colleges, professional and industrial schools; and that we call upon all friends of progress and upon the Legislature of New York, in establishing and endowing institutions, to favor pre-eminently those which seek to place males and females on a level of equal advantages in their system of education.

Resolved, That, inasmuch as universal experience proves the insepa-rable connection between dependence and degradation—while it is plain to every candid observer of society that women are kept poor, by being crowded together, to compete with and undersell one another in a few branches of labor, and that from this very poverty of women, spring many of the most terrible wrongs and evils, which corrupt and endanger society; therefore do we invite the earnest attention of capitalists, mer-chants, traders, manufacturers, and mechanics, to the urgent need, which everywhere exists, of opening to women new avenues of honest and honorable employment, and we do hereby call upon all manly men to make room for their sisters to earn an independent livelihood.

Resolved, That, whereas, the custom of making small remuneration for woman's work, in all departments of industry, has sprung from her de-pendence, which dependence is prolonged and increased by this most irrational and unjust habit of half pay; therefore do we demand, in the name of common sense and common conscience, that women equally with men, should be paid for their services according to the quality and quantity of the work done, and not the sex of the worker.

Resolved, That, whereas, the State of New York, in the acts of 1848 and 1849, has honorably and justly placed married women on the footing of equality with unmarried women, in regard to the receiving, holding, conveying, and devising of all property, real and personal, we call upon the Legislature of the State to take the next step—so plainly justified by its own precedents—of providing that husbands and wives shall be joint owners of their joint earnings—the community estate passing to the survivor at the death of either party.

Resolved, That, whereas, the evident intent of the Legislature of the State of New York has for many years been progressively to do away with the legal disabilities of women, which existed under the savage usages of the old common law, therefore we do urgently call upon the Legis-lature of this State, at its next session, to appoint a joint committee to examine and revise the statutes, and to propose remedies for the redress of all legal grievances from which women now suffer, and suitable meas-ures for the full establishment of women's legal equality with men.

Resolved, That, whereas, under the common law, the father is regarded as the guardian, by nature, of his children, having the entire control of their persons and education, while only upon the death of the father, does the mother become the guardian by nature; and, whereas, by the revised statutes of New York, it is provided, that where an estate in lands shall become vested in an infant, the guardianship of such infant, with the rights, powers, and duties of a guardian in soccage, shall belong to the father, and only in case of the father's death, to the mother;

and, whereas, finally and chiefly, by the revised statutes of New York, it is provided, that every father may, by his deed or last will, duly executed, dispose of the custody and tuition of his children, during their minority, "to any person or persons in possession or remainder"; therefore, do we solemnly protest against the utter violation of every mother's rights, authorized by existing laws, in regard to the guardianship of infants, and demand, in the name of common humanity, that the Legislature of New York so amend the statutes, as to place fathers and mothers on equal footing in regard to the guardianship of their children. Especially do we invite the Legislature instantly to pass laws, entitling mothers to become their children's guardians, in all cases where, by habitual drunkenness, immorality, or improvidence, fathers are incompetent to the sacred trust.

Resolved, That, whereas, according to the amendments of the Constitution of the United States, it is provided that "in all criminal cases, the accused shall enjoy the right to a speedy and public trial, by an impartial jury," and that "in suits at common law, where the value in controversy shall exceed twenty dollars, the right of trial by jury shall be preserved"; and, whereas, according to the revised statutes of New York, it is provided, that "no member of this State can be disfranchised or deprived of any of the rights or privileges, secured to any citizen thereof, unless by the law of the land, or the judgment of his peers"; therefore, do we demand, that women, as "members" and "citizens" of this State, equally with men, should be entitled to claim a trial by "an impartial jury of their peers." And especially do we remonstrate against the partial, mean, and utterly inequitable custom, everywhere prevalent, that in questions of divorce, men, and men alone, should be regarded as "an impartial jury."

Resolved, That, whereas, in the Declaration of Independence of the United States, one of the "injuries and usurpation" complained of is Taxation without the consent of the persons taxed; and, whereas, it is provided in the revised statutes of New York, that "no tax, duty, aid or imposition whatever—except such as may be laid by a law of the United States—can be taken or levied within this State, without the grant and assent of the people of this State; by their representatives in Senate and Assembly"; and that "no citizen of this State can be compelled to contribute to any gift, loan, tax, or other like charge, not laid or imposed by a law of the United States, or by the Legislature of the State"; therefore do we proclaim, that it is a gross act of tyranny and usurpation, to tax women without their consent, and we demand, either that women be represented by their own appointed representatives, or that they be freed from the imposition of taxes.

Resolved, That inasmuch as it is the fundamental principle of the Nation and of every State in this Union, that all "governments derive their just powers from the consent of the governed"—it is a manifest violation of the Supreme Law of the land for males to govern females without their consent; and therefore do we demand, of the people of New York, such a change in the Constitution of the State, as will secure to women the right of suffrage which is now so unjustly monopolized by men.

Resolved, That Elizabeth Cady Stanton, Samuel J. May, Ernestine L. Rose, William Hay, Susan B. Anthony, Burroughs Phillips, Antoinette L. Brown, W. H. Channing, and Lydia A. Jenkins, be a committee to prepare and to present an address to the Legislature of New York, at its next session, stating, as specifically as they shall see fit, the legal disabilities of women, and to ask a hearing before a joint committee, specially appointed to consider the whole subject of the just and equal rights of women.

Resolved, That Horace Greeley, Mary C. Vaughan, Abram Pryne, Sarah Pellet, and Matilda Joslyn Gage be a committee to prepare an address to capitalists and industrialists of New York, on the best modes of employing and remunerating the industry of women.

The President invited any one who saw errors or fallacies in the arguments brought forward, to make them apparent.

Mr. PRYNE, of Cazenovia, editor of the *Progressive Christian,* said : If women desire to enter the ordinary avocations of men, they must be brave enough to become shopkeepers and mechanics. There is no law to prevent it, neither is there to woman's voting. The men have made an arrangement by which their votes are not counted, but still they might provide ballot-boxes, and decide upon whom they would prefer as magistrates and legislators. A man who was thus voted to stay at home, by an overwhelming majority of women, even if elected by the men, would find himself in an uncomfortable position.

Mr. CHANNING said he understood that in a town in Ohio the women did so, and cast sixty votes.

Mr. PRYNE was glad to hear that there were practical women in Ohio. Man is where he is because he is what he is, and when woman gets the same elements of moral and physical power she will have no more wrongs to complain of.

Mrs. ROSE said it was a true maxim that he who would be free, himself must strike the blow. But woman could not, as things were, help herself. As well might the slaveholder say that the slave was fit for no other condition while he consents to occupy that position. To a certain extent this is true, and the same principles apply to both classes. But all human beings are not martyrs; the majority accept the conditions in which they find themselves, rather than make their lives one long struggle for freedom. Woman must be educated to take the stand which Mr. Pryne invites her to assume. The only object for which woman is now reared is to be married; and is she fitted even for that; to become a companion, an assistant, an aid, a comforter to man; and above all, a mother ? That alone; to fit a woman for that sphere; she must possess all the extended education which would fit her to take any position in life to which man aspires.

MARY F. LOVE said there might be hindrances in the way of woman too great for her to surmount. Men in their struggles for liberty have sometimes met insuperable obstacles; there have been unsuccessful revolutions at all stages of human development.

FREDERICK DOUGLASS, in discussing the injustice to woman in the world of work, said: Some one whispers in my ear that as teachers women get one-fourth the pay men do, while a girl's tuition is the same as a boy's.

The PRESIDENT observed, that the girl gets twice as much education, being uniformly more studious and attentive.

E. A. HOPKINS, a lawer of Rochester, spoke to the eighth resolution, which asks for a committee to examine the whole subject; he said: I believe if this question was properly presented to the Legislature, we might have well grounded hope for the relief of women from their legal disabilities, and indicated the amendments which ought to be made in the present laws regulating the relations of the married state. He argued against making the man and wife joint owners of property, except in certain specific cases.

Rev. Mr. CHANNING said that in Louisiana and California this joint ownership was recognized by the laws.

Mr. HOPKINS was not aware of that; and he did not see why labor, worth in the market no more than one or two dollars per week, should be paid for at the rate of, it may be, $200 per week. He thought the law should be altered so that the widow may have control of property while her children are minors. The right to vote, which was claimed under the idea that representation should go before taxation, he discussed with ability, taking ground against women voting. The arguments used by the other side were shown to be fallacious, or at least partaking of the aristocratic element. Women are already tried by "their peers," though not by those of their own sex. As to women holding office, this movement had proved the position of Dr. Channing, in his discussion with Miss Martineau, that "influence was good, and office bad." Women should be content to exercise influence, without seeking for the spoils and risking the temptations of office. He argued upon the maxim that "governments derive their just powers from the consent of the governed," contending that it was not true; those powers are derived from the majority who are brave enough to set up and sustain the government.*

---

* Mr. Hopkins further stated that, tenancy by the courtesy operates in favor of the husband, not of the wife. It is the husband's right during his life to the use of the wife's real estate from her death, in case of a child or children born of the marriage. It is defeasible now by the wife's will.—Cow. Rep. 74, 2 R. S., 4th Ed. 331. Tenancy by right of dower is the wife's right during her life to the use of one-third of the husband's real estate from his death. It operates in favor of the wife and not in favor of the husband, and is indefeasible by the husband's will or the husband's acts while living, and does not depend upon the birth of a child by the marriage.

The order of distribution of the husband's personal property on his death is as follows, viz. : 1st, the widow of a family takes articles exempt from execution as hers, also $150 worth of property besides. 2d, she has one-third of the personal property, absolutely— if there be no children, one-half, and if there be no parent or descendant, she is entitled, of the residue, to $2,000, and if also no brother, sister, nephew, or niece, all the residue. This order may be varied or defeated by his will.

The order of distribution of the wife's personal property on her death without will is as follows : It goes, after paying her debts, to her husband, if living ; if not, then 1st,

Frederick Douglass, in the course of his remarks, said he had seen two young women assistants in the County Clerk's office, also young women going into printing-offices to set type ; and he might have added the following, which we clip from the *The Una* of the same date :

Female compositors have been employed in the offices of the three Cincinnati daily papers which stood out against the demands of the Printer's Union. The Pittsburg *Daily Dispatch* is also set up entirely by females. The experiment was commenced on that paper two months ago, and the proprietors now announce its entire success. The Louisville *Courier* announces its intentions to try the experiment in the spring. Wherever the change has been made it seems to be completely success-ful.—*Courier and Enquirer.*

Mr. MAY said: If a woman should not leave her family to go to the Legislature, neither should a man. The obligation is mutual: and while children require the care of both parents, both should share the duty, and not leave them from ambitious motives. It is only those who have well discharged their duties to their families who are fit to become legis-lators. We are now giving the nation into the hands of boys and half-grown men. Had we such women as Lucretia Mott and Angelina Grimké in the Legislature, there would be more wisdom there than we have to-

---

to her children, 2d to her father, 3d to her mother, 4th to her collateral relatives. This order may be varied or defeated by her will. She may devise it as she may please.

His property before marriage continues his after marriage, subject to her inchoate rights of dower.

Her property before marriage continues hers absolutely.

Upon marriage he is liable to support her, and may be compelled to do it if he prove refractory.

She is not liable to support him, however wealthy she may be, or poor he may be.

He is liable to support the children. She is not so liable, though possessed of mil-lions.

The husband is the guardian of the wife, as against third persons. (Page 488). But he has no power to preserve, retain, or regain the custody of her against her will. (Page 47).

He may maintain his action against third persons for enticing her away or harboring her. But this harboring, to be actionable, must be more than a mere permission to her to stay with such third person. (4 Barb. 225).

If the husband seek to take away his wife by force, it is an assault and battery upon her. If a third person resists such force at her request he is not liable to any action. (Barb. 156).

The wife is not the husband's guardian, but if he will desert her he may be put under bonds for her support and the support of her children by him. (2 Rev. Stat., 4th Ed., pp. 53, 54).

The husband is liable for the debts of the wife contracted before marriage, but only now to the extent of her property received by him. (7 W. R. 237, 1st Chitty Pl., 66 to 68, laws of 1853). And he is liable for her debts contracted during marriage, if permit-ted by him, or if for necessaries which he neglected to provide.

The wife is not liable for her husband's debts contracted at any time.

The law casts the custody of the minor children upon the father and not upon the mother. But if this custody is abused, it is by the Court to the mother.

The father may appoint a guardian for his infant children. (2 Rev. Stat. 33. But the day. When I look through the nation and see the shameful mismanagement, I am convinced that it is the result, in part, of the absence of the feminine element in high stations; it is because the maternal influence is wanting that we run riot as we do. The State is in a condition of half orphanage, and needs the care and guidance of a mother.

E. A. HOPKINS, Esq.: Thought the movement was not entirely timely, wise, and practicable, though parts of it might be. He took up and answered each of the questions appended to the call for the Convention. His speech was characteristic of the lawyer, and the frequent recurrence of the idea, *it is right because it is customary*, will illustrate its moral character. He stated three several points where he thought woman was aggrieved and should have legislative redress. Office was a temptation, and he thought woman was better off without it.

Miss BROWN proposed that the men, for a while, be relieved from this great evil, and excused from the burdens of office. If this necessary duty was so burdensome, woman should be a helper and share its burdens with him. We are taught to be grateful for small favors. Our friend has been giving you milk, but to me it seems, even at that, diluted with water. There is one law, "All things whatsoever ye would that men should do to you, do ye even so to them." When our brothers are ready to be paid a dollar a week for keeping house and nursing the children, let them dictate this also to us. We women now offer to take the

---

Court will not allow such guardian to take the children out of the State against the mother's will, much less to separate them unjustly from the mother even though the father's will command it. (5, page 596).

During the separation of husband and wife, it is for the court now to decide, under the circumstances of each case, whether father or mother has such custody. (2 R. S 330, 332).

When both seek such custody, and both are equally qualified for it, that of daughters and young children is usually given to the mother, and that of the sons to the father, but this is in the discretion of the Court.

The earnings of the husband are his. The earnings of the wife are his, if she live with him and he support her.

But he can not compel her to work for him. And if she separate from him for cause, he may be restrained for intermeddling with her earnings.

The husband's abandonment and his refusal or neglect to provide for her, are good causes of separation. (2 R. S. 329, sec. 53, sub. 3).

For the husband's torts the wife is not liable. For the wife's torts, committed by her before marriage or during marriage the husband is liable jointly with the wife. If committed by the wife and husband, or committed by the wife in his presence and without objecting, the husband is liable alone. (1 Chitty Pl., 105, 7th American edition). Nay, even felonies (excepting murder, manslaughter, treason, and robbery), are excusable in the wife if committed in the husband's presence and by his coercion—and such coercion is presumed from his presence. For this he must suffer and she must be spared. (Barb. Crim. Law, 247 and 348, and cases there cited).

In actions or lawsuits between men and women, the law in theory claims to be impartial, but in practice it has not been impartial. Before a Court of male judges or a jury of men the bias is in favor of the woman; and if she is pleasing, in person and manners, such bias is sometimes pretty strong.

If the man and woman between whom litigation arises are husband and wife, the Court may accord an allowance to be advanced by her husband, to enable her to defray the expenses of the litigation.

burden and responsibility of government upon ourselves. We would be willing to save our friends for a time from temptation and care, as they have so generously done by us; if we are to be satisfied with things as they are, so should the slave be. He should be grateful for the care of his master, for according to the established price paid for labor, he does not earn enough to take care of himself. We should be satisfied with our present license laws; they are right, just, and good, judged by our friend's reasoning. If our offer to rule alone is not liked, we are ready, then, to co-operate with man in this according to the original design and arrangement of the Creator.

Mr. HOPKINS opposed with several objections, one of which was, that private stations demand as high qualifications, and more surely command a just recompense, than public offices; woman has yet taken few lucrative private employments; why, then, till these are taken, should she seek for public office ?

FREDERICK DOUGLASS again raised the inquiry, in the investment of money or the use of property, where there is joint ownership, and in regard to which there may be disagreement between husband and wife, how shall the matter be settled between them ? Law is not a necessity of human nature; if love ruled, statutes would be obsolete; genuine marriages and harmonious co-operations would prevent any such necessity.

Miss BROWN proposed to reply in a word: Law must regulate differences where there is not true union, and as a business copartnership, if the matter could not be adjusted between themselves to mutual satisfaction, let it be referred to a third person; where it is a property transaction, let the usual business custom be observed; but if there be a difficulty of a different nature, so serious that the parties, bound to each other for life, can not enjoy existence together if they can not make each other happy, but are to each other a mutual source of discomfort, why, let them separate; let them not be divorced, but let them each be content to live alone for the good of society.

Mrs. LOVE, of Randolph, read an address, flowery in style, but full of truth, upon the discord that pervades social life. Homes should be reformed; from domestic uncongeniality spring the chief evils of society. She advised men and women to beware of inharmonious alliances, and made a touching appeal in behalf of the fallen of her sex.

Mr. CHANNING said: Whenever he heard a woman, in face of existing prejudices, speak the simple truth in regard to the social wrongs of her sisters, as Mrs. Love had done, asking no leave of the Convention, and making no apology for her sincere words, however they might startle false delicacy, he felt bound as a man, and in the name of man, to offer her the tribute of his hearty respect.

Mr. Channing presented two forms of petitions—one for property rights, the other for suffrage—which were adopted. Rev. Lydia A. Jenkins read a carefully prepared address. Emma R. Coe made a full review of the laws, which, at that early day, was the burden of almost every speech. At the close of the sixth session, the audiences having grown larger and larger, until the spacious and beautiful Corinthian Hall was packed to its utmost, the Convention adjourned, to begin its real work in canvassing the State with lectures and petitions, preparing an address to the Legislature, securing a hearing, and holding a Convention at Albany during the coming session of that body.

An appeal * to the women of the State was at once issued, and all

---

* WOMAN'S RIGHTS.—*Circulate the Petitions.*—The design of the Convention held last week in Rochester, was to bring the subject of Woman's legal and civil disabilities, in a dignified form, before the Legislature of New York. Convinced, as the friends of the movement are, that in consistency with the principles of Republicanism, females, equally with males, are entitled to Freedom, Representation, and Suffrage, and confident as they are that woman's influence will be found to be as refining and elevating in public as all experience proves it to be in private, they claim that one-half of the people and citizens of New York should no longer be governed by the other half, without consent asked and given. Encouraged by reforms already made, in the barbarous usages of common law, by the statutes of New York, the advocates of woman's just and equal rights demand that this work of reform be carried on, until every vestige of partiality is removed. It is proposed, in a carefully prepared address to specify the remaining legal disabilities from which the women of this State suffer; and a hearing is asked before a joint committee of both Houses, specially empowered to revise and amend the statutes. Now is this movement right in principle? Is it wise in policy? Should the females of New York be placed on a level of equality with males before the law? If so, let us petition for impartial justice to Women. In order to ensure this equal justice should the females of New York, like the males, have a voice in appointing the law-makers and law-administrators? If so, let us petition for Woman's right to Suffrage. Finally, what candid man will be opposed to a reference of the whole subject to the Representatives of New York, whom the men of New York themselves elected. Let us then petition for a hearing before the Legislature. A word more, as to the petitions, given below. They are two in number; one for the Just and Equal Rights of Woman; one for Woman's Right to Suffrage. It is designed that they should be signed by men and women, of lawful age—that is, of twenty-one years and upwards. The following directions are suggested: 1. Let persons, ready and willing, sign each of the petitions; but let not those, who desire to secure Woman's Just and Equal Rights, hesitate to sign that petition because they have doubts as to the right or expediency of women's voting. The petitions will be kept separate, and offered separately. All fair-minded persons, of either sex, ought to sign the first petition. We trust that many thousands are prepared to sign the second also. 2. In obtaining signatures, let men sign in one column, and women in another parallel column. 3. Let the name of the town and county, together with the number of signatures, be distinctly entered on the petitions before they are returned. 4. Let every person, man or woman, interested in this movement, instantly and energetically circulate the petitions in their respective neighborhoods. We must send in the name of every person in the State, who desires full justice to woman, so far as it is possible. Up then, friends, and be doing, to-day. 5. Let no person sign either petition but once. As many persons will circulate petitions in the same town and county, it is important to guard against this possible abuse. 6. Finally, let every petition be returned to Rochester, directed to the Secretary of the Convention, Susan B. Anthony, on the first of February, without fail. In behalf of the Business Committee. WILLIAM HENRY CHANNING.

ROCHESTER, *Dec.* 8, 1853.

PETITION FOR THE JUST AND EQUAL RIGHTS OF WOMEN.- The Legislature of the State of New York have, by the Acts of 1848 and 1849, testified the purpose of the people of this editors requested to publish it with the forms of petitions. The responses came back in the form of 13,000 signatures in two months, gathered in thirty out of the sixty counties of the Empire State. The lecturers were: Susan B. Anthony, Mary F. Love, Sarah Pellet, Lydia A. Jenkins, and Matilda Joslyn Gage. Over sixty women were engaged in the work of circulating the petitions.

Horace Greeley, chairman of the Committee on Industry, published in *The New York Tribune* the following report:

WOMAN AND WORK.

Whether women should or should not be permitted to vote, to hold office, to serve on juries, and to officiate as lawyers, doctors, or divines, are questions about which a diversity of opinions is likely long to exist. But that the current rates of remuneration for woman's work are entirely, unjustly inadequate, is a proposition which needs only to be considered to insure its hearty acceptance by every intelligent, justice-loving human being. Consider a few facts:

Every able-bodied man inured to labor, though of the rudest sort, who steps on shore in America from Europe, is worth a dollar per day, and can readily command it. Though he only knows how to wield such rude, clumsy implements as the pick and spade, there are dozens of places where his services are in request at a dollar per day the year through, and he can even be transported hence to the place where his services are wanted, on the strength of his contract to work and the credit of his future earnings. We do not say this is the case every day in the year, for it may not be at this most inclement and forbidding season; but it is the general fact, as every one knows. And any careful, intelligent, resolute male laborer is morally certain to rise out of the condition of a mere shoveler, into a position where the work is lighter and the pay better after a year or two of faithful service.

But the sister of this same faithful worker, equally careful, intelligent, and willing to do anything honest and reputable for a living, finds no

State to place married women on an equality with married men, in regard to the holding, conveying, and devising of real and personal property. We, therefore, the undersigned petitioners, inhabitants of the State of New York, male and female, having attained to the legal majority, believing that women, alike married and single, do still suffer under many and grievous legal disabilities, do earnestly request the Senate and Assembly of the State of New York to appoint a Joint Committee of both Houses, to revise the Statutes of New York, and to propose such amendments as will fully establish the legal equality of women with men; and we hereby ask a hearing before such Committee by our accredited Representatives.

PETITION FOR WOMAN'S RIGHT TO SUFFRAGE.—Whereas, according to the Declaration of our National Independence, governments derive their just powers from the consent of the governed, we earnestly request the Legislature of New York to propose to the people of the State such amendments of the Constitution of the State as will secure to females an equal right to the Elective Franchise with males; and we hereby ask a hearing before the Legislature by our accredited Representatives.

N. B.—Editors throughout the State in favor of this movement are respectfully requested to publish this address and the petitions.

such chances proffered her. No agent meets her on the dock to persuade her to accept a passage to Illinois or Upper Canada, there to be employed on fair work at a dollar per day and expectations. On the contrary, she may think herself fortunate if a week's search opens to her a place where by the devotion of all her waking hours she can earn five to six dollars per month, with a chance of its increase, after several years' faithful service, to seven or eight dollars at most.

The brother is in many respects the equal of his employer; may sit down beside him at the hotel where they both stop for dinner; their votes may balance each other at any election; the laborer lives with those whose company suits him, and needs no character from his last place to secure him employment or a new job when he gets tired of the old one. But the sister never passes out of the atmosphere of caste—of conscious and galling inferiority to those with whom her days must be spent. There is no election day in *her* year, and but the ghost of a Fourth of July. She must live not with those she likes, but with those who want her; she is not always safe from libertine insult in what serves her for a home; she knows no ten-hour rule, and would not dare to claim its protection if one were enacted. Though not a slave by law, she is too often as near it in practice as one legally free can be.

Now this disparity between the rewards of man's and woman's labor at the base of the social edifice, is carried up to its very pinnacle. Of a brother and sister equally qualified and effective as teachers, the brother will receive twice as much compensation as the sister. The mistress who conducts the rural district school in summer, usually receives less than half the monthly stipend that her brother does for teaching that same school in winter, when time and work are far less valuable; and here there can be no pretence of a disparity in capacity justifying that in wages. Between male and female workers in the factories and mills, the same difference is enforced.

Who does not feel that this is intrinsically wrong? that the sister ought to have equal (not necessarily identical) opportunities with the brother—should be as well taught, industrially as well as intellectually, and her compensation made to correspond with her capacity, upon a clear understanding of the fact that, though her muscular power is less than his, yet her dexterity and celerity of manipulation are greater?

Where does the wrong originate? Suppose that, by some inexorable law in the spirit of Hindoo caste, it were settled that negroes, regardless of personal capacity, could do nothing for a living but black boots, and that red-haired men were allowed to engage in no avocation except horse-currying; who does not perceive that, though boot-blacking and horse-currying might be well and cheaply done, black-skinned and also red-haired men would have but a sorry chance for making a living? Who does not see that their wages, social standing, and means of securing independence, would be far inferior to those they now enjoy?

The one great cause, therefore, of the inadequate compensation and inferior position of woman, is the unjust apportionment of avocation. Man has taken the lion's share to himself, and allotted the residue to woman, telling her to take that and be content with it, if she don't want to be regarded as a forward, indelicate, presuming, unwomanly creature, who is evidently no better than she should be. And woman has come for the most part to accept the lot thus assigned her, with thankfulness, or, rather, without thought, just as the Mussulman's wife rejoices in her sense of propriety which will not permit her to show her face in the street, and the Brahmin widow immolates herself on the funeral pyre of her husband.

What is the appropriate remedy ?

Primarily and mainly, a more rational and healthful public sentiment with regard to woman's work; a sentiment which shall welcome her to every employment wherein she may be useful and efficient without necessarily compromising her purity or overtasking her strength. Let her be encouraged to open a store, to work a garden, plant and tend an orchard, to learn any of the lighter mechanical trades, to study for a profession, whenever her circumstances and her tastes shall render any of these desirable. Let woman, and the advocates of justice to women, encourage and patronize her in whatever laudable pursuits she may thus undertake; let them give a preference to dry-goods stores wherein the clerks are mainly women; and so as to hotels where they wait at table, mechanics' shops in which they are extensively employed and fairly paid. Let the ablest of the sex be called to the lecture-room, to the temperance rostrum, etc.; and whenever a post-office falls vacant and a deserving woman is competent to fill and willing to take it, let her be appointed, as a very few have already been. There will always be some widow of a poor clergyman, doctor, lawyer, or other citizens prematurely cut off, who will be found qualified for and glad to accept such a post if others will suggest her name and procure her appointment. Thus abstracting more and more of the competent and energetic from the restricted sphere wherein they now struggle with their sister for a meager and precarious subsistence, the greater mass of self-subsisting women will find the demand for their labor gradually increasing and its recompense proportionally enhancing. With a larger field and more decided usefulness will come a truer and deeper respect; and woman, no longer constrained to marry for a position, may always wait to marry worthily and in obedience to the dictates of sincere affection. Hence constancy, purity, mutual respect, a just independence and a little of happiness, may be reasonably anticipated.

HORACE GREELEY, MARY VAUGHAN, ABRAHAM PRYNE,
SARAH PELLET, MATILDA JOSLYN GAGE.

ALBANY CONVENTION.
FEBRUARY 14 AND 15, 1854.

Although the weather was inclement, a large audience assembled in Association Hall on the morning of the 14th, representing the different portions of the State. Susan B. Anthony called the Convention to order and read the call, which had been written by Rev. Wm. Henry Channing, and published in all the leading papers of the State.

JUSTICE TO WOMEN—CONVENTION AT ALBANY, FEB. 14 AND 15, 1854.

The petition asking for such amendments in the Statutes and Constitution of New York as will secure to the women of the State legal equality with the men, and to females equally with the males a right to suffrage, will be presented to the Legislature about the middle of February. We, the Committee appointed at the Convention held at Rochester in December—by whose authority these petitions were issued—do hereby invite all fellow-citizens, of either sex, who are in favor of these measures, to assemble in Convention, at Albany, on Tuesday and Wednesday, February 14th and 15th.

The so-called "Woman's Rights Movement" has been so much misrepresented, that it is desirable to make the appeal for justice earnest, imposing, and effective, by showing how eminently equitable are its principles, how wise and practical are its measures. Let the serious-minded, generous, hopeful men and women of New York then gather in council, to determine whether there is anything irrational or revolutionary in the proposal that fathers, brothers, husbands, sons, should treat their daughters, sisters, wives, and mothers as their peers. This reform is designed, by its originators, to make woman womanly in the highest sense of that term—to exalt, not to degrade—to perfect, not to impair her refining influence in every sphere. The demand is made only to take off burdens, to remove hindrances, to leave women free as men are free, to follow conscience and judgment in all scenes of duty. On what ground—except the right of might—do men, claiming to be Republicans and Christians, deny to woman privileges which they would die to gain and keep for themselves ? What evil—what but good can come from enlarging woman's power of usefulness ? How can society be otherwise than a gainer by the increased moral and mental influence of one-half of its members ? Let these and similar questions be fairly, candidly, thoroughly discussed in the hearing of the Legislature of New York.

Come then, fellow-citizens, to this Convention prepared to speak, to hear, to act. Lucy Stone, Wendell Phillips, Mrs. C. I. H. Nichols, and other earnest friends of the cause from New England and the West, as well as from our own State, are to be with us. And may the spirit of Truth preside over all.

ELIZABETH C. STANTON, SAMUEL J. MAY, ERNESTINE L. ROSE, ANTOINETTE L. BROWN, WILLIAM HENRY CHANNING, WM. HAY, BURROUGHS PHILLIPS, LYDIA ANN JENKINS, SUSAN B. ANTHONY.

Those having petitions in their hands will please send them to Susan B. Anthony, Rochester, until the first of February, after which they should be forwarded to Lydia Mott, Albany.

N. B.—Editors please copy.

January 23, 1854.

The officers* of the Convention being reported, Mrs. Elizabeth

---

* *President.*—Elizabeth Cady Stanton.
Vice-Presidents.—Rev. S. J. May, Ernestine L. Rose, New York ; Hon. William Hay

Cady Stanton (President) took the chair, and after returning her acknowledgments for the honor conferred, introduced Rev. Antoinette L. Brown, who read a series of resolutions :

1. *Resolved*, That the men who claim to be Christian Republicans, and yet class their mothers, sisters, wives, and daughters among aliens, criminals, idiots, and minors, unfit to be their coequal citizens, are guilty of absurd inconsistency and presumption ; that for males to govern females, without consent asked or granted, is to perpetuate an aristocracy, utterly hostile to the principles and spirit of free institutions ; and that it is time for the people of the United States and every State in the Union to put away forever that remnant of despotism and feudal oligarchy, the caste of sex.

2. *Resolved*, That women are human beings whose rights correspond with their duties ; that they are endowed with conscience, reason, affection, and energy, for the use of which they are individually responsible ; that like men they are bound to advance the cause of truth, justice, and universal good in the society and nation of which they are members ; that in these United States women constitute one-half the people ; men constitute the other half ; that women are no more free in honor than men are to withhold their influence and example from patriotic and philanthropic movements, and that men who deny women to be their peers, and who shut them out from exercising a fair share of power in the body politic, are arrogant usurpers, whose only apology is to be found in prejudices transmitted from half-civilized and half-christianized ages.

WHEREAS, The family is the nursery of the State and the Church—the God-appointed seminary of the human race. Therefore

3. *Resolved*, That the family, by men as well as women, should be held more sacred than all other institutions ; that it may not, without sin, be abandoned or neglected by fathers any more than by mothers, for the sake of any of the institutions devised by men—for the government of the State or the Nation any more than for the voluntary association of social reformers.

4. *Resolved*, That women's duties and rights as daughters, sisters, wives, and mothers, are not bounded within the circle of home ; that in view of the sacredness of their relations, they are not free to desert their fathers, brothers, husbands, and sons amidst scenes of business, politics, and pleasure, and to leave them alone in their struggles and temptations, but that as members of the human family, for the sake of human advancement, women are bound as widely as possible to give to men the influence of their aid and presence ; and finally, that universal experience attests that those nations and societies are most orderly, high-toned, and rich in varied prosperity, where women most freely intermingle with men in all spheres of active life.

5. *Resolved*, That the fundamental error of the whole structure of legislation and custom, whereby women are practically sustained, even in this republic, is the preposterous fiction of law, that in the eye of the law the husband and

Saratoga ; William H. Topp, Albany ; Lydia A. Jenkins, Geneva ; Lydia Mott, Albany ; Mary F. Love, Randolph.

Business Committee.—Rev. Antoinette L. Brown, South Butler ; W. H. Channing, Rochester ; Mrs. Catherine A. F. Stebbins, Mrs. Phebe H. Jones, Troy.

Secretaries.—Susan B. Anthony, Sarah Pellet.

Finance Committee.—Mary S. Anthony, Rochester ; Anna W. Anthony, Cayuga.

wife are one person, that person being the husband; that this falsehood itself, the deposit of barbarism, tends perpetually to brutalize the marriage relation by subjecting wives as irresponsible tools to the capricious authority of husbands; that this degradation of married women re-acts inevitably to depress the condition of single women, by impairing their own self-respect and man's respect for them; and that the final result is that system of tutelage miscalled protection, by which the industry of women is kept on half-pay, their affections trifled with, their energies crippled, and even their noblest aspirations wasted away in vain efforts, ennui, and regret.

6. *Resolved,* That in consistency with the spirit and intent of the Statutes of New York, enacted in 1848 and 1849, the design of which was to secure to married women the entire control of their property, it is the duty of the Legislature to make such amendments in the laws of the State as will enable married women to conduct business, to form contracts, to sue and be sued in their own names—to receive and hold the gains of their industry, and be liable for their own debts so far as their interests are separate from those of their husbands—to become joint owners in the joint earnings of the partnership, so far as these interests are identified—to bear witness for or against their husbands, and generally to be held responsible for their own deeds.

7. *Resolved,* That as acquiring property by all just and laudable means, and the holding and devising of the same is a human right, women married and single are entitled to this right, and all the usages or laws which withhold it from them are manifestly unjust.

8. *Resolved,* That every argument in favor of universal suffrage for males is equally in favor of universal suffrage for females, and therefore if men may claim the right of suffrage as necessary to the protection of all their rights in any Government, so may women for the same reason.

9. *Resolved,* That if man as man, has any peculiar claim to a representation in the government, for himself, woman as woman, has a paramount claim to an equal representation for herself.

10. *Resolved,* Therefore, that whether you regard woman as like or unlike man, she is in either case entitled to an equal joint participation with him in all civil rights and duties.

11. *Resolved,* That although men should grant us every specific claim, we should hold them all by favor rather than right, unless they also concede, and we exercise, the right of protecting ourselves by the elective franchise.

12. *Resolved,* That if the essence of a trial by an "impartial jury" be a trial by one's own equals, then has never a woman enjoyed that privilege in the hour of her need as a culprit. We, therefore, respectfully demand of our Legislature that, at least, the right of such trial by jury be accorded to women equally with men—that women be eligible to the jury-box, whenever one of their own sex is arraigned at the bar.

13. *Resolved,* That could the women of the State be heard on this question, we should find the mass with us; as the mother's reluctance to give up the guardianship of her children; the wife's unwillingness to submit to the abuse of a drunken husband, the general sentiment in favor of equal property rights, and the thousands of names in favor of our petition, raised with so little effort, conclusively prove.

WHEREAS, The right of petition is guaranteed to every member of this republic; therefore

14. *Resolved,* That it is the highest duty of legislators impartially to investigate all claims for the redress of wrong, and alter and amend such laws as prevent the administration of justice and equal rights to all.

Resolved, That all true-hearted men and women pledge themselves never to relinquish their unceasing efforts in behalf of the full and equal rights of women, until we have effaced the stigma resting on this republic, that while it theoretically proclaims that all men are created equal, deprives one-half of its members of the enjoyment of the rights and privileges possessed by the other.

The salient points of the question as embodied in the resolutions and the address were ably presented by William Henry Channing, Samuel J. May, Mrs. Nichols, Mrs. Rose, Mrs. Love, Miss Brown, Miss Anthony, Mrs. Jenkins, Hon. William Hay, and Giles B. Stebbins. At the evening session Mrs. Stanton read her address prepared for the Legislature, which Miss Anthony had stereotyped and published. A copy was laid on the desk of every legislator, and twenty thousand scattered like snow-flakes over the State.

MRS. STANTON'S ADDRESS.

To the Legislature of the State of New York :

" The thinking minds of all nations call for change. There is a deep-lying struggle in the whole fabric of society ; a boundless, grinding collision of the New with the Old."

The tyrant, Custom, has been summoned before the bar of Common-Sense. His majesty no longer awes the multitude—his sceptre is broken—his crown is trampled in the dust—the sentence of death is pronounced upon him. All nations, ranks, and classes have, in turn, questioned and repudiated his authority; and now, that the monster is chained and caged, timid woman, on tiptoe, comes to look him in the face, and to demand of her brave sires and sons, who have struck stout blows for liberty, if, in this change of dynasty, she, too, shall find relief. Yes, gentlemen, in republican America, in the nineteenth century, we, the daughters of the revolutionary heroes of '76, demand at your hands the redress of our grievances—a revision of your State Constitution—a new code of laws. Permit us then, as briefly as possible, to call your attention to the legal disabilities under which we labor.

1st. Look at the position of woman as woman. It is not enough for us that by your laws we are permitted to live and breathe, to claim the necessaries of life from our legal protectors—to pay the penalty of our crimes ; we demand the full recognition of all our rights as citizens of the Empire State. We are persons; native, free-born citizens ; property-holders, tax-payers ; yet are we denied the exercise of our right to the elective franchise. We support ourselves, and, in part, your schools, colleges, churches, your poor-houses, jails, prisons, the army, the navy, the whole machinery of government, and yet we have no voice in your councils. We have every qualification required by the Constitution, necessary to the legal voter, but the one of sex. We are moral, virtuous, and intelligent, and in all respects quite equal to the proud white man himself, and yet by your laws we are classed with idiots, lunatics, and negroes ; and though we do not feel honored by the place assigned us, yet, in fact, our legal position is lower than that of either; for the negro can be raised to the dignity of a voter if he possess himself of $250 ; the lunatic can vote in his moments of sanity, and the idiot, too, if he be a male one, and not more than nine-tenths a fool; but we, who have guided great movements of charity, established missions, edited journals, published works on history, economy, and statistics; who have governed nations, led armies, filled the professor's chair, taught philosophy and mathematics to the savants of our age, discovered planets, piloted ships across the sea, are denied the most sacred rights of citizens, because, forsooth, we came not into this republic crowned with the dignity of manhood! Woman is theoretically absolved from all allegiance to the laws of the State. Sec. 1, Bill of Rights, 2 R. S., 301, says that no authority can, on any prentence whatever, be exercised over the citizens of this State but such as is or shall be derived from, and granted by the people of this State.

Now, gentlemen, we would fain know by what authority you have disfranchised one-half the people of this State? You who have so boldly taken possession of the bulwarks of this republic, show us your credentials, and thus prove your exclusive right to govern, not only yourselves, but us. Judge Hurlburt, who has long occupied a high place at the bar in this State, and who recently retired with honor from the bench of the Supreme Court, in his profound work on Human Rights, has pronounced your present position rank usurpation. Can it be that here, where we acknowledge no royal blood, no apostolic descent, that you, who have declared that all men were created equal—that governments derive their just powers from the consent of the governed, would willingly build up an aristocracy that places the ignorant and vulgar above the educated and refined— the alien and the ditch-digger above the authors and poets of the day—an aristocracy that would raise the sons above the mothers that bore them ? Would that the men who can sanction a Constitution so opposed to the genius of this government, who can enact and execute laws so degrading to womankind, had sprung, Minerva-like, from the brains of their fathers, that the matrons of this republic need not blush to own their sons !

Woman's position, under our free institutions, is much lower than under the monarchy of England. "In England the idea of woman holding official station is not so strange as in the United States. The Countess of Pembroke, Dorset, and Montgomery held the office of hereditary sheriff of Westmoreland, and exercised it in person. At the assizes at Appleby, she sat with the judges on the bench. In a reported case, it is stated by counsel, and substantially assented to by the court, that a woman is capable of serving in almost all the offices of the kingdom, such as those of queen, marshal, great chamberlain and constable of England, the champion of England, commissioner of sewers, governor of work-house, sexton, keeper of the prison, of the gate-house of the dean and chapter of Westminster, returning officer for members of Parliament, and constable, the latter of which is in some respects judicial. The office of jailor is frequently exercised by a woman.

"In the United States a woman may administer on the effects of her deceased husband, and she has occasionally held a subordinate place in the post-office department. She has therefore a sort of post mortem, post-mistress notoriety; but with the exception of handling letters of administration and letters mailed, she is the submissive creature of the old common law." True, the unmarried woman has a right to the property she inherits and the money she earns, but she is taxed without representation. And here again you place the negro, so unjustly degraded by you, in a superior position to your own wives and mothers; for colored males, if possessed of a certain amount of property and certain other qualifications, can vote, but if they do not have these qualifications they are not subject to direct taxation; wherein they have the advantage of woman, she being subject to taxation for whatever amount she may possess. (Constitution of New York, Article 2, Sec. 2). But, say you, are not all women sufficiently represented by their fathers, husbands, and brothers? Let your statute books answer the question.

Again we demand in criminal cases that most sacred of all rights, trial by a jury of our own peers. The establishment of trial by jury is of so early a date that its beginning is lost in antiquity; but the right of trial by a jury of one's own peers is a great progressive step of advanced civilization. No rank of men have ever been satisfied with being tried by jurors higher or lower in the civil or political scale than themselves; for jealousy on the one hand, and contempt on the other, has ever effectually blinded the eyes of justice. Hence, all along the pages of history, we find the king, the noble, the peasant, the cardinal, the priest, the layman, each in turn protesting against the authority of the tribunal before which they were summoned to appear. Charles the First refused to recognize the competency of the tribunal which condemned him: For how, said he, can subjects judge a king? The stern descendants of our Pilgrim Fathers refused to answer for their crimes before an English Parliament. For how, said they, can a king judge rebels? And shall woman here consent to be tried by her liege lord, who has dubbed himself law-maker, judge, juror, and sheriff too?—whose power, though sanctioned by Church and State, has no foundation in justice and equity, and is a bold assumption of our inalienable rights. In England a Parliament-lord could challenge a jury where a knight was not empanneled; an alien could demand a jury composed half of his own countrymen; or, in some special cases, juries were even constituted entirely of women. Having seen that man fails to do justice to woman in her best estate, to the virtuous, the noble, the true of our sex, should we trust to his tender mercies the weak, the ignorant, the morally insane? It is not to be denied that the interests of man and woman in the present undeveloped state of the race, and under the existing social arrangements, are and must be antagonistic. The nobleman can not make just laws for the peasant; the slaveholder for the slave; neither can man make and execute just laws for woman, because in each case, the one in power fails to apply the immutable principles of right to any grade but his own.

Shall an erring woman be dragged before a bar of grim-visaged judges, lawyers, and jurors, there to be grossly questioned in public on subjects which women scarce breathe in secret to one another? Shall the most sacred relations of life be called up and rudely scanned by men who, by their own admission, are so coarse that women could not meet them even at the polls without contamination? and yet shall she find there no woman's face or voice to pity and defend? Shall the frenzied mother, who, to save herself and child from exposure and disgrace, ended the life that had but just begun, be dragged before such a tribunal to answer for her crime? How can man enter into the feelings of that mother? How can he judge of the agonies of soul that impelled her to such an outrage of maternal instincts? How can he weigh the mountain of sorrow that crushed that mother's heart when she wildly tossed her helpless babe into the cold waters of the midnight sea? Where is he who by false vows thus blasted this trusting woman? Had that helpless child no claims on his protection? Ah, he is freely abroad in the dignity of manhood, in the pulpit, on the bench, in the professor's chair. The imprisonment of his victim and the death of his child, detract not a tithe from his standing and complacency. His peers made the law, and shall law-makers lay nets for those of their own rank? Shall laws which come from the logical brain of man take cognizance of violence done to the moral and affectional nature which predominates, as is said, in woman?

Statesmen of New York, whose daughters, guarded by your affection, and lapped amidst luxuries which your indulgence spreads, care more for their nodding plumes and velvet trains than for the statute laws by which their persons and properties are held—who, blinded by custom and prejudice to the degraded position which they and their sisters occupy in the civil scale, haughtily claim that they already have all the rights they want, how, think ye, you would feel to see a daughter summoned for such a crime—and remember these daughters are but human—before such a tribunal? Would it not, in that hour, be some consolation to see that she was surrounded by the wise and virtuous of her own sex; by those who had known the depth of a mother's love and the misery of a lover's falsehood; to know that to these she could make her confession, and from them receive her sentence? If so, then listen to our just demands and make such a change in your laws as will secure to every woman tried in your courts, an impartial jury. At this moment among the hundreds of women who are shut up in prisons in this State, not one has enjoyed that most sacred of all rights—that right which you would die to defend for yourselves—trial by a jury of one's peers.

2d. Look at the position of woman as wife. Your laws relating to marriage—founded as they are on the old common law of England, a compound of barbarous usages, but partially modified by progressive civilization—are in open violation of our enlightened ideas of justice, and of the holiest feelings of our nature. If you take the highest view of marriage, as a Divine relation, which love alone can constitute and sanctify, then of course human legislation can only recognize it. Men can neither bind nor loose its ties, for that prerogative belongs to God alone, who makes man and woman, and the laws of attraction by which they are united. But if you regard marriage as a civil contract, then let it be subject to the same laws which control all other contracts. Do not make it a kind of half-human, half-divine institution, which you may build up, but can not regulate. Do not, by your special legislation for this one kind of contract, involve yourselves in the grossest absurdities and contradictions.

So long as by your laws no man can make a contract for a horse or piece of land until he is twenty-one years of age, and by which contract he is not bound if any deception has been practiced, or if the party contracting has not fulfilled his part of the agreement—so long as the parties in all mere civil contracts retain their identity and all the power and independence they had before contracting, with the full right to dissolve all partnerships and contracts for any reason, at the will and option of the parties themselves, upon what principle of civil jurisprudence do you permit the boy of fourteen and the girl of twelve, in violation of every natural law, to make a contract more momentous in importance than any other, and then hold them to it, come what may, the whole of their natural lives, in spite of disappointment, deception, and misery ? Then, too, the signing of this contract is instant civil death to one of the parties. The woman who but yesterday was sued on bended knee, who stood so high in the scale of being as to make an agreement on equal terms with a proud Saxon man, to-day has no civil existence, no social freedom. The wife who inherits no property holds about the same legal position that does the slave on the Southern plantation. She can own nothing, sell nothing. She has no right even to the wages she earns; her person, her time, her services are the property of another. She can not testify, in many cases, against her husband. She can get no redress for wrongs in her own name in any court of justice. She can neither sue nor be sued. She is not held morally responsible for any crime committed in the presence of her husband. so completely is her very existence supposed by the law to be merged in that of another. Think of it; your wives may be thieves, libelers, burglars, incendiaries, and for crimes like these they are not held amenable to the laws of the land, if they but commit them in your dread presence. For them, alas ! there is no higher law than the will of man. Herein behold the bloated conceit of these Petruchios of the law, who seem to say :

> " Nay, look not big, nor stamp, nor stare, nor fret,
> I will be master of what is mine own ;
> She is my goods, my chattels ; she is my house,
> My household stuff, my field, my barn,
> My horse, my ox, my ass, my anything ;
> And here she stands, touch her whoever dare ;
> I'll bring my action on the proudest he,
> That stops my way, in Padua."

How could man ever look thus on woman ? She, at whose feet Socrates learned wisdom—she, who gave to the world a Saviour, and witnessed alike the adoration of the Magi and the agonies of the cross. How could such a being, so blessed and honored, ever become the ignoble, servile, cringing slave, with whom the fear of man could be paramount to the sacred dictates of conscience and the holy love of Heaven ? By the common law of England, the spirit of which has been but too faithfully incorporated into our statute law, a husband has a right to whip his wife with a rod not larger than his thumb, to shut her up in a room, and administer whatever moderate chastisement he may deem necessary to insure obedience to his wishes, and for her healthful moral development ! He can forbid all persons harboring or trusting her on his account. He can deprive her of all social intercourse with her nearest and dearest friends. If by great economy she accumulates a small sum, which for future need she deposit, little by little, in a savings bank, the husband has a right to draw it out, at his option, to use it as he may see fit.

" Husband is entitled to wife's credit or business talents (whenever their intermarriage may have occurred) ; and goods purchased by her on her own credit, with his consent, while cohabiting with him, can be seized and sold in execution against him for his own debts, and this, though she carry on business in her own name."—7 *Howard's Practice Reports,* 105, *Lovett agt. Robinson and Whitbeck, sheriff, etc.*

" No letters of administration shall be granted to a person convicted of infamous crime; nor to any one incapable by law of making a contract; nor to a person not a citizen of the United States, unless such person reside within this State ; nor to any one who is under twenty-one years of age; nor to any person who shall be adjudged incompetent by the surrogate to execute duties of such trust, by reason of drunkenness, improvidence, or want of understanding, nor to any married woman; but where a married woman is entitled to administration, the same may be granted to her husband in her right and behalf."

There is nothing that an unruly wife might do against which the husband has not sufficient protection in the law. But not so with the wife. If she have a worthless husband, a confirmed drunkard, a villain, or a vagrant, he has still all the rights of a man, a husband, and a father. Though the whole support of the family be thrown upon the wife, if the wages she earns be paid to her by her employer, the husband can receive them again. If, by unwearied industry and perseverance, she can earn for herself and children a patch of ground and a shed to cover them, the husband can strip her of all her hard earnings, turn her and her little ones out in the cold northern blast, take the clothes from their backs, the bread from their mouths; all this by your laws may he do, and has he done, oft and again, to satisfy the rapacity of that monster in human form, the rum-seller.

But the wife who is so fortunate as to have inherited property, has, by the new law in this State, been redeemed from her lost condition. She is no longer a legal nonentity. This property law, if fairly construed, will overturn the whole code relating to woman and property. The right to property implies the right to buy and sell, to will and bequeath, and herein is the dawning of a civil existence for woman, for now the " femme covert " must have the right to make contracts. So, get ready, gentlemen; the " little justice " will be coming to you one day, deed in hand, for your acknowledgment. When he asks you "if you sign without fear or compulsion," say yes, boldly, as we do. Then, too, the right to will is ours. Now what becomes of the " tenant for life " ? Shall he, the happy husband of a millionaire, who has lived in yonder princely mansion in the midst of plenty and elegance, be cut down in a day to the use of one-third of this estate and a few hundred a year, as long he remains her widower? And should he, in spite of this bounty on celibacy, impelled by his affections, marry again, choosing for a wife a woman as poor as himself, shall he be thrown penniless on the cold world—this child of fortune, enervated by ease and luxury, henceforth to be dependent wholly on his own resources? Poor man! He would be rich, though, in the sympathies of many women who have passed through just such an ordeal. But what is property without the right to protect that property by law? It is mockery to say a certain estate is mine, if, without my consent, you have the right to tax me when and how you please, while I have no voice in making the tax-gatherer, the legislator, or the law. The right to property will, of necessity, compel us in due time to the exercise of our right to the elective franchise, and then naturally follows the right to hold office.

3d. Look at the position of woman as widow. Whenever we attempt to point out the wrongs of the wife, those who would have us believe that the laws can not be improved, point us to the privileges, powers, and claims of the widow. Let us look into these a little. Behold in yonder humble house a married pair, who, for long years, have lived together, childless and alone. Those few acres of well-tilled land, with the small, white house that looks so cheerful through its vines and flowers, attest the honest thrift and simple taste of its owners. This man and woman, by their hard days' labor, have made this home their own. Here they live in peace and plenty, happy in the hope that they may dwell together securely under their own vine and fig-tree for the few years that remain to them, and that under the shadow of these trees, planted by their own hands, and in the midst of their household gods, so loved and familiar, they may take their last farewell of earth. But, alas for human hopes! the husband dies, and without a will, and the stricken widow, at one fell blow, loses the companion of her youth, her house and home, and half the little sum she had in bank. For the law, which takes no cognizance of widows left with twelve children and not one cent, instantly spies out this widow, takes account of her effects, and announces to her the startling intelligence that but one-third of the house and lot, and one-half the personal property, are hers. The law has other favorites with whom she must share the hard-earned savings of years. In this dark hour of grief, the coarse minions of the law gather round the widow's hearth-stone, and, in the name of justice, outrage all natural sense of right; mock at the sacredness of human love, and with cold familiarity proceed to place a moneyed value on the old arm-chair, in which, but a few brief hours since, she closed the eyes that had ever beamed on her with kindness and affection; on the solemn clock in the corner, that told the hour he passed away; on every garment with which his form and presence were associated, and on every article of comfort and convenience that the house contained, even down to the knives and forks and spoons—and the widow saw it all—and when the work was done, she gathered up what the law allowed her and went forth to seek another home! This is the much-talked-of widow's dower. Behold the magnanimity of the law in allowing the widow to retain a life interest in one-third the landed estate, and one-half the personal property of her husband, and taking the lion's share to itself! Had she died first, the house and land would all have been the husband's still. No one would have dared to intrude upon the privacy of his home, or to molest him in his sacred retreat of sorrow. How, I ask you, can that be called justice, which makes such a distinction as this between man and woman?

By management, economy, and industry, our widow is able, in a few years, to redeem her house and home. But the law never loses sight of the purse, no matter how low in the scale of being its owner may be. It sends its officers round every year to gather in the harvest for the public crib, and no widow who owns a piece of land two feet square ever escapes this reckoning. Our widow, too, who has now twice earned her home, has her annual tax to pay also—a tribute of gratitude that she is permitted to breathe the free air of this republic, where "taxation without representation," by such worthies as John Hancock and Samuel Adams, has been declared "intolerable tyranny." Having glanced at the magnanimity of the law in its dealings with the widow, let us see how the individual man, under the influence of such laws, doles out justice to his help-mate. The husband has the absolute right to will away his property as he may see fit. If he has children, he can divide his property among them, leaving his wife her third only of the landed estate, thus making her a dependent on the bounty of her own children. A man with thirty thousand dollars in personal property, may leave his wife but a few hundred a year, as long as she remains his widow.

The cases are without number where women, who have lived in ease and ele-gance, at the death of their husbands have, by will, been reduced to the bare necessaries of life. The man who leaves his wife the sole guardian of his prop-erty and children is an exception to the general rule. Man has ever manifested a wish that the world should indeed be a blank to the companion whom he leaves behind him. The Hindoo makes that wish a law, and burns the widow on the funeral pyre of her husband ; but the civilized man, impressed with a dif-ferent view of the sacredness of life, takes a less summary mode of drawing his beloved partner after him ; he does it by the deprivation and starvation of the flesh, and the humiliation and mortification of the spirit. In bequeathing to the wife just enough to keep soul and body together, man seems to lose sight of the fact that woman, like himself, takes great pleasure in acts of benevolence and charity. It is but just, therefore, that she should have it in her power to give during her life, and to will away at her death, as her benevolence or ob-ligations might prompt her to do.

4th. Look at the position of woman as mother. There is no human love so strong and steadfast as that of the mother for her child ; yet behold how ruthless are your laws touching this most sacred relation. Nature has clearly made the mother the guardian of the child ; but man, in his inordinate love of power, does continually set nature and nature's laws at open defiance. The father may apprentice his child, bind him out to a trade, without the mother's con-sent—yea, in direct opposition to her most earnest entreaties, prayers and tears.

He may apprentice his son to a gamester or rum-seller, and thus cancel his debts of *honor*. By the abuse of this absolute power, he may bind his daughter to the owner of a brothel, and, by the degradation of his child, supply his daily wants ; and such things, gentlemen, have been done in our very midst. More-over, the father, about to die, may bind out all his children wherever and to whomsoever he may see fit, and thus, in fact, will away the guardianship of all his children from the mother. The Revised Statutes of New York provide that " every father, whether of full age or a minor, of a child to be born, or of any living child under the age of twenty-one years, and unmarried, may by his deed or last will, duly executed, dispose of the custody and tuition of such child dur-ing its minority, or for any less time, to any person or persons, in possession or remainder." 2 R. S., page 150, sec. 1. Thus, by your laws, the child is the absolute property of the father, wholly at his disposal in life or at death.

In case of separation, the law gives the children to the father ; no matter what his character or condition. At this very time we can point you to noble, virtuous, well-educated mothers in this State, who have abandoned their husbands for their profligacy and confirmed drunkenness. All these have been robbed of their children, who are in the custody of the husband, under the care of his relati es, whilst the mothers are permitted to see them but at stated intervals. But, said one of these mothers, with a grandeur of attitude and manner worthy the noble Roman matron in the palmiest days of that republic, I would rather never see my child again, than be the medium to hand down the low animal nature of its father, to stamp degradation on the brow of another innocent being. It is enough that one child of his shall call me mother.

If you are far-sighted statesmen, and do wisely judge of the interests of this commonwealth, you will so shape your future laws as to encourage woman to take the high moral ground that the father of her children must be great and good Instead of your present laws, which make the mother and her children the victims of vice and license, you might rather pass laws prohibiting to all drunkards, libertines, and fools, the rights of husbands and fathers. Do not the hundreds of laughing idiots that are crowding into our asylums, appeal to the wisdom of our statesmen for some new laws on marriage—to the mothers of this day for a higher, purer morality?

Again, as the condition of the child always follows that of the mother, and as by the sanction of your laws the father may beat the mother, so may he the child. What mother can not bear me witness to untold sufferings which cruel, vindictive fathers have visited upon their helpless children? Who ever saw a human being that would not abuse unlimited power? Base and ignoble must that man be who, let the provocation be what it may, would strike a woman : but he who would lacerate a trembling child is unworthy the name of man. A mother's love can be no protection to a child ; she can not appeal to you to save it from a father's cruelty, for the laws take no cognizance of the mother's most grievous wrongs. Neither at home nor abroad can a mother protect her son. Look at the temptations that surround the paths of our youth at every step ; look at the gambling and drinking saloons, the club rooms, the dens of infamy and abomination that infest all our villages and cities—slowly but surely sapping the very fo nda ions of all virtue and strength.

By your laws, all these abominable resorts are permitted. It is folly to talk of a mother moulding the character of her son, when all mankind, backed up by law and public sentiment, conspire to destroy her influence. But when woman's moral power shall speak through the ballot-box, then shall her influence be seen and felt ; then, in our legislative debates, such questions as the canal tolls on salt, the improvement of rivers and harbors, and the claims of Mr. Smith for damages against the State, would be secondary to the consideration of the legal existence of all these public resorts, which lure our youth on to excessive indulgence and destruction.

Many times and oft it has been asked us, with unaffected seriousness, "What do you women want? What are you aiming at?" Many have manifested a laudable curiosity to know what the wives and daughters could complain of in republican America, where their sires and sons have so bravely fought for freedom and gloriously secured their independence, trampling all tyranny, bigotry, and caste in the dust, and declaring to a waiting world the divine truth that all men are created equal. What can woman want under such a government? Admit a radical difference in sex, and you demand different spheres—water for fish, and air for birds.

It is impossible to make the Southern planter believe that his slave feels and reasons just as he does—that injustice and subjection are as galling as to him—

that the degradation of living by the will of another, the mere dependent on his caprice, at the mercy of his passions, is as keenly felt by him as his master. If you can force on his unwilling vision a vivid picture of the negro's wrongs, and for a moment touch his soul, his logic brings him instant consolation. He says, the slave does not feel this as I would. Here, gentlemen, is our difficulty: When we plead our cause before the law-makers and savants of the republic, they can not take in the idea that men and women are alike; and so long as the mass rest in this delusion, the public mind will not be so much startled by the revelations made of the injustice and degradation of woman's position as by the fact that she should at length wake up to a sense of it.

If you, too, are thus deluded, what avails it that we show by your statute books that your laws are unjust—that woman is the victim of avarice and power? What avails it that we point out the wrongs of woman in social life; the victim of passion and lust? You scorn the thought that she has any natural love of freedom burning in her breast, any clear perception of justice urging her on to demand her rights.

Would to God you could know the burning indignation that fills woman's soul when she turns over the pages of your statute books, and sees there how like feudal barons you freemen hold your women. Would that you could know the humiliation she feels for sex, when she thinks of all the beardless boys in your law offices, learning these ideas of one-sided justice—taking their first lessons in contempt for all womankind—being indoctrinated into the incapacities of their mothers, and the lordly, absolute rights of man over all women, children, and property, and to know that these are to be our future presidents, judges, husbands, and fathers; in sorrow we exclaim, alas! for that nation whose sons bow not in loyalty to woman. The mother is the first object of the child's veneration and love, and they who root out this holy sentiment, dream not of the blighting effect it has on the boy and the man. The impression left on law students, fresh from your statute books, is most unfavorable to woman's influence; hence you see but few lawyers chivalrous and high-toned in their sentiments toward woman. They can not escape the legal view which, by constant reading, has become familiarized to their minds: "*Femme covert*," "dow_er," "widow's claims," "protection," "incapacities," "incumbrance," is written on the brow of every woman they meet.

But if, gentlemen, you take the ground that the sexes are alike, and, therefore, you are our faithful representatives—then why all these special laws for woman? Would not one code answer for all of like needs and wants? Christ's golden rule is better than all the special legislation that the ingenuity of man can devise: "Do unto others as you would have others do unto you." This, men and brethren, is all we ask at your hands. We ask no better laws than those you have made for yourselves. We need no other protection than that which your present laws secure to you.

In conclusion, then, let us say, in behalf of the women of this State, we ask for all that you have asked for yourselves in the progress of your development, since the *Mayflower* cast anchor beside Plymouth rock; and simply on the ground that the rights of every human being are the same and identical. You may say that the mass of the women of this State do not make the demand; it comes from a few sour, disappointed old maids and childless women.

You are mistaken; the mass speak through us. A very large majority of the women of this State support themselves and their children, and many their husbands too. Go into any village you please, of three or four thousand inhabitants, and you will find as many as fifty men or more, whose only business is to discuss religion and politics, as they watch the trains come and go at the depot, or the passage of a canal boat through a lock; to laugh at the vagaries of some drunken brother, or the capers of a monkey dancing to the music of his master's organ. All these are supported by their mothers, wives, or sisters.

Now, do you candidly think these wives do not wish to control the wages they earn—to own the land they buy—the houses they build? to have at their disposal their own children, without being subject to the constant interference and tyranny of an idle, worthless profligate? Do you suppose that any woman is such a pattern of devotion and submission that she willingly stitches all day for the small sum of fifty cents, that she may enjoy the unspeakable privilege, in obedience to your laws, of paying for her husband's tobacco and rum? Think you the wife of the confirmed, beastly drunkard would consent to share with him her home and bed, if law and public sentiment would release her from such gross companionship? Verily, no! Think you the wife with whom endurance has ceased to be a virtue, who, through much suffering, has lost all faith in the justice of both heaven and earth, takes the law in her own hand, severs the unholy bond, and turns her back forever upon him whom she once called husband, consents to the law that in such an hour tears her child from her—all that she has left on earth to love and cherish? The drunkards' wives speak through us, and they number 50,000. Think you that the woman who has worked hard all her days in helping her husband to accumulate a large property, consents to the law that places this wholly at his disposal? Would not the mother whose only child is bound out for a term of years against her expressed wish, deprive the father of this absolute power if she could?

For all these, then, we speak. If to this long list you add the laboring women who are loudly demanding remuneration for their unending toil; those women who teach in our seminaries, academies, and public schools for a miserable pittance; the widows who are taxed without mercy; the unfortunate ones in our work-houses, poor-houses, and prisons; who are they that we do not now represent? But a small class of the fashionable butterflies, who, through the short summer days, seek the sunshine and the flowers; but the cool breezes of autumn and the hoary frosts of winter will soon chase all these away; then they, too, will need and seek protection, and through other lips demand in their turn justice and equity at your hands.

The friends of woman suffrage may be said to have fairly held a protracted meeting during the two following weeks in Albany, with hearings before both branches of the Legislature, and lectures evening after evening in Association Hall, by Mrs. Rose, Mr. Channing, Mr. Phillips, and Miss Brown, culminating in a discussion by the entire press of the city and State; for all the journals had something to say on one side or the other. Mrs. Rose, Mr. Channing, Miss Brown, and several anonymous writers taking part in the newspaper debate. As this was the first Convention held at the Capitol, it roused considerable agitation on every phase of the question, not only among the legislators on the bills before them, but among the people throughout the State.

The Albany Transcript thus sums up the WOMAN'S RIGHTS CONVENTION.— The meeting last evening was attended by the largest and most brilliant audience of the series. A large number of members of the Legislature were there, and a full representation of our most influential citizens. Indeed they could not have asked for a more numerous or talented body of hearers. Mrs. Rose was the sole speaker, owing to the necessity which had called the others away. . . . . She was listened to with the most profound attention, and encouraged by frequent and prolonged applause.

Thus has ended the first Convention of women designed to influence political action. On Monday the 6,000 petitions will be presented in the Legislature, and the address be placed on the members' tables. Whatever may be the final disposition of the matter, it is well to make a note of this *first effort* to influence the Legislature. It was originated by Miss Susan B. Anthony, and has been managed financially by her. Though a stranger amongst us, she has made the contracts for the room, advertised in the papers, employed the speakers, published the address, and performed much other arduous labor.

Mrs. Nichols, one of the speakers, has long been connected with the press, and is a woman of no mean ability. Her mild, beaming countenance and the affectionate tones of her voice, disprove that she is any less a woman than those who do not "speak in public on the stage." Mrs. Love is a new caterer to public favor, and promises well. Some have remarked that she is well named, being a "Love of a woman." Mrs. Jenkins is a fluent and agreeable speaker, and has a good degree of power in swaying an audience. But Mrs. Rose is the queen of the company. On the educational question in particular, she rises to a high standard of oratorical power. When speaking of Hungary and her own crushed Poland, she is full of eloquence and pathos, and she has as great a power to chain an audience as any of our best male speakers.

The Evening Journal (Thurlow Weed, editor): WOMAN'S RIGHTS.—Mr. Channing and Mrs. Rose pleaded the cause of woman's rights before the Senate Committee of bachelors yesterday. The only effect produced was a determination more fixed than ever in the minds of the committee, to *remain* bachelors in the event of the success of the movement. And who would blame them ?

The same champions, with others probably, will speak to the House Committee in the Assembly Chamber this afternoon; and Mr. Channing and Mrs. Rose make addresses in Association Hall this evening. Price twenty-five cents.

The Albany Register: WOMEN IN THE SENATE CHAMBER.—The Senate was alarmed yesterday afternoon. It surrendered to progress. The Select Committee to whom the women's rights petitions had been referred, took their seats on the president's platform, looking as grave as possible. Never had Senators Robertson, Yost, and Field been in such responsible circumstances. They were calm, but evidently felt themselves in great peril.

In the circle of the Senate, ranged in invincible row, sat seven ladies, from quite pretty to quite plain.

Ernestine L. Rose and Rev. William Henry Channing presented the arguments and appeals to the Committee, and Mrs. Rose invited them to ask questions. *The Register* concludes:

The Honorable Senators quailed beneath the trial. There was a terrible silence, and the audience eager to hear what the other ladies had to say, were wretched when they found that the Committee had silently dissolved—surrendered. Oh, what a fall was there, my countrymen !

The Albany Argus of March 4th, says: THE RIGHTS OF WOMEN DEFINED BY THEMSELVES.—Miss Anthony and Mrs. Rose before the House Committee, March 3d. The Committee took their seats in the clerk's desk, and the ladies took possession of the members' seats, filling the chamber, many members of the Legislature being present. Miss Anthony presented a paper prepared by Judge William Hay, of Saratoga, asking that husband and wife should be tenants in common of property without survivorship, but with a partition on the death of one; that a wife shall be competent to discharge trusts and powers the same as a single woman; that the statute in respect to a married woman's property descend as though she had been unmarried; that married women shall be entitled to execute letters testamentary, and of administration; that married women shall have power to make contracts and transact business as though unmarried; that they shall be entitled to their own earnings, subject to their proportionable liability for support of children; that post-nuptial acquisitions shall belong equally to husband and wife; that married women shall stand on the same footing with single women, as parties or witnesses in legal proceedings; that they shall be sole guardians of their minor children; that the homestead shall be inviolable and inalienable for widows and children; that the laws in relation to divorce shall be revised, and drunkenness made cause for absolute divorce; that better care shall be taken of single women's property, that their rights may not be lost through ignorance, that the preference of males in descent of real estate shall be abolished; that women shall exercise " the right of suffrage," and be eligible to all offices, occupations, and professions; entitled to act as jurors; eligible to all public offices; that courts of conciliation shall be organized as peace-makers; that a law shall be enacted extending the masculine designation in all statutes of the State to females.

Mrs. ROSE then addressed the Committee, saying: The right of petition is of no avail unless the reform demanded be candidly considered by the legislators. We judge of the intellectual inferiority of our fellow-men by the amount of resistance they oppose to oppression, and to some extent we judge correctly by this test. The same rule holds good for women; while they tamely submit to the many inequalities under which they labor, they scarcely deserve to be freed from them. . . . . These are not the demands of the moment or the few; they are the demands of the age; of the second half of the nineteenth century. The world will endure after us, and future generations may look back to this meeting to ac·

knowledge that a great onward step was here taken in the cause of human progress.

Mrs. Rose took her seat amidst great applause from the galleries and lobbies. The Committee adjourned.

Albany Register, March 7: WOMAN'S RIGHTS IN THE LEGISLATURE.— While the feminine propagandists of women's rights confined themselves to the exhibition of short petticoats and long-legged boots, and to the holding of Conventions, and speech-making in concert-rooms, the people were disposed to be amused by them, as they are by the wit of the clown in the circus, or the performances of Punch and Judy on fair days, or the minstrelsy of gentlemen with blackened faces, on banjos, the tambourine, and bones. But the joke is becoming stale. People are getting cloyed with these performances, and are looking for some healthier and more intellectual amusement. The ludicrous is wearing away, and disgust is taking the place of pleasurable sensations, arising from the novelty of this new phase of hypocrisy and infidel fanaticism. People are beginning to inquire how far public sentiment should sanction or tolerate these unsexed women, who make a scoff of religion, who repudiate the Bible and blaspheme God; who would step out from the true sphere of the mother, the wife, and the daughter, and taking upon themselves the duties and the business of men, stalk into the public gaze, and by engaging in the politics, the rough controversies, and trafficking of the world, upheave existing institutions, and overturn all the social relations of life.

It is a melancholy reflection, that among our American women who have been educated to better things, there should be found any who are willing to follow the lead of such foreign propagandists as the ringleted, glove-handed exotic, Ernestine L. Rose. We can understand how such men as the Rev. Mr. May, or the sleek-headed Dr. Channing may be deluded by her to becoming her disciples. They are not the first instances of infatuation that may overtake weak-minded men, if they are honest in their devotion to her and her doctrines. Nor would they be the first examples of a low ambition that seeks notoriety as a substitute for true fame, if they are dishonest. Such men there are always, and honest or dishonest, their true position is that of being tied to the apron-strings of some "strong-minded woman," and to be exhibited as rare specimens of human wickedness, or human weakness and folly. But, that one educated American woman should become her disciple and follow her infidel and insane teachings, is a marvel.

Ernestine L. Rose came to this country, as she says, from Poland, whence she was compelled to fly in pursuit of freedom. Seeing her course here, we can well imagine this to be true. In no other country in the world, save possibly one, would her infidel propagandism and preachings in regard to the social relations of life be tolerated. She would be prohibited by the powers of government from her efforts to obliterate from the world the religion of the Cross—to banish the Bible as a text-book of faith, and to overturn social institutions that have existed through all political and governmental revolutions from the remotest time. The strong hand of the law would be laid upon her, and she would be compelled back to her woman's sphere. But in this country, such is the freedom of our institutions, and we rejoice that it should be so, that she, and such as she, can give their genius for intrigue full sway. They can exhibit their flowing ringlets and beautiful hands, their winning smiles and charming stage attitudes to admiring audiences, who, while they are willing to be amused, are in the main safe from their corrupting theories and demoralizing propagandism.

The laws and the theory of our government suppose that the people are capable of taking care of themselves, and hence need no protection against the wiles of domestic or foreign mountebanks, whether in petticoats or in breeches and boots. But it never was contemplated that these exotic agitators would come up to our legislators and ask for the passage of laws upholding and sanctioning their wild and foolish doctrines. That was a stretch of folly, a flight of impudence which was hardly regarded as possible. It was to be imagined, of course, that they would enlist as their followers, here and there one among the restless old maids and visionary wives who chanced to be unevenly tempered, as well as unevenly yoked. It was also to be assumed, as within the range of possibility, that they might bring within the sphere of their attractions, weak-minded, restless men, who think in their vanity that they have been marked out for great things, and failed to be appreciated by the world, men who comb their hair smoothly back, and with fingers locked across their stomachs, speak in a soft voice, and with upturned eyes. But no man supposed they would abandon their "private theatricals" and walk up to the Capitol, and insist that the performances shall be held in legislative halls. And yet so it is.

This Mrs. Ernestine L. Rose, with a train of followers, like a great kite with a very long tail, has, for a week, been amusing Senatorial and Assembly Committees, with her woman's rights performances, free of charge, unless the waste of time that might be better employed in the necessary and legitimate business of legislation, may be regarded as a charge. Those committees have sat for hours, grave and solemn as owls, listening to the outpourings of fanaticism and folly of this Polish propagandist, Mrs. Ernestine L. Rose, and her followers in pantalets and short gowns. The people outside, and especially those interested in the progress of legislation, are beginning to ask one another how long this farce is to continue. How long this most egregious and ridiculous humbug is to be permitted to obstruct the progress of business before the Committees and the Houses, and whether Mrs. Ernestine L. Rose and her followers ought not to be satisfied with the notoriety they have already attained. The great body of the people regard Mrs. Rose and her followers as making themselves simply ridiculous, and there is some danger that these legislative committees will make themselves so too.

LECTURE OF THE REV. ANTOINETTE L. BROWN.—It will be seen the Rev. Antoinette L. Brown delivers a lecture at Association Hall to-morrow evening. It has been said that we have done the women's rights people injustice in charging upon them the infidelity of Mrs. Ernestine L. Rose. If we have done them injustice in this matter it is but right that we should

39

make amends by calling attention to the lecture of Miss Brown, which, as we understand, will embrace the Bible argument in favor of the measures which they advocate. Miss Brown is a talented woman, and we have no doubt an exemplary Christian.

For the Albany Daily State Register.

WOMAN'S RIGHTS.

Mr. EDITOR:—In your paper of Monday the 6th inst., I perceive you pass judgment upon the woman's rights cause, upon those engaged in it, and particularly upon myself—how justly, I leave to your conscience to decide·

Every one who ever advanced a new idea, no matter how great and noble, has been subjected to criticism, and therefore we too must expect it. And, in accordance with the spirit of the critic, will be the criticism. Whether dictated by the spirit of justice, kindness, gentleness, and charity, or by injustice, malice, rudeness, and intolerance, it is still an index of the man. But it is quite certain that no true soul will ever be deterred from the performance of a duty by any criticism.

But there is one thing which I think even editors have no right to do, namely: to state a positive falsehood, or even to imply one, for the purpose of injuring another. And, as the spirit of charity induces me to believe that in your case it was done more from a misunderstanding than positive malice, therefore I claim at your hands the justice to give this letter a place in your paper.

In the article alluded to, you say: "Ernestine L. Rose came to this country, as she says, from Poland, whence she was compelled to fly in pursuit of freedom." It is true that I came from Poland; but it is false that I was compelled to fly from my country, except by the compulsion, or dictates of the same spirit of "propagandism," that induced so many of my noble countrymen to shed their blood in the defence of the rights of this country, and the rights of man, wherever he struggles for freedom. But I have no desire to claim martyrdom which does not belong to me. I left my country, not flying, but deliberately. I chose to make this country my home, in preference to any other, because if you carried out the theories you profess, it would indeed be the noblest country on earth. And as my countrymen so nobly aided in the physical struggle for Freedom and Independence, I felt, and still feel it equally my duty to use my humble abilities to the uttermost in my power, to aid in the great moral struggle for human rights and human freedom.

Hoping that you will acede to my (I think) just claim to give this a place in your paper,

I am, very respectfully,

NEW YORK, *Mar.* 7, 1854.   ERNESTINE L. ROSE.

WILLIAM HENRY CHANNING asks the following questions in the *Albany Evening Journal :*

WOMAN'S RIGHTS.

A lady actively and prominently connected with the movement which is expected to secure "justice to woman," personally requested us to publish the following communication. It is proper to state that it is written in reply to an article of one of our morning contemporaries, published a day or two ago:

" Let us take it for granted that your pop-gun of pleasantry has killed off the six thousand ' strong-minded ' women and ' weak-minded ' men who signed the petitions to the Legislature for Justice to Woman. And thus having disposed of personalities, will you be pleased to pass on to a discussion of the following questions:

" 1. Are women, in New York, persons, people, citizens, members of the State ? If they are not, then why are they numbered in the census, taxed by assessors, and subjected to legal penalties ? If they are, then why is authority exercised over them without their consent asked or granted ?

" 2. If among the male half of the people, only criminals, aliens, and minors are excluded from the right of suffrage are all women excluded from exercising this right, on the ground of criminality, idiocy, foreign associations, or infantile imbecility ?

" 3. If the mothers, sisters, wives, and daughters of New York are the peers and equals of their fathers, brothers, husbands, and sons, why should they not enjoy all civil and political rights equally with them ? If they are, on the contrary, an inferior caste, how can a jury of men thus avowedly superior, be regarded as peers and equals of any woman whom they are summoned to try ?

" 4. Would the editor of *The Register* consider himself justly treated if he would some day find himself governed by women, without his consent, taxed by women without power of voting for his representative, tried by a jury of women under laws made and administered by women ?

" 5. If prosecuted under the law of libel before a court of women for his late remarks, does he think he would get his deserts ?

"Fair Play."

Knickerbocker, Albany, March 8, 1854: Going it Blind.—The editor of *The State Register* is going it blind on woman's rights matters. He was out on Monday with a half column leader that touched everything except the matter in dispute. We quote a paragraph:

" People are beginning to inquire how far public sentiment should sanction or tolerate these unsexed women, who make a scoff at religion, who repudiate the Bible, and blaspheme God; who would step out from the true sphere of the mother, the wife, and the daughter, and take upon themselves the duties and the business of men; stalk into the public gaze, and by engaging in the politics, the rough controversies, and trafficking of the world, upheave existing institutions, and overturn all the social relations of life."

The Register either misunderstands matters, or else willfully misrepresents them. The leading women connected with this new movement do not scoff at religion, repudiate the Bible, nor blaspheme God. Mrs. Stanton and Miss Brown are no more opposed to God and religion than the editor of *The Register* is. They are educated, Christian women, and would no sooner " overturn society " than they would bear false witness against their neighbors. Before *The Register* again attacks the reforms proposed by the Woman's Rights Conventions, it should become acquainted with them. "Going it blind," not only exposes one's prejudices, but ignorance. Many of the innovations proposed by Mrs. Stanton are such as every common-sense man would or should vote for. We mean those improvements which she would have made in the rights of property and the care of children. There are other propositions in her platform which we should dissent from. *The State Register* may do the same. All the "Woman's Rights" women claim is fair play and truthful criticism. They object, however, to any misstatements. They are willing to fall before truth, but not before detraction. *The State Register* will please notice and act accordingly.

Mrs. Stanton's address to the Legislature was laid upon the members' desks Monday morning, Feb. 20, 1854. When the order of petitions was reached, Mr. D. P. Wood, of Onondaga, presented in the Assembly a petition signed by 5,931 men and women, praying for the just and equal rights of women, which, after a spicy debate, was referred to the following Select Committee: James L. Angle, of Monroe Co.; George W. Thorn, of Washington Co.; Derrick L. Boardman, of Oneida Co.; George H. Richards, of New York; James M. Munro, of Onondaga; Wesley Gleason, of Fulton; Alexander P. Sharpe, of New York.

In the Senate, on the same day, Mr. Richards, of Warren County, presented a petition signed by 4,164 men and women, praying for the extension of the right of suffrage to women, and on his motion it was referred to the following Select Committee: George Yost, of Montgomery Co.; Ben. Field, of Orleans Co.; W. H. Robertson, of Westchester Co.

We give the report of the presentation and discussion of the petitions from *The Albany Evening Journal* of Feb. 20, 1854:

WOMAN'S RIGHTS.

ASSEMBLY, Monday, *February* 20, 1854.

Mr. D. P. Wood: I am requested by a Committee of the Woman's Rights Convention recently assembled in this city, to present to this body their address, together with a petition signed by 5,931 men and women, asking that certain withheld rights shall be granted to the women of the State. I ask the reference of these two documents to a Select Committee of seven; and in making this motion, I wish the Speaker to waive the courtesy which would require him, under ordinary circumstances, to place me at the head of this Committee. I am already on several Committees which are pressed with business, and I would not, in my present state of health, be able to give the subject that careful consideration which the importance requires. I am satisfied, sir, that these ladies are entitled to some relief. They think so, and they say so, in language equally eloquent and impressive.

Mr. Burnett: I hope the House will not act at all on this subject without due consideration. I hope before even this motion is put, gentlemen will be allowed to reflect upon the important question whether these individuals deserve any consideration at the hands of the Legislature. Whatever may be their pretensions or their sincerity, they do not appear to be satisfied with having unsexed themselves, but they desire to unsex every female in the land, and to set the whole community ablaze with unhallowed fire. I trust, sir, the House may deliberate before we suffer them to cast this firebrand into our midst. (Here was heard a " hiss " from some part of the chamber). True, as yet, there is nothing officially before us, but it is well known that the object of these unsexed women is to overthrow the most sacred of our institutions, to set at defiance the Divine law which declares man and wife to be one, and establish on its ruins what will be in fact and in principle but a species of legalized adultery. That this is their real object, however they may attempt to disguise it, is well known to every one who has looked, not perhaps at the intentions of all who take part in it, but at the practical and inevitable result of the movement.

It is, therefore, a matter of duty, a duty to ourselves, to our consciences, to our constituents, and to God, who is the source of all law and of all obligations, to reflect long and deliberatively before we shall even seem to countenance a movement so unholy as this. The Spartan mothers asked no such immunities as are asked for by these women. The Roman mothers were content to occupy their legitimate spheres; and our own mothers, who possessed more than Spartan or Roman virtue, asked for no repudiation of the duties, obligations, or sacred relations of the marital rite.

Are we, sir, to give the least countenance to claims so preposterous, disgraceful, and criminal as are embodied in this address ? Are we to put the stamp of truth upon the libel here set forth, that men and women, in the matrimonial relation, are to be equal ? We know that God created man as the representative of the race; that after his creation, his Creator took from his side the material for woman's creation; and that, by the institution of matrimony, woman was restored to the side of man, and became one flesh and one being, he being the head. But this law of God and creation is spurned by these women who present themselves here as the exponents of the wishes of our mothers, wives, and daughters. They ask no such exponents, and they repel their sacrilegious doctrines.

But again, sir, our old views of matrimony were, that it was a holy rite, having holy relations based on mutual love and confidence; and that while woman gave herself up to man, to his care, protection, and love, man also surrendered something in exchange for this confidence and love. He placed his happiness and his honor, all that belongs to him of human hopes and of human happiness, in the keeping of the being he received in the sacred relationship of wife. I say, sir, that this ordinance, sought to be practically overthrown by these persons, was established by God Himself; and was based on the mutual love and confidence of husband and wife. But we are now asked to have this ordinance based on jealousy and distrust; and, as in Italy, so in this country, should this mischievous scheme be carried out to its legitimate results, we, instead of reposing safe confidence against assaults upon our honor in the love and affection of our wives, shall find ourselves obliged to close the approaches to those assaults by the padlock. (The "hiss" was here repeated).

Mr. LOZIER: Mr. Speaker, twice I have heard a hiss from the lobby. I protest against the toleration of such an insult to any member of this House, and call for proper action in view of it.

The SPEAKER: The chair observed the interruption, and was endeavoring to discover its source, but has been unable to do so. If, however, its author can be recognized, the chair will immediately order the person to the bar of the House.

Mr. BURNETT: I have nothing further. The leading features of this address are well known; and I do not wish at present to further enter upon the argument of its character. I merely wish that members be afforded time for consideration. I therefore move to lay the pending motion on the table.

D. P. WOOD: I am surprised that the gentleman from Essex, who professes to desire light, and to afford members time for examination, should make a motion which, if carried, will preclude light and prevent examination. The gentleman sees fit to regard the memorial of these 6,000 men and women as a firebrand. I do not believe the ladies who presented it intended it as such; and they will be surprised to learn that a gentleman of his age and experience should have taken fire from it. Their requests are simple. They ask for "justice and equal rights," and this simple request is made the excuse for an attack upon them as unheard of as it is unjust. They ask only for "justice and equal rights." If the House does not see fit to grant them what they ask, let my motion be voted down, and send the memorial to the Judiciary Committee, of which the gentleman from Essex is chairman. Let such a disposition be made of it, and there will then be no danger that any one will be fired up by it, for it will then be sure to sleep the sleep of death.

Sir, when a petition like this comes before the Legislature, it should not only be respectfully received, but courteously considered; particularly when it asks, as this petition does, a review of the entire code of our statute laws. It should not be sent to a Committee adverse to its request. That would be unparliamentary and the end of it. If sent to such a Committee it would be smothered. The House, I am sure, is not prepared for any such disposition of the matter, but is willing to look candidly at the alleged grievances, and, if consistent with public policy, redress them, although in doing so we may infringe upon time-honored notions and usages.

Mr. PETERS: I am not surprised at the direction which the gentleman from Essex seeks to give this memorial. Any gentleman who would assail these ladies as he has done, would be prepared to make any disrespectful disposition of their rights. I may regret that he has sought to deny a hearing to these petitioners, but I am not surprised that he has done so. I trust that no other member on this floor will refuse, practically, to receive this petition—refuse to our mothers, wives, and sisters, what we every day grant to our fathers, brothers, and sons. These women come here with a respectful petition, and we should give them a candid and respectful hearing. If it be true, and true it is, that there are real grievances complained of, I hope they may be redressed after careful and candid consideration.

The time has gone by, sir, when we may say progress must stop. It is well known that in many particulars the laws are glaringly unjust in regard to the female sex. The education of the sex is defective; and this fact unfolds the secret germ of this movement. We should review the structure of our institutions of learning, and see whether there be not there room for reform. I do not believe it to be a part of the duty of women to sit in the jury-box, to vote, or to participate in all the tumultuous strifes of life; but I do believe that those who differ from me in opinion should have respectful hearing. Nor, because women are not allowed to vote, do I admit that they are precluded from all agency in the direction of national affairs. They, more than their husbands, have power over the future history of the country, by imparting a correct fireside education to their sons. But there are legal disabilities imposed upon women which I would be willing to see removed, in regard to property, etc. Whether those disabilities are of a character to justify affirmative action on the part of this House or not, is not now the question. The question simply is, shall this petition be received? I trust that it may be, and that it may afterward be sent to a select committee.

Mr. BENEDICT: The gentleman from Onondaga asks that this petition shall be sent to a select committee of seven, although he admits that the Judiciary Committee would be more appropriate, if it would not be sure, if sent to that Committee, to sleep the sleep of death. Sir, I am one of that Committee, and protest against any such imputation upon it. I will not only not vote to reject any petition offered the House, but I will give every petition sent to any committee of which I am a member a respectful hearing. This is a petition signed by some 6,000 men and women. They ask "justice" and relief. What kind of relief they may desire is no matter. It is enough for me to know that they ask to be heard. I shall vote to give them a hearing; and I can assure the gentleman from Onondaga that if sent to the Judiciary Committee it will sleep no sleep of death, but will be respectfully considered. A contrary intimation is an unjust reflection on that Committee.

Mr. WOOD: My remark was not intended to reflect upon that Committee. I referred merely to the great amount of business before it.

Mr. BENEDICT: There the gentleman is equally at fault. That Committee is a working Committee, and disposed of all the business before it on Friday last. I am, however, in favor of the motion for a select committee, and desire that the petition should receive legitimate and careful consideration, not only because the petition is largely signed, but because every petition from any portion of the people on any subject, should receive a respectful hearing from the people's representatives. I I hope, therefore, that not a single member may vote against the reception of this petition, whatever his views may be in regard to granting its prayer. I am in favor of the right of petition.

Mr. BURNETT: It was not my wish in the motion I made to have this petition rejected. Had I intended any such thing I should have said so; for I always go directly at what I want to accomplish, and never fail to call things by their right names. I merely wished, before any disposition was made of the petition, that the members should have time to examine the address, which is the key of the whole subject. This is all I desire; and it was simply an expression of this desire that has awakened all this windy gust of passion. After members shall examine the address which accompanies this petition, they can make such disposition of the petition itself as they shall deem wise and proper. This is the length and breadth of my object and desire.

Mr. WOOD: I think the House understands the subject sufficiently to justify action upon my motion of reference.

The motion for the Select Committee prevailed, ayes, 84; the Committee appointed, and Mr. Wood excused from serving.

REPORT OF THE SELECT COMMITTEE.

IN ASSEMBLY, MONDAY, *March* 27, 1854.

The Select Committee, to whom was referred the various petitions requesting "the Senate and Assembly of the State of New York to appoint a joint committee to revise the Statutes of New York, and to propose such amendments as will fully establish the legal equality of women with men," report: That they have examined the said petition, and have heard and considered the suggestions of persons who have appeared before them on behalf of the petitioners.

Your Committee are well aware that the matters submitted to them have been, and still are, the subject of ridicule and jest; but they are also aware that ridicule and jest never yet effectually put down either truth or error; and that the development of our times and the progression of our age is such, that many thoughts laughed at to-day as wild vagaries, are to-morrow recorded as developed principles or embodied as experimental facts.

A higher power than that from which emanates legislative enactments has given forth the mandate that man and woman shall not be equal; that there shall be inequalities by which each in their own appropriate sphere shall have precedence to the other; and each alike shall be superior or inferior as they well or ill act the part assigned them. Both alike are the subjects of Government, equally entitled to its protection; and civil power must, in its enactments, recognize this inequality. We can not obliterate it if we would, and legal inequalities must follow.

The education of woman has not been the result of statutes, but of civilization and Christianity; and her elevation, great as it has been, has only corresponded with that of man under the same influences. She owes no more to these causes than he does. The true elevation of the sexes will always correspond. But elevation, instead of destroying, shows more palpably those inherent inequalities, and makes more apparent the harmony and happiness which the Creator designed to accomplish by them.

Your Committee will not attempt to prescribe, or, rather, they will not attempt to define the province and peculiar sphere which a power that we can not overrule has prescribed for the different sexes. Every well-regulated home and household in the land affords an example illustrative of what is woman's proper sphere, as also that of man. Government has its miniature as well as its foundation in the homes of our country; and as in governments there must be some recognized head to control and direct, so must there also be a controlling and directing power in every smaller association; there must be some one to act and to be acted with as the embodiment of the persons associated. In the formation of governments, the manner in which the common interest shall be embodied and represented is a matter of conventional arrangement; but in the family an influence more potent than that of contracts and conventionalities, and which everywhere underlies humanity, has indicated that the husband shall fill the necessity which exists for a head. Dissension and distraction quickly arise when this necessity is not answered. The harmony of life, the real interest of both husband and wife, and of all dependent upon them, require it. In obedience to that requirement and necessity, the husband is the head—the representative of the family.

It was strongly urged upon your Committee that women, inasmuch as their property was liable to taxation, should be entitled to representation. The member of this House who considers himself the representative only of those whose ballots were cast for him, or even of all the voters in his district, has, in the opinion of your Committee, quite too limited an idea of his position on this floor. In their opinion he is the representative of the inhabitants of his district, whether they be voters or not, whether they be men or women, old or young; and he who does not alike watch over the interests of all, fails in his duty and is false to his trust.

Your Committee can not regard marriage as a *mere contract*, but as something above and beyond; something more binding than records, more solemn than specialties; and the person who reasons as to the relations of husband and wife as upon an ordinary contract, in their opinion commits a fatal error at the outset; and your Committee can not recommend any action based on such a theory.

As society progresses new wants are felt, new facts and combinations are presented which constantly call for more or less of addition to the body of our laws, and often for innovations upon customs so old that "the memory of man runneth not to the contrary thereof." The marriage relation, in common with everything else, has felt the effects of this progress, and from time to time been the subject of legislative action. And while your Committee report adversely to the prayer of the petitions referred to them, they believe that the time has come when certain alterations and amendments are, by common consent, admitted as proper and necessary.

Your Committee recommend that the assent of the mother, if she be living, be made necessary to the validity of any disposition which the father may make of her child by the way of the appointment of guardian or of apprenticeship. The consent of the wife is now necessary to a deed of real estate in order to bar her contingent interest therein; and there are certainly far more powerful reasons why her consent should be necessary to the conveyance or transfer of her own offspring to the care, teaching, and control of another.

When the husband from any cause neglects to provide for the support and education of his family, the wife should have the right to collect and receive her own earnings and the earnings of her minor children, and apply them to the support and education of the family free from the control of the husband, or any person claiming the same through him.

There are many other rules of law applicable to the relation of husband and wife which, in occasional cases, bear hard upon the one or the other, but your Committee do not deem it wise that a new arrangement of our laws of domestic relations should be attempted to obviate such cases; they always have and always will arise out of every subject of legal regulation.

There is much of wisdom (which may well be applied to this and many other subjects) in the quaint remark of an English lawyer, philosopher, and statesman, that " it were well that men in their innovations would follow the example of time, which innovateth greatly but quietly, and by degrees scarcely to be perceived. It is good also in states not to try experiments, except the necessity be urgent and the utility evident; and well to beware that it be the reformation that draweth on the change, and not the desire of change that pretendeth the reformation."

In conclusion, your Committee recommend that the prayer of the petitioners be denied; and they ask leave to introduce a bill* corresponding with the suggestions hereinbefore contained.

The report was signed by James L. Angle and all the members of the Committee except Mr. Richards.

Of the report on the petitions, Mr. Weed says:

Mr. Angle, from the Select Committee of the Assembly, to which the woman's rights petitions were referred, made a report last evening, which we publish elsewhere to-day. It is a compact, lucid, and ably drawn document, highly creditable to its author, and becomingly respectful to

---

* AN ACT RELATIVE TO THE RIGHTS OF MARRIED WOMEN:—*The People of the State of New York, represented in Senate and Assembly, do enact as follows:*

1. Any married woman whose husband, from drunkenness, profligacy, or any other cause, shall neglect and refuse to provide for her support and education, or the support and education of her children, and any married woman who may be deserted by her husband, shall have the right, by her own name, to receive and collect her own earnings, and apply the same for her own support, and the support and education of her children, free from the control and interference of her husband, or from any person claiming to be released from the same by and through her husband.

2. Hereafter it shall be necessary to the validity of any indenture of apprenticeship executed by the father, that the mother of such child, if she be living, shall, in writing, consent to such indentures; nor shall any appointment of a general guardian of the person of a child by the father be valid, unless the mother of such child, if she be living, shall, in writing, consent to such appointment.

the petitioners. The Committee report adversely to the petitions, but recommend one or two changes in our existing law, which will, we think, commend themselves as well to the opponents, as to the advocates of woman's rights.

The work in the State of New York was now thoroughly systematized. Susan B. Anthony was appointed General Agent, and it was decided to hold a series of Conventions in all the counties and chief cities of the State, in order to roll up mammoth petitions with which to bombard the Legislature at every annual session. Two appeals* were issued to the women of the State, one in June, prepared by Mr. Channing, and one in December, by Mrs. Stanton. A number of able speakers† joined in the work, and the State was thoroughly canvassed every year until the war, and petitions presented by the thousands until the bill securing the civil rights of married women was passed in March, 1860.

Lest our readers should think that there was no variety to our lives in these early days, that we did nothing but resolve, complain, petition, protest, hold conventions, and besiege Legislatures, we record now and then some cheerful item from the Metropolitan papers concerning some of our leading women.

NEW YORK, *March* 14, 1854.

ANNIVERSARY OF THE 83D BIRTHDAY OF ROBERT OWEN AT 600 BROADWAY.

When the reporter entered the room he found the ladies and gentlemen assembled there tripping the light fantastic toe to the music of a harp, piano, and violin. Ernestine L. Rose was president of the occasion, and gave a very interesting sketch of the life and labors of this noble man. After which they had a grand supper, and Lucy Stone replied to the toast, "Woman, coequal with man." The ladies not only danced and made speeches, but they partook of the supper. They did not sit in the galleries, as the custom then was, to look at the gentlemen eat, and listen to their after-dinner speeches, but enjoyed an equal share in the whole entertainment. Mrs. Rose and Miss Stone seemed to feel as much at home on this festive occasion, as amid the more important proceedings of a convention.

As the agitation was kept up from year to year with frequent conventions, ever and anon some prominent person who had hitherto

---

* See Appendix.

† Ernestine L. Rose, Francis D. Gage, Hannah Tracy Cutler, Lucy N. Coleman, Antoinette L. Brown, Matilda Joslyn Gage, Marietta Richmond, Sarah Pellet, Carrie D. Filkins, Lydia A. Jenkins, Susan B. Anthony, dividing their time and forces, held conventions in nearly every county of the State, traversing some new section each year. In 1859, Miss Anthony and Miss Brown made a successful tour of the fashionable resorts and the northern counties. All this work the State Committee assigned to its General Agent, giving her all honor and power, without providing one dollar. But Miss Anthony with rare executive ability, accomplished the work and paid all expenses.—E. C. S.

been silent, would concede a modicum of what we claimed, so timidly, however, and with so many popular provisos, that the concessions were almost buried in the objections. It was after this manner that Henry Ward Beecher, then in the zenith of his popularity, vouchsafed an opinion. He believed in woman's right to vote and speak in public. There was no logical argument against either, but he would not like to see his wife or mother go to the polls or mount the platform. This utterance called out the following letter from Gerrit Smith in *The Boston Liberator:*

PETERBORO, N. Y., *Nov.* 19, 1854.

DEAR GARRISON:—I am very glad to see in your paper that Henry Ward Beecher avows himself a convert to the doctrine of woman's voting. But I regret that this strong man is nevertheless not strong enough to emancipate himself entirely from the dominion of superstition. Mr. Beecher would not have his wife and sister speak in public. Of course he means that he would not, however competent they might be for such an exercise. I will suppose that they all remove to Peterboro, and that a very important, nay, an entirely vital question springs up in our community, and profoundly agitates it; and I will further suppose that the wife and sister of Mr. Beecher are more capable than any other persons of taking the platform and shedding light upon the subject. Are we not entitled to their superior light? Certainly. And certainly therefore are they bound to afford it to us. Nevertheless Mr. Beecher would have them withhold it from us. Pray what is it but superstition that could prompt him to such violation of benevolence and common-sense? Will Mr. Beecher go to the Bible for his justification? That blessed book is to be read in the life of Jesus Christ; and in that life is the fullness of benevolence and common-sense, and no superstition at all. Will Mr. Beecher limit his wife and sisters in the given case to their pens?* Such limitation would he then be bound in consistency to impose upon himself. Would he impose it? Again, it takes lips as well as pens to carry instruction to the utmost.

Your friend,   GERRIT SMITH.

SARATOGA CONVENTIONS,
AUGUST, 1854-'55.

Seeing calls for two national conventions, by the friends of Temperance, and the Anti-Nebraska movement, to be held in Saratoga the third week of August, the State Woman Suffrage Committee decided to embrace that opportunity to hold a convention there at

---

* It is pleasant to record that a few years later Mr. Beecher's vision was clear on the whole question, and he was often found on the woman's rights platform, not only speaking himself, but his sister, Mrs. Isabella Beecher Hooker, also. On one occasion he conducted Miss Kate Field to the platform in Plymouth Church as gracefully as he ever handed a lady out to dinner, introduced her to the audience, and presided during her address. Sitting there he seemed to feel as much at his ease as if Col. Robert G. Ingersoll had been the speaker.

the same time.* As it was at the height of the fashionable season it was thought much good might be accomplished by getting the ear of a new class of hearers.

But after the arrangements were all made, and Miss Anthony on the ground, she received messages from one after another of the speakers on whom she depended, that none of them could be present. Accordingly, encouraged by the Hon. William Hay, she decided to go through alone. Happily, Matilda Joslyn Gage and Sarah Pellet being in Saratoga, came forward and volunteered their services, and thus was the Convention carried successfully through.† The meeting was held in St. Nicholas Hall, which was well filled throughout, three hundred dollars being taken at the door. The following *resumé* of this occasion is from the pen of Judge William Hay, in a letter to *The North Star* of Rochester (Frederick Douglass, editor):

THE SARATOGA CONVENTION.

Miss Sarah Pellet addressed an audience of six hundred persons in the afternoon, most of whom returned with others to St. Nicholas Hall in the evening, thus manifesting their satisfaction with what they had heard and their interest in the cause, which was farther discussed by Mrs. Gage, whose address was an elaborate argument for the removal of woman's legal and social disabilities. Among other authorities she quoted with judgment, was the following from Wm. W. Story: "In respect to the powers and rights of married women, the law is by no means abreast the spirit of the age. Here are seen the old fossil prints of *feudalism*. The law relating to woman tends to make every family a

---

* As this meeting was hastily decided upon, there was no call issued; it was merely noticed in the county papers. *The Saratoga Whig*, August 18, 1854, says:

WOMEN'S RIGHTS.—The series of conventions that have been holding sessions in the village during the week, will close this day with a meeting for the discussion of the social, legal, and political rights of women, at which Miss Susan B. Anthony, Mrs. Matilda Joslyn Gage, and Miss Sarah Pellet will appear. The meetings will be held at St. Nicholas Hall this afternoon at 3½ o'clock, and in the evening at 8 o'clock.

† Any one but the indomitable Susan B. Anthony would have abandoned all idea of a meeting, but, as it was advertised, she felt bound to make it a fact. This decision may seem the more remarkable in view of other facts, that Miss Anthony had but little experience as a speaker, and was fully aware of her deficiencies in that line; her forte lay in planning conventions, raising money, marshalling the forces, and smoothing the paths for others to go forward, make the speeches, and get the glory. Having listened in St. Nicholas Hall for several days to some of the finest orators in the country, it was with great trepidation that she resolved to attempt to hold such audiences as had crowded all the meetings during the week, and would no doubt continue to do so. However, she had one written speech, which she decided to divide, giving the industrial disabilities of women in the afternoon, and their political rights in the evening, supplementing each with whatever extemporaneous observations might strike her mind as she proceeded. With Mrs. Gage to speak at one session and Miss Pellet at the other, Miss Anthony rounded out both meetings to the general satisfaction. It was thus she always stood ready for every emergency; when nobody else would or could speak she did; when everybody wished to speak she was silent.—E. C. S.

barony, a monarchy, or a despotism, of which the husband is the baron, king, or despot, and the wife the dependent, the serf, or slave. That this is not always the fact, is not due to the law, but to the enlarged humanity which spurns the narrow limits of its rules; for if the husband choose, he has his wife as firmly in his grasp and dominion, as the *hawk* has the *dove* upon whom he has pounced. This age is ahead of the law. Public opinion is a check to legal rules on this subject, but the rules are feudal and stern. It can not, however, be concealed that the position of woman is always the criterion of the freedom of a people or an age, and when man shall despise that right which is founded only on might, woman will be free to stand on an equal level with him—a friend and not a dependent."

Mrs. Gage also, and with like effect, cited from the same learned jurist, laws, which, had her lecture been a sermon, might have been prefixed as a text. Such opinions, although but seldom known to any but lawyers, and not appreciated by many of them, have frequently been printed in books, which, however, being professional, are perused by few persons only. Mrs. Gage* concluded her excellent discourse with Bryant's celebrated stanza, relative to truth and error.

Miss Anthony's situation had become embarrassing, if not critical. At a late hour of a summer night, she was to follow Mrs. Gage on the same subject, and before a fastidious audience, almost surfeited during three days with public addresses in several different conventions, and many of whom desired to contrast her expected effort with the splendid platform eloquence of Henry J. Raymond, Wm. H. Burleigh, and "their like," fearlessly advocating the redress of wrongs and the promotion of human rights. Miss Anthony, who had conciliated her audience by lady-like conduct and courtesy, in providing seats for the accommodation of those standing, commenced with an appropriate apology for unavoidable repetition, when it was her lot to follow Mrs. Gage. Sufficient here to say that she acquitted herself admirably. The simplicity and repose of her manner, the dignity of her deportment, the distinctiveness of her enunciation, her emphatic earnestness, the pathos of her appeals, and completeness of her arguments, convinced the understanding and persuaded all hearts.

The gossip of mustached dandies, and the half-suppressed giggle of bedizened beauty, soon settled down into respectful attention, if not appreciation. Indeed many of the most intelligent hearers before retiring, audibly confessed that they came to find fault, but had seen nothing to censure. So some who came to scoff remained to applaud. With such advocates there can be no retrogression of Woman's Rights. Equality is their motto, and onward their destiny.

WM. HAY.

This Convention was so successful in point of numbers and receipts, and the sale of woman suffrage literature, that it was decided

---

* *The Daily Saratogian.* August 19th, said: Mrs. Matilda Joslyn Gage, a medium-sized, lady-like looking woman, dressed in a tasty plum-colored silk with two flounces, made the first address upon some of the defects in the marriage laws, quoting Story, Kent, and Blackstone. She closed by speaking of Mrs. Marcet, an able writer on political economy, her book much used in schools. She referred to Miss Pinckney, of South Carolina, who in nullification times, wrote powerfully on that subject. It was said that party was consolidated by the nib of a lady's pen. She was the first woman in the United States who was honored with a public funeral.

to repeat the experiment the next year; accordingly the following call was issued early in the season:

A Convention will be held at Saratoga Springs on the 15th and 16th of August next, to discuss woman's right to suffrage.

In the progress of human events, woman now demands the recognition of her civil existence, her legal rights, her social equality with man.

How her claims can be the most easily and speedily established on a firm, enduring basis, will be the subject of deliberation at the coming Convention.

The friends of the movement, and the public generally, are most respectfully invited to attend.

Many of the advocates of the cause are expected to be in attendance.

ELIZABETH CADY STANTON,	LYDIA MOTT,
ERNESTINE L. ROSE,	ANTOINETTE L. BROWN,
SAMUEL J. MAY,	SUSAN B. ANTHONY.

This Convention also was held in St. Nicholas Hall, and a large audience greeted the speakers of the occasion as they appeared upon the platform.

A brief report of the secretaries in *The Una* of September, 1855, says: A large audience assembled on the morning of August 15th at St. Nicholas Hall. Susan B. Anthony called the meeting to order, and presented a list of officers* nominated at a preliminary gathering, which was accepted. Martha C. Wright, on taking the chair, made a brief statement of the object of the Convention, and invited all those who were opposed to our demands to come to the platform and state their objections.

During the absence of the Business Committee, Ernestine L. Rose briefly reviewed the rise and progress of the woman's rights movement. Antoinette Brown reported a series of resolutions, on which she commented at some length, when the Rev. Samuel J. May was introduced. Although he spoke to the entire edification of the platform, yet he was constantly interrupted by the audience. It was a novelty to hear women speak, and the audience having assembled

---

* *President.*—Martha C. Wright, of Auburn.

Vice-Presidents.—Rev. Samuel J. May, Syracuse; Lydia Mott, Albany; Ernestine L. Rose, New York; Antoinette L. Brown, New York; Susan B. Anthony, Rochester; Augusta A. Wiggins, Saratoga Springs.

Secretaries.—Emily Jaques, Nassau; Aaron M. Powell, Ghent; Mary L. Booth, Williamsburgh.

Finance Committee.—Susan B. Anthony, Marietta Richmond, Mary S. Anthony, Phebe H. Jones.

Business Committee.—Antoinette L. Brown, Ernestine L. Rose, T. W. Higginson, Charles F. Hovey, of Boston; Phebe Merritt, of Michigan; Hon. William Hay, of Saratoga Springs.

for that purpose, preferred to listen to woman's pathetic state-ments of her wrongs, than to the most gifted orators that men could boast. It was not until after repeated requests for order from the president, and assurances from several of the ladies that they would not speak until Mr. May had finished his remarks, that quiet was restored.

It was at this Convention that Mary L. Booth* made her first appear-ance on our platform, as one of the secretaries. One feature of these meetings was the freedom and warm sympathy between the audience and the platform. At the close of almost every speech, some one on the floor asked questions, or stated some objections which were quickly answered and refuted by the speakers in the most pleasant conversational manner.

Mrs. Rose presented the wrongs of woman in her most happy man-ner, demanding the ballot as the underlying power to protect all other rights. Thomas Wentworth Higginson made an address especially adapted to the fashionable audience. Many of the thoughtless ones whom idle curiosity had led to the hall, must have felt like the woman of Samaria (John iv. 29) at the well, when she reported that she had seen a man who told her all the things that ever she had done, so nearly did Mr. Higginson picture to them their thoughts and feelings, the ennui of their daily lives. Lucy Stone, whom the papers now call Mrs. Blackwell, arriving in the midst of the con-vention, was greeted with long and repeated cheers, and spoke with her wonted simplicity and earnestness. The resolutions cover-ing all the different phases of the movement were duly discussed through two entire days.

Antoinette Brown was called on as usual to meet the Bible argu-ment. A clergyman accused her of misapplying texts. He said Genesis iv. 7 did not allude to Cain and Abel, and that the language in Genesis iii. 16, as applied to Eve, did not mean the same thing. Miss Brown maintained her position that the texts were the same in letter and spirit; and that authority to all men over all women could be no more logically inferred from the one, than authority to all elder brothers over the younger could be from the other; and that there was no divine authority granted in either case.

Miss Anthony announced that woman's rights tracts and papers were for sale at the door, and urged all who had become interested in the subject to procure them not only for their own benefit, but to circulate among their neighbors. If they would be intelligent as to

---

* Now the successful editor of *Harper's Bazar.*

the real claims of the movement, they must take *The Una,* a paper owned and edited by one of its leaders. No one would expect to get temperance truths from Bennett's *Herald,* nor anti-slavery facts from *The New York Observer,* or *Christian Advocate;* no more can we look to any of the popular newspapers, political or religious, for reliable information on the woman's rights movement.

She also presented the claims of *The Woman's Advocate,* a paper just started in Philadelphia by Anna E. McDowell, devoted chiefly to woman's right to work—equal pay for equal service (she was sorry that it did not see that the right of suffrage underlies the work prob. lem); nevertheless the existence of a paper owned, edited, published, and printed all by women, was a living woman's rights fact, and she hoped every one would give it encouragement and support. She then gave a brief report of the work done in the State during the past year,* and closed by presenting the form of petition that had just been adopted.†

Mr. May moved the appointment of a committee of five‡ to engage lecturing agents and raise funds for their compensation. The president thanked the people for the respect and attention manifested during the several sessions, and adjourned the Convention.§

---

* This year Miss Anthony canvassed the State, holding conventions in fifty-four counties, organizing societies, getting signatures to petitions, and subscribers to *The Una.* At some of these meetings Mrs. Rose, Miss Brown, and Miss Filkins assisted by turn, but the chief part she carried through alone. She had posters for the entire State printed in Rochester, her father, brother Merritt, and Mary Luther folding and superscribing to all the postmasters and the sheriff of every county. The sheriffs, with but few exceptions, opened the Court Houses for the meetings, posted the bills, and attended to the advertising. Miss Anthony entered on this work without the pledge of a dollar. But with free meetings and collections in the afternoon, and a shilling admission in the evening, she managed to cover the entire expenses of the campaign.

† WOMEN'S RIGHTS PETITION.

To the Honorable, the Senate and Assembly of the State of New York:

WHEREAS, the women of the State of New York are recognized as citizens by the Constitution, and yet are disfranchised on account of sex ; we do respectfully demand the right of suffrage ; a right which involves all other rights of citizenship, and which can not be justly withheld, when we consider the admitted principles of popular government, among which are the following :

1st. That all men are born free and equal.

2d. That government derives its just powers from the consent of the governed.

3d. That taxation and representation should go together.

4th. That those held amenable to laws should have a share in framing them.

We do, therefore, petition that you will take the necessary steps so to revise the Constitution of our State, as that all her citizens may enjoy equal political privileges.

‡ The committee were Susan B. Anthony, Ernestine L. Rose, Antoinette L. Brown, Elizabeth Cady Stanton, Martha C. Wright, Lydia Mott.

§ At the close of this Convention, Charles F. Hovey, as was his usual custom, planned an excursion for those who had taken part in the meetings. He invited them to take a drive to the lake, a few miles out of Saratoga, gave them a bountiful repast, and together they spent a day rich in pleasant memories. Listening day after day to the wrongs

The Saratoga papers were specially complimentary in their notices of Ernestine L. Rose and Lucy Stone, pronouncing them logical and eloquent, and Miss Anthony was highly praised for her skill in getting contributions and distributing documents. She sold over twenty thousand pamphlets that year. As there were many Southern people always at Saratoga, this was considered a grand opportunity through tracts to sow the seeds of rebellion all through the Southern States. This Convention afforded a new theme for conversation at the hotels, and was discussed for many days after with levity or seriousness, to be laughed over and thought over by the women at their leisure.*

LETTERS TO THE CONVENTION.

BOSTON, *June* 23, 1855.

SUSAN B. ANTHONY.

DEAR MADAM:—Your note of the 20th has just come to hand. I am sorry to say that my engagements are such that it will not be possible for me to be present at the Woman's Rights Convention at Saratoga, which I should very much rejoice to attend.

Heartily and hastily yours, THEODORE PARKER.

SYRACUSE, *June* 13, 1855.

DEAR FRIEND:—I like your call to the Convention at Saratoga, and I shall endeavor to be there on my return from Massachusetts, where I deliver an oration on education on the 8th of August. By all means put Judge Hay's name on the Central Committee. Invite Theodore Parker without delay.

In great haste, but very truly yours, SAMUEL J. MAY

PHILADELPHIA, *Sixth Mo.*, 11, 1855.

MY DEAR SUSAN B. ANTHONY:—Returning home, I hasten to answer thy letter forwarded to me a week ago by sister M. C. Wright. It is always with regret that I have to answer any letter of the kind in the negative. But the time fixed for the Saratoga Convention renders it impracticable for me to be present. My husband and I hope to attend the National Convention at Cincinnati in October. Thy active interest and exertions in this cause are greatly cheering. We are doing little hereaway. Pennsylvania is always slow in every reformatory movement. We have circulated many of the pamphlets.

---

perpetrated on woman by law and Gospel of man's creation, Mr. Hovey always seemed to feel that he was in duty bound to throw what sunshine and happiness he could into the lives of women, and thus in a measure atone for the injustice of his sex, and most royally he did this whenever an opportunity offered, not only while he lived, but by bequests at his death.

* Twenty years after this Mrs. Stanton met a lady in Texas, who told her about this Saratoga Convention. She said her attention was first called to the subject of woman's rights by some tracts a friend of hers, then living in Georgia, brought home at that time, and that we could form but little idea of the intense interest with which they were read and discussed by quite a circle of ladies, who plied her aunt with innumerable questions about the Convention and the appearance and manners of the ladies who led the movement.

Wishing you all success at the convention, and sure of thy " great recompense and reward,"

I am thine affectionately,   LUCRETIA MOTT.

BOSTON, *June* 6, 1855.

DEAR FRIEND:—I have kept your letter by me, and omitted to reply, hoping, and indeed expecting, that though I give up all but two or three routine and neighboring engagements in the summer. I might plan so as to accept yours. But I find I can not come as you ask. My summer months must be devoted otherwise. I hope you will not nickname me *No*, for my so constantly using that monosyllable to you. Indeed, I will try to oblige you next winter.

With much regard, yours truly,   WENDELL PHILLIPS.

HIGH ROCK, LYNN, MASS., *August* 4, 1855.

EARNEST FRIEND:—We have just received your hearty invitation to the Convention at Saratoga. Nothing would give us more pleasure than to be with you on that occasion. We are all interested in Woman's Rights, and in liberty for all humanity.

Long submission has smothered the hope and extinguished the desire in many for any change of condition. But the light of the nineteenth century should awake all to earnest battle for their God-given rights. We will consult together. and if we can make up a quartette we will try and be with you to sing once more our songs* of freedom for another struggling class. With much esteem

I remain yours truly,   JOHN W. HUTCHINSON,

(for the family).

Following the Convention the usual attacks were made by the press, accusing the members of " infidelity and free love," which

---

* It is now over forty years that the various branches of the Hutchinson family have been singing the liberal ideas of their day on the anti-slavery, temperance, and Woman's Rights platforms, and they are singing still (1881) with the infusion of some new blood in the second and third generation. Only one year ago traveling in Kansas, on a dreary night train, with no sleeping car attached, I had worried through the weary hours until three o'clock in the morning, when the cars stopped at Fort Scott. I was slowly pacing up and down the aisle, when in came Asa Hutchinson, violin in hand, and a troop of boys and girls behind him. There we stood face to face, both well on the shady side of sixty-five, our locks as white as snow, each thinking the other was too old for such hard journeys, he still singing, I still preaching " equal rights to all." " Well," said I, " Asa, this is a very unchristian hour for you to be skylarking over the prairies of Kansas." " Ah !" said he, dolorously, " this is no skylarking ; we sung last night until near eleven o'clock, shook hands, and talked until twelve ; arose about two, waited an hour at a cold depot, and we all feel as cross as bears." " I can sympathize with you," I replied ; " I spent the hours until twelve as you did, entertaining my countrymen and women, and have been trying to rest ever since." In talking over old times until the day dawned we forgot our fatigue, and as I left the cars they gave me a parting salute with the " good time coming." How well I remember the power of the young Hutchinsons in the old mob days ; four brothers and one sister standing side by side on the platform in Faneuil Hall, Boston. So hated were the Abolitionists and their doctrines, that not even Wendell Phillips or Abby Kelly could get a hearing, but when the sweet singers from the old Granite State came forward silence reigned, to be broken, however, the moment the last notes of harmony died upon their lips.   E. C. S.

Miss Brown refuted through *The New York Tribune.* In this way, with conventions being continually held at the fashionable watering places * in the summer, and at the center of legislative assemblies in the winter, New York was compelled to give some attention to the question. A Woman's Rights meeting and a hearing were of annual occurrence as regular as the convening of the Legislature.

ALBANY CONVENTION, 1855.

The second Convention at Albany was held in the Green Street Universalist Church, February 13 and 14, 1855. Martha C. Wright presided; the usual speakers† were present, and letters of sympathy were received from Wendell Phillips, T. W. Higginson, Elizabeth Oakes Smith, Elizabeth Cady Stanton, expressing regret at not being able to attend.

LETTER FROM HORACE GREELEY.

NEW YORK, *February* 8, 1855.

SUSAN B. ANTHONY.

DEAR FRIEND:—I can not be in Albany next week, because I some time since promised to speak on Wednesday in Maine, and must keep my engagement. Nor, indeed, can I deem it of any consequence that I should attend your Convention. You know, already, that I am thoroughly committed to the principle that *woman shall decide for herself* whether she shall have a voice and a vote in legislation, or shall continue to be represented and legislated for exclusively by man.

My own judgment is that woman's presence in the arena of politics would be useful and beneficent; but I do not assume to judge for her. She must consider, determine, and act for herself. Whenever she shall in earnest have resolved that her own welfare and that of the race will be promoted by her claiming a voice in the direction of civil government, as I think she ultimately will do, then the day of her emancipation will be near. That day I will hope yet to see. Yours, HORACE GREELEY.

Of the hearings before the Legislature which followed this Convention, we give the report from

The Albany Register, February 17, 1855.

JUST AND EQUAL RIGHTS—HEARING BEFORE THE ASSEMBLY COMMITTEE.

The select Committee of the Assembly, to which was referred the petition for Woman's Rights, granted a hearing to the petitioners in the Assembly Chamber on Saturday evening. Ernestine L. Rose, Antoinette Brown, and Susan B. An-

---

* Saratoga, Niagara, and Trenton Falls; Clifton, Avon, Sharon, and Ballston Springs, Lake George, etc. In making the tour in 1859, Miss Brown and Miss Anthony had some recherché out-door meetings in the groves of Clifton and Trenton that were highly praised by the press and the people, and in the long summer days most charming to themselves.

† The speakers were Samuel J. May, Ernestine L. Rose, Antoinette L. Brown, Carrie D. Filkins, Lydia A. Jenkins, Aaron M. Powell, Hon. Wm. Hay, Susan B. Anthony.

thony represented the petitioners. The arguments were able, and well received. Members of the Committee and others sent up a number of questions which the ladies promptly answered, with a due sprinkling of wit, logic, and sarcasm, greatly to the entertainment of the audience, which did not disperse until after eleven o'clock.

Mr. Rickerson, from the Select Committee, to whom was referred "The Petition for the Right of Suffrage," stated that "after mature consideration the Committee unanimously report adversely to the prayer of the petitioners." Mr. Rickerson, from the same Committee to whom was referred the petition for the just and equal civil rights of woman, said: "The Committee have given the petition that examination which time and circumstances would allow, and report favorably thereon, as embraced in the bill," which they introduced.*

The petitions of 1856 were referred to the Judiciary Committee, Samuel A. Foote, Chairman. Mr. Foote was at one time a member of the bar of New York, associating with some of the first families in the State—a son, a husband, a father—and yet in his maturer years he had so little respect for himself, his mother, wife, and daughters as to present in a dignified legislative assembly the following report on a grave question of human rights—a piece ot buffoonery worthy only a mountebank in a circus:

LEGISLATIVE REPORT ON WOMEN'S RIGHTS.

The Register, ALBANY, *March,* 1856.

Mr. Foote, from the Judiciary Committee, made a report on Women's Rights that set the whole House in roars of laughter:

"The Committee is composed of married and single gentlemen. The bachelors on the Committee, with becoming diffidence, have left the subject pretty much to the married gentlemen. They have considered it with the aid of the light they have before them and the experience married life has given them. Thus aided, they are enabled to state that the ladies always have the best place and choicest titbit at the table. They have the best seat in the cars, carriages, and sleighs; the warmest place in the winter, and the coolest place in the summer. They have their choice on which side of the bed they will lie, front or back. A lady's dress costs three times as much as that of a gentleman; and, at the present time, with the prevailing fashion, one lady occupies three times as much space in the world as a gentleman.

"It has thus appeared to the married gentlemen of your Committee, being a majority (the bachelors being silent for the reason mentioned, and also probably for the further reason that they are still suitors for the favors of the gentler sex), that, if there is any inequality or oppression in the case, the

---

* If the intestate be a married man living, and having lived with his wife during marriage, or if the intestate be a married woman living or having lived with her husband during marriage, and shall die without lawful descendants, born or to be born of such marriage, or a prior marriage, the inheritance shall descend to the surviving husband or wife, as the case may be, during his or her natural life, whether the inheritance came to the intestate on the part of the mother or father or otherwise.

gentlemen are the sufferers. They, however, have presented no petitions for redress; having, doubtless, made up their minds to yield to an inevitable destiny.

"On the whole, the Committee have concluded to recommend no measure, except that as they have observed several instances in which husband and wife have both signed the same petition. In such case, they would recommend the parties to apply for a law authorizing them to change dresses, so that the husband may wear petticoats, and the wife the breeches, and thus indicate to their neighbors and the public the true relation in which they stand to each other."

ASSEMBLY—WOMEN'S RIGHTS.

Mr. PRENDERGAST presented several petitions asking for an extension of Women's Rights. Mr. P. stated that undoubtedly the Judiciary was the proper Committee to receive these petitions; but the petitioners had signified to him that, from a recent manifestation on the part of the Chairman of that Committee (Judge Foote), they would prefer that the petition should be referred to some other Committee. He therefore moved their reference to the Committee on Claims.

Mr. NORTHUP seconded the motion.

Mr. FOOTE remarked, that if there was any other Committee of this House that would or could unsex the female sex, he had no objection to the reference moved.

The motion prevailed.

Lydia Mott, in a letter to Susan B. Anthony, under date of Albany, March 15, 1856, says:

I mail a paper to you, containing the Hon. Samuel A. Foote's report on our petitions. I hardly expected any report this winter. I am glad he made one; am only sorry it was verbal. There ought to have been a large number printed for circulation. I hope you won't get discouraged; remember the good work goes bravely on, the Honorable Legislature to the contrary notwithstanding. We shall get all we demand one of these days. Our reform is so comprehensive, we must not expect a sudden change in public opinion. Only see how long we have been laboring to convert people to the one self-evident truth that a man has a right to himself; and where are we now after a quarter of a century? No; we must not be disheartened. Our labor has not been in vain. I see its good effects every day, and they will continue to multiply.

Only think, here in our midst we have a constant testimony borne to good audiences every Sunday. I don't know whether I wrote you what a true man we have in the Unitarian Church, and what a treat his sermons are to me. You remember A. D. Mayo, who has written letters to our Conventions; he doesn't come as an Unitarian, but as an Independent. It can not be otherwise than that he will do a world of good. He gave to day one of the boldest as well as finest sermons I have ever heard—full of noble thoughts. He always recognizes woman in every department. It amuses me to see the effect on some of the women as he portrays woman side by side with man, always making her his equal in every position. Mr. Mayo is the first minister who has filled the church, and the only one that has not seemed afraid of his own shadow. Mr.

Garrison heard him when here; said he could not wish to change one word or to add one to his sermon. That from Garrison is saying a great deal.

The Hon. Wm. Hay, who always aided us and watched the Legislature very closely in its action upon our question, in a letter to Miss Anthony, dated March 20, 1856, said:

I write this in the Assembly Chamber which has so recently been disgraced by an old fogy—Sam. A. Foote. He can not, however, prevent the agitation as to Woman's Rights. That of Suffrage has been discussed several times this week, incidentally, in both Houses, and will be up here again to-morrow directly. . . . .

March 21st, he says: The petition from Milton, Ulster County, was presented yesterday, and referred to the Committee on Claims, instead of the Judiciary or a Select Committee. It is thus manifest that the cause is not to be put down or even passed by with contemptuous silence, vulgar abuse, or conservative scorn. Foote squealed out his angry opposition, in the old stupid slang (or Shakespeare perverted from "Macbeth"), about unsexing woman with the right of suffrage, and endeavored to contrast it with property-claims; as if the revolutionary maxim concerning taxation and representation going together is not a property rule. I suspect, too, that personal rights, secured by the right preservative of all rights, are more important than mere property rights. But they need not be distinguished in that respect. The proceeding is (even if without any present beneficial result) a triumph; because it proves to Judge Foote and others that the Woman's Rights petitions (or rather demands) must receive suitable consideration and, at least, a respectful report.

Next winter we may hope to be more successful—if not then, success is merely postponed. It has become a question of time only, and perhaps of place—probably Nebraska!

THE SEVENTH NATIONAL WOMAN'S RIGHTS CONVENTION.

Pursuant to a call issued by the Central Committee, the Seventh National Woman's Rights Convention was held in New York, at the Broadway Tabernacle, November 25 and 26, 1856.

The Convention was called to order by Martha C. Wright, President of the last Convention.

The officers were duly appointed.*

---

* *President.*—Lucy Stone.

Vice-Presidents.—Lucretia Mott, of Pennsylvania ; Elizabeth Jones, of Ohio ; Rev. T. W. Higginson, of Massachusetts ; Cornelia Moore, of New Jersey ; A. Bronson Alcott, of New Hampshire ; Sarah H. Hallock, of New York.

Secretaries.—Martha C. Wright, of New York ; Oliver Johnson, of New York ; Henrietta Johnson, of New Jersey.

Business Committee.—Ernestine L. Rose, Susan B. Anthony, Wendell Phillips, James Mott, Mariana Johnson, T. W. Higginson, William Green, Jr.

Treasurer.—Wendell Phillips.

. . .—Susan B. Anthony.

LUCY STONE, on taking the chair, said : I am sure that all present will agree with me that this is a day of congratulation. It is our Seventh Annual National Woman's Rights Convention. Our first effort was made in a small room in Boston, where a few women were gathered, who had learned woman's rights by woman's wrongs. There had been only one meeting in Ohio, and two in New York. The laws were yet against us, custom was against us, prejudice was against us, and more than all, women were against us. We were strong only " in the might of our right "—and, now, when this seventh year has brought us together again, we can say as did a laborer in the Republican party, though all is not gained, " we are without a wound in our faith, without a wound in our hope, and stronger than when we began." Never before has any reformatory movement gained so much in so short a time. When we began, the statute books were covered with laws against women, which an eminent jurist (Judge Walker) said would be a disgrace to the statute books of any heathen nation.

Now almost every Northern State has more or less modified its laws. The Legislature of Maine, after having granted nearly all other property rights to wives, found a bill before it asking that a wife should be entitled to what she earns, but a certain member grew fearful that wives would bring in bills for their daily service, and, by an eloquent appeal to pockets, the measure was lost for the time, but that which has secured other rights will secure this. In Massachusetts, by the old laws, a wife owned nothing but the fee simple in her real estate. And even for that, she could not make a will without the written endorsement of her husband, permitting her to do so. Two years ago the law was so changed that she now holds the absolute right to her entire property, earnings included. Vermont, New Hampshire, and Rhode Island have also very much amended their statutes. New York, the proud Empire State, has, by the direct effort of this movement, secured to wives every property right except earnings. During two years a bill has been before the Legislature, which provides that if a husband be a drunkard, a profligate, or has abandoned his wife, she may have a right to her own earnings. It has not passed. Two hundred years hence that bill will be quoted as a proof of the barbarism of the times ; now it is a proof of progress.

Ohio, Illinois, and Indiana have also very materially modified their laws. And Wisconsin—God bless these young States—has granted almost all that has been asked except the right of suffrage. And even this, Senator Sholes,* in an able minority report on the subject, said, " is only a question of time, and as sure to triumph as God is just." It proposed that the Convention which meets in two years to amend the Constitution of the State should consider the subject. In Michigan, too, it has been moved that women should have a right to their own babies, which none of you, ladies, have here in New York. The motion caused much discussion in the Legislature, and it would probably have been carried had not a disciple of Brigham Young's, a Mormon member, defeated the bill. In Nebraska everything is bright for our cause. Mrs. Bloomer is there, and she has circulated petitions, claiming for women the right to vote. A bill to that effect passed the House of Representatives, and was lost in the Senate, only because of the too early closing of the session. That act of justice to woman would be gained in Nebraska first, and scores of

---

* At the close of chapter on Indiana, p. 315.

women would go there that they might be made citizens, and be no longer subjects.

In addition to these great legal changes, achieved so directly by this reform, we find also that women have entered upon many new and more remunerative industrial pursuits; thus being enabled to save themselves from the bitterness of dependent positions, or from lives of infamy. Our demand that Harvard and Yale Colleges should admit women, though not yielded, only waits for a little more time. And while they wait, numerous petty "female colleges" have sprung into being, indicative of the justice of our claim that a college education should be granted to women. Not one of these female colleges (which are all second or third rate, and their whole course of study only about equal to what completes the sophomore year in our best colleges) meets the demand of the age, and so will eventually perish. Oberlin and Antioch Colleges in Ohio, and Lima College in New York, admit women on terms nearly equal with men.

In England, too, the claims of women are making progress. The most influential papers in London have urged the propriety of women physicians. Also a petition was sent to Parliament last year, signed by the Brownings, the Howitts, Harriet Martineau, Mrs. Gaskell, and Mrs. Jameson, asking for just such rights as we claim here. It was presented by Lord Brougham, and was respectfully received by Parliament. The ballot has not yet been yielded; but it can not be far off when, as in the last Presidential contest,* women were urged to attend political meetings, and a woman's name was made one of the rallying cries of the party of progress. The enthusiasm which everywhere greeted the name of Jessie† was so far a recognition of woman's right to participate in politics. Encouraged by the success of these seven years of effort, let us continue with unfailing fidelity to labor for the practical recognition of the great truth, that all human rights inhere in each human being. We welcome to this platform men and women irrespective of creed, country, or color; those who dissent from us as freely as those who agree with us.

ERNESTINE L. ROSE, from the Business Committee, reported a series of resolutions.‡

---

* John C. Fremont's campaign.   † Mrs. Jessie Benton Fremont.

‡ 1. *Resolved*, That the close of a Presidential election affords a peculiarly appropriate occasion to renew the demands of woman for a consistent application of Democratic principles.

2. *Resolved*, That the Republican Party, appealing constantly, through its orators, to female sympathy, and using for its most popular rallying cry a female name, is peculiarly pledged by consistency, to do justice hereafter in those States where it holds control.

3. *Resolved*, That the Democratic Party must be utterly false to its name and professed principles, or else must extend their application to both halves of the human race.

4. *Resolved*, That the present uncertain and inconsistent position of woman in our community, not fully recognized either as a slave or as an equal, taxed but not represented, authorized to earn property but not free to control it, permitted to prepare papers for scientific bodies but not to read them, urged to form political opinions but not allowed to vote upon them, all marks a transitional period in human history which can not long endure.

The President stated that several letters had been received, one from Francis Jackson, of Boston, one of the noblest of the noble men of the age, inclosing $50, which, he says, he gives "to help this righteous cause along." Also a letter from the Rev. Samuel Johnson, of Salem, Massachusetts, which would be read by Mr. Higginson.

Rev. T. W. HIGGINSON said he was much more willing to be called upon to read the words of others at this time, than to utter poor words of his own. There were many who came into a Woman's Rights Convention and started to find men on the platform. He could only say, that in these times, and with the present light, there was no place where a man could redeem his manhood better than on the Woman's Rights Platform. Gentlemen in distant seats were perhaps trembling to think that they had actually got that far into this dangerous place. They might think themselves well off—no, badly off—if the maelstrom did not draw them nearer and nearer and nearer in, as it did him. He began, like them, hesitating and smiling on the back seats; they saw what he had got to now, and he hoped they, too, might get into such noble company before long. He was prouder to train in this band than to be at the head of the play-soldiers who were marching through the streets to-day, and immortalizing themselves by not failing, so utterly as some of their companions, to hit some easy target. Those were play-soldiers; these were soldiers in earnest.

Men talk a great deal of nonsense about the woman's rights movement. He never knew a husband who was demolished in an argument by his wife, or a young gentleman who found his resources of reason entirely used up by a young lady, who did not fall back at last when there was no retreat, and say: "It's no use; you can't reason with a woman." Well, so it would seem in their case. Others shelter themselves behind the general statement, that they don't wish to marry a woman's rights woman. I have no doubt the woman's rights women reciprocate the wish. These appear to have some anxiety about dinner—that seems to be the trouble. Jean Paul, the German, wanted to have a wife who could cook him something good; and Mrs. Frederica Bremer, the novelist, remarked, that a wife can always conciliate her husband by having something to stop his mouth. In a conversation in Philadelphia the other day, a young lawyer, when told that Mrs. Emma R. Coe was studying

---

5. *Resolved*, That the main power of the woman's rights movement lies in this: that while always demanding for woman better education, better employment, and better laws, it has kept steadily in view the one cardinal demand for the right of suffrage ; in a democracy the symbol and guarantee of all other rights.

6. *Resolved*, That the monopoly of the elective franchise, and thereby all the powers of legislative government by man, solely on the ground of sex, is a usurpation, condemned alike by reason and common-sense, subversive of all the principles of justice, oppressive and demoralizing in its operation, and insulting to the dignity of human nature.

7. *Resolved*, That while the constant progress of law, education, and industry prove that our efforts for women in these respects are not wasted, we yet proclaim ourselves unsatisfied, and are only encouraged to renewed efforts, until the whole be gained.

law with the intention of practicing, remarked, that he should never see her in Court, but she would remind him of mince pies; to which the gentleman he was in conversation with, observed that he had better not get her as his antagonist in trying a suit, or she would remind him of minced meat. Having given two or three examples of the nonsense of men upon this subject, he would now read them some sense. The letter was from one of the most eloquent and learned of the younger clergy of New England; a man possessed of powers of genius and practical wisdom which would yet make him heard in a larger sphere than that which he now occupied. It was not the old English Sam. Johnson who said that "there never was a lawsuit or a quarrel where a woman was not at the bottom of it." This was Sam. Johnson Americanized, and of course he was a woman's rights man.

LETTER FROM REV. SAMUEL JOHNSON.

SALEM, *October* 4, 1856.

DEAR FRIEND:—In complying with your desire that I should send a few words to the Woman's Rights Convention, I am quite aware that in this matter infinitely more depends upon what women do than upon what men say; nevertheless, if my confession of faith will be of the least service, it shall not be wanting.

I regard this movement as no less than the sum and crown of all our moral enterprises; as a proclamation of entire social freedom, never practicable until now. I welcome it, not merely because it aims at delivering half the human race from constraints that degrade and demoralize the whole, but also because it is opening a new spiritual hemisphere, destined to put a new heart into our semi-barbarian theology, politics, manners, literature, and law. And especially do I rejoice, that having defrauded the feminine element of its due share in practical affairs for so many ages, and found ourselves, as a natural consequence, drifting toward barbarism with all our wealth and wisdom, we are compelled at last to learn that justice to woman is simply mercy to ourselves.

Doubtless the main obstacles to this work come from her own sex. Strange if it were not so; if the meagre hope doled out to women hitherto should have unfitted them to believe that such a function awaits them. Strange if they did not fear a thousand perils in the untried way of freedom. But the unwise distrust will have to be abandoned; and so will the conventional flippancy and contempt. I think the grand duty of every honorable man toward this effort at emancipation is simply *not to stand in its way.* For how much is really covered by that duty? It means that he must wash his hands of every law or prejudice that dooms woman to an inferior position, and makes her the victim of miserable wages and fatal competitions with herself. It means that he must clear himself of this senseless twaddle about "woman's sphere," a matter surely no more for his legislation, than his "sphere" is for hers; and one upon which, at this stage of their experience, it is unbecoming in either to dogmatize; and it means that, as a simple act of justice, he must resign to her the control of her own earnings, secure her fair and full culture, and welcome her to the pulpit, the bar, the medical profession, and to whatever other posts of public usefulness she may prepare herself to fill. As long as he fails of doing this, he is unjustly interfering with her sacred rights; and *after* he has done this, he may safely leave the rest to her.

It is humiliating indeed that numbers of well-disposed persons should not recognize so plain a duty. I have no patience to argue it. The moral logic of this movement is as patent as the simplest rule in arithmetic. Every argument brought against it resolves itself into a sneer at woman's capacity, or an anxiety lest the distinction God has established between the sexes will not bear testing; or, what is more common still, though covered up in a thousand ways, the brutish assertion that "might makes right." There is but one answer to these impertinences, and that is the success of individual women in the work they set about. The current ridicule at "doing justice to women" will pass for the sheer vulgarity it is, when so many women shall do justice to themselves, that they can not be taken as exceptions to prove the rule. And this success depends on their own wills. The noble use of God's gifts shall make its mark in this world. As sure as God lives, it shall compel a becoming respect. For more and more of these lessons in true honor do we pray; for the very name of manhood must make us blush, so long as it is identified with these airs of patronage and control, these insulting obeisances, these flatterers of what is childish in women, these sarcasms upon what is noblest; worse than all, this willingness to derive gain from the degradation and suffering of the sex it professes to adore. And words are poor to express the gratitude that shall be forever due to those women whose moral energy shall rebuke this littleness, and stir true manliness in man.　　With sincere respect, I am truly your friend,

SAMUEL JOHNSON.

ERNESTINE L. ROSE remarked, that in the letter read by Mr. Higginson there was one sentence that struck her with great force, viz: that it is of far greater importance what woman does than what man thinks; and, she would add, what woman thinks. The influence of what she had done was felt not only in this country, but throughout the entire continent of Europe.

The author of that letter had expressed another sentiment to which she wished briefly to advert. He said that where ten men could be convinced of the truth of Woman's Rights, hardly one woman could be gained. At first sight it might so appear. But it should be borne in mind, that men were more accustomed to think and reflect and argue upon everything connected with the legal and political rights of men, at least, and, therefore, they were more easily convinced. Nevertheless, the subject, whenever presented to the mind of woman in its proper light, would not fail to find an echo in her heart. Whenever the subject was broached to a woman hitherto unacquainted with it, it first caused a smile, and, perchance, a sneer; but, put to her a few common-sense questions, and the smile disappeared, and her countenance assumed a serious expression. Ask her if she is not entitled to self-government, to the full development of her mental powers, to the free choice of her industrial avocations, to proper remuneration for her labor, to equal control of her offspring with that of her husband, to the possession and control of her own property, and to a voice in making the laws that impose taxes upon property that she may hold—ask her a few simple, straightforward questions like these, and see if an immediate, hearty, and warm assent is not elicited.

In spite of a violent storm a large number assembled in the evening. The speakers announced were Mrs. Elizabeth Jones and Wendell Phillips. Mrs. Jones' address was a clear and logical statement of the whole claim of woman. By her own request, it was not published.

Wendell Phillips:—Ladies and gentlemen. I am told that the *Times* of to-day warns the women of this Convention that if they proceed in their crusade they will forfeit the protection of the men. Perhaps, before it is offered, the question had better be asked whether it is needed. I do not think that I should run the risk of much difference of opinion if I claimed, that nine men out of ten would not be able to defend their right to vote as logically as the lady who has just addressed us has defended her right to vote. I question whether one-quarter of what we call the men educated by the colleges, and in active life—the better education of the two—would be able, arrogating to themselves as they do a far greater political and civil capacity, to state the grounds of civil rights and responsibilities, to mark out the limits, to vindicate the advantages, and to analyze the bases on which these rest, as we have just had it done. If participation in civil rights is based on mind—as in this country we claim it to be—then certainly to-night we have no right to deny that the cause is gained, for the friend who has preceded me has left very little for any one to say; she has covered the whole ground.

In fact this question is a question of civilization, nothing less. The position of woman anywhere is the test of civilization. You need not ask for the statistics of education, of national wealth, or of crime; tell me the position of woman, and you answer the question of the nation's progress. Utah is barbarism; we need no evidence; we read it in the single custom that lowers the female sex. Wherever you go in history this is true. Step by step as woman ascends, civilization ripens. I warn the anxious and terrified that their first efforts should be to conquer their fears, for the triumph of this crusade is written as certain on the next leaf that turns in the great history of the race, as that the twentieth century will open.

The time was when a Greek dared not let his wife go out of doors, and in the old comic play of Athens, one of the characters says, "Where is your wife?" "She has gone out." "Death and furies! what does she do out?" Doubtless, if any "fanatic" had claimed the right of woman to walk out of doors, he would have been deemed crazy in Athens; had he claimed the right of a modest married woman to be seen out of doors it would have been considered fanaticism, and I do not know but that the *Herald* of that day would have branded him as an infidel. But spite of the anchored conservatism of others, women got out of doors and the country grew, and the world turned round, and so modern Europe has progressed. Now the pendulum swung one way, and now another, but woman has gained right after right until with us, to the astonishment of the Greek, could he see it—of the Turk, when he hears it—she stands almost side by side with man in her civil rights. The Saxon race has led the van. I trample underfoot contemptuously the Jewish—yes, the Jewish—ridicule which laughs at such a Convention as this; for we are the Saxon blood, and the first line of record that is left to the Saxon race is that line of Tacitus, "On all grave questions they consult their women." When the cycle of Saxondom is complete, when the Saxon element culminates in modern civilization, another Tacitus will record in the valley of the Mississippi, as he did in the valley of the Rhine, "On all grave questions they consult their women." The fact is, there is no use of blinking the issue. It is Paul against the Saxon blood; it is a religious prejudice against the blood of the race. The blood of the race accords to woman equality; it is a religious superstition which stands in the way and balks the effort.

Europe has known three phases. The first was the dominion of force; the second the dominion of money; the third is beginning—the dominion of brains. When it comes, woman will step out on the platform side by side with her brother. The old Hindoo dreamed that he saw the human race led out to its varied fortune, and first he saw a man bitted and curbed, and the reins went back to an iron hand. Then he saw a man led on and on, under various changes, until, at last, he saw the man led by threads that came from the brain and went back to an invisible hand. The first was the type of despotism—the reign of force, the upper classes keeping down the under. The last is ours—the dominion of brains. We live in a government where *The New York Herald* and *New York Tribune*, thank God, are more really the government than Franklin Pierce and Caleb Cushing. Ideas reign. I know some men do not appreciate this fact; they are overawed by the iron arm, by the marble capitol, by the walls of granite—palpable power, felt, seen. I have seen the palace of the Cæsars, built of masses that seemed as if giants alone could have laid them together, to last for eternity, as if nothing that did not part the solid globe could move them. But the tiny roots of the weeds of Italian summers had inserted themselves between them, and the palace of the Cæsars lies a shapeless ruin. So it is with your government. It may be iron, it may be marble, but the pulses of right and wrong push it aside; only give them time. I hail the government of ideas.

There is another thing I claim. You laugh at Woman's Rights Conventions; you ridicule socialism (I do not accept that); you dislike the anti-slavery movement. The only discussion of the grave social questions of the age, the questions of right and wrong that lie at the basis of society—the only voices that have stirred them and kept those questions alive have been those of these three reforms. Smothered with gold—smothered with material prosperity, the vast masses of our countrymen were, living the lives of mere getters of money; but the ideas of this half of the nineteenth century have been bruited by despised reformers, kept alive by three radical movements, and whoever in the next generation shall seek for the sources of mental and intellectual change will find it here; and in a progressive people like ours that claim is a most vital and significant one. . . . .

I contend that woman, broadly considered, makes half the money that is made. Go the world over, take either Europe or America, the first source of money is intelligence and thrift; it is not speculation. . . . . Out of the twenty millions of American people that make money, woman does more than half of the work that insures the reward. I claim for that half of the race whose qualities garner up wealth, the right to dispose of it, and to control it by law.

Again, take thought. I know our sister has modestly told us how utterly they are deprived of what are called the institutions of education; but we know very well that book learning is a miserably poor thing, and that the best education in the world is what we clutch in the streets; and of that education, by hook or by crook, woman has so far gained enough, that, Europe and America through, where is the man presumptuous enough to doubt that the hand of woman is not felt as much on the helm of public opinion as that of man ? To be sure, she does not have an outside ambitious distinction ; but at home, in the molding hours, in youth, in the soft moments when the very balance-wheel of character is touched, we all know that woman, though she may not consciously enunciate ideas, does as much to form public opinion as man. The time has been—and every man who has ever analyzed history knows it—when in France, the mother to Europe of all social ideas; France that has lifted up Germany from mysticism, and told England what she means and what she wants; France that has construed England to herself, and interpreted to her what she was blindly reaching out for ; when in that very France, at the fountain-head of that eighteenth century of civil progress, it was in the saloons of woman that man did his thinking, and it was under the brilliant inspiration of her society that that mighty revolution in the knowledge and science of civil affairs was wrought. In this country, too, at this hour, woman does as much to give the impulse to public opinion as man does.

Wherever I find silent power I want recognition of the responsibility. I am not in favor of a power behind the throne. I do not want half the race concealed behind the curtain and controlling without being responsible. Drag them to the light, hold them up as you do men to the utmost study of public questions, and to a personal responsibility for their public settlement. Corruption—it often takes the very form of the passions of woman. In Paris, to-day, we are told, when the government approaches a man, the way is, not to give him wealth for his own enjoyment, but to dower his daughter. It is the pride of woman through which they reach him. Drag that woman forward on the platform of public life; give to her manifest ability a fair field, let her win wealth by her own exertions, not by the surrender of principle in the person of her husband; and although my friend doubts it, I believe, when you put the two sexes harmoniously in civil life, you will secure a higher state of civilization—not because woman is better, not because she is more merciful, or more just, or more pure than man, as man naturally, but because God meant that a perfect human being should be made up of man and woman allied, and it is only when the two march side by side on the pathway of civilization that the harmonious development of the race begins.

Then, again, you can not educate woman, in the sense that we use education. She has no motive. As my friend said, when she marries, education ceases. At that age the education of man commences : he has wealth, ambition, social position, as his stimulus; he knows that by keeping his mind on the alert he earns them all. You furnish a woman with books—you give her no motive to open them. You open to her the door of science : why should she enter ? She can gain nothing except in individual and exceptional cases; public opinion drives her back, places a stigma upon her of blue-stocking, and the consequence is, the very motive for education is taken away. Now, I believe, a privileged class, an aristocracy, a set of slaveholders, does just as much harm to itself as it does to the victimized class. When man undertakes to place woman behind him, to assume the reins of government and to govern for her, he is an aristocrat; and all aristocracies are not only unjust, but they are harmful to the progress of society.

I welcome this movement, because it shows that we have got a great amount of civilization. Every other movement to redress a wrong in the past genera-tions of the world has been yielded to only from fear. Bentham says truly, the governing race never yielded a right unless they were bullied out of it. That is true historically; but we have come to a time—and this movement shows it—when civilization has rendered man capable of yielding to something dif-ferent from fear. This movement has only been eight years on foot, and during that time, we who have watched the statute-book are aware to admiration of the rapid changes that have taken place in public opinion, and in legislation, all over the States. Within the last four years, in different localities, woman has been allowed the right to protect her earnings, and to make a will—two of the great points of property. Aye, and one little star of light begins to twinkle in the darkness of the political atmosphere: Kentucky allows her to vote. Yes, from the land where on one question they are so obstinate, the white race have remembered justice to their white co-equals. In her nobly-planned school system, Kentucky divides her State into districts; the trustees are annually chosen for the State funds; and it is expressly provided, that besides the usual voters in the election of trustees for the school fund, which is coveted by millions, there shall be allowed to vote, every widow who has a child betwixt six and eighteen years old, and she shall go to the ballot-box in person or by proxy. Kentucky repudiates the doctrine that to go to the ballot-box forfeits the delicacy of the sex; for she provides, in express terms, that she shall go to the ballot-box in person, or by proxy, as she pleases. It is the first drop of the coming storm—it is the first ray of light in the rising sun.

Civilization can not defend itself, on American principles, against this claim. My friend of Brooklyn claims the right to make political speeches, as well as sermons, because he is a citizen. Well, woman is a citizen too: and if a minis-ter can preach politics because he is a citizen, woman can meddle in politics and vote, because she is a citizen too. When Mr. Beecher based his right, not on the intellect which flashes from Maine to Georgia, not on the strength of that nervous right arm, but solely on his citizenship, he dragged to the platform twelve millions of American women to stand at his side. But the difficulty is, no man can defend his own right to vote, without granting it to woman. The only reason why the demand sounds strange, is because man never analyzed his own right. The moment he begins to analyze it, he can not defend it without admitting her. Our fathers proclaimed, sixty years ago, that government was co-equal with the right to take money and to punish for crime. Now, all that I wish to say to the American people on this question is, let woman go free from the penal statute—let her property be exempt from taxation, until you admit her to the ballot-box—or seal up the history of the Revolution, make Bancroft and Hildreth prohibited books, banish the argument of '76, and let Mr. Simms have his own way with the history of all the States, as well as South Carolina. Yes, the fact is, women make opinion for us; and the only thing we shut them out from is the ballot-box.

I would have it constantly kept before the public, that we do not seek to prop up woman; we only ask for her space to let her grow. Govern-ments are not made; they grow. They are not buildings like this, with dome and pillars; they are oaks, with roots and branches, and they grow, by God's blessing, in the soil He gives to them. Now man has been allowed

Very Sincerely
Yr. friend
M. C. Wright.

to grow, and when Pharaoh tied him down with bars of iron, when Europe tied him down with privilege and superstition, he burst the bonds and grew strong. We ask the same for woman. Göethe said that if you plant an oak in a flower-pot, one of two things was sure to happen: either the oak will be dwarfed, or the flower-pot will break. So we have planted woman in a flower-pot, hemmed her in by restrictions, and when we move to enlarge her sphere, society cries out, "Oh! you'll break the flower-pot!" Well, I say, let it break. Man made it, and the sooner it goes to pieces the better. Let us see how broadly the branches will throw themselves, and how beautiful will be the shape, and how glorious against the moonlit sky, or glowing sunset, the foliage shall appear.

I say the very first claim, the middle and last claim of all our Conventions should be the ballot. Everywhere, in each State, we should claim it; not for any intrinsic value in the ballot, but because it throws upon woman herself the responsibility of her position. Man never grew to his stature until he was provoked to it by the pressure and weight of responsibility; and I take it woman will grow up the same way.

The first three resolutions on the Presidential election were brought up for discussion and adopted. Those persons in the audience who desired to speak were urged to do so.

Mrs. ROSE said: In reference to this last election, though it was not my good fortune to be here during the time of that great excitement, being then on the continent of Europe; yet, even at that great distance, the fire of freedom that was kindled here spread itself across the Atlantic. The liberal, intelligent, and reformatory portion of the people of Europe, as well as in England, have most warmly, most heartily sympathized with us in the last struggle of freedom against slavery. It is a most glorious epoch. I will not enter into a political or anti-slavery lecture, but simply state this fact—the time has come when the political parties are entirely annihilated. They have ceased to exist. There is no longer Whig and no longer Democrat — there is Freedom or Slavery. We have here an equally great purpose to achieve. This, too, is not woman's rights or man's rights, but it is human rights. It is based on precisely the same fundamental truths with the other question. In the last election the general feeling prevailed that woman ought to take more interest in political affairs, and with the noble work she did during the campaign, it seems to me most extraordinary that the men who have worked thus nobly for the freedom of one class, should yet refuse freedom to the other class.

PHILLIP D. MOORE rose in the body of the building and said: During this last Presidential canvass I heard more than once the oldest member of Congress declare that Freedom was based upon the law of God, which was declared in our Bill of Rights—our Declaration of Independence—that it was the inalienable right of all mankind to life, to liberty, and to the pursuit of happiness. He placed this last Presidential struggle upon that right higher than all human law; and upon that it seems this contest in behalf of human rights is based. I think that we should adopt these resolutions, and also appeal to the legislative bodies, where, I believe, there are men who will hear and heed the voice of justice.

Rev. T. W. HIGGINSON took the floor, and expressed his hope that they would have more speaking from the floor and less from the platform. As a Republican voter, he would take his stand in support of these resolutions; and he would declare that it was true that the close of the Presidential election was the time for a woman's Convention to be held. It was true that the Republican party was pledged, if it had any manliness in it, to support the cause of women, to whom it had applied to support its cause every day; and it was positively true that, if there were such a thing in the land as a Democratic party, that party was the party of the women also. As a further illustration of the idea expressed by the gentleman who had preceded him, he would state the fact that, when he was invited to Vermont to address the Legislature in favor of the appropriation of $20,000 for Kansas,* the meeting was postponed, on the ground that the shortness of the notice would not allow time for procuring the attendance of the women of the village to fill the galleries, and by their sympathy to influence the determination of the members of the Legislature who might be present. Accordingly they waited a little longer, gave sufficient notice, got the gallery full of ladies, and ultimately got the $20,000 appropriation, too. But always when the women had given their sympathy and began to demand some in return, it was found out that they were very " dependent " creatures, and that, if they persisted in it, they would forfeit the "protection " of the men; and this in the face of the fact, that when politicians wanted votes and clergymen wanted money, their invariable practice was to appeal to the women !

The last time he had considered woman's rights he was in a place where man's rights needed to be defended—it was in Kansas. No man could go to Kansas and see what woman had done there, and come back and see the little men who squeak and shout on platforms in behalf of Kansas, and then turn to deride and despise women, without a feeling of disgust. He would like to place some of these parlor orators and dainty platform speakers where the women of Kansas had stood, and suffered, and acted. He saw, while in Kansas, a New York woman†—whose story they might remember in the newspapers—how she hospitably prepared, in one day, three dinners for the marauders who were hovering around her house, and in their starvation became respectful at last, and asked her for the hospitality they did not then quite dare to enforce; and how they ate her dinner and abused her husband, until the good woman could stand it no longer, and at last opened her lips and gave them a piece of

---

* During the struggle to extend slavery into that free State.

† Jeannette Brown Heath, daughter of Nathan Brown, of Montgomery County, New York. She traveled with Abby Kelly at one time as a companion. Jeannette was a famous horsewoman; the young ladies of the county thought themselves well off when they could purchase a steed that she had trained for the saddle. I remember many an escapade in my youth on a full-blooded black horse from Jeannette's equery, as I lived in her neighborhood; she is now residing with two sons and one daughter in Rochester, N. Y., enjoying the needed rest after such an eventful life.—E. C. S.

her mind. He saw that woman. She had lived for weeks together in the second story of a log hut, with the windows of the lower story boarded up, so that the inmates had to climb in by a ladder. She was surrounded by pro-slavery camps; and while her husband was in the army, she was left alone. The house had been visited again and again, and plundered. The wretches would come at night, discharge their rifles, and howl like demons. Her little girl, a nervous child, had sickened and died from sheer fright. But still, after the death of that child, the mother lived on, and still gave hospitality to free-soil men, and still defended the property of her husband by her presence: At last the marauders burned her house over her head, and she retreated for a time. The speaker saw her when she was on her way back to that homestead, to rebuild the house which she had seen once reduced to ashes by the enemy; and she said that if her husband was killed there in Kansas, she should preëmpt that claim, and defend the property for her children.

He saw another woman, a girl of twenty. He visited a mill which had been burnt by Missourians, where piles of sawdust were still in flames before his eyes, and there he met her; and when he asked to whom that house belonged, she said to her father. And when he inquired about her adventures in connection with that burning house, this was the story. Twenty-eight hundred Missourians were encamped around that house the morning after they had burned it. The girl had fled with her mother a mile off, but had come back to see if she could save any of the property. She walked into the midst of the crowd, and found a man she had previously known seated upon her favorite horse. Said she, "That is my horse; get off." He laughed at her. She repeated her demand. He loaded her with curses and insults. She turned to the bystanders—the herd of ruffians who had burned her father's house—and said: "This is my horse; make that man get off." Those fellows obeyed her; they shrank before that heroic girl, and made their companion dismount. She mounted the horse and rode off. When she had gone about half a mile, she heard a trampling of horses' hoofs behind her. The thief, mounted on a fleeter horse, was riding after her. He overtook her, and reining his horse in front of her, he seized hers by the bridle, and commanded her to let go. She held on. Said he, "Let go, or it will be the worse for you." She still held on. He took out his bowie-knife, and drew it across her hand, so that she could feel the sharpness of the edge. Said he, "If you don't let go, I will cut your hand off." Said she, "Cut if you dare." He cut the rope close to her hand, and took the bridle from her. It was useless to resist any longer, so she slipped off and walked away. But it was not ten minutes before she again heard trampling behind, and as she looked around, she saw two companions of this miscreant —two men less utterly villainous than he—bringing back her horse. Moved by her heroism, they had compelled him again to give up the horse, had brought it back to her, and she owns it now.

That was what great emergencies made out of woman. That girl had splendid physical proportions, and though some accident had deprived her of her left arm, she had a right arm, however, which was worth a good many. She had one arm, and the editor of *The New York Times*, he supposed, had two. He was not much accustomed to seeking defence of anybody, but he must say that, if he ever did get into difficulty as a Woman's Rights man, and had to choose between the protection of the one arm of that girl in Kansas, and the two of the New York editor, he thought his first choice would not be the Lieutenant-Governor. Seeing the heroism of the women of Kansas, he told the men of Lawrence, that when the time came for them to assert their rights, he hoped they would not imitate the border ruffians of the Eastern States, who asserted rights for man, and denied them to woman.

Mr. Higginson then reported the following resolution from the Business Committee:

Resolved, That the warm sympathies of this Convention are respectfully offered to those noble women in England, who are struggling against wrongs even greater than those of American women, but the same in kind; and we trust that they will follow on their demands in logical consistency, until they comprise the full claim for the equality of the sexes before the law.

This resolution referred, as some of them knew, to the recent action of some of the noblest women in England, in behalf of juster rights of property and a larger construction of human rights than had hitherto prevailed there. The list included a few of the very noblest of the women who had helped to make England's name glorious by their deeds in literature and in art. It included Mrs. Norton, to whom Wendell Phillips had referred, as a living proof of the intellectual greatness of woman; she had a husband who, after blasting her life by an infamous charge against her, which he confessed to his counsel he did not believe, now lived on the earnings of the brains of his wife. It included, also, Mrs. Somerville, a woman who had forever vindicated the scientific genius of her sex, by labors that caused the wonder and admiration of scientific men; a woman of whom it is said, that she is in all respects true to her sex, because while studying the motions of the heavenly bodies, she does not forget the motion of the tea-cups around her own table, and is as exquisite a housekeeper, as she is wise and accomplished as a student. It included also Harriet Martineau, that woman who, perhaps more than any other person in this age, had contributed to place the last half century in Europe in a clear light, by her admirable History, and shown in her treatise on Political Economy, a grasp and clearness which few men attain. It included also the name of Elizabeth Barrett Browning, that woman of rarest genius, of whom her husband, himself the greatest of England's living poets, had said that his wife's heart, which few knew, was greater than her intellect, which everybody knew; a woman whose inspiration had drawn from that husband, in the closing poem of his latest volume, the very highest strain which modern English poetry had struck, and the noblest utterance of emotion that ever man produced toward woman, in the speaker's judgment, since the world began. It also included Mary Howitt, whose beautiful union with her husband is a proof of what true marriage will be, when man and woman are equals, and whose genius had brought forth the wonderful powers of another woman whom we may fearlessly claim as a co-laborer, Frederica Bremer. These were the women of England to whom the resolution referred; women who had taken the first step in that movement, of which the full enfranchisement of woman will be the last.

He could not quite accept the opinion by Mrs. Jones in her admirable essay in regard to the superior education of the women of England. The women of England, as he took it, did not equal the women of America in their average education, although they did surpass them in that physical vigor of constitution which, in the end, gave greater power of action and thought. Whilst the English woman was, by the necessity of the case, taught more of the modern languages, she was not so commonly taught either the ancient languages or the mathematics, and had not, therefore, the same amount of mental training. In England, too, this Woman's Rights movement was met by more serious obstacles. It had to encounter all the thunders of *The Thunderer*—all the terrors of *The Times*—whilst here it had to undergo the very diluted thunders of *The Times the Little.* A recent traveler has remarked that he could distinguish the Massachusetts women from the women of any other State—not because they spoke through their nose, or sung psalms, but because they had "views." Every woman had her "views" upon every subject. It was true that the English women had superb frames, grand muscles, fine energies, that they spoke two or three languages, but then they usually didn't have any "views"; and he thanked God that he lived in a State where women had them.

He had spoken for woman and to woman, because he was a man. He did not dare, as a Republican voter, to throw his vote with one hand, without doing something for Woman's Rights with the other. Men and women were one before God, and this union can not be perfect until their equality be recognized. So long as woman is cut off from education, man is deprived of his just education. So long as woman is crushed into a slave, so long will man be narrowed into a despot. Without this movement, the political conventions of the present day would only prove to posterity that the nation was half civilized; but now future historians will record that in 1856, New York had not only her caucuses and her ballot-boxes, but her Woman's Rights Convention also.

Mrs. Rose wished to remark, in reference to the resolution offered by Mr. Higginson, that English women, to her knowledge, were very active in forwarding the Woman's Rights movement throughout Great Britain. And not only English women, but young and noble English girls—girls, who were too timid to take part publicly in the movement, but who were untiring and indefatigable in making converts and enlisting aid. There was Miss Smith, Miss Fox, the daughter of the celebrated W. J. Fox, the eloquent lecturer and member of Parliament for Oldham, Miss Parkes, and others. They had devoted themselves to the great work, which was more difficult in that country than this. They had no declaration of independence to appeal to, declaring that all men were created equal, and endowed with the incalculable right to life, liberty, and the pursuit of happiness. They had no such standard to appeal to there, because men there were not recognized as free. Banking interests, manufacturing interests, land monopolies, and monopolies of every other kind were represented in England, but not men. The principle of universal suffrage had not yet obtained in England, and hence the greater difficulties that woman had to encounter there.

Another obstacle was the division of the people into classes and castes. No movement could make headway in England unless it was commenced among what are termed the higher classes. Every petition to Parliament must first have some names that have a title attached to them before it can obtain other signatures. The thinking portion of the middle classes were kept silent to a great extent, because of their utter inability to do anything unless it was taken up and supported by the higher classes. But this state of things would not continue long; there was "a good time coming" there as well as here. Signatures by thousands had been obtained to the Woman's Petition, and she presumed by the time it was presented to Parliament it would contain tens of thousands of names.

Mrs. Rose then offered the following resolution from the Committee:

Resolved, That we also present our assurances of respect and sympathy to the supporters of the cause of women in Paris, the worthy successors of Pauline Roland and Jeanne Deroine, who, in the face of imperial despotism, dare to tell the truth.

In commenting on this resolution, Mrs. Rose remarked that if the difficulties surrounding English women who advocated an amelioration of woman's condition were great, how much greater were those which surrounded the French women, owing to the blight of despotism in that country. They could write their thoughts, but their writings could not be published in France. They had to send them to the one State in Italy which was not crushed by dark and bitter despotism. That bright spot is Sardinia. The works of the noble French women had to be sent to Turin, printed there, and sent back to Paris for private, secret distribution. And when these women met in consultation, they had to watch the doors and windows, to see that all was secure. She knew many of them, but dared not mention their names, for fear they might be borne across the Atlantic, and lead to their oppression and proscription. The noblest thoughts that had ever been uttered in France were by women, not only before the Revolution, but down to the present day. Madame Roland was imprisoned for uttering the truth, in consequence of which imprisonment she lost her arm. Jeanne Deroine was exiled, and now resides in London, where she supports herself, two daughters and son. She was teaching them herself, because she had no means to pay for their education. She filled their minds with noble thoughts and feelings, even to the very sacrifice of themselves for the benefit of the race, and more especially for the elevation of woman, without which she feels convinced that the elevation of man can never be accomplished.

But while the names of a few such noble women were made public, hundreds, nay, thousands, who had done as much, and even more than these, were in obscurity. They were constantly watching to find what was done in America. And there was one thing which characterized these French women, and that was, the entire absence of jealousy and envy of the talents and virtues of others. Wherever they see a man or woman of intellect or virtue, they recognize them as a brother or sister; and they never ask from whom a great thought or a virtuous action comes, but, is it good, is it noble? It seemed to her that the character of the French women was the very essence of human nobility. They are ready to welcome, with heart and hand, every reformer, without stopping to inquire whether he is English, American, German, or Turk. But poor France was oppressed as she never was before. The usurper that now disgraces the throne, as well as the name he bears, does not allow the free utterance of a single free thought. Men and women are taken up privately and imprisoned, and no newspaper dares to publish any account of it.

When Mrs. Rose had concluded, a young gentleman in the rear of the hall rose from his seat, and desired to make a few remarks. We subsequently understood he was from Virginia, and that his name was Leftwich, a theological student. He asked whether the claims of woman, which had been stated and advocated in the Convention, were founded on Nature or Revelation? He wished Mr. Higginson would enlighten him and several of his friends on that subject.

Rev. Mr. HIGGINSON said that he was very glad that it was not a place for theological discussion. He was requested to answer the query whether the claims of woman, as stated in this Convention, were founded in Nature or Revelation. To define either what Nature or Revelation was, would involve metaphysical argument and abstract considerations that would take up the entire day. The basis of the movement was not due to this or that creed. Every Woman's Rights man or woman does his or her own thinking. He (the speaker) did his own. Included in the movement were men and women of all sects. There was Wendell Phillips, who thought himself a strict Calvinist; there were on the other hand professed atheists among them, and there were, he believed, Roman Catholics, so that it would be, in the highest degree, presumptuous for any one man to speak on that peculiar topic. Antoinette L. Brown had formed her idea of Woman's Rights from the Bible, and some of her friends thought that she was wasting her time in writing a treatise on Woman's Rights, deduced from Scripture. She was an orthodox Congregational minister, ordained in a Methodist meeting-house, while a Baptist minister preached the ordination sermon. There were some of the Woman's Rights friends who believed that we could get support from the Bible, and some who believed we could not, and who did not care whether we can or not. There were, also, those who simply believed that God made man and woman, and knew what He was about when He made them—giving them rights founded on the eternal laws of nature. It was upon these laws of nature that he (Mr. H.) founded his Woman's Rights doctrines. If there was any book or teacher in the world which contradicted them, he was sorry for that book and for that teacher. Was the gentleman answered?

THE GENTLEMAN FROM VIRGINIA rose, in his place, in the rear of the building, and replied that he was not answered. Although earnestly invited to come upon the platform and address the audience, he declined to do so. His remarks, in consequence, were inaudible to about one-half the audience. He said it seemed to him that there was an inconsistency and an antagonism between theology and Mr. Higginson's views, as expressed by himself. The gentleman had contradicted himself. He refused to treat the question on the ground of revelation, and then declared that the claim of Woman's Rights was founded on the fundamental laws of God and nature. Here he took issue with Mr. H. The test of the naturalness of a claim was its universality. The principles upon which it was based must be found wherever man was found, and must have existed through all time and under every condition of life. What was found everywhere under all circumstances was natural. This Woman's Rights claim was not found everywhere even in this country, let alone others.

He knew many enlightened and refined districts which had never heard the principles of this society, much less felt them. They were not popular anywhere in the age in which they were inaugurated. Therefore they were not founded in nature, and the claim of naturalism must fall to the ground. The taste for the beautiful, and the love of right, were innate faculties of the mind, because they existed everywhere; not so with the recognition of the claim of Woman's Rights. Again, the claim was not based on revelation, which he would prove in this way: Revelation is never inconsistent with itself. The claim for woman of the right to vote, inasmuch as she would of necessity vote as she pleased, and therefore sometimes contrary to her husband, involved a disobedience of her husband, which was directly antagonistic to the injunction of the Scriptures requiring wives to obey their husbands.

AN ELDERLY QUAKER LADY in the body of the audience rose, and told the gentleman from the Old Dominion that if he wished to do any good he must come on the platform where he could be heard. The gentleman declined.

LUCY STONE said that men had rights as well as women, and she would not insist on the gentleman coming to the platform if he chose to remain where he was, but it would be more convenient if he would come.

THE GENTLEMAN FROM VIRGINIA still declined, and proceeded to quote Scripture against the Woman's Rights movement.

THE QUAKER LADY again started up, and told him he had got hold of the letter of the Bible, but not the spirit.

LUCY STONE desired that each speaker would take his or her turn, "in due order, so that all might be edified."

THE GENTLEMAN FROM VIRGINIA proceeded. Referring to a remark of Mr. Phillips on the preceding evening, in connection with a quotation from Tacitus, "that this movement was Paul against the Anglo-Saxon blood," he stood by the apostle to the Gentiles, and Mr. Phillips might stand by the corrupted Saxon blood.

A GENTLEMAN rose and requested him to go upon the platform, as half the audience were breaking their necks by trying to listen to him. Still the gentleman declined.

THE VIRGINIAN argued that woman was not fitted for the pulpit, the rostrum, or the law court, because her voice was not powerful enough. God gave her a mild, sweet voice, fitted for the parlor and the chamber, for the places for which He had designed her. God has not given her a constitution to sustain fatigue, to endure as man endures, to brave the dangers which man can brave. She was too frail, too slender—too delicate a flower for rough blasts and tempests. In her whole physical organization there was proof that she was not capable of what man was capable. Hers was a more beautiful mission than man's—a pure atmosphere was hers to breathe. Surrounded by all gentle influences, let her be content with the holy and beautiful position assigned to her by her Maker. He did not rise to make a speech. He was urged into it by the desultory, erratic, shallow, superficial reasonings of the gentleman who in one breath invited them to free discussion, and in the next defamed and scandalized the editor of *The Times*, because he took the liberty to discuss this question freely in his paper.

Mr. HIGGINSON came forward promptly to reply. He thanked the gentleman for his speech. Such speeches were just what the Convention wanted.

He was glad to hear from the applause which followed the gentleman's remarks, that there was a large number of persons present who were opposed to the views of the Convention. It was of little use talking to friends who already agreed with you, but it was always of advantage to talk to opponents, whom you might hope to convert. He was glad that those who differed with them were there, because it showed that the question was one of interest, and was beginning to excite those who probably had bestowed but little thought on it before. He did not think the gentleman could have meant what he said when he accused him of slander. He did not mean to slander anybody. And he did not think he quite meant what he said about his erratic and shallow reasonings. He would appeal to all if he had not treated the gentleman with courtesy. He thought he had answered the gentleman's inquiry, when in reply to the question whether he founded this claim on nature or on revelation, he said that he personally founded it on nature. If there was in the compass of the English language any simpler way of answering the question than that he did not know it. The gentleman, from the scope of his remarks, evinced a considerable love for metaphysical theology. His reasoning appeared to be a little dim; perhaps it was for want of comprehension on his part. He liked to plant himself on the fundamental principles of human nature, and work out his opinions from them.

In reply to the gentleman's reasoning about the universality of a thing being a test of its naturalness, he could say that there were a good many races who did not know that two and two make four. According to the gentleman's idea of natural laws, therefore, it was not natural that two and two should make four. But it had always been a question among metaphysicians, which was really the most natural condition for man—the savage or the civilized state? His own opinion was that the state of highest cultivation was the most natural state of man. He tried to develop his own nature in that way, and one of the consequences of that development was the conviction that two and two made four; while another was the conviction that his wife had as much right to determine her sphere in life for herself as he had for himself. And having come to that conviction, he should endeavor to carry it out, and he hoped by the time the young gentleman came to have a wife, he would be converted to that principle.

In reference to his attack on the editor of *The Daily Times* for the article on the Woman's Convention, which had appeared in the edition of the previous day, he remarked that he had read that article without any particular reverence for its author. He knew the quarter from which it came. There was not a man in New York who better uuderstood on which side his bread is buttered than the editor of *The Daily Times*. That gentleman always wished people to understand that his journal was *The Times*, and was not *The Tribune*, and never failed to avail himself of the Woman's Rights movement as giving him such an opportunity. Have you ever seen a little boy running along the street, and carefully dodging between two big boys? If you have, that was the editor of *The Times* between Greeley and Bennett. *The Times* seeks to be a journal and nothing else. I will always say of it, continued the speaker, that the *reports* in

The Times are very perfect and very excellent. I do not mean any disrespect to the other reporters present when I say that the report of yesterday's proceedings of this Convention, published in this morning's *Times*, was fuller and far more perfect than the report of any other paper. And so it always is with the reports of *The Times*. They are as full, as its criticisms on moral subjects are empty.

LUCY STONE vacated the chair to address the meeting. She was more than glad, for the sake of the cause, that this discussion had arisen. She was glad that the question had been asked, whether this claim was based on nature or on revelation. Many were asking the same question, and it was proper that it should be answered. If we were living in New Zealand where there is no revelation and nobody has ever heard of one, there would yet be an everlasting truth or falsehood on this question of woman's rights, and the inhabitants of that island would settle it in some way, without revelation. The true test of every question is its own merits. What is true will remain. What is false will perish like the leaves of autumn when they have served their turn.

But in regard to this question of Nature and Revelation, we found our claim on both. By Revelation I suppose the gentleman means Scripture. I find it there, "He who spake as never man spake" held up before us all radiant with God's own sunlight the great truth, "All things whatsoever ye would that men should do to you, do ye even so to them"; and that revelation I take as the foundation of our claim, and tell the gentleman who takes issue with us, that if he would not take the position of woman, denied right of access to our colleges, deprived of the right of property, compelled to pay taxes, to obey laws that he never had a voice in making, and be defrauded of the children of his love, then, according to the revelation which he believes in, he must not be thus unjust to me.

The gentleman says he believes in Paul. So do I. When Paul declares that there is neither Jew nor Greek, neither bond nor free, male nor female in Christ, I believe he meant what he said. The gentleman says he believes in Paul more than in the Anglo-Saxon blood. I believe in both. But when Paul tells us to "submit ourselves to every ordinance of man for the Lord's sake," and to "fear God and honor the king," the heavy tread of the Anglo-Saxon blood walks over the head of Paul and sweeps away from this republic the possibility of a king. And the gentleman himself, I presume, would not assent to the sway of a crowned monarch, Paul to the contrary, notwithstanding. Just as the people have outgrown the injunction of Paul in regard to a king, so have the wives his direction to submit themselves to their husbands. The gentleman intimates that wives have no right to vote against their husbands, because the Scriptures command submission, and he fears that it would cause trouble at home if they were to do so. Let me give him the reply of an old lady, gray with the years which bring experience and wisdom. She said that when men wanted to get their fellow-men to vote in the way they desire, they take especial pains to please them, they smile upon them, ask if their wives and children are well, and are exceedingly kind. They do not expect to win their vote by quarreling with them—that would be absurd. In the same way, if a man wanted his wife to vote for his candidate he will be sure to employ conciliatory means.

The golden rule settles this whole question. We claim it as ours, and whatever is found in the Bible contradictory to it, never came from God. If men quote other texts in conflict with this, it is their business, not mine, to make them harmonize. I did not quite understand the gentleman's definition of what is natural. But this I do know, that when God made the human soul and gave it certain capacities, He meant these capacities should be exercised. The wing of the bird indicates its right to fly; and the fin of the fish the right to swim. So in human beings, the existence of a power, presupposes the right to its use, subject to the law of benevolence. The gentleman says the voice of woman can not be heard. I am not aware that the audience finds any difficulty in hearing us from this platform. All Europe and America have listened to the voice of Madam Rachel and Jenny Lind. The capacity to speak indicates the right to do so, and the noblest, highest, and best thing that any one can accomplish, is what that person ought to do, and what God holds him or her accountable for doing, nor should we be deterred by the senseless cry, "It is not our proper sphere."

As regards woman's voting, I read a letter from a lady traveling in the British provinces, who says that by a provincial law of Nova Scotia and New Brunswick, women were actually voters for members of Parliament; and still the seasons come and go, children are born, and fish flock to that shore. The voting there is *viva voce.* In Canada it is well known that women vote on the question of schools. A friend told me when the law was first passed giving women who owned a certain amount of property, or who paid a given rental, a right to vote, he went trembling to the polls to see the result. The first woman who came was a large property holder in Toronto; with marked respect the crowd gave way as she advanced. She spoke her vote and walked quietly away, sheltered by her womanhood. It was all the protection she needed. In face of all the arguments in favor of the incapacity of woman to be associated in government, stood the fact that women had sat on thrones and governed as successfully as men. England owes more to Queen Elizabeth than to any other sovereign except Alfred the Great. We must not always be looking for precedents. New ideas are born and old ones die. Ideas that have prevailed a thousand years have been at last exploded. Every new truth has its birth-place in a manger, lives thirty years, is crucified, and then deified. Columbus argued through long years that there must be a western world. All Europe laughed at him. Five crowned heads rejected him, and it was a woman at last who sold her jewels and fitted out his ships. So, too, the first idea of applying steam to machinery was met with the world's derision. But its triumphs are recognized now. What we need is to open our minds wide and give hospitality to every new thought, and prove its truth.

I want to say a word upon the resolutions. The present time, just after a presidential election, is most appropriate to consider woman's demand for suffrage. The Republican party claims especially to represent the principles of freedom, and during the last campaign has been calling upon women for help. One of the leaders of that party went to Elizabeth Cady Stanton and said he wanted her help in this campaign, and before she told me what answer she made, she asked me how I would have felt if the same had been asked of me. I told her I should have felt as Samson did when the Philistines put out his eyes, and then asked that he should make merriment for them. The Republican party are a part of those who compel us to obey laws we never had a voice in making—to pay taxes without our consent; and when we ask for our political and legal rights, it laughs in our face, and only says: "Help *us* to places of power and emolument, and *we* will rule over you." I know there are men in the Republican party who, like our friend Mr. Higginson, take a higher stand, and are ready to recognize woman as a co-sovereign; but they are the exceptions. There is but one party—that of Gerrit Smith—that makes the same claim for woman that it does for man. But while the Republican and Democratic parties deny our political existence, they must not expect that we shall respond to their calls for aid.

Madame de Staël said to Bonaparte, when asked why she meddled with politics: "Sire, when women have their heads cut off, it is but just they should know the reason." Whatever political influence springs into being, woman is affected by it. We have the same rights to guard that men have; we shall therefore insist upon our claims. We shall go to your meetings, and by and by we shall meet with the same success that the Roman women did, who claimed the repeal of the Appian law. War had emptied the treasury, and it was still necessary to carry it on; women were required to give up their jewels, their carriages, etc. But by and by, when the war was over, they wished to resume their old privileges. They got up a petition for the repeal of the law; and when the senators went to their places, they found every avenue to the forum thronged by women, who said to them as they passed, "Do us justice." And notwithstanding Cato, the Censor, was against them, affirming that men must have failed in their duty or women would not be clamorous for their rights, yet the obnoxious law was repealed.

In that story of Mr. Higginson's, of the heroic woman in Kansas whose left arm was cut off, there is a lesson for us to learn. I tell you, ladies, though we have our left hand cut off by unjust laws and customs, we have yet the right hand left; and when we once demand the ballot with as much firmness as that Kansas daughter did her horse, believe me, it will not be in the power of men to withhold it—even the border ruffians among them will hasten to restore it. After all, the fault is our own. We have sat to

"Suckle fools, and chronicle small beer;"

and, in inglorious ease, have forgotten that we are integral parts in the fabric of human society—that all that interests the race, interests us. We have never once, as a body, claimed the practical application of the principles of our government. It is our own fault. Let it be so no longer. Let us say to men : "Government is just only when it obtains the consent of the governed": we are governed, *surrender to us our ballot.* If they deride, still answer: Surrender our ballot ! *and they will give it up.* "It is not in our stars that we are underlings, but in ourselves." Woman has sat, like Mordecai at the king's gate, hoping that her silent presence would bring justice; but justice has not come. The world has talked of universal snffrage; but it has made it universal only to man. It is time we spoke and acted. It is time we gave man faith in woman—and, still more, woman faith in herself. It is time both men and women knew that whatever has been achieved by woman in the realm of mind or matter, has been achieved by right womanly women. Let us then work, and continue to work, until the world shall assent to our right to do whatever the capacities God has given us enable us to do.

SUSAN B. ANTHONY rose and said that several gentlemen had handed her contributions, one $40, another $25. She trusted that all New York men and women would find they had something more to do than listen to speeches.

LETTER FROM HORACE GREELEY.

NEW YORK, *November* 22, 1856.

MY FRIEND:—You are promised to be present and speak at the approaching "Woman's Rights Convention." I, too, mean to attend its deliberations, or some portion thereof, but not to take part in them. For I find this evil apparently inseparable from all Radical gatherings: a very large and influential portion of the press, including, I grieve to say, religious as well as secular journals, are prone and eager to expose to odium those whom they would undermine and destroy, by attributing to them, not the sentiments they have personally expressed, but those of others with whom they are or have been associated in some reformatory movement. He, then, who appears as a speaker at a Woman's Rights Convention is made responsible for whatever may be uttered at such Convention—no matter by whom—which is most likely to excite popular prejudice and arouse popular hostility. I have borne a good share of this unfairly excited and unjust odium, with regard to the dietetic, anti-slavery, and social reforms suggested in our day, and shall bear on as patiently as I may; but I grow older, and do not confront the world on a fresh issue with so light a heart, so careless a defiance, as I might have done twenty years ago. Allow me, then, through you, to say what I think of the woman's rights movement, its objects, incitements, and limitations. If I may thus attain perspicuity, I can bear the imputation of egotism.

1. I deem the intellectual, like the physical capacities of women unequal in the average to those of men; but I perceive no reason in this natural diversity for a factitious and superinduced legal inequality. On the contrary, it seems to me that the fact of a natural and marked discrepancy in the average mental as well as muscular powers of men and women ought to allay any apprehensions that the latter, in the absence of legal interdicts and circumscriptions, would usurp the functions and privileges of the former.

2. I believe the range of employment for woman, in our age and country, far too restricted, and the average recompense of her labor, consequently far less than it should be. In saying this, I do not intimate a doubt that the best possible employment for most women is to be found in the care and management of their own households respectively, with the rearing and training of their children. But many women, including

some of the most noble and estimable, are never called to preside over households; while some of the called are impelled to decline the invitation. In point of fact, then, there is and always will be a large proportion of the gentler sex who are, at least temporarily, required to earn their own subsistence, and vindicate their own usefulness in some other capacity than that of the loved and honored wife and mother. The maiden or widow, blessed with opulence, ought to be insured against the worse calamities of a reverse of fortune, by the mastery of some handicraft or industrial avocation; she ought to lead a life of persistent and efficient industry, as the fulfillment of a universal duty; while her unportioned sister must do this or grovel in degrading idleness and dependence on a father's or brother's overtaxed energies, looking to marriage as her only chance of escape therefrom. For man's sake, no less than woman's, it is eminently desirable that that large portion of our women, who are not absorbed in domestic cares, should be attracted and stimulated to industry by a wider range of pursuits, and a consequent increase of recompense. I deem it at once unjust and—like all injustice—impolitic, that a brother and sister, hired by the same farmer, the one to aid him in his own round of labor, the other to assist his wife in hers, should be paid, the one twelve to twenty, the other but four to six dollars per month. The difference in their wages should be no greater than in their physical and mental ability. Still more glaring is this discrepancy, when the two are employed as teachers, and, though of equal efficiency, the one is paid five hundred dollars per annum, the other but two, or in that proportion, merely because the former is a man and the latter a woman. While such disparities exist, right here in this metropolis of American civilization and Christianity, it is in vain that Conservatism stops its ears and raises its eyebrows at the announcement of a Woman's Rights Convention.

3. Regarding marriage as the most important, most sacred, and tender of human relations, and deeming it irrevocable, save by death, it seems to me essential that woman should be proffered such a range of employments, with such adequate recompense, as to enable her at all times to support herself in honored and virtuous independence, so that marriage shall be accepted by her at the dictates of love, and not of hunger. Much might be urged on this point, but I choose simply to commend it to the consideration of others.

4. As to woman's voting or holding office, I defer implicitly to herself. If the women of this or any other country believe their rights would be better secured and their happiness promoted by the assumption on their part of the political franchises and responsibilities of men, I, a Republican in principle from conviction, shall certainly interpose no objection. I perceive what seem to be serious practical difficulties in the way of realizing such assumption; but these are difficulties, not for me, but for them. I deem it unjust that men should be so constantly and unqualifiedly impeached as denying rights to woman which the great majority of women seem quite as reluctant to claim as men are to concede. I apprehend that whenever women shall generally and earnestly desire an equality of political franchises with men, they will meet with little impediment from the latter.

5. I can not share at all in the apprehensions of those who are alarmed at the Woman's Rights agitation, lest it should result in the unsexing of woman, or her general deflection from her proper sphere. On the contrary, I feel sure that the freest inquiry and discussion will only result in a clearer and truer appreciation of woman's proper position, and a more general and rigid adherence thereto. "Let there be light!" for this is an indispensable condition of all true and healthy growth. Let all convictions find free utterance—all grievances be stated and considered. In the range of my observation, I have found those women who were conscious of defects in the present legal and social position of their sex among the most zealous, faithful, and efficient in the discharge of their household and parental duties. I feel confident that a general discussion of the subject of Woman's Rights will result in a more general recognition and cheerful performance of woman's appropriate duties.

Very truly yours,   HORACE GREELEY.

Rev. SAMUEL J. MAY.

LETTER FROM HON. WILLIAM HAY, OF SARATOGA SPRINGS.

I acknowledge, with much pleasure, the receipt of a printed circular, calling for the Seventh Woman's Rights Annual Convention. I also acknowledge, with increased pleasure, and perhaps with more pride than becomes me, the accompanying invitation to attend that Convention, and take part in its proceedings. I like this word, because it implies progress.

Pre-engagement will prevent my personal attendance at the Broadway Tabernacle, but, be assured, my heart shall be there, with all its desires and hopes for the future of humanity; because I am convinced that until the individual and social rights of our whole race, without distinction of caste or sex, shall have been universally recognized, the tyrannies of earth will not cease from oppressing it.

I wish that every woman in the United States could be at New York, throughout the continuance of your Convention, where each might see for herself, in Mrs. Lucretia Mott, what woman may be, and should be, and must be, before her sex can attain, individually and socially, "that equal station to which the laws of Nature and of Nature's God entitle" her. For physical and mental improvement of man's condition, according to his birthright and educational capacity, there must be, in America, more Marys, the mothers of Washingtons.

The great political and legal reform announced in your circular, contemplating complete development of the entire human race, is already operating, sympathetically and auspiciously, in Europe, upon pre-eminent minds, like that of Lord Brougham, and may favorably react, in practical adoption here, of Jefferson's elementary truth (almost a self-evident proposition, and yet treated as theory), that government derives its just powers from suffrage-consent of all (not half) of the governed. Partial consent (especially by and to a moiety of mankind, arrogantly claiming, like Louis XIV., to be the State) can confer only unjust power, which Heaven's higher law of liberty, equality, and justice never sanctioned.

Your Convention is most opportune, for this Continent is threatened with permanent and peculiar danger, produced by the feudal condition of women. I allude to the increasing curse of Mormonism, a consequence of woman's legalized inferiority or nonentity. With power from your local situation and undoubted sphere, to influence, for all time, the destiny of every civilized country, the members of your Convention, conscious of their duty, will never flinch from the responsibility of their position. It requires an unequivocal and uncompromising claim for perfect equality of rights in every department of manual and machine labor, of thought, of speech, of government, of society, and of life itself. Indeed, testamentary provision for assertion of that claim, by those few fortunate women who have, like Mrs. Blandina Dudley,* wealth to bestow, should become a ruling principle, instead of that passion, so strong in death, for posthumous pulpit and newspaper applause, which Protestantism has sagaciously substituted in lieu of the saving ordinances of the Roman Catholic Church.   Respectfully yours,

WILLIAM HAY.

LETTER FROM FRANCES D. GAGE.

ST. LOUIS, *November* 19, 1856.

DEAR LUCY STONE:—Most earnestly did I desire to attend this Seventh National Convention, more especially as I felt that I should be the only representative from the west side of the great Father of Waters. But it is impossible for me to remove the barriers just now opposed to so long a journey and absence from home. There is much thought in the free States of the great West—much less of conservatism and rigid adherence to the old-time customs of law and theology among the masses, than in the East. Thousands are becoming ready to be baptized into a new faith, a broader and holier recognition of the rights of humanity. The harvest-fields are ripening for the reapers.

> The gloomy night is breaking—
> E'en now the sunbeams rest
> With a bright and cheering radiance
> On the hill-tops of the West ;
> The mists are slowly rising
> From the valley and the plain,
> And a spirit is awaking
> That shall never sleep again.

But since I can not meet you in your councils, I will endeavor to allay the disappointment by striving to reach with my pen some of the sunset homes in the far West, and endeavor to arouse woman there to her duties and responsibilities, that she may sympathize more fully with her Eastern sisters, who caught the first glow of the sunrise hour of our great reform movement. With sincere and earnest wishes for your advancement in right and truth,

I am respectfully yours,   FRANCES D. GAGE.

Mr. HIGGINSON was then introduced. Mrs. President, and Ladies and Gentlemen: I think, as perhaps some of you do, that a disproportionately large

---

* She gave $100,000 to the Observatory in Albany.

portion of the time of the meeting to-day has been taken up by the speeches of men; therefore I do not intend that this man's speech shall be a very long one. I remember a certain sermon, of which it was said it had nothing good in it except its subject and its shortness. My speech is going to be like that sermon. But there is one great advantage which men enjoy in speaking on a Woman's Rights platform: they can not help doing good to the movement, no matter how they speak; for if a man speaks well, of course he helps it by his speech; and if he speaks ill on the subject, he still helps it, because there are women about him who won't speak ill, and the comparison is useful.

I wish to take up a point which, as a man, I am entitled to claim should have more prominence given it than has yet been the case; a point touched upon by me previously, in something I said yesterday, which some of you thought was not correct; and a point touched upon by Wendell Phillips this afternoon. I mean the claim of the Woman's Rights movement on woman; the wrong done by woman to that movement; and the injustice of the charge against man, that he especially resists it. And yet I can not fully accept the position taken by Rev. Mr. Johnson and Horace Greeley, that man's duty is only to stand aside and let woman take her rights. Not so. It is not so easy as that, let me tell you, gentlemen, to get rid of the responsibility of years of wrong. We men have been standing for years with our hands crushing down the shoulders of woman, so that she should not attain her true altitude; and it is not so easy, after we have cramped, dwarfed, and crippled her, to get rid of our responsibility by standing back at last, and saying, " There, we will let you go ; stand up for yourself." If it is true, as these women say, that we have wronged them for centuries, we have got to do something more than mere negative duty. By as much as we have helped to wrong them, we have got to help to right them; by as much as we have discouraged them heretofore, we have got to encourage them hereafter; and that is why I wish to speak to women to-night of their duties, as these women have spoken to us of ours. I want to remind them that the time has come when men must appeal to them; for be assured that when women are ready to claim their rights, men will be ready to grant them.

There are three special obstacles, Mrs. President, to the willingness of woman to do her simple duty to the Woman's Rights movement. The first is the obstacle of folly—sheer, unadulterated folly—the folly in which women are trained, and in which we men help to train them, and for which we then denounce them. The reason why many women don't like the Woman's Rights movement, is because they have too little real thought in them to appreciate it at all. They have been brought up as fashionable society brings up woman on one side, or as mere household drudgery brings them up on the other in each case, without power to appreciate a great principle—without power to appreciate a sublime purpose—without power to appreciate anything but a " good match," and the way to obtain it. On their entrance into life, their choice lies, for social position, for enjoyment, for occupation, for usefulness, in this narrow alternative—between a husband and nothing; and that, as Theodore Parker once said, is very often a choice between two nothings. These women may have literary culture and social polish ; but, for want of an idea to light up their eyes and strengthen their souls, these things are only glitter and worthlessness.

A certain celebrated French woman in the last century (Mlle. de Launay), who

42

made mathematical science her study, at last had a lover; whereupon she partially forgot her mathematics, and only remembered enough of it for practical purposes. And, in her Memoirs, she mentions the fact that her lover at length began to be less attentive to her; so much so, that she observed that whereas in walking home with her in the evening, he used to take pains to go round the two sides of the public square, in order to make the walk as long as possible, he now cut it short by always striking across the center; "so that his love for me," she observes, "must have decreased in the inverse ratio between the diagonal of a rectangular parallelogram and the sum of two adjacent sides." Who shall say that mathematics are wasted on a woman after that? Now, that is the sum of the science that is taught in half our institutions of education, in more than half our fashionable boarding-schools, in nearly all the most cultivated social circles in the land. How can you expect, from such women, any nobleness or appreciation of nobleness? How can you expect any from such a woman's husband, when all his thoughts of woman have been crushed down, by sad experience, to the level of his wife's capacities? When I find a man who is obstinate against Woman's Rights, I try to find out either what sort of a mother or what sort of a wife that man has, and there I find the key to his position; for how can you expect any man to have a noble and equal idea of woman, when his mother knows nothing in the universe beyond a cooking-stove, and his wife has not much experimental acquaintance even with that?

No; the first obstacle to this Woman's Rights movement is the feminine, that builds all its hopes upon the wretched adulation and flattery of men—that thinks "the gentlemen admire weakness in a woman." Well, so they do admire to flatter it and to laugh at it! Those are the women who have called out from gifted men, age after age, those terrible denunciations of which literature is full. Women who are here, who think men admire weakness in a woman, let me tell you that if you want to know what men really think of women, you must go beyond the flatteries of the ball-room; you must go beyond the compliments of the public speaker. You must follow your young admirer from the ball-room into the bar-room, where he ridicules you among his companions, and laughs at the folly he has been flattering. You must pass from the public meeting into the office or study, to learn how the man who flatters woman most may despise her in his heart.

Think what great men of the world have said of woman. Voltaire said: "Ideas are like beards—women and young men have none." Lessing, the German, says: "The woman who thinks is like a man who puts on rouge—ridiculous." Dr. Maginn, that accomplished literary man, says: "We like to hear a few words of wit from a woman, just as we like to hear a few words of sense from a parrot—because they are so unexpected." These things were never said to women, but they were said of them. In the presence of female intellect, men are very often like that Englishman who was reproached by the judge in the police-court, because he, being a very large, athletic man, allowed his wife, who was a very delicate, puny woman, occasionally to beat him. Said the judge: "How can you allow it? you have ten times her strength." "Oh," said the giant, drawing himself up to his full stature, "it is no great matter; it pleases her, and it don't hurt me." That is the way men deal with female intellect—they like to amuse themselves with it, to flatter it as an entertaining trifle. But when it comes in earnest, and shows itself, then it is that these men stand apart from the new spectacle of a woman transformed into a thinker and worker; while true men rejoice to see nobleness in a woman. There is not a man here who does not, in his own highest moments, reverence in woman the same qualities he admires in himself, if he thinks he claims them. Power of clear thought and of heroic action—every man admires these in woman in the best moments of his life. It is when he lowers himself to the level of the public meeting, or of the fashionable drawing-room, that he is changed into a flatterer, and he who flatters always despises the object of his flattery.

Another source of opposition to this movement among women is founded in Fear. It does not require much courage for a man to stand on a Woman's Rights platform. I do not say that it does not require more than a good many men have, for it would be difficult to find a thing so easy as not to do that. He, of course, has to run the gauntlet of the old nonsense of " strong-minded women and weak-minded men." Well, I am willing to be accounted weak-minded in the presence of strength of mind and heart, with which it has been my privilege to be associated in this movement. That is a small thing, and it is the experience of every man who has entered into this reform, that if he had a fiber of manhood in him heretofore, that fiber had been doubled, trebled, and quadrupled before he had been in it a year. Instead of requiring courage for a man to enter into this movement, it rather requires courage to keep out of it, if he is a logical, clear-headed man. But with a woman it is different. She needs much courage. A woman who, for instance, has been engaged in some literary avocation, and obtained some position, does not wish to risk her reputation by connecting herself with those who advocate the right of woman, not merely to write and to speak, but to vote also; hence, while admitting, secretly admitting, the justice of the claim, she will shrink back from avowing it for fear of " losing her position." How can any brave man honor such a recreant woman as that, who, having gained all she wants to herself, under cover of the bolder efforts of these nobler spirits, then settles back upon the ease and comfort of that position, and turns her small artillery on her own sisters? I feel a sense of shame for American literature, when I think how our literary women shrink, and cringe, and apologize, and dodge to avoid being taken for " strong-minded women." Oh, there's no danger. I don't wonder that their literary efforts are stricken with the palsy of weakness from the beginning. I don't wonder that our magazines are filled with diluted stories, in which sentimental heroines sigh, cry, and die through whole pages of weary flatness, and not a single noble thought relieves that Sahara of emptiness and barrenness. It is a retribution on them. A man or woman can not put in a book more than they have in themselves, and if woman is not noble enough to appreciate a great thought, she is not noble enough to write one. I don't wonder that their fame does not keep the promise of its dawn, when that dawn is so dastardly.

The time will come, let me tell you, ladies, when the first question asked about any woman in this age who is worth remembering will be, " Did that woman comprehend her whole sphere? Did she stand beside her sisters who were laboring for the right? If she did not this, it is no matter what she did." It is thus we already begin to judge the American women of the past. The time will come, when of all Mrs. Adams' letters, the passage best remembered will be that, where she points out to her great husband, that while emancipating the world, he still believes in giving men the absolute control over women. So the time will come when Harriet Beecher Stowe will be less honored, even as the authoress of "Uncle Tom's Cabin," than as the woman who in *The New York Independent*, that repository of religious thought, dared to place it among her religious thoughts, that Antoinette Brown had a right to stand in the pulpit. I wish Mrs. Stowe were yet more consistent; I wish she were not satisfied with merely wishing that others would attend Woman's Rights Conventions, and support Woman's Rights Lectures, but would join and take part in these things herself, as I believe she will when her brave spirit has gone a little further. Her heroic brother, Henry Ward Beecher, is with us already in the public advocacy of the right of suffrage for women.

The third obstacle that sets woman against this movement is *prejudice*. It is the honest feeling of multitudes of women that their "natural sphere," their domestic duties, will be interfered with by any other career. Let me tell you that so judging, you have only learned half the story we have to tell. We encourage these domestic duties most fully and amply. There is not a woman here who is not proud to claim them. Of all the women who have stood or spoken on this platform since this Convention began, there is only one who is not a married woman; there are very few who are not mothers; and among them all there is not one who does not give, by the nobleness of her domestic life, a proof of the consistency of that with the rest of the claims she makes for her sex. Some there are who doubt this; some there are who do not see how the elective franchise is any way connected with home duties and cares. I tell you there is the closest connection. If any one thing caps the sum of the argument for the rights of woman, it is the fact of those domestic duties which some idly array against it. What has a man at stake in society? What has he to risk by his ballot? Ask him at the ballot-box, and you will hear his statement. You will hear it in a thousand ways, and in a thousand voices. His own personal interest. A man invests *himself* in society; woman invests infinitely more, for she throws in *her child*. The man can run away to California with his interests, and from his duties; the woman is anchored to her home. It is important to him, you say, whether the community provides, by its statutes, schools or dram-shops. Then how vast, how unspeakable the importance to her! Deprive every man in the nation of the ballot, if you will, but demand, oh, demand its protection for the wife and the mother!

See the unjust workings of the present system. I knew in a town in Massachusetts a widow woman, who paid the highest tax bill in the town; nay, for every dollar that any man paid in the town, she paid two, and yet that woman had not the right to the ballot, which belonged to the most ignorant Irishman in her employ. She hadn't the right to protect her child from the misappropriation of his property; and if she had owned the whole town, and there had not been any other person to pay a property tax except that solitary woman, the case would have been the same, and not the slightest power of protection would have been in her hands, against the most outrageous misappropriation.

In another town of Massachusetts there is a story told of a man, a member of the Society of Friends. He was once sending his wife on a long journey. As she was about to set forth in the stage, "My dear," said she, "thee has forgotten to give me any money for my journey. "Why," said the Quaker, "thee knows very well that I paid thy fare in the stage." "But thee knows," said she, "that I am going to be away for some weeks, and perhaps it may be well for me to have some little money, in case I should have any expenses." "Rachel," said the astonished husband, "where is that ninepence I gave thee day before yesterday?" That man had gained all the money he had in the world through that wife. He obtained her property by marriage; he invested that property in real estate, and had grown richer and richer, until he grew rich enough to spare a ninepence for Rachel the day before yesterday. It is such marriages as that, that we wish to avert, by placing woman in an honorable position, by substituting an equal union in marriage; such a union as is shown in the lives of those who stand behind me now.

The movement which these women urge is sweeping on with resistless power. Within the last seven years, every legislature, every school, every industrial avocation has been reached by it. This is preliminary work. The final Malakoff, the right of suffrage, is yet to be gained. Already it has been partially conceded, in communities differing in all else, in Canada and in Kentucky. We have only to press on. Strange to say, the reform is reversing the ordinary weapons of the sexes, for the women have all the logic, and the men only gossip and slander. But it finds its answering echo in the very hostility it creates. It has a million hearts. Silence every woman on this platform, and the movement still goes on. Elevate woman at any point, and you lead directly to this. The thousand schools of New York are educating a Woman's Rights advocate in every house.

During the latter part of Mr. Higginson's remarks, a frequent disturbance was made by some of the occupants of the galleries, who were evidently curious to hear the female speakers.

The President then introduced Ernestine L. Rose, who said she wished to say to all self-respecting men, that this is the last place in which they should create a disturbance, especially in a matter which concerns their sisters, their wives, and their mothers.

Mrs. ROSE : This morning a young man made some remarks in opposition to our claims. We were glad to hear him, because he gave evidence of an earnest, sincere spirit of inquiry, which is always welcome in every true reform movement. And as we believe our cause to be based on truth, we know it can bear the test of reason, and, like gold doubly refined, will come out purer and brighter from the fiery ordeal. The young man, who, I hope, is present, based his principal argument against us, "Because," said he, "you can bring no authority from revelation or from nature." I will not enter into an inquiry as to what he meant by these terms, but I will show him the revelation from which we derive our authority, and the nature in which it is written in living characters. It is true we do not go to revelations written in books; but ours is older than all books, and whatever of good there is in any written revelations, must necessarily agree with ours, or it is not true, for ours only is the true revelation, based in nature and in life. That revelation is no less than the living, breathing, thinking, feeling, acting revelation manifested in the nature of woman. In her manifold powers, capacities, needs, hopes, and aspirations, lies her title-deed, and whether that revelation was written by nature or nature's God, matters not, for here it is. No one can disprove it. No one can bring an older, broader, higher, and more sacred basis for human rights. Do you tell me that the Bible is against our rights? Then I say that our claims do not rest upon a book written no one knows when, or by whom. Do you tell me what Paul or Peter says on the subject? Then again I reply that our claims do not rest on the opinions of any one, not even on those of Paul and Peter, for they are older than they. Books and opinions, no matter from whom they came, if they are in opposition to human rights, are nothing but dead letters. I have shown you that we derive our claims from humanity, from revelation, from nature, and from your Declaration of Independence; all proclaim our right to life, liberty, and the pursuit of happiness; and having life, which fact I presume you do not question, then we demand all the rights and privileges society is capable of bestowing, to make life useful, virtuous, honorable, and happy.

But I am told that woman needs not as extensive an education as man, as her place is only the domestic sphere; *only* the domestic sphere! Oh, how utterly ignorant is society of the true import of that term! Go to your legislative halls, and your Congress; behold those you have sent there to govern you, and as you find them high or low, great or small, noble or base, you can trace it directly or indirectly to the domestic sphere.

The wisest in all ages have acknowledged that the most important period in human education is in childhood—that period when the plastic mind may be moulded into such exquisite beauty, that no unfavorable influences shall be able entirely to destroy it—or into such hideous deformity, that it shall cling to it like a thick rust eaten into a highly polished surface, which no after-scouring shall ever be able entirely to efface. This most important part of education is left entirely in the hands of the mother. She prepares the soil for future culture; she lays the foundation upon which a superstructure shall be erected that shall stand as firm as a rock, or shall pass away like the baseless fabric of a vision, and leave not a wreck behind. But the mother can not give what she does not possess; weakness can not impart strength.

Sisters, you have a duty to perform—and duty, like charity, begins at home. In the name of your poor, vicious, outcast, down-trodden sister! in the name of her who once was as innocent and as pure as you are! in the name of her who has been made the victim of wrong, injustice, and oppression! in the name of man! in the name of all, I ask you, I entreat you, if you have an hour to spare, a dollar to give, or a word to utter—spare it, give it, and utter it, for the elevation of woman! And when your minister asks you for money for missionary purposes, tell him there are higher, and holier, and nobler missions to be performed at home. When he asks for colleges to educate ministers, tell him you must educate woman, that she may do away with the necessity of ministers, so that they may be able to go to some useful employment. If he asks you to give to the churches (which means to himself) then ask him what he has done for the salvation of woman. When he speaks to you of leading a virtuous life, ask him whether he understands the causes that have prevented so many of your sisters from being virtuous, and have driven them to degradation, sin, and wretchedness. When he speaks to you of a hereafter, tell him to help to educate woman, to enable her to live a life of intelligence, independence, virtue, and happiness here, as the best preparatory step for any other life. And if he has not told you from the pulpit of all these things; if he does not know them; it is high time you inform him, and teach him his duty here in this life.

This subject is deep and vast enough for the wisest heads and purest hearts of the race; it underlies our whole social system. Look to your criminal records—look to your records of mortality, to your cemeteries, peopled by mothers before the age of thirty or forty, and children under the age of five; earnestly and impartially investigate the cause, and you can trace it directly or indirectly to woman's inefficient education; her helpless, dependent position; her inexperience; her want of confidence in her own noble nature, in her own principles and powers, and her blind reliance in man. We ask, then, for woman, an education that shall cultivate her powers, develop, elevate, and ennoble her being, physically, mentally, and morally; to enable her to take care of herself, and she will be taken care of; to protect herself, and she will be protected. But to give woman as full and extensive an education as man, we must give her the same motives. No one gathers keys without a prospect of having doors to unlock. Man does not acquire knowledge without the hope to make it useful and productive; the highest motives only can call out the greatest exertion. There is a vast field of action open to man, and therefore he is prepared to enter it; widen the sphere of action for woman, throw open to her all the avenues of industry, emolument, usefulness, moral ambition, and true greatness, and you will give her the same noble motives, the same incentives for exertion, application, and perseverance that man possesses—and this can be done only by giving her her legal and political rights—pronounce her the equal of man in all the rights and advantages society can bestow, and she will be prepared to receive and use them, and not before. It would be folly to cultivate her intellect like that of man without giving her the same chances to use it—to give her an industrial avocation without giving her the right to the proceeds of her industry, or to give her the right to the proceeds of her industry without giving her the power to protect the property she may acquire; she must therefore have the legal and political rights, or she has nothing. The ballot-box is the focus of all other rights, it is the pivot upon which all others hang; the legal rights are embraced in it, for if once possessed of the right to the ballot-box, to self-representation, she will see to it that the laws shall be just, and protect her person and her property, as well as that of man. Until she has political rights she is not secure in any she may possess. One legislature may alter some oppressive law, and give her some right, and the next legislature may take it away, for as yet it is only given as an act of generosity, as a charity on the part of man, and not as her right, and therefore it can not be lasting, nor productive of good.

Mothers, women of America! when you hear the subject of Woman's Rights broached, laugh at it and us, ridicule it as much as you please; but never forget, that by the laws of your country, you have no right to your children—the law gives the father as uncontrolled power over the child as it gives the husband over the wife; only the child, when it comes to maturity, the father's control ceases, while the wife never comes to maturity. The father may bequeath, bestow, or sell the child without the consent of the mother. But methinks I hear you say that no man deserving the name of man, or the title of husband and father, could commit such an outrage against the dearest principles of humanity; well, if there are no such men, then the law ought to be annulled, a law against which nature, justice, and humanity revolt, ought to be wiped off from the statute book as a disgrace; and if there are such—which unhappily we all know there are—then there is still greater reason why the laws ought to be changed, for bad laws encourage bad men and make them worse; good men can not be benefited by the existence of bad laws; bad men ought not to be; laws are not made for him who is a law unto himself, but for the lawless. The legitimate object of law is to protect the innocent and inexperienced against the designing and the guilty; we therefore ask every one present to demand of the Legislatures of every State to alter these unjust laws; give the wife an equal right with the husband in the property acquired after marriage; give the mother an equal right with the father in the control of the children; let the wife at the death of the husband remain his heir to the same extent that he would be hers, at her death; let the laws be alike for both, and they are sure to be right; but to have them so, woman must help to make them.

We hear a great deal about the heroism of the battle-field. What is it? Compare it with the heroism of the woman who stands up for the right, and it sinks into utter insignificance. To stand before the cannon's mouth, with death before him and disgrace behind, excited to frenzy by physical fear, encouraged by his leader, stimulated by the sound of the trumpet, and sustained by the *still emptier sound of glory*, requires no great heroism; the merest coward could be a hero in such a position; but to face the fire of an unjust and prejudiced public opinion, to attack the adamantine walls of long-usurped power, to brave not only the enemy abroad, but often that severest of all enemies, your own friends at home, requires a heroism that the world has never yet recognized, that the battle-field can not supply, but which woman possesses.

When the Allied Powers endeavored to take Sebastopol they found that every incision and inroad they made in the fortress during the day was filled up by the enemy during the night; and even now, after the terrible sacrifice of life to break it down, they are not safe, but the enemy may build it up again. But in a moral warfare, no matter how thick and impenetrable the fortress of prejudice may be, if you once make an inroad in it, that space can never be filled up again; every stone you remove is removed for aye and for good; and the very effort to replace it tends only to loosen every other stone, until the whole foundation is undermined, and the superstructure crumbles at our feet.

The PRESIDENT: Before this Convention closes, I want to say a word to the women who hear me. This work lies chiefly in our hands. We have undertaken no child's play. It is nothing less than a change in customs hoary with age—in laws which have existed through long years—in mistaken religious interpretations and views of duty, which have received the sanction and veneration of antiquity. It is to place woman where she may make herself fit for life's duties, in whatever department she may find herself, whether as woman, daughter, wife, or mother. Every influence around us to-day tends to the reverse. The young girl stands beside her brother in the world's wide arena, and looks out to see what it shall assign her. To him, everything that power can win is open, while the world cheers him, by so much as he grasps and conquers. To her is presented, what kind of a life? There is not a man in the world, who, if such a life were offered him, would not sooner lie down peacefully in his grave, than in a paltry cage fret away a life that ought to have been broad and grand, as God who gave it intended it should be.

Horace Greeley says he thinks the intellect of woman is not equal to that of man. Horace Greeley was a poor boy, and had to make his way up in the world. He has reached a position that is attained by few. When he speaks the nation listens. Suppose that he had been told by his mother, as she placed her hand upon his little head, with all the tenderness that gushes from a mother's heart, "My son, here is your brother; he shall grow up in the world of society, and no school or college shall be closed against him; the great school of life shall be free to him; he shall have a voice in making the laws he is to obey; he shall pay taxes, and he shall direct the use of the tax; but for you, alas! none of these places will be open; you must therefore rest satisfied with helping your brother. He will win power and wealth, but none of it shall be your own; if you seek to enter into the same position that he is in, the world will scorn and deride you." And if when he came into life he had found all that his mother told him was true, what think you would have been the success of Horace Greeley, with all this mountain-weight upon him? Would he have taken the place he has now? I am glad he was not hindered; I am only sorry that woman is. It is too early for him or us to say what the intellect of woman is, till she has had the freedom to try its powers. I am reminded of what Frederick Douglass said of the negroes: "You shut us out of the schools and colleges, you put your foot on us, and then say, Why don't you know something?" That is just what is said to us.

Let us teach men who talk of the wrongs perpetrated in Kansas, that they are doing the very same thing to us here. One need not go to Kansas to find border ruffians, or bogus legislation, for they can all be found here; and when the future historian shall record that in Kansas, Missourians deprived free State men of the franchise, and that New York men deprived the women of the same, it will be said that the border ruffians of Missouri and the border ruffians of New York were very much alike —one came with the gloved hand, and smiled and bowed, saying, I can't let you vote; while the other said, If you do I will blow out your brains. The result is the same.

I look in the faces of men and marvel that they can meet us in the way they do, when they have made such laws against us. Clear-headed and far-sighted, they do not appear to realize that the outrages they condemn in Kansas, they are themselves all the while inflicting upon us. John Randolph, when the women of Virginia were making garments for the Greeks, pointed to long gangs of slaves, and said, "Ladies, the Greeks are at your doors."

In addition to the annual canvass of the State, lectures from the most popular orators were secured in the large cities. In the winter of 1856, by invitation of Miss Anthony, Theodore Parker, William Lloyd Garrison, Wendell Phillips, Ralph Waldo Emerson, lectured in Corinthian Hall, Rochester, to good audiences. In the spring of 1858, Miss Emily Howland managed a course of lectures in Mozart Hall, New York, in aid of "The Shirt-sewers' and Seamstresses' Union," viz: George Wm. Curtis, "Fair Play for Women"; Lucy Stone, "Woman and the Elective Franchise"; Hon. Eli Thayer, "Benefit to Women of Organized Emigration"; and Rev. E. H. Chapin, "Woman and her Work." In the autumn of the same year, through the enterprise of Elizabeth M. Powell, Henry Ward Beecher, James T. Brady, Solon Robinson, and others addressed a large audience in Dr. Chapin's church, Mayor Tieman presiding, to aid in the establishment of a "Free Library for Working-Women."

In January, 1859, Antoinette L. Brown gave a series of Sunday sermons in Rochester, and in 1860 she preached in Hope Chapel, New York, for six months. In Rochester during the winter of 1859, Miss Anthony had a series of lectures by George William Curtis, Wendell Phillips, Antoinette Brown, Ernestine L. Rose, and others. The following letter will show that Thomas Starr King was in full sympathy with our movement:

SUSAN B. ANTHONY.   BOSTON, *Sep.* 20, 1858.

DEAR MADAM:—It would afford me great satisfaction to be able to serve you as you request. I am compelled to say, however, that it is entirely out of my power. I have already engaged for so much work beyond my regular duties, that I shall have no leisure even to prepare a new Lyceum address. Not having any lecture upon the position of woman that is full enough, and adequate in any way to the present state of the discussion, I must reluctantly decline the opportunity you offer.

With sincere thanks, I remain truly yours,   T. S. KING.

In the autumn of 1858, Francis Jackson, of Boston, placed $5,000 in the hands of Wendell Phillips for woman's enfranchisement, as will be seen by the following letter:

BOSTON, *Nov.* 6, 1858.

DEAR FRIENDS:—I have had given me five thousand dollars, to be used for the Woman's Rights cause; to procure tracts on that subject, publish and circulate them, pay for lectures, and secure such other agitation of the question as we deem fit and best to obtain equal civil and social position for woman.

The name of the giver of this generous fund I am not allowed to tell you; the only condition of the gift is, that the fund is to remain invested in my keeping. In other respects, we three are a Committee of Trustees to spend it wisely and efficiently.

Let me ask you to write me what plan strikes you as best to begin with. I think some agitation specially directed to the Legislature very important. It is wished that we should begin our efforts at once.

Yours truly,   WENDELL PHILLIPS.

Miss SUSAN B. ANTHONY.
Mrs. LUCY STONE.

It was in the year 1859 that Charles F. Hovey of Boston left by will,* a sum of $50,000 to be expended annually in the promotion of various reforms, Woman's Rights among them.

---

*EXTRACTS FROM THE WILL OF THE LATE CHARLES F. HOVEY, ESQ.

ARTICLE 16. After setting aside sufficient funds to pay all legacies and bequests herein made, I direct my said Trustees to hold all the rest and residue of my estate, real, personal and mixed, in special trust for the following purposes, namely ; to pay over, out of the interest and principal of said special trust, a sum of not less than eight thousand dollars annually, until the same be all exhausted, to said Wendell Phillips, William Lloyd Garrison, Stephen S. Foster, Abby K. Foster, Parker Pillsbury, Henry C. Wright, Francis Jackson and Charles K. Whipple, and their survivors and survivor, for them to use and expend, at their discretion, without any responsibility to any one, for promotion of the Anti-Slavery cause and other reforms, such as Woman's Rights, Non-Resistance, Free Trade and Temperance, at their discretion ; and I request said Wendell Phillips and his said associates to expend not less than eight thousand dollars annually, by the preparation and circulation of books, newspapers, employing agents, and the delivery of lectures that will, in their judgment, change public opinion, and secure the abolition of Slavery in the United States, and promote said other reforms. Believing that the chain upon four millions of slaves, with tyrants at one end and hypocrites at the other, has become the strongest bond of the Union of the States, I desire said Phillips and his associates to expend said bequest by employing such agents as believe and practice the doctrine of " No union with slaveholders, religiously or politically " ; and by circulating such publications as tend to destroy every pro-slavery institution.

ARTICLE 17. In case chattel slavery should be abolished in the United States before the expenditure of the said residue of my estate, as stated in said sixteenth article of this Will ; then, in that case, I desire that the unexpended part of said residue be applied by said Phillips and his associates, in equal proportions, for the promotion of Non-Resistance, Woman's Rights and Free Trade ; requesting that no agents be employed by them for the promotion of said causes, except such as believe it wrong to have any voluntary connection with any government of violence, and such as believe that the natural rights

MOZART HALL,

NEW YORK, MAY 13, 14, 1858.

The year 1857 seems to have passed without a National Convention, although the work was still vigorously prosecuted in the State of New York, but in the spring of 1858, the ninth National Convention was called in New York during the week of the anniversaries when crowds were always attracted to attend the various religious and reformatory meetings. Henceforward, for many years, a Woman's Rights Convention was a marked feature of this period in the month of May. There were several persons at this Convention who had not before honored our platform.* These, with the usual familiar speakers,† filled the platform with quite a striking group of

---

of men and women are equal. Whether slavery be abolished or not, I desire that a part of the said residue of my estate may be applied to the promotion of the kindred causes of Temperance, Woman's Rights, Non-Resistance and Free Trade, at the discretion of the said Phillips and his associates.

. . . .

ARTICLE 22. I particularly request that no prayers be solicited from any person, and that no priest be invited to perform any ceremony whatever, over or after my body. The Priesthood are an order of men, as I believe, falsely assuming to be reverend and divine, pretending to be called of God; the great body of them in all countries have been on the side of power and oppression; the world has been too long cheated by them; the sooner they are unmasked, the better for humanity. As I have heretofore borne my testimony against slavery, intemperance, war, tariffs and all indirect taxation, banks and all monopolies, I desire to leave on record my abhorrence of them all. The fear of being buried before I am dead is slight, nevertheless it is greater than the fear of death itself. I therefore request my executors not to bury my body until at least three days after my decease. In witness whereof, I have hereto set my hand and seal, this twenty-eighth day of March, in the year eighteen hundred and fifty-nine.

CHARLES F. HOVEY.

Signed, sealed, published and declared by the said Testator to be his last Will and Testament, in presence of us, who, at his request, and in his presence, and in the presence of each other, have hereto subscribed our names as witnesses.

GEORGE L. LOVETT.
THOMAS MACK.
WILLIAM W. HOWE.

I do prove, approve and allow the same, and order it to be recorded. Given under my hand and seal of office, the day and year above written.

ISAAC AMES,
May 30, 1859.
Judge of Probate and Insolvency.

* George William Curtis, Mrs. Eliza W. Farnham, Parker Pillsbury, Sarah Hallock, Mrs. Sidney Howard Gay, Sarah M. Grimké, Charles Lenox Remond, Lucy A. Coleman, Sarah P. Remond, and the Hutchinson family, consisting of Jessie, his wife, and two children, and Abby, who sung among many other sweet ballads, "The Good Time Coming."

† Frederick Douglas, Thomas Wentworth Higginson, Ernestine L. Rose, Lucretia Mott, Frances Dana Gage, Wendell Phillips, Wm. Lloyd Garrison, Oliver Johnson, Susan B. Anthony, Caroline H. Dall, Lucy Stone, Antoinette Brown, Aaron M. Powell.

ladies and gentlemen. The morning session was occupied with the usual preliminary business matters, choosing officers, presenting resolutions, and planning new aggressive steps for the coming year. Susan B. Anthony was President on this occasion, and fulfilled her duties to the general satisfaction. During the evening session the hall was crowded, all the available space for either sitting or standing was occupied, the platform and steps were densely packed, and this at twenty-five cents admission.

Mr. Phillips, Mrs. Mott, Mrs. Rose, Mr. Garrison, Mr. Higginson, Miss Brown, and Lucy Stone all spoke with their usual effect. Mrs. Eliza Woodson Farnham, the author of "Woman and her Era," spoke at length on the "Superiority of Woman."

She presented a series of resolutions, recognizing the right of man in the primary era in his physical and cerebral structure, to be the conqueror, the mechanic, the inventor, the clearer of forests, the pioneer of civilization, but she looked to the dawning of a higher era, when woman should assume her true position in harmony with her superior organism, her delicacy of structure, her beauty of person, her great powers of endurance, and thus prove herself not only man's equal in influence and power, but his superior in many of the noblest virtues. In woman's creative power during maternity, she recognized her as second only to God himself. Woman should recognize man as a John the Baptist, going before to prepare the world for her coming, he recognizing her greater divinity as equal in the Godhead, as heavenly mother as well as father.

Mrs. Farnham* enforced her theory of woman's superiority in a long speech, which was received with apparent satisfaction by the audience, though several on the platform dissented from the claim of superiority, thinking it would be a sufficient triumph over the tyrannies of the past, if popular thought could be educated to the idea of the equality of the sexes.

Mrs. Sarah Hallock read an extract from the Statutes of New York, giving the items set aside by law for use of the wife and minor children, in case the husband died without a will.

(Extract from the Statutes of New York).

ARTICLES INVENTORIED, BUT NOT APPROVED, BELONGING TO THE WIDOW AND MINOR CHILDREN.

1st. All spinning-wheels, weaving-looms, or stoves put up for use.

---

* Eliza Farnham was in many respects a remarkable woman. As matron of the Sing Sing prison at one time, she introduced many humane improvements in the occupation and discipline of the women under her charge. She had a piano in the corridor, and with sweet music touched the tender chords in their souls. Instead of tracts on hell-fire and an angry God, she read aloud to them from Dickens' most touching stories. In every way, assisted by Mariana Johnson and Georgiana Bruce, she treated them as women, and not as criminals.

2d. The family Bible, family pictures, school-books, and books not exceeding in value fifty dollars.

[Mrs. Hallock here interjected, husbands had better give their wives cheap books].

3d. Ten sheep and their fleeces, and the yarn and cloth manufactured from the same; one cow, two swine, and the pork of such swine. [Laughter].

4th. All necessary wearing apparel, beds, bedsteads, and bedding; the clothing of the widow and her ornaments proper to her station (as to ornaments, tastes differ as to those proper to her station), one table, six chairs (suppose there were seven or ten children, what then ? queried Mrs. Hallock [Laughter],) six knives and forks, six tea-cups and saucers, one sugar-dish, one milk-pot, one tea-pot, and six spoons. "So great a favorite is the female sex of the laws of England and America," says Blackstone.

Mrs. ROSE protested against *one* tea-pot; the law didn't mention tea-pot at all. [Great laughter].

Mrs. HALLOCK: Oh, yes ! but not a coffee-pot. [Renewed laughter].

Mrs. GAGE: In Ohio they give twelve spoons. [Convulsive laughter].

Mrs. HALLOCK: We'll get up a delegation to Ohio, then.

Mrs. FARNHAM: I would say that I will give up all these things if the State will only give us in return one of our children. [Applause and laughter].

Mrs. HALLOCK: Isn't it a pity that our laws—are they ours ?

Mrs. ROSE: No.

Mrs. HALLOCK: Well, then, your laws. It is a pity that those statutes should not be revised so as to give a widow a carpet and other smaller articles of luxury. [Great laughter].

And such was the boasted "protection" secured to the wives and mothers by the laws of the most civilized nations on the globe, and such the law-makers in whose hands woman's interests were supposed to be secure, when we began our battle for equality. Class laws, class legislation, legalized robbery from the unborn child, down to the commonest necessaries of life, has been the "protection" woman has complained of from fathers, husbands, brothers, and sons. Those just awaking to an interest in this reform, see but the smoke of the former battles; they can not appreciate all the tyranny from which this agitation has freed them. Step by step, custom by custom, law by law, a partial victory has been wrested, and a public opinion slowly created that promises other victories in the near future.

Those who have not been through the conflict will never realize how dark the prospect was in starting. Denied education, and a place in the world of work, denied the rights of property, whether of her own earnings, or her inheritance, with the press and the pulpit, custom, and public opinion sustaining the law, was there ever a struggle entered upon, which at its beginning seemed more hopeless than this for woman? But these constant presentations of the laws, with the comments and arguments in our Conventions, gradually appealed to the understanding of sensible men and women, and opened the eyes of the community to the wrongs of woman, perpetrated under the specious name of justice.

All the sessions of this Convention were interrupted by the rowdyism of a number of men occupying the rear part of the hall.

PARKER PILLSBURY said he had attended three of these Conventions, but had not spoken in one before. He thought the ladies encroached a little on the men's rights, as in the first and second, the Methodists gave the ladies the use of their church in a city of the West, on condition that Parker Pillsbury should not be allowed to speak. [Applause and laughter]. Now that the door was open, and he had ventured in, he did not know what to say. [Laughter and cries of " Go on "]. He would recommend the women to hold their next Convention at the ballot-box, as that would do more good than a hundred such as these. If their votes were refused, let them look the tax collectors in the face and defy them to come for taxes, as long as they were not allowed a voice in the Government. And carry the war into the Church, too, demand equality there as well as in the State.

He knew an orthodox church, consisting of twelve members. One was a man and a deacon, the remainder were women. A vote had to be taken for changing the day for the prayer-meeting, but some difficulty arose between the minister and the deacon, and the only way it could be settled was by the votes of the women. So the deacon went round on tip-toe, and put his head under each bonnet, and held a little private caucus meeting with one after another, and then returned to the altar and reported to the minister that the vote was unanimous. If women had any proper self-respect, they would scorn to remain one hour in any church in which they were not considered and recognized as equals.

OLIVER JOHNSON said there was a new church formed called " Progressive Friends," in which men and women stood on perfect equality. He said there was another church (Henry Ward Beecher's) in Brooklyn, where women were expected to vote on all questions connected with the business affairs of the congregation. Another church in this city (Rev. Dr. Cheever's) had a difficulty in which the capitalists tried to dismiss the pastor, because he maintained the right of the slave to freedom, and of the woman to the elective franchise. He agreed with Mr. Pillsbury that it was woman's duty to test her equality in the Church as well as the State.

AARON M. POWELL took the same ground. As women made the large majority in the churches, they could easily secure equal rights there if united in an effort to do so. Why, said he, are there no young women sitting at the reporters' desks, taking note of the proceedings of this Convention ? He advocated the elective franchise, saying that no class could be protected in all its rights without a voice in the laws.

A Mr. WARREN said he had no objection to woman's claiming equality, but when they declared their superiority, they injured themselves and the rising generation in teaching the young to disrespect the men of the household. (Great laughter and hisses). Woman might be the savior of man, but was not God, and had no place in the Godhead. (Laughter and cheers). He spoke from experience when he said men had already suffered much from the tyrannical usurpations of women. Let woman be the true helpmate of man, religiously, politically, morally, socially; but, oh ! said he, in a sorrowful tone, it will be a sad day for the race when woman takes command, and man is pushed aside. (Convulsive laughter, and cries of " Give us your experience.")

Mrs. FARNHAM was glad the subject of woman's superiority had been broached, and only regretted that as a scientific fact it could not be more seriously discussed.

A gentleman deprecated the fact that Mr. Warren had not been more fully heard.

THE PRESIDENT said it was the audience and not the platform that laughed. Loud calls were made for

DOUGLASS, to which he responded, claiming woman's right to freedom and equality on the same grounds he based his own.

WILLIAM LLOYD GARRISON maintained woman's right to sit in Congress and the legislatures—that there should be the same number of women as men in all the national councils. He said respect for his sainted mother, love for his noble wife, and for the only daughter of his house and heart (my own Fanny), compel me to defend the rights of all women. Those who have inaugurated this movement are worthy to be ranked with the army of martyrs and confessors in the days of old. Blessings on them ! They should triumph, and every opposition be removed, that peace and love, justice and liberty, might prevail throughout the world.

A Mr. TYLER remarked that a fear had been expressed that in coming to the polls, woman would be compelled to meet men who drink and smoke. Do women encounter no such evils in their homes ? Whisky and tobacco are much greater obstacles at the marriage altar than at the polls—in the relation of wife than in that of citizen.

GEORGE WILLIAM CURTIS, then in the height of his reputation (as Howadji), spoke at length in favor of suffrage for woman, but amid constant interruptions. With a short speech from Mrs. Rose, the Convention adjourned amid great confusion.

NINTH NATIONAL CONVENTION.

In accordance with a call issued by the Central Committee, the Ninth National Woman's Rights Convention was held in the City of New York on Thursday, May 12, 1859.

The sessions commenced with a business meeting, on the afternoon of that day, in Mozart Hall. The meeting was called to order by SUSAN B. ANTHONY, of Rochester, New York, who made a few introductory remarks, after which, the question of the expediency of memorializing the Legislatures of the different States, on the subject of granting equal rights to Woman, was discussed at some length. At the close of the debate, a resolution was adopted, that it was expedient so to memorialize the several Legislatures, and a committee * was appointed for that purpose, and a series of resolutions † offered by Caroline H. Dall.

These resolutions were discussed by Mrs. Dall, Mrs. Hallock, Mrs. Elizabeth Neal Gay, Lucretia Mott, A. M. Powell, Charles C. Burleigh, and others.

EVENING SESSION.

At an early hour, Mozart Hall was crowded to overflowing, every seat being occupied, and crowds standing in the aisle, and the rear of the hall.

LUCRETIA MOTT had been chosen to preside, but was not able, on account of the crowd, to reach the platform at the hour appointed. The Convention was therefore called to order by Susan B. Anthony.

Mrs. CAROLINE H. DALL, of Boston, was the first speaker. She desired to commemorate the century which had just closed since the death of Mary Woolstonecraft, and to show that what she did in the old world, Margaret Fuller had done in the new ; but the noise and restlessness among the audience were so great (much of which, we

---

* Wendell Phillips, Elizabeth Cady Stanton, Caroline H. Dall, Caroline M. Severance, Ernestine L. Rose, Antoinette Brown Blackwell, Thomas W. Higginson, Susan B. Anthony.

† *Resolved*, That while every newspaper in the land carries on its face the record of woman's dishonor, the women who seek to elevate their sex are bound to inquire into its causes and save from its paralysis.

Resolved, That while we have no daughters too tender and pure, no sons too innocent, to escape from the influence of such tragedies as those at North Adams and Washington, the true modesty of every mother, the true dignity of every wife, should forbid her to put aside the questions they involve.

Resolved, That the dishonor of single women proceeds in great measure from destitution, and the dishonor of married women as much from their own want of education and utter absence of purpose in life as from the inability of their husbands to inspire them with true respect and help them to true living: therefore,

Resolved, That it is our bounden duty to open, in every possible way, new vocations to women, to raise their wages by every advisable means, and to secure to them an education which shall be less a decoration to their persons than a tool to their hands.

Resolved, That while courts adjourn in honor of a man like Philip Barton Key, while the whole Bar of the District of Columbia pass resolutions in his honor, and vote to attend his funeral, as a mark of respect, while the public opinion of a whole community sustains a man who could not defend his murderous indignation by the witness of an unspotted life, it is our duty to rate public opinion as a corrupting power, and to bring up our children in the knowledge and sanction of a higher law.

43

charitably hope, was attributable rather to the discomfort of their position than to any want of respect for the speaker, or for the cause which the Convention represented), that she yielded to the wish of the presiding officer, and sat down without speaking of Margaret Fuller.

Short speeches were made by Lucretia Mott, Antoinette Brown Blackwell, and Ernestine L. Rose; but as it proved to be another turbulent meeting, Wendell Phillips, who understood from long experience how to play with and lash a mob, and thrust what he wished to say into their long ears, all with one consent yielded the platform to him, and for nearly two hours he held that mocking crowd in the hollow of his hand. In closing he said:

I will not attempt to detain you longer. ["Go on"—"Go on."] I have neither the disposition nor the strength to trespass any longer upon your attention. The subject is so large that it might well fill days, instead of hours. It covers the whole surface of American society. It touches religion, purity, political economy, wages, the safety of cities, the growth of ideas, the very success of our experiment. I gave to-night a character to the city of Washington which some men hissed. You know it is true. If this experiment of self-government is to succeed, it is to succeed by some saving element introduced into the politics of the present day. You know this: Your Websters, your Clays, your Calhouns, your Douglases, however intellectually able they may have been, have never dared or cared to touch that moral element of our national life. Either the shallow and heartless trade of politics had eaten out their own moral being, or they feared to enter the unknown land of lofty right and wrong.

Neither of these great names has linked its fame with one great moral question of the day. They deal with money questions, with tariffs, with parties, with State law, and if by chance they touch the slave question, it is only like Jewish hucksters trading in the relics of Saints. The reformers—the fanatics, as we are called — are the only ones who have launched social and moral questions. I risk nothing when I say, that the anti-slavery discussion of the last twenty years has been the salt of this nation; it has actually kept it alive and wholesome. Without it, our politics would have sunk beyond even contempt. So with this question. It stirs the deepest sympathy; it appeals to the highest moral sense; it enwraps within itself the greatest moral issues. Judge it, then, candidly, carefully, as Americans, and let us show ourselves worthy of the high place to which God has called us in human affairs. (Applause).

MEMORIAL.

To the Honorable the Legislature of the State of ———

The National Woman's Rights Convention, held in New York City, May 12, 1859, appointed your memorialists a Committee to call your attention to the anomalous position of one-half the people of this Republic.

All republican constitutions set forth the great truth that every human being is endowed with certain inalienable rights—such as life, liberty, and the pursuit of happiness—and as a consequence, a right to the use of all those means necessary to secure these grand results.

1st.—A citizen can not be said to have a right to life, who may be deprived of it for the violation of laws to which she has never consented—who is denied the right of trial by a jury of her peers—who has no voice in the election of judges who are to decide her fate.

2d.—A citizen can not be said to have a right to liberty, when the custody of her person belongs to another; when she has no civil or political rights—no right even to the wages she earns; when she can make no contracts—neither buy nor sell, sue or be sued—and yet can be taxed without representation.

3d.—A citizen can not be said to have a right to happiness, when denied the right to person, property, children, and home; when the code of laws under which she is compelled to live is far more unjust and tyrannical than that which our fathers repudiated at the mouth of the cannon nearly one century ago.

Now, we would ask on what principle of republicanism, justice, or common humanity, a minority of the people of this Republic have monopolized to themselves all the rights of the whole? Where, under our Declaration of Independence, does the white Saxon man get his power to deprive all women and negroes of their inalienable rights?

The mothers of the Revolution bravely shared all dangers, persecutions, and death; and their daughters now claim an equal share in all the glories and triumphs of your success. Shall they stand before a body of American legislators and ask in vain for their right of suffrage—their right of property—their right to the wages they earn—their right to their children and their homes—their sacred right to personal liberty—to a trial by a jury of their peers?

In view of these high considerations, we demand, then, that you shall, by your future legislation, secure to women all those rights and privileges and immunities which in equity belong to every citizen of a republic.

And we demand that whenever you shall remodel the Constitution of the State in which you live, the word "male" shall be expurgated, and that henceforth you shall legislate for all citizens. There can be no privileged classes in a truly democratic government.

Elizabeth Cady Stanton,	Martha C. Wright,
Wendell Phillips,	Caroline M. Severance,
Caroline H. Dall,	Thomas W. Higginson,
Ernestine L. Rose,	Susan B. Anthony,
Antoinette Brown Blackwell,	*Committee.*

The above memorial was extensively circulated and sent to the Legislature of every State in the nation, but, owing to the John Brown raid and the general unrest and forebodings of the people on the eve of our civil war, it commanded but little attention.

FORM OF APPEAL AND PETITION CIRCULATED IN THE STATE OF NEW YORK DURING THE SUMMER AND AUTUMN OF 1859.

To the Women of the Empire State:

It is the desire and purpose of those interested in the Woman's Rights movement, to send up to our next Legislature an overwhelming petition, for the civil and political rights of woman. These rights must be secured just as soon as the majority of the women of the State make the demand. To this end, we have decided thoroughly to canvass our State before the close of the present year. We shall hold conventions in every county, distribute tracts and circulate petitions, in order, if possible, to arouse a proper self-respect in woman.

The want of funds has heretofore crippled all our efforts, but as large bequests have been made to our cause during the past year, we are now able to send out agents and to commence anew our work, which shall never end, until, in Church and State, and at the fireside, the equality of woman shall be fully recognized.

We hope much from our Republican legislators. Their well-known professions encourage us to believe that our task is by no means a hard one. We shall look for their hearty co-operation in every effort for the elevation of humanity. We have had bills before the Legislature for several years, on some of which, from time to time, have had most favorable reports. The property bill of '48 was passed by a large majority. The various bills of rights, to wages, children, suffrage, etc., have been respectfully considered. The bill presented at the last session, giving to married women their rights to make contracts, and to their wages, passed the House with only three dissenting votes, but owing to the pressure of business at the close of the session, it was never brought before the Senate.

Whilst man, by his legislation and generous donations, declares our cause righteous and just—whilst the very best men of the nation, those who stand first in Church and State, in literature, commerce, and the arts, are speaking for us such noble words and performing such God-like deeds—shall woman, herself, be indifferent to her own wrongs, insensible to all the responsibilities of her high and holy calling? No! No!! Let the women of the Empire State now speak out in deep and earnest tones that can not be misunderstood, demanding all those rights which are at the very foundation of Republicanism —a full and equal representation with man in the administration of our State and National Government.

Do you know, women of New York! that under our present laws married women have no right to the wages they earn? Think of the 40,000 drunkards' wives in this State—of the wives of men who are licentious—of gamblers—of the long line of those who do nothing; and is it no light matter that all these women who support themselves, their husbands and families, too, shall have no right to the disposition of their own earnings? Roll up, then, your petitions *

---

* FORM OF PETITION.

To the Senate and Assembly of the State of New York:

The undersigned, citizens of ——, New York, respectfully ask that you will take measures to submit to the people an amendment of the Constitution, allowing women to vote and hold office. And that you will enact laws securing to married women the full on this point, if no other, and secure to laboring women their wages at the coming session!

Now is the golden time to work! Before another Constitutional Convention be called, see to it that the public sentiment of this State shall demand suffrage for woman! Remember, " they who would be free, themselves must strike the blow! " E. CADY STANTON,
Chairman Central Committee.

Of the canvass of 1859 and '60, we find the following letter in *The New York Tribune,* February, 1860.

To the Editor of The Tribune :

SIR:—The readers of *The Tribune* who have perused its columns closely for the last six months will have noticed repeated announcements of County Conventions in different parts of the State to be addressed by certain ladies engaged in advocating equal rights for woman. It may not be uninteresting to them to know that every one of those appointments was filled by said ladies. Over fifty counties of the State have been thus visited, and petitions presented to the people for their signatures, praying for equal property rights, and for steps to be taken to so amend the Constitution as to secure to woman the right of suffrage, which have been numerously signed and duly presented to the Legislature. In the rural districts the success has been wonderful, considering the unpopularity of the subject; our most violent opposers being demagogical Democrats who frankly acknowledge that if our doctrines prevail, anti-slavery, temperance, moral reform, and Republicanism will conquer.

Large bequests have been made in the East for the furtherance of this movement, and under the direction of a committee appointed for that purpose, these ladies have gone forth to proclaim the doctrine of civil and political equality for woman. No laggards are they in their work. In the language of Mr. Greeley, they have found a work to be done, and have gone at it with ready and resolute will; they have not been able to answer all the calls made upon their time and talent. One of them (I can speak but for one) between the 11th of November and the 31st of January, has given sixty-eight lectures, not missing one appointment, resting only through the holidays and on Sundays. The others have doubtless done as well. In most instances all have been able to pay their own expenses, and in some cases their own salaries.

These ladies are not disappointed old maids, desolate widows, or unhappy wives, though there is one widow and one who has passed what is called the sunny side of twenty-five. Miss Susan B. Anthony, the general agent, resides at Rochester, and is unmarried. Mrs. Ernestine L. Rose, of New York City, is too widely known to need comment. The same may be said of Antoinette Brown Blackwell, the eloquent minister,

---

and entire control of all property originally belonging to them, and of their earnings during marriage ; and making the rights of the wife over the children the same as a husband enjoys, and the rights of a widow, as to her children, and as to the property left by her husband, the same that a husband has in the property and over the children of his deceased wife.

accomplished scholar, and amiable wife and mother. Mrs. J. Elizabeth Jones, of Ohio, is a lady in the ripeness of womanhood, to whom, equally with the above, all these adjectives apply. Mrs. Hannah Tracy Cutler, of Illinois, has been twice married, and has superintended two families of children satisfactorily; she has been teacher in a high-school in Columbus, Ohio, and matron of a deaf and dumb asylum, has taken premiums on sorghum sugar made by her own hands, and is also a physician among the poor of her neighborhood. Mrs. Lucy N. Colman, of New York, is a widow, and has fought life's battle bravely and well for herself and children. Mrs. Frances D. Gage, of Missouri, formerly of Ohio, might claim the nomination for President under the authority of Henry Ward Beecher, "having brought up six unruly boys," whose aggregate height would form a column of thirty-six feet in honor of their mother, who will all vote the Republican ticket in 1860 but one, and he is not old enough; and no one of them smokes or chews, or stimulates the inner man with intoxicating beverages. She is also the mother of two daughters.

Two years ago Mr. Greeley said to one of the ladies, "Why don't you ladies go to work?" They have gone to work; and with the help of such men as Garrison, Phillips, Parker, Giddings, Curtis, Beecher, Chapin, Brady, and a host of others whom the world delights to honor, their cause will surely triumph. It is a question of time only; not of fact. God speed the day.

The State Convention of 1860 was held in Association Hall, Albany, February 3d and 4th, with fine audiences throughout, and the usual force of speakers. As the outpourings of Miss Anthony's love element all flowed into the suffrage movement, she was sorely tried with the imperative cares that the domestic experiments of most of her coadjutors so constantly involved. Her urgent missives coming ever and anon to arouse us to higher duties, are quite inspiring even at this date. In a letter to Martha C. Wright, she says:

Mr. Bingham, the chairman of the Judiciary Committee, will bring in a radical report in favor of all our claims, but previous to his doing so he wishes our strongest arguments made before the Committee, and he says Mrs. Stanton must come. I write her this mail, but I wish you would step over there and make her feel that the salvation of the Empire State, at least the women in it, depends upon her bending all her powers to moving the hearts of our law-makers at this time. Mr. Bingham says our Convention here has wrought wondrous changes with a large number of the members who attended, and so says Mr. Mayo, of the Albanians; indeed our claims are so patent they need only to be known to be approved. Mrs. Stanton must move heaven and earth now to secure this bill, and she can, if she will only try. I should go there myself this very night, but I must watch and encourage friends here. The Earnings Bill has passed the House, and is in Committee of the Whole in the Senate. Then a Guardianship Bill must be drafted and put through if possible.

I returned from New York last evening; have taken the "Cooper Union," for our National Convention in May. Saw Miss Howland; she said Mr. Beecher's lecture is to be in this week's *Independent*. Only think how many priestly eyes will be compelled to look at its defiled page. Theodore Tilton told me that Mr. Beecher had had a severe battle to get into *The Independent*.

Mrs. Stanton, in answering Miss Anthony's appeal, says:

I am willing to do the appointed work at Albany. If Napoleon says cross the Alps, they are crossed. I can not, my dear friend, "move heaven and earth," but I will do what I can with pen and brain. You must come here and start me on the right train of thought, as your practical knowledge of just what is wanted is everything in getting up the right document. Kind regards to the anti slavery host now with you. I did not think that the easy arm-chair I occupied on the Auburn platform was to bring me so much glory. Did you know the resolutions of that meeting were read on the floor of Congress?—that pleased me greatly. I am very proud to stand maternal sponsor for the whole string. I wish our Albany resolutions had more snap in them. The Garrison clique are the only men in this nation that know how to write a resolution.

On the 18th of February Mrs. Stanton addressed the Legislature on woman's right of suffrage and the bill then pending in the Senate. A magnificent audience greeted her in the Capitol. She occupied the Speaker's desk, and was introduced by Senator Hammond, and spoke as follows:

GENTLEMEN OF THE JUDICIARY:—There are certain natural rights as inalienable to civilization as are the rights of air and motion to the savage in the wilderness. The natural rights of the civilized man and woman are government, property, the harmonious development of all their powers, and the gratification of their desires. There are a few people we now and then meet who, like Jeremy Bentham, scout the idea of natural rights in civilization, and pronounce them mere metaphors, declaring that there are no rights aside from those the law confers. If the law made man too, that might do, for then he could be made to order to fit the particular niche he was designed to fill. But inasmuch as God made man in His own image, with capacities and powers as boundless as the universe, whose exigencies no mere human law can meet, it is evident that the man must ever stand first; the law but the creature of his wants; the law-giver but the mouthpiece of humanity. If, then, the nature of a being decides its rights, every individual comes into this world with rights that are not transferable. He does not bring them like a pack on his back, that may be stolen from him, but they are a component part of himself, the laws which insure his growth and development. The individual may be put in the stocks, body and soul, he may be dwarfed, crippled, killed, but his rights no man can get; they live and die with him.

Though the atmosphere is forty miles deep all round the globe, no man can do more than fill his own lungs. No man can see, hear, or smell but just so far; and though hundreds are deprived of these senses, his are not the more acute. Though rights have been abundantly supplied by the good Father, no man can appropriate to himself those that belong to another. A citizen can have but one vote, fill but one office, though thousands are not permitted to do either. These axioms prove that woman's poverty does not add to man's wealth, and if, in the plenitude of his power, he should secure to her the exercise of all her God-given rights, her wealth could not bring poverty to him. There is a kind of nervous unrest always manifested by those in power, whenever new claims are started by those out of their own immediate class. The philosophy of this is very plain. They imagine that if the rights of this new class be granted, they must, of necessity, sacrifice something of what they already possess. They can not divest themselves of the idea that rights are very much like lands, stocks, bonds, and mortgages, and that if every new claimant be satisfied, the supply of human rights must in time run low. You might as well carp at the birth of every child, lest there should not be enough air left to inflate your lungs; at the success of every scholar, for fear that your draughts at the fountain of knowledge could not be so long and deep; at the glory of every hero, lest there be no glory left for you. . . . .

If the object of government is to protect the weak against the strong, how unwise to place the power wholly in the hands of the strong. Yet that is the history of all governments, even the model republic of these United States. You who have read the history of nations, from Moses down to our last election, where have you ever seen one class looking after the interests of another? Any of you can readily see the defects in other governments, and pronounce sentence against those who have sacrificed the masses to themselves; but when we come to our own case, we are blinded by custom and self-interest. Some of you who have no capital can see the injustice which the laborer suffers; some of you who have no slaves, can see the cruelty of his oppression; but who of you appreciate the galling humiliation, the refinements of degradation, to which women (the mothers, wives, sisters, and daughters of freemen) are subject, in this the last half of the nineteenth century? How many of you have ever read even the laws concerning them that now disgrace your statute-books? In cruelty and tyranny, they are not surpassed by any slaveholding code in the Southern States; in fact they are worse, by just so far as woman, from her social position, refinement, and education, is on a more equal ground with the oppressor.

Allow me just here to call the attention of that party now so much interested in the slave of the Carolinas, to the similarity in his condition and that of the mothers, wives, and daughters of the Empire State. The negro has no name. He is Cuffy Douglas or Cuffy Brooks, just whose Cuffy he may chance to be. The woman has no name. She is Mrs. Richard Roe or Mrs. John Doe, just whose Mrs. she may chance to be. Cuffy has no right to his earnings; he can not buy or sell, or lay up anything that he can call his own. Mrs Roe has no right to her earnings she can neither buy nor sell, make contracts, nor lay up anything that she can call her own. Cuffy has no right to his children; they can be sold from him at any time. Mrs. Roe has no right to her children; they may be bound out to cancel a father's debts of honor. The unborn child, even by the last will of the father, may be placed under the guardianship of a stranger and a foreigner. Cuffy has no legal existence; he is subject to restraint and moderate chastisement. Mrs. Roe has no legal existence; she has not the best right to her own person. The husband has the power to restrain, and administer moderate chastisement.

Blackstone declares that the husband and wife are one, and learned commentators have decided that that one is the husband. In all civil codes, you will find them classified as one. Certain rights and immunities, such and such privileges are to be secured to white male citizens. What have women and negroes to do with rights ? What know they of government, war, or glory ?

The prejudice against color, of which we hear so much, is no stronger than that against sex. It is produced by the same cause, and manifested very much in the same way. The negro's skin and the woman's sex are both *prima facie* evidence that they were intended to be in subjection to the white Saxon man. The few social privileges which the man gives the woman, he makes up to the negro in civil rights. The woman may sit at the same table and eat with the white man; the free negro may hold property and vote. The woman may sit in the same pew with the white man in church; the free negro may enter the pulpit and preach. Now, with the black man's right to suffrage, the right unquestioned, even by Paul, to minister at the altar, it is evident that the prejudice against sex is more deeply rooted and more unreasonably maintained than that against color. As citizens of a republic, which should we most highly prize, social privileges or civil rights ? The latter, most certainly.

To those who do not feel the injustice and degradation of the condition, there is something inexpressibly comical in man's "citizen woman." It reminds me of those monsters I used to see in the old world, head and shoulders woman, and the rest of the body sometimes fish and sometimes beast. I used to think, What a strange conceit ! but now I see how perfectly it represents man's idea ! Look over all his laws concerning us, and you will see just enough of woman to tell of her existence; all the rest is submerged, or made to crawl upon the earth. Just imagine an inhabitant of another planet entertaining himself some pleasant evening in searching over our great national compact, our Declaration of Independence, our Constitutions, or some of our statute-books; what would he think of those " women and negroes " that must be so fenced in, so guarded against ? Why, he would certainly suppose we were monsters, like those fabulous giants or Brobdignagians of olden times, so dangerous to civilized man, from our size, ferocity, and power. Then let him take up our poets, from Pope down to Dana; let him listen to our Fourth of July toasts, and some of the sentimental adulations of social life, and no logic could convince him that this creature of the law, and this angel of the family altar, could be one and the same being. Man is in such a labyrinth of contradictions with his marital and property rights; he is so befogged on the whole question of maidens, wives, and mothers, that from pure benevolence we should relieve him from this troublesome branch of legislation. We should vote, and make laws for ourselves. Do not be alarmed, dear ladies! You need spend no time reading Grotius, Coke, Puffendorf, Blackstone, Bentham, Kent, and Story to find out what you need. We may safely trust the shrewd selfishness of the white man, and consent to live under the same broad code where he has so comfortably ensconced himself. Any legislation that will do for man, we may abide by most cheerfully. . . . .

But, say you, we would not have woman exposed to the grossness and vulgarity of public life, or encounter what she must at the polls. When you talk, gentlemen, of sheltering woman from the rough winds and revolting scenes of real life, you must be either talking for effect, or wholly ignorant of what the facts of life are. The man, whatever he is, is known to the woman. She is the companion, not only of the accomplished statesman, the orator, and the scholar; but the vile, vulgar, brutal man has his mother, his wife, his sister, his daughter. Yes, delicate, refined, educated women are in daily life with the drunkard, the gambler, the licentious man, the rogue, and the villain; and if man shows out what he is anywhere, it is at his own hearthstone. There are over forty thousand drunkards in this State. All these are bound by the ties of family to some woman. Allow but a mother and a wife to each, and you have over eighty thousand women. All these have seen their fathers, brothers, husbands, sons, in the lowest and most debased stages of obscenity and degradation. In your own circle of friends, do you not know refined women, whose whole lives are darkened and saddened by gross and brutal associations? Now, gentlemen, do you talk to woman of a rude jest or jostle at the polls, where noble, virtuous men stand ready to protect her person and her rights, when, alone in the darkness and solitude and gloom of night, she has trembled on her own threshold. awaiting the return of a husband from his midnight revels?—when, stepping from her chamber, she has beheld her royal monarch, her lord and master—her legal representative—the protector of her property, her home, her children, and her person, down on his hands and knees slowly crawling up the stairs? Behold him in her chamber—in her bed! The fairy tale of "Beauty and the Beast" is far too often realized in life. Gentlemen, such scenes as woman has witnessed at her own fireside, where no eye save Omnipotence could pity, no strong arm could help, can never be realized at the polls, never equaled elsewhere, this side the bottomless pit. No, woman has not hitherto lived in the clouds, surrounded by an atmosphere of purity and peace—but she has been the companion of man in health, in sickness, and in death, in his highest and in his lowest moments. She has worshiped him as a saint and an orator, and pitied him as madman or a fool. In Paradise, man and woman were placed together, and so they must ever be. They must sink or rise together. If man is low and wretched and vile, woman can not escape the contagion, and any atmosphere that is unfit for woman to breathe is not fit for man. Verily, the sins of the fathers shall be visited upon the children to the third and fourth generation. You, by your unwise legislation, have crippled and dwarfed womanhood, by closing to her all honorable and lucrative means of employment, have driven her into the garrets and dens of our cities, where she now revenges herself on your innocent sons, sapping the very foundations of national virtue and strength. Alas! for the young men just coming on the stage of action, who soon shall fill your vacant places—our future Senators, our Presidents, the expounders of our constitutional law! Terrible are the penalties we are now suffering for the ages of injustice done to woman.

Again, it is said that the majority of women do not ask for any change in the laws; that it is time enough to give them the elective franchise when they, as a class, demand it.

Wise statesmen legislate for the best interests of the nation; the State, for the highest good of its citizens; the Christian, for the conversion of the world. Where would have been our railroads, our telegraphs, our ocean steamers, our canals and harbors, our arts and sciences, if government had withheld the means from the far-seeing minority? This State established our present system of common schools, fully believing that educated men and women would make better citizens than ignorant ones. In making this provision for the education of its children, had they waited for a majority of the urchins of this State to petition for schools, how many, think you, would have asked to be transplanted from the street to the school-house? Does the State wait for the criminal to ask for his prison-house? the insane, the idiot, the deaf and dumb for his asylum? Does the Christian, in his love to all mankind, wait for the majority of the benighted heathen to ask him for the gospel? No; unasked and unwelcomed, he crosses the trackless ocean, rolls off the mountain of superstition that oppresses the human mind, proclaims the immortality of the soul, the dignity of manhood, the right of all to be free and happy.

No, gentlemen, if there is but one woman in this State who feels the injustice of her position, she should not be denied her inalienable rights, because the common household drudge and the silly butterfly of fashion are ignorant of all laws, both human and Divine. Because they know nothing of governments, or rights, and therefore ask nothing, shall my petitions be unheard? I stand before you the rightful representative of woman, claiming a share in the halo of glory that has gathered round her in the ages, and by the wisdom of her past words and works, her peerless heroism and self-sacrifice, I challenge your admiration; and, moreover, claiming, as I do, a share in all her outrages and sufferings, in the cruel injustice, contempt, and ridicule now heaped upon her, in her deep degradation, hopeless wretchedness, by all that is helpless in her present condition, that is false in law and public sentiment, I urge your generous consideration; for as my heart swells with pride to behold woman in the highest walks of literature and art, it grows big enough to take in those who are bleeding in the dust.

Now do not think, gentlemen, we wish you to do a great many troublesome things for us. We do not ask our legislators to spend a whole session in fixing up a code of laws to satisfy a class of most unreasonable women. We ask no more than the poor devils in the Scripture asked, "Let us alone." In mercy, let us take care of ourselves, our property, our children, and our homes. True, we are not so strong, so wise, so crafty as you are, but if any kind friend leaves us a little money, or we can by great industry earn fifty cents a day, we would rather buy bread and clothes for our children than cigars and champagne for our legal protectors. There has been a great deal written and said about protection. We, as a class, are tired of one kind of protection, that which leaves us everything to do, to dare, and to suffer, and strips us of all means for its accomplishment. We would not tax man to take care of us. No, the Great Father has endowed all his creatures with the necessary powers for self-support, self-defense, and protection. We do not ask man to represent us; it is hard enough in times like these for man to carry backbone enough to represent himself. So long as the mass of men spend most of their time on the fence, not knowing which way to jump, they are surely in no condition to tell us where we had better stand. In pity for man, we would no longer hang like a mill-stone round his neck. Undo what man did for us in the dark ages, and strike out all special legislation for us; strike the words "white male" from all your constitutions, and then, with fair sailing, let us sink or swim, live or die, survive or perish together.

At Athens, an ancient apologue tells us, on the completion of the temple of Minerva, a statue of the goddess was wanted to occupy the crowning point of the edifice. Two of the greatest artists produced what each deemed his masterpiece. One of these figures was the size of life, admirably designed, exquisitely finished, softly rounded, and beautifully refined. The other was of Amazonian stature, and so boldly chiselled that it looked more like masonry than sculpture. The eyes of all were attracted by the first, and turned away in contempt from the second. That, therefore, was adopted, and the other rejected, almost with resentment, as though an insult had been offered to a discerning public. The favored statue was accordingly borne in triumph to the place for which it was designed, in the presence of applauding thousands, but as it receded from their upturned eyes, all, all at once agaze upon it, the thunders of applause unaccountably died away—a general misgiving ran through every bosom—the mob themselves stood like statues, as silent and as petrified, for as it slowly went up, and up the soft expression of those chiselled features, the delicate curves and outlines of the limbs and figure, became gradually fainter and fainter, and when at last it reached the place for which it was intended, it was a shapeless ball, enveloped in mist. Of course, the idol of the hour was now clamored down as rationally as it had been cried up, and its dishonored rival, with no good will and no good looks on the part of the chagrined populace, was reared in its stead. As it ascended, the sharp angles faded away, the rough points became smooth, the features full of expression, the whole figure radiant with majesty and beauty. The rude hewn mass, that before had scarcely appeared to bear even the human form, assumed at once the divinity which it represented, being so perfectly proportioned to the dimensions of the building, and to the elevation on which it stood, that it seemed as though Pallas herself had alighted upon the pinnacle of the temple in person, to receive the homage of her worshippers.

The woman of the nineteenth century is the shapeless ball in the lofty position which she was designed fully and nobly to fill. The place is not too high, too large, too sacred for woman, but the type that you have chosen is far too small for it. The woman we declare unto you is the rude, misshapen, unpolished object of the successful artist. From your stand-point, you are absorbed with the defects alone. The true artist sees the harmony between the object and its destination. Man, the sculptor, has carved out his ideal, and applauding thousands welcome his success. He has made a woman that from his low stand-point looks fair and beautiful, a being without rights, or hopes, or fears but in him—neither noble, virtuous, nor independent. Where do we see, in Church or State, in school-house or at the fireside, the much talked-of moral power of woman? Like those Athenians, we have bowed down and worshiped in woman, beauty, grace, the exquisite proportions, the soft and beautifully rounded outline, her delicacy, refinement, and silent helplessness—all well when she is viewed simply as an object of sight, never to rise one foot above the dust from which she sprung. But if she is to be raised up to adorn a temple, or represent a divinity—if she is to fill the niche of wife and counsellor to true and noble men, if she is to be the mother, the educator of a race of heroes or martyrs, of a Napoleon, or a Jesus—then must the type of womanhood be on a larger scale than that yet carved by man.

In vain would the rejected artist have reasoned with the Athenians as to the superiority of his production; nothing short of the experiment they made could have satisfied them. And what of your experiment, what of your wives, your homes? Alas! for the folly and vacancy that meet you there! But for your club-houses and newspapers, what would social life be to you? Where are your beautiful women? your frail ones, taught to lean lovingly and confidingly on man? Where are the crowds of educated dependents—where the long line of pensioners on man's bounty? Where all the young girls, taught to believe that marriage is the only legitimate object of a woman's pursuit—they who stand listlessly on life's shores, waiting, year after year, like the sick man at the pool of Bethesda, for some one to come and put them in? These are they who by their ignorance and folly curse almost every fireside with some human specimen of deformity or imbecility. These are they who fill the gloomy abodes of poverty and vice in our vast metropolis. These are they who patrol the streets of our cities, to give our sons their first lessons in infamy. These are they who fill our asylums, and make night hideous with their cries and groans.

The women who are called masculine, who are brave, courageous, self-reliant and independent, are they who in the face of adverse winds have kept one steady course upward and onward in the paths of virtue and peace—they who have taken their gauge of womanhood from their own native strength and dignity—they who have learned for themselves the will of God concerning them. This is our type of womanhood. Will you help us raise it up, that you too may see its beautiful proportions—that you may behold the outline of the goddess who is yet to adorn your temple of Freedom? We are building a model republic; our edifice will one day need a crowning glory. Let the artists be wisely chosen. Let them begin their work. Here is a temple to Liberty, to human rights, on whose portals behold the glorious declaration, "All men are created equal." The sun has never yet shone upon any of man's creations that can compare with this. The artist who can mold a statue worthy to crown magnificence like this, must be godlike in his conceptions, grand in his comprehensions, sublimely beautiful in his power of execution. The woman—the crowning glory of the model republic among the nations of the earth—what must she not be? (Loud applause).*

---

* Lydia Mott, in writing to a friend, says: "I have heard but one opinion about the merits of the address and the manner of its delivery, and the press is very complimentary. It was better that one like Mrs. Stanton should speak on the occasion than two unless

AN ACT CONCERNING THE RIGHTS AND LIABILITIES OF HUSBAND AND WIFE.

The Act of 1860* was offered by Andrew J. Colvin in the Senate as a substitute for a bill from the Assembly, which was simply an amendment of the law of 1848. Senators Hammond, Ramsey, and Colvin constituted the Judiciary Committee, to whom the bill was referred. Mr. Colvin objected to it for want of breadth in giving to married women the rights to which he thought them entitled, and urged that a much more liberal measure was demanded by the

the other might have been Wendell Phillips. Mr. Mayo expressed himself thoroughly satisfied; the whole effect was grand. Even old Father Woolworth stood the whole time, and very often he would nod assent at certain points. The House was packed, but so still that not one word was lost. It was worth as much to our cause as our whole Convention, though we could not have spared either."

* AN ACT

CONCERNING THE RIGHTS AND LIABILITIES OF HUSBAND AND WIFE.

Passed March 20, 1860.

The People of the State of New York, represented in Senate and Assembly, do enact as follows:

Section 1. The property, both real and personal, which any married woman now owns, as her sole and separate property; that which comes to her by descent, devise, bequest, gift, or grant; that which she acquires by her trade, business, labor, or services, carried on or performed on her sole or separate account; that which a woman married in this State owns at the time of her marriage, and the rents, issues, and proceeds of all such property, shall notwithstanding her marriage, be and remain her sole and separate property, and may be used, collected, and invested by her in her own name, and shall not be subject to the interference or control of her husband, or liable for his debts, except such debts as may have been contracted for the support of herself or her children, by her as his agent.

§ 2. A married woman may bargain, sell, assign, and transfer her separate personal property, and carry on any trade or business, and perform any labor or services on her sole and separate account, and the earnings of any married woman from her trade, business, labor, or services shall be her sole and separate property, and may be used or invested by her in her own name.

§ 3. Any married woman possessed of real estate as her separate property may bargain, sell, and convey such property, and enter into any contract in reference to the same; but no such conveyance or contract shall be valid without the assent, in writing, of her husband, except as hereinafter provided.

§ 4. In case any married woman possessed of separate real property, as aforesaid, may desire to sell or convey the same, or to make any contract in relation thereto, and shall be unable to procure the assent of her husband as in the preceding section provided, in consequence of his refusal, absence, insanity, or other disability, such married woman may apply to the County Court in the county where she shall at the time reside, for leave to make such sale, conveyance, or contract, without the assent of her husband.

§ 5. Such application may be made by petition, verified by her, and setting forth the grounds of such application. If the husband be a resident of the county and not under disability from insanity or other cause, a copy of said petition shall be served upon him, with a notice of the time when the same will be presented to the said court, at least ten days before such application. In all other cases, the County Court to which such application shall be made, shall, in its discretion, determine whether any notice shall be given, and if any, the mode and manner of giving it.

§ 6. If it shall satisfactorily appear to such court, upon application, that the husband spirit of the times. In one of Miss Anthony's interviews with Mr. Colvin, she handed him a very radical bill just introduced in the Massachusetts Legislature, which after due examination and the addition of two or three more liberal clauses, was accepted by the Committee, reported to the Senate by Mr. Colvin, and adopted by that body February 28, 1860.* The bill was concurred in by the Assembly, and signed by the Governor, Edwin D. Morgan. It is quite remarkable that the bill in its transit did not receive a single alteration, modification, or amendment from the time it left Mr. Colvin's hands until it took its place on the statute-book. The women of the State who labored so persistently for this measure, felt that the victory at last was due in no small degree to the deep interest and patient skill of Andrew J. Colvin. Hon. Anson Bingham, chairman of the Judiciary Committee, who did good service in the Assembly at this time, should be gratefully

---

of such applicant has willfully abandoned his said wife, and lives separate and apart from her, or that he is insane, or imprisoned as a convict in any state prison, or that he is an habitual drunkard, or that he is in any way disabled from making a contract, or that he refuses to give his consent without good cause therefor, then such court shall cause an order to be entered upon its records, authorizing such married woman to sell and convey her real estate, or contract in regard thereto without the assent of her husband, with the same effect as though such conveyance or contract had been made with his assent.

§ 7. Any married woman may, while married, sue and be sued in all matters having relation to her property, which may be her sole and separate property, or which may hereafter come to her by descent, devise, bequest, or the gift of any person except her husband, in the same manner as if she were sole. And any married woman may bring and maintain an action in her own name, for damages against any person or body corporate, for any injury to her person or character, the same as if she were sole; and the money received upon the settlement of any such action, or recovered upon a judgment, shall be her sole and separate property.

§ 8. No bargain or contract made by any married woman, in respect to her sole and separate property, or any property which may hereafter come to her by descent, devise, bequest, or gift of any person except her husband, and no bargain or contract entered into by any married woman in or about the carrying on of any trade or business under the statutes of this State, shall be binding upon her husband, or render him or his property in any way liable therefor.

§ 9. Every married woman is hereby constituted and declared to be the joint guardian of her children, with her husband, with equal powers, rights, and duties in regard to them, with the husband.

§ 10. At the decease of husband or wife, leaving no minor child or children, the survivor shall hold, possess, and enjoy a life estate in one-third of all the real estate of which the husband or wife died seized.

§ 11. At the decease of the husband or wife intestate, leaving minor child or children, the survivor shall hold, possess, and enjoy all the real estate of which the husband or wife died seized, and all the rents, issues, and profits thereof during the minority of the youngest child, and one-third thereof during his or her natural life.

* On the final passage of the bill the following Senators, as *The Journal* shows, voted in favor of the measure, viz: Senators Abell, Bell, Colvin, Conally, Fiero, Goss, Hillhouse, Kelly, Lapham, Sessions, Manierre, Montgomery, Munroe, P. P. Murphy, Truman, Prosser, Ramsey, Robertson, Rotch, Warner, Williams—21.

remembered by the women of New York. Mr. Bingham acted in concert with Mr. Colvin, both earnestly putting their shoulders to the wheel, one in the Assembly and one in the Senate, and with the women pulling all the wires they could outside, together they pushed the grand measure through.

Judge Bingham served our cause also by articles on all phases of the question over the signature of "Senex," published in many journals throughout the State. And this, too, at an early day, when every word in favor of woman's rights was of immense value in breaking down the prejudice of the ages.

In addition to this, another act of great benefit to a large number of housekeepers, called the "Boarding House Law," was secured by the same members. Miss Emily Howland, Mrs. Margaret Murray, Mrs. Manning, and Mrs. Griffith Satterlee spent some weeks in Albany using their influence in favor of this measure.

In February, 1860, Emily Howland arranged a course of lectures on Woman's Rights, to be given in Cooper Institute, New York. Henry Ward Beecher delivered his first lecture on the question in this course, receiving his fee of $100 in advance, as it was said he considered no engagement of that sort imperative without previous payment. Mr. Beecher's speech was published in full in *The New York Independent*, of which he was then editor-in-chief. The State Committee purchased a large number, which Lydia Mott, of Albany, laid on the desk of every member of both Houses. At the time we felt the speech worth to our cause all it cost.

TENTH NATIONAL WOMAN'S RIGHTS CONVENTION.

COOPER INSTITUTE, NEW YORK, MAY 10–11, 1860.

A large audience assembled in Cooper Institute at 10½ o'clock, Thursday morning. Susan B. Anthony called the Convention to order, and submitted a list of officers,* nominated at a preliminary meeting, which was adopted without dissent.

The President, Martha C. Wright, of Auburn, on taking the Chair, addressed the Convention as follows:

---

* *President.*—Martha Wright, of Auburn, New York.

Vice-Presidents.—Abby Hopper Gibbons, of New York; Asa Fairbanks, of Rhode Island; Rev. Antoinette Brown Blackwell, of New Jersey; Thomas Garrett, of Delaware; Wendell Phillips, of Massachusetts; Robert Purvis, of Pennsylvania; J. Elizabeth Jones, of Ohio; Giles B. Stebbins, of Michigan.

Secretaries.—Ellen Wright and Mary L. Booth.

Finance Committee.—Susan B. Anthony, Lucy N. Colman, and Marietta Richmond.

Business Committee.—Ernestine L. Rose, A. L. B. Blackwell, Wm. Lloyd Garrison, E. Cady Stanton, Mary Grew, and Wendell Phillips.

I have only to thank you for the honor you have conferred by electing me to preside over the deliberations of this Convention. I shall leave it to others to speak of the purposes of this great movement and of the successes which have already been achieved.

There are those in our movement who ask, "What is the use of these Conventions? What is the use of this constant iteration of the same things?" When we see what has been already achieved, we learn the use of this "foolishness of preaching:" and after all that we demand has been granted, as it will be soon, *The New York Observer* will piously fold its hands and roll up its eyes, and say, "This beneficent movement we have always advocated," and the pulpits will say "Amen!" (Laughter and applause). Then will come forward women who have gained courage from the efforts and sacrifices of others, and the great world will say, "Here come the women who are going to do something, and not talk."

There are those, too, who find fault with the freedom of our platform, who stand aloof and criticise, fearful of being involved in something that they can not fully endorse. Forgetting that, as Macaulay says, "Liberty alone can cure the evils of liberty," they fear to trust on the platform all who have a word to say. But we have invited all to come forward and speak, and not to stand aside and afterward criticise what has been said. We trust that those present who have an opinion, who have a word to say, whether they have ever spoken before or not, will speak now. If they disapprove of our resolutions, if they disapprove of anything that is said on this platform, let them oppose if they can not unite with us. (Applause.)

Susan B. Anthony was then introduced, and read the following report:

For our encouragement in laboring for the elevation of woman, it is well ever and anon to review the advancing steps. Each year we hail with pleasure new accessions to our faith. Strong words of cheer have come to us on every breeze. Brave men and true, from the higher walks of literature and art, from the bar, the bench, the pulpit, and legislative halls, are ready now to help woman wherever she claims to stand. The Press, too, has changed its tone. Instead of ridicule, we now have grave debate. And still more substantial praises of gold and silver have come to us. A gift of $5,000 from unknown hands; a rich legacy from the coffers of a Boston merchant prince—the late Charles F. Hovey; and, but a few days ago, $400,000 from Mr. Vassar, of Poughkeepsie, to found a college for girls, equal in all respects to Yale and Harvard.

We had in New York a legislative act passed at the last session, securing to married women their rights to their earnings and their children. Other States have taken onward steps. And, from what is being done on all sides, we have reason to believe that, as the Northern States shall one by one remodel their Constitutions, the right of suffrage will be granted to women. Six years hence New York proposes to revise her Constitution. These should be years of effort with all those who believe that it is the right and the duty of every citizen of a State to have a voice in the laws that govern them.

Woman is being so educated that she will feel herself capable of assuming grave responsibilities as lawgiver and administrator. She is crowding into higher avocations and new branches of industry. She already occupies the highest places in literature and art. The more liberal lyceums are open to her, and she is herself the subject of the most popular lectures now before the public. The young women of our academies and high schools are asserting their right to the discipline of declamation and discussion, and the departments of science and mathematics. Pewholders, of the most orthodox sects, are taking their right to a voice in the government of the church, and in the face of priests, crying "let your women keep silence in the churches," yes, at the very horns of the altar, calmly, deliberately, and persistently casting their votes in the choice of church officers and pastors.* Mass-meetings to sympathize with the "strikers" of Massachusetts are being called in this metropolis by women. Women are ordained ministers, and licensed physicians. Elizabeth Blackwell has founded a hospital in this city, where she proposes a thorough medical education, both theoretical and practical, for young women. And this Institute in which we are now assembled, with its school of design, its library and reading-room, where the arts and sciences are freely taught to women, and this hall, so cheerfully granted to our Convention, shows the magnanimity of its founder, Peter Cooper. All these are the results of our twenty years of agitation. And it matters not to us, though the men and the women who echo back our thought do fail to recognize the source of power, and while they rejoice in each onward step achieved in the face of ridicule and persecution, ostracise those who have done the work. Who of our literary women has yet ventured one word of praise or recognition of the heroic enunciators of the great idea of woman's equality—of Mary Woolstonecraft, Frances Wright, Ernestine L. Rose, Lucretia Mott, Elizabeth Cady Stanton? It matters not to those who live for the race, and not for self alone, who has the praise, so that justice be done to woman in Church, in State, and at the fireside—an equal everywhere with man—they will not complain, though even *The New York Observer* itself does claim to have done for them the work.

During the past six years this State has been thoroughly canvassed, and every county that has been visited by our lecturers and tracts has rolled up

---

* In the Scotch Presbyterian Church at Johnstown, N. Y., there was great excitement at one time on the question of temperance, the pastor being a very active friend to that movement. The opposition were determined to get rid of him, and called a church meeting for that purpose. To the surprise of the leading men of the congregation, the women came in force, armed with ballots, to defeat their proposed measures. When the time came to vote, according to arrangement, my mother headed the line marching up to the altar, where stood the deacon, hat in hand, to receive the ballots. As soon as he saw the women coming, he retreated behind the railing in the altar, closing the little door after him, which the women deliberately opened, and soon filled the space, completely surrounding *the inspector of election*, and, whichever way he turned, the ballots were thrown into the hat; and, when all had voted, my mother put her hand into the hat and stirred them up with the men's votes, so that it would be impossible to separate them. The pastor, representing the interests of temperance, had a large majority for his retention. But the men declared the election void because of the illegal voting, and, barricading the women out, with closed doors, voted their own measures the next day. Rev. Jeremiah Wood presided on the occasion, and whilst the women were contending for their rights under the very shadow of the altar, he recited various Scriptural texts on woman's sphere, to which these rebellious ones paid not the slightest attention. One dignified Scotch matron, looking him steadily in the face, indignant at the behavior of the men, said with sternness and emphasis: "I protest against such high-handed proceedings." The result of this outbreak, was a decree by the Judicature of the Church, "that the women of the congregation should have the right to vote in all business matters," which they have most judiciously done ever since. E. C. S.

petitions by the hundreds and thousands, asking for woman's right to vote and hold office—her right to her person, her wages, her children, and her home. Again and again have we held Conventions at the capital, and addressed our Legislature, demanding the exercise of all our rights as citizens of the Empire State. During the past year, we have had six women * lecturing in New York for several months each. Conventions have been held in forty counties, one or more lectures delivered in one hundred and fifty towns and villages, our petitions circulated, and our tracts and documents sold and gratuitously distributed throughout the entire length and breadth of the State.

A State Convention was held at Albany early in February. Large numbers of the members of the Legislature listened respectfully and attentively to the discussions of its several sessions, and expressed themselves converts to the claims for woman. The bills for woman's right to her property, her earnings, and the guardianship of her children passed both branches of the Legislature with scarce a dissenting voice, and received the prompt signature of the Governor.

Our Legislature passed yet another bill that brings great relief to a large class of women. It was called the Boarding-House Bill. It provides that the keepers of private boarding-houses shall have the right of lien on the property of boarders, precisely the same as do hotel-keepers. We closed our work by a joint hearing before the Committees of the Judiciary at the Capitol on the 19th of March. Elizabeth Cady Stanton addressed them. The Assembly Chamber was densely packed, and she was listened to with marked attention and respect. The Judiciary Committees of neither House reported on our petition for the right of suffrage, though the Chairman, with a large minority of the House Committee and a majority of the Senate Committee, favored the claim. The Hon. A. J. Colvin, of the Senate Committee, in a letter to me, says:

"The subject was presented at so late a day as to preclude action. While a majority of the Senate Committee I think were favorable, a majority of the House Committee, so far as I could learn, were opposed. So many progressive measures had passed both Houses that I felt apprehensive we might perhaps be running too great a risk by urging this question of justice and reform at this session. I did not therefore press it. Should I remain in the Senate, I may take occasion at an early day in the next session to bring up the subject and present my views at length. The more reflection I give, the more my mind becomes convinced that in a Republican Government, we have no right to deny to woman the privileges she claims. Besides, the moral element which those privileges would bring into existence would, in my judgment, have a powerful influence in perpetuating our form of government. It may be deemed best, at the next session, to urge an early Constitutional Convention. In case one should be called, your friends should be prepared to meet the emergency. Is the public mind sufficiently enlightened to accept a constitution recognizing the right of women to vote and hold office ? You should consider this."

The entire expense of the New York State work during the past year is

---

* Frances D. Gage, Hannah Tracy Cutler, J. Elizabeth Jones, Antoinette Brown Blackwell, Lucy N. Colman, and Susan B. Anthony.

nearly four thousand dollars. The present year we propose to expend our funds and efforts mostly in Ohio, to obtain, if possible, for the women of that State, the liberal laws we have secured for ourselves. Ohio, too, is soon to revise her Constitution, and we trust she will not be far behind New York in recognizing the full equality of woman. We who have grasped the idea of woman's destiny, her power and influence, the trinity of her existence as woman, wife, and mother, can most earnestly work for her elevation to that high position that it is the will of God she should ever fill. Though we have not yet realized the fullness of our hopes, let us rest in the belief that in all these years of struggle, no earnest thought, or word, or prayer has been breathed in vain. The influence has gone forth, the great ocean has been moved, and those who watch, e'en now may see the mighty waves of truth slowly swelling on the shores of time.

> "One accent of the Holy Ghost,
> A heedless word hath never lost."

ERNESTINE L. ROSE being introduced, said: Frances Wright was the first woman in this country who spoke on the equality of the sexes. She had indeed a hard task before her. The elements were entirely unprepared. She had to break up the time-hardened soil of conservatism, and her reward was sure—the same reward that is always bestowed upon those who are in the vanguard of any great movement. She was subjected to public odium, slander, and persecution. But these were not the only things that she received. Oh, she had her reward !—that reward of which no enemies could deprive her, which no slanders could make less precious—the eternal reward of knowing that she had done her duty; the reward springing from the consciousness of right, of endeavoring to benefit unborn generations. How delightful to see the molding of the minds around you, the infusing of your thoughts and aspirations into others, until one by one they stand by your side, without knowing how they came there ! That reward she had. It has been her glory, it is the glory of her memory; and the time will come when society will have outgrown its old prejudices, and stepped with one foot, at least, upon the elevated platform on which she took her position. But owing to the fact that the elements were unprepared, she naturally could not succeed to any great extent.

After her, in 1837, the subject of woman's rights was again taken hold of—aye, taken hold of by woman; and the soil having been already somewhat prepared, she began to sow the seeds for the future growth, the fruits of which we now begin to enjoy. Petitions were circulated and sent to our Legislature, and who can tell the hardships that then met those who undertook that great work ! I went from house to house with a petition for signatures simply asking our Legislature to allow married women to hold real estate in their own name. What did I meet with ? Why, the very name exposed one to ridicule, if not to worse treatment. The women said: "We have rights enough; we want no more"; and the men, as a matter of course, echoed it, and said: "You have rights enough; nay, you have too many already." (Laughter). But by perseverance in sending petitions to the Legislature, and, at the same time, enlightening the public mind on the subject, we at last accomplished our purpose. We had to adopt the method which physicians sometimes use, when they are called to a patient who is so hopelessly sick that he is unconscious of his pain and suffering. We had to describe to women their own position, to explain to them the burdens that rested so heavily upon them, and through these means, as a wholesome irritant, we roused public opinion on the subject, and through public opinion, we acted upon the Legislature, and in 1848-'49, they gave us the great boon for which we asked, by enacting that a woman who possessed property previous to marriage, or obtained it after marriage, should be allowed to hold it in her own name. Thus far, thus good; but it was only a beginning, and we went on. In 1848 we had the first Woman's Rights Convention, and then some of our papers thought it only a very small affair, called together by a few "strong-minded women," and would pass away like a nine-days' wonder. They little knew woman ! They little knew that if woman takes anything earnestly in her hands, she will not lay it aside unaccomplished. (Applause). We have continued our Conventions ever since. A few years ago, when we sent a petition to our Legislature, we obtained, with but very little effort, upward of thirteen thousand signatures. What a contrast between this number and the five signatures attached to the first petition, in 1837 ! Since then, we might have had hundreds of thousands of signatures, but it is no longer necessary. Public opinion is too well known to require a long array of names.

We have been often asked, "What is the use of Conventions ? Why talk ? Why not go to work ?" Just as if the thought did not precede the act ! Those who act without previously thinking, are not good for much. Thought is first required, then the expression of it, and that leads to action; and action based upon thought never needs to be reversed; it is lasting and profitable, and produces the desired effect. I know that there are many who take advantage of this movement, and then say: "You are doing nothing; only talking." Yes, doing nothing ! We have only broken up the ground and sowed the seed; they are reaping the benefit, and yet they tell us we have done nothing ! Mrs. Swisshelm, who has proclaimed herself to be "no woman's rights woman," has accepted a position as inspector of logs and lumber. (Laughter). Well, I have no objection to her having that avocation, if she have a taste and capacity for it—far from it. But she has accepted still more, and I doubt not with a great deal more zest and satisfaction—the five hundred dollars salary; and I hope she will enjoy it. Then, having accepted both the office and the salary, she folds her arms, and says: "I am none of your strong-minded women; I don't go for woman's rights." Well, she is still welcome to it. I have not the slightest objection that those who proclaim themselves not strong-minded, should still reap the benefit of a strong mind (applause and laughter); it is for them we work. So there are some ladies who think a great deal can be done in the Legislature without petitions, without conventions, without lectures, without public claim, in fact, without anything, but a little lobbying. Well, if they have a taste for it, they are welcome to engage in it; I have not the slightest objection. Yes, I have. I, as a woman, being conscious of the evil that is done by these lobby loafers in our Legislature and in the halls of Congress, object to it. (Loud cheers). I will wait five years longer to have a right given to me legitimately, from a sense of justice, rather than buy it in an underhand way by lobbying. Whatever my sentiments may be, good bad, or indifferent, I express them, and they are known. Nevertheless, if any desire it, let them do that work. But what has induced them, what has enabled the n, to do that work? The Woman's Rights movement, although they ₅ re afraid or ashamed even of the name "woman's rights."

You háve been told, and much more might be said on the subject, that already the Woman's Rights platform has upon it lawyers, ministers, and statesmen—men who are among the highest in the nation. I need not mention Wm. Lloyd Garrison, or Wendell Phillips; but there are others, those even who are afraid of the name of reformer, who have stood upon our platform. Brady! Who would ever have expected it? Chapin! Beecher! Think of it for a moment! A minister advocating the rights of woman, even her right at the ballot-box! What has done it? Our agitation has purified the atmosphere, and enabled them to see the injustice that is done to woman.

Mrs. ELIZABETH JONES, of Ohio, was the next speaker. She said: I wish to preface my remarks with this resolution:

Resolved, That woman's sphere can not be bounded. Its prescribed orbit is the largest place that in her highest development she can fill. The laws of mind are as immutable as are those of the planetary world, and the true woman must ever revolve around the great moral sun of light and truth.

As a general proposition, we say that capacity determines the true sphere of action, and indicates the kind of labor to be performed. I often hear women discussing this subject, much more in earnest than in jest, though they profess to be simply amusing themselves. One says: "If I were a man, I should be a mechanic"; another says: "I should be a merchant." One says: "I am sure I should be rich"; another, in the excess of her humor, thinks she should be distinguished. Why do women talk thus? Because one feels that she has mechanical genius; the power to construct, to perfect. Another understands the secrets of trade, and would like to incur the heavy responsibilities it involves. A third is conscious that she was born a financier; while a fourth has an intuitive perception of the elements of success.

Many women are beginning to judge for themselves the proper sphere of action, and are not only jesting about what they should do under other circumstances, but are already entering upon such paths as their taste and capacity indicate. Some will doubtless make mistakes, which experience will rectify, and others will perhaps persist in striving to do that which it will be very evident they have no ability to perform. This is the case with men who have had freedom in every sphere. Look at the American pulpit, for instance. Go through the country, and listen to those who claim to be the messengers of God, and if you do not say that many are destitute of capacity to fill the sphere they have chosen, we shall regard it as an act of obedience on your part to the command which says: "Judge not, lest ye be judged." (Laughter). Let adaptation be the rule for pulpit occupancy, and while it would eject some who are now no honor to the station, and no benefit to the people, it would open the place to many an Anna and Miriam and Deborah to fulfill the mission which God has clearly indicated by the talents He has bestowed.

The world says now, man is God's minister, and woman is not fit to call sinners to repentance; but let it say: "Those who have faith in the principles of eternal right, and have power to give it utterance; those who have the clearest perceptions of moral truth; those who understand the wants of the people, are the proper persons, whether they be men or women, to dispense to the needy multitude the bread of life." This would elevate the standard of pulpit qualifications, and bring into the field a far greater amount of talent to choose from, and thus would the intellectual and spiritual needs of the people be more fully answered. What is true of this profession will apply with equal force to others. Should I be told that the American bar needs no more talent, I would reply that it needs decency, and a well-founded self-respect. When you enter a court-room, and listen to a cross-examination of a delicate nature, one where woman is concerned, and she would rather die a hundred deaths, if she could, than to have the case dragged before the public, you will see it treated in the coarsest way, as if her holiest affections and her most sacred functions were fitting themes for brutish men to jeer at. And even in the most ordinary cases, gentlemen who would spurn the imputation of incivility in social life, will so browbeat and badger a witness, that the most disgusting bear-baiting would become by comparison a refined amusement. If the young aspirants for legal honors should meet among the advocates and judges sensible, dignified, and highly cultivated women, they would, if I am not much mistaken, get the benefit of certain lessons, upon manners and morals, that it is essential for all young men to learn. (Applause). It appears to me that by association of men and women in this profession, the bar might be purged of this indecorum, and possess the humanity, the wisdom, and the dignity that should ever characterize a Court of Justice.

You need not tell me that the profession would be overstocked, if women should enter it, for, like men, they must stand on their merits. Let there be no proscription on account of sex. Let talent be brought fairly into competition, and although many a young man, as well as young woman, would sit down forever briefless, having neither the capacity nor the acquirements to bring or retain clients, yet their loss would be for the public good, and for the honor and respectability of the profession. Let the talents of women be fully developed, and no man will lose any place that he is qualified to fill in consequence, and no woman will obtain that place who has not peculiar fitness. All these matters will find their own level, ultimately. I can point you to localities now where the people prefer women for teachers. A Union School in Northern Ohio, which is made up of ten departments, employs women for teachers, and a woman as superintendent of the whole. The people reason this way: We prefer women, because they bring us the best talent. Not that they have better talents than men, but with the latter, teaching is generally a stepping-stone to a profession. Woman accepts it as her highest post, and brings her best energies. With man, it is often a subordinate interest, and his best talents will be exercised upon what he regards as something higher and better. As in this, so in other things. The time will come when talent or capacity will govern the choice and not sex. It is so now in Art, to a great extent. I think there is not much known of sex there. The world does not care who wrote "Aurora Leigh." It does not recognize it as the production of a woman, but as the work of genius. Let the artists say what they please, the world does not care who chisels Zenobia, so that Zenobia be well chiseled. It does not care whether Landseer or Rosa Bonheur paints animals, so that animals are well painted. No one says this or that is well done for a woman, but he says, this is the work of an artist, that has no merit; not because a woman did it, not because a man did it, but because the author was destitute of capacity to embody the idea.

Again, read the little village newspapers, got out by little editors, and you will find, in many cases, an utter want of ability to fill the place that has been chosen. I hope young women will not make such mistakes as these young men have done, who might have been supposed to know something, if they had only kept still. (Laughter). If these papers, to which I have referred, were all in the hands of women, and so destitute of editorial pith and point as they now are, I should counsel against any further efforts for the elevation of the sex, believing the case to be hopeless. (Applause). If I mistake not, women have a peculiar fitness for trade. Mrs. Dall says, in her second lecture, that on the Island of Nantucket, women have engaged in commerce very successfully. They did it in the war, and afterward, when destitution drove the men to the whale fisheries, and again when they went to California. They have had much experience; and Eliza Barney tells of seventy women who engaged in trade, and retired with a competence, and besides brought up and educated large families of children. She says, also, that failures were very uncommon when women managed the business, and some of the largest and safest fortunes in Boston were founded by women. Whenever, therefore, one shows any ability for trade, that is her license for engaging in it—a license granted under the higher law, and therefore valid. I went into a bonnet store the other day, and saw a man-milliner holding up a bonnet on his soft white hand to a lady customer, and expatiating upon the beauties of the article with an earnestness, if not the eloquence, of an orator. She tried it on, and he went into ecstacies. (Laughter). It was so becoming ! It was so charming ! He complimented her, and he complimented the bonnet, and had she not been a strong-minded woman, I do not know how much of the flattery she would have taken for truth. I thought that man was out of his sphere; and not only that, but he had crowded some woman out of her appropriate place, out of the realm of taste and fashion. (Applause). When I passed out on the street, the harsh, discordant tone of a fish-woman fell upon my ear. I saw that she bore a heavy tub upon her head, evidently seeking by this branch of merchandise to procure a living for herself and family. So few were the avenues open to her, as she thought, and so much had men monopolized the places she could fill, that she was compelled to carry fish on her head, until she could raise money enough to procure a better conveyance.

Again, I see young men selling artificial flowers, and laces and embroidery, crinolines and balmorals, and I think to myself they had better be out digging coal or making brick. When I go back home to the West, I could take a car-load with me, and set them to work, and I would greatly benefit their condition, while the places they vacate here might be filled by the girls who are now starving in your garrets. (Applause). At a shoe-store, instead of finding a sprightly miss, to select and fit the ladies gaiters, you often see a strong, healthy man, kneeling before the customer with a gallantry that would be admirable in a drawing-room, and worth infinitely more than the price of the article he is selling; and he fusses over the gaiters and over the lady's foot, until you wonder if she is not tempted to propel him into a more appropriate sphere. (Laughter). Whatever possessed men to imagine that God designed them to fit ladies' gaiters, is more than I can imagine. (Applause). I am unable to realize how they obtained the revelation that for a woman to thus officiate would take her out of her appropriate sphere. Shall I be held to my principles here, and told that these men succeed in business, and success being the test of sphere, therefore they are in their place? It remains to be proved that they have succeeded. A man may jump Jim Crow from morning till night, or make a fool of himself in any other way, and succeed admirably in pleasing auditors and gathering pennies; but when you take into consideration his high and heavenly origin, and the noble purposes for which he was made, you can hardly call it a success. Neither should I think a woman was in suitable business, even if it were ever so lucrative and well done, unless that business developed her talents; made her stronger, more self-reliant, and better fitted her for life and its duties. These stores would be a good discipline for young girls, but not for men.

This whole question lies in a small compass. Our reform would leave woman just where God placed her—a moral, accountable being, endowed with talents whose scope and character indicate the work she is to do; and who is responsible primarily to her Creator for the use she makes of those talents. He says to every man and to every woman, Go work in my vineyard! That vineyard I understand to be the world, embracing all the varied responsibilities of life. Whether man shall pursue science, literature, or art, whether he shall engage in agriculture, manufactures, or mechanics, is for *him* to determine, and whether woman shall engage in any of these things is for *her* to determine. Nothing but an internal consciousness of power to perform certain work, and that it will be for her own good, can aid her in her choice. If a woman can write vigorous verse, then let her write verse. If she can build ships, then let her be a ship-builder. I know no reason why. If she can keep house, and that takes as much brains as any other occupation, let her be a housekeeper. They tell us that "eternal vigilance is the price of liberty"; eternal vigilance is the price of a well-ordered home, and every woman before me knows it. (Applause). I know that the conservative, in his fear, says, Surely you would not have woman till the soil, sail the seas, run up the rigging of a ship like a monkey (I use the language of one of your most distinguished men), go to war, engage in political brawls ? No ! I would not have her do anything. She must be her own judge. In relation to tilling the soil, the last census of the United Kingdom reports 128,418 women employed in agriculture. Examples are by no means rare where a woman carries on a farm which her deceased husband has left, and I have seen much skill evinced in the management. "In Media, Pa., two girls named Miller carry on a farm of 300 acres, raising hay and grain, hiring labor, but working mostly themselves." I have been on a farm in your own State where I saw, not Tennyson's six mighty daughters of the plow, but I saw three* who plowed, and not only that, but they plowed well. Doubtless, some of our fastidious young ladies would be greatly shocked at such an exhibition, and I must acknowledge that it was to me a novel sight; but the more I considered it, the more I thought that I would rather see a young woman holding the plow, than to see her leading such an aimless, silly life as many a young lady leads. I would rather see a young woman holding the plow, than to see her decked out in her finery, and sitting idle in the parlor, waiting for an offer of marriage. (Applause). I hope women will not copy the vices of men. I hope they will not go to war; I wish men would not. I hope they will not be contentious politicians; I am sorry that men are. I hope they will not regard their freedom as a license to do wrong; I am ashamed to acknowledge that men do. But we need not fear. We may safely trust the judgment of those who tell us that politics and morals, and every department into which woman may enter, will be elevated and re-fined by her influence.

So far as navigation is concerned, I think many women would not be attracted to that life. There might be now and then a Betsy Miller, who could walk the quarter-deck in a gale, and that certainly would indicate constitutional ability to become a sailor. I do not suppose so much violence would be done to her nature by navigating the seas, as by helping a drunken husband to navigate the streets habitually. (Applause). In relation to running up the rigging like a monkey, or in regard to any other monkey performance, I do not believe that women will ever enter into competition with men in these things, because the latter have shown such remarkable aptitude for that business. (Laughter and applause). But after all that may be said on this subject, we fail to reach one class in the community who have spare time, spare energies, abundance of power for work. I mean young ladies of wealth and rank. The world shows a degree of toleration now toward any young woman who from necessity has engaged in any industrial avocation to which women have not heretofore applied themselves. But there is no such toleration for the rich. Many of these are now striving to kill time with fancy-work and fiction, with flirtation and flaunting. Some are destitute of aspiration for anything better. These could be moved only by some convulsion in the social system, like the earthquake, or like the volcano that opens the ground at our feet and shows us our danger. But there are others whose convictions lead them to desire something better; who feel that they are living to no purpose; who know that their own powers, good as any God ever created, are lying in inglorious repose. Some of the advocates

---

* Mrs. Roberts and her daughters in Niagara County.

of our cause have said that for these there is no profession but marriage. If they are not literary, artistic, or philanthropic, what can they do? They are held by a cable, made up of home influence, of fashion, and of perverted Scripture, which binds them down to an insipid existence. Hence, they suppress all desire for a fuller, larger life; they smile graciously upon their fetters; they profess to be the happiest of all happy women, and thus they glide along through the thoroughfares of society with a lying tongue and an aching heart.

I wish these had enough vitality of soul and enough energy of character to rise superior to the circumstances around them, and make some approach to their own ideal. I know this is asking them to martyrize themselves. But could they see the beauty and the glory that will invest the future woman, when she shall have her proper place among the children of the Father; when she shall infuse her love, her moral perceptions, her sense of justice, into the ethics and governments of the earth; when she shall be united to man in a Divine harmony, and her children shall go forth to bless all coming generations, they would regard martyrdom but dust in the balance compared with such blessing. And when the world shall see the moral grandeur, the sublime position of a race redeemed by the sanctifying influences of this Divine harmony, it will weave for them a brighter chaplet than it has ever woven for any of its martyrs who have suffered at the stake. (Loud applause).

Rev. BERIAH GREEN, of Whitesboro', N. Y., was next introduced, and said:

It is not, I suppose, at all the design of this platform in any way to abolish what the grammarians call "the distinction of sex"; and when we speak of "woman's rights," we admit, in the very language which is thus employed, that she is a "woman"—that that is appropriately her character—that under this name she is fitly described. Now, a comprehensive description of all the rights which any member of the human family, whoever and whatever and wherever he may be, is entitled to challenge and maintain, we have in the brief and simple expression, the right to be himself; the right to be true to the nature which he has inherited; the right to the free and full development of the powers with which he is endowed; the right to lay out those resources of which he is constructed happily, effectively, properly; the right to rise to the highest position in excellence and in blessedness to which his capacities and powers may elevate him. This is a comprehensive description of man's rights, a comprehensive description of woman's rights, and a comprehensive description of human rights, under every form and phase of application of which human rights may be supposed capable.

Now, I regard it as a repulsive feature of the age, that one sex should feel itself constrained to come forward and defend itself from the other sex; to demand a redress of the wrongs to which it may be exposed, and a vindication of the rights to which it may be entitled; for, look you! most obviously and clearly, the relation between the sexes is naturally most intimate. The one lives in and through the other. They do not make two distinct classes, most obviously and certainly. They do not in nature; they do not according to the Divine arrangement; and it always seems to me to be most absurd, and in the highest degree ungrateful, to present the subject with which we are now occupied, under any such aspect. Mankind are divided, doubtless—divided now by accident, and now by arrangement—into different classes; but to make the women one class, and the men another class, seems to me to be essentially and flagrantly absurd. (Applause). Manifestly, the grand right of man (employing the term man here not generally, but specifically), in his relations to woman, as well as in all his other relations, is to be grandly, vigorously beautiful; in every way a man ; in all the relations of life to be true to whatever may be characteristic of his nature, and to whatever may be distinctive in his sex. And what may be affirmed of him in this respect may be affirmed of his mother, of his wife, of his sister.

It is a general law of our humanity, an all-comprehensive and all-controlling principle, that we belong, as human beings, to each other. Every man belongs to the whole human family, and the whole human family belongs to every one of its members. We are mutually, as a matter of course, under the controlling influence of this great law; we are mutually to contribute, as effectively and wisely as we may, to each other's improvement and welfare. This is the great general law which lies at the very basis of our being; this is the law which asserts its majesty in the depths of our consciousness. This law has manifestly a specific and beneficent application to the relation which binds man to woman, and unites woman to man. In a natural state of things, where the ordinances of our true Father were regarded, where the principles of our existence were reverently heeded, as a matter of course, individually and generally, man would devote himself, as man, generously, magnanimously, his entire self, whatever belongs to his manhood, in every department of his being—he would devote himself, as man, to woman; and woman, on the other hand, would just as characteristically, just as nobly, just as cheerfully, just as gratefully, just as effectively, devote herself to the improvement and welfare of man ; and according to the nature of the relation which unites them, the one would supply whatever might seem to be demanded in the construction of the other. A man is never completely himself until he is united to woman, and a woman is never completely herself until she is united to man ; and thus they become a beautiful unit, playing continually into each other's hands, their hearts beating in delightful harmony with each other. This is the great fundamental law of our social existence. The very germ of the social is to be found in the sexual relations which bind men and women together, and society, in all its forms and phases, is nothing under heaven but the development, the fit, symmetrical, and full development of the germ to which I have thus referred.

As has already been intimated in the beautiful thoughts which have been expressed by those who have preceded me, the great law, which was, perhaps, as intelligibly and impressively presented by Napoleon as by any other man, giving liberty to every man to use the tools who is qualified to use them—" The tools to him who can use them ! "—or, in better language still, as it fell from the lips of the Great Teacher, " Every man according to his ability "—this great law applies with equal force to woman as to man. There have been women greatly distinguished for physical power. You remember the old story of Kate Guardinier. A distinguished wrestler, who came to lay hold of her brother, her muscular and gigantic brother, and measure strength with him, found that he was absent. " Well," says Kate, " I will wrestle with you, and if I throw you, you need not wait the return of my brother." And so she did, and he went away, fully satisfied that there was no occasion for him to wait for any more vigorous arm than Kate Guardinier wielded. Now, wherever there is a strong arm, adapt its task to its powers—that is the will of High Heaven. Wherever there are well-trained powers, let these be recognized powers, and of course the general results can not be otherwise than happy.

In regard to the great question who shall take the lead in the family or the community, let me say, that I do not care through what medium wisdom may reach me, through what medium I may secure the benefit of healthful guidance. What I want is wisdom. Wisdom, goodness, and power are the soul of all government. Wherever these are combined, there you have the results of wisdom, goodness, and power. Now, then, if the mother in a household, or even if a daughter in a household, is more distinguished for these high qualities, for these grand attainments, than any other member of that family, why, it is nothing but rebellion against God, it is nothing but gibbering madness, that would make any member of that family hesitate to avail himself of the guidance thus offered, of the light of the wisdom which may thus be poured around him. In God's name, give me wisdom, give me genuine power, give me magnanimity!—as to the incidents of the matter, I do not insist upon them. Whether it be through my father or my mother that true guidance is afforded, whether it be by my wife or my daughter that good counsel is offered, very clearly, to reject these is to spurn the kindness of benignant Heaven.

WENDELL PHILLIPS said:—We are here to enforce, on the consideration of the civil state, those elements of power which have already made the social state. You do not find it necessary to-day to say to a husband, "Your wife has a right to read"; or necessary to say to Dickens, "You have as many women over your pages as men." You do not find it necessary to say to the male members of a church that the women members have a right to change their creed. All that is settled; nobody contests it. If a man stood up here and said, "I am a Calvinist, and therefore my wife is bound to be one," you would send him to a lunatic asylum. You would say, "Poor man! don't judge him by what he says; he don't mean it." But law is halting back just where that old civilization was; we want to change it.

We are not doing anything new. There is no fanaticism about it. We are merely extending the area of liberty—nothing else. We have made great progress. The law passed at the last session of the New York Legislature grants, in fact, the whole question. The moment you grant us anything, we have gained the whole. You can not stop with an inconsistent statute-book. A man is uneasy who is inconsistent. As Thomas Fuller says, "You can not make one side of the face laugh, and the other cry!" You can not have one-half your statute-book Jewish, and the other Christian; one-half of the statute-book Oriental, the other Saxon. You have granted that woman may be hung, therefore you must grant that woman may vote. You have granted that she may be taxed, therefore, on republican principles, you must grant that she ought to have a voice in fixing the laws of taxation—and this is, in fact, all that we claim—the whole of it.

Now, I want to consider some of the objections that are made to this claim. Men say, "Woman is not fit to vote; she does not know enough; she has not sense enough to vote." I take this idea of the ballot as the Gibraltar of our claim, for this reason, because I am speaking in a democracy; I am speaking under republican institutions. The rule of despotism is that one class is made to protect the other; that the rich, the noble, the educated are a sort of probate court, to take care of the poor, the ignorant, and the common classes. Our fathers got rid of all that. They knocked it on the head by the simple principle, that no class is safe, unless government is so arranged that each class has in its own hands the means of protecting itself. That is the idea of republics. The Briton says to the poor man, "Be content; I am worth five millions, and I will protect you." And America says, "Thank you, sir; I had rather take care of myself!"—and that is the essence of democracy. (Applause). It is the corner-stone of progress, also; because, the moment you have admitted that poor ignorant heart as an element of the government, able to mold your institutions, those five millions of dollars, feeling that their cradle is not safe and their life is in peril, unless that heart is bulwarked with education and informed with morality, selfishness dictates that wealth and education should do its utmost to educate poverty and hold up weakness—and that is the philosophy of democratic institutions. (Applause). I am speaking in a republic which admits the principle that the poor are not to be protected by the rich, but to have the means of protecting themselves. So, too, the ignorant; so, too, races. The Irish are not to trust to the sense of justice in the Saxon; the German is not to trust to the native-born citizen; the Catholic is not to trust to the Protestant; but all sects, all classes, are to hold in their own hands the scepter—the American scepter—of the ballot, which protects each class. We claim it, therefore, for woman. The reply is, that woman has not got sense enough. If she has not, so much the more shame for your public-schools—educate her! For you will not say that woman naturally has not mind enough. If God did not give her mind enough, then you are brutes, for you say to her: "Madam, you have sense enough to earn your own living—don't come to us!" You make her earn her own bread, and, if she has sense enough to do that, she has enough to say whether Fernando Wood or Governor Morgan shall take one cent out of every hundred to pay for fireworks. When you hold her up in both hands, and say, "Let me work for you! Don't move one of your dainty fingers! We will pour wealth into your lap, and be ye clothed in satin and velvet, every daughter of Eve!"—then you will be consistent in saying that woman has not sense enough to vote. But if she has sense enough to work, to depend for her bread on her work, she has sense enough to vote. . . . .

But men say it would be very indelicate for woman to go to the ballot-box or sit in the Legislature. Well, what would she see there? Why, she would see men. (Laughter). She sees men now. In "Cranford Village," that sweet little sketch by Mrs. Gaskill, one of the characters says, "I know these men—my father was a man." (Laughter). I think every woman can say the same. She meets men now; she could meet nothing but men at the ballot-box, or, if she meets brutes, they ought not to be there. (Applause). Indelicate for her to go to the ballot-box!—but you may walk up and down Broadway any time from nine o'clock in the morning until nine at night, and you will find about equal numbers of men and women crowding that thoroughfare, which is never still. You may get into an omnibus—women are there, crowding us out, sometimes. (Laughter). You can not go into a theater without being crowded to death by two women to one man. If you go to the lyceum, woman is there. I have stood on this very platform, and seen as many women as men before me, and one time, at least, when they could not have met any worse men at the ballot-box than they met in this hall. (Laughter and applause). You may go to church, and you will find her facing men of all classes—ignorant and wise, saints and sinners. I do not know anywhere that woman is not. It is too late now to say that she can not go to the ballot-box. Go back to Turkey, and shut her up in a harem ; go back to Greece, and shut her up in the private apartments of women ; go back to the old Oriental phases of civilization, that never allowed woman's eyes to light a man's pathway, unless he owned her, and you are consistent ; but you see, we have broken down the bulwark, centuries ago. You know they used to let a man be hung in public, and said that it was for the sake of the example. They got ashamed of it, and banished the gallows to the jail-yard, and allowed only twelve men to witness an execution. It is too late to say that you hang men for the example, because the example you are ashamed to have public can not be a wholesome example. So it is with this question of woman. You have granted so much, that you have left yourselves no ground to stand on. My dear, delicate friend, you are out of your sphere ; you ought to be in Turkey. My dear, religiously, scrupulously fashionable, exquisitely anxious hearer, fearful lest your wife, or daughter, or sister shall be sullied by looking into your neighbors' faces at the ballot-box, you do not belong to the century that has ballot-boxes. You belong to the century of Tamerlane and Timour the Tartar; you belong to China, where the women have no feet, because it is not meant that they shall walk. You belong anywhere but in America ; and if you want an answer, walk down Broadway, and meet a hundred thousand petticoats, and they are a hundred thousand answers ; for if woman can walk the streets, she can go to the ballot-box, and any reason of indelicacy that forbids the one covers the other.

Men say, "Why do you come here ? What good are you going to do ? You do nothing but talk." Oh, yes, we have done a great deal besides talk ! But suppose we had done nothing but talk ? I saw a poor man the other day, and said he (speaking of a certain period in his life), "I felt very friendless and alone—I had only God with me"; and he seemed to think that was not much. And so thirty millions of thinking, reading people are constantly throwing it in the teeth of reformers that they rely upon talk ! What is talk ? Why, it is the representative of brains. And what is the characteristic glory of the nineteenth century ? That it is ruled by brains, and not by muscle; that rifles are gone by, and ideas have come in; and, of course, in such an era, talk is the fountain-head of all things. But we have done a great deal. In the first place, you will meet dozens of men who say, "Oh, woman's right to property, the right of the wife to her own earnings, we grant that; we always thought that; we have had that idea for a dozen years." I met a man the other day in the cars, and we read the statute of your New York Legislature. "Why," said he, "that is nothing; I have assented to that for these fifteen years." All I could say to that was this: "This agitation has either given you the idea, or it has given you the courage to utter it, for nobody ever heard it from you until to-day." . . . .

What do we toil for ? Why, my friends, I do not care much whether a woman actually goes to the ballot-box and votes—that is a slight matter; and I shall not wait, either, to know whether every woman in this audience wants to vote. Some of you were saying to-day, in these very seats, coming here out of mere curiosity, to see what certain fanatics could find to say, "Why, I don't want any more rights; I have got rights enough." Many a lady, whose husband is what he ought to be, whose father is what fathers ought to be, feeling no want unsupplied, is ready to say, "I have all the rights I want." So the daughter of Louis Sixteenth, in the troublous time of 1791, when somebody told her that the people were starving in the streets of Paris, exclaimed, "What fools! I would eat bread first!" Thus wealth, comfort, and ease say, "I have rights enough." Nobody doubted it, madam! But the question is not of you; the question is of some houseless wife of a drunkard; the question is of some ground-down daughter of toil, whose earnings are filched from her by the rum debts of a selfishness which the law makes to have a right over her, in the person of a husband. The question is not of you, it is of some friendless woman of twenty, standing at the door of the world, educated, capable, desirous of serving her time and her race, and saying, "Where shall I use these talents? How shall I earn bread?" And orthodox society, cabined and cribbed in St. Paul, cries out, "Go sew, jade! We have no other channel for you. Go to the needle, or wear yourself to death as a school-mistress." We come here to endeavor to convince you, and so to shape our institutions that public opinion, following in the wake, shall be willing to open channels for the agreeable and profitable occupation of women as much as for men. People blame the shirt-makers and tailors because they pay two cents where they ought to pay fifty. It is not their fault. They are nothing but the weathercocks, and society is the wind. Trade does not grow out of the Sermon on the Mount; merchants never have any hearts, they have only ledgers; two per cent. a month is their Sermon on the Mount, and a balance on the wrong side of the ledger is their demonstration. (Laughter). Nobody finds fault with them for it. Everything according to the law of its life. A man pays as much for making shirts or coats as it is necessary to pay, and he would be a fool and a bankrupt if he paid any more. He needs only a hundred workwomen; there are a thousand women standing at his door saying, "Give us work; and if it is worth ten cents to do it, we will do it for two"; and a hundred get the work, and nine hundred are turned into the street, to drag down this city into the pit that it deserves. (Loud applause).

Now, what is the remedy? To take that tailor by the throat, and gibbet him in *The New York Tribune?* Not at all; it does the women no good, and he does not deserve it. I will tell you what is to be done. Behind the door at which those women stand asking for work, on one side stands an orthodox disciple of St. Paul, and on the other a dainty exquisite; and the one says, it is not religious, and the other says, it is not fashionable, for woman to be anything but a drudge. Now, strangle the one in his own creed, and smother the other in his own perfumes, and give to those thousand women freedom to toil. Let public opinion only grant that, like their thousand brothers, those thousand women may go out, and wherever they find work to do, do it, without a stigma being set upon them. Let the educated girl of twenty have the same liberty to use the pen, to practice law, to write books, to attend the telegraph, to go into the artist's studio, to serve in a library, to tend in a gallery of art, to do anything that her brother can do. St. Paul is dead and rotten, and ought to be forgotten — (Applause, laughter, and a few hisses) —so far as this doctrine goes, mark you ! for his is the noblest figure in all history, except that of Christ, the broadest and most masterly intellect of any age; but he was a Jew and not a Christian; he lived under Jewish civilization and not ours, and was speaking by his own light, and not by inspiration of God.

This is all we claim; and we claim the ballot for this reason; the moment you give woman power, that moment men will see to it that she has the way cleared for her. There are two sources of power: one is civil, the ballot; the other is physical, the rifle. I do not believe that the upper classes—education, wealth, aristocracy, conservatism—the men that are in—ever yielded, except to fear. I think the history of the race shows that the upper classes never granted a privilege to the lower out of love. As Jeremy Bentham says, "The upper classes never yielded a privilege without being bullied out of it." When man rises in revolution, with the sword in his right hand, trembling wealth and conservatism say, "What do you want ? Take it; but grant me my life." The Duke of Tuscany, Elizabeth Barrett Browning has told us, swore to a dozen constitutions when the Tuscans stood armed in the streets of Florence, and he forgot them when the Austrians came in and took the rifles out of the Tuscans' hands. You must force the upper classes to do justice by physical or some other power. The age of physical power is gone, and we want to put ballots into the hands of women. . . . .

Political economy puts in every man's hand, by the labor of half a day, money enough to be drunk a week. There is one temptation, dragging down the possibility of self-government into the pit of imbruted humanity; and on the other side, is that hideous problem of modern civilized life—prostitution—born of orthodox scruples and aristocratic fastidiousness—born of that fastidious denial of the right of woman to choose her own work, and, like her brother, to satiate her ambition, her love of luxury, her love of material gratifications, by fair wages for fair work. As long as you deny it, as long as the pulpit covers with its fastidious orthodoxy this question from the consideration of the public, it is but a concealed brothel, although it calls itself an orthodox pulpit. (Applause and hisses). I know what I say; your hisses can not change it. Go, clean out the Gehenna of New York ! (Applause). Go, sweep the Augean stable that makes New York the lazar-house of corruption ! You know that on one side or the other of these temptations lies very much of the evil of modern civilized life. You know that before them, statesmanship folds its hands in despair. Here is a method by which to take care of at least one. Give men fair wages, and ninety-nine out of a hundred will disdain to steal. The way to prevent dishonesty is to let every man have a field for his work, and honest wages; the way to prevent licentiousness is to give to woman's capacity free play. Give to the higher powers activity, and they will choke down the animal. The man who loves thinking, disdains to be the victim of appetite. It is a law of our nature.

45

Give a hundred women honest wages for capacity and toil, and ninety-nine out of the hundred will disdain to win it by vice. That is a cure for licentiousness. (Applause).

I wish to put into our civil life the element of woman's right to shape the laws, for all our social life copies largely from the statute-book. Let woman dictate at the capital, let her say to Wall Street, "My votes on finance are to make stocks rise and fall," and Wall Street will say to Columbia College, "Open your classes to woman; it needs be that she should learn." The moment you give her the ballot, you take bonds of wealth and fashion and conservatism, that they will educate this power, which is holding their interest in its right hand. I want to spike the gun of selfishness; or rather, I want to double-shot the cannon of selfishness. Let Wall Street say, "Look you ! whether the New York Central stock shall have a toll placed upon it, whether my million shares shall be worth sixty cents in the market or eighty, depends upon whether certain women up there at Albany know the laws of trade and the secrets of political economy"—and Wall Street will say, "Get out of the way, Dr. Adams !—absent yourself, Dr. Spring !--we don't care for Jewish prejudices; these women must have education !" (Loud applause). Show me the necessity in civil life, and I will find you forty thousand pulpits that will say St. Paul meant just that. (Renewed applause). Now, I am orthodox; I believe in the Bible; I reverence St. Paul; I believe his was the most masterly intellect that God ever gave to the race; I believe he was the connecting link, the bridge, by which the Asiatic and European mind were joined; I believe that Plato ministers at his feet; but, after all, he was a man, and not God. (Applause). He was limited, and made mistakes. You can not anchor this western continent to the Jewish footstool of St. Paul; and, after all, that is the difficulty—religious prejudice. It is not fashion—we shall beat it; it is not the fastidiousness of the exquisite—we shall smother it; it is the religious prejudice, borrowed from a mistaken interpretation of the New Testament. That is the real Gibraltar with which we are to grapple, and my argument with that is simply this: You left it when you founded a republic; you left it when you inaugurated Western civilization; we must grow out of one root.

Let me, in closing, show you, by one single anecdote, how mean a thing a man can be. You have heard of Mrs. Norton, "the woman Byron," as critics call her—the granddaughter of Sheridan, and the one on whose shoulders his mantle has rested—a genius by right of inheritance and by God's own gift. Perhaps you may remember that when the Tories wanted to break down the reform administration of Lord Melbourne, they brought her husband to feign to believe his wife unfaithful, and to sue her before a jury. He did so, brought an action, and an English jury said she was innocent ; and his own counsel has since admitted, in writing, under his own signature, that during the time he prosecuted that trial, the Honorable Mr. Norton (for so he is in the Herald's Book) confessed all the time that he did not believe a word against his wife, and knew she was innocent. She is a writer. The profits of her books, by the law of England, belong to her husband. She has not lived with him—of course not, for she is a woman !—since that trial; but the brute goes every six months to John Murray, and eats the profits of the brain of the wife whom he tried to disgrace. (Loud cries of "shame," "shame"). And the law of England says it is right; the orthodox pulpit says, "If you change it, it will be the pulling down of the stars and St. Paul." I do not believe that the Honorable Mr. Norton is half as near to the mind of St. Paul as the Honorable Mrs. Norton. I go, therefore, for woman having her right to her brain, to her hands, to her toil, to her ballot. "The tools to him that can use them"—and let God settle the rest. If He made it just that we should have democratic institutions, then He made it just that everybody who is to suffer under the law should have a voice in making it; and if it is indelicate for woman to vote, then let Him stop making women (applause and laughter), because republicanism and such women are not consistent. I say it reverently; and I only say it to show you the absurdity. Why, my dear man and woman, we are not to help God govern the world by telling lies ! He can take care of it Himself. If He made it just, you may be certain that He saw to it that it should be delicate; and you need not insert your little tiny roots of fastidious delicacy into the great giant rifts of God's world—they are only in the way. (Applause).

The first evening session was called to order at 7½ o'clock. The President in the chair. The audience was very large, the hall being uncomfortably full, and the attention unremitting and profound. The most excellent order was preserved ; the meeting, in this respect, furnishing a marked and gratifying contrast with the evening sessions of the last two years at Mozart Hall.

Mrs. Rose, from the Business Committee, presented a series of resolutions*, which were read by Miss Anthony. Elizabeth Cady

---

* *Resolved*, That inasmuch as man, in the progress of his development, found that at each advancing step new wants demanded new rights, and naturally walked out of those places, customs, creeds, and laws that in any way crippled and trammeled his freedom of thought, word, or action, it is his duty to stand aside and leave to woman the same rights—to grow up into whatever the laws of her being demand.

Resolved, That inasmuch as on woman are imposed by her Creator the duties of self-support and self-defense, and by government the responsibilities of taxation and penalties of violated law, she should be protected in her natural, inalienable rights, and secured in all the privileges of citizenship.

Resolved, That we demand a full recognition of our equal rights, civil and political—no special legislation can satisfy us—the enjoyment of a right to-day is no security that it will be continued to-morrow, so long as it is granted to us by a privileged class, and not secured to us as a sacred right.

WHEREAS, the essence of republican liberty is the principle that no class shall depend for its rights on the mercy or justice of any other class, therefore,

Resolved, That woman demands her right to the jury-box and the ballot, that she may have, as man has, the means of her own protection in her own hands.

Resolved, That woman, in consenting to remain in any organization or church where she has no voice in the choice of officers, trustees, or pastor—no right of protest against false doctrines or action—is wanting in a proper self-respect, in that dignity which, as a philanthropist and a Christian, she should ever manifest.

Stanton was the first speaker of the evening. By particular request she gave the same address recently delivered before the Legislature at Albany, and was followed by Ernestine L. Rose with one of her logical and convincing arguments.

Susan B. Anthony then read the following letters:

LETTER FROM HON. GERRIT SMITH.

ELIZABETH CADY STANTON: PETERBORO', *May* 3, 1860.

MY VERY DEAR COUSIN:—It is proper that one of the first letters which I write in my new life, should be to the cousin whose views are most in harmony with my own. I call it my new life, because I have come up into it from the gates of death. May it prove a new life also, in being a far better and nobler one than that which I had hitherto lived !

I wake up with joy to see my old fellow-laborers still in their work of honoring God, in benefiting and blessing man. Your own zeal for truth is unabated. I see that you are still laboring to free the slave from his chains, and woman from her social, civil, and political disabilities; and to preserve both man and woman from defiling and debasing themselves with intoxicating liquors and tobacco. Precious reforms are these which have enlisted your powers ! It is true that they do not cover the whole ground of religious duty. But it is also true that the religion, which, like the current one, opposes or ignores them all, is spurious; and so, too, that the religion which opposes or ignores any one of them is always sadly defective, if not always spurious.

Please add the inclosed draft for $25 to the fund for serving the cause of woman's rights. To no better cause can money, time, or talents be appropriated. I am in high health, compared with any I have enjoyed since the succession of my frightful diseases, begun two and a half years ago. My nerves, however, are still weak, and most of the year 1859 is still full of confusion and darkness to me.

Your friend and cousin, GERRIT SMITH.

LETTER FROM FRANCIS JACKSON, ESQ.

LUCY STONE: BOSTON, *May* 6, 1860.

DEAR FRIEND:—I intend to be at the annual meeting of the American Anti-Slavery Society, but my engagements are such that I shall not stop

---

Resolved, That we from this platform instruct our legal representatives to make no more appropriations to colleges for boys exclusively. Now that we are large property holders and tax-payers, we protest against the injustice of being compelled to build and endow colleges into which we are forbidden to enter.

Resolved, That we advise women to apply to the trustees and heads of public libraries, galleries of art, and similar institutions, for employment as clerks and attendants, thus securing to themselves, when admitted, a more liberal means of support, and furnishing a stepping-stone to other occupations.

Resolved, That we return thanks to the Legislature of New York for its acts of justice to woman during the last session. But the work is not yet done. We still claim the ballot, the right of trial by a jury of our own peers, the control and custody of our persons in marriage, and an equal right to the joint earnings of the co-partnership. The geographical position and political power of New York make her example supreme.; hence we feel assured that when she is right on this question, our work is done.

long enough in New York to attend your meeting of Woman's Rights. I herewith inclose you $20 to help the cause along.   FRANCIS JACKSON.

Hon. Erastus D. Culver, of Brooklyn, New York, being present among that portion of the audience seated upon the platform, was recognized and loudly called for, and came forward in response to the call, and spoke as follows:

Mrs. PRESIDENT, LADIES, AND GENTLEMEN:—They used to have, in old times, in the country where I was brought up, a minister, who, after delivering his sermon, would call upon some brother to get up and make the application. Now, I want to give you an application of what I have heard to-night, and there seems to be a sort of providence in it. This very day, since I opened my court this morning, three cases have come in review before me, each one of them directly connected with the subject matter of this evening's deliberations, and with the law which has been alluded to to-night. The first was the case of a woman who had brought a suit, in conjunction with her husband (as she had to do, as the law was) against the city of Brooklyn, for personal injuries, received by falling into a hole; and on the first trial, it was found very difficult to make out the case, because we were obliged to exclude the woman as a witness. If her husband had fallen into that hole, and hurt his side, making him a cripple for life, he might have brought a suit, and he would have been by law a competent witness: but his wife was not; and as he was not with her at the time of the accident, of course he could not testify. To-day the case came on again, and they were making a very poor show at proving the accident, when the lawyer for the lady said, "I will offer the lady as a witness." The other lawyer started up (he is an old fogy, who does not keep up with the times) and said, "She is a party out of sight in law; in law, she is one of the invisibles"; when, to my great surprise and joy (for I had lost track of it myself) the lady's lawyer pulled out from his pocket a slip from a newspaper, which contained the noble law of the 20th of March, 1860, and that law says that "any married woman may bring and maintain an action in her own name for damages against any person or body corporate for any injury to her person or character." That obviated the difficulty. The law was handed to the opposite lawyer, and when he had read it through, with a frown on his face, he said, ill-naturedly, "If your honor please, it is so; they have emancipated the women from all obligations to their husbands." Now, just look at that old presumption of the law, that a married woman could not tell the truth, even in a matter about which she knew better than any one else, on the ground that she was a *feme covert*, and was *nil*—nothing!

That was one case. Another was that of a woman who made a bitter complaint against her husband, saying that he had become a drunkard, and was squandering her estate, and threatened to take their two children away. I signed the writ, and the husband and two children were brought in. He addressed the Court in his own defence, and I have not heard such eloquence in court for many a year. He told how he loved his wife, how devoted he was, and that it would ruin him for ever to be separated from her. He said to his lawyer, "Do you keep still; I can talk better than you can." "Now," said he to the Court, "I adjure you, by the feelings of a father and a man, restore to me my wife and children ! Do not disgrace me in this way !" All present were deeply affected, and it seemed as if he had carried the people with him, whether he had the Court or not. His speech sounded admirably; but I am sorry to say, that when his wife's turn came, she had not spoken five minutes before she had taken the wind entirely out of his sails. "I was married," she said, "eleven years ago, and not a fortnight after, he beat me, and left his bruises upon me. He has pawned all my clothes, everything I have in the house has been pledged, and I am left destitute; and here, your honor, are the wounds upon my head, here are the bruises that he has left. I can not live with him any longer; I can not be reconciled, until he abjures rum and comes home resolved to live a sober life." "Well," said the husband's lawyer, "we claim our paramount rights— that the father shall have the custody of the children." Then came up this very law again, and this lawyer was as much surprised as the one to whom I first referred. There is a clause in that law which declares that, from this time forward, there shall be no such thing as "paramount rights." It is declared in that statute that from this day "every married woman is constituted and declared to be the joint guardian of her children, with equal powers, rights, and duties in regard to them, with her husband." In view of that law, I said, "I can not take the children away from the mother; she has just as much right to them as her husband, and if she says she must have them, I will let her have them." (Loud applause).

Now, ladies and gentlemen, I have never been identified with this Woman's Rights movement, but I tell you what it is, we have got to admit some things. We have got to admit that these indefatigable laborers, amid obloquy and reproach, in Church and State, by buffoons and by men, have at last set the under-current in motion. The statute-book is their vindication to-night. The last measure passed has relieved woman, to a great extent, from the disabilities under which she was placed. I am one who believes that she may go forward. There will come a time, friends, when we shall see the ballot-box open, and one particular department (as we have at the post-office) where the ladies will all march up and vote. (Applause, and a few hisses). Now, you men that hiss, you would like to have them help you elect your candidate this year, wouldn't you ? I wish most sincerely that they could help elect our Republican candidate. (Applause). There is to be a still further advance in this matter. I do not think it at all degrading to say, that there will come a time when ladies will sit in the jury-box, to pass upon certain cases that come particularly within their sphere; and I will say (now that I am off the bench) that they would make better judges than some who are on the benches now. (Laughter and applause).

Mrs. Rose added: I have been most happy to hear the remarks of Judge Culver. Who can doubt of our success, when judges, and noble ones, too—for it is only noble ones who are ready to identify themselves with this cause before it becomes fully successful—come forward to endorse our movement ! All we now have to do is, to continue in the good cause, and, depend upon it, the time will come when we shall look back to this last spring's enactment of the Legislature, as the commencement of the real " good time coming." But we have yet some duties to perform. What we have gained, has not been gained without labor. Freedom, my friends, does not come from the clouds, like a meteor; it does not bloom in one night; it does not come without great efforts and great sacrifices; all who love liberty, have to labor for it. We expect that from this hour, you will all help us to work out that glorious problem, whether or not woman can govern herself quite as well as man can govern her. Give us the elective franchise, and we ask for no more. When we have obtained that, it shall be our fault if we do not take all the rights we now claim. (Applause).

ELIZABETH JONES said: The adoption of the plans now proposed would place woman above the necessity of any mercenary marriages. She could leave her father's home if she didn't like it, and engage in business and support herself. Who cared for the husband of Jenny Lind, or of Mrs. Norton ? It was not necessary for Florence Nightingale, Harriet Hosmer, or Elizabeth Blackwell to marry to secure the world's consideration. The wife should have equal and joint proprietorship with her husband. Two brothers, John and Henry, go to California and form a partnership; John cooks while Henry digs. Henry finds one day a lump of gold worth a hundred dollars. Will he pay John fifty cents for cooking, and take the rest himself ? Of course not; he will divide with him. So the husband should regard the property that he accumulates as owned by his wife jointly and equally with himself. Woman would have her rights, let man do what he might. She asked no rights from man, for man had none to give her—none to spare from himself. Satan promised Jesus all the kingdoms of the world, and the glory of them, if He would fall down and worship him; but it was well known that the poor devil had not a foot to give. And so man could give no rights to woman. She was born with rights, and only wanted man to recognize them. Her purpose was to demand them persistently, or, if need be, like the Prince of Orange, die in the last ditch before she surrendered them. (Applause).

Rev. Samuel Longfellow, of Brooklyn, N. Y., brother of the poet, was next introduced, and spoke as follows:

Mrs. PRESIDENT:—It might seem, that on a platform like this, when a woman speaks, her presence is not merely a plea and an argument, but also a proof. When a woman speaks, and speaks well, speaks so as to interest and move and persuade men, there is no need of any argument back of that to prove that she has the liberty and the right, and that it is a part of her sphere to do it. She has done it; and that of itself is the whole argument—both premise and conclusion in one. And I think if there were none but men present here, it would be better that only women should speak; for there is a subtle power which God implanted from the first in woman over man, so that the thought of her mind and the tone of her voice are more powerful over us than almost any man, be he eloquent as he may; but not only men are here, but women, also; and as our friend who has just spoken has addressed herself to men, I will address myself to women.

I have often thought that the obstacle in the way of a full allowance and recognition of woman's right to stand side by side with man in all the departments of life, and to add her feminine influence and fiber twined in with man's influence and fiber, in all things that are thought and done, that the obstacle lay more in woman than in man. I have often thought that men were more willing to accept these ideas and grant these claims than women were even to make the claims for themselves; and I have no doubt that those women who have labored, through so much difficulty, through so much scorn and obloquy, in behalf of these simple rights, will tell you that they have often found the greatest opposition among their own sex.

The simple proposition which, it seems to me, includes the whole of this matter, is, what I should call a self-evident truth—that in all departments of life, men and women, made from the first to be co-mates and partners, should stand side by side, and work hand to hand. Not because men and women are identical, not because they are not different, but because they are different; because each has a special quality running through the whole organization of the man and the woman, which quality is needed to make a complete manhood and womanhood. And then there is another proposition, which is this: that whatever any human being can do well, that being has a right to do, and the ability of any person marks the sphere of that person. ("Hear"—"hear"). This, I say, I count to be strictly a self-evident proposition. (Applause). If you want to know what the level of water is at any particular spot upon the face of the earth, you do not force the water up with a force-pump, you do not build a great reservoir with high stone walls, to hold it, you simply leave it alone, and it finds its level. So, if you want to know what is the true sphere of man or woman, just leave the man or the woman alone, and the natural law, and the divine law, which can not be broken, and which are as sure in the moral and human world as they are in the external world, will settle the matter. If you want to know, really and sincerely, what woman's sphere is, leave her unhampered and untrammeled, and her own powers will find that sphere. She may make mistakes, and try, as man often does, to do things which she can not, but the experiment will settle the matter; and nothing can be more absurd than for man, especially, *a priori*, to establish the limits which shall bound woman's sphere, or for woman, as a mere matter of speculation, to debate what her sphere shall be, since the natural laws are revealed, not to speculation, but to action.

The obstacle to the progress of the simple ideas which underlie this movement, and to their being carried out into practice, I take to be nothing else than this—the *vis inertiæ* of prejudice, the dead-weight of the customary and familiar—that which has been; and that is simply the dead-weight which hangs upon the wheels of every movement of reform. A thing has not not been, it is not customary, it is strange, it disturbs our ordinary modes of thought, and we will have nothing to do with it. When you are driving with your carriage along the track of the horse-railroad, your wheels run very smoothly; but if you are obliged to turn out, it wrenches the wheels and jars your carriage; and the deeper the ruts, the more disturbance and trouble will you have if you are obliged to move out of them. We all move in the ruts of habit and custom; and it disturbs and troubles us to be asked to move out of them—to do or think anything unusual. This *vis inertiæ* is what stands in the way, first and most of all, of the success of this movement, of the reception of these ideas, as of every other movement of reform. And this dead-weight of prejudice, this *vis inertiæ* of old and traditional thought, is concentrated in this phrase, uttered with tones of indifference or with tones of self-satisfaction and pride, "I think, for my part, that woman's sphere is home." This phrase you hear everywhere—in the parlors, in the streets, in conventions, and in pulpits, and read in books— "Woman's sphere is home!" (Applause). "Well, is it not?" some one asks among you, perhaps. Now, I have no desire to deny that the home is for woman, as for man, the most noble sphere of life. I am sure that there is not one who will stand upon this platform, or speak or write in this cause, who will deny that; not one but will declare that they count home a sacred and noble sphere for woman, as for man—a sphere for grand and high influence, for noble consecration and devoted work; whether it be the simple duties of house-keeping, which a high and cultivated soul can make beautiful by the spirit in which they are done—or whether it be the care of children and the training up of the youthful mind into noble thought and preparation for noble action, which is a sphere so high, that none of us, perhaps, know how high it is—or whether it be as the friend and comforter, encourager and inspirer, to all things noble in thought and grand in action, of man. But if home be the sphere of woman—as none of us deny or doubt for a moment—if it be a sphere for woman high and noble, and to some altogether sufficient to bound their capacities and bound their desires, it is also a sphere for man—a sphere which he altogether too much neglects, not knowing how high and noble it is, and that his duty lies at home, however much he ignores it, with his wife and with his children. But when it is said that home is woman's only sphere—and that is what is meant—it is simply a mistake; it is simply a narrow statement. Take the very woman who says this. As she passes along the street, she sees a placard for a Woman's Rights meeting, and with scornful lip she says, "I think woman's sphere is home"—and goes promenading up and down the street to meet acquaintances, and spends all the morning in shopping—because woman's sphere is home! (Applause and laughter). And after dinner, she says to her husband, "Where shall we go this evening?" "I think we will go to the opera," he says; and so she leaves the children with the servant, and spends half the night at the opera, because woman's sphere is home! (Laughter). On Sunday she goes to church morning and evening, because woman's sphere is home! and during the week goes to concerts and lectures and balls, perhaps, because woman's sphere is home! This is the answer to be given to all those who claim that woman can do nothing but attend to household affairs, or to those duties which are called especially the duties of home. No woman attends to these utterly. No woman need neglect the duties of home in order to fulfill duties in a wider sphere. It takes as much time to sit and hear a lecture as to stand and deliver it; to sit and hear a concert as to stand before the audience and sing.

There is time enough, and if one has a talent for either, that is the sphere for him or her.

But when this claim is made that woman's sphere is at home, it is quite forgotten how many women there are who have not imposed upon them the cares of a home; what numbers there are who are not at the head of families; what numbers there are who have not these domestic ties to call upon them for effort; and it is also forgotten how many there are who can not possibly always remain at home, because upon their going forth depends the getting of the money that shall provide for the wants of the home—that shall bring the clothing and the bread that are to supply the home's outward wants. To do this, these women must go from their homes; and oh! hundreds and thousands of working-women in this city are women whose sphere can not be home alone. It is upon this ground that there is pressed home upon us the consideration of the demands for a wider sphere of work for woman, that she shall not be cut off from this and that means of getting a living, which are freely opened to man, but from which woman is excluded, through prejudices and fears. Let the wide sphere of work be opened to woman, that she may select from it, just as man does, whatever her strength and skill are sufficient for her to accomplish. She is not to be shut up, it is claimed, and justly, to a few poor, small, and wretchedly-paid employments, by which she can, with her own hands and skill, gain a living, but is to be allowed and encouraged to open to herself every variety of employment wherein she shall be paid an equal sum with that which man is paid for doing the same work; a claim which has been too long ignored and set aside, but which will press itself until its manifest justice shall compel its admission. The woman who has not the care of a family is to be encouraged to expand her powers, her talents, and genius, and to apply them to the purpose of securing a livelihood, without any obstacle whatever being put in the way; for when we talk of man's sphere and woman's sphere, it is all a farce. There is no one sphere fitted for all men, any more than for all women. Some men can not make good business men, and must fail if they try; and some men can not possibly write books, or preach, or speak in public, and must fail if they try. They do not try, because they have wisdom enough to know that they could not succeed. So it will be with women. People commonly think, that if you grant this claim of woman's right to make her own sphere, that all women will immediately rush into public speaking, and be crowding to the platform, or into the pulpit, or writing books, or carving statues, or painting pictures. There is not the slightest danger of that. Of course, if either of these is the true sphere of any woman, she ought to go there; but those who have not a talent for these things will not try them.

If the right to vote was granted to woman—from which I do not see how we can escape—I do not suppose that all women would go to the polls, for I know that many men do not, although they have much to say about the great privilege which every man enjoys, of having a voice in the government, and the responsibility of a voter. Things would remain much as now if to-morrow every obstacle were removed from woman's path. Only gradually would the change occur, as individual after individual found larger room for action than that in which she is now pent. As this discussion has been going on, woman after woman has been enlarging the sphere allowed her. Women write admirable books, paint admirable pictures, chisel admirable statues, make most excellent and well-instructed physicians. Women are doing everything which it is now claimed they have the right to do, except voting, which they are not yet permitted to do ; and I am not sure, in regard to that, that the best plan would not be, as our Platonic friend in New England once said, for the women to go quietly and vote, without waiting to be asked or told that they would be permitted to do so. To be sure, he said, their votes could not be counted, but there they would be, and they would have their force. He thought that the moral influence of those votes would go a great ways, and it is quite possible that they would have that effect. But I hope, whether in that way or some other—perhaps before that step is taken—men will be led to see, that in the sphere of politics, as well as in the sphere of literature and art, woman's influence is needed; and all the objections that are made to woman's voting are of the most trivial character, that would not stand a day before any serious desire that she should have her simple right in this matter, so far as she chooses to claim it. And her right lies simply in these old propositions, so dear to our fathers—upon which they stood and fought an eight years' war--"Taxation without representation is tyranny," and that "all just powers of government are derived from the consent of the governed." And there is nothing in these two propositions which confines their application to man ; there is nothing in them which does not demand that woman should be included as well as man. Wherever woman is taxed, she has a right to vote, by this fundamental principle of our government ; and wherever she is legislated for and governed, she is entitled to a voice in that legislation and government.

This is a very simple matter. To-day, it is only a question of time, when, from a matter of speculation, it will become a matter of fact, the details of which can be managed as well as anything in the world. Women will not be obliged to enter into a scramble with dirty and fighting men at the polls—though it is possible, if she went where such men are, they would be put on their good manners, and be as well-behaved as anybody; but she could have a separate place to vote, and go to the polls as quietly, and with as little loss of time, as she now goes to the post-office, or walks the streets, where rough, rude men congregate, but where she has enough room to go and purchase her silks and satins and laces in Broadway. (Applause). I congratulate those who, taking an interest in this cause, espoused it when it was a great cross to bear— who took it up with the simple courage of woman, the patient perseverance of woman, and have carried it through as far as it has gone now—upon the advances which it has made, upon the opening and enlightenment of the public mind, and upon its favorable reception, spite of all the obstacles that still remain. I bid them be of good cheer, and remember that the great law of progress is a law of steps ; so that we must needs all be patient, while we must also all needs be persevering. It is but a question of time and of steps. The great psalm of human progress is (to borrow a phrase from the Hebrew Bible) a psalm of degrees. By patient steps man rises out of falsehood into truth, out of wrongs into rights. So it is with woman, as a part of humanity. Let every woman be true to this as her mission; let no woman dare to place any obstacle or coldness in the way of this movement; but let all calmly consider it, hear the arguments that are made, and allow them to have their full weight; look at the simple facts, and decide. Then we may, perhaps, all of us live to see the day when, throughout all the spheres of his life, and all the departments of his action, side by side with man and the manly quality, there shall be woman and the womanly quality, and a new Eden begin on earth. (Applause).

The President said :—Before introducing the next speaker, I want to express the gratitude which we women feel to Mr. Longfellow and the other gentlemen who have identified themselves with an unpopular and ridiculed cause. Permit me to say one word in relation to this matter of woman's sphere. There is a lady in my neighborhood, who was speaking to me not long since, in the most enthusiastic terms, of this recent law that has passed through our Legislature, and of gratitude toward Susan B. Anthony, through whose untiring exertions and executive ability, aided by two or three other women, this law has been secured. After she had expatiated for a while on this subject, her husband said, " Miss Anthony had a great deal better have been at home, taking care of her husband and children." Thank Heaven ! there is one woman who has leisure to care for others as well as herself. (Applause).

Elizabeth Cady Stanton then presented a series of resolutions,* in support of which she addressed the Convention as follows :

Mrs. PRESIDENT:—In our common law, in our whole system of jurisprudence, we find man's highest idea of right. The object of law is to secure justice. But

---

* 1. *Resolved*, That, in the language (slightly varied) of John Milton, " Those who marry intend as little to conspire their own ruin, as those who swear allegiance, and as a whole people is to an ill government, so is one man or woman to an ill marriage. If a whole people, against any authority, covenant, or statute, may, by the sovereign edict of charity, save not only their lives, but honest liberties, from unworthy bondage, as well may a married party, against any private covenant, which he or she never entered, to his or her mischief, be redeemed from unsupportable disturbances, to honest peace and just contentment."

2. *Resolved*, That all men are created equal, and all women, in their natural rights, are the equals of men, and endowed by their Creator with the same inalienable right to the pursuit of happiness.

3. *Resolved*, That any constitution, compact, or covenant between human beings, that failed to produce or promote human happiness, could not, in the nature of things, be of any force or authority ; and it would be not only a right, but a duty, to abolish it.

4. *Resolved*, That though marriage be in itself divinely founded, and is fortified as an institution by innumerable analogies in the whole kingdom of universal nature, still, a true marriage is only known by its results ; and, like the fountain, if pure, will reveal only pure manifestations. Nor need it ever be said, " What God hath joined together, let no man put asunder," for man could not put it asunder ; nor can he any more unite what God and nature have not joined together.

5. *Resolved*, That of all insulting mockeries of heavenly truth and holy law, none can be greater than that physical impotency is cause sufficient for divorce, while no amount of mental or moral or spiritual imbecility is ever to be pleaded in support of such a demand.

6. *Resolved*, That such a law was worthy those dark periods when marriage was held by the greatest doctors and priests of the Church to be a work of the flesh only, and

in,asmuch as fallible man is the maker and administrator of law, we must look for many and gross blunders in the application of its general principles to individual cases.

The science of theology, of civil, political, moral, and social life, all teach the common idea, that man ever has been, and ever must be, sacrificed to the highest good of society; the one to the many—the poor to the rich—the weak to the powerful—and all to the institutions of his own creation. Look, what thunderbolts of power man has forged in the ages for his own destruction!—at the organizations to enslave himself! And through those times of darkness, those generations of superstition, behold all along the relics of his power and skill, that stand like mile-stones, here and there, to show how far back man was great and glorious! Who can stand in those vast cathedrals of the old world, as the deep-toned organ reverberates from arch to arch, and not feel the grandeur of humanity? These are the workmanship of him, beneath whose stately dome the architect himself now bows in fear and doubt, knows not himself, and knows not God—a mere slave to symbols—and with holy water signs the Cross, whilst He who died thereon declared man God.

I repudiate the popular idea of man's degradation and total depravity. I place man above all governments, all institutions—ecclesiastical and civil—all constitutions and laws. (Applause). It is a mistaken idea, that the same law that oppresses the individual can promote the highest good of society. The best interests of a community never can require the sacrifice of one innocent being—of one sacred right. In the settlement, then, of any question, we must simply consider the highest good of the individual. It is the inalienable right of all to be happy. It is the highest duty of all to seek those conditions in life, those surroundings, which may develop what is noblest and best, remembering that the lessons of these passing hours are not for time alone, but for the ages of eternity. They tell us, in that future home—the heavenly paradise—that the human family shall be sifted out, and the good and pure shall dwell together

---

almost, if not altogether, a defilement; denied wholly to the clergy, and a second time, forbidden to all.

7. *Resolved*, That an unfortunate or ill-assorted marriage is ever a calamity, but not ever, perhaps never, a crime—and when society or government, by its laws or customs, compels its continuance, always to the grief of one of the parties, and the actual loss and damage of both, it usurps an authority never delegated to man, nor exercised by God himself.

8. *Resolved*, That observation and experience daily show how incompetent are men, as individuals, or as governments, to select partners in business, teachers for their children, ministers of their religion, or makers, adjudicators, or administrators of their laws; and as the same weakness and blindness must attend in the selection of matrimonial partners, the dictates of humanity and common sense alike show that the latter and most important contract should no more be perpetual than either or all of the former.

9. *Resolved*, That children born in these unhappy and unhallowed connections are, in the most solemn sense, of unlawful birth—the fruit of lust, but not of love—and so not of God, divinely descended, but from beneath, whence proceed all manner of evil and uncleanliness.

10. *Resolved*, That next to the calamity of such a birth to the child, is the misfortune of being trained in the atmosphere of a household where love is not the law, but where discord and bitterness abound; stamping their demoniac features on the moral nature, with all their odious peculiarities—thus continuing the race in a weakness and depravity that must be a sure precursor of its ruin, as a just penalty of long-violated law.

in peace. If that be the heavenly order, is it not our duty to render earth as near like heaven as we may?

For years, there has been before the Legislature of this State a variety of bills, asking for divorce in cases of drunkenness, insanity, desertion, cruel and brutal treatment, endangering life. My attention was called to this question very early in life, by the sufferings of a friend of my girlhood, a victim of one of those unfortunate unions, called marriage. What my great love for that young girl, and my holy intuitions, then decided to be right, has not been changed by years of experience, observation, and reason. I have pondered well these things in my heart, and ever felt the deepest interest in all that has been written and said upon the subject, and the most profound respect and loving sympathy for those heroic women, who, in the face of law and public sentiment, have dared to sunder the unholy ties of a joyless, loveless union.

If marriage is a human institution, about which man may legislate, it seems but just that he should treat this branch of his legislation with the same common-sense that he applies to all others. If it is a mere legal contract, then should it be subject to the restraints and privileges of all other contracts. A contract, to be valid in law, must be formed between parties of mature age, with an honest intention in said parties to do what they agree. The least concealment, fraud, or deception, if proved, annuls the contract. A boy can not contract for an acre of land, or a horse, until he is twenty-one, but he may contract for a wife at fourteen. If a man sell a horse, and the purchaser find in him great incompatibility of temper—a disposition to stand still when the owner is in haste to go—the sale is null and void, and the man and his horse part company. But in marriage, no matter how much fraud and deception are practiced, nor how cruelly one or both parties have been misled; no matter how young, inexperienced, or thoughtless the parties, nor how unequal their condition and position in life, the contract can not be annulled. Think of a husband telling a young and trusting girl, but one short month his wife, that he married her for her money; that those letters so precious to her, that she had read and re-read, and kissed and ⁀ished, were written by another; that their splendid home, of which, on their wedding-day, her father gave him the deed, is already in the hands of his creditors; that she must give up the elegance and luxury that now surround her, unless she can draw fresh supplies of money to meet their wants! When she told the story of her wrongs to me—the abuse to which she was subject, and the dread in which she lived—I impulsively urged her to fly from such a monster and villain, as she would before the hot breath of a ferocious beast of the wilderness. (Applause). And she did fly; and it was well with her. Many times since, as I have felt her throbbing heart against my own, she has said, "Oh, but for your love and sympathy, your encouragement, I should never have escaped from that bondage. Before I could, of myself, have found courage to break those chains my heart would have broken in the effort."

Marriage, as it now exists, must seem to all of you a mere human institution. Look through the universe of matter and mind—all God's arrangements are perfect, harmonious, and complete! There is no discord, friction, or failure in His eternal plans. Immutability, perfection, beauty, are stamped on all His laws. Love is the vital essence that pervades and permeates, from the center to the circumference, the graduating circles of all thought and action. Love is the talisman of human weal and woe—the open sesame to every human soul.

Where two beings are drawn together, by the natural laws of likeness and affinity, union and happiness are the result. Such marriages might be Divine. But how is it now? You all know our marriage is, in many cases, a mere outward tie, impelled by custom, policy, interest, necessity; founded not even in friendship, to say nothing of love; with every possible inequality of condition and development. In these heterogeneous unions, we find youth and old age, beauty and deformity, refinement and vulgarity, virtue and vice, the educated and the ignorant, angels of grace and goodness, with devils of malice and malignity: and the sum of all this is human wretchedness and despair; cold fathers, sad mothers, and hapless children, who shiver at the hearthstone, where the fires of love have all gone out. The wide world, and the stranger's unsympathizing gaze, are not more to be dreaded for young hearts than homes like these. Now, who shall say that it is right to take two beings, so unlike, and anchor them right side by side, fast bound—to stay all time, until God shall summon one away?

Do wise, Christian legislators need any arguments to convince them that the sacredness of the family relation should be protected at all hazards? The family, that great conservator of national virtue and strength, how can you hope to build it up in the midst of violence, debauchery, and excess? Can there be anything sacred at that family altar, where the chief-priest who ministers makes sacrifice of human beings, of the weak and the innocent? where the incense offered up is not to the God of justice and mercy, but to those heathen divinities, who best may represent the lost man in all his grossness and deformity? Call that sacred, where woman, the mother of the race—of a Jesus of Nazareth—unconscious of the true dignity of her nature, of her high and holy destiny, consents to live in legalized prostitution!—her whole soul revolting at such gross association!—her flesh shivering at the cold contamination of that embrace, held there by no tie but the iron chain of the law, and a false and most unnatural public sentiment? Call that sacred, where innocent children, trembling with fear, fly to the corners and dark places of the house, to hide themselves from the wrath of drunken, brutal fathers, but, forgetting their past sufferings, rush out again at their mother's frantic screams, "Help, oh help"? Behold the agonies of those young hearts, as they see the only being on earth they love, dragged about the room by the hair of the head, kicked and pounded, and left half dead and bleeding on the floor! Call that sacred, where fathers like these have the power and legal right to hand down their natures to other beings, to curse other generations with such moral deformity and death?

Men and brethren, look into your asylums for the blind, the deaf and dumb, the idiot, the imbecile, the deformed, the insane; go out into the by-lanes and dens of this vast metropolis, and contemplate that reeking mass of depravity; pause before the terrible revelations made by statistics, of the rapid increase of all this moral and physical impotency, and learn how fearful a thing it is to violate the immutable laws of the beneficent Ruler of the universe; and there behol. the terrible retributions of your violence on woman! Learn how false and cruel are those institutions, which, with a coarse materialism, set aside those holy instincts of the woman to bear no children but those of love ! In the best condition of marriage, as we now have it, to woman comes all the penalties and sacrifices. A man, in the full tide of business or pleasure, can marry and not change his life one iota; he can be husband, father, and everything beside; but in marriage, woman gives up all. Home is her sphere, her realm. Well, be it so. If here you will make us all-supreme, take to yourselves the universe beside; explore the North Pole; and, in your airy car, all space; in your Northern homes and cloud-capt towers, go feast on walrus flesh and air, and lay you down to sleep your six months' night away, and leave us to make these laws that govern the inner sanctuary of our own homes, and faithful satellites we will ever be to the dinner-pot, the cradle, and the old arm-chair. (Applause).

Fathers, do you say, let your daughters pay a life-long penalty for one unfortunate step ? How could they, on the threshold of life, full of joy and hope, believing all things to be as they seemed on the surface, judge of the dark windings of the human soul ? How could they foresee that the young man, to-day so noble, so generous, would in a few short years be transformed into a cowardly, mean tyrant, or a foul-mouthed, bloated drunkard ? What father could rest at his home by night, knowing that his lovely daughter was at the mercy of a strong man drunk with wine and passion, and that, do what he might, he was backed up by law and public sentiment ? The best interests of the individual, the family, the State, the nation, cry out against these legalized marriages of force and endurance. There can be no heaven without love, and nothing is sacred in the family and home, but just so far as it is built up and anchored in love. Our newspapers teem with startling accounts of husbands and wives having shot or poisoned each other, or committed suicide, choosing death rather than the indissoluble tie; and, still worse, the living death of faithless wives and daughters, from the first families in this State, dragged from the privacy of home into the public prints and courts, with all the painful details of sad, false lives. What say you to facts like these ? Now, do you believe, men and women, that all these wretched matches are made in heaven ? that all these sad, miserable people are bound together by God ? I know Horace Greeley has been most eloquent, for weeks past, on the holy sacrament of ill-assorted marriages; but let us hope that all wisdom does not live, and will not die with Horace Greeley. I think, if he had been married to *The New York Herald,* instead of the Republican party, he would have found out some Scriptural arguments against life-long unions, where great incompatibility of temper existed between the parties. (Laughter and applause).

Our law-makers have dug a pit, and the innocent have fallen into it; and now will you coolly cover them over with statute laws, *Tribunes,* and Weeds,* and tell them to stay there and pay the life-long penalty of having fallen in ? Nero was thought the chief of tyrants, because he made laws and hung them up so high that his subjects could not read them, and then punished them for every act of disobedience. What better are

---

* Thurlow Weed, editor of *The Albany Evening Journal,* opposed the passage of the Divorce Bill before the New York Legislature in 1860.

Elizabeth Lady Stanton

our Republican legislators ? The mass of the women of this nation know nothing about the laws, yet all their specially barbarous legislation is for woman. Where have they made any provision for her to learn the laws ? Where is the Law School for our daughters ? where the law office, the bar, or the bench, now urging them to take part in the jurisprudence of the nation ?

But, say you, does not separation cover all these difficulties ? No one objects to separation when the parties are so disposed. But, to separation there are two very serious objections. First, so long as you insist on marriage as a divine institution, as an indissoluble tie, so long as you maintain your present laws against divorce, you make separation, even, so odious, that the most noble, virtuous, and sensitive men and women choose a life of concealed misery, rather than a partial, disgraceful release. Secondly, those who, in their impetuosity and despair, do, in spite of public sentiment, separate, find themselves in their new position beset with many temptations to lead a false, unreal life. This isolation bears especially hard on woman. Marriage is not all of life to man. His resources for amusement and occupation are boundless. He has the whole world for his home. His business, his politics, his club, his friendships with either sex, can help to fill up the void made by an unfortunate union or separation. But to woman, marriage is all and everything; her sole object in life—that for which she is educated— the subject of all her sleeping and her waking dreams. Now, if a noble, generous girl of eighteen marries, and is unfortunate, because the cruelty of her husband compels separation, in her dreary isolation, would you drive her to a nunnery; and shall she be a nun indeed ? Her solitude is nothing less, as, in the present undeveloped condition of woman, it is only through our fathers, brothers, husbands, sons, that we feel the pulsations of the great outer world.

One unhappy, discordant man or woman in a neighborhood, may mar the happiness of all the rest. You can not shut up discord, any more than you can small-pox. There can be no morality where there is a settled discontent. A very wise father once remarked, that in the government of his children, he forbade as few things as possible; a wise legislation would do the same. It is folly to make laws on subjects beyond human prerogative, knowing that in the very nature of things they must be set aside. To make laws that man can not and will not obey, serves to bring all law into contempt. It is very important in a republic, that the people should respect the laws, for if we throw them to the winds, what becomes of civil government ? What do our present divorce laws amount to ? Those who wish to evade them have only to go into another State to accomplish what they desire. If any of our citizens can not secure their inalienable rights in New York State, they may in Connecticut and Indiana. Why is it that all agreements, covenants, partnerships, are left wholly at the discretion of the parties, except the contract, which of all others is considered most holy and important, both for the individual and the race ? This question of divorce, they tell us, is hedged about with difficulties; that it can not be approached with the ordinary rules of logic and common-sense. It is too holy, too sacred to

46

be discussed, and few seem disposed to touch it. From man's standpoint, this may be all true, as to him they say belong reason, and the power of ratiocination. Fortunately, I belong to that class endowed with mere intuitions, a kind of moral instinct, by which we feel out right and wrong. In presenting to you, therefore, my views of divorce, you will of course give them the weight only of the woman's intuitions. But inasmuch as that is all God saw fit to give us, it is evident we need nothing more. Hence, what we do perceive of truth must be as reliable as what man grinds out by the longer process of reason, authority, and speculation.

Horace Greeley, in his recent discussion with Robert Dale Owen, said, this whole question has been tried, in all its varieties and conditions, from indissoluble monogamic marriage down to free love; that the ground has been all gone over and explored. Let me assure him that but just one-half of the ground has been surveyed, and that half but by one of the parties, and that party certainly not the most interested in the matter. Moreover, there is one kind of marriage that has not been tried, and that is, a contract made by equal parties to live an equal life, with equal restraints and privileges on either side. Thus far, we have had the man marriage, and nothing more. From the beginning, man has had the sole and whole regulation of the matter. He has spoken in Scripture, he has spoken in law. As an individual, he has decided the time and cause for putting away a wife, and as a judge and legislator, he still holds the entire control. In all history, sacred and profane, the woman is regarded and spoken of simply as the toy of man—made for his special use—to meet his most gross and sensuous desires. She is taken or put away, given or received, bought or sold, just as the interest of the parties might dictate. But the woman has been no more recognized in all these transactions, through all the different periods and conditions of the race, than if she had had no part nor lot in the whole matter. The right of woman to put away a husband, be he ever so impure, is never hinted at in sacred history. Even Jesus himself failed to recognize the sacred rights of the holy mother of the race. We can not take our gauge of womanhood from the past, but from the solemn convictions of our own souls, in the higher development of the race. No parchments, however venerable with the mould of ages, no human institutions, can bound the immortal wants of the royal sons and daughters of the great I Am,—rightful heirs of the joys of time, and joint heirs of the glories of eternity.

If in marriage either party claims the right to stand supreme, to woman, the mother of the race, belongs the scepter and the crown. Her life is one long sacrifice for man. You tell us that among all womankind there is no Moses, Christ, or Paul,—no Michael Angelo, Beethoven, or Shakspeare,—no Columbus, or Galileo,—no Locke or Bacon. Behold those mighty minds attuned to music and the arts, so great, so grand, so comprehensive,—these are our great works of which we boast! Into you, O sons of earth, go all of us that is immortal. In you center our very life-thoughts, our hopes, our intensest love. For you we gladly pour out our heart's blood and die, knowing that from our suffering comes forth a new and more glorious resurrection of thought and life. (Loud applause).

Rev. Antoinette Brown Blackwell followed, and prefaced her remarks by saying: " Ours has always been a free platform. We have believed in the fullest freedom of thought and in the free expression of individual opinion. I propose to speak upon the subject discussed by our friend, Mrs. Stanton. It is often said that there are two sides to every question; but there are three sides, many sides, to every question. Let Mrs. Stanton take her's; let Horace Greeley take his; I only ask the privilege of stating mine. (Applause). I have embodied my thought, hastily, in a series of resolutions,* and my remarks following them will be very brief."

Resolved, That marriage is the voluntary alliance of two persons of opposite sexes into one family, and that such an alliance, with its possible incidents of children, its common interests, etc., must be, from the nature of things, as permanent as the life of the parties.

Resolved, That if human law attempts to regulate marriage at all, it should aim to regulate it according to the fundamental principles of marriage ; and that as the institution is inherently as continuous as the life of the parties, so all laws should look to its control and preservation as such.

Resolved, That as a parent can never annul his obligations towards even a profligate child, because of the inseparable relationship of the parties, so the married partner can not annul his obligations towards the other, while both live, no matter how profligate that other's conduct may be, because of their still closer and alike permanent relationship ; and, therefore, that all divorce is naturally and morally impossible, even though we should succeed in annulling all legalities.

Resolved, That gross fraud and want of good faith in one of the parties contracting this alliance, such as would invalidate any other voluntary relation, are the only causes which can invalidate this, and this, too, solely upon the ground that the relation never virtually existed, and that there are, therefore, no resulting moral obligations.

Resolved, however, That both men and women have a first and inviolable right to themselves, physically, mentally, and morally, and that it can never be the duty of either to surrender his personal freedom in any direction to his own hurt.

Resolved, That the great duty of every human being is to secure his own highest moral development, and that he can not owe to society, or to an individual, any obligation which shall be degrading to himself.

Resolved, That self-devotion to the good of another, and especially to the good of the sinful and guilty, like all disinterestedness, must redound to the highest good of its author, and that the husband or wife who thus seeks the best interests of the other, is obedient to the highest law of benevolence.

Resolved, That this is a very different thing from the culpable weakness which allows itself to be immolated by the selfishness of another, to the hurt of both ; and that the miserable practice, now so common among wives, of allowing themselves, their children and family interests, to be sacrificed to a degraded husband and father, is most reprehensible.

Resolved, That human law is imperatively obligated to give either party ample protection to himself, to their offspring, and to all other family interests, against wrong, injustice, and usurpation on the part of the other, and that, if it be necessary to this, it should grant a legal separation ; and yet, that even such separation can not invalidate any real marriage obligation.

Resolved, That every married person is imperatively obligated to do his utmost thus to protect himself and all family interests against injustice and wrong, let it arise from what source it may.

Resolved, That every woman is morally obligated to maintain her equality in human rights in all her relations in life, and that if she consents to her own subjugation, either

Mrs. Blackwell continued :

I believe that the highest laws of life are those which we find written within our being ; that the first moral laws which we are to obey are the laws which God's own finger has traced upon our own souls. Therefore, our first duty is to ourselves, and we may never, under any circumstances, yield this to any other. I say we are first responsible to ourselves, and to the God who has laid the obligation upon us, to make ourselves the grandest we may. Marriage grows out of the relations of parties. The law of our development comes wholly from within ; but the relation of marriage supposes two persons as being united to each other, and from this relation originates the law. Mrs. Stanton calls marriage a " tie." No, marriage is a *relation* ; and, once formed, that relation continues as long as the parties continue with the natures which they now essentially have. Let, then, the two parties deliberately, voluntarily consent to enter into this relation. It is one which, from its very nature, must be permanent. Can the mother ever destroy the relation which exists between herself and her child ? Can the father annul the relation which exists between himself and his child ? Then, can the father and mother annul the relation which exists between themselves, the parents of the child ? It can not be. The interests of marriage are such that they can not be destroyed, and the only question must be, " Has there been a marriage in this case or not ? " If there has, then the social law, the obligations growing out of the relation, must be life-long.

But I assert that every woman, in the present state of society, is bound to maintain her own independence and her own integrity of character ; to assert herself, earnestly and firmly, as the equal of man, who is only her peer. This is her first right, her first duty ; and if she lives in a country where the law supposes that she is to be subjected to her husband, and she consents to this subjection, I do insist that she consents to degradation ; that this is sin, and it is impossible to make it other than sin. True, in this State, and in nearly all the States, the idea of marriage is that of subjection, in all respects, of the wife to the husband—personal subjection, subjection in the rights over their children and over their property ; but this is a false relation. Marriage is a union of equals—equal interests being involved, equal duties at stake ; and if any woman has been married to a man who chooses to take advantage of the laws as they now stand, who chooses to subject her, ignobly, to his will, against her own, to take from her the earnings which belong to the family, and to take from her the children which belong to the family, I hold that that woman, if she can not, by her influence, change this state of things, is solemnly obligated to go to some State where she can be legally divorced ; and then she would be as solemnly bound to return again, and, standing for herself and her children, regard herself, in the sight of God, as being bound still to the father of those children, to work for his best interests, while she still maintains her own sov-

---

in the family, Church or State, she is as guilty as the slave is in consenting to be a slave.

Resolved, That a perfect union can not be expected to exist until we first have perfect units, and that every marriage of finite beings must be gradually perfected through the growth and assimilation of the parties.

Resolved, That the permanence and indissolubility of marriage tend more directly than anything else toward this result.

ereignty. Of course, she must be governed by the circumstances of the case. She may be obliged, for the protection of the family, to live on one continent while her husband is on the other : but she is never to forget that in the sight of God and her own soul, she is his wife, and that she owes to him the wife's loyalty ; that to work for his redemption is her highest social obligation, and that to teach her children to do the same is her first motherly duty. Legal divorce may be necessary for personal and family protection ; if so, let every woman obtain it. This, God helping me, is what I would certainly do, for under no circumstances will I ever give my consent to be subjected to the will of another, in any relation, for God has bidden me not to do it. But the idea of most women is, that they must be timid, weak, helpless, and full of ignoble submission. Only last week, a lady who has just been divorced from her husband said to me—" I used to be required to go into the field and do the hardest laborer's work, when I was not able to do it ; and my husband would declare, that if I would not thus labor, I should not be allowed to eat, and I was obliged to submit." I say the fault was as much with the woman as with the man ; she should never have submitted.

Our trouble is not with marriage as a relation between two ; it is all individual. We have few men or women fit to be married. They neither fully respect themselves and their own rights and duties, nor yet those of another. They have no idea how noble, how godlike is the relation which ought to exist between the husband and wife.

Tell me, is marriage to be merely a contract — something entered into for a time, and then broken again—or is the true marriage permanent ? One resolution read by Mrs. Stanton said that, as men are incompetent to select partners in business, teachers for their children, ministers of their religion, or makers, adjudicators, or administrators of their laws, and as the same weakness and blindness must attend in the selection of matrimonial partners, the latter and most important contract should no more be perpetual than either or all of the former. I do not believe that, rightly understood, she quite holds to that position herself. Marriage must be either permanent, or capable of being any time dissolved. Which ground shall we take? I insist that, from the nature of things, marriage must be as permanent and indissoluble as the relation of parent and child. If so, let us legislate toward the right. Though evils must sometimes result, we are still to seek the highest law of the relation.

Self-devotion is always sublimely beautiful, but the law has no right to require either a woman to be sacrificed to any man, or a man to be sacrificed to any woman, or either to the good of society ; but if either chooses to devote himself to the good of the other, no matter how low that other may have fallen, no matter how degraded he may be, let the willing partner strive to lift him up, not by going down and sitting side by side with him—that is wrong—but by steadily trying to win him back to the right: keeping his own sovereignty, but trying to redeem the fallen one as long as life shall endure. I do not wish to go to the other state of being, and state what shall be our duty there, but I do say, that where there is sin and suffering in this universe of ours, we may none of us sit still until we have overcome that sin and suffering. Then if my husband was wretched and degraded in this life, I believe God would give me strength to work for him while life lasted. I would do that for the lowest drunkard in the street, and certainly I would do as much for my husband. I believe that the greatest boon of existence is the privilege of working for those who are oppressed and fallen; and those who have oppressed their own natures are those who need the most help. My great hope is, that I may be able to lift them upwards. The great responsibility that has been laid upon me is the responsibility never to sit down and sing to myself psalms of happiness and content while anybody suffers. (Applause). Then, if I find a wretched man in the gutter, and feel that, as a human sister, I must go and lift him up, and that I can never enjoy peace or rest until I have thus redeemed him and brought him out of his sins, shall I, if the man whom I solemnly swore to love, to associate with in all the interests of home and its holiest relations — shall I, if he falls into sin, turn him off, and go on enjoying life, while he is sunk in wretchedness and sin ? I will not do it. To me there is a higher idea of life. If, as an intelligent human being, I promised to co-work with him in all the higher interests of life, and if he proves false, I will not turn from him, but I must seek first to regenerate him, the nearest and dearest to me, as I would work, secondly, to save my children, who are next, and then my brothers, my sisters, and the whole human family. (Applause).

Mrs. Stanton asks, "Would you send a young girl into a nunnery, when she has made a mistake ?" Does Mrs. Stanton not know that nunneries belong to a past age, that people who had nothing to do might go there and try to expiate their own sins ? I would teach the young girl a higher way. I do not say to her, "If you have foolishly united yourself to another" (not "if you have been tied by the law"; for, remember, it was not the law that tied her; she said, "I will do it," and the law said, "So let it be !")—"sunder the bond"; but I say to her, that her duty is to reflect, "Now that I see my mistake, I will commence being true to myself; I will become a true unit, strong and noble in myself; and if I can never make our union a true one, I will work toward that good result, I will live for this great work—for truth and all its interests." Let me tell you, if she is not great enough to do this, she is not great enough to enter into any union!

Look at those who believe in thus easily dissolving the marriage obligation ! In very many cases they can not be truly married, or truly happy in this relation, because there is something incompatible with it in their own natures. It is not always so; but when one feels that it is a relation easily to be dissolved, of course, incompatibility at once seems to arise in the other, and every difficulty that occurs, instead of being overlooked, as it ought to be, in a spirit of forgiveness, is magnified, and the evil naturally increased. We purchase a house, the deed is put into our hands, and we take possession. We feel at once that it is really very convenient. It suits us, and we are surprised that we like it so much better than we supposed. The secret is, that it is our house, and until we are ready to part with it, we make ourselves content with it as it is. We go to live in some country town. At first we do not like it; it is not like the home we came from; but soon we begin to be reconciled, and feel that, as Dr. Holmes said of Boston, our town is the hub of the universe. So, when we are content to allow our relations to remain as they are, we adapt ourselves to them, and they adapt themselves to us, and we constantly, unconsciously (because God made us so) work toward the perfecting of all the interests arising from those relations. But the moment we wish to sell a house, or remove from a town, how many defects we discover ! The place has not the same appearance to us at all; we wish we could get out of it; we feel all the time more and more dissatisfied. So, let any married person take the idea that he may dissolve this relation, and enter into a new one, and how many faults he may discover that otherwise never would have been noticed ! The marriage will become intolerable. The theory will work that result; it is in the nature of things, and that to me is everything.

Of course, I would not have man or woman sacrificed—by no means. First of all, let every human being maintain his own position as a self-protecting human being. At all hazards, let him never sin, or consent to be sacrificed to the hurt of himself or of another; and when he has taken this stand, let him act in harmony with it. Would I say to any woman, " You are bound, because you are legally married to one who is debased to the level of the brute, to be the mother of his children ?" I say to her, "No ! while the law of God continues, you are bound never to make one whom you do not honor and respect, as well as love, the father of any child of yours. It is your first and highest duty to be true to yourself, true to posterity, and true to society." (Applause). Thus, let each decide for himself and for herself what is right. But, I repeat, either marriage is in its very nature a relation which, once formed, never can be dissolved, and either the essential obligations growing out of it exist forever, or the relation may at any time be dissolved, and at any time those obligations be annulled. And what are those obligations ? Two persons, if I understand marriage, covenant to work together, to uphold each other in all excellence, and to mutually blend their lives and interests into a common harmony. I believe that God has so made man and woman, that it is not good for them to be alone, that they each need a co-worker. There is no work on God's footstool which man can do alone and do well, and there is no work which woman can do alone and do well. (Applause). We need that the two should stand side by side everywhere. All over the world, we need this co-operation of the two classes—not because they are alike, but because they are unlike—in trying to make the whole world better. Then we need something more than these class workers. Two persons need to stand side by side, to stay up each other's hands, to take an interest in each other's welfare, to build up a family, to cluster about it all the beauties and excellencies of home life; in short, to be to each other what only one man and one woman can be to each other in all God's earth.

No grown-up human being ought to rush blindly into this most intimate, most important, most enduring of human relations; and will you let a young man, at the age of fourteen, contract marriage, or a young maiden either ? If the law undertakes to regulate the matter at all, let it regulate it upon principles of common-sense. But this is a matter which must be very much regulated by public opinion, by our teachers. What do you, the guides of our youth, say ? You say to the young girl, " You ought to expect to be married before you are twenty, or about that time; you should intend to be; and from the time you are fifteen, it should be made your one life purpose; and in all human probability, you may expect to spend the next ten or twenty years in the nursery, and at forty or fifty, you will be an old woman, your life will be well-nigh worn out." I stand here to say that this is all false. Let the young girl be instructed that, above her personal interests, her home, and social life, she is to have a great life purpose, as broad as the rights and interests of humanity. I say, let every young girl feel this, as much as every young man does. We have no right, we, who expect to live forever, to play about here as if we were mere flies, enjoying ourselves in the sunshine. We ought to have an earnest purpose outside of home, outside of our family relations. Then let the young girl fit herself for this. Let her be taught that she ought not to be married in her teens. Let her wait, as a young man does, if he is sensible, until she is twenty-five or thirty. (Applause). She will then know how to choose properly, and probably she will not be deceived in her estimate of character; she will have had a certain life-discipline, which will enable her to control her household matters with wise judgment, so that, while she is looking after her family, she may still keep her great life purpose, for which she was educated, and to which she has given her best energies, steadily in view. She need not absorb herself in her home, and God never intended that she should; and then, if she has lived according to the laws of physiology, and according to the laws of common-sense, she ought to be, at the age of fifty years, just where man is, just where our great men are, in the very prime of life ! When her young children have gone out of her home, then let her enter in earnest upon the great work of life outside of home and its relations. (Applause).

It is a shame for our women to have no steady purpose or pursuit, and to make the mere fact of womanhood a valid plea for indolence; it is a greater shame that they should be instructed thus to throw all the responsibility of working for the general good upon the other sex. God has not intended it. But as long as you make women helpless, inefficient beings, who never expect to earn a farthing in their lives, who never expect to do anything outside of the family, but to be cared for and protected by others throughout life, you can not have true marriages; and if you try to break up the old ones, you will do it against the woman and in favor of the man. Last week I went back to a town where I used to live, and was told that a woman, whose husband was notoriously the most miserable man in the town, had in despair taken her own life. I asked what had become of the husband, and the answer was, "Married again." And yet everybody there knows that he is the vilest and most contemptible man in the whole neighborhood. Any man, no matter how wretched he may be, will find plenty of women to accept him, while they are rendered so helpless and weak by their whole education that they must be supported or starve. The advantage, if this theory of marriage is adopted, will not be on the side of woman, but altogether on the side of man. The cure for the evils that now exist is not in dissolving marriage, but it is in giving to the married woman her own natural independence and self-sovereignty, by which she can maintain herself.

Yes, our women and our men are both degenerate; they are weak and ignoble. "Dear me!" said a pretty, indolent young lady, "I had a great deal rather my husband would take care of me, than to be obliged to do it for myself." "Of course you would," said a blunt old lady who was present; "and your brother would a great deal rather marry an heiress, and lie upon a sofa eating lollypops, bought with her money, than to do anything manly or noble. The only difference is, that as heiresses are not very plenty, he may probably have to marry a poor girl, and then society will insist that he shall exert himself to earn a living for the family; but you, poor thing, will only have to open your mouth, all your life long, like a clam, and eat." (Applause and laughter). So long as society is constituted in such a way that woman is expected to do nothing if she have a father, brother, or husband able to support her, there is no salvation for her, in or out of marriage. When you tie up your arm, it will become weak and feeble; and when you tie up woman, she will become weak and helpless. Give her, then, some earnest purpose in life, hold up to her the true ideal of marriage, and it is enough—I am content! (Loud applause).

ERNESTINE L. ROSE said:—Mrs. President—The question of a Divorce law seems to me one of the greatest importance to all parties, but I presume that the very advocacy of divorce will be called "Free Love." For my part (and I wish distinctly to define my position), I do not know what others understand by that term; to me, in its truest significance, love must be free, or it ceases to be love. In its low and degrading sense, it is not love at all, and I have as little to do with its name as its reality.

The Rev. Mrs. Blackwell gave us quite a sermon on what woman ought to be, what she ought to do, and what marriage ought to be; an excellent sermon in its proper place, but not when the important question of a Divorce law is under consideration. She treats woman as some ethereal being. It is very well to be ethereal to some extent, but I tell you, my friends, it is quite requisite to be a little material, also. At all events, we are so, and, being so, it proves a law of our nature. (Applause).

It were indeed well if woman could be what she ought to be, man what he ought to be, and marriage what it ought to be; and it is to be hoped that through the Woman's Rights movement—the equalizing of the laws, making them more just, and making woman more independent—we will hasten the coming of the millennium, when marriage shall indeed be a bond of union and affection. But, alas! it is not yet; and I fear that sermons, however well meant, will not produce that desirable end; and as long as the evil is here, we must look it in the face without shrinking, grapple with it manfully, and the more complicated it is, the more courageously must it be analyzed, combated, and destroyed. (Applause).

Mrs. Blackwell told us that, marriage being based on the perfect equality of husband and wife, it can not be destroyed. But is it so? Where? Where and when have the sexes yet been equal in physical or mental education, in position, or in law? When and where have they yet been recognized by society, or by themselves, as equals? "Equal in rights," says Mrs. B. But are they equal in rights? If they were, we would need no conventions to claim our rights. "She can assert her equality." Yes, she can assert it, but does that assertion constitute a true marriage? And when the husband holds the iron heel of legal oppres io on the subjugated neck of the wife until every spark of womahood is crushed out, will it heal the wounded heart, the lacerated spirit, the destroyed hope, to assert her equality? And shall she still continue the wife? Is that a marriage which must not be dissolved? (Applause).

According to Mr. Greeley's definition, viz., that there is no marriage unless the ceremony is performed by a minister and in a church, the tens of thousands married according to the laws of this and most of the other States, by a lawyer or justice of the peace, a mayor or an alderman, are not married at all. According to the definition of our reverend sister, no one has ever yet been married, as woman has never yet been perfectly equal with man. I say to both, take your position, and abide by the consequences. If the few only, or no one, is really married, why do you object to a law that shall acknowledge the fact? You certainly ought not to force people to live together who are not married. (Applause).

Mr. Greeley tells us, that, marriage being a Divine institution, nothing but death should ever separate the parties; but when he was asked, "Would you have a being who, innocent and inexperienced, in the youth and ardor of affection, in the fond hope that the sentiment was reciprocated, united herself to one she loved and cherished, and then found (no matter from what cause) that his profession was false, his heart hollow, his acts cruel, that she was degraded by his vice, despised for his crimes, cursed by his very presence, and treated with every conceivable ignominy—would you have her drag out a miserable existence as his wife?" "No, no," says he; "in that case, they ought to separate." Separate? But what becomes of the union divinely instituted, which death only should part? (Applause).

The papers have of late been filled with the heart-sickening accounts of wife-poisoning. Whence come these terrible crimes? From the want of a Divorce law. Could the Hardings be legally separated, they would not be driven to the commission of murder to be free from each other; and which is preferable, a Divorce law, to dissolve an unholy union, which all parties agree is no true marriage, or a murder of one, and an execution (legal murder) of the other party? But had the unfortunate woman, just before the poisoned cup was presented to her lips, pleaded for a divorce, Mrs. Blackwell would have read her a sermon equal to St. Paul's "Wives, be obedient to your husbands," only she would have added, "You must assert your equality," but "you must keep with your husband and work for his redemption, as I would do for my husband"; and Mr. Greeley would say, "As you chose to marry him, it is your own fault; you must abide the consequences, for it is a 'divine institution, a union for life, which nothing but death can end.'" (Applause). *The Tribune* had recently a long sermon, almost equal to the one we had this morning from our reverend sister, on "Fast Women." The evils it spoke of were terrible indeed, but, like all other sermons, it was one-sided. Not one single word was said about fast men, except that the "poor victim had to spend so much money." The writer forgot that it is the demand which calls the supply into existence. But what was the primary cause of that tragic end? Echo answers, "what?" Ask the lifeless form of the murdered woman, and she may disclose the terrible secret, and show you that, could she have been legally divorced, she might not have been driven to the watery grave of a "fast woman." (Applause).

But what is marriage? A human institution, called out by the needs of social, affectional human nature, for human purposes, its objects are, first, the happiness of the parties immediately concerned, and, secondly, the welfare of society. Define it as you please, these are only its objects; and therefore if, from well-ascertained facts, it is demonstrated that the real objects are frustrated, that instead of union and happiness, there are only discord and misery to themselves, and vice and crime to society, I ask, in the name of individual, happiness and social morality and well-being, why such a marriage should be binding for life?—why one human being should be chained for life to the dead body of another ? "But they may separate and still remain married." What a perversion of the very term! Is that the union which "death only should part"? It may be according to the definition of the Rev. Mrs. Blackwell's theology and Mr. Greeley's dictionary, but it certainly is not according to common-sense or the dictates of morality. No, no! "It is not well for man to be alone," before nor after marriage. (Applause).

I therefore ask for a Divorce law. Divorce is now granted for some crimes ; I ask it for others also. It is granted for a State's prison offense. I ask that personal cruelty to a wife, whom he swore to "love, cherish, and protect," may be made a heinous crime—a perjury and a State's prison offense, for which divorce shall be granted. Willful desertion for one year should be a sufficient cause for divore, for the willful deserter forfeits the sacred title of husband or wife. Habitual intemperance, or any other vice which makes the husband or wife intolerable and abhorrent to the other, ought to be sufficient cause for divorce. I ask for a law of Divorce, so as to secure the real objects and blessings of married life, to prevent the crimes and immoralities now practiced, to prevent "Free Love," in its most hideous form, such as is now carried on but too often under the very name of marriage, where hypocrisy is added to the crime of legalized prostitution. "Free Love," in its degraded sense, asks for no Divorce law. It acknowledges no marriage, and therefore requires no divorce. I believe in true marriages, and therefore I ask for a law to free men and women from false ones. (Applause).

But it is said that if divorce were easily granted, "men and women would marry to-day and unmarry to-morrow." Those who say that, only prove that they have no confidence in themselves, and therefore can have no confidence in others. But the assertion is false; it is a libel on human nature. It is the indissoluble chain that corrodes the flesh. Remove the indissolubility, and there would be less separation than now, for it would place the parties on their good behavior, the same as during courtship. Human nature is not quite so changeable; give it more freedom, and it will be less so. We are a good deal the creatures of habit, but we will not be forced. We live (I speak from experience) in uncomfortable houses for years, rather than move, though we have the privilege to do so every year ; but force any one to live for life in one house, and he would run away from it, though it were a palace.

But Mr. Greeley asks, "How could the mother look the child in the face, if she married a second time ?" With infinitely better grace and better conscience than to live as some do now, and show their children the degrading example, how utterly father and mother despise and hate each other, and still live together as husband and wife. She could say to her child, "As, unfortunately, your father proved himself unworthy, your mother could not be so unworthy as to continue to live with him. As he failed to be a true father to you, I have endeavored to supply his place with one, who, though not entitled to the name, will, I hope, prove himself one in the performance of a father's duties." (Applause).

Finally, educate woman, to enable her to promote her independence, and she will not be obliged to marry for a home and a subsistence. Give the wife an equal right with the husband in the property acquired after marriage, and it will be a bond of union between them. Diamond cement, applied on both sides of a fractured vase, re-unites the parts, and prevents them from falling asunder. A gold band is more efficacious than an iron law. Until now, the gold has all been on one side, and the iron law on the other. Remove it; place the golden band of justice and mutual interest around both husband and wife, and it will hide the little fractures which may have occurred, even from their own perception, and allow them effectually to re-unite. A union of interest helps to preserve a union of hearts. (Loud applause).

WENDELL PHILLIPS then said: I object to entering these resolutions upon the journal of this Convention. (Applause). I would move to lay them on the table; but my conviction that they are out of order is so emphatic, that I wish to go further than that, and move that they do not appear on the journals of this Convention. If the resolutions were merely the expressions of individual sentiments, then they ought not to appear in the form of resolutions, but as speeches, because a resolution has a certain emphasis and authority. It is assumed to give the voice of an assembly, and is not taken as an individual expression, which a speech is.

Of course, every person must be interested in the question of marriage, and the branch that grows out of it, the question of divorce; and no one could deny, who has listened for an hour, that we have been favored with an exceedingly able discussion of those questions. But here we have nothing to do with them, any more than with the question of intemperance, or Kansas, in my opinion. This Convention is no Marriage Convention—if it were, the subject would be in order; but this Convention, if I understand it, assembles to discuss the laws that rest unequally upon women, not those that rest equally upon men and women. It is the laws that make distinctions between the sexes. Now, whether a man and a woman are married for a year or a life is a question which affects the man just as much as the woman. At the end of a month, the man is without a wife exactly as much as the woman is without a husband. The question whether, having entered into a contract, you shall be bound to an unworthy partner, affects the man as much as the woman. Certainly, there are cases where men are bound to women carcasses as well as where women are bound to men carcasses. (Laughter and applause). We have nothing to do with a question which affects both sexes equally. Therefore, it seems to me we have nothing to do with the theory of marriage, which is the basis, as Mrs. Rose has very clearly shown, of divorce. One question grows out of the other; and therefore the question of the permanence of marriage, and the laws relating to marriage, in the essential meaning of that word, are not for our consideration. Of course I know, as everybody else does, that the results of marriage, in the present condition of society, are often more disastrous to woman than to men. Intemperance, for instance, burdens a wife worse than a husband, owing to the present state of society. It is not the fault of the statute-book, and no change in the duration of marriage would alter that inequality.

The reason why I object so emphatically to the introduction of the question here is because it is a question which admits of so many theories, physiological and religious, and what is technically called "free-love," that it is large enough for a movement of its own. Our question is only unnecessarily burdened with it. It can not be kept within the convenient limits of this enterprise; for this Woman's Rights Convention is not Man's Convention, and I hold that I, as a man, have an exactly equal interest in the essential question of marriage as woman has. I move, then, that these series of resolutions do not appear at all upon the journal of the Convention. If the speeches are reported, of course the resolutions will go with them. Most journals will report them as adopted. But I say to those who use this platform to make speeches on this question, that they do far worse than take more than their fair share of the time; they open a gulf into which our distinctive movement will be plunged, and its success postponed two years for every one that it need necessarily be.

Of course, in these remarks, I intend no reflection upon those whose views differ from mine in regard to introducing this subject before the Convention; but we had an experience two years ago on this point, and it seems to me that we might have learned by that lesson. No question —Anti-Slavery, Temperance, Woman's Rights—can move forward efficiently, unless it keeps its platform separate and unmixed with extraneous issues, unmixed with discussions which carry us into endless realms of debate. We have now, under our present civilization, to deal with the simple question which we propose—how to make that statute-book look upon woman exactly as it does upon man. Under the law of Divorce, one stands exactly like the other. All we have asked in regard to the law of property has been, that the statute-book of New York shall make the wife exactly like the husband; we do not go another step, and state what that right shall be. We do not ask law-makers whether there shall be rights of dower and courtesy—rights to equal shares—rights to this or that interest in property. That is not our business. All we say is, "Gentlemen law-makers, we represent woman; make what laws you please about marriage and property, but let woman stand under them exactly as man does; let sex deprive her of no right, let sex confer no special right; and that is all we claim." (Applause). Society has done that as to marriage and divorce, and we have nothing more to ask of it on this question, as a Woman's Rights body.

ABBY HOPPER GIBBONS, of New York City, seconded the motion of Mr. Phillips, and said that she wished the whole subject of marriage and divorce might be swept from that platform, as it was manifestly not the place for it.

Mr. GARRISON said he fully concurred in opinion with his friend, Mr. Phillips, that they had not come together to settle definitely the question of marriage, as such, on that platform; still, he should be sorry to have the motion adopted, as against the resolutions of Mrs. Stanton, because they were a part of her speech, and her speech was an elucidation of her resolutions, which were offered on her own responsibility, not on behalf of the Business Committee, and which did not, therefore, make the Convention responsible for them. It seemed to him that, in the liberty usually taken on that platform, both by way of argument and illustration, to show the various methods by which woman was unjustly, yet legally, subjected to the absolute control of man, she ought to be permitted to present her own sentiments. It was not the specific object of an Anti-Slavery Convention—for example—to discuss the conduct of Rev. Nehemiah Adams, or the position of Stephen A. Douglas, or the course of *The York Herald;* yet they did, incidentally, discuss all these, and many other matters closely related to the great struggle for the freedom of the slave. So this question of marriage came in as at least incidental to the main question of the equal rights of woman.

Mrs. BLACKWELL: I should like to say a few words in explanation. I do not understand whether our friend Wendell Phillips objects to both series of resolutions on the subject of divorce, or merely to mine.

Mr. PHILLIPS: To both.

Mrs. BLACKWELL: I wish simply to say, that I did not come to the Convention proposing to speak on this subject, but on another ; but finding that these resolutions were to be introduced, and believing the subject legitimate, I said, "I will take my own position." So I prepared the resolutions, as they enabled me at the moment better to express my thought than I could do by merely extemporizing.

Now does this question grow legitimately out of the great question of woman's equality? The world says, marriage is not an alliance between equals in human rights. My whole argument was based on the position that it is. If this question is not legitimate, what is? Then do we not ask for laws which are not equal between man and woman? What have we been doing here in New York State? I spent three months asking the State to allow the drunkard's wife her own earnings. Do I believe that the wife ought to take her own earnings, as her own earnings? No; I do not believe it. I believe that in a true marriage, the husband and wife earn for the family, and that the property is the family's — belongs jointly to the husband and wife. But if the law says that the property is the husband's, if it says that he may take the wages of his wife, just as the master does those of the slave, and she has no right to them, we must seek a temporary redress. We must take the first step, by compelling legislators, who will not look at great principles, to protect the wife of the drunkard, by giving her her own earnings to expend upon herself and her children, and not allow them to be wasted by the husband. I say that it is legitimate for us to ask for a law which we believe is merely a temporary expedient, not based upon the great principle of human and marriage equality. Just so with this question of marriage. It must come upon this platform, for at present it is a relation which legally and socially bears unequally upon woman. We must have temporary redress for the wife. The whole subject must be incidentally opened for discussion. The only question is one of present fitness. Was it best, under all the circumstances, to introduce it now? I have not taken the responsibility of answering in the affirmative. But it must come here and be settled, sooner or later, because its interests are everywhere, and all human relations center in this one marriage relation. (Applause).

SUSAN B. ANTHONY: I hope Mr. Phillips will withdraw his motion that these resolutions shall not appear on the records of the Convention. I am very sure that it would be contrary to all parliamentary usage to say, that when the speeches which enforced and advocated the resolutions are reported and published in the proceedings, the resolutions shall not be placed there. And as to the point that this question does not belong to this platform,—from that I totally dissent. Marriage has ever been a one-sided matter, resting most unequally upon the sexes. By it, man gains all—woman loses all; tyrant law and lust reign supreme with him—meek submission and ready obedience alone befit her. Woman has never been consulted; her wish has never been taken into consideration as regards the terms of the marriage compact. By law, public sentiment and religion, from the time of Moses down to the present day, woman has never been thought of other than as a piece of property, to be disposed of at the will and pleasure of man. And this very hour, by our statute-books, by our (so called) enlightened Christian civilization, she has no voice whatever in saying what shall be the basis of the relation. She must accept marriage as man proffers it, or not at all.

And then again, on Mr. Phillips' own ground, the discussion is perfectly in order, since nearly all the wrongs of which we complain grow out of the inequality, the injustice of the marriage laws, that rob the wife of the right to herself and her children—that make her the slave of the man she marries.

I hope, therefore, the resolutions will be allowed to go out to the public, that there may be a fair report of the ideas which have actually been presented here, that they may not be left to the mercy of the secular press. I trust the Convention will not vote to forbid the publication of those resolutions with the proceedings.

REV. WM. HOISINGTON, the blind preacher: Publish all that you have said and done here, and let the public know it.

The question was then put on the motion of Mr. Phillips, and it was lost.

After which, the resolutions reported by the Business Committee were adopted without dissent.

Miss MARY GREW, of Philadelphia, said: Friends, we are about to separate. This convention was called for the consideration of one of the most important questions before the American people. The press may ridicule your movement, the pulpit denounce it, but, as time rolls on, it will be seen—the press and pulpit will see—that it is one of the most important questions that has ever agitated the community. It is well that those who are engaged in this movement should go forth deeply impressed with the importance of the work that is before them. It is well that you who have assembled from curiosity, to listen to what these "fanatics" have to say, should take home with you to your souls one thought which is sufficient to settle this whole question. All the arguments that have been adduced against us, and against granting to woman all her rights, come to us in one form or another of prejudice or expediency. Talk with whom you will about it,—the priest, politician, merchant, farmer, mechanic, and one after another says, (you have heard them, I have heard them, we all hear them,) to every right which woman claims, "I grant you that, in the abstract, you are right ; but it is not expedient, nor wise, nor safe for woman nor man, nor good for the world." Let me tell you, that the man who grants that the position we assume is, in the abstract, right, has granted all we want ; and if he is not ready to take that step of abstract right, he only assumes to be wiser than He who made the world.

Mrs. President, I hear every day of my life, almost, the assertion that it is fanaticism to say that it is always safe and right to follow abstract right. This principle does not belong to any one belief ; it is the living soul of God's universe, that the absolute right is safe. If woman has the same right as man to read, to vote, to rule, to learn, to teach, there is nothing further to be said about it; and I never care to argue with the man who says it is right, but for some reason or other, it ought not to be granted, for he has granted everything, and has no ground left to stand upon.

Is it fanaticism to believe that God is wiser than man; that He, "who stretched out the heavens and laid the foundations of the earth," who "commanded the morning, and caused the day-spring to know its place," is wise enough to give laws to the universe which it shall be safe for you and me to obey? (Applause). Into this fanaticism this world is to be educated, if it is to be saved from going down to moral ruin and death. Remember, then, O man! father, husband, brother, clergyman, and politician—remember, when these words slip so easily from your tongues, as they often do, "I grant you have the same abstract right to do this that man has," you grant all that woman claims; and remember, as you stand reverently in the presence of God, that if you assert that that is not safe which He has pronounced to be right, you claim to be wiser, not than these women or these men who stand on the platform of the "Woman's Rights Convention," but you claim to be wiser than the Creator of man and woman. (Applause).

Allusion was made here this morning — well and wisely made — to the charge that when woman walks out into the avenues of public life, there to gain a living for herself and her children, or to help guide the nation, she ceases to be domestic, and faithful to the cares and shrine of home. We heard something well said this morning on the sphere of woman being the home, and we are told that this objection to our movement was altogether dishonest, contemptible, and ridiculous. It is not always such. Good men and true, and sometimes wise men, also, really in their souls believe that if a woman touches a ballot, her hand will be unfit for domestic duties; that if she teaches in the public congregation, she can not act well her part in the family circle. As I listened to what was said here, the words called to my mind the image of a woman of America, known as a religious and moral teacher, who bears a name of which this nation will one day be proud, but now slandered by a venal press, scorned by an arrogant pulpit, little appreciated by the mass of men and women, for whom the bearer of it is laboring night and day. The image of that woman rose before me. The world regards her as a public woman, as out of her sphere, and infers that she is neglectful of the cares and insensible to the loveliness of domestic life; and as I remembered her, I felt as I ever feel, that there is not a woman who, as a representative of my own sex, I would sooner show to the world as the embodiment of all domestic beauty and wifely care and motherly fidelity. I only wish that they and you might know her as I know her. I only wish that you might see in her, as I see in her, the very best possible illustration of the power of guiding and guarding all the sanctity of home, of blessing husband and children and grandchildren, and exerting in the guidance of her household an intellectual power which would be the glory of this or any other platform. Not only do husband and children "rise up and call her blessed," but in the time to come, the children and children's children of those who now scorn her name—of priests who have despised it, editors who have ridiculed and slandered it, and heaped upon it all of the ignominy of their souls—will thank God, as they reap the benefit of her exertions and her beautiful life, for the name of LUCRETIA MOTT. (Applause).

The word I would impress upon you all, as you go hence, is this—it is always safe to do right. Carry away with you from this Convention, my friends, this one thought—God is wiser than man. What He has made right, He has also made safe. His paths are paths of pleasantness, and all His ways are peace. And to those who go forward, bearing this great cause in their hands, to work for themselves, for their sisters, for their mothers—to them I would say, "Be not discouraged at any obstacles that may lie in your way! Forget, for a little while, the sneers of the press and the pulpit, the laugh of the fashionable lady. who calls you unladylike, and the scorn of arrogant men, who appreciate not your labors! You need not pay back the laughter and the scorn with scorn. Your work is too great, too high, too holy. Forgive them, and pass on! Rejoice to think that, in a few years, they, too, will rise up and thank you for it. Those who work for mankind must be content not to receive their reward in the appreciation of their services as they pass through life. It is of little consequence. The only thing is to be sure we are doing right, and living for some great purpose; for, of all the afflictions that can befall a man or woman, there is none so great as to pass through life without effecting anything—to die and leave the world no better than we found it, never being missed in consequence of any useful work we have done. (Applause). No good cause can go backward. No good cause declines. Nothing can put us down if we are right. All that we need to sustain and strengthen us in any great work is to be quite satisfied with the smile of God, and to have faith and hope that man shall at last be wholly and utterly redeemed and saved." (Applause).

The Convention then adjourned *sine die.*

47

From The New York Tribune of May 30.

MARRIAGE AND DIVORCE.

To the Editor of The New York Tribune:

SIR:—At our recent National Woman's Rights Convention many were surprised to hear Wendell Phillips object to the question of Marriage and Divorce, as irrelevant to our platform. He said: "We had no right to discuss there any laws or customs but those where inequality existed in the sexes; that the laws on Marriage and Divorce rested equally on man and woman; that he suffered, as much as she possibly could, the wrongs and abuses of an ill-assorted marriage."

Now, it must strike every careful thinker, that an immense difference rests in the fact, that man has made the laws, cunningly and selfishly, for his own purpose. From Coke down to Kent, who can cite one clause of the marriage contract where woman has the advantage? When man suffers from false legislation, he has his remedy in his own hands. Shall woman be denied the right of protest against laws in which she has had no voice—laws which outrage the holiest affections of her nature—laws which transcend the limits of human legislation—in a Convention called for the express purpose of considering her wrongs? He might as well object to a protest against the injustice of hanging a woman, because capital punishment bears equally on man and woman.

The contract of marriage is by no means equal. The law permits the girl to marry at twelve years of age, while it requires several years more of experience on the part of the boy. In entering this compact, the man gives up nothing that he before possessed—he is a man still; while the legal existence of the woman is suspended during marriage, and henceforth she is known but in and through the husband. She is nameless, purseless, childless—though a woman, an heiress, and a mother.

Blackstone says: "The husband and wife are one, and that one is the husband." Kent says: "The legal effects of marriage are generally deducible from the principle of the common law, by which the husband and wife are regarded as one person, and her legal existence and authority lost or suspended during the continuance of the matrimonial union."—Vol. 2, p. 109. Kent refers to Coke on Littleton, 112, a. 187, B. Litt. sec. 168, 291.

The wife is regarded by all legal authorities as a "*feme-covert,*" placed wholly *sub potestate viri.* Her moral responsibility, even, is merged in the husband. The law takes it for granted that the wife lives in fear of her husband; that his command is her highest law: hence a wife is not punishable for theft committed in presence of her husband.—Kent, vol. 2, p. 127. An unmarried woman can make contracts, sue and be sued, enjoy the rights of property, to her inheritance—to her wages—to her person—to her children; but, in marriage, she is robbed by law of all and every natural and civil right. "The disability of the wife to contract, so as to bind herself, arises not from want of discretion, but because she has entered into an indissoluble connection, by which she is placed under the power and protection of her husband."—Kent, vol. 2, p. 127. She is possessed of certain rights until she is married; then all are suspended, to revive again the moment the breath goes out of the husband's body.—See "Cowen's Treatise," vol. 2, p. 709.

If the contract be equal, whence come the terms " marital power "—" marital rights "—" obedience and restraint "—"dominion and control "—"power and protection," etc., etc. ? Many cases are stated, showing the exercise of a most questionable power over the wife, sustained by the courts.—See Bishop on Divorce, p. 489.

The laws on Divorce are quite as unequal as those on Marriage; yes, far more so. The advantages seem to be all on one side, and the pena'ties on the other. In case of divorce, if the husband be the guilty party, he still retains the greater part of the property. If the wife be the guilty party, she goes out of the partnership penniless.—Kent, vol. 2, p. 33; Bishop on Divorce, p. 492.

In New York and some other.States, the wife of the guilty husband can now sue for a divorce in her own name, and the costs come out of the husband's estate; but, in the majority of the States, she is still compelled to sue in the name of another, as she has no means of paying costs, even though she may have brought her thousands into the partnership. " The allowance to the innocent wife of *ad interim* alimony and money to sustain the suit, is not regarded as strict right in her, but of sound discretion in the court."—Bishop on Divorce, p. 581.

" Many jurists," says Kent, vol. 2, p. 88, " are of opinion that the adultery of the husband ought not to be noticed or made subject to the same animadver-ions as that of the wife, because it is not evidence of such entire depravity, nor equally injurious in its effects upon the morals, good order, and happiness of domestic life. Montesquieu, Pothier, and Dr. Taylor all insist that the cases of husband and wife ought to be distinguished, and that the violation of the mar-riage vow, on the part of the wife, is the most mischievous, and the prosecution ought to be confined to the offense on her part.--" Esprit des Loix," tom. 3, 186; "Traité du Contrat de Mariage," No. 516 ; " Elements of Civil Law," p. 254.

Say you, " These are but the opinions of men " ? On what else, I ask, are the hundreds of women depending, who this hour demand in our courts a release from burdensome contracts ? Are not these delicate matters left wholly to the discretion of courts? Are not young women from the first families dragged into the public courts—into assemblies of men exclusively—the judges all men, the jurors all men?—no true woman there to shield them by her presence from gross and impertinent questionings, to pity their misfortunes, or to protest against their wrongs ?

The administration of justice depends far more on the opinions of emi-nent jurists, than on law alone, for law is powerless when at variance with public sentiment.

Do not the above citations clearly prove inequality ? Are not the very letter and spirit of the marriage contract based on the idea of the su-premacy of man as the keeper of woman's virtue—her sole protector and support ? Out of marriage, woman asks nothing at this hour but the elective franchise. It is only in marriage that she must demand her rights to person, children, property, wages, life, liberty, and the pursuit of happiness. How can we discuss all the laws and conditions of mar-riage, without perceiving its essential essence, end, and aim ? Now, whether the institution of marriage be human or divine, whether re-garded as indissoluble by ecclesiastical courts, or dissoluble by civil courts, woman, finding herself equally degraded in each and every phase of it, always the victim of the institution, it is her right and her duty to sift the relation and the compact through and through, until she finds out the true cause of her false position. How can we go before the Legislatures of our respective States, and demand new laws, or no laws, on divorce, until we have some idea of what the true relation is ?

We decide the whole question of slavery by settling the sacred rights of the individual. We assert that man can not hold property in man, and reject the whole code of laws that conflicts with the self-evident truth of that assertion.

Again I ask, is it possible to discuss all the laws of a relation, and not touch the relation itself ? Yours respectfully,

ELIZABETH CADY STANTON.

HORACE GREELEY in *The New York Tribune*, May 14, 1860.

One Thousand Persons Present, seven-eighths of them Women, and a fair Proportion Young and Good-looking.—Whether the Woman's Rights Convention will finally succeed or not in enlarging the sphere of woman, they have certainly been very successful in enlarging that of their platform. Having introduced easy Divorce as one of the reforms which the new order of things demands, we can see no good reason why the platform should not be altogether replanked. We respectfully suggest that with this change of purpose there shall also be a change in name, and that hereafter these meetings shall be called not by name of Woman, but in the name of Wives Discontented. Hitherto we have supposed that the aim of this movement related to wrongs which woman suffered as woman, political and social inequalities, and disabilities with which she was mightily burdened. A settlement of the marriage relation, we conceive, does not come within this category. As there can be no wives without husbands, the subject concerns the latter quite as much as it does the former. One of the wrongs which it is charged woman suffers from man, is that he legislates for her when she is not represented. We acknowledge the justice of that plea, and, for that very reason, complain that she, under the name of Woman's Rights, should attempt to settle a question of such vital importance to him where he is supposed to be admitted only on suffrance. We believe in woman's rights; we have some conclusions (?) on the rights of husbands and wives; we are not yet, we confess, up to that advanced state which enables us to consider the rights of wives as something apart from that of husbands.

On the subject of marriage and divorce we have some very positive opinions, and what they are is pretty generally known. But even were they less positive and fixed, we should none the less protest against the sweeping character of the resolutions introduced at the Woman's Rights Convention on Friday by Mrs. Elizabeth Cady Stanton. We can not look upon the marriage relation as of no more binding force than that which a man may make with a purchaser for the sale of dry-goods, or an engagement he may contract with a schoolmaster or governess. Such doctrine seems to us simply shocking.

The intimate relation existing between one man and one woman, sanctified by, at least, the memory of an early and sincere affection, rendered more sacred by the present bond of dependent children, the fruit of that love, hallowed by many joys and many sorrows, though they be only re-membered joys and sorrows, with other interests that can be broken in upon only to be destroyed—such a relation, we are very sure, has ele-ments of quite another nature than those which belong to the shop or the counting-house. In our judgment, the balance of duty can not be struck like the balance of a mercantile statement of profit and loss, or measured with the calculations we bestow on an account current. Such a doctrine we regard as pernicious and debasing. We can conceive of nothing that would more utterly sap the foundations of sound morality, or give a looser rein to the most licentious and depraved appetites of the vilest men and women. Upon the physiological and psychological laws which govern generation, we do not care here to enter, even if Mrs. Stanton leads the way; but we believe that the progress of the world, springing out of connections formed under such a dispensation of humanity as is here indicated, with so little of duty or conscience, with so little hope or expectation of abiding affection, with so little intention of permanency as must necessarily belong to them, would be more monstrous than the world has ever dreamed of. For such a rule of married life contemplates no married life at all, and no parental relation. It destroys the family; it renders the dearest word in the Saxon tongue (home) a vague and un-meaning term; it multiplies a thousand-fold and renders universal all the evils which in the imperfections of human nature are now occasional under the binding force of a moral sense, the duty of continency, and the remnant of nothing else is left of love.

There are some other things besides in these resolutions to which we might object on the score of truth, some things which we rather marvel, modest women should say, and that modest women, in a mixed assem-bly, should listen to with patience. But these are secondary matters. The thought—more than them all—that the marriage tie is of the same nature as a mere business relation, is so objectionable, so dangerous, that we do not care to draw attention from that one point.

In asserting that marriage is an equal relation for husbands and wives, Mr. Greeley, like Mr. Phillips, begs the whole question. If it is legitimate to discuss all laws that bear unequally on man and woman in woman's rights conventions, surely those that grow out of marriage, which are the most oppressive and degrading on the statute-book, should command our first consideration. There could be no slaveholders without slaves; the one relation involves the other, and yet it would be absurd to say that slaves might not hold a conven-tion to discuss the inequality of the laws sustaining that relation, and incidentally the whole institution itself, because the slaveholder shared in the evils resulting from it. There never has been a woman's convention held in which the injustice suffered by wives and mothers has not been a topic for discussion, and legitimately so.

And if the only way of escape from the infamous laws by which all power is placed in the hands of man, is through divorce, then that is the hospitable door to open for those who wish to escape. No proposition contained in Mrs. Stanton's speech on divorce, viewed in any light, can be a tenth part so shocking as the laws on the statute-books, or the opinions expressed by many of the authorities in the English and American systems of jurisprudence.

It is difficult to comprehend that the release of the miserable from false relations, would necessarily seduce the contented from happy ones, or that the dearest word in the Saxon tongue (home) should have no significance, after drunkards and villains were denied the right to enter it. It is a pleasant reflection, in view of the dolorous results Mr. Greeley foresees from the passage of a divorce law, that the love of men and women for each other and their children in no way depends on the Statutes of New York. In the State of Indiana, where the laws have been very liberal for many years, family life is as beautiful and permanent as in South Carolina and New York, where the tie can be dissolved for one cause only. When we consider how little protection the State throws round the young and thoughtless in entering this relation, stringent laws against all escape are cruel and despotic, especially to woman, for if home life, which is everything to her, is discordant, where can she look for happiness?

APPEAL TO THE WOMEN OF NEW YORK.

WOMEN OF NEW YORK:—Once more we appeal to you to make renewed efforts for the elevation of our sex. In our marital laws we are now in advance of every State in the Union. Twelve years ago New York took the initiative step, and secured to married women their property, received by gift or inheritance. Our last Legislature passed a most liberal act, giving to married women their rights, to sue for damages of person or property, to their separate earnings and their children; and to the widow, the possession and control of the entire estate during the minority of the youngest child. Women of New York! You can no longer be insulted in the first days of your widowed grief by the coarse minions of the law at your fireside, coolly taking an inventory of your household gods, or robbing your children of their natural guardian.

While we rejoice in this progress made in our laws, we see also a change in the employment of women. They are coming down from the garrets and up from the cellars to occupy more profitable posts in every department of industry, literature, science, and art. In the church, too, behold the spirit of freedom at work. Within the past year, the very altar has been the scene of well-fought battles; women claiming and exercising their right to vote in church matters, in defiance of precedent, priest, or Paul.

Another evidence of the importance of our cause is seen in the deep interest men of wealth are manifesting in it. Three great bequests have been given to us in the past year. Five thousand dollars from an unknown hand,* a share in the munificent fund left by that noble man of Boston, Charles F. Hovey, and four hundred thousand dollars by Mr. Vassar, of Poughkeepsie, to found a college for girls, equal in all respects to Yale and Harvard. Is it not strange that women of wealth are constantly giving large sums of money to endow professorships and colleges for boys exclusively—to churches and to the education of the ministry, and yet give no thought to their own sex—crushed in ignorance, poverty, and prostitution—the hopeless victims of custom, law, and Gospel, with few to offer a helping hand, while the whole world combine to aid the boy and glorify the man?

Our movement is already felt in the Old World. The nobility of England, with Lord Brougham at their head, have recently formed a "Society for Promoting the Employments of Women."

All this is the result of the agitation, technically called "Woman's Rights," through conventions, lectures, circulation of tracts and petitions, and by the faithful word uttered in the privacy of home. The few who stand forth to meet the world's cold gaze, its ridicule, its contumely, and its scorn, are urged onward by the prayers and tears, crushed hopes and withered hearts of the sad daughters of the race. The wretched will not let them falter; and they who seem to do the work, ever and anon draw fresh courage and inspiration from the noblest women of the age, who, from behind the scene, send forth good words of cheer and heartfelt thanks.

Six years hence, the men of New York purpose to revise our State Constitution. Among other changes demanded, is the right of suffrage for women—which right will surely be granted, if through all the intervening years every woman does her duty. Again do we appeal to each and all—to every class and condition—to inform themselves on this question, that woman may no longer publish her degradation by declaring herself satisfied in her present position, nor her ignorance by asserting that she has "all the rights she wants."

Any person who ponders the startling fact that there are four millions of African slaves in this republic, will instantly put the question to himself, "Why do these people submit to the cruel tyranny that our government exercises over them?" The answer is apparent—"simply because they are ignorant of their power." Should they rise *en masse*, assert and demand their rights, their freedom would be secure. It is the same with woman. Why is it that one-half the people of this nation are held in abject dependence — civilly, politically, socially, the slaves of man?

---

* Francis Jackson. This fund was drawn upon by several of the States. $1,993.66 was expended in the campaigns in New York, the publication of 60,000 tracts, and the appropriation of several hundred to a series of sermons by the Rev. Antoinette Brown Blackwell, delivered in Hope Chapel, New York; $1,000 was expended in the Ohio canvass of 1860, and tracts in large numbers were also sent there. Both money and tracts were contributed to the Kansas campaign of 1859. Lucy Stone had $1,500 to expend in Kansas in 1867, and thus in various ways the fund was finally expended, Lucy Stone drawing out the last $1,000 in 1871. So careful had been the management of this fund, that the accumulation of the interest had greatly increased the original sum.

Simply because woman knows not her power. To find out her natural rights, she must travel through such labyrinths of falsehood, that most minds stand appalled before the dark mysteries of life— the seeming contradictions in all laws, both human and divine. But, because woman can not solve the whole problem to her satisfaction, because she can not prove to a demonstration the rottenness and falsehood of our present customs, shall she, without protest, supinely endure evils she can not at once redress? The silkworm, in its many wrappings, knows not it yet shall fly. The woman, in her ignorance, her drapery, and her chains, knows not that in advancing civilization, she too must soon be free, to counsel with her conscience and her God.

The religion of our day teaches that in the most sacred relations of the race, the woman must ever be subject to the man; that in the husband centers all power and learning; that the difference in position between husband and wife is as vast as that between Christ and the church; and woman struggles to hold the noble impulses of her nature in abeyance to opinions uttered by a Jewish teacher, which, alas! the mass believe to be the will of God. Woman turns from what she is taught to believe are God's laws to the laws of man; and in his written codes she finds herself still a slave. No girl of fifteen could read the laws concerning woman, made, executed, and defended by those who are bound to her by every tie of affection, without a burst of righteous indignation. Few have ever read or heard of the barbarous laws that govern the mothers of this Christian republic, and fewer still care, until misfortune brings them into the iron grip of the law. It is the imperative duty of educated women to study the Constitution and statutes under which they live, that when they shall have a voice in the government, they may bring wisdom and not folly into its councils.

We now demand the ballot, trial by jury of our peers, and an equal right to the joint earnings of the marriage copartnership. And, until the Constitution be so changed as to give us a voice in the government, we demand that man shall make all his laws on property, marriage, and divorce, to bear equally on man and woman.

	E. CADY STANTON, *President.*
New York State	LYDIA MOTT,* *Sec. and Treas.*
Woman's Rights Committee.	ERNESTINE L. ROSE.
	MARTHA C. WRIGHT.
November, 1860.	SUSAN B. ANTHONY.

N. B.—Let every friend commence to get signatures to the petition without delay, and send up to Albany early in January, either to your representative or to Lydia Mott.

How can any wife or mother, who to-day rejoices in her legal right to the earnings of her hands, and the children of her love, withhold the small pittance of a few hours or days in getting signatures to the petition, or a few shillings or dollars to carry the work onward and upward, to a final glorious consummation.

---

* Lydia Mott was one of the quiet workers who kept all things pertaining to the woman's rights reform in motion at the capital. Living in Albany, she planned conventions

CONVENTION IN ALBANY AND HEARING BEFORE THE JU-
DICIARY COMMITTEE IN THE ASSEMBLY CHAMBER.

FEBRUARY 7TH AND 8TH, 1861.

The last Convention before the War was held in Albany. Ernes-
tine L. Rose, Lucretia Mott, William Lloyd Garrison, Rev. Beriah
Green, Aaron M. Powell, Elizabeth Cady Stanton, and Susan B.
Anthony were the speakers. They had a hearing also before the
Judiciary Committee on the bill then pending asking divorce for vari-
ous causes.* The interest in the question was intense at this time,

---

and hearings before the Legislature. She knew a large number of the members and men of
influence, who all felt a profound respect for that dignified, judicious Quaker woman. Her
home was not only one of the depots of the underground railroad, where slaves escaping
to Canada were warmed and fed, but it was the hospitable resort for all reformers. Everything about the house was clean and orderly, and the table always bountiful, and the food
appetizing. As such men as Seward and Marcy, leaders from opposite political parties,
Gerrit Smith, Garrison, Phillips, Pillsbury, Remond, Foster, Douglass, representing all
the reforms, met in turn at Miss Mott's dinner-table, she had the advantage of hearing
popular questions discussed from every standpoint. And Miss Mott was not merely
hostess at her table, but on all occasions took a leading part in the conversation. All of
us who enjoyed her friendship and hospitality deeply feel her loss in that conservative city.

[* Introduced, on notice, by Mr. Ramsey ; read twice, and referred to the Committee on
the Judiciary ; reported from said Committee for the consideration of the Senate, and
committed to the Committee of the Whole].

AN ACT IN REGARD TO DIVORCES DISSOLVING THE MARRIAGE CONTRACT.

The People of the State of New York, represented in Senate and Assembly, do enact as follows :

SECTION 1. In addition to the cases in which a divorce, dissolving the marriage contract, may now be decreed by the Supreme Court, such a divorce may be decreed by said
court in either of the cases following :

1. Where either party to the marriage shall, for the period of three years next preceding the application for such divorce, have willfully deserted the other party to the marriage, and neglected to perform to such party the duties imposed by their relation.

2. Where there is and shall have been for the period of one year next preceding the application for such divorce, continuous and repeated instances of cruel and inhuman treatment by either party, so as greatly to impair the health or endanger the life of the other
party, thereby rendering it unsafe to live with the party guilty of such cruelty or
inhumanity.

§ 2. The foregoing sections shall not apply to any person who shall not have been an
actual resident of this State for the period of five years next preceding such application
for such divorce.

§ 3. Specifications one, two, and three of original section thirty-eight, of article three,
of title one, of chapter eight, of part two of the Revised Statutes, shall apply to these
causes for divorce as they now apply to the cause of adultery.

§ 4. The other provisions of the Revised Statutes relating to the granting of divorces
for adultery, and regulating the form and manner of proceedings and decrees, and the effects thereof, and the restrictions and defences to the application thereof, shall be applicable to the granting of divorces for causes hereinabove specified, and all proceedings
therefor and therein, so far and in such manner as the same may be capable of such
application.

§ 5. This act shall take effect immediately.

owing to several very aggravated cases among leading families, both in this country and England. The very liberal bill pending in the Legislature had drawn special attention to it in the Empire State, which not only made the whole question of marriage and divorce a topic of conversation at every fireside, but of many editorial debates in our leading journals. Among others, Horace Greeley, in *The New York Tribune*, had a prolonged discussion with the Hon. Robert Dale Owen,* in which it was generally thought that the weight of argument rested with Mr. Owen; but it was evident that Mr. Greeley did not think so, as he afterward republished the whole controversy at his own expense. *The Albany Evening Journal* also took strong grounds against the bill. But the opponents invariably discussed the question on the basis that marriage was an *equal* relation, in which man suffered as much as woman, ignoring the fact that *man* had made the laws governing it, and all to his own advantage.

From the following letter of Lucretia Mott, we see how clear she was as to the merits of the position we had taken in the discussion of this vital question:

ROADSIDE, near Philadelphia, 4th Mo., 30th, '61.

MY DEAR LYDIA MOTT:—I have wished ever since parting with thee and our other dear friends in Albany to send thee a line, and have only waited in the hope of contributing a little "substantial aid" toward your neat and valuable "depository." The twenty dollars enclosed is from our Female Anti-Slavery Society.

I see the annual meeting in New York is not to be held this spring. Sister Martha is here, and was expecting to attend both anniversaries. But we now think the Woman's Rights meeting had better not be attempted, and she has written Elizabeth C. Stanton to this effect.

I was well satisfied with being at the Albany meeting. I have since met with the following from a speech of Lord Brougham's, which pleased me, as being as radical as mine in your stately Hall of Representatives:

"Before woman can have any justice by the laws of England, there must be a total reconstruction of the whole system; for any attempt to amend it would prove useless. The great charter, in establishing the supremacy of law over prerogative, provides only for justice between man and man; for woman nothing is left but common-law, accumulations and modifications of original Gothic and Roman heathenism, which no amount of filtration through ecclesiastical courts could change into Christian laws. They are declared unworthy a Christian people by great jurists; still they remain unchanged."

So Elizabeth Stanton will see that I have authority for going to the root of the evil.

We had a delightful golden-wedding on the 10th inst. All our children and

---

* Published at the close of Mr. Greeley's "Recollections of a Busy Life."

children's children were present, and a number of our friends hereaway. Our sister Mary W. Hicks and her grand daughter May were all of James's relatives from New York. Brother Richard and daughter Cannie could not feel like coming. Brother Silas and Sarah Cornell could not come.

Love to all.   LUCRETIA MOTT.

In 1861 came "the war of the rebellion," the great conflict between the North and the South, the final struggle between freedom and slavery. The women who had so perseveringly labored for their own enfranchisement now gave all their time and thought to the nation's life; their patriotism was alike spontaneous and enduring. In the sanitary movement, in the hospitals, on the battle-field, gathering in the harvests on the far-off prairies—all that heroic women dared and suffered through those long dark years of anxiety and death, should have made "justice to woman" the spontaneous cry on the lips of our rulers, as we welcomed the return of the first glad days of peace. All specific work for her own rights she willingly thrust aside. No Conventions were held for five years; no petitions circulated for her civil and political rights; the action of State Legislatures was wholly forgotten. In their stead, Loyal Leagues were formed, and petitions by the hundred thousand for the emancipation of the slaves rolled up and sent to Congress—a measure which with speech and pen they pressed on the nation's heart, seeing clearly as they did that this was the pivotal point of the great conflict.

Thus left unwatched, the Legislature of New York amended the law of 1860, taking from the mother the lately guaranteed right to the equal guardianship of her children, replacing it by a species of veto power, which did not allow the father to bind out or will away a child without the mother's consent in writing. The law guaranteeing the widow the control of the property, which the husband should leave at death, for the care and protection of minor children, was also repealed. This cowardly act of the Legislature of 1862 * is the strongest possible proof of woman's need of the ballot

---

* PASSED APRIL 10, 1862.

SECT. 3. Any married woman, possessed of real estate as her separate property, may bargain, sell, and convey such property, and enter into any contract in reference to the same, with the like effect in all respects as if she were unmarried; and she may in like manner enter into such covenant or covenants for title as are usual in conveyances of real estate, which covenants shall be obligatory to bind her separate property, in case the same or any of them be broken.

§ 2. The fourth, fifth, sixth, ninth, tenth, and eleventh sections of the said Act are hereby repealed.

7th. Any married woman may, while married, sue and be sued, in all matters having relation to her sole and separate property, or which may hereafter come to her by

in her own hand for protection. Had she possessed the power to make and unmake legislators, no State Assembly would have dared thus to rob the mother of her natural rights. But without the suffrage she was helpless. While, in her loyalty to the Government and her love to humanity, she was encouraging the "boys in blue" to fight for the freedom of the black mothers of the South, these dastardly law-makers, filled with the spirit of slaveholders, were stealing the children and the property of the white mothers in the Empire State !

When Susan B. Anthony heard of the repeal of 1862, she was filled with astonishment, and wrote thus to Miss Lydia Mott :

DEAR LYDIA:—Your startling letter is before me. I knew some weeks ago that that abominable thing was on the calendar, with some six or eight hundred bills *before it,* and hence felt sure it would not come up this winter, and that in the meantime we should sound the alarm. Well, well; while the old guard sleep the young "devils" are wide-awake, and we deserve to suffer for our confidence in "man's sense of justice," and to have all we have gained thus snatched from us. But nothing short of this can rouse our women again to action. All our reformers seem suddenly to have grown politic. All alike say, "Have no conventions at this crisis"! Garrison, Phillips, Mrs. Mott, Mrs. Wright Mrs. Stanton, etc., say, "Wait until the war excitement abates"; which is to say,

---

descent, devise, bequest, purchase, or the gift or grant of any person, in the same manner as if she were sole ; and any married woman may bring and maintain an action in her own name, for damages, against any person or body corporate, for any injury to her person or character, the same as if she were sole ; and the money received upon the settlement of any such action, or recovered upon a judgment, shall be her sole and separate property. In case it shall be necessary in the prosecution or defense of any action brought by or against a married woman, to enter into any bond or undertaking, such bond or undertaking may be executed by such married woman, with the same effect in all respects as if she were sole ; and in case the said bond or undertaking shall become broken or forfeited, the same may be enforced against her separate estate.

8th. No bargain or contract made by any married woman, in respect to her sole and separate property, or any property which may hereafter come to her by descent, devise, bequest, purchase, or the gift or grant of any person (except her husband), and no bargain or contract entered into by any married woman, in or about the carrying on of any trade or business, under any statute of this State, shall be binding upon her husband, or render him or his property in any way liable therefor.

5th. In an action brought or defended by any married woman in her name, her husband shall not, neither shall his property, be liable for the costs thereof, or the recovery therein. In an action brought by her for an injury to her person, character, or property, if judgment shall pass against her for costs, the court in which the action is pending shall have jurisdiction to enforce payment of such judgment out of her separate estate, though the sum recovered be less than one hundred dollars.

6th. No man shall bind his child to apprenticeship or service, or part with the control of such child or create any testamentary guardian therefor, unless the mother, if living, shall in writing signify her assent thereto.

7th. A married woman may be sued in any of the courts of this State, and whenever a judgment shall be recovered against a married woman, the same may be enforced by execution against her sole and separate estate in the same manner as if she were sole.

"Ask our opponents if they think we had better speak, or, rather, if they do not think we had better remain silent." I am sick at heart, but I can not carry the world against the wish and the will of our best friends. But what can we do now, when even the motion to retain the mother's joint guardianship is voted, down? Twenty thousand petitions rolled up for that—a hard year's work!— the law secured!—the echoes of our words of gratitude in the capitol have scarce died away, and now all is lost!

And, worse still, in 1871,* after the black man was not only emancipated, but enfranchised, by the Fourteenth and Fifteenth Amendments, which, overriding State Constitution and statute law, abolished the property qualification for colored voters in the State of New York, another step of retrogressive legislation was taken against woman, in the repeal of section nine † of the Act of 1860, re-enacting the spirit and letter of the old common law, which holds that the children born in legal wedlock belong to the father alone. Had woman held the ballot—that weapon of protection—in her hand to punish legislators, by withholding her vote from those thus derelict to duty, no repeal of the law of 1860 could have possibly taken place.

ALBANY, *April* 8, 1881.

DEAR MISS ANTHONY:—Your esteemed favor of the 6th duly received.

The Statute of 1862, Laws of 1862, chapter 90, page 157, repealed the grandest and crowning section of the Statute of 1860, viz: Sections 4, 5, 6, 9, 10, and 11, copies of which sections I herewith inclose you. Had these sections remained, wives in this State would have possessed equal rights with their husbands, save simply the right of voting. It was a great mistake and wrong to repeal them. Had I been a member of the Senate at that time, as I was not, I don't think it would have been done.

I do not know who was the author of the repeal bill, nor did I know of its existence until I saw it in the statute-book. I think Judge Charles J. Folger, now Chief-Justice of the Court of Appeals, was chairman of the Senate Judiciary Committee, and the bill of 1862 must therefore have passed through the hands of that Committee, in which it originated, or through which it was reported, and by the influence of which it must have been adopted.

---

* THE GUARDIANSHIP LAW, PASSED APRIL 25, 1871.

6th. The Surrogate, to whom application may be made under either of the preceding sections, shall have the same power to allow and appoint guardians as is possessed by the Supreme Court, and may appoint a guardian for a minor whose father is living, upon personal service of notice of the application for such appointment upon such father, at least ten days prior thereto; and in all cases the Surrogate shall inquire into the circumstances of the minor and ascertain the amount of his personal property, and the value of the rents and profits of his real estate, and for that purpose may compel any person to appear before him and testify in relation thereto.

† See law of 1860.

Strange that you women, so watchful and so regardful of your rights, should have allowed the repeal of those important sections, without strenuous opposition. Very sincerely yours,

ANDREW J. COLVIN.

We were busily engaged rolling up petitions for the Thirteenth Amendment to the Federal Constitution, our hearts and hands full of work for the Government in the midst of the war, supposing all was safe at Albany. But how comes it that the author of the bill of 1860, residing at the capital, never heard of its repeal? If the bill was so slyly passed that Mr. Colvin himself did not know of it until he saw it in the statute-book, it is not remarkable that it escaped our notice in time to prevent it.

GENENA, N. Y., *April* 12, 1881.

MISS ANTHONY, DEAR MADAM:—I was chairman of the Judiciary Committee of the New York Senate in 1862-'3-'4-'5-'6-'7-'8-'9. Judge John Willard, of Saratoga County, was a member of the State Senate in that year, and a member of that Committee. He was the author of the Act of 1862. His object, as I have always understood it, was to simplify, make clear, consistent, and practical some of the legislation in regard to married women. I think, with deference I say it, that you are not strictly accurate in calling the legislation of 1862 a repealing one. The first section of the Act of 1862 (chap. 172, p. 343) *amends* the third section of the Act of 1860 (chap. 90, p. 157), by striking out the provision requiring the assent of the husband, and giving the wife the right (or privilege) to contract and convey as a *feme sole,* and to covenant for title, etc., etc. That amendment rendered unnecessary the fourth, fifth, and sixth sections of the Act of 1860. They would have fallen of themselves, that is, have been repealed by implication, as inconsistent with the greater power and freedom attained by married women by the amendment of 1862 to the Act of 1860. But *ex abundanti cautela,* as Judge Willard would have said, there was an express repeal of them. The tenth and eleventh sections of the Act of 1860, were also repealed expressly; but not to the sole detriment of married women. The tenth section gave to married men and married women a life estate in certain cases in one-third of all the real estate of which the wife or husband died seized. The wife had before the Act of 1860, and has now, that estate. The tenth section gave her nothing. The repeal of it took nothing from her. The eleventh section, so far as it gave a life estate, is the same as the tenth. So far as it gave the use of all the real estate of the intestate for the minority of the youngest child, it was an addition to the property rights of the wife, but it was also an addition to the property rights of the husband. I am not able from memory to say why it was repealed; and it is remembrance and not reasoning that you ask for. The third section of the Act of 1862 amends the seventh of the Act of 1860 by striking out the phrase, "*except her husband,*" thus enabling a married woman to protect the property given to her by the husband, in which the Act of 1860 was lame, and in other ways gave more freedom and power to married women. The fourth section of the Act of 1862 amends the eighth section of the Act of 1860, but only in its verbiage. The fifth section of the Act of 1862 does not impair the Act of 1860; it simply puts the woman before the courts, and the law as an entity able to go alone. The sixth section of the Act of 1862 increases the powers of a married woman, by giving her a veto on some acts of her husband. The seventh section is like the fifth. In no other respect than those I have named did the Act of 1862 affect the Act of 1860. In but one thing did it repeal, in the sense of taking away any right or power or privilege or freedom that the Act of 1860 gave. On the contrary, in some respects, it gave more or greater.

I am glad that you wrote to me. I am glad that I have the opportunity to defend the memory of a good man, Judge John Willard. I make bold to ask you to turn to the thirty-seventh volume of Barbour's Supreme Court Reports, Appendix, pp. 670 *et seq.*, and read the words spoken of him by his peers. I am glad also to have the opportunity to speak a word for my Judiciary Committee.

And I will not close this lengthened answer, without suggesting a suspicion, that those who have taken the notion that the Act of 1862 was a retrograde step, have done so without comparing for themselves the two acts.

For myself, I have the distinction of being one of less than half-a-dozen Senators who voted that women have the right to vote for delegates to the Constitutional Convention of 1866; and one of about a dozen and a half members of that Convention who voted to erase from the suffrage article the word "*male.*" I have never been convinced of the expediency of giving to females the privilege of suffrage; but I have never been able to see the argument by which they were not as much entitled to the *right* as males.

Trusting that you will forgive the length of this epistle,

I am with respect, yours, etc., etc.,

MISS SUSAN B. ANTHONY. CHARLES J. FOLGER.

As will be seen by the above letters, both Mr. Colvin and Mr. Folger make mistakes in regard to the effect of these bills. In speaking of the complete equality of husbands and wives under the law of 1860, Mr. Colvin said, "All the wife then had to ask was the right of suffrage," quite forgetting that the wife has never had an equal right to the joint earnings of the copartnership, as no valuation has ever been placed on her labor in the household, to which she gives all her time, thought, and strength, the absolute sacrifice of herself, mind and body, all possibility of self-development and self-improvement being in most cases out of the question. Mr. Folger in saying the repeal of section eleven affected man as much as woman, falls into the same mistake, assuming that the joint earnings belong to man. We say that the wife who surrenders herself wholly to domestic life, foregoing all opportunities for pecuniary independence and personal distinction in the world of work, or the higher walks of literature and art, in order to make it possible for the husband to have home and family ties, and at the same time, his worldly successes and ambitions, richly earns the place of an equal partner. In their joint accumulations, her labor and economy should be taken into account.

This is *the vital point* of interest to the vast majority of married women, since it is only the *few* who ever possess anything through separate earnings or inheritance. A law securing to the wife the absolute right to one-half the joint earnings, and at the death of the husband, the same control of property and children that he has when she dies, might make some show of justice; but it is a provision not yet on the statute-books of any civilized nation on the globe.

The seeming sophistry of Judge Folger may be traced to the universal fact that man does not appreciate the arduous and unremitting labors of the wife in the household, or her settled dissatisfaction in having no pecuniary recompense for her labors. No man with cultured brain and skilled hands would consider himself recompensed for a life of toil in being provided with shelter, food, and clothes while his employer was living, to be cut down in his old age to a mere pittance; yet such is the fate of the majority of wives and widows under the most beneficent provisions of our statutes in this favored republic. True, the law says "the husband shall maintain the wife in accordance with his circumstances"; he being judge, jury, executive. Though she may toil incessantly, and her duties be far more exhaustive than his, yet he is supposed to maintain her, and the joint property is always disposed of on that basis. Legislation for woman proceeds on the assumption, that all she needs is a bare support; and that she is destitute of the natural human desire to accumulate, possess, and control the results of her own labor.

p. 40-41

Locker Notes

Women were nelgected of their rights for their poperty

Matilda Joslyn Gage

CHAPTER XV.

WOMAN, CHURCH, AND STATE.

BY MATILDA JOSLYN GAGE.

Woman under old religions—Woman took part in offices of early Christian Church Councils—Original sin—Celibacy of the clergy—Their degrading sensuality—Feudalism—Marriage—Debasing externals and debasing ideas—Witchcraft—Three striking points for consideration — Burning of Witches—Witchcraft in New England — Marriage with devils—Woman s Right of property not recognized—Wife ownership—Women legislated for as slaves—Marriage under the Greek Church—The Salic law—Cromwellian era—The Reformation—Woman under monastic rules in the Protestant home—Polygamy taught by Luther and other Protestant Divines—The Mormon doctrine regarding woman its logical result—Milton responsible for many existing views in regard to woman—Woman's subordination taught to-day—The See trial—Right Rev. Dr. Cox—Rev. Knox-Little—Pan-Presbyterians—Quakers not as liberal as they have been considered—Restrictive action of the Methodist Church—Offensive debate upon ordaining Miss Oliver—The Episcopal Church and its restrictions—Sunday-school teachings—Week-day-school teachings—Sermon upon woman's subordination by the President of a Baptist Theological Seminary—Professor Christlieb of Germany—"Dear, will you bring me my shawl?"—Female sex looked upon as a degradation—A sacrilegious child—Secretary Evarts, in the Beecher-Tilton trial, upon woman's subordination—Women degraded in science and literature—Large-hearted men upon woman's degradation—Wives still sold in the market-place as "mares," led by a halter around their necks—Degrading servile labor performed by woman in Christian countries—A lower degradation — "Queen's women "—" Government women "—Interpolations in the Bible—Letter from Howard Crosby, D.D., LL.D—What is Truth?

WOMAN is told that her present position in society is entirely due to Christianity, and this assertion is then made the basis of opposition to her demands for exact equality with man in all the relations of life. Knowing that the position of every human being keeps pace with the religion and civilization of his country, and that in many ancient nations woman had secured a good degree of respect and power, as compared even with that she has in the present era, it has been decided to present this subject from a historical standpoint, and to show woman's position under the Christian Church for the last 1,500 years.

If in so doing we shall help to show man's unwarranted usurpation over woman's religious and civil rights, and the very great difference between true religion and theology, this chapter will not have been written in vain, as it will prove that the most grievous wound ever inflicted upon woman has been in the teaching that she was not created equal with man, and the consequent denial of her rightful place and position in Church and State.

Woman had acquired great liberty under the old civilizations. In Rome she had not only secured remarkable personal and property rights,* but she officiated as priestess in the most holy offices of religion. Not only as Vestal Virgin did she guard the Sacred Fire, upon whose preservation the welfare of Rome was held to depend, but at the end of every consular period women officiated in private worship and sacrifice to the *Bona Dea*, with mystic ceremonies which no man's presence was suffered to profane. The Eleusinian mysteries were attributed to Ceres herself, and but few men had the courage to dare initiation into their most secret rites. In ancient Egypt, woman bought and sold in the markets, was physician, colleges for her instruction in medicine existing 1,200 years before Christ; she founded its literature, the "Sacred Songs" of Isis being deemed by Plato literally 10,000 years old; as priestess she performed the most holy offices of religion, holding the Sacred Sistrum and offering sacrifices to the gods; she sat upon its throne and directed the civilization of this country at the most brilliant period of its history; while in the marriage relation she held more than equality; the husband at the ceremony promising obedience to the wife in all things, a rule which according to Wilkinson, wrought no harm, but, on the contrary, was productive of lasting fidelity and regard, the husband and wife sitting together upon the same double chair in life, and lying together in the same tomb after death. [Crimes against women were rare in olden Egypt, and were punished in the most severe manner.] In Persia, woman was one of the founders of the ancient Parsee religion, which taught the existence of but a single God, thus introducing monotheism into that rare old kingdom. The Germans endowed their wives upon marriage with a horse, bridle, and spear, emblematic

---

* Maine (Gaius) says of the position of woman under Roman law before the introduction of Christianity: "The juriconsulists had evidently at this time assumed the equality of the sexes as a principle of the code of equity. The situation of the Roman woman, whether married or single, became one of great personal and property independence . . . . but Christianity tended somewhat, from the very first, to narrow this remarkable liberty. The prevailing state of religious sentiment may explain why modern jurisprudence has adopted these rules concerning the position of woman which belong peculiarly to an imperfect civilization. . . . . No society which preserves any tincture of Christian institutions, is likely to restore to married women the personal liberty conferred on them by middle Roman law. Canon law has deeply injured civilization."

of equality, and they held themselves bound to chastity in the marital relation. [The women of Scandinavia were regarded with respect, and marriage was held as sacred by both men and women.] These old Berserkers reverenced their Alruna, or Holy Women, on earth, and worshiped goddesses in heaven.

All Pagandom recognized a female priesthood, some making their national safety to depend upon them, like Rome; sybils wrote the Books of Fate, and oracles where women presided were consulted by many nations. The proof of woman's also taking part in the offices of the Christian Church at an early date is to be found in the very restrictions which were at a later period placed upon her. The Council of Laodicea, A.D. 365, in its eleventh canon* forbade the ordination of women to the ministry, and by its forty-fourth canon prohibited them from entering into the altar.

The Council of Orleans, A.D. 511, consisting of twenty-six bishops and priests, promulgated a canon declaring that on account of their frailty, women must be excluded from the deaconship.

Nearly five hundred years later than the Council of Laodicea, we find the Council of Paris (A.D. 824) bitterly complaining that women serve at the altar, and even give to the people the body and blood of Jesus Christ. The Council of Aix-la-Chapelle, only eight years previously, had forbidden abbesses from taking upon themselves any priestly function. Through these canons we have the negative proof that for many hundred years women preached, baptized,† administered the sacrament, and filled various offices of the Church, and that men took it upon themselves to forbid them from such functions through prohibitory canons.

A curious old black-letter volume published in London in 1632, entitled "The Lawes and Resolutions of Women's Rights," says,

---

* Canon law is the whole body of Church decrees enacted by councils, bulls, decretals, etc., and is recognized as a system of laws primarily established by the Christian Church, and enforced by ecclesiastical authority. It took cognizance first merely of what were considered spiritual duties, but ultimately extended itself to temporal rights. It was collected and embodied in the ninth century, since which period numerous additions have been made.

† The women claimed the right to baptize their own sex. But the bishops and presbyters did not care to be released from the pleasant duty of baptizing the female converts.—*Hist. of Christian Religion from A.D. to 200, p. 23, Waite.* The Constitution of the Church of Alexandria, which is thought to have been established about the year 200, required the applicant for baptism to be divested of clothing, and after the ordinance had been administered, to be anointed with oil.—*Ibid., p.* 384–5. The converts were first exorcised of the evil spirits that were supposed to inhabit them ; then, after undressing and being baptized, they were anointed with oil.—*Bunsen's Christianity of Mankind, Vol. VII., p.* 386–393 ; *3d Vol. Analecta.*

" the reason why women have no control in Parliament, why they make no laws, consent to none, abrogate none, is their Original Sin."

This doctrine of her original sin lies at the base of the religious and political disqualifications of woman. Christianity, through this doctrine, has been interpreted as sustaining man's rights alone. The offices held by her during the apostolic age, she has been gradually deprived of through ecclesiastical enactments. To Augustine, whose early life was spent in company with the most degraded of woman-kind, is Christianity indebted for the full development of the doctrine of Original Sin, which, although to be found in the religious systems of several ancient nations, was not a primitive one of the Christian Church.* Taught as one of the most sacred mysteries of religion, which to doubt or to question was to hazard eternal damnation, it at once exerted a most powerful and repressing influence upon woman, fastening upon her a bondage which the civilization of the nineteenth century has not been able to cast off.

To this doctrine of woman's created inferiority we can trace those irregularities which for many centuries filled the Church with shame, for practices more obscene than the orgies of Babylon or Corinth, and which dragged Christendom to a darkness blacker than the night of heathendom in pagan countries—a darkness upon which the most searching efforts of historians cast scarcely one ray of light—a darkness so profound that from the seventh to the eleventh century no individual thought can be traced. All was sunk in superstition; men were bound by Church dogmas, and looked only to aggrandizement through her. The priesthood, which alone possessed a knowledge of letters, prostituted their learning to the basest uses ; the nobility spent their lives in warring upon each other ; the peasantry were the sport and victim by turns of priest and noble, while woman was the prey of all ; her person and her rights possessing no consideration only as they could be made to advance the interest or serve the pleasure of noble, husband, father, or priest—some man-god to whose lightest desire all her wishes were made to bend. The most pronounced doctrine of the Church during this period was, that through woman sin had been introduced into the world ; that woman's whole tendency was toward evil, and that had it not been for the unfortunate oversight of her creation, man would be dwelling in the paradisical innocence and happiness of Eden blessed with

---

* All, or at least the greater part of the fathers of the Greek Church before Augustine, denied any real, original sin.—" Augustinism and Pelagianism," p. 43, Emerson's Translations (Waite). The doctrine had a gradual growth, and was fully developed by Augustine, A.D. 420.—*Hist. Christian Religion to* A.D. 200 *(Waite), p.* 382.

immortality.) The Church looking upon woman as under a curse, considered man as God's divinely appointed agent for its enforcement, and that the restrictions she suffered under Christianity were but parts of a just punishment for having caused the fall of man. Christian theology thus at once struck a blow at these old beliefs in woman's equality, broadly inculcating the doctrine that woman was created for man, was subordinate to him and under obedience to him. It bade woman stand aside from sacerdotal offices, forbidding her to speak in the church, commanding her to ask her husband at home for all she wished to know, at once repressing all tendency toward her freedom among those who adopted the new religion, and by various decretals taught her defilement through the physical peculiarities of her being. It placed the legality of marriage under priestly control, secured to husbands a right of divorce for causes not freeing the wife, and so far set its ban upon this relation as to hold single women above the wife and mother in holiness. After having forbidden woman the priestly office, it forbade her certain benefits to be derived therefrom, thus unjustly punishing her for an ineligibility of its own creation; offices in the Church, learning, and property rights, freedom of thought and action, all were held as improper for a being secondary to man, who came into the world, not as part of the great original plan, but as an afterthought of the Creator.

While it took many hundred years to totally exclude woman from the priesthood, the strict celibacy of the male clergy was during the same period the constant effort of the Church. At first its restrictions were confined to a single marriage with a woman who had never before entered that relation. A Council of A.D. 347, consisting of twenty-one bishops, forbade the ordination of those priests who had been twice married, or who had married a widow. A Council of A.D. 395, ruled that a bishop who had children after ordination, should be excluded from the major orders. The Council of A.D. 444, deposed Chelidonius, Bishop of Besancon, for having married a widow; while the Council of Orleans, A.D. 511, consisting of thirty-two bishops, decided that any monk who married should be expelled from the ecclesiastical order.

In the sixth century a Council was held at Macon (585), consisting of forty-three bishops with sees, sixteen bishops without sees, and fifteen envoys. At this Council the celebrated discussion took place of which it has often been said, the question was whether woman had a soul. It arose in this wise. A certain bishop insisted that woman should not be called " homo "; but the contrary was argued by others from the two facts that the Scriptures say that God created man, male and female, and that Jesus Christ, son of a woman, is called the son of man. Woman was, therefore, allowed to remain a human being in the eyes of the clergy, even though considered a very weak and bad one.

The Church held two entirely opposing views of marriage. Inasmuch as it taught that the fall came through marriage, this relation was regarded by many priests with holy horror as a continuance of the evil which first brought sin into the world. It was declared that God would have found some method of populating the world outside of marriage, and that condition was looked upon as one of peculiar temptation and trial. Another class taught its necessity, though in it woman was under complete subordination to man. These views can be traced to the early fathers; through clerical contempt of marriage, the conditions of celibacy and virginity were regarded as those of highest virtue. Jerome respected marriage as chiefly valuable in that it gave virgins to the Church, while Augustine, although he admitted the possibility of salvation to the married, yet spoke of a mother and daughter in heaven, the mother shining as a dim star, the daughter as one of the first magnitude.

In the " Apostolic Constitutions," held by the Episcopal Church as regulations established by the apostles themselves, and which are believed by many to be among the earliest Christian records, there are elaborate directions for the places of all who attend church, the unmarried being most honored. The virgins and widows and elder women stood, or sat first of all. The Emperor Honorius banished Jovinius for asserting the possibility of a man being saved who lived with his wife, even though he obeyed all the ordinances of the Church and lived a good life.

St. Chrysostom, whose prayer is repeated at every Sunday morning service of the Episcopal Church, described woman as " a necessary evil, a natural temptation, a desirable calamity, a domestic peril, a deadly fascination, and a painted ill." The doctrine of priestly celibacy which was early taught, though not thoroughly enforced until the eleventh century, and the general tenor of the Church against marriage, together with its teaching woman's greater sinfulness, were the great causes of undermining the morals of the Christian world for fifteen hundred years. With these doctrines was also taught the duty of woman to sacrifice herself in every way to man. The loss of chastity in a woman was held as a light sin in comparison to the degradation that marriage would bring upon the priesthood, and young girls ruined by some candidate or priest, con sidered themselves as doing God service by refusing a marriage that would cause the expulsion of their lovers from this order. With woman's so-called divine self-sacrifice, Heloise chose to remain Abelard's mistress rather than destroy his prospects of advancement in the Church.*

To the more strict enforcement of priestly celibacy, the barons were permitted to make slaves of the wives and children of married priests. While by common law children were held as following the condition of their fathers, under Church legislation they were held to follow the condition of their mothers. Serf mothers have thus borne serf children to free-born fathers, and slave mothers have borne slave children to their masters; while unmarried mothers still bear bastard children to unknown fathers, the Church thus throwing the taint of illegitimacy upon the innocent. The relations of man and woman to each other, the sinfulness of marriage, and the license of illicit relations employed most of the thought of the Church.† The duty of woman to obey, not only her husband, but all men by virtue of their sex, was sedulously inculcated. She was trained to hold her own desires and even her own thoughts in complete abeyance to those of man; father, husband, brother, son, priest, alike held themselves as her rightful masters, and every holy principle of 'ler nature was subverted in this most degrading assumption. A great many important effects followed the full establishment of priestly celibacy. The doctrine of woman's inherent wickedness took new strength; a formal prohibition of the Scriptures to the laity was promulgated from Toulouse in the twelfth century; the canon law gained control of the civil law; the absolute sinfulness of divorce, which had been maintained in councils, yet allowed by the civil law, was established; the Inquisition arose; the persecution of woman for witchcraft took on a new phase, and a tendency to suicide was developed. The wives of priests rendered homeless, and with their children suddenly ranked among the vilest of the earth, were powerless and despairing, and not a few of them shortened their agony by death at their own hands. For all these crimes the Church was directly responsible.

---

* Milman says that Heloise sacrificed herself on account of the impediments the Church threw in the way of the married clergy's career of advancement. As his wife she would close the ascending ladder of ecclesiastical honors, priory, abbacy, bishopric, metropolitane, cardinalade, and even that which was above and beyond all.—" *Latin Christianity.*"

† The Christian Church was swamped by hysteria from the third to the sixteenth century.—*Rev. Charles Kingsley's Life and Letters.*

Priestly celibacy did not cause priestly purity of life,* but looking upon themselves as especially sanctified and set apart by virtue of that celibacy, priests made their holy office the cover of the most degrading sensuality.† Methods were taken to debauch the minds of women as well as their bodies. As late as the seventeenth century it was taught that a priest could commit no sin. This was an old doctrine, but received new strength from the Illumines. It was said that " The devout, having offered up and annihilated their own selves, exist no longer but in God. Thenceforth they can do no wrong. The better part of them is so divine that it no longer knows what the other is doing." The doctrine of some Protestant sects, " Once in grace, always in grace," is of the same character. The very incarnation was used as a means of weakening woman's virtue. An enforcement of the duty of an utter surrender of the soul and the will was taught by the example of the Virgin, " who obeyed the angel Gabriel and conceived, without risk of evil, for impurity could not come of a spirit."‡ Another lesson, of which the present century has some glimpse, was " that sin could be killed by sin, as the better way of becoming innocent again." The result of this doctrine was seen in the mistresses of the priests, known as " The Hallowed Ones."

Under such religious teaching as to woman, naught could be expected but that the laity would closely imitate the priesthood. Although Church and State may not be legally united, it is impossible for any religious opinion to become widely prevalent without its influencing legislation. Among the Anglo-Saxons, the priesthood possessed great influence; but after the Norman Conquest, ecclesiasticism gained greater control in England. Previous to this, a man was compelled by law to leave his wife one-third of his property,

---

* In 1874 an Old Catholic priest of Switzerland, about to follow Père Hyacinth's example in abandoning celibacy, announced his betrothal in the following manner : "I marry because I wish to remain an honorable man. In the seventeenth century it was a proverbial expression, 'As corrupt as a priest,' and this might be said to-day. I marry, therefore, because I wish to get out of the Ultramontane slough."—*Galignani's Messenger, September* 19, 1874.

† The abbot elect of St. Augustine, at Canterbury, in 1171 was found, on investigation, to have seventeen illegitimate children in a single village. An abbot of St. Pelayo in Spain in 1130 was proved to have kept no less than seventy mistresses. Henry 3d, Bishop of Liege, was deposed in 1274 for having sixty-five illegitimate children.—*Lecky, " Hist. of European Morals," p.* 350. This same bishop boasted in a public banquet, that in twenty-two months, fourteen children had been born to him. A tax called " Cullagium," which was, in fact, a license to clergymen to keep concubines, was during several centuries systematically levied by princes.—*Ibid, Vol.* 2, *p.* 349. It was openly attested that 100,000 women in England were made dissolute by the clergy. — *Draper's " Intellectual Development of Europe," p.* 498.

‡ " *Le Sorcerie," p.* 259, *Michelet.*

and could leave her as much more as he pleased. Under ecclesiastical law he was not permitted to will her more than one-third, and could leave her as much less as he pleased. Glanville laid it down as a law of the kingdom that no one was compelled to leave another person any portion of his property, and that the part usually devised to wives was left them at the dictate of affection and not of law.

Women were not permitted to testify in court unless on some question especially concerning themselves. It is but twenty years since this law was annulled in Scotland, and but three years since, that by the influence of Signor Morelli,* the Parliament of Italy repealed the old restriction upon woman's testimony.

Sisters were not allowed to inherit with brothers, the property, according to old ecclesiastical language, going "to the worthiest of blood." Blackstone acknowledges that this distinction between brothers and sisters reflects shame upon England, and was no part of the old Roman law, where the children of a family inherited equally without distinction of sex. It is but two years since the old law of inheritance of sons alone was repealed in one of the Swiss Cantons. Even in this enlightened age its repeal met much opposition, men piteously complaining that they would be ruined by this act of justice done their sisters.

The minds of people having been corrupted through centuries by Church doctrines regarding woman, it was an easy step for the State to aid in her degradation. The system of Feudalism rising from the theory of warfare as the normal condition of man, still further oppressed woman by bringing into power a class of men accustomed to deeds of violence, and finding their chief pleasure in the sufferings of others. To be a woman, appealed to no instinct of tenderness in this class. To be a woman was not to be protected even, unless she held power in her own right, or was acting in place of some feudal lord. The whole body of villeins and serfs were under absolute dominion of the Feudal Lords. They were held as possessing no rights of their own: the Priest had control of their souls, the Lord of their bodies. But it was not upon the male serfs that the greatest oppression fell.

Although the tillage of the soil, the care of swine and cattle was theirs, the masters claiming the half or more of everything even to one-half the wool shorn from the flock,† and all exactions upon them

---

* *Died in* 1880.

† In the dominion of the Count de Foix the lord had right once in his life-time to take, without payment, a certain quantity of ·oods from the stores of each tenant.—" *Histoire Universelle*," *Cesar Cantu.*

were great, while their sense of security was slight, it was upon their wives and daughters that the greatest outrages were inflicted. It was a pastime of the castle retainers to fall upon peaceful villages to the consternation of its women, who were struck, tortured, and made the sport of the ribald soldiery. " Serfs of the Body," they had no protection. The vilest outrages were perpetrated by the Feudal Lords under the name of Rights. Women were taught by Church and State alike, that the Feudal Lord or Seigneur had a right to them, not only as against themselves, but as against any claim of husband or father. The law known as *Marchetta*, or Marquette, compelled newly-married women to a most dishonorable servitude. They were regarded as the rightful prey of the Feudal Lord from one to three days after their marriage, and from this custom, the oldest son of the serf was held as the son of the lord, " as perchance it was he who begat him." From this nefarious degradation of woman, the custom of Borough-English arose, in which the youngest son became the heir. The original significa-tion of the word borough being to make secure, the peasant through Borough-English made secure the right of his own son to what in-heritance he might leave, thus cutting off the claim of the possible son of his hated lord. France, Germany, Prussia, England, Scot-land, and all Christian countries where feudalism existed, held to the enforcement of Marquette. The lord deemed this right as fully his as he did the claim to half the crops of the land, or to the half of the wool sheared from the sheep. More than one reign of terror arose in France from the enforcement of this law, and the uprisings of the peasantry over Europe during the twelfth century, and the fierce Jacquerie, or Peasant War, of the fourteenth century in France owed their origin, among other causes, to the enforcement of these claims by the lords upon the newly-married wife. The Edicts of Marly securing the Seigneural Tenure in Lower Canada, transplanted that claim to America when Canada was under the control of France.

To persons not conversant with the history of feudalism, and of the Church for the first fifteen hundred years of its existence, it will seem impossible that such foulness could ever have been part of Christian civilization. That the crimes they have been trained to consider the worst forms of heathendom could have existed in Chris-tian Europe, upheld by both Church and State for more than a thousand five hundred years, will strike most people with incre-dulity. Such, however, is the truth ; we can but admit well-attested facts of history how severe a blow soever they strike our pre-conceived beliefs.

Marquette was claimed by the Lords Spiritual* as well as by the Lords Temporal. The Church, indeed, was the bulwark of this base feudal claim. With the power of penance and excommunication in its grasp, this feudal demand could neither have originated nor been sustained unless sanctioned by the Church.

In Scotland, Margaret, wife of Malcolm Conmore, generally known, from her goodness, as St. Margaret,† exerted her royal influence in 1057, against this degradation of her sex, but despite the royal prohibition and the substitution of the payment of a merk in money instead, the custom had such a foothold and appealed so strongly to man's licentious appetite it still continued, remaining in existence nearly seven hundred years after the royal edict against its practice. These customs of feudalism were the customs of Christianity during many centuries.‡ These infamous outrages upon woman were enforced under Christian law by both Church and State.§

The degradation of the husband at this infringement of the lord spiritual and temporal upon his marital right, has been pictured by many writers, but history has been quite silent upon the despair and shame of the wife. No hope appeared for woman anywhere. The Church, which should have been the great conserver of morals, dragged her to the lowest depths, through the vileness of its priestly customs. The State, which should have defended her civil rights, followed the example of the Church in crushing her to the earth.

---

* In days to come people will be slow to believe that the law among Christian nations went beyond anything decreed concerning the olden slavery ; that it wrote down as an actual right the most grievous outrage that could ever wound man's heart. The Lord Spiritual had this right no less than the Lord Temporal. The parson being a lord, expressly claimed the first fruits of the bride, but was willing to sell his rights to the husband. The Courts of Berne openly maintain that this right grew up naturally.—"*La Sorcerie,*" *Michelet, p.* 62.

† Margaret was canonized in 1251, and made the patron saint of Scotland in 1673. Several of the Scotch feudalry, despite royal protestation, kept up the infamous practice till a late date. One of the Earls of Crawford, a truculent and lustful anarch, popularly known and dreaded as " Earl Brant," in the sixteenth century, was probably among the last who openly claimed leg-right (the literal translation of *droit de jambage*).—*Sketches of Feudalism.*

‡ At the beginning of the Christian era, Corinth possessed a thousand women who were devoted to the service of its idol, the Corinthian Venus. "To Corinthianize " came to express the utmost lewdness, but Corinth, as sunken as she was in sensual pleasure, was not under the pale of Christianity. She was a heathen city, outside of that light which, coming into the world, is held to enlighten every man that accepts it.

§ Les Cuisiniers et les marmitons de l'archevêques de Vienne avaient imposé un tribut sur les mariages ; on croit que certains feuditaires exigeaient un droit obscène de leur vassaux qui se mariaient, quel fut transformé ensuite en droit de *cuissage* consistant, de la part du seigneur, à mettre une jambe nue dans le lit des nouveaux époux. Dans d'autres pays l' homme ne pouvait couche avec sa femme les trois premières nuits sans le consentement de l'evêque ou du seigneur du feif.—*Cesar Cantu, "Histoire Universelle," Vol. IX., p.* 202-3.

God Himself seemed to have forsaken woman. Freedom for the peasants was found alone at night. Known as the Birds of the Night, Foxes and Birds of Prey, it was only at these night assemblages they enjoyed the least happiness or security. Here, with wives and daughters, they met together to talk of their gross outrages. Out of these foul wrongs grew the sacrifice of the " Black Mass," with woman as officiating priestess, in which the rites of the Church were travestied in solemn mockery, and defiance cast at that heaven which seemed to permit the priest and lord alike to trample upon all the sacred rights of womanhood in the names of religion and law.

During this mocking service a true sacrifice of wheat was offered to the Spirit of the Earth who made wheat to grow, and loosened birds bore aloft to the God of Freedom the sighs and prayers of the serfs asking that their descendants might be free. We can not do otherwise than regard this sacrifice as the most acceptable offering made in that day of moral degradation, a sacrifice and prayer more holy than all the ceremonials of the Church. This service, where woman, by virtue of her greater despair, acted both as altar and priest, opened by the following address and prayer : " I will come before Thine altar, but save me, O Lord, from the faithless and violent man ! " (from the priest and the baron).* From these assemblages, known as " Sabbat," or " the Sabbath," from the old Pagan Midsummer-day sacrifice to " Bacchus Sabiesa," rose the belief in the " Witches' Sabbath," which for several hundred years formed a new source of accusation against women, and sent tens of thousands of them to the most horrible death.

Not until canon or Church law had become quite engrafted upon the civil law, did the full persecutions for witchcraft arise. A witch was held to be a woman who had deliberately sold her soul to the Evil One, who delighted in injuring others, and who chose the Sabbath day for the enactment of her impious rites, and who was especially connected with black animals ; the black cat being held as her familiar in many countries.

In looking at the history of witchcraft, we see three striking points for consideration :

First. That women were chiefly accused, a wizard being seldom mentioned.

Second. That man, believing in woman's inherent wickedness, and understanding neither the mental nor the physical peculiarities of her being, ascribed all her idiosyncrasies to witchcraft.

---

* *Le Michelet*, " *Le Sorcerie*," p. 151.

Third. That the clergy inculcated the idea that woman was in league with the devil, and that strong intellect, remarkable beauty, or unusual sickness, were in themselves a proof of that league.

Catholic and Protestant countries alike agreed in holding woman as the chief accessory of the devil. Luther said, " I would have no compassion for a witch ; I would burn them all." As late as 1768, John Wesley declared the giving up of witchcraft to be in effect giving up the Bible. James I., on his accession to the throne, ordered the learned work of Reginald Scot against witchcraft, to be burned in compliance with the act of Parliament of 1603, which ratified a belief in witchcraft over the three kingdoms. Under Henry VIII., from whose reign the Protestant Reformation in England dates, an act of Parliament made witchcraft felony; this act was again confirmed under Elizabeth. To doubt witchcraft was as heretical under Protestantism as under Catholicism.

Even the widely extolled Pilgrim Fathers brought this belief with them when they stepped ashore at Plymouth Rock. With the " Ducking-Stool " and the " Scarlet Letter " of shame for woman, while her companion in sin went free, they also brought with them a belief in witches. Richard Baxter, the " greatest of the Puritans," condemned those who disbelieved in witchcraft as " wicked Sadducees," his work against it adding intensity to the persecution. Cotton Mather was active in fomenting a belief in this doctrine.

So convinced were those in power of the tendency of woman to diabolism that the learned Sir Matthew Hale condemned two women without even summing up the evidence. Old women, for no other reason than that they were old, were held as most susceptible to the assaults of the devil, and most especially endowed with supernatural powers for evil, to doubt which was equivalent to doubting the Bible. We see a reason for this hatred of old women, in the fact that woman was chiefly viewed from a sensual stand-point, and when by reason of age or debility, she no longer attracted the physical admiration of man, he looked upon her as of no farther use to the world, and as possessing no right to life. At one period it was very unusual for an old woman in the north of Europe to die peaceably in her bed. The persecution against them raged with special virulence in Scotland, where upon the act of the British Parliament in 17—, abolishing the burning and hanging of witches, the assembly of the Calvinistic Church of Scotland " confessed " this act of Parliament " as a great national sin." Looked upon as a sin rather than a crime, the Church sought its control, and when coming under its power, witchcraft was punished with much greater severity than when falling under lay tribunals. It proved a source of great emolument to the Church, which was even accused of fostering it for purposes of gain. A system of "witch finders" or "witch persecutors" arose. Cardan, a famous Italian physician, said of them: "In order to obtain forfeit property, the same persons acted as accusers and judges, and invented a thousand stories as proof."

Witchcraft was as a sin almost confined to woman; a wizard was rare, one writer saying: to every 100 witches, we find but one wizard. In the time of Louis XIII. this proportion was greatly increased; "to one wizard, 10,000 witches," another person declared there were 100,000 witches in France alone. Sprenger, the great Inquisitor, author of "The Witch Hammer," * through whose persecutions many countries were flooded with victims, said, "Heresy of witches, not of wizards, must we call it, for these latter are of very small account." No class or condition escaped Sprenger; we read of witches of fifteen years, and two "infernally beautiful"† of seventeen years.

The Parliament of Toulouse burned 400 witches at one time. Four hundred women at one hour on the public square, dying the horrid death of fire, for a crime which never existed save in the imagination of those persecutors, and which grew in their imagination from a false belief in woman's extraordinary wickedness, based upon a false theory as to original sin. Not a Christian country but was full of the horrors of witch persecution and violent death. Remy, Judge of Nancy, acknowledged to having himself burnt 800 in sixteen years. Many women were driven to suicide in fear of the torture in store for them. In 1595 sixteen of those accused by Remy, destroyed themselves rather than fall into his terrible hands. Six hundred were burnt in one small bishopric in one year; 900 during the same period in another. Seven thousand lost their lives at Treves; 1,000 in the province of Como in Italy in a single year; 500 were executed at Geneva in a single month. Under the reign of Francis I. more than

---

* The very word *femina* (woman) means one wanting in faith; for *fe* means faith, and *minus*, less.—*Witch Hammer.* This work was printed in 18mo, an unusually small size for that period, for the convenience of carrying it in the pocket, where its assertions, they could not be called arguments, could be always within reach, especially for those traveling witch inquisitors, who proceeded from country to country, like Sprenger himself, to denounce witches. This work bore the sanction of the Pope, and was followed, even in Protestant countries, until the eighteenth century. It based its theories upon the Bible, and devoted thirty-three pages to a proof that women were especially addicted to sorcery.

† It was observed they (devils) had a peculiar attachment to women with beautiful hair, and it was an old Catholic belief that St. Paul alluded to this in that somewhat obscure passage in which he exhorts women to cover their heads because of the angels.— SPRANGLER.

100,000 witches are said to have been put to death, and for hundreds of years this superstition controlled the Church. In Scotland the most atrocious tortures were invented, and women died "shrieking to heaven for that mercy denied them by Christian men." One writer casually mentions seeing nine burning in a single day's journey.

When for "witches" we read "women," we shall gain a more direct idea of the cruelties inflicted by the Church upon woman. Friends were encouraged to cast accusations upon friends, and rewards were offered for conviction. From the pulpit people were exhorted to bring the witch to justice. Husbands who had ceased to care for their wives, or in any way found them a burden, or who for any reason wished to dissolve the marriage tie, now found an easy method. They had but to accuse them of witchcraft, and the marriage was dissolved by the death of the wife at the stake. Mention is made of wives dragged by their husbands before the arch-Inquisitor, Sprenger, by ropes around their necks. In Protestant, as in Catholic countries, the person accused was virtually dead. She was excommunicated from humanity; designated and denounced as one whom all must shun, with whom none must buy or sell, to whom no one must give food or lodging or speech or shelter; life was not worth the living.

Besides those committing suicide, others brought to trial, tired of life amid so many horrors, falsely accused themselves, preferring a death by the torture of fire to a life of endless isolation and persecution. An English woman on her way to the stake, with a greatness of soul all must admire, freed her judges from responsibility by saying to the people, "Do not blame my judges, I wished to put an end to my own self. My parents kept aloof from me; my husband had denied me. I could not live on without disgrace. I longed for death, and so I told a lie."

Of Sir George Mackenzie, the eminent Scotch advocate, it was said:

He went to examine some women who had confessed,* and one of them

---

* One of the most powerful incentives to confession was systematically to deprive the suspected witch of her natural sleep. . . . Iron collars, or witches' bridles, are still preserved in various parts of Scotland, which had been used for such iniquitous purposes. These instruments were so constructed that by means of a loop which passed over the head, a piece of iron having four points or prongs, was forcibly thrust into the mouth, two of these being directed to the tongue and palate, the others pointing outward to each cheek. This infernal machine was secured by a padlock. At the back of the collar was fixed a ring, by which to attach the witch to a staple in the wall of her cell. Thus equipped, and day and night waked and watched by some skillful person appointed by her inquisitors, the unhappy creature, after a few days of such discipline, maddened by the misery of her forlorn and helpless state, would be rendered fit for confessing anything, in

told him "under secrecie" that she had not confessed because she was guilty, but being a poor wretch who wrought for her meat, and being defined for a witch, she knew she would starve, for no person thereafter would give her either meat or lodging, and that all men would beat her and hound dogs at her, and therefore she desired to be out of the world, whereupon she wept most bitterly, and upon her knees called upon God to witness what she said.

The death these poor women chose to suffer rather than accept a chance of life with the name of witch clinging to them,* was one of the most painful of which we can conceive,† although in the diversity of torture inflicted upon "the witch," it is scarcely possible to say which was the least agonizing.

Not only was the persecution for witchcraft brought to New England by the Puritans, but it has been considered and treated as a capital offense by the laws of both Pennsylvania and New York. Trials took place in both colonies not long before the Salem tragedy; the peaceful Quaker, William Penn, presiding upon the bench at the time of the trial of two Swedish women accused of witchcraft. The Grand Jury acting under instruction given in a charge delivered by him, found bills against them, and his skirts were only saved from the guilt of their blood by some technical irregularity in the indictment.

---

order to be rid of the dregs of her wretched life. At intervals fresh examinations took place, and they were repeated from time to time until her "contumacy," as it was termed, was subdued. The clergy and Kirk Sessions appear to have been the unwearied instruments of "purging the land of witchcraft," and *to them, in the first instance, all the complaints and informations were made.—Pitcairn*, Vol. I., Part 2, p. 50.

* The following is an account of the material used, and the expenses attending the execution of two witches in Scotland:

For 10 loads of coals to burn the witches....................£3	06	8
" a tar barrel.. 0	14	0
" towes.. 0	06	0
" hurdles to be jumps for them............................. 3	10	0
" making of them.. 0	08	0
" one to go to Tinmouth for the lord to sit upon the assize as judge 0	06	0
" the executioner for his pains........................... 8	14	0
" his expenses there...................................... 0	16	4

—Lectures on Witchcraft in Salem, Charles W. Upham.

† See an account of the tortures and death of Alison Balfour, in which not only she, but her husband and her young children were also grievously tortured in order to wring confession from the wife and mother. This poor woman bore everything applied to herself, nor did the sufferings of her husband and son compel a confession of guilt. Not until her little daughter of seven or eight years was put to the torture in her presence did the constancy of the mother give way. To spare the innocent child, the equally innocent mother confessed she was a witch. After enduring all the agonies applied to herself, and all she was made to bear in the persons of her innocent family, she was still made to undergo the frightful suffering of death at the stake. She was one of those who died calling upon God for that mercy she could not find at the hands of Christian men.

Marriage with devils was long one of the most ordinary accusations in witch trials. The knowledge of witches was admitted, as is shown in the widely extended belief of their ability to work miracles. A large part of the women termed witches were in reality the profoundest thinkers, the most advanced scientists of those ages. For many hundred years the knowledge of medicine, and its practice among the poorer classes was almost entirely in their hands, and many discoveries in this science are due to them; but an acquaintance with herbs soothing to pain, or healing in their qualities, was then looked upon as having been acquired through diabolical agency. Even those persons cured through the instrumentality of some woman were ready when the hour came to assert their belief in her indebtedness to the devil for that knowledge. Not only were the common people themselves ignorant of all science, but their brains were filled with superstitious fears, and the belief that knowledge had been first introduced to the world through woman's obedience to the devil. Thus the persecution which for ages raged against witches, was in reality an attack upon science at the hands of the Church.

The entire subordination of the common law to ecclesiasticism, dates in England to the reign of Stephen, who ascended the throne in 1135. Its new growth of power must be ascribed to avarice, as it then began to take cognizance of crimes, establishing an equivalent in money for every species of wrong-doing. The Church not only remitted penalties for crimes already perpetrated, but sold indulgences for the commission of new ones. Its touch upon property soon extended to all the relations of life. Marriages within the seventh degree were forbidden by the Church as incestuous, but those who could buy indulgence were enabled to get a dispensation. No crime so great that it could not be condoned for money.

Canon law gained its greatest power in the family relation in its control over wills, the guardianship of orphans, marriage and divorce. Under ecclesiastical law, marriage was held as a sacrament, was performed at the church door, the wife being required to give up her name, her person, her property, her own sacred individuality, and to promise obedience to her husband in all things. Certain hours of the day were even set aside as canonical after which no marriage could be celebrated.* Wherever it became the basis of legislation, the laws of succession and inheritance, and those in regard to children, constantly sacrificed the

---

* No marriage could take place after 12 M., which is even now the rule of the established Church of England.

49

interests of wives and daughters to those of husbands and sons. Ecclesiastical law ultimately secured such a hold upon family property and became so grasping in its demands, that the civil law interfered, not, however, in the interests of wives and children, but in the interests of creditors. Canon law had its largest growth through the pious fictions of woman's created inferiority.

To the credit of humanity it must be said that the laity did not readily yield to priestly power, but made many efforts to wrest their temporal concerns from ecclesiastical control. But in the general paucity of education, together with the abnegation of the will, sedulously taught by the Church, which brought all its dread power to bear in threats of excommunication and future eternal torment, the rights of the people were gradually lost. The control of the priesthood over all things of a temporal, as well as of a spiritual nature, tended to make them a distinct body from the laity, and rights were divided into those pertaining to persons and things, the rights of persons belonging to the priesthood alone; but inasmuch as every man, whatever his condition, could become a priest, and no woman, however learned or pious or high in station, could, the whole tendency of ecclesiastical law was to separate man and woman into a holy or divine sex, and an unholy or impious sex, creating an antagonism between those whose interests are by nature the same. Thus canon law, bearing upon the business of ordinary life between man and man, fell with its greatest weight upon woman; it not only corrupted the common law in England, but perverted the civil law of other countries. The denial under common law of the right of woman to make a contract, grew out of the denial of her right of ownership. Not possessing control over her own property or her future actions, she was held as legally unable to make a binding contract.

Property is a delicate test of the condition of a nation. It is a singular fact of history that the rights of property have everywhere been recognized before the rights of persons, and wherever the rights of any class to property are attacked, it is a most subtle and dangerous assault upon personal rights. The chief restrictive element of slavery was the denial to the slave of the proceeds of his own labor. As soon as a slave was allowed to hire his time, the door of freedom began to open to him. The enslavement of woman has been much increased from the denial of the rights of property to her, not merely to the fruits of her own labor, but to the right of inheritance.

The great school of German jurists* teach that ownership increases both physical and moral capacity, and that as owner, actual or possible, man is a more capable and worthy being than he would otherwise be. Inasmuch as under canon law woman was debarred from giving testimony in courts of law, sisters were prohibited from taking an inheritance with brothers, and wives were deprived of property rights, it is entirely justifiable to say ecclesiastical law injured civilization by its destruction of the property rights of women.†

The worst features of canon law, as Blackstone frankly admits, are those touching upon the rights of woman. These features have been made permanent to this day by the power the Church gained over common law,‡ between the tenth and sixteenth centuries, since which period the complete inferiority and subordination of the female sex has been as fully maintained by the State as by the Church. The influence of canon law upon the criminal codes of England and America has but recently attracted the attention of legal minds. Wharton, whose " Criminal Law " has for years been a standard work, did not examine their relation until his seventh edition, in which he gave a copious array of authors, English, German, and Latin, from whom he deduced proof that the criminal codes of these two countries are pre-eminently based upon ecclesiastical law.

Canon law gave to the husband the power of compelling the wife's return if, for any cause, she left him. She was then at once in the position of an outlaw, branded as a run-away who had left her master's service, a wife who had left " bed and board " without consent, and whom all persons were forbidden " to harbor " or shelter " under penalty of the law." The absconding wife was in the position of an excommunicate from the Catholic Church, or of a woman

---

* Science of Law.

† Gerard says the doctrines of the Canon Law most favorable to the power of the clergy, are founded on ignorance, or supported by fraud and forgery.

‡ Whoever wishes to gain insight into that great institution, Canon Law, can do so most effectively by studying Common Law, in regard to woman.—BLACKSTONE. I have arrived at conclusions which I keep to myself as yet, and only utter as Greek φωνᾶντα, συνετοῖσι, the principle of which is that there will never be a good world for woman till the last monk, and therewith the last remnant of the monastic idea of, and legislation for, woman, i. e., the Canon Law, is civilized off the face of the earth. Meanwhile all the most pure and high-minded women in England and in Europe, have been brought up under the shadow of the Canon Law, and have accepted it with the usual divine self-sacrifice, as their destiny by law of God and nature, and consider their own womanhood outraged when it, their tyrant, is meddled with.—*Charles Kingsley, Life and Letters. Letter to John Stuart Mill, of June* 17, 1849.

condemned as a witch.   Any person befriending her was held accessory to the wife's theft of herself from her husband, and rendered liable to fine and other punishment for having helped to rob the husband (master) of his wife (slave).

The present formula of advertising a wife, which so frequently disgraces the press, is due to this belief in wife-ownership.

Whereon my wife . . . . . has left my bed and board without just cause or provocation, I hereby forbid all persons from harboring or trusting her on my account.

By old English law, in case the wife was in danger of perishing in a storm, it was allowable " to harbor " and shelter her.

It is less than thirty years since the dockets of a court in New York city, the great metropolis of our nation, were sullied by the suit of a husband against parties who had received, " harbored " and sheltered his wife after she left him, the husband recovering $10,000 damages.

Although England was Christianized in the fourth century, it was not until the tenth that a daughter had a right to reject the husband selected for her by her father ;* and it was not until this same century that the Christian wife of a Christian husband acquired the right of eating at table with him.   For many hundred years the law entered families, binding out to servile labor all unmarried women between the ages of eleven and forty.

For more than a thousand years women in England were legislated for as slaves.   They were imprisoned for crimes that, if committed by a man, were punished by simple branding in the hand; and other crimes which he could atone for by a fine, were punished in her case by burning alive.   Down to the end of the eighteenth century the punishment of a wife who had murdered her husband was burning† alive ; while if the husband murdered the wife, his was hanging, " the same as if he had murdered any stranger."   Her

---

* Wives in England were bought from the fifth to the eleventh century (*Descriptive Sociology, Herbert Spencer*).   By an ancient law of India, a father was forbidden to sell his daughter in marriage.   *Keshub Chunder Sen,* who recently spent a few years in England, objected, after his return home, to the introduction of English customs in regard to woman into India, on account of their degradation of the female sex.

† Our laws are based on the all-sufficiency of man's rights ; society exists for men only ; for women, merely in so far as they are represented by some man, are in the *mundt,* or keeping of some man (*Descriptive Sociology, England, Herbert Spencer*).   In England, as late as the seventeenth century, husbands of decent station were not ashamed to beat their wives.   Gentlemen arranged parties of pleasure to Bridewell, for the purpose of seeing the wretched women who beat hemp there whipped.   It was not until 1817 that the public whipping of woman was abolished in England.—*Ibid.*

crime was petit treason, and her punishment was the same as that of the slave who had murdered her master. For woman there existed no " benefit of clergy," which in a man who could read, greatly lessened his punishment; this ability to read enabling him to perform certain priestly functions and securing him immunity in crime. The Church having first made woman ineligible to the priesthood, punished her on account of the restrictions of its own making. We who talk of the burning of wives upon the funeral pyres of husbands in India, may well turn our eyes to the records of Christian countries.

Where marriage is wholly or partially under ecclesiastical law, woman's degradation surely follows ; but in Catholic and Protestant countries a more decent veil has been thrown over this sacrifice of woman than under some forms of the Greek Church, where the wife is delivered to the husband under this formula : " Here, wolf, take thy lamb ! " and the bridegroom is presented with a whip, giving his bride a few blows as part of the ceremony, and bidding her draw off his boots as a symbol of her subjugation to him. With such an entrance ceremony, it may well be surmised that the marriage relation permits of the most revolting tyranny. In Russia, until recently, the wife who killed her husband while he was chastising her, was buried alive, her head only being left above ground. Many lingered for days before the mercy of death reached them.

Ivan Panim, a Russian exile, now a student in Harvard College, made the following statement in a speech at the Massachusetts Woman Suffrage Convention, held in February, 1881 :

A short time ago the wife of a well-to-do peasant came to a justice of one of the district courts in Russia and demanded protection from the cruelty of her husband. She proved conclusively by the aid of competent witnesses, that he had bound her naked to a stake during the cold weather, on the street, and asked the passers-by to strike her; and whenever they refused, he struck her himself. He fastened her, moreover, to the ground, put heavy stones and weights on her and broke one of her arms. The court declared the husband "not guilty." "It can not afford," it said, "to teach woman to disobey the commands of her husband." This is by no means an extreme or isolated case. Few, indeed, become known to the public through the courts or through the press.*

---

* WIVES IN RUSSIA.—A peasant in the villageof Zelova Baltia, having reason to doubt the fidelity of his spouse, deliberately harnessed her to a cart in company with a mare— a species of double harness for which the lady was probably unprepared when she took the nuptial vow. He then got into the cart in company with a friend, and drove the ill-assorted team some sixteen versts (nearly eleven English miles), without sparing the whip-cord. When he returned from his excursion he shaved the unlucky woman's head, tarred and feathered her, and turned her out of doors. She naturally sought refuge and consolation from her parish priest ; but he sent her back to her lord and master, pre

Canon law made its greatest encroachments at the period that chivalry was at its height; the outward show of respect and honor to woman keeping pace in its false pretense with the destruction of her legal rights. Woman's moral degradation was at this time so great that a community of women was even proposed, and was sustained by Jean de Meung, the "Poet of Chivalry," in his Roman de la Rose. Christine of Pisa, the first strictly literary woman of Western Europe, took up her pen in defense of her sex against the general libidinous spirit of the age, writing in opposition to Meung.

Under Feudalism, under Celibacy, under Chivalry, under the Reformation, under the principles of new sects of the nineteenth century—the Perfectionists and Mormons alike—we find this one idea of woman's inferiority, and her creation as a subject of man's passions openly or covertly promulgated.

The Salic law not only denied to women the right to reign, but to the inheritance of houses and lands. One of its famous articles was: "Salic land shall not fall to women; the inheritance shall devolve exclusively on the males." The fact of sex not only prohibited woman's inheritance of thrones and of lands, but there were forms in this law by which a man might "separate himself from his family, getting free from all obligations of relationship and entering upon an entire independence." History does not tell us to what depths of degradation this disseverance of all family ties reduced the women of his household, who could neither inherit house or land. The formation of the Salic code is still buried in the mists of antiquity; it is, however, variously regarded as having originated in the fourth and in the seventh century, many laws of its code being, like English common law, unwritten, and others showing "double origin." But our interest does not so greatly lie in its origin, as in the fact that after the conversion of the Franks to Christianity the law was revised, and all parts deemed inconsistent with this religion were revoked. The restrictions upon woman were retained.

Woman's wrongs under the Reformation, we discover by glancing

---

scribing further flagellation. An appeal to justice by the poor woman and her relatives resulted in a non-suit, and any recourse to a higher court will probably terminate in the same manner.

WOMAN'S LOT IN RUSSIA.—Here and there the popular songs bear traces of the griefs which in the rough furrows of daily life the Russian woman finds it prudent to conceal. "Ages have rolled away," says the poet Nekrasof; "the whole face of the earth has brightened; only the sombre lot of mowjik's wife God forgets to change." And the same poet makes one of his village heroines say, *apropos* of the enfranchisement of the serfs, "God has forgotten the nook where He hid the keys of woman's emancipation."

at different periods. The Cromwellian era exhibited an increase of piety. Puritanism here had its birth, but brought no element of toleration to woman. Lydia Maria Child, in her " History of Woman," says :

Under the Commonwealth society assumed a new and stern aspect. Women were in disgrace; it was everywhere reiterated from the pulpit that woman caused man's expulsion from Paradise, and ought to be shunned by Christians as one of the greatest temptations of Satan. "Man," said they, "is conceived in sin and brought forth in iniquity; it was his complacency to woman that caused his first debasement; let him not, therefore, glory in his shame; let him not worship the fountain of his corruption." Learning and accomplishments were alike discouraged; and women confined to a knowledge of cooking, family medicines, and the unintelligible theological discussions of the day.

A writer about this period, said : " She that knoweth how to compound a pudding is more desirable than she who skillfully compoundeth a poem."

At the time of the Reformation, Luther at first continued celibate, but thinking " to vex the Pope," he suddenly, at the age of forty-two, gave his influence against celibacy by marriage with Catherine Von Bora, a former nun. But although thus becoming an example of priestly marriage under the new order of things, Luther's whole course shows that he did not believe in woman's equality with man. He took with him the old theory of her subordination. It was his maxim that " no gown or garment worse becomes a woman than that she will be wise." Although opposing monastic life, the home under the reformation was governed by many of its rules for woman.

First. She was to be under obedience to the masculine head of the household.

Second. She was to be constantly employed for his benefit.

Third. Her society was strictly chosen for her by her master and head.

Fourth. This masculine family head was a general father confessor, to whom she was held responsible in thought and deed.

Fifth. Neither genius nor talent could free woman from such control, without consent.

Luther, though free from the lasciviousness of the old priesthood, was not monogamic in principle. When applied to by the German Elector, Philip,* Landgrave of Hesse-Cassel, for permission to marry a second wife, while his first, Margaret of Savoy, was

---

* One of the powerful German Electors, who formerly made choice of the Emperor of Germany.

still living, Luther called a synod of six of the principal reformers, who in joint consultation decided that as the Bible nowhere condemned polygamy, and as it had been invariably practiced by the highest dignitaries of the Church, the required permission should be granted. History does not tell us that the wife was consulted in the matter. She was held as in general subordination to the powers that be, as well as in special subordination to her husband; but more degrading than all else is the fact that the doctrine of unchastity for man was brought into the Reformation, as not inconsistent with the principles of the Gospel.*

Many Protestant divines have written in favor of polygamy. John Lyser, a Lutheran minister, living in the latter part of the seventeenth century, defended it strongly in a work entitled "Polygamia Triumphatrix." A former general of the Capuchin Order, converted to the Protestant faith, published, in the sixteenth century, a book of "Dialogues in Favor of Polygamy." Rev. Mr. Madan, a Protestant divine, in a treatise called "Thalypthora," maintained that Paul's injunctions that bishops should be the husbands of one wife, signified that laymen were permitted to marry more than one. The scholarly William Ellery Channing could find no prohibition of polygamy in the New Testament. In his "Remarks on the Character and Writings of John Milton," he says: "We believe it to be an indisputable fact, that although Christianity was first preached in Asia, which had been from the earliest days the seat of polygamy, the apostles never denounced it as a crime, and never required their converts to put away all wives but one. No express prohibition of polygamy is found in the New Testament." The legitimate result of such views is seen in Mormonism, the latest Protestant sect, which claims its authority from the Bible as well as from the Book of Mormon. We give the remarks recently made in defence of polygamy by Bishop Lunt of the Mormon Church, to a reporter of *The San Francisco Chronicle:*

God revealed to Joseph Smith the polygamous system. It is quite true that his widow declared that no such revelation was ever made, but that was because she had lost the spirit. God commanded the human race to multiply and replenish the earth. Abraham had two wives, and the Almighty honored the second one by a direct communication. Jacob had Leah and Zilpah. David had a plurality of wives, and was a man after

---

* Even as late as the sixteenth century a plurality of wives was allowed in some of the Christian countries of Europe, and the German reformers were inclined to permit bigamy as not inconsistent with the principles of the Gospel.—"*Woman in all Countries and Nations,*" *Nichols*

God's own heart. God gave him Saul's wives, and only condemned his adulteries. Moses, Gideon, and Joshua had each a plurality of wives. Solomon had wives and concubines by hundreds, though we do not believe in the concubine system. We leave that to the Gentiles. Virtue and chastity wither beneath the monogamic institution, which was borrowed from the pagan nations by the early Christians. It was prophesied that in the latter days seven women would lay hold of one man and demand to bear his name, that they might not be held in dishonor. The Protestants and Catholics assail us with very poor grace when it is remembered that the first pillars of the religion they claim to profess were men like the saints of Utah—polygamists. The fact can not be denied. Polygamy is virtually encouraged and taught by example by the Old Testament. It may appear shocking and blasphemous to Gentiles for us to say so, but we hold that Jesus Christ himself was a polygamist. He was surrounded by women constantly, as the Scriptures attest, and those women were His polygamous wives. The vast disparity between the sexes in all settled communities is another argument in favor of polygamy, to say nothing of the disinclination among young male Gentiles to marrying. The monogamic system condemns millions of women to celibacy. A large proportion of them stray from the path of right, and these unfortunates induce millions of men to forego marriage. As I have said, virtue and chastity wither under the monogamic system.

There are no illegitimate children in Utah; there are no libertines; there are no brothels, excepting where the presence of Gentiles creates the demand for them. Even then our people do what they can to root out such places. There is a positive advantage in having more than one wife. It is impossible to find a Gentile home, where comforts and plenty prevail, in which there is only one woman. No one woman can manage a household. She must have assistance. Hence we claim that when a man marries a second wife, he actually benefits the first one, and contributes to her ease, and relieves her of a large burden of care. The duties of the household are divided between the two women, and everything moves on harmoniously and peacefully. The whole thing is a matter of education. A girl reared under the monogamic system may look with abhorrence on ours; our young women do not do so. They expect, when they marry a man, that he will some day take another wife, and they consider it quite natural that he should do so. In wealthy Gentile communities the concubine system largely takes the place of the polygamous system. Any man of intelligence, observation, and travel, knows that such is the case. The fact is ignored by general consent, and little is said about it, and nothing is written about it. It is not regarded as a proper subject of conversation or of publication. How much better to give lonely women a home while they are uncontaminated, and honor them with your name, and perpetually provide for them, and before the world recognize your own offspring! The polygamous system is the only natural one, and the time rapidly approaches when it will be the most conspicuous and beneficent of American institutions. It will be the grand characteristic feature of American society. Our women are contented with it—more, they are the most ardent defenders of it to be found in Utah. If the question were put to a vote to-morrow, nine-tenths of the women of Utah would vote to perpetuate polygamy.

The Mormons claim that polygamy is countenanced by the New Testament as well as by the Old. They interpret Paul's teaching in regard to bishops, while commanding them to marry one wife, as also not prohibiting them from marrying more than one; their interpretation of this passage slightly varying from that of Rev. Mr. Madan.

Rev. C. P. Lyford, of the Methodist Church, long a resident of Utah, in a letter of February 19, 1881, to *The Northern Christian Advocate,* a Methodist paper published in Syracuse, says:

We read of the stories of India and China, and the wonder of their existence is lost in their antiquity. Mohammedanism, with its 1,200 years of existence, amazes us that it should have obtained such a footing. But here, in our day, surrounded with all the advantages of the nineteenth century, that a people should have come up from nothing; that a man of low family, himself a worthless character, should have come up with a lie in his mouth and a stolen manuscript in his hand, and be found dictating terms to a strong government, and become an absolute despot in a republic, is the most amazing fact of history. It took the Methodist Church forty years to get a membership of 138,000. Mormonism in forty-four years counted 250,000. It seems incredible, nevertheless it is a fact. In this brief space of time it has also been able to nullify our laws, oppose our institutions, openly perpetrate crimes, be represented in Congress, boast of the helplessness of the nation to prevent these things, and give the Church supremacy over the State and the people. Bills introduced in Congress adequate to their overthrow have been year after year allowed to fall to the ground without action upon them.

Our public men can only pronounce against the crime of polygamy; the press can see only polygamy in Utah; the public mind is impressed with only the heinousness of polygamy. Back of polygamy is the tree that produces it and many kindred evils more dear to the Mormon rulers. They do not care for all the sentiment or law against this one fruit of the tree, if the tree itself is left to stand. The tree—the prolific cause of so many and so great evils in Utah, the greatest curse of the territory, the strength of Mormonism, and its impregnable wall of defence against Christianity and civilization, is that arbitrary, despotic, and absolute hierarchy known as the Mormon Priesthood.

Mr. Lyford has partial insight into the truth when he says "back of polygamy is the tree that produces it and many kindred evils"; but in defining that tree as the hierarchy—the priesthood— he has not reached the entire truth. He does not touch the ground which supports the tree. Polygamy is but one development of the doctrine of woman's created inferiority, the constant tendency of which is to make her a mere slave ,under every form of religion extant, and of which the complex marriage of the Oneida Community was but another logical result.

When woman interprets the Bible for herself, it will be in the interest of a higher morality, a purer home. Monogamy is woman's doctrine, as polygamy is man's. Backofen, the Swiss jurist, says that the regulation of marriage by which, in primitive times, it became possible for a woman to belong only to one man, came about by a religious reformation, wherein the women, in armed conflict, obtained a victory over men.

In Christian countries to-day, the restrictions on woman in the married relation are much greater than upon man.* Adultery, which is polygamy outside of the married relation, is everywhere held as more venial in man than in woman. In England, while the husband can easily obtain a divorce from his wife, upon the ground of adultery, it is almost impossible for the wife to obtain a divorce upon the same ground. Nothing short of the husband's bringing another woman into the house, to sustain wifely relations to him, at all justifies her in proceeding for a separation; and even then, the husband retains control of the wife's property. A trial† in England is scarcely ended in which a husband willed his wife's property to his mistress and illegitimate children. The courts not only decided in his favor, but to this legal robbery of the wife, added the insult of telling her that a part of her own money was enough for her, and that she ought to be willing that her husband's mistress and illegitimate children should share it with her.

Milton's "Paradise Lost" is responsible for many existing views in regard to woman. After the Reformation, as women began to waken to literature, came Milton, a patriot of patriots—as patriots were held in those days, a man who talked of liberty for men— but who held man to stand in God's place toward woman. Although it has been affirmed that in his blindness Milton dictated his great epic to his daughters, and a Scotch artist has painted the scene (a picture recently purchased by the Lenox Library), yet this is one of the myths men call history, and amuse themselves in believing. This tale of blind Milton dictating "Paradise Lost" to his daughters, is a trick ‡ designed to play upon our sympathies. Old Dr.

---

* See report of the Seney trial in Ohio, 1879, in which the judge decided against the prosecuting wife, upon the ground of her lack of the same ownership over the husband that the husband possessed over the wife.

† The Birchall case .

‡ "History," says Voltaire, "is only a parcel of tricks we play with the dead."

Johnson said of Milton, that he would not allow his daughters[*]
even to learn to write. Between Milton and his wives, we know
there was tyranny upon one side and hatred on the other. He could
not gain the love of either wife or daughter, and yet he is the man
who did so much to popularize the idea of woman's subordination
to man. "He, for God; she, for God in him"—as taught in the
famous line: "God thy law, thou mine."

That the clerical teaching of woman's subordination to man was not
alone a doctrine of the dark ages, is proven by the most abundant
testimony of to-day. The famous See trial of 1876, which shook
not only the Presbytery of Newark, but the whole Synod of New
Jersey, and finally, the General Presbyterian Assembly of the United
States, was based upon the doctrine of the divinely appointed subordination of woman to man, and arose simply because Dr. See
admitted two ladies[†] to his pulpit to speak upon temperance; which
act, Rev Dr. Craven, the prosecutor, declared to have been "an
indecency in the sight of Jehovah." He expressed the general
clerical and Church view, when he said:

I believe the subject involves the honor of my God. I believe the
subject involves the headship and crown of Jesus. Woman was made
for man and became first in the transgression. My argument is that
subordination is natural, the subordination of sex. Dr. See has admitted marital subordination, but this is not enough; there exists a created
subordination; a divinely arranged and appointed subordination of
woman as woman, to man as man. Woman was made for man and became
first in the transgression. The proper condition of the adult female is marriage; the general rule for ladies is marriage. Women without children,
it might be said, could preach, but they are under the general rule of

---

[*] JOHN MILTON AND HIS DAUGHTERS.—Milton's Oriental views of the function of
woman led him not only to neglect, but to positively prevent the education of his daughters. They were sent to no school at all, but were handed over to a schoolmistress in
the house. He would not allow them to learn any language, saying, with a sneer, that
"for a woman one tongue was enough." The Nemesis, however, that follows selfish
sacrifice of others is so sure of stroke that there needs no future world of punishment
to adjust the balance. The time came when Milton would have given worlds that his
daughters had learned the tongues. He was blind, and could only get at his precious
book—could only give expression to his precious verses—through the eyes and hands of
others. Whose hands and whose eyes so proper for this as his daughters? He proceeded to train them to read to him, parrot-like, in five or six languages, which he (the
schoolmaster) could at one time have easily taught them; but of which they could not
now understand a word. He turned his daughters into reading-machines. It is appalling to think of such a task. That Mary should revolt, and at last, after repeated contests with her taskmaster, learn to hate her father—that she should, when some one
spoke in her presence of her father's approaching marriage, make the dreadful speech
that "it was no news to hear of his wedding, but if she could hear of his death, that
were something"—is unutterably painful, but not surprising.—*The Athenæum.*

[†] Mrs. Robinson, of Indiana, and Mrs. E. S. Whitney, of New York.

subordination. It is not allowed women to speak in the Church. Man's place is on the platform. It is positively base for a woman to speak in the pulpit; it is base in the sight of Jehovah. The whole question is one of subordination.

Thus, before a large audience composed mainly of women, Dr. Craven stood, and with denunciatory manner, frequently bringing his fists or his Bible emphatically down, devoted a four hours' speech to proving that the Bible taught woman's subordination; one of his statements being that "in every country, under every clime, from the peasant woman of Naples with a handkerchief over her hair, to the women before him with bonnets, every one wore something upon her head in token of her subordination." Dr. Craven's position was fully sustained by many brother clergymen, some of whom enthusiastically shouted " Amen ! "

Dr. Ballantine considered the subject too simple for an argument. Dr. Few Smith, although he admired Miss Smiley, more than almost any other orator he had ever listened to, did not want her or any other woman to permanently occupy the Presbyterian pulpit. Dr. Wilson rejoiced to see so many women crowding in the lecture-room; but Brother See should not take all the glory to himself. He was glad to see the women take so deep an interest in the subject under discussion; but as he looked at them he asked himself, " What will all the little children do, while these women are away from home ? " *

The Christianity of to-day thus continues to teach the existence

---

* While in the midst of correcting proof, March 22d, the New York press comes with an article showing how generally women are rousing to their rights. It is headed :

" WOMEN AT THE CHURCH POLL—*What Came of Reviving an Old Statute in Portchester.*— The trustees of the Presbyterian Church in Portchester, although elected on the 24th of February last, did not organize until about ten days ago. The reason for this delay lies in the claim made by some of the congregation that the election was irregular, owing to women having been allowed to vote. Some of the trustees who held over were at first inclined to resign, and the matter has been much discussed. When opposition was made to women voting, H. T. Smith produced the statute of 1813, which says that any member of the church at full age shall have a right to vote for trustees. There is nothing in the act prohibiting women from voting. There are, I believe, statutes forbidding women to vote in the Dutch Reformed and Episcopal Churches ; but this is a regular Presbyterian Church. It seems to me that the women have worked hard for this church, and that they ought to have a vote at the election of trustees and other officers. A *Sun* reporter called upon the ladies for their version of the troubles. Miss Pink, who is a school teacher, said : ' We women do four-fifths of the work, and contribute more than one-half the money to support the church. Two years ago we were allowed to vote for a minister, and we don't see why we shouldn't vote for trustees and at other elections.' Miss Camp gave similar reasons for voting. Mrs. Montgomery Lyon said : ' If the old trustees didn't know that we had a right to vote, it isn't our fault. We women do all the work, and why shouldn't we vote ?' Women will vote for President, soon."

of a superior and an inferior sex within the Church, possessing different rights, and held accountable to a different code of morals, when even woman's dress is held as typical of her inferiority. Not alone did Dr. Craven express this idea, but the Right Rev. Dr. Coxe refused the sacrament to the lady patients at the Clifton Springs Sanitarium in 1868, whose heads were uncovered. This same Right Rev. Dr. Coxe, in a speech at his installation as first President of Ingham Seminary for young ladies, declared "the laws of God to be plainly Salic."

Rev. Knox-Little, a High-Church clergyman of England, spent a few weeks in the United States during the fall of 1880. In the course of his stay in Philadelphia he preached a "Sermon to Women," in the large church of St. Clements. The following extract from the report in the *Times* of that city shows its teachings:

"God made himself to be born of a woman to sanctify the virtue of endurance; loving submission is an attribute of woman; men are logical, but women lacking this quality, have an intricacy of thought. There are those who think women can be taught logic; this is a mistake. They can never by any power of education arrive at the same mental status as that enjoyed by men, but they have a quickness of apprehension, which is usually called leaping at conclusions, that is astonishing. There, then, we have distinctive traits of a woman, namely, endurance, loving submission, and quickness of apprehension. Wifehood is the crowning glory of a woman. In it she is bound for all time. To her husband she owes the duty of unqualified obedience. There is no crime which a man can commit which justifies his wife in leaving him or applying for that monstrous thing, divorce. It is her duty to subject herself to him always, and no crime that he can commit can justify her lack of obedience. If he be a bad or wicked man she may gently remonstrate with him, but refuse him never. Let divorce be anathema; curse it; curse this accursed thing, divorce; curse it, curse it! Think of the blessedness of having children. I am the father of many children and there have been those who have ventured to pity me, 'Keep your pity for yourself,' I have replied. 'They never cost me a single pang.' In this matter let woman exercise that endurance and loving submission which with intricacy of thought are their only characteristics."

Such a sermon as the above, preached to woman, under the full blaze of nineteenth century civilization, needs few comments. In it woman's inferiority and subordination are as openly asserted as at any time during the dark ages. According to Rev. Knox-Little, woman possesses no responsibility; she is deprived of conscience, intelligent thought, self-respect, and is simply an appendage to man, a thing. As the clergy in the middle ages divided rights into those of persons and things, themselves being the persons, the laity, things, so the Rev. Knox-Little and his ilk of to-day divide the world into persons and things,—men being the persons and women the things.

It should require but little thought upon woman's part to see how closely her disabilities are interwoven with present religious belief as to her inferiority and pre-destined subordination. If she needs aid to thought, the Knox-Littles will help her. Have protests against his blasphemous doctrine been made by his brother clergymen? Not one. Has a single church denied his degrading theory? Not one. He has been allowed in this sermon to stand as the representative, not only of High-Church theology in regard to woman, but as expressing the belief of all churches in her creation and existence as an inferior and appendage to man.

There is scarcely a Protestant sect that has not, within a few years, in some way, placed itself upon record in regard to woman's subordination. The Pan-Presbyterian Council that assembled in Edinburgh a few years since, refused to admit a woman even as a listener to its proceedings, although women constitute at least two-thirds of the membership of that Church. A solitary woman who persisted in remaining to listen to the discussions of this body, was removed by force; " six stalwart Presbyterians " lending their ungentle aid to her ejection. The same Pan-Presbyterian body when in session in Philadelphia in the summer of 1880, laughed to scorn the suggestion of a liberal member, that the status of woman in the Church should receive some consideration. The speaker referred to the Sisters of Charity in the Catholic Church, and to the position of woman among the Quakers; but although the question was twice introduced, it was as often met with derisive laughter, and no action was taken upon it. A vote of the New England Society of Friends at their meeting in Newport, 1878, proves that as liberal as they have been considered toward woman, even they have not in the past held her as upon a plane of perfect equality. This body voted that hereafter " women shall be eligible to office in the management of the Society, shall sign all conveyances of real estate made by the Society, and shall be considered equal to the opposite sex."

The Congregational Church is placed upon record through laws governing certain of its bodies :

" By the word ' church ' is meant the adult males duly admitted and retained in the First Evangelical Congregational Church in Cambridgeport, present at any regular meeting of said church and voting by a majority." *

---

* The above is article xiv. of the by-laws of the society connected with the aforesaid church. Thus the society undertakes to dictate to the church who shall have a voice in the selection of a pastor. It is a matter of gratitude that the society, if it forbids females to vote in the church, yet allows them to pray and to help the society raise money.—*Independent, N. Y., Feb.* 24, 1881.

In the Unitarian and Universalist churches, which ordain women to preach and administer the ordinances, these women pastors are made to feel that the innovation is not universally acceptable.

The Methodist Church, professing to stand upon a broad basis, still refuses to ordain its most influential women preachers, and, within the year, has even deprived them of license, though one of them * has brought more converts to the Church than a dozen of its most influential bishops during the same period. To such bitter lengths has the opposition to woman's ordination been carried, that a certain reverend gentlemen, in debating the subject, declared that he would oppose the admission of the mother of our Lord into the ministry, the debate taking on a most unseemly form. The *Syracuse Sunday Morning Courier* of March 4, 1877, reported this debate as follows:

WOMEN AS PREACHERS.

The subject of permitting women to preach in Methodist pulpits was incidentally, but rather racily discussed at the Methodist ministers' meeting in New York city a few days since. A Miss Oliver—a more or less reverend lady—had been invited to preach to the ministers at their next meeting, and the question was raised, by what authority she was invited ? Thereupon Brother Buckley took the floor and gave expression to his dissent in the following terms:

I am opposed to inviting any woman to preach before this meeting. If the mother of our Lord were on earth I should oppose her preaching here. [Sensation and murmurs of disapproval]. Oh, I do not mind that, I like at the beginning of a speech to find that there are two sides to my question. There is no power in the Methodist Church by which a woman can be licensed to preach; this is history, this is the report made at the last General Conference. It is, therefore, not legal for any quarterly conference to license a woman to preach, nevertheless here is a woman who claims to have such a license, and we are asked to invite her to preach.

A BROTHER: We have the right !

BROTHER BUCKLEY: Oh, you have the right to believe the moon is made of green cheese, but yet have no right to commit the ministers of this city on an unsettled Church question. [Laughter and applause]. The tendency of men—now here is a chance to hiss—the tendency of men to endeavor to force female preachers on the Church, and the desire to run after female preachers, is, as Dr. Finney said to the students at Oberlin, an aberration of amativeness. [Roars of laughter and applause]. When men are moved by women, then by men under the same circumstances, it is certainly due to an aberration of amativeness. [Applause and more

---

* BROKEN DOWN.—Mrs. Van Cott, the woman evangelist, has retired from the field, probably forever. Her nervous system is broken down. During the fourteen years of her ministry she has traveled 143,417 miles, has preached 4,294 sermons, besides conducting 9,333 other religious meetings, and writing 9,853 letters.—*Ex.*

laughter]. For some time the male and female students at Oberlin used to have their prayer-meetings together, but after a time they divided, and the young men complained to Dr. Finney that the Holy Ghost no longer came with equal force. Dr. Finney said this showed amativeness, or that the men were back-sliding. [Applause].

BROTHER DICKINSON: As to the talk of amativeness, what about our holiness meetings and seaside meetings, where we go to hear woman, and to be moved by her words and her personality ? [Applause]. Why are there so many women in the Church ? It must be amativeness which urges them to go and hear men preach. [Laughter].

Dr. ROACH: If this meeting has any dignity, has any Christian intelligence, has any weight of character, it ought not to take this action. [Laughter]. What wildness, what fanaticism, what strange freaks will we not take on next ? [Laughter and applause].

Brother McAllister and others took part in the discussion, and finally, amid cries of "Motion," "Question," points of order, and the utmost confusion, the question was put, and the meeting refused to invite Miss Oliver to preach by a vote of 46 to 38. The result was received with ejaculations of "Amen" and "Thank God" and "God bless Brother Buckley." The Chair announced that Brother Kittrell will preach next Monday on "Entire Satisfaction," and the meeting adjourned.

Miss Oliver appealed to the General Conference of the Methodist Episcopal Church in session in Cincinnati, May, 1880, for full installment and ordination. In this appeal she said :

I am so thoroughly convinced that the Lord has laid commands upon me in this direction, that it becomes with me a question of my own soul's salvation. I have passed through tortures to which the flames of martyrdom would be nothing, for they would end in a day; and through all this time, and to-day, I could turn off to positions of comparative ease and profit. I ask you, fathers and brethren, tell me what you would do in my place ? Tell me what you would wish the Church to do toward you, were you in my place ? Please apply the golden rule, and vote in Conference accordingly.

As answer to this appeal, and in reply to all women seeking the ministry of that Church, the Conference passed the following resolution :

Resolved, That women have already all the rights and privileges in the Methodist Church that are good for them, and that it is not expedient to make any change in the books of discipline that would open the doors for their ordination to the ministry.*

An Episcopal Church Convention meeting in Boston in the sum-

* But this Conference, which could not recognize woman's equality of rights in the Church, adjourned in a body to Chicago, before its business was completed, by its presence there to influence the Republican Nominating Convention in favor of General Grant's name for the Presidency.

mer of 1877, busied itself in preparing canons upon marriage and divorce, thus aiming to reach the finger of the Protestant Church down to a control of this most private family relation. The Diocesan Convention of South Carolina, in the spring of 1878, denied women the right to vote upon Church matters, although some churches in the diocese counted but five male members.

Not alone in her request for ordination has woman met with opposition, but in her effort for any separate church work. The formation of woman's foreign missionary societies was bitterly opposed by the different evangelical denominations, although they have raised more money than the male societies have ever been able to do—even helping them pay old debts—and have reached large classes of their own sex whom the male societies were powerless to touch. By thus supplementing men's work, they have made themselves acceptable.

Not only do councils, convocations, conferences, conventions, synods, and assemblies proclaim woman's inferiority, but Sunday-schools teach the same doctrine. A letter from a correspondent of *The National Citizen and Ballot-Box* (Syracuse, N. Y.), in August, 1880, said :

> Our Sunday-schools here have just finished the lesson on the creation and fall of man, and those of us who are capable of feeling, felt keenly the thrusts at woman for her infidelity to God's laws, and her overpowering influence in dragging man from his exalted position in life into a bondage of sin and death, and that she is to be held responsible for all the accumulated sins of the ages. One man said that "had not Eve been *lurking* around where she had no business, the devil would never have tempted her." Another said, "Had it not been for woman, we might to-day be living in ease and splendor," and I listened to hear them say the fallen angel was a woman.

This same doctrine is taught in the public schools. *The Republican*, of Havre de Grace, Maryland, in its issue of August 6, 1880, gave the following report of a speech at that time :

> Thus spoke Master Showell at the Berlin (Wicomico County) High-School commencement: "By woman was Eden lost and man cursed. If you trust her, give up all hopes of heaven. She can not love, because she is too selfish. She may have a fancy, but that is fleeting. Her smiles are deceit; her vows are traced in sand. She is a thread of candor with a web of wiles. Her charity is hypocrisy; she is deception every way—hair, teeth, complexion, heart, tongue, and all. Oh, I hate you, ye cold composition of art!"

Sermons are frequently preached in opposition to woman's demand for equality of right in Church and State. On the Sunday following the Thirtieth Anniversary Woman Suffrage Convention, held in Rochester, 1878, the Rev. A. H. Strong, D.D., President of the Baptist Theological Seminary of that city, preached upon "Woman's Place and Work," saying :

In the very creation of mankind in the garden of beauty, God ordained the subordination of woman.

This president of a theological seminary, where Christian theology is taught to embryo Christian ministers, said that woman's subordination would be most perfectly seen in the "Christian humility and gentleness and endurance of her character, and in her indisposition to assume the place or do the work of man," forgetting, apparently, that subordination, humility, and endurance are precisely the qualities which tend to destroy nobleness of character.

The sermon was especially directed against the following resolutions of this Convention, which throughout the country met much clerical criticism and opposition :

Resolved, That as the duty of every individual is self-development, the lessons of self-sacrifice and obedience taught women by the Christian Church have been fatal, not only to her own highest interests, but through her have also dwarfed and degraded the race.

Resolved, That the fundamental principle of the Protestant Reformation, the right of individual conscience and judgment in the interpretation of Scripture, heretofore conceded to and exercised by man alone, should now be claimed by woman, and that in her most vital interests she should no longer trust authority, but be guided by her own reason.

Resolved, That it is through the perversion of the religious element in woman, cultivating the emotions at the expense of her reason, playing upon her hopes and fears of the future, holding this life, with all its high duties, forever in abeyance to that which is to come, that she, and the children she has trained, have been so completely subjugated by priestcraft and superstition.

Professor Christlieb, a distinguished German clergyman who was in attendance upon the Evangelical Alliance in New York, a few years since, expressed severe condemnation of the marriage relation as he saw it in this country. His criticism is a good exemplification of the general religious view taken of woman's relation to man. After his return to Germany, a young American student called, it is related, upon the professor with a note of introduction, and was cordially received by the German, who, while he praised this country, expressed much solicitude about its future. On being asked his reasons, he frankly expressed his opinion that "the Spirit of

Christ " was not here, and proceeded to illustrate his meaning. He seriously declared that on more than one occasion he had heard an American woman say to her husband, " Dear, will you bring me my shawl ? " and the husband had brought it ! Worse than this, he had seen a husband, returning home at evening, enter the parlor where his wife was sitting—perhaps in the very best chair in the room—and the wife not only did not go and get his slippers and dressing-gown, but she even remained seated, and left him to find a chair as he could. In the view of this noted German clergyman, the principles of the wife's equality with the husband, as shown in the American home, is destructive of Christian principles.*

Clerical action to-day, proves woman to hold the same place in the eyes of the Church that she did during the dark ages. Woman is as fully degraded, taking into consideration our civilization, as she ever was. The form alone has changed. She is no longer burned at the stake as a witch ; she is no longer prostituted to feudal lords. The age has outgrown a belief in the supernatural, and feudalism is dead ; yet the same principle which degraded her five hundred or a thousand years since, still exists, even though its mani-festation is not the same. The feminine principle is still looked upon as secondary and inferior,† though all the facts of nature and science prove it to extend throughout creation.

It is through the Church idea of woman that the press of the world is filled with scandals like the one that recently agitated the Romish Church, in which the dead Cardinal Antonelli's name was bandied about in courts of law. It is through Church interpreta-tion of woman's position that the suit of his putative daughter, the Countess Lambertina, for his property, was decided against her on the ground that she was "a sacrilegious child." The person who commits sacrilege steals sacred things. "Sacrilegious" means vio-lating sacred things. " A sacrilegious child " is a child who " violated sacred things " by coming into existence. Her father was holy ; he did not violate holy things when he violated and ruined a woman's life. He committed no sacrilege in the eyes of the Church. His sin was nothing ; but the unfortunate result of his sin was a violation

---

* A professor of theology said a while ago, how sorry he should be to have the law recognize that one-half of the income of the family belonged to his wife, "it would establish such a mine-and-thine relation." It evidently seemed to him, somehow, more harmonious, less of the earth, earthy, that he could say, "All mine, my love," and that she could sweetly respond, "All thine, dearest."—*State Prohibitionist, Des Moines, Ia., Jan.* 28, 1881.

† The great botanist, Linnæus, was persecuted when he first presented his sexual sys-tem in vegetation to the world.

of holy things by the mere fact of her coming into existence. What irony of all that is called holy !

It is because the Church has taught that woman was created solely for man, that in tearing asunder a recent will in New York, it was proven that the husband, indebted though he was to his wife for the beginning of his vast fortune, incarcerated her while sane in a lunatic asylum, because she objected to his practical polygamy by his introduction of a mistress into the family.

Political despotism has now its strongest hold in the theory of woman's created subordination. Woman has been legislated for as a class, and not as a human being upon a basis of equality with man, but as an inferior to whom a different code was applicable.

Our recent Secretary of State, William M. Evarts, when counsel in the Beecher-Tilton trial, defined woman's legal and theological position as that of subordination to man, declaring that notwithstanding changing customs and the amenities of modern life, women were not free, but were held in the hollow of man's hand, to be crushed at his will.

Then Mr. Evarts read from various legal authorities instances and opinions bearing upon the subjugation of weak wives by strong husbands, the gist of them being that confessions of guilt obtained by such husbands from such wives are not entitled to great weight. He continued:

RECOGNIZING THE PRINCIPLES OF MARRIAGE.

This institution of marriage, framed in our nature, built up in our civilization, studied, contemplated, understood by the jurisprudence of ages, is a solid and real institution, and for its great benefits, and as a necessary part of them, it carries not only the fact of the wife's subordination to the husband, but of the merciful interpretation of that subordination* which sensible, instructed men ever accord in practical life, and which the judges pronounce from the bench, and the juries confirm by their verdicts. Now, gentlemen, you may think that is our advanced civilization, when so much of independence is assumed for women, and such entire equality is accorded to them in feeling and in sentiment by their husbands and by the world, that the old rule of the common law interpreting this institution of marriage, by which a wife was never held responsible to the law, or subject to punishment for any crime committed in the presence or under the influence of her husband, was one of those traits of human nature belonging to ruder ages and to past times; but, gentlemen, in our own Court of Appeals, and in the highest tribunals of En-

---

* The legal subordination of one sex to another is wrong in itself, and now one of the chief hindrances to human improvement; it ought to be replaced by a principle of perfect equality, admitting no powers or privileges on the one side or disability on the other.— *Subjection of Woman, John Stuart Mill.*

gland, within the last few years, there is an explicit recognition of these principles.

Mr. Evarts cited an English case in which a wife, who participated in a robbery under the guidance of her husband, was acquitted on the ground that she was irresponsible; and he added an argument that the principle of law involved was correct. Then he called attention to a recent case in this State, which he held was a confirmation of the same sound theory.

The teachings of the Church that it was sinful for woman to use her own reason, to think for herself, to question authority, thus fettering her will, together with a false interpretation of Scripture, have been the instruments to hold her, body and soul, in a slavery whose depths of degradation can never be fathomed, whose indescribable tortures can never be understood by man.

Not only has woman suffered in the Church, in society, under the laws, and in the family by this theological degradation of her sex, but in science and literature she has met a like fate. Hypatia, who succeeded her father, Theon, in the government of the Alexandrian school, and whose lectures were attended by the wisest men of Europe, Asia, and Africa, was torn in pieces by a Christian mob afraid of her learning.

A monument erected to Catherine Sawbridge Macaulay, as " Patroness of Liberty," was removed from the Church by order of its rector. Harriet Martineau met the most strenuous opposition from bishops in her effort to teach the poor ; her day-schools and even her Sunday-schools were broken up by clerical influence. Madam Pepe-Carpentier, founder of the French system of primary instruction, of whom Froebel caught his kindergarten idea, found her labors interrupted, and her life harassed by clerical opposition.

Mary Somerville, the most eminent English mathematician of this century, was publicly denounced in church by Dean Cockburn, of York; and when George Eliot died a few weeks since, her lifeless remains were refused interment in Westminster Abbey, where so many inferior authors of the privileged sex lie buried ; the grave even not covering man's efforts toward the degradation of woman.

When Susannah Wesley dared to conduct religious services in her own house, and to pray for the king, contrary to her husband's wishes, he separated from her in consequence. The husband of Annie Besant left her because she dared to investigate the Scriptures for herself, and was sustained by the courts in taking from her the control of her little daughter, simply because the mother thought best not to train her in a special religious belief, but to allow her to wait until her reason developed, that she might decide her religious views for herself.   A woman writing in the "Woman's Kingdom" department of *The Chicago Inter-Ocean*, says:

The orthodox Church has been almost suicidal in its treatment of women (and I write as one whose name still stands on the membership list of the Presbyterian Church). Persons who have not walked with wounded, lacerated hearts through the terrible realities, can form no idea of the suffering occasioned young women whose conscience summoned them to speak for temperance and woman suffrage, by the persecutions encountered in the Church. We have known clergymen come straight from the pulpit where they have talked eloquently of "moral courage," of the heroism of Martin Luther and Calvin and Wesley, and even of Garrison and Harriet Beecher Stowe, to meet with a sneer some brave young woman, who, with the same moral courage was proclaiming the truth as revealed unto her. Our young women have been denied admittance into theological schools; they have been compelled to go out into the by-ways and hedges; they have been persecuted for righteousness' sake. The Church has decreed that two-thirds of its members shall be governed by the masculine one-third; but despite this decision, woman will preach and the world will listen.

Not only has woman recognized her own degradation, but the largest-hearted men have also seen it.   Thomas W. Higginson, in an address at the anniversary of the Young Men's Christian Union, in New York City, as long ago as 1858, in an address upon women in Christian civilization, said:

No man can ever speak of the position of woman so mournfully as she has done it for herself. Charlotte Brontë, Caroline Norton, and indeed the majority of intellectual women, from the beginning to the end of their lives, have touched us to sadness even in mirth, and the mournful memoirs of Mrs. Siddons, looking back upon years when she had been the chief intellectual joy of English society, could only deduce the hope, "that there might be some other world hereafter, where justice would be done to woman."

The essayist, E. P. Whipple, in a recent speech before the Papyrus Club of Boston, said of George Eliot:

The great masculine creators and delineators of human character, Homer, Cervantes, Shakespeare, Göethe, Scott, and the rest, cheer and invigorate us even in the vivid representation of our common humanity in its meanest, most stupid, most criminal forms. Now comes a woman endowed not only with their large discourse of reason, their tolerant views of life, and their intimate knowledge of the most obscure recesses of the human heart and brain, but with a portion of that rich, imaginative humor which softens the savageness of the serious side of life by a quick perception of its ludicrous side, and the result of her survey of life is, that she depresses the mind, while the men of genius animate it, and that she saddens the heart, while they fill it with hopefulness and joy. I do not intend to solve a problem so complicated as this, but I would say, as some approach to an explanation, that this remarkable woman was born under the wrath and curse of what our moden philosophers call "heredity." She inherited the results of man's dealings with woman during a thousand generations of their life together.

Contempt for woman, the result of clerical teaching, is shown in myriad forms. Wife-beating is still so common, even in America, that a number of the States have of late introduced bills especially directed to the punishment of the wife-beater. Great surprise is frequently shown by these men when arrested. "Is she not my wife?" is cried in tones proving the brutal husband had been trained to consider this relationship a sufficient justification for any abuse.

In England, wives are still occasionally led to the market by a halter around the neck to be sold by the husband to the highest bidder.* George Borrow, in his singular narrative, "The Rommany Rye," says:

The sale of a wife with a halter around her neck is still a legal transaction in England. The sale must be made in the cattle market, as if she were a mare, "all women being considered as mares by old English law, and indeed called 'mares' in certain counties where genuine old English is still preserved."

It is the boast of America and Europe that woman holds a higher position in the world of work under Christianity than under pagandom. Heathen treatment of woman in this respect often points the moral and adorns the tale of returned missionaries, who are apparently forgetful that servile labor† of the severest and most degrading character is performed by Christian women in highly Christian countries. In Germany, where the Reformation had its first inception, woman carries a hod of mortar up steep ladders to the top of the highest buildings; or, with a coal basket strapped to her back, climbs three or four flights of stairs, her husband remaining at the foot, pipe in mouth, awaiting her return to load the hod or basket, that she may make another ascent, the payment for her work going

---

* The *Worcester Chronicle* of recent date gives an account of a wife sale in England. Thomas Middleton delivered up his wife Mary M. to Philip Rostius, and sold her for one shilling and a quart of ale, and parted from her solely and absolutely for life, "not to trouble one another for life." Philip Rostius made his mark as a witness. A second witness was S. H. Shore, Crown Inn, Trim street.

† In the peace made by the Sabines with the Romans, after the forcible abduction of the Sabine maidens, one of the provisions was that no labor, except spinning, should be required of these Roman wives.

into the husband's hands for his uncontrolled use. Or mayhap this German wife works in the field harnessed by the side of a cow, while her husband-master holds the plough and wields the whip. Or, perhaps, harnessed with a dog, she serves the morning's milk, or drags her husband home from work at night.

In France women act as porters, carrying the heaviest burdens and performing the most repulsive labors at the docks, while eating food of so poor a quality that the lessening stature of the population daily shows the result. In Holland and Prussia women drag barges on the canal, and perform the most repulsive agricultural duties. On the Alps* husbands borrow and lend their wives, one neighbor not scrupling to ask the loan of another's wife to complete some farming task, which loan is readily granted, with the understanding that the favor is to be returned in kind. In England, scantily clothed women work by the side of nude men in coal pits, and, harnessed to trucks, perform the severe labor of dragging coal up inclined planes to the mouth of the pit, a work testing every muscle and straining every nerve, and so severe that the stoutest men shrink from it; while their degradation in brick-yards and iron mines has commanded the attention of philanthropists and legislators.†

A gentleman recently travelling in Ireland blushes for his sex when he sees the employments of women, young and old. They are patient drudges, staggering over the bogs with heavy creels of turf on their backs, or climbing the slopes from the seashore, laden like beasts of burden with the heavy sand-dripping seaweed, or undertaking long journeys on foot into the market towns, bearing weighty hampers of farm produce. In Montenegro, women form the beasts of burden in war, and are counted among the "animals" belonging to the prince. In Italy, that land which for centuries led the world in art, women work in squalor and degradation under the shadow of St. Peter's and the Vatican for four-pence a day; while in America, under the Christianity of the nineteenth century, until within twenty years, she worked on rice and cotton plantations waist-deep in water, or under a burning sun performed the tasks demanded by a cruel master, at whose hands she also suffered the same kind

---

*THE FAIR SEX IN THE ALPS.—The farmers in the Upper Alps, though by no means wealthy, live like lords in their houses, while the heaviest portion of agricultural labors devolves on the wife. It is no uncommon thing to see a woman yoked to the plough with an ass, while her husband guides it. An Alpine farmer accounts it an act of politeness to lend his wife to a neighbor who has too much work, and the neighbor in return lends his wife for a few days' labor whenever requested.

† Lord Shaftesbury bringing the subject before Parliament.

of moral degradation exacted of the serf under feudalism. In some portions of Christendom the " service "* of young girls to-day implies their sacrifice to the Moloch of man's unrestrained passions.

Augustine, in his work, " The City of God," taunts Rome with having caused her own downfall. He speaks of her slaves, miserable men, put to labors only fit for the beasts of the field, degraded below them; their condition had brought Rome to its own destruction. If such wrongs contributed to the overthrow of Rome, what can we not predict of the Christian civilization which, in the twentieth century of its existence, degrades its Christian women to labors fit only for the beasts of the field; harnessing them with dogs to do the most menial labors; which drags them below even this, holding their womanhood up to sale, putting both Church and State sanction upon their moral death; which, in some places, as in the city of Berlin, so far recognizes the sale of women's bodies for the vilest purposes as part of the Christian religion, that license for this life is refused until they have partaken of the Sacrament; and which demands of the " 10,000 licensed women of the town " of the city of Hamburg, certificates showing that they regularly attend church and also partake of the sacrament?

A civilization which even there has not reached its lowest depths, but which has created in England, as a result of its highest Christian civilization, a class of women under the protection of the State, known as " Queen's women," or " Government women," with direct purpose of more fully protecting man in his departure from the moral law, and which makes woman the hopeless slave of man's lowest nature; a system not confined to England, but already in practice in France, in Italy, in Switzerland, in Germany, and nearly every country in Europe. A system of morality which declares " the necessity " of woman's degradation, and which annually sends its tens of thousands down to a death from which society grants no resurrection.

---

* A STORY OF IRELAND IN 1880.—Recently, a young girl named Catherine Cafferby, of Belmullet, in County Mayo—the pink of her father's family—fled from the " domestic service " of a landlord as absolute as Lord Leitrim, the moment the poor creature discovered what that " service " customarily involved. The great man had the audacity to invoke the law to compel her to return, as she had not given statutable notice of her flight. She clung to the door-post of her father's cabin; she told aloud the story of her terror, and called on God and man to save her. Her tears, her shrieks, her piteous pleadings were all in vain. The Petty Sessions Bench ordered her back to the landlord's "service," or else to pay £5, or two weeks in jail. This is not a story of Bulgaria under Murad IV., but of Ireland in the reign of the present sovereign. That peasant girl went to jail to save her chastity. If she did not spend a fortnight in the cells, it was only because friends of outraged virtue, justice, and humanity paid the fine when the story reached the outer world.

In a letter to the National Woman's Suffrage Convention, held at St. Louis, May, 1879, upon this condition of Licensed Vice, from Josephine E. Butler, Hon. Secretary of the Federation and the Ladies' National Association for the Protection of Women ; a society which has its branches over Europe, and has for years been actively at work against this last most hideous form of slavery for women, Mrs. Butler says :

England holds a peculiar position in regard to the question. She was the last to adopt this system of slavery, and she adopted it in that thorough manner which characterizes the actions of the Anglo-Saxon race. In no other country has prostitution been regulated by law. It has been understood by the Latin races, even when morally enervated, that the law could not without risk of losing its majesty and force sanction illegality and violate justice. In England alone the regulations are law.

This legalization of vice, which is the endorsement of the "necessity" of impurity for man and the institution of the slavery of woman, is the most open denial which modern times have seen of the principle of the sacredness of the individual human being. An English high-class journal dared to demand that women who are unchaste shall henceforth be dealt with "not as human beings, but as foul sewers," or some such "material nuisance" without souls, without rights, and without responsibility. When the leaders of public opinion in a country have arrived at such a point of combined skepticism and despotism as to recommend such a manner of dealing with human beings, there is no crime which that country may not presently legalize, there is no organization of murder, no conspiracy of abominable things that it may not, and in due time will not—have been found to embrace in its guilty methods. Were it possible to secure the absolute physical health of a whole province or an entire continent by the destruction of one, only one poor and sinful woman, woe to that nation which should dare, by that single act of destruction, to purchase this advantage to the many! It will do it at its peril. God will take account of the deed not in eternity only, but in time, it may be in the next or even in the present generation.

The fact of governments lending their official aid to the demoralization of woman by the registration system, shows an utter debasement of law. This system is directly opposed to the fundamental principle of right, that of holding the accused innocent until proven guilty, which until now has been recognized as a part of modern law. Under the registration or license system, all women within the radius of its action are under suspicion ; all women are held as morally guilty until they prove themselves innocent. Where this law is in force, all women are under an irresponsible police surveillance, liable to accusation, arrest, examination, imprisonment, and the entrance of their names upon the list of the lewd women of a town. Upon this frightful infraction of justice, we have the sentiments of Sheldon Amos, Professor of Jurisprudence in the Law College of London University. In " The Science of Law," he says, in reference to this very wrong:

The loss of liberty to the extent to which it exists, implies a degradation of the State, and, if persisted in, can only lead to its dissolution. No person or class of persons must be under the cringing fear of having imputed to them offences of which they are innocent, and of being taken into custody in consequence of such imputation. They must not be liable to be detained in custody without so much as a *prima facie* case being made out, such as in the opinion of a responsible judicial officer leaves a presumption of guilt. They must not be liable to be detained for an indefinite time without having the question of their guilt or innocence investigated by the best attainable methods. When the fact comes to be inquired into, the best attainable methods of eliciting the truth must be used. In default of any one of these securities, *public liberty* must be said to be proportionately at a very low ebb.

Great effort has been made to introduce this system into the United States, and a National Board of Health, created by Congress in 1879, is carefully watched in its action, lest its irresponsible powers lead to its encroachment upon the liberties and personal rights of woman. A resolution adopted March 2, 1881, at a meeting of the New York Committee appointed to thwart the effort to license vice in this country, shows the need of its watchful care.

Resolved, That this committee has learned with much regret and apprehension of the action of the American Public Health Association, at its late annual meeting in New Orleans, in adopting a sensational report commending European governmental regulation of prostitution, and looking to the introduction in this country, with modifications, through the medium of State legislative enactments and municipal ordinances, of a kindred immoral system of State-regulated social vice.

From all these startling facts in Church and State we see that our government and religion are alike essentially masculine in their origin and development. All the evils that have resulted from dignifying one sex and degrading the other may be traced to this central error: a belief in a trinity of masculine Gods in One, from which the feminine element is wholly eliminated.* And yet in the

---

* The son of the late William Ellery Channing, in a recent letter to a friend on this point, says: "Religions like the Jewish and Christian, which make God exclusively *male*, consign woman logically to the subordinate position which is definitely assigned to her in Mahometanism. History has kept this tradition. The subjection of woman has existed as an invariable element in Christian civilization. It could not be otherwise. If God and Christ were both represented as male (and the Holy Ghost, too, in the pictures of the old masters), it stood to reason and appealed to fanaticism that the male form was the Godlike. Hence, logically, intellect and physical force were exalted above the

Scriptural account of the simultaneous creation of man and woman, the text plainly recognizes the feminine as well as the masculine element in the Godhead, and declares the equality of the sexes in goodness, wisdom, and power. Genesis i. 26, 27: " And God said: let us make man *in our own image, after our own likeness.* . . . . So God created man in His own image ; in the image of God created He him ; *male* and *female* created He THEM. . . . . And gave them dominion over the fish of the sea, and over the fowl of the air, and over every living thing that moveth upon the earth."

While woman's subordination is taught as a Scriptural doctrine, the most devout and learned biblical scholars of the present day admit that the Bible has suffered many interpolations in the course of the centuries. Some of these have doubtless occurred through efforts to render certain passages clearer, while others have been forged with direct intention to deceive. Disraeli says that the early English editions contain 6,000 errors, which were constantly introduced, and passages interpolated for sectarian purposes, or to sustain new creeds. Sometimes, indeed, they were added for the purpose of destroying all Scriptural authority by the suppression of texts. *The Church Union* says of the present translation, that there are more than 7,000 variations from the received Hebrew text, and more than 150,000 from the received Greek text.

These 7,000 variations in the Old Testament and 150,000 in the New Testament, are very significant facts. The oldest manuscripts of the New Testament are the Alexandrine Codex, known since the commencement of the seventeenth century, and believed to date back to the middle of the fifth century, the Sinaitic, and the Vatican Codices, each believed to have been executed about the middle of the fourth century. The Sinaitic Codex was discovered by Professor Tischendorf, a German scholar, at a monastery upon Mt. Sinai, in fragments, and at different periods from 1848 to 1859, a period of eleven years elapsing from his discovery of the first fragment until he secured the last one. The Vatican Codex has been in the Vatican library since its foundation, but has been inaccessible to scholars until very recently. It is not known from whence it came or by whom executed, but is deemed the oldest and most authentic

---

intuition of conscience and attractive charm. The male religion shaped government and society after its own form. Theodore Parker habitually addressed God as our Father and Mother. What we call God is the infinite ideal of humanity. The preposterous, ridiculous absurdity of supposing God so defined to be of the male sex, and to call God ' him,' does not need a word to make it apparent. This ideal which we all reverence, and for which we yearn, necessarily enfolds in *One* the attributes which, separated in our human race, express themselves in Manhood and Womanhood."

copy of the Bible extant. As these oldest codices only date to the middle of the fourth century, we have no record of the New Testament, in its present form, for the first three hundred and fifty years of this era.

A commission of eminent scholars has been engaged for the past eleven years upon a revision of the Bible. The New Testament portion is now about ready for the public, but so great and so many are its diversities from the old version, that it is prophesied the orthodox church will be torn by disputes between adherents of the old and the new, while those anxious for the truth, touch where it may, will be honestly in doubt if either one is to be implicitly trusted. Various comments and inquiries in regard to this revision have already appeared in the press.* The oldest codices do not contain many texts we have learned to look upon as especially holy. Portions of the Sermon on the Mount are not in these old manuscripts, a proof of their interpolation to serve the purpose of some one at a later date. In the same way additions have been made to the Lord's Prayer. Neither of these manuscripts contain the story of the woman taken in adultery, as narrated John viii. 1–11, so often quoted as proof of the divine mercy of Jesus. A letter upon this so long accepted story, from the eminent scholar, Howard Crosby, D.D., LL.D., a member of the revisory commission, will be read with interest:

Mrs. M. J. Gage:

Dear Madame:—The passage in John viii. 1–11, is *not* in the Alexandrian, nor is it in the Sinaitic, Vatican, and Ephraim Codices. It is found in twelve uncials (though marked *doubtful* in five of these) and in over 300 cursives. Yours very truly,

Howard Crosby.

116 East 19th, N. Y., *March* 14, '81.

The world still asks, What is Truth? A work has recently been published entitled, " The Christian Religion to A.D. 200." It is the fruit of several years' study of a period upon which the Church has

---

* Some person, over the signature of " A Bible Reader," writing in the *Sun* of March 16, says : " I would be sincerely glad to know what guarantee we have that ere long we shall not have another revision of Scripture ? It is not so long ago since the discovery of Tischendorf of an important manuscript of the New Testament, which gave a number of new readings. There may be in existence other and older manuscripts of the Bible than any we now have, from which may be omitted the narratives of the Crucifixion and the Resurrection. Should we then have to give these up ? If the revisers act consistently they would certainly have to do so.

" It appears that already the Calvinists and the Trinitarians have been deprived by the revisers of the texts they relied upon to uphold their peculiar doctrines. It remains to be seen how the Universalists, Baptists, and other Christian sects will fare."

but little record. It finds no evidence of the existence of the New Testament in its present form during that time; neither does it find evidence that the Gospels in their present form date from the lives of their professed authors. All Biblical scholars acknowledge that the world possesses no record or tradition of the original manuscripts of the New Testament, and that to attempt to reëstablish the old text is hopeless. No reference by writers to any part of the New Testament as authoritative is found earlier than the third century (A.D. 202). The first collection, or canon, of the New Testament was prepared by the Synod or Council of Laodicea in the fourth century (A.D. 360). It entirely omitted the Book of Revelation from the list of sacred works. This book has met a similar fate from many sources, not being printed in the Syriac Testament as late as 1562.

Amid this vast discrepancy in regard to the truth of the Scriptures themselves; with no Hebrew manuscript older than the twelfth century; with no Greek one older than the fourth; with the acknowledgment by scholars of 7,000 errors in the Old Testament, and 150,000 in the New; with assurance that these interpolations and changes have been made by men in the interest of creeds, we may well believe that the portions of the Bible quoted against woman's equality are but interpolations of an unscrupulous priesthood, for the purpose of holding her in subjection to man.

Amid this conflict of authority over texts of Scripture we have been taught to believe divinely inspired, destroying our faith in doctrines heretofore declared essential to salvation, how can we be sure that the forthcoming version of the Bible from the masculine revisers of our day will be more trustworthy than those which have been accepted as of Divine origin in the past?

This chapter is condensed from the writer's forthcoming work, " WOMAN, CHURCH, AND STATE."

APPENDIX.

CHAPTER I.

PRECEDING CAUSES.

MARGARET FULLER possessed more influence upon the thought of America, than any woman previous to her time. Men of diverse interests and habits of thought, alike recognized her power and acknowledged the quickening influence of her mind upon their own. Ralph Waldo Emerson said of her : " The day was never long enough to exhaust her opulent memory; and I, who knew her intimately for ten years, never saw her without surprise at her new powers."

William H. Channing, in her " Memoirs," says : " I have no hope of conveying to my readers my sense of the beauty of our relation, as it lies in the past, with brightness falling on it from Margaret's risen spirit. It would be like printing a chapter of autobiography, to describe what is so grateful in memory—its influence upon oneself."

Rev. James Freeman Clarke says : " Socrates without his scholars, would be more complete than Margaret without her friends. The insight which Margaret displayed in finding her friends ; the magnetism by which she drew them toward herself ; the catholic range of her intimacies ; the influence which she exerted to develop the latent germ of every character ; the constancy with which she clung to each when she had once given and received confidence ; the delicate justice which kept every intimacy separate, and the process of transfiguration which took place when she met any one on this mountain of friendship, giving a dazzling lustre to the details of common life—all these should be at least touched upon and illustrated, to give any adequate view of these relations."

Horace Greeley, in his " Recollections of a Busy Life," said : " When I first made her acquaintance she was mentally the best instructed woman in America."

When Transcendentalism rose in New England, drawing the brightest minds of the country into its faith, Margaret was accepted as its high-priestess ; and when *The Dial* was established for the expression of those views, she was chosen its editor, aided by Ralph Waldo Emerson and George Ripley. Nothing could be more significant of the place Margaret Fuller held in the realm of thought than the fact, that in this editorship she was given precedence over the eminent philosopher and eminent scholar, her associates.

She sought to unveil the mysteries of life and enfranchise her own sex from the bondage of the past, and while still under thirty planned a series of conversations (in Boston) for women only, wherein she took a leading part. The general object of these conferences, as declared in her programme, was to supply answers to these questions : " What are we born to do?" and " How shall we do it?" or, as has been stated, " Her three special aims in those conversations were, To pass in review the departments of thought and knowledge, and endeavor to place them in one relation to one another in our minds. To systematize thought and give a precision and clearness in which our sex are so deficient, chiefly, I think, because they have so few inducements to test and classify what they receive. To ascertain what pursuits are best suited to us, in our time and state of society, and how we may make the best use of our means of building up the life of thought upon the life of action."

These conversations continued for several successive winters, and were in reality a vindication of woman's right to think. In calling forth the opinions of her sex upon Life, Literature, Mythology, Art, Culture, and Religion, Miss Fuller was the precursor

51   (801)

of the Woman's Rights agitation of the last thirty-three years. Her work, "The Great Lawsuit; or, Man *vs.* Woman, Woman *vs.* Man," was declared by Horace Greeley to be the loftiest and most commanding assertion made of the right of woman to be regarded and treated as an independent, intelligent, rational being, entitled to an equal voice in framing and modifying the laws she is required to obey, and in controlling and disposing of the property she has inherited or aided to acquire. In this work Margaret said : " It is the fault of MARRIAGE and of the present relation between the sexes, that the woman *belongs* to the man, instead of forming a whole with him. . . . . Woman, self-centered, would never be absorbed by any relation ; it would only be an experience to her, as to Man. It is a vulgar error that love—*a* love—is to Woman her whole existence ; she is also born for Truth and Love in their universal energy. Would she but assume her in-heritance, Mary would not be the only virgin mother.''

Margaret Fuller was the first woman upon the staff of *The New York Tribune*, a position she took in 1844, when she was but thirty-four. Mrs. Greeley having made Margaret's acquaintance, attended her conversations and accepted her leading ideas, planned to have her become a member of the Greeley family, and a writer for *The Tribune ;* a position was therefore offered her by Mr. Greeley upon his wife's judgment. It required but a short time, however, for the great editor to feel her power, although he failed to fully comprehend her greatness. It has been declared not the least of Horace Greeley's services to the nation, that he was willing to entrust the literary criticisms of *The Trib-une* to one whose standard of culture was so far above that of his readers or his own.

Margaret Fuller opened the way for many women, who upon the editorial staff of the great New York dailies, as literary critics and as reporters, have helped impress woman's thought upon the American mind.

Theodore Parker, who knew her well, characterized her as a critic, rather than a crea-tor or seer. But whether we look upon her as critic, creator, or seer, she was thoroughly a woman. One of her friends wrote of her, " She was the largest woman, and not a woman who wanted to be a man." Woman everywhere, to-day, is a critic. Enthralled as she has been for ages, by both religious and political despotism, no sooner does she rouse to thought than she necessarily begins criticism. The hoary wrongs of the past still fall with heavy weight upon woman—their curse still exists. Before building society anew, she seeks to destroy the errors and injustice of the past, hence we find women critics in every department of thought.

CHAPTER IV.

NEW YORK.

Seneca Falls and Rochester Conventions.

WOMEN OUT OF THEIR LATITUDE.

We are sorry to see that the women in several parts of this State are holding what they call " Woman's Rights Conventions," and setting forth a formidable list of those Rights in a parody upon the Declaration of American Independence.

The papers of the day contain extended notices of these Conventions. Some of them fall in with their objects and praise the meetings highly ; but the majority either depre-cate or ridicule both.

The women who attend these meetings, no doubt at the expense of their more appro-priate duties, act as committees, write resolutions and addresses, hold much correspond-ence, make speeches, etc., etc. They affirm, as among their rights, that of unrestricted franchise, and assert that it is wrong to deprive them of the privilege to become legislators, lawyers, doctors, divines, etc., etc. ; and they are holding Conventions and making an agitatory movement, with the object in view of revolutionizing public opinion and the laws of the land, and changing their relative position in society in such a way as to divide with the male sex the labors and responsibilities of active life in every branch of art, science, trades, and professions.

Now, it requires no argument to prove that this is all wrong. Every true hearted female will instantly feel that this is unwomanly, and that to be practically carried out, the males must change their position in society to the same extent in an opposite direction, in order to enable them to discharge an equal share of the domestic duties which now appertain to females, and which must be neglected, to a great extent, if women are allowed to exercise all the " rights " that are claimed by these Convention-holders. Society would have to be radically remodelled in order to accommodate itself to so great a change in the most vital part of the compact of the social relations of life ; and the order of things established at the creation of mankind, and continued *six thousand years*, would be completely broken up. The organic laws of our country, and of each State, would have to be licked into new shapes, in order to admit of the introduction of the vast change that it contemplated. In a thousand other ways that might be mentioned, if we had room to make, and our readers had patience to hear them, would this sweeping reform be attended by fundamental changes in the public and private, civil and religious, moral and social relations of the sexes, of life, and of the Government.

But this change is impracticable, uncalled for, and unnecessary. *If effected*, it would set the world by the ears, make " confusion worse confounded," demoralize and degrade from their high sphere and noble destiny, women of all respectable and useful classes, and prove a monstrous injury to all mankind. It would be productive of no positive good, that would not be outweighed tenfold by positive evil. It would alter the relations of females without bettering their condition. Besides all, and above all, it presents no remedy for the *real* evils that the millions of the industrious, hard-working, and much suffering women of our country groan under and seek to redress.—*Mechanic's* (Albany, N. Y.) *Advocate.*

INSURRECTION AMONG THE WOMEN.

A female Convention has just been held at Seneca Falls, N. Y., at which was adopted a " declaration of rights," setting forth, among other things, that " all men and *women* are created equal, and endowed by their Creator with certain inalienable rights." The list of grievances which the *Amazons* exhibit, concludes by expressing a determination to insist that woman shall have " immediate admission to all the rights and privileges which belong to them as citizens of the United States." It is stated that they design, in spite of all misrepresentations and ridicule, to employ agents, circulate tracts, petition the State and National Legislatures, and endeavor to enlist the pulpit and the press in their behalf. This is *bolting* with a vengeance.— *Worcester* (Mass.) *Telegraph.*

THE REIGN OF PETTICOATS.

The women in various parts of the State have taken the field in favor of a petticoat empire, with a zeal and energy which show that their hearts are in the cause, and that they are resolved no longer to submit to the tyrannical rule of the *heartless* " lords of creation," but have solemnly determined to demand their " natural and inalienable right " to attend the polls, and assist in electing our Presidents, and Governors, and Members of Congress, and State Representatives, and Sheriffs, and County Clerks, and Supervisors, and Constables, etc., etc., and to unite in the general scramble for office. This is right and proper. It is but just that they should participate in the beautiful and feminine business of politics, and enjoy their proportion of the " spoils of victory." Nature never designed that they should be confined exclusively to the drudgery of raising children, and superintending the kitchens, and to the performance of the various other household duties which the cruelty of men and the customs of society have so long assigned to them. This is emphatically the age of " democratic progression," of *equality* and *fraternization*—the age when all colors and sexes, the bond and free, black and white, male and female, are, as they by right ought to be, all tending downward and upward toward the common level of equality.

The harmony of this great movement in the cause of freedom would not be perfect if women were still to be confined to petticoats, and men to breeches. There must be an " interchange " of these " commodities " to complete the system. Why should it not be so ? Can not women fill an office, or cast a vote, or conduct a campaign, as judiciously and vigorously as men? And, on the other hand, can not men " nurse " the babies, or preside at the wash-tub, or boil a pot as safely and as well as women? If they can not, the evil is in that arbitrary organization of society which has excluded them from the practice of these pursuits. It is time these false notions and practices were changed, or, rather, removed, and for the political millennium foreshadowed by this petti-coat movement to be ushered in. Let the women keep the ball moving, so bravely started by those who have become tired of the restraints imposed upon them by the antediluvian notions of a Paul or the tyranny of man.—*Rochester* (N. Y.) *Daily Advertiser*, Henry Montgomery, Editor.

" Progress," is the grand bubble which is now blown up to balloon bulk by the windy philosophers of the age. The women folks have just held a Convention up in New York State, and passed a sort of " bill of rights," affirming it their right to vote, to become teachers, legislators, lawyers, divines, and do all and sundries the " lords " may, and of right now do. They should have resolved at the same time, that it was obligatory also upon the " lords " aforesaid, to wash dishes, scour up, be put to the tub, handle the broom, darn stockings, patch breeches, scold the servants, dress in the latest fashion, wear trinkets, look beautiful, and be as fascinating as those blessed morsels of humanity whom God gave to preserve that rough animal man, in something like a reasonable civilization. " Progress ! " Progress, forever !—*Lowell* (Mass.) *Courier.*

To us they appear extremely dull and uninteresting, and, aside from their novelty, hardly worth notice.—*Rochester Advertiser.*

This has been a remarkable Convention. It was composed of those holding to some one of the various *isms* of the day, and some, we should think, who embraced them all. The only practical good proposed—the adoption of measures for the relief and amelioration of the condition of indigent, industrious, laboring females—was almost scouted by the leading ones composing the meeting. The great effort seemed to be to bring out some new, impracticable, absurd, and ridiculous proposition, and the greater its absurdity the better. In short, it was a regular *emeute* of a congregation of females gathered from various quarters, who seem to be really in earnest in their aim at revolution, and who evince entire confidence that " the day of their deliverance is at hand." Verily, this is a progressive era !—*Rochester Democrat.*

THE WOMEN OF PHILADELPHIA.

Our Philadelphia ladies not only possess beauty, but they are celebrated for discretion, modesty, and unfeigned diffidence, as well as wit, vivacity, and good nature. Whoever heard of a Philadelphia lady setting up for a reformer, or standing out for woman's rights, or assisting to man the election grounds, raise a regiment, command a legion, or address a jury? Our ladies glow with a higher ambition. They soar to rule the hearts of their worshipers, and secure obedience by the sceptre of affection. The tenure of their power is a law of nature, not a law of man, and hence they fear no insurrection, and never ex-perience the shock of a revolution in their dominions. But all women are not as reason-able as ours of Philadelphia. The Boston ladies contend for the rights of women. The New York girls aspire to mount the rostrum, to do all the voting, and, we suppose, all the fighting too. . . . . Our Philadelphia girls object to fighting and holding office. They prefer the baby-jumper to the study of Coke and Lyttleton, and the ball-room to the Palo Alto battle. They object to having a George Sand for President of the United States ; a Corinna for Governor ; a Fanny Wright for Mayor ; or a Mrs. Partington for Postmas-ter. . . . . Women have enough influence over human affairs without being politicians. Is not everything managed by female influence? Mothers, grandmothers, aunts, and sweethearts manage everything. Men have nothing to do but to listen and obey to the " of course, my dear, you will, and of course, my dear, you won't." Their rule is abso-lute ; their power unbounded. Under such a system men have no claim to rights, espe-cially " equal rights."

A woman is nobody. A wife is everything. A pretty girl is equal to ten thousand men, and a mother is, next to God, all powerful. . . . The ladies of Philadelphia, there-fore, under the influence of the most serious " sober second thoughts," are resolved to maintain their rights as Wives, Belles, Virgins, and Mothers, and not as Women."—*Pub-lic Ledger and Daily Transcript.*

WOMAN'S RIGHTS CONVENTION.

This is the age of revolutions. To whatever part of the world the attention is directed, the political and social fabric is crumbling to pieces; and changes which far exceed the wildest dreams of the enthusiastic Utopians of the last generation, are now pursued with ardor and perseverance. The principal agent, however, that has hitherto taken part in these movements has been the rougher sex. It was by man the flame of liberty, now burning with such fury on the continent of Europe, was first kindled; and though it is asserted that no inconsiderable assistance was contributed by the gentler sex to the late sanguinary carnage at Paris, we are disposed to believe that such a revolting imputation proceeds from base calumniators, and is a libel upon woman.

By the intelligence, however, which we have lately received, the work of revolution is no longer confined to the Old World, nor to the masculine gender. The flag of independence has been hoisted, for the second time, on this side of the Atlantic; and a solemn league and covenant has just been entered into by a Convention of women at Seneca Falls, to "throw off the despotism under which they are groaning, and provide new guards for their future security." Little did we expect this new element to be thrown into the cauldron of agitation which is now bubbling around us with such fury. We have had one Baltimore Convention, one Philadelphia Convention, one Utica Convention, and we shall also have, in a few days, the Buffalo Convention. But we never dreamed that Lucretia Mott had convened a fifth Convention, which, if it be ratified by those whom it purposes to represent, will exercise an influence that will not only control our own Presidential elections, but the whole governmental system throughout the world. . . . . The declaration is a most interesting document. We published it in *extenso* the other day. The amusing part is the preamble, where they assert their equality, and that they have certain inalienable rights, to secure which governments, deriving their just powers from the consent of the governed, are instituted; and that after the long train of abuses and usurpations to which they have been subjected, evincing a design to reduce them under absolute despotism, it is their right, it is their duty, to throw off such government.

The declaration is, in some respects, defective. It complains of the want of the elective franchise, and that ladies are not recognized as teachers of theology, medicine, and law. . . . . These departments, however, do not comprise the whole of the many avenues to wealth, distinction, and honor. We do not see by what principle of right the angelic creatures should claim to compete with the preacher, and refuse to enter the lists with the merchant. A lawyer's brief would not, we admit, sully the hands so much as the tarry ropes of a man-of-war; and a box of Brandreth's pills are more safely and easily prepared than the sheets of a boiler, or the flukes of an anchor; but if they must have competition in one branch, why not in another? There must be no monopoly or exclusiveness. If they will put on the inexpressibles, it will not do to select those employments only which require the least exertion and are exempt from danger. The laborious employments, however, are not the only ones which the ladies, in right of their admission to all rights and privileges, would have to undertake. It might happen that the citizen would have to doff the apron and buckle on the sword. Now, though we have the most perfect confidence in the courage and daring of Miss Lucretia Mott and several others of our lady acquaintances, we confess it would go to our hearts to see them putting on the panoply of war, and mixing in scenes like those at which, it is said, the fair sex in Paris lately took prominent part.

It is not the business, however, of the despot to decide upon the rights of his victims; nor do we undertake to define the duties of women. Their standard is now unfurled by their own hands. The Convention of Seneca Falls has appealed to the country. Miss Lucretia Mott has propounded the principles of the party. Ratification meetings will no doubt shortly be held, and if it be the general impression that this lady is a more eligible candidate for the Presidential chair than McLean or Cass, Van Buren or old "Rough and Ready," then let the Salic laws be abolished forthwith from this great Republic. We are much mistaken if Lucretia would not make a better President than some of those who have lately tenanted the White House.—*New York Herald*, James Gordon Bennett, Proprietor.

In answer to all the newspaper objections, Elizabeth Cady Stanton, in an article published in the *National Reformer*, Rochester, N. Y., Geo. G. Cooper, Editor, Sept. 14, 1848, said as follows:

There is no danger of this question dying for want of notice. Every paper you take up has something to say about it, and just in proportion to the refinement and intelligence of the editor, has this movement been favorably noticed. But one might suppose from the articles that you find in some papers, that there were editors so ignorant as to believe that the chief object of these recent Conventions was to seat every lord at the head of a cradle, and to clothe every woman in her lord's attire. Now, neither of these points, however important they be considered by humble minds, were touched upon in the Conventions. . . . . For those who do not yet understand the real objects of our recent Conventions at Rochester and Seneca Falls, I would state that we did not meet to discuss fashions, customs, or dress, the rights or duties of man, nor the propriety of the sexes changing positions, but simply our own inalienable rights, our duties, our true sphere. If God has assigned a sphere to man and one to woman, we claim the right to judge ourselves of His design in reference to *us*, and we accord to man the same privilege. We think a man has quite enough in this life to find out his own individual calling, without being taxed to decide where every woman belongs; and the fact that so many men fail in the business they undertake, calls loudly for their concentrating more thought on their own faculties, capabilities, and sphere of action. We have all seen a man making a jackass of himself in the pulpit, at the bar, or in our legislative halls, when he might have shone as a general in our Mexican war, captain of a canal boat, or as a tailor on his bench. Now, is it to be wondered at that woman has some doubts about the present position assigned her being the true one, when her every-day experience shows her that man makes such fatal mistakes in regard to himself?

There is no such thing as a sphere for a sex. Every man has a different sphere, and one in which he may shine, and it is the same with every woman; and the same woman may have a different sphere at different times. The distinguished Angelina Grimké was acknowledged by all the anti-slavery host to be in her sphere, when, years ago, she went through the length and breadth of New England, telling the people of her personal experience of the horrors and abominations of the slave system, and by her eloquence and power as a public speaker, producing an effect unsurpassed by any of the highly gifted men of her day. Who dares to say that in thus using her splendid talents in speaking for the dumb, pleading the cause of the poor friendless slave, that she was out of her sphere? Angelina Grimké is now a wife and the mother of several children. We hear of her no more in public. Her sphere and her duties have changed. She deems it her first and her most sacred duty to devote all her time and talents to her household and to the education of her children. We do not say that she is not *now* in her sphere. The highly gifted Quakeress, Lucretia Mott, married early in life, and brought up a large family of children. All who have seen her at home agree that she was a pattern as a wife, mother, and housekeeper. No one ever fulfilled all the duties of that sphere more perfectly than did she. Her children are now settled in their own homes. Her husband and herself, having a comfortable fortune, pass much of their time in going about and doing good. Lucretia Mott has now no domestic cares. She has a talent for public speaking; her mind is of a high order; her moral perceptions remarkably clear; her religious fervor deep and intense; and who shall tell us that this divinely inspired woman is out of her sphere in her public endeavors to rouse this wicked nation to a sense of its awful guilt, to its great sins of war, slavery, injustice to woman and the laboring poor. As many inquiries are made about Lucretia Mott's husband, allow me, through your columns, to say to those who think he must be a *nonentity* because his wife is so distinguished, that James Mott is head and shoulders above the greater part of *his sex*, intellectually, morally, and physically. As a man of business, his talents are of the highest order. As an author, I refer you to his interesting book of travels, "Three Months in Great Britain." In manners he is a gentleman; in appearance, six feet high, and well-proportioned, dignified, and sensible, and in every respect worthy to be the companion of Lucretia Mott.

Mrs. C. I. H. Nichols.

Miss Barber, of *The Madison* (Ga.) *Visitor*, promises to "sit in the corner and be a good girl," if we will admit her to our next "editorial *soirée*." Indeed we will, and brother Lamb, of *The Greenfield Democrat*, shall sit in the other corner and "cast sheep's (Lamb's) eyes" at her; for he copies her naughty declaration of inferiority, and adds that she "is just the editress for him"; that he "don't like Mrs. Swisshelm, Mrs. Pierson, and that class." We will let him off with a whispered reminder that there is a *Mr.* Swisshelm, *Mr.* Pierson, and more of the same sort for "*that class.*" He has nobody on his side but the musty, fusty old bachelors of the ——, and ——, and ——, who, never having wanted for anything but *puddings* and *shirts*, imagine, as Mrs. Pierson says, that "a shirt and a pudding are the two poles of woman's sphere."

But we can not let Miss Barber off so lightly. She says "it is written in the volume of inspiration, as plainly as if traced in sunbeams, that man, the creature of God's own image, is superior to woman, who was afterward created to be his companion. He has a more stately form, stronger nerves and muscles, and, in nine cases out of ten, a more vigorous intellect."

In the first place, it is paying no great compliment to man to suppose that God created an *inferior* to be his companion. But a man, "*the* creature of God's own image!*" And was the material for God's image all worked up in creating Adam? And if so, whose images are the men of to-day, who can't possibly lay claim to more of the original stock than mother Eve, who set up existence with an *entire rib!* And what has it to do with the question of her intellectual equality, that she was created *afterward?* If precedence in creation gave any advantage intellectually, the inferior animals may claim superiority of intellect over both man and woman. It would be quite as sound logic to maintain, as some do, that, as last in the series which commenced in nothing (?) and rose by grada- tions to image God, *woman's* superiority to all that preceded her in the creation, is proba- ble. . . . . Again, if women have less nerves and muscles, the ox and the ass have a great deal more—while God and angels and disembodied spirits have none at all; so that nerves and muscles are of no more significance in this question of the intellectual equal- ity or inequality of the sexes, than is the beard that grows on a man's face and not on a woman's. And arguments drawn from such premises always remind us of the profound logic of a gentleman we once met in a stage coach, and who is now holding a high office under Government at Washington. He professed to set great store by whiskers and mustaches—he had none himself—and gave as a reason why the beard should be tenderly cherished, that "it was given to man as a badge of his superiority over woman." We were young and mischievous then, and so we told him, most complacently, that the ladies would readily concede the point, and give him the full benefit of his argument and of his beard, since men shared their "badge of superiority" with goats, monkeys, and many other inferior animals. Some fifteen years have passed, but we never think of the hon- orable gentleman or see his name attached to official reports, without a laugh.

Miss Barber assumes woman's entire intellectual equality, in claiming that she "may mould the mind of the future statesman into *whatsoever* she will—that "through him she *can* and *will* make the laws." And we only regret that she should speak so lightly of "depositing a little strip of paper in the ballot-box." To us it is a serious thing, that the depositing of that strip of paper gives and takes the rights, whose possession is the means of the highest intellectual and moral culture and enjoyment.—*Windom County Democrat*, Brattleboro, Vermont.

Mrs. Jane G. Swisshelm.

A Mistake.—*Dear Brother Wright :*—In printing my former letter, there was a mistake made which I intended to let pass; but as some of your cotemporaries have taken an agony over the letter, it may be as well to set it right. The last sentence reads, "Now, I move Grace be let alone, and her moral power be no longer invoked by those who have set her and all the rest of her sex, down on a stool mid-way between free negroes and laborers." I wrote it "between free negroes and *baboons*," and meant just what I said. Man, in his code of laws, has assigned woman a place somewhere between the rational and irrational creation. Our Constitutions provide that all "free white male citizens" of a certain age shall have a right to vote. Here Indians, negroes, and women stand side by side. Our gallant legislators excluded the "*inferior* races" from the elective franchise because of their inferiority; and just threw their wives and mothers into the same heap, because of their great superiority! One was excluded because they hated them, the other because they loved them so very well. Yet one sentence covers both cases. Women and negroes stand side by side in this case, and also in that of exclusion from our colleges. A negro can not be admitted into one of our colleges or seminaries of the highest class. Neither can a woman. Witness the refusal of some half dozen of your medical colleges to admit Miss Blackwell.

But free negroes can acquire property, can sell it, keep it, give it away, or divide it. A baboon has no such rights; neither has a woman in her highest state of existence here. The right to acquire and hold property is a distinguishing trait between mankind and the brute creation. Woman is deprived of that distinction; for all that she has and all she can acquire, belongs to her master. Custom says she should be fed and clothed, dandled and fondled, her freaks borne with and her graces admired; it awards the same attentions, in a little different degree, to a pet monkey. So woman has been "set down midway between free negroes and baboons."

Your good-tempered friend and sister,　　Jane G. Swisshelm

Borders of Monkeydom, *Sept.* 28, 1848.

P. S.—There is a man who edits *The Sunday Age* of New York—H. P. Grattan—who appears to be in a peck of trouble about "Blue-Stocking Effusions" in general, and my letter to you in particular. He says, "We love woman. We bow down to them in adoration. But they have their proper place; but the moment they step from the pedestal upon which heaven *stood* them, they fail to elicit our admiration," etc. Then, to show what the pedestal is on which he adores them, he adds, "If they gave evidence of a knowledge of puddings and pies, how much happier they might be," in the sunlight of his admiration, of course. Well, freedom of conscience in this free land! The Faithful may bow to his prophet; the Persian adore his sun; the Egyptian may kneel to his crocodile; and why should not Mr. Grattan go into rhapsodies before his cook, as the dispenser of the good things of this life? The good book speaks of "natural brute beasts who make a god of their bellies," and it might be natural to transfer the homage to her who ministers to the stomach. I can see his chosen divinity now, mounted on her "pedestal," a kitchen stool, her implements before her, crowned with a pudding-pan, her sceptre a batter spoon, and Mr. Grattan down, in rapt adoration, with eyes upturned, and looks of piteous pleading! Poor fellow! Do give him his dinner! J. G. S.—*Saturday Visitor*, Pittsburg, Penn.

Here are some of the titles of editorials and communications in respectable papers all over the country: "Bolting among the Ladies," "Women Out of their Latitude," "Insurrection among the Women," "The Reign of Petticoats," "Office-Seeking Women," "Petticoats *vs.* Boots." The reader can judge, with such texts for inspiration, what the sermons must have been.

Resolutions at Rochester.

The following resolutions, which had been separately discussed, were again read. Amy Post moved their adoption by the meeting, which was carried with but two or three dissenting voices:

1. *Resolved*, That we petition our State Legislature for our right to the elective franchise, every year, until our prayer be granted.

2. *Resolved*, That it is an admitted principle of the American Republic, that the only just power of the Government is derived from the consent of the governed; and that taxation and representation are inseparable; and, therefore, woman being taxed equally with man, ought not to be deprived of an equal representation in the Government.

3. *Resolved*, That we deplore the apathy and indifference of woman in regard to her rights, thus restricting her to an inferior position in social, religious, and political life, and we urge her to claim an equal right to act on all subjects that interest the human family.

4. *Resolved,* That the assumption of law to settle estates of men who die without wills, having widows, is an insult to woman, and ought to be regarded as such by every lover of right and equality.

5. WHEREAS, The husband has the legal right to hire out his wife to service, collect her wages, and appropriate it to his own exclusive and independent benefit; and,

WHEREAS, This has contributed to establish that hideous custom, the promise of obedience in the marriage contract, effectually, though insidiously, reducing her almost to the condition of a *slave,* whatever freedom she may have in these respects being granted as a privilege, not as a right; therefore,

Resolved, That we will seek the overthrow of this barbarous and unrighteous law; and conjure women no longer to promise obedience in the marriage covenant.

Resolved, That the universal doctrine of the inferiority of woman has ever caused her to distrust her own powers, and paralyzed her energies, and placed her in that degraded position from which the most strenuous and unremitting effort can alone redeem her. Only by faithful perseverance in the practical exercise of those talents, so long " wrapped in a napkin and buried under the earth," she will regain her long-lost equality with man.

Resolved, That in the persevering and independent course of Miss Blackwell, who recently attended a series of medical lectures in Geneva, and has now gone to Europe to graduate as a physician, we see a harbinger of the day when woman shall stand forth " redeemed and disenthralled," and perform those important duties which are so truly within her sphere.

Resolved, That those who believe the laboring classes of women are oppressed, ought to do all in their power to raise their wages, beginning with their own household servants.

Resolved, That it is the duty of woman, whatever her complexion, to assume, as soon as possible, her true position of equality in the social circle, the Church, and the State.

Resolved, That we tender our grateful acknowledgment to the Trustees of the Unitarian Church, who have kindly opened their doors for the use of this Convention.

Resolved, That we, the friends who are interested in this cause, gratefully accept the kind offer from the Trustees of the use of Protection Hall, to hold our meetings whenever we wish.

SIGNATURES TO THE DECLARATION ADOPTED AT SENECA FALLS.

Firmly relying upon the final triumph of the Right and the True, we do this day affix our signatures to this Declaration:

Lucretia Mott,	Hannah Plant,
Harriet Cady Eaton,	Lucy Jones,
Margaret Pryor,	Sarah Whitney,
Elizabeth Cady Stanton,	Mary H. Hallowell,
Eunice Newton Foote,	Elizabeth Conklin,
Mary Ann McClintock,	Sally Pitcher,
Margaret Schooley,	Mary Conklin,
Martha C. Wright,	Susan Quinn,
Jane C. Hunt,	Mary S. Mirror,
Amy Post,	Phebe King,
Catharine F. Stebbins,	Julia Ann Drake,
Mary Ann Frink,	Charlotte Woodward,
Lydia Mount,	Martha Underhill,
Delia Matthews,	Dorothy Matthews,
Catharine C. Paine,	Eunice Barker,
Elizabeth W. McClintock,	Sarah R. Woods,
Malvina Seymour,	Lydia Gild,
Phebe Mosher,	Sarah Hoffman,
Catherine Shaw,	Elizabeth Leslie,
Deborah Scott,	Martha Ridley,
Sarah Hallowell,	Rachel D. Bonnel,
Mary McClintock,	Betsy Tewksbury,
Mary Gilbert,	Rhoda Palmer,

Sophronie Taylor,	Margaret Jenkins
Cynthia Davis,	Cynthia Fuller,
Mary Martin,	Eliza Martin,
P. A. Culvert,	Maria E. Wilbur,
Susan R. Doty,	Elizabeth D. Smith,
Rebecca Race,	Caroline Barker,
Sarah A. Mosher,	Ann Porter,
Mary E. Vail,	Experience Gibbs,
Lucy Spalding,	Antoinette F. Segur,
Lavinia Latham,	Hannah J. Latham,
Sarah Smith,	Sarah Sisson.

The following are the names of the gentlemen present in favor of the movement :

Richard P. Hunt,	Charles L. Hoskins,
Samuel D. Tilman,	Thomas McClintock,
Justin Williams,	Saron Phillips,
Elisha Foote,	Jacob Chamberlain,
Frederick Douglass,	Jonathan Metcalf,
Henry W. Seymour,	Nathan J. Milliken,
Henry Seymour,	S. E. Woodworth,
David Spalding,	Edward F. Underhill,
William G. Barker,	George W. Pryor,
Elias J. Doty,	Joel Bunker,
John Jones,	Isaac Van Tassel,
William S. Dell,	Thomas Dell,
James Mott,	E. W. Capron,
William Burroughs,	Stephen Shear,
Robert Smalldridge	Henry Hatley,
Jacob Matthews,	Azaliah Schooley.

Many persons signed the Declaration at Rochester, among them Daniel Anthony, **Lucy** Read Anthony, Mary S. Anthony, the officers of the Convention, and others.

————

CHAPTER VI.

O H I O.

Salem Convention, April 19, 20, 1850.

LETTER FROM ELIZABETH CADY STANTON.

SENECA FALLS, N. Y., *April* 7.

DEAR MARIANA :—How rejoiced I am to hear that the women of Ohio have called a Convention preparatory to the remodeling of their State Constitution. The remodeling of a Constitution, in the nineteenth century, speaks of progress, of greater freedom, and of more enlarged views of human rights and duties. It is fitting that, at such a time, woman, who has so long been the victim of ignorance and injustice, should at length throw off the trammels of a false education, stand upright, and with dignity and earnestness manifest a deep and serious interest in the laws which are to govern her and her country. It needs no argument to teach woman that she is interested in the laws which govern her. Suffering has taught her this already. It is important now that a change is proposed, that she speak, and loudly too. Having decided to petition for a redress of grievances, the question is, *for what shall you first petition?* For the exercise of your right to the elective franchise—nothing short of this. The grant to you of this right will secure all others ; and the granting of every other right, whilst this is denied, is a mockery. For instance : What is the right to property without the right to protect it? The enjoyment of that right to-day is no security that it will be continued to-morrow, so long as it is granted to us as a favor, and not claimed by us as a right. Woman must exercise her right to the elective franchise, and have her own representatives in our National councils, for two good reasons :

1st. Men can not represent us. They are so thoroughly educated into the belief that woman's nature is altogether different from their own, that they have no idea that she can be governed by the same laws of mind as themselves. So far from viewing us like themselves, they seem, from their legislation, to consider us their moral and intellectual antipodes ; for whatever law they find good for themselves, they forthwith pass its opposite for us, and express the most profound astonishment if we manifest the least dissatisfaction. For example : our forefathers, *full of righteous indignation*, pitched King George, his authority, and his tea-chests, all into the sea, and because, forsooth, they were forced to pay taxes without being represented in the British Government. "Taxation without representation," was the text for many a hot debate in the forests of the New World, and for many an eloquent oration in the Parliament of the Old. Yet, in forming our new Government, they have taken from us the very rights which they fought and bled and died to secure to themselves. They not only tax us, but in many cases they strip us of all we inherit, the wages we earn, the children of our love ; and for such grievances we have no redress in any court of justice this side of Heaven. They tax our property to build colleges, then pass a special law prohibiting any woman to enter there. A married woman has no legal existence ; she has no more absolute rights than a slave on a Southern plantation. She takes the name of her master, holds nothing, owns nothing, can bring no action in her own name ; and the principle on which she and the slave is educated is the same. The slave is taught what is considered best for him to know—which is nothing ; the woman is taught what is best for her to know—which is little more than nothing, man being the umpire in both cases. A woman can not follow out the impulses of her own mind in her sphere, any more than the slave can in his sphere. Civilly, socially, and religiously, she is what man chooses her to be, nothing more or less, and such is the slave. It is impossible for us to convince man that we think and feel exactly as he does ; that we have the same sense of right and justice, the same love of freedom and independence. Some men regard us as devils, and some as angels ; hence, one class would shut us up in a certain sphere for fear of the evil we might do, and the other for fear of the evil that *might be done to us ;* thus, except for the sentiment of the thing, for all the good that it does us, we might as well be thought the one as the other. But we ourselves have to do with what *we are* and what *we shall be.*

2d. Men can not legislate for us. Our statute books and all past experience teach us this fact. His laws, where we are concerned, have been, without one exception, unjust, cruel, and aggressive. Having denied our identity with himself, he has no data to go upon in judging of our wants and interests. If we are alike in our mental structure, then there is no reason why we should not have a voice in making the laws which govern us ; but if we are not alike, most certainly we must make laws for ourselves, for who else can understand what we need and desire? If it be admitted in this Government that all men and women are free and equal, then must we claim a place in our Senate Chamber and House of Representatives. But if, after all, it be found that even here we have classes and caste, not "Lords and Commons," but lords and women, then must we claim a lower House, where our Representatives can watch the passage of all bills affecting our own welfare, or the good of our country. Had the women of this country had a voice in the Government, think you our national escutcheon would have been stained with the guilt of aggressive warfare upon such weak, defenceless nations as the Seminoles and Mexicans? Think you we should cherish and defend, in the heart of our nation, such a wholesale system of piracy, cruelty, licentiousness, and ignorance as is our slavery ? Think you that relic of barbarism, the gallows, by which the wretched murderer is sent with blood upon his soul, uncalled for, into the presence of his God, would be sustained by law ? Verily, no, or I mistake woman's heart, her instinctive love of justice, and mercy, and truth !

Who questions woman's right to vote ? We can show our credentials to the right of self-government ; we get ours just where man got his ; they are all Heaven-descended,

God-given. It is our duty to assert and reassert this right, to agitate, discuss, and petition, until our political equality be fully recognized. Depend upon it, this is the point to attack, the stronghold of the fortress—*the one* woman will find the most difficult to take, *the one* man will most reluctantly give up ; therefore let us encamp right under its shadow ; there spend all our time, strength, and *moral* ammunition, year after year, with perseverance, courage, and decision. Let no sallies of wit or ridicule at our expense ; no soft nonsense of woman's beauty, delicacy, and refinement ; no promise of gold and silver, bank stock, road stock, or landed estate, seduce us from our position until that one stronghold totters to the ground. This done, the rest they will surrender *at discretion.* Then comes equality in Church and State, in the family circle, and in all our social relations.

The cause of woman is onward. For our encouragement, let us take a review of what has occurred during the last few years. Not two years since the women of New York held several Conventions. Their meetings were well attended by both men and women, and the question of woman's true position was fully and freely discussed. The proceedings of those meetings and the Declaration of Sentiments were all published and scattered far and near. Before that time, the newspapers said but little on that subject. Immediately after, there was scarcely a newspaper in the Union that did not notice these Conventions, and generally in a tone of ridicule. Now you seldom take up a paper that has not something about woman ; but the tone is changing—ridicule is giving way to reason. Our papers begin to see that this is no subject for mirth, but one for serious consideration. Our literature is also assuming a different tone. The heroine of our fashionable novel is now a being of spirit, of energy, of will, with a conscience, with high moral principle, great decision, and self-reliance.

Contrast Jane Eyre with any of Bulwer's, Scott's, or Shakespeare's heroines, and how they all sink into the shade compared with that noble creation of a woman's genius ! The January number of *The Westminster Review* contains an article on "Woman," so liberal and radical, that I sometimes think it must have crept in there by mistake. Our fashionable lecturers, too, are now, instead of the time-worn subjects of " Catholicism," " The Crusades." " St. Bernard," and " Thomas à Becket," choosing Woman for their theme. True, they do not treat this new subject with much skill or philosophy ; but enough for us that the great minds of our day are taking this direction. Mr. Dana, of Boston, lectured on this subject in Philadelphia. Lucretia Mott followed him, and ably pointed out his sophistry and errors. She spoke to a large and fashionable audience, and gave general satisfaction. Dana was too sickly and sentimental for that meridian. The women of Massachusetts, ever first in all moral movements, have sent, but a few weeks since, to their Legislature, a petition demanding their right to vote and hold office in their State. Woman seems to be preparing herself for a higher and holier destiny. That same love of liberty which burned in the hearts of our sires, is now being kindled anew in the daughters of this proud Republic. From the present state of public sentiment, we have every reason to look hopefully into the future. I see a brighter, happier day yet to come ; but woman must say how soon the dawn shall be, and whether the light shall first shine in the East or the West. By her own efforts the change must come. She must carve out her future destiny with her own right hand. If she have not the energy to secure for herself her true position, neither would she have the force or sta bility to maintain it, if placed there by another. Farewell !

Yours sincerely,   E. C. Stanton.

LETTER FROM LUCRETIA MOTT.

Dear Friends :—The call for this Convention, so numerously signed, is indeed gratifying, and gives hope of a large attendance. The letter of invitation was duly received, and I need scarcely say how gladly I would be present if in my power. Engagements in another direction, as well as the difficulty to travel at this season of the year, will prevent my availing myself of so great a privilege. You will not, however, be at a loss for speakers in your midst, for among the signers to the call are the names of many whose hearts " believe unto righteousness " ; out of their abundance, therefore, the mouth will make " confession unto salvation."

The wrongs of woman have too long slumbered. They now begin to cry for redress. Let them be clearly pointed out in your Convention; and then, not *ask* as *favor*, but *de mand* as *right*, that every civil and ecclesiastical obstacle be removed out of the way.

Rights are not dependent upon equality of mind; nor do we admit inferiority, leaving that question to be settled by future developments, when a fair opportunity shall be given for the equal cultivation of the intellect, and the stronger powers of the mind shall be called into action.

If, in accordance with your call, you ascertain "the bearing which the circumscribed sphere of woman has on the great political and social evils that curse and desolate the land," you will not have come together in vain.

May you, indeed, "gain strength" by your contest with "difficulty!" May the whole armor of "Right, Truth, and Reason" be yours! Then will the influence of the Convention be felt in the assembled wisdom of *men* which is to follow; and the good results, as well as your example, will ultimately rouse other States to action in this most important cause.

I herewith forward to you a "Discourse on Woman," which, though brought out by local circumstances, may yet contain principles of universal application.

Wishing you every success in your noble effort,

I am yours, for woman's redemption and consequent elevation,

PHILADELPHIA, *4th mo.*, 13, 1850. LUCRETIA MOTT.

LETTER FROM LUCY STONE.

For the Woman's Rights Convention :

DEAR FRIENDS : — The friends of human freedom in Massachusetts rejoice that a Woman's Rights Convention is to be held in Ohio. We hail it as a sign of progress, and deem it especially fitting that such a Convention should be held *now*, when a State Constitution is to be formed.

It is easier, when the old is destroyed, to build the *new* right, than to right it *after* it is built.

The statute books of every State in the Union are disgraced by an article which limits the right to the elective franchise to "male citizens of twenty-one years of age and upwards," thus excluding one-half the population of the country from all political influence, subjecting woman to laws in the making of which she has neither vote nor voice. The lowest drunkard may come up from wallowing in the gutter, and, covered with filth, *reel* up to the ballot-box and deposit his vote, and his right to do so is not questioned. The meanest foreigner who comes to our shores, who can not speak his mother-tongue correctly, has secured for him the right of suffrage. The negro, crushed and degraded, as if he were not a brother man, made the lowest of the low, even he, in some of the States, can vote; but woman, in every State, is politically plunged in a degradation lower than *his* lowest depths.

Woman is taxed under laws made by those who profess to believe that taxation and representation are inseparable, while, in the use and imposition of the taxes, as in representation, she is absolutely without influence. Should she hint that the profession and practice do not agree, she is gravely told that "Women should not talk politics." In most of the States the married woman loses, by her marriage, the control of her person and the right of property, and, if she is a mother, the right to her children also; while she secures what the town paupers have—the right to be maintained. The legal disabilities under which women labor have no end : I will not attempt to enumerate them. Let the earnest women who speak in your Convention enter into the detail of this thing, nor stop to "patch fig-leaves for the naked truth," but "before all Israel and the sun," expose the atrocities of the laws relative to women, until the ears of those who hear shall tingle. So that the men who meet in Convention to form the new Constitution for Ohio, shall, for very shame's sake, make haste to put away the last remnant of the barbarism which your statute book (in common with other States) retains in its inequality and injustice to woman. We know too well the stern reform spirit of those who have called this Woman's Rights Convention, to doubt for a moment that what can be done by you to secure equal rights for all, will be done.

Massachusetts *ought* to have taken the lead in the work you are now doing, but if she chooses to linger, let her young sisters of the West set her a worthy example ; and if the " Pilgrim spirit is not dead," *we'll pledge Massachusetts to follow her.*

Yours, for Justice and Equal Rights,　　　LUCY STONE.

SOUTHAMPTON, *April* 10, 1850.

LETTER FROM SARAH PUGH.

" Lawrencian Villa is extremely beautiful ; the grounds full of shrubbery and flowers ; the splendid dairy, the green-houses and conservatories—four or five of them appropriated to fruit, flowers, and rare plants in large numbers –the whole presenting great taste and skill. *Mrs.* Lawrence's improvements are not completed ; she is extending her shrubbery and walks. She is undoubtedly one of the most skillful cultivators and florists in the country (a country abounding with them), and carries off more prizes at the horticultural exhibitions than almost any one else. I am told Mr. Lawrence is an eminent surgeon in London, and that the whole of the country place is under *Mrs.* Lawrence's management."—*Colman's Letters from Europe.*

DEAR FRIENDS :—As I finished reading this paragraph, your letter, inviting me to your Convention, to be held on the 19th inst., was received. I can not, as I gladly would, be with you. That my mite may not be wanting in aid of the cause, taking the above extract for my text, I would add as a commentary, that, according to the laws and usages of a large portion of Christendom, in the event of the death of Mr. Lawrence, Mrs. Lawrence, the one whose skill and taste has formed this elegant establishment, would be left by the will of Mr. Lawrence an income from a *part* of the estate, and the "privilege " of occupying " during her natural life," two or three rooms in the large mansion, but powerless as a stranger in the beautiful demesne made valuable by her industry and skill ! This is not " supposing " a case, only in the application of it to Mrs. L. In this country, where, as a general rule, women take their full share of the labor and responsibility of a household, and thus by their constant assiduity contribute their full proportion to the means by which a comfortable competence is secured, do we not see the disposal of it assumed as a matter of right by the male partner of the firm ?

That women contribute their full share in the building-up of an estate by *labor*—the only rightful mode—no one that is capable of taking an enlightened view of the prevailing condition of things will deny. True, she may not wield the axe or guide the plough, braced by the invigorating air, for hers is the wearisome task, and the one which requires the most skill to attend to the complicated machinery within doors ; she may not handle the awl or the plane for " ten hours a day," with but a small tax on the intellectual, but by her *perpetual* oversight and unvarying labor she may make one dollar, two, or more.

This is one form of the many grievances to which women are subjected, all arising from the false assumption of their inferiority by nature and by the " ordination of Providence." May your Convention aid in dispelling this delusion from the minds of men, but chiefly from the minds of women ; for to themselves, in a great degree, is their degraded position owing. Rouse them to a belief in their natural equality, and to a desire to sustain it by cultivation of their noblest powers.

There is much that crowds on me for utterance, but there will be those among you that will be able to give a fuller and fitter expression to the thoughts that cluster around this all-important question, the " Rights and Duties of Women "—her rights equal to those of men—she alone the judge of her duties.

May your Convention hasten the day when these rights shall be acknowledged as equal to those of man and independent of him, and when men and women shall equally co-operate for the good of all mankind.

With great interest, your friend,　　　SARAH PUGH.

To the Ohio Convention of Women, Phila., April 15, 1850.

RESOLUTIONS OF THE SALEM (OHIO) CONVENTION, 1850.

6th. *Resolved,* That in those laws which confer on man the power to control the property and person of woman, and to remove from her at will the children of her affection, we recognize only the modified code of the slave plantation ; and that thus we are brought more nearly in sympathy with the suffering slave, who is despoiled of all his rights.

16th. *Resolved,* That we regard those women who content themselves with an idle, aimless life, as involved in the guilt as well as the suffering of their own oppression ; and that we hold those who go forth into the world, in the face of the frowns and the sneers of the public, to fill larger spheres of labor, as the truest preachers of the cause of Woman's Rights.

19th. *Resolved,* That, as woman is not permitted to hold office, nor have any voice in the Government, she should not be compelled to pay taxes out of her scanty wages to support men who get eight dollars a day for *taking* the right to *themselves* to enact laws *for* her.

20th. *Resolved,* That we, the women of Ohio, will hereafter meet annually in Convention, to consult upon and adopt measures for the removal of the various disabilities— political, social, religious, legal, and pecuniary—to which women, as a class, are subjected, and from which results so much misery, degradation, and crime.

After the Akron Convention in 1851, *The New York Sunday Mercury* published a woodcut covering a whole page, representing the Convention. Every woman in coat and breeches and high-heeled boots, sitting cross-legged smoking cigars (truly manly arguments for equal political rights). There was not a Bloomer present.

Elizabeth Cady Stanton.

To the Woman's Convention, held at Akron, Ohio, May 25, 1851 :

Dear Friends :—It would give me great pleasure to accept your invitation to attend the Convention, but as circumstances forbid my being present with you, allow me, in addressing you by letter, to touch on those points of this great question which have, of late, much occupied my thoughts. It is often said to us tauntingly, " Well, you have held Conventions, you have speechified and resolved, protested and appealed, declared and petitioned, and now, what next ? Why do you not do something ? " I have as often heard the reply, " We know not what to do."

Having for some years rehearsed to the unjust judge our grievances, our legal and political disabilities and social wrongs, let us glance at what we *may do,* at the various rights of which we may, even now, quietly take possession. True, our right to vote we can not exercise until our State Constitutions are remodelled ; but we can petition our legislators every session, and plead our cause before them. We can make a manifestation by going to the polls, at each returning election, bearing banners, with inscriptions thereon of great sentiments handed down to us by our revolutionary fathers—such as, " No Taxation without Representation," " No just Government can be formed without the consent of the Governed," etc. We can refuse to pay all taxes, and, like the English dissenters, suffer our goods to be seized and sold, if need be. Such manifestations would appeal to a class of minds that now take no note of our Conventions or their proceedings ; who never dream, even, that woman thinks herself defrauded of a single right. The trades and professions are all open to us ; let us quietly enter and make ourselves, if not rich and famous, at least independent and respectable. Many of them are quite proper to woman, and some peculiarly so. As merchants, postmasters, and silversmiths, teachers, preachers, and physicians, woman has already proved herself fully competent. Who so well fitted to fill the pulpits of our day as woman ? All admit her superior to man in the affections, high moral sentiments, and religious enthusiasm ; and so long as our popular theology and reason are at loggerheads, we have no need of acute metaphysicians or skillful logicians in our pulpits. We want those who can make the most effective appeals to our imaginations, our hopes and fears.

Again, as physicians. How desirable are educated women in this profession ! Give her knowledge commensurate with her natural qualifications, and there is no position woman could assume that would be so pre-eminently useful to her race at large, and her own sex in particular, as that of ministering angel to the sick and afflicted ; an angel, not capable of sympathy merely, but armed with the power to relieve suffering and prevent disease. The science of Obstetrics is a branch of the profession which should be monopolized by woman. The fact that it is now almost wholly in the hands of the male practitioner, is an outrage on common decency that nothing but the tyrant *custom* can excuse. "From the earliest history down to 1563, it was practiced by women. The distinguished individual first to make the innovation on this ancient, time-sanctified custom, was no less a personage than a court prostitute, the Duchess of Villiers, a favorite mistress of Louis XIV. of France." This is a formidable evil, and productive of much immorality, misery, and crime. But now that some colleges are open to woman, and the "Female Medical College of Pennsylvania" has been established for our sex exclusively, I hope this custom may be abolished as speedily as possible, for no excuse can be found for its continuance, in the want of knowledge and skill in our own sex. It seems to me, the existence of this custom argues a much greater want of delicacy and refinement in woman, than would the practice of the profession by her in all its various branches.

But the great work before us is the education of those just coming on the stage of action. Begin with the girls of *to-day*, and in twenty years we can revolutionize this nation. The childhood of woman must be free and untrammeled. The girl must be allowed to romp and play, climb, skate, and swim; her clothing must be more like that of the boy—strong, loose-fitting garments, thick boots, etc., that she may be out at all times, and enter freely into all kinds of sports. Teach her to go alone, by night and day, if need be, on the lonely highway, or through the busy streets of the crowded metropolis. The manner in which all courage and self-reliance is educated *out* of the girl, her path portrayed with dangers and difficulties that never exist, is melancholy indeed. Better, far, suffer occasional insults or die outright, than live the life of a *coward*, or never move without a protector. The best protector any woman can have, one that will serve her at all times and in all places, is *courage;* this she must get by her own experience, and experience comes by exposure. Let the girl be thoroughly developed in body and soul, not modeled, like a piece of clay, after some artificial specimen of humanity, with a body like some plate in Godey's book of fashion, and a mind after the type of Father Gregory's pattern daughters, loaded down with the traditions, proprieties, and sentimentalities of generations of silly mothers and grandmothers, but left free to be, to grow, to feel, to think, to act. Development is one thing, that system of cramping, restraining, torturing, perverting, and mystifying, called education, is quite another. We have had women enough befooled under the one system, pray let us try the other. The girl must early be impressed with the idea that she is to be "a hand, not a mouth"; a worker, and not a drone, in the great hive of human activity. Like the boy, she must be taught to look forward to a life of self-dependence, and early prepare herself for some trade or profession. Woman has relied heretofore too entirely for her support on the *needle*—that one-eyed demon of destruction that slays its thousands annually; that evil genius of our sex, which, in spite of all our devotion, will never make us healthy, wealthy, or wise.

Teach the girl it is no part of her life to cater to the prejudices of those around her. Make her independent of public sentiment, by showing her how worthless and rotten a thing it is. It is a settled axiom with me, after much examination and reflection, that public sentiment is false on every subject. Yet what a tyrant it is over us all, woman especially, whose very life is to please, whose highest ambition is to be approved. But once outrage this tyrant, place yourself beyond his jurisdiction, taste the joy of free thought and action, and how powerless is his rule over you! his sceptre lies broken at your feet; his very babblings of condemnation are sweet music in your ears; his darkening frown is sunshine to your heart, for they tell of your triumph and his discomfort. Think you, women *thus* educated would long remain the weak, dependent beings we now find them? By no means. Depend upon it, they would soon settle for themselves this whole question of Woman's Rights. As educated capitalists and skillful laborers, they would not be long in finding their true level in political and social life.

SENECA FALLS, *May,* 1851.   E. C. STANTON.

RESOLUTIONS OF THE MASSILON (OHIO) CONVENTION, 1852.

1st. *Resolved,* That in the proposition affirmed by the nation to be self-evidently true, that "all men are created equal," the word "MEN" is a general term, including the whole race, without distinction of sex.

2d. *Resolved,* That this equality of the sexes must extend, and does extend, to rights personal, social, legal, political, industrial, and religious, including, of course, representation in the Government, the elective franchise, free choice in occupations, and an impartial distribution of the reward of effort ; and in reference to all these particulars, woman has the same right to choose *her* sphere of action, as man to choose *his.*

3d. *Resolved,* That since every human being has an individual sphere, and that is the largest he or she can fill, no one has the right to determine the proper sphere of another.

4th. *Resolved,* That the assertion of these rights for woman, equally with man, involves the doctrine that she, equally with him, should be *protected in their exercise.*

5th. *Resolved,* That we do not believe any legal or political restriction necessary to preserve the distinctive character of woman, and that in demanding for women equality of rights with their fathers, husbands, brothers, and sons, we neither deny that distinctive character, nor wish them to avoid any duty, or to lay aside that feminine delicacy which legitimately belongs to them as mothers, wives, sisters, and daughters.

6th. *Resolved,* That to perfect the marriage union and provide for the inevitable vicissitudes of life, the individuality of both parties should be equally and distinctively recognized by the parties themselves, and by the laws of the land ; and, therefore, justice and the highest regard for the interests of society require that our laws be so amended, that married women may be permitted to conduct business on their own account ; to acquire, hold, invest, and dispose of property in their own separate and individual right, subject to all corresponding and appropriate obligations.

7th. *Resolved,* That the clause of the Constitution of the State of Ohio, which declares that "all men have the right of acquiring and possessing property," is violated by the judicial doctrine that the labor of the wife is the property of the husband.

8th. *Resolved,* That in the general scantiness of compensation of woman's labor, the restrictions imposed by custom and public opinion upon her choice of employments, and her opportunities of earning money, and the laws and social usages which regulate the distribution of property as between men and women, have produced a pecuniary dependence of woman upon man, widely and deeply injurious in many ways; and not the least of all in too often perverting marriage, which should be a holy relation growing out of spiritual affinities, into a mere bargain and sale—a means to woman of securing a subsistence and a home, and to man of obtaining a kitchen drudge or a parlor ornament.

9th. *Resolved,* That sacred and inestimable in value as are the rights which we assert for woman, their possession and exercise are not the ultimate end we aim at ; for rights are not ends, but only means to ends, implying duties, and are to be demanded in order that duties may be performed.

10th. *Resolved,* That God, in constituting woman the mother of mankind, made her a living Providence, to produce, nourish, guard, and govern His best and noblest work from helpless infancy to adult years. Having endowed her with faculties ample, but no more than sufficient, for the performance of her great work, He requires of her, as essentially necessary to its performance, the full development of those faculties.

11th. *Resolved,* That we do not charge woman's deprivation of her rights upon man alone, for woman also has contributed to this result; and as both have sinned together, we call on both to repent together, that the wrong done by both may, by the united exertions of both, be undone.

FIFTH NATIONAL WOMAN'S RIGHTS CONVENTION, CLEVELAND, OHIO, 1853.

1st. *Resolved,* That by Human Rights, we mean natural Rights, in contradistinction to conventional usages, and that because Woman is a Human being, she, *therefore,* has Human Rights.

2d. *Resolved,* That because woman is a human being, and man is no more, she has, by virtue of her constitutional nature, equal rights with man ; and that state of society must necessarily be wrong which does not, in its usages and institutions, afford equal opportunities for the enjoyment and protection of these Rights.

4th. *Resolved,* That the common law, by giving the husband the custody of the wife's person, does virtually place her on a level with criminals, lunatics, and fools, since these are the only classes of adult persons over which the law-makers have thought it necessary to place keepers.

5th. *Resolved,* That if it be true, in the language of John C. Calhoun, that "he who digs the money out of the soil, has a right to it against the universe," then the law which gives to the husband the power to use and control the earnings of the wife, makes robbery legal, and is as mean as it is unjust.

6th. *Resolved,* That woman will soonest free herself from the legal disabilities she now suffers, by securing the right to the elective franchise, thus becoming herself a lawmaker; and that to this end we will petition our respective State Legislatures to call conventions to amend their Constitutions, so that the right to the elective franchise shall not be limited by the word "male."

7th. *Resolved,* That there is neither justice nor sound policy in the present arrangements of society, restricting women to so comparatively a narrow range of employments; excluding them from those which are most lucrative; and even in those to which they are admitted, awarding them a compensation less, generally by one-half or two-thirds, than is paid to men for an equal amount of service rendered.

8th. *Resolved,* That, although the question of the intellectual strength and attainments of woman has nothing to do with the settlement of their rights, yet in reply to the oft-repeated inquiry, "Have women, by nature, the same force of intellect with men?" we will reply, that this inquiry can never be answered till women shall have such training as shall give their physical and intellectual powers as full opportunities for development, by being as heavily taxed and all their resources as fully called forth, as are now those of man.

Mr. Garrison, on being called for, replied that the resolutions would do for his speech to-night, and read as follows:

1st. *Resolved,* That the natural rights of one human being, are those of every other, in all cases equally sacred and inalienable; hence the boasted "Rights of Man," about which we hear so much, are simply the "Rights of Woman," of which we hear so little; or, in other words, they are the Rights of Humanity, neither affected by, nor dependent upon, sex or condition.

2d. *Resolved,* That those who deride the claims of woman to a full recognition of her civil rights and political equality, exhibit the spirit which tyrants and usurpers have displayed in all ages toward the mass of mankind; strike at the foundation of all truly free and equitable government; contend for a sexual aristocracy, which is as irrational and unjust in principle, as that of wealth and hereditary descent, and show their appreciation of liberty to be wholly one-sided and supremely selfish.

3d. *Resolved,* That for the men of this land to claim for themselves the elective franchise, and the right to choose their own rulers and enact their own laws, as essential to their freedom, safety, and welfare, and then to deprive all the women of all these safeguards, solely on the ground of a difference of sex, is to evince the pride of self-esteem, the meanness of usurpation, and the folly of a self-assumed superiority.

4th. *Resolved,* That woman, as well as man, has a right to the highest mental and physical development; to the most ample educational advantages; to the occupancy of whatever position she can reach, in Church and State, in science and art, in poetry and music, in painting and sculpture, in civil jurisprudence and political economy, and in all the varied departments of human industry, enterprise, and skill; to the elective franchise, and to a voice in the administration of justice, and the passage of laws for the general welfare.

5th. *Resolved,* That to pretend that the granting of these claims would tend to make woman less amiable and attractive, less regardful of her peculiar duties and obligations as wife and mother, a wanderer from her proper sphere, bringing confusion into domestic life, and strife into the public assembly, is the cant of Papal Rome as to the discordant and infidel tendencies of the right of private judgment in matters of faith; is the outcry of legitimacy as to the incapacity of the people to govern themselves; is the false allegations which selfish and timid conservatism is ever making against every new measure of reform, and has no foundation in reason, experience, fact, or philosophy.

6th. *Resolved,* That the consequences arising from the exclusion of woman from the possession and exercise of her natural rights and the cultivation of her mental faculties, have been calamitous to the whole human race; making her servile, dependent, unwomanly; the victim of a false gallantry on the one hand, and of tyrannous subjection on the other; obstructing her mental growth, crippling her physical development, and incapacitating her for general usefulness; and thus inflicting an injury upon all born of woman, and cultivating in man a lordly and arrogant spirit, a love of dominion, a disposition to lightly regard her comfort and happiness, all which have been indulged to a fearful extent, to the curse of his own soul and the desecration of her nature.

7th. *Resolved*, That so long as the most ignorant, degraded, and worthless men are freely admitted to the ballot-box, and practically acknowledged to be competent to determine who shall be in office and how the Government shall be administered, it is preposterous to pretend that women are not qualified to use the elective franchise, and that they are fit only to be recognized, politically speaking, as *non compos mentis*.

REBECCA M. SANFORD TO THE CLEVELAND CONVENTION.

NEW LONDON, HURON Co., O., *October* 3, 1853.

FRIENDS OF REFORM :—Not being present at the Convention, I can but express my interest by a few lines.

The mere question of woman's civil rights is not a deep one, for it is a natural one, and closely follows her mission in this world. She was not created anything else than a helpmeet to man, and where to limit that assistance there is no rule in nature, except her physical functions; *there is a limit in law*, but whether the law has the right to place her where she is, is the question. It must be conceded that the law has drawn too great an inference from her ancient social attitude, and from present custom and prejudice. But has the law the right to be prejudiced—ought it not to stand pure, and noble, and magnanimous, founded on the natural rights of the human soul? The law grants woman protection; it also grants negroes, animals, and property protection in their certain spheres. It gives no more to woman.

Woman's sphere is her capability of performing her duty to herself, her family, and to society, taking self-preservation as the first law of her nature. At present she does not fully act in her sphere. The lid of the ballot-box shuts out more than one-half of her duty to herself, family, and society. The eye of the law is diseased, and woman must be made assistant occulist, to render that eye pure and single-sighted. Let not this Convention close until some way and means are decided upon to secure woman's vote at the polls. The propriety or impropriety of the same place and box and other objections, can be disposed of in a short time, as occasion requires.

This done, the monster evils of society, Intemperance, etc., can be handled with ungloved hands.

At this time, as far as custom, made potent by law, permits woman to lead her sons on in the journey of life, she keeps them pure and unspotted from the world; but where she leaves off, hell's avenues are opened, and man too often leads them through.

Allow me, as one who has been obliged to look upon our Conventions from many points of observation, and to note their effects upon the community by actual communication with that community; as one who feels identified in principle and purpose, to suggest perfect unity and but few resolutions, and those well-digested and fully acted upon. Beware of *ultraisms*. Give a high tone and elevation to your deliberations; bring out the true, the beautiful, the divine of your own souls, to meet the true, the grand, the divine inspirations of this agitation.

One thing else I would strongly recommend. Let no gentleman be appointed to office in the Convention, or by the Convention. You will then secure yourselves from outside coarseness, and secure to yourselves greater respect from the public at large. If you do not come to this *now*, you will be obliged to come to it before you receive the credit for a *wisdom* you justly deserve.

May God guide you and bless you.

Yours, strong in the right,   REBECCA M. SANFORD.

SIXTH NATIONAL WOMAN'S RIGHTS CONVENTION, CINCINNATI, OHIO, 1856.

OFFICERS :

*President—*Martha C. Wright, New York.

*Vice-Presidents—*Ernestine L. Rose, New York; James Mott, Pennsylvania; Frances D. Gage, Missouri; Hannah Tracy Cutler, Emily Robinson, Ohio; Euphemia Cochrain, Michigan; Paulina Wright Davis, Rhode Island.

Business Committee—Lucy Stone Blackwell, Ohio ; Lucretia Mott, Pennsylvania ; Josephine S. Griffing, Adelaide Swift, Henry B. Blackwell, Ohio.

Secretaries—Rebecca Plumly, Pennsylvania ; Wm. Henry Smith, editor of *The Type of the Times*.

RESOLUTIONS.

WHEREAS, All men are created equal and endowed with certain inalienable rights, and that among these are life, liberty, and the pursuit of happiness ; and,

WHEREAS, To secure these rights governments are instituted among them, deriving their just powers from the consent of the governed ; therefore

Resolved, That the legislators of these United States are self-convicted of the grossest injustice and of inconsistency with their own admitted principles, while they refuse these rights to women.

Resolved, That taxation without representation is tyranny.

Resolved, That in accordance with an universally. admitted and self-evident truth, woman should possess the elective franchise, as a basis of all legal and political rights, as the only effective protection of their interests, as a remedy against present oppression, and as a school for character.

Resolved, That the right to acquire knowledge should be limited only by the capacity of the individual ; and, therefore, we deprecate, especially, that social usage, inexorable as a written statute, which excludes woman from all our best colleges, universities, schools of law, medicine, and divinity, and that we demand equal scholastic advantages for our daughters and our sons ; that while only three out of the one hundred and fifty American colleges are open to women, and while every avenue to scientific and professional culture is closed against her, it is unfair to judge woman by the same intellectual standard as man, and impossible to define a limit to her capacities and talents.

Resolved, That the inadequate compensation which the labor of women now commands, is the source of inexpressible individual misery and social demoralization ; that inasmuch as the law of supply and demand will always regulate the remuneration of labor, the diversity of female employments and her free access to every branch of business, are indispensable to the virtue, happiness, and well-being of society.

CHAPTER VIII.

MASSACHUSETTS.

First Worcester Convention, 1850.

NAMES OF PERSONS WHO SIGNED THE CALL OF 1850.

MASSACHUSETTS.

Lucy Stone,	B. S. Treanor,	Dr. Seth Rogers,
Wm. H. Channing,	Mary M. Brooks,	Eliza F. Taft,
Harriot K. Hunt,	T. W. Higginson,	Dr. A. C. Taft,
A. Bronson Alcott,	Mary E. Higginson,	Charles K. Whipple,
Nathaniel Barney,	Emily Winslow,	Mary Bullard,
Eliza Barney,	R. Waldo Emerson,	Emma C. Goodwin,
Wendell Phillips,	William L. Garrison,	Abby Price,
Ann Greene Phillips,	Helen E. Garrison,	Thankful Southwick,
Adin Ballou,	Charles F. Hovey,	Eliza J. Kenney,
Anna Q. T. Parsons,	Sarah Earle,	Louisa M. Sewall,
Mary H. L. Cabot,	Abby K. Foster	Sarah Southwick.

RHODE ISLAND.

Sarah H. Whitman,	Sarah Brown,	George Clarke,
Thomas Davis,	Elizabeth B. Chace,	Mary Adams,
Paulina W. Davis,	Mary Clarke,	George Adams.
Joseph A. Barker,	John L. Clarke,	

NEW YORK.

Gerrit Smith,	Charlotte G. Coffin,	Joseph Savage,
Nancy Smith,	Mary G. Taber,	L. N. Fowler,
Elizabeth C. Stanton,	Elizabeth S. Miller,	Lydia Fowler,
Catharine Wilkinson,	Elizabeth Russell,	Sarah Smith,
Samuel J. May,	Stephen Smith,	Charles D. Miller.
Charlotte C. May,	Rosa Smith,	

PENNSYLVANIA.

William Elder,	Jane G. Swisshelm,	Myra Townsend,
Sarah Elder,	Charlotte Darlington,	Mary Grew,
Sarah Tyndale,	Simon Barnard,	Sarah Lewis,
Warner Justice,	Lucretia Mott,	Sarah Pugh,
Huldah Justice,	James Mott,	Hannah Darlington,
William Swisshelm,	W. S. Pierce,	Sarah D. Barnard.

MARYLAND.

Mrs. Eliza Stewart.

OHIO.

Elizabeth Wilson,	Mary Cowles,	Benjamin S. Jones,
Mary A. Johnson,	Maria L. Giddings,	Lucius A. Hine,
Oliver Johnson,	Jane Elizabeth Jones,	Sylvia Cornell.

RESOLUTIONS.

Wendell Phillips presented, from the Business Committee, the following resolutions :

Resolved, That every human being of full age, and resident for a proper length of time on the soil of the nation, who is required to obey law, is entitled to a voice in its enactments ; that every such person, whose property or labor is taxed for the support of the government, is entitled to a direct share in such government ; therefore,

Resolved, That women are clearly entitled to the right of suffrage, and to be considered eligible to office ; the omission to demand which on her part, is a palpable recreancy to duty, and the denial of which is a gross usurpation, on the part of man, no longer to be endured ; and that every party which claims to represent the humanity, civilization, and progress of the age, is bound to inscribe on its banners, "Equality before the law, without distinction of sex or color."

Resolved, That political rights acknowledge no sex, and, therefore, the word "male" should be stricken from every State Constitution.

Resolved, That the laws of property, as affecting married parties, demand a thorough revisal, so that all rights may be equal between them ; that the wife may have, during life, an equal control over the property gained by their mutual toil and sacrifices, be heir to her husband precisely to the same extent that he is heir to her, and entitled at her death to dispose by will of the same share of the joint property as he is.

Resolved, That since the prospect of honorable and useful employment, in after life, for the faculties we are laboring to discipline, is the keenest stimulus to fidelity in the use of educational advantages, and since the best education is what we give ourselves in the struggles, employments, and discipline of life ; therefore, it is impossible that woman should make full use of the instruction already accorded to her, or that her career should do justice to her faculties, until the avenues to the various civil and professional employments are thrown open to arouse her ambition and call forth all her nature.

Resolved, That every effort to educate woman, until you accord to her her rights, and arouse her conscience by the weight of her responsibilities, is futile, and a waste of labor.

Resolved, That the cause we have met to advocate—the claim for woman of all her natural and civil rights—bids us remember the two millions of slave women at the South, the most grossly wronged and foully outraged of all women ; and in every effort for an improvement in our civilization, we will bear in our heart of hearts the memory of the trampled womanhood of the plantation, and omit no effort to raise it to a share in the rights we claim for ourselves.

PAULINA WRIGHT DAVIS.—*Dear Madam :*—I take the liberty of enclosing you an extract from a long epistle I have just received from Helene Marie Weber. It speaks of matter interesting to us all, and I ask of you the favor to submit it to the Convention. Miss Weber, as a literary character, stands in the front rank of essayists in France. She has labored zealously in behalf of her sex, as her numerous tracts on subjects of reform bear testimony. No writer of the present age, perhaps, has done more to exalt woman than she has by her powerful essays. My personal knowledge of Miss Weber enables me to speak confidently of her private character. It is utterly false that she is a masculine woman. Her deportment is strictly lady-like, modest, and unassuming, and her name is beyond reproach. She is a Protestant of the Lutheran order; exemplary in all her religious duties, and unaffectedly pious and benevolent.

She is, as you are doubtless aware, a practical agriculturist. The entire business of her farm is conducted by herself, and she has been eminently successful. She has proved the capacity of woman for business pursuits. Her success in this vocation is a practical argument worth a thousand theories. I find no difficulty with her because she dresses like a man. Her dress has not changed her nature. Those who censure her for abandoning the female dress, make up their judgment without proper reflection. She has violated no custom of her own country, and has merely acted according to the honest dictates of her mind—"*Honi soit qui mal y pense.*"

Miss Weber is now about twenty-five years of age. She is a ripe scholar, and has a perfect command of the English language. I am decidedly of the opinion that her visit among us will do a vast deal of good to our cause, and we ought to give her a hearty welcome when she comes. I can assure our most rigid friends that they will all be reconciled to her attire on five minutes' acquaintance. . . . .

I remain, dear madam, yours sincerely, MILDRED A. SPOFORD.

Extract from a Letter of H. M. WEBER.

LA PELOUSE, *August* 3, 1850.

. . . . Circumstances place it out of my power to visit America during the present season. . . . . The newspapers, both of England and America, have done me great injustice. While they have described my apparel with the minute accuracy of professional tailors, they have seen fit to charge me with a disposition to undervalue the female sex, and to identify myself with the other. Such calumnies are annoying to me. I have never wished to be an Iphis—never for a moment affected to be anything but a woman. I do not think any one ever mistook me for a man, unless it may have been some stranger who slightly glanced at me while passing along the street or the highway. I adopted male attire as a measure of convenience in my business, and not through any wish to appear eccentric or to pass for one of the male sex; and it has ever been my rule to dress with the least possible ostentation consistent with due neatness. I have never had cause to regret my adoption of male attire, and never expect to return to a female toilette. I am fully aware, however, that my dress will probably prejudice the great body of our friends in America against me, while present impressions on that subject exist; and it was with the view of allaying this feeling that I wished to address the assembly at Worcester.

By this means I think I could satisfy any liberal-minded person, of either sex, that there is no moral or political principle involved in this question, and that a woman may, if she like, dress in male habiliments without injury to herself or others. . . . . Those who suppose that woman can be "the political, social, pecuniary, religious equal of man" without conforming to his dress, deceive themselves, and mislead others who have no minds of their own. While the superiority of the male dress for all purposes of business and recreation is conceded, it is absurd to argue that we should not avail ourselves of its advantages.

There are no well-founded objections to women dressing, as we term it, *en cavalier.* The only two I ever heard are these: "To do so is contrary to law, both human and divine," and, "The male dress is *outre* and less graceful than our own." These objections may be answered in a few words. The human statutes on this subject should be repealed, as they surely will be in due time, or be regarded as they now are in European States—as dead letters. The practice is not contrary to divine law. The alleged prohibition, as contained in the fifth book of Moses, had reference to a religious custom of the Amorites, and was limited in its application to the children of Israel, who had by Divine command dispossessed that pagan nation of their territory, and destroyed their temples of idolatrous worship.

The context will show two other prohibitions on this subject. In the 11th and 12th verses of the same chapter (Deut. xxii.) it is forbidden to "wear garments of divers sorts, as of woolen and linen together," and to wear fringes on the vesture. These prohibitions are all of the same character, and had an obvious reference to the ceremonies used by the pagans in their worship of idols. If one of these prohibitions be binding upon nations of the present age, the others are not less so. To the second objection, it may be said that beauty and grace in matters of dress are determined by no rules, and if the fashion of men's clothes be awkward it can easily be improved.

Women who prefer the gown should, of course, consult their own pleasure by continuing to wear it; while those whose preference is a male dress, ought not to be blamed for adopting it. I close this homily by recording my prediction, that in ten years male attire will be generally worn by the women of most civilized countries, and that it will precede the consummation of many great measures which are deemed to be of paramount importance. I hope to visit America next year. Thanks to the invention of steam, a voyage across the ocean is now a mere *bagatelle.* I have not much of the spirit of travel remaining. My agricultural pursuits confine me at home nearly the whole year, but my captivity is a delightful one.

Affectionately yours,

H. M. WEBER.

William Henry Channing, from the Business Committee, suggested a plan for organization, and the principles which should govern the movement for establishing woman's co-sovereignty with man, and reported the following:

Resolved, That as women alone can learn by experience and prove by works, what is their rightful sphere of duty, we recommend, as *next steps,* that they should demand and secure:

1st. *Education* in primary and high-schools, universities, medical, legal, and theological institutions, as comprehensive and exact as their abilities prompt them to seek and their capabilities fit them to receive.

2d. *Partnership* in the labors, gains, risks, and remunerations of productive industry, with such limits only as are assigned by taste, intuitive judgment, or their measure of spiritual and physical vigor, as tested by experiment.

3d. A *co-equal share* in the formation and administration of law, Municipal, State, and National, through legislative assemblies, courts, and executive offices.

4th. *Such unions* as may become the guardians of pure morals and honorable manners— a high court of appeal in cases of outrage which can not be, and are not touched by civil or ecclesiastical organizations, as at present existing, and a medium for expressing the highest views of justice dictated by human conscience and sanctioned by holy inspiration.

Resolved, That a Central Committee be appointed by this Convention, empowered to enlarge its numbers, on (1st) Education; (2d) Industrial Avocations; (3d) Civil and Political Rights and Regulations; (4th) Social Relations; who shall correspond with each other and with the Central Committee, hold meetings in their respective neighborhoods, gather statistics, facts, and incidents to illustrate, raise funds for the movement; and through the press, tracts, books, and the living agent, guide public opinion upward and onward in the grand social reform of establishing woman's co-sovereignty with man.

Resolved, That the Central Committee be authorized to call Conventions at such times and places as they see fit, and that they hold office until the next Annual Convention.

To carry out the plan suggested by Mr. Channing, the following Committees were appointed:

MEMBERS OF COMMITTEES.

Central Committee.—Paulina W. Davis, Chairman; Sarah H. Earle, Secretary; Wendell Phillips, Treasurer; Mary A. W. Johnson, Wm. H. Channing, Gerrit Smith, John G. Forman, Martha H. Mowry, Lucy Stone, Abby K. Foster, Pliny Sexton, J. Elizabeth Jones, William Elder, William Stedman, Emily Robinson, Abby H. Price, William Lloyd

Garrison, Lucretia Mott, Ernestine L. Rose, Elizabeth C. Stanton, Angelina Grimké Weld, Antoinette L. Brown, Harriot K. Hunt, Emma R. Coe, Clarina I. H. Nichols, Charles C. Burleigh, Adin Ballou, Sarah H. Hallock, Joseph A. Dugdale.

Educational Committee.—Eliza Barney, Chairman ; Marian Blackwell, Secretary ; Elizabeth C. Stanton, Eliza Taft, Clarina I. H. Nichols, Calvin Fairbanks, Hannah Darlington, Ann Eliza Brown, Elizabeth Oakes Smith.

Industrial Committee.—Elizabeth Blackwell, Harriot K. Hunt, Benjamin S. Treanor, Ebenezer D. Draper, Phebe Goodwin, Alice Jackson, Maria Waring, Sarah L. Miller.

Committee on Civil and Political Functions.—Ernestine L. Rose, Lucy Stone, Wendell Phillips, Hannah Stickney, Sarah Hallock, Abby K. Foster, Charles C. Burleigh, Elizabeth C. Stanton, William L. Garrison.

Committee on Social Relations.—Lucretia Mott, William H. Channing, Anna Q. T. Parsons, William H. Fish, Rebecca Plumley, Elizabeth B. Chace, John G. Forman, Henry Fish, Mary Grew.

Committee on Publication.—Wm. Henry Channing, Chairman ; Ernestine L. Rose, Charlotte Fowler Wells.

MEMBERS WORCESTER CONVENTION, 1850.

Massachusetts.—James N. Buffam, W. A. Alcott, A. H. Johnson, W. H. Harrington, E. B. Briggs, A. C. Lackey, Ora Ober, Olive W. Hastings, Thomas Provan, Rebecca Provan, A. W. Thayer, M. M. Munyan, W. H. Johnson, G. W. Benson, Mrs. C. M. Carter, H. S. Brigham, E. A. Welsh, Mrs. J. H. Moore, Margaret S. Merritt, Martha Willard, A. N. Lamb, Mrs. Chaplin, N. B. Hill, K. H. Parsons, C. Jillson, L. Wait, Chas. Bigham, J. T. Partridge, Eliza C. Clapp, Daniel Steward, Sophia Foord, E. A. Clarke, E. H. Taft, Mrs. E. J. Henshaw, Edward Southwick, E. A. Merrick, Mrs. C. Merrick, Lewis Ford, J. T. Everett, Loring Moody, Sojourner Truth, E. Jane Alden, Elizabeth Dayton, Lima H. Ober, Thomas Hill, Elizabeth Frail, Eli Belknap, M. M. Frail, Valentine Belknap, Mary R. Metcalf, R. H. Ober, D. A. Mundy, Dr. S. Rogers, Elizabeth Earle, G. D. Williams, Dorothy Whiting, Emily Whiting Abigail Morgan, Susan Fuller, Thomas Earle, Allen C. Earle, Martha B. Earle, Anne H. Southwick, Joseph A. Howland, Adeline H. Howland, O. T. Harris, Julia T. Harris, John M. Spear, E. D. Draper, D. R. P. Hewitt, L. G. Wilkins, J. H. Binney, Mary Adams, Anna Goulding, E. A. Parrington, Mrs. Parrington, Harriot K. Hunt, Chas. F. Hovey, Mrs. J. G. Hodgden, C. M. Shaw, Ophelia D. Hill, Mrs. P. Allen, Anna Q. T. Parsons, C. D. McLane, W. H. Channing, Wendell Phillips, Abby K. Foster, S. S. Foster, Effingham L. Capron, Frances H. Drake, E. M. Dodge, Eliza Barney, Lydia Barney, Wm. D. Cady, C. S. Dow, E. Goddard, Mary F. Gilbert, Josiah Henshaw, Andrew Wellington, Louisa Gleason, Paulina Gerry, Lucy Stone, Mary Abbot, Anna E. Fish, C. G. Munyan, Maria L. Southwick, F. H. Underwood, J. B. Willard, Perry Joslin, Elizabeth Johnson, Seneth Smith, Marian Hill, Wm. Coe, E. T. Smith, S. Aldrich, M. A. Maynard, S. P. R., J. M. Cummings, Nancy Fay, M. Jane Davis, D. R. Crandell, E. M. Burleigh, Sarah Chafee, Adeline Perry, Lydia E. Chase, J. A. Fuller, Sarah Prentice, Emily Prentice, H. N. Fairbanks, Mrs. A. Crowl, Dwight Tracy, J. S. Perry, Isaac Norcross, Julia A. McIntyre, Emily Sanford, H. M. Sanford, C. D. M. Lane, Elizabeth Firth, S. C. Sargeant, C. A. K. Ball, M. A. Thompson, Lucinda Safford, S. E. Hall, S. D. Holmes, Z. W. Harlow, N. B. Spooner, Ignatius Sargent, A. B. Humphrey, M. R. Hadwen, J. H. Shaw, Olive Darling, M. A. Walden, Mrs. Chickery, Mrs. F. A. Pierce, C. M. Trenor, R. C. Capron, Wm. Lloyd Garrison, Emily Loveland, Mrs. S. Worcester, Phebe Worcester, Adeline Worcester, Joanna R. Ballou, Abby H. Price, B. Willard, T. Pool, M. B. Kent, E. H. Knowlton, G. Valentine, A. Prince, Lydia Wilmarth, J. G. Warren, Mrs. E. A. Stowell, Martin Stowell, Mrs. E. Stamp, C. M. Barbour, Annie E. Ruggles, T. B. Elliot, A. H. Metcalf, Eliza J. Kenney, Rev. J. G. Forman, Andrew Stone, M.D., Samuel May, Jr., Sarah R. May, M. S. Firth, A. P. B. Rawson, Nathaniel Barney, Sarah H. Earle, F. C. Johnson.

Maine.—Anna R. Blake, Ellen M. Prescott, Oliver Dennett, Lydia Dennett.

New York.—Frederick Douglass, Lydia Mott, S. H. Hallock, Ernestine L. Rose, Joseph

Carpenter, Pliny Sexton, J. C. Hathaway, Lucy N. Colman, Antoinette L. Brown, Edgar Hicks.

New Hampshire.—P. B. Cogswell, Julia Worcester, Parker Pillsbury, Sarah Pillsbury, Asa Foster.

Vermont.—Clarina I. Howard Nichols, Mrs. A. E. Brown.

Pennsylvania.—Hannah M. Darlington, Sarah Tyndale, Emma Parker, Lucretia Mott, S. L. Miller, Isaac L. Miller, Alice Jackson, Janette Jackson, Anna R. Cox, Jacob Pierce, Lewis E. Capen, Olive W. Hastings, Rebecca Plumley, S. L. Hastings, Phebe Goodwin.

Connecticut.—C. C. Burleigh, Martha Smith, Lucius Holmes, Benj. Segur, Buel Picket, Asa Cutler, Lucy T. Dike, C. M. Collins, Anna Cornell, S. Monroe, Anna E. Price, M. C. Monroe, Gertrude R. Burleigh.

Rhode Island.—Betsy F. Lawton, Paulina W. Davis, Cynthia P. Bliss, Rebecca C. Capron, Martha Mowry, Mary Eddy, Daniel Mitchell, G. Davis, Susan Sisson, Dr. S. Mowry, Elizabeth B. Chase, Rebecca B. Spring, Susan R. Harris, A. Barnes.

Iowa.—Silas Smith.

Ohio.—Mariana Johnson, Oliver Johnson, Ellen Blackwell, Marian Blackwell, Diana W. Ballou.

California.—Mrs. Mary G. Wright.

Asenath Fuller, Denney M. F. Walker, Eunice D. F. Pierce, Elijah Houghton, L. H. Ober, A. Wyman, Silence Bigelow, Adeline S. Greene, Josephine Reglar, Anna T. Draper, E. J. Alden, Sophia Taft, Alice H. Easton, Calvin Fairbanks, D. H. Knowlton, E. W. K. Thompson, Caroline Farnum, Mary R. Hubbard.

SECOND WORCESTER CONVENTION, 1851.

RESOLUTIONS.

1. *Resolved,* That while we would not undervalue other methods, the Right of Suffrage for Women is, in our opinion, the corner-stone of this enterprise, since we do not seek to protect woman, but rather to place her in a position to protect herself.

2. *Resolved,* That it will be woman's fault if, the ballot once in her hand, all the barbarous, demoralizing, and unequal laws relating to marriage and property, do not speedily vanish from the statute-book ; and while we acknowledge that the hope of a share in the higher professions and profitable employments of society is one of the strongest motives to intellectual culture, we know, also, that an interest in political questions is an equally powerful stimulus ; and we see, beside, that we do our best to insure education to an individual when we put the ballot into his hands ; it being so clearly the interest of the community that one upon whose decisions depend its welfare and safety, should both have free access to the best means of education, and be urged to make use of them.

3. *Resolved,* That we do not feel called upon to assert or establish the equality of the sexes, in an intellectual or any other point of view. It is enough for our argument that natural and political justice, and the axioms of English and American liberty, alike determine that rights and burdens—taxation and representation—should be co-extensive ; hence women, as individual citizens, liable to punishment for acts which the laws call criminal, or to be taxed in their labor and property for the support of government, have a self-evident and indisputable right, identically the same right that men have, to a direct voice in the enactment of those laws and the formation of that government.

4. *Resolved,* That the democrat, or reformer, who denies suffrage to women, is a democrat only because he was not born a noble, and one of those levelers who are willing to level only down to themselves.

5. *Resolved,* That while political and natural justice accords civil equality to woman ; while great thinkers of every age, from Plato to Condorcet and Mill, have supported

their claim ; while voluntary associations, religious and secular, have been organized on this basis, still, it is a favorite argument against it, that no political community or nation ever existed in which women have not been in a state of political inferiority. But, in reply, we remind our opponents that the same fact has been alleged, with equal truth, in favor of slavery ; has been urged against freedom of industry, freedom of conscience, and the freedom of the press ; none of these liberties having been thought compatible with a well-ordered state, until they had proved their possibility by springing into existence as facts. Besides, there is no difficulty in understanding why the subjection of woman has been a *uniform custom,* when we recollect that we are just emerging from the ages in which *might* has been always right.

6. *Resolved,* That, so far from denying the overwhelming social and civil influence of women, we are fully aware of its vast extent ; aware, with Demosthenes, that "measures which the statesman has meditated a whole year may be overturned in a day by a woman"; and for this very reason we proclaim it the very highest expediency to endow her with full civil rights, since only then will she exercise this mighty influence under a just sense of her duty and responsibility ; the history of all ages bearing witness, that the only safe course for nations is to add open responsibility wherever there already exists unobserved power.

7. *Resolved,* That we deny the right of any portion of the species to decide for another portion, or of any individual to decide for another individual what is and what is not their " proper sphere "; that the proper sphere for all human beings is the largest and highest to which they are able to attain ; what this is, can not be ascertained without complete liberty of choice ; woman, therefore, ought to choose for herself what sphere she will fill, what education she will seek, and what employment she will follow, and not be held bound to accept, in submission, the rights, the education, and the sphere which man thinks proper to allow her.

8. *Resolved,* That we hold these truths to be self-evident : That all men are created equal ; that they are endowed by their Creator with certain inalienable rights : that among these are life, liberty, and the pursuit of happiness ; that, to secure these rights, governments are instituted among men, deriving their just powers from the consent of the governed ; and we charge that man with gross dishonesty or ignorance, who shall contend that " men," in the memorable document from which we quote, does not stand for the human race ; that " life, liberty, and the pursuit of happiness," are the " inalienable rights " of *half* only of the human species ; and that, by " the governed," whose consent is affirmed to be the only source of just power, is meant that *half* of mankind only who, in relation to the other, have hitherto assumed the character of *governors.*

9. *Resolved,* That we see no weight in the argument that it is necessary to exclude women from civil life because domestic cares and political engagements are incompatible ; since we do not see the fact to be so in the case of men ; and because, if the incompatibility be real, it will take care of itself, neither men nor women needing any law to exclude them from an occupation when they have undertaken another incompatible with it. Second, we see nothing in the assertion that women, themselves, do not desire a change, since we assert that superstitious fears and dread of losing men's regard, smother all frank expression on this point; and further, if it be their real wish to avoid civil life, laws to keep them out of it are absurd, no legislator having ever yet thought it necessary to compel people by law to follow their own inclination.

10. *Resolved,* That it is as absurd to deny all women their civil rights because the cares of household and family take up all the time of some, as it would be to exclude the whole male sex from Congress, because some men are sailors, or soldiers in active service or merchants, whose business requires all their attention and energies.

GLEN HAVEN, *Feb.* 18, 1853.

PAULINA WRIGHT DAVIS.—*My Dear Friend :*—Bless you for *The Una,* and for sending me a copy. I am pleased with its appearance and with the heartiness of your correspondents. Would you find room for some of my lucubrations ? If so, I will drive my quill a little for you some of these evenings. Perhaps I might utter something readable. I do not ask you to send me *The Una,* for the dollar must go with the request, and the dollar has yet to be earned by *quill-work*, a task quite as hard as was work when a child at the *quill-wheel*, winding yarn from the reel.

Drop me a line if you would like my assistance as a correspondent, and what I can do, I will cheerfully.

Very truly, your friend,   J. C. JACKSON, M.D.*

PETITION OF HARRIOT K. HUNT TO THE MASSACHUSETTS CONSTITUTIONAL CONVENTION.

To the Constitutional Convention now sitting in Boston :

Your petitioner respectfully prays your honorable body to insert into the Constitution a clause securing to females paying town, county, and States taxes upon property held in their own right, and who have no husbands or other guardians to represent and act for them, the same right of voting possessed by male tax-paying citizens ; or, should your honorable body not deem such females capable of exercising the right of suffrage with due discretion, at least excuse them from the paying of taxes, in the appropriation of which they have no voice, thus carrying out the great principle on which the American Revolution was based—that taxation and representation ought to go together. All of which your petitioner will ever pray.

PAULINA WRIGHT DAVIS

Died August 24, 1876, after two years of great suffering. A large circle of friends gathered at her elegant residence near Providence, Rhode Island, to pay their last tributes of friendship and respect. The chief speaker on the occasion was, at her request, Elizabeth Cady Stanton. She left her noble husband, Hon. Thomas Davis, and two adopted daughters, to mourn her loss. It was a soft, balmy day, just such as our friend would have chosen, when she was laid in her last resting-place. Dr. and Mrs. Channing, Theodore Tilton, and Joaquin Miller, were among those who followed in the funeral *cortège.*

CHAPTER IX.

INDIANA.

Dublin Convention, October, 1851.

RESOLUTIONS.

Resolved, That all laws and customs having for their perpetuation the only plea that they are time-honored, which in any way infringe on woman's equal rights, cramp her energies, cripple her efforts, or place her before the eyes of her family or the world as an inferior, are wrong, and should be immediately abolished.

Resolved, That the avenues to gain, in all their varieties, should be as freely opened to woman as they now are to man.

Resolved, That the rising generation of boys and girls should be educated together in the same schools and colleges, and receive the same kind and degree of education.

Resolved, That woman should receive for equal labor, equal pay with man.

Resolved, That as the qualification for citizenship in this country is based on capacity and morality, and as the sexes in their mental condition are equal, therefore woman should enjoy the same rights of citizenship with man.

An association was organized and a constitution was adopted, to which the following names were appended : Amanda M. Way, Minerva Maulsby, Jane Morrow, Agnes Cook, Rebecca Shreves, Rebecca Williams, Wilson D. Schooley, Samuel Mitchell, Elda Ann Smith, Dr. O. P. Baer, Mrs. O. P. Baer, Hannah Birdsall, Melissa J. Diggs, Hannah

---

* At present the head of the water-cure establishment, Dansville, New York. Dr. Jackson has been identified with all the leading reforms of his generation—Anti-slavery, Temperance, Woman Suffrage—and an earnest advocate for a new dress for woman that shall give freedom to her lungs and powers of locomotion.

Hiatt, Jas. P. Way, B. F. Diggs, Mary B. Birdsall, Fanny Hiatt, Henry Hiatt, Thomas Birdsall, Elizabeth Hoover, Elijah C. Wright, Elizabeth Wright, A. W. Pruyne, Dr. Mary F. Thomas, Dr. Owen Thomas, Emi B. Swank, Joel P. Davis, Lydia P. Davis, Thursey A. Way, Rebecca A. C. Murray.

CHAPTER X.

PENNSYLVANIA.

SAXE, DANA, AND GRACE GREENWOOD.

MR. SAXE not long since, in a poem, satirized literary women very keenly, upon which Grace Greenwood wrote a severe criticism on his volume, which was published in *The Evening Post.* Mr. Saxe, after seeing the criticism, wrote a note to the editor of the *Post,* in which he makes an exception in favor of Grace. This calls forth another letter from her, from which we make the following extract :

NEW BRIGHTON, *Jan.* 22, 1850.

GENTLEMEN :— . . . . At the time of my writing, I was feeling peculiarly sensitive in regard to my womanly, as well as literary position. The grandpapaish lectures of Mr. Dana had troubled and discouraged me. I said, " If so speak and write our poets, surely the age is on the backward line of march." I had become impatient and indignant for my sex, thus lectured to, preached at, and satirized eternally. I had grown weary of hearing woman told that her sole business here, the highest, worthiest aims of her existence were to be loving, lovable, feminine, to win thus a lover and a lord whom she might glorify abroad and make comfortable at home.

We have had enough of this. Man is not best qualified to mark out woman's life-path. He knows, indeed, what he desires her to be, but he does not yet understand all that God and nature require of her. Woman should not be made up of love alone, the other attributes of her being should not be dwarfed that this may have a large, unnatural growth. Hers should be a distinct individuality, an independent moral existence—or, at least, the dependence should be mutual. Woman can best judge of woman, her wants, capacities, aspirations, and powers. She can best speak to her on the life of the affections, on the loves of her heart, on the peculiar joys and sorrows of her lot. She can best teach her to be true to herself, to her high nature, to her brave spirit ; and then, indeed, shall she be constant in her love and faithful to her duties, all, even to the most humble. Woman can strengthen woman for the life of self-sacrifice, of devotion, of ministration, of much endurance which lies before her.

A woman of intellect and right feeling would never dream of pointing out the weak and unfilial Desdemona as an example to her sex in this age ; would never dare to hold up as " our destined end and aim," a one love, however romantic and poetical, which might be so selfishly sought and so unscrupulously secured.

Thank Heaven, woman herself is awaking to a perception of the causes which have hitherto impeded her free and perfect development, which have shut her out from the large experiences, the wealth and fullness of the life to which she was called. She is beginning to feel, and to cast off the bonds which oppress her—many of them, indeed, self-imposed, and many gilded and rarely wrought, covered with flowers and delicate tissues, but none the less bonds—bonds upon the speech, upon the spirit, upon the life.

There surely is a great truth involved in this question of " Woman's Rights," and agitated as it may be, with wisdom and mildness, or with rashness and the bold, high spirit which shocks and startles at the first, good will come out of it eventually, great good, and the women of the next age will be the stronger and the freer, aye, and the happier, for the few brave spirits who stood up fearlessly for unpopular truth against the world.

I know that I expose myself to the charge of being unfeminine in feeling, of ultraism. Well, better that than conservatism, though conservatism were safer and more respectable. Senselessness is always safety, and a mummy is a thoroughly respectable personage.

But to return to Mr. Saxe. Our poet satirized rather keenly literary women, as a class, in the poem on which I remarked, but afterwards, in his communication to the *Post*, most politely intimates that he excepts me as one of the " women of real talent." But I will not be excepted. I stand in the ranks, liable to all the penalties of the calling—exposed to the hot shot of satire and the stinging arrows of ridicule. I will not be received as an exception, where full justice is not done to the class to which I belong.

Suppose, now, that I should write a poem to deliver before some " Woman's Rights Convention " or " Ladies' Literary Association," on " The Times," which should come down sharp and heavy on the literary men of the day, for usurping the delicate employ by right and nature the peculiar province of woman, " the weaker vessel " ; for neglecting their shops, their fields, their counting-houses, and their interesting families, and wasting their precious time in writing love-tales, " doleful ditties," and " distressful strains," for the magazines; for flirting with the muse, while their wives are wanting shoes, or perpetrating puns, while their children cry for " buns " ! Suppose that, pointing every line with wit, I should hold them up to contempt as careless, improvident lovers of pleasure, given. to self-indulgence ; taking their Helicon more than dashed with gin ; seekers after notoriety, eccentric in their habits and unmanly in all their tastes ! After this, should I very handsomely make an exception in favor of Mr. Saxe, would he feel complimented ?

As far as I have known literary women, and as far as they have been made known to us in literary biography, the unwomanly and unamiable, the poor wives, and daughters, and sisters, have been the rare exceptions. I mean not alone " women of genius," but would include those of mere talent, of mediocre talent even, devoted to letters as a profession, and who, by their estimable characters and blameless lives, are an honor to their calling.

I believe that for one woman whom the pursuits of literature, the ambition of authorship, and the love of fame have rendered unfit for home-life, a thousand have been made thoroughly undomestic by poor social strivings, the follies of fashion, and the intoxicating distinction which mere personal beauty confers.

GRACE GREENWOOD.

WESTCHESTER CONVENTION, JUNE 2 AND 3, 1852.

LETTER FROM MARY MOTT.

AUBURN, DE KALB COUNTY, INDIANA, *May* 17, 1852.

SISTERS :—You have called another Convention, and all who are the friends of equal rights are invited to attend and participate in the deliberations. The invitation will probably meet the eye of thousands who would gladly encourage you by their presence, did circumstances permit them to do so. Your aim is the moral, physical, and intellectual elevation of woman, and through her to benefit the whole human race. Can a Convention be called for a nobler purpose ? Have men ever aimed so high ? They have had Conventions without stint ; old men and young men, Whigs, Democrats, Abolitionists, and Slaveholders, all have had Conventions ; but how few have aimed at anything higher than political power for themselves and party. We have looked upon their contests without personal interest in their result. Some benefits might come to our husbands and brothers, but none to us. We are permitted to talk about liberty, but we may not enjoy it. We may water the tree with our tears, while our husbands pluck and enjoy the fruit. Of what advantage is it to us to live in a Republic ? Our social position is no better than it was in the days of Queen Elizabeth. Men have made great progress since that day ; from being subjects they have become sovereigns, ruling, as she professed to rule, by *divine right*. True, many of these sovereigns have not a foot of ground, and but one subject, a wife ; but then he has absolute control over that one. Yes, they have made progress ; but for that progress they are much indebted to men who, being in possession of power, were only anxious to retain and extend it. The Great Charter was extorted from King John by the barons in order to consolidate their power; they attended to the interests of the common people (who then were in a state of villanage) just so far as they could clearly see would be for their own interest, and no further. The world is much indebted to those sturdy barons ; they did more good than they ever thought of doing. There were germs in that charter that have borne excellent fruit since that day.

Error delights in obscurity; surrounded with clouds and darkness, it is comparatively secure; but let these clouds be scattered, let the light of reason fall upon it, and it is dangerous no longer. Any act that causes men to think, is so far an advantage to society. The ideas will not be lost. When King James I. talked and wrote upon the doctrine of the divine right of kings, he little thought it would result in the beheading of his son Charles, and the expulsion of his son James from the throne. Shrouded in mystery, it was approached with reverence, and seldom critically examined, until he lifted the veil and invited others to behold its beauty. What had been a mystery was a mystery no longer. He forgot what others remembered—that it might have different aspects for the sovereign and subject. It was judged unworthy of national homage, but very desirable as a household god. And men who thought Paul was in the dark when he wrote, " Let every soul be subject unto the higher powers, for there is no power but of God. The powers that be are ordained of God. Whosoever resisteth the powers resisteth the ordinance of God; and they that resist shall receive to themselves damnation ; " the men, I say, who could not and would not receive such doctrine from Paul, found him worthy of all praise when he said, " wives, obey your husbands." After a while England proposed taxing the Colonies. One party held that protection gave them the right of taxation. The other said the British Constitution gave the Government no power to tax, unless the persons were represented in Parliament. They declared their resolution to pay no taxes without representation. Much was said about the rights of man. And when at last a three-penny tax was laid upon tea, the men, being brimful of patriotism, cared nothing for the tax; it was the principle they cared for, and they would fight for their principles. How very sincere they were, let the millions of wives answer, whose very existence is ignored in law. There was one thing women gained by that contest ; they gained a clearer knowledge of their rights, a better understanding of their wrongs, which, according to Blackstone, are a deprivation of rights. A knowledge of these has produced a strong desire to seek a remedy. Hence the call for a Woman's Convention. We must expect some difference of opinion as to the extent of the reforms proposed ; but none who have carefully examined the subject will see reason to doubt that our rights run parallel with the rights of man. That being granted, we may then inquire into their expediency. Many things we have a right to do which are inexpedient ; but it is for *us* to say what rights we will waive and what we will enjoy.

We claim that the professions should be open to woman, believing she can preach as acceptably, study the law as thoroughly, and practice medicine as successfully, as man. The business of a clerk seems to us to be peculiarly feminine, and we claim the right to choose any trade or business for which we have strength and capacity. If it is true that governments derive their just powers from the consent of the governed, we would respectfully ask by what authority men legislate for us, and who gave them that authority ? If the power is a just one, from what source did they derive it ? Certainly not from the consent of the governed. We presume neither men nor women care for the privilege of voting, except as a means of securing the enjoyment of the rights with which they have been endowed by their Creator, and for the protection of which " Governments were first instituted among men." The rights of women have been long in abeyance, but no lapse of time can deprive her of them ; they are not transferable. She does not ask the law to confer upon her new rights. She only asks to have her just rights recognized and protected. A glance at the present position of women will show that the law does not effect this. It places minors, idiots, insane persons, and married women in the same category. Man takes all that the wife has to his own use, and such robberies are so common that they excite no indignation in the breasts of his fellow-men. He can spend all she has at the gaming-table, and who can hinder him ? He can spend it in dissipation, while his deceived wife is suffering at home for the necessaries of life. The law gives him the property, and with that he can usually find tools to work out his designs. The law interposes no barriers between him and his victim. If a married woman had equal protection with her husband, she would be ambitious to acquire property by her own industry, and the habit of industry and forethought thus acquired, would be found valuable in the marriage relation, and she would not be compelled to enter matrimony as a house of refuge. But we are told that marriage is a contract, voluntarily entered into by competent parties, and by this contract the rights of the woman are transferred to the man. But *marriage is not a contract*, it is an union instituted by God Himself, anterior to any contract whatever. Man was not pronounced good until woman was created, and God said, Let us make man in our image after our own likeness, and let THEM *have dominion.* But some one may meet us here with the question, did He not say to the woman, after the fall, " Thy desire shall be to thy husband and he shall rule over thee ? " Yes, the Bible says so ; and in the next chapter we are told that Adam and Eve had two sons, the eldest called Cain, the youngest Abel ; and God said to Cain when speaking of Abel, " Unto thee shall be his desire, and *thou shalt rule over him.*" You see they are the very words used to Eve ; therefore, if dominion was taken from the woman and given to the man, it was taken from all younger brothers and given to the first-born. If marriage be a contract, why is it not governed by the same rules that govern other contracts ? A consideration is necessary to the existence of a contract. In marriage, the man offers love for love and hand for hand, but what is the consideration for those personal rights of which he dispossesses her ? If a contract, why is there no remedy for its violation either in law or equity, as is the case with other contracts ? The bridegroom says in the marriage service, " With all my worldly goods I thee endow." Those who framed that impressive service no doubt considered it but just that he who received all by the courtesy of England, should endow her as liberally, and they thus reminded every bridegroom of his duty, even before the altar ; and what honest man will say he should not keep his word ?

MARY MOTT.

LETTER FROM DR. ELIZABETH BLACKWELL.

NEW YORK, *May* 27, 1852.

MRS. DARLINGTON.—*Dear Madam :*—I thank you cordially for your very kind invitation, and would willingly attend your Convention did not my duties in New York prevent my leaving the city.

The Convention could not choose a more important subject than education for discussion, and great good will be done if public attention is roused to the imperfection of our present system, in which the *physical nature* and the *duties of life* are equally neglected. I believe that the chief source of the false position of women is, the *inefficiency* of *women themselves*—the deplorable fact that they are so often careless mothers, weak wives, poor housekeepers, ignorant nurses, and frivolous human beings. If they would perform with strength and wisdom the duties which lie immediately around them, every sphere of life would soon be open to them. They might be priests, physicians, rulers, welcome everywhere, for all restrictive laws and foolish customs would speedily disappear before the spiritual power of strong, good women.

In order to develop such women, our present method of educating girls, which is an injurious waste of time, must be entirely remodeled, and I shall look forward with great interest to any plan of action that may be suggested by your Convention.

With hearty sympathy in every aspiration, and the right hand of fellowship to every conscientious worker, believe me,

Very truly yours,   ELIZABETH BLACKWELL.

LETTER FROM PAULINA WRIGHT DAVIS.

It is also often asked if women want more rights, why do they not take them ? Let us see how that may be. Does a woman desire a *thorough* medical education, where is the institution fully and properly endowed to receive her ? Two women, it is true, have made their way through two separate colleges, and when they had honorably won their diplomas, and even the voice of scandal could not cast a shadow upon them, they were publicly insulted by having the doors of those institutions closed upon all others of their sex. If she desires a course of thorough disciplinary study for any purpose whatsoever, where is she to find means or the institution to receive her ? The academic shades are forbidden ground to her, while their massive doors turn with no harsh grating sound at the magic word of man for man. If we did not feel too deeply the injustice of this, we might comfort ourselves with the idea that our brains are so superior that we do not need the same amount of study and discipline as the other sex. . . . .

When Socrates was advocating the equal education of women for governmental offices, he was met by ridicule. His words in consideration of it are full of wisdom. Says the sage, " The man who laughs at women going through their exercises, reaps the unripe fruit of a ridiculous wisdom, and seems not rightly to know at what he laughs, or why he does it, for that ever was and will be deemed a noble saying, that the profitable is beautiful and the hurtful base." . . . .

The harmony, unity, and oneness of the race, can not be secured while there is class legislation ; while one half of humanity is cramped within a narrow sphere and governed by arbitrary power. This unrecognized *half* desires these factitious restraints removed, and to be placed side by side with the other, simply that there may be full, free, and equal development in the future. The moral life which urges this claim is the God within us. The force which opposes it, it matters not whence it comes, "is of the earth, earthy." . . . .

LETTER FROM WM. H. AND MARY JOHNSON.

The influence of woman as a wife and a mother has been so often portrayed, that it would be difficult to find a moral writer who has not indulged in the fruitful theme, but we can not omit the occasion of quoting the sentiments of the eloquent Wm. Wirt on this subject : " Is not *our* conduct toward this sex ill-advised and foolish in relation to our own happiness ? Is it not to reject a boon which Providence kindly offers to us, and which, were we to embrace and cultivate it with skill, would refine and enlarge the sources of our own enjoyment, and purify, raise, and ennoble our own character beyond the power of human calculation ?

" As the companion of a man of sense and virtue, as an instrument and partner of his earthly happiness, what is the most beautiful woman in the world without a mind—without a cultivated mind, capable of an animated correspondence with his own, and of reciprocating all his thoughts and feelings ?

Is not our conduct on this head ungenerous and ignoble to the other sex ? Do we not deprive them of the brightest and most angelic portion of their character, degrade them from the rank of intelligence which they are formed to hold ; and instead of making them the partners of our souls, attempt to debase them into mere objects of sense ?

" Is not our conduct mean and dastardly ? Does it not look as if we were afraid that, with equal opportunities, they would rival us in intelligence, and examine and refute our pretended superiority ? "

We congratulate the Convention on the selection of the place for holding their deliberations. In no part of the State could a community be found better qualified to appreciate the objects of such a meeting, or the means for their accomplishment. Chester has undoubtedly taken the lead of all her sister counties in educational movements, as may be witnessed in her numerous flourishing schools for both sexes, which are attracting, as to a common focus, pupils from all parts of the country. And it affords us unmingled pleasure to observe the numerous female schools that have been established in this quarter, and the patronage that has been extended toward them. These are sure indications of an improved public sentiment in relation to the development of the female mind.

But there are other indications of advancement in this particular still more encouraging, because they exhibit fruits of the most ennobling powers of the human understanding. We allude to those benevolent associations particularly for promoting temperance, in which the females of Chester County have borne such a conspicuous and effective part. The reflection is, indeed, animating, that at a period when almost all kindred associations in the State, among the other sex, had languished, and intemperance seemed likely once more to overwhelm the land with more desolating evils than had ever yet been known, there was yet to be found in Chester County an association of females who were nobly bearing the standard of total abstinence, and by their well-timed labors giving evidence that there was yet vitality in the cause ! Thus we have seen not only in this, but in other fields of moral reform, that the progress has uniformly been commensurate with the intellectual and moral culture of the female mind. Let the sex, then, give their influence in promoting a system of education that will, if carried out, secure to every woman in the land the blessings of thorough practical instruction. May the deliberations of the Convention tend to the promotion of this most desirable object. With such developments as must result from the more general diffusion of knowledge, not only *rights*, but duties that have been hidden by the suggestions of ignorance and bigotry will be brought to light, and the sex will realize the noble sentiment of one of New England's gifted sons, that

> " New occasions teach new duties—Time makes ancient good uncouth,
> They must upward still and onward, who would keep abreast of Truth ! "

Desiring that your discussions may be guided by that spirit which has heretofore characterized them, we remain your friends,

WM. H. JOHNSON AND MARY JOHNSON.

RESOLUTIONS OF THE WESTCHESTER CONVENTION, 1852.

Resolved, That every party which claims to represent the humanity, the civilization, or the progress of the age, is bound to inscribe on its banner, " Equality before the laws, without distinction of sex."

Resolved, That the science of government is not necessarily connected with the violence and intrigue which are now frequently practised by party politicians, neither does the exercise of the elective franchise, or the PROPER discharge of governmental duties necessarily involve the sacrifice of the refinement or sensibilities of true womanhood.

Resolved, That in demanding for women that equal station among their brethren to which the laws of nature and of nature's God entitle them, we do not urge the claim in the spirit of an adverse policy, or with any idea of separate advantages, or in any apprehension of conflicting interests between the sexes.

Resolved, That while we regret the antagonism into which we are necessarily brought to some of the laws, customs, and monopolies of society, we have cause to rejoice that the exposure of the great wrongs of woman has been so promptly met by a kind spirit, and a disposition to redress these wrongs, to open avenues for her elevation, and to cooperate for her entire enfranchisement.

Resolved, That the greatest and most varied development of the human mind, and the widest sphere of usefulness, can be obtained only by the highest intellectual culture of the whole people, and that all obstructions should be removed which tend to prevent women from entering, as freely as men, upon the study of the physical, mental, and moral sciences.

Resolved, That we can not appreciate the justice or generosity of the laws which require women to pay taxes, and thus enable legislators richly to endow colleges and universities for their own sex, from which the female sex is entirely excluded.

Resolved, That the growing liberality of legislation and judicial construction, in regard to the property rights of married women, affords gratifying evidence of the equity of our demands and of their progress in public sentiment.

Resolved, That the disposition of property by law as affecting married parties, ought to be the same for the husband and the wife, " that she should have, during life, an equal control over the property gained by their mutual toil and sacrifices ; and be heir to her husband, precisely to the extent that he is heir to her."

Resolved, That the mother being as much the natural guardian of the child as the father, ought so to be recognized in law, and if it is justly the province of the court to appoint guardians for minors, want of qualification in the surviving parent should be the required condition of the appointment.

Resolved, That the inequality of the remuneration paid for woman's labor compared with that of man, is unjust and degrading, for so long as custom awards to her smaller compensation for services of equal value, she will be held in a state of dependence, not by any order of nature, but by an arbitrary rule of man.

Resolved, That the distinctive traits of female character, like its distinct physical organism, having its foundation in nature, the widest range of thought and action, and the highest cultivation and development of all its varied powers, will only make more apparent those sensibilities and graces which are considered its peculiar charm.

Resolved, That in claiming for woman all the rights of human beings we are but asserting her humanity, leaving the differences actually existing in the male and female constitutions to take care of themselves, these differences furnishing no reason for subjecting one sex to the other.

Resolved, That a Committee be appointed to prepare and circulate petitions, asking of our Legislature such a change in the Constitution and laws of this State, as shall extend to woman the privilege of the elective franchise, and equality in the division and inheritance of property.

Resolved, That said Committee be instructed to collect information upon the rights acknowledged and privileges guaranteed to women by other States and Governments, publishing it in such way as by them shall be deemed best for promoting political and legal equality between the sexes.

Resolved, That H. M. Darlington, P. E. Gibbons, Hannah Wright, Mary Ann Fulton, Sarah E. Miller, Lea Pusey, and Ruth Dugdale be the Committee.

Oliver Johnson offered a resolution expressing the satisfaction afforded to the members of the Convention by the presence and labors of those friends who had come from their distant homes in other States to be with us on this occasion. It was unanimously adopted.

The Convention adjourned *sine die*.

FOURTH NATIONAL W. R. CONVENTION, PHILADELPHIA, OCTOBER 18, 19, 20, 1854.

RESOLUTIONS.

Resolved, That we congratlate the true friends of woman upon the rapid progress which her cause has made during the year past, in spite of the hostility of the bad and the prejudices of the good.

Resolved, That woman's aspiration is to be the only limit of woman's destiny.

Resolved, That so long as woman is debarred from an equal education, restricted in her employments, denied the right of independent property if married, and denied in all cases the right of controlling the legislation which she is nevertheless bound to obey, so long must the woman's rights agitation be continued.

Resolved, That in perfect confidence that what we desire will one day be accomplished, we commit the cause of woman to God and to humanity.

Resolved, That in demanding the educational rights of woman, we do not deny the natural distinctions of sex, but only wish to develop them fully and harmoniously.

Resolved, That in demanding the industrial rights of woman, we only claim that she should have " a fair day's wages for a fair day's work," which is, however, impossible while she is restricted to few ill-paid avocations, and unable (if married) to control her own earnings.

Resolved, That in demanding the political rights of woman, we simply assert the fundamental principle of democracy—that taxation and representation should go together, and that, if this principle is denied, all our institutions must fall with it.

Resolved, That our present democracy is an absurdity, since it deprives woman even of the political power which is allowed to her in Europe, and abolishes all other aristocracy only to establish a new aristocracy of sex, which includes *all* men and excludes all women.

Resolved, That it is because we recognize the beauty and sacredness of the family, that we demand for woman an equal position there, instead of her losing, as now, the control of her own property, the custody of her own children, and, finally, her own legal existence, under laws which have all been pronounced by jurists " a disgrace to a heathen nation."

Resolved, That we urge it upon the women of every American State : First, to petition the legislatures for universal suffrage and a reform in the rights of property ; second, to use their utmost efforts to improve female education ; third, to open as rapidly as possible new channels for female industry.

Mrs. Tracy Cutler made an address upon the objects of the movement.

CHAPTER XI.

LUCRETIA MOTT'S FUNERAL.

Lucretia Mott died at her quiet home, "Roadside," near Philadelphia, Nov. 11, 1880. Notwithstanding the Associated Press dispatch said, "Funeral strictly private by special request," the attendance on that occasion was large. *The Philadelphia Times* thus describes it : The funeral of Lucretia Mott, attended by an immense concourse of people, at her residence as well as in the cemetery, was an impressive scene not soon to be forgotten. A handsome stone house, standing in tastefully laid out and carefully kept grounds studded with forest trees, just west of the old York road in Cheltenham township, Montgomery County, was the home of Lucretia Mott. On this occasion the road and grounds were densely packed with carriages, people on horseback and on foot, coming from many miles about to pay their last tributes of respect to this noble woman.

The funeral was conducted according to the custom of the Society of Friends, and was in all its appointments simple and unostentatious, in keeping with the character of the noble woman who had passed away. No set forms were observed.

The body, in her usual Quaker costume, lay in a room adjoining the library, in a plain, unpolished walnut coffin, padded and lined with some white material, but without any ornamentation whatever. There were no flowers and no uttered demonstrations of grief, but a profound sadness seemed to pervade the house, and for half an hour no sound was heard in the densely thronged rooms save the muffled tread over the thick carpets of fresh arrivals and the whispered directions of a servant, pointing the way to the room where a last look at the dead might be had.

At half-past 12 o'clock Deborah Wharton arose from her seat in the parlor, and made a brief but touching address on the life and character of the deceased. She began by a quotation from the Bible : "This day a mighty prince has fallen in Israel." She then contrasted the condition in life of Lucretia Mott and that of a prince, and showed how she had accomplished more for humanity than the most powerful princes, but without noise and tumult and the shedding of blood.

Dr. Furness paid a beautiful tribute to the dead. He quoted the beatitudes from the the fifth chapter of Matthew, and applied them to her. "We are accustomed," he said, "to speak of the dead as having gone to their reward, but Lucretia Mott had her reward here, and she shall have it hereafter a hundred fold." Dr. Furness closed with an eloquent prayer that the example of the beautiful life ended upon earth might not be lost upon the living.

Phœbe Couzins paid a tender and loving tribute that touched every heart. Then loving hands took up the little coffin—it looked hardly larger than a child's—and bore it to the gravelled drive in front of the house. The route was down York road to Fairhill, the Friends' cemetery, at Germantown Avenue and Cambria Street, in this city, which was reached about three o'clock. Here several hundred people were already gathered to witness the interment. Fairhill is a little cemetery, about the size of a city square. It is mound-shaped, sloping up from all sides to the center. It is filled with trees and shrubbery, but does not contain a single monument, the graves being simply marked with little marble blocks, which do not rise more than six inches above the ground. In the highest part of the grounds was the open grave, by the side of the husband, James Mott, who was buried about twelve years ago. Above the grave spread the branches of an aspen tree, and near it is a weeping willow. While thousands stood about, the coffin was reverently, solemnly, and silently lowered. The grave was then filled up, the friends turned away, and slowly the cemetery was deserted.

Memorial services were held the same day and hour by Liberal Germans in Milwaukie, Wisconsin, and by the City Suffrage Association in New York. Dr. Clement Lozier, president of the society, presided. Charles G. Ames, of Philadelphia ; Frederick Hinckley, of Providence ; Robert Collyer, of New York, gave memorial sermons in their respective churches.

CHAPTER XIII.

MRS. STANTON'S REMINISCENCES.

PETERBORO, *December* 1, 1855.

ELIZABETH C. STANTON.—*My Dear Friend :*—The " Woman's Rights Movement " has deeply interested your generous heart, and you have ever been ready to serve it with your vigorous understanding. It is, therefore, at the risk of appearing somewhat unkind and uncivil, that I give my honest answer to your question. You would know why I have so little faith in this movement. I reply, that it is not in the proper hands ; and that the proper hands are not yet to be found. The present age, although in advance of any former age, is, nevertheless, very far from being sufficiently under the sway of reason to take up the cause of woman, and carry it forward to success. A much stronger and much more widely diffused common sense than has characterized any of the generations, must play its mightiest artillery upon the stupendous piles of nonsense, which tradition and chivalry and a misinterpreted and superstitious Christianity have reared in the way of this cause, ere woman can have the prospect of the recognition of her rights and of her confessed equality with man.

The object of the " Woman's Rights Movement " is nothing less than to recover the rights of woman—nothing less than to achieve her independence. She is now the dependent of man ; and, instead of rights, she has but privileges—the mere concessions (always revocable and always uncertain) of the other sex to her sex. I say nothing against this object. It is as proper as it is great ; and until it is realized, woman can not be half herself, nor can man be half himself. I rejoice in this object ; and my sorrow is, that they, who are intent upon it, are not capable of adjusting themselves to it—not high-souled enough to consent to those changes and sacrifices in themselves, in their positions and relations, essential to the attainment of this vital object.

What if a nation in the heart of Europe were to adopt, and uniformly adhere to, the practice of cutting off one of the hands of all their new-born children ? It would from this cause be reduced to poverty, to helpless dependence upon the charity of surrounding nations, and to just such a measure of privileges as they might see fit to allow it, in exchange for its forfeited rights. Very great, indeed, would be the folly of this strange nation. But a still greater folly would it be guilty of, should it, notwithstanding this voluntary mutilation, claim all the wealth, and all the rights, and all the respect, and all the independence which it enjoyed before it entered upon this systematic mutilation.

Now, this twofold folly of this one-hand nation illustrates the similar twofold folly of some women. Voluntarily wearing, in common with their sex, a dress which imprisons and cripples them, they, nevertheless, follow up this absurdity with the greater one of coveting and demanding a social position no less full of admitted rights, and a relation to the other sex no less full of independence, than such position and relation would naturally and necessarily have been, had they scorned a dress which leaves them less than half their personal power of self-subsistence and usefulness. I admit that the mass of women are not chargeable with this latter absurdity of cherishing aspirations and urging claims so wholly and so glaringly at war with this voluntary imprisonment and this self-degradation. They are content in their helplessness and poverty and destitution of rights. Nay, they are so deeply deluded as to believe that all this belongs to their natural and unavoidable lot. But the handful of women of whom I am here complaining —the woman's rights women—persevere just as blindly and stubbornly as do other women, in wearing a dress that both marks and makes their impotence, and yet, O amazing inconsistency! they are ashamed of their dependence, and remonstrate against its injustice. They claim that the fullest measure of rights and independence and dignity shall be accorded to them, and yet they refuse to place themselves in circumstances corresponding with their claim. They demand as much for themselves as is acknowledged to be due to men, and yet they refuse to pay the necessary, the never-to-be-avoided price of what they demand—the price which men have to pay for it.

I admit that the dress of woman is not the primal cause of her helplessness and degradation. That cause is to be found in the false doctrines and sentiments of which the dress is the outgrowth and symbol. On the other hand, however, these doctrines and sentiments would never have become the huge bundle they now are, and they would probably have all languished, and perhaps all expired, but for the dress. For, as in many other instances, so in this, and emphatically so in this, the cause is made more efficient by the reflex influence of the effect. Let woman give up the irrational modes of clothing her person, and these doctrines and sentiments would be deprived of their most vital aliment by being deprived of their most natural expression. In no other practical forms of folly to which they might betake themselves, could they operate so vigorously and be so invigorated by their operation.

Were woman to throw off the dress, which, in the eye of chivalry and gallantry, is so well adapted to womanly gracefulness and womanly helplessness, and to put on a dress that would leave her free to work her own way through the world, I see not but that chivalry and gallantry would nearly or quite die out. No longer would she present herself to man, now in the bewitching character of a plaything, a doll, an idol, and now in the degraded character of his servant. But he would confess her transmutation into his equal; and, therefore, all occasion for the display of chivalry and gallantry toward her on the one hand, and tyranny on the other, would have passed away. Only let woman attire her person fitly for the whole battle of life—that great and often rough battle, which she is as much bound to fight as man is, and the common sense expressed in the change will put to flight all the nonsensical fancies about her superiority to man, and all the nonsensical fancies about her inferiority to him. No more will then be heard of her being made of a finer material than man is made of; and, on the contrary, no more will then be heard of her being but the complement of man, and of its taking both a man and a woman (the woman, of course, but a small part of it) to make up a unit. No more will it then be said that there is sex in mind—an original sexual difference in intellect. What a pity that so many of our noblest women make this foolish admission! It is made by the great majority of the women who plead the cause of woman.

I am amazed that the intelligent women engaged in the "Woman's Rights Movement," see not the relation between their dress and the oppressive evils which they are striving to throw off. I am amazed that they do not see that their dress is indispensable to keep in countenance the policy and purposes out of which those evils grow. I hazard nothing in saying, that the relation between the dress and degradation of an American woman, is as vital as between the cramped foot and degradation of a Chinese woman; as vital as between the uses of the inmate of the harem and the apparel and training provided for her. Moreover, I hazard nothing in saying, that an American woman will never have made her most effectual, nor, indeed, any serviceable protest against the treatment of her sex in China, or by the lords of the harem, so long as she consents to have her own person clothed in ways so repugnant to reason and religion, and grateful only to a vitiated taste, be it in her own or in the other sex.

Women are holding their meetings; and with great ability do they urge their claim to the rights of property and suffrage. But, as in the case of the colored man, the great needed change is in himself, so, also, in the case of woman, the great needed change is in herself. Of what comparative avail would be her exercise of the right of suffrage, if she is still to remain the victim of her present false notions of herself and of her relations to the other sex?—false notions so emphatically represented and perpetuated by her dress? Moreover, to concede to her the rights of property would be to benefit her comparatively little, unless she shall resolve to break out from her clothes-prison, and to undertake right earnestly, as right earnestly as a man, to get property. Solomon says: "The destruction of the poor is their poverty." The adage that knowledge is power, is often repeated; and there are, indeed, many instances to verify it. Nevertheless, as a general proposition, it is a thousandfold more emphatically true that property is power. Knowledge helps to get property, but property is the power. That the slaves are a helpless prey, is chiefly because they are so poor and their masters so rich. The masses almost everywhere are well-nigh powerless, because almost everywhere they are poor. How long will they consent to be poor? Just so long as they shall consent to be robbed of their God-given right to the soil. That women are helpless is no wonder, so long as women are paupers.

As long as woman shall be silly enough to learn her lessons in the schools of gallantry and chivalry, so long will it be the height of her ambition to be a graceful and amiable burden upon the other sex. But as soon as she shall consent to place herself under the instructions of reason and common sense, and to discard, as wholly imaginary, those differences between the nature of man and the nature of woman, out of which have grown innumerable nonsenical doctrines and notions, and all sorts of namby pamby sentiments, so soon will she find that, to no greater extent than men are dependent on each other, are women to foster the idea of their dependence on men. Then, and not till then, will women learn that, to be useful and happy, and to accomplish the high purposes of their being, they must, no less emphatically than men, stand upon their own feet, and work with own hands, and bear the burdens of life with their own strength, and brave its storms with their own resoluteness.

The next " Woman's Rights Convention " will, I take it for granted, differ but little from its predecessors. It will abound in righteous demands and noble sentiments, but not in the evidence that they who enunciate these demands and sentiments are prepared to put themselves in harmony with what they conceive and demand. In a word, for the lack of such preparation and of the deep earnestness, which alone can prompt to such preparation, it will be, as has been every other Woman's Rights Convention, a failure. Could I see it made up of women whose dress would indicate their translation from cowardice to courage ; from slavery to freedom ; from the kingdom of fancy and fashion and foolery to the kingdom of reason and righteousness, then would I hope for the elevation of woman, aye, and of man too, as perhaps I have never yet hoped. What should be the parts and particulars of such dress, I am incapable of saying. Whilst the " Bloomer dress " is unspeakably better than the common dress, it nevertheless affords not half that freedom of the person which woman is entitled and bound to enjoy. I add, on this point, that however much the dresses of the sexes should resemble each other, decency and virtue and other considerations require that they should be obviously distinguishable from each other.

I am not unaware that such views as I have expressed in this letter will be regarded as serving to break down the characteristic delicacy of woman. I frankly admit that I would have it broken down ; and that I would have the artificial and conventional, the nonsensical and pernicious thing give place to the natural delicacy which would be common to both sexes. As the delicacy, which is made peculiar to one of the sexes, is unnatural, and, therefore, false, this, which would be common to both, would be natural, and, therefore, true. I would have no characteristic delicacy of woman, and no characteristic coarseness of man. On the contrary, believing man and woman to have the same nature, and to be therefore under obligation to have the same character, I would subject them to a common standard of morals and manners. The delicacy of man should be no less shrinking than that of woman, and the bravery of woman should be one with the bravery of man. Then would there be a public sentiment very unlike that which now requires the sexes to differ in character, and which, therefore, holds them amenable to different codes—codes that, in their partiality to man, allow him to commit high crimes, and that, in their cruelty to woman, make the bare suspicion of such crimes on her part the justification of her hopeless degradation and ruin.

They who advocate that radical change in her dress which common sense calls for, are infidels in the eyes of such as subscribe to this interpretation of the Bible. For if the Bible teaches that the Heaven-ordained condition of woman is so subordinate and her Heaven-ordained character so mean, then they are infidels who would have her cast aside a dress so becoming that character and condition, and have her put on a dress so entirely at war with her humble nature, as to indicate her conscious equality with man, and her purpose to assert, achieve, and maintain her independence. Alas, how misapprehended are the true objects and true uses of the Bible ! That blessed book is given to us, not so much that we may be taught by it what to do, as that we may be urged by its solemn and fearful commands and won by its melting entreaties, to do what we already know we should do. Such, indeed, is the greatest value of its recorded fact that Jesus

Christ died to save us from our sins. We already know that we should repent of our sins and put them away; and it is this fact which furnishes our strongest possible motive for doing so. But men run to the Bible professedly to be taught their duty in matters where their very instincts—where the laws, written in large, unmistakable, ineffaceable letters upon the very foundations of their being—teach them their duty. I say *professedly*, for generally it is only so. They run to the Bible, not to learn the truth, but to make the Bible the minister to folly and sin. They run from themselves to the Bible, because they can more easily succeed in twisting its records into the service of their guilty passions and guilty purposes than they can their inflexible convictions. They run to the Bible for a paramount authority that shall override and supplant these uncomfortable convictions. They run from the teachings of their nature and the remonstrances of their consciences to find something more palatable. Hence, we find the rum-drinker, and slaveholder, and polygamist, and other criminals going to the Bible. They go to it for the very purpose of justifying their known sins. But not only may we not go to the Bible to justify what we ourselves have already condemned, but we must not take to the judicature of that book, as an open question, any of the wrongs against which nature and common sense cry out—any of the wrongs which nature and common sense call on us to condemn.

So fraught with evil, and ruinous evil, is this practice, on the part of the Church as well as the world, of inquiring the judgment of the Bible in regard to sins, which the natural and universal conscience condemns, but which the inquirer means to persist in, if only he can get the Bible to testify against his conscience and in favor of his sins; so baleful, I say, is this practice, as to drive me to the conclusion that the Bible can not continue to be a blessing to mankind in spite of it. The practice, in its present wide and well-nigh universal extent, turns the heavenly volume into a curse. Owing to this practice, the Bible is, this day, a hindrance rather than a help to civilization.

But if woman is of the same nature and same dignity with man, and if as much and as varied labor is needed to supply her wants as to supply the wants of man, and if for her to be, as she so emphatically is, poor and destitute and dependent, is as fatal to her happiness and usefulness and to the fulfillment of the high purposes of her existence, as the like circumstances would be to the honor and welfare of man, why then put her in a dress which compels her to be a pauper—a pauper, whether in ribbons or rags? Why, I ask, put her in a dress suited only to those occasional and brief moods, in which man regards her as his darling, his idol, and his angel; or to that general state of his mind in which he looks upon her as his servant, and with feelings certainly much nearer contempt than adoration. Strive as you will to elevate woman, nevertheless the disabilities and degradation of this dress, together with that large group of false views of the uses of her being and of her relations to man, symbolized and perpetuated, as I have already said, by this dress, will make your striving vain.

Woman must first fight against herself—against personal and mental habits so deep-rooted and controlling, and so seemingly inseparable from herself, as to be mistaken for her very nature. And when she has succeeded there, an easy victory will follow. But where shall be the battle-ground for this indispensable self-conquest? She will laugh at my answer when I tell her, that her dress, aye, her dress, must be that battle-ground. What! no wider, no sublimer field than this to reap her glories in! My further answer is, that if she shall reap them anywhere, she must first reap them there. I add, that her triumph there will be her triumph everywhere; and that her failure there will be her failure everywhere.

Affectionately yours,   Gerrit Smith.

Mrs. Stanton's Reply.

Seneca Falls, *Dec.* 21, 1855.

My dear Cousin:—Your letter on the "Woman's Right Movement" I have thoroughly read and considered. I thank you, in the name of woman, for having said what you have on so many vital points. You have spoken well for a man whose convictions on this subject are the result of reason and observation; but they alone whose souls are fired through personal experience and suffering can set forth the height and depth, the source and center of the degradation of women; they alone can feel a steadfast faith in their own native energy and power to accomplish a final triumph over all adverse surroundings, a speedy and complete success. You say you have but little faith in this reform, because the changes we propose are so great, so radical, so comprehensive; whilst they who have commenced the work are so puny, feeble, and undeveloped. The mass of women are developed at least to the point of discontent, and that, in the dawn of this nation, was considered a most dangerous point in the British Parliament, and is now deemed equally so on a Southern plantation. In the human soul, the steps between discontent and action are few and short indeed. You, who suppose the mass of women contented, know but little of the silent indignation, the deep and settled disgust with which they contemplate our present social arrangements. You claim to believe that in every sense, thought, and feeling, man and woman are the same. Well, now, suppose yourself a woman. You are educated up to that point where one feels a deep interest in the welfare of her country, and in all the great questions of the day, in both Church and State; yet you have no voice in either. Little men, with little brains, may pour forth their little sentiments by the hour, in the forum and the sacred desk, but public sentiment and the religion of our day teach us that silence is most becoming in woman. So to solitude you betake yourself, and read for your consolation the thoughts of dead men; but from the Bible down to Mother Goose's Melodies, how much complacency, think you, you would feel in your womanhood? The philosopher, the poet, and the saint, all combine to make the name of woman synonymous with either fool or devil. Every passion of the human soul, which in manhood becomes so grand and glorious in its results, is fatal to womankind. Ambition makes a Lady Macbeth; love, an Ophelia; none but those brainless things, without will or passion, are ever permitted to come to a good end. What measure of content could you draw from the literature of the past?

Again, suppose yourself the wife of a confirmed drunkard. You behold your earthly possessions all passing away; your heart is made desolate; it has ceased to pulsate with either love, or hope, or joy. Your house is sold over your head, and with it every article of comfort and decency; your children gather round you, one by one, each new-comer clothed in rags and crowned with shame; is it with gladness you now welcome the embrace of that beastly husband, feel his fevered breath upon your cheek, and inhale the disgusting odor of his tobacco and rum? Would not your whole soul revolt from such an union? So do the forty thousand drunkards' wives now in this State. They, too, are all discontented, and but for the pressure of law and gospel would speedily sunder all these unholy ties. Yes, sir, there are women, pure and virtuous and noble as yourself, spending every day of all the years of their existence in the most intimate association with infamous men, kept so by that monstrous and unnatural artifice, baptized by the sacred name of marriage. I might take you through many, many phases of woman's life, into those sacred relations of which we speak not in our conventions, where woman feels her deepest wrongs, where in blank despair she drags out days, and weeks, and months, and years of silent agony. I might paint you pictures of real life so vivid as to force from you the agonized exclamation, How can women endure such things!

We who have spoken out, have declared our rights, political and civil; but the entire revolution about to dawn upon us by the acknowledgment of woman's social equality, has been seen and felt but by the few. The rights, to vote, to hold property, to speak in public, are all-important; but there are great social rights, before which all others sink into utter insignificance. The cause of woman is, as you admit, a broader and a deeper one than any with which you compare it; and this, to me, is the very reason why it must succeed. It is not a question of meats and drinks, of money and lands, but of human rights—the sacred right of a woman to her own person, to all her God-given powers of body and soul. Did it ever enter into the mind of man that woman too had an inalienable right to life, liberty, and the pursuit of her individual happiness? Did he ever take in the idea that to the mother of the race, and to her alone, belonged the right to say when a new being should be brought into the world? Has he, in the gratification of his blind passions, ever paused to think whether it was with joy and gladness that she gave up ten or twenty years of the heyday of her existence to all the cares and sufferings of excessive maternity? Our present laws, our religious teachings, our social customs on the whole question of marriage and divorce, are most degrading to woman; and so long as man continues to think and write, to speak and act, as if maternity was the one and sole object of a woman's existence—so long as children are conceived in weariness and disgust—you must not look for high-toned men and women capable of accomplishing any great and noble achievement. But when woman shall stand on an even pedestal with man—when they shall be bound together, not by withes of law and gospel, but in holy unity and love, then, and not till then, shall our efforts at minor reforms be crowned with complete success. Here, in my opinion, is the starting-point; here is the battle-ground where our independence must be fought and won. A true marriage relation has far more to do with the elevation of woman than the style and cut of her dress. Dress is a matter of taste, of fashion; it is changeable, transient, and may be doffed or donned at the will of the individual; but institutions, supported by laws, can be overturned but by revolution. We have no reason to hope that pantaloons would do more for us than they have done for man himself. The negro slave enjoys the most unlimited freedom in his attire, not surpassed even by the fashions of Eden in its palmiest days; yet in spite of his dress, and his manhood, too, he is a slave still. Was the old Roman in his toga less of a man than he now is in swallow-tail and tights? Did the flowing robes of Christ Himself render His life less grand and beautiful? In regard to dress, where you claim to be so radical, you are far from consistent.

Believing, as you do, in the identity of the sexes, that all the difference we see in tastes, in character, is entirely the result of education—that "man is woman and woman is man"—why keep up these distinctions in dress? Surely, whatever dress is convenient for one sex must be for the other also. Whatever is necessary for the perfect and full development of man's physical being, must be equally so for woman. I fully agree with you that woman is terribly cramped and crippled in her present style of dress. I have not one word to utter in its defense; but to me, it seems that if she would enjoy entire freedom, she should dress just like man. Why proclaim our sex on the house-tops, seeing that it is a badge of degradation, and deprives us of so many rights and privileges wherever we go? Disguised as a man, the distinguished French woman, "George Sand," has been able to see life in Paris, and has spoken in political meetings with great applause, as no woman could have done. In male attire, we could travel by land or sea; go through all the streets and lanes of our cities and towns by night and day, without a protector; get seven hundred dollars a year for teaching, instead of three, and ten dollars for making a coat, instead of two or three, as we now do. All this we could do without fear of insult, or the least sacrifice of decency or virtue. If nature has not made the sex so clearly defined as to be seen through any disguise, why should we make the difference so striking? Depend upon it, when men and women in their every-day life see and think less of sex and more of mind, we shall all lead far purer and higher lives.

Your letter, my noble cousin, must have been written in a most desponding mood, as all the great reforms of the day seem to you on the verge of failure. What are the experiences of days and months and years in the lifetime of a mighty nation? Can one man in his brief hour hope to see the beginning and end of any reform? When you compare the public sentiment and social customs of our day with what they were fifty years ago, how can you despair of the temperance cause? With a Maine Law and divorce for drunkenness, the rum-seller and drunkard must soon come to terms. Let woman's motto be, "No union with Drunkards," and she will soon bring this long and well-fought battle to a triumphant close.

Neither should you despair of the anti-slavery cause; with its martyrs, its runaway slaves, its legal decisions in almost every paper you take up, the topic of debate in our national councils, our political meetings, and our literature, it seems as if the nation were all alive on this question. True, four millions of slaves groan in their chains still, but every man in this nation has a higher idea of individual rights than he had twenty years ago.

As to the cause of woman, I see no signs of failure. We already have a property law, which in its legitimate effects must elevate the *femme covert* into a living, breathing woman, a wife into a property-holder, who can make contracts, buy and sell. In a few years we shall see how well it works. It needs but little forethought to perceive that in due time these large property-holders must be represented in the Government; and when the mass of women see that there is some hope of becoming voters and law-makers, they will take to their rights as naturally as the negro to his heels when he is sure of success. Their present seeming content is very much like Sambo's on the plantation. If you truly believe that man is woman, and woman is man; if you believe that all the burning indignation that fires your soul at the sight of injustice and oppression, if suffered in your own person, would nerve you to a life-long struggle for liberty and independence, then know that what you feel, I feel too, and what I feel the mass of women feel also. Judge by yourself, then, how long the women of this nation will consent to be deprived of their social, civil, and political rights; but talk not to us of failure. Talk not to us of chivalry, that died long ago. Where do you see it? No gallant knight presents himself at the bar of justice to pay the penalty of our crimes. We suffer in our own persons, on the gallows, and in prison walls. From Blackstone down to Kent, there is no display of gallantry in your written codes. In social life, true, a man in love will jump to pick up a glove or bouquet for a silly girl of sixteen, whilst at home he will permit his aged mother to carry pails of water and armfuls of wood, or his wife to lug a twenty-pound baby, hour after hour, without ever offering to relieve her. I have seen a great many men priding themselves on their good breeding—gentlemen, born and educated—who never manifest one iota of spontaneous gallantry toward the women of their own household.

Divines may preach thanksgiving sermons on the poetry of the arm-chair and the cradle; but when they lay down their newspapers, or leave their beds a cold night to attend to the wants of either, I shall begin to look for the golden age of chivalry once more. If a short dress is to make the men less gallant than they now are, I beg the women at our next convention to add at least two yards more to every skirt they wear. And you mock us with dependence, too. Do not the majority of women in every town support themselves, and very many their husbands, too? What father of a family, at the loss of his wife, has ever been able to meet his responsibilities as woman has done? When the mother dies the house is made desolate, the children are forsaken—scattered to the four winds of heaven—to the care of any one who chooses to take them. Go to those aged widows who have reared large families of children, unaided and alone, who have kept them all together under one roof, watched and nursed them in health and sickness through all their infant years, clothed and educated them, and made them all respectable men and women, ask them on whom they depended. They will tell you on their own hands, and on that never-dying, never-failing love, that a mother's heart alone can know. It is into hands like these—to those who have calmly met the terrible emergencies of life—who, without the inspiration of glory, or fame, or applause, through long years have faithfully and bravely performed their work, self-sustained and cheered, that we commit our cause. We need not wait for one more generation to pass away, to find a race of women worthy to assert the humanity of women, and that is all we claim to do.

Affectionately yours,   ELIZABETH CADY STANTON.

FRANCES D. GAGE'S REPLY TO GERRIT SMITH.

[From Frederick Douglass' paper].

FREDERICK DOUGLASS.—*Dear Sir:*—In your issue of Dec. 1st, I find a letter from Hon. Gerrit Smith to Elizabeth C. Stanton, in reference to the Woman's Rights Movement, showing cause, through labored columns, why it has proved a failure.

This article, though addressed to Mrs. Stanton, is an attack upon every one engaged in the cause. For he boldly asserts that the movement "is not in proper hands, and that the proper hands are not yet to be found." I will not deny the assertion, but must still claim the privilege of working in a movement that involves not only my own interest, but the interests of my sex, and through us the interests of a whole humanity. And though I may be but a John the Baptist, unworthy to unloose the latchet of the shoes of those who are to come in *short skirts* to redeem the world, I still prefer that humble position to being Peter to deny my Master, or a Gerrit Smith to assert that truth *can* fail.

I do not propose to enter into a full criticism of Mr. Smith's long letter. He has made the whole battle-ground of the Woman's Rights Movement her dress. Nothing brighter, nothing nobler than a few inches of calico or brocade added to or taken from her skirts, is to decide this great and glorious question—to give her freedom or to continue her a slave. This argument, had it come from one of less influence than Gerrit Smith, would have been simply ridiculous. But coming from *him*, the almost oracle of a large portion of our reformers, it becomes worthy of an answer from every earnest woman in our cause. I will not say one word in defense of our present mode of dress. Not I; but bad as it is, and cumbersome and annoying, I still feel that we can wear it, and yet be lovers of liberty, speaking out our deep feeling, portraying our accumulated wrongs, saving ourselves for a time yet from that antagonism which we must inevitably meet when we don the semi-male attire. We *must own ourselves under the law first*, own our bodies, our earnings, our genius, and our consciences; then we will turn to the lesser matter of what shall be the garniture of the body. Was the old Roman less a man in his cumbrous toga, than Washington in his tights? Was Christ less a Christ in His vesture, woven without a seam, than He would have been in the suit of a Broadway dandy?

"Moreover, to concede to her rights of property, would be to benefit her comparatively little, unless she shall resolve to break out of her clothes-prison, and to undertake right earnestly, as earnestly as a man, to get property." So says Gerrit Smith. And he imputes the want of earnestness to her clothes. It is a new doctrine that high and holy purposes go from without inward, that the garments of men or women govern and control their aspirations. But do not women *now* work right earnestly? Do not the German women and our market women labor right earnestly? Do not the wives of our farmers and mechanics toil? Is not the work of the *mothers* in our land as important as that of the father? "Labor is the foundation of wealth." The reason that our women are "paupers," is not that they do not labor "right earnestly," but that the law gives their earnings into the hands of manhood. Mr. Smith says, "That women are helpless, is no wonder, so long as they are paupers"; he might add, no wonder that the slaves of the cotton plantation are helpless, so long as they are paupers. What reduces both the woman and the slave to this condition? The law which gives the husband and the master entire control of the person and earnings of each; the law that robs each of the rights and liberties that every "free white male citizen" takes to himself as God-given. Truth falling from the lips of a Lucretia Mott in long skirts is none the less truth, than if uttered by a Lucy Stone in short dress, or a Helen Maria Weber in pants and swallow-tail coat. And I can not yet think so meanly of manly justice, as to believe it will yield simply to a change of garments. Let us assert our right to be free. Let us get out of our prison-house of law. Let us own ourselves, our earnings, our genius; let us have power to control as well as to earn and to own; then will each woman adjust her dress to her relations in life.

Mr. Smith speaks of reforms as failures; what can he mean? "The Temperance Reform still drags." I have been in New York thirty-seven days; have given thirty-three lectures; have been at taverns, hotels, private houses, and depots; rode in stages, country wagons, omnibuses, carriages, and railroad cars; met the masses of people daily, and yet have not seen one drunken man, scarce an evidence that there was such a thing as intemperance in the Empire State. If the whole body has been diseased from childhood and a cure be attempted, shall we cry out against the physician that his effort is a failure, because the malady does not wholly disappear at once? Oh, no! let us rather cheer than discourage, while we see symptoms of amendment, hoping and trusting that each day will give renewed strength for the morrow, till the cure shall be made perfect. The accumulated ills of centuries can not be removed in a day or a year. Shall we talk of the Anti-Slavery Cause as a "failure," while our whole great nation is shaking as if an Etna were boiling below? When did the North ever stand, as now, defiant of slavery? Anti-slavery may be said to be written upon the "chariots and the bells of the horses." Our National Congress is nothing more or less than a great Anti-slavery Convention. Not a bill, no matter how small or how great its importance, but hinges upon the question of slavery. The Anti-Slavery Cause is no failure; RIGHT CAN NOT FAIL.

"The next Woman's Rights Convention will be, as has every other Woman's Rights

Convention, a failure, notwithstanding it will abound in righteous demands and noble sentiments." So thinks Mr. Smith. Has any Woman's Rights Convention been a failure? No movement so radical, striking so boldly at the foundation of all social and political order, has ever come before the people, or ever so rapidly and widely diffused its doctrine. The reports of our conventions have traveled wherever newspapers are read, causing discussion for and against, and these discussions have elicited truth, and aroused public thought to the evils growing out of woman's position. New trades and callings are opening to us ; in every town and village may be found advocates for the equality of privilege under the law, for every thinking, reasoning human soul. Shall we talk of failure, because forty, twenty, or seven years have not perfected all things? When intemperance shall have passed away, and the four million chattel slaves shall sing songs of freedom ; when woman shall be recognized as man's equal, socially, legally, and politically, there will yet be reforms and reformers, and men who will despair and look upon one branch of the reform as the great *battle-ground*, and talk of the failure of the eternal law of progress. Still there will be stout hearts and willing hands to work on, honestly believing that truth and right are sustained by no single point, and their watchword will be "Onward!" We can not fail, for our cause is just.

ROCHESTER, *Dec.* 24, 1855.   FRANCES D. GAGE.

The names of those who wore the Bloomer costume at that early day are : Elizabeth Smith Miller, Elizabeth Cady Stanton, Amelia Bloomer, Sarah and Angelina Grimké, Mrs. William Burleigh, Charlotte Beebe Wilbour, Lucy Stone, Susan B. Anthony, Helen Jarvis, Lydia Sayre Hasbrook, Amelia Williard, Celia Burleigh, Harriet N. Austin, Lydia Jenkins, and many patients at sanitariums, many farmers' wives, and many young ladies for skating and gymnastic exercises.

Looking back to this experiment, we are not surprised at the hostility of men in general to the dress, as it made it very uncomfortable for them to go anywhere with those who wore it. People would stare ; some men and women make rude remarks ; boys follow in crowds, or shout from behind fences, so that the gentleman in attendance felt it his duty to resent the insult by showing fight, unless he had sufficient self-control to pursue the even tenor of his way without taking the slightest notice of the commotion his companion was creating. No man went through the ordeal with the coolness and dogged determination of Charles Dudley Miller, escorting his wife and cousin on long journeyings, at fashionable resorts, in New York and Washington, to the vexation of all his gentleman friends and acquaintances.

AMELIA BLOOMER COMMENTS ON JANE G. SWISSHELM.

To the Editor of the Nonpareil :

Jane Grey Swisshelm thinks it is dare-devil independence that is ruining the women of this country.—*Nonpareil.*

And what woman of them all has shown so much "dare-devil independence" as Jane G. Swisshelm? One of the first women to wield the pen-editorial thirty years ago, she was so independent and fearless as to excite the wonder of her readers. The first woman admitted to the reporters' gallery in the Capitol of the nation, she astonished and shocked the country by her attacks upon Daniel Webster and other prominent senators at that day, and was expelled from the gallery for her "dare-devil independence." While publishing a paper at St. Cloud, she was so outspoken and offensive in her personalities, that her press and type were destroyed by indignant politicians. After the war she obtained an office in one of the departments at Washington, and started a paper called the *Reconstructionist* in that city. For her "dare-devil independence" as a writer in attacking President Johnson and charging that he had part in the assassination of President Lincoln, she was relieved of her office and her press destroyed.

And so in whatever she has part ; to whatever she sets her hand, she ever displays a reckless independence that is truly a marvel to those who watch her uncertain course. She fearlessly attacks both friend and foe, if they go contrary to her views of right; and both people and measures that to-day have her countenance and approval, are liable to-morrow to receive an unmerciful lashing from her pen. No woman has set an example of more " dare-devil independence " before "the women of this country " than Jane G. Swisshelm, and if it is proving their ruin she has much to answer for. But we are not prepared to believe her assertion, and we can not think her a ruined woman, notwithstanding her many years of " dare-devil independence." The writer has known her long, has engaged in many a pen-tilt with her, but has never met her personally. She regards her as an able, outspoken defender of the wronged and oppressed, a fearless advocate of the right as she sees it, and an " independent dare-devil " writer on whatever subject she deems worthy of her pen.

COUNCIL BLUFFS, *July* 30, 1880. AMELIA BLOOMER.

CHAPTER XIV.

NEW YORK.

NEW YORK STATE TEMPERANCE CONVENTION, ROCHESTER, APRIL 20, 21, 1852.

LETTER FROM FRANCES DANA GAGE.

MCCONNELLSVILLE, O., *April* 5, 1852.

MY DEAR MISS ANTHONY :—Yours of March 22d, asking of me words of counsel and encouragement for the friends of temperance, who are to meet at Rochester on the 20th inst., is before me. Need I tell you how earnestly my heart responds to that request, and with what joy I hail every demonstration on the part of woman that evidences an awakening energy in her mind, to the great duties and responsibilities of her being !

If we examine the statistics of crime in the United States, we shall find that a very large proportion of the criminals of our land are the victims of intemperance. The records of poverty, shame, and degradation furnish the same evidence against the traffic and use of ardent spirits. Examine those same statistics, and another great truth stares us in the face—that nine-tenths of all the manufacturers of ardent spirits, of all the drinkers of ardent spirits, and of all the criminals made by ardent spirits, are men. But we find, too, in our search, a fact equally interesting to us, that the greatest sufferers from all this crime and shame and wrong, are women. Is it not meet, then, that women should lay aside the dependent inactivity which has hitherto held them powerless, and give their strength to the cause of reform which is now agitating the minds of the people?

What is woman ? The answer is returned to me in tones that shake my very soul. She is the mother of mankind ! The living providence, under God, who gives to every human being its mental, moral, and physical organism—who stamps upon every human heart her seal for good or for evil ! Who then, but she, should cry aloud, and spare not, when the children she has borne—forgetting their allegiance to her and their duty to themselves, have assumed the power to rule over her, shutting her out from their counsels, and surrounding her, without her own consent, with circumstances which lead to misery and death ; and, in their pride and strength, trampling upon justice, love, and mercy, withering her heart by violence and oppression, and yet compelling her, in her dependence as a wife, to perpetuate in her offspring their own depraved appetites and disorganized faculties ?

It will not be denied that woman in all past ages has been made, by both law and custom, the inferior of her own children. Man has assumed to himself the power of being "lord of creation " ; yet what has he done for his kind ? Look at the present state of society and receive your answer ! He has filled the world with madness, with oppression and wrong ; he has allowed snares to be laid at every turn, to entangle the feet of our children, and lead them away into vice and crime. He has legalized the causes which fill the jails, the penitentiaries, the houses of correction, the poorhouses, and asylums with the blood of our hearts, even our children, and our children's children. There is not a drunkard in the land, not a criminal that has been made by strong drink, but is the child of a woman. Yet not one woman's vote has ever been given to legalize the sale of ardent spirits, that have maddened the brain of her child. No woman's vote ever sanctioned the rum-seller's bar, at which her husband has bartered away his manhood, and made himself more vile than the brutes that perish.

Shall I be answered that woman's home influence must keep her children and her husband in the paths of virtue and honor? What! disfranchised woman—made by her law-maker an appendage to himself, her intellect shackled, her labor underrated, her physical power dwarfed and enfeebled by custom—is she expected to do this mighty thing? I hear again an answer—"Woman is responsible for the moral atmosphere that surrounds her." Is this indeed so? Men have taken from her every power to protect herself, even the dignity and respect which the right of suffrage confers upon the lowest man in the community, and which makes his opinion worth its price among men, is denied her. Men are in the daily habit of indulging in immoralities and vices, while they enjoin it upon woman—"poor, frail, weak woman," as they call us—to destroy the influence they have created. They place the temptation before the child, then sternly demand of its suffering mother her vigilance and care to control the appetite, which he has, it may be, inherited from his fathers, back from the third and fourth generation. Perchance, even through her own breast, he has sucked the poison that is corrupting all the streams of his young life. She may have grappled with the tempter, and come off conqueror; but can she hold him, the drunkard's child—the drunkard's grandchild—with the twofold curse upon his brow, while men place this direful temptation ever within his reach, glaring out upon him in beautiful enticement at every corner of the street, and at every turn of his daily and nightly walks, and add their influence and example to draw him away from the counsels of a mother's love, and the endearments of home? Then, when, under the influence of men, he outrages society, and in his maniac madness violates the law of the land, and becomes a felon, wasting away his days in the gloomy prison, or expiating his crimes upon the gallows, they forget what they have done, and, turning to the poor, crushed, and bleeding heart, which they have pierced with a thousand sorrows, cry out, "You, O mother of that guilty man, have not done your duty, and society holds you responsible for all his suffering and for all his crimes. O God! is this not adding insult to injury? How can the weak control the strong? How can the servant, bound hand and foot by the master, do the bidding of the tyrant? But all men are not weak—all men are not oppressive—all men are not unjust. There is a strong force, ever in the field of battle, struggling for truth and right with earnest heart and firm resolve. Let us arouse, O my sisters, and add our strength to theirs. The time is coming, aye, now is, when we must shake off our dependence and inactivity, and live more true to ourselves; when we must refuse to live the wives of drunkards, perpetuating, as mothers, their vices and crimes, to pollute society.

Let us unite with the good and true among men, that our efforts may overcome the legions who have hitherto conquered on the side of wrong, and raise high the standard of love and humanity, where falsehood and hate have ruled rampant. Let every woman, everywhere, speak out her bold, free thought on the subject of temperance; and while we plead with our rulers to deliver our husbands, fathers, sons, and brothers from the temptations to sin, let us demand with earnestness the right hereafter to protect ourselves; that we may redeem ourselves from the unjust law that now taxes every woman, without her own consent, according to her property or ability to labor, to pay her proportion for the support of vice and crime—that hereafter, when such great moral questions are under public discussion, and we, as one-half of the people, send up our petitions to our law-makers for a redress of wrongs, or an abatement of evils, our voice of pleading shall not be spurned by the heartless sneer, "They are only women, and the voice of a woman can not affect us at the polls, or disturb the course of our political parties. What care we for her progress or her wrongs?" Thus have we too often been answered, and shall be again, if we do not prove worthy of the chaplet of freedom, by winning it for ourselves. Let us then unite heart and hand in this great temperance reform—laying aside all local animosities, all sectional prejudices and sectarian jealousies—and, as it were, with one voice and one spirit, take hold of the work before us, resolved, if we fail to-day, to rise with renewed energy to-morrow, and "Never give up!" be our motto, till, without bloodshed, without hate, or uncharitableness, we gain the victory over those who cater to the most uncontrollable and destructive passion that has ever cursed humanity—the passion for strong drink—and then, and not till then, will we fold our arms and take our rest, amid the hallelujahs of the redeemed.

Yours, in the cause of humanity, FRANCES D. GAGE.

S. B. ANTHONY, *Chairman of Committee.*

LETTER FROM MRS. C. I. H. NICHOLS.

BRATTLEBORO, Vt., *April* 13, 1852.

SISTERS AND FRIENDS OF TEMPERANCE :—In resorting to the pen as a medium of communication with your Convention, I feel, most sensibly, its inferiority to a *vis-à-vis* talk—it tells so little, and that so meagerly ! But, remembering that a single just thought or vital truth, communicated to intelligent minds and willing hearts, is an investment sure of increase, I will bless God for the pen, and ask of Him to make it a tongue for humanity.

The limits of a written communication will forbid me to say much, and I would address myself to a single point broached in your Albany Convention, and a point that seems to me of the first importance ; because a mistake in morals, a wrong perpetrated in the home relations, is the greatest of all wrongs to humanity. And marred, indeed, would be your triumph, if, in preventing the repeal of one unjust statute, you sanction the enactment of another. So true it is that one injustice becomes the source of another, I fear to contemplate the enactment of a trifling encroachment even upon inalienable rights or divinely sanctioned pursuits.

In addressing myself to the position that "drunkenness be made a good and sufficient cause for divorce," I am secured from any fear that you will regard me as warring with abstractions, since such a bill has found its way into your Legislature, proving that the popular sympathy for suffering women and children is already concentrating on divorce as the remedy. I have hesitated about addressing you on this subject, lest I might render myself obnoxious to the charge of diverting the objects of your meeting, to an occasion for the discussion of forbidden topics. But an irresistible conviction, that since the subject is already launched upon your reform, it is important that a just view of its bearings should be presented, impels me to throw myself upon your sympathy, trusting in the divine power of truth to commend both my motives and my positions to your judgments and your hearts.

And first, let me say, I would not be understood as opposed to emancipating the wretched victims of irremediable abuse. And if there be a benevolence, under the warm heaven of Almighty Love, it is the protecting of helplessness and innocence from the sufferings that result, inevitably, from the rum traffic. But while I fully agree with Mrs. Stanton, that no pure-hearted and understanding woman can innocently become the mother of a drunkard's offspring—while I rely upon the general diffusion of physiological truths to create a sentiment abhorrent to the idea of raising a posterity, the breath of whose life shall be derived from the animalized and morally tainted vitality of the drunkard—I differ with her in the remedy proposed.

If drunkenness were irremediable, and beyond the reach of legislation, then would I accept her remedy as the final resort. But regarding divorce as, at best, only affording a choice of evils, and drunkenness as equally with..i the power of legislation, I propose that drunkenness be legislated out of existence, and thus the necessity for divorce, which it creates, be avoided.

Let a thoroughly prohibitive law destroy the traffic, and the drunkard will be found "clothed " again and "in his right mind." It will come to this glorious consummation at last ; and, though years may intervene, it becomes us to act with reference to the discerned future, and beware that transient evils do not betray us into planting life-long regrets. Allow me to illustrate my idea by narrating incidents of a case in point, and which is inwoven with the recollections and tenderest sympathies of my whole life.

The young and lovely mother of five little ones procured a divorce from her husband, whose incompetency and unkindness was the result solely of intemperance, and that intemperance the consequence of his strong social bias and inability to resist the temptations of a period, when every man put the bottle to his neighbor's mouth as proof of his generosity, his friendship, and his good-breeding. His father, on whom the family were dependent for support, urged it upon the wife, as a duty to her children and due to her own self-respect, to procure a divorce, when, at last, the miserable husband had been sent to prison for a forgery, involving a small sum, and which he had thought to meet—before the note came to maturity—undetected.

She submitted, and, before the period of his imprisonment expired, married again, by the advice and persuasion of her kind father-in-law, to a wealthy and excellent man, who offered a father's care and home to her children, in proof of his affection for herself. But the heart never yielded its first love ; and, when more than twenty years had passed, she confessed to a friend "that, should he reform at the eleventh hour, she must be the most wretched of women." He did reform ! and for many years has exhibited those cheerful graces of the Christian, which, added to his naturally amiable disposition and unselfish deportment, make his three-score and tenth year seem rather the morning than the evening of a life, stretching far away into the glories of eternity.

And now, tell me, friends, if the picture of that youthful affection, strengthened and intensified in the hearts of both by long years of unavailing regret, does not awaken in you a conviction of some better way for protecting helpless women and children from the evils of drunkenness ? Oh, say, can you calmly contemplate the hundreds and thousands of hearts which would throb with repressed anguish, when the wretchedness which drove them to divorce shall have vanished with the doomed traffic, and reformed men, by the strong arm of law, reclaim their children from the weeping Rachels of the land ?

But think not, friends, that I am unmindful of the misery of years, or months even, when I plead that divorce shall not be made the necessity of hunted and betrayed affections, the factitious barrier against abuse and starvation. I present to your consideration a remedy equally effective, and far more grateful to the delicate sensibilities and hopeful affection of the woman and the wife—a remedy which possesses the merit of a preventive power, and the collateral security of a reclaiming influence.

The advantage proposed to be secured to the wife of the drunkard, by divorce, is the release from his control of her property and person. Secure to the innocent and suffering wife the guardianship of her children, and the control of her own earnings—in short, make her a free, instead of a bond-woman—and you secure to the family of the drunkard all the alleviation in the power of legislation, and without compelling the wife, from pecuniary necessity or self-immolating regard for her children, to sever her conjugal relation, and quench the hope of a future of rational companionship.

The pauperism and extreme degradation of the drunkard's family is mainly chargeable to the laws, which wreck the energies, by merging the means of the wife and mother in the will of the irresponsible husband and father.

With these views—gathered from facts and heart-broken confidences open to few—I appeal to you in the name of the most sacred affections—I protest, in behalf of humanity, against compelling the unfortunate of my dependent sex to choose between their present bondage of means and divorce.

To the Christian, who shrinks from divorce, as separating what God hath joined, I appeal to carry out the principle, preserving everywhere what God hath joined. Hath He not joined mother and child in body and spirit ? Sever them not. Hath He not joined in each human being necessities and ability to supply them ? But, alas ! by man's carpentry, the ability of woman to supply her wants is pressed into the service of man's carnal and wicked appetites, to supply him with liquid fire, while herself and babes become miserable paupers in body and in mind !

I leave the subject here, praying that God may bless your deliberations, and guide you into all truth.   Yours, for the oppressed, ever,   C. I. H. NICHOLS.

SYRACUSE CONVENTION, SEPT. 8, 9, 10, 1852.

ELIZABETH CADY STANTON'S LETTER.

SENECA FALLS, *Sept.* 6.

MY DEAR FRIENDS :—As I can not be present with you, I wish to suggest three points for your sincere and earnest consideration.

1. Should not all women living in States where woman has the right to hold property refuse to pay taxes, so long as she is unrepresented in the government of that State?

Such a movement, if simultaneous, would no doubt produce a great deal of confusion, litigation, and suffering on the part of woman; but shall we fear to suffer for the maintenance of the same glorious principle for which our forefathers fought, bled, and died? Shall we deny the faith of the old Revolutionary heroes, and purchase for ourselves a false power and ignoble ease, by declaring in action that taxation without representation is just? Ah, no! like the English Dissenters and high-souled Quakers of our own land, let us suffer our property to be seized and sold, but let us never pay another tax until our existence as citizens, our civil and political rights be fully recognized. . . . . The poor, crushed slave, but yesterday toiling on the rice plantation in Georgia, a beast, a chattel, a thing, is to-day, in the Empire State (if he own a bit of land and a shed to cover him), a person, and may enjoy the proud honor of paying into the hand of the complaisant tax-gatherer the sum of seventy-five cents. Even so with the white woman —the satellite of the dinner-pot, the presiding genius of the wash-tub, the seamstress, the teacher, the gay butterfly of fashion, the *feme covert* of the law, man takes no note of her through all these changing scenes. But, lo! to-day, by the fruit of her industry, she becomes the owner of a house and lot, and now her existence is remembered and recognized, and she too may have the privilege of contributing to the support of this mighty Republic, for the "white male citizen claims of her one dollar and seventy-five cents a year, because, under the glorious institutions of this free and happy land, she has been able, at the age of fifty years, to possess herself of a property worth the enormous sum of three hundred dollars. It is natural to suppose she will answer this demand on her joyously and promptly, for she must, in view of all her rights and privileges so long enjoyed, consider it a great favor to be permitted to contribute thus largely to the governmental treasury.

One thing is certain, this course will necessarily involve a good deal of litigation, and we shall need lawyers of our own sex whose intellects, sharpened by their interests, shall be quick to discover the loopholes of retreat. Laws are capable of many and various constructions; we find among men that as they have new wants, that as they develop into more enlarged views of justice, the laws are susceptible of more generous interpretation, or changed altogether; that is, all laws touching their own interests; for while man has abolished hanging for theft, imprisonment for debt, and secured universal suffrage for himself, a married woman, in most of the States in the Union, remains a nonentity in law—can own nothing; can be whipped and locked up by her lord; can be worked without wages, be robbed of her inheritance, stripped of her children, and left alone and penniless; and all this, they say, according to law. Now, it is quite time that we have these laws revised by our own sex, for man does not yet feel that what is unjust for himself, is also unjust for woman. Yes, we must have our own lawyers, as well as our physicians and priests. Some of our women should go at once into this profession, and see if there is no way by which we may shuffle off our shackles and assume our civil and political rights. We can not accept man's interpretation of the law.

2. Do not sound philosophy and long experience teach us that man and woman should be educated together? This isolation of the sexes in all departments, in the business and pleasure of life, is an evil greatly to be deplored. We see its bad effects on all sides. Look at our National Councils. Would men, as statesmen, ever have enacted such scenes as the Capitol of our country has witnessed, had the feminine element been fairly represented in their midst?. Are all the duties of husband and father to be made subservient to those of statesman and politician? How many of these husbands return to their homes as happy and contented, as pure and loving, as when they left? Not one in ten. . . . . Experience has taught us that man has discovered the most profitable branches of industry, and we demand a place by his side. Inasmuch, therefore, as we have the same objects in life, namely, the full development of all our powers, and should, to some extent, have the same employments, we need precisely the same education; and we therefore claim that the best colleges of our country be open to us. . . . . This point, the education of boys and girls together, is a question of the day; it was prominent at the late Educational Convention in Newark, and it is fitting that in our Convention it

should be fully discussed. My ground is, that the boy and the girl, the man and the woman, should be always together in the business and pleasures of life, sharing alike its joys and sorrows, its distinction and fame ; nor will they ever be harmoniously developed until they are educated together, physically, intellectually, and morally.

I hope, therefore, that in the proposed People's College, some place will be provided where women can be educated side by side with man. There is no better test of the spirituality of a man, than is found in his idea of the true woman. Men having separated themselves from women in the business of life, and thus made their natures coarse by contact with their own sex exclusively, now demand separate pleasures too ; and in lieu of the cheerful family circle, its books, games, music, and pleasant conversation, they congregate in clubs to discuss politics, gamble, drink, etc., in those costly, splendid establishments, got up for such as can not find sufficient excitement in their own parlors or studios. It seems never to enter the heads of these fashionable husbands, that the hours drag as heavily with their fashionable wives, as they sit alone, night after night, in their solitary elegance, wholly given up to their own cheerless reflections ; for what subjects of thought have they ? Gossip and fashion will do for talk, but not for thought. Their theology is too gloomy and shadowy to afford them much pleasure in contemplation ; their religion is a thing of form and not of life, so it brings them no joy or satisfaction. As to the reforms of the day, they are too genteel to feel much interest in them. There is no class more pitiable than the unoccupied woman of fashion thrown wholly upon herself. . . . . Does not the abuse of the religious element in woman demand our earnest attention and investigation ?

Priestcraft did not end with the beginning of the reign of Protestantism. Woman has always been the greatest dupe, because the sentiments act blindly, and they alone have been educated in her. Her veneration, not guided by an enlightened intellect, leads her as readily to the worship of saints, pictures, holy days, and inspired men and books, as of the living God and the everlasting principles of Justice, Mercy, and Truth.

There is the Education Society, in which women who can barely read and write and speak their own language correctly, form sewing societies, and beg funds to educate a class of lazy, inefficient young men for the ministry, who, starting in life on the false principle that it is a blessing to escape physical labor, begin at once to live on their piety. What is the result ? Why, after going through college, theological seminaries, and a brief struggle at fitting up skeleton sermons, got up by older heads for the benefit of beginners, and after preaching them for a season to those who hunger and thirst for light and truth, they sink down into utter insignificance, too inefficient to keep a place, and too lazy to earn the salt to their porridge, whilst the women work on to educate more for the same destiny. Look at the long line of benevolent societies, all filled with these male agents, living, like so many leeches, on the religious element in our natures, most of them from the ranks of the clergy, who, unable to build up or keep a church, have taken refuge in some of these theological asylums for the intellectually maimed, halt, and blind of this profession.

Woman really thinks she is doing God service when she casts her mite into their treasury, when in fact not one-tenth of all the funds raised ever reach the ultimate object Among the clergy we find our most violent enemies—those most opposed to any change in woman's position ; yet no sooner does one of these find himself out of place and pocket, than, if all the places in the various benevolent societies chance to be occupied, he takes a kind of philanthropic survey of the whole habitable globe, and forthwith forms a Female Benevolent Society for the conversion of the Jews, perhaps, or for sending the Gospel to the Feejee Islands, and he is, in himself, the law for one and the gospel for the other. Now, the question is, not whether the Jews are converted, or whether the Gospel ever reaches the islands, but, Does the agent flourish ? Is his post profitable ? And does woman beg and stitch faithfully for his support and for the promotion of his *glorious mission?*

Now, I ask women with all seriousness, considering that we have little to give, had we not better bestow our own charities with our own hands? And instead of sending our benevolent outgushings in steamers to parts unknown, had we not better let them flow in streams whose length and breadth we can survey at pleasure, knowing their source and where they empty themselves ? Instead of any further efforts in behalf of a pin-cushion ministry, I conjure my countrywomen to devote themselves from this hour to the education, elevation, and enfranchisement of their own sex. If the same amount of devotion and self-sacrifice could be given in this direction now poured out on the churches, another generation would give us a nobler type of womanhood than any yet molded by any Bishop, Priest, or Pope.

Woman in her present ignorance is made to rest in the most distorted views of God and the Bible and the laws of her being; and like the poor slave "Uncle Tom," her religion, instead of making her noble and free, and impelling her to flee from all gross surroundings, by the false lessons of her spiritual teachers, by the wrong application of great principles of right and justice, has made her bondage but more certain and lasting, her degradation more helpless and complete.

Elizabeth Cady Stanton.

To Mrs. Paulina W. Davis: Gloucester, Mass., *August* 24, 1852.

Dear Madam :— . . . . I have never questioned what I understand to be the central principle of the reform in which you are engaged. I believe that every mature soul is responsible directly to God, not only for its faith and opinions, but for the details of its life in the world. In every crisis of duty there can be consultation, at last, only between one spirit and its Creator. The assertion that woman is responsible to man for her belief or conduct, in any other sense than man is responsible to woman, I reject, not as a believer in any theory of "Woman's Rights," but as a believer in that religion which knows neither male nor female, in its imperative demand upon the individual conscience.

This being true, I know not by what logic the obligation of woman to form her own ideal of life, and pursue the career which her reason and conscience dictate, can be denied. The sphere of activity in which any person will shine, is always an open question until answered by experience. I may admire the wisdom of the mind which has discovered that half the people in the world are incompetent to act beyond one circle of duty; but until the fact has been established by the universal failure of your sex, everywhere outside that fatal line, I must admire rather than believe. Every real position in society is achieved by conquest. I must convince my people that I am a true minister of the Gospel, before I can claim their respect and support. And when a woman, in the possession of the powers and opportunities given her by God, tells me she must trade, or instruct the young, or heal the sick, or paint, or sing, or act upon the stage, or call sinners to repentance, I *can* say but one thing—just what I must say to the man who affirms the same —" My friend, show your *ability* to serve society in this way, and all creation can not deprive you of the right. If you *can do* this to which you aspire—can do it well, then you and everybody will be the gainers. And whoever says you have forfeited any essential grace or virtue of womanhood by your act, betrays, by the accusation, an utter incompetency to judge upon questions of human responsibility and obligation."

. . . . I therefore believe the method of this reform is that declared by God when He said to Adam : "In the sweat of thy face shalt thou eat bread." There is no "royal road" to womanhood, as there is certainly none to manhood. *You* must achieve what you desire. . . . . Woman must do much before man can help her. I suppose the sexes are about equally culpable ; and I make no peculiar charge, when I say that until I can see more individual consecration, more clearness of perception and firmness of conduct in regions outside of the walls of the household among the mass of women, than now, I shall not cherish extravagant hopes of the great immediate success of your noble object.

. . . . Your movement is a part of the great onward march of society, and must be exposed to the reverses from outward hostility and inward faithlessness, that have always hindered the progress of the race. . . . . This reform will be a sword of division, and you will not be surprised when those who have entered it from any motive less exalted than consecration to duty, fall away in weariness and disgust. Yet all the more honorable will it be to those who are content to remain, and abide the fatal conditions of sincere human effort. You are not very near your journey's end; but you are doing much for your sex, in a mode which will "tell" inevitably upon society. I often encounter a new spirit of self-respect and honorable independence ; a new hope, and works corresponding to it, among young women, which I can trace back to these Conventions. I believe cultivated men in all professions are becoming ashamed to treat your arguments with open ridicule or quiet contempt, and occupy a position, at least, of fair-minded neutrality, to a greater degree than ever before, while the popular sympathies are every year more enlisted in your success. . . . . With great respect, I remain your friend and fellow-laborer in the cause of truth,

A. D. MAYO.

Samuel J. May read the following extract from a letter from Wm. Lloyd Garrison, of Boston :

"Much, very much, do I regret that I can not be at the Woman's Rights Convention which is to assemble to-morrow in Syracuse ; but circumstances prevent. I shall be there in spirit, from its organization to its dissolution. It has as noble an object in view, aye, and as Christian a one, too, as was ever advocated beneath the sun. Heaven bless all its proceedings.

"Yours for all Human Rights,   WM. LLOYD GARRISON.

"Rev. S. J. MAY."

COMMENTS OF THE PRESS AFTER THE SYRACUSE CONVENTION.

The Syracuse Standard, Sept. 10*th* (a liberal Democratic paper).

Great interest was manifested in the proceedings yesterday, and the hall was densely crowded during the day and evening. Much difficulty was found in getting out of the Convention after the adjournment. Each lady covered at least three steps of the stairway with her dress, and little groups of ladies gathered in the passage-ways and went through the ceremony of shaking hands and kissing each other, as though they had been separated for years and never expected to meet again. This operates as a serious obstacle, and we noticed some ladies exhibiting a petulant spirit in being jostled by the crowd which they themselves had occasioned, as their dresses were torn and soiled by the feet of those who were using their utmost efforts to keep the crowd from pushing them all down-stairs together. This is a great annoyance to those who are not fond of going through the world at the slow and steady pace of a fashionable lady, and we suggest the practice of making the outside of the hall a place for retailing gossip. Those who sweep the dirty stairway with their dresses should don the Bloomer costume without delay.

The Star, belonging to that portion of the press called "the Satanic," held to its original character while speaking of the Convention. It was through this paper that Reverends Sunderland and Ashley made public their sermons against Woman's Rights.

The Star, September 10*th.*

The women at the Tomfoolery Convention now being held in this city, talk as fluently of the Bible and God's teachings in their speeches, as if they could draw an argument from inspiration in maintenance of their Woman's Rights stuff. . . . . The poor creatures who take part in the silly rant of "brawling women" and Aunt Nancy men, are most of them "ismizers" of the rankest stamp, Abolitionists of the most frantic and contemptible kind, and Christian (?) sympathizers with such heretics as Wm. Lloyd Garrison, Parker Pillsbury, C. C. Burleigh, and S. S. Foster. These men are all Woman's Righters, and preachers of such damnable doctrines and accursed heresies, as would make demons of the pit shudder to hear.

We have selected a few appropriate passages from God's Bible for the consideration of the infuriated gang (Bloomers and all) at the Convention : Gen. iii. 16 ; Tit. ii. 4, 5 ; Prov. ix. 13, xxi. 9, 19 ; 1 Cor. xi. 8, 9 ; 1 Tim. ii. 8–14 ; 1 Cor. xiv. 34, 35 ; Eph. v. 22–24.

Daily Star, Sept. 11*th.*

Our usual amount of editorial matter is again crowded out this morning by the extreme quantity of gabble the Woman's Righters got off yesterday. Perhaps we owe an apology for having given publicity to the mass of corruption, heresies, ridiculous nonsense, and reeking vulgarities which these bad women have vomited forth for the past three days. Our personal preference would have been to have entirely disregarded these folks *per signe de mepris*, but the public appetite cries for these novelties and eccentricities of the times, and the daily press is expected to gratify such appetites; furthermore, we are of opinion that reporting such a Convention as this, is the most effectual way of checking the mischief it might otherwise do. The proceedings of these three days' pow-wow are a most shocking commentary upon themselves, and awaken burning scorn for the participants in them.

The Convention adjourned *sine die* last evening at ten o'clock, and, for the credit of our city, we hope its members will adjourn out of town as soon as possible, and stay so adjourned, unless they can come among us for more respectable business. Syracuse has become a by-word all through the country because of the influence which goes out from these foolish Conventions held here, and it is high time that we should be looking after our good name.

When the pamphlet report of the Convention's proceedings appeared, *The Star* said :
It gives the written speeches quite full, but only the skeleton of the spoken ones, which in reality constituted the cream of the affair. . . . . This portion of the world's history in relation to these agitating questions, is very appropriately treated upon by the Lord Himself : " *The sea and the waves roaring ; men's hearts failing them for fear, and for looking after those things which are coming on earth ; for the power of heaven shall be shaken.*" We recognize the sea as symbolizing the ideas which are drifted over the earth's surface, and the waves roaring, the agitating topics which the times have brought upon us.

The New York Herald (editorial), *Sept.* 12, 1852.

THE WOMAN'S RIGHTS CONVENTION—THE LAST ACT OF THE DRAMA.

The farce at Syracuse has been played out. We publish to-day the last act, in which it will be seen that the authority of the Bible, as a perfect rule of faith and practice for human beings, was voted down, and what are called the laws of nature set up instead of the Christian code. We have also a practical exhibition of the consequences that flow from woman leaving her true sphere where she wields all her influence, and coming into public to discuss questions of morals and politics with men. The scene in which Rev. Mr. Hatch violated the decorum of his cloth, and was coarsely offensive to such ladies present as had not lost that modest " feminine element," on which he dwelt so forcibly, is the natural result of the conduct of the women themselves, who, in the first place, invited discussion about sexes ; and in the second place, so broadly defined the difference between the male and the female, as to be suggestive of anything but purity to the audience. The women of the Convention have no right to complain ; but, for the sake of his clerical character, if no other motive influenced him, he ought not to have followed so bad an example. His speech was sound and his argument conclusive, but his form of words was not in the best taste. The female orators were the aggressors ; but, to use his own language, he ought not to have measured swords with a woman, especially when he regarded her ideas and expressions as bordering upon the obscene. But all this is the natural result of woman placing herself in a false position. As the Rev. Mr. Hatch observed, if she ran with horses she must expect to be betted upon. The whole tendency of these Conventions is by no means to increase the influence of woman, to elevate her condition, or to command the respect of the other sex.

Who are these women? what do they want? what are the motives that impel them to this course of action ? The *dramatis personæ* of the farce enacted at Syracuse present a curious conglomeration of both sexes. Some of them are old maids, whose personal charms were never very attractive, and who have been sadly slighted by the masculine gender in general; some of them women who have been badly mated, whose own temper, or their husbands, has made life anything but agreable to them, and they are therefore down upon the whole of the opposite sex ; some, having so much of the virago in their disposition, that nature appears to have made a mistake in their gender—mannish women, like hens that crow ; some of boundless vanity and egotism, who believe that they are superior in intellectual ability to "all the world and the rest of mankind," and delight to see their speeches and addresses in print; and man shall be consigned to his proper sphere—nursing the babies, washing the dishes, mending stockings, and sweeping the house. This is "the good time coming." Besides the classes we have enumerated, there is a class of wild enthusiasts and visionaries—very sincere, but very mad—having the same vein as the fanatical Abolitionists, and the majority, if not all of them, being, in point of fact, deeply imbued with the anti-slavery sentiment. Of the male sex who attend these Conventions for the purpose of taking a part in them, the majority are hen-pecked husbands, and all of them ought to wear petticoats.

In point of ability, the majority of the women are flimsy, flippant, and superficial. Mrs. Rose alone indicates much argumentative power.

How did woman first become subject to man as she now is all over the world? By her nature, her sex, just as the negro is and always will be, to the end of time, inferior to the white race, and, therefore, doomed to subjection; but happier than she would be in any other condition, just because it is the law of her nature. The women themselves would not have this law reversed. It is a significant fact that even Mrs. Swisshelm, who formerly ran about to all such gatherings from her husband, is now "a keeper at home," and condemns these Conventions in her paper. How does this happen? Because, after weary years of unfruitfulness, she has at length got her rights in the shape of a baby. This is the best cure for the mania, and we would recommend a trial of it to all who are afflicted.

What do the leaders of the Woman's Rights Convention want? They want to vote, and to hustle with the rowdies at the polls. They want to be members of Congress, and in the heat of debate to subject themselves to coarse jests and indecent language, like that of Rev. Mr. Hatch. They want to fill all other posts which men are ambitious to occupy—to be lawyers, doctors, captains of vessels, and generals in the field. How funny it would sound in the newspapers, that Lucy Stone, pleading a cause, took suddenly ill in the pains of parturition, and perhaps gave birth to a fine bouncing boy in court! Or that Rev. Antoinette Brown was arrested in the middle of her sermon in the pulpit from the same cause, and presented a "pledge" to her husband and the congregation; or, that Dr. Harriot K. Hunt, while attending a gentleman patient for a fit of the gout or *fistula in ano*, found it necessary to send for a doctor, there and then, and to be delivered of a man or woman child—perhaps twins. A similar event might happen on the floor of Congress, in a storm at sea, or in the raging tempest of battle, and then what is to become of the woman legislator?

WORLD'S TEMPERANCE CONVENTION.

COMMENTS OF THE PRESS.

"*The New York Herald*" (editorial article), *September* 9, 1853.

. . . . "We are at length—praised be the stars!—drawing to the termination of the clamorous conventions, which have kept the city in a state of ferment and agitation, excitement and fun, for the past two weeks. . . . .

"The World's Temperance Convention commenced its sittings on Tuesday, and is still in session. This organization was calculated to effect much good, had it not been leavened with the elements of discord, which had brought contempt and ridicule on that of the 'Whole World.' The Rev. Miss Antoinette Brown cast the brand of disorder into it, by presenting herself as a delegate from the other association. This was a virtual declaration of Woman's Rights, and a resolute effort to have them recognized by the Convention. Neal Dow, as President and as a man of gallantry, decided on receiving Miss Antoinette's credentials, and for a time victory appeared to smile on the Amazons. The triumph, however, was only ephemeral and illusive. The motion was put and carried that none but the officers and invited guests of the Convention should be permitted to occupy places on the platform, and so, by this indirect movement, Miss Brown saw herself, in the moment of her brightest hopes, expelled from the stage, and once more the Anti-Woman's Righters were in the ascendancy.

"This was on Tuesday. Next day another stormy scene, arising from the same cause, was enacted. The meek, temperate Dow—the light of the reformation, the apostle of the Maine Liquor Law, the President of the World's Temperance Convention—no longer able to control the stormy elements which had developed themselves in the council, resolved by a *coup d'état* to give the world an instance of his temperate demeanor and of the liberality of the reformers, and accordingly directed the police officers in attendance to clear the hall. The order was enforced, and even Miss Antoinette Brown, notwithstanding she was the bearer of credentials, was compelled to evacuate with the rest of the throng, and leave Metropolitan Hall to the quiet and peaceful possession of the male delegates to the World's Temperance Convention. Thus harmony was restored in that obstreperous assembly.

"' They made a solitude, and called it peace.' "

"Herald," *September* 10, 1853.

. . . . "Thus stands the case, then. This World's Temperance, or Maine Law Convention, headed by Neal Dow, the founder of the aforesaid statute, has turned adrift the Woman's Rights party, male and female, black and white, the Socialists, the Amalgamationists, the Infidels, the Vegetarians, and the Free Colored Americans. . . . . What is to follow from these proceedings, excluding Miss Brown, Phillips, Douglass, and Smith from the holy cause of temperance? Agitation? Of course. What else? Very likely a separate Maine Law coalition movement, comprising the Abolitionists, the strong-minded women, and Free Colored Americans all over the North, in opposition to Neal Dow and the orthodox Maine Law party. Thus the house will be divided—is, indeed, already divided—against itself. What then? The Scriptures say that such a house can't stand. It can't. And thus the Maine Law is crippled in a miserable squabble with fugitive slaves, Bloomers, and Abolitionists. How strange! Great country this, anyhow."

" National Democrat," *September* 5 (Rev. Chauncey C. Burr, editor).

"Time was when a full-blooded nigger meeting in New York would have been heralded with the cry of ' Tar and feathers !' but, alas! in these degenerate days, we are called to lament only over an uproarious disturbance. *The Tribune* groans horribly, it is true, because a set of deistical fanatics were interrupted in their villainous orgies ; but it should rather rejoice that no harsher means were resorted to than ' tufts of grass.' Talk about freedom ! Is any land so lost in self-respect—so sunk in infamy—that God-defying, Bible-abhorring sacrilege will be civilly allowed? Because the bell-wether of *The Tribune*, accompanied by a phalanx of blue petticoats, is installed as the grand-master of outrages, is that any reason for personal respect and public humiliation? In view of all the aggravating circumstances of the case, we congratulate the foolhardy fanatics on getting off as easy as they did ; and we commend the forbearance of the considerate crowd in not carrying their coercive measures to extremes, because, the humbug being exploded, all that is necessary now is to laugh, hiss, and vociferously applaud. When men make up their minds to vilify the Bible, denounce the Constitution, and defame their country (although this is a free country), they should go down in some obscure cellar, remote from mortal ken, and, even there, whisper their hideous treason against God and liberty."

MOB CONVENTION, 1853.

1. *Resolved*, That this movement for the rights of woman makes no attempt to decide whether woman is better or worse than man, neither affirms nor denies the equality of her intellect with that of man—makes no pretense of protecting woman—does not seek to oblige woman any more than man is now obliged, to vote, take office, labor in the professions, mingle in public life, or manage her own property.

2. *Resolved*, That what we do seek is to gain these rights and privileges for those women who wish to enjoy them, and so to change public opinion that it shall not be deemed indecorous for women to engage in any occupation which they deem fitted to their habits and talents.

3. *Resolved*, That the fundamental principle of the Woman's Rights movement is—that every human being, without distinction of sex, has an inviolable right to the full development and free exercise of all energies ; and that in every sphere of life, private and public, Functions should always be commensurate with Powers.

4. *Resolved*, That each human being is the sole judge of his or her sphere, and entitled to choose a profession without interference from others.

5. *Resolved*, That whatever differences exist between Man and Woman, in the quality or measure of their powers, are originally designed to be and should become bonds of union and means of co-operation in the discharge of all functions, alike private and public.

6. *Resolved*, That the monopoly of the elective franchise, and thereby of all the powers of legislation and government, by men, solely on the ground of sex, is a monstrous usurpation—condemned alike by reason and common-sense, subversive of all the principles of justice, oppressive and demoralizing in its operations, and insulting to the dignity of human nature.

Resolved, That we see no force in the objection, that woman's taking part in politics would be a fruitful source of domestic dissension; since experience shows that she may be allowed to choose her own faith and sect without any such evil result, though religious disputes are surely as bitter as political—and if the objection be sound, we ought to go further, and oblige a wife to forego all religious opinions, or to adopt the religious as well as the political creed of her husband.

8. *Resolved*, That women, like men, must be either self-supported and self-governed, or dependent and enslaved; that an unobstructed and general participation in all the branches of productive industry, and in all the business functions and offices of common life, is at once their natural right, their individual interest, and their public duty; the claim and the obligation reciprocally supporting each other; that the idleness of the rich, with its attendant physical debility, moral laxity, passional intemperance and mental dissipation, and the ignorance, wretchedness, and enforced profligacy of the poor, which are everywhere the curse and reproach of the sex, are the necessary results of their exclusion from those diversified employments which would otherwise furnish them with useful occupation, and reward them with its profits, honors, and blessings, that this enormous wrong cries for redress, for reparation by those whose delinquency allows its continuance.

Whereas, The energies of Man are always in proportion to the magnitude of the objects to be obtained; and, whereas, it requires the highest motive for the greatest exertion and noblest action; therefore,

9. *Resolved*, That Woman must be recognized politically, legally, socially, and religiously the equal of man, and all the obstructions to her highest physical, intellectual, and moral culture and development be removed, that she may have the highest motive to assume her place in that sphere of action and usefulness which her capacities enable her to fill.

10. *Resolved*, That this movement gives to the cause of education a new motive and impulse; makes a vast stride toward the settlement of the question of wages and social reform; goes far to cure that widespread plague—the licentiousness of cities; adds to civilization a new element of progress; and in all these respects commends itself as one of the greatest reforms of the age.

FIRST APPEAL OF 1854.

WOMAN'S RIGHTS.—CIRCULATE THE PETITION.

The Albany Woman's Rights Convention, held in February last, resolved to continue the work of Petitioning our State Legislature, from year to year, until the law of Justice and Equality shall be dispensed to the whole people, without distinction of sex.

In order to systematize and facilitate the labors of the friends who shall engage in the work of circulating the Petitions, a Committee was appointed to devise and present some definite plan of action. In the estimation of that Committee, the first and most important work to be done is to enlighten the people as to the REAL claims of the Woman's Rights Movement, thereby dispelling their many prejudices, and securing their hearty good-will. To aid in the accomplishment of this first great object, the Committee purpose holding Woman's Rights Meetings in all the cities and many of the larger villages of the State, during the coming fall and winter, and gladly, could they command the services of Lecturing Agents, would they thoroughly canvass the entire State. But, since to do so is impossible, they would urge upon the friends in every county, town, village, and school district, to hold public meetings in their respective localities, and, if none among their own citizens feel themselves competent to address the people, invite speakers from abroad. Let the question be fully and freely discussed, both *pro* and *con*, by both friends and opponents.

Though the living speaker can not visit every hearthstone throughout the length and breadth of the Empire State, and personally present the claims of our cause to the hearts and consciences of those who surround them, his arguments, by the aid of the invaluable art of printing, may. Therefore the Committee have resolved to circulate as widely as possible the written statement of Woman's Political and Legal Rights, as contained in the Address written by Elizabeth Cady Stanton, of Seneca Falls, N. Y., and adopted by the Albany Convention—presented to our Legislature at its last session. This Address has been highly spoken of by many of the best papers in the State, and pronounced, by eminent lawyers and statesmen, an able and unanswerable argument. And the Committee, being fully confident of its power to convince every candid inquirer after truth of the justice and mercy of our claims, do urgently call upon the friends everywhere to aid them in giving to it a thorough circulation.

There is no reform question of the day that meets so ready, so full, so deep a response from the masses, as does this Woman's Rights question. To ensure a speedy triumph, we have only to take earnest hold of the work of disseminating its immutable truths. Let us, then, agitate the question, hold public meetings, widely circulate Woman's Rights Tracts, and show to the world that we are in earnest—that we will be heard—that our demands stop not short of justice and perfect equality to every human being. Let us, at least, see to it, that this admirable Address of Mrs. Stanton is placed in the hands of every intelligent man and woman in the State, and thus the way prepared for the gathering up of a mighty host of names to our petitions to be presented to our next Legislature, a mammoth roll, that shall cause our law-makers to know that the PEOPLE are with us, and that if our prayer be not wisely and justly answered by them, other and truer representatives will fill those Legislative Halls.

The success of our first appeal to our Legislature, made last winter, encourages us to persevere. That the united prayer of only 6,000 men and women should cause the reporting and subsequent passage in the House, of a bill granting two of our most special claims—that of the wife to her earnings, and the mother to her children—is indeed a result the most sanguine scarce dared to hope for. What may we not expect from our next appeal, that shall be 20,000, nay, more, if we but be faithful, 100,000 strong. To the work, then, friends, of renovating public sentiment and circulating petitions. There is no time to be lost. Our Fourth of July gatherings will afford fit opportunity for both distributing the Address and circulating the petitions. And, Women of the Empire State, it is for you to do the work, it is for you to shake from your feet the dust of tyrant custom, it is for you to remember that "he who would be free must himself strike the blow."

The petitions to be circulated are the same as last year—one asking for the JUST ANI EQUAL RIGHTS OF WOMEN, and the other for WOMAN'S RIGHT OF SUFFRAGE. The petitions are to be signed by both men and women, the men's names placed in the right column, and the women's in the left. *All* intelligent persons must be ready and willing to sign the first, asking a revision of the laws relative to the property rights of women, and surely no true republican can refuse to give his or her name to the second, asking for woman the Right of Representation—a practical application of the great principles of '76.

It is desirable that there shall be one person in each county to whom all the petitions circulated in its several towns, villages, and school districts, shall be forwarded, and who shall arrange and attach them in one roll, stating upon a blank sheet, placed between the petition and the signatures, the number of signers, the name of the county, and the number of towns represented, and forward them as early as the 1st of December next, to Susan B. Anthony, Rochester, N. Y. Where no person volunteers, or is appointed such county agent, the petitions, properly labeled, may be sent directly to Rochester.

Mrs. Stanton's Address is published in neat pamphlet form, in large type, and may be had at the following prices : $2 per 100, 37½ cts. per dozen ; or if sent by mail, $3 per 100, and 50 cts. per dozen. Packages of over 25 may be sent by express to all places on the line of the railroads at a less cost than by mail.

It is hoped that every person who reads this notice, and feels an interest in the universal diffusion of the true aim and object of the Woman's Rights agitation, will, without delay, order copies of this address to distribute gratuitously or otherwise, among their neighbors and townsmen. Should there be any wishing to aid in this work, who can not command the money necessary to purchase the Address, their orders will be cheerfully complied with free of charge.

The Committee have on hand a variety of Woman's Rights Tracts, written by S. J. May, Wendell Phillips, Elizabeth C. Stanton, Mrs. C. I. H. Nichols, Ernestine L. Rose, T. W. Higginson, and others. Also, the Reports of the several National Woman's Rights Conventions, all of which may be had at very low prices.

All correspondence and orders for Address, petitions, etc., should be addressed to

SUSAN B. ANTHONY, General Agent, Rochester, N. Y.

June 22, 1854.

SECOND APPEAL OF 1854.

To the Women of the State of New York :

We purpose again this winter to send petitions to our State Legislature—one, asking for the Just and Equal Rights of Woman, and one for Woman's Right of Suffrage. The latter, we think, covers the whole ground, for we can never be said to have just and equal rights until the right of suffrage is ours. Some who will gladly sign the former may shrink from making the last demand. But be assured, our cause can never rest on a safe, enduring basis, until we get the right of suffrage. So long as we have no voice in the laws, we have no guarantee that privileges granted us to-day by one body of men, may not be taken from us to-morrow by another.

All man's laws, his theology, his daily life, go to prove the fixed idea in his mind of the entire difference in the sexes—a difference so broad that what would be considered cruel and unjust between man and man, is kind and just between man and woman. Having discarded the idea of the oneness of the sexes, how can man judge of the needs and wants of a being so wholly unlike himself ? How can he make laws for his own benefit and woman's too at the same time ? He can not. He never has, as all his laws relative to woman most clearly show. But when man shall fully grasp the idea that woman is a being of like feelings, thoughts, and passions with himself, he may be able to legislate for her, as one code would answer for both. But until then, a sense of justice, a wise self-love, impels us to demand a voice in his councils.

To every intelligent, thinking woman, we put the question, On what sound principles of jurisprudence, constitutional law, or human rights, are one-half of the people of this State disfranchised ? If you answer, as you must, that it is done in violation of all law, then we ask you, when and how is this great wrong to be righted ? We say NOW ; and petitioning is the first step in its accomplishment. We hope, therefore, that every woman in the State will sign her name to the petitions. It is humiliating to know that many educated women so stultify their consciences as to declare that they have all the rights they want. Have you who make this declaration ever read the barbarous laws in reference to woman, to mothers, to wives, and to daughters, which disgrace our Statute Books ? Laws which are not surpassed in cruelty and injustice by any slaveholding code in the United States ; laws which strike at the root of the glorious doctrine for which our fathers fought and bled and died, "no taxation without representation" ; laws which deny a right most sacredly observed by many of the monarchies of Europe—" the right of trial by a jury of one's own peers" ; laws which trample on the holiest and most unselfish of all human affections—a mother's love for her child—and with ruthless cruelty snap asunder the tenderest ties ; laws which enable the father, be he a man or a minor, to tear the infant from the mother's arms and send it, if he chooses, to the Feejee Islands—yea, to will the guardianship of the *unborn* child to whomsoever he may please, whether to the Sultan of Turkey or the Imam of Muscat ; laws by which our sons and daughters may be bound to service to cancel their father's debts of *honor*, in the meanest rum-holes and brothels in the vast metropolis; laws which violate all that is most pure and sacred in the marriage relation, by giving to the cruel, beastly drunkard the rights of a man, a husband, and father; laws which place the life-long earnings of the wife at the disposal of the husband, be his character what it may; laws which leave us at the mercy of the rum-seller and the drunkard, against whom we have no protection for our lives, our children, or our homes; laws by which we are made the watch-dogs to keep a million and a half of our sisters in the foulest bondage the sun ever shone upon—which forbid us to give food and shelter to the panting fugitive from the land of slavery.

If, in view of laws like these, there be women in this State so lost to self-respect, to all that is virtuous, noble, and true, as to refuse to raise their voices in protest against such degrading tyranny, we can only say of that system which has thus robbed womanhood of all its glory and greatness, what the immortal Channing did of slavery, "If," said he, "it be true that the slaves are contented and happy—if there is a system that can blot out all love of freedom from the soul of man, destroy every trace of his Divinity, make him happy in a condition so low and benighted and hopeless, I ask for no stronger argument against such a slavery as ours." No! never believe it; woman falsifies herself and blasphemes her God, when in view of her present social, legal, and political position, she declares she has all the rights she wants. If a few drops of Saxon blood gave our Frederick Douglass such a clear perception of his humanity, his inalienable rights, as to enable him, with the slaveholder's Bible, the slaveholder's Constitution, a Southern public sentiment and education all laid heavy on his shoulders, to stand upright and walk forth in search of freedom, with as much ease as did Samson of old with the massive gates of the city, shall we, the daughters of our Hancocks and Adamses, we in whose veins flow the blood of the Pilgrim Fathers, shall we never try the strength of these withes of law and gospel with which in our blindness we have been bound hand and foot? Yes, the time has come.

> "The slumber is broken, the sleeper is risen,
> The day of the Goth and the Vandal is o'er,
> And old Earth feels the tread of Freedom once more."

Fail not, Women of the Empire State, to swell our Petitions. Let no religious scruples hold you back. Take no heed to man's interpretation of Paul's injunctions to women. To any thinking mind, there is no difficulty in explaining those passages of the Apostle as applicable to the times in which they were written, as having no reference whatever to the Women of the nineteenth century.

"Honor the King," heroes of '76! Those leaden tea-chests of Boston Harbor cry out, "Render unto Cæsar the things that are Cæsar's." When the men of 1854, with their Priests and Rabbis, shall rebuke the disobedience of their forefathers—when they shall cease to set at defiance the British lion and the Apostle Paul in their National Policy, then it will be time enough for us to bow down to man's interpretation of law touching our social relations, and acknowledge that God gave us powers and rights, merely that we might show forth our faith in Him by being helpless and dumb.

The writings of Paul, like our State Constitutions, are susceptible of various interpretations. But when the human soul is roused with holy indignation against injustice and oppression, it stops not to translate human parchments, but follows out the law of its inner being, written by the finger of God in the first hour of its creation.

Our Petitions will be sent to every county in the State, and we hope that they will find at least ten righteous Women to circulate them. But should there be any county so benighted that a petition can not be circulated throughout its length and breadth, giving to every man and woman an opportunity to sign their names, then we pray, not that "God will send down fire and brimstone" upon it, but that the "Napoleon" of this movement will flood it with Woman's Rights Tracts and Missionaries.

ELIZABETH CADY STANTON,
Chairman N. Y. State Woman's Rights Committee.

SENECA FALLS, *Dec.* 11, 1854.

N. B.—All orders for forms of Petitions and Woman's Rights Tracts, and all communications relating to the movement in this State, should be addressed to our General

Agent, Susan B. Anthony, Rochester, N. Y. Let the Petitions be returned, as soon as possible, to Lydia Mott, Albany, N.Y., as we wish to present them early in the session, and thereby give our Legislature due time for the consideration of this important question.

NATIONAL WOMAN'S RIGHTS CONVENTION, COOPER INSTITUTE, 1856.

LETTER FROM MRS. STANTON.

SENECA FALLS, *November* 24, 1856.

DEAR LUCY STONE:—We may continue to hold our Conventions, we may talk of our right to vote, to legislate, to hold property, but until we can arouse in woman a proper self-respect, she will hold in contempt the demands we now make for our sex. We shall never get what we ask for until the majority of women are openly with us; and they will never claim their civil rights until they know their social wrongs. From time to time I put these questions to myself: How is it that woman can longer silently consent to her present false position? How can she calmly contemplate the barbarous code of laws which govern her civil and political existence? How can she devoutly subscribe to a theology which makes her the conscientious victim of another's will, forever subject to the triple bondage of the man, the priest, and the law? How can she tolerate our social customs, by which womankind is stripped of all true virtue, dignity, and nobility? How can she endure our present marriage relations, by which woman's life, health, and happiness are held so cheap, that she herself feels that God has given her no charter of rights, no individuality of her own. I answer, she patiently bears all this because in her blindness she sees no way of escape. Her bondage, though it differs from that of the negro slave, frets and chafes her just the same. She too sighs and groans in her chains; and lives but in the hope of better things to come. She looks to heaven; whilst the more philosophical slave sets out for Canada. Let it be the object of this Convention to show that there is hope for woman this side of heaven, and that there is a work for her to do before she leaves for the celestial city.

Marriage is a divine institution, intended by God for the greater freedom and happiness of both parties—whatever therefore conflicts with woman's happiness is not legitimate to that relation. Woman has yet to learn that she has a right to be happy in and of herself; that she has a right to the free use, improvement, and development of all her faculties, for her own benefit and pleasure. The woman is greater than the wife or the mother; and in consenting to take upon herself these relations, she should never sacrifice one iota of her individuality to any senseless conventionalisms, or false codes of feminine delicacy and refinement.

Marriage, as we now have it, is opposed to all God's laws. It is by no means an equal partnership. The silent partner loses everything. On the domestic sign, the existence of a second person is not recognized by even the ordinary abbreviation, Co. There is the establishment of John Jones. Perhaps his partner supplies all the cents and the senses—but no one knows who she is or whence she came. If John is a luminous body, she shines in his reflection; if not, she hides herself in his shadow. But she is nameless, for a woman has no name! She is Mrs. John or James, Peter or Paul, just as she changes masters; like the Southern slave, she takes the name of her owner. Many people consider this a very small matter; but it is the symbol of the most cursed monopoly on this footstool; a monopoly by man of all the rights, the life, the liberty, and happiness of one-half of the human family—all womankind. For what man can honestly deny that he has not a secret feeling that where his pleasure and woman's seems to conflict, the woman must be sacrificed; and what is worse, woman herself has come to think so too. She believes that all she tastes of joy in life is from the generosity and benevolence of man; and the bitter cup of sorrow, which she too often drinks to the very dregs, is of the good providence of God, sent by a kind hand for her improvement and development. This sentiment pervades the laws, customs, and religions of all countries, both Christian and heathen. Is it any wonder, then, that woman regards herself as a mere machine, a tool for men's pleasure? Verily is she a hopeless victim of his morbidly developed passions. But, thank God, she suffers not alone! Man too pays the penalty of his crimes in his enfeebled mind, dwarfed body, and the shocking monstrosities of his deformed and crippled offspring.

Call yourselves Christian women, you who sacrifice all that is great and good for an ignoble peace, who betray the best interests of the race for a temporary ease? It were nobler far to go and throw yourselves into the Ganges than to curse the earth with a miserable progeny, conceived in disgust and brought forth in agony. What mean these asylums all over the land for the deaf and dumb, the maim and blind, the idiot and the raving maniac? What all these advertisements in our public prints, these family guides, these female medicines, these Madame Restells? Do not all these things show to what a depth of degradation the women of this Republic have fallen, how false they have been to the holy instincts of their nature, to the sacred trust given them by God as the mothers of the race? Let Christians and moralists pause in their efforts at reform, and let some scholar teach them how to apply the laws of science to human life. Let us but use as much care and forethought in producing the highest order of intelligence, as we do in raising a cabbage or a calf, and in a few generations we shall reap an abundant harvest of giants, scholars, and Christians.

The first step in this improvement is the elevation of woman. She is the protector of national virtue; the rightful lawgiver in all our most sacred relations.

Yours truly,   ELIZABETH CADY STANTON.

LETTER FROM N. H. WHITING.

MARSHFIELD, MASS., *September* 29, 1856.

DEAR FRIEND:—I do not see that I can do much to aid you in your effort for self-emancipation from the injustice your sex encounters in the present social and political arrangements of the world. You know the old maxim, "The gods help them who help themselves." This is true of all times and circumstances. The two inevitable conditions that are found in, and are essential to all bondage, are the spirit of oppression, the desire to exercise unlawful dominion on the one side, and ignorance, servility, the willingness, if not the desire to be enslaved on the other. The absence of either is fatal to the existence of the thing itself.

I apprehend the principal thing you want from our sex, as a preliminary to your growth and equal position in the great struggle of life, is what Diogenes wanted of Alexander, viz., that we shall "get out of your sunshine." In other words, that we shall remove the obstacles we have placed in your way. To this end, politically, all laws which discriminate between man and woman, to the injury of the latter, should at once be blotted out. Women should have an equal voice in the creation and administration of that government to which they are subject. This will be a fair start in that direction. The first thing to be done, socially, is to so regulate and arrange the industrial machinery that women shall have an equal chance to labor in all the departments, and that the same work shall receive the same pay whether done by man or woman. This will do much to clear the track, so that all can have a fair chance. This is all you ask, as I take it. This you should have. Justice demands it. . . . .

But, save in the removal of the outward forms of society, which now environ and hedge up your way, the active work in all this change in the most important human relations must be done by yourselves. "They who would be free, themselves must strike the blow." What woman is capable of we shall never know until she has a fair chance in the wide arena of universal human life.

If the love of frivolity and show and of empty admiration, which now so generally obtains, is an unfailing characteristic in the female sex, legislation can not help you. Encouragement, sympathy, can not help you. It is of no use to fight against the eternal laws. But if this be only a perversion or misdirection of noble and lovely powers and faculties, the result of accidental circumstances and vicious institutions, as I believe, then, when the outward pressure is removed, the elastic spring of the genuine human spirit, encased in the form of woman, shall return; the great curse of civil and domestic strife shall cease; the true marriage of the male and female heart can then take place, because that perfect equality, under which alone it can exist, will be recognized and established.

You are engaged in a great work. May you have faith and resolution to continue to the end. It is a long way before you. Man is a plant of slow growth. His education and development are the work of ages. It is only by a landmark extending far back into the dim and misty past we can trace his upward path.

But though the race grows so slow, and the forward wave is so often pressed backward by the prevailing currents of ignorance, superstition, and oppression, still, it is cheering to know that no true word was ever spoken, or good deed ever done, but it cast some rays of light into the surrounding darkness, while it gave strength and vigor to the spirit that sent it forth. That is a grand truth whose utterance is attributed to Jesus, "It is more blessed to give than to receive." By that gift we may relieve the want of others, but we gain far more to ourselves by creating from the chaos of human crime and misery a beautiful and godlike act. That act is wrought into the fibers of our own individual life, and we are nobler, better, happier than before.

So you, in the thankless task before you, subject to ribald jest, to the cold, heartless sneer, to obloquy and abuse of all sorts from our and even your sex, who are most immediately to be benefited by your labors, will have this great truth to console and stimulate you, that in every step of this grand procession in which you are marching, you will gather rich and substantial food for the sustenance and growth of your own mental and moral natures. Truly yours, N. H. WHITING.

NEW YORK, *November* 25, 1856.

To the Seventh National Woman's Rights Convention:

The central claim for Woman is her right to be, and to do, as well as to suffer. Allow her everywhere to represent herself and her own interests.

Custom and law both deny her this right. If she is too cowardly to contend with custom, and to overcome it, let her remain its slave. But the law has bound her hand and foot. Here she can not act. The law-makers have forged her chains and riveted them upon her. They alone can take them off. Shall we not, then, at once demand of them—demand of every sovereign State in the Union—the elective franchise for woman? With this franchise she can make for herself a civil and political equality with man. Without it she is utterly without power to protect herself. She does not need to be protected like a child. She does need freedom to use the powers of self-protection with which her own nature is endowed.

Each of the several States has its specific laws—statutes and constitution—varying in details, but all more or less unjust to her as wife, mother, property-holder; in short, unjust to her in all her relations as citizen. Every State denies to her the right to represent herself politically. Once give her this, and she can take all the rest.

Would it not be wholly appropriate, then, for this National Convention to demand the right of suffrage for her from the Legislature of each State in the Nation? We can not petition the General Government on this point. Allow me, therefore, respectfully to suggest the propriety of appointing a committee, which shall be instructed to prepare a memorial adapted to the circumstances of each legislative body; and demanding of each, in the name of this Convention, the elective franchise for woman.

Such a memorial, presented to the several States during the coming winter, could not fail of doing good. It would be pressing home this great question upon all the powers that be in the whole nation; and, with comparatively little effort, would, at least, create a healthful agitation. Who shall say that the just men of some State will not even accord to us the franchise we claim? With this hint to the wise, I remain, as ever,

Yours, for equal human rights, ANTOINETTE L. BROWN BLACKWELL.

Mr. HATTELLE moved that a Committee be at once appointed to draft such a memorial, which was adopted.

WENDELL PHILLIPS rose to offer as an amendment, that a recommendation go forth from this Convention to the women of each State, to inaugurate their presentation of the subject to their several Legislatures.

Thomas Wentworth Higginson proposed that the friends of Woman Suffrage should publish an almanac each year giving the advance steps in their movement. He issued one for 1858, from which we clip the following:

THE WOMAN'S RIGHTS ALMANAC.

THE HISTORY OF WOMAN IN THREE PICTURES.

I. HINDOO LAWS. 2000 B. C.—"A man, both day and night, must keep his wife so much in subjection, that she by no means be mistress of her own actions. If the wife have her own free-will, notwithstanding she be of a superior caste, she will behave amiss."

"The Creator formed woman for this purpose, that man might have sexual intercourse with her, and that children might be born from thence."

"A woman shall never go out of the house without the consent of her husband . . . . and shall act according to the orders of her husband, and shall pay a proper respect to the Deity, her husband's father, the spiritual guide, and the guests; and shall not eat until she has served them with victuals (if it is physic, she may take it before they eat); a woman also shall never go to a stranger's house, and shall not stand at the door, and must never look out of a window."

"If a woman, following her own inclinations, goes whithersoever she choose, and does not regard the words of her master, such a woman shall be turned away."

"If a man goes on a journey, his wife shall not divert herself by play, nor shall see any public show, nor shall laugh, nor shall dress herself with jewels and fine clothes, nor shall see dancing, nor hear music, nor shall sit in the window, nor shall ride out, nor shall behold anything choice or rare, but shall fasten well the house-door and remain private; and shall not eat any dainty victuals, and shall not view herself in a mirror; she shall never exercise herself in any such agreeable employment during the absence of her husband."

"It is proper for every woman, after her husband's death, to burn herself in the fire with his corpse."

It will be seen that the following laws scarcely vary at all, in *principle*, from the preceding:

II. ANGLO-SAXON LAWS. 1848.—"By marriage, the husband and wife are one person in law; that is, *the very being or existence of the woman is suspended during the marriage*, or at least is incorporated and consolidated into that of the husband, under whose wing, protection, and *covert* she performs everything; and is, therefore, called in our Law-French a *feme-covert*, is said to be *covert-baron*, or under the protection and influence of her husband, her baron, or lord; and her condition during her marriage is called her *coverture*. Upon this principle, of an union of person in husband and wife, depend almost all the legal rights, duties, and disabilities that either of them acquire by the marriage."—1 *Blackstone Com.*, 356.

"The husband also, by the old law, might give his wife moderate correction. For, as he is to answer for her misbehavior, the law thought it reasonable to intrust him with this power of restraining her by domestic chastisement, in the same moderation that a man is allowed to correct his apprentices or children. But this power of correction was confined within reasonable bounds, and the husband was prohibited from using any violence to his wife, *aliter quam ad virum, ex causa regiminis et castigationis uxoris suae licite et rationabiliter pertinet* (except as lawfully and reasonably belongs to a husband, for the sake of governing and disciplining his wife). The civil law gave the husband the same, or a larger authority over his wife, allowing him, for some misdemeanors, *flagellis et Fustibus acriter verberare uxorem* (to beat his wife severely with whips and cudgels); for others only *modicam castigationem adhibere* (to administer moderate chastisement). But with us, in the politer reign of Charles II., this power of correction began to be doubted, and a wife may now have security of peace against the husband, or, in return, a husband against his wife. Yet the lower rank of people, who were always fond of the old common law, still claim and exact their ancient privilege, and the courts of law will still permit a husband to restrain a wife of her liberty in case of any gross misbehavior."—1 *Blackstone*, 366.

" The legal effects of marriage are generally deducible from the principle of the common law by which the husband and wife are regarded as one person, and her legal existence and authority are in a degree lost or suspended during the continuance of the matrimonial union."— *2 Kent's Comm. on Am. Law*, 129.

" Even now, in countries of the most polished habits, a considerable latitude is allowed to marital coercion. In England the husband has the right of imposing *such corporal restraints as he may deem necessary*, for securing to himself the fulfillment of the obligations imposed on the wife by virtue of the marriage contract. He may, in the plenitude of his power, adopt every act of physical coercion which does not endanger the life or health of the wife, or render cohabitation unsafe."—*Petersdorff's Abridgement, note.*

" The husband hath, by law, power and dominion over his wife, and *may keep her by force within the bounds of duty, and may beat her*, but not in a violent or cruel manner." —*Bacon's Abridgement, title " Baron aud Feme," B. 9.*

" *The wife is only the servant of her husband.*"—*Baron Alderson (Wharton's Laws relating to the Women of England, p. 163.*

" It is probably not generally known, that whenever a woman has accepted an offer of marriage, all she has, or expects to have, becomes virtually the property of the man thus accepted as a husband ; and no gift or deed executed by her between the period of acceptance and the marriage is held to be valid ; for were she permitted to give away or otherwise settle her property, he might be disappointed in the wealth he looked to in making the offer."—*Roper, Law of Husband and Wife, Book I., ch. xiii.*

" A lady whose husband had been unsuccessful in business, established herself as a milliner in Manchester. After some years of toil, she realized sufficient for the family to live upon comfortably, the husband having done nothing meanwhile. They lived for a time in easy circumstances, after she gave up business, and then the husband died, *bequeathing all his wife's earnings to his own illegitimate children.* At the age of sixty-two, she was compelled, in order to gain her bread, to return to business."—*Westminster Review, Oct., 1856.*

MR. JUSTICE COLERIDGE'S JUDGMENT " *in re Cochrane.*"—The facts were briefly these. A writ of *habeas corpus* had been granted to the wife, who, having been brought into the power of the husband by strategem, had since that time been kept in confinement by him. By the return to the writ, it appeared that the parties had lived together for about three years after their marriage on terms of apparent affection, and had two children ; that in May, 1836, Mrs. Cochrane withdrew herself and offspring from his house and protection, and had resided away from him against his will, for nearly four years. While absent from her husband, Mrs. Cochrane had always resided with her mother, nor was there the slightest imputation on her honor. In ordering her to be restored to her husband, the learned judge, after stating the question to be whether by the common law, the husband, in order to prevent his wife from eloping, *has a right to confine her in his own dwelling-house, and restrain her from liberty for an indefinite time,* using no cruelty nor imposing any hardship or unnecessary restraint on his part, and on hers there being no reason from her past conduct to apprehend that she will avail herself of her absence from his control to injure either his honor or his property, stated, " *That there could be no doubt of the general dominion which the law of England attributes to the husband over the wife.*"—*8 Dowling's P. C.* 360. *Quoted in Westminster Review, Oct., 1856.*

III. SIGNS OF THE TIMES. 1857.—It is obvious that the English common law, as above stated, is scarcely a step beyond barbarism. Yet this law remained almost unaltered in the United States, as respects woman, till the year 1848—the year of the first local Woman's Rights Convention, the first National one being held in 1850. Since then every year has brought improvements, and even those who denounce the Woman's Rights Movement, admit the value of these its results.

There is near Trenton, says *The Newark Advertiser*, a woman who is a skillful mechanic. She has made a carriage, and can make a violin or a gun. She is only 25 years old.

This is told as though it were something wonderful for a woman to have mechanical genius; when the fact is, that there are thousands all over the country who would make as good mechanics and handle tools with as much skill and dexterity as men, if they were only allowed to make manifest their ingenuity and inclinations. A girl's hands and head are formed very much like those of a boy, and if put to a trade at the age when boys are usually apprenticed, she will master her business quite as soon as the boy—be the trade what it may.

SALE OF A WIFE AT WORCESTER, ENGLAND.—One of these immoral and illegal transactions was recently completed at Worcester. The agreement between the fellow who sold and the fellow who bought is given in *The Worcester Chronicle:*

"Thomas Middleton delivered up his wife, Mary Middleton, to Phillip Rostius, and sold her for one shilling and a quart of ale, and parted wholly and solely for life, not trouble one another for life. Witness, Signed Thomas ⋈ Middleton. Witness, Mary Middleton, his wife. Witness, Phillip ⋈ Rostins. Witness, S. H. Stone, Crown Inn, Friar Street."

FEMALE INVENTORS.—"Man, having excluded woman from all opportunity of mechanical education, turns and reproaches her with having invented nothing. But one remarkable fact is overlooked. Society limits woman's sphere to the needle, the spindle, and the basket; and tradition reports that she *herself invented all three.* If she has invented her tools as fast as she has found opportunity to use them, can more be asked?"—*T. W. Higginson.*

In the ancient Hindoo dramas, wives do not speak the same language with their husbands, but employ the dialect of slaves.

A correspondent of *The London Spectator* suggests:—"The employment of women *as clerks at railway stations* would not be an unprecedented innovation; they not unfrequently fill that position abroad; and I can recall at least one instance, when, at a principal station in France, a female clerk displayed under difficult circumstances an amount of zeal and intelligence which showed her to be admirably suited to her office—'the right *woman* in the right place.'"

The word courage is, in the Spanish and Portuguese languages, a *feminine* noun.

Upwards of ten thousand females in New York, forty thousand in Paris, and eighty thousand in London, are said, by statisticians, to regularly earn a daily living by immoral practices. And yet all these are Christian cities!

A widow lady of Bury, Mary Chapman, who would appear to have been a warlike dame, making her will in 1649, leaves to one of her sons, among other things, "also *my* muskett, rest, bandileers, sword, and headpiece, *my* jacke, a fine paire of sheets, and a hutche."

Addison, in *The Spectator*, refers to a French author, who mentions that the ladies of the court of France, in his time, thought it ill-breeding and a kind of female pedantry, to pronounce a hard word right, for which reason they took frequent occasion to use hard words, that they might show a politeness in murdering them. The author further adds, that a lady of some quality at court, having accidentally made use of a hard word in a proper place, and pronounced it right, the whole assembly was out of countenance for her.

SEWING IN NEW YORK.—"I am informed from one source, that based on a calculation some two years ago, the number of those who live by sewing in New York exceeds fifteen thousand. Another, who has good means of information, tells me there are forty thousand earning fifteen shillings ($1.87½) per week, and paying twelve shillings ($1.50) for board, making shirts at four cents."—*E. H. Chapin, "Moral Aspects of City Life."*

The first "pilgrim" who stepped ashore on Plymouth Rock is said, by tradition, to have been a young girl, named Mary Chilton.

The St. Louis Republican mentions that there is one feature about the steamer Illinois Belle, of peculiar attractiveness—a lady clerk. "Look at her bills of lading, and ' Mary J. Patterson, clerk,' will be seen traced in a delicate and very neat style of chirography. A lady clerk on a Western steamer! It speaks strongly of our moral progress."

George Borrow, in his singular narrative, "The Romany Rye," states that the sale of a wife, with a halter round her neck, is still a legal transaction in England. It must be done in the cattle-market, as if she were a mare, "all women being considered as mares by old English law, *and indeed called mares in certain counties where genuine old English is still preserved.*"

Testimonial to Miss Mitchell.—The fame of our talented countrywoman, Miss Maria Mitchell, of Nantucket, has spread far and wide among astronomers, and is cherished with pride by all Americans. We are glad to learn that it is proposed to present her a testimonial which will be at once an appropriate tribute to her talents, and an aid to the future prosecution of her astronomical researches. An observatory on Nantucket Island is for sale on very favorable terms, and a plan is on foot for its purchase, to be presented to her. The sum needed is $3,000, of which more than a third has been raised by ladies in Philadelphia and its neighborhood.

Miss Mitchell is now in Europe, visiting the principal observatories and astronomers there, and it is hoped that she will soon be gratefully surprised by learning that the very imperfect means hitherto at her disposal in pursuing her favorite science are to be replaced on her return by a collection of instruments which she will be delighted to possess. Drs. Bond, of Harvard College Observatory, and Hall, of Providence, have interested themselves in securing this object, and express strongly their opinion that valuable results to science can not fail to be realized by furnishing so skillful and diligent an observer as Miss Mitchell the proposed aids to her researches. Dr. Bond expresses the conviction that Nantucket enjoys special advantages as an astronomical site, on account of its comparative exemption from thermometrical disturbances of the atmosphere.

We hope this worthy tribute to our countrywoman's scientific merit will not fail to be paid. Miss Mitchell's friends have the refusal of the observatory only till September 1st, and several other purchasers are ready to take it at once. Dr. Geo. Choate, of Salem, has consented to receive the pledges of such as desire to be enrolled among the subscribers to the fund, among whose names are already the honored ones of Edward Everett, J. I. Bowditch, John C. Brown, of Providence, and F. Peabody, of Salem, besides other munificent patrons of science.—*Journal of Commerce.*

Learn to Swim.—When the steamer Alida was sinking from her collision with the Fashion, a Kentucky girl of seventeen was standing on the guard, looking upon the confusion of the passengers, and occasionally turning and looking anxiously toward the shore. A gallant young man stepped up to her and offered to convey her safely to shore. "Thank you," replied the lady, "you need not trouble yourself; I am only waiting for the crowd to get out of the way, when I can take care of myself." Soon the crowd cleared the space, and the lady plunged into the water, and swam to the shore with ease, and without any apparent fear.

A Lady Horsebreaker in France.—In consequence of the success obtained by Madame Isabelle in breaking in horses for the Russian army, the French Minister of War lately authorized her to proceed officially before a commission, composed of general and superior officers of cavalry, with General Regnault de St. Jean d'Angely at their head, to a practical demonstration of her method on a certain number of young cavalry horses. After twenty days' training, the horses were so perfectly broken in, that the minister no longer hesitated to enter into an arrangement with Madame Isabelle to introduce her system into all the imperial schools of cavalry, beginning with that of Saumur.— *Galignani's Messenger.*

Since the passage of what is called the Married Woman's Act, in 1848, in Pennsylvania, there have been brought, in the Court of Common Pleas, one thousand one hundred and thirty-five suits for divorce. A large majority of the cases are brought by the wives, on the ground of cruel treatment and desertion.

" Women ruled all, and ministers of state
Were at the doors of women forced to wait—
Women, who've oft as sovereigns graced the land,
But never governed well at second-hand."

Churchill's Satires, *A.D.* 1761.

SENATOR ANTHONY.

" A Woman's Rights Convention is in session in New York. A collection of women arguing for political rights, and for the privileges usually conceded only to the other sex, is one of the easiest things in the world to make fun of. There is no end to the smart speeches and the witty remarks that may be made on the subject. But when we seriously attempt to show that a woman who pays taxes ought not to have a voice in the manner in which the taxes are expended, that a woman whose property and liberty and person are controlled by the laws, should have no voice in framing those laws, it is not so easy. If women are fit to rule in monarchies, it is difficult to say why they are not qualified to vote in a republic ; nor can there be greater indelicacy in a woman going up to the ballot-box than there is in a woman opening a legislature or issuing orders to an army.

" We do not say that women ought to vote ; but we say that it is a great deal easier to laugh down the idea than to argue it down. Moreover, there are a great many things besides voting that are confined to men, and that women can do quite as well, or even better. There are many employments which ought to be opened to women, there are many ways in which women can be made to contribute more largely to their own independence and comfort, and to the general good of society. All well-directed plans to this end should receive the support of thinking men. The danger is that conventions of this kind are apt to overlook the present and attainable good, in their efforts for results which are of less certain value and far less practicable."—*Providence Journal, Edited by Ex-Governor Anthony.*

WISCONSIN LEGISLATURE, 1857.

WISCONSIN REPORT ON THE SUFFRAGE QUESTION.—The following extract from the report on the extension of the right of suffrage in Wisconsin, we find in *The Milwaukee Free Democrat:*

" Perhaps no question ever submitted to a community would call forth so much of its mental activity, such a crusade into the realms of history, such a balancing of good and evil, of the past with the present, such an examination of the social and political rights and relations, as the question whether the right of suffrage ought to be extended to all citizens over the age of twenty-one, which would, of course, include both sexes. The giddy devotee of fashion would be surprised in the midst of her frivolity, and be compelled to think and reason, in view of a new responsibility which is menacing her. Even if opposed to the proposition, she would be compelled to organize and inspire the public opinion necessary to defeat it. Whatever might be the event, woman's intellectual position would be changed, and changed forever, and with hers that of all. other classes. . . . .

" Let no one imagine that he can dispose of this question by a contemptuous fling at strong-minded women and hen-pecked husbands. The principle will gain more strength from the character of the arguments of its opponents than from any number of Bloomer conventions. The modern idea of the fashionable belle, floating like a bird of paradise through the soiree ; the impersonation of motion and grace in the ball-room, indulging alternately in syncope and rapture over the marvelous adventures and despair of the hero of a mushroom romance, her rapid transition from one excitement to another, to fill up the dreary vacuum of life, provoking as it does the secret derision of sensible men ; all this comes from that legislation, from that public opinion, which drives women away from real life ; from the discussion of questions in which her happiness and destiny are involved. A senseless, though a false fondness, denies her a participation in all questions of the actual world around her. The novel writers therefore create a fictitious world, filled with fantastic and hollow characters, for her to range in. Awhile she believes she is an angel, till some unfortunate husband finds her to be a moth on his fortune, and a baleful shadow stretching across his pathway, without curiosity or interests in all those practical realities, which the world, outside of her charmed existence, is attending to. These are the abortions of a false public opinion. For ages they have been regarded as the natural results of female organism. Hence, woman has become famed as a gossip, because she would degrade herself by discussing Judge A.'s qualifications for Judge of Probate, though Judge A. may yet appoint a guardian for her children. In the sewing society, she sews scandal, or reads brocades, silks, and crinolines, because it would be extremely coarse and vulgar in her to read the statutes of Wisconsin, where her rights of person and property, marriage and divorce, are regulated. In those statutes she would find that though $350,000 are appropriated to build a University, she is as effectually excluded from that institution as though it was a convent of monks. So there is some inconvenience at last in being regarded as a *bona-fide* angel, for angels have no use for Universities. Some indignant school-ma'am begins to suspect the hollow compliments of moon-struck admirers, and demands a direct voice in the laws which provide for the mutual improvement of her sex. But the grave doctor of law puts on his spectacles, and tells her she is fully and exactly represented in man, only more so. When he eats, she eats ; when he thinks, she thinks ; when he gets drunk, she gets drunk ; that it would be as absurd to provide for the board and education of one's own shadow as to provide a separate establishment for woman, who possesses all things, enjoys all things, and sways all things in man, as fully as though she did it herself. And a single woman, or widow, may pay taxes, but it would be outrageous for her to have a choice in the men who are to spend the money and then cry out for more. When married, ten years ago, her education was equal to her husband's, now she can not write a grammatical letter : her husband's mind has been enlarged by the influx of new ideas, and by contacts with the electric atmosphere of thought in the great world without ; but denied as she has been the right of expressing her will by a direct vote, she has lost all interest in passing events ; the globe has dwindled to a half-acre lot and the village church. Her partner finds the match unequal, spends his time with more congenial society, and is out-and-out in favor of Moses' law of a galloping divorce. The old stager has filled the political arena with frauds and brawls, and bruises and blood ; and having levelled the morals of the ballot-box with those of the race-ground or box-ring, he has yet virtue enough left to declare that woman shall not enter this moral Aceldama.

"Yet it may be that democracy, for self-preservation, will be compelled to invite women to the ballot-box, to restrain and overawe the ruffianism of man. Though man smiles with secret derision at the competition of woman, in dress and show, yet he is too tender of her reputation to allow her the same field with himself wherein to exercise her powers. We believe that this contortion of character is justly attributable to the denial of the right of voting, the great mode by which the questions of the day are decided in this country. Politics are our national life. As civilization advances, its issues will penetrate still deeper into social and every-day life of the people ; and no man or woman can be regarded as an entity, as a power in society, who has not a direct agency in governing its results. Without a direct voice in molding the spirit of the age, the age will disown us.

"But the objection is argued seriously. Political rivalry will arm the wife against the husband ; a man's foes will be those of his own household. But we believe that political equality will, by leading the thoughts and purposes of the sexes, to a just degree, into the same channel, more completely carry out the designs of nature. Women will be possessed of a positive power, and hollow compliments and rose-water flatteries will be exchanged for a pure admiration and a well-grounded respect, when we see her nobly discharging her part in the great intellectual and moral struggles of the age, that wait their solution by a direct appeal to the ballot-box. Woman's power is, at present, poetical and unsubstantial ; let it be practical and real. There is no reality in any power that can not be coined into votes. The demagogue has a sincere respect and a salutary fear of the voter ; and he that can direct the lightning flash of the ballot-box is greater than he who possesses a continent of vapor, gilded with moonshine.

"It is true, the right of voting would carry with it the right to hold office ; but since it is true that the sexes have appropriate spheres, the discretion of individual voters would recognize this fact, and seldom elect a woman to an office, for which she is unfitted by nature and education, as incompetent men are now elected. But the cruelty of our laws is seen in this—that where nature makes exceptions, the laws are inexorable.

"We have shown that woman is not correctly represented by man at the ballot-box. Could her voice be heard, it would alter the choice of public men and their character. With legislators compelled to respect her opinions, the law itself, constitutions, and politics reflect, to a just extent, her peculiar views and interests. Nor is it for us to decide whether these would be for the better or worse. Let the majority rule. *Vox populi vox Dei.* Woman's intellect would enlarge with her more commanding political condition, and though she might blight the hopes of many a promising aspirant, yet the Union would not be dissolved under her administration. Believing the time has come when an appeal on her behalf to the voters of this State will not be in vain, we have prepared to submit the question to the people, by our amendment to the Senate bill.

" DAVID NOGGLE.
" J. T. MILLS.

"I altogether prefer the Committee's amendment to the Senate bill.
"February 27, 1857.   HOPEWELL COXE."

ONE YEAR'S WORK.—The following are a portion of the results of the Woman's Rights petitions, presented during the winter of 1856–7 :

In Ohio and Wisconsin, Legislative Committees have reported favorably to the Right of Suffrage, and extracts from the reports are given above.

Ohio, Maine, Indiana, and Missouri have passed laws giving to married women the right to control their own earnings. The Ohio and Maine statutes are printed below ; also a Maine act, giving the husband title to an allowance from a deceased wife's property, similar to that now given by the law to widows.

The memorial presented to the New York Legislature, owing to some mistake, was not offered till too late for action.

OHIO STATUTE.—Bill passed by the Ohio Legislature, April 17, 1857.

Sec. 1. Be it enacted by the General Assembly of the State of Ohio, that no married man shall sell, dispose of, or in any manner part with, any personal property, which is now, or may hereafter be, exempt from sale upon execution, without having first obtained the consent of his wife thereto.

Sec. 2. If any married man shall violate the provisions of the foregoing section, his wife may, in her own name, commence and prosecute to final judgment and execution, in civil action, for the recovery of such property or its value in money.

Sec. 3. Any married woman, whose husband shall desert her, or from intemperance or other cause become incapacitated, or neglect to provide for his family, may, in her own name, make contracts for her own labor and the labor of her minor children, and in her own name, sue for and collect her own or their earnings.

MAINE STATUTE.—At the recent session of the Legislature of Maine, the following acts were passed :

" An Act relating to the property of deceased married women. Be it enacted," etc.

" When a wife dies intestate and insolvent, her surviving husband shall be entitled to an allowance from her personal estate, and a distributive share in the residue thereof, in the same manner as a widow is in the estate of her husband ; and if she leaves issue he shall have the use of one-third, if no issue, one-half of her real estate for life, to be received and assigned in the manner and with the rights of dower." Approved April 13, 1857.

" An Act in relation to the rights of married women.

" Any married woman may demand and receive the wages of personal labor performed other than for her own family, and may hold the same in her own right against her husband or any other person, and may maintain an action therefore in her own name." Approved April 17, 1857.

FEMALE SUFFRAGE IN KENTUCKY.—Kentucky Revised Statutes, 1852, ch. 88. "Schools and Seminaries." Art. 6, Sec. 1 :

"An election shall be held at the school-house of each school district, from nine o'clock in the morning till two o'clock in the evening, of the first Saturday of April of each year, for the election of three Trustees for the District for one year, and until others are elected and qualified. The qualified voters in each District shall be the electors, and *any widow having a child between six and eighteen years of age, may also vote in person or by written proxy.*"

[But if the suffrage is not limited to *widows* who have a child between six and eighteen, but extended to *unmarried, married,* and *childless* men, why not give it to women in those positions also ? Such a partial concession, though valuable as recognizing a principle, is not likely to be extensively used. For in this case, as in that of women who are stockholders in corporations, the female voters will be deterred by their own small numbers and by the prejudices of society. But give woman the equal right of suffrage, and the prejudice will soon be swept away].

FEMALE SUFFRAGE IN CANADA.—[The following is the Canadian law under which women vote. The omission of the word *male* was intentional, and was done to secure the weight of the Protestant property in the hands of women, against the Roman Catholic aggressions and demands for separate schools. The law works well. "A friend of mine in Canada West told me," said Lucy Stone recently, "that when the law was first passed giving women who owned a certain amount of property, or who paid a given rental, a right to vote, he went trembling to the polls to see the result. The first woman who came was a large property holder in Toronto ; with marked respect the crowd gave way as she advanced. She spoke her vote and walked quietly away, sheltered by her womanhood. It was all the protection she needed."]

XVIII. AND XIV. VICTORIA, CAP 48.—An Act for the better establishment and maintenance of Common Schools in Upper Canada. Passed July 24, 1850.

Sec. 1. Preamble—Repeals former acts.

Sec. 2. Enacts that the election of School Trustees shall take place on the second Wednesday of January in each year.

Sec. 22. And be it enacted, that in each Ward, into which any City or Town is or shall be divided according to Law, two fit and proper persons shall be elected School Trustees by a majority of all the *taxable inhabitants.*

Sec. 25. Enacts that on the second Wednesday in January there shall be a meeting of all the taxable inhabitants of every incorporated village, and at such meeting six fit and proper persons, from among the resident householders, shall be elected School Trustees.

Sec. 5. Provides that in all *Country* School Districts *three* trustees shall be similarly elected by a majority of *the freeholders or householders* of such school section.

"THE EMANCIPATION OF WOMEN."—A very curious controversy, on paper, is going on at present in the *Reveu Philosophique et Religieuse,* between M. Proudhon and Mme. Jenny D'Hericourt. The latter defends, with great warmth, the moral, civil, and political emancipation of woman. Proudhon, in reply, declares that all the theories of Mme. D'Hericourt are inapplicable, in consequence of the inherent weakness of her sex. The periodical in which the contest is going on was founded and is conducted by the old St. Simoniens.

REPORT OF THE SELECT COMMITTEE OF THE OHIO SENATE, ON GIVING THE RIGHT OF SUFFRAGE TO FEMALES.

COLUMBUS, 1858.

The following petition, numerously signed by both men and women, citizens of this State, was, at the first session of the Legislature, referred to the undersigned Select Committee :

"WHEREAS, The women of the State of Ohio are disfranchised by the Constitution solely on account of their sex ;

"We do, respectfully, demand for them the right of suffrage—a right which involves all other rights of citizenship—one that can not, justly, be withheld, as the following admitted principles of government show :

" First. ' All men are born free and equal.'

" Second. ' Government derives its just power from the consent of the governed.'

" Third. ' Taxation and representation are inseparable.'

" We, the undersigned, therefore, petition your honorable body to take the necessary steps for a revision of the Constitution, so that all citizens may enjoy equal political rights."

Your Committee have given the subject referred to them a careful examination, and now

REPORT.

Your Committee believe that the prayer of the petitioners ought to be granted. Our opinion is based both upon grounds of principle and expediency, which we will endeavor to present as briefly as is consistent with a due consideration of this subject.

The founders of this Republic claimed and asserted with great emphasis, the essential equality of human rights as a self-evident truth. They scouted the venerable old dogma of the divine right of kings and titled aristocracies to rule the submissive multitude. They were equally explicit in their claim that " taxation and representation are inseparable."

The House of Representatives of Massachusetts, 1764, declared, " That the imposition of duties and taxes, by the Parliament of Great Britain, upon a *people not represented* in the House of Commons, is absolutely irreconcilable with their rights." A pamphlet entitled " The Rights of the British Colonies Asserted," was sent to the agent of the Colony in England, to show him the state of the public mind, and along with it an energetic letter. " The silence of the province," said this letter, alluding to the suggestion of the agent that he had taken silence for consent, " should have been imputed to any cause— even to despair—rather than be construed into a tacit cession of their rights, or the acknowledgment of a right in the Parliament of Great Britain, to impose duties and taxes on a people who are not represented in the House of Commons." " *If we are not represented we are slaves !* " Some of England's ablest jurists acknowledge the truth of this doctrine. Chief Justice Pratt said : " My position is this—taxation and representation are inseparable. The position is founded in the law of nature. It is more ; it is itself an eternal law of nature." In defence of this doctrine they waged a seven years' war ; and yet, when they had wrung from the grasp of Great Britain the Colonies she would not govern upon this principle, and undertook to organize them according to their favorite theory, most of the Colonies, by a single stroke of the pen, cut off one-half of the people from any representation in the government which claimed their obedience to its laws, the right to tax them for its support, and the right to punish them for disobedience.

This disparity between their theory and practice does not seem to have excited much, if any notice, at the time, nor until its bitter fruits had long been eaten in obscurity and sorrow by thousands who suffered, but did not complain. Indeed, so apathetic has been the public mind upon this subject, that no one is surprised to see such a remark as the following by a distinguished commentator upon American institutions : " In the free States, except criminals and paupers, *there is no class of persons* who do not exercise the elective franchise." It seems women are not even a class of persons. They are fairly dropped from the human race, and very naturally, since we have grown accustomed to recognize as *universal* suffrage, that which excludes by constitutional taboo one-half of the people. To declare that a voice in the government is the right of *all*, and then give it only to a *part*—and that the part to which the claimant himself belongs—is to renounce even the appearance of principle. As ought to have been foreseen, the class of persons thus cut off from the means of self-protection, have become victims of unequal and oppressive legislation, which runs through our whole code. We first bind the hands, by the organic law, and then proceed with deliberate safety, by the statute, to spoil the goods of the victim. Whatever palliation for the past hoary custom, false theology, and narrow prejudice may furnish, it is certainly time now to remedy those evils, and reduce to practice our favorite theory of government.

The citizens thus robbed of a natural right complain of the injustice. They protest against taxation without representation. They claim that all *just* government must derive its power from the consent of the governed. A forcible female writer says : " Even this so-called free government of the United States, as at present administered, is nothing but a political, hereditary despotism to woman ; she has no instrumentality whatever in making the laws by which she is governed, while her property is taxed *without* representation."

But this feeling, it is claimed, is entertained but by few women ; on the contrary, they generally disown such claim when made in their behalf. Supposing the fact to be true to the fullest extent ever asserted, if it proves that American women ought to remain as they are, it proves exactly the same with respect to Asiatic women ; for they, too, instead of murmuring at their seclusion and at the restraint imposed upon them, pride themselves on it, and are astonished at the effrontery of women who receive visits from male acquaintances, and are seen in the streets unveiled. Habits of submission make women, as well as men, servile-minded. The vast population of Asia do not desire or value— probably would not accept—political liberty, nor the savages of the forest civilization ; which does not prove that either of these things is undesirable for them, or that they will not, at some future time, enjoy it. Custom hardens human beings to any kind of degradation, by deadening that part of their nature which would resist it. And the case of woman is, in this respect even, a peculiar one, for no other inferior caste that we have heard of has been taught to regard its degradation as their, its, honor. The argument, however, implies a secret consciousness that the alleged preference of women for their dependent state is merely apparent, and arises from their being allowed no choice ; for, if the preference be natural, there can be no necessity for enforcing it by law. To make laws compelling people to follow their inclinations, has not, hitherto, been thought necessary by any legislator.

The plea that women do not desire any change is the same that has been urged, times out of mind, against the proposal of abolishing any social evil. " There is no complaint," which is generally, and in this case certainly not true, and when true, only so because there is not that hope of success, without which complaint seldom makes itself audible to unwilling ears. How does the objector know that women do not desire equality of freedom ? It would be very simple to suppose that if they do desire it they will all say so. Their position is like that of the tenants and laborers who vote against their own political interests to please their landlords or employers, with the unique admission that submission is inculcated in them from childhood, as the peculiar attraction and grace of their character. They are taught to think that to repel actively even an admitted injustice, done to themselves, is somewhat unfeminine, and had better be left to some male friend or protector. To be accused of rebelling against anything which admits of being called an ordinance of society, they are taught to regard as an imputation of a serious offence, to say the least, against the propriety of their sex. It requires unusual moral courage, as well as disinterestedness in a woman, to express opinions favorable to woman's enfranchisement, until, at least, there is some prospect of obtaining it.

The comfort of her individual life and her social consideration, usually depend on the good-will of those who hold the undue power ; and to the possessors of power, any complaint, however bitter, of the misuse of it, is scarcely a less flagrant act of insubordination than to protest against the power itself. The professions of women in this matter remind us of the State offenders of old, who, on the point of execution, used to protest their love and devotion to the sovereign by whose unjust mandate they suffered. Griselda, himself, might be matched from the speeches put by Shakespeare into the mouths of male victims of kingly caprice and tyranny ; the Duke of Buckingham, for example, in " Henry VIII.," and even Wolsey.

The literary class of women are often ostentatious in disclaiming the desire for equality of citizenship, and proclaiming their complete satisfaction with the place which society assigns them ; exercising in this, as in many other respects, a most noxious influence over the feelings and opinions of men, who unsuspectingly accept the servilities of toadyism as concessions to the force of truth, not considering that it is the personal interest of these women to profess whatever opinions they expect will be agreeable to men. It is not among men of talent, sprung from the people, and patronized and flattered by the aristocracy, that we look for the leaders of a democratic movement. Successful literary women are just as unlikely to prefer the cause of woman to their own social consideration. They depend on men's opinion for their literary, as well as for their feminine successes ; and such is their bad opinion of men, that they believe there is not more than one in a thousand who does not dislike and fear strength, sincerity, and high spirit in a woman. They are, therefore, anxious to earn pardon and toleration for whatever of these qualities their writings may exhibit on other subjects, by a studied display of submission on this ; that they may give no occasion for vulgar men to say—what nothing will prevent vulgar men from saying—that learning makes woman unfeminine, and that literary ladies are likely to be bad wives.

But even if a large majority of women do not desire any change in the Constitution, that would be a very bad reason for withholding the elective franchise from those who do desire it. Freedom of choice, liberty to choose their own sphere, is what is asked. We have not heard that the most ardent apostles of female suffrage propose to compel any woman to make stump speeches against her will, or to march a fainting sisterhood to the polls under a police, in Bloomer costume. Women who condemn their sisters for discontent with the laws as they are, have their prototype in those men of America who, in our revolutionary struggle with England, vehemently denounced and stigmatized as fanatics and rebels the leaders and malcontents of that day. But neither their patriotism nor wisdom have ever been much admired by the American people, perhaps not even by the English.

The objection urged against female suffrage with the greatest confidence and by the greatest number, is that such a right is incompatible with the refinement and delicacy of the sex. That it would make them harsh and disputative, like male voters. This objection loses most, if not all of its force, when it is compared with the well-established usages of society as relates to woman. She already fills places and discharges duties with the approbation of most men, which are, to say the least, quite as dangerous to her refinement and retiring modesty, as the act of voting or even holding office would be. In our political campaigns all parties are anxious to secure the co-operation of women. They are urged to attend our political meetings, and even in our mass meetings, when whole acres of men are assembled, they are importunately urged to take a conspicuous part, sometimes as the representatives of the several States, and sometimes as the donors of banners and flags, accompanied with patriotic speeches by the fair donors. And in great moral questions, such as temperance, for example, in the right disposition of which woman is more interested than man, she often discharges a large amount of the labor of the campaign ; but yet, when it comes to the crowning act of voting, she must stand aside— delicacy forbids—that is too masculine, too public, too exposing, though it could be done, in most cases, with as little difficulty and exposure as a letter can be taken out or put in the post-office.

Then there is that large class of concert singers and readers of the drama, who are eulogized and petted by those who are most shocked at the idea of women submitting themselves to the exposure of voting. In fact, the whole question of publicity is settled to the fullest extent; at least every man must be silent who acquiesces in the concert, the drama, or the opera. We need not dwell on the exposures of the stage or the indelicacies of the ballet, but if Jenny Lind was " an angel of purity and benevolence " for consenting to stand, chanting and enchanting, before three thousand excited admirers ; if Madame Sontag could give a full-dress rehearsal (which does not commonly imply a superfluity of apparel) for the special edification of the clergy of Boston, and be rewarded with duplicate Bibles, it is difficult to see why a woman may not vote on questions vitally affecting the interests of herself, or children, or kindred.

But, with all our dainty notions of female proprieties, women are, by common consent, dragged into court as witnesses, and subjected to the most scrutinizing and often indelicate examinations and questions, if either party imagines he can gain a sixpence, or dull the edge of a criminal prosecution, by her testimony. The interest, convenience, and prejudices of men, and not any true regard for the delicacy of the sex, seem to be the standard by which woman's rights and duties are to be measured. It is prejudice, custom, long-established usage, and not reason, which demand the sacrifice of woman's natural rights of self-government; a relic of barbarism still lingering in all political, and nearly all religious organizations. Among the purely savage tribes, woman takes position as a domestic drudge—a mere beast of burden, whilst the sensual civilization of Asia regard her more in the light of a domestic luxury, to be jealously guarded from the profane sight of all men but her husband. Both positions equally and widely remote from the noble one God intended her to fill.

In Persia and Turkey women grossly offend the public taste if they suffer their faces to be seen in the streets. In the latter country they are prohibited by law, in common with "pigs, dogs, and other unclean animals," as the law styles them, from so much as entering their mosques. *Our* ideas of the proper sphere, duties, and capabilities of woman do not differ from these so much in kind as degree. They are all based upon the assumption that man has the right to decide what are the rights, to point out the duties, and to fix the boundaries of woman's sphere; which, taking for true, our cherished theory of government, to wit: the *inalienability and equality of human rights* can hardly be characterized by a milder term than that of an impudent and oppressive usurpation. Who has authorized us, whilst railing at miters, and crosiers, and scepters, and shouting in the ears of the British Lion, as self-evident truths, "representation and taxation are, and *shall* be, inseparable,"—"governments, to be *just*, must have the consent of the governed;" to say woman, one-half of the whole race, shall, nevertheless, be taxed without representation and governed without her consent? Who hath made us a judge betwixt her and her Maker?

It is said woman's mental and moral organization is peculiar, differing widely from that of man. Perhaps so. She must then have a peculiar fitness of qualification to judge what will be wise and just government for her. Let her be free to choose for herself, in the light of her peculiar organization, to what she is best adapted. She is better qualified to judge of her proper sphere than man can be. She knows her own wants and capabilities. Let us leave her, as God created her, a free agent, accountable to Him for any violation of the laws of her nature. He has mingled the sexes in the family relation; they are associated on terms of equality in some churches. They are active working and voting members of literary and benevolent societies. They vote as share-holders in stock companies, and in countries where less is said about freedom, and equality, and representation, they are often called to, and fill, with distinguished ability, very important positions, and often discharge the highest political trusts known to their laws. Which of England's kings has shown more executive ability than Elizabeth, or which has been more conscientious and discreet than Annie and Victoria? Spain, too, had her Isabella, and France her Maid of Orleans, her Madame Roland, yes, and her Charlotte Corday. Austria and Hungary their Maria Theresa. Russia her Catharine; and even the jealous Jewish Theocracy was judged forty years by a woman. It is too late, by thirty centuries, to put in the plea of her incompetency in political affairs.

But it is objected that it would not do for woman, particularly a married woman, to be allowed to vote. It might bring discord into the family if she differed from her husband. If this objection were worth anything at all, it would lie with tenfold greater force against religious than political organizations. No animosities are so bitter and implacable as those growing out of religious disagreements; yet we allow women to choose their religious creeds, attend their favorite places of worship, and in some of them take an equal part in the church business, and all this, though the husband is of another religion, or of no religion, and no one this side of Turkey claims that the law should compel woman to have no religion, or adopt that of her husband. But, even if that objection were a good one, more than half the adult women of the State are unmarried.

It is said, too, that as woman is not required to perform military duty, and work on the roads, she ought not to vote. None but "able-bodied" men, under a certain age, are required to do military duty, and the effect is practically the same in regard to the two days' work on the roads, whilst women pay tax for military and road purposes the same as man. A *man's* right to vote does not depend on his ability to perform physical labor, why should a *woman's*? By the exclusion of woman from her due influence and voice in the government, we lose that elevating and refining influence which she gives to religious, social, and domestic life. Her presence at our political meetings, all agree, contributes greatly to their order, decorum, and decency. Why should not the polls, also, be civilized by her presence?

Does not the morality of our politics demonstrate a great want of the two qualities so characteristic of woman, heart and conscience? The female element which works such miracles of reform in the rude manners of men, in all the departments of life where she has the freedom to go, is nowhere more needed than in our politics, or at the polls.

We have endeavored to show that the constitutional prohibition of female suffrage is not only a violation of natural right, but equally at war with the fundamental principles of the government. Let us now look at the practical results of this organic wrong. After having taken away from woman the means of protecting her person and property, by the peaceable, but powerful ballot, how have we discharged the self-imposed duty of legislating for her? By every principle of honor, or even of common honesty, we are bound to see that her interests do not suffer in our hands. That, if we depart at all from the principle of strict equality, it should be in her favor. Let us see what are the facts.

When a woman marries she becomes almost annihilated in the eyes of the law, except as a subject of punishment. She loses the right to receive and control the wages of her own labor. If she be an administratrix, or executrix, she is counted as dead, and another must be appointed. If she have children, they may be taken from her against her will, and placed in the care of any one, no matter how unfit, whom the father may select. He may even give them away by will. "The personal property of the wife, such as money, goods, cattle, and other chattels, which she had in possession at the time of her marriage, in her own right, and not in the right of another, vest immediately in the husband, and he can dispose of them as he pleases. On his death, they go to his representatives, like the residue of his property. So, if any such goods or chattels come to her possession in her own right, after the marriage, they, in like manner, immediately vest in the husband." "Such property of the wife, as bonds, notes, arrears of rent, legacies, which are termed *choses in action*, do not vest in the husband by mere operation of marriage. To entitle him to them, he must first reduce them into possession, by recovering the money, or altering the security, as by making them payable to himself. If the husband appoint an attorney to receive a debt or claim due the wife, and the attorney received it, or if he mortgaged the claim or debt, or assign it for a valuable consideration, or recover judgment by suit, in his own name, or if he release it, in all these cases the right of the wife, upon the decease of the husband, is gone."

The real estate of the wife, such as houses and lands, is in nearly the same state of subjection to the husband's will. He is entitled to all the rents and profits while they both live, and the husband can hold the estate during his life, even though the wife be dead. A woman may thus be stripped of every available cent she ever had in the world, and even see it squandered in ministering to the low appetite or passions of a drunken debauchee of a husband. And when, by economy and toil, she may have acquired the means of present subsistence, this, too, may be *lawfully* taken from her, and applied to the same base purpose. Even her Family Bible, the last gift of a dying mother, her only remaining comfort, can be lawfully taken and sold by the husband, to buy the means of intoxication. *This very thing has been done.* Can any one believe that laws, so wickedly one-sided as these, were ever honestly designed for the equal benefit of woman with man? Yet wives are said to have quite a sufficient representation in the government, through their husbands, to secure them protection.

But the cruel inequality of the laws relating to woman as wife are quite outdone by those relating to her as widow. It is these stricken and sorrowful victims, the law seems especially to have selected as its prey. Upon the death of the husband, the law takes possession of the whole of the estate. The smallest items of property must be turned out for valuation, to be handled by strangers. The clothes that the deceased had worn, the chair in which he sat, the bed on which he died, all these sacred memorials of the dead, must undergo the cold scrutiny of officers of the law. The widow is counted but as an alien, and an incumbrance on the estate, the bulk of which is designed for other hands. She is to have doled out to her, like a pauper, by paltry sixes, the furniture of her own kitchen. "One table, six chairs, six knives and forks, six plates, six tea-cups and saucers, one sugar-dish, one milk-pail, one tea-pot, and *twelve* spoons!" All this munificent provision for, perhaps, a family of only a dozen persons. Think of it, ye widows, and learn to be grateful for man's provident care of you in your hour of need !

Then comes the sale of "the effects of the deceased," as they are called ; and amid the fullness and freshness of her grief, the widow is compelled to see sold into the hands of strangers, amid the coarse jokes and levity of a public auction, articles to her beyond all price, and around which so many tender memories cling. Experience alone can fully teach the torture of this fiery ordeal. But this is only the beginning of her sorrows. If she have children, the estate is considered to belong to them, while she is but an "incumbrance" upon it. She is to have the rents and profits of one-third part of the real estate her lifetime, which, in the vast majority of cases, is so unproductive as to compel her to leave that spot, endeared to her by so many tender ties—the home of her early love, the birthplace of her children—for a cheaper and less comfortable home. But, bereaved of her husband and robbed of her property,

> "The law hath yet another hold on her."

Following up the insulting and injurious assumption of her incompetency and untrustworthiness, implied in the denial of her right of suffrage, the guardianship of her children is taken from her. Her daughter, at the age of twelve, and her son, at fifteen, are to go through the mockery of choosing for themselves a *competent* guardian—a proceeding calculated to destroy the beautiful trust and confidence in the wisdom and fitness of the mother to govern and direct them, so natural and so essential to the happiness of children. When the justifying pretext for the infliction of all this misery is the benefit of the children, her maternal nature will struggle hard to endure it with patience. But, until the passage of the law of 1853, "regulating descents and distributions," when there were no children of either parent, the law did not abate its rigor toward her, in the disposition of the real estate, which is generally all that is left, after paying the debts and costs of "settlement," though the whole of the houses and lands might have been bought with her money, two-thirds were immediately handed over to the relatives of the husband, however above need ; and though they might have been strangers, or even enemies, to her. She had but a life estate in the other third, which, at her death, also went, as the other, to her husband's heirs. She could not indulge her benevolent feelings or gratify her friendships, by devising by will, to approved charities or favorite friends, the means she no longer needed. With a bitter sense of injustice and despairing sorrow, she might well adopt the language of the unhappy Jew :

> " Nay, take my life and all, pardon not that ;
> You take my house, when you do take the prop
> That doth sustain my house ; you take my life,
> When you do take the means whereby I live."

Such is the famous right of dower, which has been the subject of so many stupid eulogies by lawyers and commentators.

Take an example of the effect of these laws upon an overburdened heart, which occurred just before the passage of the Act of 1853. A young couple, by their united means and patient industry, had secured for themselves a small, but comfortable home. It furnished the means of supplying all their simple wants. It was their own ; doubly endeared by the struggles and sacrifices it had cost them. They were content. They had no children, but they had each other, and were happy in their mutual love. Death seemed a great way off; and life—it was a real joy. They knew little of the laws of estates. Owing nothing, they feared no intrusion upon the sanctity of their home. But the husband was killed by the falling of a tree ; and, after some hours, was found dead by the agonized wife. There was no will. The wrung heart of the childless widow, in her utter bereavement, still clung to her home, which, though blighted and desolate, was still dear to her. There, at least, she would find shelter. But soon the inexorable law laid its cold, unwelcome hand upon that darkened home. There must be letters of administration had—an inventory of the "effects"—an appraisement. Everything was explained by sympathizing counsel. The "right of dower" set conspicuously in the foreground—"one equal third part"—at length she comprehended it all. Her home was to pass into other hands : henceforth she was to be counted only as an incumbrance on it. Looking from the misery of the present down the gloom of the future, she could see only widowhood and penury. And whilst the appraisers were performing their un- gracious task of overhauling cupboards and drawers, and estimating the value in cash of presents received in her courtship, she, in her quiet despair at this last bitter drop added to her full cup, arrayed herself in her best apparel (which the law generously provides "she shall retain"), and, without uttering a word of complaint or farewell, walked to the nearest water and drowned herself.

If "oppression maketh even a wise man mad," ought we to wonder that a woman, almost crazed by a sudden and terrible bereavement, upon finding that her calamity, instead of giving her the jealous and compassionate protection of the law, was to be made the pretext for robbing her of what yet remained of earthly comforts, should, in the madness of her despair, cast away the burden of a life no longer tolerable? In India she would have been burned upon the funeral pile of her dead husband; we drive her to madness and suicide by the slower, but no less cruel torture, of starvation and a breaking heart. Whilst persisting in such legislation, how could we expect to escape the woe, denounced by the compassionate and long-suffering Saviour, against the "hypo- crites who devour widows' houses"?

It is said woman can accomplish any object of her desire better by persuasion, by her smiles and tears and eloquence, than she could ever compel by her vote. But with all her powers of coaxing and eloquence, she has never yet coaxed her partner into doing her simple justice. Shall we never get beyond the absurd theory that every woman is legally and politically represented by her husband, and hence has an adequate guarantee? The answer is, that she has been so represented ever since representation began, and the result appears to be that, among the Anglo-Saxon race generally, the entire system of laws in regard to women is, at this moment, so utterly wrong, that Lord Brougham is reported to have declared it useless to attempt to amend it—"There must be a total re- construction before a woman can have any justice." The wrong lies not so much in any special statute as in the fundamental theory of the law, yet no man can read the statutes on this subject of the most enlightened nation, without admitting that they were obviously made by *man*, not with a view to woman's interest, but his *own*. Our Ohio laws may not be so bad as the law repealed in Vermont in 1850, which *confiscated to the State* one-half the property of every childless widow, unless the husband had other heirs. But they must compel from every generous man the admission, that neither justice nor gallantry has yet availed to procure anything like impartiality in the legal provisions for the two sexes. With what decent show of justice, then, can man, thus dishonored, claim a con- tinuance of this suicidal confidence? There is something respectable in the frank bar- barism of the old Russian nuptial consecration, "Here, wolf, take thy lamb." But we can not easily extend the same charity to the civilized wolf of England and America, clad in the sheep's clothing of a volume of revised statutes, caressing the person of the bride and devouring her property.

It is said the husband can, by will, provide against these cases of hardship and injus- tice. True, he can, if he will, but does he? The number is few, some of the more thoughtful and conscientious ; but this is only obtaining justice as a favor, and not as a natural right. But it is a majority of husbands who make these laws, and they generally have no desire to amend them by will. Besides, the will of the husband is sometimes even worse than the law itself. Such cases are by no means rare. Almost every man's memory may furnish one or more examples that have fallen under his immediate notice. One or two only we will mention. A woman, advanced in life, who owned a valuable farm in her own right, in the border of a flourishing town, married a man who had little or no property. The farm was soon cut up into town lots and sold at high prices. In a few years the husband died, leaving no children, but, by will, directed the division of nearly the whole of the estate among his relatives, persons who the wife never saw. The only remedy in this case was to fall back upon her right of dower, and submit to the robbery of the law, in order to escape the worse robbery of the will. This will was not the result of any disagreement between the husband and the wife. It was only the natu- ral outgrowth of the whole policy of our laws as regards the property rights of woman.

Permit us to notice one other case, which occurred in a neighboring State. Many similar ones, no doubt, have occurred in our own, the law in both States being the same.

A woman who had a fortune of fifty thousand dollars in " personal property," married. All this, by the law, belonged absolutely to the husband. In a year he died, leaving a will directing that the widow should have the proceeds of a certain part of this money, *so long as she remained unmarried.* If she married again, or at her death, it was to go to his heirs.

How different in all these cases is the condition of the husband upon the death of the wife. There is then no officious intermeddling of the law in his domestic affairs. His house, sad and desolate though it be, is still sacred and secure from the foot of unbidden guests. There is no legal " settlement " to eat up his estate. He is not told that " one equal third part " of all his lands and tenements shall be set apart for his use during his lifetime. " He has all, everything, even his wife's bridal presents too are his. If the wife had lands in her own right, and if they have ever had a living child, he has a life estate in the whole of it, not a beggarly ' third part.' "

Such is the result of man's government of woman without her consent. Such is the protection he affords her. She now asks the means of protecting herself, by the same instrumentality which man considers so essential to his freedom and security, representation, political equality—THE RIGHT OF SUFFRAGE. The removal of this constitutional restriction is of great consequence, because it casts upon woman a stigma of inferiority, of incompetency, of unworthiness of trust. It ranks her with criminals and madmen and idiots. It is essential to her, practically, as being the key to all her rights, which will open to her the door of equality and justice.

Does any one believe that if woman had possessed an equal voice in making our laws, we should have standing on our statute books, for generations, laws so palpably unequal and unjust toward her ? The idea is preposterous.

If our sense of natural justice and our theory of government both agree, that the being who is to suffer under laws shall first personally assent to them, and that the being whose industry the government is to burden should have a voice in fixing the character and amount of that burden, then, while woman is admitted to the gallows, the jail, and the tax-list, *we have no right* to debar her from the ballot-box.

Your Committee recommend the adoption of the following resolution :

Resolved, That the Judiciary Committee be instructed to report to the Senate, a bill to submit to the qualified electors at the next election for senators and representatives, an amendment to the Constitution whereby the elective franchise shall be extended to the citizens of Ohio, without distinction of sex.

J. D. CATTELL,
H. CANFIELD.